CONTEMPORARIES OF ERASMUS
A BIOGRAPHICAL REGISTER OF THE
RENAISSANCE AND REFORMATION

VOLUME 1

A–E

Contemporaries of
ERASMUS

A BIOGRAPHICAL REGISTER OF THE

RENAISSANCE AND REFORMATION

VOLUME 1

A–E

Peter G. Bietenholz
University of Saskatchewan

Editor

Thomas B. Deutscher
University of Saskatchewan

Associate Editor

University of Toronto Press

Toronto / Buffalo / London

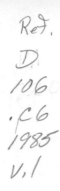

The research and publication costs of the
Collected Works of Erasmus are supported by the
Social Sciences and Humanities Research Council of Canada
(and previously by the Canada Council).
The publication costs are also assisted by
University of Toronto Press.

ISBN 0-8020-2507-2

Canadian Cataloguing in Publication Data
Main entry under title:
Contemporaries of Erasmus
Supplement to: Erasmus, Desiderius, d. 1536. Works.
Collected works of Erasmus.
Includes index.
Contents: v. 1. A–E
ISBN 0-8020-2507-2 (V. 1)
1. Erasmus, Desiderius, d. 1536 – Dictionaries,
indexes, etc. 2. Renaissance – Biography.
3. Reformation – Biography. I. Bietenholz, Peter G., 1933–
II. Deutscher, Thomas Brian, 1949–
III. Erasmus, Desiderius, d. 1536. Works.
Collected works of Erasmus.
PA8500 1974 suppl.   876'.04   c85-098027-5

Collected Works of Erasmus

The aim of the Collected Works of Erasmus
is to make available an accurate, readable English text
of Erasmus' correspondence and his
other principal writings. The edition is planned
and directed by an Editorial Board, an Executive Committee,
and an Advisory Committee.

The manuscript editors for *Contemporaries of Erasmus*
were Margaret Parker and Erika Rummel.
The book was designed by Antje Lingner.

Contents

Preface

Contemporaries of Erasmus offers biographical information about the more than 1900 people mentioned in the correspondence and works of Erasmus who died after 1450 and were thus approximately his contemporaries, if it proved possible to trace and identify them.

These volumes are the result of a decision taken early in the planning of the Collected Works of Erasmus (CWE). In the absence of standard biographical reference works for the period, Renaissance scholars had long been dependent on and indebted to the biographical notes in P.S. Allen's distinguished edition of Erasmus' correspondence for a ready source of information on personalities of the European community of learning and religion. Because of the advances in our knowledge of the period since his edition was completed, it was evident that Allen's information required massive revision, and the CWE provided the opportunity for a separate reference work that would accomplish this. Annotators of both Correspondence and Works volumes were therefore asked to restrict the biographical content of their notes to the data required for simple identification and to details pertinent to the events and circumstances mentioned in the passage under discussion. Fuller information on the subject's life, writings, and connections with Erasmus – although not necessarily the particulars required to explain each of Erasmus' references – would be made available in this separate biographical register. Ideally, work on the register might have been postponed until both the Latin *Opera omnia* sponsored by the Dutch Royal Academy (ASD) and the CWE were nearing completion, but this would have meant indefinite delay. Rather than wait to take advantage of scores of ASD and CWE volumes, the Editorial Board decided that a working index of Erasmus' contemporaries should be created, mostly on the basis of the Leiden *Opera omnia* of 1703–6 and the Allen edition of Erasmus' correspondence. In the process some few names may have been missed and some titular, anonymous, and pseudonymous references may have gone undecoded, but on the other hand the present register will not only benefit Erasmus' readers but also assist many future CWE editors and annotators in their task and greatly reduce the need for repetitive annotation.

In view of its stated objective of including all Erasmus' contemporaries who can be identified, this work is bound to differ substantially from the excellent national biographical dictionaries that are available today, and to which it is much indebted.

Whereas the latter restrict themselves to persons who were in one way or another significant, *Contemporaries of Erasmus* combines famous figures with such obscure men and women as domestic servants and commercial messengers. To aim for absolute uniformity was therefore neither possible nor desirable. In some instances no biographical data, however meagre, could be discovered despite research in local archives and in rare printed books of the early modern period. In others, encyclopaedias of every sort already provide a basic biography, frequently within limits of length not unlike those applying to the present register. Thus it was necessary to determine the length and orientation of each article in the light of the individual's importance and the accessibility of biographical data in other works of reference. For men and women in modest positions circumstantial and even trivial scraps of information warranted mention. On the other hand, in articles on those well known it was appropriate to concentrate on their contacts with, or influence upon, Erasmus. Readers will notice that the number of biographies devoted to women is exiguous; Erasmus' world was predominantly a man's world. But readers will also notice that women have written approximately half of the biographies in *Contemporaries of Erasmus*. In a way this international endeavour, involving over one hundred scholars of fifteen different nationalities, reflects not only the breadth of Erasmus' own contacts but also the constant and growing interest in his ideas.

It is impossible to name all the individuals and institutions who have contributed in various ways to this project. We should like, however, to express particular appreciation for the generous financial support given by the Social Sciences and Humanities Research Council of Canada, the Fonds national suisse de la recherche scientifique, the University of Toronto, the University of Saskatchewan, and University of Toronto Press; and finally our gratitude for the pioneering scholarship of P.S. Allen.

PGB

Editorial Notes

In assembling *Contemporaries of Erasmus*, the following principles have been applied, with an appropriate degree of flexibility in view of the diversity of available material and fields of scholarly specialization among contributors.

– No biography is offered unless the person in question could be plausibly identified. On the other hand, even persons known merely by their first names are included in the register, provided the references to them warranted investigation. It is hoped that our short notes will encourage further research and eventually lead to further identification of those so mentioned.

– Both first and second names are given in the appropriate vernacular, provided predominant forms could be established; Latin forms often seemed preferable for unidentified or obscure persons. Humanist names in Latin or Greek were preferred wherever they seemed less uncertain than their vernacular counterparts or were deemed to be more widely known.

– Persons known by place of birth rather than by family name are indexed under their first names, unless contemporaries already tended to use the place name as a surname.

– In accordance with English-language custom, popes, emperors, queens, and kings are indexed under their first names, given in English; other members of royal houses, both legitimate and illegitimate, are similarly indexed.

– All members of noble houses are listed together under the family name, with first names in the appropriate language. In some cases, however, the names of a house and a territory are identical or, as with many German princes, the territorial name, often in Anglicized form, is in general use, as with Albert of BRANDENBURG, archbishop of Mainz.

– Women are listed under their maiden names, when known, rather than under names adopted in marriage. Cross-references are provided to married names.

– Cross-references are provided to name forms and identifications proposed by Allen but now abandoned. Cross-references are also given for variant name forms, Latin or vernacular, wherever expedient.

– An asterisk has been used with the name of an individual to indicate that a biography on that individual is included in *Contemporaries of Erasmus*; the asterisk precedes the name under which the biography is indexed.

- For names of places, modern vernacular forms are used, with the exception of those for which there is a form commonly accepted in current English usage (for example The Hague, Brussels, Louvain, Cologne, Milan). Current political frontiers are respected in the choice of place names rather than historical geography; this practice was adopted as being the most acceptable to an international readership, despite the occasional anachronisms that result.
- References to the correspondence and works of Erasmus are incorporated in each article without an obligation to completeness. *Contemporaries of Erasmus* is not intended as a substitute for the indexes that complement the CWE.
- Contributors were given latitude in the preparation of the bibliographies that accompany their articles so that they could be arranged thematically, alphabetically, or chronologically, as was thought most appropriate for the particular biography.
- Abbreviated references are used for works frequently cited throughout *Contemporaries of Erasmus*. A list of these works, offering fuller data, will be found at the end of each volume. On occasion, however, the full reference to a work cited in abbreviated form in the text of an article will be found in the bibliography following that entry.

The biographies are signed with the names of their authors or co-authors. Initials identify the members of the team in the research office generously provided by the University of Saskatchewan:

| PGB | Peter G. Bietenholz | IG | Ilse Guenther |
| TBD | Thomas B. Deutscher | CFG | Catherine F. Gunderson |

The biographies contributed by members of this team frequently reflect their fields of competence, but just as often they had to be compiled with local research facilities because of limits on time and available funds.

BIOGRAPHIES

Volume 1

A–E

Henry ABINGDON d by September 1497
Abingdon (Abyndon), whose name may have
been connected with the village of Abington,
near Cambridge, is first documented in 1445.
He was succentor at Wells in 1447 and a canon
in 1458, and became master of the children's
choir of the Chapel Royal in 1456. In 1464 he
received the first bachelor of music degree
known to have been granted at Cambridge. In
the same year he was master of St Catherine's
hospital, Bedminster, Bristol.

In his youth, Thomas *More composed
three epigrams on Abingdon's death, one of
which was criticized by Germain de *Brie and
is noted in Epp 1087, 1093.

BIBLIOGRAPHY: Allen Ep 1087 / Emden BRUC
1–2 / *The New Grove Dictionary of Music and
Musicians* ed Stanley Sadie (London 1980) I 30
/ Thomas More *Latin Epigrams* ed and trans L.
Bradner and C.A. Lynch (Chicago 1953) / S.L.
Holahan 'More's Epigrams on Henry Abing-
don' *Moreana* 5 (1968) XVII 24–6
                                                    CFG

Henry ABYNDON *See* ABINGDON

Mariano ACCARDO of Noto, died c 1521
Mariano Accardo (Accardi) was born in Noto,
Sicily, during the second half of the fifteenth
century. He probably received a doctorate of
law in his youth and entered the service of
Rinaldo Montuoro, bishop of Cefalù. In 1510
Accardo accompanied the bishop in his mission as ambassador of Sicily to the court of
*Ferdinand II of Aragon. After Montuoro's
death in October 1511, the young scholar left
Spain and became secretary to the Spanish
viceroy in Sicily, Hugo de Moncada. In 1516
Moncada was driven from Palermo by a Sicilian uprising, and in 1517 the future emperor,
*Charles V, summoned him to Brussels, where
he was removed from his office. Accardo had
accompanied his master to the Netherlands
but returned to Sicily where he entered the
service of the new viceroy, Ettore Pignatelli.
Accardo died of the plague in Noto.

Guillaume *Budé was probably referring to
Accardo and to a hitherto unidentified Spanish friend of his in a letter to Erasmus of 26
November 1516 (Ep 493) in which he described
the two 'noblemen' as admirers of the Dutch
scholar. The two men visited Erasmus at

Brussels in February 1517. In his answer
Erasmus stated that he was particularly impressed by Accardo and described him as a
charming person, 'a good scholar and an
open-hearted man' (Ep 531). After Erasmus'
departure from Brussels, Accardo sent him
two letters of friendship and praise (Epp 544,
564), mentioning Erasmus' letter to Budé and
two lost letters to himself, which he believed
would give him the gift of immortality.

Little is known about Accardo's literary
activity. In 1507 at Venice he edited the
Proverbiorum liber of Ramón Lull, with a
dedication to Johannes Franciscus de Iudici-
bus, reprinted at Majorca in 1735. The same
volume contained an edition of the *Disputatio
eremitae et Raymundi super aliquibus dubiis ques-
tionibus sententiarum Magistri Petri Lombardi.*
Apparently Accardo also wrote some poetry.

BIBLIOGRAPHY: Allen Ep 544 / R. Zapperi in
DBI I 68 / E. Rogent and E. Duran *Bibliografia de
les impressiones lullianes* (Barcelona 1924) 36–7,
289 / Lucio Marineo Siculo *Epistolario* ed P.
Verrua (Bologna 1940) 73, 106 / Benedetto
Croce 'Erasmo e gli umanisti napoletani' *Aned-
doti di varia letteratura* (Bari 1953) I 176–7
                                    DANILO AGUZZI-BARBAGLI

ACCHATIUS (Ep 367, of 30 October 1515)
Acchatius brought greetings from Erasmus to
Udalricus *Zasius at Freiburg and took Ep 367
back to Basel. The verbal greetings suggest an
educated visitor rather than a commercial
messenger.

A brother Achatius of the order of St Paul,
MA, matriculated at the University of Freiburg
on 3 April 1508. There was a Pauline monastery at Bonndorf in the Black Forest.

BIBLIOGRAPHY: *Matrikel Freiburg* I-1 182
                                                    PGB

Donato ACCIAIUOLI of Florence, 15 March
1429–28 August 1478
Acciaiuoli (Acciaiolus) was born in Florence,
the son of Neri di Donato and Lena di Palla
Strozzi. He was educated partly in the Florentine lay confraternities but also at the Dominican convent of San Marco, where he studied
logic with Angelo da Lecco. Beginning in 1450
he studied Greek, first with Francesco di
Castiglione and later with Carlo Marsuppini
and Johannes *Argyropoulos.

Acciaiuoli divided his time between public duties and literary and scholarly pursuits. His service with the Medici included several embassies, and he died in Milan on his way to a diplomatic mission in France. Besides participating in the activities of the Platonic Academy, he also published various works, including commentaries on Aristotle's *Politics* and *Nicomachean Ethics*, and translated Leonardo Bruni's history of Florence into Italian. Erasmus mentioned him briefly, along with other fifteenth-century Italians, as being unacceptable to the Ciceronians (ASD I-2 662).

BIBLIOGRAPHY: A. d'Addario in DBI I 80-2 / E. Garin *Medioevo e Rinascimento* 2nd ed (Bari 1961) 211-87, trans in *Portraits for the Quattrocento* (New York 1972) 55-117

CHARLES B. SCHMITT

Benedetto ACCOLTI 29 October 1497-21 September 1549
The nephew of Cardinal Pietro Accolti, a distinguished jurist, Benedetto studied law at Pisa and entered his uncle's household in 1515, becoming an abbreviator of papal letters. On 16 March 1523 he was appointed archbishop of Cremona, on 17 August 1524 archbishop of Ravenna, and on 3 March 1527 cardinal; he also received pensions and benefices from the Emperor *Charles v. He became papal secretary in 1523, and his signature appears at the bottom of the papal letter of 8 July 1525 granting Erasmus a dispensation to make a will (Ep 1588).

There is no evidence of a direct correspondence, much less an acquaintance, with Erasmus. In 1532 the legation of the Marches excluding Ancona was bestowed on Accolti, but in September 1534 he was deprived of this office for betraying to the Anconitans *Clement VII's plan to subject them to Cardinal Ippolito de' *Medici. On 5 April 1535 Accolti was arrested on various charges and imprisoned in Castel Sant'Angelo (Ep 3011). At the end of August he was freed, but at the cost of a heavy fine (Ep 3039). Accolti retired to Ravenna; he did not return to Rome until 1544 and died there in 1549. He was the author of various juridical tracts and some mythological poetry and corresponded with Pietro Aretino, *Bembo, and other literary personalities.

BIBLIOGRAPHY: Allen Ep 1588 / E. Massa in DBI I 102-4, with full references, bibliography, and mention of unpublished material available

D.S. CHAMBERS

Mariangelo ACCURSIO of Aquila, c 1489-1546
Mariangelo Accursio was born in Aquila, the son of Giovan Francesco Accursio, chancellor of the commune. By 1513 he was in Rome, where after the accession of Pope *Leo x he composed the *Osci et Vulsci dialogus ludis Romanis actus* (1513), a witty parody of the Latin style popularized by Giambattista *Pio. In Rome Accursio numbered among his friends the humanists Tommaso Pietrasanta, Giano Vitale, and Girolamo *Aleandro, and one of his poems was published in the collection entitled *Coryciana* (Rome: L. de Henricis and L. Perusinus 1524). However, his main interests were antiquarian and philological. It was Accursio who prepared a series of corrections appended to the *Epigrammata antiquae Urbis*, an anonymous publication often attributed to Francesco Albertini (Rome: J. Mazzocchi 1521). According to Roberto Weiss, Accursio's work set new standards for epigraphy.

Accursio accepted the post of majordomo, tutor, and guide to Johann Albrecht and Gumpbert von Hohenzollern, who had taken up residence in Rome to complete their education, and in 1522 he followed them in their travels to Poland and Germany. In 1523 they returned to Rome, where Accursio published his major philological work, the *Diatribae*, containing textual emendations of the works of Ausonius, Solinus, and Ovid's *Metamorphoses* (M. Argentei 1523). For the next ten years he remained in the service of the Hohenzollern princes, following them in their travels in France and Germany and in their visit to the court of *Charles v in Spain (1525-9). Around 1532 he left their service to find hospitality in the circle of Anton *Fugger in Augsburg. In this city he edited the histories of Ammianus Marcellinus (S. Otmar 1533), with a dedication to Fugger, and the *Variarum epistolarum libri xii* and the *De anima* of Cassiodorus (H. Steiner 1533). In 1533 he returned to Italy. Having settled at Aquila, Accursio served in the government of the commune, returning to Germany three times on its business, in 1538, 1540-1, and 1544-5. Late in life he married

Caterina Lucentini Piccolomini, by whom he had a son, Casmiro, who died in 1563.

In a letter of 5 June 1533 Johann *Koler informed Erasmus about the work of Accursio on Ammianus Marcellinus and Cassiodorus, adding that the Italian intended to depart for Venice and Aquila (Ep 2814). Accursio's departure may have been prompted by recent religious turmoil in Augsburg, in which Anton Fugger, his patron, was indicted for his role in a riot on the feast of the Ascension, on 22 May (Epp 2818, 2845). Erasmus stated that he did not know whether Accursio had encouraged Fugger's intransigence (Ep 2818). By August Accursio was in Padua, where he suggested to *Viglius Zuichemus that Fugger might be following him to Italy (Ep 2854).

Accursio's epigraphic studies, including those left in manuscript form, were utilized by Lodovico Antonio Muratori in the compilation of his *Novus thesaurus veterum inscriptionum* (Milan 1739–63). Accursio's work was used in a more systematic fashion by Theodor Mommsen, Wilhelm Henzen, and Emil Hübner in the preparation of the *Corpus inscriptionum latinarum* (Berlin 1862–1931). After Accursio's death, his unpublished epigraphical and philological studies amounted to seven volumes, two of which were obtained by Gian Vincenzo Pinelli and were subsequently acquired by Cardinal Federico Borromeo for the Biblioteca Ambrosiana.

BIBLIOGRAPHY: Allen Ep 2854 / A. Campana in DBI I 126–32 / A. De Angeli 'L'umanista Mariangelo Accursio e le diatribe in Ovidium' *Bollettino della società di storia patria A.L. Antinori negli Abruzzi* 5 (1893) 170–204 / L. Ferrari *Onomasticon* (Milan 1947) 3 / P. Lehmann *Eine Geschichte der alten Fuggerbibliotheken* (Tübingen 1956–60) I 11, 20 / Esther Pastorello *Epistolario manuziano* (Florence 1957) Epp 1145, 1152, 1376, 1649 / Julius Pflug *Correspondance* ed J.V. Pollet (Leiden 1969–) I Ep 75 / Roberto Weiss *The Renaissance Discovery of Classical Antiquity* (Oxford 1969) 81, 153–4, and passim

DANILO AGUZZI-BARBAGLI

Georg ACHTSYNIT, ACHTZNICHT *See Georgius AMELIUS*

Ursula ADLER of Augsburg, documented c 1512–c 1542

Ursula was the daughter of Phillipp Adler, who had moved from Speyer to Augsburg in the early 1480s and who in 1522 ranked among those who paid the highest taxes in Augsburg. By 1512 she married Jakob *Villinger and had one son by him, Karl *Villinger, who survived his father (Ep 2497). Soon after Jakob's death she married Johann *Löble (Ep 2256), probably in January 1530. Löble assisted her in her dispositions concerning Villinger's house 'zum Walfisch' at Freiburg and his estate 'Heilig Kreuz' near Colmar (Ep 2497), which she sold to the city of Colmar in 1536. Löble died in 1536, and until 1542 his widow was involved in attempts to secure repayment of loans he had made to King *Ferdinand. Her likeness is on the stained-glass windows which she and Jakob Villinger presented to the cathedral of Freiburg in 1524.

BIBLIOGRAPHY: Clemens Bauer 'Jakob Villinger ... Ein Umriss' *Syntagma Friburgense ... Hermann Aubin dargebracht* (Lindau-Constance 1956) 9–28, esp 14–15 / G. von Pölnitz *Anton Fugger* (Tübingen 1958–) II 569, and passim / F. Geiges *Der mittelalterliche Fensterschmuck des Freiburger Münsters* (Freiburg 1931) 117–18 (with illustrations)

PGB

Pope ADRIAN VI 2 March 1454– 14 September 1523

Adriaan Floriszoon, the future pope, was born in Utrecht. His father, Florens Boeyens, was apparently a shipwright. He died early but left to his widow, Geertruid, sufficient means for Adrian to receive a good education. After attending the Latin school in Utrecht he went to a school of the Brethren of the Common Life, perhaps in Zwolle, and thus was introduced to the ideals of *devotio moderna*. At the age of seventeen Adrian entered the University of Louvain, matriculating on 1 June 1476; in 1478 he obtained his MA, on 1 August 1490 a licence in theology, and on 18 or 21 June 1491 a doctorate. He was thus ready to begin his teaching career in the theological faculty. In the same year he entered the priesthood.

Adrian was rector of the university from 28 February to 31 August 1493 and from 31

Pope Adrian VI

August 1500 to 28 February 1501. As dean of St Peter's, Louvain, from 1497, he was also chancellor of the university. He drew income from his canonry of St Peter's and the chaplaincy of the *béguinage* in Louvain, the parish of Goedereede in South Holland (from 1492), a vicarship of St Peter's in Utrecht, and further prebends at the Utrecht cathedral chapter (from 1505), St Mary's, Utrecht, and elsewhere. These multiple benefices provided him with a handsome income as well as with pastoral duties, which he took seriously. In 1502 he founded in Louvain a college for indigent students of theology, later to be known as Pope's College, which was headed by Godschalk *Rosemondt.

Adrian's theological views are determined by the Thomist concept of finality. His *Quaestiones quodlibeticae* and his commentary on the fourth book of Peter Lombard's *Sentences* show points of affinity as well as contrast with Thomas Aquinas and his school but also contain ideas derived from John Duns Scotus, William of Ockham, and the early Fathers. His eclecticism shows critical judgment. A predominant concern with moral theology prompted him to focus on the tension between divine and human law. Here he saw his opportunity for contributing to the sacramental life of the church: law, morality, and dogma were viewed in perspective, each sphere having equal importance in the treatment of a particular question. The treatment, too, followed scholastic tradition and reflected his thorough knowledge of the *Corpus iuris canonici* and its numerous commentaries.

The favourable judgment passed on Adrian by his students shows his efficiency as a teacher and his ability to generate new interest in traditional scholastic approaches to both theological and philosophical questions. When Nicolas *Ruistre, bishop of Arras, founded a new undergraduate college at Louvain for poor students from his diocese, he entrusted its direction to his friend Adrian. Another close friend was Jérôme de *Busleyden, the founder of the Collegium Trilingue, which was to have a generous patron in Adrian. Juan Luis *Vives praised his academic work and saw in him one of the great restorers of the church. Adrian also had close connections with Jan *Briart of Ath, who took over the direction of the theological faculty after Adrian's departure for Spain in 1515. Among his students were Gabriël van der Muyden, Albert *Pigghe, Jan *Driedo, Gerard *Morinck, and Ruard *Tapper.

When Erasmus came to Louvain in the autumn of 1502 Adrian persuaded the magistrate of the city to offer him a lectureship at the university, but Erasmus declined the offer (Ep 171). Later Erasmus indicated that he attended Adrian's lectures in theology and admired his integrity (Ep 1304). Perhaps one may conclude that a certain familiarity existed between them.

In 1507 the Emperor *Maximilian I appointed Adrian tutor of the future *Charles v. Adrian's influence on the boy was considerable. From 1512 on he was a councillor to Charles, and in 1515 he joined the council of *Margaret of Austria. In October 1515 he was sent to King *Ferdinand II of Aragon to secure his consent to Charles' succession in Aragon as well as Castile. His success in these negotiations was facilitated by his friendship with Cardinal *Jiménez, who also introduced him to the movement for ecclesiastical reform in

Spain. After Ferdinand's death on 23 January 1516 Charles was proclaimed king on 13 March. He instructed Adrian and Cardinal Jiménez to represent him and govern Spain until his arrival. On 18 August 1516 Adrian was appointed bishop of Tortosa and on 14 November 1516 inquisitor of Aragon, probably on Jiménez's recommendation. From 4 March 1518 he was also inquisitor of Castile. On 1 July 1517 Pope *Leo x created him cardinal at Charles' request.

Adrian did not attend the conclave after Leo's death, and his election to the papacy on 9 January 1522 was unexpected. However, he accepted on 9 February and took the name of Adrian vi, resigning the regency at the same time. His departure for Rome was delayed until August, partly because the transfer of his administrative powers proved difficult, but also for lack of funds, since it was thought necessary to assemble a whole fleet to take him to Italy. On 28 August he arrived in Rome and was crowned at St Peter's on 31 August, notwithstanding the presence of plague in the city.

Erasmus' contacts with Adrian had apparently ceased when the latter left Louvain. His remarks concerning Adrian's progress in Spain are cool (Epp 608, 713, 969), and even as Adrian ascended the papal throne he wondered in what direction his former friend would be moving (Ep 1311). He did congratulate and praise him publicly, however, by dedicating to the new pope his edition of Arnobius (Epp 1304, 1310). Adrian was delighted and, according to Erasmus, offered to find him a benefice in return, but Erasmus declined (Ep 1416; Allen I 43). Adrian also repeatedly invited him to Rome (Epp 1324, 1352). Erasmus assured his readers and correspondents that the pope, himself an eminent theologian, appreciated the New Testament edition so much that he had asked Erasmus to render the same service for the Old Testament (Epp 1571, 1581) and also claimed that Adrian had helped to silence his critics in Louvain (Epp 1331, 1342, 1581; Allen I 25).

Adrian's pontificate coincided with great political and religious upheavals. He tried to preserve the independence of the papacy amid a Franco-Spanish war and even to mediate between Charles v and *Francis I. Mean-while the Turkish threat grew, and on 21 December 1522 Rhodes was captured by the Ottoman armies, Belgrade having been lost the preceding year. Adrian's response was the bull *Monet nos* (30 April 1523), which attempted to restore the peace and unity of Christendom with threats of excommunication and interdict. But all it did was cause a breach with France. While the pro-French Cardinal Francesco *Soderini was kept under arrest, in a consistory of 29 July 1523 a large majority of cardinals advocated a protective alliance against France. On 3 August 1523 Adrian therefore joined an anti-French league with Charles v, *Henry viii, and Venice, believing that it was defensive in nature. Though gravely ill, he lived to see the renewal of hostilities in Italy.

Adrian died on 14 September 1523 and was buried initially in St Peter's. On 1 August 1533 his remains were transferred to the German church, Santa Maria dell' Anima. The funeral inscription epitomized his life: 'Alas, how much it matters in what times a man, albeit the best, must prove his skills.'

While Adrian's political endeavours failed, he contributed significantly to the advent of church reform. Amid the derision and disdain with which the Roman populace had greeted the Dutchman's election, he set out to reorient the papacy from the secular direction it had taken under his predecessors. To do so, he called for support and advice, and he received both. Erasmus, for one, expressed in two letters to Adrian his hopes that the pope would be able to restore peace and unity (Epp 1304, 1329). These hopes are also reflected in other letters (Epp 1273, 1284) and were shared by Erasmus' friends Cornelis *Gerard of Gouda and Juan Luis Vives. Gerard's *Apocalypsis* and Vives' memorandum of October 1522 are good examples of the recurrent demands for an ecumenical council and curial reform. Suggestions for reform also came from cardinals *Campeggi, *Schiner, and *Cajetanus, from Zaccaria Ferreri, and from Johann Weidemann, dean of St Mary's, Erfurt. The expectations were great, but proposals for concrete action diverged widely.

Adrian did not call a council. He saw reform at the top as his first task and made it clear that he was determined to end corruption and malpractice in the curial hierarchy. Adrian's plans were clearly formulated in the instructions to Francesco *Chierigati, his legate to the diet of Nürnberg. Adrian envisaged gradual reform, but his acknowledgment of Rome's failings and his assurances of goodwill brought no tangible results. The suspicion and hatred felt for Rome among the estates of the Empire was too great. Promises of reform from the top had often been made and never fulfilled. At least Adrian had a clear concept of the necessity of reform, although an unfortunate combination of circumstances prevented the execution of his plans.

In Luther and his followers he saw not reformers but destroyers of the unity of the church. As a cardinal in Spain he had demanded a detailed review of the new doctrine. He pressed for the implementation of the edict of Worms, and his further action against the growing Lutheran movement followed the same line. Adrian considered intellectual dispute the only correct means of dealing with the situation and asked Erasmus to write against Luther (Ep 1324), although he realized that the dispute was no longer a theological issue but was being carried on by the laity. Most likely as the result of a visit from Johannes *Fabri, the pope's special emissary, Erasmus felt encouraged to advise Adrian of his views on the best response to the new gospel. Erasmus' letter (Ep 1352) is only extant in fragments; important sections were deleted when the letter was first published. It shows, however, that he did not think the pope capable of getting to the root of the problem and remedying all corrupt church practices and that he considered this task also beyond the powers of the theologians. Adrian's reaction is not known. Despite the invitations extended to Erasmus and others, the pope was unable to draw the leading lights to Rome; on the contrary, important men left the city. The exception was Johann *Eck, who had come to Rome on business with the curia and thus was able to consult extensively with the pope on matters to do with reform. It is likely that he influenced Adrian in some measure. Although Adrian's pontificate was short, its significance is undisputed today.

Adrian's works include the *Quaestiones quodlibeticae*, reflecting academic disputations

at Louvain in the years 1488–1507. At the urging of Adrian's former students, they were edited by Maarten van *Dorp (Louvain: D. Martens 1515). The *Quaestiones in quartum Sententiarum librum* were based on Adrian's lectures on Peter Lombard and probably composed in the years 1499–1509 (Paris: J. Bade 1516, not revised by Adrian). His commentary on Proverbs 1–13:6 is preserved in manuscript in the library of the seminary of Mechelen, together with theological orations, sermons, and occasional papers.

BIBLIOGRAPHY: Allen Ep 171 / J. Coppens in NBW III 5–19 / NNBW I 25–9 / Pastor IX 1–230 / P. Berglar 'Die kirchliche und politische Bedeutung des Pontifikats Hadrians VI.' *Archiv für Kulturgeschichte* 54 (1972) 97–112 / P. Brachin 'Adrien VI et la devotio moderna' *Etudes germaniques* 14 (1959) 97–105 / C. Burmannus *Hadrianus Sextus sive analecta historica de Hadriano Sexto* (Utrecht 1727) / 'Célébration du cinquième centenaire de la naissance du pape Adrien VI' *Ephemerides theologicae Lovanienses* 35 (1959) 513–629 / J. Coppens *Paus Adriaan VI en zijn stichting te Leuven* (Louvain 1959) / A. Delvigne *Le pape Adrien VI: Sa vie et ses écrits* (Brussels 1862) / M. von Domarus 'Die Quellen zur Geschichte des Papstes Hadrian VI.' *Historisches Jahrbuch der Görres-Gesellschaft* 16 (1895) 70–91 / K.-H. Ducke *Das Verständnis von Amt und Theologie im Briefwechsel zwischen Hadrian VI. und Erasmus von Rotterdam* (Leipzig 1973) / K.-H. Ducke *Handeln zum Heil: Eine Untersuchung zur Morallehre Hadrians VI.* (Leipzig 1976) / C. von Höfler *Papst Adrian VI.* (Vienna 1880) / P. Kalkoff 'Hadrian VI. und Erasmus von Rotterdam' *Archiv für Reformationsgeschichte* 5 (1908) 313–14 / P. Kalkoff 'Kleine Beiträge zur Geschichte Hadrians VI.' *Historisches Jahrbuch der Görres-Gesellschaft* 39 (1919) 31–72 / A. Mercati *Dall' Archivio Vaticano* II: *Diarii di consistori del pontificato di Adriano VI* (Rome 1951) / R.E. McNally 'Pope Adrian VI (1522–23) and church reform' *Archivium Historiae Pontificiae* 7 (1969) 253–85 / G. Moringus *Vita Hadriani Sexti pontificis maximi* (Louvain 1536) / *Paus Adrianus VI. Herdenkingstentoonstelling: Gedenkboek, Catalogus* ed J. Coppens and M.E. Houtzager (Utrecht-Louvain 1959) / G. Pasolini *Adriano VI* (Rome 1913) / J. Posner *Der deutsche Papst Adrian VI.* (Recklinghausen 1962) / R.R. Post 'Paus Adriaan VI.' *Ephemerides*

Theologicae Lovanienses 35 (1959) 524–33 / R.R.
Post 'Studiën over Adriaan VI' *Archief voor de
geschiedenis van de katholieke kerk in Nederland* 3
(1961) 121–61 / E.H.J. Reusens *Syntagma doc-
trinae theologicae Adriani Sexti* (Louvain 1862) /
E. Rodocanachi 'La jeunesse d'Adrien VI'
Revue historique 56 (1931) 300–6 / J. Wensing
Het leven van Adriaan VI (Utrecht 1870)

K.-H. DUCKE

ADRIANUS documented November 1498–
January 1501
Adrianus was a messenger who carried a
number of letters exchanged between Jacob
*Batt in Tournehem and Erasmus in Paris and
Orléans (Epp 80, 95, 101, 130, 133). In April
1500 there was some question of sending him
to England (Ep 124). Erasmus' last reference to
him indicates extreme dissatisfaction (Ep 146).
BIBLIOGRAPHY: Allen and CWE Ep 80 / Bierlaire *Familia* 46

FRANZ BIERLAIRE

ADRIANUS (Epp 163, 165, of July–August
1501)
No sources have come to light which would
permit the identification of Adrianus, a resident of Saint-Omer. Erasmus' letters show
that he had ties with the Franciscan community of his town; twice Erasmus associates his
name with that of Jean *Vitrier, the warden of
the Saint-Omer monastery (Epp 163, 165). It is
unlikely, however, that Adrianus was himself
a friar since he was in a position to take young
*Ludovicus into his household (Epp 166, 167)
and to invite Erasmus to stay with him (Ep
163). It appears more likely that he was a
respected citizen, perhaps a bookseller (Epp
166, 168), and evidently a man of culture and
piety (Epp 167, 168). Whether or not he was a
tertiary of St Francis, he evidently belonged to
the small circle of mystical inspiration which
flourished at Saint-Omer under the spiritual
leadership of Vitrier.
BIBLIOGRAPHY: Allen and CWE Ep 166

ANDRÉ GODIN

ADRIANUS (Ep 652) *See Arnold* VYNCK

Matthaeus ADRIANUS documented 1501–21
Matthaeus Adrianus, a baptized Jew of Spanish origin, is first documented in 1501, when

he published his Hebrew grammar in Venice
(reprinted there in 1508 and 1512 and in Basel
in 1518 and 1520). In Italy he studied medicine. He laid claim to a medical doctorate when
he wrote from Strasbourg to Johann *Amerbach (AK I Ep 477, 31 January 1513), offering
his services as a Hebraist for the edition of
Jerome and announcing his intention to visit
Venice after Easter for a pilgrimage to the
Holy Land. He also sent his Hebrew translation of some prayers, recently published in
Tübingen (*Libellus hora faciendi pro Domino*, T.
Anshelm 1513), inviting Amerbach to reprint
it. Finally he enclosed recommendations by
*Reuchlin and *Pellicanus, both of whom he
claimed as his students. Subsequently he must
have gone to Basel, where he gave Hebrew
lessons to the *Amerbach sons (AK II Ep 654,
VIII Ep 654a). He was also the teacher of
Wolfgang Faber *Capito (Epp 731, 797, 798,
877), who came to Basel in 1515, but their
association may have predated Capito's arrival
there; at any rate there is no evidence to
suggest either that Erasmus met Adrianus
during his first visit to Basel (1514–15) or that
Adrianus had any part in editing Jerome.
Around 1514 Adrianus was in Heidelberg and
taught his language to Johannes *Oecolampadius and Johann *Brenz.
    Later Adrianus was practising medicine in
Middelburg when he was called to Louvain in
the autumn of 1517 to be the first professor of
Hebrew in the newly founded Collegium
Trilingue. Erasmus thought highly of his
knowledge of Hebrew and appears to have
been the driving force behind his appointment
(Epp 686, 687, 689–91, 699); he was pleased to
announce the appointment (formalized in
February 1518) to his friends in France, England, Germany, and Spain (Epp 707, 721, 722,
731, 777, 794). Although he was successful as
a teacher, Adrianus left Louvain suddenly at
the end of July 1519. He later presented his
departure as the consequence of an oration in
defence of the three languages which he had
given on 21 March and which was in fact
bound to displease the conservative theologians of Louvain. Published by Johann Rhau-
Grunenberg at Wittenberg in 1520, the oration
was edited by Henry de Vocht in CTL I 533–43.
On the other hand, Erasmus reported that
Adrianus had left Middelburg with heavy

debts and needed an advance on his salary in Louvain (Epp 732A, 798); *Dorp hinted at the inadequacy of his salary in Louvain and described him as close-fisted and suspicious (Ep 852); and Capito and others accused him of entanglement in cabbalistic magic (Ep 798) – all of which was bound to cause friction.

Erasmus was amused by Adrianus (Ep 798) but consulted him during his illness in the autumn of 1518, and at Easter of the same year he had met Edward *Lee at Adrianus' dinner table (Epp 876, 1061; *Opuscula* 243). He lost touch with him, however, when Adrianus left Louvain. Adrianus appeared in Wittenberg in October or November 1519, applying for a teaching position. He obtained an appointment eventually, but negotiations were not completed until 16 April 1520. As early as the autumn of that year he quarrelled with Martin *Luther, who complained to *Spalatinus (w *Briefwechsel* II Ep 351), and in February 1521 Adrianus resigned and left, to Luther's relief (w *Briefwechsel* II Ep 377). His movements thereafter are not known. When Adrianus went to Louvain he left a wife behind in Middelburg (Ep 691). Another marriage, at Wittenberg, is mentioned in w *Briefwechsel* II Ep 299.

BIBLIOGRAPHY: Allen and CWE Ep 686 / de Vocht CTL I 241–56, 369–75, 533–43 / AK I Ep 477, VIII Ep 654a / NDB I 87 / *Matrikel Wittenberg* I 90 / *Index Aureliensis* (Baden-Baden 1962–) I 74–5 / Luther w *Briefwechsel* I Epp 217, 218 / *Correspondance de Nicolas Clénard* ed A. Roersch (Brussels 1940–1) Ep 2 and notes

IG & PGB

AEGIDIUS *See* GILLIS

Aemilius de AEMILIIS *See Emiglio de'* MIGLI

Paulus AEMILIUS *See Paolo* EMILIO

AENEAS SYLVIUS *See Pope* PIUS II

Adriaan AERNOUT d November 1536
Aernout (Arnoldi, Arnout) made his profession at the Carmelite monastery of Bruges, possibly as early as 1483. He matriculated at the University of Louvain on 3 July 1504 and received the degree of bachelor of theology in 1507. On 18 September 1517 he was appointed to the titular see of Rhosus in Cilicia and succeeded Jean *Briselot as suffragan bishop of Cambrai in 1520. In Ep 1040 of 1519 Erasmus counted Aernout as one of the most active opponents of Martin *Luther, and to a lesser degree of himself, in the Netherlands.

BIBLIOGRAPHY: Allen and CWE Ep 1040 / *Matricule de Louvain* III-1 277 / de Vocht CTL I 434 / de Vocht *Busleyden* 321 / Eubel III 287

CFG & PGB

Jan AERTS of Nossegem, d 27 September 1537
Jan Aerts (Arnoldi) of Nossegem, between Brussels and Louvain, joined the congregation of Augustinian eremites of St Maartensdal at Louvain in 1487. He was elected the eighth prior on 2 January 1493 and served until 1497, when he retired because of ill health. He then became rector to a convent of nuns at Bethany, near Sint-Pieters-Leeuw, south-west Brussels. He returned to St Maartensdal and was re-elected the eleventh prior on 18 January 1509. He restored discipline, built a new infirmary, and made other general improvements. He came to be known as Prior 'Platteborse' because of his constant need for money and eventually died in office, leaving St Maartensdal in good order and flourishing.

Maarten *Lips, who was Aerts' friend, maintained contacts between him and Erasmus; two of Erasmus' letters to Lips (Epp 1190, 1547) acknowledged receipt of a token gift from the prior. Aerts may also be the recipient of a letter from Erasmus in 1531 (Ep 2587).

BIBLIOGRAPHY: Allen Ep 1190 / de Vocht CTL I 377 / *Monasticon Windeshemense* ed W. Kohl et al (Brussels 1976) 155, 159

CFG

Wolfgang von AFFENSTEIN d by March 1556
Wolfgang von Affenstein was descended from an old and well-respected noble family of the Rhineland. His parents were Oswald von Affenstein and Noppurg Horneck von Homberg. In about 1507 Affenstein married Margarete, duchess of Zimmern, who died by Easter 1513. Later Dorothe Kistler von Dürckheim became his second wife. From these marriages sprang five children. Affenstein had useful connections to the imperial court,

where his brother-in-law, Johannes Naves, was the vice-chancellor. This helped him to overcome an initial animosity on the part of the Zimmern family, which resented the inferior rank of Margarete's husband. Thereafter Affenstein repeatedly came to the aid of the Zimmern family in legal disputes. He had a house in Dirmstein, south-west of Worms, and lived there unless he was called away in the service of the Palatine dynasty.

As of 14 October 1510 Affenstein is listed as a doctor and procurator and as of 29 January 1522 as an advocate at the Reichskammergericht, the imperial court of justice (although his name is omitted from the lists of 1511 and 1523). In 1512, 1515, 1517, and 1534 his name appears in connection with several law suits that he conducted. In 1521 he was present at the diet of Worms. He also attended the diet of Nürnberg from January to March 1524 as councillor of the Palatinate and was a member of the commission on constitutional matters.

In July 1524 Affenstein went to Utrecht as an official of the new bishop, Henry, count *Palatine, who also held the see of Worms. As Henry's representative he attended the diet of Speyer in 1526 and the diet of Augsburg in 1530. As steward of the bishop of Worms in Ladenburg, Affenstein reorganized the library of Johann von *Dalberg (Ep 1774). In December 1526 he was approached by his physician, Theobald *Fettich, on behalf of Erasmus and was asked to supply a Greek manuscript to Hieronymus *Froben (Ep 1767). This manuscript was translated and published by Erasmus under the title *Fragmentum commentariorum Originis in Evangelium secundum Matthaeum* (Basel 1527, Ep 1844). On 13 June 1527 Affenstein wrote to Louis v, elector *Palatine, and asked him to take steps against Anabaptist preachers in Worms. When Henry surrendered Utrecht to *Charles v, Affenstein was called upon to explain the reasons for the surrender. The future elector *Palatine, Frederick II, who was elected by the German estates commander of their forces against the Turks at the diets of Speyer in 1529 and Regensburg in 1532, appointed Affenstein to his military council. On 23 September 1531 he represented the Elector Louis in the negotiations at Schmalkalden (2–3 September 1531). On Louis' behalf he also negotiated at Geln-

hausen (17–22 May 1534) with the councillors of *Ferdinand I about Württemberg. In 1535 Affenstein and Wilhelm von Renneberg were sent to Bremen by Queen *Mary of Hungary and Count Frederick. There and subsequently in Lüneburg (12 October 1535) he negotiated with the cities of Lübeck, Rostock, Stralsund, and Wismar about financial and military aid for the count of Oldenburg and also presented the claims of Frederick II to the throne of Denmark.

In 1538 Affenstein was a member of the government of the Upper Palatinate established by Frederick II, which had its seat in Neumarkt. On behalf of the Palatine elector Affenstein attended the diet of Speyer in February 1542. In 1545 he explained to the chapter of Worms that the court of Heidelberg rejected their complaints about communion services in the Protestant fashion. After the death of Cardinal Albert of *Brandenburg (24 September 1545) Affenstein represented Frederick II in negotiations over the succession to the archsee of Mainz and, against his own convictions, joined the councillors of Landgrave Philip of *Hesse in supporting Sebastian of Heusenstamm. When the Schmalkaldic League met in Frankfurt in December 1545 Affenstein was sent there to discuss the accession of the Palatinate, but the matter remained unresolved. In April 1546 Affenstein attended the diet of the Palatine estates at Heidelberg and tried with little success to argue the views of the Catholic party. In July 1546 he was dispatched to reassure Charles v about Frederick II's attitude towards the Schmalkaldic League. At the diet of Augsburg in 1548 he participated in the negotiations over the Interim, which he officially proclaimed before the assembled estates of the Upper Palatinate at Amberg (15 July) and in the chancellery of Heidelberg castle for the Rhenish Palatinate (17 August). For a short while at least the country had thus been returned to the Catholic faith. In 1549 Affenstein was a judge of the Palatine Hofgericht and in 1552 a member of the elector's privy council. He carried out his last political function in 1552, when Frederick II sent him and two other councillors to negotiate with Alcibiades of Brandenburg, whose troops had invaded the Palatinate. In March 1556

Frederick II died and was succeeded by Otto Henry, elector *Palatine, who held Affenstein responsible for the loss of the chapter of Ellwangen. The old councillor was detained in his own house at Dirmstein and dismissed from the elector's service. He died a few days later under the impact of this harsh and unfair treatment and was buried in the family chapel at the monastery of Henau.

Only two of Affenstein's writings were published: a letter to Louis V (dated 3 June 1527) and another to Erasmus (Ep 1774).

BIBLIOGRAPHY: Allen Ep 1774 / *Zimmerische Chronik* ed K. Barack and P. Herrmann (Meersburg-Leipzig 1932) II 112–14 / Johannes Maximilian Humbracht *Die höchste Zierde Teutsch-Landes und Vortrefflichkeit des Teutschen Adels* (Frankfurt 1707) no 238 / Adolf Hasenclever 'Kurfürst Friedrich II. von der Pfalz und der schmalkaldische Bundestag zu Frankfurt vom Dezember 1545' *Zeitschrift für die Geschichte des Oberrheins* n s 18 (1903) 58–85, esp 65 / Konrad Braun *Annotata de personis iudicij camerae imperialis a primo illius exordio usque ad annum Domini 1556* (Ingolstadt 1557) / Johann Heinrich Harpprecht *Staats-Archiv des Kayserl. und des H. Römischen Reichs Kammer-Gerichts* III (Ulm 1759) / *Katalog der Handschriften der Universitätsbibliothek in Heidelberg* II: *Die deutschen Pfälzer Handschriften des 16. und 17. Jhd.* ed Jakob Wille (Heidelberg 1903) 25–6 / *Deutsche Reichstagsakten* Jüngere Reihe (Gotha-Göttingen 1893–) II and IV passim / 'Hendrik van Beijeren, Bisschop van Utrecht (1525–1528)' ed A.M.C. van Asch van Wijck in *Archief voor kerkelijke en wereldlijke geschiedenis van Nederland* (Utrecht 1853), esp 125 / *Quellen zur Geschichte der Täufer* IV: *Baden und Pfalz* ed Manfred Krebs (Gütersloh 1951) 114–15 / Cornelius Paulus Hoynck van Papendrecht *Analecta Belgica* (The Hague 1743) III-1 62, 64, 84 / Hubert Thomas Leodius *Annales Palatini* 2nd ed (Frankfurt 1665) 117, 156, 209, 282 / Ernst Joachim von Westphalen *Monumenta inedita rerum Germanicarum praecipue Cimbriacarum et Megapolitensium* (Leipzig 1734–45) III / Maximilian Weigel 'Ein Gutachten des Johann Agricola von Eisleben über das Interim (1548)' *Zeitschrift für bayerische Kirchengeschichte* 14 (1941) 33 / *Politische Correspondenz der Stadt Strassburg im Zeitalter der Reformation* II ed Otto Winckelmann (Strasbourg 1887) 560 and passim / Hans Rott

Friedrich II. von der Pfalz und die Reformation (Heidelberg 1904) 24 and passim / Horst Rabe *Reichsbund und Interim* (Cologne-Vienna 1971) 262, 418 / Max Steinmetz 'Die Politik der Kurpfalz unter Ludwig V.' (doctoral thesis, University of Freiburg 1942) I 77 / Sigmund von Herberstein *Selbstbiographie* in *Fontes rerum Austriacarum* I-1 (Vienna, 1855, repr 1969) 312

KONRAD WIEDEMANN

Henricus AFINIUS of Lier,
d before 23 August 1520
Henricus Afinius (a Fine, de Fine, van den Eynde) of Lier, near Antwerp, matriculated at the University of Louvain on 31 August 1499 to begin his course in the faculty of arts. He registered for a second time on 14 June 1507, probably as a student of medicine. By 1513 he was *archiater*, or town physician, of Antwerp, where he lived until his death. His wife's name was Anna Embrechts.

On 19 December 1516 in Louvain Afinius defended three academic theses, which he subsequently had printed as *Questiones tres* (Antwerp 1519, NK 42). A complimentary letter from Erasmus inserted in this volume (Ep 542) presents the earliest evidence of a connection between the two men. Perhaps in return for this service Afinius promised Erasmus some silver cups but then was in no hurry to send them, despite many indirect and direct reminders (Epp 616, 637, 638, 681, 712, 736, 753, 754). Erasmus in turn had promised to dedicate one of his works to Afinius, and a dedication of sorts (Ep 799) was eventually published with the *Encomium medicinae* (ASD I-4 165–86). Afinius was acquainted with Pieter *Gillis and the painter Quinten *Metsys. For the year 1518 he published an almanac, *La Grande Prenostication de Louvain* (NK 2249); a similar undertaking for the year 1533 and likewise attributed to Afinius must be considered apocryphal.

BIBLIOGRAPHY: Allen and CWE Ep 542 / de Vocht CTL II 25 / *Matricule de Louvain* III-1 191, 334 / H. Brabant *Erasme humaniste dolent* (Brussels 1971) 92 / P. Boeynaems 'Afinius, een Lierse arts en vriend van Erasmus' *Land van Ryen* 9 (1959) 3–17

MARCEL A. NAUWELAERTS

AFONSO prince of Portugal, 1509–16/21 April 1540

Dom Afonso was a son of King *Manuel I and his second wife, Maria of Castile, and thus a brother of King *John III. When Erasmus *Schets mentioned the king's brother who was very generous, learned, and fond of Damião de *Gois (Ep 3042), he was referring either to Afonso or, perhaps more likely, to his brother, *Henry, the future cardinal-king of Portugal.

Afonso was bishop of Evora, archbishop of Lisbon, and ultimately cardinal. He had as a teacher the famous humanist Aires Barbosa, who had studied with *Poliziano in Italy. In his *Encomium* of Erasmus (1531) André de *Resende assured Erasmus that King John III and Dom Afonso were among his admirers. Not long before his death Afonso wrote a letter to Pietro *Bembo, congratulating him on his appointment to the college of cardinals. Gois, who had known Bembo well during his residence in Italy, may have been the intermediary between Afonso and Bembo.

BIBLIOGRAPHY: Eubel III 17, 191, 322 / Pietro Bembo *Epistolae familiares* book VI (Venice 1552) 379–80: Bembo's reply to Afonso, from Rome, 9 April 1541 / André de Resende *L'Itinéraire érasmien d'André de Resende* (Paris 1971) 60

ELISABETH FEIST HIRSCH

Hieronymus AGATHIUS *See Girolamo AIAZZA*

Augustijn AGGE of The Hague, fl 1510–25

Augustijn Agge (Aggeus), a native of The Hague, received a BA at Paris in 1506. By 1510 he was in London, where on 31 January he wrote the preface for an edition of Johannes de Burgo's *Pupilla oculi* (Paris: W. Hopyl 25 June 1510). Together with his friend Johannes *Sixtinus he returned to the Netherlands in the autumn of 1513 (cf Ep 511), taking along a letter from Erasmus to Jan *Becker (cf Ep 291). In Ep 511 Agge described himself to Erasmus as a 'physician,' so he must also have studied medicine somewhere. Allen was correct in dating Ep 511 in 1517, for it contains a reference to a mission which Agge undertook to negotiations at Cambrai, opened as a result of mediatory effort by the Parlement of Paris; on 15 November 1516 *Charles V authorized him and Arnold van Gruythuizen to represent him

there. In 1519 Agge carried a letter from Erasmus and Maarten van *Dorp's *Oratio in praelectionem divi Pauli* to Nicolas *Bérault in Paris (cf Ep 1024). On 6 November 1525 Karel van *Egmond sent him to *Henry VIII as his representative. Of his later life nothing is known. He was acquainted with Gerardus *Listrius and *Gozewijn of Halen; the later accused Agge of fraudulently keeping a copy of Suidas belonging to him.

BIBLIOGRAPHY: Allen Epp 291, 511, IV xxiii / M. van Rhijn *Studiën over Wessel Gansfort en zijn tijd* (Utrecht 1933) 151–2 / J.E.A.L. Struick *Gelre en Habsburg* (Utrecht 1960) 248

C.G. VAN LEIJENHORST

Georgius AGRICOLA of Glauchau, 24 March 1490–21 November 1555

Georgius Agricola (Bauer, Pawer) was born at Glauchau, north of Zwickau, Saxony. From 1514 to 1517 he studied the humanities and theology at the University of Leipzig, receiving a BA in 1515. In 1517 he went to Zwickau, where he at first taught in the existing town school but soon established a new Greek and Latin school. In 1520 in Leipzig he published a Latin grammar in which a text from Erasmus' translation of St Matthew was inserted for study. By 1522 Agricola was again at Leipzig, studying medicine under Heinrich *Stromer but also maintaining close contacts with the Greek scholar Petrus *Mosellanus. In 1523 he made his way to Italy, where he completed his medical training, although it is not known from which university he received his medical doctorate. In August 1525 he was in Padua and asked a fellow student, Leonard *Casembroot, to recommend him to Erasmus (Ep 1594). At that time he had joined John *Clement, Edward Wotton, and Thomas *Lupset, who along with other scholars were preparing texts for the Aldine first edition of Galen's collected works in Greek (1525).

After his return from Italy Agricola settled as a physician at Jáchymov (Joachimsthal), in the Bohemian Erz mountains, which was then at the peak of its importance as a mining centre. In 1526 or 1527 he married Anna Arnold, the widow of Matthias *Meyner. After her death Agricola married his second wife, Anna Schütz, in 1543. There is no indication that Agricola's practice of medicine was particularly

Johannes Agricola by Balthasar Jenichen

innovative; on the other hand, it may have been his pharmacological interests which initially prompted him to undertake a thorough study of metallurgy. The medical viewpoint is clearly discernible in his famous *Bermannus sive de re metallica* (Basel: H. Froben 1530). In September 1529 a manuscript of this dialogue was sent to Erasmus by Agricola's friend Petrus *Plateanus. Despite his profound admiration for the great scholar, the author himself had apparently not yet overcome his hesitation to approach Erasmus directly (Ep 2216). At this time he was in close contact with Andreas and Christoph von *Könneritz, good friends of Agricola, who were studying at Freiburg. But even without their recommendations Erasmus would not have been likely to miss the value and originality of the *Bermannus*. Froben printed the work at his suggestion together with Erasmus' letter to the Könneritz brothers (Ep 2274) and a dedicatory epistle addressed to their father by Plateanus.

Agricola was a loyal Catholic and as such was called back to his native country by Duke George of *Saxony, who in 1531 arranged for his appointment as town physician in Chemnitz

(Karl-Marx-Stadt). His knowledge of metallurgy permitted him to invest profitably in various mines and smelters. He prospered, and notwithstanding the advent of the Reformation in ducal Saxony, he was elected mayor of Chemnitz for the years 1546–7, 1551, and 1553. Meanwhile Agricola energetically pursued his scholarly work, and by March 1531, after some prodding, he had finally written to Erasmus. In his reply (Ep 2529) Erasmus offered to read the manuscript of Agricola's *De mensuris et ponderibus* (Basel: H. Froben and N. Episcopius 1533) and briefly characterized the authors of preceding works on that topic. In a letter written for publication (Ep 2803) Erasmus compared Agricola's work favourably with the studies of these same rivals, *Budé, *Alciati, and Leonardo de *Portis. In his last extant reply to Agricola in the spring of 1534 (Ep 2918), Erasmus evidently took up some topics covered in Agricola's letter, which is missing, mentioning a recent attack by *Luther and the names of *Egranus and *Witzel, with whose Erasmian outlook Agricola would have been able to identify.

In his dedicatory epistle to the *Bermannus* Plateanus wrote that Agricola had already collected a great deal of material towards further works on metallurgy. Eventually *De ortu et causis subterraneorum* (Basel 1546) was succeeded by his crowning achievement, *De re metallica* (1556), with its important illustrations that were used again for German and Italian versions of Agricola's great work (1557 and 1563 respectively). Among Agricola's medical works, *De peste* (1544) had a certain success. All of these were first printed in Basel (H. Froben and N. Episcopius). He also published an oration in support of the war against the Turks (German version, Dresden and Nürnberg 1531; Latin version, Basel 1538) and prepared a historical work on the Saxon dynasty, which, although completed in 1555, was not published until 1963.

BIBLIOGRAPHY: Allen Ep 1594 / NDB I 98–100 / ADB I 143–5 / *Dictionary of Scientific Biography* ed C.C. Gillispie (New York 1970–80) I 77–8 / Georg Agricola *Ausgewählte Werke* ed Hans Prescher (Berlin 1955–) / *Matrikel Leipzig* I 534, II 504 / Schottenloher I 4–5, VII 4–6 / *Index Aureliensis* (Baden-Baden 1962–) I 157–60
MICHAEL ERBE & PGB

Johannes AGRICOLA of Gunzenhausen,
1496–6 March 1570
Johannes Agricola (Peurle, Beuerle, Agricola
Ammonius), born in Gunzenhausen, in Middle
Franconia, south-west of Nürnberg, studied in
Ingolstadt from 1506 and, after extensive
travels, became professor of Greek (1515) and
of medicine (1531) there. He seems to have
remained in Ingolstadt until his death. He
published a work on pharmaceutical plants,
Medicinae herbariae libri duo (Basel: B. West-
heimer 1539), which is noteworthy for its
reliance on personal observation and for its
dedication to Anton *Fugger. This was
accompanied by his *Index copiosissimus simpli-
cium pharmacorum omnium* (Basel: [B. West-
heimer] 1539). Among his other works there
are translations of and commentaries on Greek
medical writers: *Hyppocratis aphorismorum et
sententiarum libri septem* (Ingolstadt 1537) and
*Commentarii novi in Galeni libros sex de locis
affectis* (Nürnberg: J. Petreius 1537). For his
*Scholia copiosa in therapeuticum methodum, id est,
absolutissimam Claudii Galeni Pergameni curandi
artem* (Augsburg: P. Ulhart 1534) Erasmus
wrote a preface, Ep 2803, referring to Matthias
*Kretz as a common acquaintance.
    BIBLIOGRAPHY: Allen Ep 2803 / NDB I 100 /
Index Aureliensis (Baden-Baden 1962–   ) I 171
                                                    IG

Rodolphus AGRICOLA of Baflo, 17 February
1444–27 October 1485
Rodolphus Agricola (Roelof or Rudolf Huus-
man or Huisman) was born at Baflo, near
Groningen, on the very day that Hendrik Vries
(d 1480), whose natural son he was, became
abbot of the neighbouring Benedictine house
of Selwert. His mother, Zycka, later married
and gave birth to his beloved half-brother,
Johannes. Agricola probably received his early
education at St Martin's, the school of the
Brethren of the Common Life in Groningen,
and from 27 March 1454 was financially
supported by a prebend from the bishop of
Münster. On 1 May 1456 he matriculated at
Erfurt, in the same semester as Rudolf von
*Langen, who became his friend. After
receiving his BA in 1458, Agricola chose to
continue his studies at Cologne, where he
matriculated on 20 May 1462, again in the
faculty of arts. From Cologne he went to

Rodolphus Agricola by Theodor Stimmer

Louvain, where he took his MA in 1465, being
first in arts.
    At the age of twenty-four Agricola travelled
to Italy. He stayed at Pavia from 1468/9 until
1474, returning to the Netherlands in the
winter of 1471 and in 1474 to visit his father;
during one of his trips north he instructed
Alexander *Hegius, later Erasmus' teacher, in
Greek. He also delivered at least three orations
– on 1 July of the years 1471, 1473, and 1474 – to
honour the new rectors, Matthias Richilus,
Paul de Baenst, and Johann von *Dalberg. He
then moved to Ferrara, where he was organist
in the court of Duke Ercole I d'Este. Here he
translated many works from Greek into Latin –
he was once even credited with Erasmus'
translations of Euripides (Epp 3008, 3032) –
and he inaugurated the academic year 1476–7
with his famous *Oratio in laudem philosophiae et
reliquarum artium*.
    Agricola returned to Germany in 1479,
spending some time at Dillingen, where he
completed his most important work, the *De
inventione dialectica* (Deventer: J. Le Febre n d),
an influential study of the proper place of logic
in rhetorical studies. He then returned to

Groningen, where he was appointed town secretary (*scriba et orator*), which gave him ample opportunity to travel and to make and renew friendships. He regularly met Wessel *Gansfort, Hegius, Antoon Vrije (see *Gang), and other men of learning at the abbey of Aduard. At Deventer he published the dialogue *Axiochus* (R. Pafraet c 1480) and the poem *Anna mater* (R. Pafraet 1483), mentioned by Erasmus in Ep 145. Agricola was not at that time content with his position at Groningen, although he declined several attractive offers of employment elsewhere. After much delay he decided to join Johann von Dalberg, then bishop of Worms, at Heidelberg, where he arrived on 2 May 1484. Here he lectured and participated in disputations at the university, learnt Hebrew (LB V 79A), and wrote *De formando studio* (1484), a defence of humanistic studies in the form of a letter to his friend Jacobus Barbirianus. He also delivered an *Exhortatio ad clerum Wormatiensem* and, at Christmas 1484, an oration *De nativitate sive immensa natalis diei Iesu Christi laetitia*. In 1485 he accompanied Dalberg to Rome, where he composed the oration which the bishop delivered before Innocent VIII on 6 July. On the return journey Agricola fell ill; he died at Heidelberg of the quartan fever and, as Erasmus recalled in the colloquy *Exequiae seraphicae* (ASD I-3 689), was buried in the Franciscan habit. Ermolao (I) *Barbaro composed an epitaph for him (Ep 174).

When he was about twelve years old, Erasmus saw Agricola at Deventer (Allen I 2). Years later Philippus *Melanchthon asserted that Agricola predicted Erasmus' great future, while in recent times Preserved Smith has argued that Agricola heard Erasmus recite his *Bucolicum carmen* (Reedijk poem 1). In fact neither story seems true, for in his letter to Johann von *Botzheim Erasmus stated that he saw Agricola and nothing more than that happened (Allen I 2). Nevertheless, Erasmus admired Agricola, calling him the first to bring a breath of better literature from Italy, and eulogizing him in *Adagia* I iv 39. He rarely mentioned Agricola without due praise (Epp 23, 480, 1237, 2073; *Ciceronianus* ASD I-2 682–3) and purchased a number of his works (Epp 174, 184, 311), keeping several of these in his library until he died (F. Husner *Gedenkschrift*

zum 400. Todestage, Basel 1936, 238, 242). Although he once remarked in passing that he owed nothing to Agricola (*Spongia* LB X 1666A), Erasmus used his translations from the Greek in preparing Eucherius of Lyon's letter to Valerianus and an exhortation of Isocrates for his edition of Cato's *Disticha moralia* (Louvain: D. Martens 1517; NK 535; Epp 676, 677), and he used Agricola's handwritten notes to his copy of the Treviso Seneca (1478) when he produced his second edition of Seneca's works (Basel: H. Froben March 1529) (Ep 2056, 2091, 2108). His only clear citation of Agricola occurs in the *De contemptu mundi* (ASD V-1 56).

Erasmus was at one time prepared to assist Matthias *Schürer in editing works by Agricola (Epp 612, 633) and later encouraged *Haio Herman, a relative of Agricola, to undertake the project (Ep 1978). In 1528 Erasmus published Agricola's first Pavia oration with the *De pronuntiatione* and *Ciceronianus* (Basel: H. Froben). Three years after Erasmus' death *Alaard of Amsterdam published the standard edition of Agricola's works in two volumes (Cologne: J. Gymnich 1539; repr 1975) This respectable achievement was supplemented in recent times from the Stuttgart manuscript (Württembergische Landesbibliothek *Cod. Poet. et Philol.* no 36), copied by order of two young friends of Agricola, Dietrich and Johann von Pleningen: his life of Petrarch was edited by Johannes Lindeboom in *Nederlandsch Archief voor Kerkgeschiedenis* n s 17 (1924) 93–106 and Ludwig Bertalot in *La Bibliofilia* 30 (1928–9) 382–404 (also in his *Studien zum ... Humanismus*, Rome 1975, II 1–29), and his *Exhortatio* by Lewis W. Spitz and Anna Benjamin in *Archiv für Reformationsgeschichte* 54 (1963) 1–15. The earliest accounts of Agricola's life are by the von Pleningens, *Gozewijn of Halen, Gerard *Geldenhouwer, and Melanchthon.

BIBLIOGRAPHY: Allen Ep 23 / J. Prinsen in NNBW IX 12–16 / ADB I 151–6 / M. Seidlmayer in NDB I 103–4 / P.S. Allen 'The letters of Rudolph Agricola' *English Historical Review* 21 (1906) 302–17 / *Matrikel Erfurt* I 255 / *Matrikel Köln* I 681 / K. Hartfelder 'Unedierte Briefe ...' in *Festschrift der Badischen Gymnasien* (Karlsruhe 1886) 1–36 / H.E.J.M. van der Velden *Rodolphus Agricola* (Leiden 1911) / M.A. Nauwelaerts *Rodolphus Agricola* (The Hague 1963) / L.W. Spitz *The Religious Renaissance of the German*

Humanists (Cambridge, Mass, 1963) 20–40 /
E.H. Waterbolk *Een hond in het bad* (Groningen
1966) / T.E. Mommsen 'Rudolf Agricola's Life
of Petrarch' *Traditio* 8 (1952) 367–86 / W.J. Ong
Ramus and Talon Inventory (Cambridge, Mass,
1958) 534–58 lists 53 editions of the *De
inventione dialectica* prior to 1590 / J.R. McNally
'An appraisal of Rudolph Agricola's *De
inventione dialectica*' (doctoral thesis, University
of Iowa 1966; cf *Dissertation Abstracts* 27 1966)
1465A-6A / J.R. McNally '*Prima pars dialecticae*:
the influence of Agricola's dialectic upon
English accounts of invention' *Renaissance
Quarterly* 21 (1968) 166–77 / Preserved Smith
Erasmus (New York-London 1923) 11

C.G. VAN LEIJENHORST

Henricus Cornelius AGRIPPA of Nettesheim, 14 September 1486–18 February 1535
Henricus Cornelius Agrippa was a son of
Heinrich, a citizen of Cologne. Although in
later life Agrippa claimed to be of a noble family
and styled himself 'von Nettesheim,' his
assumption of noble status appears to have
been unfounded, and Nettesheim was significant to him only as his father's town of origin.
On 22 July 1499 Agrippa matriculated at the
University of Cologne, studying law, medicine, and theology. Petrus Ravennas was the
most important of his teachers. In 1507 he
studied at Paris, where he may have been
known to Germain de *Brie and Symphorien
*Champier, and where he already demon-
strated a deep interest in magic and the occult.
In 1509, after a period of military service in
Catalonia, he appeared at Dole in the
Franche-Comté, lecturing on the *De verbo
mirifico*, a cabbalistic study by Johann *Reuchlin. Hoping to win the patronage of
*Margaret of Austria, regent of Netherlands
and of the Franche-Comté, he wrote the *De
nobilitate et praecellentia foeminei sexus declamatio*.
However he shelved this work – not published
until 1529 – and left Dole when the Franciscan
Jean Catilinet denounced him as a 'Judaizing
heretic.'

In 1510 Agrippa travelled to London, where
he studied the Pauline Epistles with John
*Colet. He returned to Cologne the same year,
holding theological disputations at the university. He also met Johannes *Trithemius, who
encouraged him to complete his *De occulta

Henricus Cornelius Agrippa

philosophia, a study of magic and esoteric
knowledge which circulated in manuscript for
many years. In 1511 Agrippa went to Italy as an
agent for the Emperor *Maximilian I, attending
the schismatic council of Pisa of 1511–12, and,
according to his own claim, winning knighthood on the battlefield. He also contacted
Italian intellectuals who continued the hermetic interests of Marsilio *Ficino and Giovanni *Pico della Mirandola, and gained
additional knowledge of hermetic literature
and of the Hebrew Cabbala, lecturing in these
subjects after 1515 at Pavia and Turin. In Italy
he wrote or drafted three short studies of the
role of the Cabbala in human knowledge: *De
triplici ratione cognoscendi Deum* (c 1516) and *De
originale peccato* (c 1518) – both first published
with *De nobilitate et praecellentia foeminei sexus
declamatio* (Antwerp: M. Hillen 1529) – and
Dialogus de homine (c 1516), edited by Paola
Zambelli in *Rivista critica di storia della filosofia* 13
(1958) 57–71.

By early 1518 Agrippa left Italy for the city of
Metz, where he obtained a post as public
advocate. However, he alienated the religious
orders by championing the French reformer

Jacques *Lefèvre d'Etaples in his pamphlet *De beatissimae Annae monogamia* (1519; published Cologne 1534) and by successfully defending a young girl charged with witchcraft. He moved to Geneva, where he became a physician, and from 1523 to 1524 he served as a town councillor and physician at Fribourg. In 1524 he went to the French court, then at Lyon, where he was a physician to the queen mother, Louise of *Savoy. In 1528 he moved to the Netherlands, where he failed to obtain a position as physician to Margaret of Austria but became court historian and archivist in 1530. In the same year Agrippa published his *De incertitudine et vanitate scientiarum atque artium declamatio* (Antwerp: J. Grapheus), a work in which he emphasized the tension between human knowledge and the word of God. In 1531 he published a revised first book of his *De occulta philosophia* (Antwerp: J. Grapheus); the evident contradiction between this work and the scepticism of the *De vanitate* remains the subject of debate. At any rate the furore created by the *De vanitate* and its attacks on scholastic theology forced Agrippa to flee to Cologne. Here he published a complete version of the *De occulta philosophia* (J. Soter 1533). From Cologne Agrippa travelled to Bonn and finally back to Lyon, where he was not favourably received. He died in poverty at Grenoble. He had married three times and fathered seven children; his last marriage ended in divorce. His *Opera omnia* were published around 1600, ostensibly in Lyon (repr 1970), and he is said to have been a prototype of Goethe's Faust.

Although Erasmus shunned the study of the Cabbala and was not interested in magic and the occult, Agrippa was from an early age his admirer and, as Paola Zambelli has demonstrated, shared in both his desire for a Christianity founded on the Bible and on the Fathers of the church and in his dislike of scholastic theologians. Agrippa's works contain many references to the *Adagia*, the *Apophthegmata*, and the *Antibarbari*, and he is known to have purchased copies of the *Ratio verae theologiae*, the *Farrago epistolarum*, and the *Spongia* against *Hutten. For his part, Erasmus heard of Agrippa around 1523, when Claudius *Cantiuncula and Hilarius *Bertholf spoke of him at table (Agrippa *Opera* II 751–2). The

Cologne humanist Johannes *Caesarius was another possible intermediary between the two. However, direct epistolary contact between Erasmus and Agrippa appears to have occurred only from 1531 to 1533. In August 1531 Erasmus wrote to Georgius *Agricola, expressing interest in Agrippa's new book – evidently the *De vanitate* – and stating that he was afraid that the audacity of Agrippa's attacks on monks and scholastic theologians would hurt the cause of good letters (Ep 2529). On 19 September Erasmus wrote to Agrippa himself, again stating that he wished to read his book, and introducing a certain *Andreas, a French priest who had come to Germany to meet Erasmus and Agrippa (Ep 2544). This led to a series of friendly exchanges, the majority written by Agrippa (Epp 2589, 2626, 2692, 2737, 2739, 2748, 2790, 2796). His main topic was his growing controversy with the theologians of Louvain, which he referred to in militaristic terms: he would do battle with them using the weapons forged by Erasmus (Ep 2737). In April 1533 he informed Erasmus that he had tried unsuccessfully to have his *Apologia* against the Louvain theologians printed at Basel (Ep 2790); the work appeared later in 1533 without the name of its printer or place of publication. Meanwhile Erasmus had finally borrowed a copy of the *De vanitate*, but only long enough to have a servant read several passages to him. Although he approved the work, he advised Agrippa to use caution in dealing with the theologians, citing the example of the unfortunate Louis de *Berquin (Ep 2796). Thus Erasmus' encouragement and support of Agrippa was always tempered by the fear that the younger scholar would draw him into new struggles with theologians (Ep 2800). That possibility was removed by Agrippa's departure from Germany and the evident termination of his contacts with Erasmus.

BIBLIOGRAPHY: Allen Ep 2544 / H. Grimm in NDB I 105–6 / R. Schmitz in *Dictionary of Scientific Biography* ed C.C. Gillispie et al (New York 1970–80) I 79–81 / *Matrikel Köln* II 473 / *Melanchthons Briefwechsel* II Ep 1280 / A. Prost *Corneille Agrippa* (Paris 1881–2, repr 1965) / W.D. Müller-Jahncke in *Kabbalistes chrétiens* (Paris 1979) 197–209 / C.G. Nauert 'Agrippa in Renaissance Italy: the esoteric tradition' *Studies in the Renaissance* 6 (1959) 195–222 / C.G. Nauert *Agrippa and the Crisis of Renaissance Thought* (Urbana, Ill, 1965) / E. Droz *Chemins de l'hérésie* (Geneva 1970–6) II 1–26 / Lynn Thorndike *A History of Magic and Experimental Science* (New York 1923–58) V 127–38 / D.P. Walker *Spiritual and Demonic Magic* (London 1958) 90–6 and passim / P. Zambelli 'Cornelio Agrippa, Erasmo e la teologia umanistica' *Rinascimento* 2nd series, 10 (1970) 29–88

TBD

Girolamo AIAZZA of Vercelli, c 1472–1538
Aiazza (Agathius, Agacius), of Vercelli, Piedmont, was a doctor of laws. On 7 March 1524 he was appointed president of the council of Savoy and on 27 March 1528 grand chancellor of Duke Charles II of *Savoy. In August 1528 he gave a letter for Erasmus to a ducal secretary, perhaps Amblard *Alardet, or more likely Joachim *Zasius, who planned to travel to or through Basel. Erasmus sent a brief reply which shows no special regard for the distinction of its recipient (Epp 2020, 2041). Aiazza was still in office in 1535; he was buried in the church of San Bernardo, Vercelli. A younger relative of his, Vespasiano Aiazza, abbot of Notre Dame d'Abondance (Haute-Savoie), 1597–1627, attained some prominence as a close friend of St Francis de Sales (DBF I 847–8).

BIBLIOGRAPHY: Allen Ep 2020 / *Amtliche Sammlung der älteren eidgenössischen Abschiede* ed K. Krütli et al (Lucerne 1839–86) IV-1a 1521

PGB

Stanisław AICHLER of Cracow, c 1519/20–c 1585
Stanisław Aichler (Aychler, Glandinus), was the son of Erazm, an alderman of Cracow, and Sabina, the daughter of a Poznan burgher family. At the beginning of 1531 he left Poland as a companion to the nobleman Jan *Boner under the care of Anselmus *Ephorinus. They travelled to Erfurt and then to Nürnberg. From Ep 2533 one may conclude that Aichler stayed with Erasmus at Freiburg from April to the end of August. He then moved to Basel (Ep 2545), where he stayed to the spring of 1532. Erasmus, who took note of Aichler's ability, intended to dedicate an edition of Terence's comedies jointly to Aichler and Jan Boner, but

on the advice of Ephorinus contented himself with mentioning Aichler with praise (Epp 2554, 2584). After a short visit to Augsburg, Aichler went to Padua, where he remained from the spring of 1532 to mid-1534, keeping in touch with Erasmus (Epp 2658, 2718; AK IV Ep 1739). No other traces of his contacts with Erasmus are known.

From the summer of 1534 Aichler studied law in Bologna, and in 1535 he obtained the doctorate of civil and canon law. He then accompanied Ephorinus and Boner to Rome and Naples and in 1537 returned to Poland by way of France (where he stayed in Paris), the Netherlands, and Germany. With the support of Bishop Johannes *Dantiscus he was made notary of Cracow in 1539 and later bailiff of Magdeburg law at the Cracow castle. Highly esteemed as a lawyer, he also became a protégé of the *voivode*, Piotr *Kmita. After 1550 he attached himself to the supporters of the Reformation and served as an elder of the Calvinist church in Cracow. His wife was Justina, the daughter of the historian Justus Ludovicus *Decius; they had seven children.

Several poems in Latin written by Aichler were published as an appendix to Johannes Dantiscus' *Carmen paraeneticum* (Cracow: H. Wietor 1539). He also wrote *Epithalamium Isabellae ... filiae serenissimi regis Poloniae Sigismundi, ad serenissimum maritum Joannem Hungariae regem proficiscentis ...* (Cracow: H. Wietor 1539). His edition of the work of Pomponius *Laetus, *De Romanorum magistratibus, sacerdotiis, iurisperitis et legibus libellus* (Cracow: F. Ungler 1544), is dedicated to Piotr Kmita.

BIBLIOGRAPHY: Allen Ep 2545, also Epp 2539, 2549, 2550, 2606 / PSB I 33–4 / K. Estreicher et al *Bibliografia polska* (Cracow 1870–1951) XII 79, XXI 25 / *Korespondencja Erazma z Rotterdamu z Polakami* ed M. Cytowska (Warsaw 1965) / AK IV Ep 1739 / *Akta synodów różnowierczych w Polsce* ed M. Sipayłło II (Warsaw 1972) / Cracow, Library Czartoryskich MS 1597 p 455

HALINA KOWALSKA

ALAARD of Amsterdam 1491–c 28 August 1544
Alaard (Alardus Aemstelredamus, Allard) was born at Amsterdam, the son of one Petrus, and was a kinsman of Meynard *Man. In his youth

Alaard of Amsterdam by Jacob Cornelisz van Oostsanen

Amsterdam and the famous library of Pompeius *Occo which contained the Agricola papers (Ep 485); in Utrecht he was ordained on 11 April. Subsequently he journeyed almost every year to Amsterdam or other centres of the Netherlands, and frequently also to Cologne, either in search of manuscripts or to see his many publications through the press. But Louvain, where he was to die, remained his base. There he taught and worked for Martens' press; on 22 June 1539 he was admitted as a guest to the Collegium Trilingue, in 1540–1 he appears to have attended the theological lectures of *Tapper and Jacobus *Latomus, and from 1542 he lived in the college of Pope *Adrian VI. His many publications include scholarly editions and short texts for the classroom and a number of theological treatises characterized by polemic against the reformers. His great achievement was an edition of the collected works of Agricola in two volumes (Cologne: J. Gymnich 1539).

In Alaard's relations with Erasmus crucial developments followed the exchange of friendly letters in 1516 and 1517 (Epp 433, 485, 676). In March 1519 Alaard announced publicly his intention of lecturing on Erasmus' *Ratio verae theologiae* under the auspices of the newly founded Collegium Trilingue, but his initiative was smothered by the university since he had not received the *venia legendi*. In fact he was never to become a member of the university faculty, although later that year he may have applied unsuccessfully for the Latin chair of the Trilingue (Ep 1051; cf Ep 1437). Whether it was Erasmus' lack of support for such an application or another reason that doomed the old friendship, it is clear that from this time onwards their contacts were insignificant. Erasmus' letters mentioned Alaard occasionally and with angry contempt (Epp 1889, 2587, 3052); he appears to have resented Alaard's role in the publication of his *Paraphrases in Elegantias Vallae* (Epp 2354, 2412), and an Alardus is introduced in the *Colloquia* edition of 1522, only to be characterized as a chatterbox (ASD I-3 140). There are indications that Erasmus' bitter feelings were not, or were not for long, reciprocated by Alaard, or he would not have approached the *Froben press when trying to find a publisher for his edition of Agricola (Ep 2587).

he was probably a student of Willem *Hermans of Gouda, for whom he later wrote an epitaph (published in Cornelis *Croock's *Epistola* on the Epistles of James, Cologne 1531), and perhaps of Alexander *Hegius. Not later than 1511 he began to teach in the school at Alkmaar and continued to do so when Johannes *Murmellius became headmaster. It was at Alkmaar that he first became interested in the surviving papers of Rodolphus *Agricola. By 1514 Alaard must have moved to Louvain. His name does not seem to appear in the university register, but in January 1515 he published an edition, through Dirk *Martens' press, of Agricola's *De inventione dialectica* (Ep 336). After matriculating at the University of Cologne for the winter term 1515–16 he returned to Louvain, from where he addressed letters to Erasmus in July and November (Epp 433, 485). By then he had also secured a volume of early compositions by Erasmus and Willem Hermans, from which he edited and published (in 1538) Erasmus' *Carmen bucolicum* (Reedijk poem 1). Erasmus in turn published in 1517 one or two texts supplied by Alaard and related with his interest in Agricola's papers (Epp 676, 677). In that same year Alaard had returned to

BIBLIOGRAPHY: Allen Ep 433 / M.A. Nauwe-

laerts in NBW III 21–5 / NNBW VI 19–21 / de
Vocht CTL I 316–21, 490–5, and passim
CFG & PGB

Petrus ALAMIRUS documented 1496–1534
Petrus Alamirus (Pieter van den Hove, Pierre
Alamire or La Mire), presumably a native of the
Netherlands, is first documented in 1496 in the
accounts of the St Mary's brotherhood of 's
Hertogenbosch, for which he had copied
masses and motets. He may then have been
living at 's Hertogenbosch. From 1503 to 1505
he was at Antwerp and there sold to Philip the
Handsome, duke of *Burgundy, 'a large book
of music.' In 1509 he was attached to the court
of the future *Charles v as 'scribe and keeper of
the books,' a position which he seems to have
retained for a quarter of a century, producing a
considerable number of music manuscripts. In
addition he sang in the choir and may have
held a chaplaincy. In 1516 he was at the court of
*Margaret of Austria at Mechelen, while *Mary
of Hungary granted him a pension as of 1
January 1534. He also copied music and
perhaps other manuscripts for private patrons;
it was probably for work of this kind that he
received a payment from the estate of Jérôme
de *Busleyden.
    Alamirus was also a political agent of
considerable skill. King *Henry VIII of
England, to whom he supplied musical
instruments and manuscripts in 1515, employed him until 1518 to watch the movements
of Edmund de la *Pole's brother Richard, who
had earlier been recognized by France as king
of England. On occasion he coded his
messages to England in musical notation.
Primarily, however, he seems to have acted on
behalf of his own government of the
Netherlands, which between 1517 and 1520
repeatedly sent him to the courts of Saxony. In
November 1517 Georgius *Spalatinus gave him
a letter and a verbal message for Erasmus (Ep
711). That letter was not delivered, however,
until July or August 1519, when Erasmus met
Alamirus first in Louvain and subsequently in
Mechelen (Ep 1001). At the same time he
handed Erasmus a similarly dated letter from
Willibald *Pirckheimer, who had shown
Alamirus his guest suite ready to receive
Erasmus (Ep 1095).
    BIBLIOGRAPHY: Allen and CWE Ep 711 /
Herbert Kellman in *The New Grove Dictionary of*

Music and Musicians ed Stanley Sadie (London
1980) I 192–3, with a detailed account of
Alamirus' surviving manuscripts / *Deutsche
Reichstagsakten* Jüngere Reihe (Gotha-Göttingen 1893–   ) I 416 / de Vocht *Busleyden* 67,
69–70

PGB

Johannes ALANUS *See John* ALLEN

Amblard and Claude-Louis ALARDET of
Geneva
Originally the Alardet (Allardet) family came
from Treffort (Département de l'Ain). From
1502 to 1520 Syboyet Alardet was recorded as a
secretary of the duke of Savoy as well as a
citizen and councillor of Geneva, while his
brother Pierre was a canon of Geneva. Syboyet
had two sons. Amblard, the older, was
probably named after his maternal uncle,
Amblard Goyet, canon of Geneva and
commendatory abbot of Filly, near Thonon on
Lake Geneva. Like his father, Amblard became
a ducal secretary and was thus a colleague of
Joachim *Zasius.
    Syboyet's younger son, Claude-Louis Alar-
det, succeeded his uncles as a canon of Geneva
in 1529 and abbot of Filly in 1530, but the
Geneva council prevented him from taking
possession of his prebend, and the abbey of
Filly was secularized by the conquering
Bernese in 1536–7. He may be the Louis Alardet
who held offices among the francophone
students of Padua from 1531 to 1532. In 1533 he
was an apostolic protonotary and in 1535 a
member of the Geneva chapter reconstituted at
Annecy. In 1542 he was appointed dean of
Chambéry in French-occupied Savoy, conceivably on the recommendation of his good friend
Jean de *Boysonné. On 6 June 1555 Duke
Emmanuel Philibert appointed him prior of
Entrèves; in 1559 he was elected bishop of
Mondovi, but before he could take possession
of this see he was called to that of Lausanne in
1560. As a bishop he continued to reside at
Chambéry until his death, probably in 1565.
    Claude-Louis' ecclesiastical career was
closely linked to his political activity. In 1533 he
became tutor to Emmanuel Philibert, the later
duke, and he continued to serve Duke Charles
II of *Savoy in the years of the French
occupation when he lost most of the revenue of
his benefices. In 1540 he accompanied Duke

Charles to the diet of Worms and thereafter may have remained in Germany for some time. While residing at Chambéry he joined a conspiracy against the French in 1551–2 and was banned from Savoy until the peace of Cateau-Cambrésis in 1559, when the revival of ducal Savoy permitted him to return to Chambéry. In 1559–60 he was also involved in efforts to restore Geneva to the rule of the duke, efforts that at one point included a plot to assassinate Calvin.

Erasmus' secretary, Hilarius *Bertholf, addressed some poems to an Alardet who was a canon of Geneva. Perhaps Bertholf had met members of the Alardet family in January 1524 when he visited another canon of Geneva, Philibert de *Lucinge. In August 1527 Claude-Louis wrote to Erasmus at the suggestion of Amblard, who, according to his brother, had earlier written to Erasmus in his own name. Like the missing letter by Amblard, Ep 1852 by Claude-Louis dealt with Jean *Gachi's outbursts against Erasmus. The latter replied obligingly to both brothers (Ep 1892), informing them of his steps in the matter of Gachi, and again sent greetings to them in 1529 (Ep 2084).

BIBLIOGRAPHY: Allen Ep 1852 / E. Fasano Guarini in DBI I 576–8 / DHGE II 475 / Eubel III 220 / Henri Naef *Les Origines de la réforme à Genève* 2nd ed (Geneva 1968) I 28–9 and passim / Mario Zucchi *I governatori dei principi reali di Savoia* (Turin 1925) 33–4 / H. Cornelius Agrippa of Nettesheim *Opera* (Lyon n d, repr 1970 II 1134–9 erroneous pagination) / Giuliana Toso Rodinis *Scolari francesi a Padova agli albori della Controriforma* (Padua 1970) 163

PGB

Duke of ALBA, ALVA *See Fadrique* ALVAREZ *de Toledo*

Erasmus ALBER of Buchenbrücken, c1500–5 May 1533
Erasmus Alber (Alberus) was born in Bruchenbrücken (Wetterau, near Frankfurt-am-Main), the son of Tilemann Alber. He attended the Latin schools in Nidda and Weilburg and matriculated at the University of Wittenberg in 1520. He studied theology, first under Andreas *Karlstadt and later under Martin *Luther. In 1524 he was a schoolteacher in Eisenbach (Ep 1523). After his marriage in 1527, he was a minister in Sprendlingen, near Frankfurt, from

1528 to 1539. After 1539 his life was more unsettled; he was a minister in Brandenburg, Rothenburg-ob-der-Tauber, the Wetterau, and Neubrandenburg. Opposing the conditions of the Augsburg Interim imposed by *Charles V in 1548, he retired to Magdeburg, where he remained until 1551, joining the circle of militant Lutherans there. He died in Neubrandenburg.

In 1524 Erasmus was greatly annoyed by a letter in which Alber took issue with his *Spongia* against Hutten, even though some of Alber's comments were favourable (LB X 1255D). Erasmus complained that he had seen the letter only in print, and at first he believed its author to be Hermannus *Buschius. No doubt it was the *Iudicium Erasmi Alberi de Spongia Erasmi …, quatenus illi conveniat cum M. Lutheri doctrina* (Haguenau: J. Setzer [1524]; cf Epp 1437, 1466, 1477, 1496).

Alber published a great many pamphlets, primers, and hymns, including *Ein schön lustig Gespräch zweyer Weiber* (n p, n d another ed n p 1539), apparently adapted from one of Erasmus' colloquies. He also paraphrased many of Aesop's fables in German rhymes: *Etliche Fabel Esopi verteutscht* (Haguenau 1534, and repeatedly thereafter); he wrote a *Kurtze Beschreibung der Wetterau*, which was not published until 1731.

BIBLIOGRAPHY: Allen Ep 1466 / NDB I 123 / *Matrikel Wittenberg* I 95 / *Index Aureliensis* (Baden-Baden 1962–) I 220–9

IG

Claudius ALBERICUS of Toul, documented in 1532
Claudius Albericus (presumably Aubéry, Aubry), of Toul in Lorraine, matriculated at the University of Freiburg on 28 June 1532, being a cleric and claiming to be a MA. Two months later Erasmus mentioned him as a close friend of Pierre *Du Chastel (Ep 2720). No more is known about Albericus.

BIBLIOGRAPHY: Allen Ep 2720 / *Matrikel Freiburg* I-1 282

PGB

ALBERT cardinal-archbishop of Mainz *See Albert of* BRANDENBURG

Antoine d'ALBON 1507–24 September 1574
The descendant of two prominent noble

families of the Lyonnais, Antoine d'Albon (Dalbanus) was the son of Guillaume d'Albon, seigneur of Saint-Forgeux, and Gabrielle de Saint-Priest. In 1519, at the age of twelve, he entered the Benedictine abbey of Savigny in the Lyonnais and the next year, upon the resignation of his great-uncle, became its abbot. He studied theology at the University of Paris, listening especially to the lectures of Claude Guillaud. In 1525, again following an uncle, he became abbot of the ancient abbey of Saint-Martin-de-l'Ile-Barbe, north of Lyon, whose library dated back to Carolingian times. By 1530, perhaps through the good offices of Nicolas *Maillard (Ep 2424), the young abbot was in correspondance with Erasmus and seemed to have hoped to entice him to Ile-Barbe. The communication between the two was good enough that Erasmus expressed to d'Albon his concerns about political matters in France, Germany, and elsewhere and about the progress of Zwinglianism and Lutheranism (Epp 2410, 2472). D'Albon was also in touch with literary figures in Lyon, such as the poet Nicolas *Bourbon, and may also have had contact with his former teacher Claude Guillaud when he came to edit the *Biblia sacra*, along with Michael *Servetus, for the Grande Compagnie des libraires (1545).

In 1549 d'Albon won from Pope *Paul III permission for the monks at Ile-Barbe to become secular canons, arguing that this would allow them better to work for their salvation, serve God, and attract noble and lettered persons to their house. Much criticized by pious Catholics of the seventeenth century, this secularization may have been in part a humanist effort to rethink the relation of monks to the world. D'Albon's own responsibilities increased in 1558, when for three years he became lieutenant-governor of the Lyonnais (his uncle, Jacques d'Albon de Saint-André, was the governor) and found himself ordering military action against the growing Protestant movement in Lyon. In 1564, in the wake of the reformed regime in Lyon, he was consecrated archbishop of Lyon and administered the archdiocese during a decade of intense struggle between Protestants and Catholics. The Jesuit order was firmly established in the city; the Tridentine Missal was published there with his permission; and Huguenots were slaughtered in his prisons in

the Lyon Vespers of 1572. He also had time to edit and dedicate to Pope Pius V a commentary on the Psalms by the fourth-century Rufinus of Aquileia, a manuscript he had found at Ile-Barbe (Lyon: Guillaume Rouillé 1570).

BIBLIOGRAPHY: Allen Ep 2410 / DBF I 1263–5 / *Gallia christiana* IV 185–7 and passim / Claude Le Laboureur *Les Masures de l'Ile-Barbe* (Lyon 1887) I 238–54, II 4–7 / A. Péricaud *Notes et documents pour servir à l'histoire de Lyon (1560–74)* (Lyon n d) 6, 23–4 / J. and H. Baudrier *Bibliographie lyonnaise* (Lyon 1895– 1921) II 98, 103, III 211, IV 226, 343, VIII 380, IX 332–3, 364–5, XII 257–60
NATALIE ZEMON DAVIS

Alain and Jean d'ALBRET *See* JOHN *d'Albret, king of Navarre*

Andrea ALCIATI of Milan, 8 May 1492– 12 January 1550
Andrea Alciati (Alciatus, Alciato), the great interpreter of Roman law, was born in Milan or in Alzata, near Como, from which his family took its name. He was the only son of Ambrogio Alciati and Margherita Landriani. His father, a merchant of some means, sometime Milanese ambassador to the republic of Venice, seems to have died early, since there is no mention of him in his son's extant letters. His mother, who was of aristocratic background, was alive until a few years before her son's death. From 1504 Alciati studied under the guidance of Aulus Janus Parrhasius in Milan, where he also attended the lectures of Janus *Lascaris. His precocity is attested to by a group of writings which included a collection of ancient inscriptions, begun while he was working on a history of Milan, a brief essay showing the modern value of ancient coins, and a study of a number of Milanese churches. His excellent early training in classical philology made possible his restorations and reinterpretations of the legal documents of antiquity. In 1507 Alciati began to study law in Pavia with Giasone del Maino, Filippo *Decio, and Paolo Pico da Montepico. Less than satisfied with Pavia, he went in 1511 to Bologna, where he heard the lectures of Carlo Ruini. By 1515 his first two juridical works were published in Strasbourg. According to Roberto Abbondanza he received his doctorate in 1516 in Ferrara.

Returning to Milan Alciati was admitted to

Andrea Alciati by Philippe Galle

the college or guild of jurisconsults despite his youth and practised law. In 1517 the Milanese printer Alessandro Minuziano published his annotations to Tacitus in an edition of the works of that author. The following year the same printer published a number of Alciati's works which brought him to the attention of the learned circles of Europe; among these were his *Dispunctiones* and *Praetermissa,* cited by Erasmus in his *Adagia* (I iii 59, I vii 34). Between 1518 and 1520 Claudius *Cantiuncula, in letters to *Budé and *Agrippa of Nettesheim, adding Alciati's name to that of *Zasius and Budé, called them a 'triumvirate' responsible for a new era in jurisprudence. Erasmus concurred because he was aware that, with the tools of humanistic scholarship, Alciati was attempting to do for law what he himself was striving to do for theology.

Alciati began his professorial career in 1518 in Avignon, where, except for intermittent absences caused by the plague, he lectured on civil law until the spring of 1522, when he resigned because of a dispute over his salary. Through the good offices of his childhood friend Francesco Giulio *Calvo, a bookseller

and publisher, Alciati was given the honorific title of palatine count in 1521 by Pope *Leo x. In 1519 Alciati met Budé, with whom, despite some disagreements, he managed to maintain a cordial relationship. An important factor in Alciati's relationship with Erasmus was the arrival in May 1520 of Bonifacius *Amerbach, who had come to Avignon to study with Alciati.

There is no evidence that Erasmus and Alciati ever met, but a manuscript in which Alciati criticized the monastic life brought about a written exchange between them. Calvo had given it to Erasmus without Alciati's consent. Fearful that Erasmus might allow others to read it, Alciati expressed his uneasiness to Amerbach, who relayed his apprehension to Erasmus (Ep 1201). In December 1521 Erasmus wrote to Alciati, assuring him that he had no need to worry (Ep 1250). Alciati replied gratefully, asking Erasmus to burn the manuscript (Ep 1261). Despite further reassurances Alciati's disquiet continued until March 1531, when Erasmus declared that he had burnt 'the little essay' (Ep 2468). At least one version of the work survived, for it was published in Holland in 1695.

After a second exchange of letters in April and May 1522 (Epp 1278, 1288), Erasmus wrote to Amerbach: 'You will be a letter to Alciati in my name' (Ep 1293). Although there were subsequent letters, Amerbach became the intermediary between the two.

Alciati spent the war years, 1522–7, in Milan, devoting himself to private study, polishing earlier translations of poems from the Greek Anthology and of 'The Clouds' of Aristophanes, and writing an original comedy, 'Philargyrus.' The most notable product of those difficult years was the beginning of a collection of what Alciati called 'emblems,' first mentioned by him in a letter to Calvo dated 9 January 1523. These, he explained, were epigrams describing something from history or nature, symbolizing something elegant, from which painters, goldsmiths, or sculptors might be able to derive insignia. Thus was created the Renaissance emblem book, which brought Alciati more lasting fame than his work in jurisprudence. Consisting of a motto, a woodcut, and a poem, each emblem was cleverly contrived to illustrate the virtues and vices of mankind. Into them Alciati incorporated his knowledge of Greek and Roman history, literature and mythology, echoes from the then fashionable pseudo-hieroglyphica, and his translations from the Greek Anthology. So pervasive was the influence of Erasmus in them that Augustin Renaudet called the emblems 'an ingenious complement to the *Adagia.*' The collection grew from the original 104 (1531) to 212 emblems. It was first published in Augsburg, and more than forty editions appeared during Alciati's lifetime, including translations into French, German, Spanish, and Italian. Henry Green in his unsurpassed analytical bibliography of editions listed 178.

In 1523 Alciati's house in Milan was invaded by the French; in 1526 it was occupied by Spanish mercenaries. In letters to Amerbach in 1525 (AK III Epp 1018, 1878) Alciati expressed regret that Erasmus was involved in the current religious controversies as well as his happiness in being mentioned in the writings of Erasmus. In May 1526 a new note was sounded in a letter from Erasmus concerning a new group of 'Ciceronians,' which had risen up against him 'no less feverishly than the Lutherans' (Ep 1706). He described too the inflexibility of Christophe de *Longueil, believed to be the Nosoponus in his *Ciceronianus* (Basel: H. Froben March 1528). In that work Erasmus ironically has Nosoponus state that the most erudite men characterized Alciati in Ciceronian terms as 'the ablest jurist in the ranks of the orators and the best orator in the ranks of the jurists' (ASD I-2 669). In the 1526 edition of the *Adagia* Erasmus had referred to Alciati as 'the ornament in this age, not only of civil law, but of all studies' (I v 45). Pleased by these tributes, Alciati declared to Amerbach that Erasmus had given him 'everlasting fame.' This evoked a long letter from Erasmus in which he praised Alciati for his fortitude in adversity and then lamented his own plight, referring to his enemies in Germany and in Rome as 'a monster with thousands of heads' (Ep 2051).

In a letter to Calvo of October 1527 Alciati reported his return to his teaching post in Avignon. In that letter he mentioned a wife, 'alive and well,' left behind in Milan. There is no subsequent reference to her in the Alciati correspondence. Alciati left Avignon in the spring of 1529 for Bourges, where he had been invited to teach by *Francis I. His four years at Bourges were his most glorious. His lectures were attended by admirers from all over Europe, including the king, to whom he dedicated a treatise on duelling. Among his students were Karel *Sucket, *Viglius Zuichemus, the poet Johannes Secundus (Johannes Nicolai Everardi) and Calvin, the last a less than enthusiastic pupil. In 1530 in Lyon, *Gryphius published two of Alciati's most celebrated works: *De verborum significatione* and the *Commentarii ad rescripta principum.* During this period Amerbach frequently mentioned Alciati in his letters to Erasmus, while Viglius reported to Erasmus that Alciati mentioned him daily, and that no one read his *Adagia* more thoroughly (Ep 2210). Erasmus and Alciati exchanged four letters between March 1530 and March 1531. When Erasmus complained about the attack of Alberto *Pio (Ep 2329), Alciati strongly urged silence, maintaining that Erasmus triumphed through his works (Ep 2394). Erasmus insisted that he must defend himself against his enemies, deadly monsters similar to those faced by Hercules (Ep 2468).

In 1533 Alciati returned to Italy to teach at Pavia at the command of Duke Francesco II *Sforza, who made him a senator at Milan. This occurred at a time when Pietro *Bembo was negotiating with the republic of Venice for the appointment of Alciati to a post in Padua. Alciati spent four unhappy years at Pavia, where his unruly Italian students did not appreciate his humanistic method. In the 1533 edition of the *Adagia* Erasmus added an adage culled from Alciati's recent work, referring to him as 'the most learned by far' among the jurisconsults (*Adagia* IV ix 36). In March 1535 Erasmus listed Alciati with *Sadoleto and Bembo as true Ciceronians most friendly to himself (Ep 3005). That same month Giovanni Angelo *Odoni offered as proof to Erasmus that he was read and admired among the Italians the reverence and love of Alciati, Bembo, Sadoleto, and others (Ep 3002). In June 1535 Hector van *Hoxwier, who had been recommended to Alciati by Erasmus in a letter no longer extant, informed him that Alciati spoke of him 'most lovingly' (Ep 3022). Rumours of Erasmus' death in July 1536 reached Pavia only in January 1537. In April Alciati acknowledged a letter from Amerbach confirming those rumours and enclosed two epigrams on Erasmus that Amerbach had requested.

When war broke out again between *Charles v and Francis i Alciati left Pavia for Bologna, where he taught from 1537 to 1541, despite the efforts of the Milanese authorities to recall him to Pavia. In 1542 he accepted the invitation of Duke Ercole ii d'*Este to teach in Ferrara, declining the repeated invitations of Cosimo de' *Medici to teach at Pisa. Among his friends in Ferrara was Giorgio Vasari. When he was offered a cardinalate in 1546 by *Paul iii, Alciati declined, but he did accept the title of apostolic protonotary. Called back to Pavia in 1546, at what he considered a financial loss, Alciati taught there until his death. He was buried in the church of the Holy Epiphany. The funeral oration was delivered by Alessandro Grimaldi. The elaborate monument erected by his heir, Francesco Alciati, was transferred in 1773 from the church to the University of Pavia, where it dominates the quadrangle of the law school. The inscription on it reads in part: 'He fulfilled the circle of all learning; he was the first to restore the study of law to its ancient splendour.' The monument is surmounted by a large statue of Alciati. Framing the inscription are four reliefs: balancing each other on the left and right are figures symbolizing literature and the law; below on the left, representing the family name, is an elk (*alce*); below on the right is Alciati's *impresa*, the herald's staff of Mercury, the god of eloquence, entwined by two serpents and cornucopias, around which is inscribed in Greek: 'The fruit of the just man does not perish.'

The most authentic portrait of Alciati is in the Uffizi gallery in Florence and was based on a copy of a painting by Battista Dossi done in 1544 at Ferrara. There are other portraits in Vienna, Wolfenbüttel, Versailles, and Basel. Among the numerous engravings see *Illustrium iureconsultorum imagines ... ex musaeo Marci Mantuae Benavidii* (Rome 1566); J.C.J. Bierens de Haan *L'Oeuvre gravé de C. Cort* (1533–1578) (The Hague 1948); and N. Reusner *Icones sive imagines vivae literis clarorum virorum* (Basel 1589).

BIBLIOGRAPHY: The primary sources for the life of Alciati, besides the Erasmus correspondence and AK ii–vi, are the orations of Alciati included in the 1582 edition of his collected works (Basel 1582) and *Le lettere di Andrea Alciato* ed G.L. Barni (Florence 1953). The latter should be used with the supplement of R. Abbondanza 'A proposito dell' epistolario dell' Alciato' *Annali di storia del diritto* 1 (1957) 467–500. The most recent biographies are P.E. Viard *André Alciat, 1492–1550* (Paris 1926) and H. De Giacomi *Andreas Alciatus* (Basel 1934). Of the early biographies the best is that of Giammaria Mazzucchelli in *Gli scrittori d'Italia* i-1 (Brescia 1753) 354–68. The most precise biographical and bibliographical material is that furnished by R. Abbondanza, the leading Alciati scholar, in DBI ii 69–77. See also Allen Ep 1250. For recent evaluations of Alciati as jurisconsult see D.R. Kelley *Foundations of Modern Historical Scholarship* (New York 1970) 90–106 and R. Abbondanza 'Jurisprudence: the method of Andrea Alciato' in *The Late Italian Renaissance* ed E. Cochrane (London 1970) 77–90. For Alciati's relationship with Erasmus see V.W. Callahan 'The Erasmus-Alciati friendship' *Acta Conventus Neo-Latini Lovaniensis* (Munich 1973) 133–41.

Of the several editions of the complete works of Alciati the best is the four-volume *Opera omnia* (Basel: Thomas Guarinus 1582). The only complete edition of the emblems, published by Tozzi (Padua 1621), contains the life of Alciati by Claude Mignault (Minos) and the combined commentaries of Mignault, Sanctius, Pignorius, and Johannes Thuilius. Still valuable is H. Green's *Andrea Alciati and His Book of Emblems* (London 1872). See also James Hutton's introduction to the Alciatus section of *The Greek Anthology in Italy to the Year 1800* (Ithaca, N.Y., 1935) 195–208

VIRGINIA W. CALLAHAN

Pietro ALCIONIO of Venice, c 1487–1527
Pietro Alcionio (Petrus Alcyonius, Halcyonius) was probably born at Venice, but we do not even know his family name (Alcyonius is an honorific humanist title). He perhaps acted as a corrector for the Aldine press while he was young. The first mention of him occurs in Erasmus' letter to John *Watson in 1516 (Ep 450), where he is praised for his eloquence. He studied with Marcus *Musurus and applied

unsuccessfully for the latter's chair of Greek at Padua upon his death in 1517. According to Ambrogio *Leoni (Ep 854) Alcionio translated into Latin works of Isocrates, Demosthenes, and Aristotle, but only the last are known (Venice: B. dei Vitali 1521); cf *Index Aureliensis* (Baden-Baden 1962–   ) II no 107.880. In 1522 he published *Medicus legatus de exilio*, a Ciceronian dialogue, at the Aldine press and the same year went to Florence to become professor of Greek. With the election of *Clement VII to the papacy he was called to a chair of Greek at Rome. Alcionio was wounded during the Sack of Rome in May 1527 and died later the same year, possibly as a result of his injury (Ep 2665).

BIBLIOGRAPHY: Allen Ep 450 / M. Rosa in DBI II 77–80 / Additional MS sources are listed in P.O. Kristeller *Iter Italicum* (London-Leiden 1965–   ) indices

CHARLES B. SCHMITT

Robert ALDRIDGE of Burnham, d 5 March 1556
Robert Aldridge (Aldrich, Aldrisius) was born about 1495 at Burnham, Buckinghamshire, studied at Eton College, and became a scholar of King's College, Cambridge in 1507. Having graduated BA in 1512 and MA in 1515, he was elected headmaster of Eton the same year. After vacating the post in 1521, he returned to Cambridge, where he was ordained deacon in 1522, becoming university preacher the following year and senior proctor for 1524–5. By that time Aldridge was already in the service of John *Longland, bishop of Lincoln (LP IV 1142). Aldridge's church career began in 1528, when he became vicar of Stanton Harcourt, Oxfordshire, canon of Lincoln, and prebendary of Centum Solidorum, the last of which was exchanged the following year for the prebendary of Decem Librarum. Having taken a bachelor's degree in divinity at Cambridge, he received a doctorate in theology from Oxford in 1530. On 3 January 1531 Aldridge was given the rectory of Cheriton, Hampshire, which had been vacated following the death of Thomas *Lupset. The same year he was made archdeacon of Colchester, being already the king's chaplain. Aldridge also played a role in *Henry VIII's divorce, being one of the members of convocation who signed in favour

of the divorce in April 1533. Two months later Aldridge accompanied Thomas *Howard, duke of Norfolk, in his mission to Pope *Clement VII and King *Francis I. On 23 April 1534 Aldridge was made registrar of the order of the Garter, almost immediately thereafter becoming canon of Windsor (LP VII 534, 761(4)). The following year he was present during the interrogation of John *Fisher and Thomas *More and served on the commission appointed to persuade the members of Sion College to accept the king's supremacy (LP VIII 867, IX 986). On 17 March 1536 Aldridge became provost of Eton, while the following year, when he was already chaplain and almoner to Queen Jane Seymour, he was elevated bishop of Carlisle. He supported the Act of the Six Articles of 1539 and the annulment of Henry VIII's marriage to Anne of Cleves the following year. The last sixteen years of his life were lived in relative seclusion in his bishopric. During the reign of Edward VI he resisted the introduction of the new liturgy, and consequently he faced some hardships. But following the accession of Queen *Mary he regained his former position and became a member of the commission for the suppression of heresy.

Aldridge met Erasmus while a student at Cambridge and may be identified as the 'smooth-tongued young man' who remained with Erasmus for six months (Ep 1766) and acted as his interpreter during the famous visit to the shrine of Walsingham in the summer of 1512 (*Colloquia* ASD I-3 479–80). After Erasmus' departure, the two were apparently not in contact until December 1525, when Erasmus was engaged in revising his edition of Seneca's work which had been published by Johann *Froben in 1515. In preparation for the new Froben edition of 1529 Aldridge arranged for the collation of three manuscripts in King's College and Peterhouse; unfortunately they did not include the one most important to Erasmus, which was apparently missing from the King's College Library, and thus Aldridge's efforts were largely wasted (Epp 1656, 1766, 1797, 2040, 2056). Perhaps to reward him for his trouble, Erasmus addressed to him in August 1527 an apologia in the form of a long letter written for immediate publication, justifying in particular his rendering of John

7:39 (Ep 1858). In 1534 and 1535 Aldridge is mentioned repeatedly in the correspondence of Erasmus with his banker Erasmus *Schets as a person suitable to act in the matter of Erasmus' English annuity (Epp 2913, 2924, 3028, 3042).

BIBLIOGRAPHY: Allen Ep 1656 / DNB I 252–3 / Emden BRUO 1501–40 4–5 / C.M.L. Bouch *Prelates and people of the Lake Counties* (Kendal 1948) 187, 193–5

MORDECHAI FEINGOLD

ALDUS *See Aldo* MANUZIO

Giambattista ALEANDRO of Motta, documented 1500–22

Giambattista was the younger brother of Cardinal Girolamo *Aleandro, whose career he followed in the role of a not very successful jackal. The year of his birth is unknown and was significantly not included by Girolamo in the list of important dates attached to his diary. In 1500 he is said to have been studying literature in Venice, possibly under his brother's general supervision, but there is no evidence to show that he continued to Padua, and he definitely did not join Girolamo's expedition to Paris in 1508. Only when his brother's success was assured did Giambattista hasten to share it, gaining employment under Erard de la *Marck, bishop of Liège, in 1515, a canonry of Chartres somewhat later, and a post as apostolic protonotary by 1517 (Ep 735). From the warmth of Erasmus' greeting on this occasion, and from the similarly warm response (Ep 748), we should probably conclude that the two had met in Venice. But Giambattista was to share his brother's quarrel with Erasmus as well: by 1525 Erasmus believed that the two were engaged in a sinister conspiracy against him (Ep 1585) and even said that Giambattista was the more dangerous of the two, since he could disguise his real feelings (Epp 1549, 1553). In fact, the single surviving letter that passed between the brothers and the scanty mentions in Girolamo's private journal suggest that he saw Giambattista as a dependant rather than an ally. Writing from Spain in 1522, Girolamo concentrated only on his success in wheedling six hundred ducats' worth of benefices from Pope *Adrian VI, and when bequeathing two

hundred ducats to Giambattista, he insisted that his brother should use them only for the dowry of a natural daughter, since he enjoyed an adequate income from his own ecclesiastical benefices. We may infer from this that Giambattista survived Girolamo, but the precise date of his death is unknown.

BIBLIOGRAPHY: Allen Ep 1549 / J. Paquier *Lettres familières de Jérôme Aléandre 1510–1540* (Paris 1909) Ep 55 / *Journal autobiographique du cardinal Jérôme Aléandre* ed H. Omont (Paris 1895) passim / *Le Carnet de voyage de Jérôme Aléandre en France et à Liège (1510–1516)* ed J. Hoyoux (Brussels-Rome 1969) 65 and passim

M.J.C. LOWRY

Girolamo ALEANDRO of Motta, 13 February 1480–1 February 1542

Girolamo Aleandro (Aleander) was born at Motta, some twenty miles east of Treviso, of parents who probably belonged to the minor nobility of Friuli. His father, Francesco, was a doctor who clearly had high educational ambitions for his sons: in the autumn of 1493 he took Girolamo to Venice to study under Benedetto Brugnolo at the school of San Marco, but finding it overcrowded, he moved the boy to the school of Petronillo of Rimini. When Girolamo fell ill during the summer of 1494, he was brought home to recover before being sent to study under Paulus Amaltheus in Pordenone. Here Girolamo made rapid progress and delivered his first public lecture at the age of fifteen. By 1497 he was so precocious a scholar that his father, faced with the problem of educating three sons younger than Girolamo and having recently lost his wife, urged him to settle down and teach in Motta. But Girolamo was determined to pursue his studies further.

He was first unable to find anyone who could teach him Greek, but in 1498 was able to apply himself to Hebrew under the tutelage of a Jewish refugee from Spain named Moses Perez. This association and Perez's baptism in 1499 under the name of Girolamo are the only evidence for Erasmus' later claim that Aleandro had Jewish blood (Epp 1166, 2414, 2578; LB X 1645D). During 1499 and 1500 Girolamo took short-term posts in Venice, teaching Hebrew to the archbishop of Nicosia, Sebastiano Priuli, and reading Cicero to a group of young nobles. But illness and family troubles interrupted his

studies. His father died in January 1501, and
Girolamo returned to Motta to find that his
younger brother Vincenzo had frittered away
most of their late mother's dowry. A promising
offer of a private tutorship at Padua came to
nothing, and Girolamo ended the year as
secretary to Angelo Leoni, the papal legate in
Venice, who dispatched him to the king of
Hungary with a war-subsidy. An impromptu
liaison with a Slavonic courtesan led to another
long period of illness, and it was not until the
end of 1502 that Girolamo was able to return to
his teaching in Venice and in 1503 to secure a
prestigious post in the household of Cardinal
Domenico *Grimani. Thereafter his position in
intellectual society advanced rapidly.

On 12 June 1504 Girolamo accompanied one
of his young patrician pupils, Maffeo Lion, to
Padua. In the autumn of that year Aldo
*Manuzio (Aldus) dedicated both volumes of
his edition of Homer to Aleandro, paying
tribute to his encyclopaedic learning and
implicitly inviting the sort of academic
co-operation that is in fact reflected by six
letters written from Padua by Girolamo
between 1504 and 1508. Perfecting the Greek
he had already learned from *Fortiguerra and
by attendance at *Musurus' lectures, he was
involved in editorial work on the Aldine
edition of Plutarch's *Moralia* by November 1507
and, having secured his doctorate in theology,
took up residence in Venice early in 1508,
shortly after Erasmus' own arrival. At this
stage, their relationship was both friendly and
profitable. They shared a room and a bed (Ep
2443); Aleandro offered help with a number of
passages in the *Adagia* (LB II 419C, 550B),
brought Michael *Apostolius' collection of
proverbs to Erasmus' attention, and was
among the small group of Italian advisers to
whom Erasmus paid a special tribute (LB II
405D). Aleandro later admitted that when he
left Venice for France on 5 May 1508, he did so
on Erasmus' advice (Allen Ep 256:3n) and
greeted his friend by name in the first letter he
wrote from Paris. But since the relationship can
only have lasted about five months, we may
reasonably doubt if it was quite as deep-rooted
as the polemics of both parties later implied.

By the end of July 1508 Aleandro had
established himself in Paris, made contact with
*Budé and *Lefèvre d'Etaples, and begun

Girolamo Aleandro by Agostino Veneziano

some private lessons in Greek from texts
brought or ordered directly from Aldus in
Venice. But the breakdown of relations
between France and the Republic early in 1509
cut off this supply of books, and from 30 April
1509 Girolamo embarked on a series of Greek
editions in collaboration with Gilles de
*Gourmont, beginning with a selection from
Plutarch's *Moralia* and continuing with extracts
from Isocrates and Lucian. He began his public
lectures on Plutarch on 8 October 1509, but an
outbreak of plague in Paris during that autumn
drove him to seek refuge in Orléans, where he
remained from 8 December until 14 June of the
following year, again relying on a small circle of
private pupils. Success came rapidly after his
return to Paris. His own claim that audiences at
the Collège de la Marche rose from 25 to 140 is
borne out by the letters of pupils who describe
throngs of up to 1500 waiting breathless in the
July heat for two hours before the lectures
began. He complemented his teaching by
editing a new series of publications in Paris,
including a reissue of Craston's Greek lexicon
in 1512, a Theocritus and the grammar of
Theodorus *Gaza in 1513, and Fra Urbano

*Valeriano's *Institutiones graecae grammatices* in 1514. The dependence on Aldus' program is obvious, and Aleandro's importance as a transmitter of Italian humanist scholarship into France was already obvious to his contemporaries. He was principal of the Collège des Lombards from 1511 and on 18 March 1513 was appointed rector of the university, the first Italian to hold the post since Marsilius of Padua two centuries earlier.

The privations of early manhood had left Girolamo morbidly anxious about his financial security, and throughout this apparently prosperous period he was exploring the possibilities of improving his position by entering the service of the bishop of Trieste, by teaching in Germany, or by securing ecclesiastical benefices in France itself. 'I manage to live, but only from day to day,' he complained to Erasmus in February 1512, reproaching his friend for failing to write, and regretting that he had failed to meet him in Paris (Ep 256). After accepting service as secretary to Etienne *Poncher, bishop of Paris, on 4 December 1513, Aleandro shifted his allegiance almost exactly a year later to Erard de la *Marck, bishop of Liège, and assembled benefices worth around one thousand livres per year in the process. Dispatched as the bishop's emissary to the curia on 8 March 1516, he used the patronage of Alberto *Pio, to whom he had sent a number of books, to arrange for his transfer into the service of Cardinal Giulio de' Medici on 2 December 1517. From there he was promoted to the librarianship of the Vatican on 27 July 1519. It was a fitting conclusion to a decade of determined place-seeking, and the letters in which Girolamo besought Alberto Pio to see that he was granted a room in the cardinal's palace reveal the agility and servility that had been required.

In the summer of 1520 Aleandro was sent to implement the papal bull *Exsurge Domine*, excommunicating *Luther, in Germany and the Low Countries. His own attitude appears to have been uncompromising: his letters note the support he was receiving, dwell with satisfaction on the bonfires of books in Louvain and Liège that were alarming both Erasmus and *Hutten (Epp 1135, 1157, 1161), and make oblique reference to 'the agitation of a certain unprincipled character,' who was hardening

the resistance of the Germans. Aleandro did all in his power to have Luther handed over directly to Rome and then to prevent his being heard by the diet of Worms. Failing on both counts, he remained to help the depleted diet formulate its edict against Luther on 26 May 1521, then accompanied *Charles v to the Low Countries to continue the campaign against heresy (Ep 1233). During the spring of 1522 he preceded the emperor to Spain, where he met the new pope, *Adrian vi, and rejoiced over his success in securing six hundred ducats' worth of benefices in Valencia from that parsimonious pontiff.

But Adrian's death in September 1523 and the elevation of an old patron, Giulio de' Medici, to the papal throne as *Clement vii soon brought Aleandro back to Rome. On 8 August 1524, Gianpietro Carafa, the future *Paul iv, resigned the archiepiscopate of Brindisi in his favour and on 9 October consecrated him priest. Only four days later he was dispatched as papal nuncio to the French court, which he joined near Pavia just in time to share the defeat and capture of *Francis i on 24 February 1525. Returning to Rome on 3 August, Girolamo had more time to reflect on theological questions and on the responsibilities of his archdiocese. At about this time he wrote 'Racha,' an unpublished personal attack on Erasmus and his interpretation of Matthew 10:27; a manuscript version has recently been discovered in Parisinus Latinus 3461 (Epp 1717, 1719, 1987, 2077, 2443); cf E. Massa 'Intorno ad Erasmo: una polemica che si credeva perduta' in *Classical, Medieval and Renaissance studies in Honor of Berthold Louis Ullman* (Rome 1964) ii 435–54. But since Girolamo's diary continues to note the progress of three illegitimate children and of his treatment for syphilis, there is little reason to believe that the company of the reforming prelates Carafa and Gian Matteo *Giberti brought about a fundamental change of heart in Aleandro himself. He had the luck to leave Rome on 8 March 1527, avoiding the Sack, and spent the next two years in the vicinity of Brindisi. He watched the stages of the Italian wars and the peace negotiations at Bologna from the relative security of Venice during 1529 and 1530.

At this point the valuable entries in

Aleandro's diary end altogether, and personal insights become more difficult to find. A new tour of duty as nuncio to the imperial court took him to the Low Countries in 1531, but by 4 January of the following year he had already been instructed to proceed to the nunciature of Venice. By now Aleandro was recognized as a staunch opponent of heresy. As a reward for his services, Charles v granted his family the privilege of quartering the imperial eagle with their coat of arms, and Girolamo's dispatches from Venice from 1533 to 1535 reveal his growing anxiety at the spread of Lutheranism in the republic and its territories. Probably because of his wide diplomatic experience, Aleandro was summoned to Rome by *Paul III towards the end of 1534, and in 1536 was drafted with his friends *Contarini, Carafa, *Sadoleto, and Giberti onto the pope's committee to advise on reform of the church and on a general council. Aleandro's part in framing the Consilium de emendanda ecclesia of February 1537 is not clear. Minutes he is known to have drafted about this time treat any future council as being a strictly Catholic affair rather than a means of reuniting the church. This suggests that his attitude was less liberal than that of Contarini, and it was not until 18 March 1538 that he was raised to the cardinalate with the title San Ciriaco and dispatched to the imperial court with legatine powers to summon the general council to Vicenza. After the failure of Contarini's bid for an agreement with the Protestants at Regensburg in 1541, Carafa and Aleandro were the first cardinals to be elected to a papal Inquisition with a view to initiating a more repressive policy. But by this time Aleandro's health had been completely undermined, and he died in 1542.

Girolamo's relations with Erasmus mystified even their contemporaries, since the two passed from warm friendship to bitter hostility without an open quarrel. The warmth of Aleandro's letter in 1512 (Ep 256) and Erasmus' automatic assumption in the winter of 1517–18 that his friend's promotion meant the promotion of piety and learning (Epp 735, 738, 756) do not suggest that there was any friction between them over works like the Moria or the New Testament. It seems to have been the publication of Erasmus' very guarded letter to

Luther (Ep 980) that aroused Aleandro's suspicions (Allen Ep 1167:111–23). Apart from oblique private references to 'agitators,' he certainly denounced Erasmus in his dispatches to Cardinal Giulio de' Medici; cf P. Smith Luther's Correspondence and Other Contemporary Letters (Philadelphia 1913) I 454. Rumours of this reached Erasmus and combined with Hutten's goading (Epp 1135, 1161) and Aleandro's zealous burning of books in Louvain to make Erasmus so suspicious of his former friend's duplicity that by the spring of 1521 he recalled an instance when he had feared to be poisoned by Aleandro (Ep 1188). Nevertheless, the two met accidentally at an inn called the 'Wild Man' in Louvain, apparently in October, and were able to pick up the threads of their friendship without difficulty (Epp 1244, 1342; CWE Ep 1241A = Allen Ep 2680). Aleandro even intervened to check the attacks of an outspoken Dominican on Erasmus (Epp 1271, 1281, 1342). But the reconciliation did not last. By the spring of 1522 Erasmus was again naming Aleandro as an enemy (Epp 1263, 1268): he was convinced of his dishonesty, ambition, and jealousy (Ep 1437), and he soon replied to new complaints from Girolamo with a series of new charges of his own (Ep 1482) – that Aleandro was spreading malicious gossip and attacking Erasmus' scholarship. Until the end of 1525 Erasmus made a few half-hearted gestures towards reconciliation (Ep 1621), but the simultaneous appearance of 'Racha' and the first draft of Alberto Pio's criticisms convinced Erasmus that Aleandro was hatching a conspiracy against him in Rome (Epp 1744, 2029, 2042, 2143, 2329, 2371, 2375, 2466). The publication of *Scaliger's orations in defence of Cicero during 1531 led Erasmus unhesitatingly to the conclusion that 'Scaliger' was either a satellite or a pseudonym of his old enemy (Epp 2575, 2581), who was also accused of engineering his condemnation by the Sorbonne (Ep 2585). Aleandro's justifiable plea that he had hardly written to Alberto Pio, or been anywhere near Paris, for at least seven years (Epp 2638, 2639) and *Rabelais' assurance that Scaliger was a real person (Ep 2743) carried no weight with Erasmus. Though Erasmus had some reason to consider himself the first injured party, he had rejected all efforts at reconciliation, lumped Aleandro together with other one-time friends in a wholesale rejection of all things Italian, and was in a far more uncompromising position than his adversary (Ep 2892; ASD I-3, 677–85; LB IX 1136–7).

Considering the fear and respect in which his intellect was held by contemporaries, Aleandro has left remarkably few traces of it behind. Few of his works were published in his own lifetime, and most of these were revisions of classical texts already in print. His voluminous diplomatic correspondence is only now being printed. His library, inventoried at his death and bequeathed to the church of Madonna dell'Orto in Venice, is notable chiefly for the immense quantity of Protestant writing that it appears to have contained. A single small portrait by Agostino di Musi is preserved in Biblioteca Apostolica Vaticana MS Latinus 5234 and reproduced in Paquier's biography. It depicts Aleandro as archbishop of Brindisi in 1536, with an expression of utter exhaustion mixed with ennui. Perhaps, as he repeatedly told Erasmus, Aleandro was far too worried about politics to spare much time for the things of the mind.

BIBLIOGRAPHY: Allen Ep 256 / G. Alberigo in DBI II 128–34 / J. Paquier *Jérôme Aléandre de sa naissance à la fin de son séjour a Brindes, 1480–1529* (Paris 1900 / On Aleandro's own writings, see *Lettres familières de Jérôme Aléandre, 1510–1540* ed J. Paquier (Paris 1909); F. Gaeta *Nunziature di Venezia* I (Rome 1958); *Concilium Tridentinum* XII (Freiburg 1930); *Journal autobiographique du cardinal Jérôme Aléandre* ed H. Omont (Paris 1895) / On his editions of the classics, see Paquier's biography, and for comment M. Jovy 'François Tissard et Jérôme Aléandre' *Mémoires de la Société des sciences et des arts de Vitry-le-François* 19 (1913) 318–457. / On his library, see L. Dorez 'Recherches sur la bibliothèque du Cardinal Jérôme Aléandre' and 'Nouvelles recherches …' *Revue des bibliothèques* 2 (1892) 49–68, 7 (1897) 14.

M.J.C. LOWRY

Johannes ALEMANNUS *See Jean* LALEMAND

Alessandro d'ALESSANDRO of Naples, 1461–October 1523
Alessandro d'Alessandro (Alexander ab Alexandro) was born to a family of lawyers. In his youth he studied with Giovanni *Pontano in Naples. He went to Rome in 1472–3 for further study, and divided the rest of his life between Rome, where he died, and Naples. He gave up a career in the practice of law to devote himself to legal scholarship and was given the Basilian monastery Sant' Elia and Sant' Anastasio di Carboni *in commendam*. His most important work, highly respected by his contemporaries, is the *Dies geniales* (Rome 1522), a collection of notes and discussions of philological and especially legal topics, as well as personal notes and anecdotes of his friends and experiences. Among his friends were Pontano, Raffaele *Maffei, Paolo *Cortesi, and Ermolao I *Barbaro.

Erasmus and Alessandro knew each other only through their works, and then not extensively. Erasmus' one mention of Alessandro indicates that he had only recently heard of him and that Alessandro was generally unknown, at least among northern humanists (Allen Ep 2810:109–13). Erasmus' negative attitude towards him was probably based upon Alessandro's antipathy towards Lorenzo *Valla.

BIBLIOGRAPHY: Allen Ep 2810 / E. Garin 'Alessandro d'Alessandro e Raffaele da Volterra' *Rinascimento* 1 (1950) 102–3 / Domenico Maffei *Alessandro d'Alessandro: giureconsulto umanista (1461–1523)* (Milan 1956) / Cosenza I 122–3

JOHN F. D'AMICO

Pope ALEXANDER VI 1430/2–8 August 1503
Rodrigo de Borja (Borgia), the future pope, was born at Xativa, near Valencia. His father was Jofré de Borja y Doms and his mother was Isabella, the sister of Alonso de Borja, later Pope Calixtus III. Prior to his fifteenth birthday he entered the church and began to receive numerous benefices from his uncle, then bishop of Valencia. Rodrigo followed his uncle to Rome, was a disciple of Gaspare da Verona, and studied canon law at the University of Bologna. On 8 April 1455 Alonso de Borja became pontiff, and on 10 May 1455 Rodrigo was appointed protonotary apostolic and on 20

February 1456 received a cardinalate. Within a year he was appointed vice-chancellor of the church, an office he held for thirty-five years. During his uncle's pontificate Rodrigo acquired enormous wealth and influence, which he managed to retain under succeeding popes. Under *Sixtus IV he returned to Spain as legate and assisted in the union of Castile and Aragon. A robust, eloquent man, with a reputation for immorality, he was narrowly defeated in the conclave of 1484. The conclave following Innocent VIII's death was notorious for simony, and from it Rodrigo emerged on 11 August 1492 as Pope Alexander VI.

From the first Alexander conducted the papacy like a secular state. He bestowed offices and benefices upon his supporters, arranged marriages between his children and leading allies and adversaries, and used the creation of cardinals to placate various princes, to raise immediate money, and to strengthen his own position, as he did by giving red hats to his nephew, Juan, and his son, Cesare.

In the face of the French invasion of Italy in 1494, Alexander vacillated between resistance and compromise until the situation was perilous, but he eventually joined the coalition opposing the French. Alexander's treatment of Girolamo *Savonarola shows the same pattern of equivocation which allows a bad situation to worsen until it can be resolved only by the most extreme measures. On three occasions Erasmus quotes a saying attributed to Alexander in which he asserts he would rather offend any of the reigning kings than a single monk (Ep 694; Colloquia ASD I-3, 665, 698). Alexander's hesitancy in dealing with Savonarola may have resulted from his sense of the monk's power.

Alexander financed the conquest of Romagna and the Marches that was undertaken by his son, Cesare, with a new creation of cardinals and the revenues from the jubilee of 1500. In Ep 1211 Erasmus referred to Alexander making two jubilees from one, an allusion to the scheduling of jubilees at intervals of twenty-five years, which was actually instigated before Alexander's time. Erasmus' suspicion of Alexander's avarice was shared by many who saw the pope channelling church resources into Cesare's war of conquest. Alexander created Cesare vicar of the church and in May 1501 duke of Romagna. The central

Pope Alexander VI by Pinturicchio

states of Italy – Romagna, the Marches, Urbino, Camerino – fell before the force of Cesare's army, and Ferrara was secured by his sister's marriage to its duke, Alfonso d'*Este. In 1503, when Cesare was at the pinnacle of power and eyeing new realms, Alexander died. His death was widely attributed to poison (as retribution for his alleged means of removing enemies), but a malaria was the probable cause. Stricken at the same time, the one circumstance he had not foreseen, was Cesare. His father's death and his own incapacitation spelt the end of Cesare's empire. In De bello turcico (LB V 353C) Erasmus recalled Alexander's ruthless betrayal of Prince *Djem, and elsewhere he expressed his scorn (Ep 292; Adagia III iii 1).

Alexander, so embroiled in Italian politics, performed an act of significance for the New World on 4 May 1493 when he designated the dividing line between Spanish and Portuguese interests. The flagrant immorality of the Borgias and many of the cardinals did much to diminish the spiritual authority of the papacy. Alexander, like all the Renaissance popes, was a patron of the arts and collected around him a court of renowned humanists. Pinturicchio's fresco in the Borgia apartments in the Vatican portrays the pontiff as a genial, cultured aristocrat.

BIBLIOGRAPHY: G.B. Picotti in DBI II 196–205 (with bibliography) / Giovanni Soranzo *Studi intorno a Alessandro VI* (Milan 1950) / M.E. Mallett *The Borgias* (London 1969)

DE ETTA V. THOMSEN

Alexander ab ALEXANDRO See ALESSANDRO

Augustine of ALFELD, AHLFELD See Augustin ALVELDT

ALFONSO II of Aragon king of Naples, 4 November 1448–18 December 1495
Alfonso was born in Naples, the son of Ferrante, prince of Capua and subsequently king of Naples, and of Isabella da Chiaromonte. Neapolitan humanism flourished during the reign of his grandfather, Alfonso I, and the young prince was educated by its most distinguished representatives, Antonio Beccadelli called Panormita and Giovanni *Pontano. Although Alfonso was fully aware of the debt he owed these teachers, an unfavourable historiographical tradition proposes to see in him the target of Pontano's dialogue *Asinus sive de ingratitudine.*

Alfonso was named duke of Calabria by his grandfather in 1458, and at the tender age of fourteen he directed a military expedition against the rebel barons who supported Jean d'Anjou. In 1465 in Milan he married by proxy Ippolita Maria Sforza, who later bore him two sons, Ferrandino and Pietro, and a daughter, Isabella, the future bride of Gian Galeazzo Sforza, duke of Milan. Two years after his marriage he fought for Florence against the Venetians, but in the wake of the Pazzi conspiracy of 1478 he joined papal troops in their war against Florence. Having entered Siena on 20 February 1479, he proceeded to defeat the Florentines at Poggio Imperiale and at Colle. In 1480 the Turkish threat impelled him to return home: the campaign he led from August 1480 to September 1481 succeeded in liberating Otranto from the Ottoman invaders. In the following year he joined Ercole I d'Este in his struggle against Pope *Sixtus IV and Venice but was defeated by the Venetian

commander, Roberto Malatesta, on 21 August 1482 at Campomorto in the papal states. In the same year he was elected commander for a league of princes and cities directed against Venice. He conducted the ensuing operations with considerable success and at one point even came to besiege the city of Venice.

After a peace had been concluded on 7 August 1484 Alfonso returned to Naples amid the fears of the unruly barons that his presence might strengthen the hand of his weak father. And in fact Alfonso persuaded his father to take stern measures in the face of a conspiracy against the throne and in the process incurred the lasting hatred of the nobility. This hostility survived the actual conspiracy; in the end it led not only to a negative judgment on Alfonso on the part of most contemporary chroniclers and later historians but also to the very downfall of his dynasty as a result of the French invasion headed by King *Charles VIII. When Ferrante died on 25 January 1494, Alfonso succeeded his father to rule for barely a year in a climate of recrimination and unpopularity. In January 1495 his abdication in favour of his son Ferrandino was a final attempt to save his dynasty from the French threat. The attempt failed, and Alfonso died while preparing to enter a monastery.

Alfonso's defeat by Charles VIII is mentioned by Robert *Gaguin in a letter to Erasmus (Ep 46).

BIBLIOGRAPHY: R. Moscati in DBI II 331–2 / *Regis Ferdinandi primi instructionum libri* ed L. Volpicello (Naples 1916), with a good bibliography, 225–9 / E. Pontieri *Per la storia del regno di Ferrante I d'Aragona, re di Napoli* (Naples 1947)

MARCO BERNUZZI

ALFONSO de Aragon 1470–25 February 1520
Alfonso de Aragon, the illegitimate son of *Ferdinand II, king of Aragon, was born at Cervera in Catalonia. At the age of seven he was named archbishop of Saragossa and received title to several abbeys. On 14 August 1478 *Sixtus IV reluctantly allowed him to administer the archdiocese until he reached the canonical age of twenty-five. In 1482 Alfonso was named lieutenant-general of Aragon and in 1483 chancellor. He was ordained priest on 7 November 1501 and consecrated bishop on the following day, in the presence of his two sons

and two daughters. On 24 January 1505 he added the archdiocese of Monreal to his ecclesiastical holdings, exchanging this for Valencia on 23 January 1512. On the death of Ferdinand in 1516 he served as viceroy of Aragon, while Ferdinand's widow, *Germaine de Foix, was vicereine of Valencia. Despite the less savoury aspects of his ecclesiastical career, he was a zealous administrator of the church, holding numerous diocesan synods, restoring churches, and disciplining the clergy. Various collections of synodical decrees and ecclesiastical regulations were published under his name. He died while conducting pastoral visitations and was buried in the church of La Seo at Saragossa.

On 18 July 1516 Pierre *Barbier mentioned Alfonso in a letter to Erasmus (Ep 443).

BIBLIOGRAPHY: Allen Ep 443 / DHGE II 698–9 / New Cambridge Modern History ed G.R. Potter (Cambridge 1957–) I 323

TBD

Lieven ALGOET of Ghent, d 25 January 1547 Lieven Algoet (Livinus Algotius, Omnibonus, Panagathus), a young man born at Ghent by the turn of the century, entered Erasmus' service in 1519 at Louvain. Hired at the recommendation of Marcus *Laurinus, his patron and perhaps a relative, Algoet was permitted to take courses at the Collegium Trilingue and treated, Erasmus insists, 'not as a servant but as a son' (Ep 1091). From the time Erasmus settled at Basel Algoet became known to his master's correspondents as one of his regular letter-carriers. He was sent to the Low Countries and England in the spring of 1523 (Epp 1366, 1373, 1383), in April 1524 (Epp 1430, 1434, 1437, 1452, 1457, 1458, 1463, 1467, 1470, 1478), and again in September of that same year (Epp 1486, 1488, 1489, 1491, 1494, 1531, 1537, 1547, 1549). On this latter trip Algoet carried a recommendation to Cardinal *Wolsey, who had a young relative studying at Louvain. Erasmus suggested that Algoet might join that young Englishman as a tutor and fellow student. Algoet, he said, was born to be a scholar (Epp 1486, 1491). Algoet himself, however, was not so intent on the pursuit of learning. In July 1525 Erasmus referred to him as a former famulus (Ep 1585) and in May 1526 recommended him to the papal datary, Gian

Matteo *Giberti, presumably because Algoet was then trying to obtain a benefice (Ep 1716). In July 1527 Algoet was in Paris, perhaps to study medicine (Epp 1848, 2792); subsequently he returned to the Netherlands.

Algoet often wrote to Erasmus (Epp 1871, 1922), and in March 1530 he visited Erasmus at Freiburg (Ep 2278); Erasmus sent him on an errand to Augsburg, where the court of *Charles v was expected to arrive for the diet (Epp 2294; cf Ep 2292, 2299–301). Algoet reached Augsburg early in April (Ep 2307) and from there went to Trent, where he found the court and attached himself to Cornelis de *Schepper, hoping for some employment (Ep 2336). He returned to Augsburg with the court and subsequently published his own account of the diet, Pro religione christiana res gestae in comitiis Augustae Vindelicorum habitis (Louvain: B. Gravius 1530). From 1531 Erasmus spared no effort to secure him a place in the entourage of *Mary of Hungary, recommending him to Alfonso de *Valdes (Epp 2469, 2528) and particularly to Nicolaus *Olahus, who did in fact appoint him his secretary (Epp 2567, 2570, 2582, 2583, 2587, 2607, 2613, 2646, 2693). By the end of June 1533 Algoet was sent on a mission to Freiburg, where he was to prepare the way for Erasmus' return to Brabant. Erasmus promptly used him on errands of his own, sending him to Augsburg (Ep 2856) and Dole (Ep 2860). Towards the end of August he again left for Mary's court, uncertain about the success of his mission but warmly recommended by Erasmus (Ep 2860).

In 1534 Algoet was appointed maistre d'escole des pages d'honneur at Queen Mary's court (Ep 2915) and in 1538 king-of-arms and keeper of records (greffier) in the imperial chancery. In particular he produced geographical maps, one of which was printed in several sixteenth-century atlases. He also composed an Epitaphium for *Isabella of Portugal, the wife of Charles v (Antwerp 1548). As Erasmus saw it, Algoet had a brilliant future as a scholar (Ep 2762), but he played around, neglecting his studies and applying for unsuitable positions (Epp 2587, 2792). Erasmus also found fault with Algoet's marriage (6 August 1532) to Catherine Hannot (Annoot), the grandaughter of Antonius *Clava (Epp 2707, 2735, 2759, 2792). In the same vein he accused him of

Francesco Alidosi, school of Francesco Francia

complicity with Johannes *Clauthus, but still chose to pay him – although clearly without enthusiasm – a large sum of money through Erasmus *Schets (Epp 3028, 3042, 3053).

BIBLIOGRAPHY: Allen Ep 1091 / BNB VIII 68–9 / NBW VI 1–3 / A. Roersch *L'Humanisme belge à l'époque de la renaissance* (Brussels-Louvain 1910–33) II 11–31 / de Vocht *Dantiscus* 53 and passim / de Vocht CTL II 136–9 and passim / de Vocht MHL 53–4 / de Vocht *Literae ad Craneveldium* 145–6 and passim / Bierlaire *Familia* 55–9 / Miklós Oláh *Levelezése* ed Arnold Ipolyi in *Monumenta Hungariae historica. Diplomataria* XXV (Budapest 1875) 144 and passim
FRANZ BIERLAIRE

Francesco ALIDOSI 1455–24 May 1511
The third son of Giovanni Alidosi, signore of Castel del Rio and Masso Alidosio (near Imola), Francesco was educated at Bologna, where he is believed to have studied theology. He became an apostolic scriptor under *Sixtus IV (possibly owing to the patronage of Girolamo Riario) and a papal secretary in 1493. A member of Cardinal Giuliano della Rovere's household, he accompanied him to France, and on

Giuliano's election as *Julius II became successively a papal chamberlain, treasurer, bishop of Pavia (May 1505), and a cardinal (7 December 1507). He accompanied the pope to Perugia and Bologna in 1506 and was appointed papal legate of Viterbo in March 1507 and of Bologna on 19 May 1508, arriving there on 9 June 1508 and remaining until November, when he was recalled to Rome for discussions concerning the forthcoming joint war against Venice. He returned to Bologna in April 1509, and in June his legation was extended to include Romagna and the Marches. In Bologna he proceeded ruthlessly against the partisans of the Bentivoglio; because of complaints about his repressive administration he was recalled to Rome on 5 January 1510 but returned in March. On 7 October 1510 he was arrested by Francesco Maria *della Rovere, duke of Urbino and papal commander, on a charge of conspiracy with the French in his own family interests, but Julius II, as usual, favoured him and promoted him to the bishopric of Bologna on 19 October. After the fall of Bologna to the French in May 1511, for which he was widely blamed, he first fled to Castel del Rio but then went to rejoin the pope at Ravenna, where on 24 May he was murdered in the street by the duke of Urbino.

Some doubt must be cast upon Allen's identification of Francesco as the cardinal of Bologna to whom Erasmus was grateful for his favour (Allen Ep 296:103n; CWE Epp 296:109n, 334:44n). When he arrived at Bologna in 1508 Erasmus was in Venice, but in any case Erasmus' two letters make clear that the favour was enjoyed in Rome, and Francesco left Rome at about the time Erasmus arrived there in 1509. Moreover Francesco was usually known as the cardinal of Pavia and is so identified in the *Julius exclusus* (*Opuscula* 88–9), while Stefano *Ferreri was the cardinal of Bologna, although admittedly Paris de Grassis refers to Francesco (Frati 222) as 'Bononiensis sive Papiensis.' He was cardinal protector of England from September 1508 probably until his death, though he was reported to be untrustworthy (D.S. Chambers *Cardinal Bainbridge in the Court of Rome*, Oxford 1965, 10–12, 73), but there is no evidence of any link with Erasmus through his tenure of this office.

Francesco did enjoy the reputation of being a

generous patron and was associated with the commissioning of various paintings. It has been suggested that Raphael's portrait of an unknown cardinal in the Prado Museum is of him; it bears some resemblance to the portrait medal by an anonymous Bolognese (Hill no 610). His head is preserved in the Biblioteca Classense, Ravenna.

BIBLIOGRAPHY: G. de Caro in DBI II 373–6 / *Le due spedizioni militari di Giulio II* ed L. Frati (Bologna 1886) passim / Pastor v 171 and passim / Sanudo *Diarii* v 392, 570, and passim / J. Kalcsko *Jules II* (Paris 1898) 287ff attempted to defend Alidosi

D.S. CHAMBERS

Giles ALINGTON *See Thomas* ELRYNGTON

John ALLEN 1476–27/28 July 1534
Allen (Alen, Aleyn, Alanus) studied at Oxford and then at Cambridge, where he received his MA in 1498 and later, his bachelor of laws. For several years prior to 1512 he was in Rome, acting in part as Archbishop *Warham's agent (Ep 249). While abroad he obtained a doctorate in law by 1508. He was ordained in 1499 and in the same year was acting as a commissary to the bishop of Rochester. Allen was prebendary of Lincoln in 1503 and from then until 1515 received many benefices including the vicarage of Chislet, near Canterbury, in 1503 and the living of Aldington, Kent, which he held from 1511 to 1512 and in which he preceded Erasmus. In 1512 he had been known for some time to Andrea *Ammonio (Ep 249) and probably also to Erasmus (Ep 250) who apparently disliked him. He was a friend of William *Thale and acquainted with Johannes *Sixtinus (Ep 244). Allen was one of two special legatine commissaries assigned to the probation of wills by Cardinal *Wolsey and Archbishop Warham. He acted as Wolsey's agent in the suppression of minor monasteries in 1524 and 1525, an action which led others to complain of him to the king. He also assisted Wolsey in the examination of heretics and in a suit begun in 1527 to invalidate King *Henry VIII's marriage to *Catherine of Aragon. In that same year he accompanied Wolsey to France. From 1527 to 1528 he was canon of St Paul's in London. He was appointed archbishop of Dublin in 1528 upon the king's recommenda-

tion and in the same year was made chancellor of Ireland. In 1531 he was fined for offences against the statutes of provision and *praemunire*, but received a general pardon. He was murdered in Ireland during the rebellion of Lord Thomas Fitzgerald.

Allen is said to have written two treatises: 'Epistola de pallii significatione activa et passiva' and 'De consuetudinibus ac statutis in tutoriis causis observandis'; he also compiled two registers detailing affairs of his diocese and the church, which are preserved.

BIBLIOGRAPHY: Allen and CWE Ep 244 / Emden BRUC 8–9 / DNB I 305–7 / W.E. Wilkie *The Cardinal Protectors of England* (Cambridge 1974) 167–8 / G.B. Parks *The English Traveler to Italy* (Rome 1954–) I 375

CFG

Theodoricus ALOSTENSIS, ALUSTENSIS
See Dirk MARTENS

Fadrique ALVAREZ de Toledo c 1460–1531
Fadrique Alvarez de Toledo was the second duke of Alba. He was the son of García Alvarez de Toledo and Leonor Enriquez, the sister of Juana Enriquez, the mother of *Ferdinand II of Aragon. Fadrique's eldest son, García, who died at the battle of Gelves (1510), was the father of the third duke of Alba, Fernando Alvarez de Toledo (1507–82), best known for his role in resisting the revolt of the Netherlands. As first cousin to Ferdinand, Fadrique played an important role in the reign of the Catholic Monarchs. His name is especially associated with the wars of Granada of 1482–92, in which he played an exceptional role in the sieges of Baza in 1489 and the city Granada from 1490 to 1492. He subsequently led the invasion of Roussillon, culminating in the siege of Salses in 1503. On the death of *Isabella of Castile Fadrique did not support the accession of Philip the Handsome of *Burgundy but followed Ferdinand to Aragon in 1506. He pressed Ferdinand to return to Castile in 1507 and led the Spanish army in the conquest of Navarre in 1512. In 1517 he welcomed the future *Charles v to Valladolid but actively opposed the appointment of Flemish ministers. His son Diego was a candidate for the see of Toledo, which was given to Guillaume (II) de *Croy. This moved

Fadrique Alvarez de Toledo

Fadrique to refuse to accompany Charles to Aragon. Reconciliation seems to have come shortly thereafter, since he is known to have been in Charles' following after 1518. He was made a knight of the Golden Fleece in 1519 at Barcelona and accompanied the emperor to Germany. Between 1519 and 1525 he was occasionally deputed to Italy and Flanders. In 1526 he became a member of the Spanish council of state and was present at the arrival of Princess *Isabella of Portugal, before following Charles to Seville. As Juan Luis *Vives indicated in a letter to Erasmus (Ep 2208), in 1529 the duke continued to occupy an important position on the council of state and took part in the administration of Spain, with Queen Isabella, Alonso de *Fonseca, and Francisco de *Zúñiga, during Charles' absence in Italy.

In 1522 Vives informed Erasmus of a rumour circulated by Girolamo *Aleandro that Fadrique was displeased with him (Ep 1256). Vives himself was offered a post as tutor to the duke's grandsons in Spain in the same year (Ep 1271).

BIBLIOGRAPHY: Allen Ep 1256 / *Diccionario de historia de España* (Madrid 1968–9) / *Enciclopedia universal ilustrada europeo-americana* (Barcelona-

Madrid 1907–   ) IV 1046 / Edward Armstrong *The Emperor Charles V* (London 1910) I 32 / Pedro Girón *Crónica del emperador Carlos V* ed J. Sánchez Montes (Madrid 1964) / Francisco López de Gómara *Annals of Charles V* ed R.B. Merriman (Oxford 1912) / Manuel Foronda y Aguilera *Estancias y viajes del emperador Carlos V* (Madrid 1914) / Pedro Mexía *Historia del emperador Carlos V* ed J. de Mata Carriazo (Madrid 1945) / Hernando del Pulgar *Crónicas de los reyes de Castilla* ed C. Rosell y López (Madrid 1953) III / F. Soldevila Zubiburu *Historia de España* 2nd ed (Barcelona 1962) III

LOUIS P.A. MAINGON

Augustin ALVELDT of Alfeld, c 1480–c 1535
Augustin Alveldt (Alveldianus, Alveldensis) was born in Alfeld, near Hildesheim (Hanover). He was a Franciscan and was lector in the monastery at Leipzig in 1520 when he wrote the pamphlet against Martin *Luther *Super apostolica sede* (Leipzig: M. Lotter 1520). After a reply by Johannes *Lonicerus he published several more pamphlets against Luther in the course of 1520 and others later on; see *Index Aureliensis* (Baden-Baden 1962–   ) I 422–5. Alveldt visited Italy in 1523 and 1526 and from 1524 was warden of the Franciscans in Halle, where he died. He was a good friend of Johannes *Cochlaeus and Hieronymus *Emser. In 1530 he supervised the publication of Emser's translation of the New Testament, and in 1535 he wrote an explanation of the rules of the order of St Clare. In Epp 1153, 1154, 1167, 1186 Erasmus shows some acquaintance with his writings against Luther; cf LB X 1652 C.

BIBLIOGRAPHY: Allen Ep 1167 / NDB I 230–1 / DHGE II 984–5 / LThK I 410 / Luther w *Briefwechsel* II Epp 276, 284, 297

IG

Bartolomeo d'ALVIANO 1455–7 October 1515
Bartolomeo d'Alviano was born to Francesco and the noblewoman Isabella degli Atti, probably at Todi near Perugia. Prepared for a military career from childhood, Alviano became one of Renaissance Italy's most famous *condottieri*, principally in the service of Venice. During the war of the League of Cambrai, he was defeated and captured by the French at the battle of Agnadello of 14 May 1509. Later,

allied with France, Alviano and his Venetian forces played a key role in the defeat of the Swiss at Marignano on 13 September 1515. He died of intestinal disorders several weeks later.

Erasmus mentioned Alviano only in 1535 (Ep 3032), when claiming that Pietro *Corsi in his *Defensio pro Italia ad Erasmum Roterodamum* (Rome: A. Bladus 1535) had exaggerated Alviano's victory over the invading German troops of *Maximilian I in 1508, when Erasmus himself was present in Venice.

BIBLIOGRAPHY: Allen Ep 3032 / DBI II 587–91

TBD

AMANDUS of Zierikzee documented 1503– d 1524/1534

Amandus of Zierikzee, on the island of Schouwen, is first documented as a member of the Franciscan Conventuals and rose to be the head of their Cologne province from 1503 to 1506. In 1506, however, he joined the Franciscan Observants and lived to his death in their house at Louvain, serving repeatedly as warden and also lecturing in the faculty of theology. He was knowledgeable in Hebrew, Syriac, and Greek, and devoted himself particularly to the study of history. His valuable *Chronica ... mundi* was posthumously published by Frans *Titelmans (Antwerp: S. Cocus 1534) with a continuation by Titelmans himself and some biographical material on Amandus in the introduction.

Amandus composed commentaries on Genesis, Ecclesiastes, and Job, and wrote other theological works, which were preserved in manuscript at Louvain prior to the French revolution. Two treatises, *Quaedam notatu digna de Sophi, rege Persarum* and *De septuaginta hebdomadibus Danielis scrutinium*, were appended by Titelmans to his edition of the *Chronica*. Maarten van *Dorp assured Erasmus of Amandus' admiration and confirmed his skill in languages (Ep 1044).

BIBLIOGRAPHY: Allen Ep 1044 / B. De Troeyer in NBW I 982–4

CFG

Romolo Quirino AMASEO of Udine, 24 June 1489–June 1552

Romolo Quirino Amaseo was born at Udine to the humanist teacher Gregorio Amaseo and Fiore di Marano, a nun of the convent of Santa Chiara. He was legitimized in August 1506. He spent his childhood and adolescence at Udine, Venice, Bergamo, and Padua, studying Latin and Greek under his father and his uncle, Girolamo Amaseo. By the end of 1509 he settled in Bologna, where he taught privately and became a friend of the humanists Giambattista *Pio, Achille *Bocchi, and Giovanni Campeggi. In 1512 he married Violante Guastavillani, who bore him twelve children. Pompilio, his eldest son, continued the family tradition of teaching.

In 1513 the senate of Bologna appointed Amaseo lecturer in Latin and Greek at the university. With the exception of several years spent at Padua (1520–4), he taught at Bologna until 1544, establishing himself as one of the greatest Latinists of his day. Especially memorable were two introductory lectures of 1529–30, in which he defended Latin as the only language suitable for scholars. From 1530 he also served as secretary to the senate of Bologna. In 1544, after rejecting offers to teach at Mantua and Venice and in England, Amaseo travelled to Rome to teach at the university. His many famous students included Reginald *Pole and the nephews of Pope *Paul III. In 1550 he was named papal secretary of Latin letters, but he died soon after.

In the correspondence of Erasmus, Amaseo is mentioned twice by the Dutch legal scholar *Viglius Zuichemus. On 8 June 1532 Viglius informed Erasmus of a rumour that Lazzaro *Bonamico, who taught Latin at Padua, was considering moving to Bologna, and that several of his partisans had tried without success to have Amaseo resign in his favour (Ep 2657). On 17 April 1533 Viglius informed Erasmus that Amaseo had just completed a Latin edition of Xenophon (Ep 2791). Amaseo's translation of Xenophon's *Anabasis* or *De Cyri minoris expeditione* was first published at Bologna in March 1533.

Amaseo also translated the *Graeciae descriptio* by Pausanias (Florence: L. Torrentino 1551). Amaseo's *Orationum volumen* was edited by his son Pompilio and published in 1564 (Bologna: G. Rossi).

BIBLIOGRAPHY: Allen Ep 2657 / R. Avesani in DBI II 660–6

TBD

Georges (I) d'AMBOISE 1460–25 May 1510

Georges, the son of Pierre d'Amboise, seigneur of Chaumont-sur-Loire, and Anne-Marie

Georges (1) d'Amboise, memorial sculpture in Rouen cathedral

Bueil, was intended for the church from childhood. On 8 January 1475 he was abbot of Saint-Paul in Narbonne; he became bishop of Montauban in 1484. Amboise was opposed to the regency of Anne de Beaujeu for King *Charles VIII and became involved in a plot to overthrow her. When this plot was discovered, he was imprisoned for two years; afterwards he had to retire to the diocese of Montauban. Amboise associated himself with the duke of Orléans, later King *Louis XII, and when the duke arranged the marriage of Charles VIII to Anne of Brittany, Amboise was recalled to court. With the king's support he became archbishop of Narbonne in 1492 and of Rouen in 1493.

In 1494 he accompanied Charles VIII to Italy. When Louis XII succeeded Charles in 1498, Amboise immediately came to wield great influence as his adviser. He obtained Pope *Alexander VI's permission for the king to marry Anne, the widow of Charles VIII, and obtained a cardinalate for himself on 12 September 1498. By now he was very powerful in France and strengthened his position further by ecclesiastical reforms that benefited

the country. In 1503 he was unsuccessful in his endeavour to become pope; no love was lost between him and *Julius II, who was then elected (*Julius exclusus, Opuscula* 97). Amboise returned to France, assisted the victims of plague and famine, and in 1508 played a prominent part in the negotiations leading to the treaty of Cambrai. He was extremely wealthy and was a patron of art, bringing architects, painters, and sculptors from Lombardy to France. He died near Lyon and was buried in Rouen, where his nephew, Georges (II) d'*Amboise, had a marble statue of him erected in the cathedral.

BIBLIOGRAPHY: DBF II 491–503 / DHGE II 1060–72

IG

Georges (II) d'AMBOISE 1488–1550

Georges was a nephew of the more famous prelate of the same name, Georges (I) d'*Amboise, and his successor as archbishop of Rouen (1511–50). He was the son of Jean d'Amboise, seigneur de Bussy, and of Catherine de Saint-Belin, dame de Choiseul. Under the influence of his uncle he embarked early on a clerical career in Rouen. He was made archbishop at twenty-three in accordance with the dying request of his uncle.

Amboise was very rich, a cultivated man, with a taste for art and luxury. Visitors to his châteaux were received with near-royal splendour. He was neither a very effective administrator nor a very profound theologian; his response to Protestantism was to order public prayers, join the confraternity of the Conception, reduce the number of feast days, and summon the assistance of Franciscans, Capuchins, and Dominicans. Erasmus, in his reference to Amboise (Ep 2126, 21 March 1529), reports a rumour that he was the principal member of a board of six bishops appointed to pronounce on heretical books in France, and that this board had caused the burning of Erasmus' works in the public square.

In the most dramatic event in his life, Amboise defied his king's command and, despite the fact that *Francis I was a personal friend, refused to permit the levying of what he denounced as unjust taxes upon the clergy of his archdiocese. The property of his see was accordingly sequestered, and he himself was

put in prison. Eventually he had to submit, but
on terms that limited what his clergy were
obliged to pay as a 'charitable gift.' He was
generous to the poor and a patron of the arts,
being responsible for the execution of a
number of works of art in and about Rouen,
notably the tomb of his uncle in the cathedral.
He became a cardinal in 1545 but was never to
have a role in Franco-papal diplomacy
comparable with that of his uncle.

BIBLIOGRAPHY: Allen Ep 2126 / DBF II 503–6 /
Gallia christiana I 34 for the family / DHGE II
1072–3

GORDON GRIFFITHS

AMBROGIO da Calepio *See Ambrogio*
CALEPINO

AMBROSIUS CATHARINUS *See Lancelotto*
de' POLITI

Georgius AMELIUS d 28 October 1541
Georgius Amelius (Achtznicht, Achtsynit), a
native of Moravia, registered in 1518 at the
University of Bologna, where he probably
obtained the doctorate to which he laid claim
when matriculating at Freiburg on 30 September 1521. Having taught a regular law course
since 1523, he became the first professor
ordinarius of canon law in 1525 and continued
in this position until his death, being seven
times dean of law and three times rector. His
first rectorate in the summer term of 1523
established him as a forceful spokesman for the
rights of the university, which he often
thereafter had occasion to defend. From an
initial sixty florins his annual salary had been
increased to one hundred in 1538, but he found
it entirely inadequate, as he complained in a
letter to Fridericus *Nausea, an old friend. He
was also a friend of Udalricus *Zasius,
exchanged letters with him, and was reluctantly permitted to contribute some preliminary matter to his *Intellectus iuris civilis* (Basel:
A. Cratander 1526). From 1532 he also
corresponded with Bonifacius *Amerbach.

In view of these connections it is not
surprising that Amelius was closer to Erasmus
than was his colleague Theobald *Bapst, with
whom he came to blows during a senate
meeting in 1535. Direct contacts began in 1529,
shortly before Erasmus' arrival in Freiburg

Georges (II) d'Amboise, memorial sculpture in
Rouen cathedral

(Epp 2096, 2104). Six years later, when
Erasmus returned to Basel, Amelius offered to
help his housekeeper, Margarete *Büsslin (Ep
3045). His reaction to the news of Erasmus'
death was warm and spontaneous (AK IV Epp
2080, 2083); he recalled how he had advised
him on his second will (between 1530 and 1533:
Ep 2317; Allen XI 362), going once again over
the entire question of Erasmus' illegitimacy,
remedied by papal brief. He gently regretted
seeing this will superseded by the final one,
which was made at Basel and favoured the
people and the university of that city. Amelius,
who was buried in the cathedral of Freiburg,
was married to Magdalena Nittlin of Trepp-
bach and had two sons. One of them, Martin,
became chancellor of the margraviate of Baden
(NDB I 245).

BIBLIOGRAPHY: Allen Ep 2096 / ADB I 394 /
Schreiber *Universität Freiburg* II 353–6 / *Matrikel*
Freiburg I 254 and passim / Knod 3–4 / AK III Epp
1031, 1032, and passim / *Udalrici Zasii epistolae*
(Ulm 1774) Ep 253 / *Epistolae ad Nauseam* 231–2 /
Clausdieter Schott *Rat und Spruch der Juristen-*
fakultät Freiburg i. Br. (Freiburg 1965) 137–8 and
passim

PGB

Basilius AMERBACH of Basel, 28 March
1488–8 April 1535
Basilius, the second son of Johann *Amerbach,
was seven years older than his better-known
brother Bonifacius *Amerbach. He was educated with Bruno *Amerbach, the eldest of the
three brothers. They first studied at Sélestat
from May 1497 to 21 April 1500 (AK I Ep 113);
subsequently they continued at Basel and at
Paris, where – to the disappointment of their
father – their philosophical training was
nominalist rather than realist. Basilius also
applied himself to languages, and Erasmus and
*Glareanus praised him as an expert in Latin,
Greek, and even Hebrew (Epp 334, 396, 2157;
AK II Ep 597). Still with his elder brother,
Basilius graduated BA at the beginning of 1505
(AK I Ep 256) and MA in April 1506 (AK I Epp
304, 305). He then commenced his legal studies
at Freiburg from May 1507 and continued them
to some date between April 1510 and the
summer of 1512 (AK I Epp 435, 464). For part of
this time he lodged with Udalricus *Zasius (AK I
Epp 363, 364), but eventually he left Freiburg
without a doctoral degree. His legal outlook
remained closer to the approach known as the
mos gallicus, as taught by Zasius, than to that of
his brother Bonifacius (AK II Ep 913). During
his studies at Paris, he had done less well than
Bruno (AK I Epp 185, 191, 265). He was often
sick, and initially his father may have intended
him to enter the church rather than join his
press as a scholar-collaborator (AK I Ep 480).
After his father's death he did, nonetheless,
work in Johann *Froben's printing shop from
about 1514, but it seems that he was not happy
there, as he did not get along well with
Froben, who lacked higher education.

Basilius relayed Erasmus' news to his
brother Bonifacius but never made an attempt
to become close friends with the Dutch scholar.
Only one letter of his addressed to Erasmus
survives, and that may never have been sent
(Ep 1207). Erasmus bequeathed some silver
dishes to him in his first will (Allen VI 503), but
this was mainly a token of gratitude for
Basilius' help in the production of the Jerome
and for the numerous other services rendered
in the editing of his works. Basilius' affections
were reserved for Bonifacius, his gifted young
brother, who may have named his only male
child after him, and to his little niece, Faustina

*Amerbach, born in 1530. He remained a
bachelor, and for eight and a half years he took
his meals with Bonifacius' family (AK III Ep
1480). Like his brother, he dutifully answered
letters, filled requests for books, and proved
conscientious in collating and emending texts
for Froben's press, but he was meditative by
nature and lacked initiative and the stamina to
withstand stress. It does not appear that he
ever made much use of his legal training. The
reformed creed troubled him as much as it did
Bonifacius. When taking the Eucharist was
made compulsory under the threat of excommunication, he took refuge with his relatives at
Neuenburg, on the Rhine (AK IV Ep 1556,
September 1531). His hope was that his
influential brother would be able to reach a
special arrangement that might be used as a
precedent for others like himself. He returned
for a while, then left again, and only after
Bonifacius had obtained approval of his
Buceran creed from the pastors and the
council, did he settle again at Basel. A few
months later he died (AK IV Ep 1933).
    BIBLIOGRAPHY: Allen Ep 331 / *Matrikel Basel* I
260 / AK I Ep 70 and passim
                                MANFRED E. WELTI

Bonifacius AMERBACH of Basel, 11 October
1495–24/25 April 1562
The youngest child of Johann *Amerbach,
Bonifacius spent his childhood at Basel. From
the summer of 1507 to the winter of 1508–9 his
father had him attend the humanist school of
Hieronymus Gebwiler at Sélestat. After his
return home, he matriculated at the University
of Basel, receiving his BA in 1511 and his MA on
1 February 1512 (AK I Ep 465). His schooling in
Latin and Greek was complemented by his
contacts with the scholars who were engaged
in the production of his father's edition of
Jerome. His first meeting with Erasmus must
have occurred immediately after the latter's
arrival at Basel; from 1516 onwards there is a
steady flow of correspondence between the
two.

Amerbach's training in the liberal arts was
followed by four and a half years of legal
studies under Udalricus *Zasius at Freiburg.
Zasius was basically a strong adherent of the
legal approach known as the *mos gallicus*,
although he had some reservations about the

use *Budé made of it. In 1520 Amerbach moved to Avignon, where for three years he studied under Giovanni Francesco de Ripa and Andrea *Alciati. Amerbach admired both, but his attachment to Alciati was closer and more lasting. Alciati, like Zasius in Freiburg, tended to follow the *mos gallicus* in his teaching. It is a remarkable achievement that in his legal thought Amerbach did not continue the approach of his teachers but developed an original synthesis between the two conflicting tendencies of *mos gallicus* and *mos italicus*. Although continuing to hold the French legal school in esteem, he made abundant use of the Italian glossators and commentators who focused more closely on the practical legal needs of contemporary city republics. The moderate conservatism which Amerbach showed in spite of his rather progressive teachers at Freiburg and Avignon may perhaps be connected with the emphasis placed on late medieval was well as classical texts in his father's publishing programme. At any rate, Amerbach fitted well into the intellectual atmosphere of Basel. Claudius *Cantiuncula had prepared the way for an exponent of humanistic jurispendence, and when he resigned the chair of Roman law in 1524, he recommended Amerbach as his successor. Amerbach did not accept the appointment at once, but first took the time to obtain his doctorate in Avignon (4 February 1525; AK III Epp 993–6) and permitted Johann *Sichard to take the chair, contenting himself – after his return to Basel – with teaching the *Institutiones* till 1530. For six years after that he held the chair, covering the entire field of Roman law in his teaching; then he shared the subject with some colleagues until his retirement in the 1550s (AK VII Ep 3112). In 1535, the city council appointed him to the confidential post of consultant to the city, increasing his annual salary to two hundred gold florins. He played a conspicuous role in the rebuilding of the university after its near collapse in the Reformation crisis, and was its rector five times.

As a lawyer, Amerbach proclaimed his mediating position between the two *mores* as early as 1525 in his inaugural lecture. More than half a century later, his arguments, especially his defence of the glossators and

Bonifacius Amerbach by Hans Holbein the Younger

commentators, were resumed by the Oxford professor Alberico Gentili. As Amerbach did not produce a major work of his own, the bulk of his juridical thought is contained in the more than one hundred legal pronouncements he set down for private and public clients, ranging from deeds for local patricians and merchants to an opinion on a case pending between the duke of Brunswick and the city of Goslar. In an opinion on the matrimonial laws of the Protestant duchy of Württemberg, he showed greater rigour than the duke himself in that he admitted the legality of divorce only in cases of adultery and dereliction but not in cases of physical or mental illness, and thus placed himself in the tradition of canon law. In a time when with the canon law itself traditional family law was becoming suspect, he insisted on the necessity of following the principle of equity (ἐπιείκεια) as a guideline in the elaboration of new laws. He wrote and lectured much on that principle, so that a colleague could hail him as the 'magister epieíkeias in iure nostro' (Kisch *Erasmus* 379). As legislation was to him a noble application of moral thought, it is not surprising that in 1535 he recommended the creation of a chair for moral philosophy in the university. He perceived the theoretical foundation of morals to be on the one hand the legal sources and their commentators and on the other the classical philosophers, above all Aristotle. Amerbach was a philosophical eclectic, but he certainly had a predilection for Aristotle.

Owing to the complete preservation of the Amerbach family papers in Basel, the extant letters in the correspondence between Bonifacius and Erasmus are more numerous than those of any other epistolary exchange the latter had. This exchange, which is evenly spread between the two correspondents, started when Amerbach was twenty-one and had not yet left Basel for his law studies. It is formal and circumlocutory at first, but later becomes familiar and even confidential, especially on Erasmus' side, with the common opposition of the two men to the Basel reformers. Their correspondence was complemented by an intimate personal relationship from about 1527 onwards (Ep 1914). By that date, Amerbach had already brought about contacts between his acquaintances Alciati and *Sadoleto and Erasmus (Epp 1201, 1250, 1511), and he was to serve the humanist on many other occasions later on.

The stand Amerbach took towards the Reformation was reminiscent of Erasmus' own. He disapproved of the abuses in the church and supported the reforms demanded by *Luther but withdrew his allegiance when the Reformation became a popular movement, when Erasmus was attacked and the cause of the *bonae literae* imperilled. He took an uncompromising stand against the Anabaptists and the rebelling peasants, approving of their slaughter on grounds that there has never been a utopia on earth. Although he opposed the Reformation in his native city, he stayed on in 1529, when Erasmus and others left, being attached to Basel by virtue of his family connections, his civic sentiment, and his possessions rather than his academic position; in fact he was soon offered comparable posts at Freiburg and Dole and in Italy (Ep 2267). He disliked, even detested, the turmoil brought about by the Reformation, blaming it on such leaders as *Oecolampadius and *Zwingli (Epp 2221, 2224, 2248, 2312). When the Basel council made attendance at the reformed Sunday service compulsory (1 April 1529; cf AK III Epp 1356, 1405), he claimed exemption on account of his academic liberties. On 23 April 1531, the council took severer measures at the instigation of Oecolampadius, threatening to excommunicate all those who would not receive the Eucharist. Between 25 April and 2 August 1531 Amerbach was summoned three times to appear before the disciplinary committee of his parish. He was finally saved from excommunication by Oecolampadius' death in November 1531, and in the spring of 1534 he reached an agreement with the pastors and the council on the basis of a personal creed. While he had hitherto been ἀσύμβολος, ie, not Zwinglian (Epp 2312, 2519), and had even denounced *Bucer for intending an attack against Erasmus (c 16 April 1530; Ep 2312), appealing his case to Luther for arbitration (May–June 1531; AK IV Ep 1533), he now moved towards a conciliatory attitude between the Swiss and the Lutheran conceptions of the Eucharist (Burckhardt-Biedermann 100ff, 395ff). From 1534 on he can be called a liberal Buceran. At that time Amerbach was offered the post of legal adviser to the Strasbourg council, and when six years later Basel was invited to send deputies to the colloquy of Worms, the choice fell on him and on his colleague Simon *Grynaeus (AK V Ep 2414) although Grynaeus eventually had to attend without Amerbach. Despite his Buceran leanings Amerbach was so well settled in the Basel church that he could act as an intermediary in delicate negotiations between the university and the city pastors. His relations with Erasmus did not suffer from his conversion to moderate Protestantism: the latter continued to discuss confidential matters with him and Amerbach in turn forwarded many letters to and from Freiburg and in 1535 helped Erasmus in his transfer back to Basel.

In his last will of 12 February 1536, Erasmus made Amerbach his legal heir (Allen XI 364) and charged him with the administration of a bequest amounting to five thousand florins invested with the duke of Württemburg and the city of Geneva at an interest rate of five per cent. According to Erasmus' disposition, Amerbach had to distribute the resulting revenue among the aged, the poor, the disabled, girls without dowries, and students.

He tended to favour students and needy scholars, and his administration of the Legatum Erasmianum brought him into contact with numerous persons of that kind, natives as well as foreigners. His help was requested by students coming from as far as Ireland and Hungary, and he became the chief supporter of the many religious refugees who found shelter in Basel. In that way he assisted Pietro Martire Vermigli, Celio Secondo Curione, Sebastianus Castellio, Pier Paolo *Vergerio, Johann Basilius Herold, and many others. But Amerbach was Erasmus' heir in a far wider sense, in that he lent his support to that current which made of Protestant Basel a stronghold of 'Erasmian' latitudinarianism. That the city was to be a centre of Erasmian inspiration for nearly half a century was due in large part to Bonifacius and to his son, Basilius. The main feature of Basel's humanistic culture was its religious and philosophical toleration. Amerbach contributed to the spread of this toleration in an unsystematic, quiet, but very efficient way. As a member of the commission in charge of preventive book censorship, he helped reject the most radical projects, thus ensuring the continuation of a liberal publishing policy. In 1557 he defended Curione's *De amplitudine beati regni Dei* (1554) against the attack of the Lutheran Vergerio, and a few months later he sided with the Lutheran Giovanni Bernardino Bonifacio against Curione in a dispute about two other publications. At the same time, in the course of the controversy between Basel and Geneva caused by the publication of Castellio's *De haereticis an sint persequendi* (1554), he defended the memory of Erasmus against accusations by *Farel and Bèze.

Amerbach was sober, self-confident, and reliable; he stood firm in his legal and religious views. His wife, Martha *Fuchs, bore him five children: Ursula *Amerbach and Esther, who both died in childhood, and Faustina *Amerbach, Basilius, and Juliana. Despite many opportunities, Bonifacius did not remarry after Martha's death in 1541. His physical and mental forces, which were not very robust, seem to have been absorbed in later years by his various activities as a professor, consultant, protector of scholars and students, and correspondent. By that time his correspondence may have surpassed in volume that of Erasmus. He collected everything he wrote, not only the drafts of his letters and legal opinions, but also manuscripts on history, art history, geography, and archaeology. Self-critically he denounced his passion as χαρτο-φυλαττία. On a smaller scale, he was a collector of art objects; he loved exquisite furniture and treasured the gold and silver dishes Erasmus had left him in his last will. He possessed a rich library, including many books with dedicatory inscriptions; his books all passed to the library of the University of Basel. In his spare hours he devoted himself to instrumental music and choral singing. He corresponded with musicians, for example the Strasbourg-born organist Hans Kotter and Sixt Dietrich at Augsburg.

BIBLIOGRAPHY: Allen Ep 408 / Ferdinand Buisson *Sébastien Castellion* (Paris 1892; repr Nieuwkoop 1964) / Wilhelm Merian 'B. Amerbach und Hans Kotter' *Basler Zeitschrift für Geschichte und Altertumskunde* 16 (1917) 140–206 / Frederic C. Church *The Italian Reformers 1534–1564* (New York 1932) / Walther Köhler 'B. Amerbach und die württembergische Eheordnung von 1553' in *Vom Wesen und Wandel der Kirche: Zum 70. Geburtstag von Eberhard Vischer* (Basel 1935) 60–77 / Carl Roth 'Das Legatum Erasmianum' *Gedenkschrift zum 400. Todestag des Erasmus von Rotterdam* (Basel 1936) 282–98 / Delio Cantimori *Eretici italiani del cinquecento* (Florence 1939) / Paul Burckhardt 'David Joris und seine Gemeinde in Basel' *Basler Zeitschrift für Geschichte und Altertumskunde* 48 (1949) 5–106 / Hans Thieme 'Die beiden Amerbach' in *L'Europa e il diritto romano: Studi in memoria di P. Koschaker* (Milan 1953) 139–77 / Alfred Hartmann 'Bonifacius Amerbach als Verwalter der Erasmusstiftung' *Basler Jahrbuch* (1957) 7–28 / Theophil Burckhardt-Biedermann *Bonifacius Amerbach und die Reformation* (Basel 1894) / Adrian Staehelin *Die Einführung der Ehescheidung in Basel zur Zeit der Reformation* (Basel 1957) 52–4, 173ff / Jacques V. Pollet *Martin Bucer: Etudes sur sa correspondance* (Paris 1958–62) 177–93 and passim / Peter G. Bietenholz *Der italienische Humanismus und die Blütezeit des Buchdrucks in Basel* (Basel 1959) / Peter G. Bietenholz *Basle and France in the Sixteenth Century* (Geneva-Toronto 1971) / Edgar Bonjour *Die Universität Basel* (Basel 1960) 188–98 / Myron P. Gilmore *Humanists and Jurists: Six Studies in the*

Renaissance (Cambridge, Mass, 1963) 146–77 / Andreas Burckhardt *Johannes Basilius Herold* (Basel-Stuttgart 1967) / Martin Steinmann *Johannes Oporinus* (Basel-Stuttgart 1967) 25–31, 92 / Guido Kisch *Erasmus und die Jurisprudenz seiner Zeit* (Basel 1960) / Guido Kisch *Melanchthons Rechts- und Soziallehre* (Berlin 1967) 52–9 / Guido Kisch *Gestalten und Probleme aus Humanismus und Jurisprudenz* (Berlin 1969) 62, 99–178 / Uwe Plath *Calvin und Basel in den Jahren 1552–1556* (Zürich 1974) / Manfred E. Welti *Giovanni Bernardino Bonifacio im Exil, 1557–1597* (Geneva 1976) 37–9

MANFRED E. WELTI

Bruno AMERBACH of Basel, 9 December 1484–22 October 1519
Bruno, the eldest child of the printer Johann *Amerbach, spent a large part of his short life with his brother Basilius *Amerbach. From May 1497 to 21 April 1500 (AK I Ep 113) they studied at Sélestat with Crato Hofmann, then for a short time at Basel with Hieronymus *Emser (AK I Ep 117; *Matrikel Basel* I 260), and afterwards, accompanied by a famulus, in several colleges of the University of Paris. They received their BA degrees at the beginning of 1505 (AK I Ep 256) and the MA in April 1506 (AK I Epp 304, 305). Their ways separated for some years after both had returned to Basel at the end of April 1506. While Basilius continued his studies at Freiburg, Bruno again went to Paris, where he arrived in October 1506. His father's hopes of having him study philosophy under *Lefévre d'Etaples (AK I Ep 320) seem to have been only partially realized, and other teachers had to be substituted for the famous philosopher. Also much of Bruno's time seems to have been devoted to social life, including amorous adventures. He was sociable by nature and disregarded social standing in his friendships, which was not always to the liking of his stern father (AK I Epp 331, 348, 358, 374, 416). The circle of students he belonged to seems to have fostered German patriotic sentiment (AK I Ep 423). When he went home in the summer of 1508, he had no degree but a solid knowledge of Latin, Greek, and Hebrew. He entered his father's printing shop as a scholar-collaborator, was soon engaged in the great enterprise of editing the collected works of Jerome (J. Froben 1516); he had occasion to perfect his languages when Johannes *Cono of Nürnberg joined the editorial team at the end of 1510 (AK I Epp 443, 446, 460). Unlike his brother Basilius, Bruno tended to be an extrovert, and his temperament must have agreed rather well with that of Johann *Froben, for whom he drafted letters in Latin (Ep 801). After the death of Johann Amerbach (1513), his sons retained a financial interest in the printing firm, which was now directed by Froben. Bruno's energetic collaboration became vital for the continued success of the press. He was closer to Erasmus than Basilius was, and their links anticipated in familiarity, if not in depth, the ones established later by Bonifacius *Amerbach. The letters exchanged between them are short, but they suggest close personal relations. Bruno planned to go to Italy in the spring of 1517, but it is doubtful whether he ever carried out his plan (CWE Epp 464, 595, 632, 732a; AK IV Ep 595a). In September 1518 he married Anna, the daughter of Johann *Schabler, thereby reinforcing his French connections and possibly also his links with the firm of Froben. The marriage was short-lived: Anna died by the middle of May 1519 at the age of twenty-one, and Bruno died of the plague six months later (Ep 1084; AK II Ep 695). Erasmus commemorated the tragic end of the young couple in an epitaph (Reedijk poem 108).

BIBLIOGRAPHY: Allen and CWE Ep 331 / AK I Ep 70 and passim / Verena Vetter *Baslerische Italienreisen* (Basel 1952) 69–70 / Peter G. Bietenholz *Basle and France in the Sixteenth Century* (Geneva-Toronto 1971) 27–31, 181–2

MANFRED E. WELTI

Faustina AMERBACH of Basel, 25 November 1530–19 February 1602
Faustina, the second child of Bonifacius *Amerbach, and her first husband were the founders of a lineage that is still extant, whereas the male branches of the Amerbach family have died out. As a child and a young girl, Faustina was sociable and well liked by her relatives. A marriage linking the Amerbachs with the Grynaeus family would have been welcome to Bonifacius, who was on good terms with them, but in the end the negotiations failed (AK VI Epp 2860, 2998), and on 9 July 1548 Faustina married Johann Ulrich

Iselin, who had obtained his doctorate in law from Pavia a year before and was just beginning his academic career in the University of Basel. Faustina bore him seven children. Iselin died in 1564, and in the summer of 1566, after turbulent negotiations, Faustina took as her second husband Johannes Oporinus, the editor and printer. Both with her money and with her advice she helped Oporinus to wind up his firm, which was heavily in debt. When he was sixty-one, she bore him his first son. After his death in 1568 she did not remarry, and details of her subsequent life have not yet been studied in the large collection of Amerbach papers that passed to the library of the University of Basel in the seventeenth century.

BIBLIOGRAPHY: Allen Ep 2684:80n / Martin Steinmann *Johannes Oporinus* (Basel-Stuttgart 1967) 111–14

MANFRED E. WELTI

Johann AMERBACH of Amorbach, c 1443–25 December 1513
The famous editor, printer, and bookseller later known as Johann Amerbach or Hans Fenediger, a native of Amorbach in Franconia, in the diocese of Würzburg, was probably born to the town's burgomaster, Peter Welcker. He studied at Paris with Johann Heynlin von Stein, who represented the realist tradition of scholasticism, and received his MA by 1464, having acquired a 'vigorous Latinity' (Allen) and some knowledge of Greek. He travelled to Italy, perhaps studying for a time in Rome and probably working in Venice as a printer (AK I Epp 433, 481). He settled at Basel by 1478 and prospered rapidly, joining the 'Safran' guild in 1481 and paying taxes on one thousand florins at that time. He bought a house, married the widowed Barbara Ortenberg, and in 1484 purchased the citizenship of Basel. He had five children, three sons and two daughters. In his trade, he collaborated with other printers, editors, and booksellers, corresponding with business friends and agents as far away as Paris, Nürnberg, and London. But his most fertile collaboration was with his former Paris teacher, Heynlin von Stein, who, having also moved to Basel, wrote prefaces and commentaries for him, and also collated and emended manuscripts. It was Heynlin who persuaded

Amerbach to edit the collected works of the Fathers of the church and in general fostered his predilection for the works of Christian and pagan antiquity. Heynlin was also instrumental in establishing Amerbach's close connection with the Carthusian monastery, which possessed a rich collection of manuscripts dating back to the years of the council of Basel. These Carthusian manuscripts were to serve the printer for many of his publishing ventures. Heynlin may even have exercised some influence upon Amerbach in the choice of type and other typographical material. On a smaller scale he 'was to Amerbach what Erasmus was to Amerbach's successor, Johann *Froben' (Bietenholz).

Combining his faith in realism with the new formal and thematic tendencies of humanism, Amerbach entered into contact with several scholars of his time. *Trithemius of Sponheim, *Wimpfeling, Sebastian *Brant, and *Reuchlin collaborated with him. Brant contributed poems to his editions, and Reuchlin was of great help in the publication of works of Augustine and Jerome. Amerbach died when working on his greatest enterprise, the publication of the collected works of the four doctors of the church, Ambrose, Jerome (Epp 309, 396), Gregory, and Augustine (Ep 2157). He was buried in the same Carthusian monastery whose library had supplied many manuscripts for his printing firm and which had in turn been considerably enriched by his donations of many of the books produced by his press.

BIBLIOGRAPHY: Allen and CWE Ep 309 / Percy S. Allen *The Correspondence of an Early Printing-House: The Amerbachs of Basle* (Glasgow 1932) 12–18 / AK I xix–xxiii, IV 484–486 / NDB I 247–8 / Friedrich Luchsinger *Der Basler Buchdruck als Vermittler italienischen Geistes, 1470–1529* (Basel 1953) 2ff / Lucien Febvre and Henri-Jean Martin *L'Apparition du livre* 2nd ed (Paris 1971) 211–3 / Manfred E. Welti *Der Basler Buchdruck und Britannien* (Basel 1964) 17 and passim / Grimm *Buchführer* / Peter G. Bietenholz *Basle and France in the Sixteenth Century* (Geneva-Toronto 1971) 168–70 and passim / E. Hilgert 'Johann Froben and the Basel university scholars, 1513–1523' *The Library Quarterly* 41 (1971) 141–5

MANFRED E. WELTI

Margarete AMERBACH of Basel, 14 February 1490–26 September 1541

Margarete, the second youngest child and only surviving daughter of Johann *Amerbach and Barbara Ortenberg, eloped and married as a young girl on 7 February 1506. Her husband, Jakob *Rechberger, a spice-merchant, was evidently not to her father's liking, for she was formally disinherited on 18 February 1506. The parties were reconciled in 1507, and Margarete received a dowry of five hundred florins. She had several children, some of whom died in early childhood. She was always willing to help others and was particularly attached to her youngest brother, Bonifacius *Amerbach, who did not always return her feelings. After his return from Avignon, Bonifacius lived for a time with the Rechbergers (AK III 1042, 1163). Margarete's correspondence, especially her own letters in hearty Alemannic dialect, are one of the treasures in the Amerbach family papers, and many have been published in AK. She died of the plague.

BIBLIOGRAPHY: AK I Epp 87, 297, 491a, and passim / Gertrud Lendorff *Kleine Geschichte der Baslerin* (Basel 1966) 52–61

MANFRED E. WELTI

Ursula AMERBACH of Basel, 25 December 1528–20 June 1532

Ursula was the first child (Ep 2051) of Bonifacius *Amerbach and Martha *Fuchs. She was particularly fond of her uncle, Basilius *Amerbach (AK IV Ep 1556). To judge from Erasmus' comments, Bonifacius adored her, and he suffered profoundly when she died in her fourth year. Erasmus and his other friends attempted to console him with letters and poems, and he himself composed verses to express his grief (Epp 2678, 2684; AK IV Epp 1661, 1662, 1669: 1n, and passim).

MANFRED E. WELTI

Adrien AMEROT of Soissons, d 14 January 1560

Adrien Amerot de Quenville (Amerotius, Amoury, Quennevelle) attended the Greek lectures of Girolamo *Aleandro in Paris in 1512; in 1513 he entered the College of the Lily at Louvain, where he tutored fellow students in Greek grammar even before receiving his MA in 1516. He kept in touch with Aleandro and also became a good friend of Paschasius *Berselius, both of whom were in the service of Erard de la *Marck, bishop of Liège. Dirk *Martens published Amerot's excellent *Compendium graecae grammatices* in 1520 (NK 115). In the dedicatory preface, addressed to his pupil Antoine de la *Marck, Amerot praised his former teachers Joost *Vroye of Gavere and Jan de *Neve.

After taking his MA Amerot began to study law and continued to teach Greek privately. As early as 1521 Erasmus remarked on his proficiency in literature, philosophy, and law, recommending him to Bernard Bucho van *Aytta as one of the cleverest teachers at the Lily (Ep 1237). Soon after 1522 he was taken into the service of the imperial secretary, Nicolas *Perrenot de Granvelle, as his children's tutor. In 1545 he succeeded Rutgerus *Rescius as professor of Greek in the Collegium Trilingue; he held this post with distinction until his death in 1560 and left the university half of his possessions. In a preserved legal opinion he gave qualified approval to the use of some of Erasmus' work in academic teaching. He also composed a *Libellus de dialectis graecis*; the first known edition was printed in 1534 (Paris: C. Wechel).

BIBLIOGRAPHY: Allen Ep 1237 / BNB XXIX 70 / DBF II 630–1 / de Vocht CTL IV 252–65

CFG

Petrus AMICUS *See Pierre LAMY and Pieter de VRIENDT*

Andrea AMMONIO of Lucca, c 1478– 17 August 1517

Andrea Ammonio (de Herena, della Rena) was born at Lucca. He was a member of one of the oldest families of the city, the de Herena or della Rena, but later was given the hellenized name of Ammonio. He studied at Bologna under Oliverius Jontus of Montegallorum, who taught there from 1494 to 1498. He then travelled to Rome and by 1506 was in England. He probably travelled to England in the company of Silvestro *Gigli, the Luccanese bishop of Worcester, who was sent to England in 1505 to give *Henry VII tokens of the esteem of *Julius II.

During his first years in England Ammonio

suffered from lack of money. However in 1509 he became secretary to William *Blount, Lord Mountjoy, and by 1511 he was Latin secretary to *Henry VIII. On 3 February 1512 he received a prebend in the cathedral of St Stephen, Westminster. He later received a canonry at Worcester. In 1512 Ammonio was in France with the English expeditionary force during its victory over the French at the battle of the Spurs (Ep 273). On 12 April 1514 he became an English citizen, and in 1515, after a bitter struggle with Polidoro *Virgilio, he was appointed by Pope *Leo x as subcollector of papal taxes in England. He enjoyed this position only briefly, dying suddenly of the 'sweating sickness' in London before he reached the age of forty.

Ammonio was one of Erasmus' closest friends in England. The two met when Erasmus visited the country in 1505 and 1506 (Ep 283) and renewed their friendship from 1509 to 1511, after Erasmus returned from his trip to Italy. For a time they stayed together in the household of Thomas *More (Epp 221, 232). Between 1511 and 1517 they exchanged over forty known letters. Topics ranged from domestic and personal matters such as the duplicity of English messengers (Epp 239, 240) and boatmen (Ep 295) and the bad quality of wine at Cambridge (Ep 226, 228) – where Erasmus lectured in Greek in 1511–12 – to international affairs of the highest importance in Europe, from the wars of Julius II to the Swiss defeat at Marignano in 1515 (Epp 236, 239, 247, 262, 360). Ammonio also assisted Erasmus in his quest for financial security and freedom from the bonds of his religious order, the canons regular of St Augustine. In 1511 and 1512 he constantly reminded Richard *Foxe, bishop of Winchester, and Thomas *Ruthall, bishop of Durham, of Erasmus' desire for a benefice, and was instrumental in Erasmus' receiving the parish of Aldington in Kent from Archbishop *Warham of Canterbury in March 1512, which he soon renounced for a pension (Epp 247–50, 255, 273). In order to hold ecclesiastical benfices Erasmus required a dispensation from Rome. In January 1506 Julius II had granted him permission to hold a benefice even though he was a member of a religious order (CWE Ep 187A), but he feared that this was not comprehensive enough. In

1516 Erasmus decided to approach Leo x (Epp 446, 447) for a new brief dispensing him from any censures incurred by his setting aside of the habit of the canons regular and permitting him to hold more than one benefice. In July 1516 Erasmus returned to England to consult with Ammonio in person on the content of his letter to the pope (Epp 451–3). Ammonio added a letter of his own (Ep 466), and negotiations in Rome were in the hands of his former master Silvestro Gigli, then Henry VIII's ambassador at the papal court. The petitions were presented to Leo x some time before October 1516 (Ep 479), and by December Ammonio had received a preliminary draft (Ep 498). Erasmus begged to have proceedings expedited because he expected to receive new benefices in Flanders (Ep 505). On 26 January 1517 Leo sent the requested brief to Ammonio (Ep 517), with letters to Erasmus (Epp 518, 519). On 9 April, at St Stephen's, Westminster, in the presence of Johannes *Sixtinus, Ammonio, acting on behalf of Leo x, absolved Erasmus of all censures caused by his failure to wear the habit of his order (Ep 517).

Ammonio's death was reported to Erasmus by Thomas *More on 19 August 1517 (Ep 623). Saddened by the death of his friend (Epp 637, 643), Erasmus asked Sixtinus and Pietro *Vannes to collect his correspondence with Ammonio lest it should fall into the wrong hands (Epp 655, 656).

Ammonio's literary production was small. In 1511, on a trip to Paris, Erasmus showed a collection of Ammonio's poems to Lord Mountjoy, including a dedication to the latter. Mountjoy found the dedication excessive in its praise of himself and through Erasmus (Epp 218, 219) advised Ammonio to substitute a new one (Epp 220, 221). Erasmus then had the volume published. Ammonio also wrote a 'Panegyricus ad Henricum VIII,' the object of Erasmus' friendly criticism in Ep 283, but now lost. Ammonio may also have written an account of Henry's conflict with the Scots (Ep 283), but this work is also lost. The complete poems of Ammonio were published by Clemente Pizzi in 1958. In 1511 Erasmus addressed a poem to Ammonio, partly to thank him for a gift of excellent wine (Ep 234; Reedijk poem 91).

BIBLIOGRAPHY: Allen and CWE Ep 218 / DNB I

363 / Clemente Pizzi *Un amico di Erasmo,
l'umanista Andrea Ammonio* (Florence 1956) /
Andrea Ammonio *Carmina omnia* ed Clemente
Pizzi (Florence 1958) / Denys Hay *Polydore
Vergil: Renaissance Historian and Man of Letters*
(Oxford 1952) 7, 10–13, and passim / William E.
Wilkie *The Cardinal Protectors of England: Rome
and the Tudors before the Reformation* (Cambridge
1974) 15, 40, and passim

TBD

Pietro AMMONIO *See Pietro* VANNES

Johannes AMMONIUS of Ghent, documented 1500–after 1534
Johannes Ammonius (de Arena, Harenaceus)
was a son of Jacob van den Zande, who when
widowed joined the canons of St Austin in
Courtrai. Like his brother, Levinus *Ammonius, Johannes became a Carthusian; in about
1500 he joined the convent of La Chapelle
(domus Capellae) at Hérinnes, north of
Enghien, which had been richly endowed by
his father. He was instructed in his youth by
Joost van der Cleyen (Argillanus). He wrote
poems, biographies of some members of his
order, and a description of the baptism of the
future *Charles v. In 1517 he wrote to Erasmus
(Ep 570), attempting to bring about a
connection. Subsequently he favoured the
cause of Martin *Luther and as a result was
forbidden to leave his cell and was finally
imprisoned. His brother broke off all contact
with him 1531. In the same year Johannes
addressed from La Chapelle a letter of
introduction to Johannes *Dantiscus, the
Polish ambassador, who was then in Brussels.
He also wrote a continuation (covering
1490–1534) to the chronicle of La Chapelle by
Arnold Beeltsens.
    BIBLIOGRAPHY: CWE Ep 570 / de Vocht
Dantiscus 95–6 / BNB XIV 83–4 / Arnold Beeltsens
and Johannes Ammonius *Chronique de la
Chartreuse de la Chapelle à Hérinnes-les-Enghien*
ed E. Lamalle (Louvain 1932)

PGB

Levinus AMMONIUS of Ghent, 13 April
1488–19 March 1557
Levinus Ammonius (Lieven van den Zande, de
Harena) of Ghent joined the Carthusian order,
making his profession on 18 August 1506 in the

monastery of St Maartensbos near Geraardsbergen, 30 kilometres west of Brussels. He
remained in St Maartensbos until the advent of
a new prior who was opposed to humanistic
studies drove him away. In 1533 he was
transferred to the monastery of Koningdal
outside Ghent (Ep 2817) and subsequently to
Arnhem and to Scheut, near Brussels, before
returning to Ghent, where he eventually died.
He was the brother of Johannes *Ammonius,
another Carthusian.
    Levinus was a good scholar and an eager
student of Greek and Latin authors. Although
firmly opposed to the reformers, he was an
outspoken critic of such traditional theologians
as Noël *Béda (Ep 1763) and Pierre *Cousturier
(Ep 2016). In 1524 he sent Erasmus a carefully
composed letter of admiration (Ep 1463), but
the ongoing correspondence he had hoped for
did not develop until four years later, when
Erasmus replied amicably to a second letter
from Ammonius (Epp 2016, 2062). The
subsequent exchanges have survived only
partially (Epp 2082, 2197, 2258, 2483, 2817).
Levinus' letters were long and erudite. In the
loneliness of his cell he was much given to
letter-writing, although on occasion it aroused
the suspicions of his fellow-monks (Ep 2570; cf
Ep 2016). His correspondence helped him
develop and sustain friendly relations with
other Belgian humanists, including Erasmus'
friends Karel *Uutenhove, Johannes de *Molendino, a kinsman of Ammonius (Ep 2016),
Frans van *Massemen, Omaar van *Edingen,
and Jakob *Jespersen. In 1529, when the
triumph of the reformers drove Erasmus away
from Basel, Levinus seconded Edingen, who
invited him to Flanders (Ep 2209). Erasmus in
turn invited Ammonius to join the team of
translators for his edition of Chrysostom, but
the manuscript he was expected to translate
never reached him (Ep 2258). In 1531 he and
Simon *Grynaeus were dinner guests at the
house of Marcus *Laurinus at Bruges (Ep
2499), and in his last surviving letter to
Erasmus (Ep 2817) he pleaded with him not to
waste his efforts on apologiae.
    An autograph letter-book by Ammonius is
preserved in the Bibliothèque municipale of
Besançon. Other letters are printed in the
correspondence of Nicolaus *Olahus and
elsewhere. Ammonius also composed some

poems and a biography of Willem Bibaut, the general of his order. He published a commentary on the parable of the Prodigal Son, *Tractatus in parabolam* (Brussels: P. Paulus 1542).

BIBLIOGRAPHY: Allen Ep 1463 / de Vocht CTL II 191 and passim / de Vocht *Dantiscus* 124–5 / P.N.M. Bot 'Levinus Ammonius en Erasmus' in *Postillen over kerk en maatschappij in de xv en xvi eeuw* (Utrecht 1964) 326–43 / Albert Pil 'Vijf brieven van Levinus Ammonius ... aan Johannes de Molendino' in *Horae Tornacenses* (Tournoi 1971) 157–76

PGB

Gervasius AMOENUS of Dreux, documented 1506–29(?)

A native of Dreux in Normandy, Gervasius Amoenus (Omenius Drocensis, Chuaenus) is documented in the summer of 1506 as Erasmus' amanuensis in Paris. He must have been engaged in the preceding winter or spring when Erasmus was in England translating some of Lucian's writings, among them the *Historia longaevorum*. Erasmus merely states that a dishonest secretary ('notarius suffuratus') later published this translation in Paris as his own work (Allen I 8:8–10), but the unscrupulous scribe was in fact Amoenus, for the piece is found in the latter's *Lucubratiunculae* (Paris: J. Bade October 1513), together with two unedited letters also by Erasmus, which were given the title of *Institutio liberorum* (see ASD I-3 68–70, 119–20).

Curiously, Amoenus' name never occurs in Erasmus' preserved correspondence. It is found, however, in the heading of an epigram appended to Erasmus' translation of Euripides' *Iphigenia* (Paris: J. Bade 13 September 1506: cf ASD I-1 359). Erasmus thought that these verses were a fine example of the famulus' exalted literary aspirations. To make fun of him, he gave them in Amoenus' presence to the printer Josse *Bade, precisely as the proud author had hoped. Unaware of Erasmus' joke, Bade promptly printed them, and all Erasmus could do to save face was have them removed when the *Iphigenia* was reprinted a year later by Aldo *Manuzio (Ep 209).

Little is known about Amoenus' subsequent career. Apart from the *Lucubratiunculae*, he published an edition of Valerius Flaccus'

Argonautica (Paris: J. Bade and J. Petit 7 February 1512/13). The prefatory letter addressed to Robert de *Keysere refers to seven years spent by Amoenus in England, apparently as a protégé of William *Blount. The same epistle praises the Paris humanists and printers for their contribution to the renaissance of letters. Amoenus may be identical with the Norman schoolmaster Erasmus accuses of being an accomplice of Pierre *Cousturier in a letter of 1528 (Ep 2062). At any rate the recipient of that letter, Levinus *Ammonius, seems to have thought of Amoenus at once (Ep 2082).

BIBLIOGRAPHY: Allen Ep 209 / Bierlaire *Familia* 48–9, 108 / Philippe Renouard *Imprimeurs et libraires parisiens du xvie siècle* (Paris 1964–) II 43, 100, 102–3 / Brigitte Moreau *Inventaire chronologique des éditions parisiennes du xvie siècle* (Paris 1977) II 160, 164, 171 / J. Machiels 'Robert en Pieter de Keysere als drukker' *Archives et bibliothèques de Belgique* 46 (1975) 10–12 / Franz Bierlaire *Erasme et ses Colloques: le livre d'une vie* (Geneva 1977) 25

FRANZ BIERLAIRE

AMORBACH See AMERBACH

Nikolaus von AMSDORF of Torgau, 3 December 1483–14 May 1565

Nikolaus was the son of Georg von Amsdorf (Amsdorff), an official of the dukes of Saxony at Mühlberg, and of Katharina, the sister of Johann von *Staupitz. Born in Torgau, he was educated in Leipzig, where he registered at the university in 1500. In the winter term of 1502–3 he was among the first students to matriculate at the newly founded university of Wittenberg, where he received his first degrees. In 1511 he was promoted licentiate in theology and appointed to lecture on theological and philosophical topics. In 1513 and again in 1522 he was elected rector of the University of Wittenberg.

From the beginning of *Luther's public campaign Amsdorf was among his closest supporters and accompanied the reformer to the Leipzig debate in 1519 and the diet of Worms in 1521. On Luther's recommendation he was called to Magdeburg in July 1524 as minister of St Ulrich's and first superintendent. His activities were not restricted to the region

Nikolaus von Amsdorf

of Magdeburg, however, and he played a prominent role in the reformation of Goslar, Einbeck, Meissen, and other towns as well as participating in 1540 and 1541 in the religious conferences of Haguenau, Worms, and Regensburg. After a round of difficult negotiations Luther officiated on 20 January 1542 at Amsdorf's installation as bishop of Naumberg, the first ordination of an evangelical bishop in Germany. To secure Amsdorf's appointment the Elector John Frederick of *Saxony had had to bring pressure to bear on the Naumberg chapter, which had elected Julius von *Pflug, Erasmus' friend. Five years later the outcome of the Schmalkaldic war of 1546–7 compelled Amsdorf to withdraw from his diocese. He spent his remaining years in Weimar, Magdeburg, and finally in Eisenach as a self-proclaimed religious refugee. Lacking a specific appointment, he was consulted and composed memoranda on a variety of theological problems. He took a passionate and uncompromising part in the dogmatic controversies that erupted in the years after Luther's death. He joined Matthias Flacius and Nicolaus Gallus in rejecting the Augsburg

Interim (1548) and thus saw himself obliged to oppose Wittenberg theologians, in particular *Melanchthon and the so-called Adiaphorists or Philippists. In his unyielding defence of strict Lutheran orthodoxy he was hailed by his supporters as a 'second Luther.'

Amsdorf never married. He died at Eisenach and was buried in front of the altar of the principal church of St George. Deeply committed to Lutheran orthodoxy, he believed that the tenets of Christian humanism presented a danger for the Protestant church and its doctrine. He supported Luther in his controversy with Erasmus, which he caused to flare up again in 1534, as Erasmus pointed out at the beginning of his *Purgatio adversus epistolam Lutheri* (LB X 1537C; cf Ep 2918). Writing Melanchthon on 6 October 1534 (Ep 2970), he added that Amsdorf had been described to him as lacking in gifts and learning.

BIBLIOGRAPHY: NDB I 261 / ADB I 412–15 / RGG I 333–4 / *Matrikel Leipzig* I 435, II 387 / *Matrikel Wittenberg* I 5 / N. von Amsdorf *Ausgewählte Schriften* ed O. Lerche (Gütersloh 1938) / C. Eichhorn 'Amsdorfiana … ' *Zeitschrift für Kirchengeschichte* 22 (1901) 605–45 / Weimar, Thüringische Landesbibliothek, MSS Amsdorfiana, ff 38–42: five volumes containing some two thousand leaves / Theodor Pressel *Nicolaus von Amsdorf* (Elberfeld 1862) / E.J. Meier 'H. von Amsdorfs Leben' in *Das Leben der Altväter der lutherischen Kirche* III (Leipzig 1863) / Peter Brunner *Nikolaus von Amsdorf als Bischof von Naumburg* (Gütersloh 1961) / D.C. Steinmetz *Reformers in the Wings* (Philadelphia 1971) 100–8
HARTMUT VOIT

Alardus AMSTELREDAMUS, AEMSTEL-REDAMUS *See* ALAARD *of Amsterdam*

Pierre AMY *See Pierre* LAMY

Bernard ANDRÉ of Toulouse, c 1455–c 1522
Bernard André (Andreas Tolosanus, Tholosates), born at Toulouse, entered the order of St Augustine and received degrees in civil and canon law, but it is not known from which university. He was already blind in 1485 when he crossed the Channel, probably with the future *Henry VII, who held him in high esteem and made him his poet laureate. From 1510 he

was also court historiographer. André and some other literate courtiers such as John *Skelton, Giovanni Gigli, and Cornelio *Vitelli rallied to the defence of the king against Robert *Gaguin, who had produced some undiplomatic verses during his embassy to England from 1489 to 1490. André taught at Oxford for some years, and he maintained a good relationship with prominent persons such as the bishops Richard *Foxe and John Alcock. He was eager to return to France, but Gaguin dissuaded him (Gaguin's Ep 55, to be dated April 1492), and in 1496 he was appointed tutor to King Henry's oldest son, *Arthur.

Using both Latin and French, André wrote works on grammar, rhetoric, history, and the education of princes as well as poetry and annotations to the classics. He is best known, however, as the author of a life of Henry VII. A list of his writings is preserved in Paris in a manuscript (Arsenal MS 360) containing André's commentary on St Augustine's De civitate Dei. What survives of his writings is for the most part in the British Library (Cotton MSS Domitianus A XVIII and Julius A III–IV; Royal MSS 12 A X, 12 B XIV, 16 E XI, and 16 F II). Other manuscripts are preserved in Hatfield (CP 277) and Oxford, New College (MS 287). Noteworthy is the almost constant confusion between 'Andreas' and 'Andrelinus' in the Arsenal MS 360: this confusion confirms the hypothesis that the 'B. Andrelinus' who is the writer of a letter copied in British Library MS Arundel 249, ff 81 verso–82 recto, is to be identified with Bernard André and not with Fausto *Andrelini.

Erasmus probably met André for the first time in 1499 while visiting Eltham Palace with Thomas *More. On his next visit to England in 1511 he was not very eager to see André since he owed him some money. The debt was settled shortly afterwards by Erasmus' Maecenas, William *Blount, Lord Mountjoy (Epp 248, 254). Thus André may have been the 'Cerberus' whose presence had at first discouraged Erasmus from visiting Mountjoy's house (Epp 240, 247, 248). In that same period André offered to introduce Erasmus to Richard *Bere, abbot of Glastonbury, but nothing came of it; after André's death, Erasmus recorded this episode in rather unkind terms (Ep 1490; cf Reedijk poem 49), and in Ep 2422 he also

accused André of intriguing against Thomas *Linacre. On the other hand, Erasmus had earlier written complimentary poems for André's commentary on De civitate Dei and his Hymni christiani (Paris: J. Bade 1517).

BIBLIOGRAPHY: Allen and CWE Ep 243 / Emden BRUO I 33 / J. Gairdner in DNB I 398–9 / Historia regis Henrici Septimi a Bernardo Andrea Tholosate conscripta; necnon alia quaedam ad eundem regem spectantia ed J. Gairdner (London 1858) / Roberti Gaguini epistole et orationes ed L. Thuasne (Paris 1903) / H.L.R. Edwards 'Robert Gaguin and the English poets, 1489–90' The Modern Language Review 32 (1937) 430–4 / W. Nelson John Skelton, Laureate (New York 1939; repr 1964) 14–39, 239–42, and passim / F. Roth in Augustiniana 15 (1965) 622–8 / G.B. Parks 'Pico della Mirandola in Tudor translation' in Philosophy and Humanism: Renaissance Essays in Honour of Paul Oskar Kristeller ed E.P. Mahoney (Leiden 1976) 354–5 / G. Tournoy 'Two poems written by Erasmus for Bernard André' Humanistica Lovaniensia 27 (1978) 45–51 / A major study of André is being prepared by Constance Blackwell, London

GILBERT TOURNOY

ANDREAS (Epp 2544, 2589 of September and December 1531)
Andreas was an unidentified French priest who travelled to Germany and the Netherlands in the autumn of 1531 to visit Erasmus and Henricus Cornelius *Agrippa.

ANDREAS of Hoogstraten *See* HOOGSTRATEN

ANDREAS NEAPOLITANUS *See Alessandro* D'ANDREA

Eustachius ANDREAS (Ep 1533 of 27 December 1524)
Eustachius Andreas, addressed by Erasmus in Ep 1533, has not been identified. He was a monk of Cluny and had visited Erasmus at Basel.

Fran Trankvil ANDREIS *See Tranquillus* ANDRONICUS

Fausto ANDRELINI of Forlì, c 1462–25 February 1518
Fausto Andrelini was born at Forlì, probably

in the year 1462. He left his native town at a very early age to study law at the University of Bologna. Although no supporting evidence has come to light, we can safely assume that he obtained a degree because he calls himself 'decretorum doctor' in the title of his work *De Neapolitana Fornoviensique victoria* (Paris: G. Marchant for J. Petit 1496). He then went to Rome, where he completed his humanistic studies under the guidance of *Pomponius Laetus, a rather eccentric figure and a fervent admirer of all relics of antiquity, who directed the Roman Academy. During a journey to Germany in the winter of 1482–3 Pomponius had received from the Emperor *Frederick III a privilege entitling the Roman Academy to confer the traditional poet's laurel. Fausto was the first to benefit. Although it was due to take place during the official celebration of the anniversary of Rome on 20 April 1483, Fausto's crowning had to be postponed; however it still took place in the same year rather than in 1484, as asserted in DBI I 138. For in 1484 it was the turn of Aelius Lampridius Cerva and Laurentius Bonincontrius to be crowned. In the years 1484–8 Fausto enjoyed the protection of Ludovico Gonzaga, bishop of Mantua, but life in the bishops' service did not meet his expectations and he decided to leave Italy.

In the autumn of 1488 Fausto arrived in France, where he at first enjoyed the hospitality of Chiara Gonzaga, the bishop's sister, and of her husband, Gilbert de Montpensier, count of Auvergne. In the following winter he moved to Paris. Together with two other Italian humanists, the Venetian Girolamo *Balbi and Cornelio *Vitelli of Cortona, he tried to gain a footing in the university. The appointment of the three Italian poets was discussed on 16 and 27 February and on 4 August 1489. Finally on 5 September all three were admitted to teach poetry for one hour each every afternoon. Balbi was consumed by jealousy of his colleagues because they had obtained the same position although they had arrived in Paris after him. He managed to drive away Vitelli, who left for England before the end of 1489. Then he turned on Andrelini; after the publication of Andrelini's *Livia* (Paris: G. Marchant 1490), Balbi accused the author of plagiarism and even caused a rumour to be spread in Italy that Andrelini had been burnt alive for heresy. Probably in the autumn of 1491 (rather than 1490, as was assumed by Thuasne), Fausto left Paris to teach poetry and rhetoric in Toulouse and Poitiers. On his return, he managed to rid himself of his rival: before January 1493 Balbi left for England. After his departure, Fausto consolidated his position at the university and, through the mediation of Robert Briçonnet, archbishop of Reims, he also gained access to the court. In 1496 he read from his work *De Neapolitana Fornoviensique victoria* in the presence of *Charles VIII and received a large gift of money as well as an annuity from the king's treasury. Thus began his career as poet royal, which lasted for about twenty years.

A year earlier, in the autumn of 1495, Erasmus had visited Paris, and Fausto made his acquaintance through Robert *Gaguin. Erasmus had already heard of Fausto from the Sicilian Pietro *Santeramo, one of his companions in the household of Hendrik van *Bergen (Ep 326). Then, in September 1495 he introduced himself to Gaguin with a letter and a poem. The letter is lost; the poem has been inserted in the volume *De casa natalicia Iesu* (Reedijk poem 38). In Ep 44 Gaguin asked Erasmus about Fausto's composition *De celesti vaticinatione* (obviously the same as *De influentia siderum*, published on 10 May 1496), adding that he and Fausto were old friends. In a little poem by Gaguin, preserved with some poems by Erasmus (edited in P. Smith *Erasmus* 2nd ed, New York 1962, 456), the Frenchman invites Erasmus and Fausto to a simple but amicable meal at his home. Meanwhile Erasmus was leading a cheerless existence in the Collège de Montaigu, smarting under his own poverty and the stern discipline imposed by the college principal, Jan *Standonck. Andrelini shared Erasmus' distaste for the barren disputes among the scholastic theologians of Paris; thus his friendship with the sprightly Italian humanist brought solace to Erasmus in these hard days, as is testified to in his eclogue entitled *In Annales Gaguini et Eglogas Faustinas carmen ruri scriptum et autumno* (Reedijk poem 39), composed during a short stay in the country in the autumn of 1495. It describes an encounter with Fausto's lovely Muse, Thalia, and refers to Gaguin's historical work *De*

origine et gestis Francorum compendium. When
on 30 September 1495 the Paris printer Pierre
Le Dru completed the printing of this work,
three and a half pages remained empty and
were forthwith filled with appendices, including four couplets by Fausto in praise of history
and Erasmus' elegant Ep 45.

For the next three years it seems that
Erasmus and Fausto continued to be on
excellent terms with each other (Epp 95, 136).
Erasmus encouraged Willem *Hermans, his old
friend in the monastery of Steyn, to write to
Andrelini (Ep 81); Erasmus may also have
induced Andrelini to send Hermans a character reference on his behalf (Ep 84). To this
period we may assign five short notes
exchanged between Fausto and Erasmus,
perhaps to enliven the tedium of a dull lecture
(Epp 96–100).

In the spring of 1499 Erasmus travelled to
England and from there addressed a letter to
Fausto (Ep 103) which was perfectly suited to
the character of the addressee, inviting him to
share in all the delights that England had to
offer, especially the charm of the English girls,
who were generous with soft and fragrant
kisses.

After his return to Paris Erasmus published
his *Adagia* (Paris: J. Philippi June 1500), and
Fausto wrote a letter at the printer's request to
introduce Erasmus' work to the reader (Ep 127,
cf Ep 1175). In the autumn of 1500 Erasmus fled
from Paris to avoid the plague. As Fausto had
apparently criticized his lack of courage,
Erasmus attempted to justify his move and also
humbly asked his erudite and successful friend
to promote the sale of the *Adagia* by writing a
further testimonial. At the end he revealed to
Fausto his intention to employ him 'not merely
as a critic, but also as an architect' (Ep 134).
This sentence raises the question of reciprocal
influences between the *Adagia* of Erasmus and
Fausto Andrelini's *Epistolae proverbiales et
morales.* That Fausto had begun this collection
of letters before 1490 is confirmed by his pupil
Johannes Cortiger in his letter accompanying
the first edition of Fausto's *Livia.* Erasmus
probably read them before they went to press.
On the other hand, it is possible that Erasmus'
Adagia influenced Fausto when he was putting
the final touches on his *Epistolae*, the first
edition of which dates from 1508. Contem-

porary scholars were aware of the problem;
Johann Sturm refers to it in his biography of
*Beatus Rhenanus, who was Fausto's pupil in
Paris. In Erasmus' own work we find no trace
of any controversy about this matter, a fact
which should be noted in view of the sustained
polemic between Erasmus and Polidoro *Virgilio about the relationship of his *Adagia* with
the latter's *Proverbia* (Epp 531, 1175). Judgment
in this matter should be deferred until there are
critical editions of the two works.

When Erasmus returned to Paris in 1504 he
took with him the manuscript of Lorenzo
*Valla's *Adnotationes in Novum Testamentum,*
which he had discovered in Park Abbey,
outside Louvain. This discovery redoubled his
desire to devote his whole life to the
restoration of theology. Fausto, meanwhile,
was fully occupied editing Latin poets and
composing a series of poems in praise of the
French king's Italian policy: in 1499 he edited
Ovid's *Fasti* and Octavius Cleophilus Fanensis'
De coetu poetarum, and in 1501 Ovid's *Tristia*
followed. He also became a member of the circle
of poets assembled by Queen Anne of Brittany.
At her request he wrote some complimentary
letters to her husband, *Louis XII, who was at
war in Italy. In 1505 his poetic exploits gained
him a canonry at Bayeux.

Erasmus, by contrast, was gradually turning
from poetry. Moreover his close relations with
his English friends tended to replace his ties
with Andrelini and other friends in Paris,
although when he passed through the city on
his way to Italy, in the early summer of 1506,
his old friends welcomed him with enthusiasm,
all the more so because they had feared him
dead. Writing to Thomas *Linacre in June 1506,
Erasmus claimed to harbour as much affection
for his French friends as for the English (Ep
194). But from that point on all contacts with
his Parisian friends seemed to be interrupted
until Erasmus returned to Paris in April 1511.
In this period Louis XII was fully involved in
his conflict over Gallicanism with Pope *Julius
II, and Paris was replete with anti-papal
literature. In these circumstances Erasmus may
have written the mordant epigram against
Julius II (Reedijk 392, 393) that constituted, so
to speak, the outline for the later dialogue
Julius exclusus e coelis. Fausto also contributed
to the campaign against Rome by writing to the

pope in the name of Queen Anne, accusing him of ingratitude towards the king of France. The appearance of the initials F.A.F. (Apparently the abbreviation for Faustus Andrelinus Foroliviensis) on one of the first (Parisian?) editions of the *Julius exclusus* has caused a great deal of controversy. Barring new discoveries, it may be assumed that Thomas *Lupset was responsible for the first Paris edition of the *Julius exclusus*, and that – perhaps with Fausto's knowledge – he used these initials as a ploy to protect Erasmus.

After his last stay at Paris in 1511, Erasmus' friendship with Fausto came to an end. He was gaining recognition as a dominant figure in the international scholarly world, while Fausto's career was declining. Erasmus mentioned his death only in passing (Epp 803, 855).

In an edition of the *Adagia* printed at Basel in the year of Fausto's death Erasmus created a modest literary monument to Fausto (II ii 68). Did scruples inhibit Erasmus from speaking ill of his old friend so soon after his death? Two years later, when writing to Juan Luis *Vives (Epp 1108, 1111) he changed his tone. He berated the dead Fausto severely for his levity and wondered how he had succeeded for so many years in impressing the Paris scholars despite his mediocre erudition. This judgment is doubtless inspired by the character of the addressee – Vives was an ardent moralist who disliked poetry – but also by Erasmus' rather uncomfortable situation at Louvain in those years. In a letter of 1528, however, he criticized the Paris and Louvain theologians for admitting *Bracciolini's *Facetiae* and Fausto's *Elegiae* to the curriculum, whilst his own works were excluded (Ep 2037). Erasmus' attacks on Fausto thus seem inspired not so much by personal dislike as by disappointment. Moreover, he was turning away from his early friends in Paris, especially Fausto, whose introductions to academic circles he no longer needed.

During Erasmus' years in Paris the contacts between him and Fausto were limited to good companionship, based on some common interests and their mutual distaste for traditional theology. But there was too great a difference in the ways they experienced contemporary events and personalities, even literature and humanism, for an unbreakable tie of friendship to be forged. Fausto was a typical Italian humanist, vivacious, quick, and self-confident. Erasmus was a northerner, irresolute, melancholic, and timorous, but full of high aspirations and profound ideas which were not compatible with Fausto's copious flow of glib words.

BIBLIOGRAPHY: Allen and CWE Ep 84 / R. Weiss in DBI III 138–41 / *Il diario romano di Jacopo Gherardi da Volterra* ed E. Carusi (Città di Castello 1904–6) / *Roberti Gaguini epistole et orationes* ed L. Thuasne (Paris 1903) / D. Hay *Polydore Vergil, Renaissance Historian and Man of Letters* (Oxford 1952) / J. IJsewijn 'Erasmus ex poeta theologus, sive de litterarum instauratarum apud Hollandos incunabulis' in *Scrinium Erasmianum* I 375–89 / Godelieve Tournoy-Thoen 'Deux épîtres inédites de Fausto Andrelini et l'auteur du "Iulius Exclusus"' *Humanistica Lovaniensia* 18 (1969) 43–76 / Godelieve Tournoy-Thoen 'La laurea poetica del 1484 all' "Accademia Romana"' *Bulletin de l'Institut historique belge de Rome* 42 (1972) 211–35 / Godelieve Tournoy-Thoen 'Fausto Andrelini et la cour de France' in *L'Humanisme français au début de la renaissance* (Paris 1973) 65–79 / Godelieve Tournoy-Thoen *Publi Fausti Andrelini Livia sive Amorum libri quattuor: Met een biobibliografie van de auteur* (Brussels 1981)

GODELIEVE TOURNOY-THOEN

Tranquillus ANDRONICUS Parthenius of Trogir, 1490–1571

Fran Trankvil Andreis is best known under the name of Andronicus, used before him by other members of this family of Dalmatian nobles established at Trogir on the Adriatic coast, west of Split. They aligned themselves with Venice in the fifteenth century and produced men of culture as well as administrators. One relative of Tranquillus taught Latin in Dubrovnik (Ragusa), and another joined the Dominican order and was in the diplomatic service of *Leo x. In the course of his studies Tranquillus progressed from Dubrovnik to Padua and other Italian university centres. At the time of the fifth Lateran council he was in Rome and entered the service of Jan *Łaski, archbishop of Gniezno, who attended the council between 1513 and 1515; this connection had a significant effect on the remainder of Andronicus' life. In April 1517 he matriculated in Vienna, introduced himself to *Vadianus, and offered to

lecture on Quintilian and Cicero. Vadianus
recommended him to Urbanus *Rhegius in
Ingolstadt, where in the winter of 1517–18 he
joined a circle of Polish students. *Maximilian
I's last diet attracted him to Augsburg, where
he published the first of his many books, an
oration in support of the crusade against the
Turks which was later reprinted several times.
For the spring term of 1518 he matriculated at
Leipzig, again as a member of the Polish
nation, and lectured on Quintilian (Ep 911); he
also visited Nürnberg and Erfurt, introducing
himself to *Pirckheimer, *Eobanus Hessus, and
Euricius *Cordus. Following the example of
Eobanus and other Erfurt humanists, he set out
in the spring of 1519 for a visit to Erasmus in
Louvain. Unfortunately he failed to make
contact with Erasmus either in Louvain or in
Antwerp. His desire to lecture in Louvain fell
on deaf ears, so that he finally left in anger for
Paris. Erasmus afterwards attempted to placate
him in Ep 991. In the colloquy *Convivium
poeticum* (1523; ASD I-3 344–59) he introduced a
speaker by the name of Parthenius.

Over the next twenty-five years Andronicus'
diplomatic career included many secret assignments and is not, it seems, documented with
anything approaching clarity. His principal
employer was apparently Hieronim *Łaski, the
nephew of the archbishop of Gniezno and the
right hand of *John Zápolyai, and subsequently also a Hapsburg spy in Zápolyai's
entourage. Andronicus' activities in the
Hungarian imbroglio also brought him into
contact with Alvise *Gritti and the Turkish
government. Some letters he wrote to Gritti
have survived. Hieronim Łaski seems to have
secured his release after two years' imprisonment in Vienna. Afterwards he served King
*Ferdinand as an agent and apparently also at
times the French. In 1544 he retired from
politics and henceforward devoted himself to
humanistic study, at first in Cracow and
subsequently at Trogir, where he died,
possibly under suspicion of heresy and under
investigation by the Inquisition. He left a
number of publications, among them *Oratio
contra Thurcas* (Augsburg: J. Miller 1518), *Oratio
de laudibus eloquentiae* (Leipzig: M. Lotter 1518),
Dialogus Sylla (n p 1527), *De Caesaribus
Romanorum invictissimis, Carolo et Ferdinando*
together with the *Oratio contra Thurcas* (Vienna:

J. Singren 1541), *Ad optimatos Poloniae admonitio*
and *Dialogus, philosophandum ne sit* (both
Cracow: H. Wietor 1545), and *Pia precatio ad
Deum* (Vienna: K. Stainhofer 1566). In the same
year Stainhofer printed a metric exhortation in
support of the crusade, which is reprinted with
the prose oration of 1518 in Hutten *Opera* v
203–28. Andronicus' *De rebus in Hungaria gestis
ab Ludovico Gritti* was edited by F. Banfi in
Archivio storico per la Dalmazia 18 (1934–5)
419–68. Some poems were found in Gniezno
and edited by B. Bolz in *Meander* 7–8 (Warsaw
1962) 378–97.

BIBLIOGRAPHY: Allen and CWE Ep 991 /
Enciklopedija Jugoslavije (Zagreb 1955–   ) I
101–2 / *Matrikel Wien* II-1 438 / *Matrikel Leipzig* I
564 / *Index Aureliensis* (Baden-Baden 1962–   ) I
570–1 / de Vocht CTL I 321–3 / I.N.
Goleniščev-Kutuzov *Il Rinascimento italiano e le
letterature slave dei secoli* XV *e* XVI (Milan 1973)
passim / Maria Cytowska 'Andronicus Tranquillus Dalmata – klient dworu Łaskich i Jana
Zapolyi' in *Studia z dziejów polsko- węgierskich
stosunków literackich* (Warsaw-Budapest 1969)
95–106 / A. Ritoók-Iralay 'Andronicus Tranquillus Dalmata und die Vita Aulica' *Ziva
Antika* 25 (1975) 202–9

PGB

ANGELUS (Ep 2698) of August 1532
Angelus' first name ('Engell') is confirmed in
Basler Chroniken (Basel 1872–   ) IV 98. He is
mentioned by Erasmus in Ep 2698 for his part in
the drama that ended the lives of his master,
Christoph *Baumgartner, and of other members of his family. Angelus has not otherwise
been identified.

PGB

Johannes ANGELUS *See Jean* LANGE

Pierre and Jean Pyrrhus d'ANGLEBERME
Pierre d'Angleberme (Anglebermeus) had
apparently moved to Orléans, where he
practised medicine, by the time his son, Jean
Pyrrhus, was born (c 1470–5). Pierre was still
alive and vigorous towards the end of 1517 (Ep
725). Jean Pyrrhus is known mostly from his
publications. He was one of Erasmus' students
in Paris (Epp 140, 866). By December 1510 he
had returned to Orléans and received a
doctorate in law. In his capacity as rector of the

university he engaged Girolamo *Aleandro to teach Greek at Orléans for the winter term of 1510–11. Pyrrhus continued to lecture on law in Orléans until 1515, when he was appointed to join the French administration in Milan. There he met Andrea *Alciati (Ep 1250), continued his scholarly work, and died prematurely in 1521.

Pyrrhus' publications include *Institutio boni magistratus, ubi ad iurisprudentiam nonnulla maxime conducentia* (Orléans: J. Hoys c 1500); *Index opusculorum* (Paris: A. Bocard 1517), containing, in addition to 'Sermo de musica et saltatione ex Luciano' and other translations from Plutarch, his important commentary on the customs of Orléans, which was often reprinted throughout the sixteenth century; *Militia Francorum regum pro re christiana* (Paris: J. Bade 1518); *Tres posteriores libri Codicis Iustiniani interpretati* (Paris: B. Rembolt 1518); and another collection, *Index operis* (Milan: A. Minuziano 1520), containing an 'Epistola de Mediolani laudibus.'

Erasmus had met Pierre at Orléans in 1500 and responded to his medical ministrations with Ep 140. He corresponded intermittently with Pyrrhus (Epp 256, 725). In 1518 we learn that Pyrrhus had asked his former student Adolf *Eichholz to submit some of his written work to Erasmus for review (Ep 866). When news of Pyrrhus' death reached him, probably through Alciati, Erasmus reacted with sincere shock (Epp 1250, 1278, 2468).

BIBLIOGRAPHY: Allen Ep 140 / *Index Aureliensis* (Baden-Baden 1962–) I 589–90 / A. Cioranescu *Bibliographie de la littérature française du seizième siècle* (Paris 1959) 87 / BRE Ep 369 / *Le Carnet de voyage de Jérôme Aléandre en France et à Liège (1510–1516)* ed Jean Hoyoux (Brussels-Rome 1969) 53–7

MICHEL REULOS & PGB

Wolfgang ANGST of Kaysersberg, c 1485– c 1523
A native of Kaysersberg in Upper Alsace, Angst matriculated in 1506 in the newly founded University of Frankfurt an der Oder, obtaining his BA in 1507. At Frankfurt he met Ulrich von *Hutten, who was one step ahead of Angst in his studies and soon came to exercise a lasting influence upon the young

Alsatian. Both were restless, both possessed a solid knowledge of Latin, and both were devoted to the cause of *Reuchlin. Unlike Hutten, however, Angst did not produce original compositions but employed his scholarship in the service of various printers. Among the editions he saw through the press were one of Cicero's *Tusculanae quaestiones* for Matthias *Schürer (Strasbourg 1514) and a manual of sermons by Santius de Porta, edited in the winter of 1514–15 for the Haguenau printer Heinrich Gran, who specialized in the production of works of scholastic theology. Soon thereafter, however, Gran produced anonymously the first edition of the famous *Epistolae obscurorum virorum*, most likely as a result of the connections between Angst, Hutten, and *Crotus Rubianus (cf Hutten's testimonial for Angst in the second part of the *Epistolae obscurorum virorum*, 1517, verses 124–31). Gran's first edition gave Angst a reason to approach Erasmus. On 19 October 1515 he sent him a copy of the newly published book accompanied by Ep 363.

While working for Schürer at Strasbourg, perhaps as early as 1513 (AK I Ep 487), Angst was in contact with the *Amerbach brothers, offering scholarly advice on some difficult readings in Jerome, and in May 1517 (AK II Ep 584) he had joined them at Basel and was working as a corrector for Johann *Froben's press. In the course of his employment with Froben he read the proofs for the *Adagia* of 1517–18 and corresponded with Erasmus in the name of his master (Epp 575, 594, 628, 634). On occasion he came in for his share of Erasmus' lively suspicions, but was likewise encouraged to continue his study of Greek (Epp 732, 733). By the end of September 1518 Angst had moved to Mainz (Ep 881; AK II Ep 628), where he collaborated with Hutten and the printer Johann *Schöffer on an important edition of Livy – the first to add the text of two books recently discovered in the library of the Mainz cathedral chapter (Epp 919, 951) – and also on the publication of Hutten's *De guaiaci medicina* (April 1519; Angst's epilogue is reprinted in Hutten *Opera* I Ep 96).

After this time – and without discernible reason – no further references to Angst are found in the letters of Hutten, Erasmus, and the Froben circle, although he is known to have been living at Haguenau in the spring of 1523.

BIBLIOGRAPHY: CWE and Allen Ep 363 / *Matrikel Frankfurt* I 5 / Heinrich Grimm in NDB I 296 / Heinrich Grimm *Ulrichs von Hutten Lehrjahre an der Universität Frankfurt (Oder) und seine Jugenddichtungen* (Frankfurt a.O.-Berlin 1938) 175

PGB

Nicolaus ANIANUS *See Anianus* BURGONIUS

ANNE Boleyn Queen of England, d 19 May 1536

*Henry VIII's second queen was the younger daughter of Sir Thomas *Boleyn and Elizabeth, the daughter of Thomas Howard, the second duke of Norfolk. Anne was probably born at Hever Castle, Kent, around 1507 and when she was about twelve followed her elder sister, Mary, to France, remaining there until war broke out in 1522. On her return to England she was destined to marry the heir to the earldom of Ormond, which the Boleyn family also claimed. When she was introduced at court by her father and grandfather, her looks and charm won many admirers, including the poet Sir Thomas Wyatt and Henry Percy, the son and heir of the duke of Northumberland. Mary Boleyn became the king's mistress, and in 1525 Sir Thomas was raised to the peerage. The exact chronology of Anne's own rise to prominence cannot be known, but by 1526 she had replaced her sister in the king's affections, although she refused to be his mistress. Their earliest correspondence has been ascribed to 1527. It is improbable that Anne was, as Reginald *Pole alleged, the first to implant doubts in Henry's mind about the validity of his marriage with *Catherine of Aragon; the queen's repeated failure to produce a male heir was the strongest influence on the king's desire for a new wife. In May 1527 formal investigations into the marriage began; the issue was complicated by Henry's acknowledged intercourse with Mary Boleyn, since this created a canonical impediment to marriage between him and Anne that required papal dispensation. Such a dispensation was wrung from Pope *Clement VII in 1528 but was

Anne Boleyn

naturally contingent upon the proven nullity of the first marriage.

During these first years of diplomacy and litigation Anne remained in the background, though she was used by the old nobility (headed by Thomas *Howard, third duke of Norfolk, and Charles *Brandon, duke of Suffolk) to break the power of Cardinal *Wolsey. In October 1528, when Cardinal *Campeggi arrived in London to try the case with Wolsey, Anne was deliberately kept from court, but by December she had moved into Catherine's rooms at Greenwich Palace. Anne's influence over the king's policies at this time should not be overstated, though she appears to have been genuinely friendly to the reforming party and introduced Henry to William *Tyndale's caesaropapist *Obedience of a Christian Man.* Erasmus only mentioned her in passing when commending her father (Ep 2315).

By 1531 Anne was the king's constant companion. Henry finally gave her official status on 1 September 1532 by creating her marchioness of Pembroke. In September

Thomas *Cromwell began his propaganda campaign on the king's behalf and started to prepare the Act of Appeals which would allow the marriage case to be settled in England. Only then did Anne yield to the king's demands and by the middle of January 1533 was found to be pregnant. As it was essential to Henry that his child should be born legitimate he married Anne secretly on or about 25 January. In May Archbishop *Cranmer pronounced the king's marriage with Catherine void. On 1 June Anne was crowned in Westminster Abbey with great pomp but little popular enthusiasm. Thomas *More stayed conspicuously away. On 7 September Anne gave birth to a daughter. Henry was so furious that he did not, it seems, attend the christening; but this child was now made his heir in the Act of Succession. There was no truth in a rumour which Erasmus apparently entertained in the spring of 1534 that the king intended to repudiate his new wife and return to Catherine (Ep 2915). In fact by this time Henry's eye had fallen on Jane Seymour, sometime maid to both Anne and Catherine, and the king and queen drifted apart. In January 1536 Catherine of Aragon died; on the day of her burial Anne produced a stillborn child. These events proved fatal, for Henry saw that a new wife (and a new heir) might now prove acceptable to all factions. Anne, who had never been popular, saw her family's influence at court eclipsed by the rise of the Seymours. In April the king started seeking grounds for a new divorce; Anne's previous contract with the Percy heir was found insufficient, but Henry wanted to be rid of her by any means. On 24 April Cromwell and Norfolk were told to find charges against her, and in a few days they had 'discovered' her adultery with several courtiers, including her own brother. Erasmus received news of this on 8 May (Ep 3119). Anne was doubtless indiscreet, but it is difficult to believe that she was guilty of the shocking crimes for which she was condemned at her trial on 15 May. She protested her innocence to the last but on 19 May was executed on Tower Green. Two days previously Cranmer had pronounced her marriage invalid because of the king's previous relations with her sister.

Jane Seymour, whom Henry married on 30 May, did indeed give the king a son; it was, however, Anne Boleyn's daughter who, eventually succeeding to the throne in 1558 as Elizabeth I, proved the strong and successful ruler her father had aspired to.

Anne Boleyn's portrait is in the National Portrait Gallery, London.

BIBLIOGRAPHY: DNB I 425–9 / G.E. C[ockayne] *The Complete Peerage* ed V. Gibbs et al (London 1910–59) x 403–5 / J.H. Round *The Early Life of Anne Boleyn* (London 1886) / P. Friedmann *Anne Boleyn, a Chapter of English History, 1527–1536* (London 1884) remains the most substantial biography; the most recent is M.L. Bruce *Anne Boleyn* (New York 1972) / *Letters of Royal and Illustrious Ladies of Great Britain* ed M.A.E. Green (London 1846) II 14–16, 45–9, 74–5, 186–92 / *The Letters of Henry VIII* ed M. St Clare Byrne (London 1936) 53–61 and passim / R.W. Chambers *Thomas More* (London 1935) 292 / The best general accounts of Anne and her times are in J.J. Scarisbrick *Henry VIII* (London 1968) 147–54 and passim and G.R. Elton *Reform and Reformation* (London 1977) 175–82 and passim

C.S. KNIGHTON

Johannes ANNIUS of Viterbo, d 13 September 1502
Johannes Annius (Giovanni Nanni) of Viterbo was born some time in the 1430s. Entering the Dominican order, he studied at Florence, where he drafted a theological opinion for Giovanni Rucellai. In Genoa and in his native Viterbo he had an active career as an astrologer and teacher. At some point around 1490 he began to forge inscriptions and texts that attributed a historical role of great importance to ancient Viterbo. When *Alexander VI came to Viterbo in 1493, he was most impressed by Annius' historical fantasies. He made him 'master of the sacred palace' and based the decorative scheme of the Appartmento Borgia in the Vatican partly on Annius' ideas.

Annius' most famous work was his collection of *Antiquitates* (Rome: E. Silber 1498). This much-reprinted volume included forged texts by several ancient near-eastern, Greek, and Roman historians whose names were known although their works were lost, along with enormous commentaries by Annius himself that showed that the forged texts contradicted

– and therefore discredited – the extant pagan historians of Greece and Rome. Though several of Annius' Italian contemporaries saw through the fraud, Erasmus did not. And when he reluctantly entered into the questions posed by the genealogy of Jesus given in Luke 3, he drew on Annius' text of Pseudo-Philo's *Breviarium de temporibus* as well as on his notes; see *Novum instrumentum* (Basel: J. Froben 1516) II 326–7. True, Erasmus had no love for Annius or his ideas. 'The problem of the genealogy of Christ,' he wrote in 1518, 'I know to be insoluble ... and I am not really satisfied with what I have collected out of Annius, who as a scholar, I rather suspect, is rash and pompous, and in any case a Dominican' (Ep 784). But even after Edward *Lee had subjected the relevant sections of the *Annotationes* to a searching attack in his own *Annotationes ... in Annotationes Novi Testamenti Desiderii Erasmi* (Paris: G. de Gourmont, c 1520, ff f verso – g verso), Erasmus retained the Annian material in the third and later editions of his *Annotationes* (Basel: J. Froben 1522, 147–8; LB VI 244D, 245E; V 1054BC, IX 155–6).

BIBLIOGRAPHY: Allen Ep 784 / R. Weiss 'Traccia per una biografia di Annio da Viterbo' *Italia medioevale e umanistica* 5 (1962) 425–41 / E.N. Tigerstedt 'Ioannes Annius and *Graecia Mendax*' in *Classical, Mediaeval and Renaissance Studies in Honor of Berthold Louis Ullman* (Rome 1964) II 293–310

ANTHONY GRAFTON

Thomas ANSHELM of Baden-Baden, d c 1523
Thomas Anshelm matriculated in Basel in 1485 as a poor student and left without obtaining a degree. He learnt the printing trade and on 10 January 1488 is documented as a printer in Strasbourg. By 1496 he had moved to Pforzheim and set up a printing shop that soon flourished; seventy-eight books printed by Anshelm in his Pforzheim years have been identified. He was a friend of Johann *Reuchlin, most of whose books he published, and Reuchlin encouraged him to move to Tübingen, where he matriculated on 20 March 1511. Here, Anshelm printed about seventy-five works, among them editions of classical authors, works by *Hutten, *Wimpfeling, and Johann *Stöffler, and Reuchlin's *Ars cabalistica* (1517; Ep 500), as well as his collection of letters

received from humanist scholars (*Clarorum virorum epistolae ad Ioannem Reuchlin*, March 1514). Reuchlin's nephew, Philippus *Melanchthon, worked for a while as a corrector for Anshelm.

In March 1514 Anshelm published an edition of Erasmus' *Adagia* (mentioned in Ep 492), and two years later Erasmus contributed a commendatory preface to Johannes *Nauclerus' world chronicle (Ep 397), praising Anshelm's Latin, Greek, and Hebrew types and his service to humanistic studies. In November 1516 Anshelm moved to Haguenau in Alsace, where he is documented until December 1522, producing about a hundred volumes. In 1517 Johannes *Caesarius suggested that Anshelm should publish a defence of Reuchlin which Erasmus had apparently promised to write (Ep 610), but this project was not carried out. In May 1519 Anshelm published another edition of the letters addressed to Reuchlin (*Illustrium virorum epistolae ... ad Ioannem Reuchlin*) with five letters from Erasmus among the newly added pieces, and this time Erasmus was not pleased (Ep 1041).

Many of Anshelm's books were undertaken to fill orders from international publishers and booksellers such as Franz *Birckmann in Cologne and Johann Knobloch in Strasbourg.

BIBLIOGRAPHY: Allen and CWE Ep 397 / NDB I 312 / ADB I 483 / RE Epp 256, 282, 292, and passim / Benzing *Buchdrucker* 161, 357, 436 / *Matrikel Basel* I 189 / *Matrikel Tübingen* I 182 / *Short-Title Catalogue of Books Printed in the German-Speaking Countries ... from 1455 to 1600 now in the British Museum* (London 1962) 968–9 and passim

IG

Jacob ANTHONISZOON of Middelburg, d before 16 May 1510
Jacob (Jacobus Middelburgensis), the son of Anthonie, was born at Middelburg – the date is not known – and obtained a doctorate in canon law in Italy. He was the vicar-general of Hendrik van *Bergen, bishop of Cambrai, and it was in the bishop's service that he became acquainted with Erasmus, who enjoyed his hospitality in 1498 (Epp 60, 77). He also held some offices; on 19 June 1471 he became a canon of St Gudula's, Brussels, and was the precentor from 11 June 1474 to 1 October 1502,

describing himself as a 'humble cantor' in an introductory letter published with his only known work, *De praecellentia potestatis imperatoriae* (Antwerp: D. Martens 1 April 1502; NK 120). The work is a profuse compilation, gleaned from various authors, of arguments against the position taken by Leonardo Bruni in one of his letters. The date of publication has to be 1503, new style, because Erasmus contributed to the book two poems (Reedijk poems 66 and 67), one of which is an epitaph for Hendrik van Bergen (d 6/7 October 1502). Erasmus also contributed to Jacob's book a complimentary letter which is, however, not without a critical undertone (Ep 173). In a preceding letter he expressed his obligations to Anthoniszoon and asked for the manuscript of *De praecellentia* which his servant had forgotten to take with him after a visit to Anthoniszoon's house (Ep 153, cf Ep 155). A second edition of the book, alleged to have been printed in Rome in 1503, has not been traced.

Anthoniszoon, who by 1503 was an old man (Allen Ep 173:53–4), made his will on 13 February 1508. He was buried in the oratory of St Nicholas at Brussels, which was demolished in 1533, and the accounts concerning his grave were dated 16 May 1510.

BIBLIOGRAPHY: Allen and CWE Ep 153 / J. van Kuyk in NNBW III 37–8 / P. Lefèvre 'Deux amis d'Erasme, membres du grand collège canonical à Bruxelles' *Scrinium Erasmianum* I 25–8, esp 25–7 / On Erasmus' two poems see C. Reedijk 'Erasmus' verzen op het overlijden van Hendrik van Bergen ...' *Het Boek* 30 (1949–51) 297–305

C.G. VAN LEIJENHORST

Marco Antonio ANTIMACO of Mantua, c 1473–c 1551
Marco Antonio was the son of Matteo Antimaco of Mantua, who had been a pupil of Gregorius *Tiphernas. From 1489 to 1494 he was at Sparta, studying Greek under Johannes Moschus. He taught Greek at Mantua, and by 1517 was a professor of Greek at the University of Ferrara (Ep 611). He held that position until 1545, when he was succeeded by Francesco Porto. Antimaco wrote Latin and Greek poetry and published in one volume Latin translations of the *Historia de gestis Graecorum post pugnam Mantineam* of *Gemistos Plethon, the *De re*

militari praefatio of Polyaenus, and works of Dionysius of Halicarnassus and Demetrius Phalereus (Basel: R. Winter 1540). The volume included his own oration in praise of Greek literature. His notes and preface were incorporated into Johannes Oporinus' second edition of the Sibylline books (Basel 1555).

In July 1517 Ulrich von *Hutten who had met Antimaco at Ferrara, said that he never mentioned Erasmus without praise (Ep 611).

BIBLIOGRAPHY: Allen Ep 611 / Cosenza I 203–4 / *Nuovi documenti relativi ai docenti dello studio di Ferrara nel secolo XVI* ed Adriano Franceschini (Ferrara 1970) 31, 32, 40, 45

TBD

Jacopo ANTIQUARIO of Perugia, 1444/5–1512
Jacopo was probably the son of the physician Stefano Antiquario. After studying under Giovanni Antonio *Campano, who taught at Perugia from 1452 to 1459, he entered the service of the papal governor to the city, Giovanni Battista Savello, and accompanied him to Bologna when he was transferred there in 1468. In the early 1470s he moved to Milan, possibly on the invitation of Bartolomeo Caldo, secretary to the duke, Galeazzo Maria Sforza. Antiquario served as secretary to the dukes, with supervision over appointments to ecclesiastical benefices. He chose to remain at Milan even after the French removed Ludovico (il Moro) *Sforza in 1500, and died there twelve years later.

Antiquario was a protector, adviser, and confidant of the greatest literary figures of his day, most notably of Angelo *Poliziano. Erasmus mentioned him in the *Ciceronianus* as one of the many writers who could not meet the exacting standards of the Ciceronians (ASD I-2 667).

The works of Antiquario are few; they include the *Oratio ... pro populo Mediolanensi in die triumphi ad Ludovicum regem Francorum et ducem Mediolanensium* (Milan: A. Minuziano ? c 1510) and several published *Epistolae* (Perugia: C. Bianchini 1519).

BIBLIOGRAPHY: E. Bigi in DBI III 470–2 / *Index Aureliensis* (Baden-Baden 1962–) I 610–11

TBD

Jan ANTONIN of Košice, c 1499–c 1549
Jan Antonin, the son of Anton, came from
Kassa in northern Hungary, now Košice, in
Czechoslovakia. In 1515 he began his studies at
the University of Cracow, and in 1517 he
received a BA. About 1521 he went to Italy for
medical studies and received his doctorate in
medicine from Padua. In July of 1524 he
travelled to Basel, where, assisted by the
recommendation of Udalricus *Zasius, he was
able to stay for a while. Here he made friendly
connections with Bonifacius *Amerbach,
Johann *Sichard, Claudius *Cantiuncula, Henricus *Glareanus, *Beatus Rhenanus, and
Ludwig *Baer. Above all he made the
acquaintance of Erasmus and was able to offer
him his medical services. At this time he
presented Erasmus with a magic coin called *Leo
astrologicus*, which was minted in Padua in 1523
according to the medieval formula of Pietro
d'Abano, the first professor of medicine in
Padua (Allen I 46; AK V Ep 2149). Dipped in
wine the coin was to serve its owner as a
remedy against gallstones. Although he had
received a public invitation to settle and
practise in Basel, Antonin left in November of
1524, to the great regret of Erasmus, who stated
that no one had been able to relieve his pain as
well as Antonin (Epp 1512, 1564).

Antonin first travelled to Hungary but left
his native land and in 1525 settled in Cracow.
His marriage with Anna, the daughter of the
goldsmith Jan *Zimmermann, and his successful cures brought him immediate popularity
and recognition among the dignitaries at the
royal court. He was at one time or another
physician to Bishop Piotr *Tomicki, King
*Sigismund I, and the bishop of Cracow, Piotr
Gamrat. Above all, he was closely attached to
the group of Cracow humanists, who appreciated not only his medical ministrations but also
his wide intellectual interests, his love of
classical literature, and his friendship with
Erasmus.

Antonin was one of the most active
propagators of the cult of Erasmus in Poland
and, because of his ties to the Thurzos and
other countrymen, also in Hungary. He was a
constant intermediary in the exchange of books
and letters and also brought Erasmus new
patrons. This influence caused Erasmus to
establish contact with Alexius *Thurzo (Ep

1572) and Piotr Tomicki (Ep 1919).

Of all Antonin's letters to Erasmus, only
three have been preserved (Epp 1660, 1810,
3137); they reflect his strong and admiring
attachment. Although not a wealthy man – not
until 1536 was he able to buy himself a home in
Cracow – he sent Erasmus expensive gifts: a
pearl soon after his departure from Basel, and,
perhaps in 1527, a silver-gilt cup (Epp 1698,
1916). Erasmus in turn dedicated to him his
translation from Galen (Ep 1698). He often
praised Antonin in letters to friends and
recommended him to wealthy patrons in
Poland. The news of a nervous disorder that
troubled Antonin in 1528 and 1529 filled
Erasmus with anxiety, and he rejoiced greatly
upon receiving word of his recovery (Ep 2173).

Antonin also kept in contact with Johann
Sichard, to whom he sent a recently recovered
manuscript of Quintilian's *Institutiones*; this
manuscript was then published by Sichard
(Basel: J. Froben 1528). He also corresponded
with Bonifacius Amerbach. After Erasmus'
death he wrote a eulogy and tried to have
Tomicki's last letter to Erasmus published. He
also suggested to Amerbach – unsuccessfully –
a collective publication defending Erasmus
against Etienne *Dolet (AK V Ep 2149).

From his marriage to Anna Zimmermann,
Antonin had two daughters, both of whom
became wives of physicians: Catherine married
Anton Schneeberger from Zürich, who had
settled in Cracow, and Ursula married Erasm
Lipnicki, who inherited the library of his
father-in-law, consisting largely of medical and
humanist works, among which Erasmus' books
were not lacking.

Antonin died before November 1549. Some
epitaphs by Clemens Janicius were written, as
was then customary, during Antonin's lifetime. Janicius also dedicated to him an elegy
about the occupation of Buda by the Turks
(*Tristia* I 8); after Janicius' death Antonin had in
turn edited his *Epitalamion serenissmo regi
Poloniae Sigismundo Augusto* (Cracow: Ungler-
owa 1543).

Antonin's publications include *Elegia in
mortem Petri Tomicii* ... (Cracow: H. Wietor
1535), *Elegia in mortem Erasmi Rotterodami* ...
(Cracow: F. Ungler 1536) and *De tuenda bona
valetudine* ... (Cracow: H. Wietor 1535). His
epigrams are appended to the *Libellus de*

erudienda iuventute (Cracow: H. Wietor 1526) by
Leonard *Cox, to the Cracow edition of
Erasmus' *Lingua* (Cracow: H. Wietor 1526), and
to Anrzej *Krzycki's *De afflictione ecclesiae
commentarius in psalmum xxi* (Cracow: H.
Wietor 1527).

BIBLIOGRAPHY: Allen Ep 1612 / AK III Ep 1187
and passim / PSB I 141 / *Korespondencja Erazma z
Rotterdamu z Polakami* ed M. Cytowska
(Warsaw 1965) / *Bibliografia polska* ed K.
Estreicher et al (Cracow 1870–1951) XIII 177 / E.
Major *Erasmus von Rotterdam* (Basel 1926) 71 /
Colloquia Erasmiana Turonensia I 568 and passim
/ H. Barycz 'Die ersten wissenschaftlichen
Verbindungen Polens mit Basel' *Vierteljahres-
schrift für Geschichte der Wissenschaft und Technik*
(Warsaw) 5 (1960) Sonderheft 2, 26–47, esp
31–3 / J. Fijałek 'Przekłady pim św. Grzegorza z
Nazyanzu w Polsce' *Polonia Sacra* (Cracow) 1
(1918) 74–5 / L. Hajdukiewicz *Ksiegozbiór i
zainteresowania bibliofilskie Piotra Tomickiego na
tle jego działalności kulturalnej* (Wrocław 1961) /
Archiwum do dziejów literatury i oświaty w Polsce
(Cracow 1892) VII 229–32 / *Clementis Janicii
carmina* ed J. Krókowski (Wrocław-Warsaw
1966) / Maria Cytowska 'Wegierscy wielbiciele
Erazma w Krakowie Joannes Antonius Casso-
viensis' in *Studia* dziejów *Polsko- Wegierskich
stosunków literkich* (Warsaw-Budapest 1979)
107–15

HALINA KOWALSKA

Egidio ANTONINI of Viterbo, 1469–12
November 1532
Egidio Antonini (better known as Aegidius
Viterbiensis, Giles of Viterbo) was born in 1469
at Viterbo; his parents were Lorenzo Antonini
and Maria del Testa da Canino. (A mistaken
belief that his surname was Canisio has long
prevailed.) He began studying logic with the
Augustinian friars at Viterbo and subsequently
entered the order. In June 1488 he came under
the influence of Fra Mariano da Genazzano.
He studied at the University of Padua,
attending the lectures of Agostino Nifo among
others, and reacted strongly against Aristoteli-
anism. At a hermitage in Istria, where he lived
for two years, he studied Platonic doctrines
under Domizio Gavardo. The protector of his
order, Cardinal Raffaele *Riario became
devoted to him and called him to Rome. On his

way he visited Florence and met Marsilio
*Ficino. By 1498 he had become assistant to Fra
Mariano, whom he accompanied to Naples,
entering the circle of the Academy of *Pontano
there. A narrow escape from shipwreck on his
return turned him to a life of austerity; his
inclination was to retire to a remote hermitage
in the Monti Cimini, south-east of Viterbo, but
he was continually in demand as a preacher
throughout Italy. He accompanied the papal
court from Viterbo to Perugia and later to
Bologna in 1506; on 7 October 1507 he became
general of his order and devoted himself to its
reform and expansion.

Egidio was in Rome between 22 February
and 4 July 1509, and Cardinal Riario may well
have introduced Erasmus to him. Erasmus may
also have heard him preaching at San Lorenzo
in Damaso or at St Peter's, where his sermon on
3 June contained references to moral and
disciplinary reform as well as to the Spanish
capture of Oran. Although he deplored
bloodshed, Egidio in general supported *Julius
II's wars as the necessary prologue to a crusade
and the triumphant spread of Christianity.
Early in 1510 he joined Julius II at Bologna and
preached in favour of his war against
'barbarians.' On 3 May 1512, in his oration at
the opening of the fifth Lateran council, he
approved the Holy League in principle and
uttered a famous aphorism that religion should
change men and not men religion. He was also
enthusiastic about the rebuilding of St Peter's.
Egidio welcomed the election of *Leo x, whom
he joined at Bologna in December 1515 before
being commissioned to go to Germany. He
returned to Rome to report on this mission in
May 1516. In 1517 he was perturbed by the
involvement of Cardinal Riario in the plot
against Leo x's life, but he did intercede for
him. He was also troubled by the dissidence
within his order provoked by Luther. Egidio
became a cardinal on 1 July 1517, remaining
general of the Augustinians until 25 February
1518; he was appointed bishop of Viterbo on 30
December 1523. In April 1518 he was sent as
legate to Spain to raise support for a crusade,
returning to Rome in early 1519 after visits to
Milan and Venice. He suffered greatly from
poor health and had been a regular patient at
the baths of Viterbo since 1505. He was ill

during the conclave of 1521, and also in May 1527, although he led a troop of two thousand men in an attempt to relieve *Clement VII in Castel Sant'Angelo. Afterwards he did not rejoin the curia until 5 October 1528.

Egidio was celebrated for his encyclopaedic knowledge of theology and of the Latin, Greek, Hebrew, and Chaldaic languages. He was a patron of the Jewish scholar Elias *Levita and a supporter of Johann *Reuchlin. In 1540 *Beatus Rhenanus wrote that Egidio and Erasmus had met (Allen I 62). Although Erasmus described Egidio as a friend (Ep 3032), his references to the Augustinian cardinal were relatively few. Writing to Guillaume *Budé in June 1527 Erasmus mentioned that Egidio had praised the De partu Virginis of Jacopo *Sannazaro (Ep 1640). In the Ciceronianus Erasmus mentioned Egidio's preface to a printed collection of the briefs of Leo X and Clement VII (ASD I-2 700).

Since 1502 Egidio had pressed for the publication of works by distinguished members of his order; he himself undertook an edition of the writings of Gregory of Rimini and a collection of lives of his predecessors in the generalcy. Among the most remarkable of Egidio's works is the 'Historia viginti saeculorum' (still unpublished), which contains prophetic observations. He has been identified as the writer of an anonymous polemic, Racha, which Erasmus took to be by Girolamo *Aleandro (E. Massa 'Intorno ad Erasmo: una polemica che si credeva perduta' Classical, Mediaeval and Renaissance Studies in Honor of Berthold Louis Ullman II, Rome 1964, 435–54). Egidio's own library, including many autograph manuscripts, was destroyed in 1527.

BIBLIOGRAPHY: For succinct biographical articles see Allen Ep 1840, EI XIII 535 / DHGE will shortly appear under 'Gilles,' DBI under 'Egidio.' / Basic information is in Eubel III 16 and passim, Pastor VII 153 and passim / Important recent studies include F.X. Martin (whose unpublished Cambridge PH D thesis Giles of Viterbo, 1959, is fundamental) 'The problem of Giles of Viterbo, a historiographical survey' Analecta Augustiniana IX (1959) 357–79, X (1960) 43–60 and J.W. O'Malley Giles of Viterbo and Church Reform (Leiden 1968)

D.S. CHAMBERS

St ANTONINUS archbishop of Florence, 25 March/1 April 1389–2 May 1459
St Antoninus was born at Florence to the prominent notary Niccolò Pierozzi and his second wife, Tommasa di Cenni di Nuccio. As a youth he came under the influence of Giovanni Dominici, a disciple of St Catherine of Siena, and in 1405 he entered the Dominican order. Ordained a priest around 1413, he served as prior at Cortona and Fiesole before being called to Naples in 1424 to assist in the implementation of the strict observance of the Dominican rule. He was transferred to Rome in 1430, and on 28 May 1437 was named vicar of the Observance for all Italy. From 1439 to 1444 he also served as prior of the monastery of San Marco at Florence. On 9 January 1446 Eugenius IV named him archbishop of Florence. Although frequently called upon by popes for advice, he devoted his episcopate principally to the reform and guidance of his flock and to charitable work. He was canonized by *Adrian VI on 31 May 1523.

Antoninus' writings included the Summa theologica (Venice: N. Jenson 1477–80), designed for confessors and preachers, the Chronicon (Venice 1474–9), a narrative of history since Adam, and various confessors' manuals and devotional works. In the Antibarbari (ASD I-1 110) Erasmus referred to a number of casuist works, including a Summa of Antoninus, in order to support his point that Christians were not forbidden to read secular literature.

BIBLIOGRAPHY: DBI III 524–32 / DTC I-2 1450–4
TBD

Aelius ANTONINUS Nebrissensis See Elio Antonio de NEBRIJA

ANTONIUS (Epp 1610, 1679, 1956 of 1525–8)
According to Erasmus, Antonius was the name of the procurator to the archdeacon of Besançon, Ferry de *Carondelet. It has not been possible to identify the procurator. While dining at his table during a visit to Besançon in the spring of 1524, Erasmus caused a minor scandal by inadvertently interrupting the prayers.

ANTONIUS (ASD I-3 447–8)
Antonius, a priest of Louvain and a favourite
of Philip the Good, duke of *Burgundy,
remembered by Erasmus in the colloquy
Convivium fabulosum for his indelicate jokes,
has not been identified.

ANTONIUS of Luxembourg documented at
Saint-Omer, 1500–18
Antonius, evidently a native of Luxembourg
(Antonius Lutzenburgus), was a priest and
steward of the abbey of St Bertin at Saint-Omer
until close to September 1517 (Ep 673); he also
held a canonry in the chapter of Notre Dame of
Saint-Omer (Ep 273) both during and after his
stewardship at St Bertin.

At St Bertin Antonius enjoyed the special
trust of his abbot, Antoon (I) van *Bergen,
during whose frequent absences he seems to
have been in charge of the abbey jointly with
the monks' executive council instituted by
Antoon. It is not certain, however, that he was
also Antoon's chaplain; the reference to him as
sacellanus (chaplain) in Allen Ep 143:236 may
well have resulted from a faulty transcription
of *sacellarius*, which means treasurer, as does
the term *economus* used in Ep 273.

However this may be, Antonius' services to
the abbot were not restricted to administrative
duties. In the winter of 1500–1, at Erasmus'
request, he recommended the appointment of
Jacob de *Voecht as tutor to the abbot's
brother, Dismas van *Bergen (Epp 137, 150), an
appointment which did not in the end come
about (Ep 170). Erasmus himself, who was at
that time greatly in need of a new patron (Ep
128), did not fully trust the promises made him
by the abbot and preferred to approach his
steward with requests that he present
Erasmus' case to abbot Antoon (Epp 148, 161),
and on occasion also that of his friends (Ep
762). In the same fashion he addressed himself
to Antonius when told that the abbot had
taken offence at his *Moria* in view of some
caustic remarks about monks (Ep 673). Erasmus
may have presented Antonius with a book at
some point before 1506 (Reedijk poem 77), and
in 1518 he sent him a copy of his *Paraphrasis in
Romanos* (Ep 762); in doing so, he was not only
appealing to a person of influence but also
honouring his friend as a man of culture (Epp

150, 161), although at first he had judged him
lacking in education (Ep 130).

Regrettably Erasmus' letters remain the only
source for Antonius, since the archives of the
Saint-Omer chapter have so far failed to yield
any information on his life and death, even
though as a canon he must have been more
conspicuous than others.

BIBLIOGRAPHY: Allen and CWE Ep 137
ANDRÉ GODIN

Petrus ANTONIUS (Ep 3057, of 13 September
1535)
Petrus Antonius is described as a bookseller
who was going to Basel to buy books and had
agreed to take to Erasmus Ep 3057, a letter
written from Brescia. Conceivably the carrier of
this letter was Petrus Antonius, a bookseller
established at Frankfurt am Main during the
1550s and documented as a customer of the
Basel press of Hieronymus *Froben and
Nicolaus *Episcopius in 1557. As the Frankfurt
bookseller is said to have immigrated from
France he could conceivably be a younger
relative of Johannes Antonius of Cividale del
Friuli in Venetia, who had been active in
England as a printer and bookseller and in 1501
and 1502 exercised his trade in Paris. A Pierre
Antoine, 'compagnon cordonnier,' is documented at Paris in February 1521 in association
with the bookseller Michel Antoine and other
printers and booksellers.

BIBLIOGRAPHY: Benzing *Buchdrucker* 176 /
Grimm *Buchführer* 1497 / Renouard *Répertoire* 7 /
Rechnungsbuch der Froben und Episcopius ed R.
Wackernagel (Basel 1881) 4 / Ernest Coyecque
*Recueil d'actes notariés relatifs à l'histoire de Paris
... au XVIe siècle* (Paris 1905–23) I 115

PGB

Petrus APIANUS of Leisnig, 16 April 1495–
21 April 1552
Petrus Apianus (Bienewitz, Bennewitz) was
born in Leisnig, in Saxony, and studied in
Leipzig and Vienna. At the University of
Ingolstadt he taught mathematics from 1527 to
his death. Apianus' *Cosmographicus liber*
(Landshut: J. Weissenburger 1524) became
famous (BRE Ep 401) for its important
observations concerning navigation and was
many times reprinted. Even more important is

his work on astronomy: his observation in 1531 of the comet later known as Halley's comet, his use of stereographic projection which enabled him to solve problems on spheric trigonometry, his *Quadrans astronomicus* (Ingolstadt: P. and G. Apianus 1532) and his *Astronomicum Caesareum* (Ingolstadt: P. and G. Apianus 1540), dedicated to the Emperor *Charles v. In recognition of this work Apianus was raised to the nobility on 20 July 1541 (with the title 'zu Ittlkofen'). His *Instrumentum primi mobilis* (Nürnberg: J. Petreius 1534) contains the first printed tables of sine calculations for every minute, with the radius divided decimally. Together with Bartholomaeus Amantius, he collected and published Greek and Latin inscriptions, *Inscriptiones sacrosanctae vetustatis* (Ingolstadt: P. and G. Apianus 1534). Apianus' intention to publish the *Geography* of Ptolemy in Greek and Latin is referred to in Ep 2606 (1532); it was carried out only in part.

BIBLIOGRAPHY: Allen Ep 2606 / NDB I 325–6 / *Dictionary of Scientific Biography* ed C.C. Gillispie et al (New York 1970–   ) I 178–9 / Arnold Reimann *Die älteren Pirckheimer* (Leipzig 1944) 203 / Lynn Thorndike *A History of Magic and Experimental Science* (New York 1923–58) V 352–3 / Moritz B. Cantor *Vorlesungen über Geschichte der Mathematik* 2nd ed (Leipzig 1894–1908) II 401–5 / René Talon et al *The Beginnings of Modern Science* (London 1964) 32–3 / *Index Aureliensis* (Baden-Baden 1962–   ) II 21–32

IG

Jacobus APOCELLUS of Ubstadt, d 1550
Jacobus Apocellus (Apocello, Appozeller) of Ubstadt, near Bruchsal, matriculated at Heidelberg on 5 February 1509. In 1515 and 1516 he was in Rome with Michael *Hummelberg, who in a letter associated him with the town of Pforzheim, located in the same region as Bruchsal. From 1518 he is documented as a notary in Rome. He was connected with Santa Maria dell'Anima, the German institution in Rome, and in 1526 he registered in the book of Santa Maria's confraternity, describing himself as provost and canon of St Thomas', Strasbourg, and as an apostolic protonotary and a knight of St Peter. In December 1526 and in 1530 he was *provisor*, or head, of Santa

Petrus Apianus by Philippe Galle

Maria and in 1544 and 1545 he was *comprovisor*. In a letter of December 1527 he described his experiences during the Sack of Rome, and in 1542 he witnessed the will of Girolamo *Aleandro. He was buried in the church of Santa Maria dell'Anima. His humanistic tastes are revealed by two documents published by Anthony Hobson, one of which is a list of ten Greek manuscripts from his library drawn up by Jean *Matal.

Apocellus was a relative of Justus *Diemus of Bruchsal, who in 1525 persuaded Erasmus (Ep 1630) and *Beatus Rhenanus (BRE Ep 249) to recommend him to Apocellus. He was kindly received, and Apocellus would have liked him to stay.

BIBLIOGRAPHY: Allen Ep 1630 / Cosenza I 231 / *Matrikel Heidelberg* I 469 / V. Forcella *Iscrizioni delle chiese ... di Roma* (Rome 1869–84) III 456 / A.J. Schmidlin *Geschichte der deutschen Nationalkirche in Rom, S. Maria dell'Anima* (Freiburg-Vienna 1906) 274, 361 / Aloys Schulte *Die Fugger in Rom, 1495–1523* (Leipzig 1904) I 239 / *Liber confraternitatis B. Mariae de Anima* ed C. Jaenig (Rome 1875) 133 / A. Hobson in

Transactions of the Cambridge Bibliographical Society 7 (1979) 279–83

PGB

Arsenius APOSTOLIUS of Candia, c 1468/9–30 April 1535
Arsenius (Aristoboulos) Apostolius (Apostolis, Apostolides) was born in Candia (Iraklion), Crete, the son of Michael *Apostolius and his second wife, who was a noblewoman from Monemvasia (Malvasia), on the Peloponnese. Following in his father's footsteps, he became a scribe. The earliest known manuscript that he copied and signed is dated 31 March 1489. It specifies that by this time he had been ordained a deacon. His youth notwithstanding, he began to teach, having among his pupils Johannes Gregoropoulos and probably also Marcus *Musurus. In April 1492 he was in contact with Janus *Lascaris, who was visiting Crete in search of Greek manuscripts for the library of Lorenzo (I) de' *Medici. Perhaps Apostolius accompanied Musurus on his return to Italy; at any rate he was in Venice in June 1492 and in Florence in the autumn, eager to join the entourage of Lorenzo's son, Piero de' Medici. In 1494, probably following the expulsion of the Medici, he returned to Venice and began to work for Aldo *Manuzio, who had just started his press. Apostolius' name appears in several early Aldine editions. In January 1496 he was back in Crete, as is shown by another manuscript that he signed and dated. By the turn of that year Aldus sued him for repayment of a loan which, according to Apostolius, had been paid off through the copying of a manuscript.

In 1504 Apostolius directed his attention to Monemvasia, then under Venetian domination. The inhabitants were split into an Orthodox and a Catholic congregation, both headed by an archbishop. Apostolius attempted to occupy the Orthodox see; he visited Venice and won the endorsement of the senate. He was installed in 1506, but his flock turned against him and, it seems, even before he was excommunicated by the patriarch of Constantinople in June 1509, he was forced to leave the city. He went to Venice, where he met Erasmus (CWE Ep 1232A), who was attached to the Aldine press in 1508, and where his presence is attested for 8 June 1509 by the records of the senate. Subsequently he went to Crete, but he aspired to return to Monemvasia, this time as the Catholic archbishop. He could not conceal his disappointment when on 19 June 1516 Pope *Leo X named Musurus to the vacant position. After Musurus' death in the following year, Apostolius again failed to obtain the appointment. He was, however, invited to Rome, where in 1519 he edited parts of his father's collection of proverbs with additions of his own and was appointed head of a new college for Greek students that Leo X was setting up in Florence. It was from Florence that Apostolius wrote to Erasmus on 31 August 1521, sending him a copy of the printed proverbs (CWE Ep 1232A).

In 1524 another vacancy in the Catholic see of Monemvasia created conditions that finally allowed Apostolius to return there as archbishop of both congregations, having obtained the agreement of Venice and Pope *Clement VII. He visited Venice again in 1527 and also spent the last four years of his life there from 1531. Life in Greece was precarious at best, and Italy offered better opportunities for collaboration with the printers. Among other works, in 1532 Apostolius edited for the Venetian press of Stefano da Sabbio two volumes of works by Michael Psellus, dedicating them to Cardinal Niccolò Ridolfi, and in 1534 he prepared an important first edition of commentaries on Euripides for another Venetian press, that of Luca Antonio Giunta. On 30 March 1534 he was appointed preacher of San Giorgio dei Greci in Venice, but two months later, by employing two Catholic priests to act as his assistants, he once more caused a rift in his congregation. Apostolius was buried in the courtyard of San Giorgio dei Greci.

BIBLIOGRAPHY: CWE Ep 1232A / A. Pratesi in DBI III 611–13 / D.J. Geanakoplos *Greek Scholars in Venice* (Cambridge, Mass, 1962) 167–200 / M.J.C. Lowry *The World of Aldus Manutius* (Oxford 1979) 61, 74, 305, and passim / ''Αρσενίου Μονεμβασίας τοῦ Ἀποστόλη ἐπιστολαὶ ἀνέκδοτοι (1521–34)' ed M.I. Manousakas 'Επετηρὶς τοῦ Μεσαιωνικοῦ 'Αρχείου 8–9 (1958–9) 5–56 / W.J.W. Koster 'Een brief van de humanist Arsenius an

Erasmus' *Hermeneus* 11 (1938/9) 17–20 / *La Correspondance d'Erasme* IV ed M.A. Nauwelaerts (Brussels-Québec 1970) Ep 1226A

PGB

Michael APOSTOLIUS of Constantinople, d c 1480–6

'Michael, the father of Arsenius *Apostolius, was a student of Johannes *Argyropoulos in his native Constantinople by 1448. In 1452 he succeeded to Argyropoulos' teaching position and aligned himself with those who supported the union between the Greek and Latin churches. When the Ottomans conquered Constantinople in 1453 Apostolius, like other scholars, was imprisoned. In the following year, however, he was able to make his way to Crete, where he married, and subsequently to Bologna, where he met Cardinal *Bessarion and was commissioned by him to search for Greek manuscripts. By the autumn of 1455 he had returned to Crete and opened a scriptorium in Candia (Iraklion). Some scribes who had been trained by him were later active in Venice and contributed to the city's pre-eminence in the early history of Greek printing. Apart from repeated trips to Italy he passed the rest of his life in Candia. He soon lost his first wife but married again and precariously supported himself and his family, helped by an annuity from Bessarion, part of which seems to have been paid to him even after the cardinal's death in 1472.

Apostolius gathered a large collection of Greek proverbs, the Ἰωνία, which was later continued by his son, who edited part of it as Ἀποφθέγματα ...: *Praeclara dicta philosophorum, oratorum et poetarum* (Rome: at the Greek Gymnasium 1519). A fuller edition appeared in 1538 (Basel: J. Herwagen and J.E. Froben), and the first modern edition was made by Christian Walz (Stuttgart 1832). Erasmus used the collection in manuscript during his stay in Venice and was later sent a copy of the 1519 edition (CWE Ep 1232A). He used it frequently in his own *Adagia*, but let it be known that he found it inadequate (*Adagia* I iii 99, III iii 31, 42, 66). In his preface to the *Adagia* of 1515 (Ep 269) he deplored its proneness to 'ignorance and errors' and in the preface to the 1533 edition (Ep 2773) he claimed that he had always given

due credit to his sources, even to Apostolius. In 1468 Apostolius launched an appeal for the liberation of Byzantium to the Emperor *Frederick III (edited by Marquard Freher, Frankfurt 1600, and partially translated in Geanakoplos 97–9). In another discourse (printed in Noiret 148–53 and partially translated in Geanakoplos 101–6) he offered himself to any interested Italian city as a teacher of Greek. Some verses by him appeared in the first edition of Homer's Βατραχομυομαχία (Venice: Laoconicus of Crete 1486), and Hippolyte Noiret edited his *Lettres inédites ... d'après les manuscrits du Vatican, avec des opuscules inédits* (Paris 1889).

BIBLIOGRAPHY: CWE 31:317, 323, 324, and passim / D.J. Geanakoplos *Greek Scholars in Venice* (Cambridge, Mass, 1962) 73–110 / D.S. Chambers *The Imperial Age of Venice 1380–1580* (London 1970) 151 / P.O. Kristeller *Iter Italicum* (London-Leiden 1965–   ) I 282 and passim

PGB

Gabriel AQUILINUS documented in 1520

In June 1520 (Ep 1108) Juan Luis *Vives recalled some promising Spanish scholars and students he had met on a recent visit to the University of Paris, among them Gabriel Aquilinus, who matriculated on 17 September 1520 at the University of Montpellier, laying claim to the degree of *magister* but failing to indicate his native region or town. Of the other Spaniards listed in Vives' letter, at least Juan Martín *Población was a former Montpellier student, while another, Johannes *Fortis, seems to have matriculated there in September 1523. It also appears that some Spaniards belonged to a circle of admirers of Erasmus at Montpellier that was to form a few years later around Petrus *Decimarius.

BIBLIOGRAPHY: *Matricule de Montpellier* 41

PGB

Alfonso of ARAGON *See* ALFONSO *of Aragon*

Michel d'ARANDE d March or April 1539

Michel d'Arande (Arantius, Aranda) was born at or close to Tournai, probably of Spanish decent. His birthdate is unknown. Having taken orders as an Augustinian friar, he lived for some time in a convent in the diocese of

Cambrai and was eventually ordained a priest. At the beginning of the sixteenth century he went to Paris to study theology. It is possible that he enrolled at the Collège de Saint-Michel, then under the direction of Martial Mazurier. In the spring of 1521 he left Paris to join Mazurier, Pierre Caroli, Gérard *Roussel, and *Lefèvre d'Etaples at Meaux.

In June 1521 d'Arande was sent to court at the behest of *Margaret of Angoulême. In the next few years he served as the primary intermediary between the evangelicals of Meaux and the royal family. In November and December 1522 his evangelical preaching before the ladies of the court was denounced by the royal confessor, Guillaume *Petit. Royal intervention was necessary to save him from prosecution by the Paris faculty of theology. In 1523 Margaret sent d'Arande to preach at Alençon and later at Bourges. When he was invited to preach by the canons of Bourges cathedral, his sermons were so heterodox that they led to a protest to the king by the papal nuncio, Girolamo *Aleandro. His attempt to preach at Lent 1524 led to his expulsion from the pulpit by the archbishop, François de Bueil. At the instance of Margaret of Angoulême the court interceded once again, going so far as to seize the temporalities of the archbishop in order to discipline him.

In October 1524 d'Arande was named almoner of the duchess of Angoulême and followed the court to Lyon. In December he preached at Mâcon and later at Meaux. In the spring of 1525 he rejoined the court of Lyon and tried unsuccessfully to introduce evangelical reforms in that city. By then religious reaction was in full swing, and the duchess of Angoulême had difficulty in preventing d'Arande's arrest. When he was summoned to Paris to testify before the university, d'Arande chose to flee the kingdom at the end of 1525 alongside Lefèvre d'Etaples and Gérard Roussel. In a letter to *Francis I Erasmus named d'Arande with *Papillon and *Du Blet among those who had been recent victims of the persecution of the Paris faculty of theology (Ep 1722). D'Arande remained at Strasbourg for six months and rejoined Margaret at Cognac at the beginning of May 1526. By then he had been named bishop of Saint-Paul-Trois-Châteaux. Although he faithfully carried out his episco-

pal duties in Saint-Paul, where he died, his letter to Farel of March 1536 makes it clear that he remained attached to his earlier convictions and associations.

D'Arande wrote a commentary on the Psalms, which has disappeared.

BIBLIOGRAPHY: Allen Ep 1722 / Roman d'Amat in DBF III 227–30 / Guillaume Briçonnet and Marguerite d'Angoulême *Correspondance (1521–24)* ed Michel Veissière et al (Geneva 1975–) passim / Phillip August Becker 'Marguerite, duchesse d'Alençon, et Guillaume Briçonnet, évêque de Meaux d'après leur correspondance inédite (1521–1524)' *Bulletin de la Société de l'histoire du Protestantisme français* 49 (1900) 393–477, 661–7 / Herminjard I passim / Eugène and Emile Haag *La France protestante* 2nd ed by H. Bordier (Paris 1877–8) I 296–300 / V.-L. Saulnier, 'Marguerite de Navarre aux temps de Briçonnet: étude de la correspondance générale' BHR 39 (1977) 458–9
                                                          HENRY HELLER

Remaclus d'ARDENNE, ARDUENNA *See REMACLUS ARDUENNA*

Franciscus ARETINUS *See Francesco GRIFFOLINI*

Johannes ARGYROPOULOS of Constantinople, 1415–26 June 1487
Little is known of Johannes Argyropoulos (Giovanni Argiropolo) before he arrived in Italy for the first time in 1438 on the occasion of the council of Ferrara-Florence. After briefly returning to Constantinople in 1441, he went back to Italy and received a doctorate at the University of Padua in 1444. After spending more time in his native land, he took permanent refuge in Italy after the fall of Constantinople in 1453. From 1456 until 1471 and again from 1477 to 1481 he taught Greek at the University of Florence, where he had numerous students, including Donato *Acciaiuoli, Cristoforo *Landino, and Angelo *Poliziano. He was in Rome from 1471 to 1477 and from 1481 to 1487. Besides translating much of Aristotle into Latin, he composed a number of works of his own, both in Greek and in Latin, including a work on the procession of the Holy Spirit. Erasmus refers several times to his translations of Aristotle (Epp 456, 862, 2432).

BIBLIOGRAPHY: Allen Ep 456 / E. Bigi in DBI IV 129–31 (with references to earlier literature) / J.E. Seigel 'The teaching of Argyropoulos and the rhetoric of the first humanists' in *Action and Conviction in Early Modern Europe: Essays in Memory of E.H. Harbison* ed T.K. Rabb and J.E. Seigel (Princeton 1969) 237–601 / A.F. Verde *Lo studio fiorentino 1473–1503* (Florence 1973–   ) II 316–21 (bibliography)

CHARLES B. SCHMITT

Ludovico ARIOSTO of Ferrara, 8 September 1474–16 July 1533
Ludovico was born at Reggio Emilia to Niccolò Ariosto, a nobleman in the service of the Este dukes of Ferrara, and Daria Malaguzzi Valeri. In his early years Ludovico moved frequently, since his father was transferred to Rovigo, then to Ferrara, Modena, and back to Ferrara. In the early 1490s he attended the University of Ferrara, forced by his father to study law. In 1494, however, his father relented and he was freed to devote himself entirely to humanistic studies, especially to poetry. Gregorio da Spoleto was his teacher, and Alberto *Pio of Carpi, Ercole Strozzi, and Pietro *Bembo became his friends. In 1500 the death of his father forced Ariosto, the first-born son, to look after his family. In 1501 he was appointed captain of the citadel of Canossa, and in 1503 he became secretary of Cardinal Ippolito d'*Este and took minor orders in the church. He accompanied the cardinal on missions to Rome, Florence, Mantua, and other cities, but in 1517, when Ippolito left for his bishopric of Buda in Hungary, he refused to follow, preferring instead to remain close to Alessandra Benucci, whom he married secretly in 1528. He entered the service of Alfonso I d'*Este, the duke of Ferrara, acting as governor of the rugged territory of Garfagnana from 1522 to 1525. He returned to Ferrara in March 1525 and remained there until his death.

Even in the midst of his official duties Ariosto found time to write poetry, and his masterpiece, the chivalric epic *Orlando furioso*, is held by many to be the greatest poetic work of the Italian Renaissance. Intended to continue the *Orlando innamorato* of Matteo Maria Boiardo (c 1440–94), the *Orlando furioso* followed the adventures of the knight Roland, with numerous plots and sub-plots, including

Johannes Argyropoulos

the wars between Christians and Moors and the love of Ruggero and Bradamante, who were destined to found the Este family. Begun in 1503, the *Orlando furioso* was first published in 1516 (Ferrara: G. Mazzocchi del Bondeno), with substantially revised editions appearing in 1521 (Ferrara: G.B. della Pigna) and 1532 (Ferrara: F. Rossi da Valenza). By the end of the century it had been translated into French, Spanish, and English. Ariosto's lesser works included *Satire* (Ferrara: F. Rossi da Valenza 1534), *Rime* (Venice: J. Coppa 1546), and *Carmina* (Ferrara: G.B. della Pigna 1553). He also wrote five comedies, published together in 1562 (Venice: G. Giolito): *Cassaria* (1508), *Suppositi* (1509), *Negromante* (1520), *Lena* (1530), and *Studenti* or *Scholastica* (completed after his death by his brother Gabriele and son Virginio).

Giovanni Angelo *Odoni mentioned Ariosto with praise in his letter to Erasmus of March 1535 (Ep 3002).

BIBLIOGRAPHY: N. Sapegno in DBI IV 172–88, with extensive bibliography and information on recent editions of Ariosto's works

TBD

Georges d'ARMAGNAC 1500–10 July 1585
Georges belonged to the house of the counts of
Armagnac and was tutored by Pierre *Gilles. In
the service of the French crown he obtained a
huge accumulation of ecclesiastical preferment, being bishop of Rodez (1530–61), of
Vabre (1536–48), and of Lescar (1555–6) and
archbishop of Tours (1548–51), Toulouse
(1562–82, 1584–5), and Avignon (1577–84).
Among the commendatory abbacies he received were Figeac, La Grâce, Belleperche
(1552), La Daurade (1560), and La Clarté-Dieu.
On 19 December 1544 he was named cardinal
by *Paul III.

Georges d'Armagnac represented *Francis I
as ambassador in Venice (1536–9) and Rome
(1539–45). After his return to France he
devoted his energies to the suppression of
heresy in southern dioceses and was also
appointed royal *lieutenant* of the seneschalcy of
Toulouse (1552). A man of learning, he
corresponded with Guillaume *Budé and other
scholars. In November 1531 Erasmus approached him on behalf of Hieronymus
*Froben to secure the use of a Greek
manuscript of Josephus (Ep 2569). As it turned
out, the Josephus belonged to Jean de *Pins,
who had lent it to Pierre Gilles. The latter
apparently lent a hand in getting the
manuscript to François *Rabelais for conveyance to Basel (Epp 2628, 2665, 2743). In a
Lexicon graecolatinum revised by Gilles (Basel:
V. Curio 1532) Simon *Grynaeus addressed a
dedicatory epistle (dated 1 September 1532) to
Georges d'Armagnac praising his patronage of
letters.

BIBLIOGRAPHY: Allen Ep 2569 / E.G. Ledos in
DBF III 677–9 / C. Samaran in DHGE IV 263–7 /
Eubel III 28 and passim

MICHEL REULOS & PGB

**Johannes ARMENTHERIENSIS, ARMEN-
THERIUS** *See Jan* HEEMS

ARNOLD of Tongeren *See Arnold Luyd of*
TONGEREN

Beat ARNOLD of Sélestat, 4 May 1485–4
October 1532
Beat Arnold (Batt Arnold, Arnoaldus) was
born in Sélestat, the son of an artisan. Together
with his kinsman *Beatus Rhenanus he studied
in Paris and received a BA in 1504. From 1507 to
1511 he worked for the printers in Strasbourg,
and verses by him appear in many of their
books. In 1509 Beatus Rhenanus addressed to
him a dedicatory epistle for the *Opuscula
christiana* by Ludovico Bigi Pittorio when the
book was reprinted by Matthias *Schürer in
Strasbourg (BRE Ep 5). Subsequently Arnold
entered the chancery of *Maximilian I, where
his compatriot Jakob *Spiegel was employed
from 1504, and afterwards that of *Charles V. It
seems that he was often employed as a courier,
so that his whereabouts are not easy to
establish (Ep 1467). He did, however, visit his
native Sélestat from time to time (BRE Epp 163,
255, 435), and his name is included in Erasmus'
poem in praise of Sélestat (August 1514;
Reedijk poem 98). Setting out from there with a
letter of recommendation by Johannes *Sapidus (Ep 399), he apparently visited Erasmus in
the spring of 1516 at Basel. Similar visits seem
to have taken place in the spring of 1524, and
again a year later when Arnold was returning
from Spain with letters and advice for Erasmus
(Epp 1553, 1554; cf Ep 1467). In the spring of
1526, too, his arrival from Spain was expected
in Sélestat (BRE Ep 255). On the emperor's
recommendation he received a canonry in
Saint-Dié, west of the Vosges, in 1527. In June
1531 he wrote to Beatus Rhenanus from Ghent,
promising his support in securing printer's
privileges for the *Froben press. In fact when
he met the chancellor, Matthias *Held, in
Regensburg he persuaded him to issue them,
but then the matter stalled when Arnold died
in Vienna (BRE Epp 278, 291; AK IV Ep 1719).
Erasmus' praise for Arnold (Ep 1467) was
echoed by Held and others, and Beatus
Rhenanus, who was a close friend, composed
an inscription for his tomb (BRE 10, 622).

BIBLIOGRAPHY: Allen Ep 399 / BRE Ep 5 and
passim / Schmidt *Histoire littéraire* I xx, II 84, 165

PGB

Edward and Richard ARNOLD *See Arnoldus*
EDUARDUS

Adrianus ARNOLDI *See Adriaan* AERNOUT

Johannes ARNOLDI *See Jan* AERTS

ARNOLDUS (Ep 1018, of 2 October 1519)
Arnoldus, a servant of Maximilian van
*Egmond at Louvain, has not been identified.

ARNOLDUS (Allen I 6:20) *See Arnoldus*
EDUARDUS

ARNOLDUS Coloniensis (Ep 3002 of c March
1535)
Arnoldus Coloniensis was at least occasionally
one of a group of Erasmians at Bologna who
gathered around Eusebio Renato and Giovanni Angelo *Odoni. In the early 1530s he
managed a German bookstore at Bologna (Ep
3002) and carried letters from the Erasmian
circle at Bologna to Martin *Bucer. His
identification with Arnoldo Arlenio Perassilo
or with Arnold Birckmann, presumably the son
of Franz *Birckmann, is uncertain.
  BIBLIOGRAPHY: S. Seidel Menchi 'Sulla
fortuna di Erasmo in Italia' *Revue suisse
d'histoire* 24 (1974) 537–634 / S. Seidel Menchi
'Passione civile e aneliti erasmiani di Riforma
nel patriziato genovese del primo cinquecento'
Rinascimento 18 (1978) 119–21
                        SILVANA SEIDEL MENCHI

Batt ARNOLT *See Beat* ARNOLD

ARTHUR prince of Wales, 19 September
1486–2 April 1502
Arthur was born at Winchester, the oldest son
of *Henry VII by his queen, *Elizabeth of York.
Thus he was heir to the English throne, to
which he would bring the claims of the house
of York. In 1489 he was made a knight of the
Bath and in 1491 a knight of the Garter. His first
tutor was John Rede, who was succeeded by
the blind poet Bernard *André (Epp 1490,
2422). By the age of sixteen he had studied the
grammarians and a number of the Greek and
Latin authors. Negotiations towards a marriage between Arthur and *Catherine of
Aragon began as early as 1488. In 1501 the
marriage was celebrated, but in all probability
it had not been consummated when the prince
died at Ludlow, near the border of Wales, on 2
April 1502.
  Although Arthur was not present when
Erasmus was taken to Eltham castle for a
surprise visit with the royal children in 1499

Arthur, Prince of Wales

(Allen I 6), Arthur afterwards received his
share of compliments when the event inspired
Erasmus to compose a lengthy poem (Reedijk
poem 45).
  BIBLIOGRAPHY: DNB I 603 / J.J. Scarisbrick
Henry VIII (London 1968) passim
                                                     CFG

Hieronymus ARTOLF of Mutten, d August
1541
Artolf (Artulf, Artolbius) was born at Mutten,
near Thusis in the Grisons. He matriculated at
Basel in the fall term of 1509, obtaining his BA in
1511 and his MA in 1513, and studying together
with Konrad *Brunner and Bonifacius *Amerbach. Subsequently he began to study
medicine, as is confirmed by an elegy Henricus
*Glareanus addressed to him (published in
1516). The same source mentions conversations Artolf had had with Erasmus. Although a
medical doctorate eluded him, he may on
occasion have practised as a physician.
Primarily he was a schoolmaster, teaching at
various times in two of Basel's parish schools
and heading a residence for university

students. In 1533 he was briefly jailed on account of his verbal outbursts against Protestant ministers and magistrates. Between 1537 and 1540, while registered as a candidate for a medical degree, he was once or twice dean of the faculty of arts and for 1538–9 he was elected rector of the university, in part, no doubt, thanks to the support of Bonifacius Amerbach, whose policy proposals he presented to the authorities in an attempt to reduce the academic influence of the Protestant party. In 1540 he was appointed to the chair of logic but he died a year later of the plague.

In addition to his teaching Artolf seems to have done some work for Johann *Froben and other Basel printers. In 1519 he assisted *Beatus Rhenanus in the collation of the *Germania* for Froben's great edition of Tacitus. No doubt as a reward for his editorial assistance he was allowed to add a dedicatory preface, addressed to Bonifacius Amerbach, to the first book of *Zasius' *Responsa iuris* (Basel: M. Isengrin 1538). His connections with Erasmus were probably more frequent than can be documented on the basis of the correspondence. Artolf wrote to Erasmus in 1528 (Ep 2012) while paying a visit to Besançon, and in 1534 he sent him some pens in return for some others he had previously borrowed (Ep 2907, 2908).

BIBLIOGRAPHY: CWE and Allen Ep 440 / AK II Epp 583, 817, 835, IV Epp 1537, 1868, V Epp 2188, 2250, 2269, 2271, VI 354, and passim / *Matrikel Basel* I 298, II 514 / *Vadianische Briefsammlung* XXV Ep 226, XXVI Addenda Ep 77 / Z VII Ep 99 and passim / BRE Epp 135, 143
PGB

Gerrit van ASSENDELFT of Haarlem, 1488 – 5 or 7 December 1558
Gerrit was a son of Nicolaas van Assendelft (d 1501) and Aleid van Kijfhoek (d 1530). From 1509 he was lord of Assendelft, ten kilometres north-east of Haarlem. He matriculated at Orléans on 5 May 1505 and received a licence in law, it seems on 3 April 1507. Having been injudicious enough to marry Catherine de Chasseur, an innkeeper's daughter, he only had himself to blame when she followed him on his return to Holland and the council of Holland forced him to take her into his house (2

March 1509). However, on 11 April 1532 she was bought off with a house and an allowance. She was executed exactly nine years later, after a counterfeiter's workshop had been discovered in her house.

In the mean time van Assendelft had become a member of the council of Holland in 1515, and on 9 October 1528 he became president in succession to Nicolaas *Everaerts. When Maarten van *Dorp visited The Hague in 1519, he mentioned the lord ('dominus') of Assendelft together with Everaerts, adding that Assendelft was an avid reader of Erasmus (Ep 1044). This letter could have prompted Erasmus to seek Assendelft's support against his critics (Ep 1166). It should be noted, however, that there was also an ecclesiastical member of the council of Holland, Hugo van Assendelft (1467–1540), a canon of The Hague and probably a relative of Gerrit, who could conceivably be the 'dominus' mentioned in Ep 1044. On the other hand, Gerrit was still a patron of Erasmus in 1532 and 1533, when Erasmus sent him greetings (Epp 2645, 2800) and wrote to him direct saying that he was deeply in the president's debt (Ep 2734). In response Assendelft helped to arrange for a handsome cash present on behalf of the states of Holland (Ep 2819).

Van Assendelft signed wills on 24 April 1547 and 16 February 1556. He left most of his properties to Otto Floriszoon van Assendelft (d 1580); however, the will was successfully challenged by Nicolaas (c 1514–70), his son by Catherine.

BIBLIOGRAPHY: CWE Ep 1044 / Allen Ep 2646 / W.M.C. Regt in NNBW VII 34–6 / *Matricule d'Orléans* II-1 251–2 / de Vocht MHL 95–8 / F.A. Holleman *Dirk van Assendelft, schout van Breda, en de zijnen* (Zutphen 1953) passim / *Memorialen van het Hof (den Raad) van Holland, Zeeland en West-Friesland* ed A.S. de Blécourt et al (The Hague 1929) xxxiv, xlvi
C.G. VAN LEIJENHORST

Hugo van ASSENDELFT *See Gerrit van* ASSENDELFT

Alvaro de ASTUDILLO of Burgos, documented 1530–40
Alvaro de Astudillo was probably born in

Burgos, where his family was renowned in banking and commerce. The family's operations extended to the Low Countries, Germany, and Florence, and its members were frequent benefactors of charitable and ecclesiastical institutions in their native city. There may be undiscovered references to Alvaro de Astudillo in the Consulado, or notarial archives, of Burgos, but at present all that is known of him is told in English records and in the correspondence of Erasmus.

The earliest reference to Astudillo occurs in an inventory of goods shipped by him and other Spanish merchants in 1530 (LP Addenda I 719). Thereafter, references proliferate. He was among the most important traders to Spain operating out of London and other ports, and in the 1530s he took out papers of denization in London. In 1540 he was responsible for arranging credit in Spain for the diplomat John Mason.

As early as 1532 Astudillo is found acting in partnership with Luis de *Castro, who helped to handle Erasmus' English affairs. But the first direct link between Erasmus and Astudillo occurred in April 1535, when Erasmus *Schets, who said that he always used Astudillo's good offices for business in England, proposed to use Luis de Castro and Astudillo for the collection and remittance of Erasmus' English annuity (Ep 3009). It appears from this letter that Astudillo also handled business on behalf of the imperial ambassador, Eustache *Chapuys, who had offered to help collect Erasmus' money. Though collecting annuities was a troublesome task, Astudillo seems to have coped well with his share of the job, which was to transfer to Schets the money he received from Castro and Chapuys, for in August 1535 Schets recorded the arrival of a remittance from him (Epp 3042, 3058, 3067). There are no later references in the correspondence, but it may be presumed that Astudillo continued to serve Erasmus in the same capacity, since Chapuys certainly did so (Ep 3090) and Astudillo does not appear to have left London. He was still plying his trade there in the 1540s, but of the rest of his life and the circumstances of his death nothing is known.

BIBLIOGRAPHY: G. Connell-Smith *Forerunners of Drake* (London 1954) 17 / M. Basas Fernández

'Mercaderes burgaleses en el siglo XVI' *Boletín de la Institución Fernán González* (1954) 156–69 / LP V 1065 (23), LP Addenda I 719

FELIPE FERNÁNDEZ-ARMESTO

ASULANUS See TORRESANI

Jorge de ATECA d 1545
Jorge de Ateca (Athequa), a Dominican from Ateca, west of Saragossa, replaced Diego Fernandez as confessor to Queen *Catherine of Aragon. In 1517, while remaining in attendance upon the queen, he was created bishop of Llandaff. Probably on Catherine's recommendation, he was appointed Master of St Catherine's hospital. He remained with the queen when she was divorced by *Henry VIII and in 1533 was one of two chaplains who accompanied her to Buckden. After the queen's death in 1536 he was imprisoned but was released the same year through the intervention of Eustache *Chapuys. Upon his return to Spain he was given the sees of Ampurias in Catalonia and Tempio in Sardinia in 1538.

In 1519 Erasmus saw in Ateca an unenlightened critic of his own work (Ep 948).

BIBLIOGRAPHY: Allen Ep 948 / G. Mattingly *Catherine of Aragon* (London 1941) passim / W.E. Wilkie *The Cardinal Protectors of England* (Cambridge 1974) 147, 154, 217

CFG

Johannes ATENSIS See Jan BRIART

Thomas AUCUPARIUS See Thomas VOGLER

Eleutherius AUDAX See Eleuthère HARDY

Thomas AUDLEY 1488–30 April 1544
Born into an Essex family, Thomas Audley may have studied arts at Cambridge; subsequently he studied law in the Inner Temple in London, where he was an autumn reader in 1526. After serving on various royal commissions and as attorney for the duchy of Lancaster, he joined the household of Cardinal *Wolsey in 1527. In the same year he was re-elected to parliament as a member for Essex, having previously sat for Colchester in 1523, and was also chosen Speaker of the Commons in succession to

Johannes Aventinus

Thomas *More. On 20 May 1532, probably through the influence of Thomas *Cromwell, he was given the great seal when More resigned as Lord Chancellor. Although he had assumed the duties of the office in 1532, he was not named Lord Chancellor until 26 January 1533. Audley profited from his service to *Henry VIII in the Reformation Parliament, receiving one of the 'first cuts' of monastic property, the priory of Christchurch, Aldgate (in London), suppressed before the general dissolution of the monasteries. Christchurch became his town house, while the abbey of Walden in Essex, which he received later, became his country seat. He carried out many assignments of questionable ethics, presiding over the trials of John *Fisher, More, the accomplices of *Anne Boleyn, the Yorkshire rebels of the Pilgrimage of Grace, and others. On 29 November 1538 he was created Baron Audley of Walden. In 1542 he founded Magdalen College, Cambridge. His portrait there is an eighteenth-century copy of an original at Audley End (Essex) by Hans *Holbein the Younger.

He resigned the seal on 21 April 1544

because of physical infirmity and died nine days later. He was buried in a magnificent tomb at Saffron Walden. He was married twice, the second time to Elizabeth, daughter of Thomas Grey, Marquis of Dorset, who bore him two daughters.

Although Erasmus alluded to More's successor as Lord Chancellor at least twice in his correspondence, he does not appear to have known Audley by name (Epp 2728, 2750). In Ep 2831, the last surviving piece of correspondence between Erasmus and More, More spoke of his successor as a distinguished man, giving no sign of animosity. In Ep 3079 to Damião de *Gois, an unknown Englishman gave a narrative of the trial and death of Fisher, mentioning Audley's part in that sorry business.

BIBLIOGRAPHY: DNB I 723–6 / G.E.C[okayne] *The Complete Peerage of England* ed V. Gibbs et al (London 1910–59) I 348–50 / R.W. Chambers *Thomas More* (London 1935) 247 and passim / E.E. Reynolds *The Trial of Thomas More* (London 1964) 75 / Nicholas Harpsfield *Life and Death of Sir Thomas More* ed C.W. Hitchcock (London 1932) 60 and passim / W. Roper *Sir Thomas More* ed C.W. Hitchcock (London 1935) 52 and passim / J.J. Scarisbrick *Henry VIII* (London 1968) 270, 521 / S.E. Lehmberg *The Reformation Parliament* (Cambridge 1970) 79–80 and passim / J. and J.A. Venn *Alumni Cantabrigienses* (Cambridge 1922–54) I-1 56

R.J. SCHOECK

AUGUSTINUS (Ep 3115 of 12 April 1536) Augustinus was the name of a man who appeared in Besançon claiming to be Erasmus' famulus, sent to fetch wine. It is quite uncertain whether he was identical with a young man of Antwerp who was briefly in Erasmus' service in 1535 (Ep 3052; but cf Ep 3104).

BIBLIOGRAPHY: de Vocht CTL III 394–5 / Bierlaire *Familia* 97

FRANZ BIERLAIRE

Cornelius AURELIUS *See Cornelis* GERARD

Johannes AVENTINUS of Abensberg, 4 July 1477–9 January 1534
Johannes Aventinus (Turmair, Thurmaier) was the son of an innkeeper in Abensberg, Lower

Bavaria. He attended the local school of the Carmelite monastery and matriculated at the University of Ingolstadt in 1495. In 1496 he received the lower orders and soon afterwards followed his teacher, Conrad Celtis, to Vienna, where he pursued humanistic studies. These he continued in Cracow and Paris, obtaining his MA. In 1517 he was appointed tutor to dukes Louis and Ernest of *Bavaria. In 1509 he began to gather material for a history of Bavaria, and in 1511 he sent Duke William IV of *Bavaria a first outline for such a work (not yet published). A more direct fruit of his tutorial duties was a short Latin grammar, *Grammatica omnium utilissima ac brevissima* (Munich: H. Schobser 1512, reprinted eleven times).

In 1517 Aventinus was named historiographer to the dukes of Bavaria. For two years he visited archives and convent libraries all over the Bavarian lands and then returned to Abensberg, where between 1519 and 1521 he wrote the *Annales Boiorum*. In the following year he published with the Nürnberg press of Friedrich Peypus an epitome in German of the great work *Bayrischer Chronicon ... kurzer Auszug*; from then on his reputation as one of Germany's leading historians was never in doubt. While continuing to revise the Latin *Annales*, he also wrote the *Chronik*, a work comparable with the *Annales* in size and ambition but, thanks to the German idiom, freer in expression and more involved. In 1524 Aventinus accepted an annual stipend from the dukes and in return committed himself to hand over the manuscript of the *Annales* on completion. As it turned out, both works were severely anticlerical and thus unsuited for publication under the auspices of the Catholic dukes, and the church set them on the Index. Not until 1554 was an expurgated version of the *Annales* published at Ingolstadt, while an incomplete manuscript of the *Chronik* appeared in print at Frankfurt in 1566. A modern edition of Aventinus' *Sämtliche Werke* was published in Munich, 1890–1908 (for further details of the publication history see Strauss 265–7). Later in his life Aventinus continued work on a chronicle of all Germany, the *Zeitbuch*, or *Germania illustrata* in the Latin version, of which, however, only the first book and an index were completed. In 1535 Erasmus seems to have confused this work with the

Annales when he wrote twice to the Bavarian chancellor, Leonhard von *Eck, in an effort to obtain the latter for Johann *Herwagen, who wished to print it at Basel (Epp 3030, 3035). Aventinus' admiration for Erasmus is evident from several passages in both works (Allen Ep 3030:9n).

From 1527 Aventinus lived in the free imperial city of Regensburg, which remained aloof when the dukes of Bavaria began to repress all Lutheran tendencies. In 1529 he married Barbara Fröschmann, and in 1533 he tutored Leonhard von Eck's son, Anton.

BIBLIOGRAPHY: Allen Ep 3030 / NDB I 469–70 / ADB I 700–4 / Gerald Strauss *Historian in an Age of Crisis: The Life and Work of Johannes Aventinus, 1477–1534* (Cambridge, Mass, 1963) / Eduard Fueter *Histoire de l'historiographie moderne* (Paris 1914) 239–41 / Hans Rupprich in R. Newald et al *Geschichte der deutschen Literatur* (Munich 1957–   ) IV-1 515, 672 / BRE Ep 236

IG & PGB

Stanislaus AYCHLER *See Stanisław* AICHLER

Jean AYMERY II *See Jean* EMERY

Bernard Bucho van AYTTA of Zwichem, 1465–3 December 1528
Bernard Bucho, a native of Zwichem, near Leeuwarden, was a son of Gerbrand van Aytta and Jets Bucama. He was the uncle of *Viglius Zuichemus, who never failed to express his indebtedness to him (Epp 2101, 2129, 2168) and even called himself 'Zuichemus' after him. Bernard Bucho studied arts at the College of the Falcon at Louvain, where he ranked first in the promotion to the degree of MA of 1487. He also studied law, in which he became a licentiate, in addition to attending lectures of Adriaan Floriszoon, the future Pope *Adrian VI. Having taken orders, he became pastor of several minor places in Friesland and later of St Vitus' in Leeuwarden. In 1499 he became a member of the new council of Friesland and from 1504 to 1506 was one of the region's six regents. In July 1515, the future Emperor *Charles V, to whom George of *Saxony had yielded his rights to Friesland, appointed Bernard Bucho president of the council of Friesland; he was subsequently sent on embassies to England and France and else-

where, serving so well that in 1519 he was made dean of Our Lady's of The Hague (Ep 1092) and a member of the council of Holland. He held these offices until his death. Johannes Secundus, a son of Nicolaas *Everaerts, wrote an epitaph for him. Bernard Bucho left a fine library and a considerable amount of money to Viglius Zuichemus. When Viglius founded the Aytta hospital at Zwichem in 1572 he was inspired by similar plans made by his uncle.

Only one letter from Erasmus to Bernard Bucho is preserved (Ep 1237), although there is a possibility that Ep 1166 was also addressed to him. In Ep 1237, dated 24 September 1521, Erasmus recommended several scholars of Louvain who would be suitable tutors for the 'children of a friend' of Aytta and possibly also for Viglius.

BIBLIOGRAPHY: Allen Ep 1237 / J. van Kuyk in NNBW III 47–8 / de Vocht CTL II 97–8 and passim / *Naamrol der Edele Mogende Heeren Raden's Hoffs van Friesland* (Leeuwarden 1742) 3–6 / J.S. Theissen *Centraal gezag en Friesche vrijheid* (Groningen 1907) XXVI 22, 32, 88, 90, 102, 231 / J.S. Theissen *De regeering van Karel V in de Noordelijke Nederlanden* (Amsterdam 1912) 38–41, 47, 236 / E.H. Waterbolk and Th.S.H. Bos *Vigliana* (Groningen 1975) 48, 57

C.G. VAN LEIJENHORST

Wigle van AYTTA of Zwichem See VIGLIUS ZUICHEMUS

John BABHAM documented 1512–15
After residence in Oxford for two years and a term Babham received his BA on 20 February 1514. He returned home in the same year owing to an illness in his family, cutting short his disputations, but was resident at Oxford again in 1515. Babham wrote to Erasmus, perhaps in April from Oxford (Ep 259) referring to some previous contacts between them and in appreciation of a previous kindness shown him. He is not mentioned elsewhere in Erasmus' correspondence and is not otherwise known.

BIBLIOGRAPHY: Allen Ep 259 / Emden BRUO 1501–40 19

CFG

Bartholomäus BACH of Geyer, documented 1522–36
Bartholomäus Bach (Bacchus) was born at Geyer, in the Saxon Erz mountains, the son of a miner and presumably a relative of several students from Geyer by the name of Bach who were registered at the University of Leipzig between 1466 and 1499 (a Bartholomäus Bach of Naumburg matriculated in the spring of 1497). From 1522 to 1536 Bach was town clerk of Jáchymov (Joachimsthal); in 1530 he also held the office of *Berggegenschreiber*, or mining clerk. Bach was a good friend of Georgius *Agricola, who mentioned Bach's devotion to classical literature in his *Bermannus* (Basel: H. Froben 1530). He also stated that a mine was named after Bach, in which he had given a share to *Eobanus Hessus, the neo-Latin poet. In his correspondence with Agricola, Erasmus twice returned Bach's greetings (Epp 2529, 2918).

BIBLIOGRAPHY: Allen Ep 2529 / Georg Agricola *Ausgewählte Werke* II (Berlin 1955) 80–1, 118, 269 / *Matrikel Leipzig* II 420, III 29

MICHAEL ERBE & PGB

Gerard BACHUUS d 29 June 1569
Bachuus (Gerardus Bacchusius) was a priest, a canon of St Donatian of Bruges, and teacher (*submonitor*) at the school of his chapter before becoming its rector on 4 May 1523. He directed the school until 1530 and died at Bruges.

After meeting Erasmus' secretary, Hilarius *Bertholf, Bachuus wrote to Erasmus in May 1522 (Ep 1286), reporting on the progress of Louis of *Flanders, lord van Praet, who had studied with him at Bruges for two years. Erasmus is not known to have answered. Bachuus compiled a collection of decisions passed by the chapter, which is preserved in the diocesan archives at Bruges under the title of 'Rapriarium'. He has wrongly been identified with a namesake of his who was born in Maaseik and matriculated at Louvain in 1534 (*Matricule de Louvain* IV–1 104).

BIBLIOGRAPHY: A.C. de Schrevel *Histoire du Séminaire de Bruges* (Bruges 1883–95) I 56, 66–7, 73, 113, 134, 142, 677, 718, 766 / de Vocht *Literae ad Craneveldium* 134–5 / de Vocht CTL I 218, III 262

MARCEL A. NAUWELAERTS

Josse BADE of Ghent, c 1461 –December 1535
Although very likely born in Ghent, Josse Bade
(Jodocus Badius Ascensius, probably Joost van
Assche) is best known today under the French
form of his name because France quickly
became his adoptive country. He was educated
in Ghent at the school of the Brethren of the
Common Life before perhaps moving on to the
University of Louvain. Subsequently he went
to Italy for further studies – Filippo (I)
*Beroaldo was among his teachers – and then
taught in Valence and Lyon, where he settled
in 1492. He edited a number of books for the
printer Jean Trechsel, whose corrector and
scholarly adviser he became, and published
some of his own writings with Trechsel's press.
After the latter's death in 1498 he married
Hostelye, Trechsel's stepdaughter. In 1499 he
moved to Paris, where he continued to edit
scholarly works for the presses. In 1503 he
opened his own press with the assistance of
the bookseller Jean *Petit. He continued to
work as a scholar-printer until his death, from
1515 as one of the privileged *libraires-jurés*.
Bade's eldest son, whose name may have been
Jean, died in July or August 1526 (Ep 1733). A
much younger son, Conrad, later followed in
his father's footsteps and set up a press in
Geneva.

Bade's first press was in the Rue des Carmes;
in 1507 he relocated on the rue Saint-Jacques
under the sign of the 'Praelum Ascensianum'
(actually showing a press) which he also used
on his printer's marks. His printing shop and
bookstore was a meeting place for such Paris
humanists as Jacques *Lefèvre d'Etaples,
Guillaume *Budé, Jacques *Toussain, Pierre
*Danès, and Pierre *Vitré, a former student of
Erasmus, and for foreign scholars like Thomas
*Grey and Thomas *Lupset, who had also been
Erasmus' students. Like other printers, Bade
facilitated exchanges among the international
community of scholars by forwarding letters
and books and passing on news in his own
letters; in particular, much of the correspondence between Budé and Erasmus passed
through his hands (Epp 493, 528, 609, 617, 744,
813). He travelled to Flanders in 1518 and was
the guest of Pieter *Gillis in Antwerp (Ep 849).

Bade's own literary production includes
works on grammar, moral treatises, Latin

Josse Bade at his press

poetry, and a large number of prefaces for the
books he published. Sometimes he also
annotated the texts he printed, as he did with
Budé's *De asse* (1517). This confused Erasmus,
who at first thought that the notes were Budé's
own (Ep 531).

Bade's entire production amounts to 720
works, printed, for the most part, in his own
shop, although a number of these editions
were launched jointly with other bookseller's
and printers such as Jean Petit, the brothers de
Marnef, and Jean de Roigny, Bade's son-in-
law. The majority of these were theological and
philosophical treatises, grammars and dictionaries, and texts by classical and humanistic
authors; however, in 1518 and 1519 Bade
published several contributions to the controversy around Mary Magdalen, all from the
conservative camp. In 1521 it fell to him to print
the *Determinatio* of the Paris faculty of theology
against *Luther, and in 1526 and 1527 he issued
two polemical attacks on Luther by Jérôme de
*Hangest.

Forty-three of Bade's books offer works by
Erasmus, alone or together with other authors,

and forty-eight more offer works edited or annotated by Erasmus. No other Paris printer did as much for the circulation of Erasmus' writings. Bade also belonged to the chosen few among all printers with whom Erasmus maintained close personal contact over many years.

After Erasmus' return to Paris in the winter of 1504, Bade printed for him the first edition of Lorenzo *Valla's notes on the New Testament, of which Erasmus had found a manuscript (Epp 182, 183), and two years later, before his departure to Italy, Erasmus gave Bade about twenty new adages, which were printed in Bade's edition of the *Adagia*, 1506 (Ep 1175), and his Latin translations of Euripides' *Hecuba* and *Iphigenia* as well as his own and *More's translations from Lucian (Epp 187, 188, 198, 1479). The two tragedies by Euripides sold very well, and by the autumn of 1517 Bade had proposed to print a second edition, but in view of the many errors found in his earlier edition, Erasmus preferred to have the new edition undertaken by Aldo *Manuzio in Venice (Ep 207). Bade's letter of 19 May 1512 (Ep 263) reveals a good deal about their business connections. Erasmus had sent him a considerable batch of printer's copy, including *De copia*, which had not formerly been published, but also the *Moria*, which Bade at first said he did not wish to reprint for fear of trouble with the publisher of the preceding edition but which he subsequently printed despite his concern. Bade also wondered what would be a fair price to pay the author for printed copy that had merely been revised, while offering Erasmus a specified amount for new manuscripts. He was especially keen on having the thoroughly revised text of the *Adagia*. Erasmus agreed to all his proposals (Ep 264), but the revised *Adagia* were in the end taken to the Basel printer Johann *Froben rather than to Bade, probably not without Erasmus' knowledge (Epp 269, 283). The translations from Lucian, however, were published by Bade, but only after a delay of two years which kept Erasmus worrying (Epp 261, 264, 283, 293). A revised copy of Erasmus' editions of Seneca's tragedies had also been sent to Bade in the spring of 1512, but since Seneca had just been published by Jean Petit, Bade's edition of Erasmus' text did not come out until December 1514. When it finally appeared, it annoyed Erasmus because commentaries by other scholars had been added (Ep 263, Allen I 13).

In 1516 Bade politely reproached Erasmus for providing different printers with the same copy, with or without revisions, a practice that had caused Bade heavy losses (Ep 472); one instance is *De copia*, which was reprinted by Matthias *Schürer at Strasbourg in December 1514 (Epp 311, 346, 434). To make up for this, Erasmus offered Bade the *Parabolae*, and despite his initial scruples in view of a recent edition by Dirk *Martens in Louvain, Bade eventually published them late in 1516 (Epp 312, 434, 472, 764). In another case Bade could not help harming Froben just as the Basel printer had previously harmed him, and by that time, the summer of 1517, Erasmus had definitely decided to cast in his lot with Froben (Ep 602). He confirmed this decision a year later in his last known letter to Bade (Ep 815), explaining that Bade's inadequate supply of Greek type left him no choice. Thereafter their relations seem to have been limited to the exchange of news and occasional greetings by way of common acquaintances (Epp 1713, 1733, 1842).

Despite Erasmus' decision to use Froben as his sole printer, Bade at first continued to publish new editions of Erasmus' works. In 1523, when reprinting his edition of Cato's *Disticha moralia*, together with other material, Bade even praised Erasmus, perhaps to fulfil an intention announced back in 1516 (Ep 472). In Erasmus' subsequent conflict with the Paris faculty of theology, however, Bade sided firmly with the theologians. On 28 May 1526 he published Noël *Béda's *Annotationes* against Erasmus and Lefèvre d'Etaples (Epp 1679, 1685), of which he had printed 650 copies. In August 1526, however, further sales of this book were banned by order of King *Francis I (Epp 1763, 1768). This measure did not discourage Bade, who in February 1529 published Béda's *Apologia adversus clandestinos Lutheranos*, which contained most of the letters exchanged by Béda and Erasmus since 1525. Also in February 1529 he printed Albert *Pio's *Responsio paraenetica*, directed against Erasmus, together with the latter's Ep 1634 and also a preface of his own, in which Bade took Pio's line in deploring Erasmus' influence upon

Luther. Erasmus answered Pio rather vehemently, but as far as Bade was concerned, his reaction was minimal (LB IX 1096B). On 9 March 1531 Bade printed Pio's more comprehensive rejoinder together with Erasmus' earlier *Responsio* (LB IX 1095–122; Epp 2424, 2442, 2466, 2522). Finally, in July 1531 Bade published a volume containing three consecutive condemnations of Erasmus on the part of the theological faculty, together with similar condemnations of Luther and other heretics. Erasmus again felt compelled to react but apparently saw no point in attacking the printer (LB IX 924B; cf Ep 2633). Three years earlier Erasmus' famous comparison of Bade and Budé in the *Ciceronianus* (ASD I-2 672–3), while causing a storm among the Paris humanists, should have proved rather flattering to Bade, Erasmus' former countryman.

BIBLIOGRAPHY: Allen Ep 183 / DBF IV 1138–41 / Renouard *Répertoire* 13–14 / Philippe Renouard *Bibliographie de Josse Bade Ascensius* (Paris 1908) / Philippe Renouard *Imprimeurs et libraires parisiens du XVI siècle* (Paris 1964–   ) II 6–297, with an important biographical introduction / D.J. Shaw 'Badius's octavo editions of the classics' in *Gutenberg-Jahrbuch 1973* (Mainz 1973) 276–81 / R. Wiriath 'Les rapports de Josse Bade Ascensius avec Erasme et Lefebvre d'Etaples' BHR 11 (1949) 66–71

GENEVIÈVE GUILLEMINOT

Friedrich (III) von BADEN 7 July 1458–24 September 1517
Friedrich, a son of Margrave Karl von Baden, was elected bishop of Utrecht on 13 May 1496 in succession to David of *Burgundy (d 1496) and was in turn succeeded by Philip (I) of *Burgundy. He held his solemn entry into Utrecht on 17 September 1496, but although *Maximilian I supported him as best he could, his administration of the prince-bishopric was ineffectual and hampered by an unending series of military operations. Disappointment caused him to enter into secret negotiations with King *Francis I and to seek his support in obtaining the see of Metz. When the Brussels government found out, he was prevailed upon to resign the see of Utrecht in 1516. He died in retirement at Lier but was eventually buried in the Stiftskirche of Baden-Baden, where his monumental tomb is extant.

About 1498 Erasmus seems to have hoped for his patronage but found him to be miserly (Ep 81).

BIBLIOGRAPHY: Allen Ep 81 / ADB VIII 45 / A.J. van der Ven in *Jaarboekje van 'Oud-Utrecht'* (1947–8) 62–78 / C.A. van Kalveen *Utrecht-Rome in diplomatiek en diplomatie (1516–1517)* (Groningen 1971) / C.A. van Kalveen *Het bestuur van bisschop en Staten* (Groningen 1974)

C.G. VAN LEIJENHORST & PGB

Jodocus BADIUS ASCENSIUS *See Josse* BADE

Nicolaas BAECHEM of Egmond, d 23/4 August 1526
Nicolaas Baechem (Carmelita Egmondanus, Edmondanus, or Ecmondanus) of Egmond, near Alkmaar, matriculated in Louvain on 29 October 1487. Having studied at the College of the Falcon since 1488, he ranked first in the promotion to the degree of MA in 1491 and became a doctor of divinity on 2 December 1505. In the following year he entered the Carmelite order, professed his vows on 1 March 1507 at Mechelen, and from 1510 directed the Carmelite house of studies at Louvain. He taught theology in the university and regularly preached at St Peter's with the exception of some time between 1516 and 1518 when he was prior at Brussels.

Even before Erasmus came to Louvain, when the New Testament (1516) had only just been published, Baechem preached against it as a sign of the collapse of the Christian religion and the advent of Antichrist (Epp 1162, 1196, 1581, 2045; perhaps also Epp 483, 948). This preaching, which must have originated at Louvain, may have continued in Brussels in 1517. At their first meeting in Louvain, perhaps the following year, Erasmus urged Baechem to state his objections to the edition, only to find to his surprise that the inimical preacher had neither read nor seen it (Epp 948, 1196, 1581, 2045).

Baechem was an early adversary of *Luther, and Erasmus noted his overhasty condemnation of Luther's definition of mortal sin requiring confession (Ep 1033), a remark which was to reverberate (Ep 1153) when in 1520 *Charles V appointed Baechem assistant inquisitor of the Netherlands. Baechem began to link Erasmus' name habitually with Luther's

(Epp 1144, 1147) when preaching. Erasmus appealed in this matter to Godschalk *Rosemondt, rector of Louvain (Ep 1153), whose ensuing interview (October 1520) with Erasmus and Baechem is detailed in Ep 1162 to Thomas *More. While Baechem denied having injured Erasmus' reputation and in turn accused him of ridiculing him in his books, Erasmus accused Baechem of lying about him and claimed that the Carmelite's name had never appeared in his books. Two months later Erasmus was still complaining to Rosemondt about Baechem's defamatory preaching (Epp 1164, 1172). Baechem also tended to burning Luther's books (Ep 1186).

Just as the publication of the first edition of the New Testament had provoked Baechem's wrath, so did the second (1519), and Erasmus finally had to publish in refutation an *Apologia de loco 'omnes quidem'* (Basel: J. Froben 1522; LB IX 433A–442B). The particular controversy here concerned Erasmus' substitution at 1 Corinthians 15:51 of 'Non omnes quidem dormiemus, omnes tamen immutabimur' (LB VI 740C–744A) for the Vulgate rendition 'Omnes quidem resurgemus sed non omnes immutabimur,' a point on which Erasmus has been vindicated by modern biblical scholarship. Baechem is not, however, a prominent target in the *Apologia de 'In principio erat sermo'* (Louvain: D. Martens February 1520 and enlarged Basel: J. Froben August 1520; see LB IX 111–22), although Allen so identifies him (Ep 1072). When complaining in his letters about Baechem's various attacks, Erasmus does not seem to mention the beginning of his gospel of St John. It may be that a junior 'Camelita' mentioned in the *Apologia* was a lackey of Baechem's whom he had groomed while he was prior and regent of studies at Brussels (LB IX 112C–D; cf 119A–B). Wallace K. Ferguson notes with respect to the *Dialogus bilinguium ac trilinguium* (1519) that the character Philautia, who is linked to Baechem lampooned as Momides (*Opuscula* 216–18), may refer to a second Carmelite (*Opuscula* 217:306n). If so, this is perhaps the preacher against *sermo*, conceivably Jan *Robyns.

Yet a further controversy flared when Baechem decried in the *Colloquia* (Basel: J. Froben March 1522) 'Lutheran heresies' concerning indulgences, fasting, auricular confession, and whether episcopal regulations bind under pain of hell (Ep 1299), accusations against which Erasmus defended himself to the theologians at Louvain (Ep 1301). In the *Colloquia* Erasmus openly and covertly insulted Baechem (*Apotheosis Capnionis* and Ἰχθυοφαγία ASD I-3 267–8, 521–2). He also relished punning on 'Carmelita' as 'Camelita,' because of Baechem's obtuseness, but perhaps also alluding to the camel's nasty habit of spitting in one's eye. By July 1524 Baechem was reportedly stripped of his powers by Charles V and Pope *Adrian VI – under whose earlier presidency at Louvain he had earned his doctorate – perhaps because of his association with the chief inquisitor, Frans van der *Hulst, who was also discredited (Epp 1466, 1467). Erasmus nevertheless later complained to Rome that Baechem was injuring the papal cause (Ep 1481). His appeals secured a diploma from Adrian silencing Baechem and eventually one from *Clement VII when, upon the death of the former pope, Baechem renewed his preaching against Erasmus (Epp 1359, 1509, 1515). Erasmus appealed also to *Ferdinand, and as a result *Margaret of Austria was asked to impose silence on Baechem (Epp 1515, 1553).

Although Baechem died on 23 or 24 August 1526, Erasmus still described him in September as 'mocked by all' (Ep 1747), since he had not yet received report of his demise; this finally reached him in November, with the rumour that Lutherans in s'Hertogenbosch had poisoned Baechem (Ep 1765). Erasmus' last mention of him, in 1529, recalls how Baechem mercilessly had two Augustinian friars burnt to death for heresy (Ep 2445; see also Ep 2188). The following epitaph for Baechem was attributed to Erasmus (Reedijk 394):

Hic jacet Egmondus, telluris inutile pondus:
Dilexit rabiem, non habeat requiem.

The Carmelites countered with this, inscribed on a funerary monument in the convent at Mechelen:

Hic jacet Egmundus, qui doctor in arte
profundus,
quem tremit haereticus, dum premit eximius.
Quid fert sarcasmo? Stylus est consuetus
Erasmo.
Viventem timuit; post obitum impetiit.
Maxima viventem devincere palma fuisset.
Ducere cum exanimi praelia, quale probrum!

The monument was destroyed during the sack of that city in 1580, and most of Baechem's manuscripts were lost during the religious wars in the Low Countries late in the sixteenth century.

According to ancient sources, Baechem wrote 'Oratio latina ad PP. Carmelitas in capitulo provinciali anno 1515 congregatos,' 'Praelectiones academicae,' 'Sermones de tempore et de sanctis, Bruxellis, Mechliniae et Lovanii habiti,' 'Censurae in Novum Testamentum Desiderii Erasmi, in ejusdem Colloquia et Moriam,' 'Commentarius in Evangelium Matthaei,' 'Commentarius in epistolas Paulinas,' and 'Commentarius in septem epistolas catholicas.' In addition to Erasmus' apologia against him there appeared a satirical *Vita S. Nicolai* and *Epistola de Magistris Nostris* in the *Flores siue elegantiae* of 'Nicholas Quadus' (1520). There is no record of correspondence between Erasmus and Baechem.

BIBLIOGRAPHY: Allen Ep 878 / de Vocht CTL I 460–1 and passim / NNBW I 206 / A. Bludau *Die beiden ersten Erasmus-Ausgaben des Neuen Testaments und ihre Gegner* (Freiburg 1902) 75–9 / H. de Jongh *L'Ancienne faculté de théologie de Louvain* (Louvain 1911) 152–4 / F. Bierlaire 'Le libellus colloquiorum de mars 1522 et Nicholas Baechem dit Egmondanus' *Scrinium Erasmianum* I 55–81 / Marjorie O'Rourke Boyle *Erasmus on Language and Method in Theology* (Toronto 1977) 151–2

MARJORIE O'ROURKE BOYLE

Franz (I) BAER of Basel, 1479–1543
Franz Baer (Ber, Beer) was an older half-brother of Ludwig *Baer, born to his father's first wife (Öffentliche Bibliothek of the University of Basel, MS Erasmuslade D 5 f 5 no 4). A clothier by profession, he was admitted to the 'Safran' guild in 1497 and soon thereafter to the 'Schlüssel' guild, of which he was elected master in 1516 and which he represented on the city council from 1522. He held a series of other public offices, and between 1523 and 1527 he was three times a member of the Basel delegation to the Swiss diet. From 1521 he was also Basel's member of the syndicate in charge of administering the Swiss territory south of the Gotthard.

Like his brother, Franz had high principles. In 1521 he and Heinrich *David were among the small minority of councillors who refused to accept personal pensions provided by France. A staunch member of the Catholic party, he lost his seat on the city council on 9 February 1529 and left Basel, renouncing his citizenship on 9 June. Thereafter he lived with his family and household mostly at Freiburg, the centre of the Basel émigrés, but he may at times have resided at Thann, Upper Alsace, and possibly at Lucerne. The sympathy shown to his brother by the Lucerne government after Basel's reformation was also extended to him, and in 1532 he received the citizenship of Lucerne.

In 1529 Bartholomäus *Welser recommended Franz to Erasmus as a financial agent who would be likely to cash some bills of exchange which Welser had sent (Ep 2153). In 1535 Erasmus entrusted to Ludwig and Franz Baer arrangements for the sale of his house at Freiburg (Epp 3056, 3059), and Franz himself bought some shutters which were, however, also claimed by the purchaser of the house (AK IV Ep 1989). Franz died at Freiburg; he was married first to Verena, a daughter of Heinrich *Meltinger, (d c 1504) and subsequently to Helena Iselin (d 1533).

BIBLIOGRAPHY: Allen Ep 2153 / *Basler Biographien* ed Albert Burckhardt (Basel 1900–5) I 67–9 / *Wappenbuch der Stadt Basel* ed W.R. Staehelin (Basel [1917–30]) I / R. Wackernagel *Geschichte der Stadt Basel* (Basel 1907–54) III 310 and passim / AK VII Ep 3137

PGB

Franz (II) BAER of Basel, d 1580
Franz, the youngest son of Franz (I) *Baer, was registered at the universities of Basel (1527), Freiburg (1529), and Heidelberg (1538), where he studied law. In 1534 and 1535 his uncle, Ludwig *Baer, was vigorously pursuing Franz's appointment to a canonry at Jung St Peter's, Strasbourg, and Erasmus too provided recommendations (Ep 3065 and perhaps Ep 2929). On this occasion Ludwig described Franz as a young man past twenty who had studied for several years at Paris, knew Latin and French, and hoped in years to come to obtain a legal doctorate, preferably in Italy. In 1554 Franz was steward of the lordship of Binzburg, near Offenbach, Baden, and subsequently he became the official of the bishop of Basel at Thann, Upper Alsace.

BIBLIOGRAPHY: Allen Ep 3065 / *Matrikel Basel* I 361 / *Matrikel Freiburg* I 277 / *Matrikel Heidelberg* I 568 / G. Knod in *Zeitschrift für Kirchengeschichte*

14 (1893) 129–32 / *Basler Biographien* ed Albert
Burckhardt (Basel 1900–5) I 85
                                                      PGB

Ludwig BAER of Basel, 24 May 1479–14 April
1554
The father of Ludwig Baer (Ber, Berus), Johann
(d 1502), had immigrated from Saverne, Lower
Alsace, and acquired the citizenship of Basel in
1468. Having made a fortune in banking and
grain speculation, he died as a member of the
Basel council. Seven of Ludwig's sisters were
married to notables occupying high offices in
the city; his brothers, with the exception of
Franz (I) *Baer, died young. The family lived in
the Rheingasse in the immediate neighbour-
hood of Johann *Amerbach, and as a child
Ludwig experienced much kindness from
Johann and his wife (AK I Ep 149), which he
was eager to return later on.

Ludwig had probably been intended for the
church from childhood, and, in keeping with
the family's style of living, only Paris was good
enough for his theological instruction. On 14
November 1495 he left Basel and by way of
Strasbourg and Haguenau arrived in Paris on 2
March 1496, together with one of his brothers.
At once he formed a connection with the
Collège de Saint-Barbe, where he was
subsequently to teach arts courses for seven
years (AK I Epp 304, 318). He graduated BA in
1497–8 and MA in March 1499. While teaching
arts courses he began his theological studies in
1500. At the same time he became a paying
boarder and from 1504 a fellow at the Collège
de la Sorbonne. On 28 May 1511 he ranked first
among those obtaining the theological doctorate, a distinction often noted after his return
from France (Ep 1422). He was prior of the
Sorbonne in the same year. Between academic
terms at Paris Baer frequently returned to
Basel. Such visits are documented for 1501,
1503, and b 1505; on the following visit in the
summer of 1506 he sought and received some
instruction in Hebrew from Conradus *Pellicanus, afterwards requiting his help lavishly
with gifts of new books. Although he accepted
the need for languages and textual criticism (LB
x 1648D–F) within the general field of
theological study, Baer's efforts to master the
new learning were limited in scope. His heart
belonged to formal theology in the tradition of

Paris, and it was in this field that he achieved in
his prime a reputation which was unparalleled
within the region of the Upper Rhine and
Switzerland (Ep 1539).

In Paris Baer tutored some young students
from his native region, and in 1501 Johann
Amerbach would have liked him to take charge
of his sons Bruno and Basilius *Amerbach.
However he was finally persuaded not to
pursue this aim by his sons' reluctance to
change tutors and perhaps also by some
doubts about Baer's eagerness to impart
lessons and to give prominence to the Scotist
tradition dear to Johann from his own years of
study (AK I Epp 134, 137, 154, 225, 246). Baer
accepted Amerbach's decision with a good
grace and continued to assist his sons in
practical matters such as the payment of their
bills, no doubt to prevent overcharging, but he
also provided cash when the father proved
unreasonably parsimonious (AK I Epp 274, 275,
304).

At the beginning of 1513 Baer returned to
Basel, at first intending to wind up his affairs
there and to move to Paris for good
(Friedensburg 479). However, his name
appears in the university register for the winter
term of 1513, when he began to lecture as
professor ordinarius of theology, bringing to
that faculty his prestige and sense of purpose,
which were both badly needed. By 1514–15 he
was rector of the university; he was dean of
divinity in the following year and again in
1528, and rector again in 1520. He also
discharged for many years the ceremonial
function of vice-chancellor.

His paternal inheritance provided Baer with
a handsome income, and in addition he began
to receive ecclesiastical preferment. In 1507 he
was a canon at Thann, Upper Alsace, where he
owned a house and may have spent some time
every year, his revenues being contingent
upon a residence requirement (Epp 460, 575,
594; BRE Ep 18; *Aktensammlung* IV 300;
Friedensburg 478, 480). At the time of his
return from Paris, the Basel council and his
family attempted to secure him a canonry at the
cathedral, but for the time being the chapter
refused to appoint him on account of some
legal principle rather than personal factors. As
compensation he was made canon of St Peter
on 9 March 1513 and provost of that chapter on

5 May 1518, positions which he resigned on 20 May 1527 (*Aktensammlung* I 484, II 490–2). The legal obstacles to his appointment to the cathedral chapter were finally overcome, and he was named canon by the city council on 17 March 1526 (*Aktensammlung* II 282–3). From 1535 he was the chapter's scholaster.

Baer's theological knowledge and his objectivity were much in evidence when he acted as one of the four presidents of the disputation held at Baden in 1526, but when asked a year later to preside over another disputation at Bern, he refused (*Aktensammlung* II 739–47). His support of Erasmian positions notwithstanding, he never wavered in his active defence of the papal church against all Protestant reformers. When Johann *Froben anonymously published the earliest collection of *Luther's Latin writings in October 1518, Baer lost no time in dispatching a copy to Rome (BRE Ep 118), and two years later he fought to prevent Andreas *Cratander from printing *Lutheriana* (AK II Ep 751). In 1522, when Hermannus *Buschius felt obliged to leave Basel after voicing public support of the innovators, he vowed to fight back with an apology especially against Baer (AK II Ep 878). In November 1525 Baer was requested to assist Bonifacius *Amerbach in providing the city council with an opinion as to whether an essay by Johannes *Oecolampadius on the Eucharist should go on sale. He selected ten representative passages which were bound to play a role in the eventual prohibition of the public sale, although in the view of the outspoken Udalricus *Zasius at Freiburg he had shown too much moderation (Epp 1674, 1679; AK III Epp 1063, 1065, 1066, 1070; *Aktensammlung* II 156–62).

With the triumph of the reform party in 1529 Baer left Basel for good, together with the entire chapter and many other Catholics. Like his brother Franz Baer he settled at Freiburg, which became the official seat of the Basel chapter. In 1531 the University of Freiburg offered him a vacant chair of theology, but he declined without hesitation. Shortly thereafter Erasmus mentioned new and ridiculous attacks on Baer by the Freiburg conservatives (Ep 2631). Since the Basel chapter had been deprived of much of its revenue, the government of Catholic Lucerne apparently wished to compensate Baer for his personal losses. In 1532 he received a pledge for a canonry at the chapter of Beromünster and actually held one from 1541, resigning it in 1549. In 1532 he renewed his old friendship with Girolamo *Aleandro, who invited Baer to visit him at Venice or use his cardinal's residence at Rome. Early in 1535 Baer went to Rome, keeping in touch with Aleandro and relying on the support of Ambrosius von *Gumppenberg and of Antonio *Pucci and Ennio *Filonardi, two old acquaintances from their days in Switzerland. He was received by *Paul III and, although he may have failed in a bid of his own for preferment, he succeeded in obtaining papal approval for the nomination of his nephew, Franz (II) *Baer, to a benefice at Strasbourg. Erasmus, who was offered a cardinal's hat at this time, entrusted him with personal negotiations and with letters to his friends in which he recommended him warmly. At the end of the year Baer returned to Freiburg, on the way visiting Aleandro at Venice and Lazzaro *Bonamico at Padua (Friedensburg passim; Epp 2988, 3007, 3011, 3018, 3021–7, 3043; AK IV Epp 1918, 1946, 2041). In connection with this journey Baer may have supplied Erasmus with a brief summary of the vicissitudes that had befallen him and his family (Basel MS Erasmuslade D 5 f 5 no 4).

At Freiburg Baer was plagued by occasional sickness (Epp 2321, 2322, 2827). A copy of his will is preserved at Colmar, setting out a number of charitable bequests. As early as 1545 the University of Freiburg had received a hundred books and a sum of fourteen hundred florins for scholarships. Most significantly, at the time of his burial in the cathedral it received in memory of him an altar diptych by Hans *Holbein, donated by Amalia Tscheckenbürlin, another refugee from Basel, and her second husband, Anton, a son of Franz (I) Baer, which is still in the university chapel of the cathedral.

As Baer was in contact with well-known contemporaries in many countries, greetings to or from him occur frequently in the correspondence of Erasmus. He kept in touch with old friends from his days at the University of Paris such as Luis Nuñez *Coronel (Ep 1274), Herman *Lethmaet (Ep 1320), Pierre *Richard (Ep 1610; Basel MS G I 26 ff 4, 8), Guillaume *Cop and his family (Ep 2906; Friedensburg 482), and above all Aleandro, whom he called the closest of his Paris friends. In Germany he knew Johannes *Cochlaeus (Ep 2120), Johann *Eck (Epp 2387, 2406), Johann *Koler (Ep 2406), and Ambrosius *Pelargus (Epp 2725, 2966). From among the Romans the connection with Antonio Pucci is mentioned most frequently (Epp 1580, 3059; Friedensburg passim; Basel MS Erasmuslade D 5 f 5 no 4). *Glareanus, who was a life-long friend, addressed to Baer one of his *Elegiae*, published in 1516. Gervasius *Wain dedicated to him his *Tractatus noticiarum* (Paris 1519).

With regard to his relations with Erasmus, the preserved correspondence permits no more than glimpses of contacts which were frequent at Basel, where Erasmus called the canon of St Peter his neighbour (LB X 1648D), and especially during the Freiburg years (Friedensburg 480). Baer added his voice to those inviting Erasmus to settle in Basel and even offered him one of his two prebends (Epp 456, 625, 627). Erasmus often sought the reassurance of Baer's theological expertise. In 1517 Baer and *Capito, his colleague at the time, evidently regretted the publication of Erasmus' *Apologia* against *Lefèvre d'Etaples, raising a point of theology with the author (Epp 730–3, 798). Erasmus sought Baer's advice while preparing *De libero arbitrio* (Epp 1419, 1420, 1422), and also consulted him on the *Epistola de esu carnium* (Epp 1581, 1609, 1620), on Leo *Jud's *Antwort* (Ep 1741), on the divorce of *Henry VIII (Ep 3001), and on the second and third editions of the New Testament (Ep 1571; LB IX 754A). As in the case of the controversy with Lefèvre, Baer examined Erasmus' positions carefully and sometimes critically. In the spring of 1521 he apparently asked him to explain his attitude towards Luther (Ep 1203), and in January 1529 he requested, and subsequently received, a statement suitable to be shown around, explaining Erasmus' commitment to the church of Rome and the reasons for his continued presence at Basel (Epp 2087, 2136). Baer attempted to mediate in Erasmus' conflicts with *Hutten, *Eppendorf, and Pelargus (Ep 2725; LB X 1636B, 1641E–F, 1648D–F, 1685A, 1686B). His known reactions to the news of Erasmus' death were sober, but he treasured the golden hourglass his friend had left him (AK IV Epp 2041, 2043, 2044, 2051;

Friedensburg 488). In October 1547 he was approached by Gumppenberg, who wished to receive for the benefit of *Charles V any texts by Erasmus containing proposals for religious reconciliation (AK VI Epp 3001, 3002). Erasmus' noble tribute that Baer managed to exercise his academic duties as a theologian without the slightest hostility towards classical and biblical scholarship (LB X 1648D–F) is aptly borne out by the only book Baer published (even giving it to a press in Protestant Basel) – his sensible and pious treatise *Pro salutari hominis ad felicem mortem praeparatione* (Basel: J. Oporinus 1551; reprinted Antwerp 1554 and, in Flemish translation, Louvain 1572). Frequently borrowing from Erasmus' own *De praeparatione ad mortem*, Baer adopted to the full the concept of 'Philosophia Christi' and on this occasion refrained entirely from voicing his opposition to the reformers.

BIBLIOGRAPHY: Allen and CWE Ep 488 / NDB I 525 / AK I Ep 149 and passim / BRE Ep 18 and passim / W. Friedensburg 'Beiträge zum Briefwechsel der katholischen Gelehrten Deutschlands im Reformationszeitalter' *Zeitschrift für Kirchengeschichte* 16 (1895–6) 470–99, esp 476–90 (correspondence with Aleandro) / *Epistolae ad Nauseam* 457–8 / *Matrikel Basel* I 313, 319, 368–70 / *Aktensammlung zur Geschichte der Basler Reformation* ed E. Dürr et al (Basel 1921–50) I 483–5 and passim / *Helvetia sacra* ed A. Bruckner et al (Bern 1972–) II-2 146–7 / *Basler Biographien* ed Albert Burckhardt (Basel 1900–5) I 59–89 / R. Wackernagel *Geschichte der Stadt Basel* (Basel 1907–54) III147–8 and passim / A. Kimmenauer 'Colmarer Beriana' *Festschrift für Josef Benzing* (Wiesbaden 1964) 244–51 / Farge no 22 / P.G. Bietenholz 'Ludwig Baer, Erasmus and the Tradition of the *Ars bene moriendi' Revue de littérature comparée* 52 (1978) 155–70 / A.J. Schmidlin *Geschichte der deutschen Nationalkirche in Rom, S. Maria dell'Anima* (Freiburg-Vienna 1906) 326 / J.J. Bauer *Zur Frühgeschichte der theologischen Fakultät der Universtät Freiburg i. Br.* (Freiburg 1957) 79 / Paul Ganz *Weihnachts-Darstellung Hans Holbeins des Jüngeren: Die Flügel des Oberried-Altars* (Augsburg [1923]) / Öffentliche Bibliothek of the University of Basel MS G I 26 fol 4–10 (Baer's letters to his nephew Ulrich Iselin)

PGB

BAERLAND *See* BARLANDUS

Lazare de BAÏF d 1547

Baïf (Bayfius, Bayfus) was born around 1496 of a noble family of Anjou at the Château des Pins near La Flèche. After studying law, he went to Rome with Christophe de *Longueil (c 1516) and studied with Janus *Lascaris and Marcus *Musurus, no doubt at the recently established college on the Quirinal (Budé *Opera omnia* 1 405–6, Longueil *Orationes*, etc, Florence 1524, repr 1967, f 81 verso). After several years Baïf returned to France. From a letter from *Budé to Longueil of 6 January 1521 (Budé *Opera omnia* 1 308–10), we know that Baïf then lived far from the court, presumably in his Château des Pins and that he no longer kept in touch with Longueil. A local tradition (cf Pocquet de la Livonnière) has it that Baïf taught law and letters at the University of Angers. In these years he laid the groundwork for his learned publications, investigating the practical side of ancient life on the basis of the *Corpus juris*, according to the method developed by Budé. Ep 1479 suggests that in 1524 Baïf may have made another trip to Italy and may have met *Haio Herman at Padua.

In 1525 Baïf entered the service of Cardinal Jean de *Lorraine. After taking part in the peasants' war in Alsace, he followed the cardinal to Lyon. They were on their way to Spain, but the freeing of King *Francis 1 made that further trip unnecessary. Baïf instead returned to Pins, and, profiting from this respite, he published his first work, the annotations to the law *Vestis, ff. de auro et argento legato* (Digest xxxiv ii 23–5) under the title of *De re vestiaria* (Basel: J. Bebel March 1526). Despite the modest scope of this work of only sixty-five pages, it earned Baïf the second rank after Budé among the French scholars. In 1527 he was named apostolic protonotary, a position which enabled him to receive two abbeys *in commendam*. In 1529 Francis 1 appointed him resident ambassador to Venice, and he left for his new post on 25 June.

In Venice Baïf showed great zeal in producing scrupulous diplomatic dispatches, many of which are preserved in the Bibliothèque Nationale, at Pins, and in the archives of Chantilly. Baïf received Girolamo *Aleandro, Giambattista *Egnazio, and Lazzaro *Bona-mico, and appealed to Francis 1 in favour of Michelangelo. He also corresponded with *Bembo, *Sadoleto, Germain de *Brie, and Erasmus, and continued his philological and archeological research. He even began studying Hebrew (Ep 2447), presumably with Elias *Levita. From May 1530 Baïf employed as his secretary Pierre Bunel of Toulouse. In February 1532 his illegitimate son, Jean-Antoine, was born, a future poet of the Pléiade to whose education Baïf always paid careful attention, entrusting him to excellent tutors such as Charles Estienne and Jacques *Toussain.

At the beginning of 1534 Baïf was recalled from Venice at his own request. Returning to Paris, he set up house in the suburb of Saint-Marceau, keeping his son with him. On 17 November 1530 he had been appointed clerical councillor in the Parlement. Now, on 27 March 1534, he took his oath of office. In 1538 he was named master of requests in the royal household. In 1540 he was sent to the conference of Haguenau and departed for this important mission, accompanied by Charles Estienne, his friend and disciple, and by Pierre de Ronsard. He was to accomplish a feat of diplomatic ambiguity, namely to reassure the German Protestants at the same time as their co-religionists were being persecuted in France, and he was not, it seems, very successful. He nevertheless retained royal favour and was later charged with several other missions (for example, to Champagne in May 1542 and to Languedoc and Poitou in 1544). Baïf died between 12 April and 8 November 1547.

Baïf tried his hand at French poetry and left a rhyme translation of Sophocles' *Electra* (Paris: E. Roffet 1537). From his correspondence we know that he also translated into French the first four *Lives* of Plutarch. Of these the first two may survive in a manuscript at the Bibliothèque Nationale (MS fr 1936), but the attribution to Baïf is uncertain. His scholarly reputation rests squarely on his three Latin works: *De re vestiaria* of 1526, dedicated to Jean de Lorraine; *De vasculis* (Basel: H. Froben 1531), dedicated to the chancellor, Antoine du Bourg, and accompanied by a new edition of *De re vestiaria*; and finally *De re navali* (Paris: R. Estienne 31 August 1536), dedicated to King Francis 1 and accompanied by a new edition of the first two works. This latter edition is accompanied by illustrations derived from sketches of the pillar of Trajan and other monuments which had been obtained for Baïf by the French ambassador to Rome, François de Dinteville. In 1537, Hieronymus *Froben reprinted this edition, while another, expanded and revised by the author, was published posthumously by Robert Estienne (Paris, September 1549). Charles Estienne rearranged Baïf's work for the use of young students (various editions, 1535–7). A work on architecture is mentioned in Baïf's letter to Jean de Lorraine of 14 November 1531 (Bibliothèque Nationale, MS fr 3941), but not otherwise known to exist. Finally, Robert Estienne acknowledged Baïf's help for his second edition of the *Thesaurus linguae latinae* (1536).

Baïf's studies compare somewhat poorly with Budé's *De asse* in terms of comprehensiveness and philosophical outlook, but they follow Budé's method. Budé praised Baïf in the *Annotationes posteriores ad Pandectas* and in the re-editions of *De asse* (Budé *Opera omnia* II 81, III 354). Other tributes were paid to him by Jean *Salmon, Joachim Du Bellay, and Ronsard. Jean-Antoine de Baïf remembered his father in a biographical poem addressed to King Charles IX and published as the preface to his *Oeuvres en rime*.

Erasmus' interest in Baïf seems to go back to a flattering account of the man and his work given by *Haio Herman (Ep 1479). Erasmus was impressed with Baïf's knowledge of Greek and changed the text of *Adagia* I x 100 and III iv 52 in the light of his remarks (Ep 1479). He had great esteem for *De re vestiaria* (*Ciceronianus* ASD I-2 674; Ep 2040), followed attentively the progress of Baïf's work (Ep 1962), and in 1531 revised *De vasculis* for the Froben press. In his two extant letters to Baïf (Epp 1962, 2447 – no answers are preserved) he showed an accurate and sincere appreciation for Baïf's qualities: his well-known kindness, his high offices and social rank, his sophistication, and his rigorous philological method.

BIBLIOGRAPHY: Allen 1962 / Guillaume Budé *Opera omnia* (Basel 1557, repr 1966) passim / L. Pinvert *Lazare du Baïf (1496–1547)* (Paris 1900) / V.-L. Bourrilly 'Lazare du Baïf maître des Requêtes' in *Mélanges offerts à M. Emile Picot* (Paris 1913) 121–34 / M.-M. de la Garanderie
'L'approche philologique du fait antique' in *Actes du IXe Congrès de l'Association Guillaume Budé* (Paris 1975) 705–14 / P.G. Bietenholz *Basle and France in the Sixteenth Century* (Geneva-Toronto 1971) 197–9 and passim / Angers, Bibliothèque Municipale MS 1068: Pocquet de la Livonnière 'Histoire des illustres d'Anjou'

MARIE-MADELEINE DE LA GARANDERIE

Girolamo BALBI of Venice, d after 1535

Girolamo Balbi was born at Venice about the middle of the fifteenth century, in December; the year is unknown. He studied at Rome under *Pomponius Laetus and at Ferrara under Lucas Ripa. Probably in the second half of 1485 he came to Paris, where he was admitted to the circle of humanists headed by Robert *Gaguin. Shortly after his arrival he became involved in an intense conflict with Guillaume *Tardif, severely criticizing his grammar and attacking him in the *Rhetor gloriosus*, a parody on Plautus' *Miles gloriosus*. On 5 September 1489, with two other Italian humanists, Fausto *Andrelini and Cornelio *Vitelli, Balbi was admitted to teach literature and poetry at the University for one hour every afternoon. Almost immediately afterwards a violent quarrel broke out among the three poets. Before the end of 1489 Vitelli left for England. In 1492 Balbi managed to drive away Fausto Andrelini, but after Fausto's return he himself had to leave for England, where he remained for a short while. In the summer term of 1493 he enrolled at the University of Vienna, where he taught law and literature until he was once more embroiled in a quarrel and had to leave Vienna. In 1499 he moved to Prague, where he obtained access to the court of *Vladislav II, king of Hungary, by whom he was appointed tutor to his daughter, Princess Anne, and his son, Prince Louis. When *Louis II ascended the throne in 1516, Balbi remained attached to him and in his service carried out several diplomatic missions. In 1522 Balbi entered the service of *Ferdinand I, and in 1523 he was appointed bishop of Gurk. His various diplomatic assignments were part of the struggle against the Turks. In 1524 he went to Rome, where he remained for some years as domestic chaplain to Pope *Clement VII. In 1530 he was present at the coronation of *Charles V at Bologna. He spent his last years at Rome in obscurity, and the date of his death is unknown.

In the winter of 1486–7 Balbi published a first collection of epigrams with the press of Simon Doliatoris in Paris. A second volume followed about a year later. Balbi's epigrams found an enthusiastic admirer in Cornelis *Gerard, Erasmus' correspondent in the monastery of Lopsen. He considered Balbi as the only modern poet fit to walk in the footsteps of the ancients. Erasmus did not share his opinion, and a discussion about the quality of Balbi's poetry came to form part of a broader exchange of views between Gerard and Erasmus about literature and poetry (Epp 23, 25, 27). At about the same time Erasmus wrote a poem (Reedijk poem 49) against Charles *Fernand, who had published an edition of Seneca's tragedies with Balbi.

Erasmus never met Balbi, and in his later work he mentions him only rarely. In *De conscribendis epistolis*, written during his second stay in Paris (1496–9), he cites the name 'Balbi' as an example of a 'nomen gentilicium' (ASD I-2 280). In Ep 961 he mentioned Balbi as the possible author of the *Julius exclusus*, and in Ep 2379 he recalled the quarrel between Andrelini and Balbi.

BIBLIOGRAPHY: Allen and CWE Ep 23 / G. Rill in DBI V 370–4 / Eubel III 207 / P.S. Allen 'Hieronymus Balbus in Paris' *English Historical Review* 17 (1902) 417–28 / Gilbert Tournoy 'L'oeuvre poétique de Jérôme Balbi après son arrivée dans le Saint-Empire Romain' in *L'Humanisme allemand (1490–1540), xviiie Colloque international de Tours* (Paris-Munich 1979) 321–37 / Gilbert Tournoy 'Two poems written by Erasmus for Bernard André' *Humanistica Lovaniensia* 27 (1978) 45–51 / Gilbert Tournoy 'The literary production of Hieronymus Balbus at Paris' *Gutenberg Jahrbuch* (1978) 70–7 / Godelieve Tournoy-Thoen 'La tecnica poetica di Girolamo Balbi' in *Ecumenismo della cultura* I ed G. Tarugi (Florence 1981) 101–23

GODELIEVE TOURNOY-THOEN

Pius Hieronymus BALDUNG c 1489–1539 (?)
The Baldung (Baldungus) family came from Schwäbisch-Gmünd, in Württemberg, but several members settled in Strasbourg at the turn of the sixteenth century, among them the parents of Hans Baldung-Grien, the famous

painter. Pius Hieronymus was probably the son of another Hieronymus who also went to live at Strasbourg and was given the titles of *palatinus* and physician to *Maximilian I. It is possible, however, that Pius Hieronymus had one or more other namesakes. When he matriculated in 1504 at the University of Vienna, he was already a bachelor of law. By 1507 he had obtained a legal doctorate and was teaching poetics at the University of Freiburg; in 1510 he taught civil law. But soon he moved on to legal and administrative functions in Ensisheim, the seat of the Hapsburg government for Alsace and the Breisgau. In December 1514 *Zasius gave him the title of imperial councillor and called him to witness to his own admiration for Erasmus (Ep 319). By 1515 he had become a friend of the *Amerbach brothers (AK II Ep 534), and in 1516, after a visit from Lukas *Klett, he introduced himself to Erasmus with Ep 400. In the monastery of Murbach he discovered several old manuscripts, including a codex Theodosianus, which was of great interest to his friends in Basel (AK II Ep 755). He was sent to Switzerland with Maximilian van *Bergen and Jakob *Stürzel in the summer of 1519 and gained the admiration of *Zwingli (Z VII Ep 87), and in January 1522 he was a member of another Hapsburg delegation that negotiated with the Swiss at Zürich (AK II Ep 840). It seems that as early as 1517 he had been summoned to Innsbruck by the Emperor Maximilian, and thus he is probably the Baldung whom *Ferdinand I later appointed chancellor for the Tirol and also the one who received Thomas *Lupset with great kindness when he called on him at Innsbruck with a recommendation from Johann von *Botzheim (1523, Ep 1361). He is probably also the Hieronymus Baldung addressed by Zasius in 1532 with a letter of dedication for his *Substitutionum tractatus*, published by *Faber Emmeus in Freiburg (AK IV Epp 1609, 1670).

BIBLIOGRAPHY: Allen and CWE Ep 400 / NDB I 554 / ADB II 18–19 / Schottenloher I 37 / AK II Ep 534 and passim / *Matrikel Wien* II-1 319 / *Matrikel Freiburg* I-1 168 / *Udalrici Zasii epistolae* ed J.A. Riegger (Ulm 1774) Epp 252, 257 / Winterberg 64–5 / *Deutsche Reichstagsakten* Jüngere Reihe (Gotha-Göttingen 1893–   ) I 701–2, VII-1 11

PGB

Jacopo Bannisio

Balenus had such famous students as the theologian Gulielmus Lindanus and the oriental scholar Andreas Masius, who became a correspondent and close friend. Balenus recommended his pupil Lambert *Coomans as a suitable servant for Erasmus (Ep 3037). Coomans proved satisfactory and, thanks to a bequest from Erasmus, returned to Balenus' house to continue his studies at Louvain. Erasmus sent greetings to Balenus in 1535 (Ep 3052) and apparently wrote him soon after (Allen Ep 3130).

Balenus wrote two treatises, 'De accentibus hebraicis' and 'De consensu editionis Vulgatae cum hebraica veritate,' both mentioned in the *De optimo genere interpretandi scripturas* of his pupil Lindanus. Another book, 'De investigatione thematis in hebraico sermone,' existed in manuscript about 1760. He married Roberta van Duerne, who died on 17 December 1567. Balenus himself died two months later and bequeathed all his possessions to the poor students of Louvain.

BIBLIOGRAPHY: Allen Ep 3037 / de Vocht CTL III 208–19 and passim / *Matricule de Louvain* III-1 530

CFG

BALTHASAR AUSTRIACUS *See Balthasar von KÜNRING*

Jacopo BANNISIO of Korčula, d 19 November 1532
Jacopo Bannisio (Banisius, de Bannissis) was born on the Island of Korčula, (Curzola) in Dalmatia. His father was Paolo Bannisio, perhaps of the lower nobility. In 1493 or 1494 Bannisio entered the service of the Emperor *Maximilian I and by 1502 was an imperial secretary. He was rewarded with a number of lucrative benefices, including the deanery of Trent in 1512 and that of Antwerp in 1513, and several parishes. He received holy orders in 1514.

Bannisio took part in numerous diplomatic missions and was especially prominent in efforts to ally with England. In August of 1513 he was in the English camp at Tournai after *Henry VIII defeated the French in the battle of the Spurs. From 1515 to 1522 he was frequently in contact with English emissaries, who saw him as a partisan of their cause at the imperial court. In 1521 Bannisio was at Worms and

Andreas BALENUS of Balen, d 10 February 1568
Frequently called Balenus, Andreas van Gennep of Balen, forty kilometres east of Antwerp, was probably born about 1484. He may have received one of the scholarships in the College of the Castle, Louvain, which were reserved for young men from his district. He did not matriculate until 27 May 1516 and appears to have attended the lectures of Matthaeus *Adrianus and Jan van *Campen at the Collegium Trilingue. After receiving his MA he began to study medicine; subsequently he was often praised by his contemporaries for his knowledge of medicine, botany, and physics. He pursued a career as a physician, which he did not entirely abandon when on 26 February 1532 he succeeded Jan van Campen as professor of Hebrew at the Trilingue, accepting two-thirds of the regular professor's wages. Although he suffered from a nervous illness at the turn of 1543–4 and had to take a leave, he brought the attendance of Hebrew courses to such a level that students began to demand daily lectures and the old opponents of the Trilingue in the faculty of theology recognized the excellence of the program.

helped draft the edict against *Luther. Although he continued intermittently to be involved in the diplomatic service of the Hapsburgs, in 1522 he went to live at Trent, where he later died. Between 1523 and 1527 he engaged in a mission to return Francesco II *Sforza to Milan and for his services was rewarded with an annual income. He renounced his ecclesiastical benefices in favour of his nephew and in 1530 was permitted to appoint substitutes for his missions in the imperial service.

Bannisio was a friend and patron of artists and humanists. In 1520 he met Albrecht *Dürer at Brussels and Antwerp, where he had a residence, and helped extend a pension first paid to the artist by the Emperor Maximilian. Dürer later drafted a coat of arms for Bannisio and perhaps also a portrait sketch.

On 3 November 1517 (Ep 700), Erasmus wrote to Bannisio to apologize for not seeing him at Brussels and to express anger at *Pfefferkorn's attacks on all men of learning. Erasmus suggested that he might write to Maximilian so that the madness of Pfefferkorn could be suppressed 'not by books, but by the club of Hercules,' but Bannisio replied (Ep 709) that Pfefferkorn was best left to his own devices. Later, on 21 May 1519 (Ep 970), Erasmus wrote to Bannisio to praise the level of learning attained by Henry VIII and England.

BIBLIOGRAPHY: Allen Ep 700 / DBI V 755–7 / LP II and III passim / Erwin Panofsky *Albrecht Dürer* (Princeton 1943) II nos 382, 1075 / *Deutsche Reichstagsakten* Jüngere Reihe (Gotha-Göttingen 1893–   ) I 185 and passim

TBD

Theobald BAPST of Guebwiller, 1496/7–4 October 1564
A native of Guebwiller, Upper Alsace, Bapst was already in orders when he matriculated at the University of Freiburg on 12 January 1515. He graduated MA in 1517–18 and began to teach, while at the same time studying law with Udalricus *Zasius. Bapst was a free-wheeling youth, and there are records of a lively evening in the company of Bartholomaeus *Latomus which led to some embarrassment for the faculty of arts (1519). He settled down, however, and was elected rector for a term in 1522 (Ep 1353) and for thirteen more terms between then and 1552. Between 1525 and

1528 he had to leave Freiburg to supervise a relative at the University of Dole. On 29 March 1530, during one of Bapst's terms as rector, Zasius presided at his solemn doctoral graduation. In the Freiburg faculty of law he held the chair of the codex from 1535 until 1542, when he was promoted to the senior chair of civil law; he was also dean for fourteen terms. His legal opinions were in great demand throughout the Breisgau and Alsace, and he was councillor to the Hapsburg administration in Ensisheim, but he was not a publishing scholar. Although Bonifacius *Amerbach had been his fellow-student at Freiburg, a regular correspondence between them did not begin until the 1540s. Bapst died of the plague, leaving one half of his fortune, or 10,800 florins for the foundation of a college at Freiburg named after him.

BIBLIOGRAPHY: Allen Ep 1353 / *Matrikel Freiburg* I 218–19 and passim / Schreiber *Universität Freiburg* II 332–5 / Winterberg 15–16 / Clausdieter Schott *Rat und Spruch der Juristenfakultät Freiburg i. Br.* (Freiburg 1965) 64–6 and passim / AK VI–VIII passim / BRE Ep 270 / Öffentliche Bibliothek of the University of Basel MS G² 11 66 f 6: a letter from Bapst to J.U. Iselin, Freiburg, 17 September 1562

PGB

Hieronymus BARBA (Ep 2721 of [September-/October 1532])
Hieronymus Barba, a Dominican who associated with Ambrosius *Pelargus at Freiburg, has not been identified.

Ermolao (I) BARBARO of Venice, 1453/4–c July 1493
Ermolao Barbaro gained much of his early education away from his Venetian home in the company of his father, Zaccaria, an active politician and diplomat. He studied first in Verona with his uncle, also named Ermolao Barbaro, and from 1462 in Rome, with *Pomponius Laetus and Theodorus *Gaza. His reputation grew rapidly; in 1468 he was again in Verona, this time to receive the poet's laurel crown from *Frederick III. During the 1470s he worked sporadically but intensively at Padua, taking his doctorate in the arts on 23 August 1474 and in civil and canon law on 27 October 1477. By this time a political career was beginning to open to him. He entered the

Venetian senate at an early age in 1483, completed a successful mission to the Burgundian court at Bruges (1486–7), and was promoted to the important civil post of *savio di terraferma* (1488). Election to embassies in Milan (1489) and Rome (1490) followed quickly. But this last mission brought Barbaro's life to a turning-point. On 6 March 1491 Innocent VIII appointed him patriarch of Aquileia, perhaps in an effort to assert his independence of the Venetian government in senior ecclesiastical appointments. Barbaro's acceptance left him subject to the penalty for receiving bribes from a foreign power, and he ended his life as an exile, dying of the plague, probably in July 1493.

Barbaro's composition *De coelibatu*, written in 1472, was less influential than his lectures and commentaries on the classical philosophers and scientists, which were based on a close adherence to the Greek texts and an accurate grasp of all the information needed to understand them. He expounded Aristotle's *Ethics* and *Politics* at Padua between 1474 and 1476, translated the *Rhetoric* in 1478 and 1479, and published a paraphrase of Themistius in 1481. His researches into natural philosophy, particularly the text of Dioscurides, continued during the 1480s and eventually found expression in his *Castigationes Plinianae*, published in Rome during 1492 and 1493 by Eucharius Silber and immediately saluted as the most authoritative discussion of Pliny's *Historia naturalis* available. A number of his works were published only after his death: *In Dioscuridem corolarii* appeared in 1510, the translation of Aristotle's *Rhetoric* and a paraphrase of the *Ethics* in 1544 (Venice: Camino da Trino), and a *Compendium scientiae naturalis* in 1545 (Venice: Camino da Trino). His letters to Giovanni *Pico, with their outspoken defence of the rhetorical and philological approach to the classics, were also widely circulated. Even before his death, Barbaro was being saluted as one of Italy's leading exponents of approaching classical antiquity through both Greek and Latin sources. His early death and those of *Poliziano and Pico which closely followed his led to their being grouped together as the intellectual embodiments of a vanished age of gold.

Though Erasmus cannot have known Barbaro personally, many of his Italian friends did. Erasmus cited Barbaro's works frequently, often with respect (Ep 1544; *Adagia* I iv 39, 71, 82, II iv 43, III iii 37, 80, iv 39, V 11, IV v 79, vi 18). But the Venetian was more important as a symbol than as a scholar. He was a brilliant man who made mistakes, just as Erasmus did (Epp 1482, 1558; LB IX 392E). He was a great intellect, cut off in his prime (Epp 1347, 3032). Most of all, he represented, along with Pico, Poliziano, Lorenzo *Valla, and Theodorus Gaza, that Italian leadership in humanistic studies which Erasmus liked to feel he and his colleagues were now challenging. Though the immediate reference is normally to Budé (Epp 1108, 1479, 1794, 2046), a comparison with Erasmus is often implicit (LB IX 392E). But there is no reason to suppose that Erasmus' admiration for Barbaro was anything but sincere, for a number of references single out individual works for approval or name him simply as a great scholar of the previous generation (Epp 126, 1544).

BIBLIOGRAPHY: Allen and CWE Ep 126 / E. Bigi in DBI VI 96–9 / Ermolao Barbaro *Castigationes Plinianae et in Pomponium Melam* ed Giovanni Pozzi (Padua 1973) / V. Branca 'Ermolao Barbaro and late Quattrocento Venetian humanism' in *Renaissance Venice* ed J.R. Hale (London 1973) 218–43

M.J.C. LOWRY

Ermolao (II) BARBARO of Venice, c 1493–3 November 1556
Ermolao, the son of Alvise, was the nephew of his more famous namesake Ermolao (I) *Barbaro. Still a schoolboy at the time of Erasmus' visit to Venice, he apparently came to share a number of acquaintances with him and joined Giambattista *Egnazio in welcoming Ulrich von *Hutten to Venice in 1517 (Ep 611). But his literary interests seem to have been limited to his youth, and most of his life was devoted to public service. From the junior civil post of *savio agli ordini* (1528), he worked his way laboriously through a series of naval and diplomatic posts up to the senior governorships of Verona (1544–5) and Padua (1548–50) without, however, gaining access to the inner ring of office-holders in Venice itself. His was the colourless career of a moderately successful Venetian patrician.

BIBLIOGRAPHY: Allen Ep 611 / DBI VI 99–100

M.J.C. LOWRY

BARBAROSSA *See* KHAIR AD-DIN *Pasha*

Nicolas BARBIER of Arras, documented
1517–30
So far Nicolas, a brother of Pierre *Barbier,
seems to be known only from references in the
correspondence of Erasmus; moreover, as his
name is not always given, it is not certain –
although it is very likely – that all the
references concern one and the same brother of
Pierre.

Erasmus seems to have met Nicolas in the
early days of his association with Pierre and
Guy *Morillon (Ep 565). When Pierre had left
for Spain, Nicolas gave Erasmus a sum of
money on his behalf (Epp 608, 652). Between
1521 and 1524 transactions concerning the
Courtrai prebend were discussed and apparently completed, by which some of Pierre's
benefices were transferred to Nicolas (Epp
1245, 1287, 1470), perhaps to prevent problems
in case Pierre were to die abroad (Ep 1458).
Erasmus liked and respected Nicolas (Ep 1431)
and in 1527 was glad to hear from Jan de
*Hondt that he had escaped some peril (Ep
1862). Finally we learn of an illness which had
threatened Nicolas' life in the summer of 1530
but from which he had recovered (Ep 2404).
PGB

Pierre BARBIER of Arras, d 7 December
1551/13 January 1552
Pierre Barbier (le Barbier, Barbirius, Tonsor)
was conceivably a younger relative of, but most
probably not identical with, another Pierre
Barbier, documented as chaplain to the future
*Maximilian I in 1486, to Philip the Handsome,
duke of *Burgundy, in 1501, and to the future
*Charles V between 1515 and 1517. The
younger Barbier probably matriculated at the
University of Louvain on 3 August 1510,
perhaps as a MA of another university. In 1513
he worked as a corrector for the Louvain
printer Dirk *Martens, as did Gerard *Geldenhouwer. In Martens' circle he met *Dorp and
*Broeckhoven; it is reasonable to assume that it
was there also that he became acquainted with
Erasmus (Epp 476, 496). By 1516 Barbier was
chaplain and secretary to Chancellor Jean *Le
Sauvage (Epp 443, 585) and closely associated
with Guy *Morillon, another young newcomer
to the chancellor's service (Epp 532, 565, 588).
It seems that Le Sauvage lost no time in

securing for Barbier a benefice in the Spanish
Indies (Epp 476, 532, 913), which, far from
making its titular rich, became something of a
standing joke among his friends. In 1517
Barbier accompanied Le Sauvage to Spain and,
when the chancellor died there the following
year, found a new master in the future Pope
*Adrian VI, in whose retinue he reached Rome
in August 1522. When Pope Adrian too died
prematurely, in September 1523, Barbier's
appointment as dean of the Tournai chapter
had been confirmed by the curia (Epp 1458,
2407, 2961), but a lengthy litigation followed,
and not until 1527 or 1528 could he take up
residence at Tournai in possession of the
deanery (Epp 1862, 2015). In the intervening
years he had briefly served Girolamo *Aleandro, whom he accompanied in 1524 and 1525
on his legateship to the French court (Ep 1548),
and from April 1525 the Spanish viceroy of
Naples, Charles de Lannoy. The remainder of
Barbier's life was spent for the most part in his
deanery at Tournai. He had to provide for
several orphaned nephews (Epp 2239, 2404),
and in 1532 he pleaded extreme poverty when
asking Aleandro for his help in securing an
additional benefice. Erasmus too was fully
aware of Barbier's serious financial strain (Epp
1862, 2842), which apparently obliged the dean
to take in paying guests, such as Cornelis van
Auwater and his private students in 1548. The
date of Barbier's death is given as either 7
December 1551 or 13 January 1552.

Barbier never faltered in his admiration for
Erasmus and his desire to be of service to him.
He was clearly sincere when in his earliest
extant letter to his older, more experienced
friend he asserted that he loved Erasmus as a
father (Ep 443). For his part, Erasmus greatly
enjoyed his association with Barbier (Epp 2295,
2613) and Morillon, which soon produced a
flurry of letters full of gay informality and
jokes, such as Erasmus' reference to the 'wife'
of his clerical friend (Ep 695). Barbier clearly
did his best to advance Erasmus' fortunes, and
his master, Chancellor Le Sauvage, became
instrumental in securing for Erasmus both his
pension from the Hapsburg court and his
annuity settled upon a Courtrai canonry.
These financial benefits provide the dominating theme of Erasmus' correspondence with
Barbier and, ironically, led in the end to
unjustified bitterness on the part of Erasmus.

While not an active scholar, Barbier still had a taste for learning and Latin authors (Ep 2239); Erasmus informed him of his progress in preparing the second and third editions of the New Testament (Epp 847, 1235) and also of his controversy with *Lefèvre d'Etaples in 1517, sending him a copy of his *Apologia ad Fabrum* (Epp 652, 752). Especially in the period of Barbier's service in the curia of Adrian VI, Erasmus was anxious to inform his friend at length of his troubles with *López Zúñiga, *Baechem Egmondanus, and the conservative Louvain theologians in general (Epp 1216, 1225, 1302). It seems that Barbier occupied a central position among Erasmus' sundry friends in Rome (Epp 1294, 1345) and no doubt played his part in securing such favours to Erasmus as Pope Adrian would grant.

The complicated business of Erasmus' Courtrai annuity and Barbier's involvement in it still awaits investigation by an expert. After considerable negotiations (Epp 436, 443) a vacated Courtrai prebend was assigned to Erasmus as of 1 January 1517. It seems that Erasmus resigned it to Barbier on the same date, and Barbier in turn resigned it – or at least most of the benefices of which it was composed – to Jan de *Hondt, who became a resident member of the Courtrai chapter and was responsible for Erasmus' annuity. Barbier himself, however, retained some financial interest and also a legal function in the substitution agreement – his death abroad would have jeopardized the claims of both Erasmus and de Hondt (Ep 1458) – and pro forma at least de Hondt's payments to Erasmus had to pass through Barbier's account (Epp 1094, 2404). In addition Barbier had helped to secure for Erasmus in the winter of 1516–17 an advance of his unpaid court pension coming from the coffers of Le Sauvage. When Charles' treasury finally made a payment, Barbier was authorized to receive it and, after repaying Le Sauvage's advance, forwarded to his friend a disappointingly small balance (CWE Ep 621 introduction). Erasmus may have suspected Barbier of cheating but for the time being did not permit that suspicion to interfere with his longstanding affection for his useful friend (Epp 1548, 2961). His misgivings were reinforced, however, when Johannes de *Molendino, Barbier's agent in Tournai, was unable to remit to Erasmus his annuity for the

second half of 1523, the money having been used by Barbier for his litigation about the deanery (Ep 1548). Barbier always recognized his debt and repeatedly promised payment (Epp 1458, 1470, 1471, 1695, 2239, 2404, 2407). Although Erasmus never forgot the matter (Epp 1769, 2015), he wrote to Barbier frankly about his ambiguous relationship with Aleandro and asked him to reassure the cardinal on his behalf (Epp 1605, 1621). Late in 1529 the relationship was still good enough for Barbier to participate in Jean de *Carondelet's efforts to bring about Erasmus' return to the Netherlands (Ep 2239). Thereafter, however, Erasmus became greatly agitated when de Hondt, who had begun to delay his payments, stopped them altogether after 1530. His litigation had left Barbier heavily in debt, and de Hondt, who was apparently among his creditors, reasonably decided that it was now up to Barbier to settle Erasmus' annuity directly (Epp 2527, 2704). In addition to Barbier's new financial failings, Erasmus constantly remembered the old ones, both the real and the imagined, with bitterness, if not hatred, although Barbier's pleas in 1533 seem at least to have persuaded him to drop the further insinuation that the dean of Tournai was acting in collusion with his enemies Aleandro and Jacobus *Latomus (Epp 2799, 2842). In August 1535 Erasmus stated that Barbier had appropriated the annuity for more than five years running (Ep 2965). While clearly exaggerated, the claim was a reflection of Erasmus' exasperation with his former friend.

BIBLIOGRAPHY: Allen Ep 443 / *Matricule de Louvain* III-1 393, cf 363 / P. Gorissen 'Het Kortrijkse pensioen van Erasmus' *De Leiegouw* 13 (1971) 107–51 / Cornelis van Auwater *Epistolae et carmina* ed H. de Vocht (Louvain 1957) Ep 28 and passim / de Vocht *Literae ad Craneveldium* Ep 89 and passim / de Vocht CTL III 274 and passim

PGB

Adrianus Aelius BARLANDUS d 1535
Adrianus Aelius Barlandus (Jacobszoon, van Baerland), the son of Jacob, was born at Baarland, south of Goes; he was a cousin of Hubertus *Barlandus. He should not be confused with the more famous Adrianus Cornelii *Barlandus, with whom he was acquainted (cf Daxhelet 255) and who wrote an

epitaph for him, now lost. Together with his brother Nicolaus he matriculated at Louvain in December 1504; in June 1515 he was in Brussels. Before January 1518 (Ep 760) he became the private teacher of Antoon (III) van *Bergen, and in 1519 he accompanied his pupil to England. Erasmus, who undoubtedly had come into touch with Barlandus at Louvain, mentioned him several times in letters contemporary with his tutorship (Epp 760, 969, 1028, and perhaps 1106). After his return to the Netherlands, Barlandus became a member of the council of the University of Louvain on 28 February 1526. Through Antoon van Bergen he obtained a prebend at Bergen op Zoom, where he lived until his death, shortly before 6 September 1535. Hubertus Barlandus discussed the disease which killed his cousin in *Epistola medica* (Antwerp: J. Steelsius 1536; NK 2370).

BIBLIOGRAPHY: Allen Ep 760 / *Matricule de Louvain* III-1 286 nos 130–1 / de Vocht *Literae ad Craneveldium* 154–5 / de Vocht CTL I 256–7, II 518, 521–2 / E. Daxhelet *Adrien Barlandus* (Louvain 1938 repr 1967) 254–5

C.G. VAN LEIJENHORST

Adrianus Cornelii BARLANDUS 28 September 1486–30 November 1538
Adrianus, the son of Cornelius, was a native of Baarland, on Zuid-Beveland, whence he is generally known as Barlandus. He and Hubertus *Barlandus were relatives; he is not to be confused with Adrianus Aelius *Barlandus. At the age of eleven he became a pupil of Pieter de *Schot at Ghent (Ep 492). He continued his studies at the University of Louvain, probably in 1501, but without matriculating: this omission may have been remedied on 27 November 1503, when the name Adrianus Cornelii de Blandia appears on the university register. Having studied at the College of the Pig, Barlandus received the degree of MA in 1505 and began teaching Latin. In 1509 he was appointed professor of philosophy, and on 6 June 1510 he presided at the promotion of his friend Willem *Zagere to the degree of MA. Barlandus' star was clearly in the ascendant: he had just been elected procurator of the Dutch nation on 1 June 1510 – a position which he would hold again in 1516, 1530, 1532, and 1538. He also served terms as *quodlibetarius* in 1512 and 1520 and as dean of

the faculty of arts in 1518 and 1531. In addition his pure Latin style and pedagogical abilities helped him attract a great number of private students, among the most notable of whom were Cardinal Guillaume (II) de *Croy in 1517 and Joris, Filips, and Maximiliaan van *Egmond.

Meanwhile Barlandus had become, along with Maarten van *Dorp, one of the most ardent supporters of Erasmus and the new learning at the University of Louvain. In the autumn of 1516 he composed a catalogue of Erasmus' writings for his brother, Cornelius *Barlandus (Ep 492), later sending a copy to Erasmus (Ep 510). Erasmus had frequently been asked to prepare such a list and was pleasantly surprised by Barlandus' work (Ep 512), which was published in the *Epistolae elegantes* (Louvain: D. Martens April 1517; NK 819) and in many later collections of Erasmus' letters. In 1518 Barlandus was offered the chair of Latin in the new Collegium Trilingue, a post recently refused by Jan *Becker (Ep 852). He accepted and delivered the college's inaugural Latin lecture on 1 September 1518. However, he resigned on 30 November 1519, at least in part because he was not satisfied with the renumeration and could earn more as a private teacher, but perhaps also because of friction between the faculty of arts, of which he was still a member, and the new college. Conradus *Goclenius succeeded him, which was a matter of annoyance to Barlandus, who seems to have supported the candidature of *Alaard of Amsterdam. When Barlandus openly criticized Goclenius, he brought upon himself a mild rebuke from Erasmus (Epp 1050, 1051). However, this does not appear to have affected their friendship, for Barlandus soon edited a selection of Erasmus' letters (Louvain: D. Martens December 1520; NK 820; cf Allen III App 12 and Ep 1163), as well as an *Epitome* of the *Adagia* (Louvain: D. Martens June 1521; NK 2844; cf Ep 646). The latter was prefaced by a letter from Erasmus (Ep 1204) and was dedicated to Pieter *Zuutpene, who had entertained Barlandus when he visited Zeeland early in 1521. In June 1525 Barlandus seems to have written to Erasmus about the death of Dorp, receiving Ep 1584 in reply.

On 20 February 1526 Jean *Desmarez, the professor of eloquence (*rhetor publicus*) of Louvain, died, and the next day Barlandus was appointed to the post, which he held until his death. Erasmus wrote to congratulate him on the appointment (Ep 1694). For the use of his students he composed his *Compendiosae institutiones artis oratoriae* (Louvain: R. Rescius for B. Gravius February 1535; NK 2369) and *De amplificatione oratoria* (Louvain: S. Zassenus April 1536; NK 221), dedicated to Jan van *Fevijn and Jan Becker respectively. As professor of eloquence, Barlandus enjoyed the revenues of a prebend in the church of St Peter's. Having been ordained a priest in or before 1515, he grew more dependent on benefices after his properties in Zeeland had been destroyed by a flood in 1530; on 20 April 1534 he accepted the parish of Werhem from the abbot of Bergues Saint-Winoc. On 30 September 1538 he was again chosen to be procurator of the Dutch nation, but only two months later he died.

Barlandus, who was happy to see his merits recorded in the *Ciceronianus* (ASD I-2 680; Ep 2025) was a prolific writer. In both spirit and subject-matter his work reveals a strong Erasmian influence. In addition to the works mentioned above he published an anthology of Lucian's dialogues in Erasmus' translation (Louvain: D. Martens 14 August 1512; NK 3434), a collection of elegant sayings, the *Ioci* (Louvain: D. Martens June 1524; NK 229), and the *Dialogi XLII* (Louvain: D. Martens March 1524; NK 2360), written for and dedicated to his pupil Charles (II) de *Croy and expanded to sixty-six dialogues by June 1532 (Antwerp: M. Hillen; NK 2362). He also wrote several historical works, among them *De Hollandiae principibus* (Antwerp: J. Thibault July 1519; NK 235), dedicated to his pupils Joris, Filips, and Maximilian van Egmond, the *Rerum gestarum a Brabantiae ducibus historia* (Antwerp: H. Tilianus and J. Hoochstraten 1526; NK 236), and the *Libelli tres* (Antwerp: M. Hillen January 1520; NK 232), which included *De Hollandiae principibus* as well as a catalogue of the bishops of Utrecht and a life of Charles the Rash, duke of *Burgundy. Finally Barlandus composed pedagogical and moralistic works such as *De ratione studii* (c 1525), addressed to Zagere and first printed in the *Historica* (Cologne: B. Gualterus 1603), and *Institutio christiani hominis* (Antwerp: H. Tilianus and J. Hoochstraten c 1526; NK 2368).

BIBLIOGRAPHY: Allen Ep 492 / E. Reussens in BNB I 718–22 / M. van Rhijn in *Nederlands Archief voor kerkgeschiedenis* 35 (1946) 85–90 / M.A. Nauwelaerts in NBW III 51–5 / *Matricule de Louvain* III-1 268 / E. Daxhelet *Adrien Barlandus* (Louvain 1938 repr 1967) / de Vocht *Literae ad Craneveldium* 153–5, 658–9 / de Vocht CTL vols I-IV ad indicem / de Vocht MHL 24, 94, and passim / P.J. Meertens *Letterkundig leven in Zeeland* (Amsterdam 1943) 40–1 and passim
C.G. VAN LEIJENHORST

Cornelius BARLANDUS documented c 1516
Cornelius was the younger brother of Adrianus Cornelii *Barlandus, who addressed to him Ep 492, containing an early list of Erasmus' writings (cf Epp 510, 513). A few remarks made by Adrianus in Epp 492 and 510 appear to be the only sources of information for Cornelius. Like Adrianus, he had attended the school of Pieter de *Schot at Ghent and was devoted to good literature. He had taken up the study of law but was still living with his mother in Zeeland.

BIBLIOGRAPHY: E. Daxhelet *Adrien Barlandus* (Louvain 1938; repr 1967) 2–3, 241, 265–7
CFG

Hubertus BARLANDUS d after 1 August 1544
Hubertus Barlandus was a native of Baarland, south of Goes, and a kinsman of Adrianus Aelius *Barlandus and Jan *Becker. Becker and Juan Luis *Vives taught him the humanities at Louvain, but he later applied himself to medicine, becoming a licentiate at the same university. He then went to France, studying mathematics in Paris and, in 1526, medicine at Montpellier. Fear of a possible war led him to abandon France; he travelled as far south as Italy before returning north in 1528 via Basel and Strasbourg. At Basel he stayed with Erasmus, whom he had first seen at the College of the Lily in Louvain. Erasmus was pleased with his visit (Ep 2079), and when Barlandus moved on to Strasbourg he sent his former host Ep 2081 (30 December 1528). At Strasbourg he edited Giovanni *Manardo's *Medicinales epistolae* (J. Schott 17 February 1529), sending a copy to Erasmus, who had recommended the work to him. Erasmus thanked him in Ep 2172, which was his delayed response to Diego

*López Zúñiga's *Apologia ecclesiasticae transla-tionis Novi Testamenti* (Rome c 1524).

In January 1531 Barlandus settled at Namur. Here he attacked his former professor of medicine, Arnold Noots, in the *Velitatio* (Antwerp: H. Peetersen 1532), dedicated to his patron Antoon van *Bergen. In the *Velitatio* Barlandus, who liked to call himself 'philiat-rius,' argued that medicine should be founded on verified facts rather than on Avicenna or any one school of medicine. In 1533 he succeeded Reyner *Snoy as the personal physician of Adolph of *Burgundy; at Veere he dedicated his translation of Galen's *De paratu facilibus libellus* (Antwerp: J. Steelsius 1533; NK 950) to Jan van *Fevijn. In addition he wrote an *Epistola medica* (Antwerp: J. Steelsius 1536; NK 2370) dedicated to the Antwerp physician Petrus Morbecanus and discussing the fatal illness of his cousin Adrianus Aelius Barlan-dus, and he translated St Basil's *De agendis Deo gratiis sermo et in Iulittam martyrem* (Louvain: R. Rescius June 1541), dedicated to Maximilian of *Burgundy. In the latter work he referred to his marriage and the recent death of his wife. It is known that Barlandus was still alive on 1 August 1544, because he wrote a letter to his old friend Morbecanus on that day.

BIBLIOGRAPHY: Allen Ep 2081 / C. de Waard in NNBW I 220–1 / E.H.J. Reusens in BNB I 722–3 / P.J. Meertens *Letterkundig leven in Zeeland* (Amsterdam 1943) 36–7 / de Vocht CTL II 518–24 / *Matricule de Montpellier* 48

C.G. VAN LEIJENHORST

Jacobus BARTHOLOMAEUS, BARTHELEMY
See Jacques BERTHÉLEMY

Lorenzo BARTOLINI Salimbeni of Florence, c 1494–May 1533
Lorenzo Bartolini Salimbeni was a member of a prominent Florentine family and was born to Bartolomeo and Piera Tebaldi around 1494. His brothers, Zanobi (1485–1533) and Gherardo (1487–1551), served both the Florentine repub-lic and the Medici as governors and soldiers. In 1502 Gherardo, who had originally embarked on an ecclesiastical career, renounced the commendatory Augustinian house of Entre-mont in Savoy to Lorenzo, who later acquired other benefices. In 1519 Lorenzo was named an apostolic protonotary.

In the summer of 1519 Lorenzo Bartolini travelled north with the French humanist Christophe de *Longueil, visiting *Budé at Marly and Erasmus at Louvain on 15 October. In parting with Erasmus, Bartolini expressed a desire to correspond with him, and Erasmus responded on 1 March 1521 with a simple letter of friendship (Ep 1187). There is no evidence of further correspondence.

In 1522 Lorenzo was in Florence, and according to Giulio Landi, who admired and shared his philosophical interests, he died in Venice. Bartolini left no known works but received dedications for Antonius Francinus' translation of the first volume of the Giunta Homer (Florence 1519) and for Gérard *Roussel's edition of the *Arithmetica* of Boethius (Paris: S. de Colines 1521).

BIBLIOGRAPHY: Allen Ep 1187 / Louis Delaruelle *Répertoire analytique et chronologique de la correspondance de Guillaume Budé* (Toulouse 1907) 84 / DBI VI 630–3 (for Lorenzo's brothers only) / Rice *Prefatory Epistles* Ep 132

TBD

Riccardo BARTOLINI of Perugia, c 1475–c 1529
Riccardo Bartolini (Bartholinus), the son of Antonio, completed a program of humanistic and theological studies in his native Perugia prior to 1500, when the Perugia cathedral chapter conferred upon him the parish of saints Severo and Agata. From 1504 to 1506 his uncle, Mariano Bartolini, was papal legate at the court of *Maximilian I, and Riccardo followed him to Germany, establishing con-tacts with many of the humanists in Maximil-ian's entourage. From 1507 to 1514 he again lived in Perugia, where he received a canonry and in 1513 substituted for his former teacher, Francesco Maturanzio, as professor of Latin and Greek. In this period he composed an epic in twelve books, *Ad divum Maximilianum ... de bello Norico Austriados* (Strasbourg: M. Schürer 1516). Based in part on the author's personal experiences in Germany, it treated the war of the Bavarian succession of 1504–5 and narrated Maximilian's deeds in mythological glorifica-tion. It was reprinted in 1531 with an extensive commentary by Jakob *Spiegel.

In 1514 Bartolini returned to the imperial court, until 1519 serving officially as a chaplain to Cardinal Matthäus *Lang and less officially as a court poet and historiographer. In his *Odeporicon* (Vienna: H. Wietor 1515) he described Lang's journey from Augsburg to Vienna and Bratislava in preparation for the crucial gathering at Vienna of Maximilian, *Sigismund I of Poland, and *Vladislav II of Hungary-Bohemia, as well as the splendour of the following 'summit.' His own narrative in prose was accompanied by the verse contributions of his friends Johannes *Dantiscus and Caspar *Ursinus Velius. His *De conventu Augustensi concinna descriptio* (Augsburg: [Hans of Erfurt] 1518) is the only comprehensive account of the diet of 1518 (Ep 863), which also occasioned his *Oratio de expeditione contra Turcas suscipienda* (Augsburg: S. Grimm and M. Wirsung 1518). Bartolini maintained close connections with such Vienna humanists as Georgius Collimitius and Joachim *Vadianus and was a good friend of Spiegel and Ursinus, his colleagues in the service of Lang. In March 1517 he accompanied the emperor to Antwerp and there found occasion to approach Erasmus. With extempore verse of his own he suggested a meeting which, however, failed to take place. Subsequently he sent Erasmus a *Genethliacon* composed by Ursinus and received in return a letter of thanks in which Erasmus mentioned Paulus *Ricius as a common friend and asked for an introduction to Cardinal Lang (Ep 547–9).

Maximilian died in January 1519; he had bestowed the poet's laurel upon Bartolini but otherwise failed to provide him with any office or benefice. Bartolini therefore decided to leave Lang's service and return to Perugia, where Maturanzio had recently died. Bartolini succeeded him in the prestigious chair of rhetoric, which he held from 1520 to 1526. In 1522 and 1527 he also served his native city on embassies to Florence and to *Adrian VI and *Clement VII. Earlier he had composed an *Idyllium* to celebrate the election of their predecessor, *Leo X, in 1513, but the major part of his literary creation dates from his five years in Germany. His poems exhibit lyrical talent and a thorough knowledge of the Latin classics; they are also valuable as a historical source. In 1528 a new priest was appointed to the parish of saints Severo and Agata, and in 1529 Niccolò Scevola succeeded to his chair; it may be presumed that he died in that year.

BIBLIOGRAPHY: Allen and CWE Ep 547 / Ingeborg Walter in DBI VI 625–7 / Friedrich Hermann Schubert 'Riccardo Bartolini' *Zeitschrift für bayerische Landesgeschichte* 19 (1956) 95–127 / Giovanni Battista Vermiglioni *Biografia degli scrittori perugini* (Perugia 1828) I 188–97 / Giuseppe Ermini *Storia dell'Università di Perugia* (Florence 1971) I 610–12 / Gustav Bauch *Caspar Ursinus Velius* (Budapest 1886) 18–37 / Conradin Bonorand *Joachim Vadian und der Humanismus im Bereich des Erzbistums Salzburg* (St Gallen 1980) passim / Stephan Füssel 'Ein humanistischer Panegyriker aus dem Umkreis Maximilians I. – Studien zum Leben und Werk des Riccardus Bartolinus Perusinus' (doctoral thesis in preparation for the University of Göttingen) / Perugia, Archivio episcopale MS Francesco Riccardi 'Memorie istoriche della chiesa perugina' II f 3 recto / Perugia, Archivio di Stato MSS Comune di Perugia 'Consigli e Riformanze' vols 127, 129–31 and 'Depositario tesoriere' vols 110–20

STEPHAN FÜSSEL

Nicolaus BASELLIUS of Bad Dürkheim, documented 1496–1529

Nicolaus Basellius was born in Bad Dürkheim, north-west of Speyer. Nothing is known about his family, the date of his birth, or the date and place of his death. He was a monk of the Benedictine abbey in Hirsau, north of Calw in Württemberg. Conradus *Pellicanus, who met him in Hirsau in 1496, referred to him as the abbey's librarian and his personal friend. He called him a man of great learning and a historian, so he may then have been engaged in the composition of his historical works. Johannes *Trithemius, who was also in Hirsau at this time, claimed Basellius as his pupil in the 1509 additions to his *Catalogus illustrium virorum Germaniae*. In September 1496 Basellius was staying in Speyer, according to Peter Drach, who mentions the taking of priestly vows, but it is unclear whether he was referring to Basellius' companion only or to both men. In 1500 he copied at Hirsau the gospel according to St John. In 1501 he visited Sponheim, where Trithemius was abbot (RE Ep 80, not in Geiger's excerpt). According to Trithemius, the abbot of Hirsau had sent him to Sponheim to be instructed in Greek and Latin literature. In September 1508 Basellius finished copying Reuchlin's *Colloquia graeca*.

In 1509 Trithemius listed the following works composed by Basellius: 'Cryphiographia' (an abridgment of the history of Hirsau), a work on the famous men of Hirsau, another on the instruction of novices, and a number of letters to various persons. While none of these writings are extant, we do have the manuscripts of his copy of Reuchlin's *Colloquia graeca* and an introductory letter to Trithemius' *Sermones et exhortationes ad monachos* (Strasbourg: J. Knobloch and J. Haselberger 1516). In the chronicle of Johannes *Nauclerus (Ep 397) the events of the period from 1500 to 1514 are described by Basellius. In 1514 *Reuchlin honoured him by including two of his letters in the *Clarorum virorum epistolae ... ad Ioannem Reuchlin* (Tübingen: Thomas Anshelm 1514; RE Epp 80, 104). Other letters are published in the correspondence of Trithemius and Erasmus.

By June 1515 Basellius had met Erasmus in Speyer. They shared the same lodgings, as Basellius recalled in his letter of February 1516 (Ep 391, probably carried by Thomas *Rapp), suggesting that they should continue to exchange letters. Another letter from Basellius to Willibald *Pirckheimer, dated 5 November 1519 (Heumann 31–2), indicates that he lent a manuscript of Fulgentius to Pirckheimer, who based his subsequent edition of that author on it. However, Pirckheimer was so indignant about Basellius' apparent lack of trust in him while he was using the manuscript that he purposely omitted Basellius' name from the dedication. In 1524 and 1529 Basellius is listed among the monks of Hirsau, but his name does not occur in the list of 1535. From 1524 to 1527 he was priest of St Mary's in Ditzingen, near Stuttgart.

BIBLIOGRAPHY: Allen Ep 391 / W. Irtenkauf 'Bausteine zu einer Biographie des Nikolaus Basellius' *Zeitschrift für Württembergische Landesgeschichte* 21 (1962) 387–91 / Johann Heumann *Documenta literaria varii argumenti* (Altdorf 1758) 31–2 / St Fulgentius *Opera* ed W. Pirckheimer (Haguenau: Thomas Anshelm 1520) / BRE Epp 179, 207 / Johannes Trithemius *Opera historica* (Frankfurt 1601) II 527

KONRAD WIEDEMANN

Lucas BATHODIUS of Strasbourg, d 6 April 1554
Bathodius (properly Batodius from the Greek ἡ βάτος) was the Latin name used by Lukas

Hackfurt (Hugfordus). Born in Strasbourg in the last decade of the fifteenth century, Bathodius matriculated at Heidelberg in 1511, receiving his MA in 1513. He took holy orders, was appointed chaplain at Obernai (Oberehnheim), and also received a benefice in Strasbourg. An early convert to the Reformation movement, he renounced the priesthood, resigned his benefice, and opened a private school in Strasbourg in 1522. In 1525 he asked Erasmus to write a Latin textbook (Ep 1617).

Bathodius was acquainted with Erasmus as early as 1518 (Ep 883), and in 1523 Erasmus reported that he had seen Bathodius during his recent visit to Strasbourg (Ep 1342). In 1523, when a new system of poor relief was established, Bathodius was appointed welfare administrator for the city and served in this capacity until his death. The diary which he kept from 1524 to 1554 is an important source on welfare policy and legislation in the city and reflects the problems of providing for the poor and the religious refugees.

Bathodius was drawn to Anabaptism but formally renounced his ties to the movement before *Capito and *Bucer in 1531. He was awarded a benefice in the chapter of Alt St Peter in 1554 in recognition of his services to the city. His son, also called Lucas Bathodius, was a doctor and astrologer and an enthusiastic disciple of *Paracelsus.

BIBLIOGRAPHY: Allen Ep 883 / AK II Ep 775 / *Matrikel Heidelberg* I 480 / Johann Ficker and Otto Winckelmann *Handschriftproben des sechzehnten Jahrhunderts* (Strasbourg 1905) II 78 / Otto Winckelmann *Das Fürsorgewesen der Stadt Strassburg* (Leipzig 1922; large sections of Bathodius' diary are published in the document section) / Manfred Krebs and Hans Georg Rott *Elsass I, Stadt Strassburg 1522–1532* Quellen zur Geschichte der Täufer 7–8 (Gütersloh 1959–60) 334 / Miriam Usher Chrisman 'Urban poor in the sixteenth century, the case of Strasbourg' in *Social Groups and Religious Ideas in the Sixteenth Century* (Kalamazoo 1978) 59–67 / George H. Williams *The Radical Reformation* (Philadelphia 1962) 253

MIRIAM U. CHRISMAN

John BATMANSON d 16 November 1531
Batmanson (Bathmanson, Batemanson) may have been a son of John Batmanson, a Cambridge doctor of laws and a diplomat. He

was ordained deacon on 31 March 1510 by Bishop Richard *Fitzjames and by 1520 had joined the Carthusian order, apparently staying in London (Ep 1099). He was prior of the charterhouses of Hinton, Somerset, from 1523 and London from 1529. Erasmus claimed that Edward *Lee solicited Batmanson's support in his controversy with Erasmus; he certainly received it (Epp 1099, 1113). Erasmus referred to Batmanson as unlearned and boastful in the former letter and called him 'another Lee' in the latter. His works, none of which are known to exist in print or manuscript, included 'De unica Magdalena contra Fabrum Stapulensem' (which may be referred to in Ep 1113), 'Contra annotationes Erasmi Rotterdami,' and 'Contra quaedam scripta Martini Lutheri.'

David Knowles has identified Batmanson as the unnamed monk addressed in Thomas *More's famous letter of 1519/20 (Rogers Ep 83).

BIBLIOGRAPHY: CWE Ep 1099 / DNB I 1334–5 / E. Margaret Thompson *The Carthusian Order in England* (London 1930) 342–3 and passim / David Knowles *The Religious Orders in England* (Cambridge 1948–59) III 469 / St Thomas More *Selected Letters* ed E.F. Rogers (New Haven-London 1961) Ep 26 / Emden BRUC 44–5
CFG & PGB

Cornelis BATT of Bergen op Zoom, documented 1502–18

When Erasmus' old friend Jacob *Batt died prematurely in 1502, he was survived by Cornelis, a son, for whom Erasmus felt some responsibility. It seems that in 1514 they had met in London, where Erasmus had given Cornelis letters of introduction to Jan *Becker of Borssele and Adolph of *Burgundy (Ep 573). In April 1517 Cornelis wrote to Erasmus from Groningen (Ep 573), where he was teaching, both privately and in the seventh form of the public school (the first form being the highest). He was still at Groningen a year later when Erasmus recommended him to Marcus *Laurinus, dean of St Donatian at Bruges (Epp 839, 840).

Cornelis Batt may have been the author or translator of a cosmography, now lost. Allen wondered whether he could be the Cornelius who went to Rome in 1521 with letters of recommendation from Erasmus but on his way back was robbed and imprisoned by the French near Alessandria, finally returning to Brabant and Erasmus without the letters *Bombace and *Campeggi had given him in Rome (Ep 1236).

BIBLIOGRAPHY: Allen and CWE Ep 573 / A.A. Fokker *Levensberichten van Zeeuwsche medici* (Middelburg 1901) 6–7 / P.J. Meertens *Letterkundig leven in Zeeland* (Amsterdam 1943) 51
C.G. VAN LEIJENHORST

Jacob BATT of Bergen op Zoom, c 1466–1502

Jacob Batt was born around 1466 (ASD I-1 88) at Bergen op Zoom, or rather at the village of Bat(h), on the east point of Zuid-Beveland, not far from Bergen. After studying in Paris, probably in the faculty of arts, (ASD I-1 43, 107), he returned to his native country and was registered as a citizen of Bergen on 1 February 1494, a likely terminus post quem for his friendship with Erasmus, who was in the service of Hendrik van *Bergen at that time. Batt probably used his influence with the bishop to free Erasmus for study in Paris (Epp 42, 159). Erasmus made Batt the principal character of his revised *Antibarbari* (ASD I-1 38ff; CWE 23 16 ff), set at Halsteren, near Bergen, in the spring of 1495 (rather than 1494). Batt had recently been appointed town secretary (ASD I-1 40, 50), but after his return from Paris he had first become rector of the local municipal school, perhaps for two semesters (ASD I-1 51). According to the Bergen accounts of 1494–5, however, Batt did not serve his term as a secretary but must have resigned soon after his appointment. By 1496 he had left Bergen (Allen I Ep 38:4n), and by 1498 he had entered the service of Anna van *Borssele as tutor to her son, Adolph of *Burgundy, 'scarcely yet weaned' (Epp 93, 1005). As tutor he lived at the castle of Tournehem, where Erasmus visited him in February 1499 (Epp 80, 87) and July 1501, while working on his *Enchiridion* (Allen I 19). By the autumn of 1501 Batt was under pressure to leave his post (Ep 166), and when he died, before 2 July 1502 (Ep 170), Erasmus suggested it was by poison (cf Ep 172). Batt left a son, Cornelis *Batt.

In spite of occasional misunderstandings, especially in the period from December 1500 to March 1501 (Epp 139, 146, 148, 150), Jacob Batt was undoubtedly one of Erasmus' most faithful friends. Twenty of Erasmus' letters have survived (Epp 42, 80, 90, 91, 95, 101, 102, 119, 123, 124, 128–30, 133, 135, 138, 139, 146, 151, 163). Batt introduced Erasmus to Anna van Borssele, for some time his patroness, and her circle. Erasmus in turn acquainted Batt with Willem *Hermans (Epp 38, 92; *Antibarbari* ASD I-1 39) and William *Blount, Lord Mountjoy (Ep 120). On occasion Batt gave Erasmus financial support (Epp 138, 146, 148). Plans to live together at Louvain (Epp 95, 101) were never realized. Erasmus composed a short verse for Batt's *ex libris* and two epitaphs for him (Reedijk poems 61–3).

BIBLIOGRAPHY: Allen Ep 35 / C. Slootmans 'Erasmus en zijn vrienden uit Bergen op Zoom' *Taxandria* 35 (1928) 113–23 and NNBW VIII 57 / C.G. van Leijenhorst 'A note on the date of the "Antibarbari"' *Erasmus in English* 11 (1981–2) 7

C.G. VAN LEIJENHORST

Christoph BAUMGARTNER of Basel, d 4 August 1532
Baumgartner was a respected, well-to-do cloth merchant and a member of the 'Schlüssel' guild, said to be still 'young' at the time of his death. His residence was the house 'zum Eberstein' in the Freie Strasse at a location now occupied by the central post office.

Baumgartner was a member of the great council in 1519 and was one of the leaders of his guild and of Basel's military contingent dispatched for the so-called first Kappel war in June 1529. Under investigation in 1530 when he failed to partake of the Protestant Eucharist, he pleaded negligence and promised participation forthwith. At the time of his death he had several children from a previous marriage and a daughter aged four or five called Elisabeth after her mother, Elisabeth *David, Christoph's wife of seven years.

The tragic events culminating in Christoph's murder of his wife and daughter followed by his suicide on 4 August 1532 were widely noted and most points of Erasmus' account in Ep 2698 are confirmed by several chroniclers. The most detailed narrative in print is by Fridolin Ryff (*Basler Chroniken* I), who seemed to think that the wife was innocent, and indicated as one cause of the passionate drama the fact that Christoph and his servant were both involved with the same maid-servant.

BIBLIOGRAPHY: *Basler Chroniken* (Basel 1872–) I 140–2, IV 98–9, VI 161–3, 337–8 / *Aktensammlung zur Geschichte der Basler Reformation* ed E. Dürr et al (Basel 1921–50) III 546, IV 483 / Markus Lutz *Baslerisches Bürger-Buch* (Basel 1819) 47 / For minor references to Christoph and his estate: *Urkundenbuch der Stadt Basel* ed R. Wackernagel et al (Basel 1890–1910) X 20; *Aktensammlung* IV 253, VI 151, 228

PGB

Jakob BAUMGARTNER of Basel, documented 1511–38
Jakob, the brother of Christoph *Baumgartner, was a cloth merchant like Christoph, but he was more in the public eye than his brother and, in fact, was notorious for his merry and undisciplined way of life, which led him to participate in many brawls and to organize several mercenary expeditions. Without authorization he recruited soldiers in the territory of Basel, in 1521 for the pope and in 1526 for the king of France. In 1528 he was fined for a similar offence. His illicit activities notwithstanding, he commanded the small regular unit dispatched to Montbéliard in 1525.

Erasmus' references (Ep 2698) to Jakob's mental breakdown after tragedy struck Christoph's family in August 1532 are not repeated by the other printed sources. It may be noted, however, that in the spring of 1532 Jakob was unable to pay a large debt, so that the authorities took steps to liquidate his possessions. Jakob was married twice (to Scolastica Rul and Agnes Haller) and owned a house on the Kornmarkt.

BIBLIOGRAPHY: R. Wackernagel *Geschichte der Stadt Basel* (Basel 1907–54) III 294, 308–9, 408, 56* / *Basler Chroniken* (Basel 1872–) I 28–9 / *Urkundenbuch der Stadt Basel* ed R. Wackernagel et al (Basel 1890–1910) X 122, 153 / *Aktensammlung zur Geschichte der Basler Reformation* ed E. Dürr et al (Basel 1921–50) II 76, 368, III 110

PGB

BAUMGARTNER *See also* PAUMGARTNER

Ernest, duke of BAVARIA 13 June 1500–7 December 1560
Ernest, the third and most gifted son of duke Albert IV of Bavaria and Kunigunde, a

Ernest, duke of Bavaria, engraving by
J.A. Zimmermann

daughter of the Emperor *Frederick III, received his early education from Johannes *Aventinus, who was his tutor from 1508 on and accompanied him to Italy in 1515 where Ernest attended lectures at Pavia. Subsequently he also visited Paris and Saxony. In 1515 he matriculated at the University of Ingolstadt; he became rector in 1516 and together with Aventinus inaugurated a literary society. He also became coadjutor and in November 1516 administrator of the see of Passau (until 1540). After some initial hesitation, Ernest emerged a firm adherent of the Catholic faith and in 1524 joined in a league with his neighbours to enforce the edict of Worms in southern Germany. He was present at the diets of Augsburg in 1530 and Regensburg in 1532 and administered his territories in the spirit of Catholic reform. In 1540 he became administrator of Salzburg in succession to Matthäus *Lang but resigned in 1554 because he did not want to take the higher orders. He retired to Hallein and later to the county of Glatz, which he had acquired in 1549, devoting himself to the study of mathematics and astronomy.

In 1516 Ernest of Bavaria invited Erasmus to accept a chair at the University of Ingolstadt (Ep 386) with a generous salary (Ep 413), but Erasmus had to decline (Epp 392, 394) since he was attached to the service of the future *Charles v. In 1517 Erasmus dedicated an edition of Quintus Curtius' history of Alexander the Great to Ernest of Bavaria (Ep 704, cf Ep 844), and later they exchanged greetings through Rudbert von *Mosham (Epp 1450, 1512).

BIBLIOGRAPHY: Allen and CWE Ep 386 / NDB IV 619 / ADB VI 249–50 / Max Spindler *Handbuch der Bayerischen Geschichte* (Munich 1967–75) II passim / Gerald Strauss *Historian in an Age of Crisis: The Life and Work of Johannes Aventinus* (Cambridge, Mass, 1963) 48, 54, 64–8, 253, and passim

IG

Henry of BAVARIA *See Henry, count*
PALATINE

Louis, duke of BAVARIA 18 September 1495–22 April 1545
Louis, the second son of Duke Albert IV of Bavaria and Kunigunde of Austria, received his education from Johannes *Aventinus, together with Ernest of *Bavaria. In spite of the law of primogeniture introduced by Albert IV to ensure the unity of Bavarian lands, Louis succeeded in becoming co-regent with his older brother, William IV of *Bavaria (1514), and governed the districts of Landshut and Straubing from his residence at Landshut. He hoped to marry into a wealthy house of princely status to further his hopes for power and influence, but his plans did not materialize. Christopher of *Württemberg received refuge and help from him and William IV in 1532 when he fled from the emperor's court in Innsbruck to Landshut. Louis is mentioned in Ep 2947 as one of the participants of the peace of Kadan leading to the restoration of Christopher's father, duke Ulrich of *Württemberg in 1534, and in Ep 2993 with William IV as a signatory of the treaty of Donauwörth.

BIBLIOGRAPHY: Allen Ep 2947 / ADB XIX 513–16 / Sigmund von Riezler *Geschichte Baierns* 3rd ed (Aalen 1964) IV passim / Max Spindler *Handbuch der Bayerischen Geschichte* (Munich 1967–75) II passim / Gerald Strauss *Historian in an Age of*

Crisis: The Life and Work of Johannes Aventinus
(Cambridge, Mass, 1963) 48 and passim

IG

William IV, duke of BAVARIA 13 November
1493–6 March 1550
William, the eldest son of duke Albert IV of
Bavaria and Kunigunde of Austria, had
Leonhard von *Eck as his tutor and became
duke on 18 March 1508. He married Jakobäa
von Baden on 5 October 1522. In 1515 his sister
Sabina, who was married to Duke Ulrich of
*Württemberg, fled to him because her
marriage had failed. William commanded the
army of the Swabian League that defeated
Ulrich in 1519. A staunch adherent of the
Catholic faith (Epp 1258, 2437), he prevented
the spread of the Protestant reform in Bavaria.
In 1534 he supported his nephew, Christopher
of *Württemberg, in his claims to the duchy of
Württemberg (Ep 2917).

Duke William is mentioned in the correspondence of Erasmus as having offered to Matthias
*Kretz a position as a preacher in Munich
which Kretz later accepted (Ep 2430) and,
together with Duke Louis of *Bavaria, as
accepting financial assistance from *Francis I
(Ep 2937). In Ep 2993 he is associated with the
treaty of Donauwörth (31 January 1535), which
followed the model of the earlier Swabian
League and sealed the reconciliation between
Bavaria and the Hapsburgs. Erasmus requested Leonhard von Eck to obtain the duke's
permission to print a work by Johannes
*Aventinus at Basel (Ep 3030).

BIBLIOGRAPHY: Allen Ep 1258 / Sigmund von
Riezler in ADB XLII 705–17 / Sigmund von
Riezler *Geschichte Baierns* 3rd ed (Aalen 1964) IV
passim / Max Spindler *Handbuch der Bayerischen
Geschichte* (Munich 1967–75) II passim / Gerald
Strauss *Historian in an Age of Crisis: The Life and
Work of Johannes Aventinus* (Cambridge, Mass,
1963) 48 and passim

IG

BAVENTIUS (Ep 1407 of 1 January 1524)
Baventius studied in Paris in the colleges of
Harcourt and Lisieux. Nothing is known about
him except that he edited a small volume of
*Epigrammata ... ex optimis quibusque authoribus
selecta* (Paris: J. Bade Easter 1523) and was
mentioned by Jean *Lange among the defend-

William IV, duke of Bavaria by Barthel Beham

ers of Erasmus in Paris (Ep 1407). Conceivably
he might have been a native of Bavent,
Département Calvados, arrondissement de
Caen, canton de Troarn.

BIBLIOGRAPHY: Allen Ep 1407 / *Index Aureliensis* (Baden-Baden 1962–   ) III 354

MICHEL REULOS

Christian BAYER *See Christian* BEYER

BAYEZID II Ottoman sultan, d 26 May 1512
Bayezid (Pazaites) was born in December 1447
or January 1448. During the lifetime of his
father, *Mehmed II, he was the governor of the
province of Rum, residing at Amasya. On the
death of Mehmet II in 1481 a conflict broke out
between Bayezid and his younger brother,
*Djem. The support of the janissaries and of a
powerful faction amongst the great officials at
the Porte ensured Bayezid's succession, while
Djem was eventually forced to take refuge at
Rhodes with the knights of St John.

In 1483 Bayezid completed the subjugation
of Herzegowina. In the following year the
fortresses of Kilia in the Danube estuary and
Belgorod (Akkerman) were taken, thus giving

the Ottomans control of the land route to the
Crimea; only in the war of 1485–91 against the
Mamelukes in Egypt were they unsuccessful.
In a series of campaigns between 1492 and 1495
the Ottomans pushed across the Danube and
the Sava, suffering defeat in 1492 near Villach
in Carinthia, but decisively defeating the Croat
forces at Adbina in 1493. In the latter part of the
1490s the centre of hostilities shifted from
Hungary to Poland, as the Poles attempted to
secure access to the Black Sea by subjugating
Moldavia. The Moldavians appealed to
Bayezid for support, and their joint forces
defeated the Poles near Suceava and at Koźmin
in October 1497. After a truce with Poland in
1499, Bayezid turned his attention to Venice.
He fought the Venetians all the way from the
Peloponnese (Morea) to Friuli, and the war
ended in complete victory for the Ottomans. It
demonstrated the effectiveness of Bayezid's
military and naval preparations and marked
the emergence of the Ottomans as a formidable
sea-power. Navpaktos (Lepanto) fell to the
Ottomans in 1499, Koroni (Coron) and Pylos
(Navarino) in 1500 and Durres (Durazzo) in
1501, and all were ceded by Venice in the peace
of 1503. Erasmus summarized Bayezid's military exploits in De bello turcico (LB V 351–2).

The emergence of Safavid power in Persia
and eastern Anatolia posed a grave religious
and political danger to the Ottomans. In 1502
Bayezid took the precaution of deporting
numerous Shiite subjects to the Morea; yet in
1511 a great revolt in the region of Tekke in
Asia Minor led by Shah Kuli resulted in much
death and destruction before it was suppressed.

As Bayezid grew older there developed a
struggle for the throne amongst his sons, the
main contenders being Ahmed and *Selim.
Bayezid himself and the grand vizier, Ali
Pasha, both favoured Ahmed. As there was no
formal rule of succession, the prince who was
the first to reach Istanbul after the death of
Bayezid was virtually certain to secure the
throne. In 1510 Selim sailed from Trebizond to
Feodosiya (Kaffa, on the Crimea) and thence
moved across the Danube, demanding the
government of a province in the Balkans so as
to be nearer to Istanbul. Bayezid conferred on
him the province of Semendria, but the
apprehension that Ali Pasha might attempt to

raise Ahmed to the throne induced Selim to
march on Edirne. He was defeated and obliged
to seek refuge in the Crimea. Then Ahmed
advanced towards Istanbul, but the hostility of
the janissaries drove him into rebellion, and
this together with the fear that he might form
an alliance with Shiite Persia strengthened the
position of Selim, who now made a new bid to
secure the throne. With the support of the
janissaries, Selim obliged Bayezid to abdicate
on 24 April 1512. Bayezid decided to retire to
Didymoteikhon (Demotika) but died while
travelling to his destination.

BIBLIOGRAPHY: M. Süreyya Sicill-i Osmânî
(Istanbul 1890–7) / I.H. Uzunçarşili in Islam
Ansiklopedisi (Istanbul 1940–   ) II 392–8 / V.J.
Parry in Encyclopaedia of Islam new ed
(Leiden-London 1960–   ) I 1119–21 / The best
account is S. Tansel Sultan II. Bayezid'in Siyasî
Hayati (Istanbul 1966)

FEHMI ISMAIL

Lazarus BAYFIUS See Lazare de BAÏF

BEATUS Rhenanus of Sélestat, 22 August
1485–20 July 1547
Beatus Rhenanus (Rinower, properly Bild) was
born in Sélestat, Upper Alsace, the third son of
Anton *Bild and Barbara Kegel. Barbara's
brother, Reinhard Kegel, was a priest, and
when he died in 1519 Beatus was his heir. After
the early death of his mother and, it would
seem, his two brothers, Beatus grew up in the
care of his father and an elderly housekeeper.
In the famous Latin school of his native town
he was taught by Crato Hofmann and
Hieronymus *Gebwiler. His school work is
reflected by a notebook, still extant, which
Beatus kept at the age of thirteen or fourteen.
Soon Gebwiler came to rely on him to instruct
his younger pupils, one of whom, Johannes
*Sapidus, later recalled Beatus' lessons – and
his cane (BRE 3). His father persistently
encouraged him to become a scholar and in
1501 provided him with the means to buy his
first books.

In May 1503 Beatus went to Paris to study
the quadrivium. Among his teachers were
Fausto *Andrelini, Josse *Clichtove, Jacques
*Lefèvre d'Etaples, and Georgius *Hermony-
mus. The instruction he received was based
on Aristotle and was not well suited to

encourage the humanistic and historical
interests which were later to dominate his
scholarly work, although his textbooks and
notebooks reveal that Lefèvre had considerable influence on him. In 1505 he is mentioned
as one of the correctors in a volume of works by
Ramón Lull, edited by Lefèvre and published
by Jean *Petit (Rice Ep 45) – the earliest
reference of this kind – while in 1506 and 1507
he was permitted to contribute some introductory verse to books printed by Henri Estienne
(BRE 592–3). From an important letter to
*Reuchlin (BRE Ep 11) we know that by the age
of twenty Beatus had shown himself worthy of
the personal confidence of Lefèvre. In Paris
Beatus also came to form a lifelong friendship
with his fellow student Michael *Hummelberg;
it can further be assumed that he maintained
contact with Bruno and Basilius *Amerbach.

   From the time of his return from Paris in the
autumn of 1507 Beatus led the life of an
independent scholar; for the first twenty years
Basel was the centre of his activities, while
from 1527 to his death in 1547 he lived in his
native Sélestat. His earlier and more lively
years were devoted to philological and
editorial work amid the humanist circles of the
Upper Rhine. His adherence to the literary
society of Strasbourg (Ep 302) was somewhat
marginal, but among the printing firms of Basel
he quickly secured a privileged position, and
he moved frequently back and forth between
Sélestat, Strasbourg, and Basel where he
eventually came to spend most of his time. It
was, however, in Sélestat that he began his
career as an editor, collaborating with his
compatriot Matthias *Schürer to produce an
edition of Andrelini (Strasbourg 1508). In 1509
he spent a good deal of time at Strasbourg but
also visited Mainz to see the famous collection
of antiquities gathered by Gresamundus.
During the summer of 1510 at Sélestat he wrote
his life of Johann Geiler von Kaysersberg. He
was eager to master Greek, and the presence at
Basel of the distinguished Greek scholar
Johannes *Cono induced him to move to that
city in 1511. By the time Cono died in 1513
Beatus had become his close friend. A year
later Erasmus arrived in Basel, and soon a
relationship developed between them that was
bound to intensify Beatus' contacts with the
press of Johann *Froben that had been initiated

Beatus Rhenanus

earlier by Cono. Until 1519 Beatus appears to
have lived in Froben's house. As a result he
could hardly fail to form connections with such
men as Ludwig *Baer, *Cantiuncula, *Zasius,
*Glareanus, Wilhelm *Nesen, and Nikolaus
Briefer (BRE 6). The first Froben edition seen
through the press by Beatus was Paolo
*Cortesi's *Sententiarum libri quattuor* (1513),
which contained a dedicatory letter from
Konrad *Peutinger to Beatus and a preface by
the latter (BRE Epp 33, 35). From the following
year dates his first edition of Pliny's letters
(Strasbourg: M. Schürer). His first major
contribution to classical scholarship was his
commentary to Seneca's *Ludus* (Basel: J. Froben
1515); this had been suggested by Erasmus,
and it permitted Beatus to make considerable
use of his knowledge of Greek. It may also have
been Erasmus who drew his attention to
Platonic philosophy and inspired him to
prepare an edition of Maximus Tyrius (Basel: J.
Froben 1519), among others. When Erasmus
returned to the Netherlands Beatus was
empowered to act on his behalf in editorial as
well as in personal matters. Working so closely
with Erasmus was bound to set back his own

scholarly enterprises, but at the same time it enhanced his prestige. Erasmus instructed Froben to refer all matters to Beatus, and Bonifacius *Amerbach advised the printer Andreas *Cratander to do likewise (Ep 885; AK II Epp 604, 766). Among the many scholars to show great admiration for Beatus was Zasius (AK Ep 659), who was known for his critical judgments.

Not later than 1519 Beatus moved to a house of his own located on the Rosenberg in Klein-Basel. He was joined by his famulus Albert Burer, who also took care of Beatus' affairs during his many absences. He visited Sélestat frequently, for instance in 1519 when the plague caused him to leave Basel, and in 1520 when his father died. On Erasmus' suggestion he edited Tertullian (Basel: J. Froben 1521) as his last major contribution to patristic studies. His earliest historical work of note had already appeared: in 1520 he published the first edition of Velleius Paterculus' Roman history, prepared on the basis of a manuscript (now missing) which he had discovered in the abbey of Murbach. The series of editions of ancient texts which he had merely seen through the press came to an end with Froben's *Autores historiae ecclesiasticae* of 1523, and from that point on his scholarly interests centred on history.

By 1527 Beatus left Basel for good and, accompanied by his famulus Rudolf Berz, settled in Sélestat. His first biographer, Johann Sturm, attributed the move to his pacific nature, which could no longer cope with the growing religious strife at Basel, and consequently stressed the philosophical bent of the last two decades of his life, spent in his family home in the company of his famulus and a maid. A privilege from *Charles v freed him from all civic duties. Among the Sélestat humanists he was the recognized master; he also composed a number of Latin inscriptions for public display which caused Sélestat to resemble a Roman town.

Beatus' attitude towards the Reformation was dictated by his desire to avoid identification with any religious or political faction. At least in his heart, however, he favoured the evangelical teachings and probably took an active part in the preparation of the famous first collection of *Luther's Latin writings. On

this point the statements of Erasmus himself (Epp 967, 1526) and of his contemporaries Caspar *Hedio and Johann Sturm deserve credence in spite of Beatus' harsh condemnation of the peasant rebellion (BRE Ep 240), which caused Adalbert Horawitz and subsequent modern biographers to rank him among the opponents of reform. It would seem, however, that his life in Sélestat required a degree of accomodation with the Catholic rites prevailing in that city after his earlier manifestations of sympathy with the reformers. Beatus' qualified and cautious support of the Reformation is strongly reminiscent of the attitude of Bonifacius Amerbach. The two Erasmians corresponded frequently with one another, paying close attention to the religious and political developments from 1530 onwards. Beatus' messages to Amerbach from the time of the colloquy of Regensburg (1541) appear to confirm that by then he counted himself among the evangelicals (AK v Ep 2442). Finally, three Strasbourg ministers attended him on his deathbed.

During the last twenty years of his life Beatus established his reputation as a leading German historian. In 1526 he edited and annotated for Froben's press a Pliny, which he dedicated to Jan *Łaski (BRE Ep 252). In 1530 he undertook his last major journey, visiting Augsburg in the year of the diet; this visit permitted him to examine Peutinger's famous road atlas of the Roman Empire and also the art collection of the Fugger family. In the following year he was ready to present to the public his *Rerum germanicarum libri tres* (Basel: H. Froben 1531), intending them as an homage to King *Ferdinand, to whom they were dedicated (BRE Ep 273), but also as a challenge to other German historians. His *magnum opus* was followed by his Froben editions of Tacitus (1533) and Livy (1535). Apart from these the flow of significant publications halted during the last twelve years of his life. He was then preparing a sequel to his *Res germanicae* despite deteriorating health. After 1540 he apparently planned to marry one Anna Braun, a widowed niece of his famulus Berz; he made some pledge to her but matters did not proceed beyond that. (After his death, the inadequacy of his will led to lengthy litigation over the respective claims of Anna and Berz.) In the spring of 1547

Beatus' bladder troubles intensified and caused him to seek relief in the spa of Wildbad in the Black Forest. The waters failed to help, however, and on his way home to Sélestat he died at Strasbourg.

Turning to Beatus' relations with Erasmus, it may be noted that they could have met each other for the first time in Paris during the years 1504–6; no personal contacts are recorded, however, although both concurred later in their unfavourable opinion of Hermonymus' talents as a teacher of Greek (Allen I 7; BRE Ep 11). Their personal acquaintance may well have dated from Erasmus' arrival at Basel in August 1514 (BRE Ep 40). *Wimpfeling introduced Beatus in his formal letter to Erasmus on behalf of the Strasbourg literary society, and the latter did not fail to praise him in his reply (Epp 302, 305). Soon he was one of Erasmus' most esteemed friends, and in 1515 Erasmus dedicated to him his commentary on the first psalm (Epp 326B, 327); to Pirckheimer Erasmus wrote: 'Beatus Rhenanus ... is a friend after Pythagoras' own heart, that is, one soul with me' (Ep 362). Beatus in turn had mentioned Erasmus for the first time in a letter of 1512 to Lefèvre d'Etaples (BRE Ep 24); in fact he seems to have transferred to Erasmus the fervent admiration (BRE Ep 132) which he had earlier reserved for Lefèvre, referring to Erasmus repeatedly as his 'pater et praeceptor' (Ep 556; Ep 63 and passim). From 1515 Beatus was regularly empowered to act in Erasmus' name when the latter was absent from Basel. In August 1517 Erasmus assured Bishop Christoph von *Utenheim that any favour shown to Beatus was valued by Erasmus as a favour shown to himself (Ep 625), and similar formulas occur repeatedly thereafter. In October 1517 Erasmus' famous description of his journey back to Louvain and his ensuing illness was appropriately addressed to Beatus (Ep 867), who is frequently praised in letters to illustrious correspondents (Epp 869, 874, 1342). The true measure of Erasmus' esteem may be found in his admonitions to Froben, who did not always rely on Beatus to the degree Erasmus would have wished (Ep 885; cf CWE Ep 594 introduction). Beatus' services were so invaluable that his rash action in the case of a dedicatory letter was not met with the kind of resentment Erasmus might have shown

to another (Ep 976). Whenever Froben published a work by Erasmus Beatus normally did some measure of editing; in particular he looked after Froben's editions of the *Moria*, the *Colloquia*, and consecutive collections of Erasmus' correspondence (CWE 3 349–53). In short he acted as Erasmus' *alter ego* (Ep 1206). In 1521 Erasmus, who was on his way to Basel, called on him at Sélestat (Epp 1302, 1342), where Beatus later installed a stained-glass window in the parish church in his memory (1537, AK V Ep 2151). Together they travelled to Basel, while their subsequent joint visit to Johann von *Botzheim at Constance prompted Erasmus to sketch Beatus in a most attractive fashion in a letter to Konrad *Heresbach (Ep 1316). No finer literary portrait of Beatus exists; he is described as witty, always good-humoured, and in short the most endearing of friends.

From 1525 on Beatus' emergence as a classical scholar and historian in his own right tended to loosen somewhat his attachment to Erasmus. In that year Erasmus noted that he had no time to share Beatus' indulgence in antiquarian topics (Ep 1635) and a year later he mentioned Beatus' work on Pliny in slightly contemptuous terms: 'Nescio quid annotatiuncularum in Plinium' (Ep 1674). In 1528 Beatus and Amerbach took on the unpleasant task of arbitrating Erasmus' quarrel with *Eppendorf, and their judgment largely vindicated the latter (Epp 1933, 1937). Erasmus consulted Beatus on whether he should mention him in his *Ciceronianus*, and they eventually agreed that he should not (Epp 2008, 2305, 2446). In 1529 Beatus agreed to accompany the Basel burgomaster, Jakob *Meyer zum Hirzen, on a mission to Erasmus, but they failed to persuade him to delay his departure for Freiburg (Ep 2158). *Herwagen's Seneca of 1529 is the last edition jointly undertaken by Erasmus and Beatus. There is no evidence that they corresponded with each other after 1529, but they kept in touch through common friends. It is not known what Erasmus thought about the *Res germanicae*, but in each of his three wills Beatus figures among his closest friends.

After Erasmus' death Beatus wrote the earliest authoritative life of his friend (Allen I 53–71); dedicated to Charles V, it was published with Erasmus' translations from

Origen in 1536 and again as preface to the collected works of Erasmus published in 1540. In view of the static character of their later relationship, it is hardly surprising that Beatus' life fails to express Erasmus' historical significance in a way that would today be considered appropriate. Beatus' text may have been worked over by Bonifacius Amerbach; in any event it does not bring to life the intimacy between its author and its subject in the early years. Although Beatus offers some passages of lively biographical narrative, he does no more than touch upon Erasmus' literary work. Erasmus is presented as the apostle of nordic humanism, well aware of the need to reach broad sections of the population; he is praised, moreover, as a courageous critic of religious abuses and of the self-seeking greed of princes, and finally as a faithful friend.

Beatus' philological and historical achievements were outstanding. Since no less than half of his life's work was devoted to the emendation of classical texts, he came to develop a secure understanding of textual criticism as well as to reject roundly the fabrications and excessive rhetoric of some other humanists (BRE Epp 243, 273). Considering himself unprejudiced he wished to stand apart from the 'vulgus historicorum' whose accounts tended to be either compiled or invented; cf Res germanicae (Basel 1531) 40, 124. His own style is concise and lively. He discussed the authenticity, or lack thereof, of his texts with great enthusiasm. As a historian he emphasized the existence of a 'media antiquitas' between the classical and modern ages, thus forming a notion which helped to bring about that of the 'Middle Ages' (Joachimsen Geschichtsauffassung 127). In like manner he prepared the way for the historical notion that a nation might migrate and eventually disappear. He went beyond classical authors by including in his notion of historical sources such fields as archaeology, philology, and even local history and folklore. Joachimsen emphasizes several significantly Erasmian aspects of Beatus' historiography, such as his lack of enthusiasm for military exploits and the forging of empires, his eye for the interaction between culture and peace on the one hand and culture and religion on the other, and finally his consistent preference for

the sources of late antiquity and early Christendom over the monastic chronicles.

Beatus was not a German historian after the heart of patriotic humanists. Dispassionate and aloof from all hero-worship, he felt no need to idealize the Germanic nation, and in general he had no use for panegyrics and polemics in the humanist fashion. Of the historians of his own day perhaps only *Aventinus met with his approval. His passion for linguistics may have led him to propose many unscientific etymologies, but on the other hand he was the first historian to quote a source in old German (Res germanicae 107, citing the Otfried). There were plans for both a continuation and a German translation of the Res germanicae, but neither was carried out; as a result the popular appeal of Beatus' magnum opus remained limited, with the last edition appearing in 1693. Thereafter two remarkable Alsatians, Johann Daniel Schoepflin and Philippe Grandidier are credited with having saved his fine library and his letters and papers. The first efforts to preserve what is today the jewel of Sélestat and a prime historical monument of Alsace date from 1754. Comprising 761 volumes containing more than a thousand works spread over all disciplines, it is an almost unique example of the fully preserved library of a noted humanist – and of one who was a scholar rather than a collector, as is indicated by the multitude of Beatus' marginal notes. Beatus' funeral inscription is lost, and the only preserved portrait is a woodcut in the collection of Nikolaus Reusner (Strasbourg 1587; reproduced in CWE 5 3).

Surprisingly one must go back to the sixteenth century for the only effort ever made to analyse Beatus' character. In the pedestrian fashion of a schoolmaster, his first biographer, Johann Sturm, dwelt comfortably on Beatus' moral qualities, material existence, and religious convictions as well as his medical and social problems. His solitary and celibate way of life was bound to pose problems of comprehension for his contemporaries and even more so for the puritanical mind of the following generation, to which Sturm belonged. The same is true of his abhorrence of all religious zeal. It is evident, nevertheless, that his appealing and conciliatory nature was sufficient to protect him from controversies and violent attacks. More recent biographies are characterized by a steadily increasing measure of uncritical glorification.

BIBLIOGRAPHY: Allen Ep 327 / ADB XXVIII 383–6 / NDB I 682–3 / AK I Ep 470 and passim / Rice *Prefatory Epistles* Epp 67, 87, and passim / Johann Sturm 'Beati Rhenani vita' in Beatus Rhenanus *Rerum Germanicarum libri III* (Basel 1551, repr in BRE) / J.D. Schoepflin *Alsatia illustrata* (Colmar 1751–61) / Jacob Maehly 'Beatus Rhenanus' *Alsatia* (1856–7) 201–61 / J. Rathgeber 'Beatus Rhenanus' *Revue d'Alsace* n s 1 (1872) 384–97 / A. Horawitz 'Beatus Rhenanus: Ein biographischer Versuch' *Sitzungsberichte der [Wiener] Akademie der Wissenschaften, Phil.-Hist. Klasse* 70 (1872) 189–244 / A. Horawitz 'Des Beatus Rhenanus literarische Tätigkeit' *Sitzungsberichte der [Wiener] Akademie der Wissenschaften, Phil.-Hist. Klasse* 71 (1872) 643–90 and 72 (1872) 323–76 / A. Horawitz 'Die Bibliothek und Correspondenz des Beatus Rhenanus zu Schlettstadt' *Sitzungsberichte der [Wiener] Akademie der Wissenschaften, Phil.-Hist. Klasse* 78 (1874) 313–40 / Gustav Knod 'Zur Biographie und Bibliographie des Beatus Rhenanus' *Centralblatt für Bibliothekswesen* 2 (1885) 253–76 and 3 (1886) 265–74 / Gustav Knod 'Aus der Bibliothek des Beatus Rhenanus' in *Die Stadtbibliothek zu Schlettstadt* ed J. Gény and G. Knod (Strasbourg 1889) / *Der Briefwechsel des Beatus Rhenanus* ed A. Horawitz and K. Hartfelder (Leipzig 1886, repr 1966); cf review by G. Knod in *Centralblatt für Bibliothekswesen* 4 (1887) 305–15 / Max Lenz *Geschichtsschreibung und Geschichtsauffassung im Elsass zur Zeit der Reformation* (Halle 1895) passim / W. Teichmann 'Die kirchliche Haltung des Beatus Rhenanus' *Zeitschrift für Kirchengeschichte* 26 (1905) 363–81 / Paul Joachimsen *Geschichtsauffassung und Geschichtsschreibung in Deutschland unter dem Einfluss des Humanismus* (Leipzig 1910) passim / K. Stenzel 'Beatus Rhenanus und Johann von Botzheim' *Zeitschrift für Geschichte des Oberrheins* 68 (1914) 120–9 / H. Kaiser 'Aus den letzten Jahren des Beatus Rhenanus' *Zeitschrift für Geschichte des Oberrheins* 70 (1916) 30–52 / Rudolf Wackernagel *Geschichte der Stadt Basel* (Basel 1907–54) III passim / Eduard Fueter *Geschichte der neueren Historiographie* 3rd ed (Munich 1936) 190–2 / A. Hartmann 'Beatus Rhenanus: Leben und Werke des Erasmus' in *Gedenkschrift zum 400.*

Todestage des Erasmus von Rotterdam (Basel 1936) 11–24 / Joseph Walter *Hommage à Beatus Rhenanus à l'occasion du quatrième centenaire de sa mort* (Sélestat 1948) / Paul Adam *L'Humanisme à Sélestat: L'école, les humanistes, la bibliothèque* 2nd ed (Sélestat 1967) / Paul Adam 'Le 420e anniversaire de la mort de Beatus Rhenanus' *Annuaire de la Société des Amis de la Bibliothèque de Sélestat* 17 (1967) 150–7 / *Wimpfeling und Rhenanus: Das Leben des Johann Geiler von Kaysersberg* ed O. Herding with D. Mertens (Munich 1970) / H. Meyer 'Beatus Rhenanus et sa bibliothèque' *Librarium* (1976) 21–31 / G. Von der Gönna 'Beatus Rhenanus und die Editio princeps des Velleius Paterculus' *Würzburger Jahrbücher für Altertumswissenschaft* Neue Folge 3 (1977) 231–42 / F.L. Borchardt *German Antiquity in Renaissance Myth* (Baltimore 1971) 155–7 / Gerald Strauss *Sixteenth Century Germany: Its Topography and Topographers* (Madison 1959) 42–4 / Henri Meylan 'Beatus Rhenanus et la propagande des écrits luthériens' *Colloquia Erasmiana Turonensia* II 859–65

BEAT VON SCARPATETTI

Margaret BEAUFORT countess of Richmond and Derby, 31 May 1443–29 June 1509
The Lady Margaret was the daughter and heiress of John Beaufort, duke of Somerset, and thus a descendant of Edward III in a bastard line. She was brought up by her mother, the heiress of Lord Beauchamp of Bletsoe, learning French and a little Latin. As a child she was nominally married to the heir of the duke of Suffolk, but Henry VI intervened and made her the wife of his half-brother Edmund Tudor, earl of Richmond (the son of Henry V's widow) in 1455. Edmund died the following year, leaving Margaret carrying the future *Henry VII, who was born posthumously in January 1457. Within three years Margaret had taken as her husband Henry Stafford, second son of the first duke of Buckingham. During the civil war she retired to Pembroke Castle, returning to court during Henry VI's brief restoration in 1470. The death of the king and his son in 1471 made Margaret's son, the young earl of Richmond, the Lancastrian heir, and he was sent to Brittany for safety. Stafford also died in this year, and by 1473 Margaret had made her last marriage, to Thomas, Lord Stanley. He was briefly

Lady Margaret Beaufort

she was said to dominate the new queen, *Elizabeth of York. Later she presided over the royal nursery, bringing John *Skelton and William Hone from Cambridge as tutors for the future *Henry VIII and Princess *Mary. But Lady Margaret's appearances were mainly confined to ceremonial and family occasions, since she preferred to devote her time to the spiritual and educational concerns for which she remains celebrated.

As early as 1464 Margaret had been admitted to the fraternity of Crowland Abbey, and long before her last husband's death in July 1504 she had separated from him and taken a vow of chastity. On 1 March 1497 she endowed a perpetual chantry in Wimborne Minster, where her parents were buried. On the same day she was given licence to found a chantry in St George's Chapel, Windsor, and to endow lectureships in her name at Oxford and Cambridge, each worth twenty pounds a year. For some reason the Windsor scheme was abandoned in 1499 and the endowments transferred to Westminster Abbey. A daily mass had been said there for her since 1496, and over the subsequent twenty years her substantial benefactions, together with those of the king, secured the abbey from the effects of the growing inflation. But John *Fisher, whom Margaret probably met for the first time in 1495 when he was senior proctor of Cambridge University and who became her chaplain, confessor, agent, and executor, persuaded her to use her bounty in a way which would combine chantry prayers with the stimulation of learning and, in particular, the training of a learned preaching ministry. In February 1504 she was licensed to endow a preachership based at Cambridge, and by agreement with the abbot and convent of Westminster on 2 March 1506 the payment of the preacher and of the two university lecturers was to be discharged by the abbey in return for her grants of land worth eighty-seven pounds a year. The elaborate chantry arrangements were finalized at the same time. Fisher had, from 1502, been the first holder of the Cambridge chair, and his successor from 1511 to 1514 was Erasmus (Ep 245). The Lady Margaret's preacher was required to deliver sermons in London and in various parts of East Anglia; he was to be an unbeneficed divine,

imprisoned in 1483 but was released to be high steward at Richard III's coronation, when Margaret bore the queen's train. Her reconciliation with the Yorkists was temporary, for in 1484 she was deeply involved in the abortive rebellion of her nephew, the second duke of Buckingham; her agent was her chaplain, Christopher *Urswick, a friend of Erasmus. As a result her lands were forfeited to her husband, who was too powerful for Richard III to alienate with stronger measures. Yet it was Stanley's treachery on Bosworth Field which gave the crown to Henry Tudor in 1485; on 27 October Stanley himself received the earldom of Derby.

There was no question of Margaret becoming queen regnant, but she was naturally restored to her honours and received many further grants of land. She was also given custody of the lands of her son Edward *Stafford, third duke of Buckingham, which she administered with ability. The Spanish ambassador claimed in 1497 that she was among the most influential members of the English court; her son seems to have taken her advice on some episcopal appointments, and preferably a fellow of Christ's College. This, the first of two colleges which Margaret established at Cambridge, was begun in 1505 and received its statutes the following year. The larger foundation of St John's was incomplete at the time of Margaret's death, and Fisher had to struggle (with only partial success) to secure the funds left for its endowment; the college finally opened in 1516 (cf Ep 432). Margaret also patronized Bishop William Smith of Lincoln, the founder of Brasenose College, Oxford (1509), and Bishop Hugh Oldham of Exeter, who was to help found Corpus Christi College there in 1517.

Margaret encouraged the first English printers; Caxton issued a work at her request in 1489 (STC 3124), and in 1494 Wynkyn de Worde produced for her a translation of Hylton's *Scala perfectionis* (STC 14042). At her suggestion Fisher wrote a treatise on the penitential Psalms (STC 10902). Margaret herself translated from the French the fourth book of Atkinson's version of the *Imitatio Christi* (1503, 1504?: STC 23954.7, 23955), and in about 1506 another translation of hers appeared, *The mirroure of golde for the synfull soule*, which was reprinted several times (STC 6894.5, 6895–8). Her English renderings have been commended for their skill and directness. Margaret's literary interests were not exclusively religious; we hear of a poet in her entourage in 1497, and she may have had a hand in a treatise on apparel. Among her secular protégés was William *Blount, Lord Mountjoy, who later recalled the cheerfulness and devotion of her household. In view of her matriarchal position in English humanism it is perhaps surprising to learn little of her from Erasmus' pen; he praised her in Ep 3036 and in *Vidua christiana* extolled her as the ideal of widowhood (LB V 755E-F).

Margaret Beaufort died in the abbot's house at Westminster, outliving her son by three months. She was buried in the south aisle of Henry VII's chapel, on which occasion twenty pounds was taken in alms. A splendid tomb was erected, the figure carved by Pietro Torrigiani and the inscription composed by Erasmus (Cooper *Memoir* 124), for which he was paid twenty shillings. She left books to Westminster, Durham, and other monasteries. What influence she might have had in her grandson's reign is hard to guess; it is said that she chose Henry VIII's first ministers and commended him to the counsel of Bishop Fisher.

BIBLIOGRAPHY: DNB II 48–9 / G.E. C[okayne] *The Complete Peerage* ed V. Gibbs et al (London 1910–59) IV 207 x 825–7 XII-1 40–1, 46–8 / C.H. Cooper *Memoir of Lady Margaret, Countess of Richmond and Derby* ed J.E.B. Mayor (Cambridge and London 1874) / S.B. Chrimes *Henry VII* (London 1972) 15–16 and passim / J.J. Scarisbrick *Henry VIII* (London 1968) 6, 516 / C. Rawcliffe *The Staffords, Earls of Stafford and Dukes of Buckingham, 1394–1521* (Cambridge 1978) 21 and passim / B.F. Harvey *Westminster Abbey and Its Estates in the Middle Ages* (Oxford 1977) 29 and passim / J.H.T. Perkins *Westminster Abbey, its Worship and Ornaments* (London 1938–52) II 210–13 / J. Simon *Education and Society in Tudor England* (Cambridge 1966) 47, 81, 192 / McConica 55–8 and passim / T. Baker *History of the College of St John the Evangelist, Cambridge* ed J.E.B. Mayor (Cambridge 1869) I 55–74 / G.R. Elton *Studies in Tudor and Stuart Politics and Government* (Cambridge 1974) I 316 / W.E.A. Dixon 'The Lady Margaret as a lover of literature' *The Library* 2nd series 8 (1907) 34–41 / R.F. Scott 'On the contracts for the tomb of the Lady Margaret Beaufort' *Archaeologia* 66 (1914–15) 365–76 / *Calendar of Patent Rolls, Henry VII* (London 1914–16, repr 1970) II 79, 371 / *Calendar of Close Rolls, Henry VII* (London 1955–) II 594, 770

C.S. KNIGHTON

Martin de BEAUNE d 2 July 1527

Martin, the son of Jacques de Beaune (Fournier de Beaune), count of Semblançay, and of Jeanne Ruzé, was born into a noble family with traditional claims to ecclesiastical preferment. He was first chancellor and then dean of Tours and prior of Grand-Montain de Bois-Rahier, near Tours. Nominated by *Francis I under the terms of the concordat of Bologna, 1516, he became archbishop of Tours on 24 August 1520 and received the pallium on 5 December. He died a month before the family was disgraced by the execution of his father. When writing to Erasmus, Pierre *Vitré had conveyed greetings from the dean of Tours, and Erasmus returned them early in 1518 (Ep 779).

BIBLIOGRAPHY: Allen Ep 779 / Eubel III 321 / *Gallia christiana* XIV 132–3 150 / DHGE VII 222–3

PGB

Heinrich BEBEL of Ingstetten, 1472–31 March 1518

Heinrich Bebel (Bebelius, Henricus de Bewinden, Bewindanus), the son of a farmer, was born in 1472 in Ingstetten, near Justingen (Swabia). He attended the school in Schelklingen, near Ulm, and from 1492 studied in Cracow under Laurentius Corvinus, whose *Cosmographia dans manuductionem in tabulas Ptolemaei* (Basel 1496) he later published. While a student he acquired a reputation as a poet. In 1495 he matriculated in Basel and studied under Sebastian *Brant. In 1496 he was called to Tübingen to teach rhetoric, and there he remained for the rest of his life, highly respected as a teacher and an enthusiastic advocate of German patriotic sentiment. In 1501, when he received the poet's laurel from the Emperor *Maximilian I in Innsbruck, he delivered his *Oratio ... de laudibus atque amplitudine Germaniae*, which was well received; it was published in Pforzheim (T. Anshelm 1504) and reprinted several times together with other works by him. He had connections with Hieronymus *Emser, *Beatus Rhenanus, Johann *Reuchlin, Konrad *Peutinger, and Johannes *Nauclerus; Philippus *Melanchthon and Johann *Eck were among his students. In 1515 Bebel wrote Erasmus a letter (Ep 321) full of admiration, asking him to declare himself a German. Bebel wrote such works of Latin instruction as *Commentaria epistolarum conficiendarum* and *Ars versificandi*, both frequently reprinted; a *Dialogus de optimo studio scholasticorum* (Zwolle: P. van Os c 1506); a collection of German proverbs, *Proverbia germanica*; and above all his popular *Facetiae* (Strasbourg: J. Grüninger 1506), reprinted until 1750 (re-edited by H. Berbermeyer, Leipzig 1931). His *Triumphus Veneris* is a verse satire, especially of monastic vices. A precise reference to the date of Bebel's death ('at six o'clock in the morning') was discovered by Allen, noted in a contemporary hand on the title-page of a copy of Terence (Strasbourg: J. Grüninger 1503) in the Bibliothèque du Collège, Porrentruy. The same title-page has some verse by Bebel.

BIBLIOGRAPHY: Allen Ep 321 and IV xxiv / NDB I 685–6 / ADB II 195–9, XI 793 / BRE Ep 24 and passim / RE Ep 56 and passim / *Matrikel Basel* I 237 / *Matrikel Tübingen* I 109 / J. Haller 'Heinrich Bebel als deutscher Dichter' *Zeitschrift für deutsches Altertum* 66 (1929) 51–4 / G. Berbermeyer *Tübinger Dichterhumanisten* (Tübingen 1927) 8–46 / Karl Hartfelder *Philipp Melanchthon* (Berlin 1889) 35–6 and passim / AK II Ep 597 / Rudolf Wackernagel *Geschichte der Stadt Basel* (Basel 1907–54) III 15 / H. Rupprich in R. Newald et al *Geschichte der deutschen Literatur* (Munich 1957–) IV-1 593ff / Georg Ellinger *Geschichte der neulateinischen Literatur Deutschlands im sechzehnten Jahrhundert* (Berlin and Leipzig 1929-33) I 435ff / *Index Aureliensis* Baden-Baden 1962–) III 399–409

JUDITH RICE HENDERSON & IG

Johann BEBEL of Basel, documented 1517–38

It seems reasonable to assume that references to the printers Johann Bepli or Bepler and Hans Welsch or Welsch-Hans all concern the young Johann Bebel (but cf *Matrikel Basel* I 190). If so, he was born at Strasbourg and is documented in Basel from 1517, at first as a journeyman in the press of Johann *Froben. In 1523 Bebel began to produce books with his own imprint, and on 20 June 1524 he was admitted to the citizenship of Basel, having married there a Margarete Thorer. Although not an accomplished scholar, Bebel was well educated, and his production soon assumed scholarly significance. His printing shop was small, it seems, and for many undertakings, especially major editions, he joined forces with other Basel printers such as Andreas *Cratander, another native of Strasbourg, and Michael Isengrin, Bebel's son-in-law. In 1538 these three produced a Greek Galen in five volumes. In 1533 Bebel and Cratander issued a Greek Plutarch, while Sebastian *Münster's Hebrew and Latin Bible (1534) was produced jointly with Isengrin and Henricus Petri. Of particular interest is Bebel's relationship with the Basel booksellers trading at Lyon and Paris. He printed Greek and French New Testaments for Johann *Schabler, and Konrad *Resch commissioned him to print Erasmus' *Precatio dominica* (c 1523) and *Budé's *Commentaria linguae graecae* (1529–30), an enterprise which aroused Erasmus' special interest (Epp 2221, 2223, 2224, 2231). However, Bebel served Italian as well as French markets. In 1531 and 1532 he maintained his own agent at Venice and afterwards undertook many trips south. He published major historical texts as well as works by *Zwingli and *Oecolampadius. In fact at the beginning of his independent career, when orders for the printing of whole editions were welcome, his religious publications caused problems. Between September and December 1524 he was investigated for having printed four German pamphlets by *Karlstadt that were paid for by Gerhard Westerberg and Konrad Grebel, both known later as leading Anabaptists. Together with Thomas *Wolff, another printer who had obliged them in the same way, Bebel was imprisoned for a short time (Epp 1522, 1523, 1530) while the government issued new censorship regulations. It may be noted that earlier in the same year Bebel and Wolff were called to testify before another judicial investigation, involving a Basel parish priest accused of Anabaptism. While the Karlstadt pamphlets were being investigated, Erasmus denounced Bebel and *Farel before the city council, alleging that Bebel had printed some of Farel's pamphlets directed in part against Erasmus (Ep 1508). However, by 1527 Bebel had learned to avoid similar risks and was awarded a government contract to print an official brochure.

After the incident with Farel, it was not easy for Erasmus to trust Bebel (cf Ep 2356), but the printer henceforward proved obliging (Epp 2231, 2312), and in 1531 Erasmus contributed a dedicatory preface (Ep 2432) and some verses (Reedijk poem 130) to Bebel's edition of the Greek Aristotle in three volumes (reprinted 1535 and 1550). This was by Bebel's standards a very major undertaking, and Erasmus did his best to recommend it to potential buyers. Because of this edition and other business, such as his promising connection with Polidoro *Virgilio, Bebel travelled to England in the spring and summer of 1531 by way of the Netherlands; his companion on this trip was Simon *Grynaeus. In England Bebel was given sums of money for Erasmus, paying him an equivalent after his return. Rightly or wrongly, Erasmus gradually formed the conviction that he had been short-changed by Bebel (Epp 2488, 2499, 2512, 2527, 2530, 2552, 2558). Never again was he to trust the printer, although he cleared him of any suspicion of wrongdoing in a letter to Grynaeus (Ep 2576) and handed Bebel some more letters and commissions when

he went again to England in the following spring and to Italy at frequent intervals between 1533 and 1536 (Epp 2644, 2662, 2704, 2761, 2854, 2956, 3085). Erasmus frequently made accusations against him, as in September 1531, when he claimed that Bebel got drunk on his way from Basel to Freiburg and left letters intended for Erasmus in the inn (Epp 2535, 2541, 2542). On another occasion, however, evident contradictions in his charges against Bebel cast doubt on the truth of his allegations (Epp 2704, 2761). Bebel's name is not found on new imprints after 1538, although it does occur in the reprint of Aristotle in 1550.

BIBLIOGRAPHY: Allen Ep 1508 / Benzing *Buchdrucker* 33 / R. Wackernagel *Geschichte der Stadt Basel* (Basel 1907–54) III 443 and passim / K. Stehlin 'Regesten zur Geschichte des Basler Buchdrucks ... ' III *Archiv für Geschichte des deutschen Buchhandels* 14 (1891) nos 1998–2000, 2095 / *Aktensammlung zur Geschichte der Basler Reformation* ed E. Dürr et al (Basel 1921–50) I 138–9, 174–6, 178, II 499 / AK III Epp 1347, 1396, 1401, 1473, 1481, IV Epp 1707, 1848, 1865, V Ep 2542, VII Ep 3179 / H. Barge 'Zur Chronologie und Drucklegung der Abendmahlstraktate Karlstadts' *Zentralblatt für Bibliothekswesen* 21 (1904) 323–31 esp 325–30
                                                        PGB

Antonio BECCARIA of Verona, d 4–6 April 1474
Antonio Beccaria, born to Taddeo of Verona around 1400, was a Greek and Latin scholar of considerable importance for the transmission of Renaissance humanism from Italy to England. Destined for an ecclesiastical career from adolescence, he studied the humanities in the school of Vittorino da Feltre at Mantua. Between October 1438 and November 1439 he travelled to England, to succeed Tito Livio Frulovisi of Ferrara as secretary to Humphrey, duke of Gloucester. Duke Humphrey, the brother of Henry V and uncle of Henry VI, was a patron of the new learning and commissioned Beccaria to translate several works of St Athanasius from Greek to Latin and Boccaccio's *Corbaccio* from Italian to Latin. Beccaria also composed a number of orations while in England. It is not known precisely when he left England; the existing evidence suggests that he was back in Italy in 1446. There he entered

the service of Ermolao Barbaro, bishop of
Verona from 1453 to 1470 and uncle of the
humanist Ermolao (I) *Barbaro, and attained
the position of treasurer of the cathedral.

Most of Beccaria's work was as a translator.
In addition to those listed above, he translated
numerous works of Plutarch and the *De situ
orbis* of Dionysius Periegetes (Venice: B. Maler
and E. Ratdolt 1477).

Erasmus mentioned Beccaria in the *Ciceronianus* as one of the many authors unacceptable
to the Ciceronians (ASD I-2 662).

BIBLIOGRAPHY: Cosenza I 474–5 / C. Vasoli in
DBI VII 447–9 / Roberto Weiss *Humanism in
England During the Fifteenth Century* 2nd ed
(Oxford 1957) 45–6 and passim

TBD

Petr BECHYNĚ of Lažany, documented
1524–58
Petr Bechyně of Lažany, (Bechinie, Bechinius,
Bechinicius, a Lazan, Lazian, Lusan) descended
from a noble family originally from Seidlitz in
Brandenburg (near Gorzów, Poland) but from
1414 established at Bechyně in Bohemia. His
father Oldřich had four other sons: Jan,
Bedřich, Mikuláš, and Václav. Petr matriculated at the University of Vienna in December
1524, at Leipzig in the spring of 1528, and in
Bologna in 1530; the following year he was
procurator of the German nation there. He also
studied at Ferrara, where he met Celio
*Calcagnini, and presumably in Padua. In a
letter to Georgius *Loxanus of 27 July 1536
Pietro *Bembo mentioned Bechyně as a friend.
On his return from a journey to Italy Ludwig
*Baer handed Erasmus a letter from Bembo,
dated Padua 20 June 1535 (Ep 3026), and
another from Bechyně, dated Bassano, 40
kilometres north of Padua, 24 June 1535 (Ep
3027). Perhaps Bechyně, was on his way home
when he wrote this short letter of introduction.

By 1530 Bechyně was the provost of
Vyšehrad (Prague), and from 1536 he seems to
have resided in Prague, since he is variously
documented in the records of his chapter. In
1541 King *Ferdinand gave him permission for
a gradual redemption of assets that the chapter
had earlier been obliged to pawn. Subsequently the chapter took him to court, alleging
that he had appropriated these assets to

himself. In 1547 he resigned the provostship in
return for financial compensation. Meanwhile
he had begun to fill positions in Ferdinand's
administration of Bohemia; in 1544 he was
secretary and in 1545 chamberlain (*Unterland-
kämmerer*). In 1546 and 1547 he participated in
Ferdinand's campaign against Saxony in
support of *Charles v's war against the
Schmalkaldic League. Following the Hapsburg
victory he was named to a royal commission set
up to confiscate part of the property of the
Protestant cities and towns in Bohemia as a
penalty for their support of the Schmalkaldic
League. In 1548 he was a member of a special
court appointed to hear appeals against such
confiscations. In 1554 he held the office of
captain of the Old Town of Prague and in the
same year was appointed one of four *defensores*
for the Catholic consistory of Prague. In June
and July 1558 he took part in an ecclesiastical
visitation of the county of Glatz adjoining
Bohemia (now in the region of the Polish city of
Kłodzko), where Anabaptists and other
Protestants had been noted. The commission's
report to Ferdinand was dated from Glatz on 5
July 1558.

BIBLIOGRAPHY: Allen Ep 3027 / *Matrikel Wien*
III-1 38 / *Matrikel Leipzig* I 599 / Knod 34 / *Ottuv
slovník naufičný (Prague 1888–1909)* III 627 /
Jednání a dopisy konsistoře katolické i utrakvistické
ed Klement Borový (Prague 1868–9) II 229–35 /
Ferdinand Hrejsa *Dějiny křest'anství Českoslo-
vensku* 5 (Prague 1948) 117, 204 / Karel Tief-
trunk *Odpor stavuv českých proti Ferdinandovi I
1547* (Prague 1872) 201, 286, 344

J.K. ZEMAN & PGB

Marino BECICHEMO of Shkodēr, c 1468–1526
Marino Becichemo was born in the Venetian
town of Scutari (Shkodēr in Albania); hence he
is also called Scodrensis. His father, Marino,
was a Venetian agent at Scutari for over thirty
years, while his mother, Bianca Pagano, was
probably of a Milanese merchant family. In
1477 the Turks laid siege to Scutari, and
Becichemo was sent to nearby Dulcigno
(Ulcinj) on the coast. His father probably died
when the Turks took Scutari. Becichemo
travelled to Brescia, where he studied Latin
and Greek under Giovanni Calfurnio and
Cristoforo Barzizio. Shortly after 1484 he
returned to Dulcigno, where he married

Caterina Dabro, the daughter of one of the leading citizens of the town; they had nine sons.

Although Becichemo served as secretary to Melchiorre Trevisan, a Venetian admiral, from 1496 to 1499, his main occupations were as a teacher, a commentator on the classics, and an orator. He taught at grammar schools at Ragusa (Dubrovnik in Dalmatia, 1492–6), Venice (1500–1), Padua (1501–3), Brescia (1503–9), and again Venice (1509–17). His students included Filippo Donato, Gian Antonio Cattaneo, and Marcantonio Contarini. In 1517 he was appointed reader of rhetoric at the University of Padua. Although the humanists Gregorio Amaseo and Pietro *Bembo were critical of Becichemo and stated that his teaching was unpopular, they may have been motivated by jealousy, for they were at odds with certain Venetian patricians who supported Becichemo. Marino Sanudo, the Venetian diarist, spoke favourably of Becichemo, and the senate voted him a number of increases in pay and made his appointment permanent in 1524.

In 1519 Erasmus skimmed through Becichemo's commentary on the first book of Pliny's *Historia naturalis*, edited by Nicolas *Bérault (Paris: P. Vidoue for R. Resch 1519, cf Ep 1016). However, Erasmus did not know Becichemo personally, and in 1525 stated that he had learned his name only through Leonard *Casembroot of Bruges, then a student at Padua (Epp 1594, 1626).

Other works by Becichemo included commentaries on the *Familiares epistolae* of Cicero (Venice: G. Tacuino 1526) and on the *Rhetorica ad Herennium* (Milan: J.A. Scinzenzeler 1512), at that time attributed to Cicero. Many of Becichemo's orations were also published.

BIBLIOGRAPHY: Allen Ep 1594 / C.H. Clough in DBI VII 511–5

TBD

BECK, BECKER *See Simon* PISTORIS, *Christophorus* PISTORIUS

Jan BECKER of Borsele, d after April 1536
Jan Becker (Iohannes Becar Borsalus, de Bursalia), a native of Borsele, in Zeeland, and a kinsman of Hubertus *Barlandus and Adrianus Aelius *Barlandus, matriculated at Louvain on 30 August 1495. After his promotion to MA on

10 April 1498 he studied theology for some time, but on 22 December 1502 he was admitted to the university council as a professor of philosophy. Erasmus probably saw him often when he was at Louvain in 1502 and 1503; the two became close friends and corresponded frequently in later years. Probably in the summer of 1507 Becker left the College of the Lily, where he had hitherto lived, but remained at Louvain to teach Cornelius Erdorf, a nephew of his patron Jérôme de *Busleyden, and no doubt other young pupils, for Erdorf soon gave up his intellectual aspirations. Becker then returned to Zeeland, where in the spring of 1513 he obtained a prebend at Middelburg through the influence of Filips van *Spangen. He wrote to Erasmus in April 1514, replying to three of the latter's letters of the previous summer, now lost, and describing his situation under the patronage of Spangen (Ep 291). In the autumn of 1514, however, Busleyden employed him as tutor for a second nephew, François de *Busleyden. He took up residence at Arlon and Luxembourg, where, according to his letters to Erasmus (Epp 320, 370), he felt rather isolated.

The death of his pupil in the summer of 1517 enabled Becker to return to Louvain (Ep 687), and for several months he was with Erasmus at the Lily (Ep 717). In December 1517 Erasmus recommended Becker to a certain nobleman, probably Jan (III) van *Bergen, as a private teacher (Ep 737); more important, he supported a move to install his friend as the first professor of Latin in the new Collegium Trilingue (Epp 794, 805). Although Becker was offered the post, he did not find the conditions satisfactory, and he left Louvain in June 1518, having received the deanery of Zanddijk or Zandenburg, near Veere (Epp 849, 852). He was now under the patronage of Adolph of *Burgundy, serving as tutor to his son, Philip (III) of *Burgundy (Ep 1005). In 1522 Becker was elected dean of St Peter's at Middelburg, but the imperial court opposed his appointment on the grounds that it had the right to name the dean, and Becker had to be content with the living of Brouwershaven, granted to him by Adolph (Ep 1321).

Late in 1522 Becker accompanied Philip (III) to Louvain, where the latter matriculated on 4 December 1522. Unfortunately the young man died within a few years, and Becker returned to Veere, where he remained for eighteen months, in part owing to serious illness (Ep 1787). By February 1525 he was again at Louvain, this time as tutor to Adolph's younger son, Maximilian II of *Burgundy, staying with him at the house of Robertus *Virulus, presumably from October 1526 to the summer of 1529 (Epp 1984, 2200). Thereafter Becker remained in Zeeland and was apparently still alive in April 1536, when Adrianus Cornelii *Barlandus dedicated his *De amplificatione* (Louvain: S. Zassenus) to him. Earlier Barlandus, as co-editor of the *Pluscule Esopi ... fabulae* (Antwerp: D. Martens 22 April 1512; NK 26), had included in that book a dedicatory letter to Becker (and another letter from Becker to himself) as well as praising him in his preface to the *Libelli tres* (Antwerp: M. Hillen 5 January 1520). Gerard *Geldenhouwer, another friend (Epp 727, 759), inscribed the seventh and eighth satires of his *Satyrae octo* (Louvain: D. Martens 13 June 1515; NK 3122) to him.

Although their correspondence was often intermittent, Erasmus always held Becker in high regard (see also the colloquy *Epithalamium Petri Aegidii*, ASD I-3 416). Becker had a measure of influence on Erasmus' work, encouraging him to arrange his published letters chronologically (Epp 1787, 1851) and repeatedly urging him to write a 'Ratio concionandi' (a manual for preachers; Epp 932, 952, 1321, 1787, 1851). Although Erasmus long intended to undertake the latter work (Allen I 34), his *Ecclesiastes* did not appear until 1535 (Basel: H. Froben). At Becker's request (Epp 1860, 1898, 1984) Erasmus sent two letters to his pupil Maximilian of Burgundy (Epp 1859, 1927).

BIBLIOGRAPHY: Allen Ep 291 / J. Fruytier in NNBW VI 169 / A. Roersch in BNB XXVI 217–19 / *Matricule de Louvain* III-1 126 / de Vocht CTL I 256–67, II 82, and passim / de Vocht *Literae ad Craneveldium* Ep 12

C.G. VAN LEIJENHORST

Noël BÉDA c 1470–8 January 1537
Noël Béda (Bedda, Bédier), an inveterate critic of Erasmus, was the best-known member of the faculty of theology of Paris during the period 1520–36. He was born around 1470, probably at Mont Saint-Michel, although Erasmus thought him to be from Picardy. He probably studied

arts at the Collège de Montaigu in Paris, and taught there during the last decade of the century. From at least 1495 he was a member of the Paris reformist group around Jan *Standonck, and this experience was a formative influence in his later career. Erasmus probably knew Béda at Montaigu and later indulged in scathing criticism of the regime there. Béda succeeded Standonck as principal in 1504 and remained its director until 1535, even though he relinquished the title of principal in 1514. Under Béda's direction Montaigu became famous and wealthy, but his detractors say he merely presided over its decadence and ruin. His reformist tendency earned him censure from the faculty of theology in 1506, when he argued in his Sorbonic disputation against plurality of benefices and said that church livings could only be held by those in the state of grace. (Some authors have misinterpreted his position in the opposite sense). Béda received his licence in theology on 5 January 1508, ranking fifth of eighteen, and took his doctorate on 17 April 1508. His doctoral disputations were presided over by Thomas *Warnet, another acquaintance of Erasmus at Montaigu. He was only moderately active on the faculty of theology from 1510 to 1516 and does not appear at all in the faculty registers from 1516 until 1520. During the latter period, he wrote three books against *Lefèvre d'Etaples and Josse *Clichtove, formulating the position that the critical exegetical methods and ideas of humanists were dangerous to the essential unity of the church. He was also active at that time in the university's protest against the adoption of the concordat between King *Francis I and Pope *Leo X. All through his career Béda was called upon by the university to represent it before civil and ecclesiastical authorities and visiting dignitaries.

It was in the faculty of theology, however, that Béda was most active and influential from 1520 on. He personally suggested the creation of the office of syndic in that year – almost certainly in response to the danger he saw in Lutheran doctrine – and held the position until 1535. Reluctant at first to serve more than one year (he resigned the office at least three times), he gradually settled into the position permanently and became increasingly dominant over faculty affairs. From 1520 until his first exile in 1533 he directed faculty business by argument, suits in the Parlement of Paris, intimidation, and the sheer force of his personality. He diligently pursued and prosecuted humanists and reformers; he censored books; he enforced or reformed university statutes. Only a reading of the faculty's register of its meetings can give an appreciation of the indefatigable efforts and the importance of Béda in Paris.

Under Béda's aegis the Paris faculty of theology first attacked Erasmus' views as presented in the faulty and tendentious translations by Louis de *Berquin in 1523. A general condemnation of Bible versions and translations in August 1523 included Erasmus' New Testament. King Francis I warned the theologians in November of that year against pursuing a general condemnation of Erasmus. But the king's captivity in 1525 opened the way for another attack on Berquin, and Erasmus' *Querela pacis* was condemned on 1 June 1525. Pierre *Cousturier's violent attack, *De tralatione Bibliae*, partly based on notes Béda sent to him, prompted Erasmus to write to Béda. The eleven letters exchanged between them (Epp 1571, 1579, 1581, 1596, 1609, 1610, 1620, 1642, 1679, 1685, 1906) from April 1525 to November 1527, described by Renaudet as 'long and useless,' are nevertheless a good indication of Erasmus' strong desire to forestall further censure from the Paris faculty of theology and of Béda's persistent view of Erasmus as one who was doing harm to the church. Erasmus' attempts to prove his orthodoxy and moderation in no way moved Béda, who ended his last letter to Erasmus with the observation that someone who is suffering under the attacks of both Catholics and Lutherans is merely suffering for his own cause and not for the cause of truth (Ep 1685). Béda's *Annotationes* against Erasmus and Lefèvre d'Etaples appeared in 1526. The book contained excerpts and censures of propositions drawn from Erasmus' paraphrases on the Gospels and Epistles, the preface to the edition of Cyprian, the *De interdicto esu carnium*, and the *Enchiridion*. Erasmus complained about Béda's attacks for several years. More important, he succeeded in having Béda's *Annotationes* withdrawn from sale, although Josse *Bade reported that half of the 625 copies he had printed were already

dispersed throughout Europe, and a Cologne edition appeared shortly thereafter. Erasmus also wrote against Béda a *Prologus in supputationem calumniarum Bedae*, followed by replies to Béda's criticisms of various books of Erasmus' New Testament (LB IX 441–96); the *Elenchus in censuras Bedae* (LB IX 495–514); and the *Supputatio errorum in censuris Natalis Bedae* (LB IX 515–702) in 1526 and 1527. Béda replied only in 1529 with his *Adversus clandestinos Lutheranos* (Paris: Josse Bade), which Erasmus immediately answered with his *Responsio ad notulas Beddaicas* (LB IX 701–20) in March 1529. Meanwhile, Béda had pressed the faculty of theology for a general censure of Erasmus' works. Under Béda's direction the faculty devoted numerous committee meetings and general sessions towards that end, resulting in a formal condemnation of the *Colloquia*, paraphrases, and other works on 16 December 1527, although this was not released in print until 1531. In the latter year, Béda had Julius Caesar *Scaliger's *Oratio pro M. Tullio Cicerone contra Desiderium Erasmum Roterodamum* printed in Paris (Gilles de Gourmont and Pierre Vidoue 1531). Erasmus' *Declarationes ad censuras Lutetiae* in 1532 (LB IX 813–954) was his final answer to Béda and the faculty of theology of Paris.

Throughout these events Béda's adversaries fought back. He was satirized in several college plays and in reformist literature and letters. Berquin composed his *Duodecim articuli infidelitatis Bedae*, but Béda and the faculty claimed a leading role in his final arrest and execution in 1529. Erasmus wrote to King Francis I that Béda's actions marked a conspiracy of monks and theologians to assume political power (Ep 1722). *Rabelais satirized Béda in several places.

Béda led the opposition within the faculty to a favourable decision for *Henry VIII's consultation about his marriage – much to the displeasure of King Francis I, who needed a loan from Henry to ransom his sons. He wrote to Johann *Eck in 1533 to inform him of the Paris faculty's condemnation of *Cajetanus' commentaries on the New Testament and the Psalms. Béda's exile in 1533 to Montargis was caused proximately by the explosive atmosphere in Paris resulting from rival Lenten preaching. Recalled from exile for an investigation of the spurious Protestant propaganda piece *Confession et raison de la foy de maistre Noel Beda*, he immediately set about attacking the king's professors in the nascent *collège royal* (Collège de France). This, added to Béda's long record of opposition to the policies of Francis I (who informed the papal nuncio that there were a 'hundred reasons' why he should order Béda's head cut off), led to several months of imprisonment in 1534, to a public degradation on 31 January 1535, and to a subsequent exile to Mont Saint-Michel.

Béda made provision in 1536 to endow six scholarships at the Collège de Montaigu, leaving 1800 livres tournois, invested in rents yielding 160 livres tournois a year. He died on 8 January 1537, probably at Mont Saint-Michel, where he was buried in a chapel of the parish church. Various forms of his epitaph have come down to us. A large painting of Béda and about twenty other benefactors of the Collège de Montaigu still existed at the college in 1694, but an observer at that time wrote that the painting was in very bad condition.

The Scottish theologian John Mair (Major), who taught at Montaigu during Béda's term of office, dedicated works to Béda in 1510 and 1528, as did Johannes Basaverianus, a former pupil, in 1532.

Béda's works include: (with Thomas Warnet) *La doctrine et instruction nécessaire aux chrestiens et chrestiennes* (Paris: Jean Trepperel c 1509); (ed, with Thomas Warnet) *La petite Dyablerie dont lucifer est le chef et les membres sont tous les ioueurs iniques et pecheurs reprouvez, intitule Leglise des mauvais* (trans, with alterations, from Sermon 42, 'De alearum ludo,' from the *Quadragesimale de christiana religione* of San Bernardino of Siena) (Paris: Widow of Jean Trepperel and Jean Jehannot [1511], Alain Lotrian c 1525; English trans London: Wynken de Worde or Charles Somerset [1511]); *Scholastica declaratio sententiae et ritus ecclesiae de unica Magdalena ... contra magistrorum Jacobi Fabri et Judoci Clichtovei contheologi scripta* (Paris: Josse Bade 1519); *Apologia pro filiabus et nepotibus beatae Annae ... contra magistri Jacobi Fabri scriptum* (Paris: Josse Bade 1520); *Restitutio duarum propositionum necessitatem peccati Adae, et felicitatem culpae eiusdem indicantium, a sacra caerei Paschalis benedictione solertia Jodoci Clichtovei ... relegatarum* (Paris: Josse Bade 1520);

Annotationum Natalis Bede ... in Jacobum Fabrum Stapulensem libri duo, et in Desiderium Erasmum Roterodamum liber unus qui ordine tertius est. Primus, in commentarios ipsius Fabri super Epistolas beati Pauli. Secundus, in ejusdem commentarios super IV Evangelia. Tertius, in Paraphrases Erasmi super eadem quatuor Evangelia et omnes apostolicas Epistolas (Paris: Josse Bade 1526; Cologne: Petrus Quentel 1526); *Apologia ... adversus clandestinos Lutheranos* (Paris: Josse Bade 1529). A list of five manuscript articles by Béda appears in Farge no 34.

BIBLIOGRAPHY: Allen VI 65–7 note / ASD I-3 131 / W. Bense 'Nöel Beda and the Humanist Reformation in Paris, 1504–1534' (unpublished thesis Harvard 1967) / Clerval, passim / *Commentaires de la Faculté de Médecine de l'Université de Paris (1516–1560)* ed M.-L. Concasty, (Paris 1964) passim / DBF V 1255 / Delisle, passim / DHGE VII 391–3 / C.-E. Du Boulay *Historia universitatis Parisiensis* (Paris 1673, repr 1966) VI passim / Farge no 34 / P.-Y. Féret *La Faculté de théologie de Paris et ses docteurs les plus célèbres. Epoque moderne* (Paris 1900–10) I 134–40, II 4–17 / M. Godet *La Congrégation de Montaigu* (Paris 1912) / M.-M. de la Garanderie *Christianisme et lettres profanes (1515–1535)* (Lille-Paris 1976) I 238–53 / J. Larmat 'Picrochole, est-il Nöel Beda?' in *Etudes Rabelaisiennes* VIII (Geneva 1969) / J.-P. Massaut 'Erasme, La Sorbonne et la nature de l'église' in *Colloquium Erasmianum* (Mons 1968) 89–116 / Renaudet *Etudes Erasmiennes (1521–1529)* (Paris 1939) 49–50, 240–80

JAMES K. FARGE

Noël BÉDIER *See Nöel* BÉDA

Thomas BEDYLL c 1486–September 1537
Thomas Bedyll (Bedellus, Bidellius) became a scholar of Winchester College in 1498 and of New College, Oxford, in 1500, becoming a fellow of New College two years later. He graduated as a bachelor of civil law on 5 November 1508, although that same year he was expelled from his college for neglect of his academic duties. Bedyll was installed as rector of Halton, Buckinghamshire, in 1512. In 1514 he was given the chapels of Bockyngfold and Newstede, in the diocese of Canterbury, and by 1516 had been appointed secretary to Archbishop William *Warham. Although Bed-

yll received various preferments during the following years, it was only after Warham's death in 1532 that his star rose. That same year he was appointed chaplain to King *Henry VIII and secretary to his council, while the following year he was given the archdeaconry of London, which in 1535 was exchanged for that of Cornwall; he was also the recipient of numerous smaller livings. From 1532 until his death five years later Bedyll was increasingly occupied in the matter of Henry VIII's divorce, obtaining Oxford's favourable opinion in 1533 and being present with Thomas *Cranmer at Dunstable in May of that year when the latter pronounced the king's marriage invalid. Later he was employed in obtaining the submission of the various religious houses to Henry's supremacy and acted as one of the interrogators of John *Fisher and Thomas *More. Following the suppression of the minor monasteries in 1536, Bedyll supervised the surrender of the houses in the vicinity of London. In his devotion to the king's cause, Bedyll was accused of intolerance and cruelty.

Bedyll's relations with Erasmus were confined mainly to the payment of the latter's Aldington pension. As secretary to Warham, Bedyll was responsible for the transfer of the annuity to Erasmus, and before Warham's death he is frequently mentioned whenever payment was due or delayed (Epp 387, 782, 892, 1176, 1647, 1828, 1993) or in the event of a misunderstanding (CWE Ep 823 introduction). Owing to his close relations with both Cranmer and Thomas *Cromwell, Bedyll continued to act as the avenue for Erasmus' pension even after Warham's death (Epp 3037, 3042, 3052, 3058, 3104, 3107, 3108).

BIBLIOGRAPHY: Allen and CWE Ep 387 / DNB II 120–1 / Emden BRUO I 148–9 / LP III–XII passim / David Knowles *The Religious Orders in England* (Cambridge 1948–59) III 273–4 and passim
MORDECHAI FEINGOLD

Herman van BEEK or van der BEEKE *See* Hermannus TORRENTIUS

Georg BEHAIM of Nürnberg, c 1461–1/2 June 1520
Georg Behaim (Behem, Peham, Boëmus), a descendant of a patrician family in Nürnberg, was the nephew of the architect Hans Behaim

the Elder and Brother Lorenz Behaim, who was master of the papal artillery and from 1496 canon at Bamberg and was noted as a friend of Willibald *Pirckheimer. Georg Behaim matriculated at the University of Leipzig in the summer of 1482. Having obtained his BA in 1484 and his MA in 1488 and 1489, he became a canon of St Mariengraden, Mainz, and from 1513 to 1520 was the provost of the St Lorenz chapter in Nürnberg. As he is probably the Georgius Boëmus who was recalled by Agostino *Steuco among the learned Germans whose acquaintance he had made (Ep 2513), Georg may have visited Italy.

Erasmus mentioned in Ep 1001 a letter from Georg Behaim that reached him after a long delay. There is no evidence to suggest that the correspondence was continued.

BIBLIOGRAPHY: Allen Ep 1001 / NDB I 748–9 / *Matrikel Leipzig* I 329 / Hutten *Opera* I Ep 64 / *Christoph Scheurl's Briefbuch* ed F. von Soden and J.K.F. Knaake (Potsdam 1867–72) I Epp 60, 66, II Ep 130, and passim
IG

Judocus BEISSEL of Aachen, d 1514
At the beginning of September 1500 Erasmus expected a certain Judocus to return to Saint-Omer and intended to write him a letter (Ep 129). Two months later he sent his former servant-pupil *Ludovicus to Jacob *Batt at the castle of Tournehem, near Saint-Omer, with the intention that Ludovicus should enter the service of Judocus, whom he supposed to be back by then (Ep 135).

Erasmus' friend Judocus may be the Judocus Beysellius who wrote on 27 – the month is missing – 1500 from Saint-Omer to Julianus Carbonicus (Carbo, Cools), canon regular of St Augustine and prior of the monastery of St John's outside the walls of St Truiden. In his letter Beysellius mentioned his recent pilgrimage to the tomb of Arnoldus *Bostius, a Carmelite who had died in 1499 in his native Ghent. That pilgrimage may thus be the reason for the temporary absence of Erasmus' friend Judocus, who was away from Saint-Omer for some weeks in the autumn of 1500. Beysellius' letter is known from a contemporary copy in the Bibliothèque Mazarine. According to the copyist's heading, Beysellius was himself a Carmelite, but this assumption is not confirmed by the text of the letter. The author of the Mazarine letter may thus be identified with Judocus Beissel, who had been connected with Bostius a few years earlier, although he can hardly have been a Carmelite monk in those years. In October 1485 Beissel dedicated to Bostius his edition of the *Commentum super decem praeceptis decalogi* (Louvain: A. van der Heerstraeten 19 April 1486), composed by another Carmelite, Nicolaas Beetz (d 17 July 1476). The dedicatory letter reveals that Beissel was a councillor to the future Emperor *Maximilian I, who was then in the Netherlands, and that Beetz had formerly been Beissel's professor in Louvain.

Judocus was a son of Johann Beissel, burgomaster of Aachen. Early in 1471 he matriculated at the University of Cologne as a canon of Maastricht and a bachelor of law. It is possible that he had taken that degree in Louvain, where a Judocus Beisel had matriculated on 20 August 1465. According to the register this man's home, however, was in Gravelines, between Calais and Dunkirk. It is certain that the son of the burgomaster of Aachen studied at Louvain a few years later, receiving licences in civil law (1474) and canon law (12 December 1476). From 1494 to 1496 he was in Antwerp and Brussels in connection with an important law suit; in 1496 he also went to Rome. He was married to Katharina Speiss and died childless in 1514. He wrote several devotional and historical works as well as letters to well-known literary figures. Some of these survive in manuscript while others were printed. In his *Rosacea augustissimae christiferae Mariae corona* (Antwerp: G. Bac 1495) he is described as a licentiate in both laws of the University of Louvain, a councillor to Maximilian I, and a patrician of Aachen.

BIBLIOGRAPHY: Allen Ep 129 / W. Kaemmerer in NDB II 21–2 / *Matricule de Louvain* II-1 156 / *Matrikel Köln* I 825 / de Vocht *Busleyden* 303–4 / Gilbert Tournoy 'I manoscritti petrarcheschi in Belgio' to be published in *Italia medioevale e umanistica* / Paris, Bibliothèque Mazarine MS 1565 f 450

GILBERT TOURNOY

Arnoldus BEKA (poem 73, c 1502–4)
The names Arnold van der Beken, Beeck, Beca, Arnold of Beka (Hilvarenbeek), etc, are found often in the matriculation register of the University of Louvain. The Arnold mentioned by Erasmus in his epitaph for Wilhelmina *Beka as that lady's father could be the Arnoldus of Beka of the diocese of Cambrai who matriculated at Louvain on 14 October 1463 and the Arnoldus de Beca who obtained there a doctorate of civil and canon law on 4 July 1481, occupying Louvain's senior legal chair from that time until 1487. If the law professor is also identical with his namesake who was councillor-in-ordinary of Brabant from 6 February 1477 to 25 September 1493, it could perhaps be assumed that he was still living at Louvain in 1502 when Erasmus took up residence there.

BIBLIOGRAPHY: Reedijk poem 73 / *Matricule de Louvain* II-1 122 and passim / de Vocht CTL II 74–5

CFG & PGB

Wilhelmina BEKA d c 1502–4
Wilhelmina was the daughter of Arnoldus *Beka, whom Erasmus may have met in Louvain, perhaps during his residence there from 1502 to 1504. She married Antoon *Ysbrandtsz, who was 'pensionary,' or legal consultant, to the city of Antwerp and survived his wife. Erasmus composed an epitaph for Wilhelmina (Reedijk poem 73), first printed in the *Adagia-Epigrammata* of 1506–7, mentioning that she had given her husband eight children and died prematurely at about the age of thirty-five.

BIBLIOGRAPHY: Reedijk poem 73 / de Vocht CTL II 74–5

CFG

Pietro BEMBO of Venice, 20 May 1470–18 January 1547
Pietro Bembo was born in Venice, the son of Bernardo, a member of the Venetian aristocracy, and Elena Marcello. Having begun his education in Venice under the guidance of private tutors, Bembo continued his classical studies in Messina, at the school of Constantinus *Lascaris (1492–4) and followed courses of philosophy at the University of Padua (academic year 1494–5) and at the school of Niccolò *Leoniceno in Ferrara (1497). He gave evidence of the depth and novelty of his philological skill when he prepared editions of Petrarch's *Rime* (1501) and Dante's *Commedia*

(1502) for the Aldine press. In 1506 Bembo left
his native city to accept the hospitality of the
dukes of Urbino; except for occasional visits to
other cities, he remained at the court of the
Montefeltro until his departure for Rome
(spring 1512). There he became involved in the
controversy with Gianfrancesco *Pico on the
theory of imitation. Three epistles, including
Bembo's *De imitatione* (1 January 1513), were
first published without authorization, probably in Rome, between 1516 and 1518. In March
1513 Pope *Leo x appointed Bembo, together
with his friend *Sadoleto, to the office of
domestic secretary of the apostolic secretariat.
Probably during the same year Bembo met
Morosina (Fausta Morosina della Torre), who
later became the mother of his three children
(Lucilio, Torquato, and Elena) and remained
his faithful companion until her death (6
August 1535). In 1521 Bembo left Rome and
retired to his villa near Padua, and in this
splendid residence he began a new period of
intense intellectual activity. This comprised the
composition and publication of *Benacus* (1524),
the completion and publication of *Prose della
volgar lingua* (Venice: G. Tacuino 1525), the
preparation of the critical edition of the
Novellino (1525), the completion of the revised
edition of *Asolani* (Venice: G.A. Sabbio 1530,
first edition A. Manuzio 1505), the publication
of the *Rime* (Venice: G.A. Sabbio 1530), and the
publication of the earlier Latin works, which
included separate editions of *De Aetna, De
imitatione, De Virgilii Culice et Terentii fabulis, De
Guido Ubaldo Feretrio deque Elisabetha Gonzaga
Urbini ducibus* (Venice: G. A. Sabbio 1530). Also
in 1530 Bembo was nominated librarian and
historian of the Venetian republic and zealously worked to fulfil the assigned task of
writing the *Historiae Venetae libri xii* (published
posthumously by the Aldine press in 1551).
Bembo had been ordained 6 December 1522;
nominated cardinal *in pectore* on 20 December
1538, he was proclaimed three months later. He
died in Rome on 18 January 1547 and was
buried in the church of Santa Maria sopra
Minerva.

Scattered references suggest that Erasmus
had only the slightest acquaintance with
Bembo before 1529. A favourable comment in
Adagia ii i 1 shows that while he was with Aldo
*Manuzio Erasmus became aware of Bembo's

Pietro Bembo

intellectual activities; modern scholarship
questions his assertion that Bembo intervened
for him during his visit to Rome in 1509, when
he was seeking an interview with Domenico
*Grimani (Ep 2465). Petrus *Mosellanus linked
the names of Bembo and Erasmus in a letter of 6
January 1519 (Ep 911), and, responding to a
reference to Bembo in a letter from Leonard
*Casembroot from Padua, 25 August 1525,
Erasmus stated that he knew Bembo at that
time by repute and from reading his works
(Epp 1594, 1626).

This vague and indifferent attitude greatly
changed in the splendid letter addressed by
Erasmus to Sadoleto, after the Sack of Rome, on
1 October 1528 (Ep 2059). Here the Dutch
humanist expressed his concern for Bembo's
safety and significantly added that he 'began to
love and admire' the Venetian writer as he was
reading his correspondence with Christophe
de *Longueil (see Longolius *Epistolae* books i,
iii, v). This declaration is in essential agreement with the content of a passage added to
the second edition of *Ciceronianus* (ASD I-2
697–8). Here the humanist affirms that he
knows nothing written by Bembo, except 'a

few letters'; nevertheless he identifies the Ciceronianism of Bembo and Sadoleto as a unique form of expression of superior intellects, not to be confused with the Ciceronianism of uninspired imitators like Longeuil. In a letter to Johann von *Vlatten of 24 January 1529 (Ep 2088), also included in this edition, Erasmus stated that he had read the epistles containing the Bembo-Pico controversy after the completion of the dialogue. Moreover the humanist declared that the position of the Venetian scholar did not dissent 'too much' from his own. Rather than demonstrating that Erasmus was attempting 'un rapprochment tactique avec les plus valables des Ciceroniens' (ASD I-2 698n), this affirmation shows a remarkable degree of critical acumen when it is considered in the light of the most advanced contemporary interpretations of Bembo's attitude on the problem of authority and imitation.

On 22 February 1529 Erasmus wrote directly to Bembo to recommend his friend Karel *Uutenhove (Ep 2106). The cordial answer (Epp 2144, 2290) marks the beginning of an epistolary relationship that was always dignified, became increasingly warmer, and was terminated only by the death of the Dutch scholar. Besides Uutenhove (Epp 2106, 2144, 2209, 2290), Erasmus asked Bembo to assist *Viglius Zuichemus in his studies in Padua (Epp 2594, 2604, 2632, 2657, 2681, 2682, 2708, 2716, 2767, 2791, 2810, 2829, 2854). Later he introduced to his Italian friend the young Portuguese historian Damião de *Gois (Epp 2958, 2987, 3043). Bembo and Erasmus exchanged letters about a manuscript of Livy that might be used in revising the Froben edition of 1531. Unfortunately Bembo could not supply such a text (Epp 2925, 2975), but he helped Viglius Zuichemus to consult a manuscript of the *Institutiones* (Epp 2791, 2925) and warmly received other friends of Erasmus, including Ludwig *Baer (Ep 3026). In the same spirit the Dutch humanist praised Bembo's achievements to friends and acquaintances (Epp 2201, 2209, 2337, 2453, 3005, 3032), studied his writings in Latin (Ep 2810), and continued to be informed about the success (Epp 2154, 2165, 3002) and the progress (Ep 2829) of his other works. News about Bembo's activity reached Erasmus until the last months of his life (Ep 3085), and in December 1535 he saluted the

Venetian as one of the heroes of the literary world (Ep 3076).

The writings of Bembo also include several collections of letters: *Epistolarum Leonis x P.M. nomine scriptarum libri xvi* (Venice: G. Padovano and V. de Roffinellis 1536). In their second edition of 1552 these are followed by *Epistularum familiarium libri vi* (Venice: G. Scoto). A first volume of *Lettere* in the vernacular was published in Rome (C. Gualteruzzi 1548); a second volume appeared in Venice (1550); a third volume, containing the preceding and including two additional books, was published in Venice by Gualtiero Scoto in 1552. The *Nuove lettere famigliari* appeared in Venice (F. Rampazetto 1564). The eighteenth-century edition of Bembo's works remains the most comprehensive: *Opere del Card. Pietro Bembo ora per la prima volta in un corpo riunite* (Venice 1729). Recently Francesco Pellegrini included Bembo's *Avertimenti nella Siphili di Hieronimo Fracastoro* in his edition of *Fracastoro's *Scritti inediti* (Verona 1955); Carlo Dionisotti published the correspondence of the years 1500–1 between Bembo and Maria Savorgnan in his edition of *Carteggio d'amore* (Florence 1950).

The library and the splendid art collection gathered by Bembo began to be dispersed during the lifetime of his son Torquato, and more so after his death (1 March 1595). The library was subdivided into three main portions; the first is now in the Vatican library, the second in the Biblioteca Ambrosiana (Milan), the third (acquired by Sir Henry Wotton from 1617 to 1620) in Eton College. Other material once belonging to Bembo's library may be found in Paris, London, Vienna, and Oxford.

The two most famous portraits of Bembo, painted by Titian, are now in the Museo Nazionale of Naples and in the National Gallery of Washington; a third portrait is in the Uffizi, Florence. A medal with Bembo's portrait was cast by Valerio Belli, another is attributed to Cellini, and a third, attributed to Tommaso Perugino, is in the British Museum. The sculpted bust in Padua is the work of Danese Cattaneo.

BIBLIOGRAPHY: Allen Ep 2106 / An intelligent selection of the vast bibliography may be found in Carlo Dionisotti's article in DBI VIII 133–51 / Vittorio Cian *Un decennio della vita di M. Pietro Bembo* (Turin 1885) / Vittorio Cian 'Pietro

Bembo (quarantun anni dopo)' *Giornale storico della letteratura italiana* 88 (1926) 225–55 / Mario Santoro *Pietro Bembo* (Naples 1937) / Paolo Simoncelli 'Pietro Bembo e l'evangelismo italiano' *Critica storica* 15 (1978) 1–63

DANILO AGUZZI-BARBAGLI

Henricus BEMYNGUS *See Heinrich* BEYMING

Johannes BENEDICTI *See Jan Benedykt* SOLFA

Giorgio BENIGNO Salviati d 1520
Giorgio Benigno Salviati (Juraj Dragišić) was born in Bosnia but as a child fled with his family to Ragusa (Dubrovnik) to escape the Turks. He entered the Franciscan order and studied philosophy in France and England. He taught the Scriptures at Florence for approximately thirty years, at times serving as warden of the convent of Santa Croce. He was a member of the circle of intellectuals surrounding Lorenzo (I) de' *Medici, and on 22 June 1489 maintained in a public debate, and later at a banquet in the Medici palace, the proposition that the sin of Adam was not the greatest of sins. Benigno served as one of the tutors of Piero de' Medici and was so loved by the Salviati family of Florence that they gave him their name.

Benigno later returned to Ragusa to teach philosophy and theology. In 1507 Pope *Julius II made him bishop of Cagli in Umbria, and in 1513 *Leo x made him titular archbishop of Nazareth.

Benigno served on a commission to examine the *Augenspiegel* of Johann *Reuchlin and in January 1515 composed a short dialogue in defence of Reuchlin, the *Defensio praestantissimi viri Johannis Reuchlin*. Martin *Gröning, a lawyer appointed to defend Reuchlin's cause in Rome, presented the manuscript to *Maximilian I, and it was printed, with a dedication to the emperor, in September 1517 at Cologne. Johannes *Caesarius sent two copies to Erasmus on 22 September 1517 (Ep 680). When the Dominican theologian Jacob of *Hoogstraten attacked Reuchlin and the *Defensio* of Benigno, Erasmus replied with Ep 1006, which, among other things, criticized Hoogstraten for lack of balance and objectivity.

Benigno also wrote a study of the nature of angels: *De natura caelestium spiritum quos angelos vocamus* (Florence: Bartolomeo di Libri 1499). For the disputation of 1489 see Nicolaus Mirabilis *Disputatio nuper facta in domo magnifici Laurentii Medices* (Florence: Francesco di Dino 1489).

BIBLIOGRAPHY: Allen Ep 680 / EI VI 642 / Ludwig Geiger *Johann Reuchlin* (Leipzig 1871, repr 1964) 400–4 and passim

TBD

Nikolaus BENSROTT of Üffeln, documented 1500–9
Nikolaus Bensrott (Benseradus), born in Üffeln, on the Weser, east of Osnabrück, was brought up in the household of the counts of Virneburg near Koblenz. After studying law at Bologna he stayed in Orléans in 1500 as one of the students of Augustinus Vincentius *Caminadus (Epp 136, 156) and came into contact with Erasmus, who was one of his teachers either at Orléans or at Paris; he assisted Erasmus financially, shared his interest in Greek literature (Epp 158–60), and was eager to build up his own library. After obtaining a legal doctorate he returned to Virneburg as secretary to Count Dietrich. Johann Butzbach, prior of the Benedictine monastery of Maria Laach in the Eiffel, west of Koblenz, became one of his friends and had access to Bensrott's valuable library, which he used to write his 'Auctarium de scriptoribus ecclesiasticis' (1508–13, manuscript in Bonn), which contains a biographical note on Bensrott. Although he was highly esteemed for his knowledge of legal affairs, Bensrott suddenly decided to retire from court life and entered the Franciscan monastery in Marburg; some books from his library were distributed among his friends, but the majority were given to the monastery of Maria Laach. In 1509 Butzbach was expecting Bensrott's return from Marburg to Koblenz.

BIBLIOGRAPHY: Allen and CWE Ep 158 / G. Knod summarized and in part published Butzbach's 'Auctarium' in: *Annalen des Historischen Vereins für den Niederrhein* 52 (1891) 175–234; for Bensrott see 179–80, 214–16

IG

Michael BENTINUS d November 1527
Michael Bentinus (Bentius, Bentinius) was born in Flanders around 1495; nothing is known regarding his parents or his education.

In 1520 he was in Basel, where he worked for the press of Johann *Froben as a corrector of Latin texts, among them Erasmus' *Adagia* (published October 1520) and a translation of the Greek grammar of Theodorus *Gaza (published February 1521). He gained the friendship of *Beatus Rhenanus and the *Amerbach brothers and was later remembered in their circle with genuine admiration. Erasmus, however, was not pleased with Bentinus' handling of the *Adagia*, complaining of his misplaced zeal in correcting and collating (Ep 1437). Some time afterwards Bentinus returned to Flanders and from there wrote to Erasmus by March 1524; he reported hostility towards Erasmus and criticism of his writings on the part of Canon Jan de *Hondt at Courtrai (Ep 1433). Erasmus wrote twice to de Hondt and assured him that he had never placed much reliance in Bentinus (Epp 1433, 1471). During his stay in Flanders Bentinus visited Levinus *Ammonius a few months prior to July 1524 (Ep 1463) and spread the teachings of the reformers, whose doctrines he had embraced (Ep 1514).

By the fall of 1524 Bentinus was again in Basel, working for the presses of Valentinus *Curio and Andreas *Cratander. He married and thought that he might be summoned to France to preach the new religious beliefs (Epp 1514, 1548; Erasmus' references suggest that he was in orders). He established relations with Guillaume *Farel, Johannes *Oecolampadius, and the Strasbourg reformers and suggested to Anémond de Coct that they jointly start a press to publish French translations of the Gospels (Herminjard I Ep 120).

In 1525 Bentinus went to Zürich and Lyon in search of a better position, but he was unsuccessful and returned to Basel, where he resumed his work with Curio. In the autumn of 1527 he enjoyed the confidence of the Anabaptist Hans *Denck, who was visiting the Basel region (BA *Oekolampads* II 104). In a letter of 25 November 1527 addressed to Farel, Oecolampadius reported that Bentinus had died of the plague the previous week and that his wife and child had died earlier (BA *Oekolampads* II 112). Erasmus mentioned Bentinus' death in a letter of 1 March 1528 written to Lazare de *Baïf (Ep 1962). Perhaps on account of Bentinus' contacts with *Eppendorf (Ep 1437) and Farel (Ep 1548), Erasmus had never quite trusted him (Ep 1840).

Bentinus' literary output reflects the kind of work he performed for the Basel printers. He compiled brief commentaries on Varro (*De lingua latina*), Festus, and Nonius Marcellus which were published together with the texts of these authors and the *Cornucopia* of Niccolò *Perotti (Basel: V. Curio 1526), and prepared editions of Horace (Basel: V. Curio 1527) and Claudian (Basel: J. Bebel and M. Isengrin 1534). He assisted Andreas Cratander in an edition of Cicero which was published in 1528 and contains a preface by Cratander lamenting Bentinus' untimely death. Bentinus also edited Froben's edition of the poems of Caspar *Ursinus Velius (1522), which contained many of the Greek epigrams in translation, and he may have been responsible for the verse translations of the epigrams in Curio's edition (Basel 1524) of Traversari's Latin version of Diogenes Laertius' *Lives of the Philosophers*.

BIBLIOGRAPHY: Allen Ep 1433 / AK I Ep 746, II Ep 1162, IV Ep 2082, and passim / BRE Epp 58, 166 / BA *Oekolampads* I 395–7 and passim / P.G. Bietenholz *Basle and France in the Sixteenth Century* (Geneva-Toronto 1971) 81–2, 263, and passim / Herminjard I Epp 103, 120, 153, 164, 181–5, II Ep 207 / F. Hoefer *Nouvelle Biographie générale* (Paris 1855–70) V 415 / J. Hutton *The Greek Anthology in Italy to the Year 1800* (Ithaca, NY-London 1935) 89–91 / C.G. Jöcher *Allgemeines Gelehrten-Lexicon* Ergänzungsband I (Leipzig 1784, repr 1960) 1683

VIRGINIA BROWN & PGB

Annibale (II) BENTIVOGLIO of Bologna, 1469–24 June 1540
Annibale was the first son of Giovanni (II) *Bentivoglio, the leading citizen and lord of Bologna, and of Ginevra Sforza, a kinswoman of the dukes of Milan. In 1474 the senate of Bologna obtained permission from *Sixtus IV for him to succeed his father as Bologna's leading citizen. In 1478 he was betrothed to Lucrezia d'Este, a natural daughter of Ercole, lord of Ferrara, and the wedding was celebrated on 28 January 1487. In 1489 his father made him *gonfaloniere* of justice, to strengthen his claim to the leadership of the commune. In the diplomatic schemes of his father,

Annibale served primarily as a *condottiere*, participating in campaigns for Florence, Milan, and Venice. He also helped his father resist Cesare Borgia, who attempted to carve a secular dominion out of the Romagna at the turn of the sixteenth century. In 1506, however, he and his father were unable to prevent Pope *Julius II from conquering Bologna, which they abandoned on the night of 1–2 November. When his father proved reluctant to reconquer Bologna by force of arms, Annibale assumed leadership of his family and, after abortive attempts in 1507, 1508, and 1510, succeeded in winning the city in May 1511. His rule was short-lived, however, and he relinquished the city to papal armies on 10 June 1512. Negotiations with popes *Leo X and *Adrian VI and military expeditions in 1522 and 1527 failed to return the city to the Bentivoglio family. Annibale died in Ferrara.

Erasmus was in Bologna late in 1506, but during the critical days of the siege took refuge at Florence (Epp 200, 203, 205). In November and December 1511, Andrea *Ammonio (Ep 247) and Paolo *Bombace, who was in Bologna (Ep 251), reported news of the return of Annibale ('Bononiensis') and his relatives to Bologna, and of the second siege by papal troops.

A fresco of the members of the family of Giovanni (II) Bentivoglio, by Lorenzo Costa, is found in the church of San Giacomo Maggiore at Bologna.

BIBLIOGRAPHY: CWE Ep 247 (rejecting Allen's suggestion that Bononiensis referred to Achille de' Grassi, bishop of Bologna) / G. De Caro in DBI VIII 595–600 / Cecilia M. Ady *The Bentivoglio of Bologna* (Oxford 1937) / Albano Sorbelli *I Bentivoglio signori di Bologna* (Bologna 1969)

TBD

Giovanni (II) BENTIVOGLIO of Bologna, 15 February 1443–February 1508
Giovanni (II) Bentivoglio was born at Bologna to Donnina Visconti, a kinswoman of Filippo Maria Visconti, duke of Milan, and Annibale (I) Bentivoglio, the leading citizen of Bologna and the chief protagonist in a long struggle in defence of Bolognese autonomy against Milan, the papacy, and the *condottieri* Niccolò and

Giovanni (II) Bentivoglio by Ercole Roberti

Francesco Piccinino. When Annibale was assassinated on 24 June 1445, the Bolognese invited Sante Bentivoglio, an illegitimate cousin of Annibale, to rule the city during Giovanni's minority. Although Sante was only twenty-one in 1445, he governed Bologna with wisdom and extended the power of the Bentivoglio faction. Meanwhile, Giovanni was gradually being involved in the government of the city. In 1452 the Emperor *Frederick III made him a knight, and shortly thereafter the Bolognese elevated him to the senate.

When Sante died on 1 October 1463, Giovanni became *gonfaloniere* of justice and ruler of Bologna. The next thirty years witnessed the gradual increase of the power of the Bentivoglio and allied families over Bologna and the decline of the influence of the papal legate. Giovanni Bentivoglio enhanced his personal position by marrying Ginevra Sforza, the widow of Sante and a niece of Francesco I Sforza, duke of Milan. The union produced seven daughters and four sons – Annibale (II) *Bentivoglio, Antongaleazzo, Alessandro, and Ermes. Giovanni strengthened his control over

Bologna by contracting marriage alliances with neighbouring lords and by having his sons serve as *condottieri* for Florence, Milan, Venice, and other states. He was also a patron to artists and humanists. His power produced enemies, and in 1488 members of the Malvezzi family plotted his assassination. The conspirators were discovered and suffered death, exile, and confiscation of goods.

In 1494 *Charles VIII of France invaded Italy and began a series of events which led to the end of the Bentivoglio signory at Bologna. Although Giovanni Bentiviglio opposed Ludovico *Sforza's decision to involve France in Italian affairs, he adopted a policy of neutrality and thus spared his city from the worst effects of Charles' invasion. However, the fall of the Sforza of Milan and the Medici of Florence and the efforts of Cesare Borgia to carve out a personal dominion in the Romagna destroyed the traditional system of alliances on which the Bentivoglio depended, while the massacre of the Marescotti family, perpetrated by Ermes Bentivoglio and left unpunished by his father, undermined the loyalty of the Bolognese. The Bentivoglio regime weathered the Borgia threat but could not resist Pope *Julius II when he continued and extended the policy of removing petty despots from the papal states. On the night of 1–2 November 1506, encircled by papal and French armies and without allies, Giovanni Bentivoglio led his family from Bologna. Reluctant to attempt a counter-attack without support from *Louis XII of France, he left expeditions for the recovery of Bologna to his sons.

Erasmus was in Bologna briefly in the autumn of 1506 (Epp 200, 203, 205) but sought refuge in Florence when word arrived that Julius II and the French intended to lay siege to the city. He later lampooned Julius' motives for conquering Bologna in the *Julius exclusus* (*Opuscula* 83–5) and mentioned Giovanni Bentivoglio in *Adagia* III i 92: 'Spes alunt exules.'

A fresco of the members of the family of Giovanni (II) Bentivoglio, by Lorenzo Costa, is found in the church of San Giacomo Maggiore at Bologna. A portrait of Giovanni (II) by Costa is found in the Uffizi, Florence.

BIBLIOGRAPHY: Allen and CWE Ep 200 / G. De Caro in DBI VIII 622–32 / Cecilia M. Ady *The Bentiviglio of Bologna* (Oxford 1937) / Albano

Sorbelli *I Bentiviglio, signori di Bologna* (Bologna 1969)

TBD

Paolo BENZI of Como, documented 1516–54
Paolo Benzi was a resident of Como and a relative of Benedetto *Giovio through the latter's mother, Elisabetta Benzi. In 1525 he encouraged Benedetto to write to Erasmus (CWE Ep 1634A). Paolo's name appears regularly on the list of officials of Como between 1516 and 1554, and in 1537 he and a brother were listed on the tax rolls as living in the parish of Santa Maria, the cathedral of Como, and as possessing property and business interests at Como and Rome. In 1501 a Paolo Benzi was named in a notarial document at Milan.

BIBLIOGRAPHY: *La Correspondance d'Erasme* ed A. Gerlo et al (Brussels 1967–   ) VI 584 / Ida Calabi Limentani 'La lettera di Benedetto Giovio ad Erasmo' *Acme* 25 (1972) 25, 28–9

ANNA GIULIA CAVAGNA

Nicolas BÉRAULT of Orléans, c 1470–c 1545
Nicolas Bérault (Beraldus) was born into a family from the Bas-Poitou, established at Orléans since the fifteenth century. He studied the arts and civil law in his native Orléans. After a voyage to Italy (c 1494) he returned to Orléans and founded a private school. It says much for the reputation of this school that Erasmus spent a few days with Bérault on his way to Italy in the autumn of 1506.

The exact date when Bérault began to study Greek is unknown, but he was taught by Girolamo *Aleandro, who visited Orléans from December 1510 to June 1511 at the invitation of Jean Pyrrhus d'*Angleberme, a friend and fellow-student of Bérault. At about the same time, Bérault lectured at the University of Orléans on the *Corpus juris* (Digest I 2: *De origine juris*), and Guillaume *Budé saw in him a disciple who would continue his own work (Budé *Opera omnia*, Basel 1557, I 260–1).

In 1512 Bérault left for Paris both to give personal attention to a lawsuit and to continue his studies. At first as an *avocat* and later as a *conseiller* in the Parlement, he became one of the most important members of the Paris humanist circle, which included other men from Orléans such as François *Deloynes, Louis *Ruzé,

Guillaume *Hué, Louis de *Berquin, and Claude Brachet. At his home and in different colleges he gave public lectures on the classical authors, many of which were subsequently published: those on Cicero's *De legibus* in 1512, on Aristotle's *Oeconomica* in 1514, on Suetonius in 1515, and on Poliziano's *Rusticus* in 1518. He also edited, translated from Greek to Latin, or at least prefaced a considerable number of publications of which a nearly exhaustive inventory can be found in the articles by Louis Delaruelle. Bérault is notably the first editor of Lucretius in France (Paris: J. Bade and J. Petit 1514). His edition of Pliny's *Historia naturalis* (Paris 1516), on which he collaborated with Louis de Berquin, gained the admiration of Erasmus (Ep 1544). While this edition was being printed late in 1514, the printer, Jean Barbier, died. Bérault took charge of his press and later married Barbier's widow, but his career as a printer was short-lived. However, he remained in business as a bookseller until 1518, when Bishop Etienne *Poncher engaged him as his secretary and took him with him on his diplomatic missions to England (August 1518) and Montpellier (April 1519). He was also in contact with Michel *Boudet, the bishop of Langres, who asked him to publish the commentaries on St Paul attributed to Athanasius but actually by Theophylactus, an edition supplemented with the *Paraclesis* of Erasmus (Paris: J. Petit 1518–19). Around 1525 Bérault resumed his teaching, and Etienne *Dolet, Melchior Wolmar, and François *Poncher were among his students.

When Etienne Poncher died in February 1525 Jean d'Orléans, archbishop of Toulouse, became Bérault's new protector. In 1528 Bérault was in Orléans (Ep 2075), and in 1529 he succeeded Paolo *Emilio as the royal historiographer and, on the occasion of the treaty of Cambrai, published an *Oratio de pace restituta* (Paris: C. Wechel 1529) dedicated to Chancellor Antoine *Duprat.

In 1531, Louise de Montmorency, the widow of Gaspard de Coligny, chose Bérault to tutor her three sons. He stayed several times at Châtillon-sur-Loing in the Orléanais and remained particularly attached to the eldest Coligny son, Odet, the future cardinal of Châtillon. With Odet he followed the movements of the court, accompanying him in

1533–4 to the south of France, on the occasion of the marriage of the future *Henry II to *Catherine de' Medici. A speech entitled *De vetere ac novitia jurisprudentia* that Bérault had in vain hoped to deliver to the students of Toulouse was printed in no fewer than four editions in 1533. For a part of the summer of that year, Bérault resided near Avignon at the home of François de Clermont-Lodève and there wrote his most personal work, a dialogue entitled *Dialogus quo rationes quaedam explicantur quibus dicendi ex tempore facultas parari potest deque ipsa dicendi ex tempore facultate* (Lyon: S. Gryphius 1534). In this his last known work he advocated a living Latin, a language spontaneously spoken and capable of expressing the realities of modern life. In doing so, he denounced Ciceronianism as a sterile discipline which stifled invention. While proclaiming his admiration of Cicero, Bérault primarily recommended the study and imitation of the Latin poets.

The Burgerbibliothek of Berne owns some manuscript letters that Bérault wrote in the same period. They show him deeply affected by the tragic turn of politico-religious events and above all, weary of his restless life in the cardinal's entourage. While he was on a visit to Toulouse with Odet from 1535 to 1536 he became acquainted with Jean de *Pins (Ep 3083). In the spring of 1537 he participated in a banquet given to celebrate Etienne Dolet's release from jail. Little is known about him after this date, and the year of his death remains uncertain.

Although his close association with the Coligny provided many contacts with the new religion, Bérault appears to have kept a cautious balance; he never exceeded the critical evangelism of Budé or Erasmus. His son, François, however, was to adopt Calvinism.

Erasmus' acquaintance with Bérault dates from his visit to Orléans in 1506 and was renewed in 1516 by a postscript which Bérault added in a letter from François Deloynes (Ep 494). Warm and helpful by nature, Bérault had many friends. Always eager to join Erasmus in the battle with conservative theologians (Ep 925), Bérault once came close to endangering Erasmus' good relations with Maarten van *Dorp (Epp 994, 1002, 1024; CWE Ep 1000A) and was also cautioned in the course of Erasmus' controversy with Edward *Lee (Ep 1058). He was the intermediary between Erasmus and Nöel *Béda (Epp 1571, 1579, 1581, 1685); he also suggested to Erasmus that he dedicate to Jean de *Selve the *Apologia adversus Petrum Sutorem* (Ep 1598) and may have urged him to prolong the controversy with *Cousturier (Epp 1893, 2443). In 1522 Erasmus dedicated to Bérault *De conscribendis epistolis* (Ep 1284). He was well aware of Bérault's affectionate and congenial nature, his pedagogical gifts (Ep 535), and his scholarly qualities (Ep 1544) but may not have considered him as an outstanding writer (*Ciceronianus* (ASD I-2 674).

BIBLIOGRAPHY: Allen Ep 925 / Eugène and Emile Haag *La France protestante* 2nd ed by H. Bordier (Paris 1877–) II 297–302 / Herminjard III Ep 483 and passim / Louis Delaruelle 'Notes bibliographiques sur Nicolas Bérault, suivies d'une bibliographie de ses oeuvres et de ses publications' *Revue des Bibliothèques* 12 (1902) 420–45 / Louis Delaruelle 'Nicolas Bérault (c 1470–c 1552) ...' *Le Musée belge* 13 (1909) 253–312 / Louis Delaruelle 'Notes complémentaires sur deux humanistes' *Revue du seizième siècle* 15 (1928) 311–18 / Louis de Berquin *Declamation des louenges de mariage* ed E.V. Telle (Geneva 1976) 11–17, 103–5 / M.-M. de la Garanderie *Christianisme et lettres profanes* (Lille-Paris 1976) I 56–75 / M.-M. de la Garanderie 'Comment parler couramment le latin: Un dialogue de Nicolas Bérault (1534)' *Acta conventus neo-latini Turonensis* (Paris 1980) 481–93

MARIE-MADELEINE DE LA GARANDERIE

Antoine BERCIN of Besançon, c 1490–26 February 1537/1538
Antoine Bercin was a student at Dole in 1506, when at the age of seventeen he presented himself for the academic exercise of a public disputation on the *Institutes* of Justinian and recorded this event in his copy of Justinian (Paris 1499), which is now in the Bibliothèque publique of Besançon. On 13 September 1505, though still a student, he was appointed canon and scholaster, thus occupying a prominent rank within the chapter. Erasmus met him during his visit to Besançon in 1524 (Ep 1610), and in the spring of 1529, when he had decided to leave Basel and was considering moving to Besançon, he sent Bercin a polite letter together with a book as a present; the canon

sent him a letter of thanks (Epp 2138, 2148).

BIBLIOGRAPHY: Allen Ep 2138 / Auguste Castan *Catalogue des incunables de la Bibliothèque publique de Besançon* (Besançon 1893) 473 / Archives du Doubs, Besançon MS G 250 / Gauthier 131

PGB

BERCKMANNUS See BIRCKMANN

Richard BERE d 20 January 1525
Bere (Beere, Berus) probably came from the Somerset village of Beer; he entered the great Benedictine abbey of Glastonbury by February 1478, when he received minor orders. He doubtless held several monastic offices before his appointment as abbot, made by Richard *Foxe, bishop of Winchester, on 12 November 1493 after quashing a previous election. Four years later Abbot Bere entertained *Henry VII on his way to suppress Warbeck's rising. In 1503 he supplicated doctor of divinity at Oxford and in the same year was one of a delegation sent to the newly elected Pope Pius III to seek dispensation for Prince Henry (later *Henry VIII) to marry his late brother's widow, *Catherine of Aragon. The mission was terminated by the pope's death, but in the following year Bere was sent to his successor, *Julius II. Bere's greatest achievement was as a builder in and around Glastonbury. He enriched the now destroyed abbey church, erecting inverted strainer arches similar to those found in Wells Cathedral. He built several new chapels, including one honouring the cult of the 'Holy House' of Loretto (the first such in England, and clearly prompted by his Italian travels) and one to house the supposed remains of Saxon kings. He was an enthusiastic supporter of the cult of Joseph of Arimathea, Glastonbury's legendary founder, and in 1508 was involved in an acrimonious dispute with Archbishop William *Warham over the authenticity of his abbey's relics of St Dunstan – also claimed by the monks of Warham's cathedral.

Despite this rather excessive zeal for Glastonbury's misty past, Bere was well regarded by men of the new learning. Erasmus wrote to him in September 1524 regretting that they had not met and praising his kindness and liberality to fellow scholars, particularly Richard *Pace and Zacharias *Deiotarus; but he took

occasion to recall that Bere's chaplain had at
one time caused offence by criticism of his work
as an editor of St Jerome (Ep 1490). Bere may
also have befriended John *Claymond, the first
president of Corpus Christi College, Oxford,
who held a living in the gift of Glastonbury
Abbey. In the archives at Corpus is a letter from
Bere to Bishop Foxe concerning a land transaction in 1519 (Foxe *Letters* 119–20). Bere died on
the anniversary of his enthronement.

BIBLIOGRAPHY: Allen Ep 1490 / DNB II 323–4 /
Emden BRUO I 150 / *Victoria County History
Somerset* II (London 1911) 93 / C.A. Raleigh
Radford *Glastonbury Abbey* (1973) 14, 19 / David
Knowles *The Religious Orders in England* (Cam-
bridge 1948–1959) III 23 / P.S. and H.M. Allen
Letters of Richard Fox 1486–1527 (Oxford 1929)
106, 108, 117, 118 / F.A. Gasquet 'Blessed
Richard Bere' *Downside Review* 9 (1890) 158–63
(an account of Abbot Bere's nephew, one of the
martyred London Carthusians)

C.S. KNIGHTON

Jan Arentszoon BEREN of Amsterdam, d
before 9 April 1559
Johannes Berius or Ursus, the rector of the
municipal school of Rotterdam mentioned in
Ep 1668 with the implication that Erasmus
knew and esteemed him, was probably Jan
Arentszoon Beren (Berens), a priest of
Amsterdam. Beren, then, became rector in or
before 1525 after studying at Louvain, where
he seems to have matriculated on 19 January
1521. In 1534 he conferred a vicarage in the
Nieuwe Kerk of Amsterdam on *Alaard of
Amsterdam, to which the latter was admitted
on 8 August. On 2 April 1535 Beren himself
obtained Randenbroek, an estate south of
Amersfoort, from the bishop of Utrecht. At his
death he left three natural children: Jan, Anna,
and Trijn.

Beren was a friend of Cornelis *Gerard, who
dedicated to him for use in his school an edition
of Cornelis *Croock's *Farrago sordidorum
verborum*, printed in one volume with Erasmus'
paraphrase of Lorenzo *Valla's *Elegantiae*
(Cologne: J. Gymnich 1529). Alaard of
Amsterdam included some verses by Beren in
his edition of Erasmus' *Carmen bucolicum*
(Leiden: P. Balenus, 13 February 1538; NK 786).
Only one pupil of Beren is known: a son of
Floris *Oem van Wijngaarden and younger

Anna van Bergen, copy after Jan Mabuse

brother of Jan *Oem (Ep 1668), whom he taught
Latin and Greek.

BIBLIOGRAPHY: Allen Ep 1668 / *Matricule de
Louvain* III-1 640 / J.G. Kam in *Jaarboek van het
Centraal Bureau voor Genealogie* 16 (1962) 61
VIII-2 / J.G. Kam in *Jaarboek Amstelodamum* 54
(1962) 38, 47 / N. van der Blom *Erasmus en
Rotterdam* (Rotterdam-The Hague 1969) 73–94

C.G. VAN LEIJENHORST

Anna van BERGEN 16 September 1492–
15 July 1541
Anna was a daughter of Jan (III) van *Bergen
and Adriana van Brimeu. On 18 June 1509 she
married Adolph of *Burgundy, lord of Veere
(Ep 291). She bore him several children, among
them Maximilian, born on 28 July 1514. When
Erasmus was on visit shortly afterwards, she
had not yet recovered from the birth (Ep 301).
A portrait of Anna, now in the Isabella Stewart
Gardner Museum, Boston, is reproduced in
CWE 3 10.

BIBLIOGRAPHY: Allen Ep 93 / NNBW X 50 /
C.J.F. Slootmans *Jan metten lippen* (Rotterdam-
Antwerp 1945) 190–1

C.G. VAN LEIJENHORST

Antoon (I) van Bergen by Jacques le Boucq

Antoon (I) van BERGEN 4 July 1455–
12 January 1532

Antoon, the fourth son of Jan (II) and younger
brother of Jan (III) and Hendrik van *Bergen, is
said to have studied in Louvain. Having joined
the Cistercian order, he was abbot of
Mont-Sainte-Marie in Burgundy from 1480 to
1483. In 1483 the Benedictines of St Truiden
elected him to be their next abbot, but this was
done under duress while his brother Cornelis
was on hand with an armed force. During the
following years of civil strife St Truiden was
sacked on 20 January 1486 and Antoon was
detained for some time in Liège. He remained
commendatory abbot of St Truiden until 1516
or 1517. Meanwhile the abbacy of St Bertin at
Saint-Omer fell vacant, and on a free vote one
Jacques Duval was elected abbot and consecrated on 2 July 1493. But the Bergen family had
other plans for the rich abbey and, using
Duval's reputation as a Francophile, obtained
the support of Philip the Handsome, duke of
*Burgundy, for an appeal to Rome. Duval's
election was annulled, and owing to pressure
from Bishop Hendrik van Bergen and, once
again, the presence of a military force, Antoon

was installed as abbot on 18 July 1493 and
retained the position until his death. In 1495 he
succeeded in ending an old quarrel between
the abbey and the chapter of Saint-Omer
concerning the public display of the relics of St
Bertin and St Omer, which were kept in the
same chest. In 1518 he arbitrated the conflict
between three ecclesiastics each claiming the
abbacy of Clairmarais, a Cistercian house near
Saint-Omer.

As the most powerful abbot of the region and
a member of the very influential Bergen family,
Antoon soon took a hand in the affairs of the
entire country. In May or June 1500 Philip the
Handsome visited Saint-Omer; Antoon received
him with great pomp and was named a ducal
councillor, a function he retained under
*Charles v. In the following year he escorted
*Margaret of Austria to Dole for her marriage to
Philibert ii, duke of *Savoy. It is a mark of his
growing influence in the following decade that
in 1514 Erasmus addressed to him Ep 288, the
argument of which was later expanded in the
adage *Dulce bellum inexpertis* (*Adagia* iv i 1).
He also held splendid receptions for Charles v
at Saint-Omer in 1520 (cwe Ep 1106) and 1528,
and in the following year helped to negotiate
the 'Ladies' Peace' at Cambrai. St Bertin,
however, remained a prominent concern of
his. In 1520 the construction of the abbey
church was completed; the ruins of its tower
are still an imposing sight. In 1511 he
appointed his nephew, Engelbert van *Spangen, coadjutor. The following year, to
compensate for Engelbert's lack of experience,
he appointed a board to manage the temporal
affairs of the abbey. The *grand cartulaire* of St
Bertin conserves 432 acts relating to his abbacy
which show him to have been a good
administrator but also evidence an increasing
desire for power and pomp as Antoon himself
grew older.

According to *Beatus Rhenanus, Erasmus
first met Antoon while in the service of
Hendrik van Bergen (Allen i 58). He also saw
him in 1500 at Tournehem (Ep 128) and
probably met him in 1501 when he composed
Ep 162 on his behalf. He saw more of the abbot
in 1502 (Epp 169, 170), 1514 (Ep 301), 1515 (Ep
332), and 1516, taking to him a horse donated
by Archbishop *Warham (Epp 412, 477, 781),
but apparently missed him in 1517 (Ep 739).

After that, contacts seem to have broken off, perhaps because Antoon took offence when shown the *Moria* in a French translation (Epp 673, 739), although in January 1518 Erasmus clearly believed that he could still count on Antoon's good will (Ep 761). At the suggestion of Erasmus, Thomas *More visited Antoon in 1517 and was very well received (Epp 683, 761).

Erasmus considered the abbot to be a patron of sorts (Epp 128, 138, 143, 149, 301). Apart from six preserved letters, he addressed to him in 1502 his epitaphs for Hendrik van Bergen (Reedijk poems 64–6) and may have had Antoon in mind when composing his epigram on a stingy patron (Reedijk poem 74; cf also poem 77).

BIBLIOGRAPHY: Allen Ep 143 / H. de Laplane *Les Abbés de Saint-Bertin* (Saint-Omer 1854–5) II 59–88 / A.J. Fruytier in NNBW IX 50–1 / A.J. Fruytier in *Taxandria* 31 (1924) 102–10, 220–7 / Saint-Omer, Bibliothèque Municipale MS 803: *Le grand cartulaire* of St Bertin vols VIII and IX
ANDRÉ GODIN & C.G. VAN LEIJENHORST

Antoon (II) van BERGEN d 17 April 1540
Antoon van Bergen was a half-brother of Dismas van *Bergen, with whom he was probably studying at Orléans in 1501–2 (Ep 170). Antoon, a natural son of Jan (II) van *Bergen and Maria Goossens, pursued an ecclesiastical career. A chaplain to Philip the Handsome of *Burgundy and subsequently to *Charles V, he became canon and dean of the chapter of St Servatius at Maastricht in 1494 and held canonries at St Gummarus', Lier, from 1503, and at St Gertrude's, Bergen op Zoom, from 1510, together with other benefices. In 1522 he accompanied the emperor to England and – presumably – afterwards to Spain.

Another identification of the Antoon who studied at Orléans is proposed in Allen and CWE Ep 170.
BIBLIOGRAPHY: *Matricule d'Orléans* II-1 219 / LP III-2 968–9
PGB

Antoon (III) van BERGEN 13 May 1500–27 June 1541
Antoon was the third son of Jan (III) van *Bergen and Adriana van Brimeu; his mother failed to recover from his birth and died on 1 June 1500. In November 1517 he was studying

in Louvain (Ep 717) and there came into personal contact with Erasmus (Epp 760–2). Erasmus was favourably impressed by him but may have declined to act formally as his tutor (Ep 737). In 1518 Juan Luis *Vives dedicated to him his *Fabula de homine* and an introduction to Virgil's *Georgica*, both published in Vives' *Opuscula varia* (Louvain: D. Martens [1519]; NK 2172). In November 1519 Antoon set out for England, taking along recommendations from *Margaret of Austria and also a series of letters of introduction from Erasmus (Epp 1025, 1026, 1028, 1029, 1031, 1032). He was appointed cup-bearer to *Henry VIII but returned before long to marry Jacqueline, the sister of Cardinal Guillaume de *Croy (12 March 1521).

In 1526 Antoon was appointed to the privy council of *Charles V, and in 1531 he was made a knight of the Golden Fleece. As his two elder brothers died prematurely – Jan in 1514 and Phillips in 1525 – Antoon succeeded to all his father's titles when he died in 1532. Having formerly been lord of Grimbergen and Walhain, he now became lord of Bergen and a year later was created marquis of Bergen by Charles V. He rendered faithful and indispensable service to *Mary of Hungary, regent of the Netherlands, just as his father had done to her predecessor, Margaret of Austria, but died suddenly in 1541. Five of his six children were alive at the time of his death, among them Jan (b 6 February 1528), the heir to his titles. Given the date of his birth, Antoon cannot be identified with Antoon (II) van *Bergen, mentioned in Ep 170.
BIBLIOGRAPHY: Allen and CWE Ep 760 / C.J.F. Slootmans *Jan metten lippen* (Rotterdam-Antwerp 1945) 194–6, 309–68 / NNBW X 50–1
C.G. VAN LEIJENHORST

Dismas van BERGEN d before 1535
Dismas, a natural son of Jan (II) van *Bergen, was registered at the University of Louvain on 31 August 1497. He continued his studies at Orléans, where he matriculated on 14 August 1500. Erasmus met him in 1500 when visiting Orléans and staying with Jacob de *Voecht (Ep 133). Erasmus quickly took a liking to the young man (Epp 137, 147) and went to great lengths to have his current tutor, probably Jacques *Daniel, replaced by Voecht, who knew Dismas from Louvain and in Erasmus'

Hendrik van Bergen

view was far more capable than the other man. To this effect he wrote repeatedly to *Antonius of Luxembourg (Epp 137, 147, 150; cf Ep 143) and also to Jacob *Batt (Ep 138). Both were asked to use their influence with Antoon (I) van *Bergen, abbot of St Bertin, who was apparently responsible for Dismas' education. Erasmus' efforts succeeded only for a short while (Ep 157), because the abbot insisted that Dismas was not to be given any opportunity to speak his native Dutch (Ep 170).

In 1513 Dismas was appointed master of requests to *Margaret of Austria and in July 1517 a member of the privy council of the future *Charles V. He died in Barcelona while on an embassy. On 22 April 1510 he had married Marie, the daughter of the Burgundian treasurer-general, Hieronymus *Laurinus; one son, Maximiliaan van Bergen, became the first archbishop of Cambrai from 1562 to 1570, and another, Jan, lord of Waterdijck, became president of the grand council of Mechelen.

BIBLIOGRAPHY: Allen Ep 137 / C.J.F. Slootmans *Jan metten lippen* (Rotterdam-Antwerp 1945) 69 / *Matricule de Louvain* III-1 159 / *Matricule d'Orléans* II-1 207–8

C.G. VAN LEIJENHORST

Hendrik van BERGEN 20 July 1449–6/ 7 October 1502

Hendrik was the second son of Jan (II) van *Bergen and Margaretha van Rouveroy. He matriculated at Louvain on 22 June 1465 and at Orléans in March 1466, and was already a doctor of laws when he was appointed canon of Liège in 1473; he became abbot of St Denis-en-Broqueroie near Mons on 3 May 1477 and bishop of Cambrai on 17 May 1480, the consecration taking place at Brussels on 1 October. After lengthy resistance he was forced to give up his abbey in 1487 and perhaps in the same year went on a pilgrimage to Jerusalem, returning by way of Rome (cf Reedijk poems 64:7 and 65:6).

In April 1493 Hendrik was named chancellor of the order of the Golden Fleece and in July he again resorted to force to support the claim of his brother Antoon (I) van *Bergen to the abbey of St Bertin. Around this time, and at any rate after 25 April 1492 when Erasmus was ordained a priest, Hendrik took him into his service as a secretary (Allen I 57:40; it is impossible to suggest a date that would tally with the chronological indications made by Reyner *Snoy in his introduction to Erasmus' *Silva carminum*). To Erasmus this meant deliverance from the tedium of monastic life, particularly since Hendrik expected to be made a cardinal, which would have required him to travel to Italy. It was in the bishop's country house at Halsteren, near Bergen, that Erasmus revised the *Antibarbari* (Ep 37, Allen I 588). Hendrik's hopes of receiving the red hat were dashed, however, and so were Erasmus' hopes of visiting Italy; but before September 1495 (Ep 43) Hendrik released Erasmus so that he could take up theological studies in Paris and also pledged him some form of financial support (Allen I 58:63). In Paris Erasmus edited Willem *Hermans' *Sylva odarum*, inserting a letter of praise addressed to Hendrik (Epp 49, 51). Although their relationship was already cooling (Allen I 50; CWE 4 408) Hendrik continued to be his patron, or rather his 'anti-Maecenas' (Ep 135). On several occasions Erasmus complained about the bishop's failure to provide money (Epp 75–7, 81, 128). In the summer of 1498 Erasmus returned to Bergen to recover from the hardship of his life in Paris, but on 3 July soon after his arrival, the bishop left for an embassy to England, leaving

Erasmus to speculate that he hoped to enlist English help in his bid for the cardinalate (Epp 76, 77). By 1501 the relations between Hendrik and Erasmus were clearly under a cloud. Erasmus, who had again interrupted his studies in Paris, made great efforts to restore them (Epp 153, 154) and also visited the bishop (Ep 157), who asked him to compose a letter in his name (Ep 162), addressed to the future Pope *Leo x. After this there is no evidence to suggest that Hendrik had any further use for Erasmus or continued to support him.

As a leading prelate attached to the court of Burgundy Hendrik celebrated the wedding of Philip the Handsome of *Burgundy and *Joanna of Spain on 21 October 1496, and in November 1501 he accompanied the couple to Spain. But after a quarrel with the powerful François (I) de *Busleyden he was sent home in disgrace, as was his brother Jan (III) of *Bergen. He died a few weeks after his return to Cambrai. Erasmus wrote four epigrams for him (Reedijk poems 64–6; one, in Greek, is now missing) and received a renumeration of only six livres 'pour avoir fait aulcuns épitaphes et en aulmonne,' as the accounts specify; Erasmus commented in Ep 178 that this had been done 'so as to keep up in death the character [Hendrik] had in life.'

An anonymous portrait of Hendrik and Jan (III) van Bergen is in the Gemeentemuseum of Bergen op Zoom, and is reproduced in CWE 1 100.

BIBLIOGRAPHY: Allen Ep 49 and I 587–90 / C.J.F. Slootmans *Jan metten lippen* (Rotterdam-Antwerp 1945) 43–8 / *Matricule de Louvain* II-1 152 / *Messager des sciences historiques* (Ghent 1862) 415–17 / *Matricule d'Orléans* II-1 77–9 / A. Walther *Die Anfänge Karls v.* (Leipzig 1911) 25–6

C.G. VAN LEIJENHORST

Jan (II) van BERGEN 9 October 1417–7 September 1494
Jan (II) may be the lord of Bergen mentioned in Ep 42, provided that that letter can be assigned a date prior to his death.

BIBLIOGRAPHY: C.J.F. Slootmans *Jan metten lippen* (Rotterdam-Antwerp 1945) 9–106 / A.J. van der Aa et al *Biographisch Woordenboek der Nederlanden* (Haarlem 1852–78) VII 204–5

C.G. VAN LEIJENHORST

Jan (III) van Bergen

Jan (III) van BERGEN 15 October 1452–20 January 1532
Jan, the third son of Jan (II) van *Bergen ('Jan metten lippen') and Margaretha van Rouveroy, was born at Wouw, near Bergen op Zoom. His elder brother, Hendrik van *Bergen, had already entered the church when their oldest brother, Filips, died on 25 November 1475; thus it was Jan (III) who in 1494 inherited his father's estates of Glimes and Bergen op Zoom and the corresponding titles. Before that came to pass he was already a grand seigneur in his own right, being lord of Walhain (9 May 1472), knight of the Golden Fleece in 1481, and first chamberlain to *Maximilian I in 1485 and to Philip the Handsome, duke of *Burgundy, in 1493. He and Hendrik accompanied Duke Philip to Spain in 1501, but after a quarrel with François (I) de *Busleyden the brothers fell into disgrace and Jan lost his official appointment.

Under the new regency of *Margaret of Austria, however, Jan recovered his position of influence, becoming a member of her privy council. At court he represented a pro-English faction which opposed the policies of Guillaume de *Croy, lord of Chièvres, who sought reconciliation with France. At a time when the political orientation of the Burgundian court seemed to be constantly shifting, Jan undertook several embassies to England, and he lived to share in the triumph of Margaret's policies when prior to the 'Ladies' Peace' of Cambrai the war between England and *Charles v (1528–9) was quickly ended under pressure of commercial interdependence. As one of her intimate councillors Jan was appointed executor to Margaret's will, but he did not survive her for long. He died at Brussels and was buried at Bergen. In 1487 he had married Adriana van Brimeu (d 1500), who bore him three sons, among them Antoon (III) van *Bergen, his heir, and three daughters, one of whom, Anna van *Bergen, was to marry Adolph of *Burgundy. Seven natural children are known by name. On an anonymous painting in the Gemeentemuseum of Bergen op Zoom Jan is pictured kneeling by the side of Hendrik (reproduced in CWE 1 100).

Erasmus' acquaintance with Jan was probably a result of his close connections with Jan's brothers, Hendrik and Antoon. Although it was probably of long standing (Ep 42), it was never more than superficial. Jan, a 'man of great and well-deserved influence' (Ep 1025), probably tried in 1517 to recruit Erasmus as a tutor to his son Antoon (Ep 737). But although Erasmus felt indebted to Jan (Ep 969) and assisted Antoon as best he could, he declined the tutorship. And he declined again when Jan and some others tried to persuade him to become tutor to Prince *Ferdinand (Ep 952). In 1524 Erasmus was aware of Jan's protection of Frans van der *Hulst (Ep 1467).

BIBLIOGRAPHY: Allen and CWE Ep 737 / L.M.G. Kooperberg in NNBW X 43–51 / C.J.F. Slootmans *Jan metten lippen* (Rotterdam-Antwerp 1945) passim / de Vocht CTL I 260 and passim / Michel Baelde *De Collaterale Raden onder Karel v en Filips II* (Brussels 1965) 230–1 and passim

C.G. VAN LEIJENHORST

Maximiliaan van BERGEN d 1522
Maximiliaan was the eldest son of Cornelis and a grandson of Jan (II) van *Bergen. His mother was Maria Margaretha van Stryen, from whose family Maximiliaan inherited title to the lordship of Zevenbergen. He matriculated at

Louvain on 7 March 1498. On the death of his father in 1509 he inherited most of the family estates, which had, however, greatly suffered during the war in Gelderland of 1512–13. In 1516 he was made knight of the Golden Fleece. An outstanding diplomat, from 1518 he was intimately involved in the efforts of the house of Hapsburg to secure the emperorship for the future *Charles v and was sent to Germany for negotiations with the electors. To his disappointment he was not included when on 20 February 1519 Charles named his official representatives in Germany, but his indignant reaction ensured that he was granted a similar appointment on 4 March. He was sent to Switzerland, and on 12 April his presence at Constance is documented. He is probably the ranking diplomat who arranged for the conveyance of Ep 953 to Erasmus. In the year of his death, 1522, he was sent on an embassy to Rome. He was married to Anna van der Gracht (d 1545) but had no children.

BIBLIOGRAPHY: Allen and CWE Ep 953 / L.M.G. Kooperberg in NNBW X 51–2 / C.J.F. Slootmans *Jan metten lippen* (Rotterdam-Antwerp 1945) 197–200 / *Matricule de Louvain* III-1 169

C.G. VAN LEIJENHORST

BERGHES *See* BERGEN

Jindřich BERKA of Dubá, d 8 January 1541
Some time before 10 December 1524 Erasmus was visited at Basel by two young men recommended to him by his friend Heinrich *Stromer, professor of medicine at Leipzig. The visitors, 'a Duba' and 'ab *Haubitz' made an excellent impression (Ep 1522). The former was no doubt Jindřich Berka (Henricus Bircko, Byrck) of Dubá (Dauba), a member of a large and influential family of Bohemia. On 24 March 1520 he matriculated at the University of Wittenberg. He studied Greek with *Melanchthon, and when he left for Leipzig a year later Melanchthon dedicated to him his translation of Lucian's *De calumnia* (Wittenberg n d), a text on which he lectured in the summer term of 1521 (*Melanchthons Briefwechsel* I Ep 133). In the summer term of 1521 Berka matriculated at Leipzig, paying a fee far higher than was usual or required.

Berka subsequently returned to his native

country and served as chief justice and captain of Bohemia under King *Ferdinand I. His estates included Heřmanice, Kumburk, and Dřevenice. He was twice married and had six sons. He remained loyal to the Catholic faith and was buried in the cathedral of St Vitus, Prague. The Berka family of Dubá had several branches, and Erasmus' visitor, who is the only Berka then documented in Leipzig, should not be confused with his relative Jindřich Berka of Dubá at Drahobuz (1488–1545).

BIBLIOGRAPHY: Allen Ep 1522 / Matrikel Wittenberg I 88 / Matrikel Leipzig I 578 / Ottuv slovnik naučný (Prague 1888–1909) III 816–19 / Antonín Truhlář and Karel Hrdina Rukovět' k písemnictyí humanistickému I (Prague 1908)

J.K. ZEMAN

Cornelia BERNUY See Frans van der DILFT

Filippo (I) BEROALDO of Bologna,
7 November 1453–17 July 1505
The elder Filippo Beroaldo studied with Francesco dal Pozzo and subsequently became professor of rhetoric and poetry in Bologna in 1472. In 1476 he went to Paris, where his lectures on classical texts attracted large audiences and won him the respect and friendship of such early humanists as Robert *Gaguin. By 1479 he was back in Bologna, where he remained a highly successful teacher in the Studio until his death.

A prolific lecturer and writer, Beroaldo was known for a series of small-scale treatises on moral questions, for an Oratio on proverbs that inspired his pupil Polidoro *Virgilio to compile his collection of them, and, above all, for his enormous commentary on the Golden Ass of Apuleius, which included not only philological comments but vast excursuses on literary, historical, and artistic matters.

Erasmus came to Italy just too late to meet Beroaldo but noted the high regard in which he was held (Epp 1347, 3032; cf Ep 256). He criticized Virgilio implicity for deriving proverbs from Beroaldo rather than directly from the classical sources (Epp 1175, 2773), and in the Hieronymi vita he vigorously refuted the criticisms that Beroaldo, in an excursus in the Apuleius commentary, had made against the purity of St Jerome's Latinity (Opuscula 188–9). Among the other works by Beroaldo men-

tioned in Erasmus' correspondence are his commentary on Suetonius (Ep 648) and De terraemotu et pestilentia (Bologna: Benedictus Hectoris 1505, Ep 1803).

BIBLIOGRAPHY: Allen Ep 256 / R. Sabbadini in EI VI 771 / Myron P. Gilmore in DBI IX 382–4 / Konrad Krautter Philologische Methode und humanistische Existenz: Filippo Beroaldo und sein Kommentar zum Goldenen Esel des Apuleius (Munich 1971)

ANTHONY GRAFTON

Filippo (II) BEROALDO of Bologna,
1 October 1472–30 August 1518
Filippo, the nephew of Filippo (I) *Beroaldo, studied with his uncle and with Antonio Codro *Urceo at the Bologna Studio and became secretary to Cardinal Giovanni de' Medici, later Pope *Leo X. By 1516 he had become head of the reconstituted Roman Academy and prefect of the Vatican library. He died in Rome.

Beroaldo's published works included Latin poems that attained some popularity and a careful editio princeps of Tacitus' Annals books 1–6 (Rome: S. Guiberetus 1515). He and Erasmus became friends in Rome (Epp 1347, 3032). In the Ciceronianus Nosoponus ranks him above his uncle as a Ciceronian, despite his small output (ASD I-2 666–7).

BIBLIOGRAPHY: Allen Ep 1347 / R. Sabbadini in EI VI 771 / E. Paratore in DBI IX 384–8

ANTHONY GRAFTON

Louis de BERQUIN d 17 April 1529
Louis de Berquin (Deberquinus) was a Flemish nobleman, the son of Jean de Berquin, from whom he inherited the fiefs of Jumelles and Berquin, in what is now Vieux-Berquin, eleven kilometres south-east of Hazebrouck in the Département du Nord. The income, according to Erasmus, was a modest six hundred écus per year (Ep 2188).

The first mention of Berquin occurs in humanist prefaces: in June 1512 Josse *Bade dedicated the second volume of his edition of *Poliziano's Opera to him. Berquin seems to have taken a doctorate in civil law at Orléans, where he was associated with Nicolas *Bérault, who recommended him to Erasmus in 1519 as a 'very learned man' (Ep 925).

Berquin was tried three times for heresy, in

1523, 1526, and 1529. He escaped punishment after the first two trials thanks to the personal intervention of *Francis I, who was urged to do this, during the second trial, by his sister, *Margaret of Angoulême, and by Erasmus. After the third trial Berquin was burned at the stake, before there was time for royal intervention.

The first trial began when he was found on 1 May 1523 to be in possession of Lutheran books and manuscripts, in violation of an edict of the Parlement. These included *Luther's *De captivitate babylonica*, *Melanchthon's *Loci communes*, a work of *Karlstadt, Berquin's translations of Luther's complaint against the bull *Exsurge Domine*, of *Hutten's *Trias romana*, and of the *Paradisus Julii pape* (evidently the *Julius exclusus*, often attributed to Erasmus), and original works by Berquin, including an *Apologia ad calumniatores Lutheri* (D'Argentré I-2 404–6; Delisle 1523).

Asked by the Parlement to assess the seized materials, the faculty of theology found them to be obviously Lutheran and recommended they be burnt. The king's request to postpone the assessment arrived too late, and the books were publicly burnt on 8 August 1523.

As for Berquin himself, the faculty recommended that 'inasmuch as he is such a vigorous advocate of Lutheran impiety ... he should be required by process of law to make public abjuration of the works he has written and translated, and should be prohibited by the authority of the Parlement to write or to translate from Latin into the vernacular anything in justification of the Lutheran poison, or which is prejudicial to the Catholic faith' (D'Argentré I-2 406). The Parlement considered the faculty's recommendations, but, after permitting Berquin to appear several times to plead his case, finally turned him over to the bishop of Paris for the completion of his trial (5 August). At this point the king evoked the case to his council, which eventually released Berquin (November 1523), after he had signed the following declaration: 'I Louis, Seigneur de Berquin, detest, abominate, and anathematize every kind of heresy and particularly the heresies of Master Martin Luther, his adherents and partisans. Of his works I have made some extracts and translations, but I declare that I do not wish to

support or abide by them, as I intend to follow and adhere to evangelical and apostolic teaching and to that of Holy Church exclusively, and never to contradict it, nor to translate the books of the said Luther ... Should I pertinaciously and obstinately uphold Luther's heresies, or those of his adherents and supporters, in that case I submit to the judgment of Holy Church and to such coercion and punishment as the law requires' (*Bulletin de la Société de l'histoire du Protestantisme français* 67, 1918, 180–1).

Meanwhile the faculty was examining the writings of Erasmus. On 20 May 1525 French translations (in manuscript) of four of his works were condemned: a *Declamation des louenges de mariage* (Erasmus' *Encomium matrimonii*), a *Briesve admonition de la manière de prier* (from Erasmus' paraphrases of Matthew and Luke), a *Symbole des apostres* (Erasmus' colloquy *Inquisitio de fide*), and, in June, a *Complainte de la paix* (Erasmus' *Querela pacis*). The faculty recommended that, on account of their impious or heretical contents, these works should not be printed (D'Argentré II-1 42). Nevertheless they were, in October of the same year. Such defiance of the faculty of theology may have been what provoked the authorities to look for the translator.

Erasmus was immediately informed of the condemnations by Noël *Béda, the syndic of the faculty, who added his suspicion that the translator was Berquin (Ep 1579). Erasmus replied that he knew Berquin only from letters, and pointed out that the translator might well have added something to the text (Ep 1581). To Berquin he complained that by translating his little books into the vernacular and subjecting them to the cognizance of the theologians he was greatly increasing the ill will which the latter already felt for Erasmus (Ep 1599).

In January 1526 Berquin was back in the Parlement's prison. His new trial began in the absence of the king, a prisoner of *Charles V from his capture at the battle of Pavia, 24 February 1525, until his return to France on 18 March 1526. The Parlement had seized the opportunity to pursue the advocates of reform, especially those who had enjoyed favour at the royal court. At the request of the Parlement, the king's mother, Louise of *Savoy, acting as regent, had invited the pope to establish a special tribunal of four judges delegate to root out heresy. After arresting Berquin, the Parlement turned him over to these judges delegate for trial. They in turn asked the faculty of theology for its opinion on a collection of books and manuscripts that had been seized in a new search of Berquin's possessions.

The judges delegate received orders from the king's mother, based upon letters from the king, still a prisoner in Madrid, to release Berquin and to suspend his trial until the king's return. Despite their papal commission the judges turned to the Parlement for advice (20 February) and were told to proceed to trial pursuant to the authority which had been delegated to them (Archives Nationales MS x^{1a} 1529, f 124 verso).

Berquin attempted to challenge the authority of the judges delegate and succeeded in obtaining a hearing before the Parlement. He asked to see a copy of the judges' papal commission, but he was not challenging the jurisdiction of the church, for he was willing to be judged by the bishop of Paris, or alternatively by other judges appointed by the pope. He claimed that the present ones were prejudiced against him, and this was true enough. He asked for an opportunity to confront witnesses and for assistance of counsel. All that the Parlement was willing to concede, however, was a postponement until the following morning, to give Berquin that hardly adequate time to make out a case for his contention that the judges had abused their authority. Such an *appel comme d'abus* was the only kind of appeal the Parlement would recognize (Archives Nationales MS x^{1a} 1529, ff 149 verso–150 recto, session of 27 February 1526). A few days later, the Parlement decided to 'permit' the judges delegate to proceed with the trial, without regard to Berquin's appeal (Archives Nationales MS x^{1a} 1529, f 155 verso, session of 5 March).

On 12 March 1526 the faculty unanimously condemned certain propositions which their examiners had collected. Some of these were remarks which Berquin presumably had written in the margins of various works in his possession, including Luther's *Opera*, but also an anti-Lutheran tract by John *Fisher, bishop

of Rochester. In the margin of the latter, for example, had been found a notation that 'faith alone justifies,' which the faculty duly labelled as a heresy of Luther. Also condemned were certain books found in Berquin's possession, including the four translations of Erasmus that had been condemned the previous year. Berquin was now blamed for having translated these (D'Argentré II-1 40–2).

On the basis of the faculty's findings, the judges delegate declared on 23 March 1526 that Berquin was a relapsed heretic and turned him over to the Parlement, as the secular arm, for punishment (Béda to Erasmus, Ep 1685).

The Parlement, however, did not act. The king had returned to France on 7 March and had immediately let the court know of his displeasure over their conduct during his absence. He expressed astonishment that his mother's order to postpone the trial had not been obeyed, and he ordered them to refrain from imposing sentence and to suspend the case until he could examine it (Archives Nationales MS x^{1a} 1529, ff 198 verso–199 recto, letter dated Mont-de-Marsan, 1 April 1526).

Reporting his situation to Erasmus (Ep 1692, 17 April), Berquin asserted that the only reason why the hornets were buzzing at him again was because he had put some of Erasmus' erudite works into the vernacular. The judges, he said, had tried, but in vain, to get him to abjure Erasmus' works as heretical. They had based their case on translations which were not his: there were omissions, corruptions, and additions to the text, and differences of style. He had invited them to prove the truth of his assertions by comparing their copy with his autograph copy.

The autograph is not extant for us to examine, but printed versions of the *Mariage*, the *Symbole* and the *Briesve admonition* have survived in one copy in Geneva. Margaret Mann Phillips has found that they contain verbatim the passages condemned by the faculty (*Erasme* chapter 5). She also found that the translations were faithful to Erasmus' original, but that material had been added: 1 / explanatory elaborations involving no heresy, 2 / a preface to the *Briesve admonition*, which we now know was taken from a letter of *Farel (Herminjard I 246), and 3 / three passages from Luther's *Betbüchlein* inserted in the *Symbole*. Of the seven passages in the latter which the faculty condemned as the work of Erasmus, we can now recognize five as in fact translations of Luther. The faculty's charge of 'Lutheranism' was therefore justified – better justified than it knew. But was Berquin responsible for the insertions?

Berquin's appeal reached Erasmus at a time when his own works were being condemned. Béda had sent him some two hundred condemned passages (Ep 1717). Erasmus responded by attacking Béda, in letters to the Parlement (Ep 1721), to the king (Ep 1722), and to the faculty of theology (Ep 1723). In the letter to the king, he came to Berquin's defence and ridiculed the attacks which Béda had made upon them both. As for the translations, he defended the passages which he recognized as his own, but made no comment on those that were not, and which he attributed to Berquin (Ep 2188). The effect of Erasmus' intervention was to silence Béda for a time, but Berquin remained in prison.

The Parlement continued to obstruct the king's orders regarding Berquin. 'We find your response amazingly strange,' the king wrote on 5 October. 'By it you give us to understand that you do not take much notice of our letters and commands ... For this reason we order and enjoin you expressly, once and for all, with no more excuses, to hand Berquin over' to the bearers to be transferred to the Louvre (Archives Nationales MS x^{1a} 1529, ff 442 verso–443 recto). Nevertheless, the Parlement refused to release the prisoner, citing the nature of the crime of which he was accused, and instead sent a delegation with their remonstrances to the king. On 19 November the provost of Paris appeared before the Parlement with another letter from the king demanding Berquin's immediate release. Even now, the Parlement avoided taking such action, though it allowed the provost to take the prisoner on his own responsibility (Archives Nationales MS x^{1a} 1530, ff10 verso–11 verso).

Margaret, the king's sister, had been working constantly on Berquin's behalf, and her letters reveal the powerful impression he had made on her. To the king she wrote that she was 'sure that He for whom I believe he has suffered will approve the mercy you have in

His honor shown to His servant and yours' (Nouvelles Lettres, ed François Génin, Paris 1842, Ep 35). She thanked Anne de Montmorency for his part in bringing about the release of 'poor Berquin, whom I think of as myself, so much so that I could say that it is me you have delivered from prison.' Lettres, ed François Génin, Paris 1841, Ep 54). After his release, she took Berquin into her service. When he was again in trouble with the 'heretic-forgers,' she asked her brother to give him an audience and urged Francis to take Berquin's cause to heart (Nouvelles Lettres Ep 51).

Following his release, Berquin determined to attack his persecutors. It was probably he who extracted from Béda's writings against Erasmus twelve propositions that were allegedly heretical. Margaret brought them to the attention of the king, who asked the combined faculties of the University of Paris to examine them (Allen VII 234–5). That the university neither condemned nor approved the twelve propositions was an unsatisfactory conclusion for both parties.

The sentence of the judges against Berquin had not been invalidated by his release, and he decided to appeal against it. At the king's request, a special commission of twelve was appointed by the pope to hear the appeal. Official records of what was to be Berquin's third trial have not survived, except for the sentence handed down on 16 April 1529 (published by Bourilly 423–6). This includes a review of the case since 1523. The commission found that Berquin had clearly fallen into the Lutheran heresy, but in view of his asserted willingness to submit to the judgment of the church, limited his punishment to deprivation of his doctoral degree, burning of his books, public abjuration, and perpetual imprisonment. Berquin tried to appeal against this sentence, demanding that the commissioners specify the points on which he had been charged with heresy. Under the terms of their commission, however, there was no opportunity for appeal. Berquin was given several chances to withdraw it, but the fact that he 'obstinately' stood by his intention to appeal was interpreted by the commissioners as a refusal to obey the church, and thus further evidence of Lutheran heresy. He was failing to show penitence and revealing that his heart was still obdurate. Accordingly they declared him to be a pertinacious heretic and a defender of Luther's errors, who should be relinquished to the secular court to be punished with the usual penalties used against pertinacious heretics. He was strangled and burnt on 17 April 1529. Erasmus gives an account of the execution and the history of his relations with Berquin in Ep 2188.

Erasmus admitted that Berquin was his intellectual 'offspring.' In his contempt for ignorant monks and theologians, in his desire to make religion accessible to the people in their own language, and in his piety, Berquin was but following the example of Erasmus. Like Erasmus, he chose not to break the laws of the church, as Luther had done. Erasmus' insistence that Berquin disapproved of Lutheranism is thus understandable.

On the other hand Berquin differed from Erasmus in his assessment of political reality and in temperament. Berquin thought that the time had come to overthrow the faculty of theology, and felt it his duty in court to refuse to recant. Perhaps Luther's example at Worms was before his mind, as Théodore de Bèze suggests in his *Icones* when he says that Berquin might have been another Luther, if he had found in Francis what Luther had found in Frederick the Wise, elector of *Saxony.

BIBLIOGRAPHY: Nothing of Berquin's original work survived the flames, except two letters to Erasmus (Epp 1692 and 2066) and one to Anne de Montmorency: V.-L. Bourrilly 'Une lettre inédite de Louis de Berquin: 26 déc. 1526' *Bulletin de la Société de l'Histoire du Protestantisme français* 51 (1902) 634–7.

Research on Berquin since 1931, which has entailed a revision of our estimate of both Berquin and Erasmus, has been based upon analysis of Berquin's translations. Margaret Mann Phillips, in articles published in the *Revue du seizième siècle* 18 (1931), argued on stylistic grounds that Berquin was not the translator of the *Enchiridion*, as suggested by Erasmus (Ep 1581), but probably was the author of the three tracts in the Bibliothèque publique et universitaire of Geneva: the *Declamation des louenges de mariage*, the *Briesve admonition de la manière de prier*, and the *Symbole des apostres*, all believed to have been published by Simon Dubois, Paris, 1525 (facsimile eds,

with full notes and bibliography by Emile V. Telle, Geneva 1976, 1979). A fuller development of the argument may be found in her *Erasme et les débuts de la réforme francaise* (Paris 1934) 113–49. Now it was possible to read the extracts condemned by the faculty against the complete text of three of the four translations. The fourth translation, the *Complainte de la paix* has since been discovered in the Houghton Library of Harvard University by James E. Walsh and edited by Emile V. Telle (Geneva 1978).

To find a full account of Berquin's career one must go back to B. Hauréau 'Louis de Berquin' *Revue des deux mondes* 79 (1869) 454–81. This article was based on what are still our main sources: the letters of Erasmus, Paris, Archives Nationales MS x^{1a} 1529–30, the register of the Parlement of Paris, and the determinations of the faculty of theology, published by Duplessis d'Argentré in his *Collectio judiciorum de novis erroribus* ... (Paris 1728–36, 3 vols). This must now be supplemented by the more recently discovered calendar of its actions published by Léopold Delisle 'Notice sur un régistre des procès-verbaux de la Faculté de Théologie de Paris pendant les années 1505–1533' in *Notices et extraits des manuscrits de la Bibliothèque Nationale et autres bibliothèques* 36 (1899) 315–408 (see also Clerval).

Other important contributions to knowledge of Berquin since Hauréau are, in chronological order: Eugène and Emil Haag *La France protestante* 2nd ed H. Bordier (Paris 1879–) II 418–34 / Herminjard passim, who first recognized the authorship of the insertions in the Genevan translations / Romain Rolland 'Le dernier procès de Louis de Berquin' in *Mélanges d'archéologie et d'histoire* (Ecole Française de Rome) 12 (1892) 314–25, containing new information on the origin of the new papal tribunal of twelve, from the Salviati letters in the Vatican Archives, MS *Nunziatura di Francia* I / *Le Journal d'un bourgeois de Paris* ... ed V.-L. Bourilly (Paris 1910) 142, 234, 317–22, and, in appendix, the text of the sentence of 1529, 423–7 / Allen Ep 925 / P. Imbart de la Tour *Les Origines de la réforme* III (Paris 1914) 196–202 and passim / N. Weiss 'Louis de Berquin, son premier procès et sa rétractation d'après quelques documents inédits (1523)' *Bulletin de la Société de l'Histoire du Protestantisme francais*

67 (1918) 162–83, and the text of a 'Lettre de la Sacrée Faculté de Théologie à Guillaume Petit, évêque de Troyes, confesseur du roi, au sujet de Berquin' 209–11 / Roger Doucet *Etude sur le gouvernement de François ier dans ses rapports avec le Parlement de Paris* (Paris 1921–6) I 319–47 and passim / E. Lanoire 'Louis de Berquin' Société dunkerquoise pour l'encouragement des sciences, des lettres, et des arts *Mémoires* 65 (1929–30), 147–97, based on local archives, includes as Annex 1 the act of December 1529 by which Berquin's properties, which had escheated to Charles v, were sold for four thousand livres. This document offers the best description of the fief of 'Noord Berquin'

GORDON GRIFFITHS

Paschasius BERSELIUS of Liège, c 1480–late May 1535

Berselius was probably the son of Jean de Bierset, commissioner of the city of Liège. Since he made his profession at the Benedictine abbey of Saint-Laurent at Liège in 1501 it may be assumed that he was born around 1480, even though Louis *Ruzé calls him a young man in 1519 (Ep 926).

Berselius remained in Liège for most of his life but is documented in Louvain between 1518 and 1520, as a student and perhaps also as a corrector for the printer Dirk *Martens. In particular he wished to improve his knowledge of Greek, which he had earlier studied at Liège with Girolamo *Aleandro (Ep 674). Later he also corresponded with the Greek scholar Johannes *Guinterius (Ep 2876).

For some years Berselius belonged to the retinue of Erard de la *Marck, prince-bishop of Liège. In this capacity he exchanged several letters with Erasmus, who sent him a copy of his *Paraphrasis in Romanos* for personal presentation to the bishop (Ep 946). Three letters each from Berselius to Erasmus (Epp 674, 748, 1077) and from Erasmus to Berselius (Epp 718, 735, 756) are known today, and others are known to be missing. A note from Berselius was copied by *Goclenius in one of his own letters to Erasmus (Ep 2369). It tells of the confiscation of works by Erasmus in the Liège school of the Brethren of the Common Life (1530). In 1534 Berselius paid a visit to Guillaume *Budé in Paris. He died at Liège the following year.

Berselius left verse and prose compositions which were preserved for a time in the abbey of St Laurent at Liège but are now lost, with the exception of some distichs and his 'De excidio civitatis Leodinensis' (Brussels, Bibliothèque Royale, MS II 1184). He also tried his hand as a painter and was a sophisticated art collector, as is shown by the statue of the Virgin of Dalhem which was carved for him by Daniel Mauch and has engraved on its base a distich with Berselius' name.

BIBLIOGRAPHY: Allen and CWE Ep 674 / de Vocht CTL I 493–500, II 15 / J. Ceyssens 'Berselius et la statue de la Vierge de Dalhem' *La Vie Wallonne* 5 (1925) 341–55 / Y. Charlier *Erasme et l'amitié* (Paris 1977) 209 / J. Hoyoux 'Les relations entre Erasme et Erard de la Marck' *Chronique archéologique du pays de Liège* 36 (1945) 7–22

J. HOYOUX

Jacques BERTHÉLEMY of Paris, documented 1497–6 June 1543

Jacques Berthélemy (Barthelemy, Bartholomeus) has been said to be an Auvergnac, but the Parisian origins of his brother Michel, also a Paris theologian, are well documented. In Paris, Berthélemy probably studied arts at the Collège de Montaigu and certainly later taught there. He was a *socius* of the Collège de Sorbonne from 1497 and was the prior there in 1504. He ranked seventh of fifteen licentiates in theology on 9 May 1506 and obtained his doctorate on 10 December 1506. Berthélemy was extremely active on the faculty of theology, appearing in its proceedings in almost every year between 1506 and 1543. In 1514, his name was added to the faculty's previously constituted committee investigating *Reuchlin. He later sat on committees investigating the early books of Martin *Luther, the translations of Erasmus by Louis de *Berquin, and the writings of Aimé Maigret, *Cajetanus, and Gérard *Roussel. He examined and reported on at least twenty-one books for the faculty, among them Erasmus' *Querela pacis*, which he judged 'worthy of flames' in 1525 and the *Paraphrases* on the Gospels in 1527. In 1528 Gervasius *Wain was unable to examine the faculty's censures of Erasmus' books because these were in Berthélemy's safe keeping (Allen Ep 2027). On 23 June 1528, Berthélemy and

Noël *Béda succeeded in obtaining a formal censure of the *Colloquia* by the whole University of Paris.

Much of Berthélemy's time and efforts were devoted to the Collège de Sorbonne, where his position as *conscriptor* from 1520 until 1543 obliged him to take part in several hundred transactions of the college. Berthélemy was the first of seven Paris doctors to whom the early Jesuits sent greetings in a letter from Rome in 1538. He died between 6 June and 14 August 1543 and was buried in the chapel of the Sorbonne.

BIBLIOGRAPHY: Allen Ep 2027 / Clerval passim / Delisle passim / Farge no 42

JAMES K. FARGE

Hilarius BERTHOLF of Ledeberg, d c August 1533

Hilarius Bertholf (Berthulphus) of Ledeberg, near Ghent, was a pupil of Eligius Houckaert at Ghent and was permitted to publish some verse in the latter's *Divi Livini vita* (Paris: J. Bade 1511). Subsequently he studied in Paris together with Juan Luis *Vives (Ep 1281) and wrote some verse for Johannes Dullardus' edition of Paulus Venetus' *Summa philosophiae naturalis* (Paris: T. Kees 1513). For some years he taught in Toulouse (Ep 1403). He may have been recommended to Erasmus by Vives and taken on as a famulus prior to Erasmus' departure from the Netherlands in October 1521. From Basel he was frequently sent on missions, travelling back to the Low Countries in January 1522 (Ep 1257), again in April–June (Epp 1275, 1276, 1281, 1286, 1287, 1293, 1296), and in October–November (Epp 1317, 1322, cf Epp 1303, 1306), as well as in the spring of 1523 (Ep 1362; Allen Ep 1342:1n) and the autumn of the same year (Ep 1388). He also went to Besançon for wine (Ep 1359) and to Zürich with a verbal message for *Zwingli (Ep 1384). In December 1523 Bertholf was sent to the French court at Blois, where he delivered to *Francis I a presentation copy of Erasmus' *Paraphrasis in Marcum*, dedicated to the king, and was most generously rewarded (Ep 1403; Allen I 44). From Blois Bertholf went to Lyon (Ep 1426), where he saw an edition of Elio Antonio de *Nebrija's grammar through the press, adding some notes of his own (Lyon: J. Moylin 20 April 1524). He visited Geneva in January 1524,

possibly on his way back from Lyon, meeting Philibert de *Lucinge (Ep 1413) and the *Alardet family. Among Bertholf's epigrams printed in the *Opera* of his friend Cornelius *Agrippa some seem to be connected with this visit to Geneva; there are three anonymous letters from Bertholf to Agrippa, the first dated Basel 10 November [1523]. 'Totus Gallus, totus aulicus' (Ep 1413), he finally made his way back to Basel (Ep 1434) and, greatly esteemed by his master (Ep 1437), was sent back to Lyon in the autumn to explore the conditions for Erasmus' own resettlement in France (Epp 1487, 1516, 1527; AK II Ep 980). Bertholf found France so attractive that he only returned to Basel in December and took off again as soon as he had delivered his letters (Ep 1527). He entered the service of *Margaret of Angoulême, the king's sister, but remained in touch with Erasmus, who in May 1526 would have liked him to visit Basel and wished to learn from him how Francis I should be congratulated on his return from captivity in Spain (Epp 1711, 1712). Around 1526 Bertholf also visited Italy, fell sick in Pavia, and was cured in Trent by Hieronymus *Ricius (*Vadianische Briefsammlung* IV appendix Ep 11).

By 1527 Bertholf returned to Ghent and got married (Epp 2049, 2581). In 1531, if not earlier, he entered the service of Johannes *Dantiscus, Polish ambassador to the court of *Charles V (Ep 2570). Erasmus, who clearly remained in confidential contact with him, advised him in December 1531 to abandon the itinerant life of the court. He saw better prospects for his former famulus at Lyon, where he could tutor students and work for the printers (Ep 2581). Bertholf took his advice and moved with his family to Lyon, where he knew François *Rabelais and apparently worked for him (Epp 2735, 2743) as well as for the printer Sebastianus *Gryphius, whom he provided with a copy of Nicolas *Bérault's *De vetere et novitia iurisprudentia oratio* (Lyon, 1 July 1533). In the summer of 1533 he, his wife, and their three children died of the plague in Lyon (Ep 2805).

Bertholf's relations with Erasmus were always excellent. Erasmus introduced him as a character in his colloquies *Diversoria* and *Convivium poeticum* and gave his name to a speaker in the colloquy *Synodus grammaticorum*

Cardinal Bessarion

(ASD I-3 333–8, 344–59, 585–90). In turn Bertholf defended Erasmus and his views on religion in a letter to Guillaume *Farel of late April 1524 (Herminjard I Ep 99), and in 1525 in his edition of Girolamo *Vida's *Scacchia* (n p) he endorsed Erasmus' pacifism, even though he was writing in light vein. No doubt it was his sunny temper which permitted Bertholf to be so close to such leading minds of his time as Vives, Erasmus, Agrippa, Margaret of Navarre, and Rabelais; wherever he went, he was liked: 'ubicunque erit, Hilarius erit' (Ep 2735).

BIBLIOGRAPHY: Allen Ep 1257 / A. Roersch *L'Humanisme belge à l'époque de la Renaissance* (Brussels-Louvain 1910–33) I 69–82 / A. Roersch 'Nouvelles indications concernant Hilarius Berthulphus' in *Mélanges Paul Thomas* (Ghent 1930) 605–17 / M.A. Nauwelaerts 'Erasme et Gand' in *Commémoration nationale d'Erasme: Actes* (Brussels 1970) 156–7 / H. Naef *Les Origines de la Réforme à Genève* I (Geneva-Paris 1936) 317, 321–2 / Henricus Cornelius Agrippa *Opera* (Lyon n d, repr 1970) II 751–2, 774–5, 1129–39 erroneous pagination / de Vocht *Dantiscus* 54–5 and passim / de Vocht *Literae ad Craneveldium* Ep 19 and passim /

Vocht CTL II 100 and passim / René Hoven and Jean Hoyoux *Le Livre scolaire au temps d'Erasme et des humanistes* (Liège 1969) 12 / Bierlaire *Familia* 59–61 / Herminjard I Ep 99, III 413–14 / L. de Berquin tr *La Complainte de la paix* ed E. V. Telle (Geneva 1978) 47–9 / L. Delaruelle in *Annales du Midi* 36–7 (1925) 42–7

FRANZ BIERLAIRE & PGB

BERTRANDUS (Ep 1271 of 1 April 1522) Bertrandus has not been identified. A nobleman, he visited Erasmus at Anderlecht in 1521 and in the following year was connected with Fadrique *Alvarez de Toledo, duke of Alba, and with Juan Luis *Vives.

BERUS *See* BAER, BERE, BEREN

BESSARION of Trebizond, 2 January 1403–18 November 1472
Bessarion was born at Trebizond to a family of artisans and probably received the baptismal name of Basilius. At an early age he was entrusted to the bishop of Trebizond by his parents, and at thirteen he was sent to Constantinople for instruction in grammar, rhetoric, and philosophy. Manuel Chrysococcus was among his teachers. On 30 January 1423 he entered the Basilian order, taking the name Bessarion after an Egyptian anchorite of the fourth century. He was ordained in 1431 and from 1431 to 1433 went to Mistra to study under the neo-Platonist Georgius *Gemistos Plethon. Meanwhile, as early as 1426 he was in the service of the Emperor John VIII Palaeologus, participating in a number of diplomatic missions. He became bishop of Nicea in 1437 and in 1438 and 1439 was one of the principal Greek spokesmen for unity with the Latin church at the council of Ferrara and Florence. He returned to Constantinople after the council, but news soon arrived that Pope Eugenius IV had elevated him to the rank of cardinal on 18 December 1439. Bessarion returned to Florence in December 1440 and followed the papal court to Rome in 1443. He was appointed to a series of bishoprics, including Siponto in 1447, Mazzara and Tusculo in 1449, Pamplona in 1458, and Negroponte in 1463. On 15 May 1463 he was named patriarch of Constantinople. He also served as legate to Bologna and the Romagna

from 1450 to 1455 and as protector of the Basilian order in Italy. His principal concern, however, was promoting a crusade against the Turks, who captured Constantinople in 1453 and relentlessly extended their control over the Balkans. In 1459 he participated in a congress at Mantua for a crusade and in 1460 and 1461 he visited Nürnberg and other German cities to win the support of the German princes. In 1464 he travelled to Ancona with *Pius II to launch the long-awaited expedition, only to see the project collapse after the death of the pope. A final mission to the rulers of France, England, and Burgundy in 1472 proved equally frustrating. He died at Ravenna, shortly after his return from France, and was buried at the basilica of the Santissimi XII Apostoli at Rome.

Bessarion was a man of learning who did much to promote Greek studies in Italy and to preserve the intellectual heritage of the fallen Byzantine empire. He extended his protection to numerous Greek exiles in Italy, including George of *Trebizond, Theodorus *Gaza, Michael *Apostolius, Demetrius *Chalcon-dyles, and Constantinus *Lascaris. His circle, often called the 'Academy,' also encompassed Italian scholars such as Julius *Pomponius Laetus, Flavio *Biondo, Bartolomeo *Platina, Domizio *Calderini, and Niccolò *Perotti, who was his secretary for sixteen years. Bessarion's library, which consisted of a core of works brought from the east and other works sought out during his travels in Europe, was renowned among scholars. In 1468 the cardinal donated it to Venice, where today it is the basis of the Biblioteca Nazionale Marciana.

Erasmus was familiar with Bessarion's activity in favour of a crusade (Ep 2285, LB V 359F) and with his library (Epp 2340, 2716). The theologian Hieronymus *Dungersheim mentioned Bessarion in his letter taking issue with a passage in Erasmus' 1516 edition of the New Testament (Ep 554).

Bessarion's most important work was In calumniatorem Platonis libri IV (Rome: C. Sweinheym and A. Pannartz 1469) written in response to George of Trebizond's attack on Plato. He also wrote polemics on the doctrine of the Holy Spirit and on the question of the unity of the Latin and Greek churches, including an encyclical to the Greeks on his

nomination as patriarch (Viterbo 1470). His Orationes ad principes Italiae contra Turcos were first published in 1470 (Venice: C. Valdarfer); other orations are preserved in the Biblioteca Nazionale Marciana.

BIBLIOGRAPHY: Allen Ep 554 / L. Labowski in DBI IX 686–96 / L. Bréhier in DHGE VIII 1181–99 / L. Mohler Kardinal Bessarion als Theologe, Humanist und Staatsmann (Paderborn 1923–42) includes, in addition to a biography, Greek and Latin texts of Bessarion's most important works and letters / Also useful is Henri Vast Le Cardinal Bessarion 1403–1472 (Paris 1878, repr 1977)

TBD

Zofia BETHMANN of Cracow, d 5 May 1532
Zofia was the daughter of Seweryn Bethmann (Betman), a wealthy merchant and alderman of Cracow, and of Dorota Kletner. She was married 23 October 1515 to Seweryn *Boner and was the mother of Jan and Stanisław *Boner. Jan announced her death to Erasmus in Ep 2717.

BIBLIOGRAPHY: Allen Ep 2717 / PSB I 477, II 300–1

HALINA KOWALSKA

Karel de BEUCKELAER See Nicolaas de BEUCKE-LAER

Nicolaas de BEUCKELAER of Antwerp, d 22 September 1549
Nicolaas de Beuckelaer (Boeckelaer, Boeucke-le, Buekeler, Buclerius) was the son of Arnold, secretary of the city of Antwerp, and of Catherina van de Berghe. He matriculated at the University of Orléans on 23 March 1491 and was promoted licentiate in law two years later. From 1500 he was canon of Notre Dame, Antwerp, and from 1512 to 1534 he was the chapter's treasurer. Along with his brother Filips, who was a city councillor and later the treasurer of the city of Antwerp, Nicolaas retained a list of the silverware of Jérôme de *Busleyden, which had been deposited with a jeweller when Erasmus' friend left for Spain in 1517. In the year of his death Nicolaas endowed a prebend at the church of St Andrew's, Antwerp.

Leonard *Casembroot, who was then living with Nicolaas's nephew, Karel de Beuckelaer, believed that Nicolaas and Erasmus were old friends. Of Karel no more is known than that in 1525 he shared a house in Padua with Casembroot and other Flemish students (Ep 1594).

BIBLIOGRAPHY: *Matricule d'Orléans* II-1 162–3 / F.H. Mertens and K.L. Torfs *Geschiedenis van Antwerpen* (Antwerp 1845–53) IV 29, 117–18 / Floris Prims *Geschiedenis van Antwerpen* (Antwerp 1927–49) XVIII 194 / de Vocht *Busleyden* 323 / de Vocht CTL II 230

MARCEL A. NAUWELAERTS

Jan BEUCKELSZOON or BEUKELS *See JAN of Leiden*

BEVEREN, BEVRES *See BURGUNDY*

Christian BEYER of Klein-Langheim, c 1482–21 October 1535

Christian Beyer (Baier, Bayer, Peyer, Bowarius), born in Klein-Langheim, near Kitzingen in Franconia, matriculated at Erfurt in 1500 and obtained a BA in 1502. From 1503 he studied at Wittenberg, obtained an MA on 12 August 1505, and began to teach in 1507 in the faculty of arts. He had obtained a legal doctorate by the time he married Magdalena, a daughter of Wittenberg's burgomaster, Ambrosius Gertitz, on 3 October 1510. By 1511 he had joined the law faculty. He was a councillor at the electoral court from 1513 and repeatedly burgomaster of Wittenberg (in 1513, 1516, 1519, 1522, and 1525). By 1517 he was receiving a comparatively high salary of eighty florins annually, but he had to finance the rebuilding of his house, which had burnt down in 1512. Soon he came to support *Luther, and in October 1520 he advised the authorities to ignore the papal bull against him. He was involved in various negotiations on behalf of the Elector Frederick the Wise of *Saxony, but in spite of his absences he took his teaching duties seriously. He retained his position at the University of Wittenberg until late in 1528, when he became chancellor to the Elector John the Steadfast of *Saxony. At the diet of Augsburg he read out the German text of the Augsburg Confession on 25 June 1530. On 21 January 1529 he moved with his family to Weimar, and there he died in 1535.

Beyer was godfather to Martin Luther's eldest son; he was also a friend of Christoph Scheurl, Justus *Jonas, and *Melanchthon, who acted as guardian to Beyer's younger children between 1535 and 1544. In 1532, when Felix *Rex returned to Freiburg after a year of service at the Saxon court, Beyer and *Spalatinus gave him letters of reference addressed to Erasmus (Epp 2609, 2610).

BIBLIOGRAPHY: Allen Ep 2609 / NDB II 204, 653 / ADB II 596–7 / Luther W *Briefwechsel* V Ep 1451 and passim / *Melanchthons Briefwechsel* II Epp 897, 898, and passim / *Der Briefwechsel des Justus Jonas* ed Gustav Kawerau (Halle 1884–5) I Epp 150, 238, and passim / Walter Friedensburg *Geschichte der Universität Wittenberg* (Halle 1917) 110, 140 / Nikolaus Müller *Die Wittenberger Bewegung 1521 und 1522* (Leipzig 1911) 246–9 / *Matrikel Erfurt* II 217 / *Matrikel Wittenberg* I 8

IG

Heinrich BEYMING of Butzbach, documented 1502–after 1518

Heinrich Beyming (Beymigk, Bemyngus, de Bemingen), of Butzbach, 45 kilometres north of Frankfurt, matriculated in the University of Erfurt for the summer term of 1502. From Erfurt he seems to have gone to the University of Mainz, and in the autumn of 1509 he was registered at Wittenberg (*Matrikel Wittenberg* I 30 b 28, read 'de Bemingen'). Also in 1509 he returned to Erfurt and was received into the faculty of arts as a Mainz BA. At Erfurt he graduated MA in 1515 and subsequently became headmaster of the school at Butzbach. Among his pupils there was Daniel Greiser, who later wrote a chronicle in which he praised Beyming highly, adding that he remained a Catholic and died as the priest of a rural parish near Mainz. When *Eobanus Hessus visited Erasmus in 1518 he brought a letter from Beyming. Erasmus answered briefly with Ep 873, also returning the greetings of Jodocus *Winsheim that had been conveyed in Beyming's letter.

BIBLIOGRAPHY: Allen Ep 873 / Daniel Greiser *Historia und Beschreibunge des ganzen Lauffs und Lebens* (Dresden 1587) / G. Bauch *Die Universität Erfurt im Zeitalter des Frühhumanismus* (Wrocław 1904) 162–3 / E. Kleineidam *Universitas Studii Erffordensis* (Leipzig 1964–80) I 395, II 236, 309 / *Matrikel Erfurt* II 225

ERICH KLEINEIDAM

Judocus BEYSSELLIUS *See Judocus* BEISSEL

Willem BIBAUT of Tielt, d 24 July 1535
Willem, the son of Steven Joosz Bibaut
(Biebuyck, Bibaux, Bibaucus) and Margriet
Oudaris (d 1527), was born about 1475 in Tielt,
in Flanders. He was educated at Louvain, but
apparently did not matriculate in the university. Afterwards he taught school at Ghent
until about 1499, when he entered the
Carthusian monastery of that city. By 1507 he
occupied the office of procurator in his
convent. Shortly after 1514 he was appointed
prior of the charterhouse near Geertruidenberg, north of Breda, a position which he held
until 1521. At the same time he continued to
hold office as *covisitator* (1511–13) and *visitator*
(1513–21) of the Dutch province of his order. In
1516 he succeeded in settling a dispute
between the Carthusians of Louvain and
Henry III, count of *Nassau, which concerned
the ownership of some land near Breda.
Bibaut's intervention won him the lasting
gratitude of the Louvain brethren, and in 1521
he was called a great benefactor of the Louvain
charterhouse. In that same year he was elected
prior-general of the entire order and henceforward resided in the Grande Chartreuse near
Grenoble, where he died. In spite of the great
flourishing of the order at that time – there
were more than two hundred charterhouses –
Bibaut's tenure of the highest office was by no
means an easy task. Among the problems with
which he had to deal were the rise of
Protestantism, the Turkish threat to Hungary
and Austria, and the peasant rebellion in
Saxony. Bibaut also lent his support to
intellectual ventures undertaken within the
order such as the collected works of *Denis the
Carthusian edited by the Carthusians of the
flourishing Cologne house in thirteen folio
volumes (1532–40). In general, his stewardship
of the Carthusian order may be termed
well-balanced.

In April 1526 Erasmus wrote to the
Carthusian prior-general, asking him to
discipline Pierre *Cousturier, who was by then
his most unrelenting critic among the
Carthusians (Ep 1687). A year later he
indicated in a letter to Thomas *More (Ep 1804)
that Bibaut had complied with his request.

Bibaut's works include *Ad fratres Carthusiae*

sacrae conciones (Erfurt: M. Sachse 1539), edited
by Judocus Hessius, prior of the Erfurt
charterhouse, and *Carmen sapphicum in honorem
S. Joachim patris B.M.V.*, published repeatedly
together with the *Vita Jesu Christi* by Ludolph
of Saxony, which it complements (Paris 1534,
etc).

BIBLIOGRAPHY: Allen Ep 1687 / J. De Grauwe
in NBW VI 34–6 / H.J.J. Scholtens 'De kartuizers
bij Geertruidenberg' *Bossche Bijdragen* 18 (1941)
82–92 / Ghent, Rijksarchief MSS files 'Kartuizers' and a number of unclassified documents
                                          JAN DE GRAUWE

Theodorus BIBLIANDER of Bischofszell, d
26 September 1564
Theodorus Bibliander (Buchmann) was born in
Bischofszell, Thurgau. He was educated at
Zürich under the care of *Myconius and began
to study Hebrew, continuing his studies from
1525 at Basel under *Pellicanus and *Oecolampadius. On the recommendation of *Zwingli
and with the consent of the Zürich council he
was recruited in the summer of 1527 to join the
new academy of Duke Frederick II of Silesia.
He went to Legnica (Liegnitz), but the academy
did not for long live up to its promising
beginnings, and in the autumn of 1529 he
returned to Zürich. He lived as a private
scholar until the death of Zwingli, whom he
succeeded as professor of Old Testament in
November 1531. In Ep 3072 Pellicanus paid him
the compliment that his lectures were superior
to those of Zwingli although he was not yet
thirty years old (1535).

Bibliander composed many works, some of
which remain unpublished. Of significance are
his Hebrew grammar (Zürich: C. Froschauer
1535); a basic study of comparative linguistics
and exegesis, *De ratione communi omnium
linguarum et literarum* (Zürich: C. Froschauer
1548); and his controversial first edition of a
twelfth-century Latin translation of the Koran
together with a group of related texts (Basel: J.
Oporinus 1543). The Koran edition was
intended to serve both the student of religion
and the Christian missionary on whose work
Bibliander set great store. His studies in the
periodization of history also deserve attention,
but his chief distinction among the Zürich
theologians remains his great knowledge of
Semitic, Slavic, and other languages. Despite

his mild and kindly manner he eventually became involved in a bitter controversy with another Zürich theologian, Pietro Martire Vermigli, and their disagreement was carried into the lecture rooms. It concerned Bibliander's view of predestination, which had been linked to that of Erasmus and was judged by his colleagues in Zürich to be too compromising. In March 1560 mental fatigue was invoked as a pretext when he was asked to retire from his chair. He died four years later of the plague.

BIBLIOGRAPHY: Allen Ep 3072 / *Religion in Geschichte und Gegenwart* (Tübingen 1957–65) III 1251 / E. Egli *Analecta reformatoria* (Zürich 1899–1901) II 1–144 / z IX Epp 607, 633, and passim / AK V Ep 2554 and passim

PGB

Johannes BIBLIOPEGUS *See Hans* BOGBINDER

Gerardus de BIE *See Petrus* MELLIS

Willem van BIEBUYCK *See Willem* BIBAUT

Gabriel BIEL of Speyer, d 7 December 1495
Gabriel Biel, born in Speyer perhaps around 1418, was registered at the University of Heidelberg (1432), where he obtained his BA and MA (1438) before becoming a licentiate in theology, probably at Erfurt. In 1453 he matriculated at the University of Cologne, which adhered to the Thomist or realist tradition. In the early 1460s he was preacher at the cathedral of Mainz and thereafter joined the congregation of the Brethren of the Common Life at Marienthal, in the Rheingau, remaining there until 1568, when he became the provost of the brethren's new house at Butzbach, in Hesse. In 1477 he joined Count Eberhard the Bearded of Württemberg in his efforts to advance ecclesiastical reforms and from 1479 was the provost of the brethren's house at Urach. From 1484 he taught theology at Tübingen and was rector of the university in 1485 and 1489. After his retirement he directed another new house of the brethren, St Peter at Einsiedel, near Tübingen.

A leading representative of nominalist theology, Biel wrote and compiled a number of important works, among them his *Sermones*, a *Sacri canonis missae ... expositio*, and his

Collectorium, a commentary on the *Sentences* of Peter Lombard, based on Ockham. Often reprinted, his writings had considerable influence on Martin *Luther. In 1517 Wolfgang *Lachner planned a new Basel edition of the *Collectorium* (Ep 575), while Erasmus used Biel's name in summary references to the work of scholastic theologians (Epp 844, 2143).

BIBLIOGRAPHY: Allen and CWE Ep 575 / NDB II 225–6 / Heiko A. Oberman *The Harvest of Medieval Theology: Gabriel Biel and Late Medieval Nominalism* (Cambridge, Mass, 1963) / *Matrikel Heidelberg* I 191 / *Matrikel Köln* I 561 / *Matrikel Tübingen* I 54 / *Index Aureliensis* (Baden-Baden 1962–) IV 222–8

IG

Peter BIENEWITZ *See Petrus* APIANUS

Theobaldus BIETRICIUS *See Thiébaut* BIÉTRY

Thiébaut BIÉTRY of Porrentruy, documented 1516–26
Biétry (Theobaldus Bietricius) came from a family established at Porrentruy, in the Jura, since the fourteenth century. He was parish priest of Porrentruy from 1516 and, like Georges *Ferriot, was a member of the Confrèrie Saint Michel. When and where Biétry came to know Erasmus is not known. In the autumn of 1523 Erasmus good-humouredly complied with his request that he write a mass (*Liturgia Virginis Matris*) in honour of the Virgin of Loreto, near Ancona, dedicating it to Biétry (Epp 1391, 1573). As the cult of Loreto was not well known in the Jura, Biétry may perhaps have visited the shrine in the course of a journey to Italy. That he was a man of a certain standing is indicated by his relations with Léonard de *Gruyères and Ferry *Carondelet (Epp 1534, 1749, 1760). His enthusiasm for Erasmus' mass succeeded in drawing it to the attention of the archbishop of Besançon, Antoine de *Vergy, who granted an indulgence for those who used it. When Erasmus visited Besançon in the spring of 1524 he made his way there through Porrentruy, where his patron, Christoph von *Utenheim, bishop of Basel, was residing, and Biétry accompanied him from Porrentruy to Besançon (Ep 1610). He may also have visited Erasmus at Basel and helped to keep him supplied with

Burgundian wine (Epp 1468, 1749). No more is heard about him after his last letter to Erasmus of October 1526 (Ep 1760).

BIBLIOGRAPHY: Allen Ep 1391 / A. Chèvre 'Erasme ... et ses amis à Porrentruy' *Actes de la Société jurassienne d'émulation* 77 (1974) 369–92

PGB

Jan BIJL of Louvain, d 2 November 1540

Jan Bijl (Byl, Bijlkens, Bilhemius) was born in Louvain towards the end of the fifteenth century. He joined the order of St Francis and at different times served as warden of several Franciscan houses, including Mechelen. He is probably the Jan of Louvain who was warden at Amsterdam and had communicated some misgivings about the *Moria* to Erasmus in such a kindly fashion as to draw a friendly reply (Ep 749, 2 January 1518). Writing from The Hague on 28 November 1519 (Ep 1044), Maarten van *Dorp mentioned a Franciscan warden at Mechelen who was experienced, learned, and a great admirer of Erasmus; probably he too is referring to Bijl, who composed two works that remained unpublished: 'De curis et anxietatibus guardianorum' and 'De ruina observantiae.' In 1529 he was elected provincial of the new Franciscan province of Lower Germany, which covered in part today's Belgium.

BIBLIOGRAPHY: Allen Ep 1044 / BNB III 226–7 / de Vocht MHL 224 / A. van Puymbrouck *De franciscanen te Mechelen 1291–1893* (Ghent 1893) 157 / A. Sanderus *Chorographia sacra Brabantiae* (The Hague 1726) III 183 / S. Dirks *Histoire littéraire et bibliographique des Frères Mineurs de l'Observance de Saint François en Belgique et dans les Pays-Bas* (Antwerp 1885) 41 / *De godsdienstvriend* 87 (1861) 210–11

MARCEL A. NAUWELAERTS

Anton BILD of Sélestat, d 21 November 1520

Anton (Theny) Bild (or Rinower) was the father of *Beatus Rhenanus. In 1400 (or 1398) Anton's father, Eberhard Bild, had moved to Sélestat because his previous home town in Alsace, referred to as Rheinau, was plagued by recurrent flooding. Born by the middle of the fifteenth century, Anton obtained the citizenship of Sélestat before 1472. He practised the trade of butcher with some success, acquired property, and enjoyed general respect. He was elected to the offices of *Statmeister* in 1499 and

Schultheiss in 1506. His wife, Barbara Kegel, bore him three sons and died when the youngest, Beatus, was two years old. In the funeral inscription which Beatus composed for his father after his death, he gratefully acknowledged the strong encouragement Anton had given to his studies.

In Ep 382 Erasmus was asked to convey a message to Beatus from his father, who longed to see his son.

BIBLIOGRAPHY: Allen Ep 382 / BRE 621 / Gustav Knod 'Aus der Bibliothek des Beatus Rhenanus' in *Die Stadtbibliothek zu Schlettstadt* ed J. Gény and G. Knod (Strasbourg 1889) 1–4

BEAT VON SCARPATETTI

BINTIUS (LB IX 110D)

Bintius, mentioned in Erasmus' *Apologia de laude matrimonii* in conjunction with Maarten van *Dorp and Gillis van *Delft, has been tentatively identified by Henry de Vocht as Jean Lengherant of Binche in Hainaut, who matriculated in Louvain on 31 August 1498, received his doctorate of divinity on 4 July 1514 and was elected dean of the theological faculty on 28 February 1517. He must have died soon afterwards.

BIBLIOGRAPHY: *Matricule de Louvain* III-1 176 / H. de Jongh *L'Ancienne Faculté de théologie de Louvain* (Louvain 1911) 176 / de Vocht MHL 195 / de Vocht CTL I 453

PGB

Flavio BIONDO of Forlì, 1392–4 June 1463

Flavio Biondo (Blondus Forliviensis) was born at Forlì in Romagna in November or December 1392 to the notary Antonio di Gaspare Biondi and his wife, Francesca. He studied grammar, poetry, and rhetoric under Giovanni Balestrieri of Cremona and attended the university then at Piacenza, probably in preparation for a career as a notary. From 1420 to late 1432 he travelled through northern and central Italy serving as secretary to several governors and town councils. In 1423 he married Paola di Jacopo Maldenti, by whom he had ten children by 1440. At the end of 1432 he travelled to Rome to become a notary of the apostolic camera under Eugenius IV. He added the offices of apostolic secretary in early 1434 and *scriptor* of apostolic letters in 1436. With the exception of a brief period of disgrace (1449–53) under *Nicholas v, he served in the curia until his death. One of his sons, Gaspare (d 1493), succeeded him as apostolic secretary.

Although Enea Silvio Piccolomini (*Pius II) and other humanists had little esteem for his style, Biondo was one of the most important historians and antiquarians of Renaissance Italy. His *Historiarum ab inclinatione Romani imperii decades,* composed between 1435 and 1453 and printed at Venice in 1483 by Ottaviano Scoto, covered the period from the Sack of Rome by the Goths (410) to his own day (1441) and helped develop the idea of a break between classical and modern times. The *Roma instaurata,* completed in 1446 and printed at Rome in 1471 (n p), and the *Italia illustrata,* completed in 1453 and printed at Rome in 1474 by Johannes Philippus de Ligamine, catalogued the ruins and monuments of Rome and Italy and proved indispensable to the antiquarian and archeological studies that blossomed in Italy in the fifteenth and sixteenth centuries. Biondo's *Roma triumphans* (Brescia: Georgius and Paulus Teutonici 1473–5) was a systematic reconstruction of public and private life in ancient Rome. His lesser works included *De verbis Romanae locutionis* (1435), the *Borsus sive de militia et iurisprudentia* (1460), and the *Additiones correctionesque Italiae illustratae* (1462), all published with his letters by Bartolomeo Nogara at Rome in 1927.

In the *Ciceronianus* Erasmus stated that Biondo was inferior to Petrarch in style and understanding of Latin and thus, by implication, was not a Ciceronian (ASD I-2 661).

BIBLIOGRAPHY: R. Fubini in DBI x 536–59 / Roberto Weiss *The Renaissance Discovery of Classical Antiquity* (Oxford 1969) 59–60 and passim

TBD

Maurice BIRCHINSHAW documented 1511–35

When writing to Erasmus from Louvain in January and July 1522 Juan Luis *Vives mentioned a favourite student of his named Mauritius, who was clearly well known to Erasmus and was supposed to receive a letter from him, but by July had gone to England, evidently his native country (Epp 1256, 1303). Vives' student was very likely Maurice Birchinshaw (Byrchynsa), who may have been at Oxford as early as the turn of the century

and in 1513 was second usher at Magdalen school. In Oxford he graduated bachelor of grammar on 11 December 1511 and bachelor of civil law on 2 July 1515, and in the same year he left to teach at St Paul's School, London. On a visit to Oxford he dined on the last day of 1516 with a master of Magdalen School and Thomas *Lupset. At St Paul's, Thomas *Winter, the son of Cardinal *Wolsey, was one of his pupils, and on 30 August 1518 the boy and Birchinshaw as his tutor both matriculated at the University of Louvain as students of the College of the Pig. Whether or not they stayed in Louvain for all of the next four years, it seems evident that Birchinshaw must have known Erasmus there before the latter left for Basel. At the time of Vives' letters to Erasmus in 1522, Birchinshaw was following the Spaniard's lectures in company with his fellow countrymen Richard *Warham and William *Thale. There does not seem to be any evidence that Birchinshaw accompanied Winter, Lupset and their party to Italy in 1523. The 'Bequinsalus' mentioned by Vives in an undated letter of 1529 or 1530, who was then apparently in Paris with John Mason and Winter, must be John Bekinsau. Meanwhile his connections with Wolsey may have assisted Birchinshaw in his efforts to obtain benefices. On 31 December 1517 he was rector of Snargate, Kent, and in 1525 and 1535 he is documented as a canon of Wells. It seems that he held other benefices, but there is a danger of confusing him with men with similar names.

BIBLIOGRAPHY: Allen Ep 1256 / Emden BRUO I 190 / *Matricule de Louvain* III-1 592 / de Vocht MHL 15–16 and passim / de Vocht CTL II 404 / de Vocht *Literae ad Craneveldium* Ep 136 / McConica 50–1, 110 / J.L. Vives *Opera omnia* (Valencia 1782–90, repr 1964) VII 141

PGB

Sixtus BIRCK *See Sixt* BIRK

Arnold BIRCKMANN of Cologne, documented 1508–d 28 April 1541/2

Arnold, the brother of Franz *Birckmann, was a bookseller in Cologne from 1508. In 1511 the two brothers bought the house 'Unter der fetten Hennen,' which remained the firm's address in Cologne. Since Franz was able to build up a large business with connections and branches in many countries, both brothers had to travel extensively. Arnold was in charge of a bookstore in London from 1515 to 1518. On a trip to the continent in 1516 he carried Ep 413 from Paris to Cologne. By 1519 he seems to have been in charge of the firm's Cologne operations. In 1523 he sold his share to his brother, and in 1525, after his marriage to Agnes of Gennep, he started a flourishing book business of his own in Cologne, acquiring the citizenship of Cologne on 19 March 1526. When Franz died in 1530, Arnold took over the management of his brother's business and acted as guardian of his nephew and niece, who both received a handsome sum of money when they came of age in 1540. After Arnold's premature death the business was successfully carried on by his widow, who published two editions of *More's Utopia, and after 1550 by his two elder sons, Arnold and Johann; the youngest son became a physician. The family firm continued to run branches in Antwerp and London until 1582 and 1585 respectively.

While in London, Arnold Birckmann occasionally acted as agent for Erasmus and his friends, forwarding cash, bills of exchange, books, and letters, not always to Erasmus' satisfaction (Epp 332, 437, 885, 892, 895). There is no record of business connections between them after 1518, but Conradus *Goclenius enclosed in Ep 2573 a letter from Arnold Birckmann for the Froben press. In 1535 Birckmann was in England on business when *Fisher, More, and several Carthusian monks were put to death. After his return to Cologne he described these executions, some of which he had witnessed, to his friends (Ep 3041).

BIBLIOGRAPHY: Allen Ep 437 / ADB II 663–4 / Grimm *Buchführer* 1528–30 / Benzing *Buchdrucker* 225 / E.G. Duff *A Century of the English Book Trade* (London 1905) 13–15 / Anne Rouzet et al *Dictionnaire des imprimeurs, libraires et éditeurs des xve et xvie siècles dans les limites géographiques de la Belgique actuelle* (Nieuwkoop 1975) 16–18

IG & PGB

Franz BIRCKMANN of Hinsbeck, documented 1504–d between 7 February and 21 June 1530

Franz Birckmann, a descendant of a family from Hinsbeck, near Venlo (Gelderland), learnt the book trade in Cologne and is documented in 1504 as a stationer in London; by 1505 he was the efficient manager of a large-scale book business. In 1511 he married Gertrud, a daughter of Gerhard Amersfoort, a bookseller in Cologne. They had two children, a daughter, Anne, who seems to have remained unmarried, and a son, Franz, who is documented in Italy (1544–50) as a student and doctor of law.

On 29 December 1511, Franz and his younger brother Arnold *Birckmann, bought a large house originally called 'Blankenburg' but soon to be known as 'Unter der fetten Hennen' after the fat hen shown on the ensign of the Birckmann bookshop. The local trade was generally supervised by Arnold, while Franz directed the international operations, branch outlets, and partnership arrangements. By 1512 the firm had business connections in the Netherlands, France, and England; Franz maintained agencies in Antwerp, Paris, and, at least temporarily, in London in the book traders' district in St Paul's yard. In 1513 Erasmus saw in Franz a principal supplier of books for the English market, which was still heavily dependent on imports (Ep 283). While Arnold Birckmann managed the London agency from 1515 to 1518 and thereafter the store at Cologne, Franz had his headquarters in Antwerp between 1515 and 1526, when he moved to Cologne.

By 1512 Franz Birckmann had become a large scale publisher as well as a bookseller, ordering whole editions to be produced for him by such printers as Wolfgang Hopyl, Nicolas Prévost, and Berthold Rembolt in Paris, by Heinrich Gran in Haguenau, by Hero Fuchs and Eucharius *Cervicornus in Cologne, and by Jean *Thibault, Christoffel of Roermond, and Johannes *Grapheus in Antwerp. After his return to Cologne in 1526 Franz established a press of his own, but it never attained much importance.

By 1512 Birckmann was serving as an agent for Josse *Bade in Paris, but he had especially close connections with Wolfgang *Lachner in Basel; Lachner was the father-in-law of Johann *Froben and the driving force of his printing house. Birckmann had a large stake in the distribution of Froben's products (Epp 475, 483) in England, the Netherlands, and the Cologne area. The association continued after the death of Lachner in 1518 (AK II Ep 654) and at least until Birckmann's return to Cologne in 1526. In his last years his business ventures took a new turn; he is last documented on 7 February 1530, when the Cologne city council warned him not to offer Lutheran books for sale.

Like other booksellers Birckmann used his widely flung business to offer his customers courier and transport services (Epp 437, 464, 477, 511, 573, 827, 1256, 1258, 1778, 1788). He also acted as a banker (Epp 481, 491, 892, 1254, 2227; AK II Ep 654): it was often through him that Erasmus received his pension from England (Epp 712, 775, 782, 823, 892, 1488, 1931), an arrangement that sometimes gave Erasmus cause for grumbling but was evidently acceptable because of Birckmann's efficiency. His activities as a bookseller, publisher, and banker entailed extensive travelling. Not only did he regularly attend the Frankfurt book fair (Epp 464, 469), he was frequently on the road between Antwerp, Paris, London, Basel, and Cologne. A few examples from Erasmus' correspondence show this clearly. Birckmann, arriving in London in March 1512, returned to Paris shortly afterwards (Epp 258, 263) and in the autumn of 1513 travelled to England and Basel (Ep 283). From his base at Antwerp he travelled to London in March 1517 (Ep 543) and was again in England from February to March 1518 (Epp 772 introduction, 825) before visiting Paris in May (Ep 846).

In 1512 and 1513 Erasmus was working on a revised and enlarged edition of his *Adagia* which Josse Bade was hoping to print. In the autumn of 1513 Franz Birckmann, who repeatedly came to England as Bade's agent (Ep 258), took charge of the revised text and also some new translations from Plutarch, but instead of going to Paris he took them to Basel for the Froben press, where they were eventually published (Epp 263, 264, 269, 283, 284). Erasmus may not have been unaware of this manoeuvre (Allen I 63), but since it left him open to criticism, he claimed that Birckmann had acted on his own initiative and without consulting him (Ep 283). Bade himself exonerated Birckmann (Ep 346), while Erasmus' connection with the Froben press proved advantageous for both sides. Birckmann's services were required because Erasmus was to receive his honoraria partly in the form of

books (cf Epp 464, 469, 629, 885), but the arrangement did not always work out to his satisfaction (Epp 464, 629, 704A, 732, 885). Serious problems arose in 1523 and 1524 (Epp 1388, 1437, 1507); thereafter Erasmus often expressed his annoyance with Birckmann. His revenge took the form of the colloquy *Pseudocheus et Philetymus* (ASD I-3 321–4; Epp 1560, 1696) depicting Birckmann as a dishonest businessman.

BIBLIOGRAPHY: Allen and CWE Ep 258 / Grimm *Buchführer* 1523–8 / Benzing *Buchdrucker* 224–5 / Benzing in NDB II 254 / E.G. Duff *A Century of the English Book Trade* (London 1905) 13–15 / Anne Rouzet et al *Dictionnaire des imprimeurs, libraires et éditeurs des xve et xvie siècles dans les limites géographiques de la Belgique actuelle* (Nieuwkoop 1975) 19–20

IG & PGB

Henricus BIRCKO or BYRCK A DUBA *See* Jindřich BERKA

Sixt BIRK of Augsburg, 24 February 1501–19 June 1554

After studies at Erfurt and Tübingen (BA in 1523), Sixt Birk (Birck, Xystus Betuleius), a native of Augsburg, went to Basel on the advice of Konrad *Peutinger and matriculated there on 31 December 1523. Among his teachers at Basel was Bonifacius *Amerbach, to whom he subsequently addressed a considerable number of letters (1535–50). Remaining at Basel until 1536, he worked as a corrector for the Basel printers, taught at various schools, and lodged and supervised students. On the point of leaving Basel he graduated MA and then settled down at Augsburg as the head of Saint Anne's school. He wrote didactic dramas in both German and Latin, as well as commentaries to Cicero and Lactantius, and produced a concordance of the Greek New Testament.

At Basel he married Ursula Glaser, his landlady, in 1528, and after her death he married Barbara Schenk in Augsburg in 1538. In 1527 Birk was a witness to Erasmus' first will (Allen VI 506); he reacted to the news of Erasmus' death at Basel with appropriate rhetoric (AK IV Epp 2082, 2088, 2091).

BIBLIOGRAPHY: AK IV Ep 1994 and passim / A. Hartmann in NDB II 256 / BA *Oekolampads* II 235–6 and passim / *Simonis Grynaei ... epistolae* ed G.T. Streuber (Basel 1847) Ep 18 / *Index Aureliensis* (Baden-Baden 1962–) IV 265–9 / *Matrikel Erfurt* II 319 / *Matrikel Tübingen* I 238 The Öffentliche Bibliothek of the University of Basel has manuscript letters exchanged with C.S. Curione, J. Herwagen, and W. Musculus

PGB

Edmund BIRKHEAD d April 1518
Birkhead (Bricotus, Brigott, Brygate, Birkenhead) joined the Franciscan friars and is documented at their house of Cambridge in 1501 and 1503. After eight years of study he proceeded to the degree of bachelor of theology and subsequently received his doctorate in 1502–3. He was bishop of St Asaph from 16 April 1513 until his death and was shown other favours by *Henry VIII. He preached before the king each Lent between 1511 and 1516. He was buried in Wrexham church, the rebuilding of which he had promoted.

In Ep 1211 Erasmus recalled an episode in which Birkhead and his friends were humiliated by the king for having opposed John *Colet.

BIBLIOGRAPHY: Allen Ep 1211 / Emden BRUC 93

CFG

Nikolaus BISCHOFF *See* Nicolaus EPISCOPIUS

Peter BITTERLIN of Ehingen, d 1544
Bitterlin (Bitterle, Butterlin, Pitrellius, Picraeus) was born at Ehingen on the Danube, west of Ulm, and registered at the University of Basel in 1520, graduating BA in 1522 and MA in 1524. In 1525 he was master of the Latin school attached to the cathedral chapter. In 1527 he was among the witnesses of Erasmus' first will, perhaps in some official function since he is given the title of diocesan collator of wills (Allen VI 506). Although he had to forgo a scholarship since he was unwilling to commit himself to the priesthood he continued to study the law and was a licentiate in 1529 and a doctor of laws in 1541.

Like Erasmus Bitterlin left for Freiburg in 1529 when Basel introduced the Reformation. Bonifacius *Amerbach had earlier recommended him to Udalricus *Zasius, and Bitterlin was most likely the experienced law student

recommended by Erasmus when Antonio *Hoyos required a tutor (Ep 2098). It seems that at least a temporary connection resulted from this suggestion (Ep 2118). In January 1530 Bitterlin was in Augsburg, waiting for the diet to open, perhaps in the hope of employment. He received encouragement from Konrad *Peutinger and in November was preparing to enter the service of Henry, count *Palatine, who was then suffragan bishop of Worms and also prince-provost of Ellwangen, a rich former Benedictine abbey in Württemberg. From 1531 to 1536 Bitterlin was chancellor of Ellwangen. In 1536 he was called back to Basel and given a chair of Roman law (codex) at the newly reorganized university, but he returned to Ehingen in August 1538 when Basel was infested with plague. Despite Amerbach's efforts to retain him at Basel he soon moved to Ulm, married into a highly regarded family (apparently his second marriage, since he was married at the time he lived at Augsburg), and was appointed legal consultant to the city of Ulm.

BIBLIOGRAPHY: AK III Epp 1102, 1331, 1338, 1344, 1404, 1478; IV Epp 1731, 2074, 2091; V Epp 2165, 2232, 2245–7, 2316, 2434; VIII Ep 2434a and passim / *Matrikel Basel* I 346 / *Matrikel Freiburg* I 273 / R. Thommen *Geschichte der Universität Basel 1532–1632* (Basel 1889) 321–2 / Winterberg 16–17 / H. Pfeifer *Verfassungs- und Verwaltungsgeschichte von Ellwangen* (Stuttgart 1959) 219

PGB

Ambrosius BLARER of Constance, 4 April 1492–6 December 1564
Ambrosius Blarer von Giersberg (Blaurer) was the son of Augustin Blarer, a town councillor of Constance (d 1504). He matriculated in 1505 in Tübingen, where he obtained his BA on 23 December 1511 and his MA on 24 January 1513. In 1510 he had entered the Benedictine monastery at Alpirsbach in the Black Forest, and after completing his studies at Tübingen, he returned to his cell at Alpirsbach. His brother, Thomas *Blarer, who had come under the influence of the reformers while studying in Wittenberg from 1520 to 1522, sent him books by *Luther and *Melanchthon. This caused a conflict with the abbot, and in July 1522 Ambrosius fled to Constance. The council

Ambrosius Blarer

---

opposition and external pressures. He went to Winterthur, east of Zürich (1549–51), and then was a preacher in Biel, northwest of Berne (1551–9). Finally he returned to Winterthur, where he died.

Erasmus probably met Ambrosius during his visit to Constance in 1522 when he was fêted in the presence of Ambrosius' uncle, the burgomaster, Bartholomäus *Blarer. On 6 August 1522 Ambrosius wrote to Thomas, expressing concern about Luther's radical stance and divergence from Erasmus. Nothing, he thought, could resist these two, if they were to take a common stand (*Blarer Briefwechsel* I Ep 43). Six months later Erasmus sent greetings to the brothers through Johann von *Botzheim (Allen I 46), while Thomas conveyed Ambrosius' greetings when he wrote to Erasmus in December 1523 (Ep 1396). In 1527 Botzheim referred with a touch of irony to the subtle Reformation politics of Ambrosius Blarer (Ep 1782).

Ambrosius wrote hymns, some of which are contained in the *Konstanzer Gesangbuch*. The voluminous correspondence of Ambrosius and Thomas (*Briefwechsel der Brüder Ambrosius und Thomas Blaurer* ed Traugott Schiess, Freiburg 1908–12) is an indispensable source of information about humanism and religious reform in southern Germany.

appointed him and Johann *Zwick evangelical preachers, and soon he became the theological leader of the reform movement in Constance. A friend and admirer of Ulrich *Zwingli, he encouraged a political pact with Zürich (from 1527 until the defeat of Zürich in the second Kappel war of 1531). Blarer married a former nun in 1533. He enjoyed great prestige among the evangelicals in southern Germany, and in 1528 and years following he was invited to organize the reform movement in Memmingen, Ulm, and Esslingen. In 1534 the reinstated Duke Ulrich of *Württemberg summoned him to his duchy, but Ulrich's Lutheran advisers brought about his dismissal in 1538. At the same time his sister, Margarete *Blarer, who had always assisted her brothers' efforts, lost the bulk of her fortune, so that Ambrosius had to depend on his salary as a preacher in Constance. From 1541 he directed his attention to the improvement of the educational system. After the defeat of the Schmalkaldic League he opposed an accomodation with the victorious *Charles v, manoeuvering Constance into a position of complete isolation and finally having to leave in the face of internal

BIBLIOGRAPHY: Allen Ep 1396 / NDB II 287–8 / Rublack *Reformation in Konstanz* passim / Bernd Moeller *Johannes Zwick und die Reformation in Konstanz* (Gütersloh 1961) passim / H. Buck and E. Fabian *Konstanzer Reformationsgeschichte in ihren Grundzügen* (Tübingen 1965–) I 56, 186–93 and passim / *Matrikel Tübingen* I 146

IG

Bartholomäus BLARER of Constance, d June 1524

Bartholomäus, the influential uncle of Ambrosius and Thomas *Blarer, was first elected burgomaster of Constance in 1497. From 1511 to 1514 and again from 1519 to his death he occupied the two highest offices of burgomaster and *Reichsvogt* in alternating years. When Erasmus and *Beatus Rhenanus visited Constance in the autumn of 1522 he attended a banquet in their honor (Allen I 66).

BIBLIOGRAPHY: Rublack *Reformation in Konstanz* 166 and passim

IG

Margarete BLARER of Constance, 1493–
15 November 1541
Margarete was the daughter of Augustin
Blarer (d 1504), a town councillor of Constance,
and the sister of Ambrosius and Thomas
*Blarer von Giersberg. She received a humanist
education from Johann Jung and throughout
her life assisted her brothers in their work for
the reform movement. She also corresponded
frequently with Martin *Bucer (1531–9). In 1537
she lost a great deal of money; only after this
did Ambrosius Blarer accept a salary for his
position as a preacher. When the plague broke
out in 1541 she worked as a nurse in the
Inselkloster, a convent that had been converted into a hospital, and died there. In the
colloquy *Abbatis et eruditae* (ASD I-3 407)
Erasmus mentioned her along with the sisters
and daughters of Willibald *Pirckheimer as
models of humanist education.

BIBLIOGRAPHY: NDB II 287 / Bernd Moeller
Johannes Zwick und die Reformation in Konstanz
(Gütersloh 1961) 178, 196–9 / *Blarer Briefwechsel*
II 789–839 and passim
                                                        IG

Thomas BLARER of Constance, d 19 March
1567
Thomas Blarer von Giersberg (Blaurer) belonged to a patrician family. His father,
Augustin Blarer, was a town councillor of
Constance. Thomas matriculated in Freiburg
on 27 November 1514 and studied law under
Udalricus *Zasius. Because of an outbreak of
plague, he left Freiburg without obtaining a
degree. From 1520 to 1522 he studied theology
and Hebrew in Wittenberg and came under the
influence of the reformers. He sent books by
Martin *Luther and Philippus *Melanchthon to
his elder brother, Ambrosius *Blarer, who was
then a monk in the monastery at Alpirsbach. In
1521 he accompanied Luther to the diet of
Worms. After 1522 Thomas returned to
Constance, married, and began a civic career.
In 1525 he was a member of the town council,
and between 1536 and 1548 he was alternately
burgomaster and *Reichsvogt*. He was closely
involved with the Constance reform movement
from 1524; he took part in the unsuccessful
peace negotiations with *Charles v after the
defeat of the Schmalkaldic League (Augsburg
1548), and in 1549 he had to flee from

Constance. For his remaining years he resided
on his estate, Neugiersberg, in the Swiss
Thurgau.
    Erasmus probably met Ambrosius Blarer
during his visit to Constance in the autumn of
1522. Writing to *Botzheim on 30 January 1523,
he sent greetings to the brothers (Allen I 46).
Later that year Thomas wrote to him after
reading Ep 1342 and assured him of his
affection in spite of their opposing positions in
the religious debate (Ep 1396). Writing to
Damião de *Gois in 1534, Erasmus mentioned
two letters recently forwarded by Thomas. He
expressed respect for Thomas and asked Gois
to greet him if he passed through Constance.
    Apart from several unpublished pamphlets,
Thomas Blarer wrote seven hymns contained
in the *Konstanzer Gesangbuch*.

BIBLIOGRAPHY: Allen Ep 1396 / NDB II 288 /
Rublack *Reformation in Konstanz* passim /
Matrikel Freiburg I 218 / *Matrikel Wittenberg* I 110
/ *Blarer Briefwechsel* passim / AK II Ep 526 and
passim / D. Heuschen *Reformation, Schmalkal-
discher Bund und Österreich in ihrer Bedeutung für
die Finanzen der Stadt Konstanz 1499–1648*
(Tübingen-Basel 1969) 190–1, and passim /
Bernd Moeller *Johannes Zwick und die Reformation in Konstanz* (Gütersloh 1961) passim / H.
Buck and E. Fabian *Konstanzer Reformationsgeschichte in ihren Grundzügen* (Tübingen
1965–) I 436–7
                                                        IG

BLAURER, BLAURERUS *See* BLARER

Hermannus BLAUIUS (Epp 1481, 1482 of 2
September 1524)
Hermannus Blauius took Erasmus' letters from
Basel to Rome; he has not been identified.

BLET, BLETUS *See* Antoine DU BLET

Anton BLETZ of Zug, documented October
1528–July 1533
Anton Bletz, of Zug (Switzerland), was a
professional messenger who regularly carried
letters between Basel, Freiburg, and Paris, on
one occasion (Ep 1922) apparently losing his
mail at Thann. He appears to have had a
brother (Ep 2065), perhaps the Bernhard
mentioned in Ep 2422 (unless Erasmus
confused Christian names). There is also an

Andreas Bletz of Zug documented at Basel until 1552. He was a saddler and could conceivably be referred to in Ep 2065 and in AK III Ep 1395.

BIBLIOGRAPHY: AK III Epp 1303, 1311; IV Epp 1602, 1615, 1674, 1762; VI xxvii–viii

PGB

Bernhard BLETZ *See Anton* BLETZ

BLOSIUS PALLADIUS *See Blosius* PALLADIUS

Charles BLOUNT fifth Baron Mountjoy, 28 June 1516–10 October 1544

Charles, fifth Baron Mountjoy, was the son and heir of Erasmus' patron, William *Blount, fourth Baron Mountjoy, by his third wife, Alice *Kebel. He was born at Tournai during Mountjoy's tenure as governor there. On the advice of Erasmus, Mountjoy brought Petrus *Vulcanius from Germany to be Charles' tutor. Erasmus took an interest in Charles' education (Epp 2367, 2794) and dedicated an important edition of Livy (Basel: H. Froben 1531) to him, as well as the last three editions of the *Adagia* (Epp 2023, 2215, 2295, 2435, 2459, 2726, 2830, 3092). On his father's death in 1534 Charles became a royal ward. He later married a daughter of his stepmother, Dorothy Grey, by her first husband, Lord Willoughby. Like his father, Charles was a patron of humanists; he was praised by John Leland and Roger Ascham. He lived in London and remained in close attendance on the court. In 1544 he took an active part in the siege and capture of Boulogne.

BIBLIOGRAPHY: Allen Ep 2023 / DNB II 701–2 / G.E. C[okayne] *The Complete Peerage of England* ed V. Gibbs et al (London 1910–59) IX 341–2

STANFORD E. LEHMBERG

William BLOUNT fourth Baron Mountjoy, c 1478–8 November 1534

William Blount, fourth Baron Mountjoy, Erasmus' student and patron, was a member of a family which had distinguished itself in military and administrative pursuits for several generations. William's grandfather, Walter, had been ennobled by Henry VI for loyal service during the wars of the Roses. Walter's son John, the third baron, died in 1485, leaving William a minor heir to the title and estates.

William was born at Barton in Staffordshire; the date of his birth is not known. Polidoro *Virgilio states that he was created a privy councillor in 1486, but since it is known that he was not yet of age in 1488 this is unlikely; see *Calendar of Patent Rolls: Henry VII* (London 1914–16) II 198. He sued out livery of his lands in January 1500 (ibid I 192).

Little is known of Mountjoy's early life. It is often supposed that he was a student in Paris as early as 1496 (Nichols *The Epistles of Erasmus* I 115), but Allen (I 207) is probably correct in believing that he made a single sojourn beginning in the spring of 1498: in March of that year Richard *Whitford, a fellow of Queens' College, Cambridge, received a grace to be absent from college in order to accompany Mountjoy abroad (Ep 89). At this time Erasmus was helping support himself by teaching young Englishmen in Paris; in 1497 he had lived in a boarding-house with Thomas *Grey and Robert *Fisher (Epp 58, 62, 63, 71). By November 1498 he was acting as tutor to Mountjoy (Ep 79), and when Mountjoy returned to England in 1499 he invited Erasmus to accompany him. Erasmus had intended to visit Italy, where Fisher was studying, but (as he wrote to Fisher) 'Lord Mountjoy swept me away to his native England when I was just on the point of leaving. Where, indeed, would I not follow a young man so enlightened, so kindly, and so amiable? I would follow him, as God loves me, even to the lower world itself' (Ep 118).

During his first stay in England Erasmus was closely associated with his noble protégé and patron. Mountjoy was a friend and tutor of the future *Henry VIII, and it was while staying at Mountjoy's country house that Erasmus was first taken to visit *Henry VII's court at Eltham (Allen I 6; Reedijk poem 45).

Although Erasmus cherished his English friends and, surprisingly, found the English climate pleasant and wholesome (Ep 118), he returned to Paris in January 1500. At Dover almost all his money was confiscated by customs agents despite assurances from Mountjoy and *More that there would be no problem unless he attempted to export English coin. The loss rankled for some years (Epp 119, 120, 123, 135; Allen I 16).

Erasmus probably conceived the idea of

compiling his *Adagia* during discussions with Mountjoy, who encouraged the project (Ep 181). The first edition (Paris 1500) carried a dedicatory preface addressed to Mountjoy (Ep 126); Erasmus soon expressed disappointment that this dedication produced a smaller gift than he had anticipated (Ep 135). At about the same time Mountjoy had asked for a 'fuller and more finished' version of *De conscribendis epistolis*, which Erasmus had compiled for his pupils in Paris (Ep 117). This revision formed the basis for an unauthorized edition published by John *Siberch at Cambridge in 1521. Erasmus also wrote an oration in praise of matrimony for Mountjoy, probably at the time of Mountjoy's first marriage, but the original text is lost and that included in Siberch's *De conscribendis epistolis* is taken from the *Encomium matrimonii* published by Erasmus as a separate work in 1518; see James D. Tracy 'On the composition dates of seven of Erasmus' writings' BHR 31 (1969) 359–60.

In 1504 Erasmus wrote John *Colet suggesting indirectly that he would welcome renewed patronage from Mountjoy (Ep 181). This approach produced an invitation for Erasmus to return to England. By December 1505 Erasmus was again with Mountjoy; he remained in England, chiefly in London, until June 1506. 'The sun never shone on a truer friend of scholars,' Erasmus wrote effusively (Ep 186).

As early as 1503 Mountjoy had been appointed captain of the castle at Hammes, near Calais (Nichols *The Epistles of Erasmus* I 231, 370), a position his father had held before him. Erasmus evidently visited Mountjoy here in 1506, just after leaving England; a letter to Christopher *Urswick, written at Hammes, is probably of this date (Ep 193).

The accession of Henry VIII in 1509 called forth Mountjoy's famous panegyric: 'Oh, Erasmus, if you could only see how happily excited everyone is here ... you would be bound to weep for joy' (Ep 215). It is possible that the letter was actually written by Erasmus' friend Andrea *Ammonio, who was acting as Mountjoy's secretary. Anticipating royal patronage (for according to Mountjoy 'generosity scatters wealth with unstinting hand') Erasmus decided to return immediately to England. But Mountjoy was no longer Erasmus' chief

support, for he was kept busy on the continent throughout most of the latter's stay. In addition to serving as captain of Hammes he was master of the mints at Calais and in London (LP I 139).

When Erasmus visited Paris in the spring of 1511 he took with him a small volume of verse written by Ammonio to be published there. This was dedicated to Mountjoy; but Mountjoy did not like the original preface, which was evidently too fulsome, and Erasmus prevailed upon Ammonio to substitute another praising English liberality more generally (Epp 218–21).

In October and November 1511 Erasmus, now at Cambridge, wrote Ammonio and Colet inquiring whether Mountjoy had returned to London: Erasmus did not wish to be too long apart from his 'personal Jupiter' (Epp 231–3, 238). Mountjoy was back in England early in November (Ep 239), but Erasmus decided to avoid his house so long as 'Cerberus' – perhaps Bernard *André – lay in wait there (Epp 240, 243, 247, 248), to whom Erasmus owed some money (Epp 243, 248). Mountjoy finally paid the debt for him (Ep 254). During the next two years Mountjoy was principally occupied as chamberlain to *Catherine of Aragon, to which office he was appointed in May 1512 (LP I 1221:29).

In the preface to his enlarged and revised edition of the *Adagia*, written in 1513, Erasmus expressed his indebtedness to Mountjoy and to Archbishop *Warham, who had given him the benefice of Aldington (Ep 269). During this period Erasmus was dissatisfied with the patronage which he had found in England because it was not so liberal as Mountjoy had promised (Epp 281, 283). Erasmus decided to return to Basel in 1514, but before doing so he paid his respects to Mountjoy and Warham (Epp 287, 294). In July he visited Mountjoy at Hammes (Epp 295–7), and he later wrote him from Basel describing a painful accident which had occurred near Ghent (Ep 301).

When Henry VIII invaded France in 1513 Mountjoy was placed in charge of transport (LP I 1889, 2226, 2326), and in January 1515 he was appointed governor and bailiff of Tournai, which Henry had captured (for the date see Cruickshank *The English Occupation of Tournai* 189n). He seems to have laboured diligently at this post, but since he had to deal with mutinies and chronic shortages of funds he heartily disliked it. Erasmus visited him at Tournai in the spring of 1515 (Ep 332); it was perhaps on this occasion that Mountjoy gave him a manuscript of Suetonius from St Martin's monastery (Epp 332, 586). Erasmus now complained that Mountjoy, 'the oldest patron of my studies, has been so overwhelmed by the burdens of the war that his help fell short of his affection' (Ep 334). Mountjoy did persuade Cardinal *Wolsey to offer Erasmus a prebend at Tournai, but the conditions did not please Erasmus, and by the time he had decided to accept it Wolsey had made another appointment (Epp 360, 388). In June 1516 Erasmus planned to visit Mountjoy again at Hammes, but he may not have done so (Ep 410). Mountjoy did not return to England until 1517 (LP II 2825).

In 1520 Mountjoy attended Henry VIII at the Field of Cloth of Gold (LP III 704). In the following year Erasmus saw him, as well as More, *Tunstall, and Wolsey, at Bruges, where they were meeting with *Charles V (LP III 629; Ep 1233). By this time Mountjoy was urging Erasmus to declare his position with regard to *Luther (Ep 1219). Several writers suspected that Erasmus was the true author of Henry VIII's *Assertio septem sacramentorum* (Ep 1298), but Erasmus insisted that it was the king's own work and that Mountjoy had taught Henry to write in an Erasmian style (Ep 1313). During 1523 Mountjoy was briefly in France again at the head of an army of six thousand in the campaign of Charles *Brandon, duke of Suffolk. In 1525, in his position as Catherine of Aragon's chamberlain, he asked Erasmus to write on the topic of marriage (Ep 1624). The result was the *Christiani matrimonii institutio* published by *Froben in 1526 and dedicated to Catherine (Ep 1727). For some time after this Erasmus did not hear from Mountjoy, and he may have been referring to his old patron in a letter commenting upon a friend who seemed to have changed upon marrying (Ep 1740). In 1527 Erasmus and Mountjoy did exchange letters, and Mountjoy admitted his negligence in not writing earlier (Ep 1816).

Mountjoy retained the office of chamberlain to Catherine throughout her divorce trial in 1529. In 1533 he had the unpleasant duty of attempting to persuade her to accept the title of princess dowager. In October 1533 he begged

Thomas *Cromwell to release him from the office (LP VI 1252), and he was discharged in December. He died the next year and was buried in the Grey Friars' Church, London. He had been steward of Cambridge University from about 1529 and a knight of the Garter since 1526.

Mountjoy married four times. His first wife (Ep 105) was Elizabeth, a daughter of Sir William *Say. She died before 21 July 1506, leaving a daughter, Gertrude (afterwards the wife of Henry Courtenay, marquis of Exeter, attainted with him in 1539 but pardoned). Mountjoy's second wife was Agnes de Vanegas, a Spanish attendant of Catherine of Aragon: Henry VIII wrote to *Ferdinand II of Aragon in 1509 supporting her claim to a legacy from Queen *Isabella (LP I 128; *Calendar of State Papers Spanish* II 20; DNB fails to note this marriage). Not later than 1516 Mountjoy wed Alice *Kebel, daughter of Henry Kebel and widow of William Brown, a former lord mayor of London. She died in 1521. Mountjoy's last wife was Dorothy, daughter of Thomas Grey, marquis of Dorset, and widow of Robert Lord Willoughby. They were married before 29 July 1523; she lived until 1553. Mountjoy's heir was his son Charles *Blount, in whose education Erasmus took an interest. By his third wife Mountjoy also had a daughter, Catherine; his fourth wife bore him a son, John, who died without issue, and two daughters, Dorothy and Mary.

No portrait of Mountjoy is known to survive.

BIBLIOGRAPHY: DNB II 721–2 / G.E. C[okayne] *The Complete Peerage of England* ed V. Gibbs et al (London 1910–59) IX 338–41 / *The Epistles of Erasmus* ed and trans F.M. Nichols (London 1901–18) passim / F.M. Nichols *The Hall of Lawford Hall* (London 1891) 193–351 / C.G. Cruickshank *The English Occupation of Tournai 1513–1519* (Oxford 1971) passim / Garrett Mattingly *Catherine of Aragon* (London 1942) passim / McConica 6–7 and passim
STANFORD E. LEHMBERG

Sebastian von BLUMENECK of Freiburg, documented 1484–1542
Sebastian von Blumeneck's family belonged to the lesser nobility and derived its name from the castle and village of Blumegg, in the Black Forest. In the city and region of Freiburg

members of the family were to be found from the early fourteenth century. Sebastian is documented for the first time in 1484 for holding in fee jointly with others the village of Riegel. In 1498 he gave up the citizenship of Freiburg and moved to Strasbourg, where the same year he married Beatrix, daughter of Wilhelm Betschold. In the following year he purchased the citizenship of Strasbourg, which he exchanged again for that of Freiburg at the time of his return there in 1502. It is possible that this move followed the death of Beatrix; at any rate in 1506 Blumeneck took as his second wife Apollonia von Reischach. Both wives, together with Sebastian, are portrayed on the stained-glass windows which he donated to the Blumeneck chapel in the cathedral at Freiburg and which were executed after designs made by Hans Baldung in 1517.

During the three decades of his outstanding public career Blumeneck served from 1508 to 1530 with few interruptions on the Council of Twenty-four (*Vierundzwanziger*) as well as being burgomaster in 1509–10, 1512–13, 1515–16, 1518–19, 1521–2, and 1528–9 (Ep 2112), each term beginning and ending in June, and *Schultheiss* in 1513–15. From 1510 to 1542 he headed the overseers of cathedral works. It may be due to his initiative that Hans Baldung was chosen to paint a triptych for the cathedral's high altar. In 1512 Baldung completed a votive picture for the Betschold family of Strasbourg, and in the same year he paid the large sum of 380 florins into Blumeneck's account with the Freiburg municipal exchange bank, apparently as a savings deposit. Baldung subsequently portrayed Blumeneck and his fellow overseers, including Ulrich *Wirtner, on the predella of his altar piece. In 1511 Blumeneck also donated a stained-glass window panel for the central choir, which showed St Sebastian and his own coat of arms. Other offices he held included the stewardships of the Augustinian monastery (1517–42) and of the nunnery of St Agnes (1530–5). After 1542 his name is no longer found in the public records. He may have retired, and Kindler assumes that he was still alive in 1545. Apart from a daughter, Anastasia (d 1581), his descendants have not so far been traced reliably.

BIBLIOGRAPHY: Allen Ep 2112 / J. Kindler von Knobloch *Oberbadisches Geschlechterbuch* (Heid-

Sebastian von Blumeneck

elberg 1898–1919) I 69, 112, 118, III 481 / F. Hefele *Freiburger Urkundenbuch* III (Freiburg 1957), index / C. Wittmer *Le Livre de bourgeoisie de la ville de Strasbourg* (Strasbourg 1948–61) II 505, 513 / F. Thiele *Die Freiburger Stadtschreiber im Mittelalter* (Freiburg 1973) 89 / F. Baumgarten *Der Freiburger Hochaltar* (Strasbourg 1904) 43ff / J. Krummer-Schroth *Glasmalereien aus dem Freiburger Münster* (Freiburg 1967) 138ff and passim / H. Perseke *Hans Baldungs Schaffen in Freiburg* (Freiburg 1941) 2, 33 / Freiburg, Stadtarchiv MSS A 1 XIV, S V von Blumeneck; B 5 1f no 1 f 3; B 5 Ia no 2; B 5 VIIIa no 1

HANS SCHADEK

Josse BLYSSEL *See Judocus* BEISSEL

Achille BOCCHI of Bologna, 1488–6 November 1562
The humanist Achille Bocchi was born at Bologna to Giulio Bocchi and Costanza Zambeccari. He studied under Giambattista *Pio and before 1508 married Taddea Grassi, niece of Achille de' Grassi, bishop of Bologna. In 1508 he was appointed reader of Greek at the University of Bologna, and in 1514 reader of poetry and rhetoric. Although Bocchi

remained at Bologna until his death, his teaching was not continuous, for the senate commissioned him to write the history of Bologna. He completed seventeen books, up to the year 1263, and his son Pirro added an eighteenth, covering 1264–73.

Bocchi was a friend of Jacopo *Sadoleto, Marco Antonio Flaminio, Leandro Alberti, and many other humanists, philosophers, and dignitaries. Shortly after 1564 he founded his academy, where discussions centred on philology and other topics.

Erasmus mentioned Bocchi in the *Ciceronianus*, listing him among the many writers unworthy of the name 'Ciceronian' (ASD I-2 662).

Bocchi's first notable work was the *Apologia in Plautum, cui accedit vita Ciceronis auctore Plutarco nuper inventa* (Bologna: J.A. de Benedictis 1508), a defence of the *Commentaria in Plautum* of his master, Giambattista Pio. His most famous work was the *Symbolicarum quaestionum de universo genere quas serio ludebat libri quinque* (Bologna: Accademia Bocchiana 1555), a collection of 551 epigrams on oriental and biblical themes, illustrated with woodcuts by Giulio Bonosoni. The *Symbolicarum quaestionum* was modelled on the *Emblemata* of Andrea *Alciati. Bocchi's history of Bologna is to be found in manuscript at Bologna.

BIBLIOGRAPHY: A. Rotondò in DBI XI 67–70
TBD

Johan BOCKELSON *See* JAN *of Leiden*

Andreas BODENSTEIN *See Andreas* KARLSTADT

Hector BOECE of Dundee, c 1465–1536
Hector Boece (Boethius) was born to Alexander Boyis, a burgess of Dundee. After receiving his early education at a local grammar school, Boece matriculated at the Collège de Montaigu, University of Paris, received a BA in 1493 and a MA in 1494, and served as procurator of the German nation in 1495–6. He probably left Paris in 1496 for Aberdeen, where he assisted William Elphinstone, bishop of Aberdeen, in the foundation of a new university. He served as the first principal of the College of St Mary in Aberdeen, later to be known as King's College, successfully building up a fine teaching body and attracting many scholars.

In addition to the formative role he played in the founding of the University of Aberdeen, Boece gained renown as the first great Scottish historian. In 1522 in Paris Josse *Bade printed Boece's *Episcoporum Murthlacensium & Aberdonensium vitae*, which was followed by his publication of Boece's *Scotorum historiae a prima gentis origine* in 1527. This last work helped to secure Boece a royal pension of fifty Scots pounds in 1527, an identical sum being awarded to him again some two years later. Bade had also published Boece's *Explicatio quorundam vocabulorum* in 1519. In 1528 Boece's university conferred on him the degree of doctor of divinity, again in recognition of his studies. His small emolument as a principal was supplemented by some ecclesiastical posts; by 1509 he was rector of Tyrie and a canon of Aberdeen Cathedral, while by 1528 he had been made vicar of Tullynessle. He died before 22 November 1536.

Boece met Erasmus in the Montaigu, where both scholars had been students. The two befriended each other and Erasmus dedicated to Boece (Ep 47) his *Carmen de casa natalitia Iesu* (Paris: A. Denidel, January 1496?; Reedijk poem 33). Following Boece's return to Scotland, the two apparently lost contact until Boece wrote a letter of praise to Erasmus on 26 May 1528 (Ep 1996), reminding the latter of their earlier acquaintance and asking him for a list of his works. Erasmus replied some two years later, on 15 March 1530 (Ep 2283), acknowledging his memory of their days at the Montaigu as well as enclosing the requested 'Index omnium lucubrationum,' his last catalogue of his writings.

BIBLIOGRAPHY: Allen Ep 47 / DNB II 759–62 / University of Aberdeen *Quatercentenary of the Death of Hector Boece* by William Douglas Simpson et al (Aberdeen 1937) / Philippe Renouard *Imprimeurs et libraires parisiens du XVIe siècle* (Paris 1964–) II nos 500, 565, 743
MORDECHAI FEINGOLD

Georgius BOËMUS *See Georg* BEHAIM

Giovanni Battista, Giovanni, and Bernardo BOERIO of Genoa
Giovanni Battista Boerio, a native of Genoa,

settled in England and was physician to *Henry VII and afterwards to *Henry VIII. In 1506 he sent his sons, Giovanni and Bernardo, to Italy under the tutelage of a certain *Clyfton (Ep 194) and the supervision of Erasmus (Allen I 56, 59). Erasmus praised the Boerio boys, noting that they were intellectually advanced for their years (Epp 194, 195). Between 1511 and 1513 Boerio was intimately known to Erasmus and Andrea *Ammonio, who were then in England. In 1512 Erasmus dedicated his edition of Lucian's *Astrologia* to Boerio (Ep 267; ASD I-1 371–2, 618–22), but by April 1514 relations had become strained (Epp 289, 292, 293). The nature of the quarrel is obscure; Erasmus mentioned that Thomas *Ruthall, bishop of Durham, shared his hostility towards his former friend (Ep 282).

Meanwhile Giovanni Battista called his sons back to England in 1513 (Ep 283:60). He and Bernardo travelled to Italy in the spring of 1515 with letters of recommendation from Henry VIII to various important personages in Rome (LP II 542, 634–5). By 1518 Giovanni was also in Italy, and he and Bernardo exchanged greetings with Erasmus through Paolo *Bombace (Epp 865, 905), who had met the brothers in Bologna in 1507.

In 1530 Erasmus wrote to the brothers, whom he knew to be in Genoa, recalling his friendship with their father and mentioning their brief antagonism (Ep 2255). Bernardo replied and Erasmus wrote again in 1531, praising his achievements and wondering whether Giovanni had died in the mean time (Ep 2481). Writing at the suggestion of Antonio de' *Vivaldi, Bernardo addressed a letter to Thomas *Cromwell, signing himself as apostolic protonotary, knight of St Peter, and canon (?) of Genoa (LP V 1057). In December 1538 he was apparently in Rome (LP XIV 1).

BIBLIOGRAPHY: Allen Ep 267 / LP I 132 (102) and passim

CFG

Jacob BOGAERT See BOGARDUS and Jacob van CASTERE

BOGARDUS Ep 1347 of 1 March 1523
In Ep 1347 Erasmus recalled a physician named Bogardus whom he associated with *Gronsellus, a 'senator Mechliniensis.' Both lived to an

advanced age, with Bogardus dying a few years ahead of the other. Conceivably he could be identical with Jacob Bogaert (Bogardus), a learned physician and professor of medicine at Louvain, who entered holy orders after the death of his wife. Bogaert was a doctor of medicine at Louvain on 13 June 1480 and thus must have been fairly old when he died on 17 July 1520.

BIBLIOGRAPHY: Allen Ep 932 / de Vocht CTL I 443 / *Matricule de Louvain* II-1 466(77)

PGB

Hans BOGBINDER of Copenhagen, d circa 1564
Hans Meissenheim Bogbinder (Bibliopegus, Missenhom, Johannes Danus) was the son of another Hans Meissenheim Bogbinder, the burgomaster of Copenhagen, and his wife, Birgitte. The year of his birth is unknown; the year of his marriage probably is 1527 (Ep 1883). The future King *Christian II of Denmark was brought up with Hans in the latter's home. On 29 August 1517 Bogbinder matriculated at Louvain as a paying student of the College of the Castle; his friendly contacts with Erasmus may well date back to the time when they were both residents of Louvain. It is not known where Bogbinder obtained his MA.

When Christian II was forced to seek exile in the Netherlands (1523) Bogbinder accompanied the monarch and in years to come undertook many diplomatic errands in efforts to gain support for his cause, including a trip to Scotland in 1528 (Ep 1996). In 1550 Bogbinder was amnestied and permitted to return to Denmark, where he entered the service of King *Christian III and was sent on an embassy to England from 1522 to 1523. At about the same time he was expected to undertake an embassy to Muscovy; whether he actually went there is doubtful, however. Bogbinder's great admiration for Erasmus (Ep 1996) was rewarded by the latter with trust and warmth. 'Danus meus,' he called Bogbinder in Ep 1780, and Erasmus' Ep 1883, the only letter addressed to Bogbinder that survived, is written in a tone of confidence and pleasantry. On his many journeys undertaken in part perhaps for commercial ends, Bogbinder carried letters and greetings to and from Erasmus (Epp 1769, 1775, 1778, 1781, 1783, 1788). Erasmus' letters show

Bogbinder to have been in personal contact with Frans van der *Dilft and Johannes *Oecolampadius (Epp 1996, 2147).

BIBLIOGRAPHY: Allen Ep 1769 / *Dansk Biografisk Leksikon* 3rd ed (Copenhagen 1979–) II 302–3 / *Matricule de Louvain* III-1 564 / K. Rasmussen 'Hans Bogbinder and Muscovy: a contribution to the question of Danish influence on Russian printing in the mid-sixteenth century' *Scando-Slavica* 18 (1972) 199–203

MARTIN SCHWARZ LAUSTEN & PGB

Antoine BOHIER d 27 November 1519
Antoine, a son of Austremoine Bohier, intendant of finance, and Béraude Duprat, was born around 1460. While his brothers served in the royal administration, Antoine took monastic vows at the abbey of Fécamp, received a theological doctorate from the University of Paris, and was regent of the university. From 1492 he was abbot of St Ouen at Rouen, from 1494 of Saint-Georges-de-Boscherville, from 1499 of Issoire in the Auvergne, and from 1505 of Fécamp. He was a favourite of Cardinal Georges (I) d'*Amboise, who named him vicar-general of his archdiocese of Rouen. He also held administrative offices in Normandy and in 1499 was temporarily president of the Parlement of Rouen. From 1515 he was archbishop of Bourges, and on 1 April 1517 he was created cardinal in deference to the wishes of Louise of *Savoy and chancellor Antoine *Duprat.

Thomas *More claimed in 1520 that Bohier had at one time tried to restrain Germain de *Brie, More's literary opponent (Epp 1087, 1094).

BIBLIOGRAPHY: Allen Ep 1087 / DBF VI 780–1 / DHGE IX 511–13 / Bernard Chevalier *Tours ville royale (1356–1520)* (Paris-Louvain 1975) 505–6 / *L'Abbaye bénédictine de Fécamp: Ouvrage scientifique du XIII centenaire, 658–1958* (Fécamp 1959–63) II 284, 333, and passim

MICHEL REULOS

Nicolas BOISSEL documented at Paris c 1521–8 November 1533
Allen (Ep 2037: 150n; cf Ep 2126:145) conjectures that the rector of the University of Paris who pronounced the condemnation of the *Colloquia* was Bertinus Myss, because Du Boulay says Myss was elected on 23 June 1528, the very day of the condemnation. Little is known of Myss except that he was the principal of the Collège de Beauvais from 1527 to 1528. His term as rector expired on 11 October 1528. Contrary to Allen and Du Boulay, however, the manuscript register of the English-German nation reports that the election of the new rector took place on 24, not 23, June ('octavo calend. Julii'). After reporting the condemnation of the *Colloquia* on 23 June ('nono calend. Julii'), the register states that the German-English nation met privately on 24 June at its normal place of assembly (the church of saints Côme-et-Damien) before moving to Saint-Julien-le-pauvre, where the electors of the four nations met to choose the new rector. Immediately prior to the election, the faculty of arts thanked the outgoing rector, Nicolas Boissel, for his labours in the domain of literature – an unusual phrase for this occasion and almost certainly a reference to the preceding day's condemnation of the *Colloquia*. It was, then, Nicolas Boissel, not Bertinus Myss, who presided over the condemnation of Erasmus' *Colloquia* at the University of Paris.

Boissel was from the diocese of Rouen. He received his MA at the University of Paris around 1521 and was regent in arts as well as procurator of the nation of Normandy in 1524. He was rector of the university 25 March–24 June 1528. Boissel was a *bursarius theologus* and prior of the Collège d'Harcourt by 1529. He ranked tenth of twenty-eight in the licentiate class of the faculty of theology on 20 January 1532 and received his doctorate in theology on 14 June. In Lent 1533 he was present for the famous reformist sermons of Gérard *Roussel at the Louvre but was reluctant to co-operate with the faculty of theology's investigation.

During his student years, Boissel held a living from the parish of Notre-Dame de l'Epine in the diocese of Rouen. He was perhaps the Canon Boissel of Le Mans whose thirteen propositions on sin, baptism, and saints were condemned by the faculty of theology of Paris in 1537.

BIBLIOGRAPHY: Farge no 51 / Paris, Archives de l'Université (Sorbonne), MS Registre 15 f 149 verso–150 recto, 150 recto–verso

JAMES K. FARGE

Artus de BOISY *See Artus* GOUFFIER

Andronius BOLANUS (ASD I-2 478–80)
Andronius Bolanus, given the title of *antistes*,
or presiding priest, is the addressee of a model
letter in *De conscribendis epistolis*. No identification has been proposed, and the name may be
fictitious.

Anne BOLEYN *See* ANNE *Boleyn, queen of*
England

Thomas BOLEYN earl of Wiltshire and
Ormond, 1477–13 March 1539
Boleyn (Bulleyn, Rochefordus, Wiltiserius)
was the heir of Sir William Boleyn of Blickling,
Norfolk, in which county his ancestors had
lived since the twelfth century; his mother was
co-heiress to the Irish earldom of Ormond,
which fell vacant in 1515. Boleyn served with
his father against the Cornish rebels in 1497
and in about 1500 married Elizabeth, the eldest
daughter of Thomas *Howard, second duke of
Norfolk. He was present at the marriage of
*Catherine of Aragon to Prince *Arthur in 1501
and two years later accompanied another royal
bride, *Margaret Tudor, to Scotland. At
*Henry VIII's coronation he was made a knight
of the Bath and became one of the closest
companions of the new king. In the first year of
the reign he was made keeper of the Calais
exchange and of the foreign exchange in
England, thereafter receiving many grants of
office and property in Norfolk and Kent; he
served as sheriff for the latter county from 1511
to 1512 and from 1517 to 1518. From 1512 he
was frequently employed on diplomatic missions, being one of the negotiators of the Holy
League against France in 1513 and serving in
the subsequent campaign. When peace came in
1514 his elder daughter, Mary, went to the
French court in the suite of *Mary Tudor.
Boleyn became a privy councillor in 1518, and
from January 1519 to February 1520 he was
ambassador in France, taking with him his
younger daughter, *Anne. In 1521 and 1523 he
was sent on embassies to the emperor, from
whom he received a pension in 1525. At home
he was appointed comptroller of the king's
household in 1520, and from 1522 to 1525 he
was treasurer.
When his daughters returned from France to

the English court and successively captured
the king's affections Boleyn's rise to prominence accelerated. He was given the garter in
1523 and 18 June 1527 was created Viscount
Rochford. By the late summer of that year he
was among the king's chief ministers, handling
state affairs with Norfolk and Charles *Brandon, duke of Suffolk, to the exclusion of
Cardinal *Wolsey. On 8 December 1529 he was
advanced to the earldom of Wiltshire and also
received that of Ormond in the peerage of
Ireland. In the following January he became
keeper of the privy seal and was entrusted
with a delicate embassy to *Francis I of France,
Pope *Clement VII, and the Emperor *Charles
V, allegedly being preferred to Norfolk because
of his fluency in Latin and French; however,
the mission was a failure and he returned to
England in some disgrace.
  Another side to Boleyn's activities appears at
this time. On the day after the Reformation
parliament assembled on 3 November 1529 he
sent a request to Erasmus (whom he may have
met in England) for a commentary on Psalm 23
(Ep 2232). Erasmus promptly complied with his
Enarratio triplex in psalmum XXII (Basel: H.
Froben 1530) and in the dedication commended
his patron's erudition and devotion to letters,
even divinity (Ep 2266). He could not explain
why Boleyn had approached him. Noting that
the king wished to make Anne Boleyn queen,
he recalled his earlier commission from
Catherine of Aragon and claimed satisfaction
at having admirers in both camps (Ep 2315). It
seems that a reward from Boleyn duly followed
(Epp 2512, 2576). Boleyn also patronized the
Hebrew scholar Richard *Wakefield, a convert
to the king's cause; it may be that his courtship
of Erasmus owed more to politics than to
humanism.
  Meanwhile Boleyn was playing a leading
role in the king's affairs. He and his son were,
with the duke of Norfolk, involved in securing
the submission of the clergy in May 1532. In
March 1533, two months after the king had
secretly married Anne Boleyn, Erasmus dedicated another work, *Explanatio symboli* (Basel:
H. Froben 1533), to her father, again with an
effusive preface (Ep 2772). This work proved
very popular: Erasmus wrote with evident
satisfaction that it sold out within three hours
at the Frankfurt spring fair (Ep 2845). Boleyn

may also have commissioned the English translation (STC 10504). Fourteen years later Edward VI's Protestant commissioners would order its use in Winchester College. Boleyn received the work gratefully, passing it for consideration to the newly appointed archbishop of Canterbury, Thomas *Cranmer (Ep 2815). He thanked the author personally in a letter of 19 June, requesting a further work, on preparation for death (Ep 2824). The third work written for Boleyn, *De praeparatione ad mortem*, appeared in January 1534 (Basel: H. Froben; Ep 2884). Appended to it was a letter firmly indicating that Erasmus had never expressed approval of the king's matrimonial proceeding (Ep 2846). By 1535 Erasmus may have regretted writing at Boleyn's behest (Ep 3028), and in February 1536 he received some sour comments from Eustache *Chapuys for having done so (Ep 3090). Boleyn himself was naturally prominent during his daughter's brief consortship. One of his last major duties was at the trial of Thomas *More in July 1535. In June 1536, shortly after Anne Boleyn and her brother George, Lord Rochford, were executed, their father relinquished the privy seal and retired to Hever Castle, where he died.

BIBLIOGRAPHY: Allen Ep 2266 / DNB II 783–5 / G.E. C[okayne] *The Complete Peerage of England* ed V. Gibbs et al (London 1910–59) X 137–40, XII-1 739 / J.H. Round *The Early Life of Anne Boleyn* (London 1886) / P. Friedmann *Anne Boleyn, a chapter of English history, 1527–1536* (London 1884) / M.L. Bruce *Anne Boleyn* (New York 1972) / J.J. Scarisbrick *Henry VIII* (London 1968) 18 and passim / J.K. McConica 61, 123, 134, 137

C.S. KNIGHTON

Willem BOLLART of Brussels, d 14 November 1532

Willem Bollart (Bolart, Bolais) was born around 1470 in Brussels in very modest circumstances. Of small stature and darkish complexion, he was given to fits of anger and was generally of delicate health, although this did not prevent him from acquiring a good education. According to his biographer, Gerard *Morinck, he was, apart from his Flemish mother tongue, fluent in French and a respectable Latin scholar. Erasmus came to know him when both joined the service of Hendrik van *Bergen,

bishop of Cambrai (Ep 761), and in a probable reference to Bollart he spoke of 'great attachment through our devotion to the same pursuits' (Ep 671). While Erasmus soon left for Paris, Bollart accompanied the bishop to England in 1498 and to Spain in 1501. After Hendrik's death in 1502 Bollart joined the Cistercian order at the abbey of Clairvaux. In 1505 he was sent by his abbot, Jean Foucauld, to supervise as rector the Cistercian nunnery of Flines, near Tournai. He succeeded in restoring discipline in this house and thus came to the attention of Charles de Haultbois, bishop of Tournai and abbot of the nearby Benedictine house of Saint-Amand. Following the recommendations of Canon Eleuthère *Hardy, Bollart was chosen to reform Saint-Amand, a task which he accomplished to the satisfaction of all concerned. Shortly before Haultbois' death on 10 June 1513, Bollart received papal permission to move from the Cistercian to the Benedictine order and was nominated abbot of Saint-Amand. Known as a 'bon bourguignon,' in the days of the English occupation of Tournai in 1513 Bollart successfully argued the neutrality of his abbey in the conflict between England and France and thus saved it from the threat of a siege. Five years later he resigned the abbacy to Gérard d'Ovinghien, who in turn passed it on to Cardinal Louis de Bourbon. As this latter transaction was opposed by Bollart, a long litigation ensued until in 1526 Louis de Bourbon resigned in favour of Joris van *Egmond and also accorded Bollart an annuity.

Meanwhile, on 17 September 1517, Antoon (I) van *Bergen ceded to Bollart, the protégé of his late brother Hendrik, the rich abbey of St Trudo at St Truiden. As previously at Flines and Saint-Amand, Bollart was called in to end grave disorders, and he lost no time in doing so. He renovated the existing buildings and added new ones. From 1517 he purchased four additional houses in Louvain for the abbey and completely restored another one which the abbey had bought in 1470 as a refuge in emergencies. Bollart liked living in Louvain and after a fire destroyed the old shelter house on 24 August 1525 he had it magnificiently rebuilt. Despite the heavy expense involved, he was still able to lend Henry of *Nassau twelve thousand French silver caroli.

The eminent qualities of Bollart were recognized by Erasmus' friend Jérôme de *Busleyden, and in 1517 and 1518 Erasmus himself in the course of his residence at Louvain came to renew his acquaintance with his old colleague (Ep 761; cf Epp 671, 672, 720). From 1529 failing health caused Bollart to withdraw from his abbacy in favour of Georges Sarens, whom he chose to be his coadjutor. Papal confirmation of this choice, however, was not forthcoming until 2 October 1532, and Bollart died six weeks later in Louvain without having received word from Rome. Paschasius *Berselius composed his epitaph in the Louvain charterhouse, where his heart and entrails were buried, while the body was sent on for interment at St Truiden. His portrait is on a stained-glass window in the Louvain charterhouse.

BIBLIOGRAPHY: Allen Ep 761 / *Chronique de l'abbaye de Saint-Trond* ed C. de Borman (Liège 1877) II 357–70: an account of Bollart's activities by the continuator of the chronicle, Gerard Morinck / de Vocht *Busleyden* 454–6 / de Vocht CTL I 500 and passim / de Vocht MHL 475–9 / H. Platelle *La Justice seigneuriale de l'abbaye de Saint-Amand* (Louvain 1965) 227, 233 / E. Hautcoeur 'Documents sur la réforme introduite a l'abbaye de Flines en 1506' *Analectes pour servir a l'histoire ecclésiastique de la Belgique* 9 (1872) 210–27 / G. Simenon *L'Organisation économique de l'abbaye de Saint-Trond* … (Brussels 1913) 96 and passim / G. Simenon 'Suppliques adressées aux abbés de Saint-Trond' *Bulletins de la Commission Royale d'Histoire* 73 (1904) 408–31 / A. Louant *Le Journal d'un bourgeois de Mons* (Brussels 1969) 164 / G. Moreau *Le Journal d'un bourgeois de Tournai: le second livre des chroniques de Pasquier de le Barre* (Brussels 1975) 77, 99

GÉRARD MOREAU

Hugo BOLONIUS (documented 1515–21)
In his introduction to Ep 1178 Allen draws attention to a New Year's gift made to Erasmus on 1 January 1521 by one Hugo Bolonius, who is not otherwise known. His gift was a copy of *Scriptores rei rusticae* (Venice: A. Manuzio 1514), apparently extant. The donor is probably identical with a Hugo de Bolonia of Lille who matriculated at the University of Louvain on 26 August 1515. Allen also found

his name in a list of learned Dominicans drawn up by Philipp Wolf of Seligenstadt (d 1529).

BIBLIOGRAPHY: Allen Ep 1178 / *Matricule de Louvain* III-1 513 / R.L. Poole 'Philip Wolf of Seligenstadt' *English Historical Review* 33 (1918) 500–17, esp 515

PGB

Urbanus BOLZANIUS *See Urbano* VALERIANI

Paolo BOMBACE of Bologna, 11 February 1476–6 May 1527
The destruction of his library in the Sack of Rome has left us with little information about the early life of Paolo Bombace (Bombasius), but his close connection to the University of Bologna and to the Bentivoglio regime suggests that he may have been educated at least partly in his home town, perhaps under Filippo (I) *Beroaldo and Codro *Urceo. In 1505 he received a lectureship in rhetoric and poetry, to which the chair of Greek at Bologna was added a year later. He gave Erasmus a warm welcome in Bologna at the end of 1506, offering him lodgings, helping him with his study of Greek, and providing detailed advice on his translations from Euripides and on certain problematic passages later used in the *Adagia*. Erasmus responded by calling Bombace one of his dearest friends and paying tribute to his 'many-sided learning' (*Adagia* I vi 2).

There is nothing to show that Bombace played any direct part in introducing Erasmus to Aldo *Manuzio but by the spring of 1508 he was reporting the sale of Erasmus' versions of Euripides in Bologna and enquiring when the Aldine Plutarch was going to appear (Ep 210). By the end of the year he was receiving confidential reports from Venice (Ep 213); and in 1509 he looked to Aldus for the texts of Horace's *Odes* and Caesar's *Civil War*, on which he was about to lecture (E. Pastorello *Inedita Manutiana*, Florence 1960, 6–7).

However, a succession of personal and political misfortunes soon overtook Bombace. Stricken with acute headaches he went to Siena for a cure during 1510 and 1511, apparently meeting Erasmus as the latter travelled north (Epp 217, 223, 251). Returning to Bologna, he found that he had been replaced in the chair of Greek, though he derived some consolation from retaining his lectureship in rhetoric and the past year's salary. Deeply implicated in the defence of the Bentivoglio regime against the attacks of *Julius II, he determined to leave Bologna for Venice. During 1512 Bombace considered a number of academic situations, in Milan, or Padua, or even in England, at Erasmus' invitation (Ep 251). He eventually went to Naples, where he taught successfully for about a year before accepting a post as secretary to Cardinal Lorenzo *Pucci in the summer of 1513, thus fulfilling his desire for a permanent place in Rome. It was here that Ulrich von *Hutten met him and passed on Erasmus' greetings in 1517 (Ep 611).

This Roman idyll was soon interrupted, however, by Bombace's posting as assistant to his patron's nephew, Antonio *Pucci, who was dispatched as papal nuncio to Switzerland in the autumn of 1517 (Ep 729). Despite the company of Richard *Pace (Ep 787), as well as Erasmus' reminders of the virtue that wandering brought to Odysseus and his assurance that experience would bring further advancement (Ep 800), it is plain that Bombace found his mission very trying. He felt himself 'among barbarians' after Pace's departure (Ep 787). However, he was able to return to Rome before Pucci during the summer of 1518 (Epp 855, 860), and from this moment he became Erasmus' principal friend and academic contact at the papal court. He received news of Erasmus' ill health, comments on his disagreement with *Lefèvre d' Etaples, and some more general gossip about affairs in England (Ep 855). He was asked to secure a papal brief expressing approval of the revised edition of the New Testament (Ep 860) and had to apologize for credulously entrusting the document to a sick messenger who failed to collect it when it had been signed (Epp 865, 905). Erasmus wrote to him to deny his authorship of *Julius exclusus*, later forwarding a copy of his letter to Thomas *More in case rumours were spreading in England (Ep 908).

As late as 1521 the friendship still had a scholarly flavour: in that year Bombace checked passages in the first epistle of St John for Erasmus and sent him variant readings for chapters 4 and 5 derived from a 'very ancient' manuscript in the Vatican library (Ep 1213; LB

VI 1080E). But as the Lutheran crisis deepened and Bombace's influence at the curia grew, his function became increasingly that of a mediator between Erasmus and members of the papal court who believed him to be a Lutheran. In the letter carrying the passage from the epistle of St John, Bombace mentioned that he was now deriving four hundred ducats per year from ecclesiastical benefices, and urged Erasmus both to avoid disparaging references to Girolamo *Aleandro and to write directly against *Luther. Erasmus replied evasively that Bombace would have to obtain papal permission for him to read Luther's works (Ep 1236), and Bombace continued to defend him (Ep 1260). By 1523 Erasmus was so depressed by the attacks on him from both sides of the religious controversy that he considered visiting Bombace in Rome to defend himself (Ep 1342) and wrote to his friend a year later (Ep 1411) to enquire whether this might be worthwhile. The last direct contact between them was a letter of 9 October 1525 in which Erasmus congratulated Bombace on his 'increased fortune' – presumably the apostolic secretariate conferred during the previous year (Ep 1631). Bombace was killed in the Sack of Rome.

Apart from an oration to cardinal Sanseverino in praise of *Louis XII (Bologna: H. de Benedictis 1512), an introduction to Pace's *De fructu qui ex doctrina percipitur* (Basel: J. Froben 1517), two epigrams in Blosius *Palladius' collection *Coryciana* (Rome: L. de Henricis and L. Perusinus 1524), and scattered personal letters, Bombace's works and his library perished with him. Erasmus rather pathetically wondered about his long silence in 1532 (Ep 2628), hoped that a rumour that he had escaped to Bologna before the Sack might be true (Ep 2665), and even asked for detailed news two or three years later, when it was clear that Bombace was dead (Epp 2963, 3018). There was perhaps a hint of criticism in Erasmus' comment in the *Ciceronianus* that Bombace preferred to 'increase his fortune rather than grow old as a writer' (ASD I-2 669), but Erasmus' verdict was that he counted Bombace among the 'purest minds' he had met in Italy or elsewhere (Epp 2874, 3032).

BIBLIOGRAPHY: Allen and CWE Ep 210 / E.

Mioni in DBI XI 373–6 / G. Fantuzzi *Notizie degli scrittori bolognesi* II (Bologna 1782)

M.J.C. LOWRY

BONA Sforza, queen of Poland 2 February 1494–19 November 1557

Bona Sforza, the wife of King *Sigismund I, was born in the town of Vigevano, in northern Italy, the daughter of the duke of Milan, Gian Galeazzo Sforza, and Isabel of Aragon. Her education was comprehensive and included humanistic studies as well as statecraft. Her engagement to King Sigismund was arranged by the Emperor *Maximilian I, and the marriage and coronation took place in Cracow on 18 April 1518 (cf Allen v 620).

Bona came to exercise an influence on Sigismund and played a substantial part in national politics. She could depend on the loyalties of wholly devoted collaborators for whom she secured high positions in church and state. In foreign policy she opposed closer ties with the Hapsburgs, while favouring a French alliance and peace with Turkey. She argued against the Cracow treaty of 1525 with Albert of *Bradenburg-Ansbach, master of the Teutonic Order, and would have preferred to obtain the lands of the order. Wishing to prevent the Hapsburgs from occupying all of Hungary, she supported *John Zápolyai after 1526. In a further move against *Ferdinand of Hapsburg she married her daughter Isabel to Zápolyai in 1539 and tried in this fashion to strengthen Poland's hand in the affairs of Hungary. After Zápolyai's death Bona did her best to ensure the Hungarian succession for Isabel and her young son, John Sigismund. When this failed, Bona proposed a plan to exchange Isabel's claims to Transylvania for the duchy of Silesia.

In domestic politics Bona's aim was the strengthening of royal power. Owing to her initiative her ten-year old son, *Sigismund Augustus, was crowned king of Poland in Sigismund I's lifetime, in 1530. By means of agricultural reform and the repurchase of crown lands earlier given to the magnates and the gentry, she tried to ensure the financial independence of the dynasty. As a result she came to own large estates and accumulated a huge amount of capital, which she deposited in Venetian banks. Her greed in accumulating a fortune and in collecting fees from candidates for ecclesiastical and secular offices and her growing influence in national affairs, particularly in the last years of King Sigismund's rule, generated strong opposition to her on the part of the landed magnates. Bona further failed to appreciate the rising political aspirations of the lesser nobility opposed to the magnates and consequently did not enlist their support in her own conflict with the magnates, who leaned towards the Hapsburgs.

Bona showed some interest in religious problems, being a devout Catholic and an enemy of the reformers. She collected paintings, works of goldsmithery, jewels, and antique vases. Her loving patronage also extended to architecture, sculpture, embroidery, and music, and was always closely linked to her appreciation of the Italian Renaissance style. Although she showed some personal interest in literature and scholarship, her patronage in these fields was less extensive. She did, however, support Andrzej *Krzycki, Johannes *Dantiscus, and later Mikotai Rej, who used the Polish language for his poems and prose works.

Bona was a loyal and good wife. She bore Sigismund a number of children: Isabel (18 January 1519), Sigismund Augustus (1 August 1520), Sophia (13 July 1522), Anne (18 October 1523), Catherine (1 November 1526), and Olbracht, who died on the day of his premature birth (23 September 1527).

After the death of her husband and numerous clashes with her son, whose policies she opposed, Bona left Poland in November 1556 and retired to her family estate, the duchy of Bari in Italy. There she died three years later, poisoned by Papacoda, one of her advisers, who may have been acting on orders from the Spanish government, since Philip II was determined to force Bona to cede to him her domains in the kingdom of Naples. She was buried in the basilica of San Nicola in Bari, where in 1593 her daughter Anne erected a marble tomb in her memory.

Erasmus sent his compliments to Bona in Epp 1753 and 1819.

BIBLIOGRAPHY: Allen Epp 1753, 1954 / PSB II 288–94 / H. Barycz in DBI XI 430–6 / W. Pociecha

Krolowa Bona: Czasy i ludzie Odrodzenia (Poznan 1949–58) 4 vols

HALINA KOWALSKA

Cyprianus BONACCURSIUS (Ep 2959 of 20 August 1534)
Bonaccursius was an otherwise unidentified friend of Primo de' *Conti who delivered a letter from him to Erasmus at Freiburg.

Lazzaro BONAMICO of Bassano, 1477/8–10 February 1552
Lazzaro was born to Amico Bonamico and his wife, Dorotea, in the Venetian town of Bassano del Grappa in 1477 or early 1478. He attended schools at Bassano and by 1499 was a student of arts at the University of Padua. He studied Latin under Giovanni Calfurnio, Greek under Marcus *Musurus, and philosophy under Pietro *Pomponazzi, who became his friend and later named him an executor of his will. From 1510 to 1527 Bonamico served as a private tutor at Mantua, Bologna, Genoa, and finally Rome. Among his students was Alessandro *Campeggi, the son of Cardinal Lorenzo *Campeggi and later bishop of Bologna (Ep 2657). In Rome Bonamico's friends included the humanists Angelo *Colocci and Jacopo *Sadoleto.

Bonamico returned to Venetian territory before the Sack of Rome in 1527. He was appointed lecturer in Latin and Greek at the University of Padua and on 29 September 1530 was given the lucrative salary of three hundred ducats a year. Despite frequent attempts to lure him to Bologna, Rome, Vienna, and other centres, he remained at Padua until his death. He was married to Caterina Tamagnini.

Bonamico, one of the most renowned teachers of his day, was an exponent of Ciceronian style and a vigorous defender of the use of Greek and Latin rather than Italian, which he saw as a corruption of Latin. Although Leonard *Casembroot (Ep 1720) and *Viglius Zuichemus (Epp 2568, 2632) on several occasions stated or implied that Bonamico was a critic of Erasmus, there was no animosity between the two. Erasmus always spoke with admiration of Bonamico (Epp 2477, 2987, 3076), while Bonamico praised Erasmus' reply to the *Defensio pro Italia ad Erasmum Roterodamum*

(Rome: A. Bladus 1535) by Pietro *Corsi (Ep 3085).

Bonamico's works were few and were published posthumously. These included the *Concetti della lingua latina* (Venice 1562) and the *Carminum liber* (Venice: G.B. Somasco 1572). Fifteen letters were published in the *Epistolae clarorum virorum selectae* (Venice: P. Manuzio 1556) and three in the *Aliquot opuscula* (Louvain: R. Rescius 1544) by Damião de *Gois, the Portuguese historian and student of Bonamico. Commentaries on Cicero and Demosthenes are found in manuscript at the Biblioteca Ambrosiana in Milan. Sperone Speroni made Bonamico the spokesman for Latin and Greek against the vernacular in his *Dialogo delle lingue* (Sperone *Opere*, Venice 1740, I 166), an important work on the Italian vernacular of the 1540s.

BIBLIOGRAPHY: Allen Ep 1720 / R. Avesani in DBI XI 533–40

TBD

Johannes Baptista BONCANTUS (Ep 243 of 18 November [1511])
Boncantus, an Italian who apparently resided in London, has not been identified.

Jan BONER of Cracow, 1516–12 September 1562
Jan was the eldest son of Seweryn *Boner and Zofia *Bethmann and the brother of Stanisław. In 1531 his father sent him abroad in the care of Anselmus *Ephorinus and in the company of Stanisław *Aichler. The first stage of their journey took them to Germany: after a short visit to Erfurt they stayed for a time in Nürnberg before departing for Freiburg. Ep 2533 shows that they arrived at the beginning of April and stayed at Erasmus' house for five months. From the end of August 1531 to the spring of 1532 they were in Basel, remaining in contact with Erasmus (Epp 2548–50). Boner expressed his warm affection for Erasmus and promised a token of gratitude from his father. In December Erasmus dedicated to Jan and Stanisław an edition of Terence's comedies (Ep 2548). In the spring of 1532 Boner, Aichler, and Ephorinus departed for Augsburg and subsequently Padua, where they remained until the middle of 1534. Jan's last known contacts with

Erasmus were his letters written from Padua on 8 June and 9 September 1532 (Epp 2658, 2717). Their travels took Boner and his companions to Bologna in August 1534 (Ep 2961); from April 1535 they were in Rome, and from there made a journey to Naples, returning to Rome at the end of 1535. In the spring of 1537 they set out on their journey home to Poland. Ephorinus led his wards through France, where they stayed in Paris, then through the Netherlands and Germany; they reached Cracow in the autumn of 1537.

Boner began his career by attending the royal court. In 1546 he became castellan of Oświec, in 1552 he was promoted to castellan of Chełm, and finally, in 1555, he was made castellan of Biecz. In addition he is documented as the governor of Cracow Castle on 12 December 1551. From an early date he showed interest in the reformation. After leaning initially towards *Luther's teachings he became a devout Calvinist and protector of Calvinism in Cracow and Little Poland. In 1556 he was among those who invited the reformer Jan *Łaski to return to Poland, and he received Łaski hospitably in his own home in Cracow and his other residences in Little Poland (Balice and Osiek). His wife was Łaski's niece, Katarzyna, the daughter of the *voivode* of Sandomierz, Jan Tenczyński, and of Katarzyna Łaski. Boner died suddenly in Cracow and left no heirs.

BIBLIOGRAPHY: Allen Ep 2533; cf Epp 2520, 2521, 2554, 2600, 3010 / Korespondencja Erazma z Rotterdamu z Polakami ed M. Cytowska (Warsaw 1965) / PSB II 299–300 / H. Barycz Z dziejów polskich wędrówek naukowych za granicę (Wrocław 1969) / H. Kowalska Działalność reformatorska Jana Łaskiego w Polsce (Wrocław 1969) / Matricularium regni Poloniae summaria ... (Warsaw 1905–19) V-2 5434, 5447 / Akta synodów różnowierczych w Polsce ed M. Sipayłło (Warsaw 1966–72) I-II / G. Schramm Der Polnische Adel und die Reformation (Wiesbaden 1965)

HALINA KOWALSKA

Seweryn BONER of Cracow, 1466–12 May 1549

Seweryn Boner was the son of Jakub from Landau, in the Palatinate, who had settled in Cracow in 1512, and Barbara Lechner, the

Seweryn Boner by Melchior Baier the Elder

daughter of a burgher of Nürnberg. He owed his start in life to his uncle, Jan Boner, who was the first of the family to settle in Cracow and became an important citizen, owning a large estate. Seweryn's career was also helped by his marriage, on 23 October 1515, to Zofia *Bethmann, the daughter of a wealthy Cracow merchant.

A brilliant financier, Boner organized an impressive banking house in Cracow, keeping up his commercial contacts in Germany and Italy. He granted a loan to *Sigismund I, thus gaining the king's favour and as a result obtaining several important positions. In 1520 he was appointed prefect (*burgrabius*) of Cracow castle, and in 1523 he inherited the other offices held by his deceased uncle: governor (*magnus procurator*) of Cracow castle and administrator of the salt mines of Cracow. From this moment he became the court banker and financed all the more important royal expenditures. Among other tasks, he directed the enlargement of the castle and other works on Wawel hill. In place of loan repayments he received the tenure of royal estates in Little

Poland and was appointed prefect of Biecz, Rabsztyn, Ojców, Oświecim, Zator, and Czchów. He also held some positions usually reserved for Polish noblemen: in 1532 he was castellan of Żernów, in 1535 he became castellan of Biecz, and he was finally appointed castellan of Sacz in 1547. He held these offices despite the fact that he did not hold the rank of a member of the Polish gentry until his naturalization on 16 February 1537.

Boner owned large estates in Little Poland with castles at Balice, Ogrodzieniec, and Kamieniec. He also owned many buildings in Cracow, where his main residence was a home in the market square. The furnishings and appearance of his home resembled those of a magnate's mansion. Boner was a patron of the arts and gave shelter and patronage to a growing number of wandering German humanists who came to Cracow, mostly from Silesia.

After the death of his first wife in 1532, Boner married Jadwiga, the daughter of Mikolaj Kościelecki, *voivode* of Kalisz, and Anna, the sister of Jan (II) *Łaski. He had two sons from his first marriage, Jan and Stanisław *Boner, and two more from his second marriage, Frederyk and Seweryn. He died in Cracow and was buried in the Boner chapel at the church of Our Lady in Cracow. His effigy was carved on the gravestone, probably by Hans Vischer of Nürnberg.

Boner began his correspondence with Erasmus when his son Jan was travelling abroad. When he learnt that Jan had gone to Freiburg to stay with Erasmus, he managed to secure letters of recommendation for the boy from the king (Ep 2520), from Piotr *Tomicki (Ep 2521) and other dignitaries. In a letter to Boner of 1 September 1531 Erasmus praised the boy (Ep 2533), and on 12 December he dedicated an edition of Terence's comedies to Boner's two oldest sons (Ep 2584). Erasmus had to wait some time for Boner's thanks since a presentation copy of the book (Basel: H. Froben March 1532) did not reach Cracow until 1535. When he finally received it, Boner wrote a long letter to Erasmus explaining the delay (Ep 3010, 12 April 1535). He sent with it a gift of two gold medals especially made for the occasion, one with a portrait of King

Sigismund I, and the other with his own likeness. Both of these may be found in the Historisches Museum of Basel.

BIBLIOGRAPHY: Allen Ep 2533; cf Epp 2539, 2548, 2606, 2874, 2961 / PSB II 300–1 / *Korespondencja Erazma z Rotterdamu z Polakami* ed M. Cytowska (Warsaw 1965) / W. Pociecha *Królowa Bona. Czasy i ludzie Odrodzenia* (Poznań 1949–58) II–IV / E. Major *Erasmus von Rotterdam* (Basel 1926) 72, plate 24 / *Materiały do biografii, genealogii i heraldyki polskiej* (Buenos Aires-Paris 1971) V 70–1

HALINA KOWALSKA

Stanisław BONER of Cracow, c 1523–14 November 1560

Stanisław was the second son of Seweryn *Boner and Zofia *Bethmann. He studied at the University of Vienna in 1540 and the following year was a student at Johann Sturm's Gymnasium in Strasbourg. In 1542 he was in Paris, and upon returning to Poland, that same year he was given an appointment at the royal court. On 28 June 1550 he received the prefecture of Biecz. He was heir to the extensive domain of Ogrodzieniec in Little Poland, and in 1557 he married Elżbieta, daughter of Spytek Jordan from Zakliczyn, *voivode* of Sandomierz. In 1560 he travelled to Italy in the hope of restoring his ailing health but died in Bologna, leaving no offspring.

At the suggestion of Anselmus *Ephorinus (Ep 2554), Erasmus honoured Stanisław and his brother Jan *Boner by dedicating to them an edition of Terence's comedies (Basel 1532; Epp 2584, 3010).

BIBLIOGRAPHY: PSB II 302 / *Korespondencja Erazma z Rotterdamu z Polakami* ed M. Cytowska (Warsaw 1965) / H. Barycz *Z dziejow polskich wedrówek naukowych za granice* (Wrocław 1969) / *Matrikel Wien* III 66 (Andreas Boner Cracoviensis)

HALINA KOWALSKA

BONETUS de Lattes *See Samuel* SARFATI

Luca BONFIGLIO of Padua, c 1470–July 1540

Luca Bonfiglio (Bonfius) was born at Padua, where the noble Bonfiglio family had fled after being expelled from Bologna around 1450. His education was probably humanistic, for contemporaries praised his Latin style, and one of them, Janus Parrhasius, compared his eloquence to that of Livy (*Epistolae*, Naples 1771, 34–6). The fact that he possessed two Greek manuscripts suggests that he may have known Greek. He embarked on an ecclesiastical career, becoming a priest and obtaining the church of Santa Sofia at Padua. On the recommendation of Pietro *Bembo, he became *cubicularius*, or chamber servant, of Pope *Leo x around 1515. For many years he sought to be named a canon of the cathedral of Padua, but did not succeed until 1526, when he himself provided an endowment for a new prebend. In 1529, after further pressure was placed on Pope *Clement VII, he was named the first dean of the chapter of Padua. In the same year he also became secretary to Cardinal Lorenzo *Campeggi, whom he accompanied to the diet of Augsburg in 1530. It was probably on Campeggi's behalf that he asked Erasmus to attend the diet. Erasmus declined, giving as reasons poor health and the belief that he would not be able to accomplish much (Ep 2347). In 1531 Bonfiglio accompanied Campeggi and the imperial court to Brussels. On his return to Italy in 1532 or 1533 he resigned his deanery at Padua to a nephew and asked Clement VII to transfer him to Rome, evidently without success. He spent the rest of his life at Venice and Padua, where he died.

Bonfiglio was a friend or acquaintance of many prominent ecclesiastics and scholars, including Cardinal Marco Cornaro, Pier Paolo *Vergerio, Georgius *Sabinus, Henricus Cornelius *Agrippa, Francesco Arsilli, and Niccolò *Leoniceno. Niccolò *Leonico Tomeo, mentioned by Erasmus in his letter to Bonfiglio (Ep 2347), dedicated his translation of 'De somno et vigilia' from Aristotle's *Parva naturalia* (Venice: B. dei Vitali 1523) to Bonfiglio, and made him an interlocutor in his dialogue *Alverotus sive de tribus animorum vehiculis* (Venice: G. de Gregoriis 1524). Pierio Valeriano dedicated to him a Latin translation of Lucian's *De aulicorum erumnis* (Rome: J. Mazochius 1516).

BIBLIOGRAPHY: Allen Ep 2347 / E. Mioni in DBI XII 25–6 / *Epistolae ad Nauseam* 112–13 / *Melanchthons Briefwechsel* I Ep 955 and passim
ANNA GIULIA CAVAGNA

Pietro BONOMO of Trieste, 1458–15 June 1546
Pietro Bonomo was born into one of the oldest and most powerful families of Trieste. His father, Giovanni Antonio, was assassinated in 1468, and Pietro accompanied his family into a brief exile. He studied the humanities and law at Bologna, and after returning to his native city so impressed several ambassadors of the Emperor *Frederick III by translating Pliny at sight that they took him into the imperial service. In 1478 Frederick III appointed him chancellor of Trieste.

Around 1480 Bonomo married Margarete von Rosenburg, a lady-in-waiting at the imperial court, who died only four years later after bearing a son, Ludovico. Bonomo became an ecclesiastic and after 1490 received a number of benefices, beginning with a prebend in the cathedral of Aquileia and culminating in 1502 with the bishopric of Trieste. The low income of the diocese, reduced by pensions, forced him to keep other benefices.

Meanwhile, Bonomo continued in the imperial service as secretary and ambassador. From 1496 to 1500 he was the Emperor *Maximilian's emissary to Ludovico *Sforza, duke of Milan. In 1509, during the war of the League of Cambrai, he attempted to rally Trieste against the Venetians. On 23 July 1519 Archduke *Ferdinand named Bonomo to a regency council which governed the Austrian dominions of the Hapsburgs, and on 7 July 1521 Bonomo became chancellor of the Austrian dominions.

On 29 October 1523 Bonomo resigned as chancellor and returned to Trieste. His long episcopate was a period of toleration for Lutherans and other heretics. Although Bonomo never abandoned the Catholic faith, he sympathized with and protected exiles from other areas of Italy and employed reformers, such as Primus Truber, as chaplains and preachers.

Bonomo was in contact with a number of humanists in the employ of the imperial court and through them met Conrad Celtis and Johann *Reuchlin, who included two of his letters in the *Clarorum virorum epistolae* of 1514 (RE Epp 39, 42). Bonomo appeared in the correspondence of Erasmus in 1518 (Ep 863), when Jakob *Spiegel reported that he was present at a speech given by Erazm *Ciołek bishop of Płock in Poland.

Bonomo wrote a number of poems, many of which dealt with the personalities of the Hapsburgs, which have been preserved in manuscript. Nine of his letters were published in Giuseppe Mainati's *Dialogi piacevoli in dialetto vernacolo triestino* (Trieste 1828).

BIBLIOGRAPHY: Allen Ep 863 / G. Rill in DBI XII 341–6

TBD

BONT (Ep 275 of October 1513)
In Ep 275 Erasmus mentioned the recent death of Bont, an otherwise unknown physician at Cambridge. As the name is common both in England and in the Low Countries, this Bont may be identical with a physician and fellow-countryman at Cambridge, whom Erasmus had mentioned in 1511 (Ep 225), without giving a name.

PGB

François BONVALOT of Besançon,
d 14 December 1560
François Bonvalot was born in Besançon into a bourgeois family recently risen to wealth and now rising to power. From 1513 he was the brother-in-law of Nicolas *Perrenot de Granvelle, councillor of *Charles v. When Perrenot received the office of judge of Besançon in 1527, his functions were carried out by Jacques Bonvalot, François' father. François himself had meanwhile obtained a legal doctorate from the University of Dole and the title of apostolic protonotary. On 26 May 1510 he became a canon of Besançon, succeeding a kinsman. On 9 July 1522 he was appointed treasurer of the chapter, on 26 June 1532 abbot of Saint-Vincent at Besançon, and in 1542 abbot of Luxeuil. In the struggle for power between the town council, the chapter, and the archbishop, François used the full weight of his family connections to oppose the city. In 1532 he persuaded his father to refuse all dealings with the city hall and in 1536 he held out in resistance against an agreement reached between chapter and town. Acting in conjunction with Perrenot at the imperial court, the Bonvalots were instrumental in breaking the power of Simon Gauthiot d'Ancier, Jean

*Lambelin, and their party. Meanwhile François too was employed in the service of the emperor, undertaking missions to Rome in 1528 and to the court of France from 1530 to 1532 (Epp 2348, 2401A) and in 1538, 1541, and 1544.

On 16 May 1544 his fellow canons elected Bonvalot archbishop of Besançon, while Pope *Paul III nominated Claude de la Baume, a seven-year-old boy from an influential family, to the same position. Bonvalot immediately travelled to the court at Brussels (AK VI Ep 2674), but the conflict was resolved in favour of his opponent when Charles V ruled on 4 January 1545 that Bonvalot was to be no more than administrator of the see until his rival came of age. As a result of this decision Bonvalot administered his see with a firm hand, until April 1556, when he retired with an annual pension of four thousand florins. He spent his last years in the delightful Hôtel Bonvalot which he had built for himself a decade earlier behind the cathedral. He was a lover of music and art and developed humanistic tastes, but above all he was a skilled politician. Like other Besançon canons he had fathered children, in his case two sons.

Erasmus was not unaware of François' commitment to politics (Epp 2241, 2397); in 1529 Bonvalot, like others, advised him against a move to Besançon because of the political unrest (Ep 2112). Much of their correspondence, however, turned around Bonvalot's shipments of Burgundian wine to Erasmus (Epp 2142, 2348, 3102, 3122). Erasmus sent Bonvalot a copy of the *Apophthegmata* (Epp 3075, 3103); he also recommended to him Philippus *Montanus and Gilbert *Cousin, who needed benefices (Ep 2890). Cousin was subsequently eager to lavish praise on Bonvalot (Epp 3080, 3123).

BIBLIOGRAPHY: Allen Ep 1534 / DBF VI 1057–8 / Claude Fohlen et al *Histoire de Besançon* (Paris 1965) I 606, 651, and passim / A. Castan 'Granvelle et le petit empereur de Besançon 1518–1538' *Revue historique* 1 (1876) 78–139, esp 107, 111 / A. Castan 'La rivalité des familles de Rye et de Granvelle' *Mémoires de la Societé d'émulation du Doubs* VI-6 (1891) 13–130, esp 20–9, 97–8 / L. Febvre 'L'application du Concile de Trente et l'excommunication pour dettes en Franche-Comté' *Revue historique* 103 (1910)

225–47, esp 229–31 / AK V Ep 2595 and passim / *Gallia christiana* xv 104, 160, 193–4 / Gauthier 126, 128, 135–6 / *Correspondenz des Kaisers Karl v.* ed Karl Lanz (Leipzig 1844–6) I 517 / Pflug *Correspondance* II Ep 148 and passim

PGB

Girolamo BONVISI documented 1508–11
Girolamo Bonvisi (Buonvisi) grew up as a member of the London branch of a merchant family of great influence in its native Lucca. By 1508 he was in Rome as solicitor for the English crown. In 1509 he was named an apostolic protonotary and sent back to England by *Julius II in connection with Thomas *Ruthall's succession to the vacant see of Durham, for which Bonvisi himself was a candidate. A relative of his, Antonio Bonvisi, a merchant in London, was a close friend of Thomas *More for over forty years and was also known to *Henry VIII. In 1511, while Julius II was endeavouring to persuade Henry to enter a coalition against France, Girolamo Bonvisi was charged with holding treasonous communication with the French ambassador, and was found guilty. Erasmus' report of the incident in the *Lingua* (ASD IV-1 277), possibly coloured by More's relations with the Bonvisi family, questions his guilt, but J.S. Brewer (LP I) believes that letters to France from someone in the papal service with the code-name Abbatis are proof of Bonvisi's treachery.

BIBLIOGRAPHY: Marino Berengo *Nobili e mercanti nella Lucca del cinquecento* (Turin 1965) / W.E. Wilkie *The Cardinal Protectors of England* (Cambridge 1974) 33, 37–8, 78, and passim / LP I index / Rogers Ep 34 and passim

JAMES D. TRACY

Katharina von BORA 29 January 1499–20 December 1552
Katharina was born in Lippendorf, near Leipzig, a daughter of Hans von Bora. Her mother died in 1504, and after her father's second marriage she entered the Cistercian convent of Nimbschen near Grimma in ducal Saxony in 1508 or 1509, taking the veil in 1515. On 4 April 1523 she fled from the convent with eight other nuns, and Martin *Luther helped them to find refuge with some families in Wittenberg. After her desire to marry a young patrician from Nürnberg was thwarted by his

Katharina von Bora, workshop of Lucas Cranach

family, Luther suggested that she marry one Dr Kaspar Glatz, but she refused. On 13 June 1525 she married Luther himself, who was sixteen years older than her (W *Briefwechsel* III Ep 890). The sudden marriage aroused interest because of her youth and grace (Ep 1624) and also because of a rumour that the bride was pregnant (Epp 1633, 1653, 1655), which circulated in Germany until 1528 (W *Briefwechsel* IV Ep 1305) although it was known to be false by 1526 (Ep 1677). When Luther published *De servo arbitrio* in reply to Erasmus' *De libero arbitrio*, the latter noted that the young wife had failed to have a moderating influence on her husband (Epp 1677, 1697). She did, however, help Luther to make their home a model of domestic contentment that had a lasting effect on social patterns in Germany. Katharina Luther had six children, two of whom died quite young. After her husband's death in 1546 and the devastations wrought by the Schmalkaldic war, the family encountered financial difficulties, but Katharina, who was competent and hard-working, insisted on managing her affairs personally.

BIBLIOGRAPHY: Allen Ep 1624 / NDB II 454 /

Luther *W Briefwechsel* III Ep 599 and passim /
R.H. Bainton *Women of the Reformation in
Germany and Italy* (Boston 1974) 23–43

IG

Francesco BORGIA c 1441–4 November 1511
Believed to be the natural son of Juan de
Borgia, Francesco was a cousin of Cardinal
Rodrigo Borgia (Pope *Alexander VI), to whom
he owed his advancement. Having at first been
a canon of Valencia, by 1492 he was a solicitor
of apostolic letters in the papal chancery and
became a papal chamberlain and treasurer of
the church in 1493. After being appointed
bishop of Teano on 19 August 1495 and
archbishop of Cosenza on 6 November 1499, he
was made a cardinal on 28 September 1500. He
became generally known as the cardinal of
Cosenza. Francesco took an active part in the
papal campaign against the Colonna, Savelli,
and Caetani, taking possession of their
confiscated fiefs in June 1501; in 1502 he was
associated with Cesare Borgia's administration
in the Romagna. He remained in Rome after
*Julius II's accession but was too ill to
accompany the expedition to Perugia and
Bologna in 1506.

According to Albertini, Francesco lived at
Sant'Agostino in Rome and improved the
palace there, but whether Erasmus met him in
Rome in 1509 is unknown. In October 1510
Francesco joined the other rebel cardinals,
proceeding from Florence to Milan instead of
joining Julius II at Bologna, and he played an
active part in calling the schismatic council of
Pisa. For this he was deprived of his dignities
on 24 October 1511, as Andrea *Ammonio
reported to Erasmus (Ep 247). However, before
he could reach Pisa for the rebel council,
Francesco died at Reggio Emilia.

BIBLIOGRAPHY: Allen Ep 247 / G. De Caro in
DBI XII 709–11 / DHGE IX 1229 / See in general F.
Albertini *Opusculum de mirabilibus novae et
veteris urbis Romae, 1510* ed A. Schmarsow
(Heilbronn 1866) passim / J. Buchardus *Liber
Notarum* ed E. Celani (Città di Castello
1906–59) passim / Eubel II 24, 142 / Pastor VI 92,
102, and passim / Sanudo *Diarii* III 92–3 and
passim / A. Renaudet *Le Concile gallicane de
Pise-Milan* (Paris 1922) passim

D.S. CHAMBERS

Andrea da BORGO of Cremona, 7/8 September 1467–1 January 1533
The son of a merchant of Cremona, Andrea da
Borgo (Burgo, Burgus) was eleven years old
upon joining the court of Ludovico *Sforza,
duke of Milan. He received a good education
and in 1490 was appointed head of the 'secret'
chancery (*cancelleria segreta*). In 1496 he was
sent on a mission to meet the Emperor
*Maximilian I at Vigevano, thus beginning his
lifelong career as a diplomat. After the French
conquest of Milan in 1500 he left for Germany,
and in 1502 he entered the service of
Maximilian I, initially as a secretary, but from
1506 to 1509 he was employed exclusively on
diplomatic missions to Spain, England, and
France. On 12 December 1512 he signed on
behalf of his master the treaty of Blois between
Maximilian and *Louis XII of France. At the
court of Castile he was assigned an annuity
and in 1507 and 1508 he also represented the
interests of Spain. In 1511 and 1512 he was
with cardinals Matthäus *Lang and Matthäus
*Schiner in Italy working towards the expul-
sion of the French. From December 1515 to
September 1516 he was at Brussels negotiating
in Maximilian's name over the Spanish
succession. Subsequently he undertook missions to Prague (Ep 1297) and Hungary, where
in May 1517 King *Louis II took him into his
service. In October 1523 he participated in the
conference of Wiener Neustadt attended by
Austria's new ruler, *Ferdinand, Hungary,
and Poland. In 1525 he was living at Trent in
temporary retirement when he lost his first
wife, Dorothea von Thun. Later he married
Caterina Anguissola of Piacenza. The disaster
of Mohács in 1526 led to the loss of his position
as well as his property in Hungary. He found a
new master in Ferdinand, who in 1528 sent him
to Ferrara and the following year to Rome,
where he remained until his death, achieving
his last major success when papal subsidies
were granted for the war against the Turks. He
died in Bologna during another round of
negotiations between the emperor and the
pope.

Contemporaries varied in their opinion of
Borgo. Some thought him to be an intriguer,
haughty and venal. But more often he was said
to have served his masters faithfully and

skilfully. Among other inedited letters and dispatches by Borgo, those relating to his mission to Rome are now for the most part in the Haus-, Hof- und Staatsarchiv of Vienna.

BIBLIOGRAPHY: Allen Ep 1297 / G. Rill in DBI XII 749–53 / ADB III 610 / Karl Stoegmann 'Über die Briefe des Andrea da Borgo ... an ... Bernhard Cles' *Sitzungsberichte der kaiserlichen Akademie der Wissenschaften*, philosophisch-historische Klasse 24 (Vienna 1857) 159–252 / Edward Le Glay *Correspondance de l'empereur Maximilien I et de Marguerite d'Autriche* (Paris 1839) I–II passim / Karl Brandi *Kaiser Karl v.* new ed (Darmstadt 1959–67) I 229 and passim / Pastor x 44–5 and passim

ROSEMARIE AULINGER

Michaël BORMANUS (Ep 2054 of 1 October 1528)

On 1 October 1528 Erasmus informed Erard de la *Marck, bishop of Liège, that he had previously sent him 'by a certain Michaël Bormanus' another letter together with the second part of *Hyperaspistes*. The wording suggests that the messenger was not well known to Erasmus, whom he must have visited or encountered at Basel. Other copies of the *Hyperaspistes* were sent to some of Erasmus' friends early in September (Ep 1853 introduction). The letter sent with Bormanus is missing today, and so is any reply Erard may have sent.

There was a Michiels Borman who was a canon of the collegiate church of St Denis of Liège and parish priest of Wilderen, near St Truiden, and was thus probably of Flemish descent. He is known from his unpublished will, dated 9 April 1533, preserved in Liège (Archives de la Paroisse Saint-Denis, MS 'Liber testamentorum'). The 'Liber testamentorum' gives him the title of 'maître.' The date of his death is not known.

BIBLIOGRAPHY: J. Deckers 'Le chapitre de la collégiale Saint-Denis de Liège' *Bulletin de l'Institut archéologique liégeois* 84 (1972) 179

LÉON-E. HALKIN

Martin BORRHAUS *See* BORUS

Johannes BORSALUS or BORSSELE *See Jan BECKER*

Anna van Borssele by Michiel Yssewyn

Anna van BORSSELE lady of Veere, c 1471–8 December 1518

Anna van Borssele was the daughter and heiress of Wolfart VI van Borssele (d 29 April 1486) and Charlotte de Bourbon. Her first marriage was to Philip of Burgundy, a son of Anthony of *Burgundy, 'le Grand Bâtard.' Their marriage contract was notarized on 4 July 1485, and less than a month after the death of Anna's father, on 19 May 1486, the young couple was installed as lord and lady of Veere. They had four children, including Adolph of *Burgundy, who was to succeed his mother. Philip died on 4 July 1498. At about this time Erasmus was invited to the castle of Tournehem through the influence of Jacob *Batt, Adolph's tutor (Ep 80), and indeed in February 1499 he stayed there for some time 'loaded ... with favours' (Ep 88). Later, however, Erasmus questioned Anna's willingness to fulfil her promises of patronage (Epp 128, 129), although some of the money confiscated from Erasmus on his departure from England on 27 January 1500 must have been from her (Ep 139). For his part, Erasmus was not above scheming with

Batt to obtain money from the lady (Ep 139). Further, the flattering tone of Ep 145 to Anna, which accompanied a poem celebrating St Anne, the mother of Mary (Reedijk poem 22), stands in sharp contrast to the critical comments about her in Ep 146 to Batt. Erasmus again visited Tournehem in July 1501, but by then Anna had already come under the spell of Lodewijk van *Montfoort, and Erasmus expressed a concern (justified by the outcome) that their marriage would end Anna's patronage (Epp 145, 172). In 1502 Anna married Montfoort, who died three years later. By 1512 Erasmus seems to have transferred his hopes to Adolph (Ep 266). Anna died at the castle of Zandenburg, near Veere. Erasmus was informed of her death by Jan *Becker (Ep 932) and remembered her fondly in Ep 1949 to her grandson, Maximilian (II) of *Burgundy. A wooden statue of her, by Michiel IJssewijn, is represented in CWE 1 158.

BIBLIOGRAPHY: Allen Ep 80 / A.J. van der Aa et al *Biographisch woordenboek der Nederlanden* (Haarlem 1852–78, repr 1965) II-2 961 / L.M.G. Kooperberg in *Archief* of the *Zeeuwsch Genootschap der Wetenschappen* (1938) 1–88

C.G. VAN LEIJENHORST

BORUS (Ep 2233A of 6 November 1529) In a short letter to Bonifacius *Amerbach (Ep 2233A, not known to P.S. Allen) Erasmus expressed curiosity about one 'Borus.' The reference may be to Martin Borrhaus, whose name is also spelled Borraus, Burrhus, and Burraus, and who was also known as Martinus Cellarius. Borrhaus (1499–1564) was born in Stuttgart. In 1527 Amerbach and Jan (II) *Łaski corresponded about him and his book *De operibus Dei* (Strasbourg: n pr 1527), which aroused considerable interest in Basel and Zürich because of its critical views on infant baptism and other tenets shared between the 'magisterial' Roman and Protestant churches. From 1527 Borrhaus lived in Strasbourg and on a property his wife owned in Lower Alsace. In 1536 he moved to Basel, where he received academic appointments to teach rhetoric (1541) and the Old Testament (1544).

BIBLIOGRAPHY: AK III Ep 1210, VIII xxviii, and passim / BA *Oekolampads* II 91–2 and passim / Erasmus' letter was published by J.C. Margolin

in BHR 32 (1970) 107–13 / See also *La Correspondance d'Erasme* ed M. Delcourt et al (Brussels 1967–) VIII Ep 2233A / NDB II 474 / *The Mennonite Encyclopedia* (Scottdale 1955–9) I 538–9

PGB

Arnoldus BOSCHIUS *See Arnoldus* BOSTIUS

Arkleb of BOSKOVICE d 10 March 1528 Arkleb (Archleb, Artleb, Artlebus de Boskowicz, Vranovský, Třebíčký) was the second most influential member of the Moravian noble oligarchy during the Jagiellonian period after Jan of Pernstein at Tovačov. He was one of eight children born to Oldřich (d 1500), from whom the Trnávka-Bučovice line of the large noble family of Boskovice issued. Arkleb had five brothers, Vaněk, Jetřich, Bohuslav, Jaroslav, and Václav, and two sisters, Johanka and Apolonie. The latter were both abbesses, Johanka at the queen's nunnery in Old Brno (1508–May 1532) and Apolonie at the Cistercian convent in Tišňov (1516–40), and both died in 1540.

Nothing is known about Arkleb's life until 1508, when he served as a member of the supreme court of Moravia. In 1516 he became a regional governor (in the district of Brno), and from 1519 to 1524 he occupied the highest office of governor (*supremus capitaneus*) of the margraviate of Moravia. He was elected supreme chamberlain for the years 1526–8. In November 1526 he was a member of a delegation sent by the Moravian estates to Vienna to invite Archduke *Ferdinand to become their king and margrave on the basis of the hereditary rights of his wife. Arkleb took part in many other diplomatic missions during the difficult years of the reign of the young king *Louis II and the transition to Hapsburg rule after his death at Mohács on 29 August 1526. Arkleb resided first at Buchlov and from 1515 at Vranov (Frain), west of the city of Znojmo (Znaim) in southwestern Moravia, and hence was called Vranovský. In 1525 he exchanged the domain of Vranov for Pernstein's estate at Třebíč, west of Brno, and was known as Třebíčký. His wife, Ludmila (d 1515), bore him one son, Jan Jetřich (d 1562).

Arkleb's sister Johanka embraced Protestant

convictions, resigned from her post as abbess on 9 May 1532, and the following year financed the publication of the first edition of the Czech New Testament printed in Moravia. The translation was made from Erasmus' Latin text, and the book was dedicated to Johanka (19 November 1533). Arkleb's unmarried aunt, Marta of Boskovice, was among the first members of the nobility who openly joined the Czech or Bohemian Brethren. She lived at Litomyšl, in eastern Bohemia, and in December 1507 sent King *Vladislav II a letter of protest against the persecution of the Brethren. Arkleb himself belonged to the Utraquist (Hussite) church, which in Moravia maintained close contact with the German-speaking minority and came under strong Lutheran and Zwinglian influence. Personally he leaned towards Lutheranism. At his request, the young Czech humanist printer Oldřich Velenský of Mnichov (Ulricus Velenus Mnichoviensis), who in 1519 had translated into Czech and printed Erasmus' *Enchiridion* at his press in Bělá in Bohemia, prepared an abbreviated Czech translation of Luther's *Responsio* to Lancellotto de' *Politi (called Ambrosius Catharinus; cf Josef Benzing *Lutherbibliographie*, Baden-Baden 1966, 104–6). The book appeared in Prague in March 1522 with Velenský's dedicatory preface to Arkleb. Later in that year and again in 1523 Arkleb pleaded as governor before King Louis for the life of the Lutheran preacher Paulus Speratus (1484–1551), who sought refuge in the city of Jihlava (Iglau) after his expulsion from Vienna on 20 January 1522.

Concerned about the growth of the Unity of Brethren in Moravia, Arkleb wrote to Erasmus by October 1520 (Ep 1154) asking for his opinion of their teachings, and apparently sent another copy of the *Apologia sacrae scripturae* (Nürnberg 1511), which had already been presented to Erasmus by Mikuláš *Klaudyán and Laurentius *Voticius. Arkleb also mentioned the wide circulation of Erasmus' books and those of Luther in Moravia. In his reply of 28 January 1521 Erasmus treated Arkleb's request as a continuation of his earlier exchange of letters with Jan *Šlechta. He promised Arkleb a full reply as soon as time permitted; he pleaded for the reunification of the three branches of the church in Bohemia

and Moravia (Catholic, Utraquist, and Brethren), but also insisted that he himself was pursuing a course different from that of Luther (Ep 1183). No more is heard about subsequent contacts between Arkleb and Erasmus, except that in March 1522 the latter wrote that he had replied to the overtures of the 'captain-general of Bohemia' in such a way as to give offence (Ep 1263). There is little doubt that he meant Arkleb, the *capitaneus* of Moravia, (in Bohemia a comparable office does not exist). Since Erasmus was aware of Arkleb's Lutheran leanings, he may have thought that Ep 1183 had offended him, but the reference in Ep 1263 could also refer to a second letter, now missing; Erasmus himself allowed Epp 1154, 1183 to be published in 1521.

The plea for unity went unheeded, and within a decade Moravia displayed both a greater variety of religious groups and a higher degree of religious toleration than any other region in Europe at that time. It thus became a haven for heretics from many lands. One of them, Balthasar *Hubmaier, dedicated to Arkleb his last book, *Von dem Schwert* (Mikulov c 1527). The protection which the Moravian nobility, including Arkleb, willingly extended to many refugees did not prevent Hubmaier's execution in Vienna on 10 March 1528. Arkleb died peacefully in the same city and on the same day. He was buried in the chapel of the Augustinian monastery of St Dorothy in Vienna. Apart from Arkleb's letter to Erasmus (Ep 1154) and a few official letters written by him as governor and chamberlain, no writings are extant.

BIBLIOGRAPHY: Allen Ep 1154 / *Ottuv slovnik naucny* (Prague 1888–1909) IV 427 / Anna Císařová Kolářová *Žena v Jednotě bratrské* (Prague 1942) 219–20, 265–73, 405–6 / William R. Estep Jr *Anabaptist Beginnings* (Nieuwkoop 1976) 108–9 / A.J. Lamping *Ulrichus Velenus (Oldřich Velenský) and his Treatise against the Papacy* (Leiden 1976) 66–73 / Amedeo Molnár *Bratří a král* (Železný Brod 1947) 3–5 / Alois Vojtěch Šembera *Páni z Boskovic* ... (Vídeň 1870) 100–3, 122–6, 188–9 / Jarold Knox Zeman *The Anabaptists and the Czech Brethren in Moravia 1526–1628* (The Hague-Paris 1969) 71, 138–40, 165, 169–71, and passim

J.K. ZEMAN

Arnoldus BOSTIUS of Ghent, 1446–4 April 1499

Bostius (Boschius, de Bost) entered the Carmelite monastery in his native Ghent and was elected prior several times. It has not been established where he studied or what degrees he obtained, and in general very little is known about his life.

Bostius soon earned a reputation as a theologian, poet, and historian and was on friendly terms with a large number of scholars and humanists of the time, among them Ermolao *Barbaro, Baptista *Mantuanus, Johannes *Trithemius, Conrad Celtis, Robert *Gaguin, Charles and Jean *Fernand, Cornelio *Vitelli, Cornelis *Gerard (Ep 81), and Willem *Hermans (Ep 65A). Bostius encouraged their literary activity and always asked for copies of their works; thus he became a pivotal figure in the exchanges between the Italian and Parisian humanists and the Netherlands. Bostius himself wrote several theological and historical works focused on the Virgin Mary and on the Carmelite order. He died at Ghent.

Bostius' connection with Erasmus is known from two surviving letters, probably dated from the last years of his life. In the first (Ep 53) Erasmus replied to the unfounded suspicion that he was angry with Bostius; in the second (Ep 75) he revealed his state of mind and his plans for the future.

It is possible that Erasmus' poem in honour of St Anne (Reedijk poem 22) was inspired by Bostius, whose devotion to Anne and Joachim must be seen within the framework of his controversy with Vincenzo Bandello concerning the Immaculate Conception of the Blessed Virgin. Bostius asked all his friends to write against Bandello and organized a kind of poetical contest among them in honour of St Joachim and St Anne (see British Library, MS Add. 19.050: poems by Judocus *Beissel, Jacobus Keimolanus, Trithemius, Willem *Bibaut, etc). There does not appear to be much reason for identifying Bostius with the Arnoldus appearing in Erasmus' *Colloquia* of 1522 (ASD I-3 147–9).

BIBLIOGRAPHY: Allen and CWE Ep 53 / BNB II 762–4 / DHGE IV 555–8 / B. Zimmerman *Monumenta historica carmelitana* (Lérins 1907) passim / P.S. Allen 'Letters of Arnold Bostius' *The English Historical Review* 34 (1919) 225–36 /

E.R. Carroll *The Marian Theology of Arnold Bostius, O. Carm (1455–1499): A Study of his Work 'De patronatu et patrocinio Beatissimae Virginis Mariae in dicatum sibi Carmeli ordinem'* (Rome 1962) with further bibliography / Christine Jackson-Holzberg *Zwei Literaturgeschichten des Karmelitenordens: Untersuchungen und kritische Edition* (Erlangen 1981)

GILBERT TOURNOY

Hieronymus BOTHANUS of Massevaux, d 24 October 1531

Bothanus (Bottan, Gethan), a native of Massevaux, Upper Alsace, was registered at the University of Basel for the winter term of 1521–2 and graduated BA in 1523. From December 1525 he was the deacon of *Oecolampadius' parish of St Martin. In 1526 he married Elsbeth of Hallwil, a former nun. From 1529, the date of Basel's reformation, which he had zealously advanced, he was minister of St Alban. He was appointed chaplain to the Basel troops in the second war of Kappel and equipped with a sword at the government's expense. As Erasmus noted (Ep 2615), he was killed on the battlefield, like *Zwingli.

BIBLIOGRAPHY: Allen Ep 2615 / R. Wackernagel *Geschichte der Stadt Basel* (Basel 1907–54) III 474, 518, 101*–2* / *Matrikel Basel* I 350 / *Aktensammlung zur Geschichte der Basler Reformation* ed E. Dürr et al (Basel 1921–50) II – V passim / AK IV Ep 1596

PGB

Henri de BOTTIS of Beynost, d 1544

Henri de Bottis (Botteus) has mistakenly been called Enrico Botteo by some bibliographers. He was born at Beynost, ten kilometers north-east of Lyon, and took his MA at the Collège de Montaigu in Paris. He later claimed to have been disciplined by Noël *Béda, the unsparing master of that college (Ep 1963). Bottis still considered himself a young man in 1528, while Béda did rule the college directly until 1514 and indirectly until about 1535. Bottis became a doctor of both laws, and thus studied civil law at some university other than Paris. He became the official of the short-lived diocese of Bourg-en-Bresse and held this office during the construction of the celebrated church of Brou nearby, at which time he was on familiar terms with the sculptor Konrad *Meit. Bottis' only known work is a *Tractatus de synodo episcopi et de statutis episcopi synodalibus* (Lyon: Jean David for Vincent de Portonario 1529). It is accompanied by a poem and a letter addressed to all the bishops of Christendom and was dedicated to a certain Benedictus Faber, vicar of the bishop.

Treating Bottis as an old friend, Erasmus reassured him in December 1527 in view of rumours reporting Erasmus' death (Ep 1921). Two months later Bottis answered from Bourg-en-Bresse (Ep 1963), and Erasmus replied with a further denunciation of Béda (Ep 1985).

BIBLIOGRAPHY: Allen Ep 1921 / J. and H. Baudrier *Bibliographie lyonnaise* (Lyon 1895–1921) V 437

JAMES K. FARGE

Johann von BOTZHEIM d March 1535
Johann von Botzheim (Botzemus, Abstemius) was born around 1480 to a family of the lesser Alsatian nobility at Sasbach (Baden), where his father, Michael, was bailiff of the bishop of Strasbourg. Matriculating at the University of Heidelberg on 23 October 1496, he became a student of Jakob *Wimpfeling. In 1500 he went to Italy for further study. He returned to Germany four years later with a doctorate in civil and canon law, which he had obtained from the University of Bologna. From 1500 Botzheim held a prebend at the cathedral of Strasbourg as *vicarius chori maioris*. On 28 June 1510 he was appointed to a canonry of the cathedral chapter of Constance, and on 17 July 1511 he was installed with full rights, being described on this occasion as a priest of the diocese of Strasbourg. He spent the rest of his life as a resident canon of Constance and, although he never rose to any of the higher dignities of his chapter, he was put in charge of the workshop for the maintenance of the cathedral and of almsgiving; moreover, from 1523 to 1535 he may have been the secretary (*scriba*) of the chapter, and in 1533 he was coadjutor to the dean. From time to time he undertook missions on behalf of his chapter and the bishop, most of them concerned with collecting ecclesiastical revenues in northern Switzerland which had gone unpaid. Primarily, however, his attention was devoted to the ideal of Christian scholarship and its realization. His house in Constance was described as a 'real home of the Muses' by Erasmus (Ep 1342). In 1526 and 1527 the Reformation triumphed at Constance, and the chapter was obliged to move to Überlingen. Botzheim had been among the last canons to leave, in April 1527, and henceforward he resided in Überlingen until his death, which occurred between 24 and 29 March 1535.

Botzheim corresponded with such prominent humanists as Urbanus *Rhegius, Udalricus *Zasius, *Beatus Rhenanus, and Joachim *Vadianus and was the central figure of a humanist circle in Constance, whose outlook was bound to benefit the cause of the reformed party; a case in point is their support of the appointment of Johann *Wanner as cathedral preacher. Beyond this, an enthusiastic letter Botzheim addressed to *Luther in March 1520 (Luther w *Briefwechsel* II Ep 264) and his criticism of the concubinage of Bishop Hugo von *Hohenlandenberg raised the question of Botzheim's own orthodoxy and caused him to be accused before the Roman court of the Rota. Although he was summoned to Rome (Ep 1519), he did not go, and the suit was successfully averted, partly thanks to the efforts of Erasmus (Epp 1519, 1540, 1555) and Bonifacius *Amerbach. He was obliged, however, to admit in 1524 that he had previously been sympathetic to the Lutheran movement, vowing at the same time that he had not meant to deviate from the laws and the spirit of the Roman church and would not do so in future. It must be assumed that he was unwilling to give up his canonry and a life style which at one time had permitted him to maintain at least amicable relations with a noble nun. Later he professed abhorrence of the Anabaptist movement and the eucharistic controversy that pitted the reformers against one another (Ep 1574).

In May 1520 Erasmus responded warmly to a first approach by Botzheim that had been encouraged by Rhegius and Zasius (Ep 1103). From then on their friendship found expression in frequent letters and permitted Erasmus to follow the various phases of the reformation struggle at Constance while at the same time imparting to the Constance canon Erasmus' views on major current affairs elsewhere. Of particular interest is an exchange of 1522–3 about the dilemma posed by the pursuit of truth on the one hand and concord on the other (Epp 1331, 1335). In January 1523 Erasmus addressed to Botzheim a *catalogue raisonné* of his works, (greatly enlarged in 1524; Allen I 1–46); Botzheim had asked for such a list because he wished his impressive library to include copies of the best editions of each. In August 1529 Erasmus sent Botzheim at his request part of a reply he was then preparing to the attacks of Frans *Titelmans (Ep 2206). The full reply was published soon thereafter as *Responsio ad collationes* (LB IX 965–1016).

The climax of their friendship, however, was Erasmus' visit to Constance in the autumn of 1522, which he narrated at length in a letter intended for a speedy publication (Ep 1342). Botzheim proved to be a congenial host and, on the eve of open conflict, the divergent group among Constance's prominent citizens met for the last time in common admiration for Erasmus. In due course Botzheim's hospitality was experienced by many friends and visitors of Erasmus, including Thomas *Lupset, Reginald *Pole, Heinrich *Eppendorf, Simon *Schaidenreisser, and Kilian *Praus (Epp 1285, 1360, 1437, 1454, 1761, 2117, 2977). Botzheim remained a sincere friend, whose death Erasmus mourned in Epp 3012, 3018, while Botzheim never ceased to see in Erasmus the lodestar of humanism.

Botzheim was by no means prolific; his publications include an edition of *Speculum vitae humanae* by Rodericus Sancius, bishop of Zamora (Strasbourg: J. Prüss 1507), undertaken with Wimpfeling.

BIBLIOGRAPHY: Allen I 1 / NDB II 490–1 / LThK II 626 / *Matrikel Heidelberg* I 422 / Knod 58 / Manfred Krebs *Die Protokolle des Konstanzer Domkapitels* (Karlsruhe 1952–9) nos 3976, 4202, and passim / Hermann Baier 'Aus Konstanzer Domkapitelsprotokollen' *Zeitschrift für die Geschichte des Oberrheins* 66 (1912) esp 216–17 / AK II Ep 991 and passim / BRE Ep 227 and passim / Manfred Krebs 'Notizen zur Biographie des Humanisten Johann von Botzheim' *Zeitschrift für die Geschichte des Oberrheins* 100 (1952) 749–52 / Karl Walchner *Johann von Botzheim, Domherr zu Constanz, und seine Freunde* (Schaffhausen 1836) / Bernd Moeller *Johannes Zwick und die Reformation in Konstanz* (Güter-sloh 1961) passim / Rublack *Reformation in Konstanz* 17–18 and passim / Jörg Vögeli *Schriften zur Reformation in Konstanz* ed Alfred Vögeli (Tübingen-Basel 1972–3) II-2 873–81 and passim / Hermann Buck *Die Anfänge der Konstanzer Reformationsprozesse* (Tübingen 1964) passim / August Willburger *Die Konstanzer Bischöfe ... und die Glaubensspaltung* (Münster 1917) 253 and passim / Karlsruhe, Badisches Generallandesarchiv MS 209/1189 ff 134, 154–5

HANS-CHRISTOPH RUBLACK

Michel BOUDET of Blois, 1469–22 July 1529
Michel Boudet (Bodet, Buda) was born in Blois, the son of Jean, an official of the treasury for Brittany, and Jacquette de Garaudeau. In 1500 he was appointed to the Parlement of Paris as one of the ecclesiastical councillors, and in 1508 he was promoted to *président aux enquêtes*. From 1505 he was also canon of Langres, and in 1510 he was appointed first to the deanery of the chapter and subsequently to the episcopal see. He took possession of his diocese in 1511, and in 1516 he was named almoner to Queen *Claude, dividing his time henceforward between the court and his episcopal residences (Epp 1612, 1784). In 1517 he contributed to the rebuilding of the abbey church of St Victor in Paris and in consequence was portrayed in the stained glass of St Michael's chapel.

Boudet was a friend of Guillaume *Budé, who praised him in *De asse* (Paris 1515), and, as dedications addressed to him show, a patron of many other French humanists. Among others Josse *Bade dedicated to him a volume of *Allegoriae morales* (Paris 1520), and Jean Chéradame did likewise with an edition of Adrianus Cornelii *Barlandus' *Epitome* of Erasmus' *Adagia* (Paris: n p 1526). Boudet especially wished to see the Greek Fathers rendered more accessible through editions in Latin. Theophylactus, who had been translated by *Oecolampadius and was greatly appreciated by Erasmus, was further disseminated through several Paris editions. In these latter Erasmus' friends Philippus *Montanus and Nicolas *Bérault took an active interest; according to Allen, Bérault acknowledged Boudet's encouragement in a Latin Theophylactus, printed or reprinted at Paris in 1543. In 1523 Oecolampadius' translation of St John

Chrysostom's homilies on Genesis were also reprinted in Paris; this edition was dedicated to Boudet by Pierre Petit, a young relative of the printer Jean *Petit and a student of Bérault (BA *Oekolampads* I 293–4).

In 1523 King *Francis I appointed Boudet and two other bishops to scrutinize the examination of the works of Erasmus, *Lefèvre d'Etaples, and Louis de *Berquin undertaken by the Paris faculty of theology. When Erasmus published his *Lingua* in 1525 he was induced to send Boudet a copy and received a polite word of thanks (Ep 1612). He sent his reply by Pierre *Toussain, recommending the bearer and announcing his intention of taking issue with Oecolampadius' view of the Eucharist (Ep 1618). The same point is taken up in Erasmus' next letter to Boudet (Ep 1678; cf LB X 1617C–D), which was accompanied by another presentation copy containing the *Hyperaspistes*. By 1527 he included Boudet in a list of his patrons (Ep 1874), while his connection with Boudet's circle is further reflected in his correspondence with the bishop's chaplain, Nicolaus *Vesuvius (Ep 1784), and his physician as well as in greetings exchanged with Boudet's vicar-general, Claude *Félix (Ep 1827). In the following year Erasmus requested Boudet's advice in determining his reaction to *Béda and his other opponents in the Paris faculty of theology. The events of the 1530s might have shown more clearly how far Boudet was prepared to go in his support of his reform-minded friends, but by then the bishop of Langres had died.

BIBLIOGRAPHY: Allen Ep 1612 / DBF VI 1254 / DHGE IX 1489–90 / Clerval 356, 358 / *Catalogue général des livres imprimés de la Bibliothèque Nationale, Auteurs* (Paris 1897–) CLXXXV 816–18

PGB

Nicolas BOURBON of Vendeuvre, c 1503–c 1550

The Latin poet Nicolas Bourbon the Elder was born at Vendeuvre, near Bar-sur-Aube, to Jean Bourbon, the master of a forge, and Marie Gaulard, who had six sons and two daughters; both parents died in 1535. Nicolas Bourbon was educated at Troyes and at Paris, where he resided at the Collège de Montaigu and later at the trilingual Collège royale, studying Greek under Jacques *Toussain. He claimed to have written *Ferraria*, a poem celebrating his father's forge, at the age of fourteen, and while a student he sought patrons among the de Créqui, d'Amboise, and de Dinteville families. By 1530 he had come to the attention of Henri de Lautrec in the circle of *Margaret of Angoulême, and about 1532 he entered the service of Charles de Tournon, bishop of Viviers.

The first edition of Bourbon's *Nugae*, or poetic 'trifles' (Paris: M. de Vascosan 1533), drew a complimentary letter from Erasmus (Ep 2789), to whom Bourbon had sent a copy. This letter mentions that Bourbon had written an epitaph on hearing false rumours of Erasmus' death. Two such epitaphs appear in the second edition, expanded into eight books (Lyon: S. Gryphius 1538), but none in the first. An epigram in the 1533 edition echoes the usual Ciceronian comparison (see Ep 914) of Guillaume *Budé and Erasmus: 'hic dictis allicit, ille rapit' ('The style of Erasmus allures, that of Budé arrests us'). However, the 1538 edition attacked the Ciceronianism of Christophe de *Longueil and perhaps of his defender Etienne *Dolet, with whom Bourbon had meanwhile quarrelled. A third edition appeared in the poet's lifetime (Basel: A. Cratander 1540) and several after his death.

In 1534, shortly after the publication of the *Nugae*, Bourbon was arrested on suspicion of heresy, but he was released by order of the king. Having been appointed tutor to Henry Norreys, Thomas Harvey, and Henry Carey before his arrest, Bourbon spent the following year in the English court, where Hans *Holbein the Younger painted his portrait (Royal collection, Windsor Castle). On his return he resided at Lyon. There he addressed *Paidagogeion* (Lyon: Philippus Romanus 1536) to his pupils, among whom was probably Paul-Antoine Gadagne. Bourbon may have written the French quatrains accompanying Holbein's woodcuts in *Les Simulachres et historiées faces de la mort* (Lyon: J. Frellon 1538) and *Historiarum Veteris Testamenti icones* (Lyon: M. and G. Trechsel 1538).

About 1539 Bourbon became tutor to Jeanne d'Albret, the daughter of Margaret of Angoulême, and for her wrote *Tabellae elementariae pueris ingenuis pernecessariae* (Paris: S. de

Colines 1539). When she married Antoine de Bourbon in 1548 – an event the poet celebrated in *Epithalamion* (Paris: M. de Vascosan 1549) – Bourbon retired to a benefice at Candé. In this period he also published *In Francisci Valesii Regis obitum, inque Henrici, eius filii, Regis adventum, dialogus* (Paris: M. de Vascosan 1547) and two Latin epitaphs in *Le Tombeau de Marguerite de Valois* (Paris: M. Fezandat and R. Granjon for V. Sertenas 1551). Bourbon is last mentioned as living in 1549. His literary reputation declined with the advent of the Pléiade. Joachim du Bellay wrote of Bourbon's *Nugae* that in the entire book there was nothing better than the title.

BIBLIOGRAPHY: Allen Ep 2789 / Roman d'Amat in DBF VI 1413 / *Nouvelle Biographie générale* (Paris 1855–6) VII 42–3 / Two modern editions of Bourbon's works include biographies: *Der Eisenhammer: Ein technologisches Gedicht des 16ten Jahrhunderts* ed and trans L.H. Schütz (Göttingen 1895), and *Les Bagatelles de Nicolas Bourbon* ed and trans V.-L. Saulnier (Paris 1945) / J.-P. Nicéron *Mémoires* (Paris 1727–45) XXVI 48–51 / N.-T. Des Essarts *Les Siècles littéraires de la France* (Paris 1800–3) I 349 / J.-P. Finot 'Notice biographique sur Nicolas Bourbon (l'Ancien), poète latin du XVIe siècle' *Annuaire du Département de l'Aube* 29 (1854) 17–22 / J.-A. Jaquot *Notice sur Nicolas Bourbon de Vandoeuvre* (Troyes 1857) / Baron Alphonse de Ruble *Le Mariage de Jeanne d'Albret* (Paris 1877) 6–7 / G. Carré *De vita et scriptis Nicolai Borbonii Vandoperani* (Paris 1888) / R.C. Christie *Etienne Dolet* rev ed (London 1899) esp 318–21 / A.-S. Det 'Hans Holbein et Nicolas Bourbon, de Vendeuvre' *Mémoires, Société académique de l'Aube* 73 (1909) 47–77 / L.-E. Marcel *Le Cardinal de Givry* (Dijon 1926) I 113, II 199–205 / J. Hutton *The Greek Anthology* (Ithaca, NY, 1946) 84–7 / V.-L. Saulnier 'Recherches sur Nicolas Bourbon l'Ancien' BHR 16 (1954) 172–91 / L. Febvre *Le Problème de l'incroyance au XVIe siècle* (Paris 1962) 19–104 / *L'Erasmianus sive Ciceronianus d'Etienne Dolet* ed E.-V. Telle (Geneva 1974) 450, 452

JUDITH RICE HENDERSON

Georges de BOURBOURG *See Georges de* BRABANT

Henry BOURCHIER second earl of Essex, 1472–13 March 1540

Henry Bourchier was the son of William Bourchier and Ann Woodville, the sister of Edward IV's queen. He married Mary, the daughter of Sir William *Say and sister of Elizabeth, the first wife of William *Blount, Baron Mountjoy. He was a member of *Henry VII's privy council; he served at the siege of Boulogne in 1492 and in 1497 led a force against the rebels at Blackheath. He was captain of *Henry VIII's bodyguard and in 1511 was appointed constable of Windsor Castle. In 1514 he was raised to the position of chief captain of the English forces.

Bourchier accompanied Henry VII and Queen Elizabeth to Calais in May 1500 for their meeting with Philip the Handsome, duke of *Burgundy, and was appointed to meet *Catherine of Aragon upon her arrival in England in 1501. He continued to be a prominent figure in many official ceremonies and court entertainments. On the Field of Cloth of Gold in 1520 he was the king's marshal, and in 1521 he was one of the judges of Edward *Stafford, duke of Buckingham, from whose estates he received the manor of Bedminster. In 1526 he was appointed a member of the subdivision of the council that dealt with matters of law. In 1530 he signed the English nobles' letter to Pope *Clement VII urging him to annul the king's marriage. As he died without a male heir, the earldom of Essex and viscountcy of Bourchier became extinct.

In Ep 1595 Thomas *Lupset noted that Thomas *Winter, the natural son of Cardinal *Wolsey, was to marry Bourchier's only daughter, Anne, but this marriage was never realized. On 9 February 1527 Anne married William Parr, afterwards a marquis of Northampton, who repudiated her in 1543 after she had eloped. In the same year Parr was created earl of Essex. Anne died on 28 February 1571.

BIBLIOGRAPHY: Allen Ep 1595 / DNB II 919 / G.E. C[okayne] *The Complete Peerage of England* ed V. Gibbs et al (London 1910–59) II 249–50, V 138–40, IX 671–2

CFG

Philippe BOURGOIN d October 1514 Bourgoin, who became prior major of the abbey of Cluny in 1505, may be the 'Philippus

coenobita Cluniacensis' honoured by Erasmus with an epitaph (Reedijk poem 99).
BIBLIOGRAPHY: Reedijk poem 99 / Renaudet *Préréforme* 455

PGB

Henricus **BOVILLUS** *See Henry* BULLOCK

Lazarus **BOVOLINUS** of Mesocco, 30 August 1514–26 December 1550
Lazarus, a son of Martinus *Bovolinus, registered at the University of Basel in the winter term of 1526–7. He became a student of Henricus *Glareanus and after the Basel reformation emigrated with him to Freiburg, where he matriculated in the summer of 1529 with Johannes Baptista Bovolinus, no doubt a relative. Like his father, who recommended him to Erasmus in 1530 (Ep 2337), he became a notary at Mesocco.
BIBLIOGRAPHY: Allen Ep 2102 / *Matrikel Basel* I 360 / *Matrikel Freiburg* I 276

PGB

Martinus **BOVOLINUS** of Mesocco, d before 13 March 1531
Martinus Bovolinus (Bovollinus, Bonolinus, Bonelin, Bonalini, Boelini) belonged to a prominent family in the Mesolcina valley in the southern part of the Grisons, north of Bellinzona. As a doctor of laws he was a notary at Mesocco, but in 1529 he acted as the representative of the three Grisons leagues in the Valtelline, residing at Sondrio (Ep 2102). In February 1523, February 1524, and June 1530 (Ep 2337) he is documented in Venice, negotiating on behalf of the leagues; in 1530 he also went to Rome (Ep 2337). When returning from a mission to Milan shortly before 13 March 1531 he was murdered, together with one of his sons, by the men of Gian Giacomo de' Medici, who was trying to establish his rule in the Valtelline.
Having remained a Catholic, Bovolinus urged Erasmus to leave the reformed city of Basel and wrote to him again at Freiburg, asking him to take his son Lazarus *Bovolinus into his house and service.
BIBLIOGRAPHY: Allen Ep 2102 / *Actensammlung zur schweizerischen Reformationsgeschichte* ed J. Strickler (Zürich 1878–84) I 198, 268, III 109 / F. Sprecher von Bernegg *Pallas Rhaetica* (Basel

1617) 129 / M. Fara in *Periodico della Società storica comense* 40 (1957–9) 104

PGB

Jean de **BOYSSONÉ** of Castres, d after 1 July 1558
Jean de Boyssoné, humanist, jurisconsult, and poet, was born at Castres (Tarn) about 1500. His great wealth suggests that he belonged to the aristocratic Boysson family of Languedoc, although his biographers disagree about this connection. He earned a doctorate in civil and canon law at the University of Toulouse and by 1526 had succeeded to the chair of his uncle, Jean de Boyssoné, surnamed Luscus. He took minor orders but was not ordained priest. In a period of religious persecution at Toulouse, Boyssoné's humanist erudition in the law, his Ciceronian eloquence, his friendship with such reformers as Clément Marot and *Melanchthon, and perhaps his wealth brought him to the attention of the authorities. In 1532 he was arrested on a charge of heresy, imprisoned, forced to recant his alleged errors in a public ceremony before the Inquisition, and subjected to a heavy fine and confiscation of his property. He travelled to Padua, Bologna, Venice, Modena, Rome, and Turin before reoccupying his chair at Toulouse in 1533. In 1534 Boyssoné was one of the regents accused of fomenting student riots; he was condemned by the Parlement but in 1536 won his appeal to the grand council.
In 1539 Boyssoné declined an appointment as secretary to Guillaume *Péllicier, ambassador to Venice, in order to become a councillor in the Parlement of Chambéry in French-occupied Savoy. From 1540 on the Parlement was troubled by attacks made by the attorney general, Julien Tabouet, on his colleagues. In 1550 Boyssoné was imprisoned at Dijon with his fellow councillors. On 14 August 1551 he was convicted of falsehood and condemned by the Parlement of Dijon to pay heavy fines. Charges of violating clerical celibacy, eating meat in Lent, and frequenting suspected heretics, however, were referred to ecclesiastical jurisdiction and not, it seems, pursued. From 1551 Boyssoné taught law at the University of Grenoble but resigned before his three-year term had expired in order to pursue his appeal against Tabouet. On 16 May 1555

and 15 October 1556 the Parlement of Paris
nullified the decisions of Dijon and condemned Tabouet. Boyssoné returned to the
bench at Chambéry in 1556 and is last
mentioned in the records on 1 July 1558. In 1559
his nephew, Pierre Olivier, as his sole heir
claimed to be Tabouet's creditor for fines and
expenses imposed by the Parlement, and on 6
May 1560 a successor was appointed to the
office of *mainteneur* of the floral games at
Toulouse, which Boyssoné had held since
before 1535.

Although he was a friend and correspondent
of Etienne *Dolet, Boyssoné nevertheless
admired Erasmus (Ep 3082) and expressed his
regret at Dolet's attack in the *Dialogus de
imitatione Ciceroniana* (Lyon: S. Gryphius 1535)
on 'an old man who has rendered such great
services to literature' (Christie 218). He wrote
to Erasmus twice in 1536 at the suggestion of
Jacobus *Omphalius (Epp 3082, 3094). Boyssoné's correspondence and his Latin and
French poems are preserved in the Bibliothèque de Toulouse.

BIBLIOGRAPHY: Allen Ep 3082 / DBF VII 120–1 /
Henri Jacoubet has edited the French poems,
Les Trois Centuries (Toulouse 1923), and
summarized and annotated *Les Poésies latines*
and *La Correspondance* (both Toulouse 1931) /
Some Latin letters have been published:
Gatien-Arnoult 'Cinq lettres de Boyssoné à J.
de Coras' *Revue du Département du Tarn* 3 (1881)
180–4; Joseph Buche 'Lettres inédites de Jean
de Boyssoné et de ses amis' *Revue des langues
romanes* 38 (1895) 176–90; John Gerig 'Deux
lettres inédites de Jean de Boyssonné' *Revue de
la Renaissance* 7 (1906) 228–32; H. Jacoubet,
'Alciat et Boyssoné d'après leur correspon-
dance' *Revue du seizième siècle* 13 (1926) 231–42 /
The principal biographers of Boyssoné are
Georges Guibal 'Jean de Boysson ou la
Renaissance à Toulouse' *Revue de Toulouse et
du Midi de la France* 20 (1864) 5–33, 81–123;
François Mugnier *Jehan de Boyssonné et le
Parlement français de Chambéry* (Paris 1898); R.C.
Christie *Etienne Dolet* rev ed (London 1899)
80–9, 294–8, 392–6, and passim; Richard de
Boysson *Un Humaniste toulousain, Jéhan de
Boysson (1505–1559)* (Paris 1913); H. Jacoubet
Jean de Boyssoné et son temps (Toulouse 1930) /
For other studies see Alexandre Cioranescu
Bibliographie de la littérature française du seizième

siècle (Paris 1959) 153 / *Melanchthons Briefwechsel*
II Epp 1402, 1426

JUDITH RICE HENDERSON

Georges de BRABANT of Bourbourg, documented 1459–d 1504
Georges de Brabant (Georgius), of Bourbourg,
near Dunkirk, was no doubt a young man in
1459 when he made his profession at the
Benedictine abbey of St Bertin at Saint-Omer;
the abbey's matriculation register records his
name in the above form. He rose to occupy
important offices in his community, beginning
as *frumentarius* in charge of the grain supplies
and subsequently becoming prior (Ep 161).

BIBLIOGRAPHY: Allen Ep 161 / H. de Laplane
Les Abbés de Saint Bertin (Saint-Omer 1855) II 28

ANDRÉ GODIN

Poggio BRACCIOLINI of Terranuova,
11 February 1380–30 October 1459
Born at Terranuova in Tuscany, Poggio
Bracciolini (Poggius) studied at Arezzo and
then at Florence, where his abilities as a copyist
attracted the attention of the chancellor,
Coluccio Salutati, and of Leonardo Bruni. In
1403 he became a scribe in the curia at Rome,
and after the council of Pisa in 1409 he became
apostolic secretary under popes Alexander v
and John XXIII. In 1414, while attending the
council of Constance, he made the first of his
many remarkable discoveries of lost works of
Roman literature. Among the manuscripts
which he systematically unearthed in various
monasteries and libraries were the *Institutiones
oratoriae* of Quintilian, Cicero's oration for
Caecina, Asconius Pedianus' commentaries on
Cicero's orations, and works of Livy and
Lucretius.

In 1417, upon the election of Martin v,
Poggio lost his post as secretary and went to
London in the service of Cardinal Henry
Beaufort, bishop of Winchester. He took minor
orders, enabling him to enjoy benefices, but he
never became a priest. He hated life in England
and in 1423 returned to Rome, where he
regained his papal post and resumed his search
for lost manuscripts. He was also interested in
archaeology, studying ancient buildings, collecting coins and sculpture, and copying
inscriptions. In the 1430s and early 1440s he
accompanied Eugenius IV during his sojourns

at Florence, Bologna, and Ferrara, and in 1435
he married Vaggia de' Buondelmonte, a
Florentine girl of eighteen, by whom he had six
children. In 1453 he resigned his curial position
and returned to Florence as chancellor of the
republic. He resigned in 1458 and was
succeeded by Benedetto Accolti. He was
buried in Santa Croce; a statue by Donatello
and a portrait by Antonio del Pollaiulo
preserve his likeness.

In addition to his contributions towards the
recovery of classical works, Poggio left many
original writings. In his moral dialogues and
treatises he dealt with the purpose of human
life and the vagaries of the human condition:
De avaritia (1428–9), *An seni sit uxor ducenda*
(1436), *De infelicitate principum* (1440), *De
nobilitate* (1440), *Contra hypocritas* (1447–8), *De
varietate fortunae* (1448), *De miseria humanae
conditionis* (1445), and *Historia tripertita discep-
tativa convivalis* (1450). His *Facetiae* (1438–52)
were a collection of humorous and lascivious
tales, often satirizing the clergy. His controversies with Francesco *Filelfo and Lorenzo
*Valla, which concerned not only stylistic and
methodological issues but also petty jealous-
ies, were notorious not only in his own day but
also among humanists of later generations. His
last great work, unfinished at his death, was
the *Historiae Florentini populi*, a narrative of the
wars of 1350–1455 modelled on the technique
of Sallust. Poggio's *Opera omnia* were published at Strasbourg by Johann Knobloch and
Johann *Schott between 1511 and 1513 and at
Basel by Heinrich Petri in 1538. His letters were
edited in three volumes by Tommasso Tonelli
(Florence 1832–61), and many of his works
have appeared in modern editions.

Erasmus' attitude towards the work of
Poggio was conditioned by his preference for
Lorenzo Valla, who of all Italian humanists was
his greatest source of inspiration. He frequently referred to the controversy between
Poggio and Valla (Ep 26; ASD I-2 537, 663),
lamenting that Poggio, although he was 'a
petty clerk, uneducated, indecent,' continued
to enjoy greater popularity than Valla (Ep 182).
Elsewhere Erasmus took issue with Poggio's
Facetiae, stating that their slanders of the clergy
were dangerous reading for the young (LB IX
92E) and complaining that Poggio was widely
read despite the fact that he wrote 'filthy

Poggio Bracciolini

pestilent godless stuff,' while theologians
condemned his own *Moria* (Ep 337). Erasmus'
ire about these inequities made him overlook
Poggio's invaluable work in salvaging classical
manuscripts.

BIBLIOGRAPHY: Allen and CWE Ep 23 / A.
Petrucci in DBI XIII 640–6 / Vespasiano da
Bisticci *Le vite* ed A. Greco (Florence 1970) I
539–52 / E. Walser *Poggius Florentinus: Leben
und Werke* (Leipzig 1914) / James D. Folts 'In
search of the "Civil Life": an intellectual
biography of Poggio Braccilini (1380–1459)'
(doctoral thesis, University of Rochester, 1976)
/ Phyllis Gordan *Two Renaissance Book Hunters:
The Letters of Poggius Braccilini to Nicolaus de
Niccolis* (New York 1974) / Charles Trinkaus
*Adversity's Noblemen: The Italian Humanists on
Human Happiness* (New York 1940, repr 1965)
44, 53–6, and passim / Donald J. Wilcox *The
Development of Florentine Humanist Historio-
graphy in the Fifteenth Century* (Cambridge,
Mass, 1969) 130–76 and passim

DE ETTA V. THOMSEN & TBD

Albert of Brandenburg by Albrecht Dürer

well-known and cultured Portuguese family with interests in the arts. Erasmus *Schets had urged Erasmus to dedicate some work of his to the Portuguese king, *John III (Epp 1681, 1769), and although Erasmus followed this advice, his dedication of the Chrysostom to John III did not bring the hoped-for result. Schets thought, however, that if Brandão had still been alive at the time, he would have seen to it that Erasmus received his reward (Ep 2243).

BIBLIOGRAPHY: Allen Ep 2243 / *Dicionário de história de Portugal* ed Joel Serrão (Lisbon 1975–8) IV 219 / *Dürer's Diary of a Journey in the Netherlands July 1520–July 1521* ed Roger Fry (Boston 1913) 39–41, 68–9, and passim / M. Goris *Étude sur les colonies marchandes méridionales à Anvers de 1488–1567* (Louvain 1925) 216–7, 223–4, 230–1, and passim / A. Braamcamp Freire *Noticias da Feitoria da Flandres* (Lisbon 1920) 93 / Arthur Moreira de Sá *De re Erasmiana* (Braga 1977) 143–5, 161

ELISABETH FEIST HIRSCH

Alvise BRAGADIN of Venice, d 1560

Alvise Bragadin (Bragadino, Aloisius or Angelus Bragadenus), a youth who greeted *Hutten on his arrival in Venice (Ep 611), can be identified from the fact that his age was apparently comparable with that Ermolao (II) *Barbaro. Alvise di Andrea Bragadin of the Santa Maria branch of this prolific Venetian noble family was the son of a well-known procurator of San Marco, Andrea di Alvise, who in 1497 married Laura di Daniele Barbaro. If this was his father's first marriage, Alvise must have been born soon afterwards. He joined the Dominican order and was bishop of Vicenza from 17 March 1550 to his death.

BIBLIOGRAPHY: Allen and CWE Ep 611 / Eubel III 333 / Sanudo *Diarii* LVIII 51 / Venice, Archivio di Stato MS 'Arboro dei patritii veneti' (by Marco Barbaro) II 138 (kindly checked for us by Paul F. Grendler)

PGB

João BRANDÃO d 1527

Brandão was the factor of the Portuguese Indiahouse in Antwerp from 1509 to 1514 and again from 1520 to 1525. He came from a

Albert of BRANDENBURG 28 June 1490– 24 September 1545

Albert of Brandenburg (Albrecht, Markgraf von Brandenburg) a son of the Elector John Cicero and of Margaret of Saxony, belonged to a dynasty that had branched out to many regions of Germany. He was consequently a kinsman of numerous princes of the Empire. In 1513 he was ordained priest and in the same year, after careful diplomatic steps undertaken by his brother, the Elector Joachim of Brandenburg, was elected archbishop of Magdeburg and administrator of Halberstadt. In the following year he was elected archbishop-elector of Mainz; his elevation to the college of cardinals (Ep 891) followed on 1 August 1518 during the diet of Augsburg, giving him a position in the Empire of unsurpassed political and ecclesiastical authority, which in the years of crisis ahead was to tax his abilities to the full. When the imperial election of 1519 was called Albert from the beginning supported the future *Charles V, thus reaping major financial concessions and other pledges on the part of the Hapsburg dynasty. Twelve years later he was reluctant to cast his vote for *Ferdinand to be the Roman king, and great sums of money as well as political effort were needed to secure his support. Moreover, a sequence of diets offered Albert almost continual opportunities for exerting his influence. During the three decades of his reign the political concept underlying his interventions underwent significant changes, either as a result of modifications in his own outlook or through the influence of his advisers.

As a student at the University of Frankfurt an der Oder, Albert was first introduced to the intellectual concerns of humanism. At this time and subsequently in the early years of his reign he surrounded himself with men such as Eitelwolf von Stein, Ulrich von *Hutten, his personal physician Heinrich *Stromer, Sebastian von *Rotenhan, and Wolfgang *Capito, all of whom stood for the principles of humanistic education – especially as applied to church reform – and for Erasmus' 'philosophia Christi.' These men succeeded in creating around him a climate of open-mindedness and critical reasoning as well as in motivating Albert himself along these lines. As a result he lent his support to the cause of *Reuchlin and his friends. The irenic aspects of the humanistic program appealed to him particularly, since he was by nature opposed to controversy and radicalism. Supported by his humanistic advisers, he strove to prevent the radicalization of the religious conflict touched off by *Luther, as far as this could be done without offence to the traditional order of ecclesiastical and political priorities which he felt bound to respect, at least in their formal and juridical aspects. It must be assumed that the pliable cardinal, like so many of his contemporaries, was slow in recognizing the theological implications of Luther's teachings. This slowness was probably the principal reason for a certain ambiguity often attributed to his policy in the early years of the Reformation.

The Roman curia offered Albert a financial arrangement by which he was permitted to raise through an indulgence the sums due to the pope for the approval of his election, such as pallium fee and annates. Albert accepted this arrangement and condoned the indulgence sermons of Johann Tetzel in the diocese of Magdeburg. He also followed regular procedure in forwarding to Rome a copy of Luther's Ninety-five Theses and did not voice explicit disapproval when the curia found Luther guilty of heresy. On the other hand, he used his influential position to stall the execution of the papal sentence and, in general, to delay the persecution of religious offenders, thus defying the urgent wishes of Rome and instead following the advice of Capito, who hoped to prevent open rebellion on the part of the adherents of Luther.

Albert endeavoured not to give Rome any reason to doubt his loyalty, but at the same time he thought it politically inadvisable to countersign the edict of Worms in his capacity as arch-chancellor of the Empire. In December 1521 Capito even persuaded him to write to Luther, who was by then a confirmed heretic and outlaw; in doing so Albert humbly referred to himself as an erring sinner (Luther w *Briefwechsel* II Ep 448). Not until the knights' revolt and the peasant rebellion (1524–5), when the consequences of Lutheran preaching seemed to be jeopardizing ecclesiastical jurisdiction and the established order, did Albert begin to steer a new course. Initially it was apparently Valentin von *Tetleben, the vicar-general of Mainz, who persuaded Albert to oppose the expanding activity of evangelical preachers in his diocese. This course of action did not, however, prevent Albert from continuing his meditation between Catholic and reformed estates of the Empire, as in fact he did at the diet of Augsburg in 1530 and at Schweinfurt and Nürnberg in 1532. Not until the failure of the religious colloquy of Leipzig in 1534 were Albert's hope for a compromise effectively set aside. As recently as 1532 he had advocated temporary retention of the status quo until a general council or an imperial diet could resolve all the contentious issues. Now he came to realize that the Protestant movement was too dynamic for this. From the end of the 1530s he was convinced that the only means of saving the Catholic church from final destruction were a union of all anti-Protestant forces of the Empire, strict implementation of the decrees of the diet of Augsburg, and the immediate convening of a general council by the pope. Having earlier joined the conservative leagues of Dessau (1525) and Halle (1533), he now took a leading part in the formation of the Nürnberg union (1538), which united Charles v, King Ferdinand, and the Catholic estates in efforts to co-ordinate the struggle against the Protestants. No sooner was he committed to a policy of firm retention of the old order than he found himself in sharp conflict with the Hapsburg rulers, who were just then beginning to advocate flexibility and reconciliation. He firmly rejected the Frankfurt concordat of 1539, and at the diets of 1541–4 he was the spearhead for the conservative Catholics' refusal to compromise at the expense of the traditional ecclesiastical order.

Meanwhile Albert suffered a series of setbacks in his own territories, starting with the termination – thought to be temporary – of his ecclesiastical jurisdiction in Hesse and culminating in the removal of his residence to Aschaffenburg when Halle joined the Reformation in 1541. Others who defied him in turning towards Lutheranism were the region of Halberstadt, the chapter and city of Magdeburg, the city of Erfurt, and the district of Eichsfeld, while the Catholic leagues he had joined proved ineffectual.

It should be added that Albert continued to doubt the wisdom of political suppression, and, as the years passed by, he again set his hopes on a program of church reform such as he had advocated from the beginning of his reign to the 1520s, at least in theory. Typical of this change of policy were his appointment of Fridericus *Nausea to be the preacher of the cathedral of Frankfurt am Main, his plan to create a theological college and even a university on the basis of the New Chapter he had founded at Halle, and his support for Michael Helding, the suffragan of Mainz, and Johann Wild, the preacher at its cathedral. Owing to the influence of his chancellors, Jakob Jonas and Konrad Braun, as well as of the Jesuit Peter Faber, this new tendency became more sharply accentuated and more practical.

With all that, Albert did not set into operation a thorough reform of his dioceses. It is true that he lacked initiative and drive, but to do him justice one must point out that he had exceedingly little freedom of action. For one thing, he was plagued by massive debts, only a fraction of which was the legacy of his predecessors. The troubled state of his finances greatly reduced his options in domestic policy. For example, once the Magdeburg chapter had predominately opted for Protestantism it was politically unacceptable to saddle it with new financial burdens while trying to wean it from its Protestant leanings. Military action too had to be ruled out on practical grounds. Albert's true lack of power is demonstrated by the fact that both in the war against *Sickingen and during the turmoil caused by Otto von *Pack he was obliged to pay heavy subsidies, which had no justification in law.

In fields where his lack of funds was immaterial, Albert's domestic policies scored significant achievements. He modernized the administration and replaced poorly educated officials with properly qualified men. He reformed the juridical system and in the wake of the peasant war was able to strengthen his princely authority in the regions along the Rhine and of Aschaffenburg, with long-lasting benefits for the state of Mainz. His financial worries were caused in no small measure by his love of luxurious surroundings. Endowed with a fine taste for art and display, he spent lavishly on both the construction and the furnishings of the New Chapter house at Halle as well as on many other projects. Among those who worked for him were Grünewald, Simon of Aschaffenburg, *Dürer, Cranach, Hans Sebald Behaim, Nikolaus Glockendon, and Peter Vischer. His collections of fine art were soon broken up, however; a few days before his death at Mainz in September 1545, penury forced him to authorize the Mainz cathedral chapter to sell them.

Albert's contacts with Erasmus over more than twenty years were brought about primarily by Stromer, Hutten, and Capito, who informed Erasmus of Albert's interest in humanistic studies and his liberal support of scholars. Although for various reasons Erasmus was unable to accept Albert's repeated invitations, he pinned great hopes on the young archbishop who in his personal letters to him (Epp 661, 988) showed such genuine admiration. In 1517 he dedicated to Albert his *Ratio verae theologiae* and in return received a silver-gilt cup (Epp 745, 986, 999, 1038, 1365). In his letter of thanks (Ep 1033, 19 October 1519) Erasmus chose to present a careful analysis of the controversy around Luther, reducing it in large measure to another conflict in the continuing battle between scholasticism and humanism. The letter was bound to bolster Albert's natural inclination to restraint in this matter. In the early 1520s Albert seems to have acquired some understanding of Erasmus' theological views, evidently under the guidance of Capito, and thus a place on the fringe of the evangelical movement of the pre-Reformation years. As Erasmus' views could be interpreted as a third option between scholasticism and Lutheran reform and thus as a basis for reconciling the two religious parties, it is highly probable that his influence upon Albert's policy of mediation was far greater than has been assumed hitherto.

Two more aspects of Albert's policies suggest the influence of Erasmus and his school of thought. One was his growing awareness, theoretical at first, but later translated into practice, of the need for ecclesiastical reform within the framework of the traditional church. The other was his commitment to humanistic education, which found expression in his hiring of qualified administrators, in his plans for reforming the University of Mainz (abortive though they turned out to be), in his foundation of the New Chapter of Halle, and in the subsequent plans to upgrade it into a university. These latter plans were based on the new awareness that Catholic church reform depended in large measure on improved educational standards among the clergy. This, after all, was precisely the postulate that had survived the waning of his earlier and broader hopes for universal church reform and reconciliation between the religious camps. The patron of Hutten had become the supporter of Peter Faber, the Jesuit. Not without an inner struggle, the Erasmian ideals of his younger years had given way to faithful adherence to the program of Catholic reform as laid down by the council of Trent.

Albert's funeral monument in the cathedral of Mainz is by Dietrich Schro. There are oil portraits of him by Lucas Cranach the Elder in the Landesmuseum of Darmstadt, the Gemäldegalerie of East Berlin, the Staatliche Gemäldesammlung of Munich, and in Leningrad. Other portrait paintings are in Halle and Aschaffenburg, and drawings by Dürer exist in

the Louvre in Paris, the Albertina in Vienna (reproduced in CWE 5 116), and the Kunsthalle of Bremen.

BIBLIOGRAPHY: Allen and CWE Ep 661 / NDB I 166–7 / ADB I 268–71 / RGG I 218 / LThK I 291–2 / Theodor Brieger 'Über den Prozess des Erzbischofs Albrecht gegen Luther' *Kleinere Beiträge zur Geschichte von Dozenten der Leipziger Hochschule* (Leipzig 1894) 191–203 / Anton Philipp Brück 'Die Instruktion Kardinal Albrechts von Brandenburg für das Hagenauer Religionsgespräch 1540' *Archiv für mittelrheinische Kirchengeschichte* 4 (1952) 275–280 / Ludwig Cardauns *Zur Geschichte der kirchlichen Unions- und Reformbestrebungen 1538–1542* (Rome 1910) / Walter Delius 'Kardinal Albrecht und die Wiedervereinigung der beiden Kirchen' *Zeitschrift für Kirchengeschichte* 62 (1943–4) 178–89 / Hans Goldschmidt *Zentralbehörden und Beamtentum im Kurfürstentum Mainz vom 16. bis zum 18.Jahrhundert* (Leipzig and Berlin 1908) / H. Gredy *Kardinal-Erzbischof Albrecht II. von Brandenburg in seinem Verhältnisse zu den Glaubensneuerungen* (Mainz 1891) / J.H. Hennes *Albrecht von Brandenburg, Erzbischof von Mainz und Magdeburg* (Mainz 1858) / Paul Kalkoff *Wolfgang Capito im Dienste Erzbischof Albrechts von Mainz. Quellen und Forschungen zu den entscheidenden Jahren der Reformation (1519–1523)* (Berlin 1907) / Jacob May *Der Kurfürst, Cardinal und Erzbischoff Albrecht II. von Mainz und Magdeburg, Administrator des Bistums Halberstadt, Markgraf von Brandenburg und seine Zeit. Ein Beitrag zur deutschen Cultur- und Reformationsgeschichte* (Munich 1865–7) / Paul Redlich *Cardinal Albrecht von Brandenburg und das Neue Stift zu Halle 1520–1541. Eine kirchen- und kunstgeschichtliche Studie* (Mainz 1900) / Wilhelm Schum *Cardinal Albrecht von Mainz und die Erfurter Kirchenreformation (1514–1533)* (Halle 1878)

ALBRECHT LUTTENBERGER

Albert (I), margrave of BRANDENBURG-Ansbach 17 May 1490–20 March 1568

Albert, the third son of Frederick, margrave of *Brandenburg-Ansbach, was elected grand master of the Teutonic order in 1511. The new grand master avoided swearing allegiance to *Sigismund I of Poland, liege lord of the order's territory in Prussia. Albert negotiated with the Hapsburgs and even Muscovy in an attempt to win their support, but in the inevitable war (1520–1), the order had to face the Polish forces without outside assistance. The war ended with an agreement to observe a truce for a period of four years. Albert continued his diplomatic efforts; in the spring or summer of 1522 Jacobus *Piso met him in the course of a ceremonial visit to the court of young King *Louis II at Prague (Ep 1297), but the sympathetic reception he was given at the Hungarian court proved of little value in his conflict with Poland (Hubatsch 102–3). Meanwhile Albert prepared for the secularization of the state of the Teutonic order by opening Prussia to the influence of Lutheran preachers, and in 1523 he visited *Luther in Wittenberg. On 8 April 1525 the peace of Cracow was concluded by virtue of which the last grand master of the Teutonic order became the first duke of a secular duchy of Prussia under Polish suzerainty. On 1 July 1526 Albert married Dorothea, a daughter of King Frederick I of Denmark. In the remaining four decades of his long reign Duke Albert re-organized the administration of Prussia, and in 1544 he founded the University of Königsberg, now Kaliningrad.

BIBLIOGRAPHY: Allen Ep 1297 / Walther Hubatsch *Albrecht von Brandenburg-Ansbach* (Heidelberg 1960) / Walther Hubatsch in NDB I 171–3 / ADB I 293–310 / Fritz Gause *Geschichte der Stadt Königsberg* (Cologne-Graz 1965–   ) I 291–4 and passim

MICHAEL ERBE & PGB

Albert (II), margrave of BRANDENBURG-Ansbach 28 March 1522–8 January 1557
Albert, later known as 'Alcibiades,' was a son of Casimir, landgrave of Brandenburg-Ansbach-Kulmbach, ruler of the Franconian territories of the house of Brandenburg, which had been split from Brandenburg proper in 1473. After the early death of his father (21 September 1527) he was brought up in Ansbach by his uncle, George of *Brandenburg-Ansbach, who was his guardian, while Christophorus *Pistorius acted as the boy's tutor (Ep 1881). In 1541 the Brandenburg lands in Franconia were divided between George and Albert, with the nephew receiving the south-western region around Kulmbach and Bayreuth. His Protestant faith notwithstand-

ing, Albert fought in the Schmalkaldic war (1546–7) on the side of *Charles V but subsequently joined Maurice of Saxony in turning against the emperor. Albert was instrumental in negotiating with France the treaty of Chambord (January 1552), which enabled the Protestant princes to make their surprise attack upon the emperor in the Tirol four months later.

BIBLIOGRAPHY: Allen Ep 1881 / NDB I 163 / ADB I 252–7 / Bruno Gebhardt et al *Handbuch der deutschen Geschichte* 8th ed (Stuttgart 1954–   ) 102 and passim

MICHAEL ERBE & PGB

Frederick, margrave of BRANDENBURG-Ansbach 2 May 1460–4 April 1536
Frederick was the second son of margrave Albert, also known as 'Achilles.' In 1495, after the death of his younger brother, Sigismund, he united all the Franconian possessions of his house under his rule. His government of Ansbach and Bayreuth was chaotic and left a legacy of financial ruin. On 25 March 1515 he was deposed by reason of insanity. He spent the remainder of his life in confinement, while his two eldest sons, Casimir and George of *Brandenburg-Ansbach, were nominally instituted as co-rulers; in practice, however, for the following twelve years the government was in the hands of Casimir. After Casimir's death in 1527, another of Frederick's sons, Albert (I) of *Brandenburg-Ansbach, intervened to have the harshness of his father's treatment mitigated. Margrave Frederick was apparently the previous owner of a gilt-laminated cup 'made from the horn of a unicorn,' which was given to Erasmus by Johann *Henckel (Ep 2309).

BIBLIOGRAPHY: Allen Ep 2309 / ADB VII 480; cf IV 44–5 / Walther Hubatsch *Albrecht von Brandenburg-Ansbach* (Heidelberg 1960) 13–15, 55, 236, and passim

MICHAEL ERBE & PGB

George, margrave of BRANDENBURG-Ansbach 4 March 1484–27 December 1543
In 1505 George, the second son of Frederick of *Brandenburg-Ansbach, joined the court of *Vladislav II, king of Bohemia and Hungary, where he met Beatrix, Countess Frangipani – the widow of a natural son of King *Matthias

George of Brandenburg-Ansbach

Charles Brandon

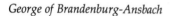

Corvinus – who in 1509 became his first wife. The wealth George inherited on her early death enabled him to acquire vast estates in Silesia. In 1521 he mediated an end to the war between *Sigismund I of Poland and his own younger brother, Albert (I) of *Brandenburg-Ansbach, master of the Teutonic order. In the following year Jacobus *Piso met the two brothers at the court of *Louis II in Prague (Ep 1297). From 1515 George had nominally been co-ruler with his eldest brother, Casimir, of the Brandenburg-Ansbach territories in Franconia, but not until after Casimir's death (21 September 1527) did he return to Franconia. During the minority of his nephew, Albert (II) of *Brandenburg-Ansbach, George governed the entire lands of his family and ensured the victory of the Reformation, earning himself the epithets 'the Pious' and 'the Confessor.' In 1530 he was among the Lutheran princes who presented *Melanchthon's 'confessio Augustana' to *Charles v at the diet of Augsburg (Ep 2333). When the Brandenburg-Ansbach territories were partitioned in 1541 between George and Albert (II), George retained Ansbach.

BIBLIOGRAPHY: Allen Ep 1297 / NDB VI 204–5 / ADB VIII 611–14

MICHAEL ERBE & PGB

Charles BRANDON duke of Suffolk, c 1485–22 August 1545
Charles was the son of William Brandon, *Henry VII's standard-bearer at the battle of Bosworth. He was born shortly before or after his father's death in that battle. As a favourite of *Henry VIII he received many grants and stewardships. He was considered an upstart by many of the nobles, and also by Erasmus (Ep 287). In 1509 he was Esquire for the Body at the funeral of Henry VII and chamberlain of North Wales, in 1511 he was marshal of the royal household, and by 1512 he had been knighted. He was marshal of the army which invaded France in 1513 and was created Viscount L'Isle. In the following year he was created duke of Suffolk and sent to France to arrange a meeting between Henry VIII and *Louis XII, king of France, and to plot the expulsion of *Ferdinand II of Aragon from Navarre.

Erasmus mentioned a rumour that Brandon was to have married the Emperor *Maximilian's

Sebastian Brant by Albrecht Dürer

daughter, *Margaret of Austria (Ep 287), but this marriage did not come about. After the death of Louis XII Suffolk was sent as an ambassador to his successor, *Francis I. In France he secretly married *Mary Tudor, the widow of Louis XII and sister of Henry VIII, although he had already been married twice and his first wife was still alive. He was later able to legalize his position with a dispensation from *Clement VII, and Henry VIII's displeasure at the marriage was soothed by the gift of Mary's jewels and plate and by Brandon's promise of further payments.

Suffolk accompanied Henry VIII to the Field of Cloth of Gold in 1520. Two years later he received him and the Emperor *Charles V at his home in Southwark. He was commander of the English army that invaded France in 1523, and he later housed Cardinal Lorenzo *Campeggi when he arrived to investigate the king's request for a divorce. In 1529 Suffolk sided against his former patron, Thomas *Wolsey, on the divorce issue, and with Thomas *Howard, duke of Norfolk, secured a warrant for Wolsey's arrest. He also signed the nobles' letter to Clement VII which warned the pope of

impending dangers if he were not to give in to the king's wishes and dissolve his marriage. In 1533 Suffolk was chosen to inform *Catherine of Aragon of the king's marriage to *Anne Boleyn; he was both lord high constable and lord high steward for the occasion of Anne's coronation in that year. When his wife, Mary, died in the same year he married Katherine Willoughby. In 1534 Brandon was commissioned to receive the oaths of the English people on the Act of Succession; he was also chief justice of Eyre, south of the river Trent. In 1536 he suppressed rebellions in Lincolnshire and Yorkshire, and for the following three years was instrumental in the suppression of the larger monasteries, retaining some of their lands for himself. He was a commissioner to treat for marriage between the king and Anne of Cleves in 1539, and in 1541 was a judge of the accomplices of Queen Catherine Howard. When he died at Guildford it was a mark of the king's favour that his body was removed to Windsor for burial.

BIBLIOGRAPHY: Allen and CWE Ep 287 / DNB II 1126–30 / G.E. C[okayne] *The Complete Peerage of England* ed V. Gibbs et al (London 1910–59) XII 454–60

CFG

Sebastian BRANT of Strasbourg, c 1458–10 May 1521
Sebastian Brant was born in Strasbourg of respectable burgher parents; his grandfather was a member of the city council, his father ran a large inn. He matriculated at Basel in 1475, early showing an interest in the law and in letters. He received his BA in 1477 and his doctorate in civil and canon law in 1489. He began to teach at the university by 1483, first literature and later law. He married Elisabeth Bürgi in 1485. He published legal texts and also worked for various Basel publishers, making the final revisions for Johann *Froben and Johannes *Petri's edition of the biblical concordance by Conrad of Halberstadt (1496). A prolific writer of verse and panegyrics, in 1494 Brant published his *Narrenschiff* (Nürnberg: P. Wagner), a vernacular satirical poem depicting the moral and religious failures of mankind, which brought him instant fame. He did not approve of Basel's accession to the Swiss Confederacy (1499) and returned to

Strasbourg, where in 1500 he was nominated syndic of the city, thus entering on a new political career. With Jakob *Wimpfeling he was a leader of the Alsatian humanist movement which centred in the city, although he wrote little after he was established there. Always conservative, Brant was deeply involved in the quarrel over the Immaculate Conception (1494–9), defending the tenet against the attacks of the Dominicans. Nevertheless in 1513 he did nothing to defend *Reuchlin, who was a personal friend, against the Dominicans. He died in 1521; a plaque in the cathedral commemorated him as a lawyer, poet, and orator.

Erasmus expressed his appreciation of Brant in an epigram written in August 1514 (Reedijk poem 95). They had met at a banquet given by the Strasbourg literary society in Erasmus' honour while he was passing through the city (Epp 302, 305). In 1520 Erasmus may have met Brant in Antwerp (Ep 1132 introduction) when Brant was there as ambassador from the town of Strasbourg to the Emperor *Charles v and he was sketched by Albrecht *Dürer (reproduced in CWE 3 14).

Brant wrote a legal textbook, Expositiones ... omnium titulorum iuris civilis at canonici (Basel: H. Furter 1490); more important are his editions of Layenspiegel (Augsburg: J. Otmar 1509) and Clagspiel (Strasbourg: M. Hupfuff 1516), legal manuals written in German for use by lay men. His earliest poems, Rosarium (1492–3) and In laudem gloriosae Mariae (Basel: J. Bergmann 1494), have religious themes. Poems on political topics are included in his Varia ... carmina (Basel: J. Bergmann 1498). Brant's moralistic-didactic writings such as Tischzucht (Basel: J. Bergmann 1490) and Liber faceti (Basel: J. Bergmann 1496) became quite popular. An edition of Terence's plays was planned by Brant and Jakob *Locher in 1496, but only six plays were published (Strasbourg 1503).

BIBLIOGRAPHY: Allen and CWE Ep 302 / NDB II 534–6 / Matrikel Basel I 138 / Schmidt Histoire littéraire I 189–333; a full bibliography of all editions of Brant's works is provided II 340–73; see also Index Aureliensis (Baden-Baden 1962–) V 126–37 / Mary Alvarita Rajewski Sebastian Brant; Studies in Religious Aspects of His Life and Works ... (Washington, DC, 1944) / Edwin H. Zeydel Sebastian Brant (New York

1967) / H. Rupprich in R. Newald et al Geschichte der deutschen Literatur (Munich 1957–) IV-1 580–5 / RE Ep 44 and passim
MIRIAM U. CHRISMAN & IG

Wolfgang BRANTNER d 28 September 1541
Wolfgang Brantner (Brandner, Prantner) was born of a noble family (Prantner zu Prandeck und Kreuzenstetten) and indicated Carinthia as his native region when matriculating at Vienna for the spring term of 1508. In 1513 he registered at the University of Bologna, where he was syndic of the German nation and became a doctor of laws in May 1516. After his return from Italy he entered the chancery of *Maximilian I and afterwards became a secretary and councillor of *Charles v, who in turn recommended him warmly to his brother *Ferdinand. On 16 December 1527 he was appointed councillor to King Ferdinand for Carinthia. In the same year he was also coadjutor to the grand master of the order of St George and was assigned the task of recruiting soldiers in Constance for the Hapsburg armies in Italy. He was a good friend of Jakob *Spiegel, who praised him in his Lexicon iuris civilis (Strasbourg 1539), while Fridericus *Nausea dedicated to him the first book of his Conciones Pragenses (Cologne: P. Quentel 1538). He died in Vienna and was buried in Trautmannsdorf.

In 1529 Erasmus' famulus, Felix *Rex, met Brantner during the diet of Speyer and found him eager to transmit Erasmus' letters to Spain. Rex described him as a close associate of Johann von *Vlatten (Ep 2130).

BIBLIOGRAPHY: Allen Ep 2130 / Matrikel Wien II-1 349 / Knod 61–2

PGB

Johannes Alexander BRASSICANUS of Tübingen, d 25 November 1539
Johannes Alexander Brassicanus (Köl, Köll) was born at Tübingen in 1500 or 1501, the son of Johannes Brassicanus, a schoolmaster descended from a family from Constance. He studied at the University of Tübingen, where he received his MA on 21 July 1517. Until 1519 he taught at Tübingen, and then he was attached to the household of Maximiliaan van *Bergen, heer van Zevenbergen, with whom he was at Constance in February 1520

(*Vadianische Briefsammlung* II Ep 81). Without waiting for the publication of his Latin poems, Πᾶν: *omnis* ([Haguenau]: T. Anshelm 1519; inspired by *Hutten's Nemo*), the Emperor *Maximilian I crowned him poet laureate (before 4 March 1518; Ep 1146). Escaping from an outbreak of the plague at Tübingen, he stayed with Johannes *Fabri at Constance from December 1520 to January 1521 (BRE Ep 189; *Vadianische Briefsammlung* II Epp 233, 235, 238), but by May he had returned to his university and was studying law. In the autumn of 1522 he succeeded Johann *Reuchlin as professor in Ingolstadt, at the same time obtaining a doctoral degree in civil and canon law. Upon Fabri's recommendation *Ferdinand I appointed him to a chair of rhetoric in the University of Vienna (9 February 1524); subsequently he also taught Greek and civil law. He died in Vienna.

A manuscript copy of the *Julius exclusus* in Brassicanus' own hand is dated 24 August 1517. Personal contacts between him and Erasmus began in September 1520, when Brassicanus visited Erasmus in Antwerp, obtaining a letter of commendation (Ep 1145). They met again in Louvain during October and in Cologne during November (BRE Ep 189). Erasmus honoured him in the colloquy *Apotheosis Capnionis* (1522, ASD I-3 267–73), where Brassicanus appears as one of the speakers. Friendly relations continued intermittently until 1531, through both Johannes Fabri and Johann *Koler, who in 1530 was asked to forward to Brassicanus a letter from Erasmus which is now lost (Ep 2406). Brassicanus sent Erasmus his book of proverbs, *Brassicani proverbiorum symmicta* (Vienna: H. Wietor 1529), which annoyed Erasmus (Ep 2810), who claimed that material had been taken from the *Adagia*. Brassicanus' numerous publications contain such poems as an elegy on the death of Maximilian I, *In mortem Divi Maximiliani ... epicedion* (Augsburg: J. Miller 1519) and editions of such patristic authors as Gennadius, Eucherius, and Salvianus, many of them based on rare manuscripts he had found in the libraries of Melk and Buda. A report on the contents of the famous library of King *Matthias Corvinus in Buda, contained in a letter and published by J.J. Maderus in 1666, is especially valuable

since this library was destroyed by the Turks only a few years after Brassicanus had inspected it.

BIBLIOGRAPHY: Allen and CWE Ep 1146 / ADB III 260 / BRE Ep 189 / *Matrikel Tübingen* I 199 / *Matrikel Wien* III 35 / Georg Ellinger *Geschichte der neulateinischen Literatur Deutschlands im sechzehnten Jahrhundert* (Berlin 1929–33) I 441 / *Johann Cuspinians Briefwechsel* ed Hans Ankwicz von Kleehoven (Munich 1933) Ep 47 and passim / Oscar Hase *Die Koberger* 2nd ed (Leipzig 1885) 166, 414

IG

Georg BRATZEL See Georgius PRECELLIUS

BRAUNSCHWEIG See BRUNSWICK

Jan BRECHT, BRECHTIUS See *Johannes CUSTOS*

Friedrich BRECHTER See Friedrich PRECHTER

Georg von BREITENBACH of Leipzig, d 1541
Georg von Breitenbach (Breyttenbach, Braitenbach) matriculated at the University of Leipzig in the winter term of 1501 and in 1506 studied at the newly founded University of Frankfurt an der Oder. He returned to Leipzig to receive his doctorate in civil and canon law, and from 1517 he taught civil law at the university. In 1524 he succeeded Simon *Pistoris as professor *ordinarius*, or head of the faculty of law. Another Breitenbach, Johann, had held that same position at the turn of the sixteenth century. Georg occupied it until after the death of Duke George of *Saxony in April 1539, when he retired and was succeeded by Pistoris on a temporary basis. He also served as vice-chancellor of the university for a term in both 1520 and 1535. After some initial indecision he became a supporter of Duke George's Catholic policy and as a result incurred the wrath of Martin *Luther. As Albertine Saxony moved officially into the Protestant camp, he was subjected to a humiliating interrogation in August 1539. In May 1540 he accepted an appointment as chancellor to the Elector Joachim II of Brandenburg. He was married to Barbara von Bernstein (d 1546).

Breitenbach was a friend of Heinrich *Stromer, who dedicated to him and Julius

*Pflug an edition of *De curialium miseriis* by
Aeneas Sylvius (Pope *Pius II), published by
Johann *Schöffer (Mainz 1517). Pflug and
Breitenbach corresponded later. It was proba-
bly Stromer who had drawn Erasmus' attention
to Breitenbach. In a letter to Duke George in
1520, Erasmus praised Breitenbach, Petrus
*Mosellanus, Stromer, and Pistoris as luminar-
ies of the University of Leipzig (Ep 1125).
    BIBLIOGRAPHY: Allen Ep 1125 / ADB III 288 /
Matrikel Leipzig I 443, III 89, and passim / Pflug
Correspondance I Ep 108 (reproducing a portrait)
and passim / *Der Briefwechsel des Justus Jonas* ed
Gustav Kawerau (Halle 1884–5, repr 1964) I Ep
444

PGB

Andrea BRENTA of Padua, d 11 February
1484
Andrea Brenta was born at Padua about 1454
and studied under Demetrius *Chalcondyles,
who taught at Padua from 1463. He travelled to
Rome as secretary to Cardinal Oliviero Carafa,
and after 1475 taught Greek and Latin at the
university. One of the first scholars to benefit
from the opening of the Vatican library to the
public in 1475, he translated *De insomniis, De
victu*, and other fragments of Hippocrates from
Greek into Latin. He died prematurely of the
plague.
    In the correspondence of Erasmus Brenta's
name appears in 1527. The physician Jan
*Antonin, suggesting that Erasmus should
translate some more works by Galen, criticized
Andreas *Cratander's edition of Hippocrates
(Basel 1526), adding that only the sections by
Brenta, Guillaume *Cop and Niccolò *Leoniceno were good (Ep 1810).
    The Biblioteca Apostolica Vaticana pos-
sesses a number of orations by Brenta as well as
introductory lectures for courses on Aristophanes, the *Commentaries* of Caesar, and the
trivium and quadrivium ('In disciplinas et
bonas artes ...'). His translations of Hippocrates were first published without place or date
under the title *Hippocrates de natura hominis*. His
In pentecostem oratio was printed in Rome by
Eucharius Silber after 18 May 1483.
    BIBLIOGRAPHY: Allen Ep 1810 / M. Miglio in
DBI XIV 149–51

TBD

Johann Brenz

Johann BRENZ of Weil der Stadt, 24 June
1494–11 September 1570
Johann Brenz (Brentius) was born in Weil der
Stadt, west of Stuttgart, the son of a judge. In
1514 he matriculated at Heidelberg and in 1518,
upon graduating MA, he began to give lectures.
*Oecolampadius instructed him in the Greek
language, and in turn he taught Greek to
*Bucer (BRE Ep 79). Deeply impressed by
Martin *Luther, who debated publicly during
the general chapter of his order at Heidelberg
(1518), Brenz turned to the study of Augustine
and Paul. From 1522 to 1548 he was, with some
interruptions, in charge of the parish of
Schwäbisch Hall, where he gradually introduced the Reformation. In 1526 he composed
the first church ordinance for Hall, and in 1532
he took part in the drafting of church
ordinances for Magdeburg and Nürnberg.
From 1534 he advised Duke Ulrich of
*Württemberg on the establishment of a
reformed church throughout his duchy and on
the reorganization of the University of
Tübingen. He was opposed to radical measures and did not favour the formation of the
Schmalkaldic League; but after its defeat he

was temporarily forced to seek refuge in Basel (1548) as the imperial troops entered Hall. When he became provost and preacher of the chapter church in Stuttgart (1553), Brenz was the leading official of the Lutheran church in Württemberg. He displayed great organizational talent and, in the face of Calvinist opposition, maintained a moderate Lutheran orthodoxy.

Brenz does not appear to have had any personal contacts with Erasmus. Oecolampadius mentioned him in March 1517 (Ep 563) as a promising young scholar and admirer of Erasmus, sharing Oecolampadius' work on Jerome at Weinsberg. In his reply (Ep 605) Erasmus showed polite interest in Brenz. Much later, in his *Epistola ad fratres Inferioris Germaniae* (1530; LB X 1599F) he referred to Brenz's book *An magistratus iure possit occidere ... haereticos* (1528; published in P. Melanchthon *Adversus anabaptistas* n p, n d) as an impressive testimony against the execution of heretics. In his later years, however, Brenz did not maintain his stance in favour of toleration. In 1530 Brenz married Margarete Gräter (d 1548), and in 1550 Katharina Isemann or Eisenmenger, the niece of a close friend. He wrote the first reformed catechism in 1527 and 1528 as well as numerous exegetical sermons.

BIBLIOGRAPHY: Allen and CWE Ep 563 / NDB II 598–9 / ADB III 314–16 / Julius Hartmann *Johannes Brenz: Leben und ausgewählte Schriften* (Elberfeld 1862) / James Martin Estes *Christian Magistrate and State Church: The Reforming Career of Johannes Brenz* (Toronto 1982) / Sebastian Castellio *Concerning Heretics* ed and trans R.H. Bainton (New York 1935) 50–8 and passim / David Steinmetz *Reformers in the Wings* (Philadelphia 1941) 109–18 / *Matrikel Heidelberg* I 497, II 438 / F.W. Kantzenbach 'Der Beitrag des Johannes Brenz zur Toleranzidee' *Theologische Zeitschrift* 21 (1965) 38–64 / *Johannes Brenz 1499–1570* ed G. Schäfer and M. Brecht (Stuttgart 1970)

IG

Lambert de BRIAERDE of Dunkirk, c 1490–10 October 1557

Lambert de Briaerde (Lambertus Briardus), knight, was the son of Adrien and Marie d'Esperlecques. He studied law and obtained a doctorate, probably in Paris. On 1 January 1521

he was appointed councillor and master of requests at the grand council of Mechelen; he was subsequently privy councillor, and on 27 November 1532 he succeeded Erasmus' friend Nicolaas *Everaerts as president of the grand council. Briaerde, who carried out several important missions for *Charles V and *Mary of Hungary, resigned the presidency a year before his death but was given the title of president on his funeral monument. A relative of Florens van *Griboval, treasurer of Flanders, Briaerde married Marie, a daughter of Philippe *Haneton, treasurer of the Golden Fleece, and after her death, in 1526 Marguerite, a daughter of the influential Jean *Micault (Epp 2571, 2767). His second wife survived him and died in 1596.

In 1531 Maarten *Davidts, canon of Brussels, suggested to Erasmus, who had met Briaerde at Paris, that he compose for the latter a commentary on Psalm 50, 'Miserere mei, Deus' (Ep 2571). Davidts suggested that Briaerde could be useful to Erasmus in securing payment of his annuity from the imperial court, and the same was pointed out in 1533 by *Viglius Zuichemus (Ep 2767). In the same year Conradus *Goclenius repeated the request that Erasmus comment on Psalm 50 for Briaerde (Ep 2851).

A treatise on legal procedure according to written law, which Briaerde had composed partly in Flemish and partly in Latin, was published after his death: *Tractaet hoe en in wat manieren dat men nae dispositie van geschreven rechten schuldich is en behoort te procederen* (Antwerp: H. de Laet 1562, copy in the Bibliothèque Royale of Brussels). Another work in Latin, 'Consilia sive responsa juris,' was never published, and the manuscript now seems to be lost. Some of Briaerde's letters survive in the Archive du Nord, Lille, and in other archives. Frans van *Cranevelt dedicated to him a Latin translation of three homilies by St Basil (Louvain: R. Rescius 1534).

BIBLIOGRAPHY: Allen Ep 2571 / F. Sweertius *Athenae Belgicae* (Antwerp 1628) 178, 508 / Valerius Andreas *Bibliotheca Belgica* 2nd ed (Louvain 1643) 611 / J. Britz in BNB III 44–6 / de Vocht *Literae ad Craneveldium* 49–50 / de Vocht CTL III 115

MARCEL A. NAUWELAERTS

Jan BRIART of Ath, 1460–8 January 1520
Jan Briart (Briaert, Briard) was later known in
Louvain as Atensis, a name derived from Ath,
in Hainaut, a city in the proximity of his native
village of Beloeil. His lifelong association with
the University of Louvain began with his
matriculation on 30 August 1478. By 1482 he
had taken his MA, apparently as the top
graduand. While teaching undergraduate
classes in the College of the Falcon – on 1
October 1492 he was admitted to the university
council as an arts teacher – he began to study
theology. He was ordained priest and by 1490
joined the entourage of Margaret of York, the
widow of Charles the Rash, duke of *Burgundy, who resided at Mechelen. As her
chaplain and later her councillor he served the
duchess until her death in 1503. She paid the
expenses for his theological doctorate, conferred on 11 February 1500, as she had done
nine years earlier in the case of Adrian of
Utrecht, the future Pope *Adrian VI, who was a
close friend of Briart. In 1506 Briart was
appointed to a chair of theology combined with
a canonry at St Peter's. For the summer terms of
1516 and 1518 he was elected dean of the
theological faculty (de Jongh 40*, 42*), and in
1505 and 1510 he served for the winter term as
rector of the university. Above all, he
substituted regularly for his friend Adrian of
Utrecht, the chancellor of the university, who
was frequently absent. From 1515, when
Adrian was sent to Spain and left Louvain for
good, Briart came to occupy a position of
prominence, often referred to as the vice-
chancellorship.

Five *quaestiones quodlibeticae*, disputed by
Briart between 1508 and 1510, were published
in reprints of the *Quaestiones quodlibeticae* of
Adrian of Utrecht (Louvain 1518, Paris 1522);
another *quodlibeticum*, dealing with an indulgence recently granted to the Netherlands,
was debated by Briart in 1516 and subsequently published: *Quaestio quodlibetica contra
dispensationes vel magis dissipationes commis-
sariorum in negocio indulgentiarum* (Leipzig: n pr
1519). The title chosen in Leipzig, reminiscent
of *Luther's position, does not appear to be
justified; although it recommends some restraint in the sale of indulgences, Briart's text
cannot be considered an attack upon the
customary practice (de Jongh 97). Apart from

these works, his teaching and continual
engagement in the administration of the
university seem to have left him no time for
publications. Of his many students some
became noted theologians, among them Jacobus *Latomus, Ruard *Tapper, Maarten van
*Dorp, and Gerard *Morinck, who left a
manuscript biography of his teacher. Among
the works dedicated to him were Nicolaas van
*Broeckhoven's edition of Hugo of St Victor's
commentary on St Paul (Louvain: D. Martens
1512), Dorp's sermon on the Assumption
(Louvain: D. Martens, 18 February 1514), and
Juan Luis *Vives' *Genethliacon Iesu Christi*
(Louvain: D. Martens 1519).

When Dorp criticized Erasmus in 1515 and
1516 on account of the *Moria* and some
passages of the New Testament, Erasmus
believed that, as Dorp's mentor, Briart was
partly responsible for the attack, although
ostensibly he had always been friendly (CWE
Epp 337:393–4, 539). But as his relations with
Dorp improved, Erasmus also seems to have
dropped his suspicions of Briart, at least for a
time. When he settled at Louvain in July 1517
Briart was prominent among those who
endeavoured to make the famous scholar
welcome and even co-opt him into the faculty
of theology (Epp 509, 536, 637, 641, 650, 651).
Erasmus responded with flattering praise for
Briart in a letter quickly released for publication (Ep 675). In September 1517 he submitted
to the vice-chancellor an elusive matter said to
be of great importance politically, which called
for consultation with the university authorities
(Epp 669, 670). Before publishing his *Paraphrasis in Romanos* in November 1517, he
showed the work to Briart, who liked it
'wonderfully' (Ep 695). In later years he also
insisted (Ep 1225) that he had obtained
Briart's approval of the second edition of the
New Testament (1518–19) before sending the
revised copy to the printer (Epp 1225, 1571,
1581; LB IX 798B, 985C; *Opuscula* 271). The
last-mentioned of these statements, in his
Apologia invectivis Lei, was published two
months after Briart's death and apparently
remained uncontradicted. Briart was one of
the first of Erasmus' friends to visit him in
September 1518, when he had been to Basel to
oversee the reprinting of the New Testament

and had returned to Louvain severely ill (Ep 867).

It is doubtful whether Erasmus' visitor realized at the time that the patient had once again begun to suspect the sincerity of his friendship. Since November 1517 Erasmus had noted that some Louvain theologians were adamantly opposed to the newly founded *Collegium Trilingue* (Epp 691, 695), and although he did not say that they had Briart's support, the minutes of a council meeting (8 March 1519) show that as the spokesman for the theological faculty Briart argued against granting *Alaard of Amsterdam permission to lecture under the auspices of the new college on Erasmus' *Ratio verae theologiae* (de Jongh 12*). Full recognition of the new college did not come until after Briart's death. Another dispute involved Briart and Erasmus directly but was at least partially resolved. In February 1519 the vice-chancellor had used his address during a graduation ceremony to attack Erasmus' *Encomium matrimonii*, although he refrained from naming the work or the author. Common friends brought the two men together; it was agreed that Briart had not fully understood Erasmus' text (LB IX 770B) and that Erasmus would reply with a short *Apologia pro declamatione de laude matrimonii* (LB IX 105–12), also without mentioning a name. Unfortunately some of Briart's disciples would not let the matter rest, so that Erasmus felt compelled to lodge a further complaint (CWE Ep 946).

For the most part it was Erasmus' controversy with Edward *Lee which caused him to suspect Briart of sinister machinations against him, or even of an actual conspiracy. In the spring of 1518, in his first public retort to Lee's criticisms of his New Testament, which again did not mention names, Erasmus dropped hints of his growing conviction that Lee was merely Briart's henchman (CWE Ep 843:538n). Later, as the controversy with Lee continued to agitate Erasmus beyond measure, his suspicions of Briart exploded in grave accusations, often veiled with transparent puns upon his name: Atensis ... Ate ... Noxus (Epp 948, 991, 993, 998, 1029). Additional attacks on Briart are to be found in the lampoons *Dialogus bilinguium ac trilinguium* and *Epistola de magistris nostris Lovaniensibus* (CWE 7 appendix; de Vocht CTL I 556–62, 571–2, 585–6, 594). As Erasmus was

ostensibly on good terms with Briart, he found no reason to object when the vice-chancellor was proposed as an arbiter in the bitter feud with Lee. Briart's health was failing, however, and despite the ministrations of his physician, Jan van *Winckele, he died in January 1520 without having pronounced a judgement. As a result both opponents were free to give their own interpretations of his presumed findings (CWE Ep 998 introduction).

It seems doubtful whether Briart deserved Erasmus' ire. If he was at all aware of the humanist's suspicions, he certainly did not allow himself to be diverted from his efforts at mediation. Although he again distrusted Briart's motives, Erasmus himself acknowledged his role in bringing about a truce with the Louvain theologians in the autumn of 1519 (CWE Epp 1022, 1028, 1029) and a few months earlier in permitting the sale in Louvain of his *Apologia contra Latomi dialogum* (Ep 960). When Briart was dead and the quarrel with Lee had abated Erasmus chose his *Spongia* against *Hutten (1523) to pay tribute to the vice-chancellor's fairness towards himself and the *bonae literae*, even though he called him irritable and suggested that he had been egged on by other theologians and by monks to play a sinister part (LB X 1649A–C; cf Allen I 22). As early as July 1520 and again later, he claimed that it had really been Jacobus Latomus who had stirred Briart to support his opponents (Epp 1123, 1804).

BIBLIOGRAPHY: Allen Ep 670 / *Matricule de Louvain* II-1 380, III-1 302, 400 / de Vocht CTL I 301–3, 313–14, and passim / H. de Jongh *L'Ancienne Faculté de théologie de Louvain* (Louvain 1911) 95–7, 149–51 / Karel Blockx *De verordeling van Maarten Luther door de theologische faculteit te Leuven in 1519* (Brussels 1958) 25–7, 30–2, and passim

PGB

Guillaume (I) BRIÇONNET d 13/14 December 1514

The son of Jean Briçonnet, treasurer of France, and Jeanne Berthelot, Guillaume was born in the mid-fifteenth century. He married Raoulette de Beaune, had three sons, and in 1483 was appointed *général des finances extraordinaires* in Languedoc and the Dauphiné, and later in Provence. His financial power,

personal influence over *Charles VIII, and
the high positions of many of his relatives
already gave him great political importance.
After his wife's death Guillaume embraced an
ecclesiastical career, becoming bishop of Saint-
Malo on 10 October 1493. He played a significant role in persuading Charles VIII to invade
Italy. Accompanying him there in 1494, he
was appointed a cardinal in Rome on 16
January 1495, and at Naples Charles VIII made
him a member of the royal council. In March
1495 he was sent to Florence to collect money
under the terms of the treaty the Republic had
made with the king of France. When Charles
VIII returned north, Guillaume was nearly
captured by Venetian *stradiotti* at the battle of
Fornovo (6 July 1495). He obtained the
bishoprics of Nîmes on 26 October 1496 and
Reims on 24 August 1497.

Unsatisfactory evidence has been used to
suggest that Guillaume was in Rome and
supervising the building of Santa Trinità dei
Monti in 1502, having stone sent from
Narbonne (of which he was not yet bishop); he
certainly was not in Rome in 1500 (Sanudo
Diarii III 844) or for the two conclaves of 1503;
in January 1504 he was at Lyon, and in
September 1505 was said to be going to
Brittany. By the autumn of 1506, however, he
had arrived in Milan and in November joined
*Julius II at Bologna. Erasmus may have seen
him there. He was present at the meeting in
Savona (June 1507) between *Louis XII and
*Ferdinand II of Aragon; some time after this he
went to Rome, being appointed cardinal
bishop of Albano on 17 September 1507, of
Frascati on 22 September 1508, and of
Palestrina on 3 June 1509. Meanwhile, on 17
December 1507, he also received the French see
of Narbonne. Guillaume was reported to be ill
in early October 1508 when Cardinal de
Clermont was staying with him in Rome
(Sanudo *Diarii* VII 647, 653); it is possible that
Erasmus met him there in 1509. In February
1510 Guillaume was again ill in Rome, with
gout (Sanudo *Diarii* x 13). In July 1510 he tried
to secure Cardinal de Clermont's release from
papal imprisonment and in August opposed
Julius II's excommunication of Alfonso I
d'*Este, duke of Ferrara. Subsequently he
disobeyed the pope's summons to join him at
Bologna, going from Florence to Genoa and

Guillaume (1) Briçonnet

then to Milan to join the other rebel cardinals
there and take a leading part in calling a
schismatic council under Louis XII's sponsor-
ship. In June 1511 he told the Florentine envoy
that if Pisa was not going to be made available,
the council could be held elsewhere. Deprived
on 24 October of all his dignities, as Andrea
*Ammonio reported to Erasmus (Ep 247),
Guillaume arrived at Pisa on 30 October. There
on 4 November he remonstrated with Niccolò
*Machiavelli about Florentine policy and on 12
November quarrelled with Cardinal Bernardino de *Carvajal; he left Pisa on 13 November
and on 1 December arrived back at Milan,
where the council resumed. Guillaume pronounced the deposition of Julius II in April
1512, but the worsening situation of the French
in Lombardy caused him to flee to Lyon. *Leo x
absolved and reinstated Guillaume on 7 April
1514, but on 13 or 14 December he died at the
episcopal palace of Narbonne.

Guillaume composed a breviary for Nîmes
in 1499 and a missal in 1511, and at his request
Paris de Grassis, papal master of ceremonies,
wrote and dedicated to him his *Ordo Romanus*.
A stained-glass window at Santa Trinità dei

Monti in Rome is said to be a contemporary portrait of him kneeling before Christ the Good Shepherd and St Juste.

BIBLIOGRAPHY: Allen Ep 247 and DHGE X 677–9 offer cursory treatment / Essential information is in Eubel II 23 and passim; Pastor v 455, 459, and passim; *Le due spedizioni militari di Giulio II* ed L. Frati (Bologna 1886) passim; Sanudo *Diarii* III 844, 1037, and passim / See also A. Renaudet *Le Concile gallican de Pise-Milan* (Paris 1922) and Y. Labande-Mailfert *Charles VIII et son milieu* (Paris 1975), which contains further bibliographical references / The statements about Santa Trinità dei Monti, apparently based on a friar's notes of documents pillaged in 1798, are in P. Clamet 'Une fondation française à Rome' *Annales de St. Louis des Français* 9 (1904) 202–3; they are repeated, with information about the stained glass, in F. Bonnard *Histoire du Couvent royal de la Trinité du Monte Pincio* (Paris-Rome 1933) 18, 55

D.S. CHAMBERS

Guillaume (II) BRIÇONNET 1472–24 January 1534

Guillaume was the son of Guillaume (I) *Briçonnet and Raoulette de Beaune. Raoulette's father, Jean de Beaune, started out as a draper in the city of Tours and became financial adviser to *Louis XI. His son Jacques became baron de Semblançay and superintendant of royal finances. The Briçonnet family likewise came from Tours and first established themselves in trade. Briçonnet's father ended his illustrious career in the church, as cardinal and archbishop of Reims.

The younger Guillaume Briçonnet studied in Paris at the Collège de Navarre. He was appointed a *président* of the Chambre des comptes and then became successively canon of the cathedral of Tours, canon of Reims, bishop of Lodève, and vicar-general of Reims. In 1507 he was sent to Rome on a diplomatic mission. The same year he was invested with the abbey of Saint-Germain-des-Prés. With the help of *Lefèvre d'Etaples he undertook to reform the abbey and to affiliate it with the reformed Benedictine congregation of Chezal-Benoît. In 1511 he took a leading role in the council of Pisa. Five years later he was sent to Rome again to conclude the negotiation of the

concordat of Bologna as well as a political alliance between France and Rome. This embassy coincided with his elevation to the bishopric of Meaux.

In 1518 Briçonnet began the reform of his diocese, reconstituting the Hôtel-Dieu, enforcing residence on the secular clergy, and restricting the activities of the Franciscans. At the beginning of 1521 he called Lefèvre d'Etaples, Pierre Caroli, Martial Mazurier, Gérard *Roussel, and other reformers into the diocese to assist with the work of reform. Briçonnet established preaching stations throughout the diocese to promote a more evangelical approach to Christianity and encouraged Lefèvre's translation of the New Testament (1523). He maintained ties to the court through *Margaret of Angoulême, the sister of *Francis I. His initiatives at Meaux were closely tied to the policy of the French court, particularly to its relationship with Rome. Through his close ties to Margaret of Angoulême he urged the king to extend the Meaux reform to the whole kingdom. In 1523 Francis I had appointed him and two other bishops to scrutinize the examination of the works of Erasmus, Lefèvre, and Louis de *Berquin conducted by the Paris faculty of theology (Clerval 356, 358), but in 1524 the monarchy began to lose interest in the Meaux reform. Moreover, popular unrest, which had been simmering since 1521, boiled over into radical preaching, dissemination of heretical literature, and ultimately iconoclastic acts. The Franciscans of Meaux and the faculty of theology of Paris had made complaints against Briçonnet as early as 1521, and the outbreak of radicalism in the town at the end of 1524 and beginning of 1525 and the king's captivity following the battle of Pavia now provided the occasion for his disgrace. At first artisans were arrested and imprisoned. In October 1525 the Parlement of Paris issued warrants against Lefèvre, Roussel, Caroli, and other leading evangelicals. Briçonnet himself was brought to trial before the Parlement by the Franciscans, rebuked for interfering with them, and fined for allowing heresy to spread through his diocese. In a letter to Erasmus in 1525 Noël *Béda noted Briçonnet's discomfiture (Ep 1579), arguing that it had occurred as a result of the publication of Lefèvre's New Testament.

In his response (Ep 1581), Erasmus bemoaned Briçonnet's fate and regretted that there were not more bishops like him. In the event, the return of the king marked Briçonnet's swift rehabilitation. An observer noted his reappearance at court in the spring of 1526, when he was said to have preached in a conservative manner (Herminjard I Ep 181), and in the same conservative manner he continued to administrate his diocese. Briçonnet died at the priory of Esmans, near Montereau.

Two works published by Briçonnet are essential for an understanding of the objectives of his reforms at Meaux, particularly in its initial stages. These are the sermons he delivered at synods of his diocese, convoked at Meaux in 1519 and 1520. The first of these had been translated and printed by H. Tardif and M. Veissière as 'Un discours synodal de Guillaume Briçonnet, évêque de Meaux (13 Octobre 1519)' Revue d'histoire ecclésiastique 71 (1976) 91–108. The second issued from the Paris press of Simon de *Colines in 1522 in Latin and in 1523 in French.

BIBLIOGRAPHY: L. Febvre 'Le Cas Briçonnet' in Au Coeur religieux du XVIᵉ siècle (Paris 1957) 145–61 / DBF VII 286 / M. Veissière 'Guillaume Briçonnet, abbé rénovateur de Saint-Germain-des-Prés (1507–1534)' Revue d'histoire de l'église de France 55 (1974), 65–84 / Guillaume Briçonnet and Marguerite d'Angoulême Correspondance (1521–1524) I ed M. Veissière et al (Geneva 1975) / H. Heller 'The Briçonnet case reconsidered' Journal of Medieval and Renaissance Studies 2 (1972) 223–58 / E.F. Rice ed The Prefatory Epistles of Jacques Lefevre d'Etaples (New York 1972) Ep 43 and passim

HENRY HELLER

Thomas BRICOT of Amiens, d 10 April 1516 Hubert Elie's conclusion that Thomas Bricot should be identified with Thomas Tricot, mentioned in François Villon's Grand Testament as 'a young priest from Meaux,' must be disputed: Bricot was from the diocese of Amiens, and furthermore a Thomas Tricot of Meaux did exist and received his BA in Paris around 6 March 1452. Thomas Bricot took his BA at Paris in February 1478 and his MA in March 1479 under Pierre Donville and incepted in 1480 under Pierre Bonnart. He taught philosophy at the Collège de Sainte-

Barbe in Paris for the nation of Picardy. He was a bursarius of the Collège des Cholets when he took his licence in theology on 13 January 1490 (ranking first among twenty-two) and his doctorate in March of that year. At that time, Bricot was the leading figure in Parisian philosophical studies, especially through his editions of Jean Buridan's versions of Aristotle's works and of Peter of Spain. These editions went through many printings in Paris, Lyon, Rouen, Caen, Basel, and even Venice.

On 23 November 1491, Bricot was named vice-chancellor of Sainte-Geneviève (that is, of the faculty of arts). He was dean of the church of Dammartin (diocese of Meaux). In 1492 he vigorously opposed the archbishop of Sens and fought against acceptance of the new bishop of Paris, and he was later fined heavily for this. In the same year he became a canon of the cathedral of Amiens and was diocesan théologal by 1497, when the chapter insisted that he lecture twice weekly there. Bricot donated funds for a statue of St Thomas in the cathedral altar retable. By 1502 he was back in Paris and was a canon of Notre-Dame, where he was also penitentiary from 1503 to 1516. Aside from participation in the affairs and decisions of the faculty of theology, where he often served as dean between 1506 and 1516, Bricot devoted his efforts towards the clerical and monastic reform movement instigated by his 1490 classmate Jan *Standonck, and to certain political and ecclesiastical interventions. On 14 May 1506, at the estates-general at Plessis-les-Tours, Bricot spoke for all the deputies in urging the marriage of King *Louis XII's daughter *Claude to the future King *Francis I, and Bricot was apparently the first to dub Louis XII 'père du peuple.' Bricot later officially welcomed Francis I in the name of the university at his royal entry into Paris in 1515. In 1511 he had supported the anti-papal council of Pisa-Milan. He was on the 1514 panel of Paris theologians investigating *Reuchlin and reported on suspect propositions in the Augenspiegel on 20 May 1514. Bricot was the butt of letter 54 in the Epistolae obscurorum virorum. Erasmus referred to him as a prime example of decadent learning (Ep 1304; ASD I-2 220). Bricot died in Paris.

Bricot's major works include Tractatus insolubilium (Paris: Antoine Caillaut 1489, Jean

Petit and François Regnault 1511); an edition of Jean Buridan *Textus summularum* (Paris: Jean Carcham 1487); *Textus abbreviatus totius logices* (Paris: Georges Mittelhus 1489); *Logicales questiones super duobus libris posteriorum Aristotelis* (Paris: Antoine Caillaut c 1490, Pierre Le Dru, Denis Roce 1504); *Textus abbreviatus Aristotelis super octo libris Physicorum et tota naturali philosophia* (Paris: Jean Higman and Wolfgang Hopyl 1494, Henri I Estienne et al 1504, Regnault Chaudière et al 1517); *Textus suppositionum logicae Petri Hispani* (Lyon 1494); an annotated edition of Georgius Bruxellensis *Expositio in logicam Aristotelis* (Paris, Caen, Rouen 1509, 1516); *Textus logices magna cum vigilantia castigatus* (Paris: Denis Roce c 1513, Jean de Gourmont c 1520).

BIBLIOGRAPHY: Allen Ep 1304 / *Auctarium chartularii universitatis Parisiensis* ed Charles Samaran et al III 780, IV 106–7, V 473 / Clerval 9, 92, 152, 175, and passim / H. Elie 'Quelques maîtres' *Archives d'histoire doctrinale et littéraire* 18 (1950–1) 197–200 / B. Moreau *Inventaire chronologique des éditions parisiennes* 2 vols (Paris 1972, 1977) / C. Prantl *Geschichte der Logik im Abendlande* (Leipzig 1927) IV 199–204 / Renaudet *Préréforme* 95–8, 438–9, and passim / Paris, Archives de l'Université (Sorbonne) Régistre 89 f lxvi recto

JAMES K. FARGE

BRICOTUS *See Edmund* BIRKHEAD

Germain de BRIE of Auxerre, d 22 July 1538
Germain de Brie (Brixius; the name form Brice is incorrect) was born in Auxerre around 1490. After he had studied law, his good fortune led him to Italy and Janus *Lascaris, whose guest and disciple he was at Venice in 1508. He met Girolamo *Aleandro and Erasmus, who were both attached to the press of Aldo *Manuzio, and also *Bembo. Leaving Venice in November of the same year, he went to Padua, where he studied with *Musurus, and subsequently to Rome, where he was a protégé, and perhaps the secretary, of Louis d'Amboise, bishop of Albi, the nephew of Cardinal Georges d'Amboise. It was very likely due to Louis' influence that Brie chose an ecclesiastical career and was made archdeacon at Albi.

After the death of his protector in May 1510,

Brie returned to France, where he entered the service of the chancellor, Jean de Ganay. When Ganay too died, in June 1512, Brie gained the protection of the queen, Anne of Brittany, by presenting to her an epic poem of 350 hexameters celebrating a recent episode in the naval war against England. It glorified the Breton captain Hervé de *Portzmoguer, who died aboard his ship on 10 August 1512. This poem, the *Chordigerae navis conflagratio* (Paris: J. Bade 13 January 1513, with an enthusiastic preface by Aleandro), became a target for Thomas *More's irony in his *Epigrammata*. Brie probably learned of More's verse in the summer of 1517 (Ep 620). He was so enraged that he published a pamphlet in verse against More, the *Antimorus* (Paris: P. Vidoue 1519). This edition of the pamphlet was accompanied by a page-by-page listing of the mistakes in More's poems and by the text of Epp 620 and 1045. Stunned by such acrimony (Ep 1087), More immediately prepared a retort, *Epistola ad Germanum Brixium* (London: R. Pynson 1520). Erasmus was greatly concerned by this quarrel which was dividing the republic of letters. When Brie first took offence Erasmus tried to prevent him from publishing his pamphlet (Ep 620). Afterward he intervened to calm tempers – with Brie both personally (Ep 1117) and through the good offices of his French friends, most notably Guillaume *Budé (Epp 1131, 1133), and also with More (Ep 1093), who agreed to suppress his reply (Epp 1096, 2379). After the end of 1520 the two protagonists accepted an uneasy truce, which was largely due to the efforts of Erasmus (Epp 1184, 1185, 1233).

Towards 1522, Brie returned to his Greek studies with Girolamo *Fondulo of Cremona. He was particularly attracted to St John Chrysostom and began to translate several of his works. Brie's translation of *De sacerdotio* in May 1525 (Ep 1733) – despite the faults of Josse *Bade's first edition – attracted the attention of Erasmus, who invited Brie to collaborate with him in his efforts to make Chrysostom more accessible (Ep 1736). Brie agreed (Ep 1800) and translated *De Babyla martyre, Contra gentiles*, the *Comparatio regis et monachi*, and later the first eight sermons on the Epistle to the Romans (Ep 2727), apparently with encouragement from

*Francis I (Ep 2405). In 1536, Brie was one of the two editors of the Chrysostom published in Paris by Claude Chevallon.

Brie's life was one of peaceful and refined ease. He combined the positions of secretary to the queen and almoner to the king. He also held several benefices in addition to the archdeaconship of Albi, being canon of Auxerre (1514–20), canon of Notre Dame of Paris (from 1519), and prior of Notre Dame of Duchaco and of Notre Dame of Brétancourt. In Paris, he owned two contiguous houses, where he received his friends in style. In 1526 Brie acquired a country property at Gentilly, where he could devote himself fully to his studies and where his old teacher, Lascaris, may have joined him during a last visit to France in 1526 and 1527 (Ep 1733).

Brie's many friends included Aleandro, Agostino *Trivulzio, Jacopo *Sadoleto, Girolamo *Vida, Jean de Tournon, Guillaume Budé (with whom he corresponded in Greek), Guillaume and Jean *Du Bellay, and Jean *Salmon. Of all the neo-Latin French poets, Brie was, in the opinion of the humanists, the most important.

The beginning of Brie's friendship with Erasmus at Venice was reflected in the publication of three epigrams by Brie – two in Greek, one in Latin – as prefatory pieces to Erasmus' *Adagia* in 1508. In November of the same year, Brie's presence at Padua induced Erasmus to stop there for a while (Ep 212). They were not to see each other again thereafter, but in 1517 their correspondence began when Brie, thinking that Erasmus was going to move to France, wrote to express his enthusiasm (Ep 569). The ensuing quarrel between Brie and More imposed a certain reserve on Erasmus, but his friendship for Brie was genuine, and he did his best to calm Brie down, while Brie apparently always considered himself a disciple of Erasmus. Not until 1526 and the work on Chrysostom, however, was their relationship truly one of master and disciple. Their letters on the subject of translating and editing Chrysostom (especially Epp 1736, 2291, 2379, 2405, 2422) are of great interest for our understanding of the humanist mind as well as of scholarship.

In 1528 and 1529, when the *Ciceronianus*

created a stir in France and caused a rift between Budé and Erasmus, Brie retained his friendship with the latter and laboured to clear up misunderstandings on both sides (Ep 2021). Thus he seems to have played a role in reconciling Erasmus with Jacques *Toussain, who had criticized Erasmus over the *Ciceronianus* (Ep 2340). In the *Ciceronianus* Erasmus showed his awareness of the many talents of Brie, who was at ease in Greek as well as Latin, in poetry as well as prose (ASD I-2 675–6; cf also Ep 1131). While deploring his slowness as a translator (Epp 2379, 2599), Erasmus held Brie in great esteem.

The poetical work of Brie includes, besides the *Chordigerae navis conflagratio* and the *Antimorus*, a number of elegies, encomia, and epitaphs; there are no modern editions of these. He also left a number of Greek and Latin letters. The major part of his writings is among the manuscripts of the Bibliothèque Mazarine, Paris. In September 1536 Brie composed an obituary for Erasmus in the form of a letter addressed to Guillaume Du Bellay as well as three epitaphs. These texts were printed in *Catalogi duo operum Des. Erasmi* (Basel 1537, reprinted among the preliminary pieces in LB I).

BIBLIOGRAPHY: Allen Epp 212, 2359 / CWE Ep 569 / DBF VII 294–5 / Jean Lebeuf *Mémoires concernant l'histoire civile et ecclésiastique d'Auxerre* (Paris 1743) II 501–2 / L. Delaruelle *Répertoire … de la correspondance de Guillaume Budé* (Toulouse-Paris 1907) Epp 8, 30, and passim / L. Delaruelle 'L'étude du grec à Paris de 1514 à 1530' *Revue du seizième siècle* 9 (1922) esp 143–5 / D. Murarasu *La Poésie nèo-latine et la renaissance des lettres antiques en France* (Paris 1929) 55–63 / M.-M. de la Garanderie 'Les épitaphes latines d'Anne de Bretagne par Germain de Brie' *Annales de Bretagne* 74 (1967) 377–96 / M.-M. de la Garanderie 'Un érasmien français, Germain de Brie' *Colloquia Erasmiana Turonensia* I 359–79 repr in *Christianisme et lettres profanes* (Lille-Paris 1976) I 171–203 / Guy Lavoie 'La fin de la querelle entre Germain de Brie et Thomas More' *Moreana* 13 no 50 (1976) 39–44 / Guillaume Budé *Correspondance* trans Guy Lavoie (Sherbrooke 1977) 45–84 / Yvonne Charlier *Erasme et l'amitié* (Paris 1977) 214–15, 244–8, and passim / P.G. Bietenholz *Basle and France in the Sixteenth Century* (Geneva-Toronto

1971) 194–5 and passim / David O. McNeil *Guillaume Budé and Humanism in the Reign of Francis I* (Geneva 1975) 54–5, 72–5, and passim

MARIE-MADELEINE DE LA GARANDERIE

René de BRIE *See René de* PRIE

Guilielmus BRIELIS (Ep 422 of 20 June [1516])
Brielis, the author of Ep 422, has not been identified. Perhaps his name was Willem van den Brielle, or conceivably he was a native of Brielle, a small town in Holland. He may have been a Carthusian monk.

E.J.M. VAN EIJL

Jean BRISELOT of Valenciennes, d 11 September 1520
Jean Briselot, of Valenciennes, in Hainaut, was a protégé of Guillaume de *Croy, lord of Chièvres, whose patronage marked him out for later promotion. In Paris, Briselot ranked third of twenty in the faculty of theology's licentiate class of 13 January 1500 (not 1502, as some sources assert), and his doctorate was completed on 18 March 1500. Briselot had joined the Carmelite order and in 1501, probably with a reform of discipline in mind, he tried to supplant the prior of the Paris Carmelite convent, but the Parlement of Paris ruled against him. He subsequently became prior in Valenciennes, where he carried out a reform in 1504. On 4 April 1505, he was made auxiliary bishop of Cambrai and administered the diocese until 1517. Briselot became a Benedictine after accepting the priory of Saint-Saulve, near Valenciennes, and the abbey of Saint-Pierre de Hautmont. In 1513, the abbot of St Médard of Soissons tried to excommunicate Briselot for failing to attend a synod of priors at Soissons. Briselot was also a canon of Ste Waudru, in Mons. In 1517, he became the confessor of the future *Charles V and on 23 December received the archbishopric of Oristano, in Sardinia. He resigned the latter benefice on 16 April 1520, reserving half the revenue for himself, and died five months later. Funeral monuments marked both his grave at Hautmont and the vault at the Carmelite priory of Valenciennes where his heart was interred.
    Briselot left several theological treatises in

manuscript, among them commentaries on the *Sentences* and on the penitential psalms. Josse *Bade dedicated to Briselot his edition of Baptista Mantuanus' *De calamitatibus suorum temporum* (Paris: Thielman Kerver 1499).
    From the time he left the Burgundian court and settled down at Louvain (the summer of 1517) Erasmus considered Briselot as one of his prominent enemies, doubly dangerous because of his influence with Charles (Epp 608, 628, 641, 1040) and especially critical of the *Moria* (Epp 597, 739); in consequence he spoke of him with frank animosity and also irony (Epp 695, 794).

BIBLIOGRAPHY: Allen Ep 597 / DHGE X 761 / Farge no 61 / P.-Y. Féret *La Faculté de theologie de Paris et ses docteurs les plus célèbres. Epoque moderne* (Paris 1900–10) II 364–5 / Irenaeus Rosier *Biographisch en bibliographisch overzicht van de vroomheid in de Nederlandse Carmel* (Tielt 1950) 67–8

JAMES K. FARGE

Johannes BRISGOICUS of Broggingen, d 31 October 1539
Johannes Brisgoicus (Calceatoris) of Broggingen, in the Breisgau, north of Freiburg, already had his MA when he matriculated at the University of Freiburg on 24 August 1499. He moved on to Paris, where he presided over the German student nation in 1500 and became a bachelor of theology. Johann *Amerbach considered asking him to tutor his sons, but on 17 February 1502 he accepted a position at the University of Freiburg. On 20 July he became regent of a residence, on 7 February 1503 a doctor of theology, and on 9 May a member of the theological faculty, receiving a chair in 1504. As he represented the Paris tradition of nominalism, his appointment was intended to help redress the balance between realists and nominalists at Freiburg, and in his first course of lectures he expounded Ockham. Until 1505 he also taught Aristotle in the faculty of arts, thereafter moving completely into the theological faculty. His annual salary of eighty florins initially was raised to a hundred in 1510. As dean for twenty-one terms and rector for another five, he was considered a leading academic, although he published nothing. In 1518 he prepared in the name of the university a submission on the reform of the calendar

which had been requested by *Maximilian I. In 1520 he established a scholarship in theology, with two more to follow in 1529, and in his will left another small sum to the university.

When Erasmus went to Freiburg in 1529 Brisgoicus offered him the use of his garden (Ep 2156) and may also have lent him some furniture, which after Erasmus' death caused a dispute between Brisgoicus and Margarete *Büsslin. He also brought about formal links between Erasmus and the university. Bonifacius *Amerbach wrote him a letter, now unfortunately lost, describing in some detail the death of Erasmus at Basel. In his reply Brisgoicus mentioned that he had sometimes heard Erasmus' confession and could attest to his Christian conduct. In his last will Erasmus left him a silver decanter.

BIBLIOGRAPHY: *Matrikel Freiburg* I 136–7, and passim / Schreiber *Universität Freiburg* I 150–4 / J.J. Bauer *Zur Frühgeschichte der theologischen Fakultät der Universität Freiburg i. Br.* (Freiburg 1957) 28, 45, 119–20, and passim / AK I Epp 132, 154, 157; IV Epp 2044, 2067; V Ep 2045a, and passim / H. Mayer in *Zeitschrift der Gesellschaft zur Beförderung der Geschichts- … und Volkskunde Freiburgs* 23 (1907) 294–300 / Öffentliche Bibliothek of the University of Basel MS G II 13a f 88: partial text of a letter (recommendation of Bruno *Amerbach) from Brisgoicus to Jacques *Lefèvre d'Etaples, about August 1506 (cf AK I Ep 315)

PGB

Pierre BRISSOT of Fontenay-le-Comte, 1478–d before 1 June 1525
Pierre, the son of Jean Brissot, a lawyer, was born in Fontenay-le-Comte in the Vendée. He studied and from 1504 also taught at the University of Paris, where he received a medical doctorate in 1514. A follower of the Greek medical authorities, he set out in 1518 to visit America in quest of new medicinal plants but was somehow detained in Evora, Portugal, where he practised for some years. His treatment of pleurisy aroused controversy in Portugal, and after his death his pupil Antonio *Lúcio of Evora published in Paris (S. de Colines, with a preface of 1 June 1525) his *Apologetica disceptatio* on blood-letting in the treatment of pleurisy, which was subsequently reprinted at Basel (1529) and Venice (1539). It is commonly asserted that he died at Evora in 1522, but in a letter of 1 January 1524 Jean *Lange lists him among the admirers and supporters of Erasmus in Paris (Ep 1407).

BIBLIOGRAPHY: Allen Ep 1407 / DBF VII 367–8 / *Index Aureliensis* (Baden-Baden 1962–) V 289–90

MICHEL REULOS

BRIXIUS Nordanus *See* PUISTUTH

Germanus BRIXIUS *See Germain de* BRIE

István BRODARICS d 8 November 1539
István Brodarics (Stephanus Brodericus, also Broderyth, Brodarich) was born of noble parents around 1471, probably in Slavonia. He became a protégé of György Szathmári, bishop of Pécs (Fünfkirchen, Quinqueecclesiae), who sent him to Italy for a university education; he entered the University of Padua and in 1506 obtained a doctorate in canon law. Upon his return to Hungary Brodarics became personal secretary to Szathmári. He was also canon of Zagreb and provost of Pécs (1521), and received another canonry at Esztergom (Gran) in 1524. Brodarics served on a number of diplomatic missions: in 1521 he was dispatched to Poland and in 1522 to Italy in an effort to secure help against the Turks from Venice and the papacy. In early 1524 he returned to Hungary but was almost immediately sent to Prague. He visited Rome again in 1525. In Italy he established friendly relations with many scholars, among them Paolo Giovio, *Bembo, and *Sadoleto. He left Rome in the spring of 1526 and returned to Hungary, where he was named royal chancellor and elevated to the bishopric of Szerém (Sirimium).

Brodarics accompanied King *Louis II on the ill-fated campaign against the Turks in August of 1526. He was present on the battlefield of Mohács (29 August) and was among the fortunate few who escaped, while King Louis, six bishops, and the flower of the Hungarian nobility perished in the battle. Brodarics made his way to join *Mary, the widowed queen, who had fled to Bratislava (Pressburg, Pozsony) after the news of the disaster had reached Buda. Brodarics was devoted to the queen and at first supported the claim of her brother, *Ferdinand of Hapsburg, to the

Hungarian throne. In the spring of 1527, however, he switched his allegiance to King *John Zápolyai, the candidate of the Hungarian national party; as a result he lost his position as chancellor. Brodarics remained in the service of John Zápolyai for the remainder of his life and was active in both the diplomatic and the ecclesiastical life of the kingdom. He was entrusted with crucial diplomatic missions to Poland (1527-39), Italy (1536), and the Empire and signed the important treaty of Várad between Ferdinand and John Zápolyai in 1538. Brodarics was rewarded for his services with the bishoprics of Pécs in 1532 and Vác in 1536. He died at his episcopal residence at Vác.

As early as 1505 Brodarics showed an interest in literature when he tried, unsuccessfully, to have the poems of *Janus Pannonius published by Aldo *Manuzio. Later he became a member of the Erasmian circle which developed at the Hungarian court around Jacobus *Piso. In 1529 he wrote to Erasmus, and the Dutch humanist replied (Ep 2178). He also carried on an active correspondence with Piotr *Tomicki, bishop of Cracow, with King *Sigismund of Poland, and others. His most important work was the eyewitness account of the battle of Mohács entitled *De conflictu Hungarorum cum Turcis ad Mohatz verissima descriptio* (Cracow: H. Wietor 1527). An important source of Hungarian history, this work was written to some degree as a defence against the attacks of some western European writers, especially Johannes Cuspinianus, who had charged that the Hungarians abandoned their king in battle. Some fifty letters were published by Gábor Kujani in 'Brodarics István levelezése' in *Történelmi tár* (1908) 258–93, 321–46 and by Sándor V. Kovács in *Magyarországi humanisták levelei* (Budapest 1971) 553–96. The most recent Hungarian edition of his account of the battle of Mohács is in *Humanista történetírok* ed Péter Kulosár (Budapest 1977) 289–328.

BIBLIOGRAPHY: Allen Ep 2178 / *Magyar irodalmi lexikon* (Budapest 1963–5) I 186–87 / *Magyar életrajzi lexikon* (Budapest 1967–9) I 266 / Pongrác Sörös *Jerosini Brodarics István, 1471–1539* (Budapest 1907) / Gábor Kujani *Adalékok a Brodarics család és Brodarics István életéhez* (Budapest 1913) / János Horváth *Az irodalmi*

müveltség (Budapest 1944) / *Acta Tomiciana* (Poznan-Wrocław 1852–   ) VI–XVII passim / W. Pociecha *Królowa Bona* (Poznan 1949–58) I–IV passim

L. DOMONKOS

Nicolaas van BROECKHOVEN of 's-Hertogenbosch, c 1478–d before 21 October 1553

Nicolaas van Broeckhoven (Brouchoven, Bruchhofen, Buschendorp, Nicolaus Buscoducensis, Klaas van den Bossche, etc) was born at 's-Hertogenbosch. He received the degrees of BA (1503) and MA at Louvain, where he afterwards worked for the printer Dirk *Martens and taught at St Martin's school. Around 1510 Maarten *Lips was one of his pupils. Broeckhoven was already a priest in 1514, when he was appointed rector of the municipal school of Middelburg; there he tutored Ludolf *Cock (Ep 2687). In 1517 he succeeded Johannes Custos Brechtanus as headmaster of the so-called Papenschool of Antwerp. Erasmus sent him greetings in the same year (Ep 616), and, although this was the first time Broeckhoven's name appeared in Erasmus' correspondence, the two had doubtless met long before, perhaps in the years when Erasmus was studying at 's-Hertogenbosch (c 1484–7). On 31 August 1521 Erasmus wrote to Broeckhoven in an attempt to dissuade him from abandoning his teaching position (Ep 1232), a step which Broeckhoven was evidently contemplating because of his growing sympathies for Lutheranism. On 9 February 1522 he was imprisoned by the Inquisition, along with his friend Cornelius *Grapheus. Erasmus was informed of these developments but continued to praise Broeckhoven as a good teacher and a morally upright man (Epp 1299, 1302, 1317?, 1318, 1351). In the spring Broeckhoven recanted and was released; he travelled to Basel, where, according to Erasmus, he was involved in the delivery of certain books (Ep 1431). He is also said to have been a professor of Latin and Greek at Basel, but this cannot have lasted long, for by November 1523 he had returned to Antwerp, intending, as he wrote to Erasmus, to remain under the eyes of his enemies, gaining vengeance on them by living virtuously (Ep 1394). He took up his old profession and, with several intermissions, lived at

Antwerp until August 1528. In 1525 he supported Robert de *Keysere in a new but unsuccessful attempt to found a university at Tournai.

In August 1528 Broeckhoven suddenly disappeared from Antwerp to turn up at Bremen, an open adherent of the Reformation. He married (cf Ep 2063) and had several children, including Hendrik (d 1576), court chaplain of Denmark from about 1553, and Anna (d 1552). By 1536 Broeckhoven had left Bremen; after a stay in Denmark he was appointed rector of the Latin school of Wesel on 29 July 1540 and became superintendent of Wesel on 23 June 1543. In 1548 he returned to Bremen and later he served as pastor of Blankenburg, in the Harz, where he died.

Nicolaas van Broeckhoven prepared many editions – for example, Richard of St Victor's commentary on the Apocalypse (Louvain: D. Martens 7 September 1513; NK 1803), Erasmus' translations of several dialogues of Lucian (Antwerp: M. Hillen 1517; NK 3436), and Plautus' *Curculio* and *Rudens* (Antwerp: M. Hillen c 1519–20; NK 3743–4). The abusive pamphlet called *Manipulus florum collectus ex libris Jac. de Hochstraten* (c 1520; NK 1485), several editions of which appeared under the pseudonym Nicolaus Quadus, is thought by some to have been Broeckhoven's work. While he was in Germany he composed a Lutheran creed, which was not published until the nineteenth century. He was among those addressed in Jan de Spouter's (Despauterius') *Syntaxis* (3rd ed, Paris: C. Chevallon c 1516–17), and Gerard *Geldenhouwer dedicated his *De Batavorum insula* (Antwerp: M. Hillen 19 September 1520; NK 978) to him.

BIBLIOGRAPHY: Allen Ep 616 / F. Rahlenbeck in BNB III 197–9 / A. Van Schelven in NNBW III 183–5 / M.A. Nauwelaerts in NBW I 282–3 / P. Kalkoff 'Der Inquisitionsprozess des Antwerpener Humanisten Nikolaus von Herzogenbusch i. J. 1522' *Zeitschrift für Kirchengeschichte* 24 (1903) 416–29 / P.J. Meertens *Letterkundig leven in Zeeland* (Amsterdam 1943) 48–9 / de Vocht CTL II 350

C.G. VAN LEIJENHORST

Antoine BRUGNARD documented 1522–47
Antoine Brugnard (Brugnarius, Brognard, 'Le Grec') bore the name of a village near

Montbéliard and was evidently a native of that region. In 1522 he had just ended an assignment as private tutor in the Netherlands, perhaps in part at Louvain, and was on the point of returning to Montbéliard when he left Antwerp precipitately for fear of being caught by the Inquisition, which had just arrested Nicolaas van *Broeckhoven (Ep 1318). He obtained a canonry at Montbéliard, and in October 1524 Erasmus, who clearly knew him well and trusted him, sent him an account of his troubles with Guillaume *Farel, who had by then moved to Montbéliard (Ep 1510). On 15 March 1532 Brugnard was appointed principal of the grammar school of Dole, and at about the same time he received a university appointment which carried the title of *rhetor*. Also in the spring of 1532 he negotiated on behalf of the university with Bonifacius *Amerbach, to whom he offered a legal chair at Dole. In April Brugnard visited Amerbach at Basel, but he eventually declined. After March 1540 Brugnard left Dole and taught for a while at Orléans, but in 1542 he had returned to Dole and until 1547 he resumed the direction of the grammar school. He maintained a correspondence with Amerbach, ordering scientific and other books from Basel, including Vesalius' *Fabrica*, and on one occasion passing on to Amerbach a medical prescription.

BIBLIOGRAPHY: Allen Ep 1318 / AK IV Ep 1611 and passim / Julien Feuvrier *Un Collège franc-comtois au milieu du XVIe siècle* (Dole 1889) 18–20, 22–4, 65–7 / Auguste Castan *Catalogue des incunables de la Bibliothèque publique de Besançon* (Besançon 1893) 649 / John Viénot *Histoire de la réforme dans le pays de Montbéliard* (Paris 1900) I 12–13

PGB

Stephanus BRULIFER of Saint-Malo, d c 1497–9
Born in Saint-Malo, Brittany, and professed in the Franciscan monastery of Dinan, Etienne Pillet, who called himself Brulifer (Brulefer), received a theological doctorate in Paris. His promising teaching career in Paris ended abruptly when he moved to Metz and subsequently to Mainz. Later in life he returned to Brittany and helped reform the houses of his order. He founded the monastery of Saint-Brieuc and died at Bernon, Morbihan.

Otto Brunfels

Among his works were widely used glosses on Duns Scotus and St Bonaventure's commentary on the *Sentences* of Peter Lombard.

In 1517 *Beatus Rhenanus used Brulifer's name among others to indicate Wolfgang *Lachner's interest in the commercial potential of voluminous scholastic compilations (Ep 575), but none of Brulifer's works were published by the press of Lachner and Johann *Froben.

BIBLIOGRAPHY: Allen and CWE Ep 575 / DTC II 1146–7 / DBF VII 500 / DHGE X 916–17 / Renaudet *Préréforme* 95 and passim

PGB

BRUMUS (Ep 106 of [October 1499])
John *Colet stated that Brumus had written to him, warmly recommending Erasmus. Brumus has not been identified. Allen suggested that the name may be a misprint for Grocinus, William *Grocyn.

Otto BRUNFELS of Mainz, c 1488–23 November 1534
Otto Brunfels was born in Mainz, the son of a cooper. Having obtained his MA by 1510, he entered the Carthusian monastery in Strasbourg and through Nikolaus *Gerbel was introduced to the Strasbourg humanist circle, including Ottmar *Nachtgall and *Beatus Rhenanus (BRE Epp 145, 165). Brunfels pursued his humanist studies and came to know *Hutten, *Capito, and Wilhelm *Nesen. In 1519 he published his first pedagogical treatises, which show the influence of Erasmus, whom he then admired sincerely (BRE Ep 176).

Brunfels was drawn to Luther and attempted to obtain a regular dispensation from monastic residence. He failed, however, to secure the support of Jakob *Spiegel and thus failed to secure the dispensation. In August 1521 he fled the monastery with his friend Michael Herr, under the protection of Hutten and the Strasbourg printer Johann *Schott. Hutten arranged an appointment for Brunfels as parish administrator of Steinau, where the latter became a close friend of Johannes ab Indagine, the parish priest of nearby Steinheim, on the Main. A secret Lutheran, Johannes was greatly interested in scientific studies, particularly mathematics and astrology. Forced to leave the region of Steinheim because of his Lutheranism, Brunfels started for Zürich, equipped with a recommendation to *Zwingli by Wilhelm Nesen, but on the way he was appointed pastor of Neuenburg, in the Breisgau. He continued to write polemics against the mass and embroiled himself in controversy with Erasmus.

Despite Hutten's death Erasmus had persisted in the publication of his *Spongia*, 'a sponge to mop up the spittle of Hutten.' Brunfels was grieved by this attack on his dead friend and wrote a response to Erasmus (Ep 1405), vehement in tone but attempting to keep open the possibility of a dialogue between the two sides. Erasmus responded only to the vehemence (Epp 1432, 1437, 1445) and complained to the Strasbourg magistrates, demanding that they take action against Brunfels and Schott, the printer (Ep 1477). Although Erasmus continued to react angrily to reprints of Brunfels' response and also held him responsible for other attacks, including a supposed caricature of himself on a title-page (Epp 1459, 1466, 1543, 1645, 1700, 1804, 2293, 2294, 2615), there was no complete rift between

them. Erasmus sent a reserved reply to a
conciliatory letter from Brunfels (Ep 1614), and
when he heard from Bonifacius *Amerbach
about Brunfels' doctoral promotion he complimented the University of Basel rather than
Brunfels (Ep 2788, spring of 1533).

Brunfels became a burgher of Strasbourg in
April 1524, married Dorothea Helg of Strasbourg, and opened a school in the city at the
request of Capito and *Bucer. His Lutheranism, tinged with the spiritualism of *Karlstadt,
kept him from forming close ties with the
Strasbourg reformers. He was always an
outsider and a target of complaint. He
continued to write prolifically, publishing one
of the first Protestant biblical concordances and
several volumes on the lives of men and women
of the Old and New Testaments. After 1530 he
was increasingly drawn to scientific work. His
Kreuterbuch published by Johann Schott was a
major contribution to botanical work. In 1532
he re-entered the University of Basel and
promptly received his degree as doctor of
medicine. He was appointed city physician of
Bern on 3 October 1533 and died there in the
following year.

The following is a list of selected works by
Brunfels, arranged chronologically by date of
publication (cf Index Aureliensis, Baden-Baden
1962– , v 337–52): De corrigendis studiis
severioribus praeceptiunculae (Strasbourg: J.
Schott 1519); Aphorismi institutionis puerorum
(Strasbourg: J. Schott 1519); Von der Zucht und
Underweisung der Kinder (Strasbourg: W.
Köpfel 1525); Vereum [sic for Verbum] Deo multo
magis expedit audire quam missam, ad episcopum
Basiliensem (Strasbourg: J. Schott 1524); De
ratione decimarum (Strasbourg: J. Schott 1524);
Pro Ulricho Hutteno vita defuncto ad Erasmi
Roterodami Spongiam responsio (Strasbourg: J.
Schott 1524); Catalogi virorum illustrium Veteris
et Novi Testamenti (Strasbourg: J. Schott 1527,
1528); Pandectarum Veteris et Novi Testamenti
libri xii (Strasbourg: J. Schott 1527); Loci omnium
fere capitum Evangelii secundum Matthaeum,
Marcum, Joannem (Strasbourg: J. Schott 1527,
1528, 1529, 1534); Pandectarum libri xxiii de
tropis, figuris et modis loquendi scripturarum
(Strasbourg: J. Schott 1528); Pandectarum
Veteris et Novi Testamenti libri xxii (Strasbourg: J.
Schott 1528, 1529, 1530, 1532); Precationes
Bibliae, sanctorum patrum, illustrium virorum et

mulierum utriusque Testamenti (Strasbourg: J.
Schott 1528); Annotationes in quattuor Evangelia
et Acta Apostolorum (Strasbourg: G. Ulricher
1535); Pandect Büchlin, beyläuffig aller Sprüch
beyder Testament Usszugk (Strasbourg: J. Schott
1529); Helden Büchlin ... der hohen gotterwölten
Männern und Weiberen ... beyder Testament
(Strasbourg: J. Schott 1529); Catechesis puerorum
in fide, in litteris et in moribus ex Cicerone,
Quintiliano, Plutarcho, Angelo Politiano, Rudol-
pho Agricola, Erasmo ... (Strasbourg: J. Schott
1529; Strasbourg: C. Egenolff 1529); Herbarum
vivae eicones ad naturae imitationem ... cum
effectibus earundem (Strasbourg: i J. Schott 1530,
ii J. Schott 1532, iii J. Schott 1536, i–iii J. Schott
1537); Contrafayt Kreuterbuch (Strasbourg: i J.
Schott 1532, 1534; ii J. Schott 1537 [a German
version of the Herbarium]); Catalogus illustrium
medicorum sive de primis medicinae scriptoribus
(Strasbourg: J. Schott 1530); Theses seu communes loci totius rei medicae (Strasbourg: G.
Ulricher 1532); Iatrion medicamentorum simpli-
cium libri iv (Strasbourg: G. Ulricher 1533);-
Neoticorum aliquot medicorum in medicinam
practicam introductiones (Strasbourg: J. Albrecht
1533); Ὀνομαστικὸν medicinae (Strasbourg: J.
Schott 1534, 1544).

BIBLIOGRAPHY: Allen Ep 1405 / NDB II 677–8 /
Johann Ficker and Otto Winckelmann Handschriftenproben des sechzehnten Jahrhunderts
(Strasbourg 1902–5) II 77 / Jean-Claude
Margolin 'Otto Brunfels dans le milieu
évangélique rhénan' in Strasbourg au coeur
religieux du xvie siècle (Strasbourg 1977) 111–41 /
Carlo Ginzburg Il nicodemismo (Turin 1970)
3–84 and passim (reproducing a portrait
etching of Brunfels by Hans Baldung Grien) /
P.W.E. Roth 'Otto Brunfels nach seinem Leben
und litterarischen Werken' Zeitschrift für
Geschichte des Oberrheins NF 9 (1894) 284–321
                                    MIRIAM U. CHRISMAN

Konrad BRUNNER of Weesen, d c 23 October
1519
When registering at the University of Basel in
1509, Brunner (Fonteius, Fontanus) indicated
that his home town was Weesen on the
Walensee, north of Glarus; but it seems that he
grew up at Brugg, between Zürich and Basel,
and that the town's mayor, Johann Grulich,
paid for his education. When first sent to Basel
in 1505 he was received into the house of

Johann *Amerbach and throughout his short life he remained closely connected with the Amerbach family and through them with the press of Johann *Froben. Even though he was dependent on them, the Amerbachs treated him rather like a member of the family, and he preferred to remain at Basel despite the prospect of a benefice in his native region of Glarus. When Erasmus went to Basel in 1514 Brunner enjoyed familiar contacts with him (Epp 313, 331; Epp 326, 338, 391 introductions) and after Erasmus' return to the Netherlands Brunner was remembered in his letters to Basel (Epp 464, 595, 630, 632). Much later Erasmus recalled Brunner's role in a prank his young Basel friends had played on a naïve caller (Ep 2486).

Meanwhile Brunner had entered the University of Basel in 1509 and graduated BA in 1511 and MA in 1513, studying together with Bonifacius *Amerbach and Hieronymus *Artolf. A year later Erasmus recommended him to *Zasius at Freiburg (Ep 313), where Bonifacius Amerbach was studying law, possibly because Brunner hoped to do likewise, supported by a scholarship. However, he remained at Basel and when *Glareanus left for Paris in 1517 Brunner, following his example, began to take on private pupils (Ep 632). Even Cardinal Matthäus *Schiner entrusted two nephews to his care. Brunner was also in regular contact with *Zwingli, since he was responsible for filling Zwingli's frequent orders for new books. He died suddenly of the plague.

BIBLIOGRAPHY: Allen and CWE Ep 331 / R. Wackernagel Geschichte der Stadt Basel (Basel 1907–54) III 180–1 and passim / AK I Ep 255 and passim / BRE Ep 71 (the author is Brunner) and passim / Zwingli VII Epp 15, 31, and passim / Martin Brunner 'Martin Schiner, ein Schüler des Conrad Fonteius zu Basel?' in Der Schweizer Familienforscher 18 (1951) 49–54 / Matrikel Basel I 297 / Öffentliche Bibliothek of the University of Basel MS C VI^a 30: Brunner's notebook, also containing personal accounts.

PGB

Ernest and Francis, dukes of BRUNSWICK-Lüneburg d 1546 and 1549 respectively
Ernest (later called 'the Confessor') was born on 26 June 1497, the second son of Duke Henry II (d 1532) of Brunswick-Lüneburg. Between 1512 and 1518 he studied at the University of Wittenberg under the supervision of Georgius *Spalatinus. From 1518 to 1521 Ernest attended the court of King *Francis I of France. His father supported Francis in his bid for the imperial crown (1519) and was forced to leave his duchy after the election of *Charles V. On 22 July 1522 Henry abdicated in favour of his sons. When Otto, the eldest brother, withdrew in 1527, Ernest shouldered the burden of governing the impoverished duchy, which was initially under the imperial ban. He married Sophia, the daughter of Duke Henry III of Mecklenburg-Schwerin, in 1528. From 1536 to 1539 Ernest ruled with his younger brother, Francis (1508–49). Both were staunch supporters of the Reformation and signed the 'Protestant' petition at the diet of Speyer in 1529. In 1530 Urbanus *Rhegius became the duchy's first superintendent. Ernest also joined the Schmalkaldic League, and in 1535 he founded a ducal court of justice based on Roman law. When Francis retired to Gifhorn, north of Brunswick, in 1539, Ernest remained the sole ruler. He died on 11 January 1546 in Celle. The dukes of Brunswick-Lüneberg are mentioned in Ep 2333 (1530) as signatories of the Augsburg Confession.

BIBLIOGRAPHY: Allen Ep 2333 / NDB IV 608 / Matrikel Wittenberg I 38

IG

Johannes BRUXELLANUS or BRUXELLENSIS See JAN of Brussels

John BRYAN of London, 1493–c October 1545
Bryan was born in London and from 1505 was educated at Eton. On 17 August 1510 he was admitted to King's College, Cambridge, where he was a fellow from 1513 to about 1526. In 1512–13 he met Erasmus at Cambridge, and occasionally served as his secretary (Ep 282). He received his BA in 1514–15 and his MA in 1518. He was ordained in 1517.

Bryan taught logic for two years in the university. In 1518 he seems to have lectured on Aristotle from the Greek texts. He became rector of Shellow-Bowells, Essex, in 1523. Bryan also wrote a history of the French (Ep 282) which was probably not published and has not survived. He was an acquaintance of

Pietro *Vannes and Petrus *Carmelianus (Ep 262). Erasmus sent Bryan greetings in letters to Henry *Bullock (Epp 456, 777, 826).

BIBLIOGRAPHY: Allen Ep 262 / DNB III 152–3 / J. and J.A. Venn *Alumni Cantabrigienses* (Cambridge 1922–54) I 43 / McConica 80

CFG

Johannes BRYSGOICUS *See Johannes* BRISGOICUS

Martin BUCER of Sélestat, 11 November 1491–27/8 February 1551

Martin Bucer (Butzer, 'Bucephalus,' 'Aretius Felinus'), the leader of the Strasbourg reform movement, was born to a shoemaker's family in Sélestat, in Alsace, and attended the famous Latin school there. Prompted by a desire for further learning he joined the Dominican order in 1506 and received a thorough training in scholastic thought. In 1516 he was sent to Heidelberg, the Dominican centre for theological studies, to continue his education. He studied Greek with Johann *Brenz, read the works of Erasmus, and was drawn to the humanist. Kohls suggests that Erasmus created a rationalist framework for Bucer's theology. Bucer received his BA and MA degrees from Heidelberg. In 1518 Bucer was present when *Luther presided over a disputation on his theses before the Augustinian order in Heidelberg, and Luther became the second major influence on his thought. Shortly thereafter Bucer began the canonical procedure for release from his monastic vows and, before a properly constituted ecclesiastical tribunal, was released from his order to become a member of the secular clergy.

Under the patronage of Franz von *Sickingen Bucer was given a preaching post at Landstuhl, west of Kaiserslautern. After Sickingen's defeat he resigned his post, planning to join Luther in Wittenberg, but on the way he was asked by Heinrich Motherer to join with him to establish the Reformation in Wissenbourg, in Lorraine. When the war against Sickingen was renewed, Bucer's presence compromised the town council since they were harbouring a protégé of Sickingen and the war was moving closer to their gates. In May 1523 Bucer took leave of his parishioners and went to Strasbourg to seek

Martin Bucer by Friedrich Hagenauer

the protection of the city as the son of a burgher (his father having become a citizen during Martin's childhood). Since he had married, the Strasbourg church could not appoint him to a pulpit, so he lectured on the Bible and on 31 March 1524 was chosen by the boisterous gardeners of the parish of Ste Aurélie as their pastor. From 1523 he played a major role in the development of the reformation in Strasbourg, evolving a theology influenced by Erasmus and Luther.

In his concept of baptism and confirmation Bucer remained close to the formulations of Erasmus, including the reaffirmation of baptism through confirmation, the *repraesentatio pristini baptismi*. Bucer and his fellow Strasbourg reformers wrote to Luther on 23 November 1524 (Luther W *Briefwechsel* III Ep 797) about the Eucharist, stating their accord with Luther's stress on the biblical words of institution, 'This is my body.' In this letter Bucer affirmed the authority of the Bible on the question and noted that Erasmus, 'enslaved by fame, preferred the spittle of his own opinion to the Holy Scripture.' This early agreement with Luther on the doctrine of communion was short-lived. Bucer later accepted Zwingli's interpretation that the words of institution were to be taken figuratively; in 1525 he suggested to Luther that the question of the meaning of the Eucharist should be allowed to rest, and that the reformers should be satisfied that the congregation participated in communion. While Luther and later Calvin became increasingly doctrinaire with regard to the Eucharist, Bucer continued to believe that it must be left a mystery, its true nature veiled.

During the early years of the reform movement Bucer and his colleagues continued to be influenced by Erasmus; indeed their indefatigable efforts in the direction of ecumenicism stemmed from his teaching and the attitudes they had learnt from him. When Otto *Brunfels and Erasmus quarrelled and were sharply divided in 1523 and 1524, the other Strasbourg reformers were not involved because they were not closely tied to Brunfels. As late as 1527 Bucer was attempting to win Erasmus over to the Reformation. Erasmus replied that he refused to pass judgment on the new tenets or to condemn Bucer, but his conscience would not let him join the evangelicals; there were too many hypocrites in the new churches and too much quarreling among them (Ep 1901).

In 1529, however, a controversy developed which created a serious rift between the two men. Gerard *Geldenhouwer, a Dutch refugee living in the city, who was a friend of Erasmus and had joined the reformers in 1525, published Erasmus' Apologia adversus ... monachos without asking his permission. He added to the tract his own plea for toleration towards the evangelicals. Erasmus was deeply angered and responded with his Epistola contra pseudevangelicos, which attacked not only Geldenhouwer but also the Strasbourg and other South German and Swiss reformers. He condemned them for having destroyed the cause of the Gospel among the princes and those in authority. He also took issue with Bucer for publishing his exposition of the Psalms (1529) under a transparent pseudonym, presenting it as the work of a Frenchman from Lyon (LB X 1581D, 1592A, 1602D). The Strasbourg reformers attempted to defend themselves in their letter Epistola apologetica, published jointly but written by Bucer. They

pointed out to Erasmus that in his own letters he had urged the necessity of reform and that any reform based on the principles of the Gospel demanded relinquishing the status quo. Bonifacius *Amberbach reported the imminent publication of the Strasbourg Epistola to Erasmus in April 1530 (Ep 2312). Letters from Erasmus in the following month reflect his scorn and contempt for the Strasbourg reformers (Epp 2321, 2324, 2365). Throughout the summer of 1530 Erasmus was obsessed by the affair, attempting to track down through his friends anyone who had aided the Strasbourg reformers in writing the apology (Epp 2371, 2392). In August 1530 Erasmus published his counter-attack, Epistola ad fratres inferioris Germaniae, bitter with hatred, which condemned the reformers for breaking with the continuous tradition of the universal church and for their inability to come to an agreement among themselves with regard to the Eucharist. Bucer and his colleagues made no attempt to reply, in part because they still maintained their respect and esteem for Erasmus. Erasmus, however, did not find it easy to forgive Bucer.

In 1531 Sebastian *Franck published his Chronica, in which Erasmus was listed among the heretics opposing the corrupt papal church. Erasmus did not accept this as a compliment but saw his position threatened by this unbridled radical. Since it was published in Strasbourg, Erasmus at first charged Bucer with responsibility for the book and later with at least encouraging the author, and he met Bucer's overtures in an unforgiving spirit (Epp 2587, 2615). In March 1530 Erasmus, while insisting that he had never met Bucer personally, grudgingly admitted to his earlier regard for him (Ep 2441). Bucer in turn remained conciliatory. When passing through Basel early in 1536 after talks on the first Helvetic Confession, Bucer and *Capito paid a courtesy visit to Erasmus. The conversation they had together was described by Sigismundus *Gelenius as jovial and intent on avoiding serious topics; see O. Clemen in Basler Zeitschrift für Geschichte und Altertumskunde 43 (1944) 17–33; Melanchthons Briefwechsel II Ep 1709.

Meanwhile the Strasbourg church drew up its own articles of faith, which were confirmed by a synod held in 1533. A new church organization was established, and Bucer later became the president of the ministers of all the churches in the city. In 1531 he had assumed the pulpit of St Thomas' church and was appointed deacon of the St Thomas chapter. He played an important role in political and religious affairs outside the city: in 1532 he was at Schweinfurt, in 1536 he participated in the Wittenberg concord, and in 1537 he was at Schmalkalden. Closely associated with Philip of *Hesse, he assisted in the organization of the new territorial church in Hesse. At the invitation of Hermann von *Wied, he was also active in the archdiocese of Cologne between 1541 and 1543, collaborating with *Melanchthon. During the 1540s he took part in the colloquies which attempted to reunite Catholics and Protestants, composing with Johann *Gropper the articles which were debated at Regensburg (1541). When the Augsburg Interim was introduced in Strasbourg (1548) Bucer was forced to leave. He was invited to England by Archbishop *Cranmer and assisted in the revision of the Anglican Book of Common Prayer. He was given an appointment at Cambridge University and wrote his major theological work, *De regno Christi*. He died in February 1551 and was buried in Cambridge. When Mary Tudor ascended the throne she ordered his bones exhumed, and his remains were excommunicated with bell, book, and candle. Elizabeth redressed this by a second reburial with the full ceremonial of the Anglican church.

A critical edition of Bucer's complete works is now in progress: *Deutsche Schriften* ed R. Stupperich (Gütersloh 1960–   ); *Opera latina* ed C. Augustijn et al (Gütersloh-Leiden 1954–   ); *Correspondance* ed J. Rott et al (Leiden 1979–   ). The following is a list of selected works by Bucer (cf also *Index Aureliensis*, Baden-Baden 1962–   , V 412–34): *An ein christlichen Rath und Gemeyn der Statt Weissenburg Summary seiner Predig daselbst gethon: mit anhangender Ursach seins Abscheydens* (Strasbourg: J. Schott 1523); *Das ym selbs niemant, sonder anderen leben soll* (Strasbourg: J. Schott 1523); *Verantwortung uff das im seine Widerwertigen, ein Theil mit der Worheit, ein Theil mit Lügen, zum ärgsten zumessen* (Strasbourg: J. Schott 1523); *Erhaltung christlicher Leer bitzhär zu Straszburg gepredigt* (Strasbourg: J. Schott 1524); *Praefatio in quartum*

tomum Postillae Lutheranae, continens summam doctrinae Christi (Strasbourg: J. Herwagen 1527); *Epistola D. Pauli ad Ephesios ... in eandem commentarius* (Strasbourg: J. Herwagen 1527); *Enarrationes in evangelia Matthaei, Marci et Lucae* (Strasbourg: J. Herwagen 1527); *Commentaria in librum Job* (Strasbourg: n pr 1528); *Vergleichung D. Luthers unnd seins Gegentheyls vom Abentmal Christi* (Strasbourg: W. Köpfel 1528); *Enarratio in evangelion Iohannis* (Strasbourg: J. Herwagen 1528); *Epistola apologetica ad syncerioris Christianismi sectatores per Frisiam orientalem ... in qua evangelii Christi vere studiosi ... iis defenduntur criminibus, quae in illos Erasmi Roterodami epistola intendit* (Strasbourg: P. Schöffer and J. Schwintzer 1530); *Confessio religionis christianae* (Strasbourg: G. Ulricher 1531); *Bekandtnusz der vier Frey und Reichstätt, Straszburg, Constanz, Memmingen und Lindaw* (Strasbourg: J. Schwintzer 1531; Strasbourg: T. Rihel 1579); *Commentarius in Ecclesiasten* (Strasbourg: n pr 1532); *De vera ecclesiarum in doctrina, ceremoniis, et disciplina reconciliatione et compositione* (Strasbourg: W. Rihel 1542); *Acta colloquii in comitus imperii Ratisponae habiti* (Strasbourg: n pr 1541); *Alle Handlungen und Schrifften zu Vergleichung der Religion auff jüngst gehaltnen Reichstag zu Regenspurg* (Strasbourg: W. Rihel 1541); *Ein summarischer Vergriff der christlichen Lere und Religion zu Straszburg gelehret* (Strasbourg: W. Köpfel 1548); *Vom Reich Christi unsers Herren* (Strasbourg: W. Rihel 1563); *De regno Christi* ed François Wendel (Paris 1955).

BIBLIOGRAPHY: Allen Ep 1901 / R. Stupperich in NDB II 695–7 / C. Augustijn 'Strasbourg, Bucer et la politique des colloques' in *Strasbourg au coeur religieux du xvie siècle* (Strasbourg 1977) 197–206 / Heinrich Bornkamm *Martin Bucers Bedeutung für die europäische Reformationsgeschichte* (Gütersloh 1952) / *Bucer und seine Zeit: Forschungsbeiträge und Bibliographie* ed Marijn de Kroon and Friedhelm Krüger (Wiesbaden 1976) / Jacques Courvoisier *La Notion d'église chez Bucer dans son développement historique* (Paris 1933) / Hastings Eells *Martin Bucer* (New Haven 1931) / Johannes Ficker and Otto Winckelmann *Handschriftenproben des sechzehnten Jahrhunderts* (Strasbourg 1902–5) II 58–9 / J.V. Pollet *Martin Bucer, études sur la correspondance* (Paris 1958–62) / Ernst-Wilhelm Kohls 'Martin Bucer: Erasmien et Martinien' in *Strasbourg au coeur religieux du xvie*

siècle (Strasbourg 1977) 167–83 / Ernst-Wilhelm
Kohls *Die Schule bei Martin Bucer in ihrem
Verhältnis zu Kirche und Obrigkeit* (Heidelberg
1963) / Ernst-Wilhelm Kohls *Die theologische
Lebensaufgabe des Erasmus und die oberrheinische
Reformation* (Stuttgart 1969) / Friedhelm Krüger
*Bucer und Erasmus: Eine Untersuchung zum
Einfluss des Erasmus auf die Theologie Martin
Bucers* (Wiesbaden 1970) / Jean Lebeau
'Erasme, Sébastien Franck et la tolérance' in
Erasme, l'Alsace et son temps Exposition 1970
(Strasbourg 1971) 117–38 / Nicole Peremans
Erasme et Bucer d'après leur correspondance (Paris
1970) / Bernard Roussel 'Martin Bucer exégète'
in *Strasbourg au coeur religieux du XVIe siècle*
(Strasbourg 1977) 153–6 / David C. Steinmetz
Reformers in the Wings (Philadelphia 1971)
121–32

MIRIAM U. CHRISMAN

Philipp BUCHAMMER
See Philipp PUCHAIMER

Bernardus BUCHO *See Bernard Bucho van*
AYTTA

BUCKINGHAM *See Edward* STAFFORD

BUCLERIUS *See* BEUCKELAER

Michael BUDA *See Michel* BOUDET

Dreux (I) BUDÉ of Paris, 1 March 1456–1528
Dreux, the elder brother of Guillaume *Budé,
inherited by right of primogeniture one half of
the estate of his father, Jean *Budé (Ep 583),
including the seigneuries of Yerres and Marly,
and in 1497 succeeded to the offices of *trésorier
des chartes* and *audiencier de la chancellerie*, which
his father had held for a time. Soon after their
father's death Dreux ceded the Marly estate to
Guillaume, who acknowledged Dreux's support and encouragement when he had
returned to court and felt oppressed by his
duties (Delaruelle Ep 105). When Dreux died
he left an estate worth fifty thousand livres.
His son Jean continued the family tradition and
became a royal secretary.
   BIBLIOGRAPHY: CWE Ep 583 / D.O. McNeil
*Guillaume Budé and Humanism in the Reign of
Francis I* (Geneva 1975) 4, 59, and passim / L.
Delaruelle *Répertoire de la correspondance de*

Guillaume Budé (Toulouse-Paris 1907) Epp 6,
105, 136

PGB

Dreux (II) BUDÉ of Paris, b circa 1507
Dreux (Draco) was the eldest son of Guillaume
*Budé and Roberte *Le Lieur. His father had
great expectations for him and entrusted his
tuition to a noted Greek scholar, Guillaume du
Maine. Among Budé's letters of the years
1519–21 there are seven in Latin to Dreux and
fifteen to Guillaume du Maine entirely in
Greek. Bartholomaeus *Latomus did not, as is
sometimes claimed, tutor Dreux but his
younger brothers. The father at times took
personal charge of Dreux's education; in 1524
Dreux was said to be Guillaume du Maine's
only pupil apart from Jacques *Toussain (Ep
1407). It seems that Dreux was talented but not
overly diligent. Josse *Bade dedicated to him
his edition of Cicero's *Orationes* (Paris: 13
January 1522, reprinted 1527 and 1531).
   Dreux became a royal secretary and master of
requests (*avocat aux requêtes de l'hôtel*). After
his father's death he endeavoured to succeed
to Guillaume's position in the secretariat of the
city of Paris but was turned down in August
1540 and again in July 1541, despite a petition
submitted by three of his brothers and the
support of the chancellor, Guillaume Poyet.
While his mother and two of his brothers, Jean
and Louis, embraced Calvinism, Dreux remained a Catholic. He did not leave behind any
writings.
   BIBLIOGRAPHY: E. de Budé *Vie de Guillaume
Budé* (Paris 1884) 297 / L. Delaruelle *Répertoire de
la correspondance de Guillaume Budé* (Toulouse-
Paris 1907) Ep 31 and passim / Budé's Greek
letters to Guillaume du Maine were translated
into French by Guy Lavoie: Guillaume Budé
Correspondance (Sherbrooke 1977) 223–44 / D.O.
McNeil *Guillaume Budé and Humanism in the
Reign of Francis I* (Geneva 1975) 85 and passim
M.-M. DE LA GARANDERIE

Guillaume BUDÉ of Paris, 26 January 1468–
22 August 1540
Guillaume Budé (Budaeus) was descended
from a bourgeois family that in the fifteenth
century had moved from Auxerre to Paris and
attained noble rank while occupying positions
in the royal treasury and chancery on a

quasi-hereditary basis. Guillaume, the second son of Jean *Budé, had an elder brother, Dreux (I) *Budé, and two younger brothers, Etienne (d 1501) and Louis *Budé, Guillaume's favourite.

By 1483 Budé went to Orléans, where he studied law for three years – without enthusiasm and accordingly with little profit. Thereafter he lived a life of leisure for five years during which the hunt seems to have been his greatest pastime. By 1491, however, with the suddenness of a religious conversion, Budé decided to devote himself totally and whole-heartedly to the pursuit of learning. In later years he would recall this turning point with pride and self-satisfaction (notably in Ep 583 and in the *De philologia, Opera omnia* I 35). It is on the basis of this conversion that he came to be seen as a sort of pioneer of the new culture, a hero or symbol. Budé's humanist culture was not handed down to him – he acquired it through his own application. He learnt Greek without a teacher (except for a few mediocre lessons given him by Georgius *Hermonymus) and often lacked suitable books (except for a few manuscripts provided by Janus *Lascaris). To the pursuit of learning he sacrificed both his social ambitions and his health. Throughout his life he suffered from violent headaches which were accompanied by fits of anxiety and were, of course, incurable at that time. He also represented a new type of man of letters in that he was not a member of the clergy but a married man; while he never knew poverty, he was nonetheless burdened with the responsi-bilities of a family man and the management of his properties. By 1505 he married Roberte *Le Lieur and they had twelve children, of whom at least eight survived. To an estate at Marly which he had received from his brother Dreux, he added an estate at Saint-Maur, building a country house on each of them. In 1519 he purchased a house on the rue Saint-Martin in Paris (Ep 915). In addition to these private burdens he had to shoulder duties in the service of his king, especially after 1522.

Budé had been a secretary to King *Charles VIII but retired from the royal court during the reign of *Louis XII, although he did serve on two embassies to Italy, one in 1501, the other in 1505. With the ascent to the throne of *Francis I, Budé saw a chance of gaining royal support

Guillaume Budé by Jean Clouet

for the humanist cause and let it be known (cf the epilogue of *De asse, Opera omnia* II 314–15) that he was available for service. It is unlikely that as early as 1515 Budé took part in a mission to Pope *Leo X, as was claimed by Francesco Guicciardini (cf McNeil 45). For the first three years of the new reign, Budé remained in the wings, and in 1517 he participated in the negotiations between Erasmus and the French court, but only in a semi-official capacity (Epp 522, 568). In 1519 Budé presented to the king a manual of advice based on examples from ancient history. Written in French, this work was published after his death under the title *L'Institution du prince* in three different and conflicting editions. In May 1519 Budé went with an embassy to Montpellier (Ep 924). In June 1520 he participated in the meeting on the Field of Cloth of Gold (Ep 1106) and there met Thomas *More, with whom he had corres-ponded since 1518. The two men discovered that they had much in common. Afterwards Budé followed the court to Amboise, Blois, Romorantin, Dijon, Autun, Troyes, and Reims.

In 1522, more honours and responsibilities fell to him. In July, when the court was in Lyon and Budé had taken the liberty of returning to his family, news of his appointment as master of requests in the royal household reached him. He was sworn in by the Parlement on 21 August and retained this position throughout his lifetime. On 16 August he was elected provost of Paris merchants, an appointment given to him for a term but conceivably renewed. In any case, at the time of his death he still retained his seat in the administration of the city of Paris. Finally, the post of royal librarian (maître de la librairie du roi) was created especially for him and granted him for life; there is no record, however, of his duties and actions in this capacity.

As a master of requests, Budé followed the king's court; in September 1523 and again from October to December 1524 he was in Lyon. In 1523 he participated in the investigation of the accomplices of Constable Charles de Bourbon. According to an unconfirmed tradition Budé was one of the judges of Louis de *Berquin during the last trial in 1529, and possibly also in the 1523 trial. After the battle of Pavia there was a rupture of relations between the chancellor, Antoine *Duprat, and the Budé family, and Guillaume ceased following the court from 1525, allegedly for reasons of health. Ten years later, when Duprat was succeeded by Guillaume Poyet, Budé was again greatly in favour and became the chancellor's inseparable adviser. He fell ill in the course of a royal visit to Normandy in July 1540 and died in Paris. In his will, which removes any doubt as to his Catholic orthodoxy, he asked to buried at night, without ceremony, in his parish church of St Nicolas-des-Champs.

Budé does not seem to have been very active in the execution of his official functions. His offices had been given to him largely on account of his status as the most important French scholar. He constantly complained that they interfered with his studies, but they nevertheless provided him with a forum in which he could more readily and more effectively plead the cause of higher learning. In effect, the advancement of learning was the only public cause he ever had at heart. He untiringly promoted the foundation of a trilingual college and, although he did not actually found the Collège de France, his

pleas, both oral and written (especially in the Greek preface to Commentarii linguae graecae, 1529, Opera omnia III f α 2–3), demonstrated a stubbornness of purpose which greatly helped to bring about the creation of the royal lectureships (1529). He returned to the same cause in 1532 in De philologia, when he reminded the king of his promise to erect a splendid building dedicated to Minerva and the Muses (Opera omnia I 94–5). After the placards affair of October 1534 it seems that Budé wished to demonstrate his orthodoxy. Especially in De transitu Hellenismi ad Christianismum (1535) he sought to dissociate the cause of learning from that of heresy. After all, the bonae literae, philological scholarship, had always been the passion of his life.

Budé had first forged his skills by translating into Latin four treatises of Plutarch (De placitis philosophorum, De fortuna Romanorum, 1503; De tranquillitate et securitate animi, De fortuna vel virtute Alexandri, 1505) and St Basil's letter to St Gregory of Nazianzus on solitude (1505). Next he turned to the study of law and published the Annotationes in quattuor et viginti Pandectarum libros (1508). Budé approached the law not as a practitioner but rather as a philologist anxious to disencumber the text of its numerous glosses which obscured the meaning and encouraged quibbling. He also approached the law philosophically (tackling the broad questions of the origin and nature of law from the first books of the Digest, or Pandects) and historically (rediscovering through legal texts the everyday realities of ancient life).

De asse et partibus ejus (1515, second edition 1516) is likewise addressed to the facts of ancient life. The aim of this substantial work, which again uses a law of the Digest as a point of departure, is to rediscover the value of all measures and monies of antiquity and to make an inventory of the wealth of the ancients. But it also attempts to make the reader reflect on the wealth of the modern age, its social injustices, and the abuses of the church. Above all, it suggests a set of values ranging from material goods and profane knowledge to sacred study and divine wisdom. The philosophical import of the work mostly derives from a crowning epilogue of a hundred pages. De asse is thus universal in its appeal, but its complex structure discouraged many readers, including Erasmus (Ep 480). In order to dedicate this work to his best friend, François *Deloynes, Budé concluded with a dialogue between them on the role of philosophers at court and in the market-place. After the publication of *De asse*, Budé was celebrated as the principal French humanist, equal to Erasmus, or indeed superior. Comparing them became a popular pastime (Epp 571, 914).

After *De asse*, Budé's work developed in the two directions that his first works had suggested: scholarly study and the philosophical essay. He pursued his studies on the Pandects with deliberateness and in 1526 published the *Annotationes posteriores*. In 1529 he provided future lexicographers with his substantial *Commentarii linguae graecae* (reprints appeared as early as 1530 in Cologne, Basel, and Venice, an enlarged edition in 1548). At his death Budé left unfinished a book on ancient procedural terms entitled *Forensia* (included in *Opera omnia* III), seven large notebooks of 'Adversaria' (collections of sayings and quotations), and some lexicographical notes which all authors of Greek dictionaries of that century would consult.

Budé's philosophical thought – already largely in evidence in several passages of *De asse* – was further developed in *De contemptu rerum fortuitarum* (1520). In November 1532 he published *De philologia* (a dialogue on eloquence and a plea in favour of the *bonae literae*), together with *De studio literarum recte ac commode instituendo*. The latter work extends the treatment given in *De asse* of the relationship between secular and sacred learning (*Christianismus*) and introduces the mystical notion of *transitus*, which would be central to *De transitu Hellenismi ad Christianismum* (1535). Budé's philosophy is above all a philosophy of culture, the crucial question being when and how to insert ancient culture into the intellectual and spiritual life of the Christian. Despite a number of analogies with Erasmus, the autonomy of Budé's thinking cannot be in doubt. Budé is a difficult author; he presents his arguments in a style which is excessively flowery and obscure. In fact the effort required to read him has always tended to discourage even serious scholars. The only edition of his collected works that we possess

was edited in Basel by an Italian religious exile, Celio Secondo Curione, in 1557.

Budé and Erasmus kept up a copious correspondence – begun in 1516 at the initiative of Erasmus – of which forty-eight letters remain. Except for one ambiguous reference in Ep 906 there is no evidence that the two men had ever met in Paris. The friendship which they pledged each other – and in which they wanted to include some of their best friends: *Tunstall, *Deloynes, *Ruzé, and *More (Ep 1233) – was purely literary and theoretical; neither of them ever recalled a shared moment or experience. Their correspondence began when both men were at the peak of their fame. The second edition of *De asse* was about to be published; Erasmus had just completed his New Testament, and in many places in his accompanying *Annotationes* he made reference to points clarified by Budé in the *Annotationes* to the Pandects or *De asse* (LB VI 30E [misnumbered 28] 103E, 288F, 295E, 299E, 1102F). Above all, Erasmus inserted after his note on Luke 1:4 a long commendation of Budé. François Deloynes discovered and showed this to Budé on 27 April 1516 (Ep 403, *La Correspondance* ed M.-M. de la Garanderie 269–70; this commendation was omitted from editions after 1527).

The correspondence thus began in an atmosphere of enthusiasm and was at first concerned with questions of biblical exegesis (Epp 403, 441). Subsequently, with that frankness of opinion which would prove nearly fatal to their friendship, the two authors compared and contrasted their respective virtues and weaknesses in infinite detail. If their views were generally compatible, their approaches to the common philological task and their styles were not (Epp 435, 480, 493). Budé felt that Erasmus wasted his time and his genius on minor *opuscula*; Erasmus found Budé's works obscure and overloaded with erudition and flowery rhetoric. Personal incompatibility led increasingly to misunderstandings; neither was sure that he could tell the other's jokes from his jabs. Thus, during the first two years, their long and frequent letters became marred by bitterness and sensitivity. A crisis was reached in the autumn of 1518 when Budé dramatically announced a rupture, which Erasmus refused to accept (Epp

896, 906; cf CWE 6 preface). The correspondence then became prolonged, continuing intermittently for almost ten years.

This conflict-ridden correspondence also reflected the state of relations between Erasmus and France. When it began, Erasmus and Budé both had a vested interest in this bond of their friendship. Correspondence with Erasmus gave Budé international fame. For Erasmus, who already had an international reputation and had recently returned from England, the correspondence might lead to new national roots. It would help him to assess the situation in France, where the new king, Francis I, seemed to think that Erasmus' presence would add to the prestige of his reign. The terms of an invitation for Erasmus were discussed from February 1517 (Ep 522). In letters set aside for publication Budé merely echoed the proposals officially presented to Erasmus at Brussels by Bishop Etienne *Poncher. But we can infer from Ep 568 that Erasmus also used Budé as a private source of information. Budé scrupulously informed Erasmus of the progress of the king's project and the reaction of the influential courtiers, even though from the summer of 1517 the quarrel between *Lefèvre d'Etaples and Erasmus and particularly Erasmus' unsparing *Apologia ad Fabrum* displeased the French in general and Budé and his friends in particular (Epp 744, 778, 810, 906). The royal invitation was renewed in 1524, this time with Budé as spokesman (Epp 1439, 1446), but Erasmus did not appear to be interested. Gradually Budé and his friends seemed to reach the conclusion that Erasmus disliked the French (Ep 1812). This explains the hostile reaction that greeted the *Ciceronianus* when the first edition appeared in Paris in August of 1528.

The *Ciceronianus* seemed to casually relegate Budé, the national glory of France, to the modest station of a Josse *Bade (ASD I-2 672–3). French indignation reached a peak and was reflected in pamphlets of verse, which were attributed to Lascaris and Jacques *Toussain. Erasmus was informed by Germain de *Brie (Ep 2021) and Gervasius *Wain (Ep 2027). He seemed surprised and always protested his innocence (Epp 2046–8, 2291, 2302). In the revised edition of the *Ciceronianus* (March 1529), Erasmus eliminated Budé's name from the incriminating passage. He also assured Brie and Toussain that he was ready to resume the dialogue with Budé (Epp 2379, 2449). But Budé had long tired, it seems, of a correspondence fraught with bitterness and tension and remained silent. Daniel *Stiebar reported a rumour that Budé refused even to open Erasmus' conciliatory Ep 2047 (AK III Ep 1303). In 1530 Brie tried to persuade Erasmus that Budé was again friendly, but a visitor from Basel interpreted Budé's silence less optimistically (AK IV Ep 1490).

Although it was the *Ciceronianus* that led to the estrangement between Budé and Erasmus, Erasmus was further disappointed by Budé's *Commentarii linguae graecae*, published in 1529. Since March 1527 (Ep 1794), he had let it be known that he expected Budé to include in this work a eulogy of his own writings in return for his praise of Budé in the New Testament. In 1528 this hope changed to a fear that Budé would seize the opportunity to get even with Erasmus after the slighting remark in the *Ciceronianus* (Ep 2052). But once again Budé simply kept silent.

BIBLIOGRAPHY: Allen and CWE Ep 403 / DBF VII 611–12 / Budé's earliest biography, by Louis Le Roy (Paris 1540), is reprinted in *Opera omnia* (Basel 1557, repr 1966), which also offers an excellent analytical preface by the editor, C.S. Curione / Other works by Budé available in anastatic reproductions are *De philologia* and *De studio literarum* (Paris 1532, repr 1964) and *De transitu* (Paris 1535; repr with a French translation by Maurice Lebel, Sherbrooke 1973) / For an English translation by Daniel Penham see *Dissertation Abstracts* 1953, 2193 / M.-M. de la Garanderie produced a French translation of Budé's correspondence with Erasmus, with introduction and notes (Paris 1967), and with More (*Moreana* 5 nos 19–20, 1968, 41–68) / A complete French translation of Budé's correspondence, by Guy Lavoie and Roland Galibois, is in progress (Sherbrooke 1977–   ) / *L'Institution du prince* had been re-edited from the manuscript by C. Bontems in *Le Prince dans la France des XVIe et XVIIe siècles* (Paris 1965); there is also an anastatic reprint of the 1547 edition (1966).

Eugène de Budé *Vie de Guillaume Budé, fondateur du Collège de France* (Paris 1857) / Abel Lefranc *Histoire du Collège de France* (Paris 1893, repr 1970) passim / Louis Delaruelle *Guillaume Budé: Les origines, les idées maîtresses* (Paris 1907) / Louis Delaruelle *Répertoire analytique et chronologique de la correspondance de Guillaume Budé* (Toulouse-Paris 1907, repr n d) / J. Plattard *Guillaume Budé et les origines de l'humanisme français* (Paris 1923) / Josef Bohatec *Budé und Calvin* (Graz 1950) / David O. McNeil *Guillaume Budé and Humanism in the Reign of Francis I* (Geneva 1975) / M.-M. de la Garanderie *Christianisme et lettres profanes* (Lille-Paris 1976) II: 'La pensée de Guillaume Budé' / M.-M. de la Garanderie 'Qui etait Guillaume Budé?' *Bulletin de l'Association Guillaume Budé* 4th series 2 (1967) 192–211 / M.-M. de la Garanderie 'L'harmonie secrète du *De asse*' *Bulletin de l'Association Guillaume Budé* 4th series 4 (1968) 473–86 / M.-M. de la Garanderie 'Le style figuré de Guillaume Budé et ses implications logiques et théologiques' in *L'Humanisme français au début de la Renaissance* (Paris 1973) 343–59 / Additional bibliography in Guy Gueudet 'Etat présent des recherches sur Guillaume Budé' in *Actes du VIIe Congrès de l'Association Guillaume Budé* (Paris 1969) 597–627.

Specifically on Erasmus and Budé see Louis Delaruelle 'Une amitié d'humanistes ... ' *Le Musée belge* 9 (1905) 321–51 / Pierre Mesnard 'Erasme et Budé' *Bulletin de l'Association Guillaume Budé* 4th series 3 (1965) 307–31 / André Stegmann 'Erasme et la France' in *Colloquium Erasmianum* (Mons 1968) 275–97 / P.G. Bietenholz *Basle and France in the Sixteenth Century* (Geneva-Toronto 1971) 187–201 and passim / Yvonne Charlier *Erasme et l'amitié* (Paris 1977) 205–9 and passim

MARIE-MADELEINE DE LA GARANDERIE

Jean BUDÉ of Paris, d 28 February 1502
Jean, the father of Guillaume *Budé, owned three seigneuries near Paris: Villiers-sur-Marne, Yerres, and Marly. By 1471 he had succeeded his own father, Dreux, as the king's *trésorier des chartes*, an office which he held under *Louis XI until 1482, when a series of scandals and lawsuits caused him to lose it. In 1477, after the death of Charles the Rash, duke of *Burgundy, Jean was sent to Dijon on an official mission.

In 1454 Jean Budé married Catherine, the daughter of Jean Le Picart, a royal secretary.

Catherine survived her husband by four years (Ep 583) and died on 2 August 1506.

BIBLIOGRAPHY: Allen and CWE Ep 583 / D.O. McNeil *Guillaume Budé and Humanism in the Reign of Francis I* (Geneva 1975) 3–5 and passim / L. Delaruelle *Répertoire de la correspondance de Guillaume Budé* (Toulouse-Paris 1907) Ep 47 and passim

PGB

Louis BUDÉ of Paris, 1470–19 November 1517
Louis, a younger brother of Guillaume *Budé, was canon (from 1494) and subsequently archdeacon of Troyes, where he died (Epp 744, 778). In 1513 he was also a non-residing canon of Auxerre. Guillaume encouraged him to study Greek, and they corresponded in that language. The only surviving letter indicates their close and affectionate relationship.

BIBLIOGRAPHY: Allen Ep 744 / Louis Delaruelle *Répertoire de la correspondance de Guillaume Budé* (Toulouse-Paris 1907) Ep 6 / D.O. McNeil *Guillaume Budé and Humanism in the Reign of Francis I* (Geneva 1975) 4–5 and passim / *Gallia christiana* XII Instrumenta 221

PGB

Roberte BUDÉ *See Roberte* LE LIEUR

Johann BUGENHAGEN of Wolin, 24 June 1485–20 April 1558
Johann Bugenhagen (Pomeranus) was born in Wolin (Wollin) in Pomerania, the son of an alderman. After attending the local school run by the Cistercian nuns, he studied from 1502 to 1504 at the University of Greifswald, where he received a solid grounding in Latin according to the curriculum that Hermannus *Buschius had introduced when he was teaching in Greifswald. When Bugenhagen became rector of the school in Trzebiatów (Treptow an der Rega) in Pomerania (1504), he laid comparable emphasis on the reading of classical authors. The school flourished, and Bugenhagen won the support of two of the teachers working under him who had studied with Johannes *Murmellius in Münster. In 1509 Bugenhagen took orders and became vicar of St Mary's church in Trzebiatów, and in 1517 he lectured privately on the Bible. At that time the influence of Martin *Luther began to reach Pomerania. Among others, Barnim, the son of

Johann Bugenhagen by Lucas Cranach the Elder

Duke Boguslaw of Pomerania, who was studying in Wittenberg, sent enthusiastic reports home. After reading Luther's *Babylonian Captivity* (1520), Bugenhagen began to exchange letters with Luther, and in 1521 he went to Wittenberg, arriving shortly before Luther and his party set out for Worms. He matriculated at the university on 29 April 1521 and began to give private lectures on the Psalms, which were well received and were attended on occasion by *Melanchthon. From 1525 he was pastor of the town of Wittenberg.

Between 1526 and 1542 Bugenhagen received numerous invitations to reform churches and schools in other regions of northern Germany. He was granted leaves from Wittenberg to visit Hamburg (October 1528 to June 1529), Lübeck (October 1530 to April 1532), Pomerania (1534), and Schleswig-Holstein (1542). He drew up ordinances for these churches and also for Minden, Osnabrück, Soest, Bremen, and Brunswick. In 1533 he obtained a doctorate of theology in Wittenberg; from 1535 he was also a member of the theological faculty. In response to an invitation from King *Christian III of Denmark, he stayed in Copenhagen

between 1537 and 1539 to organize the reformed church, at the same time assisting in the reorganization of the University of Copenhagen. After his return to Wittenberg he was made superintendent of Electoral Saxony. Considering it his duty to remain in Wittenberg, he declined calls to Schleswig in 1541 and Pomerania in 1544 (Bugenhagen *Briefwechsel* Epp 95, 98, 140). Being a close friend of Luther, he ministered at the reformer's wedding and also at his funeral in 1546. When during the Schmalkaldic war Wittenberg fell to the imperial troops after a siege (1547), Bugenhagen stayed. The fact that he accepted the terms of the Augsburg Interim (1548) rather than move elsewhere alienated him from many of his former friends and associates.

Apart from the numerous church ordinances written between 1533 and 1543, Bugenhagen wrote sermons, several missives, including one to the city of Hamburg, *Von dem christlichen Glauben und rechten guten Wercken* (Wittenberg: G. Rhau 1527), and *Ain christlicher Sendprieff* to the duchess of Pomerania [Augsburg: S. Ruff 1525]. He also wrote *De coniugio episcoporum et diacanorum* (Nürnberg: J. Petri 1525), *Oratio ... de Eucharistia* (1527), and Bible commentaries such as *Annotationes ... in Deuteronomium* (Nürnberg: J. Petri 1524) and *In librum Psalmorum interpretatio* (Basel: A. Petri 1524). He helped in translating the New Testament into Low German in 1534, and with Melanchthon he assisted Luther in a revision of the German Bible in 1539.

Bugenhagen's admiration for Erasmus was aroused by Johannes Murmellius in 1512 (Bugenhagen *Briefwechsel* Ep 2); from 1517 to 1518 Bugenhagen edited in Trzebiatów a volume that contained Erasmus' *Christiani hominis institutio* (Reedijk poem 94). Even after the publication of Erasmus' *De libero arbitrio*, Bugenhagen did not wish to attack him in public (BA *Oekolompads* I Ep 221; Bugenhagen *Briefwechsel* Ep 9). There is no record of any direct connection between Erasmus and Bugenhagen, but Erasmus referred to him occasionally in his letters (Epp 1539, 1644, 2315, 2615), in the *Hyperaspistes* (LB X 1304A, 1308C), and in the *Epistola contra pseudevangelicos* (LB X 1602B, E). Several references concern Bugenhagen's commentary on the Psalms, which Erasmus seems to have read with

attention; others concern the quarrel Bugenhagen and Luther had with *Bucer over his free
translations from their works.

BIBLIOGRAPHY: Allen Ep 1539 / NDB III 9–10 /
David C. Steinmetz *Reformers in the Wings*
(Philadelphia 1971) 82–90 / Walter M. Ruccius
John Bugenhagen Pomeranus (Philadelphia n d) /
Dr. Johannes Bugenhagens Briefwechsel ed Otto
Vogt (Stettin 1889–99, repr with additions
1966) / Leonid Arbusow *Die Einführung der
Reformation in Liv-, Est- und Kurland* (Leipzig
1921, repr 1964) 170–84, 247–50, 607–11, and
passim / *Matrikel Wittenberg* I 104

IG

Giovanni Antonio BUGLIO of Burgio, d 1545
Giovanni Antonio Buglio (Puglione, Pulione,
Pulio, Pulleo) was born in Sicily, the son of the
baron of Burgio. He inherited the barony in
1494, while still a minor. Little is known about
his youth; he may have studied in Rome,
although the first evidence definitely placing
him there dates from 1522. By that year,
however, he was already well respected and
favoured by the papal court and the Farnese
family.

Buglio's first diplomatic mission came in 1522
as well. He was sent to Poland to represent
papal interests in the negotiations for a
possible marriage alliance between the houses
of Jagiello and Gonzaga. The following year
saw the beginning of his important connections with the kingdom of Hungary. Together
with Cardinal *Cajetanus, legate to Germany,
Hungary, and Poland, he was to assist the
Hungarians in their efforts to develop defences
against the Turks and establish a Christian
alliance composed of *Louis II of Hungary, the
Archduke *Ferdinand, *Sigismund I of Poland,
and the Emperor *Charles V. After Cajetanus
was recalled to Rome Buglio was named nuncio
to Hungary in January 1524. Fortified with a
generous subsidy to hire a papal contingent for
the Christian forces and allowed great independence and initiative (in part because the
new legate, Cardinal Lorenzo *Campeggi, was
in Germany until December 1524), Buglio
worked tirelessly to build up strong resistance
to the Ottoman threat, even stopping at Venice
early in 1524 while returning from a brief trip to
Rome in an effort to persuade the Republic to
join the defensive league. However Buglio's

experience with the kings of Hungary and
Poland and the lukewarm attitude of the
Hungarian magnates to his attempts to defend
the east convinced him of the impossibility of
success in his mission. The accuracy of this
prediction was confirmed in August 1526 at the
battle of Mohács, in which the Turks destroyed
the Christian army. Buglio escaped to Bratislava in the company of the queen, *Mary of
Hungary, and from there returned to Rome.

In October 1526 *Clement VII appointed
Buglio commander of all papal forces in and
around Rome to combat the incursions of the
Colonna. After his armies were disbanded in
March 1527, he was again sent to Hungary for a
brief period and then to Venice. On 12 June
1529 Buglio was named papal nuncio to the
kingdom of Sicily with special responsibility to
oversee the administration of certain ecclesiastical properties.

The following year Buglio began his next
diplomatic mission of great importance, as
papal nuncio to England. Arriving at Dover on
3 September, Buglio was commissioned principally to work against the divorce of *Henry VIII
from *Catherine of Aragon, despite the statement in his letters of credence that his primary
objective was to secure English support for a
Christian alliance against the Turks. Initially,
Buglio worked closely with the imperial ambassador, Eustache *Chapuys, but the latter felt
that the Italian handled the king too gently and
began to suspect him of anti-imperial sympathies. Buglio's attempts to frustrate the king's
great matter were unsuccessful; indeed he
drew increasingly closer to Henry, hunting
with him and receiving generous gifts.

After his recall from England in 1533, Buglio
was appointed by Pope Clement to a number of
important posts in his native Sicily. Later, in
1536, he became governor of the city and the
archiepiscopal territory of Monreale, acting as
agent for Cardinal Alessandro *Farnese. Finally, in August of that year he was reappointed
nuncio to Sicily. He probably died at Mineo,
where he owned a residence.

Agostino *Scarpinelli, the Milanese ambassador in England, described Buglio as 'a
well-mannered person and learned.' He was
celebrated for his great diplomatic skill in
difficult circumstances and his ability to identify with those nations among whom he lived.

Still, he was an ardent papalist, believing in the necessity of all Italy's accepting the overlordship of the Holy See, and consequently he vigorously opposed *Luther and the Protestant revolt. His relations with the Empire were always ambiguous. Despite his frequent professions of loyalty to Charles v, he was suspected of conspiring against him at Venice and of aiding the Sicilian revolt of 1527–8. Certainly Chapuys thought him capable of double-dealing. Although he was a layman, married, and the father of children, Buglio was primarily an instrument of papal policy and loyal exclusively to Rome and the church.

In 1525 Andrzei *Krzycki wrote a letter to Buglio explaining Sigismund I's reasons for permitting the secularization of the Teutonic order in Prussia (Epp 1629, 1652). It was published under the title De negotio prutenico epistola (Cracow: H. Wietor 1525).

BIBLIOGRAPHY: Allen Ep 1652 / DBI XV 413–17 / LP III-2 no 1471, IV-1 no 2048, and passim / G. Fráknoi Le Baron Burgio, nonce de Clément VII en Hongrie (1523–1526) (Florence 1884) / Calendar of State Papers, Venetian IV no 621

KENNETH R. BARTLETT

Henry BULLOCK c 1497–1526

Perhaps the closest of Erasmus' Cambridge friends, Henry Bullock (Boloke, Bovillus, Bullocus) was from the diocese of Coventry and Lichfield and commenced BA from Queens' College, Cambridge, in 1504. He was elected fellow in 1506, and was made MA in the academic year 1506–7. He lectured in mathematics in 1510–11 and was dean of chapel in 1511–12. In 1517 he became a bachelor of divinity and in 1520 a doctor. He played a significant role in establishing a printing press at Cambridge in 1520 or 1521, but was one of the commissioners who supervised the burning of *Luther's books in front of St Paul's, London, on 12 May 1521. He took holy orders, and from 29 April 1522 was rector of St Martin's, Ludgate. In 1520 and 1524 he delivered orations welcoming *Wolsey to Cambridge; the first was published by John *Siberch in 1521. Siberch also printed Bullock's translation of a work of Lucian into Latin in 1521 (STC 16896). Bullock was vice-chancellor of Cambridge in 1524–5 but died before 4 July 1526. In his will, dated 24 May 1526, he left

twenty-four books to Queens', among them Erasmus' editions of the New Testament and of Jerome, the Annotationes to the New Testament of 1518–19, the Adagia, and other humanistic and patristic works.

Erasmus and Bullock may have first met when the royal party visited Cambridge in 1506. Bullock was one of the members of Erasmus' small class in Greek in 1512 and was frequently mentioned in Erasmus' correspondence with John *Colet, Andrea *Ammonio and Johannes *Sixtinus from 1511 to 1513 (Epp 225, 234, 236, 239, 240, 243, 244, 247–9, 282). When Erasmus visited England in 1516, Bullock invited him to Cambridge and praised his recent edition of the New Testament (Basel: J. Froben 1516; Ep 449). In August 1516 Erasmus replied with Ep 456, a lengthy defence of his New Testament. In May 1517 Bullock wrote to Erasmus twice, describing his recent sickness and commenting on the usefulness of Erasmus' New Testament for his lectures on Matthew (Epp 579, 580). In 1518 Erasmus sent his friend three letters, each progressively shorter than the one before, discussing the opposition to his New Testament and in particular his controversy with Jacques *Lefèvre d'Etaples (Epp 777, 826, 890). After 1518 no correspondence between the two is extant.

BIBLIOGRAPHY: Allen Ep 225 / DNB III 254–5 / Emden BRUC 105 / A. Tilley 'Greek studies in England in the early sixteenth century' English Historical Review 53 (1938) 228 / D.F.S. Thomson and H.C. Porter Erasmus and Cambridge (Toronto 1963) 218 and passim

R.J. SCHOECK

Lazzaro BUONAMICO See Lazzaro BONAMICO

William BURBANK d c January 1532

Burbank (Bourbank, Burbanke) entered Cambridge as a student of civil law on 6 July 1496. In 1509 he served as secretary to Christopher Bainbridge, archbishop of York, who undertook an embassy to the papal court. At Rome Burbank met Erasmus (Ep 1138). In 1514, after the death of Cardinal Bainbridge, Burbank was recommended by *Leo x and two cardinals to *Henry VIII (LP I 3125, 3164, 3177, 3183, August 1514), and thereafter he continued to enjoy Henry's confidence (LP IV 5783). He had been canon of York and prebendary of Fenton since

1512, and he subsequently received many other benefices. He was canon of Lincoln from 1517 to 1527 and was archdeacon of Carlisle from 1523 until his death. He was Cardinal Thomas *Wolsey's chaplain and secretary in 1516 and acted as his agent in the dissolution of the lesser monasteries. Burbank received a degree of bachelor of canon and civil law by 1519 and, when Wolsey visited Cambridge in 1520, he received a doctorate in canon law.

Erasmus wrote Burbank in 1520 (Ep 1138), recalling his many friends in England. The continuation of friendly relations between the two is documented for 1524 (Ep 1492) and 1526 (Ep 1745).

BIBLIOGRAPHY: Allen Ep 1138 / Emden BRUC 106–7 / LP I 3203–4 and passim

CFG

Johann BURCHARD of Guebwiller, documented 1503–36

A native of Guebwiller, Upper Alsace, Johann Burchard (Burkhard, 'Doctor Jhesus') studied at Heidelberg in 1503 and from 1505 at Freiburg, where he obtained a theological doctorate on 30 August 1513. When he matriculated at Freiburg he was already a Dominican, and in 1515 he was sent to his order's house in Strasbourg, where he acquired the nickname 'Doctor Jesus.' He was forced to leave Strasbourg early in 1517, when he was accused of theft and other offences. His controversial reputation assured him of a mention in the *Epistolae obscurorum virorum*.

Burchard entered the service of Girolamo *Aleandro, who had him preach at the occasion of the burning of *Luther's books in Mainz (1520) and Worms (1521). Aleandro also recommended him in Rome but failed to secure his return to Strasbourg. In the autumn of 1524 the Basel chapter called him to the pulpit of the cathedral, obviously impressed by his reputation as a militant opponent of the reformers, but in August 1525 he insulted the town clerk and was expelled from Basel amid rumours of immoral conduct. Next he obtained a position at Bremgarten, in the Aargau, where he did battle with the reform-minded priest Heinrich Bullinger. In 1526 he attended the Baden disputation and debated against *Oecolampadius. At Bremgarten he faced economic troubles, and in 1528, accused of insulting the

governments of Bern and Zürich, he had to flee once again. In 1530 he was vicar-general of the Upper-German province of his order when he attended the diet of Augsburg. In 1531 the chapter of Speyer appointed him parish priest of Esslingen, but the town council opposed him and won. In 1536 he is documented at Freiburg.

According to Ambrosius *Pelargus (Ep 2723) the name of Doctor Jesus was mentioned in conversation by Erasmus' servant when he delivered Ep 2722 from his master. As Pelargus pointed out, it is impossible to identify Burchard with the unnamed Dominican mentioned by Erasmus in Ep 2211.

BIBLIOGRAPHY: NDB III 31 / N. Paulus *Die deutschen Dominikaner in Kampf gegen Luther* (Freiburg 1903) 325–30 / z VIII Epp 428, 434; IX Epp 703, 729 / *Matrikel Freiburg* I 167 / *Aktensammlung zur Geschichte der Basler Reformation* ed E. Dürr et al (Basel 1521–50) I 224–7 / *Basler Chroniken* (Basel 1872–) VII 273 / R. Wackernagel *Geschichte der Stadt Basel* (Basel 1907–54) III 357, 469 / H. Bullinger *Werke* (Zürich 1972–) *Briefwechsel* I Ep 14 and passim / Hutten *Operum supplementum* I 298–9, II 400–1

PGB

BURCHARDUS (Epp 1890, 1897, 1899 of October–November 1527)

Burchardus has not been identified: he had worked for the *Froben press and took Erasmus' letters to the Netherlands.

Nicolas BUREAU d 1551

Bureau (Burellus, de Burellis) was a Franciscan and a bachelor of theology at the time of his appointment as suffragan bishop of Tournai on 2 December 1519. Like his predecessors he received the titular see of Sarepta, and until his death he carried out many of the practical duties of two consecutive bishops, Louis *Guillard, who generally resided in France, and Charles de *Croy, who was appointed bishop of Tournai in 1524 but did not take possession of his see until 1539. In the execution of his duties Bureau frequently preached in Bruges and in other towns. In sermons preached at Bruges in 1520 he attacked Erasmus and *Luther together and, according to the reports reaching Erasmus, called them a variety of names until he was silenced by the pensionary of Bruges, Frans van *Cranevelt. Bureau allegedly suspected there were some heresies in the *Moria* because, he said, the Latin had proved too difficult for him to understand. In 1527 Bureau attacked Juan Luis *Vives' *De subventione pauperum* in a similar fashion, calling it heretical and Lutheran, but he did not pursue the matter any further. In 1542 he submitted to the theological faculty of Louvain a question about 'the four conditions of souls,' and in 1544 he desired the same body to confirm his suspicions of heresy in three books, one of which was a French translation from Urbanus *Rhegius. Bureau died at Bruges and was buried in the Franciscan chapel.

Erasmus protested to Bishop Louis Guillard about Bureau's attacks (Ep 1212) and never tired of repeating the suffragan's alleged reply to Cranevelt (Epp 1144, 1183, 1192, 1471, 1581, 1967, 2045). There was perhaps a recollection of it when Vives, in addressing his own complaints to Cranevelt, spoke ironically of Bureau's accomplished Latinity and his familiarity with patristic literature. According to de Vocht, the story eventually found its way into an English jest-book, the *Mery Tales, Wittie Questions and Quicke Answeres* of 1567.

BIBLIOGRAPHY: Allen Ep 1144 / de Vocht *Literae ad Craneveldium* 631–4, 636 / de Vocht CTL I 524, II 197 / U. Berlière *Les Evêques auxiliaires de Cambrai et de Tournai* (Bruges 1905) 144 / *Gallia christiana* III 239, 452

PGB

Benedikt BURGAUER of St Gallen, 1 August 1494–10 January 1576
Benedikt Burgauer (Burgower) was corresponding with *Vadianus around 1512–13 when he had gone to Cracow (*Vadianische Briefsammlung* I Ep 22), presumably to study there. He took holy orders in 1515, and in the same year he became the parish priest of Marbach, in the St Gallen Rhine valley. On 30 September 1519 he was appointed to the parish of St Laurence in the city of St Gallen, where he soon came to adopt the tenets of the reformers. But to a greater extent than Vadianus he hesitated between the Lutheran and Zwinglian positions, and in general he was indecisive and lacking in leadership. He maintained the traditional views on purgatory and oral confes-

sion; as a result he was suspended in his ministry, and on 17 June 1524 he was replaced as a member of the commission created in St Gallen to supervise the introduction of the new religious order. After deferring to Vadianus and the city council in 1525 he was allowed to resume his pastoral duties. He attended the second disputation of Zürich in 1523 and that of Baden in 1526 and also appeared at the Bern disputation of 1528, although he was not a member of the official delegation of St Gallen. Once again the views he professed were criticized as inherently Catholic, and after admitting to error he was glad to move in 1528 to a parish in the city of Schaffhausen. Again he was accused of erring, this time on the side of Lutheranism, and at Christmas 1531 he was induced to make a public act of submission. In 1532 he married, but his difficulties continued, and in 1536 he lost his position at Schaffhausen. There followed short-lived appointments to St Margrethen in the St Gallen Rhine valley in 1536, to Tuttlingen in Swabia in 1537, and to Lindau in 1541, where once again he was dismissed. In 1545 he moved to Isny, in the Allgäu, where he remained to his death. In 1528 he was glad to forward to Erasmus some letters from Spain which had been given to Burgauer's brother (Ep 2067).

A Dominik Burgauer studied from 1520 in Freiburg and Basel, where he graduated MA in 1523; in 1526 he matriculated in Wittenberg; see *Matrikel Basel* I 343; Näf II 103; *Vadianische Briefsammlung* III Ep 334 and Nachträge Ep 66.

BIBLIOGRAPHY: Allen Ep 2067 / DHBS II 438 / Werner Näf *Vadian und seine Stadt St. Gallen* (St Gallen 1944–57) I 195, II 209–20, and passim / *Vadianische Briefsammlung* I Ep 22 and passim / H.M. Stückelberger *Die evangelische Pfarrerschaft des Kantons St. Gallen* (St Gallen 1971) 25–6, 146

PGB

Dominik BURGAUER *See Benedikt* BURGAUER

Andrea da BURGO *See Andrea da* BORGO

Anianus BURGONIUS of Orléans, d January 1535
Anianus Burgonius (Aignan Bourgoin ?, presumably named after St Anianus of Orléans) came from Orléans, where Jan *Łaski met him

in 1524. Impressed by the intelligence of the young lad, Łaski took him under his care. Anianus was with Łaski during the latter's visit to Erasmus in 1525 (Ep 1502) and afterwards became attached to Łaski's court in Cracow. His epigrams were written at this time. In 1527 he was placed under the care of Leonard *Cox, who reported on his progress to Erasmus (Ep 1803). Erasmus responded by expressing his good opinion of Anianus (Ep 1824). In 1530 Anianus travelled to Italy to study, funded by Łaski, and stayed in Venice, Bologna, and Padua. On his return journey to Poland he visited *Melanchthon in Wittenberg (20 November 1533). In the spring of 1534 Łaski sent him back to Wittenberg in the care of Andrzej Frycz Modrzewski. Anianus was housed by Melanchthon, who in December 1534 took him to a congress of Protestant nobles and theologians in Kassel. On the return journey Anianus fell ill and died in Leipzig. Friends took his body to Wittenberg, where he was buried in the castle church.

Anianus' poem in honour of Cox was added to *Statii Papini ... sylvae cum scholis a Leonardo Coxo ... adiectis* (Cracow: M. Scharffenberg 1527). An epigram is to be found in *Statuta nova inclite provinciae Gnesnensi ...* (Cracow: M. Scharffenberg 1527), and another was published by K. Miaskowski (*Andreae Cricii Carmina*, 1888, 157–8).

BIBLIOGRAPHY: PSB I 113–14 / O. Bartel *Jan Łaski* (Warsaw 1955) 87–8, 110–12 / *Melanchthons Briefwechsel* II Epp 1378, 1445, 1447, 1536

HALINA KOWALSKA

Adolph of BURGUNDY d 7 December 1540
Adolph was born by 1489–90 at the castle of Veere, the son of Anna van *Borssele and Philip of Burgundy (d 1498), admiral of Flanders, governor of Artois, and chamberlain to Duke Philip the Good of *Burgundy. Adolph grew up in the castle of Tournehem, carefully educated by his widowed mother, who was Erasmus' patroness, and tutored by Erasmus' good friend Jacob *Batt. Erasmus himself, through his visits to Tournehem and his correspondence with Batt, took a lively interest in Adolph's progress; he wrote for him an *Oratio de virtute* and some prayers (Epp 93, 145, 181, 492, 1927) and may have remembered

Adolph of Burgundy by Jacques le Boucq

him elsewhere (ASD I-3 325–32; Reedijk poem 48). He also intended at one time or another to dedicate to Adolph *De conscribendis epistolis, De copia*, and even the earliest *Adagia* (Epp 95, 123, 124, 147), but was finally content with sending him a printed copy of the latter (Ep 129). In 1502 Anna van Borssele remarried and Batt died; as a result the close contacts between Erasmus and Adolph seem to have ceased.

As early as 1504 Adolph was installed in his father's lordship of Flushing, while Veere and Beveren were added later. In 1505 the young grand seigneur was part of an embassy to *Ferdinand II of Aragon which was to discuss the future of Castile. In 1508, following the relocation of the Scottish staple from Bruges to Veere, Adolph sent his own envoys to Scotland and was named a knight of the order of St Andrew. In 1515 he was added to the exclusive order of the Golden Fleece. When his relative Philip (I) of *Burgundy became bishop of Utrecht, Adolph succeeded him in 1517 as admiral and in this capacity commanded the fleet that took the future *Charles v to Spain. He returned with Prince *Ferdinand, whom he formally welcomed on his arrival at Flushing,

Anthony of Burgundy, Flemish school

---

as he welcomed Charles on his return from Spain in 1520. In 1523 he received *Christian II of Denmark and his wife, *Isabella of Austria, at Veere and generally maintained close contacts with them.

In 1521 Adolph was in charge of naval operations against France. In 1527 he equipped two ships of his own for an expedition to discover new lands; the emperor had granted him title to any territories that might be discovered, but the expedition was unsuccessful. On 15 June 1528 the treaty of Hampton Court was signed after Adolph had drawn up his fleet off Calais and in the estuary of the Thames. He was also active in the later wars against France, and in 1536 he was given the command of a planned naval operation against Denmark. When not at sea he directed his attention to the naval facilities and fortifications of Zeeland. He was also involved in politics, undertaking an embassy to England in 1525 (LP IV 1213) and joining the council of state in 1540. Shortly before his death in 1540 he received the monarch once more at Veere on his return to the Netherlands.

In 1512 Erasmus attempted to re-establish the former cordial relations with Adolph (Ep 266). He visited Adolph in July 1514 at Bergen just after the birth of his second son, Maximilian (II) of *Burgundy, who in later years became the principal link between Erasmus and his father. Other connections were provided by Adolph's physician, Reyner *Snoy, and by Jan *Becker, Maximilian's tutor, who made sure that Adolph received copies of Erasmus' letters to Maximilian (Ep 1984). In addition to Maximilian, Adolph and his wife, Anna van *Bergen, had three daughters and two more sons, Philip (III) and Henry of *Burgundy, both of whom died before their parents.

BIBLIOGRAPHY: Allen and CWE Ep 93 (and CWE 2 236 for a portrait of Adolph) / L.M.G. Kooperberg in NNBW VIII 189–94 / *Collection des voyages des souverains des Pays-Bas* ed L.P. Gachard and C. Piot (Brussels 1874–82) II 57, III 212 / Alexandre Henne *Histoire du règne de Charles-Quint en Belgique* (Brussels-Leipzig 1858–60) I 78, V 261, VI 151–3, and passim / LP I 1594 and passim / de Vocht *Literae ad Cranevel-dium* Epp 54, 209, and passim / Karl Brandi *Kaiser Karl v.* new ed (Darmstadt 1959–67) I 356–7, and passim / Michel Baelde *De collaterale raden onder Karel v en Filips II* (Brussels 1965) 240–1 and passim

PGB

Anthony of BURGUNDY 1420/1–5 May 1504
One of the many natural sons of Philip the Good, duke of *Burgundy, Anthony, called 'le Grand Bâtard' or 'de Groote Bastaard,' played a fairly important and certainly conspicuous role as a soldier and diplomat. He fought in the wars of both his father and his brother, Charles the Rash, duke of *Burgundy, and may have contributed to the reconciliation between father and son. The chivalresque fashion of the time is reflected in many episodes of his life (and also in his famous library). In 1453 Anthony was among those who took a crusading vow at the famous feast of the pheasant; in obedience to his vow he took the cross in 1464 and led an expedition of fellow-crusaders as far as Marseille, where they received news of the death of Pope *Pius II at Ancona and the consequent collapse of the Italian crusading plans. In May 1456 he was made a knight of the Golden Fleece, and in

1458 he rode with a thousand horse to assist his brother David of *Burgundy in his troubles with the unruly principality of Utrecht. In 1470 he was appointed forester of Holland; in 1467 and again in 1475 he went to England to fight briefly in the wars of the Roses.

In the disastrous battle of Nancy (1477), where Charles the Rash was killed, Anthony was captured by the Swiss and sold to Duke René de Lorraine; afterwards he was retained in France, it seems for more than a decade. On his return to the Netherlands he served the future *Maximilian I but without enthusiasm. He was assumed to be a partisan of the French court; in fact he seems to have returned there repeatedly. During the last period of his long life the castle of Tournehem in the Pas-de-Calais was his principal residence. It is there that Erasmus came into superficial contact with him during his visits to Anna van *Borssele, Anthony's widowed daughter-in-law (Epp 153, 155, 166). Shortly before his death Anthony succeeded in clearing himself of suspicions about his loyalty to Hapsburg-Burgundy, which around 1501 seem to have led to some form of surveillance, or worse, for the family (Ep 157).

Anthony was count of La-Roche-en-Ardenne, lord of Beveren, etc. His wife, Marie de la Viefville, bore him a son, Philip (d 1498), and several daughters; there was also an illegitimate son, Nicolas of *Burgundy.

BIBLIOGRAPHY: Allen Ep 80 / L.M.G. Kooperberg in NNBW VIII 194–201 / BNB I 837–42 / L.P. Gachard and C. Piot Collection des voyages des souverains des Pays-Bas (Brussels 1874–82) I 272, 527 / Karl Brandi Kaiser Karl v. new ed (Darmstadt 1959–67) I 22, II 63

PGB

Charles, duke of BURGUNDY 10 November 1433–5 January 1477
Charles, called the Rash or Bold ('le Téméraire'), was the last of the Valois dukes of Burgundy. The only son of Duke Philip the Good of *Burgundy and Isabella of Portugal, he was born at Dijon and styled count of Charolais. He was to marry Catherine, the daughter of King *Charles VII of France, but she died before the wedding could take place; in February 1457 he married Isabelle de Bourbon (d 26 September 1465). In 1465 Charles joined the revolt of

Charles, duke of Burgundy by Roger van der Weyden

French noble families against King *Louis XI and forced him to restore to Burgundy the towns on the Somme which had been in French hands since 1463 (treaty of Conflans, October 1465). Thereafter Duke Charles and King Louis remained enemies until death.

When his father died on 15 June 1467, Charles became duke of Burgundy and moved to achieve his grand design of gaining for Burgundy the status of a great power, fully independent of both France and the Empire. In July 1468 he married Margaret of York, the sister of King Edward IV of England, and, needing a strong ally in his campaigns against the French king (1470–2), he met the Emperor *Frederick III at Trier in 1473, urging that a comprehensive kingdom of Burgundy should be created of all his possessions. These negotiations failed and led Charles to seek expansion by military means; yet they also laid the groundwork for the future *Maximilian I's marriage to Charles' only daughter, Mary. To enhance his power, Charles acquired some territories in Alsace and secured his succession to Gelderland. He allied himself to Savoy and tried to conquer Lorraine. In 1474 he entered

David of Burgundy by the Master of Delft

Charles le Téméraire rev ed (Brussels 1970) / Richard Vaughan *Charles the Bold* (London-New York 1974)

IG

David of BURGUNDY d 16 April 1496

Born around 1427, David was one of the many natural sons of Philip the Good, duke of *Burgundy. When he matriculated at the University of Louvain at an uncertain date before 1453 he was stated to be a native of Arras, chancellor of Flanders, and provost of St Donatian's, Liège, but not yet bishop of Thérouanne, a see which he held from 13 September 1451. Before obtaining it, he had apparently been coadjutor of Cambrai for a few years. On 12 September 1457 he was transferred to the see of Utrecht, which his predecessor had been forced to resign to him after only two years in office. His appointment clearly reflected his father's desire to forge closer links between the prince-bishopric and his own states. Twenty years later the death of Charles the Rash, duke of *Burgundy, led to an insurrection in Utrecht; Bishop David had to flee and was unable to return until 1492.

On David's character and pastoral commitment we have the testimony of Erasmus, who always felt that the see of Utrecht had special relevance for him because his birthplace lay in that diocese; moreover it was Bishop David who ordained him on 25 April 1492 (LB X 1573A) and subsequently authorized him to join Bishop Hendrik van *Bergen (Allen I 50; CWE 4 408). Erasmus saw in Bishop David a man of peace and learning; he noted how the bishop subjected his clergy to a theological examination and dismissed those found to be wanting (*Ecclesiastes* LB V 808; Ep 645) and how in his old age he wisely refused to take a coadjutor (*Adagia* III ix 38; although Philip (I) of *Burgundy did eventually become David's coadjutor). Erasmus may have composed some verses in honour of the bishop (Ep 28) and after his death composed two epitaphs for him (Reedijk poems 41, 42). He kept as a souvenir a cap worn by David, and treasured a precious ring that had belonged to David and was given to Erasmus by Philip (I) of Burgundy (LB X 1573; Allen I 43). David had also been a patron, and a patient, of Wessel *Gansfort.

the old Burgundian capital of Dijon, and in 1475 he took Nancy. Meanwhile, however, his enemies had reached an understanding with the Swiss; as a result the Swiss fought two major campaigns against Charles, defeating him in the battle of Nancy, where he met his death.

As a native of Rotterdam, Erasmus was born in the jurisdiction of Charles the Rash. He regularly characterized the duke as a warrior (*Panegyricus* ASD IV-1 52, 82). In a ringing denunciation he mentioned him in the same breath as Xerxes and Alexander the Great and criticized Charles for following a policy of aggrandizement while in Holland civil strife between the cod and hook factions went unattended and ruined the people; he also blamed the duke for his premature death in battle (*Adagia* II v 1), which was followed by domestic anarchy on an even wider scale and the corruption of monetary standards (*Institutio principis christiani* ASD IV-1 192). Erasmus was also puzzled by the irrationality of some people who obstinately refused to believe the news of Charles' death (*Adagia* IV i 63).

BIBLIOGRAPHY: DBF VIII 554–6 / Jean Bartier

BIBLIOGRAPHY: Allen Ep 603 / *Matricule de*

Louvain I 31 / Eubel II 129, 217, 278 / *Monasticon Belge* ed U. Berlière et al (Maredsous-Liège 1890–) III-3 908, III-4, 1100-3 / Henry Pirenne *Histoire de Belgique* (Brussels 1902–32) III 96–7, 177, 322 / de Vocht CTL I 55, 141 / S.B.J. Zilverberg *David van Bourgondie, bisschop van Terwaan en van Utrecht* (Groningen 1951)

PGB

Henry of BURGUNDY 26 September 1519– after March 1530

Henry was the youngest son of Adolph of *Burgundy, lord of Veere. Born at the castle of Zandenburg in Walcheren, he was tutored at home by Jacobus *Ceratinus (Ep 2209) and later probably sent to Louvain; he must have died as a child. In 1530 Erasmus dedicated to him his *De civilitate* (Ep 2282; LB I 1033–44).

BIBLIOGRAPHY: Allen Ep 2282 / NNBW VIII 193

PGB

Maximilian (I) of BURGUNDY d 1535

Maximilian of Burgundy was a son of Baldwin, one of the numerous natural children of Duke Philip the Good of *Burgundy; his mother was descended from the royal blood of Portugal. In September 1506 he matriculated at the University of Louvain; like his uncles David and Philip (I) of *Burgundy he was evidently intended for an ecclesiastical career. On 12 November 1518 Pope *Leo x appointed him abbot of the Premonstratensian house at Middelburg, in Zeeland, where he had recently become a monk, having apparently spent a number of years at court (Ep 1563). On 13 August 1525 *Charles v wrote to Pope *Clement VII in support of Maximilian's appointment as coadjutor to the aged abbot of Saint-Ghislain, in Hainaut, but this effort remained fruitless.

From 1520 Maximilian resided at Middelburg and gave his attention to the state of repair of his abbey, which had burnt down in 1492. Among the artists whom he sponsored was Jan Gossaert, called Mabuse, the creator of a great altar-piece at Middelburg. He also supported the new learning and counted among his friends Frans van *Cranevelt, Jan van *Fevijn, and Marcus *Laurinus. It thus seems natural that he was also acquainted with Erasmus, although not much is known about their contacts. They dined together late in 1520,

probably at Louvain (Ep 1164), and in 1525 Erasmus dedicated to the abbot his translation of St John Chrysostom's *De orando Deum* (Ep 1563). A copy of the first Froben edition of Erasmus' *Adagia* (1515) belonged to Maximilian before it came to be part of the library of Jan de *Hondt at Courtrai. Adrianus Cornelii *Barlandus dedicated to Maximilian his *Jocorum veterum et recentiorum duae centuriae* (Louvain: P. Martens 1524), encouraged to do so by Erasmus' praise of the abbot's open mind and hand. Also in 1524 Gerard *Geldenhouwer became the abbot's secretary after the death of his previous master, Philip (I) of *Burgundy. Cranevelt and Fevijn had recommended him for the post, and Erasmus expressed his delight at the appointment (Ep 1545); Gossaert, the painter, was also a friend of Geldenhouwer.

BIBLIOGRAPHY: Allen Ep 1164 / *Matricule de Louvain* III-1 323 / de Vocht *Literae ad Craneveldium* Epp 10, 121, 124, 125, and passim / Etienne Daxhelet *Adrien Barlandus* (Louvain 1938) Epp 49, 58, and passim / *Monasticon Belge* ed U. Berlière et al (Maredsous-Liège 1890–) I 263 / *Jan Gossaert genaamd Mabuse: Catalogus ...* ed H. Pauwels et al (Bruges-Rotterdam 1965) 18

PGB

Maximilian (II) of BURGUNDY 28 July 1514– 4 June 1558

Maximilian was born at Bergen op Zoom, the second son of Adolph of *Burgundy and Anna van *Bergen. In 1526, if not earlier, he was sent to Louvain and there was tutored by Erasmus' friend Jan *Becker of Borsele. Erasmus himself had visited Maximilian's father at Bergen soon after the boy's birth (Ep 301) and continued to take an interest in Maximilian, who became the heir apparent to his father's titles following the death of his elder brother, Philip (III) of *Burgundy (Ep 1787). Ep 1859 is a reply to a letter the thirteen-year old boy had written him at Becker's suggestion, and Erasmus wrote again when the first letter failed to reach Maximilian. He also dedicated to the young grand seigneur *De pronuntiatione* (Ep 1949; LB I 910–68). It remained for Becker to assure Erasmus in March 1528 that his gift had been received with great enthusiasm; at that time Becker expected the boy's studies in Louvain to continue for another year (Ep 1984). In July 1529 Maximilian had moved to the court, or was about to do so,

Philip (the Good), duke of Burgundy by Roger van der Weyden

when Erasmus wrote again, asking him to persevere in his interest in learning (Ep 2200). Encouragement of this kind was apparently not lost on Maximilian, who in addition to Erasmus' *De pronuntiatione* had several more works dedicated to him, including Jan Reigersberch's *Cronijcke van Zeelandt* (Antwerp: widow of H. Peetersen 1551).

From 1530 Maximilian began to be drawn into naval service by his father, the admiral, and in 1536 he fought against the French. After his father's death he received the lordships of Beveren, Veere, and Flushing and in 1542 succeeded his father as the admiral. On 10 May of the same year he married Louise, the daughter of Philippe de *Croy, but they had no children. In 1546 Maximilian was admitted to the order of the Golden Fleece and in the following year he was appointed *stadhouder* of Holland, Zeeland, and Utrecht. In recognition of twenty-five years of faithful service to the crown he was created marquis of Veere in 1555.

Maximilian devoted himself to naval matters more exclusively than his father had done and was repeatedly engaged in naval actions against the French; for example in 1543 he

sailed into the estuary of the Garonne and appeared off Bordeaux. On this and other occasions when rich booty was brought back to Veere, his actions could perhaps be termed privateering as much as official warfare.

BIBLIOGRAPHY: Allen Ep 1859 / L.M.G. Kooperberg in NNBW VIII 201–5 / de Vocht CTL II 461–4 and passim / de Vocht *Dantiscus* 394–5 and passim / Alexandre Henne *Histoire du règne de Charles-Quint en Belgique* (Brussels-Leipzig 1858–60) III 235 and passim

PGB

Nicholas of BURGUNDY d by November 1522
Nicholas was a natural son of Anthony of *Burgundy ('le Grand Bâtard') and thus a brother-in-law of Erasmus' patroness, Anna van *Borssele. On 23 May 1493 Nicholas matriculated at the University of Louvain. In 1498 he was appointed provost of St Peter's church, Utrecht; he also held livings in Brouwershaven (Zeeland) and Gapinge (?). In 1501 he was apparently imprisoned (Epp 151, 157), probably in connection with the political troubles of his father. At this time he resided in his father's castle of Tournehem, where Erasmus made his acquaintance. In 1500 and 1501 Erasmus wrote to him – one letter (Ep 144) is extant – and sent him a copy of the first edition of the *Adagia* (Epp 129, 130, 138). Nicholas may have resided in 1515 in Louvain since he was in touch with Maarten van *Dorp (Ep 337). Nicholas must have died before 23 November 1522, when Jan *Becker of Borsele informed Erasmus that the Brouwershaven living had been conferred upon himself (Ep 1321).

BIBLIOGRAPHY: Allen Ep 144 / *Matricule de Louvain* III-1 96 / de Vocht MHL 370

PGB

Philip (the Good), duke of BURGUNDY
31 July 1396–15 June 1467
Philip, third Valois duke of Burgundy, was born in Dijon, the son of John the Fearless and Margaret of Bavaria. Since his father was assassinated in 1419, Philip began his rule when he was still quite young. In 1421 he recognized young Henry VI of England as king of France but seldom took an active part in the war against King *Charles VII of France. After the treaty of Arras in 1435, by which he

recognized Charles VII as king of France and gained Auxerrois, Bar, the city of Boulogne, and other cities on the Somme, his subjects were able to enjoy long-lasting peace and prosperity. Mostly by way of conquest he acquired Hainaut (1427), Brabant (1430), Holland and Zeeland (1424–33), and Luxembourg (1443).

Philip loved magnificent festivities and favoured the arts; he encouraged Flemish painters, engaged famous musicians for his chapel, and collected a library of valuable manuscripts. He was married three times; his first wife, Michelle of France, the daughter of Charles VI, died in 1422. His second wife was Bonne d'Artois, after whose death he married Isabella of Portugal in 1429. By 1463 tensions developed between Philip and his son, Charles the Rash of *Burgundy, because of Philip's favouritism to the Croy family. Philip suffered a stroke in 1465 and died two years later in Bruges. He had a large number of illegitimate children, of whom Anthony, David, and Philip (I) of *Burgundy in particular were personally known to Erasmus at one time or another.

Although not unaware of Philip's warring (*Panegyricus* ASD IV-1 52, 82), Erasmus never criticized the duke and emphasized his devotion to the peaceful arts (Ep 604). He praised Philip with evident sincerity as truly deserving to be known as 'the Good,' said he was in fact the best of the four Valois dukes, and called the venerated bishop David a son worthy of such a father (*Epistola contra pseudevangelicos* LB X 1573A; Reedijk poems 41, 42).

BIBLIOGRAPHY: Joseph Calmette *The Golden Age of Burgundy* trans D. Weightman (London 1962) 128–69 / Richard Vaughan *Philip the Good: The Apogee of Burgundy* (London 1970)

IG

Philip (the Handsome), duke of BURGUNDY
22 July (or June) 1478–25 September 1506
Philip, called the Handsome, was the only son of *Maximilian of Hapsburg and Mary of Burgundy. He was born in Bruges amid the crisis following the defeat and death of his grandfather, Charles the Rash, duke of *Burgundy. As a Hapsburg Philip was an archduke of Austria, and he inherited the various titles of a duke of Burgundy after the sudden death of his mother on 27 March 1482. While Maximilian

was battling with the provincial estates for control of the Burgundian lands, Philip's education at Mechelen was supervised by Margaret of York, the widow of Charles the Rash. In 1494 he was declared of age and invested as duke, and on 21 October 1496 he married *Joanna, the daughter of *Ferdinand II of Aragon and *Isabella of Castile. Between 1498 and 1507 six children were born to Philip and his wife; *Eleanor, a future queen of France; the future *Charles V; *Isabella, who was to be queen of Denmark; the future Emperor *Ferdinand I; and *Mary and *Catherine, future queens of Hungary and Portugal respectively. In 1498, as a special distinction, Pope *Alexander VI sent Philip a golden rose, which was presented to him at Brussels with great solemnity (Epp 76, 77).

In 1500 Joanna became the heiress of the Spanish kingdoms. To establish her claims, Philip left with her for Spain on 4 November 1501. They passed through France, where King *Louis XII arranged splendid festivities in their honour (ASD IV-1 39–41); next, they were hospitably received by *John d'Albret, king of Navarre (ASD IV-1 42), and they eventually arrived in Spain in May 1502 to receive the homage of the Cortes of Castile and Aragon. Early in 1503, Philip set out on his return journey, while Joanna was detained in Spain by her fourth pregnancy. He passed through Savoy, where he was received by his sister *Margaret and her husband, Philibert II of *Savoy (ASD IV-1 46), and then travelled to Innsbruck to meet his father. In November 1503 he arrived back in the Low Countries, and Joanna returned in the spring of 1504.

In 1504 and 1505 Philip undertook a campaign against Karel van *Egmond, duke of Gelderland, and achieved at least temporary success. Meanwhile Queen Isabella had died on 26 November 1504. Even though Joanna's claims to the crown of Castile were not in doubt, her absence and the state of her health raised legal and political questions; friction arose when Ferdinand of Aragon attempted to retain the regency in Castile. The presence of Joanna and Philip was imperative; they therefore set out by sea on 10 January 1506, but a storm drove them to England, where they were detained until 23 April by King *Henry VII until negotiations for political and commercial agree-

Philip (1) of Burgundy

composition offered an opportunity to stress the beneficial aspects of peace. The *Panegyricus* (ASD IV-1 3–93) was presented to Philip at Brussels at Epiphany 1504 and was well received; not only was Erasmus handsomely rewarded (Ep 180; Allen I 44), but the composition was highly praised and many times reprinted. Erasmus himself relied on it to deny allegations of animosity against the French (Epp 1840, 2046). Praise for the returning prince is also the theme of a poem in Latin and another in Greek (Reedijk poems 78–9). Praise of Philip was again called for in the context of the *Vidua christiana* (LB V 726C), while even slight criticism of Philip (ASD IV-1 184–5) is noticeably rare in Erasmus' work.

BIBLIOGRAPHY: L.M.G. Kooperberg in NNBW VII 956–75 / ADB XXV 754–7 / BNB XVII 178–200 / Hermann Wiesflecker *Kaiser Maximilian I.* (Munich 1971–) I 167–71 and passim / Karl Brandi *Kaiser Karl V.* new ed (Darmstadt 1959–67) I 32–6 and passim / James D. Tracy *The Politics of Erasmus* (Toronto 1978) 17–19 and passim

IG & PGB

ments between England and the Low Countries had been completed (Ep 189). After their arrival in Spain, Joanna and Philip were proclaimed queen and king consort; a few months later, however, Philip died suddenly in Toledo after a brief illness (Epp 204–6, 393, 2143; LB V 230F). Mentally deranged, Joanna survived him until 1555. Philip, who was indeed handsome, had a reputation for pleasure-seeking and preferred to leave policy decisions to his advisers. His evident lack of sensitivity may have contributed to Joanna's illness and certainly led to alienation among all ranks of the Castilian population during the final months of his life.

Erasmus followed the short life of his sovereign with interest; hopes for a closer connection with the court arose when in 1503 Nicolas *Ruistre suggested that Erasmus should write a panegyric on Philip's first journey to Spain. Erasmus claimed that this particular type of literary composition did not appeal to him very much; moreover he was working under pressure, since Philip's return journey proceeded more quickly than expected (Epp 178–80). What did appeal to him was the fact that the

Philip (1) of BURGUNDY bishop of Utrecht, d 7 April 1524
A natural son of Philip the Good, duke of *Burgundy, and Margriet Post, the daughter of a respected Brussels family, Philip was born around 1464 and left with his mother's family until the age of twelve, when he was transferred to the court of duchess Mary of Burgundy. He may be the Philippus de Burgundia who matriculated at the University of Louvain on 7 December 1484. He then joined the future *Maximilian I and was knighted at Aachen during Maximilian's coronation as king of the Romans in 1486. Later that year he fought as one of Maximilian's captains in Flanders and Artois; however, Maximilian's captivity at Bruges (1487–8) caused him to re-examine his prospects in the King's service. He joined his brother David of *Burgundy, prince-bishop of Utrecht, and became a priest and David's coadjutor. His hopes for a speedy succession in Utrecht were dashed, however, when Maximilian managed to have Friedrich von *Baden appointed to the see after David's death in 1496. Philip returned to the court of Brussels; handsome himself and much involved with

women, he found favour with Philip the Handsome, duke of *Burgundy, and was named admiral of the Netherlands. In this capacity he accompanied the duke on his first journey to Spain from 1501 to 1503 and subsequently fought in the war against Gelderland. In 1508 he went on an embassy to Rome, taking with him the painter Jan *Gossaert, called Mabuse; Gossaert's art was transformed by his Italian experiences, and through him Italian influences left their mark on the development of Flemish painting. Philip of Burgundy himself would later employ Italian architects at great cost. He also remained an outstanding patron to Gossaert, who worked at the castle of Wijk, near Duurstede, for him as well as for his successor as admiral, Adolph of *Burgundy.

In 1510 two of Philip's natural sons matriculated together at the University of Louvain. Philip's attention again became focused on Utrecht, where from 1511 Bishop Friedrich was clearly losing his war against Gelderland. In 1516 he was forced by the court of Brussels to resign in Philip's favour and, with papal approval, the latter was duly elected prince-bishop of Utrecht on 18 March 1517, resigning in turn as admiral. After a temporary pause the war with Gelderland flared up again in 1521, preparing the way for a more general war with France. Philip had to defend his principality and did so with varying success. A resurgence of the pro-Gueldrian party within Utrecht after Philip's death finally led to decisive action on the part of *Charles v, and in 1528 Utrecht was integrated in the Hapsburg-Burgundian state.

Bishop Philip's entry into Utrecht on 19 May 1517 (Ep 584) was described by his new secretary, Gerard *Geldenhouwer, in an *Epistola ... de triumphali ingressu*, which appeared in print together with a congratulatory letter by Erasmus (Ep 645). R.R. Post suggested that it was for Philip's benefit on this occasion that Erasmus prepared his *Declamatiuncula* (LB IV 623–4), a short speech by a bishop in response to congratulatory addresses on behalf of his flock. At the same time Erasmus dedicated to the new bishop his *Querela pacis*, together with a preface, which, alluding both to Philip's martial past and to the current lull in the fighting, encouraged 'our new bishop' to 'be more diligent to preserve the peace' (Ep 603). Erasmus later commented that in his advanced

years Philip conducted the subsequent operations much against his personal wishes at the request of Charles v (*Epistola contra pseudevangelicos* LB X 1573). Not only did Geldenhouwer, the secretary, turn out to be a compulsive letter-writer, the bishop himself also responded with letters and invitations (Epp 695, 728), which greatly pleased Erasmus (Epp 751, 761, 763, 783, 794, 809), although he was at first too busy to hurry off to the bishop's presence (Epp 758, 759) and subsequently was not prepared to go out of his way to meet Philip (Epp 811, 812, 837, 867). Eventually they met at Mechelen in March 1519 (Ep 952) and again in August (Ep 1001), and in 1524 Erasmus recalled that as a reward for the *Querela pacis* Philip had offered him a prebend, which he declined, and a valuable ring, which he accepted (Allen I 43). In November 1519 he followed this up by dedicating to Philip his paraphrase of the shorter Pauline Epistles (Ep 1043), and ten months later he may momentarily have had second thoughts about the declined prebend (Ep 1141). It does not seem that personal contacts with Philip continued after Erasmus' move to Basel, but on Philip's death Erasmus remembered him gratefully (Ep 2299). He saw in the bishop a liberal churchman and a friend of the new learning (Ep 1165; LB VI f ***3 verso, X 1573). A contemporary portrait drawing is reproduced in CWE 5 22.

BIBLIOGRAPHY: Allen Ep 603 / Eubel III 336 / Henri Pirenne *Histoire de Belgique* (Brussels 1902–32) III 97–8, 292–3, and passim / de Vocht *Literae ad Craneveldium* Ep 10 and passim / J. Prinsen *Gerardus Geldenhouer Noviomagus* (The Hague 1898) 37–51 and passim / *Collectanea van Gerardus Geldenhouer Noviomagus* ed J. Prinsen (Amsterdam 1901, including *De triumphali ingressu* and Geldenhouwer's Latin *vita* of Philip first published in 1529) / *Matricule de Louvain* II-1 492, III-1 391 / Alexandre Henne *Histoire du règne de Charles-Quint en Belgique* (Brussels-Leipzig 1858–60) I 123–4, II 188, IV 330–2, and passim / LP II 3015 and passim / R.R. Post 'Een ontwerp van een bischoppelijke toespraak gemaakt door Erasmus' *Archief voor de geschiedenis van de Katholieke Kerk in Nederland* 9 (1967) 322–9

PGB

Philip (II) of BURGUNDY d June 1527
Philip, the eldest of the three natural sons of
Philip (I) of Burgundy, matriculated at the
University of Louvain on 27 April 1510,
together with his brother Jan. Philip held a
canonry of Our Lady's in Antwerp and after
his father's death he took Gerard *Geldenhouwer into his household there. He died
young at Venice. He may be identical with the
Philip mentioned by Erasmus in November
1517 in a letter to Geldenhouwer (Ep 714).

BIBLIOGRAPHY: Allen Ep 714 / Matricule de
Louvain III-1 391 / de Vocht Literae ad Craneveldium Epp 117, 238, and passim

PGB

Philip (III) of BURGUNDY 1 October 1512–
1525/6
Philip, the eldest son of Adolph of *Burgundy,
was tutored at home by Erasmus' friend Jan
*Becker of Borsele, probably as early as 1519
(Ep 1005). In the autumn of 1522 both were sent
to Louvain, as Becker told Erasmus, not on
account of the university so much as on
account of the climate, which was deemed to be
beneficial to the boy's weak health (Ep 1321).
Philip matriculated on 4 December 1522 but
died before February 1527, by which time
Becker had returned to Louvain with Philip's
younger brother, Maximilian (II) of *Burgundy, who had become the heir-apparent to
his father's title (Ep 1787).

BIBLIOGRAPHY: Allen Ep 1005 / Matricule de
Louvain III-1 688 / de Vocht CTL I 264

PGB

Andreas BURGUS See Andrea da BORGO

Rienck van BURMANIA of Friesland, d 1563
Rienck (Irenicus Phrysius), the son of the
Frisian noble Rienck van Burmania and Eeck
Hania, studied in 1530 at Dole, where his
relative *Viglius Zuichemus had spent some
years. In 1535 he became a doctor of law under
Andrea *Alciati at Pavia. In June 1535 he
returned home via Basel, delivering Ep 3022
from Hector van *Hoxwier to Erasmus and
continuing his journey before the end of the
month, carrying letters from Erasmus to Erasmus *Schets (Ep 3025; cf Ep 3028), Tielmannus
*Gravius – a letter he evidently entrusted to
another (cf Ep 3041) – and Viglius Zuichemus

(cf Ep 3060). He became a member of the council
of Friesland, and afterwards lord of the manor
(grietman) of Leeuwarderadeel, an office he still
held in 1555. In the late thirties he was the
deputy of Georg *Schenck von Tautenburg as
governor (stadhouder) of Drenthe and bailiff
(drost) of Coevorden. On Schenck's death
(1540) he was appointed bailiff of Coevorden,
Maximiliaan van *Egmond being charged with
the governorship of Drenthe. When Willem
van der Lindt (Lindanus) entered Friesland as
inquisitor (1557), Burmania was among his
foremost opponents and played an important
part in his removal. His wife, Deytzen van
Unema, who survived him by three years, bore
him two sons, Upcke and Jan.

BIBLIOGRAPHY: Allen Ep 3022 / A.J. van der
Aa et al Biographisch woordenboek der Nederlan-
den (Haarlem 1852–78, repr 1965) II 1612–3 /
W.M.C. Regt in NNBW VII 245

C.G. VAN LEIJENHORST

von dem BUSCHE, von BÜSCHEN See
BUSCHIUS

Burchardus BUSCHIUS documented from
1496, d before 31 December 1541
Burchardus (Borchardus) was a younger
brother of Hermannus *Buschius. Like
Hermannus he was probably born at the castle
of Sassenberg, east of Münster in Westphalia.
On 11 April 1496 he matriculated at the
University of Rostock. At an early age he was
directed towards an ecclesiastical career and
was ordained sub-deacon on 23 April 1519
(Münster, Staatsarchiv, MSS Urkunden des
Mindener Domstifts 402a). In the same year he
was appointed precentor of the cathedral
chapter of Minden and archdeacon of Apelern,
between Minden and Hannover. On 16 April
1526 he was elected dean of the Minden
chapter. In 1532 Ludolf *Cock mentioned him
to Erasmus as a member of the entourage of
Franz von *Waldeck, bishop of Minden,
Münster, and Osnabrück (Ep 2687).

An epigram by Hermannus Buschius is
entitled 'Borchardo Buschio fratri iuris stu-
dioso' (Carmina f e 6 recto); it suggests that
Burchardus had an interest in scholastic
theology as well as canon law. Although he
went on to become a determined opponent of
the Reformation, his relations with Hermannus

remained friendly. He arranged for Hermannus to lecture in Minden, and Hermannus chose Macrobius and Ovid as his topics. After Hermannus' death in 1534, Burchardus presented his brother's library to the cathedral of Münster. He seems to have died in 1541, and on 31 December 1541 Pope *Paul III appointed a successor to his canonry. As he had never been ordained priest his contemporaries did not criticize him for having three illegitimate sons.

BIBLIOGRAPHY: *Matrikel Rostock* I 278 / Hermann Hamelmann *Geschichtliche Werke* ed H. Detmer et al (Münster 1902–13) I-2 37, I-3 88, 228–9, and passim / Hermannus Buschius *Carmina* (Deventer 1496/7 repr in his *Vallum humanitatis* ed J. Burckhard, Frankfurt 1719)
ROBERT STUPPERICH

Hermannus BUSCHIUS d April 1534
Buschius (von Büschen, Busch, von dem Busche, Pasiphilus) was descended from a noble Westphalian family with estates in the territory of Schaumburg. The son of Burchardus, he was born around 1468 at the castle of Sassenberg, east of Münster in Westphalia. He received his first instruction from Rudolf von *Langen, a relative, in Münster, then studied with Alexander *Hegius in Deventer, Rodolphus *Agricola in Heidelberg (1484), *Pomponius Laetus in Rome, and the older Filippo *Beroaldo in Bologna (until 1491). He joined the court of Heinrich von Schwarzburg, bishop of Münster, but was soon dissatisfied with his position and in 1495 matriculated at Cologne intending to study law. During the following ten years he taught in Münster, Osnabrück, Bremen, Hamburg, Lübeck, Wismar, Rostock, and other cities. The new curriculum he introduced while he was teaching at Greifswald later enabled the young student Johann *Bugenhagen to lay the foundation for his solid knowledge of Latin.

In 1502 Buschius taught rhetoric and poetry in the newly founded University of Wittenberg, and in 1503 at Leipzig, where he obtained a bachelor's degree in law. Meanwhile his first poems, such as the *Hecatostichon* (Leipzig: M. Landsberg 1503) in honour of the Virgin Mary, had been well received. When he returned to Cologne in 1507 he wrote a pessimistic Sapphic ode, *De contemnendo mundo*, and a eulogy in honour of the city, *Flora* (Cologne: heirs of H. Quentel 1508). Soon he ran into opposition to humanist studies at the University of Cologne, where outdated textbooks were still in use; Ortwinus *Gratius was one of his main opponents. In 1511 the University of Cologne declared Johann *Reuchlin's *Augenspiegel* to be heretical, and from then on Buschius emerged as one of the leading spokesmen in defence of Reuchlin.

Erasmus met Buschius, *Hutten, and Reuchlin in the spring of 1515 in Frankfurt am Main (Hutten *Opera* I Ep 26). This meeting was the beginning of a friendship between Erasmus and Buschius that lasted for almost ten years. They met again in Cologne in 1516, when Hermannus wrote a poem in honour of Erasmus' arrival (published by Erasmus and reprinted in LB III-1 198–9; cf Epp 440, 463, 490), and at Speyer in 1518 (Epp 867, 877). Erasmus printed with his *Querela pacis* two of Buschius' elegies dealing with the destruction caused by war. Buschius was probably not involved in the writing of the *Epistolae obscurorum virorum*, although he may have supplied some of the details mentioned in the first letters. Because of rising tensions in Cologne, in 1516 or 1517 he accepted the position of rector of the Latin school in Wesel. He was at that time writing his most important work, the *Vallum humanitatis* (Cologne: N. Caesar 1518), a defence of humanism dedicated to Hermann von *Neuenahr; accepting Erasmus' advice (Ep 1196; cf LB X 1639E), Buschius used only moderate irony and refrained from bitter sarcasm. The book was highly esteemed and received warm praise from Erasmus (Ep 1110). Among other works Buschius wrote between 1516 and 1518 were an ode against Cologne (1516) and an *Epicedion* for his friend Johannes *Murmellius (Cologne: E. Cervicornus 1517; Ep 838). Between 1517 and 1519 Erasmus may have tried repeatedly to secure for Buschius the chair of Latin at the Collegium Trilingue of Louvain, but on one occasion it did not fall vacant and subsequently it was given to Conradus *Goclenius (Epp 722, 884, 1050, 1051; Ep 722 refers to a scholar introduced to Erasmus by Neuenahr, without giving a name). Buschius supported Erasmus in 1520 in his confrontation with Edward *Lee (Ep 1109) and during a stay with Johann *Froben at Basel he had a letter and some verses against Lee printed, efforts that were appreciated by Erasmus (Ep 1126). From 1520 Buschius lived for some years in Worms, where Erasmus failed to meet him in November 1522 (Epp 1109, 1342). Meanwhile, at the diet of Worms in 1521 Buschius had joined Hutten and his friends in their stand for *Luther. On a visit to Basel Buschius insulted conservative feelings on 13 April 1522 when he took part in a feast of pork during Lent. He also indulged in heated debates with the opponents of reform. When he left Basel five weeks later Erasmus apologized on his behalf to Christoph von *Utenheim, bishop of Basel (Ep 1496).

From the summer of 1523 Erasmus was suddenly incensed against Buschius (Ep 2961). Although nothing of the kind was ever published, he heard and believed various rumours about attacks that Buschius was said to be preparing against him (Epp 1386, 1406, 1466, 1496). In the *Epistola ad fratres Inferioris Germaniae* (LB X 1607 A-E) and elsewhere Erasmus vented his disappointment as he felt betrayed by a friend and protégé, and the two men lost track of each other in the following years (but cf *Ciceronianus* ASD I-2 683). Buschius received a call to the University of Marburg in 1527 and taught poetry and classical authors there until 1533. He was the main advocate of the Lutheran view at the public discussion in Münster in 1533, opposing the Anabaptist heresies of Bernhard *Rothmann (Ep 2957). When the Anabaptists burnt the library of Münster, Buschius bequeathed his own books to the dean and the chapter. Shortly afterwards, in April 1534, he died at Dülmen in Westphalia (Epp 2957, 2961, 2976, 3031A). Verses by Buschius in praise of Erasmus are printed in LB I (22).

BIBLIOGRAPHY: Allen Ep 830 / NDB III 61–2 / L. Geiger in ADB III 637–40 / L. Geiger *Johann Reuchlin* (Leipzig 1871, repr 1964) 361, 413–15, and passim / Georg Ellinger *Geschichte der neulateinischen Literatur Deutschlands im sechzehnten Jahrhundert* (Berlin 1929–33) I 419ff / Hans Rupprich in R. Newald et al *Geschichte der deutschen Literatur* (Munich 1957) IV-1 613–15 / AK II Epp 844, 878 / *Matrikel Leipzig* II 41 / Knod 82 / de Vocht CTL I 478–84 and passim
IG

Nicolaus BUSCIDUCENSIS, BUSCODUCEN-SIS *See Nicolaas van* BROECKHOVEN

Petrus BUSCONIUS *See Pieter* GHERINX

François (I) de BUSLEYDEN of Arlon d 22 August 1502
François de Busleyden (Buslidius, Busleiden), the second son of Gilles de Busleyden of Arlon and a brother of Jérôme de *Busleyden, matriculated at Louvain on 22 January 1482. He went to Italy for further studies, probably to Pavia, and obtained a doctorate of canon law in 1484–5. After his return he entered the service of Philip the Handsome, duke of *Burgundy, as chamberlain and tutor; he later became councillor and chancellor of Flanders (1490). He also received ample ecclesiastical preferment, becoming canon of St Lambert's, Liège, in 1483 and provost in 1485, and provost of St Donatian's at Bruges on 23 December 1490. When both his parents died (before 1489), François supervised the education of his brothers Jérôme and Valérien de *Busleyden. As preceptor and experienced 'Nestor' of Philip (*Panegyricus* ASD IV-1 61–2) François had considerable influence on the policy of Burgundy and prevented the Netherlands from becoming a mere tributary to Austria, while keeping good relations with France. He was appointed archbishop of Besançon on 12 September 1498 and dean of Our Lady's, Antwerp (taking possession on 1 October 1498); in addition to this he was canon of Cambrai and of St Gudula's, Brussels, where he was also treasurer. In November 1501 he accompanied Philip to Spain and died in Toledo just after he had been made a cardinal by Pope *Alexander VI. He was buried in the Cistercian abbey in Toledo, but his heart was taken to Besançon. His portrait is on a side altar in the chapel of Our Lady in the cathedral of Besançon.

François de Busleyden generously supported scholars, and Erasmus, who would have liked to gain his support as a patron (Ep 172, 1502), regretted his early death (cf Epp 180, 205). There is no evidence that Erasmus met François personally while he was in the service of Hendrik van *Bergen; he was, however, well informed about François' methodical way of working and his keeping of a diary (Ep 476). In addition to praising him in the *Panegyricus* (Ep 180), Erasmus mentioned him in an epitaph for his brother Jérôme and also in the new *Colloquia* of the autumn of 1524 (ASD I-3 413).

BIBLIOGRAPHY: Allen and CWE Ep 157 / de Vocht *Busleyden* 4–10, 205–7, and passim

IG

François (II) de BUSLEYDEN of Arlon, documented 1515–22 June 1517
François, the son of Valérien de *Busleyden, remained in Arlon and nearby Luxembourg with his mother after his father's death in 1514 and received instruction from his tutor, Jan *Becker of Borsele. He was mentioned in Jérôme de *Busleyden's will, where grave concern was expressed about his poor health; since he was not mentioned in the execution of the will he must have died in the summer of 1517.

BIBLIOGRAPHY: CWE Epp 320, 737 / de Vocht *Busleyden* 12–14, 342–3, and passim

IG

Gilles de BUSLEYDEN of Arlon, c 1465–14 July 1536
Gilles was the eldest son of Gilles de Busleyden, a commoner of Arlon, knighted in 1471 by Charles the Rash of *Burgundy, and of Jeanne (or Elisabeth) de Musset (Mussey) of Marville. Introduced by his father to the court of Philip the Handsome, duke of *Burgundy, he was appointed receiver for Luxembourg, Arlon, and Thionville on 20 March 1490. Eight years later he resigned this office in favour of his brother Valérien de *Busleyden and became master of the Chambre des comptes, whose president he was by 1510. From his father he had inherited some rents and properties at Bauschleyden (now in Luxembourg) and elsewhere; to these he added in the course of his successful career the estates of Over- and Nederheembel, Guirsch, Ter-Tommen, Rumelingen, and Ter-Bocht.

After the death of his brother Jérôme de *Busleyden in 1517, Gilles generously helped to carry out his brother's plan for the foundation of a Collegium Trilingue at Louvain (*Ratio verae theologiae* LB V 78; *Colloquia* ASD I-3 413). To the end of his life, the Trilingue continued to benefit from his advice and protection; he also

watched closely over the purse strings (Ep 2352). His six sons all studied at the Trilingue. His relations with Erasmus were cordial and trusting (Ep 1437). He frequently consulted Erasmus about the appointment of suitable instructors for the college, notably in the case of Matthaeus *Adrianus in 1517 (Epp 686, 691, 699) and also in 1531, when a replacement for Jan van *Campen was needed (Epp 2573, 2588). Busleyden helped Erasmus to collect his annuity as imperial councillor (Ep 1437) and in 1527 supported Erasmus' friends at court in their efforts to silence his enemies in Louvain (Ep 1802). He sent greetings to the ailing scholar in March 1536 (Ep 3111).

BIBLIOGRAPHY: Allen and CWE Ep 686 / de Vocht *Busleyden* 4, 16–25, and passim / de Vocht CTL I 40, 48, and passim

IG

Jérôme de BUSLEYDEN of Arlon, c 1470–27 August 1517
Jérôme was the third son of Gilles de Busleyden of Arlon, who became chamberlain of Charles the Rash of *Burgundy, and of Jeanne (or Elisabeth) de Musset (Mussey) of Marville. He was born around 1470 at Arlon. He probably received his first instruction in his native town but was sent at an early age to another school and by 1485–6 to the University of Louvain. When his parents died (before 1489), his brother François de *Busleyden saw to it that Jérôme continued to receive an excellent education; he was sent to Orléans to study law. Here he met Erasmus, who had fled from the plague in Paris (Ep 157). In 1501 Jérôme studied in Padua under Marcus *Musurus and Pietro *Pomponazzi and made the acquaintance of Cuthbert *Tunstall. On 8 February 1503 he obtained a doctorate of civil and canon law at Padua. François' death (22 August 1502) was a severe blow to Jérôme, who composed an epitaph for him (de Vocht *Busleyden* poem 1). No longer able to count on François' protection, Jérôme appealed to Philip the Handsome, duke of *Burgundy, for a suitable appointment (de Vocht *Busleyden* Ep 5, September 1502). Soon after his return from Italy, in 1504 he became councillor and master of requests in the reinstated grand council of Mechelen. At this time Busleyden, who had been archdeacon of Cambrai in 1503 (Ep 178)

Jérôme de Busleyden

composed three poems in praise of the house and its treasures. More's *Utopia* was published in 1516 with a dedication to Busleyden by Pieter *Gillis and a laudatory letter from Busleyden to More (Ep 484; de Vocht *Busleyden* Ep 81). Although never as influential as his late brother François, Busleyden was now a prominent figure, welcoming important visitors such as the Emperor *Maximilian I in 1508 and being delegated to congratulate *Henry VIII (1509) and *Francis I (1515) on their accessions to the throne. In 1516 he was one of the representatives of the future *Charles V sent to Luxembourg to receive the duchy's homage. On 24 June 1517 he was appointed to Charles' council, which was to accompany him to Spain (Ep 628). Two days earlier he made his will, providing above all for the foundation of the Collegium Trilingue in Louvain, an institution devoted to the teaching of the three languages and literature (Ep 683). While travelling to Spain by land in the company of Chancellor Jean *Le Sauvage, Busleyden fell ill in Bordeaux and died (Ep 650).

Busleyden wrote poems, a few speeches, and numerous letters, eighty-two of which have been collected. His most important contribution to culture was, however, the founding of the Collegium Trilingue according to a plan worked out with Erasmus, who by 1516 had become a close friend. Of the letters exchanged between them, unfortunately, very few remain (Epp 205, 244A, 470, 484). After their encounter in Orléans, they met again in 1503 in Brabant, when Busleyden assured Erasmus that his late brother François would have become his patron had he not died so suddenly (Ep 178), and Erasmus gave Jérôme a book with a dedicatory epigram (Reedijk poem 76). In 1506 he dedicated to Busleyden his translation of some of Lucian's dialogues (Ep 205). After his return from Basel in the spring of 1516, Erasmus resumed his close relations with Busleyden, as can be gathered from Ep 470, in which he invites his rich friend to relieve him of his horses, at a favourable price. It was at this time that the plans for the Collegium Trilingue were consolidated. Busleyden's departure for Spain and his death are frequently mentioned in Erasmus' letters, and of course he continued to take the liveliest interest in the development of the Trilingue.

and provost of St Peter's at Aire, in Artois, since 17 February 1500, decided on an ecclesiastical career and received more ecclesiastical preferment. He became canon of St Simon's, Trier, canon and treasurer of St Gudula's, Brussels, and canon of St Rombaut's at Mechelen, St Lambert's at Liège, St Waldetrudis' at Mons, and Our Lady's in Cambrai, as well as parish priest in Steenbergen in North Brabant. In the winter of 1505–6 he was one of the ambassadors sent to Rome to compliment *Julius II on his election. Busleyden delivered the formal address to the new pope.

After his return he settled in Mechelen in the house he inherited from François. Through Jérôme's additions it became an impressive mansion, beautifully adorned and furnished by craftsmen both from the Netherlands and from Italy. It is now a museum. Jérôme was very fond of music and a patron of Petrus *Alamirus; he possessed numerous musical instruments, and the organ he installed in his house became famous. His library contained a fine collection of books and manuscripts. Thomas *More, who was in the Netherlands on an embassy in 1515 (Ep 388), was a guest in his house and

In his writings Erasmus honoured Busleyden in the *Ratio verae theologiae* (1518, LB V 77–8) and composed epitaphs for him in both Latin and Greek (Epp 699, 804). He also paid tribute to his memory in the *Colloquia* edition of the autumn of 1524 (*Epithalamium Petri Aegidii* ASD I-3 413).

BIBLIOGRAPHY: Allen and CWE Ep 205 / de Vocht *Busleyden* / de Vocht CTL I passim

IG

Valérien de BUSLEYDEN of Arlon, documented 1489–1514

Valérien, the youngest brother of Gilles, François, and Jérôme de *Busleyden, studied in the College of the Lily at Louvain from the autumn of 1488 but did not matriculate until 25 February 1489. Gilles secured his appointment to the financial administration of Luxembourg. On 5 December 1498 Valérien was receiver-general for Luxembourg, Arlon, and Thionville and in 1501 councillor of the duchy of Luxembourg. In this capacity he gathered troops for the war against Karel van *Egmond, duke of Gelderland (March 1505). From his father he inherited the manors of Guirsch and Aspelt; he married Anne de Kempf (Keymich) and died prior to the summer of 1514.

In Ep 320 Valérien is mentioned as the father of François (II) de *Busleyden.

BIBLIOGRAPHY: Allen Ep 320 / de Vocht *Busleyden* 11–12 and passim

IG

Margarete BÜSSLIN documented at Basel and Freiburg, c 1522–1536

For information on Erasmus' housekeeper one must rely mostly on his correspondence and the *Colloquia*, but at least her family name is revealed by Staatsarchiv Basel-Stadt MS St Peter AAA 4 f 40 recto.

Margarete was looking after Erasmus' household in 1522 and 1523, when Heinrich *Eppendorf lived under his roof, or at least before he left Basel (Epp 1371, 2897). There is no doubt that she inspired Erasmus' characterization of the maid Margarete – ugly, outspoken, independent-minded – in *Convivium poeticum*, a colloquy first published in August 1523 (ASD I-3 344–59), and also gibes at maids in other colloquies. When Erasmus left Basel for Freiburg in 1529 she was, his outbursts

notwithstanding, indispensable enough to him to be moved along with his household (Epp 2151, 2158). In Ep 2202 he accused her of using her own discretion in giving away his things and painted a splendid picture of the self-reliant woman dauntlessly standing up to the male members of the household as well as the master who was trying to shelter behind them. He vented his feelings again in Ep 2735 ('Margarete furax, rapax, bibax, mendax, loquax') when reporting how he had tried, for the first time and the last (Ep 2897), to replace her with a younger woman, who promptly began stealing from his drawers in collusion with his servant *Jacobus. When Erasmus dissolved his household in 1535 and returned to live as a guest of Hieronymus *Froben at Basel, Margarete, who was by then quite elderly, was in a difficult position. Although three Freiburg professors had offered to help her (Ep 3045), it was left to *Glareanus, Bonifacius *Amerbach, and *Cousin to resolve her claims against her former master; while Margarete was apparently satisfied, Erasmus grumbled about the settlement (Epp 3054, 3055, 3059). After his death she is last heard of at Freiburg, where true to form, she was involved in a dispute with Johannes *Brisgoicus over some furniture from Erasmus' household (AK IV Ep 2067).

BIBLIOGRAPHY: Bierlaire *Familia* 90–1 and passim / Rudolf Wackernagel *Geschichte der Stadt Basel* (Basel 1907–54) III 86*

PGB

Martin BUTZER See Martin BUCER

Gerard de BYE See Petrus MELLIS

Jan BYL or BYLKENS See Jan BIJL

Luis CABEZA DE VACA See Luis NÚÑEZ *Cabeza de Vaca*

Diego CABRERA d c 1528

Diego Cabrera was a priest of the diocese of Orihuela in 1512, when he was consecrated titular bishop of Pulati in Albania. In 1528 he received the bishopric of Huesca but died before he could take possession of his see. He was a prominent defender of Erasmus at the conference of Valladolid in 1527, and Bataillon supposes him to be the auther of an anonymous letter in support of Erasmus which apparently circulated widely (Epp 2126, 2198).

BIBLIOGRAPHY: Bataillon *Erasmo y España* 245, 323, *and passim*

PGB

Diego de la CADENA *See Iacobus a* CATENA

Henricus CADUCEATOR of Aschaffenburg, documented 1524–9

Henricus Caduceator – only the Latin form of his name is known – was born in Aschaffenburg, on the Main, east of Mainz. He matriculated at the University of Erfurt in the summer term of 1524 and in March 1525 received his BA. Not much more is known about him except what he told Erasmus in his letter of 18 April 1527 (Ep 1811). There he claimed – surprisingly, in view of the date of his matriculation – that he had studied at Erfurt for eight years under the guidance of *Eobanus Hessus. It may thus be expected that he was still in Erfurt when the rebelling peasants occupied the city in April 1525. Soon thereafter he went to Frankfurt am Main and was appointed tutor of the five children of the patrician Philipp von *Schwalbach. Caduceator further stated that from childhood he had been afflicted with an eye disease which hindered his studies. He appealed to Erasmus for help, assuming that the famous scholar had read the works of Hippocrates, Galen, Averroes, Celsus, and other physicians. Erasmus replied with some consoling words and encouraged him to bear his condition with greater courage. Caduceator is documented in Frankfurt and Aschaffenburg for two more years through his correspondence with Fridericus *Nausea.

BIBLIOGRAPHY: Allen Ep 1811 / *Matrikel Erfurt* II 329 / *Epistolae ad Nauseam* 62–9

ERICH KLEINEIDAM

CAELIUS Rhodiginus *See Ludovico* RICCHIERI

Robertus CAESAR *See Robert de* KEYSERE

Johannes CAESARIUS of Jülich, c 1468–19 December 1550

Caesarius matriculated at Cologne on 9 November 1491 as a poor student from Jülich; he continued his studies in Paris under Jacques

*Lefèvre d'Etaples, graduating BA in 1496 and MA in 1498. During the next decade he taught at St Lebuin's school in Deventer and also published works by Lefèvre and *Clichtove in collaboration with local printers, especially Richard Pafraet. In 1508 he accompanied Hermann von *Neuenahr to Italy and used this opportunity to study Greek at Bologna. After his return in 1510, he began to teach Greek and Latin privately in Cologne. In 1512–13 he was in Münster teaching a course of Greek. He was to visit Münster again in 1518 (Ep 866); first, however, he returned to Italy and obtained a doctorate of medicine in Siena on 12 October 1513. After his return to Cologne he practised on occasion as a physician. By that time he was known as a very successful teacher; a number of his students became reputed scholars, especially Henricus *Glareanus, who in 1515 dedicated to him his *Panegyricus* for the Emperor *Maximilian I; Petrus *Mosellanus, who in 1517 dedicated to him his translation of Aristophanes' *Plutus* (Haguenau: T. Anshelm); and also *Agrippa of Nettesheim, Gerardus *Listrius, and Heinrich Bullinger. He mainly taught or tutored at Cologne, although he was at Mainz in 1524 and 1529 and at Leipzig in 1527. The sons of the noble houses of Solms, Wied, Stolberg, Isenburg, and Neuenahr were his students, and some of them supported him in his old age. From 1548 he lived in the house of the Brethren of the Common Life in Weidenbach, near Cologne, where he died two years later.

Johannes Caesarius edited a number of classical texts, such as Horace's *Epistulae* (Cologne 1523), which he dedicated to his pupils Anton and Valentin von *Isenburg; Diomedes Grammaticus (Haguenau: J. Setzer 1526); Celsus' *De re medica libri octo* (Haguenau: J. Setzer 1528); and Pliny's *Historia naturalis* (Cologne: E. Cervicornus 1524; Ep 1544). He also wrote successful manuals, especially *Rhetorica in VII libros sive tractatus digesta* (Cologne: J. of Aich 1529) and *Dialectica in x tractatus digesta* (Cologne: E. Cervicornus 1520). The latter was highly praised by *Melanchthon.

The relationship between Caesarius and Erasmus began in 1515 when Erasmus was in Basel and had recently met Glareanus, one of Caesarius' former students (Ep 374); the circle

was soon extended to include another of
Caesarius' pupils, Neuenahr, who was to
remain a close friend of both men (Epp 428,
442). In 1516 Erasmus dedicated to Caesarius
his translation of the first book of *Gaza's
Greek grammar (Ep 428), to be followed by the
dedication of the second book (Ep 771). In Ep
610 Caesarius thanked Erasmus for the first
dedication and asked him to write something in
support of *Reuchlin, to whose cause Caesarius was committed (RE Ep 244). Caesarius' next
letter (Ep 615) contains a report of Martin
*Gröning's visit to Cologne in 1517. The
controversy around Reuchlin continued to be
discussed in their correspondence (Epp 653,
701); Erasmus confided to Caesarius his unease
about the *Epistolae obscurorum virorum* (Epp
622, 808) and also his embarrassment when
the *Julius exclusus* turned up in Cologne (Ep
622); later he shared with him his worries over
the controversies with *Lee (Ep 1053) and
*Luther (Ep 1258). Caesarius in turn was
saddened by the quarrel between Erasmus and
his venerated teacher, Lefèvre (Ep 680), but
had no sympathy for another opponent of
Erasmus, Diego *López Zúñiga (Ep 1291).

By 1520 Caesarius had come into contact
with some of the Wittenberg reformers and
their friends, especially *Spalatinus, Johann
*Lang in Erfurt, and Melanchthon, who visited
him in 1528. He corresponded with Heinrich
Bullinger in the later years of his life. Caesarius
was to some extent sympathetic to the views
held by Wilhelm von *Isenburg, but like
Neuenahr and Erasmus he remained within
the fold of the traditional church. After 1518
few letters of the correspondence between him
and Erasmus have been preserved, but it is
obvious that they continued to write to each
other as good friends. Ep 2304 contains a
reference to a letter from Erasmus to Caesarius
that is now lost. In Ep 3006 Caesarius deplored
recent attacks by the Carthusians of Cologne
on Erasmus' views and wrote with appreciation of his *De praeparatione ad mortem*.

BIBLIOGRAPHY: Allen and CWE Ep 374 / NDB III
90–1 / ADB III 689–91 / Knod 83 / RE Ep 178 and
passim / J. Hashagen 'Die Hauptrichtungen
des rheinischen Humanismus' *Annalen des
historischen Vereins für den Niederrhein* 106 (1922)
1–56 esp 36–8 / Rice *Prefatory Epistles* Ep 32 and
passim / de Vocht CTL I 281 and passim

IG

Henrique CAIADO of Lisbon, d 1509
Caiado (Hermicus) was born in Lisbon; his
father, Alvaro, was a military captain. Caiado
started his education at the University of
Lisbon, then went to Italy. In Bologna he met
the humanist Cataldo Parisio Siculo, whom
King John II had summoned to Portugal in 1485
as teacher of his natural son Jorge and some
nobles. Caiado had hoped to study with
Angelo *Poliziano, but since he had recently
died, Caiado took his doctorate in law in
Padua, where his presence is documented
several times between 1503 and 1506. His fame
rests on his poetry.

Erasmus met Caiado in Rome, where the
latter died in 1509. Erasmus mentioned him in
Adagia IV viii 2, attributing his death to
excessive drinking, but had admiring words
for him in his *Ciceronianus* (ASD I-2 692). André
de *Resende referred to this in his speech at the
University of Lisbon in 1534. It is possible that
Erasmus also composed an epitaph for Caiado
(Ep 216, Reedijk poem 84), although Marcel
Bataillon does not think so.

BIBLIOGRAPHY: Marcel Bataillon 'La mort
d'Henrique Caiado' in *Etudes sur le Portugal au
temps de l'humanisme* (Coimbra 1952) 1–8 / *The
Eclogues of Henrique Cayado* ed Wilfred P.
Mustard with introduction and notes (Baltimore 1931) / André de Resende *Oração de
Sapiência* ed A. Moreira de Sá (Lisbon 1956) 54,
87–90 / Tomas da Rosa 'As éclogas de Henrique
Caiado' in *Humanitas* 3–4 (Coimbra 1953–4)
103–87 / Arnaldo Momigliano 'Enrico Caiado e
la falsificazione di *C.I.L.* II, 30' in *Terzo
contributo alla storia degli studi classici e del mondo
antico* (Rome 1966) I 111–19

ELISABETH FEIST HIRSCH

Tommaso de Vio, Cardinal CAJETANUS of
Gaeta, 20 February 1469–10 October 1534
Tommaso de Vio, better known as Cajetanus,
was born in Gaeta, the son of Francesco and
Isabella de' Sieri. The name he received at
baptism, Giacomo, was changed to Tommaso
when he entered the Dominican order (1484).
In 1488 he went to Bologna to study theology;
after being ordained in 1491 he was sent to
Padua to complete his studies. Here he
obtained the chair of theology in the Dominican convent (1493) and later taught at the
University of Padua. On 18 May 1494, during

Tommaso de Vio, Cardinal Cajetanus

the general chapter of his order in Ferrara, Cajetanus held a memorable debate with Giovanni *Pico della Mirandola and immediately afterwards was nominated *magister sacrae theologiae*. His academic career continued at the universities of Pavia (1497–9) and Rome (1501–8), where he taught thomistic theology. His ecclesiastical career included important posts in his order (procurator-general in 1501, vicar-general from 20 August 1507, master-general from 11 July 1508 until 22 May 1518) and in the church. Cajetanus strongly supported *Julius II; he opposed the positions promoted at the schismatic council of Pisa (1511–12) and expressed his views on papal authority in the treatise *De comparatione auctoritatis papae et concilii*, completed on 12 October 1511. Also highly relevant are his contributions to the Lateran council (1512–17), during the course of which he wrote the *Apologia de comparata auctoritate papae et concilii* in answer to Jacques Almain's criticism of the previous tract. On 1 July 1517 Cajetanus was proclaimed cardinal priest of San Sisto and later of Santa Prassede. On 26 April 1518 Pope *Leo x sent him as legate to the Emperor *Maximilian I and

to *Christian II of Denmark; it was during the course of this legation that the memorable encounter between Cajetanus and Martin *Luther took place at the diet of Augsburg (12 October 1518). While still in Germany Cajetanus was nominated bishop of Gaeta, and upon his return he was solemnly received by Leo x (5 September 1519). During the conclave following Leo's death, Cajetanus supported the candidacy of Adriaan Floriszoon, who after his accession as *Adrian VI sent him (in the summer of 1523) as legate to Hungary, Bohemia, Poland, and Germany, whence he was recalled by *Clement VII. Taken prisoner during the Sack of Rome, Cajetanus was obliged to pay a ransom of five thousand ducats. When Clement VII consulted him on the question of the divorce of *Henry VIII of England, Cajetanus advised against granting the king's request (13 March 1530) and later repeated his view in a letter to the English monarch (27 January 1534). On 13 October 1530 Cajetanus wrote his will and made his nephew Sebastiano de Vio his heir. According to his wishes, he was buried outside the church of Santa Maria sopra Minerva.

The name of Cajetanus begins to appear rather late in the correspondence of Erasmus. In two letters in the winter of 1518–19 Erasmus revealed that he was informed about the cardinal's activity at the diet of Augsburg and condemned his attitude towards Luther (Epp 891, 939). Erasmus continued to follow Cajetanus' mission in Germany with considerable attention (Epp 999, 1041) and showed his familiarity with his tracts on papal authority (Epp 1006, 1033). Soon Erasmus became aware of Cajetanus' antagonism towards *Reuchlin (Epp 1006, 1033), and his general disapproval of the conduct of the cardinal is epitomized in the letter of March 1521 to Nicolaas *Everaerts (Ep 1188). Here Cajetanus is depicted as an unbearably proud and arrogant individual, in terms which are later resumed and reinforced in the anonymously published tract *Acta Academiae Lovaniensis contra Lutherum* (*Opuscula* 323).

A sudden change of attitude is revealed by Erasmus' letter to Pierre *Barbier of 13 August 1521 (Ep 1225), in which he praised as exemplary for its penetration and objectivity Cajetanus' *De divina institutione pontificatus*

Romani pontificis, completed on 17 January 1521 and published during that year in Rome, Milan, and Cologne. From the letter to Barbier may be dated a new kind of respectful and friendly relationship between Erasmus and Cajetanus, the austere Dominican, philosopher, theologian, and constant advocate of ecclesiastical reform. The Dutch humanist continued to refer in his letters to the work of Cajetanus (Epp 1275, 1412), was informed about his legation to Hungary (Ep 1417), and recalled some negative remarks about the cardinal made by the Dominican Johannes *Faber (Epp 2205, 2445). From Ep 2619 we learn that Erasmus received Cajetanus' anti-Lutheran tracts *De communione sub utraque specie, De integritate confessionis, De satisfactione,* and *De invocatione sanctorum adversus Lutheranos,* all completed on 25 August 1531. The humanist praised these works for their erudite brevity and sobriety in argument, and in turn sent the cardinal his *De concordia.* Epistolary exchanges between the two are mentioned in Epp 2728, and 2729, but it is evident that part of their correspondence is lost (Epp 2929, 2935). The only letter from Erasmus to Cajetanus that is still extant is dated 23 July 1532 (Ep 2690). In answer to Cajetanus' pleas for moderation in reaction to his critics and detractors, Erasmus discussed the actions of his antagonists in a deferential but unforgiving manner and expressed the wish that the pope would recognize his merits. Subsequently Cajetanus intervened in favour of Erasmus and showed the pope either Ep 2690 or a subsequent letter (Ep 2779).

On 4 April 1533 (Ep 2787) Christoph von *Stadion commented on some of the 'errors' found in Cajetanus' work by the theologians of Paris. Cajetanus himself replied in his *Responsiones ad quosdam articulos nomine theologorum Parisiensium editos ad magistrum Ioannem studii Moguntini regentem missae,* which were not completed until 30 December 1533. After the cardinal's death Erasmus denounced the attacks against himself which the Dominican Lancellotto de' *Politi had included in his polemic against Cajetanus (Ep 3127).

Erasmus quotes the works of Cajetanus or otherwise mentions him in the *Apologia contra Stunicam* (LB IX 387C), the *Declarationes ad censuras Lutetiae* (LB IX 866A, 920D), the *Respon-* *sio ad disputationem de divortio* (LB IX 958A), and the *Responsio ad epistolam Pii* (LB IX 1105, 1119D, 1136A).

The one hundred and fourteen volumes published by Cajetanus during his lifetime are usually divided into pamphlets, theological works, philosophical works, exegetical works, and orations. A first collection of *Opuscula aurea* was published in 1511 (Paris: J. Petit) and was followed in 1558 by *Opuscula omnia* (Lyon: heirs of J. Giunta). Particularly significant are *Commentaria in de ente et essentia S. Thomae* (1494–5); the commentaries to Aristotle's *Metaphysics* (1493–6), *De interpretatione* (1496), *Posterior analytics* (1496), *Praedicamenta* (1498), and *De anima* (1509); the commentary to Porphyry's *Isagoge* (1497); and the philosophical treatises *De nominum analogia* (1498) and *De conceptu entis* (1509). The most important works completed during the period when Cajetanus was master-general of his order and papal legate are his commentaries to the *Summa theologia* of St Thomas Aquinas, published in Rome in four separate parts in 1507, 1511, 1517, and 1520. With a *motu proprio* of 18 January 1880 Pope Leo XIII ordered that the commentaries of Cajetanus be included in the *Editio Leonina* of the works of St Thomas. During the last part of his life Cajetanus devoted much of his effort to the rebuttal of Lutheran positions and to biblical exegesis. Particularly notable among the latter are *Ientacula Novi Testamenti* and the series of the *Commentaria in Epistulas et Acta Apostolorum,* composed between October 1528 and August 1529.

BIBLIOGRAPHY: Allen Ep 891 / Bio-bibliographical research was begun shortly after Cajetanus' death through the efforts of J.B. Flavius (cf M.H. Laurent 'Les premières biographies de Cajétan' *Revue Thomiste* 86–7, XVII (1934–5)) and continued by V.M. Fontana (Rome 1675), A. Ciacconius (Rome 1675), A. de Altamura (Rome 1677), Quétif-Echard (Paris 1719), A. Touron (Paris 1743), and G. Contarini (Venice 1769) / One of the most relevant twentieth-century biographies is A. Cossio *Il Cardinale Gaetano e la Riforma* (Cividale 1902) / See also P. Mandonnet in DTC II 1313–29; the biographical study prefacing the edition of Cajetanus' *Commentaria in Porphryii Isagogen ad Aristotelis Praedicamenta* (Rome 1934) by P. Isnardus M. Marega; J.F. Groner *Kardinal Kajetan: Eine*

Gestalt aus der Reformationszeit (Fribourg-Louvain 1951); P. Kalkoff 'Kardinal Kajetan auf dem Augsburger Reichstage von 1518' in *Quellen und Forschungen aus italienischen Bibliotheken und Archiven* 10 (Rome 1907) Heft 1; the articles in the commemorative issue dedicated to Cajetanus of the *Revue Thomiste* quoted above; and Jared Wicks 'Thomism between Renaissance and Reformation: the case of Cajetan' *Archiv für Reformationsgeschichte* 68 (1977) 9–32

DANILO AGUZZI-BARBAGLI

Jan CALABER of Louvain, d 14 July 1527
Calaber was born in Louvain. He entered the university there and received his medical doctorate in 1489, becoming a professor the same year. He resigned the professorship in 1522. He was elected rector of the university on 31 August 1514 and again on 28 February 1517. During his third term as rector between 31 August 1519 and 29 February 1520, his two sons, Jan and Hendrik, matriculated in the university. It was also while he was rector that a student prank brought him into conflict with Rutgerus *Rescius who was later arrested (Ep 1046). When Calaber's term as rector had ended Rescius brought suit against him. Jan *Briart tried to bring about a settlement (Ep 1225), but legal proceedings appear to have dragged on for many months (Ep 1240). Erasmus advised Rescius not to settle without receiving full satisfaction from the former rector. The outcome of that suit is not known, but it is possible that Calaber had not acted out of ill will but out of deference to the influential opponents of the Collegium Trilingue.

Calaber died at an advanced age; he was buried in the convent of the White Nuns where he had founded a benefice. Among his heirs was Joost *Vroye of Gavere.

BIBLIOGRAPHY: Allen Ep 1240 / de Vocht CTL I 412, 476–7, and passim / H. de Jongh *L'Ancienne Faculté de théologie de Louvain* (Louvain 1911) 201–3, 24*–25*, and passim / *Matricule de Louvain* III-1 83, 499, 556, 616–18

CFG

Celio CALCAGNINI of Ferrara, 17 September 1479–24 April 1541
Celio Calcagnini, the natural son of Calcagnino and Lucrezia Constantini, was born and educated in Ferrara. After about ten years (c 1496–1506) of service in the Ferrarese armies he was given a chair of Greek and Latin at the University of Ferrara in 1507 or 1509, was ordained in 1510 and admitted to the chancery of Cardinal Ippolito d'*Este. He distinguished himself on several diplomatic missions (1512–13), was nominated historiographer of the Este family (1517), and followed Ippolito to Hungary when the cardinal left Ferrara to take possession of the diocese of Eger (4 December 1517). Despite the brevity of his residence in their country, Calcagnini was able to establish close relations with leading representatives of Hungarian humanistic culture (Ferenc Perény, László Szalkán, and Sebestyen Mághy). In Hungary Calcagnini met the mathematician and astronomer Jakob *Ziegler, who exerted considerable influence on his thought. After attending the wedding of *Sigismund I of Poland and *Bona Sforza in the spring of 1518, he travelled extensively in the Ukraine. In October 1519 Calcagnini met Raphael of Urbino in Rome and became interested in the studies of the great painter and his associate Marco Fabio *Calvo on the topography of ancient Rome. After the death of Ippolito d'Este (2 September 1520) Calcagnini resumed his teaching at the University of Ferrara and his philological, philosophical, scientific, and archaeological studies. One of the recognized leaders of Ferrarese intellectual life (and thus mentioned by *Ariosto in *Orlando Furioso* XLII 90 and XLVI 14), Calcagnini developed strong anti-Lutheran positions, best revealed in the treatise *De libero animi motu* (1525), inspired by Erasmus' *De libero arbitrio.* Subsequently he became involved in the controversy on imitation originated by Giambattista Giraldi Cinzio's *Epistola super imitationem,* and expressed his firm opposition to the Ciceronians. He was consulted by Richard *Croke on the juridical problems relative to the divorce of *Henry VIII of England (1530), played a primary role in the legation sent by Ercole II d'*Este to Pope *Paul III (May 1539), and participated in the foundation of the Ferrarese Accademia degli Elevati in 1541. He died in the same year.

Erasmus met Calcagnini in the house of Richard *Pace during his visit to Ferrara in December 1508 (Ep 1578). Calcagnini is mentioned honourably in *Adagia* (II i 34, II iv 91) and in a letter of Ulrich von *Hutten (Ep 611), but it is questionable whether the 'Caelius' who appears in Ep 1407 may be identified with the Ferrarese scholar. The most important events in the relationship between Erasmus and Calcagnini centre around the composition and publication of the latter's *De libero animi motu*. On 22 February 1525 Floriano *Montini sent to Erasmus a manuscript copy of this treatise (Ep 1552). The Dutch humanist suggested its publication to Johann *Froben and allowed his answer to Montino (Ep 1578) to become a preface to Calcagnini's work. Shortly before the printing of the volume in June 1525, he wrote to Calcagnini informing him of the forthcoming edition; he criticized a passage of the work and suggested an amendment (Ep 1576). Calcagnini promptly replied with a long and obliging letter (Ep 1587).

In the *Ciceronianus* (ASD I-2 671) Erasmus praised the culture and the eloquence of Calcagnini as superior to that of *Ricchieri. But while he considered Calcagnini's style 'elegant and ornate,' he found in it traces of scholasticism sufficient to preclude the Italian humanist from being classified among the real Ciceronians. In the absence of other statements the ambivalence of these lines does not seem sufficient to justify Renaudet's conclusion: 'Erasme ne semble jamais avoir eu un gout très vif pour l'éloquence fleurie, prolixe, inépuisable de Calcagnini' (*Erasme et l'Italie* 221). Indeed, Erasmus' repeated references to Calcagnini's 'oration' in the Ferrarese residence of Pace (Epp 1576, 1578) seem by themselves adequate to prove the opposite. Calcagnini intelligently and sincerely thanked Erasmus for the observations concerning him in the *Adagia* and in the *Ciceronianus* (Ep 2869). Meanwhile the Dutch scholar continued to express an admiration for his 'old friend' (Epp 2956, 3043) that was shared by some of his correspondents (Ep 3002); Erasmus sent him greetings (Epp 3043, 3076) and received from him amicable expressions of care and concern (Epp 3085, 3113).

The first comprehensive edition of Calcagnini's works was published by Hieronymus *Froben: *Opera aliquot* (Basel 1544). Besides the letters it contains forty-eight varied works, including dialogues, apologiae, and a collection of moral maxims. The *Carmina* were

published by Giovanni Battista Pigna in a volume that included his own Latin poems and also those of *Ariosto (Venice: V. Vaugris 1553). While his projected history of the Este family was never completed, Calcagnini's catalogue of the Este medals and coin collections is still in manuscript at Modena. The commentary on Cinzio's essay on imitation appears in Giambattista Giraldi's *De obitu Alphonsi Estensis* (Ferrara: F. Roscius 1537) and the *Disquisitiones aliquot in libros Officiorum Ciceronis* in M.T. Ciceron *De somnio Scipionis fragmentum* (Basel: R. Winter 1538).

BIBLIOGRAPHY: Allen Ep 611 / DBI XVI 492–8 / E. Renaudet *Erasme et l'Italie* (Geneva 1954) 221 and passim / T.G. Calcagnini *Della vita e degli scritti di Mons. Celio Calcagnini* (Roma 1818) / E. Piana *Richerche ed osservazioni sulla vita e sugli scritti di Celio Calcagnini* (Rovigo 1899) / G. Huszti 'Celio Calcagnini in Ungheria' *Corvinia* 2 iii (1922) 57–71 / A. Lazzari 'Un enciclopedico del sec. XVI: Celio Calcagnini' *Atti e memorie della deputazione ferrarese di storia patria* 30 (1936) 83–164 / For the discussions on the treatise *Quod caelum stet, terra moveatur*, possibly the best known among Calcagnini's works, where the author defends from a philosophical standpoint the rotation of the earth on its axis, see F. Hipler 'Die Vorläufer des Nikolaus Copernicus, insbesondere C. Calcagnini' *Mitteilungen des Copernicus-Vereins zu Thurn* 4 (1882) 51–80; G. Righini *La laurea di Copernico allo Studio di Ferrara* (Ferrara 1932) / On the question of the divorce of Henry VIII see A. Roncaglia 'La questione matrimoniale di Enrico VIII e due umanisti italiani contemporanei' *Giornale storico della letteratura italiana* 90 (1937) 141–50

DANILO AGUZZI-BARBAGLI

Jacobus CALCAR See Jakob RIDDER

Johannes CALCEATOR See Johannes BRISGOICUS

Demetrius CALCONDILES See Demetrius CHALCONDYLES

Domizio CALDERINI of Torri del Benaco, 1446–June 1478
Calderini was born at Torri del Benaco, on Lake Garda, to Antonio Calderini and Mar-

gherita Pase. His baptismal name was Domenico, but this was later Latinized to Domizio. During his childhood the family moved to Verona, where his father became a successful notary; here he studied the classics under the humanist Antonio Brognanigo (or da Brognoligo). Later he travelled to Venice to study under Benedetto Brugnoli da Legnano.

In 1466 or 1467 Calderini went to Rome, where he joined the circle of humanists around the Greek Cardinal *Bessarion, becoming his secretary. In 1470 he began to teach Greek and rhetoric at the University of Rome, and in 1471 he became an apostolic secretary. In 1472 Pope *Sixtus IV sent Cardinal Bessarion to France to persuade *Louis XI to undertake a crusade against the Turks, and Calderini travelled in his train. After Bessarion died at Rome in November 1472, Calderini lived under the protection of cardinals Pietro Riario and Giuliano della Rovere (the future *Julius II), nephews of Sixtus IV. In November 1476 he accompanied della Rovere to France, where the latter was sent to curb an uprising at Avignon and to forestall a threatened council at Lyon. Calderini died of the plague at Rome.

Calderini wrote numerous commentaries on Juvenal, Martial, Ovid, Ptolemy, Virgil, and other classical authors, and engaged in a number of polemics with the humanists Niccolò *Perotti and Angelo Sani Salvini. He is mentioned in the correspondence of Erasmus as a member of a past age of literary excellence (Ep 1587), and Erasmus cited his works in the *Adagia* (II v 80, III v 76, IV v 35). In the *Ciceronianus* Erasmus stated that Calderini would have attained a Ciceronian style had not the dissipation at Rome killed him at an early age (ASD I-2 668).

BIBLIOGRAPHY: Allen Ep 1587 / A. Perosa in DBI XVI 597–605

TBD

Ambrogio CALEPINO of Calepio, c 1435–c 1510

Ambrogio Calepio, called 'il Calepino' (Calepinus), was the natural son of Count Trussardo, first feudatory of the Calepio valley near Bergamo. Born around 1435, he was baptized Giacomo and was legitimized with his brother, Marco, in 1452. In 1458 he entered the order of the Augustinian hermits, taking the name Ambrogio. After a novitiate at Milan he was transferred in turn to Mantua, Cremona, and Brescia. He was ordained priest in 1466 and returned to the convent at Bergamo, where he dedicated himself to study until his death in late 1509 or early 1510.

The most important product of Calepino's study was his Latin dictionary, first published in 1502 by Dionigio Bertocchi at Reggio, in Lombardy. Although it contained many gaps, the dictionary was an attempt to return to pure, classical Latin and was inspired by the *Elegantiae* of Lorenzo *Valla and the *Cornucopia* of Niccolò *Perotti. It proved immensely successful; nine editions appeared between 1502 and 1509, fifteen between 1509 and 1520, and many thereafter. Italian, French, and other vernacular translations were later added, and the name of Calepino became synonymous with dictionary.

Erasmus spoke highly of Calepino's dictionary (Epp 1725, 2446) but did not cite it often in his own work (LB VI 137F, IX 811C).

BIBLIOGRAPHY: Allen Ep 1725 / DBI XVI 669–70

TBD

Zacharias CALLIERGIS of Rethymnon, c 1473–after October 1524

Zacharias Calliergis was born at Rethymnon, in Crete, not later than 1473. He claimed descent from an old imperial Byzantine dynasty, and one of his ancestors, Georgius Calliergis, was honoured by Venice for his role in the war of Chioggia (1378–81) against Genoa. In his twenties he travelled to Venice, and around 1493 he founded a Greek press with the financial backing of a fellow Cretan, Nicolaus Vlastus. He published several volumes of excellent workmanship, including the *Etymologicum magnum*, a medieval Greek dictionary, completed on 8 July 1499. Early in 1501 Calliergis moved to Padua, where he copied by hand a number of Greek manuscripts. In 1509 he resumed printing at Venice, issuing several Greek devotional works. The economic difficulties Venice suffered because of the war of the League of Cambrai and the possibility of patronage in Rome led Calliergis to move to the papal city, where there was no Greek press. On 13 August 1515 he published the first Greek volume to appear in Rome, an edition of Pindar. Other publications followed until 27

May 1523, when his press completed the
Magnum dictionarium graeco-latinum of Guarino
Favorino. Calliergis then returned to his work
as a copyist, finishing in all over thirty
manuscripts, the last dated October 1524.

Erasmus recalled that in 1508 he had met a
Zacharias (probably Calliergis) at a meal in the
house of Marcus *Musurus at Padua and
described him as an exceptionally learned
young man.

BIBLIOGRAPHY: Allen Ep 1347 / DBI XVI 750–3 /
Deno John Geanakoplos *Greek Scholars in
Venice* (Cambridge, Mass, 1962) 201–22 and
passim

TBD

Florent de CALONNE documented 1489–1524
Florent (Flour) de Calonne, seigneur of Courtebourne, Hermelinghem, Austruicq, Quatre-
vans, and Akembon, was the son of Baron Jean
de Calonne and Jacqueline de Hondscoot. In
1489 he married Claude d'Humières, and in
1524 he was mayor of Saint-Omer. In this
capacity he presided over the twelve town
councillors who were responsible for police
and ordinary jurisdiction. Erasmus spent the
winter of 1501–2 in Florent's castle at Courtebourne, thirty kilometres north of Saint-Omer.
Only a short distance from Tournehem, the
castle was situated on an elevation on the road
from Licques to Ardre; today only a few ruins
of it are to be seen in the middle of the woods.

BIBLIOGRAPHY: Allen and CWE Ep 165 /
Anselme de Sainte-Marie *Histoire générale et
chronologique de la maison royale de France* 3rd ed
(Paris 1726–33) IX 278 / H. de Laplane *Les
Mayeurs de Saint-Omer* (Saint-Omer 1860) 19 / J.
Hadot 'Erasme à Tournehem et à Courtebour-
ne' *Colloquia Erasmiana Turonensia* I 87–96
ANDRÉ GODIN

Jean CALUAU of Angoulême, d June 1522
Jean Caluau may have been the son of Renaud,
procurator-general of Louise of *Savoy, the
mother of *Francis I. Licensed in law, he was
canon of Angoulême and abbot of La Couture
and La Couronne. He became councillor of the
Parlement of Paris on 16 January 1515, bishop
of Senlis on 16 March 1515, and master of
requests to Francis I in February 1516. In
December 1521 he was part of an embassy to
Switzerland led by René the Bastard of Savoy.

He returned to France in February 1522 and
died soon after at the royal court at Lyon.

In 1522 and 1523 Guillaume *Budé informed
Erasmus that he had succeeded Caluau as one
of the eight masters of requests (Epp 1328,
1370).

BIBLIOGRAPHY: Allen Ep 1328 / R. d'Amat in
DBF VII 927–8 / *Gallia christiana* x 1439

TBD

Francesco Giulio CALVO of Menaggio,
d February 1548
Francesco Giulio Calvo was born in Menaggio,
near Como. Little is known about the early
years of his life. In 1516, when still very young,
he opened a bookshop in Pavia, and by 1519 he
had travelled extensively through Europe in
search of manuscripts. He gained a considerable reputation as a humanist and numbered
among his friends Andrea *Alciati, Romolo
*Amaseo, Paolo and Benedetto *Giovio, and
Gian Matteo *Giberti. In May 1517 *Beatus
Rhenanus sent Erasmus a copy of a letter from
Calvo to Johann *Froben (Ep 581). In 1518 or
1519 Calvo changed his middle name from
Giulio to Minuzio, after his native town. For a
long time Calvo has been considered one of the
first Italian intellectuals responsible for introducing into Italy the early works of Martin
*Luther. However, Calvo's enthusiasm for the
Lutheran movement did not extend beyond the
year 1521, when he edited the anti-Lutheran
tract *Oratio in Martinum Lutherum* by Luigi
*Marliano. After 1519 he moved to Rome,
where he edited several works for the press of
Eucharius Silber. Around 1523 he established a
printing press of his own, and in 1524 he
succeeded Silber as printer for the apostolic
see. He continued his activities as a publisher
in Rome until 1534, despite serious losses
suffered during the Sack of 1527. In 1535 Calvo
moved to Milan, where he established another
printing house, tried to help friends like Giulio
*Camillo, and became interested in the prog-
ress of the council of Trent. Calvo died shortly
before 18 February 1548 and named as his sole
heir his servant, Antonio Chelucci da Colle.

Calvo met Erasmus at Louvain in the spring
of 1518, giving him editions of Theocritus and
Pindar and fragments of other works (Ep 832).
Calvo impressed Erasmus with his learning
and congeniality and insisted that he write to

Jean *Grolier (Ep 831). Calvo also gave Erasmus a copy of a letter by Andrea Alciati against monasticism, which Alciati later accused him of pilfering from his bookshelf (Ep 1261); the letter caused Alciati considerable concern because of its compromising contents, and he asked Bonifacius *Amerbach to write to Erasmus to prevent its dissemination (Epp 1201, 2464). In addition, Calvo was supposed to give Erasmus letters from Nicolas *Bérault in Paris but was accused by Bérault of being negligent in their delivery (Epp 925, 989, 994), and Erasmus could not recall receiving them (Ep 1002).

On his return to Italy Calvo visited Lodovico *Ricchieri at Milan and suggested to his host that Erasmus was displeased with his *Antiquarum lectionum libri* (Venice: Aldo Manuzio 1516), thus prompting an apologetical letter from Ricchieri to Erasmus (Ep 949). In later years, Erasmus was well informed about Calvo's activity as a printer in Rome. Having seen Jacopo *Sadoleto's *Interpretatio in psalmum 'Miserere mei Deus,'* published by Calvo in 1525 (Ep 1586), he wrote a brief but cordial note to the printer (Ep 1604), thanking him for publishing good books. Erasmus also heard that Calvo had published the works of Hippocrates in Latin in 1525 (Ep 1912), although he confused Calvo the publisher with Marco Fabio *Calvo, the translator of the work (Ep 1825).

Calvo wrote numerous prefaces to the editions issued by his presses; these, however, are the only writings of the Lombard scholar which have come down to us. Nonetheless his role in Italian cultural history is quite notable. The number of editions printed by Calvo surpassed one hundred and fifty, including medical, juridical, theological, and literary works. The works of Hippocrates were among the most famous of his publications. Another interesting enterprise was a series of comedies by Ludovico *Ariosto, Niccolò *Machiavelli, and other contemporary authors, published in 1524 and 1525. It is also interesting to note that during his period of activity in Rome Calvo was one of several publishers of short pamphlets containing letters from various personages from abroad, news concerning political and military events, and announcements of recent geographical discoveries.

These publications have a journalistic character and could well be considered as antecedents of modern magazines and journals.

BIBLIOGRAPHY: Allen Ep 581 / F. Barberi 'Le edizioni di Francesco Minuzio Calvo' in *Miscellanea di scritti di bibliografia ed erudizione in memoria di Luigi Ferrari* (Florence 1952) 57–98 / F. Barberi in DBI XVII 38–41 / *Le cinquecentine alla Biblioteca Trivulziana* ed G. Bologna (Milan 1965–) vol I *Le edizioni milanesi* / AK II Ep 767 and passim / BRE Ep 120 / *Le lettere di Andrea Alciato giureconsulto* ed G.L. Barni (Florence 1953) 3–18 and passim / Giovanni Mercati 'Su Francesco Calvo da Menaggio primo stampatore e Marco Fabio Calvo primo traduttore del corpo ippocratico in latino' in *Notizie varie di antica letteratura medica e di bibliografia* (Rome 1917) 47–71 / A. Prosperi *Tra evangelismo e Controriforma: G.M. Giberti (1495–1543)* (Rome 1969)

DANILO AGUZZI-BARBAGLI

Marco Fabio CALVO of Ravenna, died c 1527

Little is known of the early years of Marco Fabio Calvo, a native of Ravenna. Celio *Calcagnini, in a letter to Jakob *Ziegler of 1519 or 1520, described Calvo, then at Rome, as an impressive old man of eighty years, as austere as a Stoic philosopher, indifferent to riches, and extremely frugal and temperate. Calvo had probably been in Rome from 1510, labouring over the works of Hippocrates. On 24 July 1512 he completed a transcription of Hippocrates from Greek manuscripts, which is now in the Biblioteca Apostolica Vaticana (MS Graecum 278). On 14 August 1524 his Latin translation of Hippocrates was issued by the press of Francesco Giulio *Calvo at Rome.

In the first decade of his years in Rome Calvo spent a considerable amount of time in the household of the painter Raphael, where he completed a translation into Italian of Vitruvius' *De architectura*, so that his friend could read it with greater ease. Calvo and Raphael were planning to produce a pictorial reconstruction of ancient Rome, but the painter's sudden death in 1520 ended this grandiose antiquarian project. Calvo continued his studies of architectural remains on a much more modest scale and in 1527, a few weeks before the Sack of Rome, published the *Antiquae urbis Romae cum regionibus simulachrum* at the press of Ludovico

de Henricis of Vicenza. The work was published again in Rome in 1532. According to
Ginanni, Calvo lived until 1532. However,
more recent biographers tend to accept the
account of his death provided by Giovanni
Pierio Valeriano: captured during the Sack of
Rome by imperial soldiers and unable to pay
the ransom demanded, Calvo was left to die in
a hospital outside the city.

Erasmus was not well acquainted with
Calvo's activities. In a letter to him of 1 April
1527 Jan *Antonin criticized Calvo's translation
of Hippocrates (Ep 1810); in his reply Erasmus
confused Marco Fabio with the printer Francesco Giulio Calvo (Ep 1825).

BIBLIOGRAPHY: Allen Ep 1810 / Celio Calcagnini *Opera aliquot* ed A.M. Brasavola (Basel
1544) 101 / Pietro Canneti *Monumenta genealogica
nobilis familiae ravennatis De' Guiccioli* (Ravenna
1713) 11–14 / Vincenzo Fontana 'Elementi per
una biografia di M. Fabio Calvo ravennate' in
*Vitruvio e Raffaello: il 'De architectura' di Vitruvio
nella traduzione inedita di Fabio Calvo ravennate* ed
V. Fontana and Paolo Morachiello (Rome 1975)
45–61, containing an edition of Calvo's translation of Vitruvius based on MS Cod. It. 37–37a
of the Bayerische Staatsbibliothek of Munich /
Pietro Paolo Ginanni *Memorie storico-critiche
degli scrittori ravennati* (Faenza 1769) 403–8 /
Rodolfo Lanciani 'La pianta di Roma antica e i
disegni archeologici di Raffaello' *Rendiconti
della R. Accademia dei Lincei. Classe di scienze
morali* series V 3 (1894) 794–804 / Rodolfo
Lanciani *Storia degli scavi di Roma* (Rome 1902) I
240–1 / Giovanni Mercati 'Su Francesco Calvo
da Menaggio primo stampatore e Marco Fabio
Calvo da Ravenna primo traduttore del corpo
ippocratico in latino' *Notizie varie di antica
letteratura medica e di bibliografia* (Rome 1917)
47–71 / Giovanni Mercati 'Altre notizie di M.
Fabio Calvo' *Bessarione* 35 (1919) 159–63 /
Giovanni Pierio Valeriano *De litteratorum infelicitate* ed E. Brydges (Geneva 1821) 62–3 /
Roberto Weiss *The Renaissance Discovery of
Classical Antiquity* (Oxford 1969) 95–8

                              DANILO AGUZZI-BARBAGLI

Antonius CAMERANUS *See Petrus DECI-
MARIUS*

Joachim Camerarius

Joachim CAMERARIUS of Bamberg, 12 April
1500–17 April 1574
Joachim Camerarius (Kammermeister), the son
of Johann, a nobleman, episcopal official, and
councillor of Bamberg, matriculated in Leipzig
in the winter term of 1512 and studied mainly
under Georg Helt, acquiring a thorough
knowledge of Greek from Richard *Croke and
Petrus *Mosellanus. In 1518 he moved to
Erfurt, where he renewed his friendship with
*Eobanus Hessus, whom he had formerly met
in Leipzig. After obtaining his MA in Erfurt, he
went to Wittenberg, where he matriculated on
14 September 1521 and gave lectures on
Quintilian. He became a close friend of
Philippus *Melanchthon, whom he accompanied in the summer of 1524 on a visit to his
native Bretten, west of Karlsruhe. Camerarius
went on to visit Erasmus at Basel, bringing him
letters from Martin *Luther and Heinrich
*Stromer (Epp 1443, 1444). Erasmus regretted
that Melanchthon had not also come but
enjoyed meeting Camerarius (Epp 1445, 1452,
1466). In 1526 Camerarius became rector of the
newly founded Latin school in Nürnberg; he
married Anna, a daughter of Martin Truchsess

von Grünsberg, on 7 March 1527. Attending the diet of Augsburg with Melanchthon in 1530, Camerarius faced the Catholic theologians in a basically conciliatory spirit. After Ulrich of *Württemberg had regained possession of his duchy, Camerarius was asked in 1535 to help reorganize the University of Tübingen, and he stayed there until 1541. Thereafter he joined the University of Leipzig and to the end of his life served recurrently as dean of arts and rector.

A devoted classical scholar, Camerarius edited, annotated, and translated a great many ancient authors, among them Homer, Sophocles, Cicero, and Plautus. He also wrote works on grammar and style, which were often reprinted, and poems. He assisted Albrecht *Dürer in the publication of some of his books and composed a poem on the occasion of his death. Camerarius also wrote lives of Eobanus Hessus (Nürnberg: J. Montanus and U. Neuber 1553) and Melanchthon (Leipzig: E. Vögelin 1566). His historical writings include a work on the Bohemian Brethren (*Historica narratio de fratrum ... ecclesiis in Bohemia*, Heidelberg: G. Vögelin 1605) and a history of the Schmalkaldic war (*Belli Smalcaldici commentarius*, Frankfurt 1611). His letters to numerous friends, especially to Eobanus Hessus, are an important source of information on many contemporary issues. Two collections were published (Frankfurt: heirs of A. Wechel 1583, and Z. Palthenius 1595), but many letters, now in Munich, remain unpublished.

After his visit to Basel in the summer of 1524, Camerarius wrote to Erasmus on 30 September (Ep 1501) in terms of sincere admiration, thanking him for a kind reception. Erasmus replied in Ep 1524; he had heard of Wilhelm *Nesen's death by drowning and was glad that Camerarius, his companion at the time of the accident, had been able to swim to safety. Their further correspondence appears to have been sporadic; in 1528 Erasmus inquired about Camerarius' school and his literary success in Nürnberg (Ep 1945). They remained in contact through common friends such as Eobanus (Ep 2446) and Daniel *Stiebar (Ep 2745). Camerarius' literary output, especially his edition of works by late Greek astrologers and of a Greek syntax by Varennius, between 1531 and 1534, was severely criticized by Erasmus in a letter to

Eobanus that is now missing. Camerarius' reply was a mild reproof in his pamphlet *Erratum* (Nürnberg: J. Petreius 1535), in which he gathered evidence that all great men, including Erasmus had occassionally made mistakes. Together with Julius *Pflug, Camerarius took exception to Erasmus' *Ciceronianus* (1528) but delayed any public reaction until well after Erasmus' death, when his *Disputatio de imitatione* was published with his commentary on Cicero's *Tusculanae disputationes*, which were dedicated to Pflug (1538; cf *Melanchthons Briefwechsel* I Epp 693, 696, 714, II Ep 2018). When Camerarius heard the news of Erasmus' death he wrote very warmly of him in a letter to Stiebar.

BIBLIOGRAPHY: Allen Ep 1501 / NDB III 104–5 / ADB III 720–4 / *Matrikel Leipzig* I 522, II 496, and passim / *Matrikel Erfurt* II 302 / *Matrikel Wittenberg* I 107 / Carl Krause *Helius Eobanus Hessus* (Gotha 1879) I 87, and passim / Eva Mayer 'Daniel Stiebar von Buttenheim und Joachim Camerarius' *Würzburger Diözesangeschichtsblätter* 14–15 (1952–3) 485–500, especially 495 / *Der Briefwechsel des Justus Jonas* ed Gustav Kawerau (Halle 1884–5) Ep 314 and passim / *Melanchthons Werke in Auswahl* ed R. Stupperich et al (Gütersloh 1951–) VII Ep 79 and passim / Pflug *Correspondance* I Ep 126 and passim

IG

Giulio CAMILLO d 15 May 1544
Giulio Camillo Delminio was born about 1480 at Portogruaro or near San Vito di Tagliamento in Friuli. According to Francesco Patrizi, his cognomen Delminio refers to an ancient city of Dalmatia, his father's original home. Camillo studied at Venice and Padua, possibly without taking a degree. During Erasmus' visit to Italy (1506–9) he sometimes roomed with Camillo (Ep 3032); in the *Ciceronianus* (ASD I-2 637) Camillo is mentioned in juxtaposition with the Good Friday sermon which Erasmus heard in Rome in 1509. Camillo attended Celso Mellini's oration against Christophe de *Longueil in Rome on 16 June 1519. Before 1520 he taught at San Vito and Udine and about 1521–3 at Bologna. In these years of teaching, Camillo began designing a wooden theatre to provide a setting for the orator practising the ancient art of memory. He believed that in contemplating

the Hermetic and cabbalistic symbolism of his theatre the orator could master all knowledge by rising, perhaps through solar magic, to the eternal world of ideas (see Yates 135–74).

Absorbed in perfecting the design for the theatre, Camillo travelled feverishly for the rest of his life; he is found at Padua, Genoa, Venice, Portogruaro, San Vito, Gemona in Friuli, Bologna, Rome, Milan, and Pavia. In 1530 he journeyed to France with his friend Girolamo Muzio and secured the patronage of King *Francis I. While in France he wrote the *Trattato della imitatione*, which in the incomplete form in which it was published posthumously in *Due trattati* (Venice: Farri 1544) is a polite reply to Erasmus' *Ciceronianus*. After Camillo's return to Italy, Erasmus heard of this treatise from *Viglius Zuichemus (Ep 2632) and assumed (Ep 2682) that it was the scurrilous *Oratio pro M. Tullio Cicerone* of Julius Caesar *Scaliger (Paris: P. Vidoue 1531). Viglius questioned Camillo (Epp 2657, 2716). Although he concluded correctly that Camillo had written, as a gift to the French king, only a short work in Italian that he did not intend to publish, Erasmus continued to suspect Camillo of contributing to the *Oratio* (Ep 2736).

In spite of Erasmus' doubts about the king's generosity (Ep 2810), Camillo received additional grants to complete the theatre on his return to France in 1533 or 1534. Thereafter, although Camillo visited France at least twice more, Francis I began losing interest in the unfinished project. Some time after Ercole II d'*Este became duke of Ferrara (31 October 1534), Camillo dedicated to him a *Trattato delle materie che possono venire sotto lo stile dell'eloquente* (published in *Due trattati*) and visited his court, but not until early in 1544 did Camillo find a new patron in Alfonso d'Avalos, marchese del Vasto, the Spanish governor of Milan. For the marchese he dictated to Muzio *L'idea dell'theatro*. Camillo died unexpectedly at Milan.

When the *Idea* was published in 1550 (Florence: L. Torrentino), the editor, Ludovico Domenichi, could not find the wooden theatre which Camillo had built, but a painting or fresco of it was reported to exist in the villa of Pomponio Cotta, near Milan, in 1559 (Bartolomeo Taegio *La villa, dialogo* Milan 1559). The disdain felt by Erasmus and his friends for the magical theatre was shared by Camillo's fellow-Ciceronian Étienne *Dolet, but Camillo was defended by Francesco Florido Sabino, hailed as divine by Francesco Patrizi, and befriended by Johann Sturm. Yates has suggested that Camillo may even have been 'the real initiator of some of the new rhetorical and methodological movements of the sixteenth century' associated with Sturm and Ramus (Yates 235).

None of Camillo's works were published during his lifetime. In addition to the *Due trattati*, the *Idea*, and *Due orationi al re christianissimo* (Venice: n pr 1545, and Venice: V. Vaugris 1545), which first appeared separately, other works were collected in the frequently augmented and reprinted editions of *Tutte le opere*. The *Opere*, edited first by Ludovico Dolce (Venice: G. Giolito 1552), included *Discorso in materia del suo theatro*, *Lettera del rivolgimento dell'huomo a Dio*, and *Rime*. Later *De' verbi semplici*, *Topica*, *Discorso sopra Hermogene*, *Espositione sopra il primo e secondo sonetto del Petrarca*, *Grammatica*, poems and letters were added (Venice: G. Giolito 1560). Camillo's annotations on Petrarch's *Rime*, which survive in manuscript in a copy of the 1501 Aldine edition (Biblioteca Vaticana, Aldine III 2), may antedate those of Bembo, although as published in *Il Petrarca novissimamente revisto, e corretto da M. Ludovico Dolce* (Venice: G. Giolito 1553) they appear derivative to V. Cian ('Le cosiddette "Annotazioni" di M.G.C. Delminio sopra le rime del Petrarca' *Giornale storico della letteratura italiana* 100 (1932) 259–63). Two works on the theatre, *Pro suo de eloquentia theatro ad Gallos oratio* and *Ad Petrum Bembum carmen* (the poem which Camillo recited to Viglius Zuichemus, Ep 2716), were published in 1587 (Venice: G.B. Somaschi). Of the works which have survived only in manuscript (P.O. Kristeller *Iter Italicum* London-Leiden 1965–), *De transmutatione* has been published recently by L. Bolzoni ('Eloquenza e alchimia in un testo inedito di Giulio Camillo' *Rinascimento* 2nd series 14 (1974) 243–64).

BIBLIOGRAPHY: Allen Ep 2632 / G. Stabile in DBI XVII 218–30, with extensive bibliography / Frances A. Yates *The Art of Memory* (London-Chicago 1966) / E. Garin *Medioevo e Rinascimento* (Bari 1954) 144–9 / E.M. Hajós 'References to Giulio Camillo in Samuel Quicchelberg's "Inscriptiones vel tituli theatri amplissimi"' *BHR* 25 (1963) 207–11 / A.R. Cirillo 'Giulio Camillo's *Idea of the Theatre*: the enigma of the Renaissance' *Comparative Drama* 1 (1967) 19–27 / D. Radcliff-Umstead 'Giulio Camillo's emblems of memory' *Yale French Studies* 47 (1972) 47–56 / The mysterious fact that Camillo was at Geneva in 1542, observed with suspicion by Calvin, has inspired C. Vasoli to investigate Camillo's ties with reformers in France and Italy: 'Il "Luterano" Giovanni Battista Pallavicini e due orazioni di Giulio Camillo Delminio' *Nuova rivista storica* 58 (1974) 64–70 and 'Noterelle intorno a Giulio Camillo Delminio' *Rinascimento* 2nd series 15 (1975) 293–309

JUDITH RICE HENDERSON

Augustinus Vincentius CAMINADUS of Viersen, d 1511

Augustinus Vincentius Caminadus was from Viersen, near Cologne, and matriculated at Cologne on 25 October 1488 in arts. He met Erasmus at Paris in early 1497. To earn his livelihood, Caminadus publicized new releases on sale at bookstores and gave private instruction to young Zeelanders (BRE Ep 80), and also to two sons of a merchant from Lübeck, Christian and Heinrich *Northoff, whom Erasmus himself had also agreed to tutor (Epp 54–6). In July 1497, when Christian returned to Lübeck, Erasmus moved into the lodgings which Caminadus shared with Heinrich Northoff. Heinrich thus lived 'in the heart of the Muses' (Ep 61) until his return to Lübeck in February 1498. At the time Caminadus was preparing public lectures to promote the sale of the *Sylva odarum* of Willem *Hermans (Epp 70, 81). During one summer, while Erasmus was travelling, he looked after another young man from Lübeck in Erasmus' charge, perhaps Bernhard *Schinkel (Ep 82). An obliging friend, Caminadus did not hesitate to lend money to Erasmus (Ep 130), who permitted him in return to use a number of his manuscripts, notably that of his treatise *De conscribendis epistolis* (Ep 80).

On his return from the Netherlands, Erasmus was alienated from Caminadus, writing to Willem Hermans that 'there is no vestige of genuine affection between us, nor ever was, so different are we in temperament' (Ep 81). In February 1499, however, Caminadus accompa-

nied Erasmus to the Netherlands, but left him during the trip with the intention of joining him again on his route to Paris (Ep 91). Caminadus failed to appear at the rendezvous point, and on 2 May Erasmus angrily awaited him at Paris: 'Augustinus is not back yet. While he was away he caused general confusion, intercepting money sent to me and sending a threatening letter since he was afraid I had got my talons on it' (Ep 95). It is not known whether the two men saw each other again before Erasmus' departure for England, but on his return to Paris he once again lodged with Caminadus, 'living the literary life, on slender means' (Ep 119; see also Epp 124, 127, 129). It was at this time that Caminadus gave public lectures before a large audience to launch the first edition of the *Adagia*, of which he had corrected the proofs for the printer Johannes *Philippi (Epp 128, 129).

In early 1500 an epidemic forced Erasmus, Caminadus, and two of the latter's pupils to take refuge at Orléans. One of the young men fell ill, and Erasmus accepted provisional accommodation with Jacob de *Voecht: 'The terms on which I live with Master Jacob amount to living in solitude, hence I ardently look forward to the time when you and I may resume the intercourse we used to have,' he wrote to his friend (Ep 131), who was, it seems, angered by Erasmus' departure and envious of his new host. On his part, Erasmus suspected Caminadus of wanting to intercept one of his messengers in order to appropriate the money and the letters he bore: 'In short I discovered in him the spirit of an enemy, a traitor, a robber and, to sum everything up, an Augustinus, I mean the old Augustinus whom I have partly described to you,' he wrote to Jacob *Batt (Ep 133). This new rupture between the two men was short-lived: reconciliation was brought about 'by force of circumstances' (Ep 135). Caminadus returned to Paris, and Erasmus, even though he did not know whether to consider him a friend or an enemy (Ep 138), wrote to him humbly from Orléans on 9 December 1500 to propose a resumption of their life together (Ep 136). Erasmus needed Caminadus, who had an apartment and no doubt assumed most of the expenses. Furthermore, Erasmus wanted to recover the papers he had entrusted to his friend (Ep 138). Thus once again Caminadus became an 'intimate friend,' carrying letters for Erasmus (Ep 141). Erasmus, who was staying at Saint-Omer, sought news of him (Epp 155, 157, 158, 160, 170) and asked him to rejoin him on his return (Ep 156). It is not known whether they saw each other again.

In 1502 Caminadus went to Orléans to study law (Epp 170, 172), matriculating on 4 May. He received a licence the same year after interpreting the chapter 'de origine juris' of the Digest before the assembly of the doctors. The story of his relations with Erasmus ended with a final misunderstanding about several copies of the *Adagia*, which he had doubtless been promised in payment for publicity work in Paris: 'Augustinus writes to me in abusive terms on the subject of his copies of the *Adagia*; you on the other hand merely laugh,' Erasmus wrote to Willem Hermans (Ep 172; see also Epp 138, 139, 142).

On 4 November 1505 Caminadus became a burgher of Middelburg and soon after 'pensionary' of the town. When he was seriously ill in 1510, he was retired from this post, but the town later gave him a pension in return for legal consultation. Erasmus remembered his friend only when he prepared the *Familiarium colloquiorum formulae* for publication in the winter of 1518–19. He accused his former companion of having compiled from their discussions a book on the subject of formulas to be used in daily conversation and at table, and of having added personages and titles of chapters of his own liking to the trifles spoken in jest at the fireside (Ep 909). The reality was more complex. At Orléans in 1500 Caminadus was already in possession of 'a few daily conversational sentences, such as we use on meeting each other and at table' (Ep 130), a sort of manual of Latin conversation no doubt used in Paris to teach 'the humane letters, as they are called' (Ep 141). In the *Formulae* (ASD I-3 20–117) Augustinus was presented in the role of the teacher, replying to questions from Christian Northoff. The exchanges were based on the discussions both had had with Erasmus in the cordial and studious atmosphere described in Heinrich Northoff's letter to his brother in August 1497 (Ep 61). Caminadus also benefited from the lessons of Erasmus (Ep 136) and was probably assisted by him in his own work, for

example his edition of Virgil (Paris: J. Philippi 19 February 1498), which Erasmus praised in a short poem (Reedijk poem 44).

Twenty years later, Caminadus was the only one involved in the publication of the *Formulae* to be criticized harshly by Erasmus: 'With this sad stuff he imposed on certain foolish people without my knowledge, with a view to scraping together some coin, the poor starveling creature' (Ep 909). Erasmus was never very fond of Caminadus, but he depended financially on this rather narrow humanist, who may sometimes have deceived him (Ep 138) but was often very useful (Ep 146).

BIBLIOGRAPHY: Allen Ep 131 / *Matricule d'Orléans* II-1 221–2 / *Matrikel Köln* II 244 / P.J. Meertens *Letterkundig leven in Zeeland in de zestiende en de eerste helft van de zeventiende eeuw* (Amsterdam 1943) 32–3 / Franz Bierlaire 'Érasme et Augustin Vincent Caminade' BHR 30 (1968) 357–62 / Franz Bierlaire *Erasme et ses Colloques: le livre d'une vie* (Geneva 1977) 13–20 / Yvonne Charlier *Erasme et l'amitié d'après sa correspondance* (Paris 1977) 102–4

FRANZ BIERLAIRE

Haio CAMMINGHA d 1558

Haio Cammingha (Cammyngha), who was born into a noble family in Friesland, studied in Louvain and may have attended the lectures of *Goclenius and *Rescius in the Collegium Trilingue. He had his lodgings in the same house as Maximilian (II) of *Burgundy and his tutor, Jan *Becker. When he set out in the spring of 1528 to join his friend *Viglius Zuichemus, who was then studying at Dole, Becker gave him a letter for conveyance to Erasmus at Basel (Ep 1984). Cammingha found Dole disappointing and stayed for only one term. On 12 November 1528 Erasmus agreed to receive him into his household as a paying guest (Ep 2073), and by February 1529 Cammingha had moved in (Ep 2108). He stayed until the end of January 1530 (Epp 2129, 2130, 2191, 2229) and, to judge from Erasmus' recommendations, was well liked by his host (Epp 2261, 2262). He owed Erasmus a sum of money when he left and promised to settle this debt with the banker Erasmus *Schets at Antwerp; he also intended to return to Erasmus in the spring (Epp 2286, 2325, 2356). Erasmus learnt that he had gone to Italy (Ep

2587, 2624), and not until the end of May was it confirmed that he had reached Louvain (Epp 2351, 2352). Above all, he did not settle his debt until November 1531 and thus incurred the lasting wrath of Erasmus (Epp 2356, 2364, 2403, 2413, 2552, 2573, 2587, 2593). A commendatory reference to him in Ep 2586 was suppressed when Erasmus published that letter in September 1532 (Ep 2810). On his part, Cammingha made many efforts to appease Erasmus; he wrote to him directly and he asked Viglius Zuichemus to mediate, but the known correspondence offers no indication of success (Epp 2851, 2866, 2957). In his only preserved letter (Ep 2766) he even invited Erasmus to move to Friesland and be a guest in his house and garden at Leeuwarden, where he apparently lived as a lawyer and was eventually to die a violent death.

BIBLIOGRAPHY: Allen Ep 2073 / Bierlaire *Familia* 88–90 / de Vocht CTL II 455–60 and passim

FRANZ BIERLAIRE

Giovanni Antonio CAMPANO of Cavelli, 1429–15 July 1477
Giovanni Antonio was born in Cavelli, in the province of Caserta, in 1429 (27 February?) of obscure parents; he later assumed the name Campano. From 1452 to 1455 he studied Greek under Demetrius *Chalcondyles at Perugia, where he obtained the chair of rhetoric on 16 November 1455. Meeting *Pius II there on the latter's journey to Mantua in 1459, Giovanni soon became a favoured member of the pope's literary circle. He was appointed bishop of Crotone, in Calabria on 20 October 1462 and bishop of Teramo, in the Abruzzi, on 23 May 1463. He joined the household of Cardinal Alessandro Oliva (d 1463) and from 1465 to 1471 belonged to that of Cardinal Francesco Todeschini Piccolomini, whom he accompanied to Germany in 1471; Cardinal Giacomo Ammanati was a close friend and Campano wrote to him disparaging Germany. Famous for his Latin epigrams, verses, orations, and biographical and historical writing, Campano also read and corrected Pius II's *Commentarii*. He was protected during the persecution of the humanists in Rome in 1468 in spite of a dubious moral reputation. In 1469–70 he was a proofreader for the printing press of Ulrich Han in Rome and also worked for Giovanni Filippo di Legnano. After being appointed governor of Todi in 1472 and of Città di Castello in 1474 by *Sixtus IV, he fell into disgrace for his opposition to papal military policy in Umbria and died at Siena.

Giovanni's lasting fame is owed to a former pupil's collection of his *Opera omnia* (Rome: E. Silber 1495). Erasmus described him in 1497 as a man born for jesting (Ep 61) and reported from Paris in 1499 that his works, which were in any case too expensive, were no longer obtainable (Ep 101). Among other comments on his works (ASD I-2 145; *Adagia* IV v 62), Erasmus suggested that students would do better to read Pliny's letters (*De conscribendis epistolis* ASD I-2 265–6; cf 480), but he knew Campano's own well enough to quote one (Ep 1336). He also referred to his *Libellus de dignitate et fructu matrimonii* (*Dilutio* ed E.V. Telle, Paris 1968, 80). Maarten van *Dorp praised Campano as a stylist, suggesting (wrongly) that he knew no Greek (Ep 347).

BIBLIOGRAPHY: Allen Ep 61 / F.R. Hausmann in DBI XVII 424–9 (full bibliography includes important studies by the same author) / Flavio di Bernardo *Un vescovo umanista alla corte pontificia, Gianantonio Campano, 1429–77* (Rome 1975)

D.S. CHAMBERS

Alessandro CAMPEGGI of Bologna, 12 April 1504–21 September 1554
Alessandro, a son of Lorenzo *Campeggi, was born at Bologna. He received a humanistic education as a youth and subsequently studied law at the University of Padua. On 19 March 1526, having obtained a dispensation for his lack of canonical age, he was elected bishop of Bologna to replace his father, although his father continued to administer the diocese. *Clement VII and *Paul III permitted him to delay ordination and consecration as a bishop until 1541, thus leaving the way open to marriage should it be necessary for him to continue the Campeggi name. On 19 October 1541 Cardinal Alessandro *Farnese named him lieutenant-governor and vice-legate for the papal territories of Avignon, where he was faced with a difficult situation in dealing with the forces of *Francis I of France. Jacopo *Sadoleto, who disagreed with the harsh

methods employed by Campeggi, accused him
of corruption and misgovernment. Campeggi
returned to Italy in 1545. He attended the early
sessions of the council of Trent (1545–7), and in
1547 was himself host to the council, which had
been transferred to Bologna. Although for the
most part an absentee bishop, he took some
interest in the suppression of Lutheranism and
in monastic reform in Bologna. He was created
a cardinal on 20 November 1551 and died in
Rome.

In 1532 Erasmus was informed that Lazzaro
*Bonamico, a former tutor of Campeggi, was
considering going to Bologna because Campeggi was bishop there (Ep 2657).

BIBLIOGRAPHY: Allen Ep 2657 / A. Prosperi in
DBI XVII 432–5

JOHN F. D'AMICO

Lorenzo CAMPEGGI of Bologna, 1474–
25 July 1539
Lorenzo Campeggi was born in Milan to
Giovanni Zaccaria Campeggi, from a prominent Bolognese family of jurists, and Dorotea
di Tommaso Tebaldi. Following family tradition he studied law at Padua and Bologna and
became a respected law professor at Bologna.
In 1500 he married Francesca Guastavillani; he
had five legitimate and illegitimate children.
Upon his wife's death in 1509 he decided on an
ecclesiastical career. *Julius II supported his
entry into the curia, and he became an auditor
of the sacred rota and a papal diplomat. A
successful mission to *Maximilian I in 1511 and
1512, in which he persuaded the emperor not
to attend the council of Pisa, earned him the
bishopric of Feltre. A second mission to
Germany from 1513 to 1517 resulted in his
creation as cardinal on 1 July 1517 and his
nomination as cardinal protector of Germany in
the curia.

In April 1518 *Leo x appointed Campeggi
legate to England to win *Henry VIII to his
project of peace among Christian princes and a
crusade against the Turks. Campeggi was not
allowed to enter England until Cardinal
*Wolsey, Henry's chancellor, received co-
legatine powers. Although constantly up-
staged by Wolsey and only partially successful
in his mission, he was able to win royal favour
and became one of England's major representatives in Rome. While in England he helped

Lorenzo Campeggi

Wolsey establish colleges at Oxford and
Ipswich.

Campeggi left England in August 1519 and
spent the next four years in Rome. In 1522 he
submitted a reform plan, 'De depravato statu
ecclesiae,' to the newly elected *Adrian VI,
who confirmed him in his curial offices.
Campeggi's position was advanced when
Giuliano de' Medici was elected pope as
*Clement VII in November 1523. In 1523
Clement translated him to the diocese of
Bologna, which he transferred to his son
Alessandro *Campeggi in 1526. Campeggi also
received the bishoprics of Salisbury (1524),
Huesca (1530), Porec (1533), and Candia
(1534). Early in 1524 he succeeded Clement as
cardinal protector of England.

With the continued threat of a Turkish
advance and the added problem of Lutheranism, Campeggi was sent to Germany, Hungary, and Bohemia as legate from 1524 to 1525.
His attendance at the diet of Nürnberg in
March 1524 allowed him to urge stronger
Catholic opposition to Lutheran demands, and
he supported the formation of a Catholic
league at Regensburg in June. He spent six

months in Hungary beginning in December 1524, trying to organize resistance to the Turks. Recalled by Clement, he again entered Rome in October 1525. Always a loyal servant, Campeggi accepted Clement's pro-French policies of the mid-1520s, even though he personally favoured following the imperial lead. He was therefore chosen to negotiate with the imperial army after the Sack of Rome in 1527.

The pressing matter of Henry VIII's intention to divorce his queen, *Catherine of Aragon, necessitated Campeggi's return to England in 1528. Commissioned to hear Henry's suit with Cardinal Wolsey, he faithfully implemented Clement's policy of procrastination. The case was transferred to Rome in the summer of 1529, and Campeggi's mission came to an end. Henry was angered at what he considered Campeggi's betrayal and later deprived him of his English protectorship. An act of Parliament of 1534 deprived him of the bishopric of Salisbury. After the deaths of Catherine of Aragon and *Anne Boleyn, Campeggi tried unsuccessfully to reconcile himself with the king and to end the English schism.

After participating in the coronation of *Charles v at Bologna on 24 February 1530 Campeggi was once again sent as legate to Germany. He set out with Charles in March, with instructions to oppose all compromise with the Lutherans and to avoid all calls for a council. At the diet of Augsburg in June he unsuccessfully opposed the Lutheran demand to be able to read the Augsburg Confession in the presence of the emperor. Campeggi's advocacy of the use of force against the Lutherans was met by the formation of the Schmalkaldic League. After Augsburg Campeggi accompanied Charles to Flanders, where he was joined by Cardinal Girolamo *Aleandro in urging the emperor to pursue a hard line against the Protestants. Campeggi's policy was ultimately a failure. Because of the Turkish threat, the Lutherans were granted concessions by the religious peace of Nürnberg on 25 July 1532.

Campeggi departed for Rome in August 1532. In 1536 *Paul III appointed him to the commission on the proposed council, and he was also appointed one of the presidents of the abortive council planned for Vicenza in 1538. He died in Rome.

Campeggi had shown himself to be a faithful supporter of papal policy in several difficult diplomatic missions. He was generally conservative in reform matters and shared the curial suspicion of a council. His desire to improve the fortune of his family made him fawning in his attitude towards princes. He was, however, a good jurist, and his opposition to the divorce of Henry VIII appears to have been sincere. Despite his special pleading with monarchs, he acquitted himself honestly in his duties.

Campeggi was one of the highest ranking ecclesiastics to befriend Erasmus. Erasmus used Campeggi's good will and high position in Rome as a conduit to express his position on the religious upheavals of the day to the pope and curia and the Catholic group in Germany. In turn Campeggi tried to exploit his relations with Erasmus by urging him to assume a more active stance against the Lutherans (Ep 1433).

Erasmus' first known contacts with Campeggi were in 1519, when the cardinal was on his first mission to England. Erasmus wrote to him on 1 May sending a copy of the recently published second edition of his New Testament and praising his learning and support of *bonae literae* in England (Ep 961). Campeggi replied with a letter of praise for Erasmus and the gift of a diamond ring (Epp 995, 996). The two met at Bruges in October 1519 (Epp 1025, 1029, 1031). In February 1520 Erasmus dedicated to Campeggi his paraphrase on the letter to the Ephesians (Epp 1062, 1081).

Erasmus wrote to Campeggi several times discussing the religious situation and the concomitant civil unrest. He urged a moderate and conciliatory policy towards the Lutherans (Epp 1167, 1422, 2328, 2341, 2366, 2411). Erasmus also appealed to Campeggi against his attackers in Rome: Diego *López Zúñiga, Alberto *Pio, Juan Ginés de *Sepúlveda, and others (Epp 1410, 1415, 1422, 2328, 2779). In these letters Erasmus reiterated his fidelity to Catholic teachings and complained of the bad faith and mendacity of his opponents. The cardinal did personal favours for Erasmus, such as passing on a present from the pope (Ep 1438) and helping him obtain a dispensation to eat meat during Lent (Ep 1542).

Erasmus referred to his good relations with Campeggi in many of his letters to show his

important connections and as an advertise-
ment to others of his advocacy of moderation
and conciliation (Epp 1466, 1469, 1515, 1806,
2355, 2687). Erasmus even urged *Melanchthon and other reformers to write to Campeggi in order to obtain a hearing for their
views (Epp 1496, 1523). He felt close enough to
Campeggi to intercede for friends (Epp 1519,
1632, 2529, 2587). There was also some contact
between Erasmus and members of Campeggi's
familia such as Floriano *Montini (Ep 1552),
Daniel *Mauch (Ep 1633), Jacopo *Canta (Ep
2636), and Gabriel *Verinus (Ep 2660).

BIBLIOGRAPHY: Allen Ep 961 / S. Skalweit in
DBI XVII 454–62 / DNB III 850 / Gerhard Müller
'Duldung des deutschen Luthertums? Erwä-
gungen Kardinal Lorenzo Campeggios vom
September 1530' ARG 68 (1977) 158–72 / Gerhard
Müller 'Die Besetzung des Bistums Münster im
Jahr 1532: Eine Stellungnahme Kardinal Lo-
renzo Campeggios' in *Römische Kurie, kirchliche
Finanzen, Vatikanisches Archiv: Studien zu Ehren
von Hermann Hoberg* ed Erwin Gatz (Rome 1979)
545–52 / William E. Wilkie *The Cardinal Protec-
tors of England: Rome and the Tudors before the
Reformation* (Cambridge 1974) 1, 3, and passim
JOHN F. D'AMICO

Jan van CAMPEN of Kampen, c 1 August
1491–7 September 1538
Jan van Campen (Campensis), who was
descended from a respected family from Kampen, in Overijssel, completed his education in
the University of Louvain, where he may have
been preparing for a theological degree and the
priesthood as early as 1509. The independent
and scholarly bent of his mind led him to focus
on the study of the Bible and of Hebrew. He
was already learning Hebrew in 1517 when
Matthaeus *Adrianus was called to Louvain to
begin formal instruction under the auspices of
the Collegium Trilingue. By the end of 1519
Campen himself was offered the chair of
Hebrew at the Trilingue and accepted on
condition that he was first granted leave to go
to Germany and perfect his knowledge of the
subject. On his return to Louvain he commenced his lectures on 18 October 1521 and
was admitted to the university council on 27
February 1522. Erasmus probably knew him
already; from Basel he conveyed his congratulations in February 1522 (Ep 1257), and a month

later he praised Campen among the 'Trilin-
gues' in a new edition of his *Colloquia* (ASD I-3
130). By 1525 Campen had also been ordained
priest. He had shown interest in the early
works of *Luther and *Melanchthon, but it
does not seem that even the Louvain theologians found any reason to question his
orthodoxy.

Although scrupulous as a scholar, Campen
was unpopular as a teacher. A skin disease and
financial difficulties (possibly stemming from
the need to provide for the education of his
natural son) further added to his discomfort.
When personal intrigues were added and
*Clenardus and Erasmus' enemy Frans *Titel-
mans succeeded in stalling the publication of
his learned paraphrase of the Psalter and
Ecclesiastes, Campen resigned his academic
chair in November 1531 (Ep 2573) – a turn
regretted by Erasmus (Ep 2588) – and entered
the service of the Polish ambassador, Johannes
*Dantiscus, whom he was to follow on his
diplomatic missions. To Dantiscus he dedicated his valuable *Psalmorum omnium iuxta
Hebraicam veritatem interpretatio* when it was
finally published (Nürnberg: J. Petreius May
1532). In the autumn of 1532 he accompanied
Dantiscus to Poland and Prussia and was soon
in touch with the leading intellectual circles of
the region. He joined in the efforts of *Krzycki
and *Tomicki to attract Melanchthon to
Cracow, and in the course of his own studies
he perused and criticized Melanchthon's commentary on Romans. In a letter to Dantiscus of
10 May 1533 Justus Ludovicus *Decius reported
that Erasmus had recommended Campen and
suggested that he be found a teaching position
in Poland. After a visit to Tomicki in January
1534 Campen went on to Cracow, where he
lectured at the university on Romans and
published his *Commentariolus* on Romans and
Galatians and his *Proverbia* (both Cracow: M.
Scharffenberg 1534), the former dedicated to
*Aleandro, the latter to Tomicki. Scharffenberg
also published a revised edition of Campen's
Hebrew grammar composed with the help of
works by Elias *Levita, which had previously
been printed in Louvain (D. Martens July
1528).

Before the new edition appeared Campen
had left Cracow for Italy. On 25 May 1534 he
arrived in Venice, where he joined the

household of Aleandro (Epp 2876, 2961) and finally fulfilled an ambition of long standing by discussing Hebrew with the celebrated Elias Levita (Ep 2876). As a result Elias dedicated to him his *Logica Rabi Simeonis* (de Vocht CTL III 201). In October 1534 Campen joined the household of Reginald *Pole in Padua; a year later he joined that of Gian Matteo *Giberti in Verona, and at the end of February 1536 that of Gasparo *Contarini in Rome (Ep 2998). In each of these positions he continued his scholarly work on the Scriptures in relation to Hebrew and also lectured to select circles. Finally he decided to return to Brabant, but on the way there he died suddenly at Freiburg.

Erasmus was aware of the quality of Campen's Hebrew scholarship and kept track of, and conceivably facilitated, his movements among men who were often his own friends and patrons. His direct relations with Campen, however, seem to have been limited. Apart from greetings and reports in letters to and from *Goclenius (Epp 1257, 1507, 2063, 2573, 2644, 2876, 2998), one letter from Campen to Erasmus is known today (Ep 2629, March 1532); it is a message on behalf of Erard de la *Marck. By September 1533 Erasmus had received profuse thanks from Campen after praising him in a letter to Dantiscus. It seems that a sustained lack of similar greetings in preceding letters had much troubled Dantiscus (Ep 2876).

BIBLIOGRAPHY: Allen Ep 1257 / de Vocht CTL I 503–5, III 154–208, and passim / de Vocht *Dantiscus* 66–72 and passim / *Correspondance de Nicolas Clénard* ed A. Roersch (Brussels 1940–1) Ep 31 and passim

PGB

Symphorianus CAMPERIUS See Symphorien *CHAMPIER*

Lambertus CAMPESTER documented 1516–38

Information about Lambertus Campester is limited to his own publications, a papal brief addressed to him in 1525, and remarks made by Erasmus, who was hostile to Campester for good reason and had to rely on such casual reports about him as he could obtain.

Campester was a German – according to Erasmus a Saxon – who had joined the Dominican order and laid claim to a theological doctorate. It seems that he was residing in Lyon for some years before editing there, among other works, the *Legenda aurea* of Jacobus de Voragine (Lyon: C. Fradin 1516), a collection of patristic homilies dedicated to Symphorien *Champier (2nd ed, Lyon: J. Crespin 1525), the *Opera omnia* of St Bernard (Lyon: J. Clein 1520), and several works by Thomas Aquinas including the *Summa theologica* (Lyon: J. Myt for J. and F. Giunta 1520).

In 1523 Campester published with the Paris press of Simon de *Colines two attacks upon *Luther, his *Heptacolon* and *Apologia in Martinum Lutherum*, the latter with a dedication to Jean de *Selve. Also at Paris he published with Pierre *Gromors towards the end of 1523 an adulterated edition of Erasmus' *Colloquia*. No copy of this edition is known today, but there is no reason to question the information given by Erasmus in his letters and, for the first time at some length, in the second edition of his *Catalogus lucubrationum* of September 1524 (Allen I 9–12). Campester had added a spurious preface in which Erasmus promised to expurgate his own writings, and he had made changes in the text, some of them stultifying and others dictated by French patriotism and bias for the religious orders.

By 1525 Campester returned to Lyon and by papal brief of 2 November was authorized to leave the Dominican order and join the Augustinian chapter of Saint-Amable at Riom in the Auvergne or any other establishment of the canons regular. Some scandalous circumstances reported to Erasmus may perhaps shed some light on Campester's motives for this change of order. He was said to have stolen three hundred crowns from his patron, an unnamed protonotary at Lyon; when caught he was squandering this money in female company (Epp 1655, 1686, 1697). In 1532 Erasmus added that only the Dominican cowl, which he was still wearing at the time of his failings, had saved him from capital punishment. By then Erasmus further reported that Campester had joined the Anabaptists and was living in the duchy of Jülich (Ep 2728). These later indications must be viewed with scepticism, for in 1538 Campester was in fact at Riom as a canon of Saint-Amable's, where he composed an *Oratio* *laudatoria* for King *Francis I (n p, n pr). In this work he referred to himself as a 'Germano-gallus' and reasserted his hatred of Luther and his enthusiastic admiration for France; he also mentioned some unpublished works he had written on French history and in praise of the king of France.

BIBLIOGRAPHY: Allen Ep 1581 / M.-H. Laurent in *Revue d'histoire ecclésiastique* 35 (1939) 283–90 / A. Roersch in *Gedenkschrift zum 400. Todestag des Erasmus von Rotterdam* (Basel 1936) 113–29

PGB

Paolo CANAL of Venice, c 1481–16 May 1508
Paolo Canal was born to one of the most illustrious families of Venice in late 1480 or 1481. His father was Alvise of the Santa Marina branch of the Canal family, his mother Maddaluzza, a daughter of Paolo d'Arpin. Little is known about his early education except that he studied Greek and the humanities at Venice and possibly philosophy at Padua. In about 1500 he became a member of the philhellenic circle around the humanistic publisher Aldo *Manuzio. A youth of boundless energy, he transcribed and corrected a number of Greek manuscripts, including books III to xv of the *Deipnosophistai* of the Greek rhetorician Atheneus (fl c AD 200), now at the Universitätsbibliothek of Heidelberg, and the *Hipparchicus* of the Greek historian Xenophon, now at the Bayerische Staatsbibliothek of Munich. Although his manuscripts contained a number of errors, they were more than simply the work of a copyist and included Latin notes to explain the text.

Canal was also a member of the religious and poetic circle of the Venetian youths Pietro *Bembo, Gasparo *Contarini, Tommaso (Paolo) Giustiniani, and Vincenzo Querini. Indicative of his friendship with Bembo was a trip the two made to Rome in the spring of 1505, in the company of Bernardo Bembo and other emissaries to the papal court. Canal shared the desire of his friends for religious renewal and often visited the Camaldolese monastery of San Michele di Murano, where Giustiniani had retreated to a life of prayer and meditation. On 17 April 1508 Canal entered the monastery to begin a series of Easter devotions but fell ill and

on 24 April accepted the habit of the Camaldolese monks. He died twenty-one days later.

Canal probably met Erasmus between 1507 and 1508, when the latter stayed at the house of Andrea *Torresani (Allen I 61). In the Aldine edition of the *Adagia* (II iii 48) of 1508 and in Ep 1347 Erasmus lauded Canal as a brilliant youth, snatched away by an early death.

Canal also prepared a text, today lost, of Ptolemy's *Geography*, and composed a number of Latin and vernacular poems, scattered in the *Rime diverse di molti eccellentissimi autori* (Venice 1546) and other collections.

BIBLIOGRAPHY: Allen Ep 1347 / F. Lepori in DBI XVII 668–73

TBD

Johannes CANIS or CANIUS *See Jan de* HONDT

Egidio CANISIO *See Egidio* ANTONINI

Nicolaus CANNIUS *See Nicolaas* KAN

Ludovico CANOSSA of Verona, c May 1475–30 January 1532
Count Ludovico Canossa was born in Verona, a son of count Bartolomeo and Elisabetta degli Uberti. In April 1496 he entered the service of Guidobaldo da Montefeltro, duke of Urbino, and was subsequently assigned to the entourage of the duchess, Elisabetta Gonzaga, serving on both public and private missions. From 1504 he represented Urbino at the court of *Julius II and soon came to enjoy the pope's confidence. Some diplomatic errands which he undertook on behalf of the pope led to his appointment as commendatory abbot of Sant'Andrea di Bosco, near Oderzo in the territory of Venice (1509), and as bishop of Tricarico, in Lucania (1511). He never visited this diocese, which he resigned in 1529, but he did become a priest at this time, and his moral conduct was never the object of criticism. From 1512 to 1514 he lived mostly at Rome, where he attended sessions of the fifth Lateran council. His career continued under *Leo x and brought him additional abbeys and other benefices. On 20 May 1514 the pope dispatched him as his nuncio to France and England, and he contributed substantially to the conclusion of a peace treaty in August.

While in London Canossa met Erasmus in early June at the house of Andrea *Ammonio, an occasion that left an indelible impression in Erasmus' memory (Epp 2421, 2599). In view of his success Canossa was appointed permanent legate to King *Francis, whom he accompanied in 1515 on his Italian campaign. In 1516 Francis nominated him bishop of Bayeux under the terms of the concordat of Bologna. He took advantage of his new position to issue an invitation to Erasmus, who had clearly impressed him most favourably (LP II 2619, 2621), but the scholar replied in dilatory terms (Epp 489, 538). Canossa spent the winter of 1517–18 mostly at Bayeux, editing the diocesan statutes with the assistance of Germain de *Brie. For the next few years he succeeded, despite repeated disagreements between France and the papacy, to render services to, and retain the favours of, Francis I as well as Leo x and *Clement VII. He repeatedly visited his French diocese, and in 1520 he was present at the meetings on the Field of Cloth of Gold (Ep 1106). During the crucial years of 1525–8 he spent much time at Venice, trying to persuade the Republic to take the side of the opponents of the house of Hapsburg. Thereafter he seems to have retired gradually to his villa at Grezzana, near Verona, where he died.

Canossa's interest in scholarship generally and in the reforming ideas of Christian humanism particularly was not restricted to his admiration for Erasmus. In Rome he was closely associated with Gian Matteo *Giberti and Alberto *Pio. The latter connection may have led him to judge Erasmus' work more critically during his last years than he had in earlier years (Ep 2599). Scholars such as Agostino Nifo dedicated works to him, and Brie inscribed to him his edition of Chrysostom's homily Contra gentiles (Paris: S. de Colines 1528; cf Ep 2599). Jacques *Toussain was in his service in 1529 (Ep 2421). Canossa left a manuscript treatise, 'Del governo di Francia,' and a great number of letters now preserved in Verona and elsewhere. His friend Baldasar *Castiglione immortalized him by introducing him as a principal spokesman in his Cortegiano.

BIBLIOGRAPHY: Allen and CWE Ep 489 / C.H. Clough in DBI XVIII 186–92

PGB

Jacopo CANTA of Asti

Little is known of Jacopo Canta. He was from Asti and became chamberlain to Cardinal Lorenzo *Campeggi. While in Germany in the early 1530s he learnt Greek from Jakob *Jespersen (Ep 2570). Nicolaus *Clenardus dedicated his Meditationes graecanicae (Louvain: R. Rescius 1531) to him, stating that Canta had encouraged him to do the work. Erasmus wrote to Canta from Freiburg in 1532, mentioning the visit of his servant Aegidius *Vannonius, sending greetings to Cardinal Campeggi, and praising Canta's devotion to learning (Ep 2636).

BIBLIOGRAPHY: Allen Ep 2570 / Correspondance de Nicolas Clénard ed A. Roersch, Ep 8 and notes

JOHN F. D'AMICO

Antonius CANTER See Jan CANTER

Jacob CANTER of Groningen, c 1471–after 1529

Jacob Canter (Cantor), the third son of Jan *Canter, was educated at the abbey of Aduard and the Deventer school of the Brethren of the Common Life before being sent to Cologne, where his father had studied. Jacob matriculated at the University of Cologne on 11 May 1487. By 1489 he was a schoolmaster at Antwerp and also worked with the printer Gerard *Leeu, for whom he edited an Opusculum vitae et passionis Christi ... ex revelationibus beatae Birgittae compilatum, together with Petrach's Secretum (Antwerp, 14 March 1489) and Proba's Cento (Antwerp, 12 September 1489). In his monastery at Steyn, Erasmus eagerly awaited a copy of Proba's work, and though it disappointed him when it arrived, he seized the opportunity to send Canter a letter in praise of his editorial efforts and his erudite family background (Ep 32).

By the end of 1489 Canter was in Italy, where he remained for a year or so. In the spring of 1491 he was in Augsburg editing Guido Bonatti's Decem tractatus astronomiae for the press of Erhard Radolt. In the following year he visited Conrad Celtis at Ingolstadt. It seems that next he went to Český Krumlov (Krummau) on the Moldau and to Vienna, where in 1494 *Maximilian I honoured him with the poet's laurel. In 1496 he can be traced to Mainz, where he edited Rodolphus *Agricola's translation of Plato's *Axiochus,* but he subsequently returned to Český Krumlov and taught there from 1497 to 1500. The next five years he spent in Cologne and elsewhere, but from 1506 he settled down at Emden as one of the vicars of the Grosse Kirche until the repression of the papal church under Edzard II and Enno II *Cirksena, counts of Eastern Friesland, drove him away in 1528 (the year of the latter's succession) or soon after. Canter's whereabouts thereafter are not known.

Canter, who also had contacts with Johannes Cuspinianus, Johannes *Trithemius, and other German humanists of that time, enjoyed a certain reputation as a neo-Latin poet, mostly on account of his 'Osculum' (c 1495), which is not known to exist today.

BIBLIOGRAPHY: Allen Ep 32 / Heinrich Grimm in NDB III 127–8 / NNBW I 559 / de Vocht CTL I 133–5 / Hutten *Opera* III 75 / *Matrikel Köln* II 212

PGB

Jan CANTER of Groningen, d 1497

Jan Canter, a contemporary and friend of Wessel *Gansfort and Rodolphus *Agricola, matriculated on 14 October 1440 at the University of Cologne. Having graduated BA (2 November 1442), he proceeded to Italy, attended lectures at the universities of Turin and Ferrara, and received his MA. From 1445 he continued his studies at Louvain. Although he seems to have pursued studies in many areas, he eventually obtained a doctorate in civil and canon law and returned to his native Groningen, where he settled down as a lawyer. With his congenial wife, Abele, he established a household where Latin was spoken at all times and the children were brought up to share the learned interests of their father, who continued to study astronomy and other subjects. Much praised by contemporary humanists as a model of refined culture, Jan's home seems to have helped promote scholarly interests among other branches of the Canter family as well. Although he mistakenly referred to Jan as Antoon, the young Erasmus noted that the 'family's fine reputation is common talk on all sides' (Ep 32). In the 1480s Jan seems to have attended the gatherings of the 'Academy' at the Cistercian abbey at Aduard, and he seems to have published an astrological *Prognosticatio* for the year 1489, a

copy of which he sent to Conrad Celtis. Celtis later wrote a Latin epitaph for him at the request of his son Jacob *Canter. In later years Erasmus mentioned the Canter family when recalling the cultural prominence of Friesland (Epp 1237, 2073).

BIBLIOGRAPHY: Allen and CWE Ep 32 / NNBW I 559 / NDB III 127 / de Vocht CTL I 132–5 / *Matrikel Köln* I 430 / *Matricule de Louvain* I 156

PGB

Claudius CANTIUNCULA of Metz, d October 1549

Claudius Cantiuncula (Chansonnette) was born around 1490 in Metz, the son of the notary and episcopal secretary Didier Chansonnette. He studied law at Louvain, a law school open to modern methods. He matriculated on 18 October 1512 and was elected dean of the college of bachelors of both laws in 1516. By the end of that year he was back in Metz, where he received a stipend to complete his studies on condition that he serve the town council after his graduation. In the summer of 1517 he registered at Basel and immediately sought to make contact with Erasmus, to whom he was warmly recommended by Maarten van *Dorp, a common friend in Louvain (Ep 852). Cantiuncula rose rapidly at the University of Basel, so that he was already professor of civil law in the autumn of 1518, though he did not achieve a doctorate until March 1519; in October 1519 he was elected rector. Soon he also became involved in local community affairs, pleading cases before the episcopal court and working in the municipal chancery as secretary to the clerk of the town council and as a notary, and in 1522 he became syndic to the town council. In 1523 he went to Paris on an embassy and was received by King *Francis I, who gave him a letter inviting Erasmus to France (Ep 1375). Besides his professorial and chancery duties at Basel, he also helped administer the university, transcribed medieval manuscripts, and wrote or edited works for Basel presses.

In his Basel writings Cantiuncula expounded the relationship between secular and canon law, but he also committed himself firmly to juristic humanism, the study of Latin legal sources, and the methodology of legal scholarship usually described as the *mos gallicus.* Glosses, commentaries, and repertories were to be avoided 'as if they were poisoned fruits and vain dreams.' Cantiuncula's first publication at Basel was the *Topica,* printed by *Cratander in 1520 with a splendid title-page cut by Hans Frank based on a design by Ambrosius Holbein. This treatment of the doctrine of method was described by Udalricus *Zasius as 'a golden book' and 'a book to be kissed.' It was followed by *Paraenesis de ratione studii legalis* (Basel: A. Cratander 1522).

In the winter of 1523–4 Cantiuncula obtained release from his commitments to the municipal government of Basel, and in early 1524 he resigned his professorship and departed. His ostensible reason for leaving was his father's ill health, but in fact he was no longer able to bear the tensions of living in a town which was becoming increasingly committed to the Reformation. In later times he was to regret this decision, and he said as much to his friend Bonifacius *Amerbach, an equally conservative man who had chosen to stay on in Basel (AK II Ep 944, III Ep 1168). Cantiuncula also came to curse the man who had encouraged his decision to depart, who is thought to have been Ludwig *Baer.

The rest of Cantiuncula's life brought him honours, status, travels, and important offices, but little time for serious scholarship. First he returned to his native Metz, where he worked for about a year as syndic and legal consultant to the town council; then he moved to Vic-sur-Seille, seat of the episcopal administration, to serve Cardinal Jean de *Lorraine, bishop of Metz, after 1527 as his chancellor (Epp 1841, 2063). Besides numerous visits abroad on behalf of the bishop, Cantiuncula participated in the diet of Speyer (1529). In 1529 he also began serving Duke Antoine de *Lorraine, and he continued to do so until 1532, when he returned to Germany as a member of the Reichskammergericht (imperial law court) at Speyer. From 1533 on he served King *Ferdinand I, first at Vienna, then (after 1540) as chancellor of the Hapsburg government Vorderösterreich at Ensisheim, in Alsace. A call to a professorship at Vienna in 1536 failed, apparently on financial grounds. After his Basel years, Cantiuncula published little, but the *Paraphrases in tres libros Institutionum* I and II (Haguenau: J. Setzer 1533 and 1534) and

III (Nürnberg 1538) and *De officio iudicis* (Basel: M. Isingrin 1543) deserve mention. In his later writings he protested against unacknowledged borrowings others had made from his earlier writings on equity. A posthumous selection of Cantiuncula's many legal judgments was published by Cnutelius in Cologne in 1571.

The admiration which Erasmus and Cantiuncula had for one another found expression above and beyond their personal friendship. Perhaps even before its first appearance in Latin, Cantiuncula had translated Erasmus' *Exomologesis* into French as *Manière de se confesser* (Basel 1524) (Ep 1426; Herminjard V 377–9). Guido Kisch has shown how Cantiuncula's doctrine of equity was influenced by that of Erasmus, to the extent that he used the same citations and examples. They were still corresponding in 1529 (Ep 2240), but although the two preserved letters witness to the warmth and intimacy of their relationship, they do not measure up to the depth of the intellectual interests which joined them, nor do they serve as an adequate gauge of the personalities of the two men. When Cantiuncula tried to persuade Erasmus to take a position against *Oecolampadius' doctrine of the Eucharist, Erasmus begged off with threadbare excuses (Epp 1616, 1674). Fortunately we also possess some statements from Erasmus which demonstrate his genuine respect for Cantiuncula, particularly in his dedicatory letter to Cardinal Jean de Lorraine (Ep 1841). Among Cantiuncula's further contributions to the humanist cause one should note his translation of Sir Thomas *More's *Utopia* into German, published in effect as a farewell gift to Basel in 1524 (Basel: J. Bebel). In 1529 Cantiuncula was seriously learning Greek, as Erasmus and Bonifacius Amerbach noted with admiration (Ep 2320; AK III Ep 1452). He was a friend of Juan Luis *Vives (Epp 1732, 2061) and *Beatus Rhenanus, and corresponded with Guillaume *Budé in 1519 and 1520. In 1529 Cantiuncula asked Erasmus to intervene in favour of one of his relatives. This young man, known only as Henricus, had been a pupil of *Glareanus but had recently been removed from his studies by the abbot of Murbach, *George of Masseveaux (Ep 2240).

Claudius Cantiuncula died at Ensisheim at the beginning of October 1549, following a period of chronic illness. Neither a funeral oration nor a genuine portrait survives, though the Basel university registration roll does preserve a coloured coat of arms painted on his instructions. The portrait of his character which emerges from his letters and works remains impressive. Kisch emphasizes 'an almost fanatical confession of truth, honour and justice, of the aequitas which comprehends all three of these, which served him in all times and places as his ideal and as his guiding star' (Kisch *Cantiuncula* 38).

BIBLIOGRAPHY: Allen and CWE Ep 852 / NDB III 128 / DBF VII 1053 / AK II Ep 772 and passim / de Vocht MHL 54–7 and passim / *Matricule de Louvain* III-1 452 / *Matrikel Basel* I 334, 341 / BRE Ep 121 and passim / Louis Delaruelle *Répertoire ... de la correspondance de Guillaume Budé* (Toulouse-Paris 1907) Epp 38, 63 / Guido Kisch *Claudius Cantiuncula: Ein Basler Jurist und Humanist des 16. Jahrhunderts* (Basel 1970), with reference to Kisch's many other publications on Cantiuncula / Jean Schneider 'Claude Chansonette (Cantiuncula) jurisconsulte et humaniste messin (vers 1490–1550) au service de la maison de Lorraine' in *Hommage à Lucien Febvre* (Paris 1954) 231–9 / Wenzel Hartl and Karl Schrauf *Die Wiener Universität und ihre Gelehrten 1528–1565* (supplement to Joseph Ritter von Aschbach *Geschichte der Wiener Universität* vol 3) I-1 (Vienna 1898) 156–260

HANS THIEME & STEVEN ROWAN

Wolfgang Faber CAPITO of Haguenau, d 2 November 1541
Wolfgang Faber Capito (Köpfel, Fabricius) was born in Haguenau, north of Strasbourg, around 1478. His father, Hans, a smith, and his mother, Agnes, were highly enough placed in the artisan class for Hans to be a member of the city government. Of Capito's early life, little more can be said than that he was educated first in the Latin school at Pforzheim, then in the universities of Ingolstadt (BA by 1505) and Freiburg (MA in 1506, licence in theology on 17 May 1512). He took minor orders as a Benedictine late in his Freiburg period and preached at the order's house in Bruchsal from 1512 to 1515. He was such a zealous theology student at Freiburg that he was named *professor extraordinarius*, but of these studies he later

Wolfgang Faber Capito, engraving by Peter Aubry

remarked that they amounted to 'two-times-a-thousand nonsensical chatterings.'

Although he was trained in the nominalist tradition, Capito very early showed a preference for the humanistic studies of the northern Renaissance and soon became a devotee of the *bonae literae*. During a leave from Freiburg (1506–9), he was associated with the Rhenish humanist society of *Wimpfeling, *Brant, and *Beatus Rhenanus. He served as proof-reader for Heinrich Gran's press in Haguenau and worked on a new edition of Conrad Summenhardt's commentary on the physics of Albertus Magnus, to which Wimpfeling wrote a preface and he an afterword. Upon his return to Freiburg he became part of the circle around Udalricus *Zasius, and while at Bruchsal he was visited by Conradus *Pellicanus, who listened to his doubts about transubstantiation and started him in the study of Hebrew.

In mid-1515, Bishop Christoph von *Utenheim called Capito to Basel as cathedral preacher, and at the same time he was appointed professor of theology at the university. There he spent five years in the company of Johannes *Oecolampadius, Pellicanus, the

*Amerbachs, and the other scholars collected about the presses of *Froben and *Cratander. Above all, he made the acquaintance and secured the patronage of Erasmus himself. Although the two men do not appear to have been in one another's company often (Ep 459), Capito seems to have become almost Erasmus' *alter ego.* He termed Erasmus 'the author of such intelligence as I have,' and Erasmus replied that Capito had 'a fertile mind, keen judgment, no ordinary skill in the three tongues, and sufficient gifts of style to adorn your subject and not merely to convey it' (Epp 459, 541). In a published letter to Henry *Bullock, Erasmus termed Capito 'a man who besides the other liberal disciplines has no ordinary proficiency in the three tongues, Greek, Latin, and Hebrew, and is of such integrity, so upright a character that I never saw anything more invulnerable' (Ep 456). Erasmus frequently appealed to Capito as a Hebrew scholar in support of the 1516 New Testament (Epp 998, 1581), and Capito freely defended his mentor at every opportunity (Ep 1083), even to the detriment, occasionally, of his own work (AK II Ep 619). It was to Capito that Erasmus passed the 'torch' of the new learning and the work of restoring 'sacred literature' (Ep 541). And it was to Erasmus, whom he termed 'the ornament of Christendom,' that Capito consistently directed his students.

The remainder of Capito's career is well known. As soon as he had heard of *Luther, he came to the reformer's defence. In October 1518 he persuaded Froben to publish a Latin edition of Luther's early works (Ep 904; Luther w *Briefwechsel* I Ep 147), and he intervened with Erasmus on Luther's behalf (Ep 938). Then, in the spring of 1520, he moved to Mainz, first as cathedral preacher, then as confessor and adviser on ecclesiastical matters to Archbishop Albert of *Brandenburg. He became increasingly suspicious of the public unrest that followed the spread of Luther's message, and of the message itself. On 14 March 1522, after a particularly blunt exchange with Luther (Luther w *Briefwechsel* II Epp 447, 451) he came to Wittenberg and talked with the reformer. This conversation, which began his genuine conversion to the evangelical doctrines, came to fruition in mid-1523, when Capito, now

provost of the chapter of St Thomas in Strasbourg, encountered Matthäus Zell, the city's first evangelical preacher. With Martin *Bucer, he then became co-architect of reform in Strasbourg, where he remained until his death from the plague. Although at heart he was in agreement with *Zwingli on the Eucharist and was the author of the original article on the Lord's Supper in the *Confessio Tetrapolitana,* he signed the Wittenberg concord (1536) and spent his declining years in an effort to draw the Swiss into the agreement. With Zell, he was responsible for the city's relatively lenient policy towards the Anabaptists; and yet he helped Bucer in establishing the new church order that evolved from the synod of 1533 and that provided the basis for expelling them from the city. He was an early proponent of establishing what became Strasbourg's famous Gymnasium and repeatedly represented this city in consultations with the new churches in Bern, Zürich, Basel, and Frankfurt. It was with some accuracy, if with malice too, that Erasmus called the later Capito a 'bishop of the new gospel' (Ep 1459), for his life marked the transition from humanism to the Reformation.

Without question, Capito's conversion to Luther's evangelical religion ruptured his personal relationship with Erasmus. Indeed, his two letters to Erasmus of 18 June and 6 July 1523 (Epp 1368, 1374) contain such contrasting attitudes towards Erasmus that they establish the *termini* between which his conversation with Zell must have occurred. In the first, he was still Erasmus' faithful disciple; of *Hutten's *Expostulatio* he declared, 'I don't know what came into the man's head that he should decide that you are the person to attack, you, the founder of the rebirth of learning and no less of the return to personal religion.' In the second, while still offering to take up the pen against Hutten, he bitterly rejected as irresponsible Erasmus' having three years earlier called him a courtier (Ep 1158); and for the first time he bluntly exhorted Erasmus to declare himself for the party which maintained the freedom of a Christian within the limits conceded by the Scriptures. In June 1524 Erasmus complained to Caspar *Hedio that Capito had admonished him at length about grave matters, namely *De libero arbitrio* (Ep 1459), and in September he complained to Capito himself, 'I work for the Gospel cause much more whole-heartedly than you suppose' (Ep 1485). But Capito had changed. The same month he wrote Nikolaus Prugner, the reformer of Mulhouse, 'Regarding Erasmus' *Free Will*, it quite frankly flatters the flesh and human strength sufficiently.'

The breach between the two men went far. Erasmus became deeply suspicious of Capito (Epp 1496, 1497, 1991, 2341, 2615) and flatly accused him of instigating the attacks of *Eppendorf and *Brunfels (Ep 1485). The depth of the bitterness on both sides is evident from the fact that Erasmus continued to correspond with Bucer, Hedio, and Melanchthon – other reformers with whom he had never been equally close – but not with Capito, and that Capito reciprocated. He may, in fact, have added insult to injury when, in 1533, he translated Erasmus' *De concordia* into German, but with a preface in which he utterly destroyed Erasmus' irenic appeal. In words similar to those Luther once wrote him (w *Briefwechsel* II Ep 451), Capito declared, 'We insist only upon the necessary justification through faith in Christ alone ... and upon the true worship service that leads everyone to the Lord Christ.' In sum, in equally irenic form, he did his utmost to make of Erasmus' ecumenical overture a condemnation of Rome. When passing through Basel early in 1536, Bucer and Capito called upon Erasmus and were admitted, but the conversation was jovial and avoided serious topics (O. Clemen in *Basler Zeitschrift für Geschichte und Altertumskunde* 43 (1944) 17–33, *Melanchthons Briefwechsel* II Ep 1709).

It is indeed possible to underline too strongly the break in the two men's relationship. In the first place, Capito had never been Erasmus' utterly unquestioning disciple. In September 1516 he both reproved Erasmus for sloppiness in the first edition of the New Testament and pressed upon him his own abhorrence of allegorical interpretations (Ep 459). More important, there is a sense in which, through Capito, Erasmus came to influence the mainstream of the Reformation. Granted that Capito narrowed the range of acceptable religious opinion, he nevertheless within that range sought peace and unity in much the manner of Erasmus. He always opposed the

Anabaptists on doctrinal grounds, but, in agreement with Erasmus (Ep 2149), he insisted that 'their heart should be examined and the gift of God by which they were strengthened against the flesh and Satan should be acknowledged.' In 1535 he chided Heinrich Bullinger for his obdurate attitude on the Eucharist with the declaration that 'not just any truth has to be attested by one's life and blood, but precisely that truth which avails for attaining salvation.' Here, albeit within narrower limits, were echoes of Erasmus' sceptical position in *De libero arbitrio*. Here, too, were the pacifistic consequences of such a position, as Capito himself assumed them in 1519 in his lectures on Romans: 'Listen carefully: Christ, who put aside the sword, does not want you to disagree with your neighbour, and he does not like contentious people.' In his attitude towards controversy within the anti-Roman party, he replicated Erasmus' approach to religious controversy in general.

It should not, however, be concluded that Erasmus continued to influence Capito in the realm of specific doctrines. Even his ecumenical approach to relations among Protestants was more a matter of tendency than of dogma. Throughout, the weight of his admonition to unity fell upon the reformers' agreement that God's grace in Christ, apprehended through faith, was the sole source of salvation, rather than upon a more general appeal to the dictates of brotherly love. By 1524, Capito was theologically a Lutheran, save for his doctrine of the Lord's Supper. And even here, his sacramental identification of the body and blood of Christ with the bread and wine of the Eucharist harked back more to Scotus and Wyclif than to Erasmian spiritualism. Most fundamentally, he abandoned Erasmus' effort to inculcate enlightened piety in exchange for Luther's insistence upon true doctrine. While Erasmus continued to refine his *Adagia*, Capito published two catechisms.

Yet certain Erasmian tendencies were indisputably present in more than a yearning for unity. These tendencies are evident both in some of the reforms Capito sought and in how he sought them. His first reform petition, in August 1524, called upon Strasbourg's ruling councils not only to abolish the mass but also to provide for schools and closer supervision of morals. He thus continued to believe that good learning supported both civil society and true religion. He continued his own Hebrew studies and published biblical commentaries as well as polemical works. Finally, the manner in which he sought reform bespeaks a continuing indebtedness to Erasmus. He always abhorred public unrest, and he remained suspicious of the common man for his proclivity to create it. A certain élitism, which he shared with Erasmus, is surely evident in his remark that 'the common people ... have the reasoning power of a dimwit.' The 'lawlessness of the commoners' was to his mind sufficient reason to establish public schools. The other side of the coin, then, is that, even as a reformer, he gave the Christian prince the same high moral position that Erasmus gave him in the *Institutio principis christiani*. Consequently, he never allowed himself to become the leader of a popular movement against the authorities. Although doctrinally in agreement with Luther, he therefore helped create a church so closely intertwined with the Christian magistrates of Strasbourg as to render Luther's doctrine of the two kingdoms inconsequential.

Capito dedicated his translation of Erasmus' *De concordia* to his former patron, Albert of Brandenburg. Appropriately, he reflected upon his own career with the words 'I am accordingly inclined even as before in Your Princely Grace's service, although, God be praised, the understanding is brighter and my activity is more public.' Had they not become so estranged, he might well have written in the same manner to Erasmus, for both continuity and discontinuity marked their relationship, although discontinuity prevailed.

BIBLIOGRAPHY: Allen and CWE Ep 459 / NDB III 132–3 / *Matrikel Freiburg* I 161–2 / James M. Kittelson *Wolfgang Capito: from Humanist to Reformer* (Leiden 1975) / Beate Stierle *Capito als Humanist* (Heidelberg 1974). Both works contain complete listings of Capito's published works and notes on manuscript sources
                                    JAMES M. KITTELSON

Marino CARACCIOLO of Naples, 1469– 27 January 1538

Marino was born at Naples to Domizio Caracciolo, lord of Ruodi, and Martuscella di Lippo Caracciolo. His father was an important official in the government of the kingdom of Naples, serving for a time as governor of Calabria. In 1482 Marino entered the service of Ascanio Sforza when Ascanio was at Naples because of a conflict with Ludovico *Sforza, duke of Milan. When Ascanio became a cardinal in 1484 Caracciolo followed him to Rome as secretary. He served the cardinal through the vicissitudes of the next eleven years and was with him when he was taken prisoner by the Venetians on 10 April 1500 after the battle of Novara. After being transferred to the French they endured imprisonment in the tower of Bourges until January 1502 and returned to Rome only in September 1503.

Shortly after Ascanio Sforza's death in 1505 Pope *Julius II made Caracciolo commendatory abbot of Santa Maria di Teneto at Reggio Emilia. He also became apostolic protonotary with duties in the curia. In early 1513 he was named ambassador of Massimiliano Sforza, duke of Milan, at Rome, and subsequently he helped persuade *Leo x to enter into an anti-French alliance with Milan, the Emperor *Maximilian I, *Henry VIII of England, and *Ferdinand II of Aragon. Although the French were checked in 1513, their victory at Marignano in 1515 cost Massimiliano Sforza his duchy. Caracciolo remained with him for a time, but he eventually entered the papal diplomatic service and on 27 February 1517 was named to replace Lorenzo *Campeggi as nuncio to the Emperor Maximilian. His departure was delayed until March 1518, and in July he was joined by Cardinal *Cajetanus, acting as a special nuncio. Their mission was to deal with the Turkish threat to eastern Europe and the question of the succession to the imperial crown.

After Maximilian's death on 12 January 1519 Caracciolo and Cajetanus worked against the election of *Charles v, attempting to have Frederick of *Saxony chosen instead. In January 1520 Caracciolo was named nuncio to Charles, and he was joined by another special nuncio, Girolamo *Aleandro, sent to deal with the question of Martin *Luther. They could not prevent the discussion of the religious question or the appearance of Luther at the diet of Worms in the spring of 1521. Caracciolo then followed the imperial court to Spain, where he was confirmed as nuncio by the recently elected *Adrian VI. In 1523, however, Charles V sent him on a mission to Venice, and on Adrian's death he completed the transition to imperial service. *Clement VII named him bishop of Catania at the request of the emperor on 18 January 1524. Charles sent Caracciolo to Milan in 1524 to act as ambassador to Duke Francesco II *Sforza, who gave him control of the territory of Vespolate as a gift. From 1526 to 1529 he acted as the *de facto* governor of the city of Milan during the disgrace and exile of the duke but resumed his normal duties as imperial ambassador when Sforza was reinstated in January 1530. When Sforza died in 1535 Caracciolo was absent from Milan, having gone to Rome to receive the cardinalate to which he was named on 31 May 1535. On his return in July 1536 he was designated chancellor, and later he became governor of the duchy. He died in office.

Erasmus' first known contact with Caracciolo occurred in late 1518, when the nuncio relayed to him Leo X's brief supporting his work on the New Testament (Epp 865, 905). Erasmus met Caracciolo and Aleandro at Brussels in the summer of 1521 (Ep 1342), and it was probably then that the two nuncios exhorted him to write against Luther (Allen I 35; LB X 1647F–1648A). By March 1522, however, Erasmus was convinced that Caracciolo had been turned against him by Aleandro because he seemed to be protecting Luther (Epp 1263, 1268). Relations between Erasmus and Caracciolo appear to have ended on this sour note, with Erasmus suspecting the nuncio of stirring up trouble for him at the imperial court (Ep 1302), and including him in his blanket denunciation of papal agents sent to deal with Luther (Ep 1188).

BIBLIOGRAPHY: Allen Ep 865 / G. De Caro in DBI XIX 414–25 / Federico Chabod *Lo stato di Milano e l'impero di Carlo V* (Rome 1934) repr in *Lo stato e la vita religiosa a Milano nell'epoca di Carlo V* (Turin 1971) 3–225 esp 30–3 and passim

TBD

Roberto CARACCIOLO of Lecce, c 1425–6 May 1495

One of the most celebrated Italian preachers of the fifteenth century, Roberto Caracciolo (Robertus Liciensis, Roberto da Lecce) was born in Lecce and received his early education there in the monastery of the Franciscan Conventuals. However, when the time came to embrace a religious vocation, he entered a house of the Franciscan Observants. His first successes as a preacher took place in 1448 in Perugia, where he organized processions of devout followers clad in white, prayers against the plague, and public reconciliations of rival parties. By the autumn of 1448 he was in Rome, where he preached in the church of Ara Coeli and was chosen in 1450 to deliver the official eulogy during the ceremonies for the canonization of Bernardino da Siena, whose sermons he had carefully studied during his formative years. His duties as a preacher then took the Franciscan to Bologna, Padua, Milan, Siena, and other cities. After the general chapter of the Observants in San Giuliano dell'Aquila (May 1452), Caracciolo joined the Conventuals, thus fuelling the disputes between the two families of the Franciscan order. Caracciolo was influential in the curia, and on 30 May 1454 a bull of *Nicholas V granted him practically full freedom of movement. Callixtus III summoned Caracciolo's help to promote the crusade against the Turks and nominated him apostolic collector for the Roman region (1455) and then for Lombardy and Monferrato. This responsibility led Caracciolo to establish close relations with Francesco Sforza. In 1458 the friar was in Rome and Naples, and in 1464 he preached the crusade as an apostolic sub-delegate for Cardinal *Bessarion in Treviso, Padua, Vicenza, Verona, Bergamo, and Crema. After 1470 Fra Roberto preached mainly in southern Italy (Naples and Lecce). On 25 October 1475 he was named bishop of Aquino by *Sixtus IV. On 22 February 1484 he was transferred to the diocese of Lecce, which he retained until July 1485, when Innocent VIII returned him to Aquino. Caracciolo died in Lecce and was buried in the church of San Francesco della Scarpa.

In his *Ecclesiastes* Erasmus gave several anecdotes from the life of Caracciolo which depicted the friar as shrewd and witty but also vainglorious and self-centred. In one anecdote Erasmus was critical of the boast attributed to Caracciolo that he could reduce any member of his audience to tears (LB V 982C–F). In another Erasmus deplored Caracciolo's melodramatic gesture of preaching a crusade while clad in knight's clothing and girt with a sword (LB V 985F–986A). Erasmus' ambivalent attitude towards Caracciolo was shared by others. Masuccio Salernitano, for instance, has some words of high praise for the Franciscan in the commentary to his eigth novella, but in the novella itself the witty and lascivious preacher, who becomes one of the protagonists of its action, is clearly modelled after Caracciolo (see Masuccio Salernitano *Il novellino* ed A. Mauro, Bari 1940, 77–8).

The published works of Caracciolo consisted mainly of collections of sermons such as the *Sermones quadragesimales* (Milan 1474), *Sermones de laudibus sanctorum* (Naples: M. Moravus 1489), and *Specchio della fede* (Venice: J. Rubeus 1495). These went through over one hundred editions in Italy and northern Europe.

BIBLIOGRAPHY: Z. Zafarana in DBI XIX 446–52 / S. Bastanzio *Fra Roberto Caracciolo da Lecce predicatore del secolo XV* (Isola del Liri 1947) / A. Galletti *L'eloquenza (dalle origini al XVI secolo)* (Milan 1938) 150 and passim / Bonaventura von Mehr 'Über neuere Beiträge zur Geschichte der vortridentinischen franziskanischen Predigt' *Collectanea Franciscana* 18 (1948) 254 and passim

DANILO AGUZZI-BARBAGLI

Gianpietro CARAFA *See Pope* PAUL IV

Nikolaus Fabri of CARBACH c 1485–c 1534 Nikolaus Fabri of Carbach (Carbachius) was born around 1485 in Karbach, Lower Franconia. He matriculated at the University of Leipzig in 1503 and soon was noted for his knowledge of Latin and Greek. In 1512 he was appointed lecturer of ancient history at the University of Mainz, where he taught until 1533, lecturing on poetry as well as expounding Livy, Florus, Valerius Maximus, Sallust, Justinus, Suetonius, and Caesar. Around 1515 he belonged to a circle of humanists which included Ulrich von *Hutten, Johann *Huttich, and other pupils of Johannes Rhagius Aesticampianus. In the library of Mainz cathedral he discovered a manuscript of Livy, books 33–40, including two sections which had been missing so far. It served as the basis for an edition of Livy together with the epitome of Florus (Mainz: J. Schöffer 1518), which Car-

bach produced in collaboration with Wolfgang *Angst, who was editor and corrector for the Schöffer printing house. Other publications by Schöffer include an edition of Prosper of Aquitaine (*Sancti Prosperi ... adversus inimicos gratiae Dei libellus*), for which Carbach wrote a preface in 1524, and a new edition of an earlier German translation of Livy, which Carbach had revised and enlarged with fresh translations of his own (*Titi Livii Römische Historien*, 1551). Erasmus, who may have met him in the autumn of 1518 (Ep 881), wrote the preface to the Livy edition of 1518 (Ep 919), praising Carbach's scholarship.

BIBLIOGRAPHY: Allen and CWE Ep 919 / Heinrich Grimm in NDB III 137–8 / *Matrikel Leipzig* I 452 / Hutten *Opera* I Ep 110

IG

Ludovicus CARINUS of Lucerne, d 17 January 1569 Ludovicus Carinus (Kiel) was born around 1496, the son of Hans Kiel, a member of the great council and second secretary of the town of Lucerne. He was named after his uncle and godfather, Ludwig Kiel, who was a canon at Beromünster, 21 kilometres north of Lucerne. The family had often been represented in this chapter, and Ludovicus himself had a canonry reserved for him when he was still a child (1504); he took possession of it in 1513 and thus came to enjoy an annual income of a hundred ducats while not being required to become a priest or reside at Beromünster for more than five days each year. In the winter term of 1511–12 he matriculated at the University of Basel, obtaining a BA in 1514. The Basel humanist circle quickly recognized in him a bright young hope, and as such he was introduced to Erasmus during his first visits to Basel, between 1514 and 1516 (Ep 630). *Glareanus addressed him in one of his elegies, published in 1516, and Wilhelm *Nesen became his teacher and friend. In the autumn of 1517 Nesen took Carinus and his other pupils, the *Stalburg brothers, to Paris (Ep 920) and then to Louvain in the summer of 1519 (Epp 994, 1026). Meanwhile, on a visit to Beromünster in August 1518 Carinus learnt about the death of Wolfgang *Lachner and addressed a letter of condolence to Bruno *Amerbach (AK II Ep 621). At Louvain he lived with his companions in the

College of the Lily, as did Erasmus, who commended him as an exemplary young scholar (Epp 1034, 1091). On the other hand, he was bound to become involved in Nesen's unsparing battles against the conservative theologians and their supporters elsewhere in the university (Epp 1046, 1165; z VII Ep 111).

In September 1520 Carinus was at Cologne, studying with Erasmus' friend Johannes *Caesarius, when he met *Spalatinus. Hoping for a position at the court of electoral Saxony, he referred proudly to his connection with Erasmus. On 22 October he sent Spalatinus a gift copy of the satire Hochstratus ovans (Ep 1165) and in the accompanying letter showed high regard for the cause of *Luther. He was at Mainz serving as a secretary to *Capito (Epp 1165, 1215) from the end of 1520 until the autumn of 1521, when he attached himself as tutor to a noble student, Erasmus Schenk von Limpurg, whom he accompanied to Tübingen and perhaps to Paris and Louvain (Ep 1257). In July 1522 he was in Basel, living with Erasmus as his famulus and associating with Heinrich *Eppendorf and others (AK II Ep 877). Erasmus introduced him as a speaker in his colloquy Convivium poeticum, first published in August 1523 (ASD I-3 344–59). On 8 January 1523 the Frankfurt council granted leave to Nesen, their schoolmaster, and appointed Carinus his substitute and subsequently, on 9 July, his successor for a term of three years. But in October 1524 he had already returned to Switzerland in the company of *Gelenius (Melanchthons Briefwechsel I Ep 351). In 1525–6 Carinus resumed his travels in the company of Erasmus Schenk von Limpurg, writing to *Camerarius repeatedly from Bamberg and also from Strasbourg after a visit to Bourges. Shortly after Erasmus had written to him at Koblenz, where he seems to have tutored Valentin *Furster and Erasmius *Froben (Ep 1799), he matriculated in the newly founded University of Marburg for the spring term of 1527, conceivably in the hope of a teaching position. But in the autumn he was again at Basel in the circle of Erasmus and the Froben press (Ep 1946).

From July 1528 one notes a dramatic change in the relations between Erasmus and Carinus. Erasmus henceforward refers to him as the young viper he had carried in his bosom, and he and his friends twist Ludovicus Carinus' name in several slighting ways, such as calling him Lucius Catilina (Epp 2048, 2063, 2101, 2111, 2130, 2196, 2779). Carinus is just as angry, threatening to attack Erasmus in printed pamphlets (Epp 2063, 2101, 2231, 2779; AK III Ep 1292, V Ep 1291a). Common friends show some surprise but no desire to rush to Carinus' defence (Epp 2085, 2120). Such reasons as can be deduced from the preserved letters – Carinus' friendship with Eppendorf (Epp 2048, 2101, 2111, 2120, 2129, 2130) and also with the late Nesen, whom Erasmus later remembered with sudden criticism (Ep 2085), and a fight with Erasmus' servant, Felix *Rex (Epp 2112, 2130) – may or may not reveal the primary cause for Erasmus' wrath.

Meanwhile Carinus seems to have resumed his life as a private tutor. From the autumn of 1528 (Epp 2063, 2085), or possibly earlier, he was at the University of Dole, occasionally visiting Besançon (Ep 2112) and Basel (Epp 2151, 2231). He may have been at Basel early in 1529 when the Catholic faith was suppressed. Perhaps as a result, Carinus' canonry at Beromünster was in jeopardy, but his personal interventions (Epp 2085, 2152) may have been able to delay final action on the part of the chapter until the summer of 1531, when the Swiss were drifting closer to religious war and the representations of Bern and Zürich in his favour no longer had any effect. On 5 October 1531 he was deprived of his benefice, and a successor was appointed (z XI Epp 1197, 1210, 1220, 1276). By now he lived at Strasbourg as an affirmed Protestant, a step that he had so far avoided for the sake of his aged mother and his paternal inheritance (Ep 2779). At Strasbourg he renewed his friendship with Capito and also won the confidence of *Bucer. In May 1533 he was at Paris, living with Johann Sturm of Strasbourg and gladly agreeing to tutor the sons of Eucharius *Holzach (AK IV Ep 1780). Some ties to the circle of *Margaret of Angoulême are revealed by an epigram addressed to him by Nicolas *Bourbon in his Nugae of 1533. The same volume contains a letter by Carinus praising Bourbon along with *Budé and, indeed, Erasmus. After another visit to Strasbourg and Basel we find him in May 1535 with a group of German students at Louvain, where he remained for at least two years. From February 1539 to the summer of 1541 he is documented at Padua, with Ulrich Fugger among the young people in his charge. Attending the Catholic universities of Louvain and Padua as well as tutoring a member of the Fugger family cast sufficient doubt on his Protestant allegiance for the government of Lucerne to offer him the headship of their Latin school combined with a handsome benefice, but after some negotiations in 1539 and 1540 Carinus declined, and in 1544 he matriculated with Ulrich Fugger in Bologna.

In 1546 he was made a canon of the now evangelical chapter of St Thomas at Strasbourg. This appointment was facilitated by his cordial relations with Bucer on the one hand and on the other with the bishop of Strasbourg, who was his former pupil Erasmus Schenk von Limpurg. Carinus' intervention helped in bringing back to Strasbourg his friend Johann Sturm. After the Schmalkaldic war, when Bucer was compelled to leave Strasbourg in 1549, Carinus left too and for the next two years accompanied another Fugger son, Hans, during his studies and travels in France. In 1555 he resigned his Strasbourg canonry for an annuity of eighty florins; by this time he had settled down in Basel, occasionally practising the medical skills he had acquired during his many years at various universities, including Padua. His will of 20 December 1563 indicates that he was reconciled to his family in Lucerne and probably in possession of his inheritance, also that he had been treated generously by the Fuggers. He was clearly well-to-do and, apart from many other bequests, endowed nine scholarships in the University of Basel, six of them reserved for members of his family. When he died at Basel he left a library which was purchased by a member of the Fugger family for six hundred florins.

During the last part of his life Carinus gave a great deal of support to scholarly projects, securing manuscripts in the possession of the Fugger family and also subsidies for the printing of costly books. His efforts were acknowledged by his friend Hieronymus Wolf, who with the Basel printer Johannes Oporinus produced an important corpus of Byzantine historians, and also by Gelenius in the preface to his Latin translation of Josephus (Basel 1548). Wolf dedicated to him a commentary on Cicero's *De senectute* (Basel 1569) and Melanchthon an edition of Demosthenes' first Olynthiac speech (Haguenau 1524). Among the many friends and correspondents he shared with Erasmus were Camerarius, *Carlowitz, *Cochlaeus, Glareanus, *Gobler, *Goclenius, *Harst, Georg *Hörmann, and *Viglius Zuichemus.

BIBLIOGRAPHY: Allen Ep 920 / Willy Brändly in *Innerschweizerisches Jahrbuch für Heimatkunde* 19–20 (1959–60) 45–100 (with a portrait, using unpublished letters in Basel and Zürich) / BRE Ep 132 / AK II Ep 621 and passim / z VII Ep 111 and passim / *Melanchthons Briefwechsel* I Epp 314, 335 / Knod 236 / *Matrikel Basel* I 309 / de Vocht CTL I 392–3, II 26–8, and passim

PGB

Angelo CARLETTI of Chivasso, c 1414– 11 April 1495
Angelo Carletti was born to a wealthy family of Chivasso, in Piedmont, and at baptism received the name Antonio. He obtained a doctorate in civil and canon law at Bologna. At the age of thirty he entered the Franciscan Observant order, taking the name of Angelo. He served his order as canonist, moral theologian, and, on several occasions, vicar-general. In 1480 *Sixtus IV commissioned him to preach a crusade against the Turks, who had taken the city of Otranto on Italy's east coast, and in 1491 Innocent VIII sent him to arrest the progress of Waldensians in Savoy. He died at Cuneo, in Piedmont. He is usually referred to as Blessed, and his cult was approved by Benedict XIII in 1753.

Carletti is best known as a casuist. His *Summa casuum conscientiae* (Venice: C. Arnoldus 1486), popularly called the *Summa Angelica*, was published twenty times between 1486 and 1500 and frequently through the sixteenth century. In 1520, when Luther burnt the papal bull of excommunication, the *Summa theologica* of Aquinas, and the decretals, he included a copy of Carletti's work, calling it the 'Summa diabolica.' In the *Antibarbari* Erasmus stated that Carletti and other authors of casuist works were not authors but 'congestores' (ASD I-1 110).

BIBLIOGRAPHY: DBI XX 136–8 / DTC I-1 1271–2

TBD

Christoph von CARLOWITZ 13/14 December
1507–8 January 1578
Christoph von Carlowitz (Karlewitz, Carlebitzius) was born into a noble family on the estate
of Hermsdorf, north of Dresden. After attending the Holy Cross school at Dresden he
matriculated at the University of Leipzig for the
spring term of 1520. Among his teachers Petrus
*Mosellanus seems to have influenced him the
most; in 1521 and 1523 Carlowitz edited two
school books by Mosellanus for Leipzig publishers. Carlowitz was probably the student of
Mosellanus who visited Erasmus at Basel in the
autumn of 1524, delivering to him letters from
*Melanchthon and *Camerarius in Wittenberg
(Epp 1500, 1501) and returning with Erasmus'
answers (Epp 1523, 1524). Camerarius had met
him at Dresden in August 1524 and corresponded about him with Melanchthon in 1526
(*Melanchthons Briefwechsel* I Epp 337, 473). In
1527 he was in Cologne, editing for the press of
Hero Fuchs the *Antidoti* of Lorenzo *Valla
against Poggio *Bracciolini. In the same year he
is also documented as a student of Conradus
*Goclenius at Louvain, whence he departed on
26 October for another visit with Erasmus,
carrying an introduction from Goclenius (Epp
1899, 1912). By December he had become a
member of Erasmus' household (Epp 1923,
1924, 2121, 2122). These letters reflect Erasmus'
high opinion of his visitor, who seemed to him
unusually mature for his twenty years. The
Ciceronianus, published in March 1528, also
referred to Carlowitz in the most flattering
terms as a young man of great promise (ASD I-2
684). By February 1528 Carlowitz was studying
at Dole in the Franche-Comté (Epp 1956, 1983),
apparently using his spring vacation for
another trip to Cologne and Louvain (Ep 2063;
AK III Ep 1255). After his return to the
Franche-Comté he divided his time between
Dole, where he was surrounded by German-speaking fellow students and spied on Ludovicus *Carinus, and Besançon, where he was
obliged to speak French and was able to assist
Erasmus in obtaining supplies of Burgundian
wine (Epp 2010, 2058, 2085). Erasmus recommended him repeatedly to Duke George of
*Saxony (Epp 1924, 1983), who had a German
treatise on the eucharistic controversy sent to
him, requesting that he translate it into Latin

for the benefit of Erasmus (Epp 1951, 2085; cf
Ep 1313).

In March 1529 Carlowitz took leave of
Erasmus, who warmly recommended him for
employment at the courts of King *Ferdinand
(then at Speyer for the diet) and Duke George
of Saxony (Epp 2121–3, 2130, 2141, 2166). He
also visited Frankfurt am Main (Ep 2130),
where, as at Speyer, the outlook was unpromising (Ep 2166); he therefore returned to
Saxony, where Duke George employed him in
August 1529 on an embassy to England and in
March 1530 on another to Poland. His appointment to the duke's council prompted congratulations on the part of Erasmus in July 1530 (Ep
2342), but otherwise the correspondence
between them seems to have continued intermittently at best (Epp 2324, 2498).

Carlowitz is a notable representative of that
group of German politicians committed to the
ideals of Erasmus. Devoted to the Hapsburg
emperors, though wary of the Spanish influence, he was also a moderate Protestant and
worked for religious conciliation. He was most
influential under Duke and Elector Maurice of
Saxony (1541–53), but in keeping with the
precedent set by Duke George he was also
employed on many domestic assignments and
foreign missions by the Elector Augustus of
Saxony, as well as the emperors Ferdinand I
and Maximilian II. From 1534 to 1540 and from
1542 to 1553 he rented the stewardship of the
Saxon district of Zörbig, north of Halle, in 1541
and 1542 he represented Saxony in the imperial
law court (Reichskammergericht), and from
1543 was for a few years the duke's official at
Leipzig. In 1553 he acquired the estate of
Červeny Hrádek (Rothenhaus), in Bohemia,
which included the town of Jirkov (Görkau) as
well as some villages and mines. From 1557 to
1565 he was in charge of the mining centre of
Jáchymov (Joachimsthal). In 1549 Georgius
*Agricola had dedicated to him *De mensuris
quibus intervalla metimur* in *De mensuris et
ponderibus* (Basel: H. Froben and N. Episcopius
1550). Carlowitz died on his estate and was
buried in Jirkov.

BIBLIOGRAPHY: Allen Ep 2010 / NDB III 145–6 /
ADB III 788–90 / de Vocht CTL II 390–3 and
passim / Pflug *Correspondance* III Ep 382 (with
portrait engraving) and passim / AK III Ep 1228
and passim / Heinz Scheible 'Melanchthons

Brief an Carlowitz' ARG 57 (1966) 102–30 /
Bierlaire *Familia* 77–9 and passim / Schottenloher I 112–13, V 48

HEINZ SCHEIBLE

Andreas CARLSTADT, CAROLOSTADIUS
See Andreas KARLSTADT

Petrus CARMELIANUS of Brescia, 1451–
18 August 1527
Carmelianus(PietroCarmeliano, Carmigliano),
born in Brescia, was an Italian humanist who
spent many years travelling, especially in the
east, before he decided he should also see some
countries in the west. Starting from Rome in
1481, he visited France, England, and Germany, and finally settled down in England.

In 1482 Carmelianus produced a very erudite
verse description of spring, which he dedicated to the prince of Wales, afterwards
Edward v. He was also involved for some years
in Oxford printing: in 1483 he edited for
William Caxton the correspondence between
Pope *Sixtus IV and Giovanni Mocenigo, doge
of Venice, about the contemporary war of
Ferrara, and in 1484 and 1485 he worked as an
editor for the Oxford printers Theodore Rood
and Thomas Hunt. During the reign of Richard
III he wrote a poem on the life of St Catherine of
Alexandria, and in 1486 he composed a
historical narrative in verse in which he
celebrated the end of the civil war and the birth
of Prince *Arthur. In 1490 Carmelianus joined
some other poets living at the English court
(Bernard *André, Giovanni Gigli, and Cornelio
*Vitelli) in answering Robert *Gaguin, who
had directed satirical verse against the English.
In 1486 *Henry VII granted Carmelianus a
pension and gave him another in 1488;
subsequently he made him his Latin secretary,
probably by 1495, and his chaplain by 1500.
Carmelianus was canon and prebendary of St
Stephen's Chapel, Westminster, from 1493,
archdeacon of Gloucester in 1511, and canon of
St Paul's, London, and prebendary of Ealdland
in 1519; in addition he held several other
benefices. In 1508 he celebrated the betrothal
of *Mary, the daughter of Henry VII, to the
future *Charles V with a Latin epithalamium
and a Latin and English prose text, both
printed by *Pynson (copies at the British
Library, G 6118 and C 21.b.12). On the other
hand he also rendered valuable service as a
secret agent for his native republic of Venice.

Erasmus probably met Carmelianus for the
first time when he returned to England in 1505,
and about that time he wrote a short poem
acknowledging a gift from Carmelianus (Reedijk poem 81). Some years later he thanked
Carmelianus for recommending him to John
*Bryan (Ep 262). In 1513 Carmelianus wrote a
Latin epitaph for *James IV of Scotland in which
a false quantity of syllables occurred (the
epitaph is in the British Library, Add. MS 29506
f 14 recto, but the false quantity does not
appear in it). This poem was sharply criticized
by Andrea *Ammonio and Erasmus (Epp 280,
282, 283). Ammonio had replaced Carmelianus
as the king's Latin secretary in July 1511,
although the latter continued occasionally to
write letters for the king. His last poetical
composition known today is a Latin epigram on
Dominicus Mancinus' poem *De quattuor virtu-
tibus* that was published in 1518 and several
times thereafter, together with the English
translation by Alexander Barclay (STC
17242–4).

BIBLIOGRAPHY: Allen and CWE Ep 262 / M.
Firpo in DBI XX 410–13 / Emden BRUO I 358–9 /
DNB III 1036–7 / *Roberti Gaguini epistolae et
orationes* ed L. Thuasne (Paris 1903) / P.
Guerrini *Pietro Carmeliano da Brescia, segretario
reale d'Inghilterra* (Brescia 1918) / H.L.R.
Edwards 'Robert Gaguin and the English
poets, 1489–90' *The Modern Language Review* 32
(1937) 430–4 / C.F. Bühler 'Three letters from
Henry VII to the Dukes of Milan' *Speculum* 31
(1956) 485–90

GILBERT TOURNOY

Gulielmus CARMELUS *See Guillaume*
CARVEL

Pietro CARMIGLIANO *See Petrus*
CARMELIANUS

CAROLUS (Ep 1092 of 17 April 1520)
In Ep 1092 addressed to Nicolaas *Everaerts,
president of the council of Holland, Erasmus
sent greetings to Joost *Sasbout, Jacob
*Mauritszoon, and Bernard Bucho van *Aytta,
who were all councillors, and to a certain
Carolus. Evidently Carolus belonged to the
same circle, and perhaps he can be identified

with Karel Grenier, the council's attorney-general from 28 June 1494 until his death. Since Grenier died a few months after Ep 1092 was written (14 July 1520), it is not strange that Erasmus' overture was never followed up.

BIBLIOGRAPHY: E.H. Korvezee in A.S. de Blécourt and E.M. Meijers *Memorialen van het Hof (den Raad) van Holland, Zeeland en West-Friesland* (Haarlem-The Hague 1929) XLV, LV

C.G. VAN LEIJENHORST

CAROLUS documented at Saint-Omer, 1517–18

Carolus, who was sent greetings by Erasmus in Epp 673 and 762 addressed to *Antonius of Luxembourg, has not otherwise been identified. As Erasmus called him 'economus' (steward) one might assume that he succeeded Antonius as steward of the abbey of St Bertin, if it was possible for a layman – Carolus was married (Ep 762) – to hold that office.

ANDRÉ GODIN

Ferry de CARONDELET c 1473–15/27 June 1528

Ferry, the youngest brother of Erasmus' patron Jean (II) de *Carondelet, archbishop of Palermo, was born at Mechelen and grew up in the Netherlands, where his father, Jean (I) de *Carondelet, rose to be chancellor of Burgundy in times of exceptional trouble. Ferry's connections with the Burgundian homeland of his family are documented for the first time when he registered at the University of Dole on 21 September 1498 at an age well past the normal years for university attendance. In 1502 or earlier he was at Bologna, and it may have been there or at Dole that he obtained a legal doctorate. By 1508 he had returned to Flanders, where he was a member of the grand council of Mechelen and enjoyed the confidence of *Margaret of Austria. In 1509 Erasmus met him in Rome (Ep 1359), and on 12 May 1510 *Maximilian I appointed him legal agent for the Hapsburg and Burgundian lands at the papal court. In 1511 he signed the register of Santa Maria dell'Anima, the German confraternity of Rome.

Meanwhile Ferry had begun to receive ecclesiastical preferment (Ep 1350), although he never became a priest. On 19 December 1504 the chapter of Besançon elected him canon and

Ferry de Carondelet by Sebastiano del Piombo

archdeacon, thus conferring upon him the highest rank after the deanship; the latter position had been occupied for more than a decade by his brother Jean, who resided in the Netherlands. Not for a long while, however, did Ferry fulfil the hopes of his fellow-canons that he would move to Besançon and take charge of their defence against the municipality, which kept infringing the chapter's rights. Meanwhile he obtained a second major benefice in 1511, when he succeeded his brother as commendatory abbot of Montbenoît, 65 kilometres south-east of Besançon. When his mission to the papal court ended early in 1513 he returned to Flanders; he is documented at Mechelen in 1513 and 1514 but probably remained there for some time afterwards.

It is easier to follow Ferry's whereabouts from the spring of 1520, when he finally settled down in Burgundy to apply himself energetically to the problems of the Besançon chapter and his abbey of Montbenoît. In Besançon he succeeded in ending the confrontation between the town and the archbishop and his chapter. An agreement was signed on 9 January 1528, but when Ferry died a few months later trouble soon returned. At Mont-benoît he carried out a program of restoration and new construction to which the abbey owes most of its surviving splendour. He was generous by nature and had already been a patron of artists during his years in Italy. In Rome Raphael may have painted a portrait of him which was mentioned in an anonymous biography of Raphael edited by Angelo Co-molli (Rome 1790). A painting in the Thyssen-Bormemisza collection, Lugano, portraying Ferry Carondelet dictating to Guicciardini is now attributed to Sebastiano del Piombo. At Viterbo in about 1511 Fra Bartolommeo painted for him a Virgin surrounded by saints, with Ferry himself in the foreground, which was presented in his absence to the Besançon chapter on 26 May 1518 and is now in the cathedral of St Jean.

Erasmus' connections with Ferry resumed at the time he dedicated an edition of St Hilary to Carondelet's brother Jean (1523, Ep 1334). Herman *Lethmaet reported from Mechelen that Ferry had just arrived there on a visit and might well be gained as a patron (Ep 1350). Erasmus did not let the matter rest (Epp 1359, 1534) and soon received an invitation on the part of Ferry. When Erasmus actually visited Besançon in the spring of 1524 Ferry hurried over from his abbey and treated him with elaborate kindness (Ep 1610). In 1526 Erasmus asked him for wine and any scriptural manu-scripts that might prove useful in revising the New Testament for *Froben's new edition of 1527 (Ep 1749). Finally, two days before Ferry's death, he dedicated to him an edition of Faustus of Riez for which he had been asked to write a preface (Ep 2002). When he received word of Ferry's painful death at Montbenoît, resulting from a stone ailment (Epp 2010, 2012), Erasmus, himself a sufferer from the stone, did not conceal his sense of loss (Epp 2013, 2057, 2329). Ferry was a friend and correspondent of Jérôme de *Busleyden, whom he had met repeatedly in Italy.

BIBLIOGRAPHY: Allen Ep 1350 / DBF VII 1204–5 / de Vocht Busleyden 283–4 and passim / A. Castan 'La Vierge des Carondelets' Mémoires de la Société d'émulation du Doubs IV 8 (1873) 129–56 / A. Castan 'Granvelle et le petit empereur de Besançon' Revue historique 1 (1876) 78–139, esp

92–3 / Besançon, Archives du Doubs, MS G 250 / [Jean-Marie] Suchet in Académie des sciences, belles-lettres et art de Besançon Procès-verbaux et mémoires 1901 (Besançon 1902) 124–62 / Jules Gauthier 121–2, 127–8, 134 / Richard Cooke and Pierluigi de Vecchi The Complete Paintings of Raphael (London 1969) 124 / A.J. Schmidlin Geschichte der deutschen Nationalkirche in Rom, S. Maria dell'Anima (Freiburg-Vienna 1906) 303

PGB

Jean (I) de CARONDELET of Dole, 1428–2 March 1502
Jean (I) de Carondelet, of Dole in the Franche-Comté, was the father of Jean (II) and Ferry de *Carondelet, who were friends and patrons of Erasmus. The elder Carondelet had a long and distinguished career in the service of the dukes of Burgundy. Charles the Rash, duke of *Burgundy, named him president of the council for the Netherlands which he estab-lished in 1473. The future Emperor *Maximilian I appointed him chancellor of Burgundy in 1480 (Epp 1345, 1350). He was married to Marguerite de Chassey and the father of a large family; Erasmus knew and praised five of his sons (Ep 1334).

BIBLIOGRAPHY: Allen Epp 1335, 1350 / BNB III 341–8

JOHN C. OLIN

Jean (II) de CARONDELET of Dole, 1469–7 February 1545
A son of Jean (I) de *Carondelet, Jean belonged to a prominent family of the Franche-Comté whose members served the dukes of Burgundy and later the Hapsburgs in many posts. He was born at Dole and subsequently studied law at the local university, took holy orders, and in 1493 was made dean of the metropolitan church of St Etienne in Besançon. Duke Philip the Handsome of *Burgundy appointed him master of requests in his household in 1497 and later a member of his grand council and privy council at Mechelen. He was a councillor to the future *Charles V and accompanied him to Spain in 1517. Returning in 1519 he resided henceforth at Mechelen and served as one of the highest officials in the court there during the regencies of *Margaret of Austria and *Mary of Hungary. Erasmus addressed him as

'consiliarius summus' (Ep 1334). In 1540 he retired as president of the privy council of the Netherlands, a post he had held since 1531.

Carondelet was appointed archbishop of Palermo in 1519 and obtained the pallium the following year. His appointment, however, was contested by Cardinal *Cajetanus, who had previously been named archbishop and refused to resign. He never visited his distant see. He held several other ecclesiastical bene- fices, including the deanship of Besançon and the provostship of St Donatian in Bruges. He was buried in the latter church.

Erasmus' relations with him were close, and he considered Carondelet a staunch friend and one of his chief defenders at the Hapsburg court in the Netherlands. The first reference to him extant in the correspondence of Erasmus is in a letter of 26 March 1518 where Erasmus speaks of him, perhaps erroneously, as an 'old friend' (Ep 803). Erasmus wrote to him fre- quently about his pension as a councillor to Charles v and often sought his support against those who were attacking him (Epp 1276, 1434, 1703, 1806, 2055). In 1523 he dedicated to the archbishop his edition of the works of St Hilary of Poitiers (Ep 1334). In later years, after Erasmus had retired to Freiburg, Carondelet sought to induce him to return to the Nether- lands (Epp 2689, 2784, 2912).

Carondelet wrote several legal treatises and a work entitled *De orbis situ* which was published at Antwerp in 1562. A bequest in his will restored the college of St Donat at Louvain. There are several portraits of Caron- delet, including one by Jan Gossaert (*dit* Mabuse) at the Louvre, one by Bernard van Orley in Munich, and one by Jan Cornelisz Vermeyen at the Brooklyn Museum.

BIBLIOGRAPHY: Allen Ep 803 / BNB III 348–50 / DHGE XI 1108–9 / J.M. Suchet *Etude biographique sur Jean et Ferry Carondelet (1469–1544)* (Extrait des Mémoires de l'Académie de Besançon 1901) / Ep 1334 in English translation is in John C. Olin *Six Essays on Erasmus and a Translation of Erasmus' Letter to Carondelet, 1523* (New York 1979) / Michel Baelde *De collaterale raden onder Karel v en Filips II* (Brussels 1965) 245–6 and passim

JOHN C. OLIN

Jean (II) de Carondelet by Jan Cornelisz Vermeyen

Sancho CARRANZA de Miranda d 6 July 1531

Born at Miranda de Arga in Navarre, Sancho Carranza was the uncle of Bartolomé de Carranza, the famous archbishop of Toledo whose trial for heresy was a *cause célèbre* in the 1560s and 1570s. After studying both in Spain and in Paris, he became canon of Calahorra. As chaplain to Bartolomé Martí, bishop of Seg- orbe, he visited Rome during the pontificate of *Alexander VI, before whom he preached a sermon on 22 May 1496 entitled 'De divino amore.' After his return to Spain he occupied a chair at Alcalá from 1510–11 until 1518. On 13 June 1513 he became a member of the College of San Ildefonso by order of Cardinal *Jiménez de Cisneros. He taught arts at first and later theology. Juan Ginés de *Sepúlveda was his pupil there for three years and referred to him in later years as 'doctor eruditissimus.' From 1520 to 1522 he was again in Rome on a mission for the Spanish church.

In 1522 Carranza published in Rome a critique of Erasmus' New Testament scholar- ship, the *Opusculum in quasdam Erasmi Rotero-*

Bernardino López de Carvajal, Roman school

Inquisition. Carranza was himself inquisitor of Navarre from 1528 and of Calahorra. In late 1528 or early 1529 he was elected canon (*canónigo magistral*) of Seville, the archdiocese of the inquisitor-general, Alonso *Manrique, who was noted for his Erasmian sympathies. His occupancy of this position was brief, from 22 March 1529 until his death.

Carranza also published a major work entitled *De alterationis modo ac quiditate adversus Paradoxon Augustini Niphi* (Rome: J. Mazochius 1514) and a small volume entitled *Progymnasmata logicalia* (Alcalá: A. Guillen de Brocar 1517). A defence of the virgin birth made by him before *Leo x was published at Alcalá in 1523 by A. Guillen de Brocar.

BIBLIOGRAPHY: Allen Ep 1277 / Nicolás Antonio *Bibliotheca Hispana nova* (Madrid 1783–8) II 275–6 / Bataillon *Erasmo y España* xli, 16, 122–4, and passim / Joaquín Hazañas y la Rúa *Maese Rodrigo (1444–1503)* (Seville 1909) 367 / J.J. Tellechea Idígoras *El Arzobispo Carranza y su tiempo* (Madrid 1968)

WILLIAM B. JONES

dami annotationes (A. de Trino). He dedicated the book to Juan de *Vergara in the hope that Vergara would explain the scholarly intention of the work to Erasmus, which he did in Ep 1277. In polite and respectful terms Carranza's *Opusculum* invited Erasmus to explain better certain points 'to close the mouths of the murmurers.' Erasmus was annoyed by the criticisms (Ep 1312), especially since they came at a time when he was under the scathing attack of Diego *López Zúñiga. However he made an effort, which was not entirely successful, to reply courteously in an *Apologia* (LB IX 401–32) published with his *Epistola de esu carnium* (Basel: J. Froben 1522). Relations between the two men soon improved, and Erasmus came to see Carranza as a friend and supporter (Epp 1701, 1805). Meanwhile Carranza intervened in favour of Erasmus at the conference of Valladolid in 1527 which discussed the orthodoxy of his works (Ep 1814). He also approved the *Diálogo de las cosas ocurridas en Roma* (1529?) of Alfonso de *Valdés and the *Diálogo de doctrina cristiana* (Alcalá 1529) of Juan de *Valdés, although the latter work was eventually condemned by the

Johann von CARSENBROCK *See Johann von KERSSENBROCK*

Andreas CARTANDER *See Andreas CRATANDER*

CARTEROMACHUS *See Scipione FORTIGUERRA*

Bernardino López de CARVAJAL of Plasencia, 1455–17 December 1522
Bernardino López de Carvajal was born in Plasencia. He is believed to have been the nephew of Cardinal Juan de Carvajal. He received his MA at the University of Salamanca, where he was professor of theology and later rector. In 1488 he was named Spanish ambassador to the Holy See and bishop of Astorga, being promoted to the diocese of Badajoz in 1489, to that of Cartagena in 1493, and to those of Sigüenza and Plasencia in 1495. Carvajal also served as nuncio of Innocent VIII in Spain, and in 1493 he was made cardinal of San Marcello and later of Santa Croce by *Alexander VI, for whom he undertook several diplomatic missions. His services were rewarded with the bishoprics of Albano, Fras-

cati, Palestrina, and Sabina. An opponent of *Julius II's anti-French policies, Carvajal joined the cardinals who called the schismatic council of Pisa to depose the pope (5 November 1511). His leadership at Pisa was noted in the *Julius exclusus* (*Opuscula* 97–8). As a result of his involvement at Pisa Julius dispossessed Carvajal of his title of cardinal (Ep 247) while King *Ferdinand II of Aragon deprived him of the revenues of the diocese of Sigüenza. Between 1511 and 1513 Carvajal unsuccessfully tried to reconcile Ferdinand and *Louis XII of France and regain his power. Despite rumours of his reconciliation with Julius (Ep 239) he was pardoned only on 19 November 1513, with the other schismatic cardinals, after the elevation of *Leo X to the papacy. Shortly afterwards Carvajal's former possessions were restored to him and in addition he was made bishop of Ostia. He retained his pre-eminence under *Adrian VI and died in Rome as dean of the college of cardinals.

A number of Carvajal's orations and sermons were published, including orations to *Sixtus IV and Alexander VI (Rome: S. Plannck 1483 and 1493) and a sermon before the Emperor *Maximilian I (Rome: J. Besicken 1508).

BIBLIOGRAPHY: Allen Ep 239 / DHGE XI 1239–40 / J.M. Dussinague *Fernando el Católico y el Cisma de Pisa* (Madrid 1946) / Pastor V–VII index

ARSENIO PACHECO

Luis de CARVAJAL of Orosio, c 1500–August 1552

Luis de Carvajal was the only son of noble Andalusian parents from Orosio and joined the Franciscan Observants at the age of fifteen. He studied for thirteen years at Salamanca and at the theological faculty of Paris through the patronage of the nobleman Lorenzo *Suárez de Figueroa. His teachers in theology were the Franciscans Etienne Formon and Petrus de *Cornibus. Bataillon reports that for a time Carvajal admired Erasmus, but that Josse *Clichtove became his model, teaching him to unite scholastic culture with patristic erudition and a knowledge of ancient languages. He became warden of the convent of Jerez in 1535 and of that of Seville in 1541. In 1546 and 1547 he attended the early sessions of the council of Trent, where he was noted for his defence of

the Immaculate Conception of the Virgin Mary. On his return to Spain he resumed his duties as warden of the house of Seville (1548–51) and became provincial of Andalusia. He died at Jódar.

Carvajal began a controversy with Erasmus by writing the *Apologia monasticae religionis diluens nugas Erasmi* (Salamanca n pr 1528 and Paris n pr 1529). According to Bataillon, in spite of its weak points the attack had the merit of delving deeply into the reasons why Erasmus and the monks opposed each other. Erasmus obtained a copy of the Paris edition, which had been dedicated to Cardinal Francisco de *Quiñones, and replied with the *Responsio ad cujusdam febricitantis libellum* (Basel: H. Froben 1529; LB X 1673–84), in which he gave Carvajal the name Pantabulus after the buffoon of Horace's *Satires* 1.8.11. He later received the Salamanca edition, along with advice from Alfonso de *Valdés and other friends not to court trouble by publishing a reply (Epp 2126, 2198, 2301). Carvajal answered with the *Dulcoratio amarulentiarum Erasmicae responsionis* (Paris: S. de Colines 1530). It was condemned, unless amended, but the prohibition was later removed. Erasmus, who argued that the *Dulcoratio* was published illegally, replied indirectly to it in an open letter to the Franciscans (Ep 2275) published at Freiburg and in letters to Pero and Cristóbal *Mexía (Epp 2299, 2300) which were soon published in the *Epistolae floridae* (Basel: J. Herwagen 1531). However, as his death drew nearer, Erasmus tired of such controversies (Ep 2892) and according to Bataillon sent Carvajal a conciliatory letter in 1533.

Carvajal's other works included the *Declamatio expostulatoria pro immaculata conceptione genitricis Dei Mariae* (Paris 1541), the *Oratio habita in Concilio Tridentino*, delivered on 6 March 1547 (Antwerp 1548), and *De restituta theologia liber unus* (Cologne: M. von Neuss 1545), later revised to produce the *Theologicarum sententiarum liber unus* (Antwerp 1548). The last was his major work. It was a methodical inventory of the sources of Christian belief from revelation, followed by a synopsis of Catholic dogma. Wadding lists separately his *Epistola insignis ad Laurentium Suarez Figueroam* (Salamanca 1528), his dedication to the *Apologia monasticae religionis*.

BIBLIOGRAPHY: Allen Ep 2110 / Niccolás Antonio *Bibliotheca Hispana nova* (Madrid 1783–8) II 27 / Bataillon *Erasmo y España* 228, 318–28, and passim / DHGE XI 1242–3 / DTC II 1811–12 / Luis Wadding *Scriptores ordinis minorum* (Rome 1610)

WILLIAM B. JONES & TBD

Guillaume CARVEL documented 1523–32
Guillaume Carvel (Le Carvel, Carmelus), of the diocese of Coutances (archdiocese of Rouen, Départment Manche), was a cleric by 1523 when a dispute about a benefice at Saint-Nazaire-de-Ladarès (diocese of Béziers, Département Hérault) was settled in his favour. He matriculated at the University of Montpellier in December 1525, was still a cleric by the time he took his degrees, and eventually concluded his studies with a medical doctorate on 5 March 1532. In 1528 and 1529 he was prosecuted for heresy with his friend Etienne *Des Gouttes. Carvel also held the office of procurator in the royal chamber of accounts and took advantage of his official position to obtain an early release from prison; he then filed charges against the prosecutors. In the end he was found not guilty. Nothing is known of his whereabouts after his doctoral promotion.

It is possible that Carvel and his friend Petrus *Decimarius had visited Erasmus in Basel. When Decimarius wrote to Erasmus, Carvel and Des Gouttes sent greetings, which Erasmus returned in March 1528 (Ep 1986). In September Erasmus informed Decimarius that Carvel had written to him from Lyon (Ep 2050).

BIBLIOGRAPHY: *Matricule de Montpellier* 48 / Louise Guiraud *La Réforme à Montpellier* (Montpellier 1918) I 41–5, II 331–6, and passim

PGB

Battista CASALI of Rome, c 1473–13 April 1525
Battista or Giambattista Casali (Casalius) was born to an old Roman family and studied letters under *Pomponius Laetus and law under his uncle, the jurist Luca Casali. In 1496 he began teaching letters at the Roman university, the Sapienza. Renowned for his oratorical ability, he was often called upon to deliver sermons on solemn feast-days before Pope *Alexander VI and his successors. On 2 September 1508

*Julius II made him a canon of St John Lateran; *Leo X rewarded him with a number of chaplancies and on 6 July 1517 with a prebend in the basilica of St Peter, in exchange for that of St John Lateran. Casali participated in the Roman Academy, and a number of his poems were printed in such collections as the *Suburbanum Augustini Chisi* (Rome: G. Mazzocchi 1512) and the *Coryciana* (Rome: L. de Henricis 1524), both edited by Blosius *Palladius. He was a friend of Angelo *Colocci, who on his death gathered his writings for publication; however, the project was abandoned and today Casali's works are found in manuscript in the Biblioteca Apostolica Vaticana and the Biblioteca Ambrosiana of Milan (MS G 33 inf I & II).

Erasmus did not meet Casali when he visited Rome in 1509, but he may have heard of him at that time or in 1519, when Casali supported the French humanist Christophe de *Longueil in his quest for Roman citizenship. In 1522 Erasmus, alarmed by the attacks which Diego *López Zúñiga was making on him in Rome, wrote to Casali asking for support and sending a copy of his recently published paraphrases on Matthew (Basel: J. Froben 1522). Although Erasmus' letter has been lost, Casali's reply has been printed by Aloïs Gerlo and Paul Foriers in the French-language edition of Erasmus' correspondence as Ep 1270A. In his letter, Casali expressed his esteem for Erasmus but was reserved in dealing with the important question of Erasmus' relationship with *Luther. By 1524 Casali's opinion of Erasmus had changed drastically: he composed a brief but violent 'Invectiva in Erasmum Roterodamum' (Biblioteca Ambrosiana MS G 33 inf II ff 82 verso–87 verso), accusing him of belittling Italian humanists and their Ciceronianism and of undermining the Christian faith. Erasmus heard of the mounting opposition in Rome through *Haio Herman, who was then visiting Italy. In Ep 1479 he responded to a number of the criticisms made of him, mentioning Casali and Colocci by name but denying that he knew either. He attributed to Colocci an invective that was probably the above-mentioned work of Casali. By August 1525 he had heard of Casali's death, which he noted with sadness in letters to *Brie (Ep 1597) and *Pirckheimer (Ep 1603). In the *Ciceronianus* he praised Casali's eloquence, mentioning specifically his *In legem agrariam pro communi utilitate et ecclesiastica libertate tuenda oratio* (Rome: L. de Henricis and L. Perusinus 1524), delivered before *Clement VII in defence of Roman landowners (ASD I-2 698).

BIBLIOGRAPHY: Allen Ep 1479 / *La Correspondance d'Erasme* ed A. Gerlo and P. Foriers (Brussels 1967–) V Ep 1270A / G. Ballistreri in DBI XXI 75–8 / Silvana Seidel Menchi 'Alcuni atteggiamenti della cultura italiana di fronte a Erasmo' in *Eresia e riforma nell'Italia del Cinquecento* Miscellanea I (Florence 1974) 69–133 / John W. O'Malley 'The Vatican Library and the Schools of Athens: a text of Battista Casali, 1508' *The Journal of Medieval and Renaissance Studies* 7 (1977) 271–87 gives the text of Casali's sermon before Julius II on the feast of the Circumcision, 1 January 1508

TBD

Gregorius CASELIUS
(Ep 1962 of 1 March 1528)
In Ep 1962 Erasmus mentioned that the man who succeeded Michael *Bentinus as a corrector for some Basel presses died shortly after Bentinus' own death of the plague. The successor's name is not given and he has not been identified. Up to his death Bentinus had been employed by Andreas *Cratander on his comprehensive edition of Cicero. In his dedicatory preface, addressed to Ulrich *Varnbüler (13 March 1528), Cratander mentioned Bentinus and added that his death brought to mind a similar loss suffered by the people of Strasbourg in the persons of two young teachers recently appointed by the Strasbourg council, Johannes Chelius and Georgius Casselius. Rather unconvincingly, Allen identified Chelius with Hans *Denck and suggested that Caselius might be the successor to Bentinus mentioned by Erasmus. For Gregorius Caselius see J.-V. Pollet *Martin Bucer* (Paris 1958–62) I 18, II 60–1, and passim; *Blarer Briefwechsel* I Ep 98 and passim

PGB

Leonard CASEMBROOT of Bruges,
2 November 1495–26 December 1558
Leonard Casembroot (Casibrotius, Casperotus) was born into a respectable family of Bruges; his father too was named Leonard and

his mother was Barbe Clemence of Nieuwkerke. He may have held some benefice in his native town, where he also taught Latin and Greek. By 1525 he undertook to tutor the sons of Guillaume de *Moscheron who were leaving for Padua; he himself studied civil law at the famous Italian university (Epp 1626, 1720). When he returned to Bruges with his doctoral degree (c 1527–8) he entered upon an impressive career in the administration of his home town, serving from 1535 to 1539 as pensionary, and between 1542 and 1557 repeatedly as alderman and burgomaster. In 1540 he became a member of the Society of the Knights of St George, and besides his official duties he found time not only for correspondence with *Agrippa of Nettesheim and other humanists but also for the composition of verse and orations. His first wife, Maria Reyvaert, died by 1530; his second wife, Godelieve Brest, survived him.

Erasmus' good friend Marcus *Laurinus kept a fatherly eye on Casembroot and took charge of his modest inheritance when his mother died while he was in Padua (Ep 1720). It may thus have been through Laurinus that Casembroot first became acquainted with Erasmus. It seems very likely that he renewed this acquaintance by calling on Erasmus when passing through Basel on his way to Italy. After his arrival in Padua an exchange of letters developed (Epp 1594, 1626, 1650, 1705, 1720) which illustrates Casembroot's life amid the brilliant international society gathered around the famous university. The young Netherlander enjoyed the fruits of the southern climate and also the free manners of the elegant city, or at least the freedom of joking about them. When Guillaume de Moscheron suddenly appeared in Padua in November 1525 and removed his sons from Casembroot's care, the latter found himself in a delicate financial position. Erasmus twice recommended him to Reginald *Pole (Epp 1627, 1675). The resulting contacts apparently did not meet Casembroot's needs for employment, but afterwards he found some German students who were prepared to engage him as their tutor. He also met Degenhart Haess (AK III Ep 1126), *Lupset, and Jan *Łaski, and asked Erasmus for an introduction to *Pace, who was the English ambassador in Venice. Through Casembroot,

Georgius *Agricola sent greetings to Erasmus for the first time (Ep 1594). When Erasmus' amanuensis Karl *Harst arrived to negotiate with Gianfrancesco *Torresani of Asola about a new edition of Erasmus' *Adagia,* Casembroot was eager to support his efforts and subsequently disappointed when they failed. After Casembroot's return to Bruges there is another trace of continued contact and mutual affection in 1533 (Ep 2794). Allen suggested that these warm feelings might conceivably have developed twelve years earlier in Anderlecht, where in the summer of 1521 Erasmus met one Leonard who was then the tutor of the sons of Maximiliaan van *Horn (Ep 1208).

BIBLIOGRAPHY: Allen Ep 1594 / de Vocht *Literae ad Craneveldium* Ep 55 and passim

PGB

Franciscus CASSANDER of Colmars, documented 1530–1
Franciscus Cassander of Colmars (Département Alpes-de-Haute-Provence), addressed by Erasmus in two letters of 1530 and 1531 (Epp 2296, 2442), has not been identified. It is clear that he then lived in Provence and was connected with Jean-Baptiste de *Laigue, bishop of Senez, and his brother Antoine d'*Oraison and had an interest in the Fathers of the church.

Georgius CASSELIUS *See*
Gregorius CASELIUS

Bernardus CASTELLANUS (Allen Ep 1555 introduction)
Bernardus (Bartholomaeus) Castellanus, archdeacon of Avignon and until 1524 vicar for Jacopo *Sadoleto, bishop of Carpentras, was a friend of Bonifacius *Amerbach and Andrea *Alciati. He is known to have corresponded with Erasmus in 1525.

BIBLIOGRAPHY: Allen Ep 1555 introduction / AK II Ep 930, III Epp 997, 1012

PGB

CASTELLANUS, a CASTELLO *See also* DU CHASTEL

Adriano CASTELLESI of Corneto, c 1461–1521(?)
Adriano Castellesi (Castelli, Corneto) was born at Corneto, in Tuscany. By 2 March 1480

he was in Rome, where he had a minor post in the curia and was a friend of Raffaele *Maffei and Jacopo Gherardi. He married in 1485, but the marriage was annulled by Innocent VIII on 4 April 1489 on the grounds that it was not consummated, thus permitting Castellesi to pursue an ecclesiastical career. When on an abortive mission to Scotland in 1488, he met *Henry VII of England at his court and was made papal collector in England in 1489. He enjoyed the good will of Henry, who granted him denization and secured for him various benefices, including a prebend in St Paul's Cathedral on 10 May 1492. On 5 June 1493 *Alexander VI confirmed his appointment as collector and made him nuncio.

In the summer of 1494 Castellesi returned to Rome on business for Henry. Here he enjoyed the favour of Alexander VI and rose rapidly in ecclesiastical rank. He became bishop of Hereford in England in 1502 and cardinal on 31 May 1503. Meanwhile he began to encroach on the duties of Silvestro *Gigli, ambassador for England at Rome, earning Gigli's undying enmity. After the election of *Julius II on 1 November 1503 Castellesi sought to be named cardinal protector of England at the curia. However his former attachment to Alexander VI was a liability in Julius' court. This factor, combined with the intrigues of Gigli, led to the selection of Galeotto della Rovere as cardinal protector, while in compensation Castellesi was translated from Hereford to the wealthy diocese of Bath and Wells on 2 August 1504. Although Castellesi was involved in obtaining the dispensation which allowed *Henry VIII to marry *Catherine of Aragon, his influence in England and Rome was on the wane. In 1507 he abruptly fled Rome. The most plausible explanation for this action is that Gigli had informed Julius of derogatory comments made about him by Castellesi in letters to Henry. Castellesi spent the rest of Julius' pontificate in self-imposed exile at Venice and in the court of the Emperor *Maximilian I.

Castellesi returned to Rome after the death of Julius II in 1513. He managed to resume his post as papal collector for England, to the chagrin of Gigli, Thomas *Wolsey, and Cardinal Christopher Bainbridge, who resented this intrusion into their spheres of influence. In 1514 Gigli, Wolsey, and Andrea *Ammonio made a concerted effort to remove him from the post of collector. In April 1515 Polidoro *Virgilio, Castellesi's subcollector, was imprisoned after the interception of letters he wrote to Castellesi that were critical of Wolsey. The issue was settled by the end of 1515 by a compromise, which saw Castellesi continuing as collector and Ammonio replacing Virgilio as subcollector.

In May 1517 Castellesi was implicated in the plot of Cardinal Alfonso *Petrucci to assassinate *Leo x. Although his involvement in the plot was insignificant, Castellesi confessed his guilt and in punishment was fined and restricted to his house in Rome. Fearing further reprisals he again fled Rome, settling in Venice. Although Leo x appears to have been inclined to clemency, the continuing vendetta waged against Castellesi by Wolsey and Gigli resulted in his being stripped of the rank of cardinal and of all his benefices on 5 July 1518. Wolsey became bishop of Bath and Wells and Gigli papal collector. When Leo died on 1 December 1521 Castellesi once again set out for Rome. He disappeared en route, probably a victim of murder, although it was rumoured that he had fled to the Ottoman Turks.

In addition to his ill-fated career as a churchman and diplomat, Castellesi was a poet and philosopher of modest renown in the early sixteenth century. In the De copia Erasmus mentioned his poem on hunting, the Venatio (Venice: Aldo Manuzio 1505), adding that scholars denied that he wrote it (CWE 24 581). Castellesi also wrote the Iter Iulii Pontificis (Basel: J. Froben 1518), a poem celebrating the conquest of Bologna by Julius II in 1506, De vera philosophia ex quattuor doctoribus ecclesiae (Bologna: A. de Benedictis 1507), and two stylistic works designed for use in schools, De sermone latino (Rome: M. Silber 1514/15) and De modis latine loquendi (published with the second edition of De sermone latino, Rome: M. Silber 1515). Castellesi was a friend and defender of Johann *Reuchlin, who dedicated his De accentibus et orthographia to the cardinal in 1518 (RE Ep 250).

BIBLIOGRAPHY: CWE 24 581 / G. Fragnito in DBI XXI 665–71 / DNB I 146–7 / Denys Hay Polydore Vergil, Renaissance Historian and Man of Letters (Oxford 1952) 2–3 and passim / D.S. Chambers Cardinal Bainbridge in the Court of Rome (Oxford 1965) 4, 7–10, and passim / William E. Wilkie The Cardinal Protectors of England: Rome and the Tudors before the Reformation (Cambridge 1974) 15, 24, and passim

TBD

Jacob van CASTERE of Hazebrouck, documented 1504–29
Castere (Carstere, Castricius) of Hazebrouck, in the Pas-de-Calais, registered at the University of Louvain on 28 February 1504 as a paying student at the College of the Lily, where Maarten van *Dorp became his tutor. Castere himself stayed on to teach philosophy at the Lily from 1511 to 1519 while completing his medical training, although he is not known to have received a medical doctorate. He was procurator of the Flemish nation for two three-month periods beginning on 2 June 1516 and 30 September 1518. He appears to have left Louvain after 1519, presumably to practise medicine. He may be the physician mentioned in Ep 1355 among the executors of Jan de *Neve. Castere was perhaps identical with Jacobus Castricus, an Antwerp physician at the time of an epidemic of the sweating sickness in 1529. At the request of the Ghent council, Castricus wrote a brief, lucid account of its nature, symptoms, and most successful treatment. This work, De sudore epidemiali (Antwerp 1529), was considered the best on its subject for many decades.

'Jacob the physician' greeted as his 'messmate' by Erasmus in March 1519 (Ep 932) is very likely Castere rather than Jacobus Bogardus or Bogaert, as assumed by Allen.

BIBLIOGRAPHY: de Vocht CTL I 215, II 82–3, 88, 524–6 / Matricule de Louvain III-1 273

CFG & PGB

Baldesar CASTIGLIONE of Casatico, 6 December 1478–17 February 1529
Baldesar Castiglione was born in Casatico, near Mantua, and through his mother, Luigiana Gonzaga, was related to the ruling family of that city. He was educated in Mantua and Milan before taking service as a diplomat and courtier in turn with Francesco and later Federico *Gonzaga and with Guidobaldo da Montefeltro, duke of Urbino, and his wife, Elisabetta Gonzaga. In 1506 Guidobaldo sent him to England, and from 1513 he represented the Gonzagas at the papal court; from 1521 he also represented the duke of Urbino there. In 1524 *Clement VII appointed him nuncio to the

Baldesar Castiglione by Raphaël

imperial court, and in March 1525 he arrived in Spain, where he remained until his death in Toledo. Already defined by *Ariosto in 1518 (*Satires* 3.91) as 'the man who fashioned the courtier,' Castiglione owes his wider reputation exclusively to *Il libro del cortegiano*, the final version of which was completed on 28 May 1524, and published in Venice by Andrea *Torresani of Asola in 1528. It was quickly translated into Latin and, before the end of the sixteenth century, into practically all the major European languages. According to a widespread tradition, after hearing the news of his death in Toledo, the Emperor *Charles v exclaimed: 'Yo vos digo que es muerto uno de los mejores caballeros del mundo.'

Despite this reputation and the fact that Castiglione was known throughout continental Europe and England as one of the foremost Italian writers, diplomats, and members of the aristocratic élite, his name appears only briefly and indirectly in the works of Erasmus. In Ep 1791 of 13 March 1527 Pedro Juan *Olivar describes Castiglione as a member of a group of Italian diplomats apparently busy deriding the style of the Dutch humanist and rating it as

inferior to the style of *Pontano. The frivolity of these remarks – accentuated further by Olivar's superficial comment on Pontano's *Actius* – is in sharp contrast with the seriousness of the concerns uppermost in Castiglione's mind during this period, which preceded by only a few months the Sack of Rome. Castiglione had been specifically instructed by Clement vii to appraise the intentions of Charles v. When the Sack occurred, he was deeply moved by its horrors and much perturbed by the pope's severe reprimand for his supposed failure to foresee it. His reply to Clement vii came from Burgos on 10 December 1527; the admirable way in which Castiglione kept his dignity, despite his conviction of the injustice of the charges, is a demonstration of gentlemanly conduct and political wisdom. While Castiglione was still disturbed by these events, Alfonso de *Valdés began to circulate his *Diálogo de las cosas ocurridas en Roma*, which offended Castiglione, not only in his capacity as pontifical envoy, but also as an orthodox believer and a compassionate man. He wrote a *Risposta a Valdés* which, in contrast to the elegant, harmonious calm of the prose of the *Cortegiano*, ranges in tome from biblically inspired condemnation to personal abuse. These antecedents may help to explain the unforgiving attitude shown by Valdés, when – after the death of his Italian opponent – he narrated to Erasmus (Ep 2163) the origins and developments of the conflict. In the surviving letters Erasmus did not comment on Castiglione's attack on Valdés.

BIBLIOGRAPHY: Allen Ep 1791 / C. Mutini in DBI XXII 53–68 / EI IX 374–6 / For the problem of the relations between Castiglione and Alfonso de Valdés see B. Castiglione and G. Della Casa *Opere* ed G. Prezzolini (Milan-Rome 1937) 841–7; G. Prezzolini 'Castiglione and Alfonso de Valdés' *Romanic Review* 29 (1938) 313–20; Alfonso de Valdés *Diálogo de las cosas ocurridas en Roma* ed J.F. Montesinos (Madrid 1928) intro xxxix–xlii; Vittorio Cian *Un illustre nunzio pontificio: Baldesar Castiglione* (Vatican City 1951); Bataillon *Erasmo y España* 180n, 232, 385–7

DANILO AGUZZI-BARBAGLI

Francisco CASTILLO of Salamanca, documented 1527–47
Francisco Castillo was a Franciscan theologian of Salamanca. In 1527 he attended the Valladolid conference called to deal with the opposition of the religious orders in Spain to Erasmus; he was one of the opponents of Erasmus at the conference (Epp 1814, 1847). According to Luis de *Carvajal, the compilers of a collection of alleged errors drawn from the works of Erasmus before the conference were Castillo and Francisco de *Meneses, and not Edward *Lee as Erasmus supposed (Epp 1828, 2094). Nicolaus *Clenardus, who met Castillo at Salamanca in 1530–1, praised his knowledge of Latin and Greek. Almost certainly he was the same Francisco de Castillo, provincial of Burgos, to whom the bishop of Mexico, Juan de Zumárraga, addressed a letter on the censorship of Erasmus' works on 2 November 1547.
BIBLIOGRAPHY: Allen Ep 1814 / Bataillon *Erasmo y España* 219, 245, and passim
TBD

Alvaro and Luis de CASTRO of Burgos
Little is known of the brothers Alvaro and Luis (sometimes misnamed Johannes), though there may be undiscovered references in the Consulado or notarial archives of Burgos, their native city, where their numerous and wealthy family formed an important part of the banking and commercial community. In the early 1520s, Alvaro had settled in London and handled trade between England and Spain through London and Bristol. Though he knew no Latin he sympathised with humanism and befriended Juan Luis *Vives, who stayed in his house and composed De officio mariti (Bruges: H. de Crook 1529), partly at his request. Alvaro wrote to Vives on a number of occasions: in 1527 for example, he informed him of his marriage to a woman from Burgos and sent a copy of a letter in Spanish written by Alonso Ruiz de *Virués in support of Erasmus (Ep 1847).

Against this background it is not surprising that in 1525 Alvaro eagerly accepted Erasmus *Schets' proposal that he should act on Erasmus' behalf in the difficult matter of collecting and remitting the annuity from the living of Aldington (Epp 1590, 1647). He served in this capacity until at least March 1526, with some success (eg Epp 1651, 1658, 1671). But the collection of the annuity was a task fraught with difficulties, as Luis would discover when he succeeded his brother in the role from about October 1526 (Epp 1758, 1764, 1769).

According to Schets, Luis abounded in good will towards Erasmus (Ep 2001) though there is no evidence that his zeal was enlivened by the particular humanist interests which Alvaro had nurtured. As Schets observed, his efforts on Erasmus' behalf were impeded not by any personal dishonesty but by his unfamiliarity with English, by the hostility of rival agents, and by the sheer complexity of making international payments. For example, Cuthbert *Tunstall, bishop of London, was slow to use Castro's services to pay Erasmus because he did not know that this was Erasmus' wish (Epp 1866, 1993). In 1528, Quirinus *Talesius was obliged to collect some of the money which had not found its way to Castro and to publicize Luis' role to Erasmus' English friends (Epp 2014, 2270). Erasmus himself frequently wrote to English friends acquainting them with Castro's credentials (Epp 1769, 1965, 2972). But although Luis gradually became better known, the distrust which dogged him was hard to dispel. A hint of this was conveyed to Erasmus in a letter from Archbishop *Warham in March 1528 (Ep 1965), and it was to the low standing of Luis' reputation that Erasmus attributed some of his difficulty in collecting his English annuity (Epp 2159, 2487). Warham's payments proved particularly hard to collect. Though Castro came close to prising some money from Warham in July 1532 (Epp 2512, 2527), it was around the archbishop that distrust of Castro seems to have been strongest. In part, this may have been due to the influence of self-interested rival agents in the archiepiscopal entourage. Erasmus had to stress to Warham that Castro was his sole agent and that money should not be entrusted to other intermediaries (Epp 2072, 2325), and both Erasmus and Schets believed that dishonest men around the archbishop – 'harpy-like agents' – were responsible for Castro's frustration (Epp 2413, 2487, 2704). Similar trouble had occurred earlier in 1527 (Ep 1993).

Early in 1534 Luis left England (Ep 2913). Thereafter collecting and remitting the pensions was the responsibility of his partner, Alvaro de *Astudillo, and the imperial ambassador, Eustache *Chapuys. His successors were better placed to accomplish the task, partly, perhaps, as a result of Luis' years of effort, though the suspicion that he may not have exerted himself sufficiently lingers because of his apparent inefficiency in forwarding correspondence (Ep 2530). Nothing is known of him after his departure.

BIBLIOGRAPHY: G. Connell-Smith *Forerunners of Drake* (London 1954) 18, 63 / M. Basas Fernández 'Mercáderes burgaleses del s. xvi' *Boletín de la Institución Fernán González (1954)* 156–69

FELIPE FERNÁNDEZ-ARMESTO

Iacobus a CATENA (Ep 2163 of 15 May 1529) Alfonso de *Valdés mentions among the dispersed Spanish Erasmians Iacobus a Catena, who had gone to Burgos. Bataillon renders the name as Diego de la Cadena, but no identification has been offered.

BIBLIOGRAPHY: Bataillon *Erasmo y España* 363, 383

Ambrosius CATARINUS or CATHARINUS *See Lancellotto de'* POLITI

CATHERINE, CATHARINA paternal grandmother of Erasmus *See* ERASMUS' *family*

CATHERINE sister of Charles v, 1507–78 Catherine, the youngest daughter of *Joanna of Spain and Philip the Handsome of *Burgundy, bore the name of her aunt *Catherine of Aragon. Unlike her brother (the future *Charles v) and her sisters (*Isabella, *Mary, and *Eleanor), who came to maturity in the Netherlands, she was brought up at the castle of Tordesillas by the councillors of her disturbed mother. In the imperial negotiations for political control of the Empire, her brother at first promised her in marriage to the heir of Brandenburg, the future elector Joachim II; however, she was eventually married to *John III of Portugal and, in her early widowhood, acted as regent of Portugal for her grandson, Don Sebastian. Although Charles attempted to force her to accede in principle to the succession of Don Carlos (his grandson by Philip II) as potential heir to the throne of Portugal

through his mother, Catherine adamantly refused to co-operate with these plans for the unification of the Iberian peninsula. This goal was, however, ultimately achieved by Philip, who gained control of all Spanish and Portuguese possessions, not only in Europe but around the world.

Erasmus mentioned Catherine in passing at the beginning of his *Vidua christiana* (1529), which was written for her sister Mary (LB V 726E).

BIBLIOGRAPHY: Karl Brandi *Kaiser Karl v.* new ed (Darmstadt 1959–67) passim / Manuel Fernández Alvarez in *Historia de España* ed Ramón Menéndez Pidal xviii (Madrid 1966) passim / T. Miller *The Castles and the Crown* (New York 1963)

ALICE TOBRINER

CATHERINE of Aragon queen of England, 16 December 1485–7 January 1536 Catherine was born at Alcalá de Henares, north-east of Madrid; she was the youngest child of *Isabella of Castile and *Ferdinand II of Aragon and was named after her mother's grandmother, Catherine of Lancaster. Under her mother's direction Catherine was taught the usual womanly arts and in addition horsemanship and falconry. She was also tutored in Latin, in the Christian and pagan authors, and in civil and canon law. Her learning was often praised by Erasmus (Epp 855, 968, 1313, 1381, 1404, 2133). Catherine was also deeply influenced by Isabella's zeal for religion.

In 1488 negotiations were opened concerning a marriage between Catherine and Prince *Arthur of England. To place his succession on a firm basis *Henry VII looked to the power and prestige of the Spanish monarchy, while the Spanish looked to England for an ally against France. The marriage treaty was finally concluded in May 1501, and Catherine embarked for England. The marriage was celebrated at St Paul's in November. Despite objections Catherine accompanied Arthur to Ludlow on the Welsh border, where in 1502 the prince fell ill and died, leaving her a virgin widow, as she later attested. Both her return to Spain and a match with Henry VII himself were quickly ruled out. In 1503 a formal treaty was signed which provided for her marriage to Arthur's

younger brother, later *Henry VIII, on his
fourteenth birthday. At the same time application was made to Rome for a dispensation
which would remove the legal obstacles to the
marriage between brother and sister-in-law.

Political intrigues by both Henry VII and
Ferdinand at first prevented the implementation of the marriage treaty, and in 1505 Prince
Henry formally protested the betrothal and the
treaty was annulled. Owing to lack of support
from her father, Catherine was forced to
remain in England, where she was ignored.
The English king did little to support her; her
poverty and ill-treatment compelled her to
support Henry VII's bid for a marriage to her
sister *Joanna, the widowed queen of Castile.
The devotion to duty that she had acquired
early in life led her to seek the reinstitution of
the marriage treaty, and her fear of abandonment was increased by the alternative marriages being proposed for Henry.

While Henry VII lived Catherine had to
endure years of political intrigue and shabby
treatment, but after his death the new king,
Henry VIII, showed his desire for the match. In
June 1509 Catherine was married to Henry and
was later crowned queen at Westminster. At
first she was the king's constant companion,
and their mutual devotion cannot be doubted.
In 1513 Catherine was appointed regent of
England during Henry's invasion of France.
She achieved great success, as in that year the
Scots under King *James IV were defeated at
Flodden. Between 1510 and 1514 Catherine
witnessed the deaths of four of her children in
infancy. In 1516 princess *Mary was born, but
Henry desired a male heir. Perhaps as early as
1514 rumours of the king's diminishing affection for Catherine and of a possible divorce
were circulating.

In 1517 Catherine intervened on behalf of
the London apprentices who had rioted on Evil
May day and had subsequently been condemned to death. She began an extensive
program for the relief of the poor which won
her widespread admiration. In 1520 the visit of
her nephew, *Charles V, improved the long-
strained relations between her family and
Henry VIII. Catherine accompanied the king to
the Field of Cloth of Gold for a meeting with the
French king and queen, a function for which
she had little liking. She supported *Wolsey's

Catherine of Aragon

proposal to found a humanistic college at
Oxford in 1524. In 1525 she and her daughter,
Mary, suffered the first of many insults when
Henry's natural son by Elizabeth Blount,
Henry Fitzroy, was created duke of Richmond
and first peer of England with precedence over
Mary. Presently Mary was sent to Ludlow,
ostensibly to fulfil her duties as princess of
Wales. Secret preparations for the king's
divorce were begun in 1526; in May Wolsey
instituted the suit, summoning Henry to
Westminster to answer charges of living
unlawfully with his brother's wife. In June of
the same year Henry personally informed
Catherine of his wish for a separation, perhaps
to appease his feelings of guilt. When she
resisted she was forbidden to speak to the
Spanish ambassador unless Wolsey was in
attendance. Wolsey also had her mail opened
to prevent any hint of the divorce from
reaching the Spanish court.

The papal legate, Lorenzo *Campeggi,
attempted to persuade Catherine to retire to a
nunnery, but her conscience and legal position
compelled her to refuse. Henry forced all
Catherine's advisers to disclose their conversa-

tions with her in an attempt to discredit her position, but to no avail; Catherine had only urged Juan Luis *Vives to ask the Spanish ambassador to write the emperor, thus ensuring a fair hearing of the case in Rome. Catherine appealed to Henry in vain before the papal court of Blackfriars in 1529. Bishop *Fisher of Rochester preached and wrote on her behalf. The case was deferred to Rome, but meanwhile Henry's attachment to *Anne Boleyn led to Catherine's isolation and confinement.

An ineffectual brief from Rome was ignored by Henry, and Catherine's constant appeals to emperor and pope dispatched through the imperial ambassador, the faithful Eustache *Chapuys, were met with delays. Henry forbad Mary to see her mother, hoping thus to weaken Catherine's determination to resist his wishes. Finally, in July 1531, Henry abandoned her at Windsor, never to see her again. She was moved to various country estates in turn, and finally in May 1534 to Kimbolton in Huntingdonshire, formerly the property of Sir Richard *Wingfield. By this time she had been deserted by many of her counsellors and servants, and perhaps her only friend during this period was Chapuys, whom for a time she was forbidden to contact (Ep 3090).

In 1533 Henry secretly married Anne Boleyn. Thomas *Cranmer archbishop of Canterbury, declared his marriage to Catherine invalid, yet she refused to dispense with the title of queen and denied the authority of Cranmer's court at Dunstable. Catherine constantly maintained the validity of her marriage, and finally, in 1534, Rome decided in her favour; however, the Act of Supremacy had already superseded papal authority in England. Catherine was confined at Kimbolton until her death in 1536. Chapuys, who wrote to Erasmus about her death (Ep 3090), intimated elsewhere that she had been poisoned. In her final hours she dictated a letter to Henry, granting him her pardon. Mary was forbidden to attend her mother's funeral.

Catherine is often mentioned in Erasmus' letters, always with warm praise. Upon his recommendation, she cultivated the friendship of Juan Luis Vives (Ep 1222), who became her confidant. In 1526 (Ep 1727) Erasmus, probably still unaware of her impending predicament, dedicated his Christiani matrimonii institutio (LB v 613–724) to Catherine, who had requested the work. In spite of hints given by his friends (Epp 1770, 1816) the queen did not at first respond, causing Erasmus to fear that his discussion of divorce might have offended her, for by then he evidently knew of her problems (Ep 1804). Only another letter of spiritual consolation brought the expected gift (Epp 1960, 2040). Erasmus refused to express a view on the divorce issue (Epp 2256, 2846). Initially, at least, he was not always sympathetic towards Catherine; he may not have understood her tenacity with respect to the divorce but he did say that it was preferable for 'Jupiter' to be permitted a second 'Juno' rather than have the first – namely Catherine – removed (Ep 2040). Catherine, however, was impressed by Erasmus' De libero arbitrio (Ep 1513), and a few months before her death she read with approval his De praeparatione ad mortem (Ep 3090).

BIBLIOGRAPHY: DNB III 1199–1212 / G. Mattingly Catherine of Aragon (New York 1941)

CFG

CATHERINE de' Medici queen of France, 13 April 1519–5 January 1589
Catherine, the daughter of Lorenzo de' *Medici, duke of Urbino, was born in Florence. Her birth was followed within weeks by the deaths of both her parents. As an infant Catherine was taken to Rome and placed in the care of her great-uncle, Pope *Leo x. In 1525, accompanied by her cousins Alessandro and Ippolito de' *Medici, she returned to Florence. When the Medici were expelled in 1527 Catherine was left behind; she spent the next few years as a hostage within a convent. Another Medici pope, *Clement vii, arranged for her to marry a younger son of the ruling house of France (Ep 2917), and on 28 October 1533 at Marseille, in a service performed by the pope, Catherine, then fourteen years old, married the future *Henry ii.

Catherine's affection for her husband was not reciprocated. Besides her husband's mistress, Catherine, the foreign 'merchant's daughter,' had to contend with court and public hostility, exacerbated by her inability for ten years to produce offspring. Henry was rumored to be ready to repudiate her, but Catherine was saved by the support of her father-in-law, *Francis I. In 1544 Catherine's first child, Francis, was born, and eventually she bore ten children.

Catherine's influence continued to be minimal during the reigns of her husband (1547–59) and her eldest son, Francis II (1559–60). At Francis II's death, however, Catherine's ten-year-old son became Charles IX, and Catherine, as queen regent, took control. She appointed a moderate Protestant as chancellor and, with the edict of 1 January 1561, instigated a policy of toleration. At the same time she invited Protestant and Catholic leaders and theologians to meet at Poissy to resolve their differences. This early act typifies Catherine's conduct in the turbulent years to come. She sought to reconcile the opposing factions by personal diplomacy which, however, could not deal with profound religious convictions and differences. Nevertheless, in the wars that inevitably ensued, her role as moderator provided respite that perhaps prevented total havoc.

Catherine's responsibility for the infamous massacre of St Bartholomew's day, 24 August 1572, has been furiously debated. A balanced view is that she struggled to maintain equilibrium between the religious factions and only in this instance, in desperation at the possibility of seeing herself supplanted, acquiesced in the slaughter. Charles IX died in 1574 amid continued civil wars, and Catherine's favourite son succeeded him as Henry III. Another of her sons, Francis Hercules, duke of Alençon, openly opposed Henry and joined the Huguenots. Again Catherine tried to mediate. Despite her advanced age and physical infirmities she toured the realm incessantly. Faced with the duke of Guise's Catholic League, Catherine attempted to draw away from Spain and sought a marriage between the duke of Alençon and Elizabeth I of England. Her influence rapidly declined during her last years when Paris was controlled by the Catholic League.

Portraits of Catherine include Vasari's frescoes in Florence (Palazzo Vecchio) of her marriage ceremony; the portrait by François

Catherine de' Medici by François Clouet

Clouet in the Musée Condé in Chantilly; the portrait of Catherine in old age in the Louvre; and the baroque tomb by Germain Pilon in the abbey of St Denis.

BIBLIOGRAPHY: Allen Ep 2917 / DBF VII 1418–21 / *Lettres de Catherine de Médicis* ed H. de la Ferrière and Baguenault de Puchesse (Paris 1880–1909) / Lucien Romier *Le Royaume de Catherine de Médicis* (Paris 1922) / Nicola M. Sutherland 'Catherine de' Medici: The legend of the wicked Italian queen' *Sixteenth Century Journal* 9 (1978) 45–56

DE ETTA V. THOMSEN

Ludovico CATO of Ferrara, 1490–19 March 1553
Ludovico Cato (Cati) was born at Ferrara to Renato Cato, a member of an old family originating in Lendinare. He studied at Bologna under Carlo Ruino and at Ferrara under Celio *Calcagnini. On 7 August 1516 he became a doctor of civil and canon law at Ferrara. Several years later he became fiscal procurator at Ferrara and lector in civil law at its university, posts which he held until his death.

In the 1520s, as Alfonso I d'*Este struggled to maintain Ferrara amid the turbulence of the wars in Italy, Cato was entrusted with a series of diplomatic posts of the highest importance. In 1522 he was sent to Spain to offer homage to the recently elected *Adrian VI. He subsequently served as ambassador to Rome until 1524, to the commanders of the imperial forces in Italy in May 1524, to the court of *Charles V in Spain from 1525 to 1527, and to the court of *Francis I of France from 1529 to 1530. Duke Alfonso was displeased by his failure to return quickly from his mission to France in order to participate in talks with Charles V, then in Italy. In 1532, according to a letter of *Viglius Zuichemus to Erasmus (Ep 2594), an attempt was made to recruit him as a professor for the University of Padua. If he did go to Padua, as Allen suggests, he did not stay long. He returned to Ferrara as secretary to Ercole II d'*Este, who succeeded his father in October 1534. Cato's later diplomatic missions were relatively minor. He went to Venice in 1534, 1539, and 1545, to Massa Lombarda in 1535, and to Bologna in 1543 and 1544. He married Ippolita Nigrisoli, by whom he had four sons, including the jurists Renato and Sigismondo and the humanist Ercole. Cato died at Ferrara.

A friend of Andrea *Alciati, Cato published a friendly critique (Ferrara: F. Rosso da Valenza 1533) of his De quinque pedum praescriptione. A number of his legal responses and consultations are found in the Biblioteca Ariostea of Ferrara and in the Consilia ... in causis criminalibus edited by Giovanni Battista Ziletti (Venice 1572) and other printed collections.

BIBLIOGRAPHY: Allen Ep 2594 / T. Ascari in DBI XXII 392–4

TBD

Verena de CATOMARINO See VERENA zur Meerkatzen

Giovanni Maria CATTANEO of Novara, died c 1529–30
Giovanni Maria Cattaneo (Cataneo, Cathaneus) was born at Novara and studied at Milan under Giorgio *Merula and Demetrius *Chalcondyles. At Milan he published his most important work, an edition of the letters and the panegyric to Trajan of Pliny the Younger with commentary (A. Minutianus 1506), fre-

quently reprinted in the sixteenth century. Also published at Milan were his dedicatory epistle to Alberto *Pio, prince of Carpi, for Chalcondyles' edition of the Greek Suda Lexicon (G. Bissoli and B.M. Dolcibelli 1499) and two epigrams included in Janus Parrhasius' commentary on the De raptu Proserpinae of Claudianus (Milan: G.A. Scinzenzeler 1505). Cattaneo entered the service of Bandinello *Sauli of Genoa, took holy orders, and received ecclesiastical benefices. He accompanied Sauli to Rome, where in 1509 he published a Latin translation of the Oratio panegyrica of Isocrates (J. Mazzocchi). He was a member of the literary circle of Johannes *Corycius, and, encouraged by Sauli, he wrote the Genua, a mediocre poem in 446 hexameters celebrating Genoa, dedicated to Stefano Sauli, apostolic protonotary (Rome: J. Mazzocchi c 1514). He planned to write an epic on the first crusade, but was dissuaded by the ironical comments of Pietro *Bembo, who read an early draft. Three of his epigrams were included in the Coryciana collection (Rome: L. de Henricis 1524), dedicated to Corycius. His prose works included the dialogues 'De potestate et cursu solis' and 'De ludis Romanis,' now lost. He also published Latin translations of the Progymnasmata of Aphthonius the Sophist (Rome: J. Mazzocchi 1517) and of three dialogues of Lucian, and among his own writings the Amores, De conscribenda historia (Venice: Gregorius de Gregoriis 1522), and Lapithae (Rome: J. Mazzocchi n d), the last dedicated to Corycius. The death of Sauli in 1518 does not appear to have harmed his position in Rome; his dedication of a new edition of the letters of Pliny the Younger (Venice: J. Rubeus 1519) to Jacopo *Sadoleto was more indicative of his good relations with the powerful cardinal than of a desire for patronage. His death occurred in late 1529 or early 1530 but was for a time kept secret by those who sought his benefices. He was praised by Paolo Giovio, Francesco Arsili, Andrea *Alciati, and others, and Piero Valeriano made him an interlocutor in his De litteratorum infelicitate (Venice 1620) on the Sack of Rome of 1527.

A friend of Benedetto *Giovio, Cattaneo was mentioned by him in his discussion of John 8:25 in Ep 1634A to Erasmus. In 1525 Cattaneo's translation of Aphthonius' Progymnasmata was published at Cologne (J. Soter) in the same volume as Philippus *Melanchthon's *Eloquentiae encomium,* Petrus *Mosellanus' *De primis apud rhetorem exercitationibus praeceptiones,* and Erasmus' translation of the *Declamationes* of Libanius.

BIBLIOGRAPHY: *La Correspondance d'Erasme* ed A. Gerlo and P. Foriers (Brussels 1967–) VI 585 / G. Ballistreri in DBI XXII 468–71 / G. Bertolotto '"Genua" poemetto di Giovanni Maria Cattaneo' *Atti della Società ligure di storia patria* 24 (1895) 728–818

PAOLO PISSAVINO

CAUILLOTUS (Ep 885 of 22 October [1518]) Writing to Johann *Froben, Erasmus mentioned that 'Cauillotus tuus dissutus' ('your friend Cavillotus with his mouth wide open') was a Franciscan at Bruges. No plausible identification has been suggested.

Enrique CAYADO *See Henrique* CAIADO

Johannes CELLARIUS of Burgkundstadt, c 1496–1542
Johannes Cellarius Gnostopolitanus, of Burgkundstadt (Gnodstadt), on the Main, west of Bayreuth, had apparently studied in Bologna and obtained his MA before he matriculated at the University of Heidelberg on 24 January 1519. Before that date he had taught Hebrew privately in Mainz and Tübingen, and perhaps also in Liège and Louvain. In 1517 Paschasius *Berselius, writing from Liège, may be referring to him (Ep 674). He probably met Erasmus in Louvain and *Melanchthon in Tübingen. In May 1518 he visited *Reuchlin in Bad Zell, in the Black Forest, together with the Erfurt humanist Christoph *Hack. Cellarius showed Reuchlin his *Isagogicon in hebraeas literas* which was printed by Thomas *Anshelm (Haguenau 1518). One year later, in May 1519, Cellarius tried to obtain a teaching position in Wittenberg, but when negotiations stalled he went to Leipzig, where he taught Hebrew for two years; in 1521 he moved to Frankfurt an der Oder.

Cellarius was at first attracted by the views of *Zwingli but later became a Lutheran. He took up theology and became a minister in Frankfurt am Main from August 1529 to September 1532, when he was forced to yield to his Zwinglian opponents. For the remaining years of his life he was a superintendent in Dresden, where he died.

BIBLIOGRAPHY: Allen and CWE Ep 877 / Luther W *Briefwechsel* I Ep 179 and passim / RE Epp 259, 260 / *Melanchthons Werke in Auswahl* ed R. Stupperich et al (Gütersloh 1951–) VII Ep 22 / *Matrikel Heidelberg* I 517 / *Matrikel Leipzig* I 59 / de Vocht CTL I 496 / Heinrich Ulbrich *Friedrich Mykonius, 1490–1546* (Tübingen 1962) 52

IG

Martinus CELLARIUS (Borrhaus) *See* BORUS

Michael CELLARIUS of Burgheim, d February 1548
Michael Cellarius (Keller) of Burgheim, 30 kilometers west of Ingolstadt, apparently graduated MA from the University of Leipzig and became parish priest at Wasserburg, on the Inn, east of Munich. As he favoured the reformers he was forbidden to preach and, with the permission of Duke William IV of *Bavaria, left his parish in 1524 to go to Wittenberg. On the recommendation of Urbanus *Rhegius he was appointed preacher at the Franciscan monastery in Augsburg; there he engaged in a disputation with Matthias *Kretz on 22 November 1524, later publishing an account of it in the pamphlet *Krätz: Frag und Antwort* ... (Augsburg 1525). As a popular preacher, outspoken and uncompromising, Cellarius gained considerable influence in Augsburg. On 18 October 1526 he married Felicitas, a daughter of the merchant Hans Österreicher. From 1526 Cellarius was inclined towards the dogmatic views of *Zwingli and succeeded in checking the influence of Lutheranism in Augsburg; he also helped to introduce the reformed cult in Kaufbeuren. In 1539 he suffered a stroke; he died in Augsburg.

In Ep 2310 Johann von *Botzheim reported a rumour that Cellarius had fled from Augsburg in 1530 when *Charles V was due to arrive for the diet.

BIBLIOGRAPHY: Allen Ep 2310 / NDB III 181 / ADB IV 82 / Z VIII Ep 527 / F. Roth *Augsburgs Reformationsgeschichte* (Munich 1901–11) I 142–3 and passim / J.V. Pollet *Martin Bucer* (Paris 1958–62) I 81 and passim / *Blarer Briefwechsel* I Ep 258, II Epp 821, 1164

IG

Robert CÉNEAU of Paris, 1483–27 April 1560
Robert Céneau (Cénau, Cenalis) was born into
a family of the region of Autun. He studied in
Paris, receiving his MA in 1510 and his licence
and doctorate in theology on 26 January and 5
April 1514 respectively while teaching in the
Collège de Montaigu, where he was a
colleague of Jan *Standonck, Noël *Béda, John
Mair (Mayor), and Thomas *Warnet. His first
appointment as a theologian was to a faculty
committee investigating the writings of Johann
*Reuchlin. A protégé of Louise of *Savoy, he
was appointed her almoner and received a
canonry at Soissons. In 1525 he was appointed
canon and treasurer of the Sainte-Chapelle in
Paris. On 9 August 1529 he preached a solemn
sermon on the occasion of the 'Ladies' Peace'
concluded at Cambrai with the assistance of
Louise and *Margaret of Austria. Meanwhile,
in 1522, *Francis I had appointed him bishop of
Vence, in the Alpes-Maritimes. He divided his
time between the court and his diocese until
1530, when he was transferred to the see of
Riez. Since he was opposed by the chapter of
Riez he sought another transfer and in 1532
received the bishopric of Avranches, in Normandy, taking possession of his see on 10
January 1533. Apart from attending some
sessions of the council of Trent, he devoted the
rest of his life to the administration of his
diocese and to literary polemics against the
Protestants. He died in Paris and was buried in
the church of St Paul.

Among his many publications were a treatise
advocating the unification of French measure-
ments, *De liquidorum leguminumque mensuris*
(Paris: R. Estienne 1532), an excellent edition of
the statutes of the diocese of Avranches (1533),
and his *Appendix ad coenam domini* (Paris: J. Petit
1534) directed against *Bucer, which came to
the attention of Erasmus when Bucer replied
with his *Defensio ... adversus ... criminationem
R.P. Roberti episcopi Abrincensis* (Strasbourg: M.
Apiarius 1534; Epp 2972, 3127).

BIBLIOGRAPHY: Allen Ep 2972 / DBF VIII 47 /
DHGE XII 134–5 / Bernard Jacqueline in *Revue de
l'Avranchin* 49 (1972) 79–100 / Farge no 89
MICHEL REULOS

Jacobus CERATINUS of Hoorn, d 20 April
1530
Jacob Teyng, who was born in Hoorn, in North
Holland, probably in the last years of the
fifteenth century, called himself Ceratinus
after his native town. In 1517 he studied at
Cologne, probably under Johannes *Caesarius
(Epp 610, 622), although his matriculation is
not recorded. While continuing his studies
afterwards in Paris, he was introduced to
Guillaume *Budé in June 1519 by *Glareanus.
Budé was quick to note Ceratinus' solid
knowledge of Latin and Greek (Ep 992).

Erasmus received a letter from Ceratinus in
1517 (Ep 622) and could conceivably have met
him when passing through Cologne on his way
to and from Basel in 1516 or 1518. From Paris
Ceratinus may have gone directly to Basel,
perhaps to work for the press of Johann
*Froben, but by September 1519 the plague had
driven him away and he returned to the
Netherlands (BRE Ep 125). No doubt he wished
to avoid the fate of his countryman *Menard of
Hoorn, who had been sent to Froben by
Erasmus but had died of the plague late in 1518
(Ep 904). There is speculation that Ceratinus
went straight to Louvain and was perhaps
Erasmus' choice for the chair of Greek at the
new Collegium Trilingue, and even that
Erasmus encouraged the successful candidate,
*Rescius, to seek private tuition from the more
knowledgeable Ceratinus (de Vocht CTL I 294,
491, 505, II 100–1). It seems that Ceratinus was
still in Louvain a year later and applied
unsuccessfully for the Trilingue's chair of
Latin, losing the position to *Goclenius. Late in
1520 or early in 1521 he went to Tournai, where
a new college of Greek and Latin was being
founded by the archdeacon, Pierre *Cotrel,
according to a proposal made by Robert de
*Keysere. Ceratinus was, in fact, appointed
professor of Greek, but in the autumn war and
the plague drove him back to Louvain.

In September 1521 Erasmus recommended
Ceratinus to Bernard Bucho van *Aytta as a
tutor for his nephews (Ep 1237) if they were to
study in Louvain. After his own move to Basel
Erasmus arranged for him to undertake a new
edition of Craston's Greek dictionary for the
press of Froben (Ep 1460). Not only did
Erasmus see to it that he was paid for his work
(Allen Ep 1437:155–8, Allen X 409), but he also
set out a bequest for him (Allen Ep 1437:122–4).
The Greek dictionary was published in July
1524 with a preface by Erasmus. By that time
Ceratinus had moved to Brussels, where he
was tutoring the children of Gilles de *Bus-

leyden. Erasmus had recommended him for this position and Busleyden expressed great satisfaction with the new tutor (Ep 1461), but Erasmus still believed that Ceratinus should be teaching in a university. When Duke George of *Saxony consulted him about a successor for Petrus *Mosellanus, who had died in the spring of 1524, he recommended Ceratinus for the chair of Greek at Leipzig and also provided him with introductions to his friends there when he passed through Basel on his way to Saxony (April 1525; Epp 1561, 1564-8). Ceratinus received the appointment, and when he matriculated at Leipzig at the beginning of the summer term, specific reference was made in the register to Erasmus' intervention.

As early as 1 September, however, Ceratinus left Leipzig again to return to the Netherlands. Understandably Erasmus was upset, and he was inclined to blame Ceratinus' premature departure on his Lutheran leanings at a time when the University of Leipzig was still solidly Catholic (Ep 1611). In reply to his inquiries it transpired that Duke George had shown displeasure with Ceratinus, who was thought to be concealing the fact that he was a priest (Epp 1683, 1693). Although he was in fact not yet ordained, the report confirmed Erasmus in his opinion that Ceratinus inclined towards the reformers. But he continued to wish him well and recommended him promptly to *Pirckheimer at Nürnberg, where the council had recently opted for the Reformation (Ep 1717). Erasmus' suspicions were disproved, however, by Ceratinus' ordination as a priest, which took place at Utrecht early in 1527. It was Ceratinus' turn to be upset when he learned about a letter Erasmus had written to Duke George (Ep 1951).

Meanwhile Tournai had been incorporated in the Hapsburg Netherlands, and from 1523 new efforts were undertaken to set up a college as proposed by Robert de Keysere and Cotrel. In September 1525, when Ceratinus returned from Leipzig, he was again appointed to teach Greek. His second stay in Tournai is documented above all in the unpublished correspondence of the Carthusian Levinus *Ammonius (Ep 1763). Soon, however, he resumed his wanderings. By December 1526 he had left Tournai and, after a visit to his native region (Ep 1768) culminating in his ordination at Utrecht, he probably returned to Louvain. In

November 1527 he was in touch with Goclenius and had recently written to Erasmus (Ep 1899). In October 1528 Erasmus recommended him for a position at the University of Cologne (Ep 2058). In the summer of 1529 a false rumour of his death was reported to Erasmus (Ep 2197), who was clearly saddened and once more recalled his high regard for Ceratinus' learning (Ep 2209). Ceratinus had recently been in Zeeland as tutor to Henry of *Burgundy, the son of Adolph of *Burgundy, lord of Veere, but he must have left Veere at just about this time to return to Louvain, where he died and was buried in the Franciscan church. Epitaphs for him were composed by *Cranevelt and Jacob *Jespersen (Ep 2570). Erasmus had earlier praised him in the Ciceronianus (ASD I-2 682).

Apart from the Greek dictionary, Ceratinus published a Latin translation of the first two dialogues of Chrysostom's De sacerdotio (Antwerp: M. Hillen 12 August 1526; reprinted in David Hoeschel's edition, Augsburg 1599). The Greek text of De sacerdotio had been published by Erasmus in 1525. Ceratinus also wrote De sono literarum praesertim graecarum libellus (Antwerp: J. Grapheus 1527), prefaced by an elegant and cordial letter to Erasmus (Ep 1843). This work was reprinted several times until 1736 (cf Dufrane-Isaac 136-9).

BIBLIOGRAPHY: Allen and CWE Ep 622 / NNBW VI 293-4 / BNB XXIV 734-5 / Matrikel Leipzig I 591 / de Vocht CTL I, II, IV passim / O. Dufrane and M.-T. Isaac 'Un Helléniste hollandais à Tournai: Jacques Ceratinus et son dictionnaire (1524)' in Ecoles et livres d'école en Hainaut du XVIe au XIXe siècle (Mons 1971) 121-55
MARIE-THÉRÈSE ISAAC & PGB

Paolo CERRATO of Alba, c 1485-1541
Paolo Cerrato, son of Benedetto, was from Alba, south-east of Turin, and received a doctorate in law at the University of Pavia. In May 1529 *Viglius Zuichemus mentioned him in a letter to Erasmus as the source of his information about the movements of Andrea *Alciati (Ep 2168).

A number of poems by Cerrato were published, including an Epithalamium (Turin: F. de Silva 1508) on the marriage of the marquis of Monferrato, three epigrams in the Coryciana collection edited by Blosius *Palladius (Rome: L. de Henricis 1524), and De virginitate (Paris:

Demetrius Chalcondyles

S. de Colines 1528). His *Opera* were published by G. Vernazza at Vercelli in 1778.

BIBLIOGRAPHY: Allen Ep 2168 / N. Longo in DBI XXIII 805–6

TBD

Eucharius CERVICORNUS documented 1513–47
Cervicornus (Hirtzhorn, Eucharius Agrippinas), probably born in Cologne, matriculated at the University of Cologne in 1513 and engaged in the book trade at approximately the same time. In 1516 he bought the house and printing press of Martin of Werden. His interest in humanistic writings is evident in the choice of the books he published; among others the anonymous edition of *Benigno's Defensio* of Reuchlin (1517; cf Ep 680) is attributed to him, and his editions of works by Erasmus are numerous. Johannes *Murmellius and Hermannus *Buschius worked for him as editors. From 1520 to 1521 Cervicornus printed in partnership with Hero Fuchs; sometimes he produced books to be published by Gottfried Hittorp, Peter Quentel, and Johann Gymnich. He opened a press in Marburg which he

operated from November 1535 to September 1538 with his son Gottfried, but the firm's headquarters remained in Cologne. On 26 May 1538 he sold his former house in Cologne and moved his press to the house 'zum Schwan' in the Marzellenstrasse. In 1518 Johann *Froben and his partners took legal action against him because he had reprinted portions of their great edition of Jerome (Ep 802).

BIBLIOGRAPHY: Allen and CWE Ep 802 / NDB III 184–5 / ADB IV 92 / Benzing *Buchdrucker* 222, 305 / Grimm *Buchführer* 1533 / *Short-Title Catalogue of Books Printed in German-Speaking Countries ... from 1455 to 1600 now in the British Museum* (London 1962) 991–2 and passim

IG

Ivan ČESMIČKI *See* JANUS *Pannonius*

Philippe CHABOT *See Laurent de* GORREVOD

Demetrius CHALCONDYLES of Athens, August 1423–9 January 1511
Demetrius was born at Athens, the son of Basilius Chalcondyles, a member of a powerful noble family. In 1435 members of his family were banished from Athens as a result of civil strife, many of them taking refuge at Mistra. It is not known whether Demetrius accompanied the exiles or remained at Athens. The precise nature of his studies is also unknown, although they included instruction in Greek, Latin, and Platonic philosophy. In 1449 he travelled to Rome via Athens and Ragusa. From 1450 to 1452 he studied under Theodorus *Gaza, and in 1452 he taught Greek language and philosophy at Perugia, where one of his students was Giovanni Antonio *Campano. He soon returned to Rome, where he was a member of Cardinal *Bessarion's circle and where around 1462 he defended the Aristotelian Gaza against the attacks of the Platonist Michael *Apostolius. In October 1463, through the influence of Bessarion, Gaza, and others, he became the first professor of Greek at the University of Padua, a post he held until 1472. At Padua his more famous students included Janus *Lascaris and Niccolò *Leonico Tomeo. In 1475 Chalcondyles moved to Florence to assume the chair of Greek recently held by Johannes *Argyropoulos. Here his students included Angelo *Poliziano, Giovanni de'

Medici (*Leo x), Johann *Reuchlin, William *Grocyn (Ep 520), and possibly Marcus *Musurus and Giovanni *Pico della Mirandola. In 1484, at the age of sixty-one, he married a Florentine woman, by whom he had ten children. In 1491, after complex negotiations involving Ludovico *Sforza, duke of Milan, and Lorenzo de' *Medici, Chalcondyles moved to Milan, where he delivered his inaugural lecture on 6 November. At Milan he taught, among others, Baldesar *Castiglione, Benedetto *Giovio, and again Reuchlin. He was at Ferrara briefly in 1500 because of the conquest of Milan by *Louis xii but returned to Milan at the request of the French.

In the preface to his Latin translation of the Greek grammar of Theodorus Gaza, Erasmus stated that Chalcondyles was an honest man and a good scholar, but of average ability and unable to keep abreast of Gaza's critical insight (Ep 428). Whether or not this assessment of the relative merits of Gaza and Chalcondyles was justified, Chalcondyles cannot be dismissed as a mediocrity. Not only was he among the outstanding teachers of Greek in Italy for several generations, but he also published a number of important works, including the first edition of Homer (Florence: P. Demila 1488), an edition of the orations of Isocrates (Milan: U. Scinzenzeler 1493), a manual for learning Greek (Milan: U. Scinzenzeler 1494) and an edition of the Byzantine Suda lexicon (Milan: G. Bissoli and B.M. Dolcibelli 1499). Further, he was consulted by Marsilio *Ficino before the publication of his edition of Plato's dialogues (Florence: L. de Alopa 1484).

BIBLIOGRAPHY: Allen Ep 428 / A. Petrucci in DBI XVI 542–7 / Deno John Geanakoplos 'The discourse of Demetrius Chalcondyles on the inauguration of Greek studies at the University of Padua in 1463' Studies in the Renaissance 21 (1974) 118–44 / Deno John Geanakoplos Interaction of the 'Sibling' Byzantine and Western Cultures in the Middle Ages and Italian Renaissance (300–1600) (New Haven-London 1976) 231–64 and passim

TBD

René de CHALON November 1518–July 1544
René de Chalon, prince of Orange, count of Nassau, was born in Breda, the son of Henry III of *Nassau and his second wife, Claude de

René de Chalon, Netherlands school

Chalon. After the death of his father he inherited the extensive family estates in the Netherlands, and, after the death of his uncle, Philibert de Chalon, on 3 August 1536, he became prince of Orange. He married Anne, duchess of Lorraine, on 22 August 1540, and received the order of the Golden Fleece on 27 October. Four years later, however, on 21 (or 14–15) July 1544, he died of a wound he received in a battle near Saint-Dizier, in Champagne. Since he had no children, William (the Silent), the son of his uncle William (the Rich) of Nassau, became his heir.

Erasmus may have written to René in support of Gilbert *Cousin's appointment to a canonry in Nozeroy (Ep 2985).

BIBLIOGRAPHY: Allen Ep 2985 / NNBW I 1434–5 / de Vocht CTL III 246, 515 / Michel Baelde De collaterale raden onder Karel v en Filips ii (Brussels 1965) 288–9 and passim

IG

Symphorien CHAMPIER of Saint-Symphorien-le-Château, c 1474–1539
Symphorien Champier (Camperius), the son of André Champier of the Lyonnais village of

Saint-Symphorien-le-Château, studied at the University of Paris before 1495, when he matriculated at the medical school of Montpellier, which granted him his doctorate in 1504. By 15 May 1496, however, Champier had begun to widen his experience of the world – travelling in France, teaching in the region around Lyon, and seeking patronage among the nobility of the area. In 1503 he married Marguerite de Terrail, the cousin of the warrior Pierre Terrail de Bayard, and until 1509 he seems to have spent most of his time in Lyon. In that year his appointment to the post of *primarius medicus* to Antoine, duke of *Lorraine, brought him to Nancy, and in the same year he followed Antoine to Italy and the battlefield of Agnadello. He fought again in Italy in 1515, this time at Marignano, where he won his knighthood; he also won recognition as an academic teacher from the University of Pavia. He became an alderman in Lyon in 1519, and, despite his unpleasant experiences in the Rebeine rebellion of 1529, seems to have spent most of the last two decades of his life in Lyon, where he died in the latter part of 1539.

The only trace of any correspondence between Champier and Erasmus is Ep 680A of 1517, but there is no evidence that Erasmus ever saw this letter or that he ever took notice of Champier's effort to intervene in his quarrel with *Lefèvre d'Etaples over Psalm 8. Years later, Champier took offence at Erasmus' rough handling of Christophe de *Longueil in the *Ciceronianus* but withheld his criticisms of Erasmus until the publication of his *De monarchia Gallorum* in 1537. It may be that Erasmus had wounded Champier doubly, not only by having wronged Longueil but also by having omitted Champier from his roster of French humanists in the *Ciceronianus*.

With nearly fifty titles to his credit, Champier was a very prolific author, editor, and compiler. His most important writings were in medicine, pharmacy, philosophy, and occultism, but he also worked in theology, history, biography, genealogy, poetry, patristics, and other fields. His earliest work, *Janua logicae et phisicae* (1498), was a handbook of elementary philosophy and science which owed its inspiration to similar productions of Lefèvre d'Etaples. The *Janua* frequently cites the authority of Marsilio *Ficino, whose influence on Champier's *Nef des princes* (1502) and *Nef des dames* (c 1503) is even more evident. Around 1500 he published a critique of occultist beliefs and practices, the *Dyalogus ... in magicarum artium destructionem*, but a commitment to his own understanding of the occultist tradition remains a constant theme in his later work, especially in *De quadruplici vita* (1507), *De triplici disciplina* (1509), *Symphonia Platonis cum Aristotele* (1516), and *Pronosticon libri tres* (1518). The variety of his work in medicine and pharmacy may be represented by *Le Guidon en françoys* (1503), *Libelli duo: primus de medicinae claris scriptoribus* (1506), *Rosa gallica* (1514), *Cribratio, lima et annotamenta in Galeni, Avicennae et Consiliatoris opera* (1516), *Medicinale bellum inter Galenum et Aristotelem gestum* (1516/17), *Castigationes seu emendationes pharmacopolarum* (1532), and *Le Myrouer des apothiquaires* (c 1532). The work in which Champier criticizes Erasmus, the *De monarchia*, is only one of his many treatments of political and historical and mythological issues, the least investigated topics in all his *oeuvre. Tropheum Gallorum* (1507), *Le Recueil ou croniques des histoires des royaulmes d'Austrasie* (1510), *Les Grans Croniques ... de Savoye et Piemont* (1516), and *L'Antiquité de la cité de Lyon* (1529) deal with similar questions.

BIBLIOGRAPHY: Allen and CWE Ep 680A / DBF VIII 325 / Rice *Prefatory Epistles* Epp 17, 55, 58, and passim / Paul Allut *Etude biographique et bibliographique sur Symphorien Champier* (Lyon 1859) / Brian P. Copenhaver *Symphorien Champier and the Reception of the Occultist Tradition in Renaissance France* (The Hague 1978) / M.C. Guigue 'Notes sur la famille de Symphorien Champier' in *Du Royaume des Allobroges ...* (Lyon 1884) / Margaret I. Holmes (Brunyate) 'Italian Renaissance influence in the early 16th century, with particular reference to the work of Symphorien Champier' (London MA thesis 1963) / Walter Mönch *Die italienische Platonrenaissance und ihre Bedeutung für Frankreichs Literatur- und Geistesgeschichte (1450–1550)* (Berlin 1936) / Jean Tricou 'Le testament de Symphorien Champier' *Bibliothèque d'Humanisme et Renaissance* 18 (1956) 101–9 / James B. Wadsworth *Lyons, 1473–1503* (Cambridge, Mass, 1962) / D.P. Walker *The Ancient Theology* (London 1972)

BRIAN P. COPENHAVER

Jean Simon de CHAMPIGNY *See Jean* SIMON

Claude CHANSONNETTE *See Claudius* CAN-
TIUNCULA

Eustache CHAPUYS of Annecy, d 21 January
1556
Eustache Chapuys (Chapuis, Eustathius Cha-
pusius) was born at Annecy, in Savoy, the
youngest but one of six children known to
have survived infancy, to Louis, a local notary
and town syndic, and the nobly born Gui-
gonne Dupuys. The date was probably not as
late as 1499 (as suggested by the only known
copy of the inscription on his tomb), since this
would make his subsequent career implausibly
precocious. Informed speculations range from
1486 to 1491/2. Chapuys first appears in a
document of 26 August 1506 as a litigant in
company with his mother in a case against his
uncle, Pierre Chapuys, for the recovery of
some property. For legal purposes, his age is
here declared to be more than fourteen and less
than twenty-six years, which gives us *termini*
for his birth of 1480–92.

After beginning his education locally Chapuys proceeded in 1507 to Turin, where
Erasmus had received a degree in 1506, and
where Eustache probably made the acquaintance of Henricus Cornelius *Agrippa, a lifelong friend, and François Bonivard, a future
political adversary, who praised his prudence
and eloquence. Adopting law as his career, he
continued his studies, in or after 1512, at
Valence and, by early 1515, in Rome, where –
we learn from a letter of his brother Philibert
(printed by Duparc 31) – he was admitted to the
degree of doctor and received the pope's
blessing. The assumption of most authorities
that he held a doctorate from Turin is possible,
but not proven.

At unknown dates over the next two years
Chapuys was ordained and made a canon of
Geneva and dean of Viry. In August 1517 he
became the official of the diocese of Geneva,
deputising for the bishop in the episcopal
court. The bishop, John of Savoy, was closely
related to Duke Charles III of *Savoy, whom
Chapuys soon came to serve as secretary,
displaying his diplomatic skills on missions to
Fribourg, Bern, and Zürich between 1517 and

Eustache Chapuys

1519 and helping to prevent collusion between
the cities against the duke. In 1521 he withdrew to Annecy but was back in Geneva in
1522. In 1523 or 1524 the new bishop, Pierre de
la Baume (whose candidacy he had opposed in
favour of the humanistically inclined Aymon
de *Gingins, abbot of Bonmont), lent Chapuys'
services to Constable Charles de Bourbon; in
the latter's company Chapuys visited Spain in
1525 and was present at the signing of the
treaty of Madrid the following year. Probably
at about the time of the constable's death at the
siege of Rome, Chapuys joined the service of
*Charles v, attaining the positions of councillor
and master of requests by July 1527, just before
the definitive triumph of the anti-ducal party in
Geneva. At Valladolid, on 25 June 1529, he was
appointed Charles' ambassador to England.
Arriving in August, he remained there – except
for brief absences from 1539 to 1540 and in 1542
– until 1545, holding plenipotentiary credentials from 1529 to 1536 and from 1542 onwards,
handling the delicate diplomacy associated
with *Henry VIII's great matter, remaining
thereafter to keep Charles v informed of
English affairs, and returning after his short

recall to restore Anglo-imperial relations and negotiate the alliance of February 1543.

In 1545, when his dispatches record his poor health, he retired to Louvain – a fitting haven for one with his humanistic interests, albeit the dwelling of some of Agrippa's enemies in the previous decade. He enjoyed great wealth thanks to his ambassadorial and personal pensions, the inheritance of an estate at Annecy, and various ecclesiastical sinecures – the deanery of Vuillionex, canonries at Toledo, Osma, and Malaga, ecclesiastical posts in Flanders, and the lucrative abbacy of Sant' Angelo di Brolo in Sicily, which he obtained in 1545. He increased this fortune through prudent investments in Antwerp and deployed the proceeds in founding the College of Savoy in Louvain in May 1548 and a grammar school in Annecy to feed it with scholars in December 1551. The death of his illegitimate son in 1549 ensured that his foundations would be enriched at his own demise, which followed at Louvain in January 1556. To judge from the alumni they produced and the statutes he gave them, the atmosphere in Chapuys' colleges was humanistic, anti-Protestant, and in the early stages hostile to France.

Chapuys' own humanist inclinations were evinced early. In his youth he was a friend to the Annecy humanists Claude Blancherose and Claude Dieudonné, who called Chapuys 'the glory and honour of all Savoy' in a letter of 1521 (Charvet 75). Chapuys' brief exile from Geneva in 1521 was a result of the odium he incurred by favouring humanists (his support of Gingins has already been noted). In 1523 his influence helped to protect Agrippa in Fribourg, where Chapuys counted Hans Reyff as a political adversary but a respected acquaintance. Chapuys was the guardian of Agrippa's son, Aymon, in Geneva and made arrangements for the boy's education. Among various humanist tracts on behalf of *Catherine of Aragon which Chapuys, the unfaltering champion of the spurned queen, helped to inspire in the early 1530s, the anonymous Non esse (1532) was dedicated to him; so was Agrippa's personal defence, the Querela super calumnias ([Cologne: J. Soter] 1533). The former work may have been by *Vives, who was almost certainly well known to Chapuys (de Vocht

MHL 42–3), as were, among others, *Cochlaeus, with whom he corresponded on the divorce question, Pietro di Bardi, whom he entertained in London, Erasmus *Schets, with whom he corresponded concerning Erasmus, and English members of the humanist world, among whom he was particularly close to Thomas *More from the time when the latter's chancellorship brought them into professional contact. He probably frequented humanist circles in retirement. His ambassadorial prose, in which most of his surviving correspondence is written, was highly businesslike and economical, but his few extant private letters abound in allusions to classical literature, ancient history, and even the occasional modern humanist, as well as Scripture and – less frequently – law. His role in the humanist world may be said to have been as friend and correspondent of scholars and patron of institutions, rather than as a direct contributor in his own right.

His friendship with Erasmus, though begun late, was of considerable mutual importance. His dispatches first refer to Erasmus in June 1531, when he records the visit of the Basel professor Simon *Grynaeus seeking old manuscripts in England for the press (Calendar of State Papers: Spanish IV-2 178). In 1533 a visit from Quirinus *Talesius appears to have brought Chapuys a much-desired direct introduction to Erasmus (Ep 2798). Although, to Chapuys' regret, they never met, they continued to correspond, expressing deep mutual admiration: for Eustache, Erasmus was 'a phoenix without equal' (Agrippa Opera II 980); for Erasmus, Eustache was 'the best of friends' (Ep 2997). The Savoyard's roles in Erasmus' life were as purveyor of English news or intermediary between Erasmus and some of his English admirers, particularly in the delicate matter of collecting his English annuities. Erasmus was certainly grateful for Chapuys' news – of the deaths of friends or great ones or the identity of such potential patrons as Thomas *Cromwell (Epp 2997, 3090, 3107). He decided in February 1535 to refer to Chapuys any business he had in England (Ep 2997), and in February and April of that year we find Chapuys acting as a 'post office' for Erasmus' English correspondence (Epp 2992, 3009), a role he was still discharging in May 1536 (Ep

3119). Of comparable importance, no doubt, was the part he played in 1536 in the collection of Erasmus' English annuities, in which the energies of so many and varied agents were employed. Thomas More had possessed stature enough to encounter some success in this connection, but the money brokers and commercial agents on whom Erasmus generally relied rarely gave satisfactory service, usually because their standing in society was not sufficient to inspire adequate trust. In April 1535 Erasmus Schets proposed that Chapuys' good offices should be used for the collection of amounts due, which should then be transmitted to Schets via the Spanish merchant Alvaro de *Astudillo (Ep 3009). This proposal was not approved by Erasmus, who felt that Chapuys was too busy with affairs of the state to be troubled with his business; a less exalted friend, such as Robert *Aldridge, Erasmus suggested, would do instead (Epp 3025, 3028, 3042). Nevertheless, Chapuys' willingness to act and the uniquely advantageous position he enjoyed as a friend or acquaintance of most of Erasmus' English patrons seem to have combined to overcome the scholar's scruples. On February 1536 the ambassador, in his only surviving letter to Erasmus, gave his assurance that he had the matter of collecting the annuities in hand (Ep 3090; cf Ep 3119). In the same letter he informed Erasmus of the death of his beloved queen, Catherine of Aragon, reprimanding him indirectly for the dedication of *De praeparatione ad mortem* to Thomas *Boleyn.

It is surprising that a man of Chapuys' disposition should have left neither creative nor scholarly writings. His ambassadorial correspondence is printed or abstracted in *Calendar of State Papers: Spanish* IV–VIII and LP IV–VII and XX. Apart from his letter to Erasmus, already cited, his published private correspondence was with Agrippa and may be found in the sixth book of the latter's published letters. There are some unpublished letters in the Archives de la Haute-Savoie and Archives de l'État de Genève, and copies in Vienna, Haus-, Hof- und Staatsarchiv (where there may be more such material) of twenty-nine unpublished official reports, addressed to the emperor, in the library of the University of Lyon. There is a portrait, probably contemporary, in the Musée d'Annecy.

BIBLIOGRAPHY: Allen Ep 2798 / H.C. Agrippa of Nettesheim *Opera* (Lyon c 1600, repr 1970) II 959–63, 977–86, 990–1 / *Calendar of State Papers, Spanish* / L. Charvet 'Correspondance d'Eustache Chapuys et d'Henri Cornélius Agrippa de Nettesheim' *Revue savoisienne* 15 (1874) 25–98 / P. Duparc 'Naissance et jeunesse d'Eustache Chapuys' *Revue savoisienne* 84 (1943) 27–32 / G. Mattingly 'A humanist ambassador' *Journal of Modern History* 4 (1932) 175–85 / H. Naef *Les Origines de la réforme a Genève* 2nd ed (Geneva 1968) passim / J. Orsier 'Notes et documents inédits pour servir à l'histoire d'Eustache Chapuys d'Annecy' *Revue de Savoie* 1 (1912) 37–63, 125–38 / J. Orsier *Eustache Chapuys et ses deux collèges* (Paris 1912) / F. Perron 'Les instructions de Charles-Quint a messire Eustache Chapuys' *Revue savoisienne* 95 (1954) 103–10 / J.G. Ritz 'Un ambassadeur de Charles-Quint à la cour d'Henri VIII' *Cahiers d'histoire publiés par les Universités de Clermont-Lyon-Grenoble* 11 (1966) 163–79 / U. Schwarzkopf 'Zur Familie des Eustache Chapuys in Annecy' BHR 28 (1966) 521–52

FELIPE FERNÁNDEZ-ARMESTO

Emperor CHARLES V 24 February 1500–21 September 1558
Charles was born in Ghent, the eldest son of Philip the Handsome, duke of *Burgundy and *Joanna, the future queen of Castile. When his parents left for Spain in 1506 Charles and his sisters *Eleanor and *Isabella remained at Mechelen in the care of their aunt, *Margaret of Austria. Thus he grew up in the culture of his Burgundian ancestors. His religious education was entrusted to Adrian of Utrecht (the future Pope *Adrian VI) and influenced in some measure by both the *devotio moderna* and humanistic ideals, while Guillaume de *Croy, lord of Chièvres, was primarily responsible for his training in courtly etiquette and statesmanship.

Soon the weight of his unique dynastic inheritance was laid on Charles' shoulders. With the death of his father in 1506 he came to share the hereditary rights of his insane mother to the crown of Castile and ten years later also to the crown of Aragon, following the death of his grandfather, *Ferdinand II. In 1517 he was

Charles v by Bernart van Orley

the peace of Cambrai in 1529 the new approach led in the 1530s to the advocacy of partnership with France. However, with the outbreak of another war in 1544, that second concept too was seen to be unpractical and the struggle for European hegemony continued.

While the political and military conflict with France at all times remained a central concern for Charles and his advisers, it was in many ways linked both with the religious problems of Germany and with the Turkish threat to the Balkans frontier and the Mediterranean. Not until the diet of Augsburg in 1530 did Charles and his closest councillors realize the full extent of the problems posed by the Lutheran Reformation. While his understanding of German affairs in general remained deficient, Charles came to identify in large measure with the traditional political priorities of Aragon and Castile in such areas as Italy, the Mediterranean, and America. In marked opposition to Germany he even adopted a crusading ideology which had Burgundian as well as Iberian roots. It was not Germany but the economic and financial resources of Spain and the Netherlands that provided the means for his political actions. In the face of military co-operation between France and the Turks, Charles directed his own efforts to the Mediterranean sphere; through his expeditions to Tunis (1535) and Algiers (1540) he attempted unsuccessfully to wrest control of the Barbary coast from *Khair ad-Din Barbarossa, whereas the task of fighting the Turks in central Europe was delegated to his brother *Ferdinand. Charles' personal identification with Iberia was further accentuated by his marriage to *Isabella of Portugal in 1526.

After an absence of nearly a decade Charles returned to Germany in 1529. Confronted with an alliance of princely and Protestant opposition, Charles chose to act as the *vicarius ecclesiae*, but his attempted arbitration at the diet of Augsburg (1530) ended in failure. His hands were tied by the French and Turkish threat, he lacked the means to coerce the Protestant princes, and in 1532 he was obliged to offer them a truce in the hope that an ecumenical council would be able to resolve the religious issues. Notwithstanding some efforts at achieving lasting concord (especially in 1540 and 1541), Charles could never really set his

formally invested and began to rule the Spanish kingdoms. From 1518 the royal house of France was competing with the Hapsburgs for the imperial succession. Following the death of *Maximilian I (12 January 1519), Charles was eventually elected emperor (28 June 1519; Ep 1001), but the resulting antagonism between the Hapsburgs and France lasted for more than three decades, the dominant political conflict in Europe. For some time Charles v was influenced by a concept of *dominium mundi*, which can be termed modern and rational in its opposition to the pluralism of the later Middle Ages. Based largely on the tradition of Roman law and the personal experiences and views of Mercurino *Gattinara, Charles' chancellor, this program made war inevitable since it required the dismemberment of France. The defeat and capture of *Francis I at Pavia in 1525 seemed to be a turning point. However, by 1526, following Francis I's repudiation of the peace of Madrid, Charles grew wary of the concept of *dominium mundi* which had failed to bring the desired results. Although never fully abandoned, it was united to a concept of dynastic alliances based on Christian solidarity. After sights higher than interim solutions. As a result he was forced to make concessions which proved to be irrevocable, even though he was inclined to appease his Catholic conscience by assuming that they were temporary. His long-term goal of restraining the territorial states through an appropriate reform of the Empire's constitution made no headway since even the advantage gained in 1547 by defeating the Schmalkaldic League proved short-lived. Between 1548 and 1556 the revolt of the Protestant princes spearheaded by Maurice of Saxony, combined with renewed French aggression, led to Charles' personal defeat before Metz in 1552 and to a general decline of the imperial authority. Charles' gradual abdication (1555–6) was marked by rivalries within the Hapsburg family over his dominions. A tenuous compromise stipulated that the imperial dignity would alternate between the successors of King Philip II of Spain and of the Emperor Ferdinand. This too proved unworkable.

'You owe it to Heaven that your empire came to you without the shedding of blood ... your wisdom must now ensure that you preserve it without bloodshed and at peace.' Thus Erasmus addressed Charles in his dedicatory epistle to the *Institutio principis christiani* early in 1516 (Ep 393). And after Charles was proclaimed king of Castile in May 1516 Erasmus commented: 'A wonderful success, but I pray it may turn out well for our country [the Netherlands] and not only for the prince' (Ep 413).

These two statements epitomize Erasmus' view of Charles' role. Both were written at a time when Erasmus was closely and continually connected with Charles' court (CWE 4 preface). In January 1516 Chancellor Jean *Le Sauvage had obtained for him an honorary appointment as councillor to Charles, with an annual stipend of two hundred florins (Ep 370). This appointment continued to provide a formal link with the ruler, although securing payment of the stipend – an ever-recurring topic of Erasmus' letters – often proved impossible. The *Institutio principis christiani* was apparently written in response to his appointment as councillor (Ep 393 introduction; Otto Herding in ASD IV-1 106–7). It is difficult to say whether the *Institutio* should be credited with influence upon Charles' concept of the rights and duties of a ruler (cf Herding 110–12). The question is inextricably linked to an assessment of the relations between some of Charles' prominent advisers (Le Sauvage, Gattinara, *Glapion, Alfonso de *Valdés, etc) with the ruler on the one hand and with Erasmus on the other. It is, however, worth comparing Charles' own instructions to his son Philip, which were drawn up in the course of the 1540s when the future king repeatedly acted as his father's regent in Spain, and when his age was similar to that of Charles himself at the time the *Institutio* was written. It can be stated that Erasmus' principal concerns in the *Institutio* are reflected in Charles' instructions.

A year after the *Institutio* Erasmus published the *Querela pacis* (ASD IV-2 1–100; CWE Ep 603 introduction), undertaken at the suggestion of Chancellor Le Sauvage, who had probably influenced the *Institutio* as well (Ep 853). While the *Querela pacis* may well be accentuated by the personal views of Le Sauvage and Chièvres, the promoters of peace with France (Allen I 18–19), it should also be recognized that at the time of its composition it expressed and served the official policy of the Hapsburgs, reluctantly accepted even by Maximilian I (ASD IV-1 98–9). Erasmus himself was soon to announce his enthusiastic, though short-lived, expectation of 'a new kind of golden age' (Ep 541).

When Charles left the Netherlands for Spain in 1517 Erasmus chose not to accompany him (Ep 596 introduction). At the time he was disenchanted with court life because it interfered with his scholarly pursuits, but soon he also had reason for disaffection with Hapsburg politics. As new claims were added to old ones, conflicts escalated, the antagonism with France became permanent, and the rift within the church failed to be healed. Erasmus doubted that Charles would be able to solve the problems of the Low Countries as an absentee ruler (Epp 948, 969, 970); nonetheless he made a loyal effort to join in the general enthusiasm occasioned there by Charles' election to the imperial office (Ep 1001) by writing a letter for immediate publication (Ep 1009). Between Charles' return from Spain in June 1520 and the summer of 1521 (Ep 1342), Erasmus again attended his court on many occasions, including the meeting at Calais with *Henry VIII of England in July 1520 and perhaps the coronation at Aachen on 23 October (CWE Epp 1106, 1148, 1155). Thereafter, in the years of his residence at Basel and Freiburg, he did not see the emperor again. During the diet of Augsburg in 1530, when many of his friends were anxious for him to come to that city, Erasmus denied that he had been invited by Charles or that he was otherwise directly in touch with him (Epp 2358, 2365). Beginning with the two dedications of the *Institutio* and the *Paraphrasis in Matthaeum* (1522; Epp 1255, 1270), however, an intermittent exchange of letters between Erasmus and the emperor continued, while the epistolary contacts between Erasmus and members of Charles' court remained frequent at any time.

While attending Charles' court at Cologne in November 1520, Erasmus had a meeting with the Elector Frederick the Wise of *Saxony that led to the composition of the famous *Axiomata pro causa Lutheri* (*Opuscula* 329–37). These summarized the proposals for independent arbitration in the conflict between *Luther and the papal court which were spelled out more fully in the *Consilium* jointly drafted by Erasmus and the Dominican Johannes *Faber (*Opuscula* 338–61). The *Consilium* too had been shown to the Elector Frederick, and there is evidence that for some time the idea of independent arbitration entered into the negotiations of Charles V and Gattinara with the elector. The proposal was doomed, however, for after the arrival of the papal nuncio, Girolamo *Aleandro, Charles' court began to align itself firmly with Rome. Possibly in the last days of September 1520 Charles issued an edict in the Netherlands based on the papal bull *Exsurge domine*: it ordered the burning of Luther's books, as was done in October both at Louvain and at Liège (CWE Ep 1141). By the time the diet of Worms met in the first half of 1521 the conciliatory approach was largely reduced to a ploy on the part of Charles' confessor, Glapion. Erasmus consequently saw no point in going to Worms, although it had been suggested to him that he attend (Ep 1342). But on the election of Adrian VI to the papacy (January 1522) Erasmus perceived another opportunity of gaining the secular and religious heads of Christendom jointly for his program of reform and conciliation. Following friendly overtures by the new pope, he wrote to him as well as to Charles

(Epp 1496, 1526, 1566), although discretion did not permit him to divulge these letters and they are now lost. Eventually, however, and with great reluctance, he accepted that his own position towards Luther ought to be aligned to the official Hapsburg policy – rather than the opposite – and he prepared to attack the reformer in *De libero arbitrio* (August 1524; cf Ep 1731).

At all times Erasmus feared the sinister influence of intolerant theologians and monks upon the pious emperor (Epp 597, 608, 1353, 2383, 2406, 2906), but after the diet of Augsburg in 1530 he was worried that Charles was preparing for the military subjugation of the German Protestants (Epp 2605, 2612, 2620). In fact the emperor proceeded to grant them important concessions at Nürnberg (23 July 1532). The Nürnberg settlement must have encouraged Erasmus to appeal to his friends at court for support against his critics. As a result Charles issued an edict to the University of Louvain (Epp 1690, 1700, 1716, 1717, 1784A, 1785, 1806, 1897) and prevented any official censure of Erasmus by the Spanish clergy at the conference of Valladolid in 1527 (Epp 1814, 1847, 1920, 2004). In the early 1530s, however, Erasmianism in Spain suffered a series of striking reversals. It is true that the first manifestations of new toughness coincided with Charles' absence from Spain from 1529 to 1533, and that by the time of his return some staunch supporters, in particular Alfonso de Valdés, were dead, while others, like Alonso *Manrique, were to die soon afterwards. While Charles' personal attitude remains to be clarified, he did not or could not prevent the condemnation of Juan de *Vergara in 1535 or the further suppression of Erasmianism in Spain.

In view of his connections with the court of Francis I, Erasmus on the whole showed great reluctance to comment on Charles' policy against France. Even so he could not always avoid criticism from various quarters for being unduly friendly to the arch-enemy of his monarch (ASD IV-2 15; LB X 1675C–76A). He followed the Italian wars with deep sorrow and in the new *Colloquia* published in February 1526 had an interlocutor criticize Charles' desire for universal monarchy (ASD I-3 454). Nonetheless Charles' advisers believed that Erasmus could play a useful role in the imperial propaganda. To an expression of Charles' favour (Ep 1731) Erasmus replied in polite but guarded terms which were nevertheless seen as a declaration of loyalty and were published in a Spanish translation following the Sack of Rome in May and June 1527. Gattinara's request for a more direct attack upon Pope *Clement vii, who was allied with the French, was apparently ignored by Erasmus (Ep 1790A), who in 1529 even published a letter expressing in clear terms his shock and disgust at the fate of the eternal city (Ep 2059). These feelings, however, gave way to elation over the peace treaties of Cambrai and Barcelona in 1529. Now Charles was seen as truly fulfilling the duties of his imperial office (Epp 2205, 2211). Erasmus continued, nevertheless, to eye Spanish intentions in Italy with scepticism (Ep 2201), and in a letter of April 1531, which he published without delay, he severely criticized Charles, now more powerful than ever before, for his subservience to the Medici pope in the subjugation of the Florentine republic (Ep 2472). Erasmus' attitude had no visible ill-effect on the monarch and his advisers. In 1529 Erasmus claimed that Charles had invited him to Spain (Ep 2029), while in May 1530 and October 1531 official letters were drawn up in Charles' name to assist the aged humanist in practical matters (Epp 2318, 2553).

In 1540 the Basel press of Hieronymus *Froben completed its authorized edition of Erasmus' *Opera omnia*. In his dedicatory preface of the first volume to Charles v (dated Sélestat, 1 June 1540) *Beatus Rhenanus referred at the end to the renewed emphasis on conciliation which was just then beginning to dominate the imperial policy in Germany. If Erasmus were still alive, Beatus mused, how eagerly would he now commend the emperor's course of action (LB I preliminary pieces).

BIBLIOGRAPHY: A. Kohler in NDB XI 191–211 / Manuel Fernández Alvarez *Charles v* trans J.A. Lalaguna (London 1975) / Karl Brandi *Kaiser Karl v.* new ed (Darmstadt 1959–67) / Heinrich Lutz 'Karl v. – Biographische Probleme' in *Biographie und Geschichtswissenschaft* (Vienna 1979) 151–82 / Marcel Bataillon *Erasmo y España* trans A. Alatorre, 2nd ed (Mexico-Buenos Aires 1966) / L.-E. Halkin 'Erasme entre François i et Charles v' *Bulletin de l'Institut historique*

belge de Rome 44 (1974) 301–19 / *Fêtes et cérémonies au temps de Charles Quint* ed Jean Jacquot (Paris 1960), especially a paper by P. Mesnard 'L'expérience politique de Charles Quint et les enseignements d'Erasme' 45–56 / Otto Herding in ASD IV-2 23 and passim / J.D. Tracy *The Politics of Erasmus* (Toronto 1978) passim / J.M. Headley 'Gattinara, Erasmus, and the imperial configurations of humanism' ARG 71 (1980) 64–98 / Giovannangelo di Meglio *Carlo v e Clemente vii* (Milan 1970) / *Confessio Augustana und Confutatio: Der Augsburger Reichstag und die Einheit der Kirche* ed E. Iserloh (Münster 1980), especially the papers by H. Lutz 'Kaiser, Reich und Christenheit: Zur weltgeschichtlichen Würdigung des Reichstages 1530' 7–35 and W. Reinhard 'Die kirchenpolitischen Vorstellungen Kaiser Karls V., ihre Grundlagen und ihr Wandel' 62–100 / *Charles-Quint, le Rhin et la France: Droit savant et droit pénal à l'époque de Charles-Quint* Actes des journées d'études de Strasbourg 2–3 mars 1973 (Strasbourg 1973), especially a paper by J.-C. Margolin 'Charles-Quint et l'humanisme 157–82 / Ferdinand Geldner *Die Staatsauffassung und Fürstenlehre des Erasmus von Rotterdam* (Berlin 1930)

ALFRED KOHLER & PGB

CHARLES vii king of France, 22 February 1403–22 July 1461

Charles, the youngest son of King Charles vi and Isabella of Bavaria, was betrothed to Mary, the daughter of Louis ii of Anjou, in 1413 and went to live at her mother's court in Anjou and Provence. He became dauphin in 1417 and was appointed *lieutenant-général* for his insane father. With the arrival of Henry v of England in Paris and the signing of the treaty of Troyes in May 1420, he saw himself deprived of his legitimate rights to succession, and after his father's death in October 1422 he resided mostly at Chinon on the Loire, trying to rally to his cause what little support he could obtain. The military situation improved after Joan of Arc joined his forces before Orléans and succeeded in relieving the city. Reluctantly he joined his army for the triumphant campaign to Reims and his coronation on 17 July 1429. After renewed fighting and the peace treaty of Arras with Burgundy (1435) he was able to enter Paris officially on 12 November 1437. Thereafter he divided his attention between the re-

Charles VII by Jehan Fouquet

maining phases in the military reconquest of his country and administrative reorganization (Pragmatic Sanction of Bourges and 'Grande Ordonnance' in 1438). With the capitulation of Bordeaux on 8 October 1453 the war against England was virtually ended. Charles' remaining years were marked by over-indulgence and tensions with his son, the future *Louis XI.

Erasmus mentioned Charles VII in Ep 45 (1495) as the recipient of a letter from *Filelfo.

BIBLIOGRAPHY: DBF VIII 526–30

PGB

CHARLES VIII king of France, 30 June 1470–7 April 1498

Charles VIII, the son of King *Louis XI and Charlotte of Savoy, received little education because of his poor health. According to the peace of Arras, he was engaged to marry *Margaret, the daughter of the emperor *Maximilian I and Mary of Burgundy (23 June 1483). When Louis XI died on 30 August 1483, Charles' elder sister and her husband, Anne and Pierre de Beaujeu, governed in Charles' name. He was crowned at Reims on 30/31 May 1484. After the death of Duke Francis II of Brittany a

marriage by proxy was arranged between the Emperor Maximilian and Anne, the heiress of Brittany (19 December 1490). As it jeopardized French aspirations, Charles' engagement to Margaret was repudiated, he invaded and occupied Brittany, and on 6 December 1491 Anne married him. Charles now began to rule in his own right, entering the field of European politics. In virtue of his claims, inherited from Anjou ancestors, to the kingdom of Naples, he set out with an army on 23 August 1494 (Ep 46), reaching Rome in December 1494 and Naples in February 1495. Leaving behind a garrison at Naples, Charles soon turned north again, but now he had to brave a hostile league of the Italian states with the Emperor Maximilian and Spain. In the battle of Fornovo, near Parma (6 July 1495), he fought bravely against the Italians and seemed successful for the moment, but after his return to France, his troops were driven from Naples early in 1496. During the last three years of his life Charles continued to make plans for another Italian campaign and began negotiations with Spain to bring about the partition of Naples-Sicily. However, before these plans could be carried out the king died, leaving no heirs because his sons had died in infancy.

Although he was mainly interested in hunting and waging war, Charles VIII invited to his court such scholars as Janus *Lascaris (Ep 583) and Galeotto *Marzio. In the *Adagia* (II v 1) Erasmus pointed out that Charles lived to regret his abortive conquest of Naples, and in *De bello turcico* (LB V 353C) he recalled the king's seizure of prince *Djem.

BIBLIOGRAPHY: DBF VIII 530–3 / *The New Cambridge Modern History* ed G.R. Potter (Cambridge 1957) I 350–4 and passim .

IG

Richard CHARNOCK d c April 1505

Charnock was a canon regular of St Augustin and prior of the house of his order at Dunstable, in Bedfordshire, from 1482 until 1495. He was prior of St Mary's College, Oxford, around 1496, and Eramus was his guest there (Epp 106, 108). In 1495 the bishop of London appointed Charnock prior of the Austin house of Holy Trinity, Aldgate, London, in place of Thomas Percy, whom he had expelled for misconduct. After an interval during which he was displaced by Percy, Charnock held the post until his death.

Erasmus noted that he had been recommended to John *Colet by Charnock (Ep 106) and mentioned the latter's kindness and his presence at a dinner party given by Colet (Epp 115, 116). Charnock recommended Johannes *Sixtinus to Erasmus (Ep 113). Erasmus spoke of Charnock as 'a civilized and honourable man' in the preface to the *Adagia* (Ep 126) and mentioned him in other places too, for the last time in a letter of December 1504 (Ep 181).

BIBLIOGRAPHY: Allen and CWE Ep 106 / Emden BRUO I 394

CFG

Francesco CHIERIGATI of Vicenza, d 5 December 1539

Francesco Chierigati (Chiericati, Chieregatus, Cheregatus), the son of Belpietro and of Mattea Corradi, who was of Austrian descent, was born at Vicenza after 1482. He studied law at Padua, Bologna, and Siena, receiving a degree in civil and canon law at Siena. Around 1512 he became apostolic protonotary and entered the service of Cardinal Matthäus *Schiner. In 1513 he went to Rome, where he served Cardinal Adriano *Castellesi. He found favour with Pope *Leo x, who sent him as nuncio to England from 1515 to 1517, Spain in 1519, and Portugal in 1521. Under Leo x he also served for ten months as governor of Fabriano, in the Marches. In 1522 Pope *Adrian vi, who first met Chierigati in Spain, made him bishop of Teramo, in the Abruzzi. That autumn Adrian entrusted Chierigati with his most important mission, that of nuncio to the diet of Nürnberg, where he presented the pope's pleas for united action against the Turks and for enforcement of the edict of Worms against Martin *Luther. Under Pope *Clement vii Chierigati's diplomatic missions became fewer and less important, although he took part in embassies to Prussia and Muscovy. He survived the Sack of Rome of 1527 and died at Bologna twelve years later. His friends and associates included Silvestro *Gigli, Egidio *Antonini of Viterbo, and Paolo Giovio.

Chierigati may have met Erasmus during his nunciature to England. In August 1517 he wrote to Erasmus after trying unsuccessfully to see him at Antwerp (Ep 639). Erasmus wrote to Chierigati in September 1520, denouncing the monks who were clumsily attacking Luther and who tried to associate himself with the reformer (Ep 1144). When Chierigati was sent to Nürnberg, Erasmus sent him greetings, recommending Willibald *Pirckheimer to him (Ep 1336). However Pirckheimer and Chierigati were never to be friends, for the former was soon alienated by the nuncio's lack of moderation in calling for the punishment of the Lutheran preachers of Nürnberg, Andreas *Osiander, Dominik *Schleupner, and Thomas *Venatorius (Ep 1344). Erasmus again wrote to Chierigati in April 1526, sending a copy of his *Hyperaspistes* against Luther and discussing the peasant's revolt in Germany as well as his personal tribulations (Ep 1686).

BIBLIOGRAPHY: Allen Ep 639 / A. Foa in DBI XXIV 674–81 / B. Morsolin 'Francesco Chiericati vescovo e diplomatico ... ' *Atti Accademia Olimpica ... Vicenza* 3 (1873) 121–235 / *Calendar of State Papers, Venetian* II 294 and passim / Paolo Giovio *Opera: Epistolae* I and II ed G.G. Ferrero (Rome 1956–) I Ep 58 and passim / Pastor IX 112, 127–40, and passim

TBD

CHIÈVRES *See Guillaume de* CROY

CHILIANUS Praus *See Kilian* PRAUS

Adrianus CHILIUS of Maldeghem, d before 15 June 1569

Adrianus Chilius, of Maldeghem in western Flanders, may have received a MA at Louvain, although there is no record of his matriculation. In 1529 he was assistant teacher (*submonitor*) at the school attached to St Donatian's of Bruges and at the same time offered board and supervision to a number of students. After the death of his predecessor, Gerard *Bachuus, he was appointed master of the school on 19 September 1530 and the following year he was ordained. In the autumn of 1533 he resigned his position at Bruges and went to Louvain, probably for further study in the classical languages, while earning his living as a private tutor. In Louvain he formed a close friendship with the Oriental scholar Andreas Masius. In April 1540 he returned to Maldeghem to look after his sick mother and was soon appointed parish priest, an office he held for the remain-

Christian II of Denmark by Michel Sittow

scripta (Lille 1641–3) I 151 / A. Roersch *Biblio-theca Belgica* ed M.-Th. Lenger (Brussels 1964) I 103–4

MARIE-THÉRÈSE ISAAC

CHIMAY *See* CROY

Johannes CHOLERUS *See Johann* KOLER

Jan CHRISTIAANSE or CHRISTIAAN *See* CHRISTIANUS *(Ep 1)*

CHRISTIAN II king of Denmark, 2 July 1481–25 January 1559
Christian (Christiernus), the son of King John and his wife, Christina, succeeded to the Danish throne in 1513. On 12 August 1515 he married *Isabella, a sister of the future *Charles v. He began his rule by attempting to limit the powers of both the council of the realm and the church and soon faced solid opposition from nobility and clergy alike. In 1520 he recon-quered Sweden and was crowned king of the Swedes. In violation of his own amnesty he had close to eighty Swedish leaders, including noblemen and bishops, executed in Stockholm. A national uprising followed, and in 1523 Gustavus Vasa was elected king of Sweden. In Denmark Christian lent his support to the forces of Catholic reform in church and univer-sity from 1520; new ordinances were intro-duced which show the influence of Christian humanism. In 1521 Andreas *Karlstadt was invited to Copenhagen, but when he arrived his approach to reform turned out to be incom-patible with Christian's (Ep 1241).
   In the summer of 1521 Christian visited the Netherlands to win the support of Charles v against the Swedes and the Hansa cities. At Bruges Albrecht *Dürer sketched his likeness; he also met Cardinal *Wolsey and, repeatedly it seems, Erasmus, with whom he discussed *Luther and church reform (Ep 1228). Each of them was clearly impressed with the other (Epp 1263, 1342); Erasmus subsequently men-tioned how the king had read his paraphrase of Matthew (Ep 1381), and later he was saddened at the thought of Christian's misfortunes (Ep 1601 and the colloquy *Puerpera*, ASD I-3 454). He did not, however, point out that Christian's own actions were largely responsible for his troubles, nor did he comment on the ignoble

der of his life. His successor was appointed on 15 June 1569. It does not seem that Chilius ever met Erasmus, but in the early summer of 1531 the Basel professor Simon *Grynaeus and the printer Johann *Bebel were passing through Bruges and were entertained at dinner by Marcus *Laurinus. Chilius was among those invited and afterwards felt encouraged to send Erasmus a letter of compliment (Ep 2499).
   In 1533 Chilius published at Antwerp Latin verse translations of Aristophanes' *Plutus* and of Lucian's *Podagra posterior* or *Ocypus*. He also translated, allegedly from a Semitic language, perhaps from Syriac, a paraphrase of the Psalms. This work is now missing, but a manuscript, perhaps the autograph, remained in the Ter Duinen (Dunes) abbey and is men-tioned in a catalogue of the manuscripts of the abbey compiled in 1628.
   BIBLIOGRAPHY: Allen Ep 2499 / BNB IV 76 / de Vocht MHL 129 / de Vocht CTL III 262–3 and passim / V. Andrè *Bibliotheca Belgica* ed J.F. Poppens (Brussels 1739) II 11. / F.W. Sweerts *Athenae Belgicae* (Antwerp 1628) 94 / J. Meyerus *Flandricarum rerum tomi decem* (Bruges 1531) f 42 recto / A. Sanderus *Bibliotheca Belgica manu-*

treatment the king accorded his wife. On one occasion he seems to suggest that he had expected to receive a present from Christian (Ep 1883).

Having lost all support in his states, Christian was forced in April 1523 to seek refuge in the Netherlands, eventually settling down with his family at Lier. Meanwhile the Danish *Rigsraad* elected his uncle, Duke Frederick of Schleswig-Holstein, to the throne. The failure of Christian's policies was followed by personal disappointments and financial difficulties. For a time he came to sympathize with the teachings of Luther, but by 1530 he had returned his allegiance to Rome. In 1531 he persuaded Charles v to provide him with a fleet and money; he attempted to reconquer his kingdom (Ep 2570) but was captured and spent the rest of his life in captivity. There are portrait paintings of Christian by Michael Sittow in Copenhagen and by Lukas Cranach (1523) and Jan Gossaert (1526) in Frederiksborg.

BIBLIOGRAPHY: Allen Ep 1228 / *Dansk Biografisk Leksikon* 3rd ed (Copenhagen 1979–) III 293–7 / J. Oskar Andersen *Overfor Kirkebruddet* (Copenhagen 1917) 62–138 / Else Kai Sass *Studier i Christiern II's ikonografi* (Copenhagen 1970) / Michael Venge *Når vinden føjer sig* (Copenhagen 1977) / Palle Lauring *A History of the Kingdom of Denmark* trans D. Hohnen (Copenhagen 1960) 125–36 / Karl Brandi *Kaiser Karl v.* new edition (Darmstadt 1959–67) I 116–17, 156–8, and passim

MARTIN SCHWARZ LAUSTEN

CHRISTIAN III king of Denmark, 12 August 1503–1 January 1559
The son of King Frederick I of Denmark, Christian was brought up in German-speaking Holstein and in 1521 accompanied his uncle Joachim, elector of Brandenburg, to the diet of Worms, meeting *Luther in Wittenberg on the way there. In 1528 he introduced the Reformation in the territory of Haderslev, in Schleswig, of which he had been given charge. In 1533 he succeeded his father as duke of Schleswig-Holstein, but the *Rigsraad* of Denmark, under pressure from the Catholic bishops, at first refused to recognize him as king, and the Danish towns, assisted by Lübeck, rose in support of the detained King *Christian II. A

bitter civil war followed, combined with the 'Count's War' against Lübeck and her allies. After his victory near Assens, on the island of Fyn (Ep 3041), Christian III succeeded in taking Copenhagen in 1536 and holding his coronation. He began his rule by outlawing the Catholic church and confiscating its property. He also introduced the Reformation to Norway, which was reduced to the status of a Danish province. Subsequently Christian III managed to pacify his kingdom and to consolidate the position of his dynasty.

BIBLIOGRAPHY: *Dansk Biografisk Leksikon* 3rd ed (Copenhagen 1979–) III 297–302 / NDB III 233–4 / F.C. Dahlmann and D. Schäfer *Geschichte von Dänemark* (Gotha 1840–1902) IV 207–496 / Palle Lauring *A History of the Kingdom of Denmark* trans D. Hohnen (Copenhagen 1960) 138–45

PGB

CHRISTIANUS (Ep 1, [end of 1484])
Christianus has not been identified. Allen suggested that he might be Jan Christiaanse (d 8 August 1496), the fifth prior of Steyn (1464–91?), but one would expect Erasmus to refer to the prior with greater reverence. Nor can the prior be identified with the 'dominus Johannes' mentioned in Epp 20, 21, 23, for whom see Jan Dirksz van der *Haer.

BIBLIOGRAPHY: Allen Ep 1 / Dalmatius van Heel OFM *De reguliere kanunniken van het klooster Emmaus* (Gouda 1949) 23

C.G. VAN LEIJENHORST

CHRISTIANUS Hieronymita (Allen Ep 2566:167, [November 1531])
Maarten *Lips, canon of Lens-Saint-Rémy, wrote to Erasmus that *Willem of Haarlem, a brother of the Common Life at Liège, was accusing another member of his order ('Hieronymita') by the name of Christianus of resolute animosity towards Erasmus. His critical theses had been sent to Erasmus enclosed in a preceding letter by Lips which is now missing.

Perhaps Christianus may be identified with Christiaan Heusden of Mielen, near St Truiden, who is listed among the Brethren of the Common Life at Liège in 1548, 1556, and 1558 and died early in 1581. He does not, however, figure on the list for 1531, and thus no positive identification is possible.

BIBLIOGRAPHY: L.-E. Halkin 'Les Frères de la vie commune de la maison Saint-Jérôme de Liège' *Bulletin de l'Institut archéologique liégeois* 65 (1945) 12–13, 47

LÉON-E. HALKIN

Caterina CIBO duchess of Camerino, 14 September 1501–11 February 1557
Caterina Cibo (Cybo) was the daughter of Franceschetto Cibo, count of Anguillara, and Maddalena, the daughter of Lorenzo ('il Magnifico') de' *Medici. In 1520 she married Giovanni Maria Varano, duke of Camerino, a tiny and embattled principality in the Marches. Following his death in 1527 she assumed the government of Camerino after escaping from the captivity in which she was being held by her husband's relatives. After *Paul III deposed her in 1545 she spent the last twenty-two years of her life in Florence. Caterina is credited with knowledge of Greek and Hebrew as well as Latin. With her relative *Clement VII, she interceded repeatedly in favour of the Capuchin order and became a close friend of the Capuchin general, Bernardino *Ochino, who made her a principal speaker in his *Dialoghi sette* and may have been in touch with her even after his flight to Geneva.

In Ep 2968 Bonifacius *Amerbach repeated a false rumour he had read in a recent letter from Andrea *Alciati (AK IV Ep 1842) according to which Caterina had married Ippolito d'*Este, who supposedly wished to resign his cardinalate.

BIBLIOGRAPHY: Allen Ep 2968 / EI XII 201–2 / R.H. Bainton *Women of the Reformation in Germany and Italy* (Minneapolis 1971) 187–98

PGB

Francesco CIGALINI of Como, 1489–c June 1551
Francesco Cigalini (Cigalino) was a physician of Como, learned in the Greek and Hebrew languages. He was a friend of Benedetto *Giovio, who sent him a letter encouraging him to publish his studies, which employed astrology in the service of medicine. Two of his medical disputations in the form of letters were published with those of Taddeo Duni at Zürich around 1555, while the Biblioteca comunale of Como possesses copies in manuscript of his 'De nobilitate patriae,' on the history of Como. Cigalini wrote to Erasmus offering criticisms

of his interpretation of Luke 2:14, and the latter replied at length with Ep 1680, dated 15 March 1526.

BIBLIOGRAPHY: Allen Ep 1680 / S. Monti 'Lettere di Benedetto Giovio' *Periodico della Società Storica Comense* 8 (1891) 113 / P.O. Kristeller *Iter Italicum* (London 1965–) I 46, 48

TBD

Erazm CIOŁEK bishop of Płock, c 1474–9 September 1522
Erazm Ciołek, called Vitellius, came from the same family as Erazm *Ciołek, abbot of Mogiła. He was the son of Stanisław and Agnieszka, burghers of Cracow and owners of a wineshop. From 1485 he studied at the University of Cracow, obtaining his BA in 1487 and his MA in 1491. During the years 1491–3 he lectured at the University of Cracow. From 1495 he worked in the chancery of Alexander, the grand duke of Lithuania, in Vilno and saw his ability and industriousness rewarded by his master's confidence. In 1499 he was appointed canon of Vilno; later he was made dean and finally provost. He was appointed to the Cracow cathedral chapter after securing legal recognition of his status as a member of the gentry on 14 April 1502. Alexander, who had become king of Poland in 1501, nominated him to the bishopric of Płock on 29 November 1503. In 1501 Ciołek undertook his first embassy to Rome, to be followed by a second in 1505 that brought wide recognition of his diplomatic and rhetorical talents.

Besides being highly cultivated himself, Ciołek was a patron of scholars, artists, and writers. He also collected an impressive library, especially acclaimed for its illuminated manuscripts, and enlarged his episcopal palace in Płock and his house in Cracow. In 1518 Alexander's successor, King *Sigismund I, sent him on an important mission to the German diet at Augsburg and then to Rome. In Augsburg he delivered on 20 August a harangue in support of a crusade against the Turks which was well received and was published by Jakob *Spiegel with a dedication to Erasmus (Ep 863). From Augsburg Ciołek travelled to Rome, where he remained for almost two years as a representative of Sigismund I, living in great state. He died in Rome and was buried in the choir of Santa Maria del Popolo.

Ciołek's address to Pope *Alexander VI of 1505

appeared in print: *Obedientia Alexandri ... oratio* (n d, n p). His address at Augsburg was published three times in 1518 (Augsburg: J. Miller; Basel: P. Gengenbach; and Rome: J. Mazzocchi), in the last case together with an address to Pope *Leo x under the title *Orationes*. Parts of Ciołek's library, including the famous illuminated manuscripts, are preserved in the chapter library of Płock. Filippo *Beroaldo dedicated to Ciołek his *Opusculum de terremotu et pestilentia* (Bologna 1505).

BIBLIOGRAPHY: Allen Epp 863, 1803 / PSB IV 78–81 / *Bibliografia polska* ed K. Estreicher et al (Cracow 1870–1951) XIV 288–9 / *Bibliografia literatury polskiej Nowy Korbut* (Warsaw 1963–) II 96–7 / K. Hartleb *Dzialalność kulturalna biskupa dyplomaty Erazma Ciołka (Lvov 1929)* / H. Folwarski *Erazm Ciołek biskup-dyplomata* (Warsaw 1935)

HALINA KOWALSKA

Erazm CIOŁEK abbot of Mogiła, d 6 December 1546
Ciołek came from the same family as Erazm *Ciołek, bishop of Płock. His parents, Maciej, a soapmaker, and Agnieszka, were burghers of Cracow. Erazm began his studies at the University of Cracow in 1507, receiving his BA in 1509 and his MA in 1512. He then entered the Cistercian abbey of Mogiła (*Clara Tumba*) and was chosen abbot in 1522. Under his administration Mogiła experienced a great cultural upswing. The church and monastery were restored, and a large library was built to house the monastery's collection of books, which was greatly enlarged by Ciołek. In 1531 he was sent to Rome as an ambassador of King *Sigismund I; there he received a special privilege from Pope *Clement VII (28 December 1531) permitting the abbot of Mogiła to be a member of the Cracow cathedral chapter. In virtue of this privilege he was appointed canon of Cracow in 1536. In 1544 the chapter elected him suffragan bishop of Cracow, and on 14 November 1544 he received papal confirmation as titular bishop of Laodicea. He died two years later and was buried in the church of Mogiła.

When returning to Poland from Rome in the winter of 1532 Ciołek stopped at Freiburg at the beginning of February and called upon Erasmus, who hastened to write letters for him to take to Erasmus' friends in Poland (Ep 2600). After returning to Mogiła, Ciołek wrote to

Erasmus in May 1533. This letter, now missing, was accompanied by another (Ep 2811) from Jakub *Groffik, who had been with Ciołek during the visit the preceding year. As a gift Ciołek sent Erasmus a knife and fork of gilded silver – beautiful specimens of craftsmanship that are preserved at the Historisches Museum of Basel. In November 1533 Erasmus included Ciołek's name in a list of Polish patrons and friends he wished to warn against callers presenting forged letters of recommendation (Ep 2874).

BIBLIOGRAPHY: Allen Ep 2600 / PSB IV 81–2 / F. Kopera 'Dary z Polski dla Erasma z Rotterdamu' in *Sprawozdania Komisji do Badania Historii Sztuki w Polsce* VI (Cracow 1900) 117, 128–33

HALINA KOWALSKA

Enno II CIRKSENA count of Eastern Friesland, 1505–24 September 1540
Enno II, the eldest son of Edzard I (the Great) and Elisabeth von Rietberg, inherited a county that his father had consolidated into a coherent territorial state and that in its heyday reached from the Weser as far west as the city of Groningen and had its capital in Emden. When Enno succeeded his father, who had died in February 1528, he turned out to be a weak ruler but still managed to preserve the homogeneous character of his county and continued the church reform initiated by his father, secularizing all monasteries (Ep 2366). On 6 March 1530 he married Anna of Oldenburg (d 1575), who took on the regency after his death and became the patroness of Jan (II) *Łaski.

BIBLIOGRAPHY: Allen Ep 2366 / NDB I 301, III 255, IV 317, 537

PGB

CISNEROS *See Francisco JIMÉNEZ DE CISNEROS*

CLAUDE queen of France, 13 October 1494–c 20 July 1524
A daughter of *Louis XII of France and Anne of Brittany, Claude was promised in 1501 to Philip the Handsome, duke of *Burgundy, as a bride for his son, the future *Charles V. However, political and dynastic circumstances intervened, and on 18 May 1506 Claude was engaged to the future *Francis I in a solemn ceremony. They were married at Saint-Germain, near Paris, on 18 May 1514. Claude

Claude, queen of France

was not noted for particular beauty and intelligence, but she managed to retain the respect and even the affection of her husband, despite his infidelities. In 1520 she was present with her husband at the royal rendezvous on the Field of Cloth of Gold (Ep 1096). Having borne seven children in ten years of her marriage, Claude died of pleurisy at Blois between 20 and 26 July 1524 (Ep 1484). Her death may have inspired *Margaret of Angoulême to compose her *Dialogue en forme de vision nocturne*.

BIBLIOGRAPHY: Allen Ep 1096 / Charles Terrasse *François 1er, le roi et le règne* (Paris 1945–70) I 27, 52–4, 296, and passim / DBF VIII 1380–1

PGB

Nicolaus CLAUDIANUS *See Mikuláš KLAUDYÁN*

CLAUDIUS (Ep 1330 of 23 December 1522) Claudius, a bookseller whom Erasmus knew to move between Basel and Rome, has not been identified.

CLAUDIUS (Epp 2412, 2433, 2434, 2779 of 1530–3)
Between December 1530 and February 1531 Erasmus and Simon *Grynaeus refer to Claudius, a youth who had recently come to Basel from Paris and knew little German. He was associated with Grynaeus and Hieronymus *Froben, but failed to gain a place in Erasmus' household at Freiburg. He must have descended from a good family; perhaps he was a Frenchman attracted by the Reformation. It should be further noted that in March 1533 Erasmus sent a letter to Paris with a Claudius of Lorraine.

Among the students who were offered lodgings in Grynaeus' house at Basel were some Frenchmen. Moreover, several students by the name of Claudius, both from Lorraine and from other Francophone regions, were registered in the Universities of Basel, Freiburg, and Heidelberg between 1529 and 1535. P.S. Allen suggested that the references in Erasmus' correspondence might all concern the same young man and proposed a tentative identification: Allen Ep 2779:1n; see also AK IV Epp 1952, 2095, 2178.

PGB

Johannes CLAUTHUS d 10 September 1534 Clauthus, a native of the Low Countries, was recruited by Cornelius *Grapheus and entered the service of Erasmus at Freiburg in the spring of 1534 (Epp 2916, 2981, 3053). At the end of July his master sent him to England by way of Antwerp; his tasks included collecting Erasmus' annuity and gathering information on Thomas *More and John *Fisher, who had been arrested (Epp 2955, 2961). For more than four months Erasmus was waiting for news from Clauthus, and he began to wonder whether the young man had taken off for good (Ep 2980; AK IV Ep 1889). In fact he was not to see him again because Clauthus had died at Rochester in the course of his mission. Erasmus reacted to the news with anger and was only conscious of his own loss. Clauthus had been tight-lipped, he recalled; there were allegations that he was an Anabaptist (Epp 2981, 2983). Erasmus' ire knew no limits: the young man had preyed upon him; he had lost his letters and an important document (Epp 2992, 2997, 2998,

3009). These reproaches were clearly unjustified, as were the charges against Lieven
*Algoet, whom Erasmus accused of complicity
with Clauthus (Epp 3028, 3042, 3053).

BIBLIOGRAPHY: Allen Ep 2955 / Bierlaire
Familia 95–6

FRANZ BIERLAIRE

Antonius CLAVA of Bruges, d 31 May 1529
Antonius Clava (Clave, Colve) matriculated at
the University of Louvain on 29 August 1479.
In 1487 he became legal consultant or
'pensionary' to the city of Bruges, and from
1493 to 1496 and from 1499 to 1502 he served
the city of Ghent in the same capacity. He was
appointed to the council of Flanders in
succession to Bartholomeus van Massemen,
who had died on 30 March 1502 or 1503. Clava
continued to reside in Ghent, where he was a
burgher and an alderman, until his death. With
his wife, Catherina, a daughter of Joris Boreel,
he had a daughter, Margareta, who married
Willem Hannot (Annoot) and, after his death,
the physician Damiaan van *Vissenaken. From
her marriage to Hannot she had a daughter,
Catherina, who became the wife of Erasmus'
former famulus Lieven *Algoet. By 1532
Margareta, Vissenaken, and Catherina Hannot were all living in the house formerly owned
by Clava (Ep 2693).

Erasmus apparently knew Clava as early as
1503 (Ep 175) through the latter's good friend
Robert de *Keysere, who is frequently
mentioned in the subsequent correspondence
between Erasmus and Clava. In the summer of
1514 they met at Ghent (Ep 301), and three
years later Erasmus was again in Clava's house
when he received the first payment from his
imperial annuity (Ep 2404). Meanwhile they
had begun to exchange frequent letters (Epp
524, 530) and continued to do so until Erasmus'
departure for Basel in 1521; afterwards they
remained in touch until Clava's death (Ep
1373). Like de Keysere, Clava was eager to
improve his Greek, and in the spring of 1518
Erasmus presented him with a Greek Herodotus (Ep 841). During the previous summer
Clava had hoped to go to Louvain and benefit
from Erasmus' presence (Ep 617), but he did
not succeed in doing so until the summer of
1522, when he was attracted by the presence of

*Vives (Ep 1306). It was on Clava's suggestion
that Erasmus wrote to Louis of *Flanders (Ep
1191).

When informed of Clava's death (Ep 2197),
Erasmus paid glowing tribute to his memory
(Ep 2260) and composed an epitaph for him
(Reedijk poem 129). Levinus *Ammonius
inherited Erasmus' old Herodotus and two
other Greek books from Clava's library (Ep
2197). Much earlier Eligius Houcarius of Ghent
had dedicated to him his *Livini vita ... carmine
descripta* (Paris: J. Bade 1511, with a letter from
Bade to Clava), and Pieter *Gillis did likewise
with Erasmus' *Aliquot epistolae sanequam elegantes* (Louvain 1517; the dedicatory preface is
translated in CWE 3 351–2).

BIBLIOGRAPHY: Allen Epp 175, 524 / *Matricule
de Louvain* II-1 399 / NBW VI 106–7 / de Vocht CTL
I 279–80, II 138, 491, III 442, and passim / M.A.
Nauwelaerts 'Erasme et Gand' in *Commémoration nationale d'Erasme, Actes* (Brussels 1970)
162–9 / P. van Peteghem 'Centralisatie in
Vlaanderen onder keizer Karel (1515–1555)'
(doctoral thesis, Rijksuniversiteit Ghent 1980)

MARCEL A. NAUWELAERTS & PGB

Margareta CLAVA *See Antonius* CLAVA *and
Damiaan van* VISSENAKEN

CLAVUS physician at Ghent, documented
1517–18
The physician whose name is given as Clavus
in Epp 650, 681, 788 has not been identified; his
first name may have been Adrian (Epp 755,
818). See also Damiaan van *Vissenaken.

John CLAYMOND of Frampton, d 19 November 1537
John Claymond (Claimond) was born in
Frampton, Lincolnshire, to John and his wife,
Elizabeth. He may have attended the grammar
school attached to Magdalen College, Oxford,
and in 1484 was a student of Magdalen
College, becoming a fellow on 26 July 1488 and
in 1507 president of the college. He was
ordained priest in 1499, received his MA in
1504, and became a bachelor of theology in
1508 and a doctor in 1510.

Claymond was appointed canon of Wells in
1509 and was master of St Cross Hospital in
Winchester from 1517 to 1524; he owed this

Pope Clement VII by Sebastiano del Piombo

benefice to Bishop Richard *Foxe, who in 1517 persuaded him to move from Magdalen to his new Corpus Christi College as the first president; Erasmus warmly approved of this choice (Ep 990). Claymond received the rectory of Bishop's Cleeve, Gloucestershire, in the same year and later accepted other preferments. He probably met Erasmus in Oxford about 1499, and they remained loosely connected, in part through Juan Luis *Vives, who taught at Corpus Christi from 1523 to 1525 and became one of Claymond's friends (Ep 1455). In 1526 Erasmus dedicated to him a Greek edition of Chrysostom's *De fato et de providentia Dei* (Ep 1661).

When Simon *Grynaeus visited Oxford Claymond helped him obtain manuscripts for printing in Basel. Thomas *Linacre wrote Claymond while he was president of Magdalen, recommending a student to him and urging him to learn Greek. Erasmus mentioned that Cuthbert *Tunstall, Thomas *More, and Richard *Pace were Claymond's good friends (Ep 990).

Claymond founded six scholarships at Brasenose College; he also bequeathed lands

to Magdalen College and land, money, and his valuable library to Corpus Christi. The latter included a number of manuscripts purchased from the executors of William *Grocyn. Claymond's own works left in manuscript to Corpus Christi are known to have included a commentary on Pliny's *Historia naturalis* in four volumes and others on Aulus Gellius and Plautus; also included were letters and a treatise on repentance.

BIBLIOGRAPHY: Allen Ep 990 / Emden BRUO I 428–30 (with a list of the books he left to Corpus Christi) / DNB IV 467 / McConica 50, 81–2

CFG

Johannes CLEBERGIUS *See Johann* KLEBERGER

Pope CLEMENT VII 26 May 1478–25 September 1534

Giulio de' Medici was born in Florence. The misfortune and violence which was to mark his pontificate already accompanied his birth; it was illegitimate, and it occurred a month after the murder of his father, Giuliano, by the Pazzi conspirators. Cared for by his uncle, Lorenzo (I) de' *Medici, the fatherless child developed an enduring concern for the Medici family and a life-long attachment to his cousin Giovanni, the future Pope *Leo X, two and a half years his senior. The boys shared a humanist education, the study of canon law at Pisa, and summer holidays at the abbey of Passignano (1488–91) in company with Giovanni's brother Giuliano, the future duke of Nemours. By enrolling among the knights of St John of Jerusalem and accepting the rich priorate of Capua, granted at his uncle's wish by Ferdinand I of Naples, Giulio was already uniting military and priestly functions by 1492. His uncle's death in April did not disrupt his association either with Giovanni or with Florence and Rome: in March he had ridden as a knight of St John in his cousin's triumphal entry as cardinal into the holy city; he returned with him for the conclave which elected *Alexander VI. On the expulsion from Florence of Lorenzo's successor, Piero de' Medici in 1494, Giulio joined his cousins in Pisa, accompanied them to Bologna en route for exile in Rome, and from there played an active role in the family's attempts to return; however, three failures determined them to travel abroad. With Giovanni, Giuliano, and a group of friends, Giulio visited countries north of the Alps, met the future Pope *Julius II at Savona, and returned with his cousins to Rome on 18 May 1500. In the war of the Holy League directed by Pope Julius against the French, Giulio accompanied Giovanni, the papal legate, to Lombardy. On his cousin's capture he took peace proposals to Rome, following the French victory at Ravenna on 11 April 1512. By stressing the demoralization of the French army after the loss of its leader, Gaston de Foix, Giulio encouraged Julius to continue fighting. His presence at the allies' discussions at Mantua in July and August involved him in the league's invasion of Tuscany and sack of Prato, and, as head of its foreign military guard, in the defence of the restored Medici regime in Florence.

The election of Giovanni de' Medici to the papacy on 19 March 1513 caused a rapid rise in the fortunes of Giulio. On 9 May he was made archbishop of Florence. He succeeded Leo as cardinal of Santa Maria in Dominica in the pope's first creation of cardinals on 23 September and was successively titulary of San Clemente (26 June 1517) and San Lorenzo in Damaso (6 July 1517). For Giulio, as for Erasmus, illegitimacy was a canonical impediment. A dispensation was granted before his appointment as archbishop; prior to his cardinalate the further step was taken of declaring him legitimate on the grounds that his parents had been secretly married before his birth. Between 1513 and 1523 Giulio held one Hungarian, two French, and three Italian bishoprics. Early in 1514 *Henry VIII had him made cardinal protector of England, and in 1521 he succeeded Silvestro *Gigli as bishop of Worcester. After his appointment as papal vice-chancellor on 9 March 1517 Giulio became the predominating influence on Leo's policies. His association with the papal armies continued, linked since 1512 with his concern for Florence, whose new ruler, Lorenzo (II) de' *Medici, duke of Urbino, the young son of Piero, he advised from Rome. In 1515 he served as legate with the papal and Florentine forces sent to resist *Francis I of France; his slow advance – at least partly due to his sensitivity to the pro-French sympathies of Florence – contributed to the French victory at Marignano in 1515. In 1517, when Lorenzo was wounded

in the war to gain the duchy of Urbino (Ep 521), Giulio assumed command of the army, and on Lorenzo's death he was appointed papal legate for Florence with wide powers for the settlement of its affairs (May 1519). His able administration and generous expenditure on the city's fortification won universal acclaim. In October 1519 he left for Rome to help judge the works of *Luther; he returned to Florence only intermittently, but the city remained loyal to the Medici even during the critical months of Leo's unpopular anti-French offensive of May to November 1521. Giulio assisted in the conquest of Milan as legate with the papal-imperial forces. On the death of Leo on 2 December he failed to secure either his own election in the ensuing conclave or the confidence of the new pope, *Adrian VI. He left Rome for Florence and, by his feigned acceptance of schemes for political reform, foiled a plot against him in May 1522. Re-established in Rome and in the papal confidence before Adrian's death on 14 September 1523, he advocated an imperial alliance and thus won *Charles V's favour. On 19 November 1523 he was elected pope and took the title Clement VII.

Erasmus shared the rejoicing at Clement's accession (Epp 1418, 1422). Punning on the Medici name, he underlined the need for a distinguished doctor to heal the contemporary discords (Epp 1416, 1418). As a cardinal Clement had already acted on the religious divisions caused by Luther's revolt, but neither the bull Exsurge Domine (1520) nor the publication of the papal excommunication (1521) had stemmed the tide of heresy. Cardinal Lorenzo *Campeggi, sent by Clement to Germany soon after his accession, likewise failed, as Erasmus thought he would, even though he approved the personal qualities of his old friend (Epp 1422, 1432). Erasmus himself had lost his early sympathy for Luther (Ep 1526) but remained conciliatory, urging moderation on Clement (Epp 1452, 1506) and pointing out to the reformers that Clement was not as averse to a return to the religion of the Gospels as they thought (Ep 1523).

Erasmus was not alone in his belief in the pope's moral earnestness (ASD I-3 505). As archbishop of Florence he had introduced the reforming decrees of the fifth Lateran council into his diocese. In Rome he had founded in 1519 a charitable confraternity for the care of the poor and prisoners. But he constantly put off calling a general council, desired by many. Erasmus wrote quite frankly to Clement on the Lutheran problem (Epp 1418, 1496). His own position was, however, perilous. If he supported Luther he would be persecuted in Rome as a Lutheran; if he opposed him he would be hated in Germany as anti-Lutheran (Epp 1411, 1415, 1435, 1576, 1596). A rumour spread of the burning of Erasmus' books and his image in Rome (Epp 1494, 1518). He nevertheless remained loyal both to the concept of papal authority in the church and to the pope from whom he sought protection (Epp 1410, 1416, 1526, 3141).

Clement silenced the Spanish theologian Diego *López Zúñiga, Erasmus' persistent opponent (Epp 1431–3, 1488). The hostility towards Erasmus of the University of Louvain evoked a papal response, and Theodoricus *Hezius, formerly secretary to Adrian VI, was sent to request Nicolaas *Baechem, prior of the Carmelites at Louvain, to desist from his slanders (Epp 1467, 1589, 1589A). Clement's regard for Erasmus extended to inviting him to Rome (Epp 1408, 1417, 1418, 1422), accepting the dedication of his paraphrases on the Acts of the Apostles (Epp 1414, 1438), and rewarding him with two hundred florins (Epp 1466, 1486, 1488). He urged him to take up his pen against Luther (Epp 1438, 1495), and Erasmus thought of dedicating his *De libero arbitrio* to Clement (Ep 1486). The Lutheran problem remained unsolved. During Clement's pontificate – as Erasmus, Gaspare *Contarini (Pastor x 36), and others saw – the problems besetting the church were being approached by the means of the world, its arms, and its alliances (Epp 2211, 2249, 2445) and subordinated to secular interests. Clement would do better to rely on the protection of Christ than on a crowd of cardinals and wicked monks and the arms of princes (Ep 2249). However, territorial independence was a prerequisite of spiritual independence. Clement's misfortune was to achieve neither. By 1525, in expectation of French success in the continuing Hapsburg-Valois wars, he had abandoned his professed neutrality, advocated by Erasmus for the spiritual father of all Christians (Epp 1417,

1831), and the imperial victory at Pavia threatened the papal states and the Medici regime in Florence. In joining the League of Cognac (22 May 1526) against Charles V, Clement exposed Rome to the Colonna raid (Ep 1762) and the subsequent Sack of 1527. Erasmus, judging the imperialists' treatment of Rome as worse than that of the Gauls and Goths, lamented the loss of precious books and libraries (Ep 2059). He regarded Italy's troubles as signs of the wrath of God and a call to penitence (Ep 1603) but expressed confidence in Clement's ability to steer the ship to port and censured his 'inclement' treatment at the hands of the imperial forces (Ep 2059). He did not mention that the Florentines took advantage of the pope's misfortunes to revolt against his unpopular deputy, Cardinal Silvio *Passerini. However, after Clement had become reconciled with Charles V in the treaty of Barcelona of 1529 and the imperial forces had besieged Florence to restore the Medici, Erasmus criticized Clement for his 'inclemency' (Epp 2445, 2472). He held Clement VII rather than Charles V responsible for the bitter war against Florence (Epp 2371, 2375), which was well fortified as a result of the pope's earlier administration. Erasmus was not aware of this ironical twist or of the effrontery with which the anti-Medici citizens had treated Clement.

Erasmus did not criticize Clement's concern for his family. However he regarded marriage alliances between princes as a cause of war (ASD I-3 506), and their terms interested him. *Viglius Zuichemus informed him of the proposals of 1529 for a marriage between Charles V's illegitimate daughter, *Margaret (of Parma), and Alessandro de' *Medici, rumoured to be Clement's bastard (Ep 2753). After Clement had travelled to Marseille in 1533 to officiate at the wedding between *Catherine de' Medici and the future *Henry II of France, Erasmus was again kept informed (Ep 1917). Five months after his return from Marseille Clement declared Henry VIII's marriage to *Catherine of Aragon valid and lawful. As Clement had already ordered (Ep 2810), Henry was to remain with his wife. The infuriated king refused to recognize the pope as more than bishop of Rome (Ep 2915). The breach between England and the papacy was complete before Clement died (Ep 2961).

The famous portrait by Raphael of Cardinal Giulio at Leo x's elbow is in the Palazzo Pitti, Florence. Those by Sebastiano del Piombo (Museo Nazionale, Capodimonte, Naples) and by Bronzino (Uffizi, Florence) depict him as pope. There are medals by Cellini, whom Clement appointed engraver in the Roman mint. Raphael is also credited with the plan for the cardinal's magnificent villa (later called Madama) on the slopes of Monte Mario, Rome, executed by Antonio da San Gallo the Elder and Giulio Romano. Michelangelo designed both the library now known as the Laurenziana to house his cousin Leo's books from Rome and the tombs for Lorenzo, duke of Urbino, and Giuliano de' Medici in the new sacristy of San Lorenzo, Florence. Clement's tomb, by Baccio Bandinelli, faces Leo's in Santa Maria sopra Minerva, Rome.

BIBLIOGRAPHY: R. Mols in DHGE XII 1175–1244 / Important primary sources include E. Alberi *Relazioni degli ambasciatori veneti al Senato* (Florence 1839–   ) ser 2, III; Sanudo *Diarii* xxxv 208–9, and passim; and LP I-ii 2639–40, 2653; III-i 1334–5 / See also Pastor IX and X / S. Ammirato 'Ritratti d'huomini illustri di casa Medici' *Opusculi* (Florence 1642) III 108–34 / C. Pieraccini *La stirpe de' Medici di Cafaggiolo* (Florence 1924) I 285–317 / E. Rodocanachi *Les Pontificats d'Adrien VI et de Clément VII* (Paris 1933) / G. Müller *Die römische Kurie und die Reformation 1523–1534* (Heidelberg 1969) / R. Devonshire Jones *Francesco Vettori: Florentine Citizen and Medici Servant* (London 1972) 64, 91, and passim / J.N. Stephens 'Pope Clement VII, a Florentine Debtor' *Bulletin of the Institute of Historical Research* 49 (1976) 138–41 / A.F. Verde *Lo studio fiorentino* (Pistoia 1977) III-1 556 / J.R. Hale *Florence and the Medici: The Pattern of Control* (New York-London 1977) 79, 84–7, and passim / G. di Meglio *Carlo V e Clemente VII* (Milan 1970) / Cecil Roth *The Last Florentine Republic* (New York 1925, repr 1968) 7–11 and passim / Hubert Jedin *A History of the Council of Trent* trans E. Graf (London 1957–   ) I 192, and passim / Karl Schätti *Erasmus von Rotterdam und die Römische Kurie* (Basel 1954)

ROSEMARY DEVONSHIRE JONES

John CLEMENT d 1 July 1572

Nothing certain can be established about the family of John Clement (Clements, Clemens).

He was one of the first students of St Paul's School, London, under its first master, William *Lily. While at St Paul's he may have met Thomas *More, who by 1514 took him into his household as a servant-pupil. Clement accompanied More on the embassy to Bruges in 1515 and afterwards to Antwerp, where plans for More's *Utopia* were discussed with Erasmus (Ep 388). In 1516 he was tutoring John *Colet in Greek (Ep 468) and in 1517 More's children and wards. By 1518 he had entered the service of Cardinal Thomas *Wolsey (Epp 820, 1138), who appointed him the first reader of rhetoric and humanity for his newly founded Cardinal College at Oxford. While the college was under construction, Clement resided until 1520 in Corpus Christi College. More informed Erasmus that he was the most popular lecturer at Oxford and that even Thomas *Linacre praised him (Ep 907); in 1520 More reported that he was devoting himself entirely to medicine (Ep 1087). Subsequently Clement pursued his medical training in Louvain, where he had arrived before Erasmus left for Basel in October 1521 and where he associated with Juan Luis *Vives. He was unaware of Erasmus' departure; otherwise he would have gone with him to Basel for the winter (Ep 1256). Thus it was not until the spring of 1522 that he set out for Italy by way of Basel (Ep 1271). In Padua he was joined by Thomas *Lupset, who had replaced him as Greek reader at Oxford. They both assisted in the Aldine edition of Galen in Greek and were commended for their efforts in a dedicatory letter to the fifth volume (1525). Clement also received his doctorate in medicine by 1528, probably from the University of Padua.

Clement returned to England, where he was admitted as a fellow of the Royal College of Physicians, London (1 February 1528), and was appointed physician to the king. He attended the dying Wolsey at Esher in 1529 and was lecturing at Oxford about 1530. About this time he married More's ward, Margaret *Giggs, who was skilled enough in Greek and Latin to aid in her husband's translations. In 1544 he was elected president of the Royal College of Physicians.

In 1547 the rise of Protestantism under Edward VI forced Clement and his family into exile. They settled at Louvain in an English recusant community. Clement matriculated at the university in January 1551. The Clements returned to England in 1554 during *Mary's reign and settled in Essex. After the accession of Elizabeth in 1559 they left England permanently, settling in Mechelen, where Clement died in 1572 and is buried next to his wife in St Rombout's cathedral.

Clement's unpublished works included an 'Epigrammatum et aliorum carminum liber' and translations from Greek into Latin of the letters of Gregory of Nazianzus and those of Pope Celestine I to Cyril, bishop of Alexandria, and of the homilies of Nicephorus Calixtus on Greek saints. Erasmus was devoted to him (Epp 820, 1138), but no further relations are recorded after Clement had gone to Italy. Simon *Grynaeus dedicated his edition of Proclus' De motu to Clement (Basel: J. Bebel and M. Isengrin 1531). Clement and his wife were paid tribute for their prestige in the humanistic community in one of John Leland's Epithalamia (published in 1589, STC 15447).

BIBLIOGRAPHY: Allen and CWE Ep 388 / DNB IV 489 / McConica 269–72 and passim / Emden BRUO (1501–40) 121–2 / de Vocht Literae ad Craneveldium 425–6 / Giovanni Mercati 'Sopra Giovanni Clement e i suoi manoscritti' La Bibliofilia 28 (1926) 81–9

CFG & PGB

Nicolaus CLENARDUS of Diest, 6(?) December 1495–5 November 1542
Nicolaas Cleynaerts or Beken of Diest, in Brabant, better known as Clenardus, matriculated on 31 August 1512 at the University of Louvain. After graduating MA in 1515 he taught arts courses in his college, the Pig, while taking up the study of theology. He obtained a theological baccalaureate in 1521 and a licence in 1527. Having received a sound humanistic training under such teachers as Adrianus Cornelii *Barlandus, as a student of theology he came under the influence of Jacobus *Latomus, who was to remain his friend for life. A priest from about 1521, Clenardus in that year succeeded Jan *Driedo as president of Houterlee's College, a position tenable for ten years. This appointment permitted him to pursue his humanistic studies with the help of *Goclenius, *Rescius, and Jan van *Campen, professors of the Collegium

Trilingue. He taught privately (Ep 2352) and established his reputation as a Hebrew scholar with a Tabula ad grammaticen hebraeam (Louvain: D. Martens 1529). He also published two textbooks for students of Greek, the Institutiones in linguam graecam (Louvain: R. Rescius 1530) and the Meditationes graecanicae in artem grammaticam (Louvain: R. Rescius 1531), both of which met with great success and were used by generations of students. Despite these achievements Clenardus' career in Louvain was beset with disappointments. The faculty of arts had nominated him for the benefices of parish priest at the chapter of St Peter's, Louvain, and of rector of the Diest béguines, but when these positions actually fell vacant other claimants secured them. Clenardus had no more luck in his efforts to succeed Campen, who resigned in 1531 as professor of Hebrew at the Trilingue.

Clenardus' ambition to join the Trilingue may have been thwarted by a lack of reverence and prudence, which weighed against his undoubted ability. An example of his irreverent attitude was later provided by his letters commenting on Erasmus' death. During Erasmus' years at Louvain, 1517–21, Clenardus had been close to Latomus, his teacher, who was critical of Erasmus; it is therefore not surprising that Clenardus did not approach the famous man either. There is no good reason to identify the young student at Louvain with an erudite resident of Diest who had written to Erasmus in 1514 (Ep 291). Even though Clenardus' interest in humanism did not lead to any personal ties with Erasmus, de Vocht points out that he owed a considerable debt to Erasmus' epistolary style and general views and that he borrowed occasionally from the Adagia and Colloquia.

When his term as president of Houterlee's college had ended and Louvain did not seem to offer any further prospects for the time being, Clenardus was compelled to look elsewhere. Juan Luis *Vives seems to have convinced him that Muslims could be converted to Christianity by force of persuasion, and he resolved to learn Arabic. He entered the service of Hernando Colón, the son of the discoverer of America, whom he accompanied back to Spain towards the end of 1531. He taught Greek and Latin in Salamanca until 1533, when he joined

Prince *Henry of Portugal, who at the age of twenty-one was already archbishop of Braga. Under Henry's auspices, Clenardus founded a humanist college at Braga which he directed until 1538. Thereafter Henry's support enabled him to study Arabic in Granada and for a while in 1540 at Fez in Morocco. He was still in Granada at the time of his death.

Clenardus is chiefly known today from his correspondence. A series of accomplished and important letters from 1532 to his death was published in 1566 and is now available in a critical edition by Alphonse Roersch (Brussels 1940–1).

BIBLIOGRAPHY: Allen Ep 2352 / NBW II 120–3 / de Vocht MHL 411–23 / de Vocht CTL II 220–34, III 185–90, and passim / de Vocht *Danticus* 78–80 / H. de Jongh *L'Ancienne Faculté de théologie de Louvain* (Louvain 1911) 47*, 54*, and passim / *Matricule de Louvain* III-1 449

PGB

CLERICUS *See John* CLERK *and Nicolas* LE CLERC

John CLERK d January 1541
John Clerk (Clerke, Clericus) is first documented when he was admitted to the University of Cambridge on 14 December 1498. Clerk became a BA at Cambridge in 1499 and a MA in 1502. He gained a doctor's degree in law at Bologna in 1510 and stayed in Rome with Cardinal Christopher Bainbridge until 1514. He had been instituted to a benefice in Kent in 1508, the first of many preferments to come. Within ten years he had gained a place in Cardinal *Wolsey's entourage and thenceforth enjoyed his patronage. In 1516 he was dean of the chapel royal and in 1519 dean of St George's, Windsor, and in the same year he became a judge in the court of the star-chamber. It was at this point in his career that he received the single passing notice by Erasmus that we know of, as one of the ornaments of the king's court (Ep 999). Clerk went on several royal missions to France and Rome and in 1521 presented the king's *Assertio* against *Luther to *Leo x. He was master of the rolls for one year but resigned in 1523 when he succeeded Wolsey as bishop of Bath and Wells. He was one of the councillors for Queen *Catherine but later joined in pronouncing the king's divorce. He became ill at Dunkirk of

suspected poisoning when returning from a mission to William v, duke of *Cleves in 1540. He survived to return to England, where he died on either 3 (DNB; Emden BRUC) or 31 (Le Neve) January 1541 and was buried in St Botolph's, Aldgate.

Clerk's oration on presenting the king's book to Leo x was translated and prefixed to later editions. He may have assisted with other literary works, possibly including some by *Cranmer.

There seems little doubt that the Clerk mentioned by Erasmus was the above protégé of Wolsey, although, as Allen points out, Knight identifies him with another John Clerk, d 1552: S. Knight *Life of Erasmus* (Cambridge 1726) 220–1.

BIBLIOGRAPHY: Allen and CWE Ep 999 / DNB IV 495–6 / Emden BRUC 139, 673 / John Le Neve et al *Fasti ecclesiae Anglicanae* 2nd ed (London 1962–) VIII 3 / George B. Parks *The English Traveler to Italy* (Rome 1954–) I 311–14, 316–18, and passim / *The Registers of the Bishops of Bath and Wells, 1519–1559* ed H. Maxwell-Lyte (Frome-London 1940; Somerset Record Society no 55)

ELIZABETH CRITTALL

Bernhard von CLES 11 March 1485–30 July 1539
Bernhard von Cles (Gless, Glöss) was born in his ancestral castle of Cles in the Val di Non, north of Trent. He was the son of Hildebrand, captain of Trent, and Dorothea Fuchs von Fuchsberg. He studied first at Verona and from 1504 at Bologna, where he was a syndic (1506) and procurator (1508) of the German nation and on 15 May 1511 obtained a doctorate in civil and canon law. From 6 February 1512 he was a canon of Trent, and, although not yet a priest, was elected bishop of Trent in the summer of 1514, taking possession of the see on 25 September. Also from 1514 he was a councillor of the Emperor *Maximilian I. In 1519 he helped to bring about the election of *Charles v and was present at the coronation in Aachen. In 1521 and 1522 he was involved in determining the powers assigned to Charles' brother, *Ferdinand. He remained at Ferdinand's court and became his most trusted adviser. During the peasant revolt he returned temporarily to his see; otherwise he continued

Bernhard von Cles

to represent Ferdinand on successive diets, and in 1527 he helped crown his master king of Bohemia. From then on he was Ferdinand's chancellor (Ep 1936) and from 1531 governor of the Hapsburg lands along the Upper Rhine. While attending Charles' coronation in Bologna, he was made a cardinal on 9 March 1530 (Ep 2326); later that year he accompanied the emperor to the diet of Augsburg, where he was instrumental in securing Ferdinand's election as Roman king. In 1534 he was Ferdinand's candidate for the papacy. In December 1536 he went to Naples to impress upon Charles v how seriously the Turks were threatening Austria's eastern borders. Thereafter deteriorating health forced him to resign the chancellorship and retire to his bishopric of Bressanone (Brixen), whose administrator he had become in May 1539. There he died two months later.

His court duties notwithstanding, Cles showed great concern for the ecclesiastical principality of Trent. Several diocesan visitations were held, the diocesan archives were reorganized, and the holdings of the library increased (Ep 2797). A great builder, Cles improved streets and buildings and lavishly

renovated the episcopal residence as well as the cathedral, where later the council was to meet. He also patronized writers and scholars. He encouraged such Catholic polemicists as *Eck, *Cochlaeus, and Johannes *Fabri, and also *Nausea, the Erasmian, for all of whom he endeavoured to obtain financial support from *Clement vii between 1530 and 1533. He employed the poet *Ursinus Velius and maintained connections with such humanist scholars as *Brassicanus and Cuspinianus.

Erasmus probably met him during his court attendances in 1520 and 1521. They evidently knew one another when Erasmus wrote to him in April 1523, asking him to present to Ferdinand a copy of the *Paraphrasis in Matthaeum* (Ep 1357). From then on an important part of Erasmus' correspondence with the court in Vienna lay in the hands of Bernhard von Cles or his secretary, Johann *Hornburg. Cles was personally interested in the famous Dutch scholar and relations between them grew stronger over the years. By June 1524 he had invited Erasmus to visit him, and although Erasmus declined (Ep 1409) he renewed his invitation many times, offering him a residence at Trent and generous terms (Epp 1771, 2159, 2295, 2299, 2383). In 1526 Cles was delighted to receive the dedication of Erasmus' edition of Irenaeus (Epp 1738, 1755) and in return sent him one hundred pieces of gold (Epp 1771, 1793), followed by another fifty in 1533 (Epp 2808, 2821). Erasmus was also encouraged to approach Cles on behalf of Heinrich *Schürer of Waldshut (Epp 1689, 1710) and Henricus *Glareanus (Ep 2655), while Felix *Rex found employment with Ferdinand through Cles' intercession (Ep 2211). Said to be a constant reader of Erasmus' works (Ep 1935), Cles was aware of the controversies surrounding him. He reassured Erasmus about the sermons of *Medardus (Ep 2504; ASD I-3 665–6) and was the first to alert him to the undesirable way in which his name and work were being used in Sebastian *Franck's *Zeytbuch* (Ep 2587). However in 1534 he seems to have excused Erasmus on grounds of his age and health when it was suggested at court that he reply to *Luther once again (Ep 2921). He also seems to have been instrumental in settling Erasmus at Freiburg in the spring of 1529 (Ep 2107; Allen I 69). As late as February

1536 Erasmus wrote to him in support of a démarche undertaken by the city council of Basel (Epp 3095, 3110).

BIBLIOGRAPHY: Allen Ep 1357 / ADB IV 324–5 / NDB II 115–16 / LThK II 1234 / Knod 159–60 / Pflug *Correspondance* I Ep 68 and passim / Pastor X 82, 318, XI 49–51, and passim / Giulio Briani 'Carteggio tra Bernardo di Cles ed Erasmo di Rotterdam' *Studi trentini di scienze storiche* 25 (1946) 24–39, 26 (1947) 151–64

IG

John II, duke of CLEVES and Mark 13 April 1458–15 January 1521
John II of Cleves, the son of Duke John I and Elizabeth, the daughter of John of Burgundy (1415–91), count of Nevers, grew up at the Burgundian court and followed Charles the Rash of *Burgundy on his campaigns. He married Mathilde, a daughter of Henry, landgrave of Hesse, on 3 November 1489. He negotiated the marriage of his eldest son, *John III, to Maria, the heiress of Jülich-Berg in 1510; subsequently this brought about the union of the territories of Cleves-Jülich-Berg. A second son, Adolf, died in Spain in 1525. Mismanagement in the country led to discontent being voiced in the estates, and in 1501 John II was obliged to submit to their control of the finances. His policies, which were often in opposition to those of *Maximilian I, were generally unsuccessful; in particular, his plans (1514–18) for the marriage of his daughter, Anna, to Karel van *Egmond, duke of Gelderland, had to be dropped on account of Maximilian's opposition. Anna then secretly married Count Philipp von Waldeck, which caused general resentment in the family until a reconciliation was achieved on 20 November 1518.

John II of Cleves is mentioned in Ep 829.

BIBLIOGRAPHY: Allen Ep 829 / NDB X 493 / ADB XIV 210–13

IG

John III, duke of CLEVES-Mark-Jülich-Berg 10 November 1490–6 February 1539
John III (the Peaceful) of Cleves was the eldest son of John II, duke of *Cleves, and of Mathilde of Hesse. He married Maria, the only daughter of William IV (1475–1511), duke of Jülich-Berg-Ravensberg, on 1 October 1510 and succeeded

to the states of his father-in-law on 6 September 1511. After his own father's death on 15 January 1521 he was able to unite the two duchies on 21 May 1521. John was not at first particularly interested in the religious movements of his time; he did not attend the imperial diets, nor did he enforce the edict of Worms in his duchies. Subsequently, however, in an edict of 26 March 1525 he prohibited the distribution of *Luther's writings; at the same time he realized that reform within the church was necessary and had a church ordinance drawn up, which was proclaimed on 11 January 1532. All preaching was to be based on Scripture and the early Fathers and was to avoid polemics; the preachers should be educated and properly appointed priests. An 'Interpretation,' clearing up points of uncertainty, was issued on 9 April 1533, and thereafter visitations were held to ensure observance of the new rules (1533–4).

John III played an active part in the defeat of the Anabaptists of Münster in 1534–5 (Ep 2956) and, together with his son William V of *Cleves, joined the bishop of Münster, Franz von *Waldeck, in plans for rebuilding the captured city (Ep 3041). He was a good administrator and was helped in his task by his conciliatory attitude. In 1534–5 he served as a mediator in a conflict between the city of Utrecht and Karel van *Egmond, duke of Gelderland. After the latter's death in 1538 William V was elected to be his successor in Gelderland. This led to conflict with the Emperor *Charles V, but before a decisive breach occurred John died in Cleves.

Duke John III is mentioned briefly in Ep 829; however, the subsequent appointment (1523) of Konrad *Heresbach as tutor to William on Erasmus' recommendation (Ep 1390) was the beginning of a close connection between Erasmus and the ducal court that left a lasting impression on the church ordinance of 1532. Erasmus was repeatedly invited to settle in Cleves under favourable conditions (Epp 2146, 2248, 3031), and the duke granted him an annuity in 1533 (Ep 2804). Not only was he consulted in the drafting of the 'Interpretation' of the church ordinance by Heresbach, who visited him at Freiburg in September 1532 (Epp 2728, 2804, 2845), but the basic ideas it expressed and much of the wording follow

William v, duke of Cleves by Heinrich Aldegraver

William v, duke of CLEVES-Mark-Jülich-Berg 28 July 1516–5 January 1592

Duke William, the son of John III of *Cleves and Maria of Jülich-Berg, succeeded his father on 7 February 1539. According to an agreement dated 27 February 1538 he had also succeeded Karel von *Egmond as duke of Gelderland and count of Zutphen. This arrangement caused a conflict with the Emperor *Charles v, who laid claim to Gelderland according to a previous agreement (3 October 1528). William tried to uphold his claims by an alliance with King *Francis I of France, married Jeanne d'Albret, the twelve-year-old daughter of King Henry of Navarre, and temporarily joined the Schmalkaldic League. Defeated by the emperor in 1543, he had to ask for pardon at Venlo (Brabant) and give up his claims to Gelderland and Zutphen. On 2 January 1544 at Brussels he signed an agreement creating a closer alliance with the emperor, who granted him a substantial annuity; the marriage with Jeanne d'Albret was annulled by papal dispensation (12 October 1545), and he married Maria, a daughter of King *Ferdinand I of Austria, the next day.

Educated by Konrad *Heresbach along humanistic lines, William strove to improve the educational system of his territories and in 1545 founded the humanistic gymnasium in Düsseldorf. Administration of justice was also improved by means of a police ordinance of 1554 and new regulations for legal procedure in 1555. In religious matters William upheld the famous 'Erasmian' church ordinance of his father but did not effectively prevent the spread of Lutheranism among the urban population and the nobility. Charles v reproved him for this in 1548. After Charles v's abdication, William showed even greater tolerance towards the Lutherans and appointed a Lutheran court preacher, who was also entrusted with the education of his sons. In 1566 he suffered a stroke from which he never fully recovered. In 1567 he proposed modifications to the church ordinance of 1532, but these were rejected on 28 April 1568 by his councillors. A system of inquisition in religious matters was suggested in 1574 but rejected by the estates. While William v grew increasingly helpless, John William, his heir, became insane, and quarrels arose between other

Erasmus' way of thinking and writing. Erasmus hesitated to write statements on the Lord's Prayer, the Creed, and the Ten Commandments, as suggested by Johann von *Vlatten, considering these to be superfluous, but he encouraged the duke's visitations and his measures against Anabaptist preachers (Ep 2845). Erasmus praised John's moderate approach to reform (Ep 2853) but thought that Lambertus *Campester's activity in the duchy should be checked (Epp 2728, 2780). The duke's lenient attitude towards the Lutherans was criticized by Erasmus *Schets in Ep 2413. A plan to make Erasmus a provost in John's city of Xanten is mentioned in Ep 3061.

BIBLIOGRAPHY: Allen Epp 829, 2804 / NDB X 493–4 / ADB XIV 213–15 / John Patrick Dolan *The Influence of Erasmus, Witzel, and Cassander in the Church Ordinances and Reform Proposals of the United Duchies of Cleve during the Middle Decades of the 16th Century* (Münster 1957) / August Franzen *Die Kelchbewegung am Niederrheim im 16. Jahrhundert* (Münster 1955) 38–49 and passim

IG

members of his family that continued after William's death.

Erasmus dedicated to young Duke William his *De pueris instituendis* and his appended edition of St Ambrose's *Liber de apologia David* (Basel: H. Froben September 1529). In his dedicatory prefaces (Epp 2189, 2190) he praised both the boy's zeal for study and Heresbach, his tutor. In return William sent him a letter of thanks and a silver goblet (Epp 2222, 2234, 2246, 2277, 2298, 2299, 2346). In 1531 Erasmus dedicated to him his *Apophtheg-mata* (Basel: H. Froben March 1531) with a longer dedicatory preface (Ep 2431) that dealt with the sources from which the proverbs were taken and sent a presentation copy with Ep 2458 (cf Ep 2459). After the dedication had been gratefully acknowledged by Johann von *Vlatten on behalf of the duke (Ep 2654), Erasmus also dedicated to him the two additional books (Ep 2711) printed in the second edition of *Apophthegmata* (Basel: H. Froben 1532); William's thanks are expressed in Ep 2804. Finally, in Ep 3041, William's presence at a conference for the pacification of Münster is mentioned.

BIBLIOGRAPHY: Allen Ep 2189 / ADB XLIII 106–13 / Cf John III of Cleves

IG

Nicolaas CLEYNAERTS *See Nicolaus* *CLENARDUS*

Josse CLICHTOVE of Nieuwpoort, d 22 September 1543
Josse Clichtove (Joost van Clichthove, Judocus Clichtoveus) was born in 1472/3 at Nieuw-poort, Flanders, a descendant of a family of petty nobles. In 1488 he is found studying at the University of Paris amid a circle of Christian humanists motivated by the spirit of monastic reform. Probably at the Collège de Boncour he was a pupil of Charles *Fernand, who retired to the abbey of Chezal-Benoit in 1492. Between 1490 and 1492 Clichtove was admitted to the Collège du Cardinal Lemoine and became a disciple of *Lefèvre d'Etaples, whose princi-pal collaborator he remained until 1520. On 4 December 1506 he received his doctorate in theology after taking the preliminary degrees at the Collège de Sorbonne and the Collège de Navarre, where he continued to teach

theology. It is not known by what date he was ordained priest.

Clichtove began his literary career as an editor of Latin textbooks; between 1500 and 1517 he composed and published a number of commentaries to Lefèvre's expositions of works by Aristotle. From 1506 he also devoted himself to the movement of monastic reform, editing such spiritual writers as Hugo of St Victor and encouraging editions of others such as St Bernard. He served this same cause with his sermons and his defence of monasticism, *De laude monasticae religionis* (Paris: H. Estienne 1513). This work, which was dedicated to his pupil Geoffroy d'Amboise, future abbot of Cluny, may well present Clichtove's first critical response to Erasmus, who tended to find fault with the monastic way of life. In 1513 and 1519 he also contributed several small works to Marian devotion, expounding such topics as the Immaculate Conception, the Annunciation, and the Assumption. Continu-ing his close collaboration with Lefèvre, he worked to make the writings of the Christian Fathers more accessible, publishing Latin texts such as the sermons of St Cesarius (Paris: J. Marchand for J. Petit 1511) and especially Greek Fathers in Latin translation (he himself had no Greek). Quite generally, he was more concerned with pastoral theology than with critical scholarship. In *De mystica numerorum significatione* (Paris: H. Estienne 1513) he gathered a medley of patristic citations, and in his edition of the *Allegoriae in utrumque Testamentum* by Richard of St Victor (Paris: H. Estienne 1517) he inserted some quotations without alerting readers – and not always exact ones at that. In 1509 he had produced a first edition of the commentary on St John's gospel by St Cyril of Alexandria (Paris: W. Hopyl); in the second edition of this work (Paris: W. Hopyl 1520) he substituted for Cyril's missing books v to VII the annotations of John Chrysostom and Augustine, as Erasmus sarcastically noted in his *Responsio ad annota-tiones Lei* (LB IX 132F). In 1514 he published under Cyril's name the *Thesaurus* (Paris: W. Hopyl) and some homilies on Leviticus, although the latter actually belonged to Origen. In 1513 and 1515 he added many notes of his own to St John Damascene's *De fide orthodoxa* (Paris: H. Estienne) and the writings attributed to Dionysius the Areopagite, works previously published by Lefèvre.

Meanwhile Clichtove had gained a wide reputation in intellectual circles as the representative of theology among Lefèvre's collaborators. In particular, *Wimpfeling and his disciples, such as *Beatus Rhenanus, showed great appreciation for his work. Ecclesiastics of Tournai and Courtrai, such as Jan de *Hondt, who were themselves often in contact with the University of Louvain and sometimes also with Erasmus, consulted him when faced with difficult problems. In this way he was prompted to write in February 1515 a defence of Lefèvre's commentary on the Pauline Epistles, although he did not in the end publish this work. In 1517 he was offered the position of confessor to the future *Charles v but apparently declined; he did not lose the appointment because of the intrigues of his rivals, as Erasmus claimed (Epp 597, 628).

Clichtove maintained close connections with leading dignitaries of the French church, earning their patronage as a teacher, counsellor, and collaborator. Thus he was a client of Jacques d'Amboise, abbot of Cluny and bishop of Clermont, and his family. He was called upon to supervise the education of two of Jacques' nephews: François, for whom he wrote De vera nobilitate (Paris: H. Estienne 1512), and also Geoffroy, as previously mentioned. The *Briçonnets he served in like capacity, notably being the first teacher of Guillaume, the future bishop of Meaux. He was, moreover, consulted by the royal confessor, Guillaume *Petit, by Louis *Guillard, bishop of Tournai and subsequently Chartres, and even by Jan Goszton of Zelest, bishop of Győr in Hungary, who had sat at his feet in Paris in 1514 and 1515 and afterwards corresponded with him. At his request Clichtove composed his Elucidatorium ecclesiasticum (Paris: H. Estienne 1516), an exposition of liturgical texts for the benefit of priests. The work proved very successful and was reprinted by Johann *Froben on the advice of Wolfgang *Capito (Basel 1517; Ep 594).

Increasingly Clichtove's efforts were devoted to a reform of the secular clergy. In sermons before diocesan synods in Paris (1515), Tournai (1520), and Chartres (1526) and especially in his influential De vita et moribus sacerdotum

(Paris: H. Estienne 1519) he developed a new and comprehensive concept of the priestly office that anticipated the spirit of Trent. It also defended clerical celibacy and the fast, in opposition to Erasmus, although the latter is not mentioned by name. Meanwhile Clichtove had attached himself permanently to Guillard, who called him to his diocese of Tournai in 1518. He was successively canon of the cathedral chapter (18 April 1518), rector of Wazemmes (18 July 1519), and rector of St Jacob, Tournai, but resigned each benefice before accepting another. In Tournai he discovered how widely *Luther's writings were in circulation and attacked them vehemently in a diocesan synod held in April 1520.

At the same time Clichtove was engaged in a controversy with Noël *Béda and the theological faculty of Paris, who denounced his defence of Lefèvre's position on Mary Magdalen, Disceptationis de Magdalena defensio (Paris: H. Estienne 1519), a work which permitted Clichtove to develop rules of historical criticism. The Paris theologians also attacked him for his omission in the Elucidatorium of two verses in the Easter hymn Exultet that he judged to be an impious interpolation since they applied to Adam's sin the adjectives 'necessary' and 'happy.' He defended his view in De necessitate peccati Adae (Paris: H. Estienne 1519) but six years later retracted his stand on Magdalen as well as the Exultet and invited Erasmus to follow the example he had set by his retraction (Propugnaculum ecclesiae, Cologne: P. Quentel 1526, 414–15). In that same period he wrote his De regis officio (Paris: H. Estienne 1519), dedicated to *Louis ii of Hungary, and De doctrina moriendi (Paris: S. de Colines 1520), dedicated to Count Johann von Henneberg.

Compelled to leave Tournai with Guillard, Clichtove had returned to Paris by the beginning of 1521. By that time Lefèvre, his old master, had left Paris to join Briçonnet in his diocese of Meaux. In fact a break developed between Lefèvre and Clichtove, which proved to be definitive. Never again would Clichtove be found lacking in his respect for the church hierarchy; instead he devoted all his energies to the struggle against the Lutheran heresy and, through Guillard, may conceivably have invited Erasmus to join him in this effort. Erasmus pointedly replied that this was

Clichtove's business, not his (Ep 1212).
Clichtove's *De bello et pace* (Paris: S. de Colines
1523) advocated both a crusade against the
Turks and a pacifism far less radical than
Erasmus'. He went on to publish *De veneratione
sanctorum* (Paris: S. de Colines 1523), *Antilutherus* (Paris: S. de Colines 1524; Epp 1526,
1550, 1620, 1642, 1653, 1679), the *Propugnaculum ecclesiae* mentioned above (Ep 1642), and
De sacramento Eucharistiae contra Oecolampadium
(Paris: S. de Colines 1527; Epp 1780, 1893; LB IX
1124F). From 25 June 1527 he was a canon in
Guillard's new diocese of Chartres and soon
came to serve his chapter in several offices
including that of *théologal*, which he held from
12 August 1528 until his death. Also in 1528 he
participated prominently in the synod of the
archdiocese of Sens, held at Paris, and
subsequently published its decrees accompanied by his own explanations and a dedication
to *Francis I: *Compendium veritatum ad fidem
pertinentium* (Paris: S. de Colines 1529).

In France Clichtove was the first author of
any prominence to oppose Luther. Erasmus
himself saw this clearly (Epp 1526, 1893, 2615;
LB X 1249B, 1537B–D, 1624D), but at the same
time he knew Clichtove to be prominent among
the host of his own opponents (Epp 1679, 2443,
2445). It is not unreasonable to assume that
they had met one another in Paris, but there is
no evidence for such an encounter, nor is there
any trace of correspondence between them.
Despite an occasional display of friendly
feelings (Epp 621, 1620, 1805; LB IX 449B; *Dilutio*
ed Telle 69) and even though each was
prepared to grant the other some merit, they
never had a particularly high opinion of one
another, and the advent of the Reformation
could only widen the gulf between them.
Erasmus was the target of Clichtove's reproaches
in 1513 and 1519, but his name is mentioned
only in a text of 1517, which remained
unpublished; not until 1524 did he attack
Erasmus openly in his *Antilutherus* for having
questioned the authenticity of Dionysius the
Areopagite. Erasmus was right in this case and
Clichtove's criticism disturbed him, especially
since it was taken up by Noël Béda and the
Paris faculty of theology (Ep 1620; LB IX 449B,
676A, 916–17). In the same *Antilutherus*
Erasmus and particularly his *Epistola de esu
carnium* are criticized along with Luther over

his stand on fasting, priestly celibacy, and
monastic vows; and although Clichtove had
declined to mention him by name, Béda
triumphantly brought the attack to Erasmus'
attention (Ep 1642). While Erasmus refused to
admit that Béda had identified Clichtove's
target correctly (Epp 1653, 1679; LB IX 449B), the
latter repeated his charges, this time explicitly,
in the *Propugnaculum ecclesiae* of 1526, singling
out the *Encomium matrimonii*. Erasmus promptly
wrote a short defence and published it with his
replies to *Cousturier and Béda: *Appendix de
scriptis Clichtovei* (LB IX 811–14). For several
years he hesitated to reply at greater length (Ep
1780; LB IX 1089F), but after the Paris theological
faculty had published its *Censurae* Erasmus was
moved to act, and in February 1532 he
published along with his answer to the faculty
a *Dilutio eorum quae Iodocus Clithoveus scripsit
adversus declamationem Des. Erasmi suasoriam
matrimonii* (Ep 2604; new edition by E.V. Telle,
Paris 1968). Clichtove did not reply. However,
under the title *Improbatio* (Paris: S. de Colines
1533) he published an attack upon the
Erasmian Joris van *Halewijn, who had
criticized Luther in a work written in French
and now lost. Clichtove believed that Halewijn's critique left much to be desired, and so
did the Paris theologians. Finally, in 1534,
Clichtove published a collection of his *Sermones*
(Paris: widow of T. Kerver).

By 1524 Clichtove was drawing closer to
Béda, who in turn encouraged him to oppose
Erasmus (Epp 1609, 1642, 1805; LB IX 449B, 602F,
612E). It cannot be said, however, that in
criticizing Erasmus he succumbed to Béda's
influence. Faced with Clichtove's attacks,
Erasmus reacted with slighting judgements of
his opponent (Epp 1653, 1780, 2604), although
on balance he acknowledged that Clichtove
was clearly superior to Béda and Cousturier,
his *bêtes noires* at Paris. Thus he acknowledged
Clichtove's honesty (LB IX 1124E), sincerity
(*Dilutio* ed Telle 69), and moderation (LB IX
602–3) and his humanistic beginnings (Epp
1794, 1805). Clichtove's writings also gained
the attention of *Zwingli, *Oecolampadius,
*Capito, *Cranmer, and Calvin as well as their
Catholic opponents, and also of St Ignatius of
Loyola and the Fathers of the Council of Trent.

BIBLIOGRAPHY: Allen Ep 594 / Rice *Prefatory
Epistles* passim / Farge no 101 / A. Merghelynck

Recueil de généalogies inédites de Flandre I (Bruges 1877) 149–53 / J.-A. Clerval De Judoci Clichtovei Neoportuensis vita et operibus (1472–1543) (Paris 1894) / A. Salembier 'Josse Clichtove, docteur en Sorbonne, curé de Wazemmes en 1519' Revue de Lille 20 (1908–9) 419–31 / Renaudet Préréforme passim / A.L. Gabriel 'Gosztonyi püspök és Párizsi mestere' in Egyetemes Philológiai Közlöny (Budapest 1936) 15–29 / A.L. Gabriel 'The academic career of Blasius de Varda, Hungarian humanist at the University of Paris' Manuscripta 20 (1976) 219–43 / E.-V. Telle Erasme de Rotterdam et le septième sacrement (Paris 1954) / Erasmus Dilutio ed E.-V. Telle (Paris 1968) / L. de Berquin Declamation des louenges de mariage ed E.-V. Telle (Geneva 1976) / L. de Berquin La Complainte de la paix ed E.-V. Telle (Geneva 1978) / J.-P. Massaut Josse Clichtove, l'humanisme et la réforme du clergé (Paris 1968) / J.-P. Massaut 'Vers la Réforme catholique: Le célibat dans l'idéal sacerdotal de Josse Clichtove' in Sacerdoce et célibat ed J. Coppens (Gembloux-Louvain 1971) 459–506 (English trans, Milan 1973) / J.-P. Massaut Critique et tradition à la veille de la Réforme en France (Paris 1974) / J.-P. Massaut 'Histoire et allégorie dans les évangiles d'après Lefèvre d'Etaples et Clichtove' in Histoire de l'exégèse au XVIe siècle ed P. Fraenkel (Geneva 1978) 186–201 / J.-P. Massaut 'Théologie universitaire et requêtes spirituelles à la veille de la Réforme: Echo d'une controverse dans un texte inédit de Clichtove' in La Controverse religieuse ed M. Péronnet (Montpellier 1980) / J. Hourlier 'L'Eglise de France au XVIe siècle: Josse Clichtove et Jacques Lefèvre d'Etaples à Solesme' Revue historique et archéologique du Maine 44 (1969) 71–95 / F.J. Kötter Die Eucharistielehre in den katholischen Katechismen des 16. Jahrhunderts bis zum Erscheinen des Catechismus Romanus 1566 (Münster 1969) / M.J. Kraus 'Patronage and reform in France of the prereform: the case of Clichtove' Canadian Journal of History 6 (1971) 45–68 / J. Hutton 'Erasmus and France: the propaganda for peace' Studies in the Renaissance 8 (1961) 103–27 / W.F. Bense 'Paris theologians on war and peace, 1521–1529' Church History 41 (1972) 168–85 / Ch. G. Nauert 'The clash of humanists and scholastics: an approach to pre-Reformation controversies' The Sixteenth Century Journal 4

(1973) 1–18 / F.T. Bos Luther in het oordeel van de Sorbonne (Amsterdam 1974) / A. Tenenti La Vie et la mort à travers l'art au XVe siècle (Paris 1952) / A. Tenenti Il senso della morte e l'amore della vita nel Rinascimento (Turin 1957) / A. Jouanna L'Idée de race en France au XVIe siècle et au début du XVIIe siècle (1498–1614) III (Lille 1976) / G. Bedouelle Lefèvre d'Etaples et l'intelligence des Ecritures (Geneva 1976) / G. Bedouelle Le Quincuplex Psalterium de Lefèvre d'Etaples: un guide de lecture (Geneva 1979) / J.M. Victor Charles de Bovelles, 1479–1553: An Intellectual Biography (Geneva 1978) / J. Meier Der priesterliche Dienst nach Johannes Gropper (1503–1559) (Münster 1977)

JEAN-PIERRE MASSAUT

Gamaliel and William CLIFTON See CLYFTON

CLYFTON (Ep 194 of [June] 1506)
Clyfton's name is given only in Ep 194, where Erasmus, writing from Paris, described him as the tutor of Giovanni and Bernardo *Boerio and had nothing but praise for him. Shortly afterwards Erasmus travelled with Clyfton and his charges to Italy, and later he recalled a violent brawl between Clyfton and an English herald who was escorting the party (Allen I 4); perhaps this was a reason for Erasmus' bitter remarks when he abused Clyfton under the name of 'Scarabaeus' (Epp 2255, 2481).

A positive identification of Clyfton has not yet been offered. In 1540 *Beatus Rhenanus recalled that Erasmus had received his theological doctorate in Turin with an English companion (Allen I 59); this Englishman may well have been Clyfton. P.S. Allen thought he might have been Dr William Clifton, d 1548, Archbishop *Wolsey's vicar-general in the diocese of York (Emden BRUO I 143). Wallace K. Ferguson suggested Gamaliel Clifton or Clyfton, d 1541. Gamaliel is documented in Cambridge from 1500 and studied canon law at Turin in 1508. Thus it may have been at Turin that he acquired his doctorate in canon law. In 1513 he obtained a papal dispensation on account of a charge of homicide incurred in Cambridge. He was canon of York (from 1522) and canon (1528) and dean (from 16 May 1529) of Hereford. His will is dated 29 April 1541.

BIBLIOGRAPHY Allen and CWE Ep 194 / Emden BRUC 141

PGB

Andreas CNOPHA *See Andreas* KNOPKEN

Johannes COBERGIUS *See Johann* KOBERGER

Jean de COBLENCZ documented 1495–1517
Jean (Hanse) de Coblencz (Coblentz, Cow-
lance, Confluentinus), whose family was from
Koblenz, on the Rhine, although it is not
certain that he himself was born there, was a
bookseller in Paris from 1495 to 1517. Generally
in association with Jean *Petit, he published a
few classical texts, often printed or edited by
Josse *Bade.

Coblencz had a son, also called Jean, to
whom Bade addressed a letter printed in his
1501 edition of Virgil. In 1512 (Ep 263), Bade
asked Erasmus to send an eagerly expected
reply with Jean de Coblencz, who happened to
be in England and could take it back to Paris.
We do not know whether Bade was referring to
the father or the son. A Philippe de Coblencz,
presumably another son, did business with a
London bookseller in 1515.

BIBLIOGRAPHY: Allen Ep 263 / Renouard
Répertoire 87 / A. Claudin *Histoire de l'imprimerie
en France* (Paris 1901) II 541–3
                              GENEVIÈVE GUILLEMINOT

Johannes COCHLAEUS of Wendelstein,
d 10 January 1552
Johannes Cochlaeus (Dobnek), the son of a
peasant in Wendelstein, south of Nürnberg,
received some basic instruction from his uncle,
Hirspeck, attended school in Nürnberg, and
matriculated at the University of Cologne on 26
April 1504. In 1505 he obtained his BA and in
1507 his MA and adopted the name Cochlaeus,
as suggested by his friend *Remaclius Arduenna
(Ep 2120). On the recommendation of Willibald
*Pirckheimer, Cochlaeus was appointed rector
of the Latin school of St Lorenz in Nürnberg in
1510 and held the post until 1515. He wrote a
short Latin grammar, *Quadrivium grammatices*
(Strasbourg 1511); two textbooks on music
Tetrachordum Musicae (Nürnberg: J. Weissenburger 1511, ninth edition 1526) and *Musica*
([Cologne]: J. Landen 1507); and prepared a
new edition of the *Cosmographia* of Pomponius
Mela (Nürnberg: J. Weissenburger 1512). In
1515 he accompanied as their tutor three
nephews of Pirckheimer who went to study in
Italy; he himself studied law in Bologna and

Johannes Cochlaeus

maintained close contacts with *Hutten, whose
humanistic tastes he shared to the full at this
time. In March 1517 he obtained a doctorate of
theology in Ferrara. From 1518 to 1519 he was
in Rome, where he was ordained priest and
appointed dean of St Mary's in Frankfurt am
Main. He went there in 1520 and, as soon as he
had settled down, began working on an
edition of Maxentius and Fulgentius from a
manuscript that Pirckheimer had acquired from
the library of Johannes *Trithemius.

Having read *Luther's *An den christlichen
Adel* and *Captivitas Babylonica*, he planned a
refutation that was finished by December 1520
but never printed for lack of the required
funds. While attending the diet of Worms,
Cochlaeus did translations for *Aleandro, and
on 24 April 1521 had two meetings with
Luther. The final discussion in Luther's room
convinced both of their basic differences of
opinion. Thereafter Cochlaeus considered it
his duty to preserve the unity of the church by
attacking the reformers in his writings.
Although this caused him to lose many of his
former friends, he soon emerged as one of
Germany's leading Catholic controversialists.

In penning his numerous pamphlets he disregarded Aleandro's advice to proceed cautiously and often had difficulty in finding publishers. His *Assertio pro Emsero*, written in 1521, was not printed until 1545, when it appeared in the collection *In causa religionis miscellaneorum libri tres* (Ingolstadt: A. Weissenhorn). In September 1523 Cochlaeus travelled to Rome, hoping to interest Pope *Adrian vi in his plans for church reunification; but Adrian died on 14 September. On 28 February 1524 Cochlaeus returned to Nürnberg with his new friend, Fridericus *Nausea; next he stayed for a while in Stuttgart, Regensburg, and Mainz and finally went to Frankfurt again by the end of 1524; there he met with strong opposition and on 8 April 1525 had to flee to Cologne. When the peasant rebellion broke out Cochlaeus attempted to blame it on Luther. At about this time he began corresponding with John *Fisher and Thomas *More (Epp 1863, 1928).

Since return to Frankfurt was impossible, Cochlaeus accepted a prebend at St Victor in Mainz in 1526. In the summer of 1527 the Danish bishops invited him to their country, but he declined (Ep 1863) and on 22 January 1528 succeeded Hieronymus *Emser as the secretary and chaplain of Duke George of *Saxony (Ep 1923). Cochlaeus could have lived comfortably on his income at the duke's court, but his constant endeavours to finance the printing of his attacks on Luther made it difficult for him to make ends meet. In 1530 he attended the diet of Augsburg as a prominent member of the group of anti-Lutheran theologians. Luther's absence caused him to hope that he might be able to win *Melanchthon's approval for his views on reconciliation. When this failed, Cochlaeus' resentment against Melanchthon found expression in his *Philippicae quattuor* (Leipzig: N. Schmidt 1534) and similar pamphlets. In 1535 Cochlaeus became a canon of Meissen, and in 1536 he financed the establishment of the Wolrab press in Leipzig. Upset by news of the execution of his friends in England, John Fisher and Thomas More, Cochlaeus published a crude attack on King *Henry viii together with *Antiqua et insignis epistola Nicolai Papae i* (Leipzig: M. Lotter 1536); but interventions by Nausea and the papal nuncio Morone induced him to show more restraint in his *Scopa* against Richard *Morison (Leipzig: N. Wolrab 1538). After the death of Duke George (April 1539) Cochlaeus moved to Wrocław as canon at the cathedral. He took part in the conferences at Worms and Haguenau in 1540 and 1541, became a canon in Eichstätt, and continued his intensive production of polemical writings. When obliged to resign his Eichstätt prebend in 1548, Cochlaeus returned to Wrocław, where he died in 1552.

Cochlaeus' numerous writings – over two hundred are listed by Spahn – include German translations of works by his friends Johann *Dietenberger and John Fisher and a great many letters, through which he maintained personal relations with a wide range of friends and scholars. Even Erasmus, who disliked and occasionally criticized the violent tone of some of Cochlaeus' polemical writings, kept up a lively and frank correspondence with him between 1525 and 1535. The earliest letters are missing (Epp 1577, 1863), but Erasmus mentioned Cochlaeus in Epp 1688 and 1729. Cochlaeus' letter of 8 January 1528 (Ep 1928) exhibits some typical features, such as a tender concern for his aged mother, a strong sense of duty, and naivety in requesting Erasmus to write a treatise against the Anabaptists, a request that Erasmus ignored in his answer (Ep 1974). In the opening lines of his *Purgatio adversus epistolam Lutheri* (1534) Erasmus claimed that he had tried to restrain Cochlaeus' polemical zeal (LB x 1537B). Heinrich *Stromer addressed to Cochlaeus an account of the death and burial of Erasmus (Ep 3134).

BIBLIOGRAPHY: Allen Ep 1863 / NDB III 304–6 / Martin Spahn *Johannes Cochlaeus* (Berlin 1898, repr 1964) / Rogers Epp 162, 164–6 / Pflug *Correspondance* I Ep 103 and passim / *Matrikel Köln* II 557 / Cochlaeus' *Brevis Germaniae descriptio*, published in 1512 as an appendix to his edition of Pomponius Mela, has been re-edited, with an introduction and German translation, by Karl Langosch (Darmstadt 1960)

IG

Petrus a COCHLEARI (Ep 3115 of 12 April 1536)
Cochleari was an unidentified merchant or messenger recommended to Erasmus by Etienne *Desprez.

COCI, COCIUS, COCCIUS *See Ludolf* COCK, *Helius* EOBANUS *Hessus, and Conradus* WIMPINA

Ludolf COCK of Bielefeld, documented 1508–32
Ludolf Cock (Coccius, Kock) was born in Bielefeld, Westphalia. He matriculated at Erfurt in the summer term of 1508 and obtained his BA in the autumn of 1509 and his MA in 1513. Information about his further life is derived for the most part from his letter to Erasmus (Ep 2687, 9 July 1532), written from Regensburg, where he had gone at the time of the diet, perhaps in the hope of finding a new position, and where he had met Erasmus' amanuensis, Felix *Rex Polyphemus.

From Erfurt Cock had gone to Paris by way of the Netherlands, failing to meet Erasmus but staying for a while with Nicolaas van *Broeckhoven, then rector of the school at Middelburg. In Paris he took Greek lessons from Girolamo *Aleandro. His next preceptor was Rutgerus *Rescius, with whom he had kept in touch until the time of his letter to Erasmus. Perhaps through Rescius he became acquainted with Johannes *Murmellius, to whose edition of Tibullus, Propertius, and Catullus and other works he added some introductory verses when it was reprinted by Matthes Maler in Erfurt in 1514.

When Cock wrote to Erasmus he had been teaching for several years at the Latin school of Osnabrück. He urged Erasmus to recommend him to Franz von *Waldeck, bishop of Minden, Münster, and Osnabrück and mentioned several dignitaries in Waldeck's entourage. He also reported that he had travelled to Nürnberg and Augsburg at the time of the diet of 1530 and there had made friends with Willibald *Pirckheimer and Hermann von *Neuenahr as well as being honoured by the nuncio Lorenzo *Campeggi.

BIBLIOGRAPHY: Allen Ep 2687 / *Matrikel Erfurt* II 256 / de Vocht CTL I 277–8, III 109–10 / Martin von Hase 'Bibliographie der Erfurter Drucke, 1501–1550' *Archiv für Geschichte des Buchwesens* 8 (1967) 655–1096, specifically no 353

ERICH KLEINEIDAM & PGB

Theodericus COELDE *See Dietrich* KOLDE

Jorge COELHO d 28 August 1563
Jorge Coelho (Georgius Coelius) was the son of Nicolaus, who went with Vasco da Gama on his first voyage to India. Coelho studied at the University of Salamanca, and after his return to Portugal (not later than 1535) he eventually became secretary to *Henry, archbishop of Braga, later cardinal-king of Portugal. From a letter he wrote to Damião de *Gois concerning the publication of the latter's *Commentarii rerum gestarum in India* (Louvain: R. Rescius 1539) and another letter, dated 1541, both from Lisbon, it appears that he had not yet moved to Evora to join Henry's court there. On the other hand, Nicolaus *Clenardus made his acquaintance in Evora before leaving for Africa in 1542. Thus Coelho must have become Henry's secretary before 1545, the date given by Allen. Coelho, who corresponded with Clenardus, was known as an admirer of Erasmus and a poet. In a letter to Gois Coelho reported the critical reception of a poem he had written in praise of Dom *Afonso, the cardinal and Henry's brother. Nevertheless, he had more confidence in his poetic talent than he admitted and sent his best-known poem, *De patientia christiana*, to Gois for his comments, and at the same time sent it to *Sadoleto and *Bembo. In his answer Bembo noted Coelho's fame as a poet and orator. Like other Erasmians in Portugal Coelho wrote an encomium on the occasion of Erasmus' death.

BIBLIOGRAPHY: Allen Ep 3043 / M. Gonçalves Cerejeira *O Renascimento em Portugal* new ed (Coimbra 1974–5) passim / Elisabeth Feist Hirsch *Damião de Gois* (The Hague 1967) 153–5, 176–7 / José da Silva Terra 'O Humanista português Jorge Coelho e a sua correspondência con os cardeias Bembo e Sadoleto' in *Mélanges à la mémoire d'André Joucla-Ruau* (Aix-en-Provence 1978) II 1133–60

ELISABETH FEIST HIRSCH

Gilbertus COGNATUS *See Gilbert* COUSIN

Christian COLET *See Christian* KNYVET

Henry COLET d 1 October 1505
Sir Henry, the father of Erasmus' friend John *Colet, was born about 1430, the third son of Robert Colet of Wendover, Buckinghamshire. He was apprenticed to a member of the London

John Colet, bust probably by Pietro Torrigiano

Mercers' Company and by 1465 had married Christian *Knyvet. In the city of London he was alderman of Farringdon Without in 1476, sheriff in 1477, and alderman of Bassishaw in 1478, of Castle Baynard 1482–3, and of Cornhill 1486–7. He was elected mayor of London on 13 October 1486 and knighted on 13 January 1487, on the occasion of the marriage of *Henry VII to *Elizabeth of York. His London house was in the parish of St Anthony (St Antholin Budge Row); he later bought Great Place at Stepney, east of London. On 2 July 1495 he was elected mayor for the second time (Ep 1211). His will is dated 27 September 1505 and was proved on 20 October. His tomb in St Dunstan's, Stepney, is extant.

BIBLIOGRAPHY: Allen Ep 1211 / DNB IV 777 / J.H. Lupton *Life of Dean Colet* 2nd ed (London 1909) index / *Acts of Court of the Mercer's Company, 1453–1527* ed L. Lyell and F.D. Watney (Cambridge 1936) index / John B. Gleason 'The birth dates of John Colet and Erasmus of Rotterdam' *Renaissance Quarterly* 32 (1979) 73–6, esp 75 / S. Knight *The Life of Dr John Colet* new ed (Oxford 1823) 398–400
J.B. TRAPP

John COLET of London, 1467– d 16 September 1519

Colet (Colette, Collet, Coletus) was born at the beginning of 1467 (Ep 1347), almost certainly in the London parish of St Anthony (St Antholin Budge Row), where his father lived. According to Erasmus, he was the first child and the only survivor of eleven sons and eleven daughters born to Sir Henry *Colet and his wife, Dame Christian *Knyvet (Allen Ep 1211: 254–61). A brother, Richard, died in 1503.

Colet may have been a scholar at St Anthony's Hospital, Threadneedle Street, London, and his university education may have begun about 1483 at Cambridge, where a John Colet is recorded between 1484 and 1488. He was a BA by 29 September 1488. The Oxford University registers for 1464 to 1504 being lost, there is no contemporary evidence for the traditional view that he passed his early university years at Oxford or was incorporated MA there by 1490. Erasmus is silent about this; Polidoro *Virgilio (*Anglica Historia* ed D. Hay, London 1950, 146–7) records that he studied at both Oxford and Cambridge and travelled in Italy; Erasmus mentioned that he travelled in France and then in Italy (Allen Ep 1211:268–70).

Ecclesiastical preferments apart, the first contemporary document unequivocally relating to our John Colet, shows him in Rome from 14 March until at least 3 May 1493. No explicit evidence of a visit to Florence is extant, so that he may never have made the acquaintance of either Giovanni *Pico della Mirandola or Marsilio *Ficino, whose works he read and used. He also corresponded with Ficino: a first letter, by Colet, is missing, but three letters dating from about 1499 have been preserved in part (edited and translated in Jayne 81–3, who also lists the other surviving letters, 152–8). In France, Colet was at Orléans, where he got to know François *Deloynes (Epp 480, 494, 535) and, perhaps in 1495, at Paris (Ep 106). According to Erasmus, his study abroad chiefly concerned the sacred authors (Allen Ep 1211:270).

On his return to England, Colet seems to have gone to Oxford, where he lectured 'publice et gratis' on all the Epistles of St Paul. The lectures were highly regarded (Allen Ep 1211:281–90). Although he remained at Oxford from about 1495 to about 1503, no record survives of Colet's having taken a degree. Two commentaries on Romans and one on 1 Corinthians are extant in transcripts by Pieter *Meghen. From these Oxford years also probably date the so-called *Abstracts of the Celestial and Ecclesiastical Hierarchies* of the Pseudo-Dionysius, made from the second edition (1499) of Ambrogio Traversari's Latin translation (E.F. Rice in *Renaissance News* 17, 1964, 108–9); the *Letters to Radulphus on the Mosaic Account of the Creation*; and *De sacramentis ecclesiae* and *De corpore Christi mystico*. All were edited from manuscript by J.H. Lupton in 1867–76; see the bibliography of Colet's works in Jayne, who also suggests a tentative chronology (36–7, 149–52). Colet is usually said to have been admitted bachelor of theology 1501 and incorporated doctor 1504, the year he left Oxford, it seems, for London. Only one later Oxford contact – two dinners at Exeter College in 1519 – is recorded.

Colet may have been appointed to act in London for the absent dean of St Paul's, Robert Sherborne, from 1503 (but see John Le Neve *Fasti*, London 1962– , v 7n). Erasmus congratulated him on his doctorate and his deanship towards the end of 1504 (Ep 181; cf Allen Ep 1211:290–2). He was certainly dean by 1505 and collated prebendary of Mora by 5 May 1505. His first benefice was Dennington, Suffolk, to which he was admitted on 6 August 1485 and which he held until his death, though he was not ordained deacon until 17 December 1497 and priest until 25 March 1498. He was also rector of the Free Chapel of Hilberworth, Norfolk (1486), and of Thurning, Huntingdonshire (1490–4); canon of York and prebendary of Botevant (1494–1519); canon of St-Martin's-le-Grand, London, and prebendary of Goodeaster (by 1497–1504); vicar of Stepney (after 1499–1505); canon of Salisbury and prebendary of Durnford (1502–19); rector of Lambourn, Berkshire (1505); and treasurer of Chichester, Sussex (after 1508–1519).

In London Colet set about reform of the cathedral clergy by statute and sermon, his zeal in this, and perhaps in the foundation of St Paul's School, setting him at odds with his chapter. He made new statutes, and in 1518 he exhibited articles for reform to Cardinal *Wolsey. He gained a great reputation as a preacher

(Ep 855, 1229). Erasmus said that Colet shaped his English preaching style on the English poets (Allen Ep 1211:279–80). From 1510 to 1517, perhaps with an interval in 1514, he regularly received twenty shillings for the Good Friday sermon at court, his anti-war discourse of 25 March 1513 also earning him an investigatory interview with *Henry VIII (Allen Ep 1211:576–616). On 18 November 1515 Colet preached in Westminster Abbey on the occasion of Wolsey's receiving the red hat, the subject being the spiritual and temporal significance of the office of cardinal. His famous 'reform' sermon on Romans 12:2 was preached at the opening of the convocation of Canterbury on 6 February 1512 (printed in Latin c March 1512, STC 5545, and in English c 1530, STC 5550; cf Ep 258). The Latin text is the only work of Colet's printed in his lifetime of which a copy is extant. Colet was delated for heresy by his bishop, Richard *Fitzjames, to William *Warham, archbishop of Canterbury. Although Warham did not proceed with the charge, Erasmus later accused him of siding with Colet's enemies (Ep 414). Fitzjames continued to harass Colet (Ep 314; Allen Ep 1211:528–56).

On 4 November 1511 Colet seems to have made a will intended for the court of Husting of the City of London; a longer and fuller will, similarly disposing, was proved in that court on 10 June 1514. These may represent stages in his endowment of St Paul's School and may also – especially the second – be evidence of his wish to retire from public life about 1514. In that year he announced this intention and built himself a house ('nidus') for the purpose in the precincts of the Charterhouse at Sheen (Ep 314; Allen Ep 1211:372–4). It is not known that he occupied it. He was one of the five-man committee appointed by convocation at the request of Henry VIII to enquire into the dispute which eventually led to the removal of Warham from the chancellorship in 1516. He was drawn into royal service perhaps soon after this (Epp 457, 976). His appointment to the king's council predated that of Thomas *More; it may have been made by 25 January 1517, and he certainly attended meetings on 25 June, 13 July, and 6 November 1517. Colet also served on two committees of the council in 1517–18.

During and after 1517, Colet suffered three attacks of the sweating sickness that eventually caused his death (Allen Ep 1211:378–86) in 1519. He was buried in St Paul's Cathedral. Contrary to his wishes an elaborate tomb, now no longer extant, was later erected over his remains. His third will, dated 22 August 1519, was proved 5 October 1519 (printed in Knight 400–9). On 25 October 1519 Richard *Pace was elected to succeed Colet as dean.

When Erasmus first came to England in the summer of 1499, he seems to have had a letter of introduction to Colet, who welcomed him from Oxford, having already heard good things of him there and in Paris (Ep 106). Erasmus' grateful reply (Ep 107) began a close and fruitful friendship, based on a common concern for the significance of the New Testament in letters and in life. Almost at once the two were in disagreement, in the presence of Erasmus' host Richard *Charnock, about Christ's agony in the Gethsemane garden (Epp 108–11). A second dispute concerning Cain's sin is described by Erasmus in Ep 116.

In 1501, Erasmus contemplated a return to England to study divinity with Colet (Ep 159) and about December 1504 he wrote to him (Ep 181), sending the Lucubratiunculae and asking him to see to the distribution of a hundred copies of the Adagia sent three years before. He added that he wished to devote the rest of his life to the Scriptures but he needed financial help. Within three months of Colet's coming into his patrimony, by the end of 1505, and having meanwhile published Lorenzo *Valla's Adnotationes, Erasmus was in London, where Greek studies were flourishing. Colet himself was Greekless (Ep 423), though later, at the age of nearly fifty, he made the attempt to learn the language, with the help of More's servant-pupil John *Clement (Epp 468, 471). At this time he encouraged Erasmus, especially in translating the New Testament and writing commentaries (Ep 258). He provided two Latin manuscripts (Ep 373; LB VI 14E, 578C), supported Erasmus' interpretations (LB VI 58F, 973D), and was delighted with the Novum Instrumentum when it was published a decade later (Ep 423). He interested himself in the progress towards the second edition (Epp 786, 825, 891) and in 1519 was one of those who tried to persuade Edward *Lee to abstain from

attacking Erasmus (Apologia invectivis Lei, Opuscula 299; Edward Lee Annotationes 1520 f CC1 verso).

Pieter Meghen transcribed Erasmus' translation of the Epistles and Gospels in manuscript (London, British Library, MS Royal IEV, 2 vols and Cambridge, University Library, MS Dd vii 3). The Vulgate text which is in parallel columns with the Erasmus was written by Meghen for Colet (colophon dated 1 Nov 1506, 8 May and 7 Sept 1509). Colet's pupil *Lupset later helped Erasmus collate the New Testament (Ep 270), and Colet had a copy of Matthew belonging to Erasmus in 1513 (Ep 278). Erasmus told Colet that he had written a commentary on Romans (Ep 181). Later Colet reminded him of his vow to finish this (Epp 314, 423); when he finally published his paraphrase, Colet had criticisms to offer (Ep 825). Erasmus also sent Colet a translation of the office of St John Chrysostom (Epp 227, 230), announcing his intention of translating St Basil on Isaiah (Ep 237). On 20 June 1516, Colet wrote of his anxiety to see Erasmus' Jerome, as well as the Institutio principis christiani; on 2 October Erasmus arranged for a copy of Jerome to be sent to Colet (Epp 423, 474).

In 1508 Colet made his first move towards applying his inheritance from his father to the establishment in St Paul's Churchyard of a school for 153 boys to be instructed free in 'good Maners and litterature ... both laten and greke' (Statutes, in Lupton Life 271, 279; Allen Ep 1211:339–59). The school building was complete in 1512. Colet made the Mercers' Company, not the chapter, 'patrones and defenders gouernours and Rulers' of the school (Lupton 271), finding more virtue in them than in the clergy (Allen Ep 1211:360–70). He drafted statutes, appointed William *Lily first high master, and saw to the provision of textbooks. He himself wrote for the school a catechism in English, part of which was translated into Latin verse by Erasmus as Institutum christiani hominis (Reedijk poem 94; cf Ep 298; Allen I 6), and a Latin accidence in English, entitled Aeditio, composed in 1509 (first extant edition 1527). From Lily, he probably commissioned Rudimenta (a Latin syntax in English, later frequently printed with the Aeditio), and certainly De constructione (ASD I-4 105–43), a more advanced syntax in Latin.

This was given to Erasmus for revision. Erasmus performed his task throroughly, and thereafter Lily would not, and Erasmus could not, own it as his. It was first printed as an anonymous work in 1513 (Ep 341). Erasmus wrote other poems for the school (Reedijk poems 86–90; Ep 258), as well as *Concio de puero Jesu* (LB V 599–610; cf Allen I 21), besides suggesting an inscription for the schoolroom (Allen Ep 1211:350–3). *De copia* (CWE 24 279–659) was written for the school and dedicated to Colet when first published in 1512 (Ep 260). Erasmus later complained that Colet had promised money for the dedication and failed to pay it (Ep 270). *De ratione studii*, too, was intended for the school, as a blueprint for the aims and methods of education (CWE 24 661–91; cf Ep 227). Erasmus also lent support in other matters, defending the school – which Colet told him a bishop had called 'a house of idolatry' (Ep 258) – against university men, 'Thomists and Scotists' (Epp 227, 237, 260), helping to find a suitable surmaster, or second master (Epp 227, 230, 231, 237), and advising on how to deal with Thomas *Linacre, whose Latin grammar Colet had rejected as too advanced for his purposes (Epp 227, 230).

Sixteenth-century Europe's image of Colet owes everything to Erasmus. Much is still today known only from that source. Erasmus' encomium in his memorial letter to Justus *Jonas of 13 June 1521 (Ep 1211) is the fullest and most explicit portrait, but he left a large number of other testimonies to the nature and the strength of one of the most famous friendships of northern humanism. Immediately after Colet's death Erasmus wrote of his sense of irreparable loss to *Budé and friends in England (Epp 1023, 1025–30); later, he renewed his grief on many occasions (Epp 1064, 1075, 1103, 1110, 2684). Marquard von *Hattstein, as yet unaware of Colet's death, wrote an admiring letter to him on 26 April 1520. In life Colet had been made so familiar in Europe by Erasmus as the pattern of a Christian that *Oecolampadius noted the resonance of his name in Erasmus' writings (Ep 563). There are praises of him in several of Erasmus' letters (Epp 855, 976, 999). In the *Colloquia* (ASD I-3 180–1, 488–93), in *De pronuntiatione* (ASD I-4 24), in *Modus orandi Deum* (ASD V-1 154), he appears as the truly good man. *De*

conscribendis epistolis uses him as an example of correct forms of address (ASD I-2 281). *Reuchlin, whom Colet admired, with reservations, was encouraged by Erasmus to write and to send his works to Colet (Epp 300, 457, 593, 653, 713). Henricus Cornelius *Agrippa came to England in 1510, staying in the house of Colet's mother at Stepney and labouring with Colet on the Pauline Epistles; Jean *Vitrier paid England a visit solely in order to meet the man whom Erasmus had so lauded (Allen Ep 1211:246–51).

Among Colet's English friends, the most notable is Thomas More, who calls him 'vitae meae magister' in the first of two extant letters (Rogers Ep 3, 23 October [1504]). Colet's possible disapproval of the publication of *Utopia* (Ep 467) did not extend to the book's author: for him, says Erasmus, More was England's one genius (Allen Ep 999:269). More and Colet must have been jointly responsible with William *Blount, lord Mountjoy, for introducing Erasmus to the Oxford-London humanist circle – *Grocyn, Lily, Linacre, *Tunstall, Warham, William *Latimer, *Foxe, *Urswick, Pace, *Clerk, and Lupset. Colet himself was by 1511 a fellow-member with More of Doctors' Commons, a self-governing society of civil and canon lawyers, to which also belonged Grocyn, Tunstall, *Yonge, Andrea *Ammonio, and Polidoro Virgilio.

The portrait of Colet by Erasmus in his letter to Jonas was first translated into English by Matthew Tyndall in 1533 (Donald W. Rude in *Papers of the Bibliographical Society of America* 71 [1977] 61–5). It has been much drawn on above and is the chief source of what follows. Colet was impressive in appearance, tall and handsome, sober in dress, frugal in food and drink, grave in manner, and intolerant both of undue pomp and of slovenliness. He subdued his own bodily affections and his tendency to frivolity, but he was less harsh towards offenders against continence than towards those who sinned in other regards. His delight was in sacred reading and holy conversation, especially with friends. He was somewhat self-willed (Ep 468) but kept a naturally quick temper under control (Allen 1347:31–56). His definite and strongly held views (Epp 108–11, 116, 431) were the index of a powerful mind. His bias was against scholasticism, and he mistrusted monasteries and colleges for their falling away from the ideals they ought to embody. As guides to goodness of life he inclined, outside the Scriptures, to the early Fathers and the pseudo-Dionysius in particular, but he was suspicious of Reuchlin's 'Pythagorical and Cabalistic philosophy' as a way to holiness, preferring 'the love and imitation of Christ' (Ep 593). His impatience with mere observance made him intolerant of pilgrimage and the cult of relics as practised (*Modus orandi Deum* ASD V-1 154; and the colloquy *Peregrinatio religionis ergo* ASD I-3 488–93), but he did not entirely disapprove of holy images or auricular confession, though he preferred not to celebrate mass daily in the English fashion.

Colet's eloquence did not lead him to underrate goodness (Ep 593; and *Adagia* I x 74). This seems to have left him open to deception by the arguments of one of the interlocutors in the *Antibarbari* (Ep 1110; CWE 23 16). To hear him speak was to fancy oneself listening to Plato (Ep 118), but his Latin was not always pedantically correct, and this may have been the reason why he did not publish. He had from boyhood the English habit of pronouncing Latin *ie* as if it were *ii* ('*faciibat*'), and retained this peculiarity in spite of admonition (*De pronuntiatione* ASD I-4 53).

Colet seems not always to have come up to Erasmus' financial expectations, being 'not entirely immune from the love of money' (Allen Ep 1211:393). Sometimes he had to be reminded of his duty (Ep 270) or instructed in the correct modes of giving and receiving (Ep 237). But he provided much material as well as spiritual and intellectual help himself and was active to secure it from others (Epp 218, 225, 227, 244, 255, 260, 270, 278, 455, 461, 543; CWE Ep 834 introduction). Erasmus was always anxious to know if Colet and his friends in England were well-disposed to him (Epp 225, 248, 543, 966), and, if necessary, to conciliate them (Epp 231, 278).

There is a portrait bust of Colet by or after Pietro Torrigiano (c 1520?) in the possession of St Paul's School, London (on loan to the Victoria and Albert Museum); the portrait drawing at Windsor Castle of Colet was made from the bust by *Holbein during his second visit, and before 1535. A representation of Colet's tomb, including a portrait of Colet, was painted by Sir William Segar about 1585–6 on the cover of a copy of the school statutes at Mercers' Hall.

BIBLIOGRAPHY: Emden BRUC 148 / Emden BRUO I 462–4 / J.H. Lupton *Life of John Colet* 2nd ed (London 1909) is still standard / Clara Collet 'The family' *Genealogists' Magazine* 7 v (1936) 242–3, esp 243 / S. Knight *The Life of Dr John Colet* new ed (Oxford 1823) / Sears Jayne *John Colet and Marsilio Ficino* (London 1963) / W. Robert Godfrey 'John Colet of Cambridge' ARG 65 (1974) 6–18 / *Calendar of Papal Letters relating to Great Britain and Ireland* 15 (London 1980) nos 31, 335 / John B. Gleason 'The birth dates of John Colet and Erasmus of Rotterdam' *Renaissance Quarterly* 32 (1979) 73–6 / J.A. Guy *The Cardinal's Court* (Hassocks 1977) 41–2 / J.B. Trapp 'John Colet, his manuscripts and the Ps.-Dionysius' in *Classical Influences in European Culture 1500–1700* ed R.R. Bolgar (Cambridge 1976) 205–21 / F. Grossman 'Holbein, Torrigiano and some portraits of John Colet' *Journal of the Warburg and Courtauld Institutes* 13 (1950) 202–36 / John B. Gleason 'The earliest evidence for censorship of printed books in England' *The Library* 6th series, 4 (1982) 135–41 / A bibliography of Colet's works is in Jayne, 149–59; see also Carl S. Meyer 'A John Colet bibliography' *Bulletin of the Library, Foundation for Reformation Research* 5 xiii (September 1970) 23–7 and Trapp 'Colet and his MSS' passim (mistaken about date of STC 5545) / *New Cambridge Bibliography of English Literature* ed G. Watson 1 (Cambridge 1974) 1790–92 / Andrew J. Brown 'The Date of Erasmus's Latin New Testament' (forthcoming)

J.B. TRAPP

Odet de COLIGNY cardinal of Châtillon, 10 July 1517–21 March 1571

Odet was the eldest son of Gaspard de Coligny and of Louise de Montmorency, and a nephew of the powerful Constable Anne de Montmorency. As tutor to Odet and his brothers, Nicolas *Bérault was an important early influence, as he had been in the life of Louis de *Berquin. In Ep 3083 Bérault referred to Odet as his patron.

Although he was the eldest son, Odet surrendered his primogenital rights and pursued a brilliant career in the church, becoming cardinal (1533), archbishop of Toulouse (1534) and bishop of Beauvais (1535), as well as titular head of several abbeys and priories, including Vézelay and St Benoît-sur-Loire. In his diocese of Beauvais he built churches, hospitals and colleges, and created cloth manufactories. His mansion in Paris was a centre for the world of arts and letters: the poets of the Pléiade, the painter Jean Clouet, the sculptor Jean Goujon, the philosopher Petrus Ramus, and the jurist Michel de l'Hospital gathered there. The most eloquent testimonials are those of *Rabelais, who dedicated his *Quart Livre* (1552) to the cardinal, with its daring chapter LIII on the persecution of heretics, and of Ronsard, who remained loyal even after 1560, when Odet had embraced the reformed religion.

Coligny had attended the council of Trent in 1545 and had been appointed grand inquisitor by the pope in 1557, alongside the cardinals Charles de Bourbon and Charles de Lorraine. In 1564, however, he married Elisabeth de Hauteville, and he served the Huguenot cause on important diplomatic missions during the first decade of the civil wars. He even put on armour and fought bravely at Saint-Denis in 1567. In England he was well received by Elizabeth I but was poisoned by a servant on the eve of returning to France in 1571. His more famous brother, the admiral, Gaspard, was assassinated on St Bartholomew's eve of the following year.

An oil and wood portrait of Odet is in the Musée national du château de Versailles and a painting of the three Coligny brothers is in the Mauritshuis, The Hague. Both are reproduced in *Coligny: Protestants et Catholiques en France au XVIe siècle*, the catalogue of an exhibition (October 1972–January 1973) in the Archives Nationales in Paris, commemorating the fourth centenary of Admiral Coligny's death. There is also a drawing of Odet attributed to the Clouet school in the Musée Condé in Chantilly.

BIBLIOGRAPHY: Allen Ep 3083 / DHGE XIII 250–1 / DBF VIII 816–17 / E.G. Atkinson 'The Cardinal of Châtillon in England, 1568–71' *Huguenot Society Proceedings* 3 (1888–91) 172–85 / Marguerite Christol 'Odet de Coligny, cardinal de Châtillon' *Bulletin de la Société de l'histoire du Protestantisme français*, 107 (1961) 1–12 (based on contemporary testimonials, in the absence of his own writings, which were systematically destroyed)

GORDON GRIFFITHS

Willem COLGHENENS of Bergen op Zoom, d June 1518
Guihelmus Conradus, one of the interlocutors in the *Antibarbari*, is regularly referred to in that dialogue as 'consul,' a term which strongly suggests that he was one of the two mayors of Bergen op Zoom, elected annually. No other character in the *Antibarbari* being fictitious, it would be strange if Conradus was. He has been identified by Slootmans as Willem Colghenens (Coelgheenens, Coligheens, Colini), who often served as mayor of Bergen between 1477 and 1505, but not, however, on the date of the conversation described in the *Antibarbari* (probably 1495). This need not present a real difficulty, as it is stated that he held the mayoralty 'subinde' (ASD-I-1 41; CWE 23 21).

The son of another Willem Colghenens and Marie Bouwens, and perhaps a godchild of Jan (II) van *Bergen, he matriculated at the University of Louvain on 24 February 1458, and at Orléans in March 1462, where he received his MA in 1463, was twice procurator of the German nation (1463 and 1465), and finally became a licentiate in civil and canon law. He returned to his native Bergen and was appointed town secretary (for instance in 1469 and 1474) and pensionary (1478 and 1481), but it was probably in the cloth trade that he earned the handsome fortune which allowed him to make many charitable bequests in his will, dated 1515. He frequently represented the lords of Bergen on diplomatic missions, supervised the *béguines* of Bergen, and was clearly one of the leading figures of the region. Towards the end of his life Jan (II) van Bergen also made him *stadhouder* of the feudal court of Bergen (cf ASD I-1 41; CWE 23 21). He was survived by his wife, Catharina Knopper, who died in 1527.

BIBLIOGRAPHY: *Matricule de Louvain* II-1 49 / *Matricule d'Orléans* II-1 68-9 / C. Slootmans 'Erasmus en zijn vrienden uit Bergen op Zoom' *Taxandria* 35 (1928) 113–23 / G.C.A. Juten in *Taxandria* 35 (1928) 123–30

C.G. VAN LEIJENHORST

Jacques COLIN of Auxerre, d 1547
Jacques Colin was born in Auxerre between
1485 and 1495. From 1521 to 1522 he was in Italy
as secretary of Odet de Foix, sieur de Lautrec.
From 1523 he began to occupy royal offices,
being *valet de chambre du roi* in 1526. In 1526 and
1527 he undertook several diplomatic missions
to Savoy, to the Swiss cantons, and again to
Lautrec in Italy. From 1533 to 1536 he carried
out a further round of missions, negotiating
with Karel van *Egmond, duke of Gelderland,
and John III of *Cleves. Meanwhile he had
been appointed *secrétaire de la chambre du roi* as
well as *lecteur* and from 1534 until his disgrace
by 1537 he enjoyed a position of great confidence as royal almoner. He also reaped
the rewards of his service in the form of
ecclesiastical preferment, being named commendatory abbot of St Ambrose, Bourges, in
1531 and prior of Chantilly and abbot of
Issoudun in 1532.

Colin, who was also principal of the Collège
des Bons-Enfants, had literary and humanistic
interests. He corresponded with Guillaume
*Budé and translated into French portions of
Homer and works by Claude de Seyssel as well
as Baldesar *Castiglione's *Cortegiano*. By 1532
Gérard *Morrhy was discussing with him
Julius Caesar *Scaliger's attack upon Erasmus
(Ep 2633).

BIBLIOGRAPHY: Allen Ep 2633 / DBF IX 235–6 /
V.-L. Bourrilly *Jacques Colin, abbé de Saint-
Ambroise* (Paris 1905) / Louis Delaruelle *Répertoire ... de la correspondance de Guillaume Budé*
(Toulouse-Paris 1907) Ep 165 / *Gallia christiana* II
161 / *La Correspondance du cardinal Jean du Bellay*
ed Rémy Scheurer (Paris 1969–) I Epp 167,
169, II Ep 344

MICHEL REULOS & PGB

Simon de COLINES documented 1520–46
In 1520 Simon de Colines (Colinaeus) took over
the press and bookstore of Henri (I) Estienne,
whose widow, Guyonne Viart, he married in
1522. In 1526 he handed the firm over to her
son, Robert (I) Estienne, and established his
own business under the sign of the 'Soleil-
d'Or' in front of the Collège de Beauvais. In
1539 he transferred the bookstore to Regnault
Chaudière, the husband of his wife's daughter, but continued his publishing business. He

often printed for other booksellers, among
them his other stepson, François Estienne.

In all, Colines published in excess of 730
works. At first he followed the lead of Henri
Estienne in publishing the great philosophers
and medical authorities of antiquity as well as
contemporary scientific authors, but gradually
he came to concentrate on student texts in
pocket size. Apart from the Latin classics, he
published essays on pedagogics and ethics and
many editions of individual parts of the Bible,
both in Latin and in French, which were
repeatedly banned by the theological faculty of
the University of Paris. On seventy-three
occasions Colines published works written or
edited by Erasmus, among them an edition of
the *Colloquia* (1527) which according to Erasmus went to prove that his writings could
circulate freely in Paris (Ep 1875). That same
edition, however, was banned three months
later, on 17 December 1527. In 1529 Erasmus
mentioned that, as far as he knew, it had been
printed 'ad vigintiquatuor milia' (Ep 2126).
Since a printing of 24,000 copies seems
excessive, perhaps some misunderstanding
was involved; it may be noted that the book's
size is 24°. In 1530 Colines published *Carvajal's *Dulcoratio* directed against Erasmus (Ep
2412).

BIBLIOGRAPHY: Allen Ep 1875 / Renouard
Répertoire 88–9 / Philippe Renouard *Bibliographie des éditions de Simon de Colines* (Paris
1894)

GENEVIÈVE GUILLEMINOT

Angelo COLOCCI of Iesi, 1467–1 May 1549
Born at Iesi, in the Marches, Colocci made
contact with the Neapolitan literary circle of
Giovanni *Pontano during his formative years.
In 1497 he bought his way into papal service
and settled in Rome; over the next three
decades he became an associate of *Sadoleto,
*Bembo, Aldo *Manuzio, and many lesser
figures. Colocci was known chiefly as a
collector of antique coins, sculpture, and
inscriptions, but he also possessed a fine
library and became the centre of a kind of
literary circle. The Greek college of Janus
*Lascaris operated in his villa on the Quirinal
between 1516 and 1521. In 1524 Colocci was
mentioned as the author of an invective against

Erasmus (Epp 1479, 1482). However, such a work by Colocci has not survived, and Silvana Seidel Menchi has argued that the invective was really the work of Colocci's friend Battista *Casali that is found in the Biblioteca Ambrosiana of Milan (MS G 33 inf II ff 82 verso–87 verso). Since Colocci was an amateur writer and a committed patron of the pure antiquarianism ridiculed in the *Ciceronianus*, it is likely that, if he did not write an invective, he at least supported Casali's and perhaps helped circulate it. Impoverished by ransoms paid after the Sack of Rome in 1527, Colocci became bishop of Nocera in 1546 and died in 1549. A few of his books are preserved in the Biblioteca Apostolica Vaticana (A.M.P.G. de Nolhac *La Bibliothèque de Fulvio Orsini* Paris 1887, 79–81, 249–59), and Cod. Vat. Latini nos 8492–4 appear to be his archaeological scrapbooks. However his collections were lost in the Sack.

BIBLIOGRAPHY: Allen Ep 1479 / F. Ubaldini *Vita di Mons. Angelo Colocci* ed V. Fanelli (Vatican City 1969) provides copious notes and bibliography / G. Lancellotti *Poesie italiane e latine di Mons. Angelo Colocci* (Iesi 1772) gives bibliography, a selection of writings, and extracts from contemporary writers / Vittorio Fanelli *Richerche su Angelo Colocci e sulla Roma cinquecentesca* (Vatican City 1979) / Atti del Convegno *Studi su Angelo Colocci* (Iesi 1972) / Silvana Seidel Menchi 'Alcuni atteggiamenti della cultura italiana di fronte a Erasmo' in *Eresia e riforma nell'Italia del Cinquecento, Miscellanea I* (Florence 1974) 69–133

M.J.C. LOWRY

Pompeo COLONNA 5 May 1479–28 June 1532
Pompeo Colonna (Columna, Columnensius) was the son of Girolamo, prince of Salerno. One of his uncles, Prospero Colonna, a famous military captain, introduced him to the court of King Ferrante of Naples, though Paolo Giovio also relates that he was educated in the Colonna country estates near Tusculum (where he enjoyed disputing with his cousin Marcantonio about military enterprises in antiquity). Pompeo served with the Spanish armies in the south and was praised for his valour in their victory against the French at the battle of Garigliano (December 1503). He entered an ecclesiastical career in order to promote family interests, supposedly after seeing a vision of his father. He became master of the household of his uncle, Cardinal Giovanni Colonna, in Rome and a papal protonotary. Pompeo was proficient in Latin and avidly pursued his literary interests, keeping company with Pietro da Volterra, Camillo Porzio, and others; there is no evidence, however, that Erasmus met him in Rome in 1509.

Upon Cardinal Giovanni's death in September 1508, Pompeo was appointed bishop of Rieti and also obtained the abbacies of Grottaferrata and Subiaco. Indignant at *Julius II's neglect of himself and of the Roman nobility in general, he took the opportunity of the pope's severe illness in August 1511 to exhort the people of Rome to rise and regain their liberty, delivering a harangue on the Capitol in which, according to Guicciardini's amplified version, he compared the pope to the Mameluke Sultan. Julius' recovery put an end to the rebellion; Pompeo fled to Subiaco, refusing the offer of a papal pardon because it omitted reinstatement as bishop of Rieti. He was barely restrained by his uncle Prospero from joining the French forces marching on Rome in April 1512. After the death of Julius, Pompeo entered the city in March 1513 and attacked the house of Antonio Ciocchi, cardinal del Monte, who had assumed the bishopric of Rieti, but he agreed to give protection to the conclave. After *Leo X's election, and thanks to Fabrizio Colonna's intercession, he enjoyed papal favour, sharing Leo's love of hunting. In 1516 Pompeo travelled to France and obtained the release of his uncle Prospero, who had been captured at the battle of Marignano. Subsequently he went to Germany and the Emperor *Maximilian sent him on a mission to his grandson, the future *Charles V, in Flanders. It was probably on this occasion that Erasmus met him at Brussels (Ep 1432). He may also have gone to England but was again in Flanders when appointed cardinal in July 1517; by November he had returned to Rome.

In October 1519 Leo X sent Pompeo as legate to pacify Rieti and Terni, of which he also became bishop in 1520. He strongly opposed the election of Cardinal Giulio de' Medici as pope in the conclaves of 1521 and 1523, but

Abel van Colster by Jan Mostaert

Monreale on 14 December 1530. Pompeo died near Naples on 28 June 1532, allegedly because he had consumed unripe figs and wine chilled with snow. According to Giovio he had enjoyed studying during his last years at Naples and had composed writings in praise of the beauty of women. There is a portrait of him by Lorenzo Lotto in the Galleria Colonna, Rome.

BIBLIOGRAPHY: Allen Ep 1432 / EI x 855 / Eubel III 15–16 and passim / Pastor VI 371–2 and passim / Sanudo *Diarii* XIV 244 and passim / The basic source remains Paolo Giovio's biography, printed together with his lives of Leo x and Adrian VI in many editions; but this is complemented by P. Consorti *Il Cardinale Pompeo Colonna secondo documenti inediti* (Rome 1902)

D.S. CHAMBERS

Abel van COLSTER of Dordrecht, 1477–21 September 1548

Abel (Aelbert) van Colster (de Coulster) was a son of Ysbrand van Colster, sometime treasurer of Dordrecht, and Machtelt Florysdochter van Alkemade. He studied at Cologne (matriculation 31 March 1490, licence of arts 14 March 1493) and at Orléans (matriculation April 1494). With one short intermission (29 October 1515–23 July 1516) he was councillor in the council of Holland at The Hague from 3 November 1506 until his death. In 1516 he married Ysabeau Longin. Jan Mostaert painted his portrait, now in the Musée d'art ancien, Brussels.

On 25 April 1533 Erasmus sent a letter to van Colster (Ep 2800) that was clearly part of a more extensive correspondence (Ep 2645). In 1535 van Colster was present when Erasmus' orthodoxy was questioned by Quirinus *Talesius. Initially he agreed with the others present that Quirinus' charges were absurd; on the other hand, a year earlier he had been engaged in the suppression of Anabaptists, and we do not know whether Talesius' charges eventually impressed him.

BIBLIOGRAPHY: Allen Ep 2800 / *Matricule d'Orléans* II-1 176 / *Matrikel Köln* II 275 / A.F. Mellink *De wederdopers in de Noordelijke Nederlanden 1531–1544* (Groningen 1953) 156–7, 165

C.G. VAN LEIJENHORST

ultimately switched his support on the latter occasion, being rewarded by Giulio, now *Clement VII, with the office of vice-chancellor on 11 January 1524. Erasmus heard in March 1524 that Pompeo had been sent as legate to the imperial court and praised his integrity (Ep 1432). In May 1526 Pompeo joined with the imperial envoy Ugo de Moncada in protesting against Clement VII's pro-French alliance, the League of Cognac, and on 20 September led an armed attack on Rome, calling for a general council against the pope. Two days later he had to withdraw, going first to Grottaferrata and then to Naples (Ep 1762).

Pompeo was deprived of his dignity and benefices on 21 November 1526, but he did not pursue his vendetta during the Sack of Rome in May 1527, shutting himself up in his palace and recommending terms for Clement's safe departure. On 26 December 1527 Clement VII reinstated him, and he enjoyed literary praises as a second founder of Rome. Summoned to Naples by Philibert of Chalon, prince of Orange, he became papal legate there, and in July 1529 he became the imperial *luogotenente generale*. He obtained the archbishopric of

Jane COLT d July/August 1511

The eldest daughter of John *Colt, Jane married Thomas *More, probably late in 1504 or early in 1505. Their children were Margaret, Elizabeth, Cecily, and John *More. Two decades after her death, in 1532 Thomas More moved her body to Chelsea (Ep 2831).

Andrea *Ammonio told Erasmus about More's 'most agreeable wife, who never mentions you without blessing your name' (Ep 221). In Erasmus' account of the More family (Ep 999) Jane is mentioned in such a way as to suggest that Erasmus also recalled her in his colloquy *Uxor μεμψίγαμος* (ASD I-3 301–13). According to Erasmus, More had deliberately chosen for his wife a very young girl who had always lived in the country so as to educate her in his own fashion.

BIBLIOGRAPHY: Allen Ep 221 / E.E. Reynolds *St Thomas More* (London 1953) passim / W. Roper *Life of More* ed E.V. Hitchcock (London 1935) / R.W. Chambers *Thomas More* (London 1935) 95–6 / G. Marc'hadour *L'Univers de Thomas More* (Paris 1963) 473

R.J. SCHOECK

John COLT of Netherall, d 22 October 1521

John was the son of Thomas Colt (Colte), chancellor of the exchequer under Edward IV. He lived at Netherall, near Roydon on the border of Hertfordshire and Essex, and owned extensive properties in East Anglia. He was married twice and had eighteen children. His eldest daughter, Jane *Colt, married Sir Thomas *More.

Colt bequeathed to Thomas More his best colt and ten marks per year, to care for his own son Thomas Colt. He was reputed to have been a consummate actor with whom More often contrived to play jokes, and Erasmus may have introduced him under the name of Polus in his colloquy *Exorcismus sive spectrum* (ASD I-3 418–23). Erasmus wrote More in 1518 (Ep 829), referring to negotiations between Colt and Thomas *Grey over some land.

BIBLIOGRAPHY: Allen Ep 829 / E.E. Reynolds *The Field is Won – The Life and Death of St. Thomas More* (Milwaukee 1968) 53–5, 75–6 / R.W. Chambers *Sir Thomas More* (London 1935) 94–6 / *The Colloquies of Erasmus* ed C.R. Thompson (Chicago 1965) 230

CFG

Antoon COLVE *See Antonius* CLAVA

Arnoldus COMES (Ep 1316 of 18 October 1522)

Arnoldus Comes, who had apparently been recommended to Erasmus by Konrad *Heresbach, has not been identified. The family name of Graf is encountered frequently in Freiburg and other cities of the Upper Rhine region, but cf the biography of Primo de' *Conti.

PGB

COMES *See also Etienne* LECOMTE *and Primo de'* CONTI

Georg von COMMERSTADT *See Georg von* KOMERSTADT

Paulus COMMODUS Bretannus

In the *Hyperaspistes* (LB X 1255A) Erasmus refers to an epilogue published with *Luther's commentary on Galatians (first Latin ed, Leipzig 1519; Luther W II 436–618; Josef Benzing *Lutherbibliographie*, Baden-Baden 1966, nos 416–30). The epilogue is signed by Paulus Commodus Bretannus or Britannus; this is no doubt a pseudonym, perhaps for Philippus *Melanchthon of Bretten.

Johannes CONO of Nürnberg, c 1463– 21 February 1513

Cono (Conon, Cuno, Kuno, originally Kühn?) joined the Dominicans in his native city of Nürnberg at an early age. He devoted his entire life to humanistic studies, becoming one of Germany's best Greek scholars of his generation. By 1494 he was using in Nürnberg Greek manuscripts belonging to the Basel Dominicans, and by that time he seems to have studied Greek with Johann *Reuchlin at Heidelberg. At the turn of the century he was at Speyer, and in 1501 he is documented as the schoolmaster of the Dominican house of Liebenau, near Worms. He must have gone to Italy for the first time prior to 1499. In 1504 he went there again, studying until 1510, mostly at Padua under Johannes Gregoropoulos, Scipione *Fortiguerra, and especially Marcus *Musurus, but also visiting Ferrara, Rome, and Venice. In Venice he lent assistance to Aldo *Manuzio in a curious scheme to move the Aldine press to Germany in connection with a new academy to be founded under the patronage of *Maximilian I.

In 1510 Johann *Amerbach induced Cono to come to Basel, a move that was widely noticed among those interested in Greek studies. He helped in the preparation of patristic text editions, especially the monumental *Opera* of Jerome, on which Reuchlin too was working and which would eventually be published by Johann *Froben in 1516 under the direction of Erasmus (Ep 335; Allen I 63). While he had no connections with the university, he instructed the three *Amerbach sons in the Greek language, and also *Beatus Rhenanus, who in the summer of 1511 was attracted to Basel largely by Cono's presence, as he wrote (BRE Ep 21), and who soon gained Cono's special affection. After Cono's premature death it was Beatus who erected a funeral monument to him. He was left most of Cono's papers, although other manuscripts remained in the hands of the Amerbach brothers (Ep 885; AK II Ep 571) and probably of Cono's friend and compatriot Willibald *Pirckheimer (cf Ep 318).

Besides the edition of Jerome, Cono's scholarly work survived in an edition of Basil the Great (Padua 1507), in Beatus Rhenanus' editions of Gregory of Nyssa (Strasbourg: M. Schürer 1512), and Synesius of Cyrene (Basel: J. Froben 1515), and also in Cono's important letters to Pirckheimer, Beatus Rhenanus, and Reuchlin. A considerable number of manuscripts in Cono's hand have been identified, catalogued, and analysed by Sicherl, among them translations from the Greek Fathers. On 7 January 1511 Cono dedicated to Christoph von *Utenheim, bishop of Basel, a partial translation of St Basil's letter 197 to St Ambrose. Although Italy had inspired him to take a keen interest in Platonism, Cono's remarkable legacy to northern humanism lies rather in the promotion of Greek studies in general.

BIBLIOGRAPHY: Allen and CWE Ep 318 / *Pirckheimer Briefwechsel* I Epp 86, 139 / BRE Ep 25 and passim / Martin Sicherl *Johannes Cuno* (Heidelberg 1978) / Herbert Meyer 'Ein Kollegheft des Humanisten Conon' *Zentralblatt für Bibliothekswesen* 53 (1936) 281–4 / R. Wackernagel *Geschichte der Stadt Basel* (Basel 1907–54) III 140–1, *22–3 / AK I Ep 443, II Epp 551, 571, and passim / J. Tonjola *Basilea sepulta* (Basel

1661) 282 (funeral inscription) / H.O. Saffrey 'Un humaniste dominicain, Jean Cuno de Nuremberg, précurseur d'Erasme à Bâle' BHR 33 (1971) 19–62 (publishing documents and letters)

PGB

CONRADUS (Ep 1449 of 27 May 1524)
Conradus, said to be a servant of Heinrich *Eppendorf and a former servant of Ulrich von *Hutten, has not been identified.

CONRADUS Thuringus *See Conradus* THURINGUS

Guilhelmus CONRADUS *See Willem* COLGHENENS

CONRITZ *See* KÖNNERITZ

CONSTANTINE, duke of Ostrog *See Konstanty* OSTROGSKI

Angelo CONTARINI (Ep 611 of 20 July 1517)
The Angelo Contarini (Conterrenus) who met Ulrich von *Hutten at Venice in the spring of 1517 cannot be identified with certainty. For suggestions see the notes in Allen and CWE Ep 611.

Gasparo CONTARINI of Venice, 16 October 1483–24 August 1542
The son of the Venetian patrician Luigi Contarini (Contarenus) and Polissena Malipiero, Gasparo studied Latin under Marcantonio *Sabellico and Giorgio *Valla and learnt Greek from Marcus *Musurus. He studied philosophy and theology at the University of Padua; when the war of the League of Cambrai caused the university to be closed, he turned to intensive scriptural studies, withdrawing to the monastery of Camaldoli in the Apennines, near Arezzo, in 1510. At Easter 1511 a mystical experience convinced him that only faith in the expiatory passion of Christ could ensure justification. He decided to pursue his own evangelical mission, not in a religious order but in the world.

Gasparo held numerous important offices in the Venetian government, including *avogador del comun* in 1515, ambassador to *Charles V from 1521 to 1525, captain of Brescia in 1525, and head of the Council of Ten in 1530. In 1524 he wrote an influential book on the Venetian constitution and system of government, *De magistratibus et republica Venetorum* (Paris: M. Vascosan 1543). He also remained committed to the reform of the church, writing in 1516 *De officio episcopi* on the duties of a bishop and in 1518 *De immortalitate animae*, a reply to Pietro *Pomponazzi's book of the same name (1516). Another pressing concern for him was healing the schism caused by the Reformation, although he wrote a *Confutatio articulorum seu questionum Lutheranorum* in 1530.

Still a layman, Gasparo was created a cardinal on 21 May 1535 by Pope *Paul III. His appointment drew praise from many quarters (Ep 3066), and he soon established himself as a leader of Catholic reform and the spokesman of moderation and conciliation in dealing with the Protestant reformers. He headed the commission of 1536 which prepared the *Consilium de emendanda ecclesia* and later participated in the reform of the datary and of the penitentiary. In January 1538 he was among the cardinals named to begin preparations for a general council of the church. He also sought to reform the administration of the diocese of Belluno, which he received on 23 October 1536. In 1541 Contarini was sent as papal legate to the diet of Regensburg, where he led the Catholic delegation in an important meeting with the Lutherans, led by Philippus *Melanchthon. Although agreement was reached on the question of justification – an agreement which Rome later refused to ratify – the colloquy failed to reach a consensus on the Eucharist and other theological questions. The failure at Regensburg, soon followed by the death of Contarini, helped to stiffen the Catholic stance towards Protestantism, and leadership in Rome passed increasingly to the conservative faction led by Gianpietro Carafa, the future Pope *Paul IV.

Erasmus and Contarini held many views in common, and they may have met at Venice or Padua in 1507-8, but there is no evidence to suggest that they did, or that they corresponded.

Other writings of Contarini, dealing with justification, predestination, papal power, and

Gasparo Contarini by Allesandro Vittoria

many other theological and philosophical problems, were published after his death, both separately and among his *Opera* (Paris: S. Nivelle 1571).

BIBLIOGRAPHY: Allen Ep 3066 / Hubert Jedin's article in DHGE XIII 771-84 is the best biographical sketch of Contarini, and includes information about his writings and correspondence and an extensive bibliography / See also Jedin's *History of the Council of Trent* trans E. Graf (London 1957-) I, and Pastor X-XI / A recent contribution with useful references about Contarini's early life is J.B. Ross 'Gasparo Contarini and his friends' *Studies in the Renaissance* 17 (1970) 192-232

D.S. CHAMBERS

Primo de' CONTI of Milan, c 1498-1593
Primo, the son of Aloys de' Conti, was probably born in Milan. He studied Latin, Greek, Hebrew, and Chaldaic, and by 1532 was teaching rhetoric at Como. One of his pupils was his cousin the humanist Marcantonio Majoragio (1514-55). At an early date he came under the influence of St Girolamo

Emiliani (1481–1538), the founder of the Somaschi, and he eventually entered this congregation. From 1543 to 1546 he was in Milan, where he taught theology. The bishop of Como sent him to the Valtellina to preach to heretics, and Pius IV chose him to attend the final sessions of the council of Trent from 1562 to 1563 for the bishop of Padua. Gregory XIV extended many offers of preferment which Conti refused.

An admirer of Erasmus, Conti sent him a letter through Cyprianus *Bonaccursius on 20 August 1534, praising his De praeparatione ad mortem (Ep 2959). According to an anecdote of Majoragio, Conti visited Erasmus in Germany between 1529 and 1535. Erasmus, misunderstanding the signature 'Primus Comes Mediolanensis' on Conti's letter, expected a great noble. Although he made elaborate preparations for the visit he was delighted to find that Conti was a mere scholar.

Virtually nothing has survived of Conti's work. However Majoragio made him a principal speaker in his dialogue Antiparadoxon (Lyon: S. Gryphius 1546), and in 1572 Conti published Majoragio's edition of Aristotle's De arte rhetorica (Venice: F. dei Franceschi).

BIBLIOGRAPHY: Allen Ep 2959 / Quirinus Breen 'The Antiparadoxon of Marcantonius Majoragius ... ' Studies in the Renaissance 5 (1958) 37–48, esp 39 / Cosenza II 1064 / O.M. Paltrinieri Notizie intorno alla vita di Primo del Conte Milanese, della congregazione di Somasca, teologo al Concilio di Trento ... (Rome 1805)

TBD

Lambert COOMANS of Turnhout, d 1583
Lambert Coomans (Comannus) of Turnhout, in Brabant, was in Louvain by 1532, attached to Andreas *Balenus, a native of the same region, whose private student or perhaps amanuensis he was. Balenus recommended the young man to Cardinal Willem van *Enckenvoirt, who took Coomans with him to Rome. After two years of faithful service (Ep 3037), Coomans was present at the old cardinal's death (19 July 1534) and closed his eyes. He returned to Louvain and in August 1535 was recommended to Erasmus by Balenus and his colleague at the Collegium Trilingue, Conradus *Goclenius (Ep 3037). He arrived in Basel by the end of that month to become Erasmus' last famulus; after Gilbert *Cousin's departure,

he also assumed the functions of nurse and secretary (Epp 3097, 3104, 3115, 3122). Erasmus was greatly pleased with his services (Epp 3052, 3061, 3104) and left him a bequest of two hundred gold florins (Allen XI 364). After his master's death Coomans undertook a journey to the Low Countries on behalf of the executors of Erasmus' will (AK IV Epp 2052, 2056). With his return to Basel his duties ended, and he went back to Louvain, where he lived in Balenus' house and seems to have studied at the Trilingue. In March 1537 he successfully lodged a complaint about the loss he had suffered because Erasmus' two hundred gold florins were remitted to him at an unfavourable rate of exchange (AK V Ep 2122). Subsequently he returned to his native Turnhout, where he was appointed canon of the chapter of St Peter's and in 1559 was elected dean. His claims that Erasmus had died in his arms, commending himself to the Holy Virgin, cannot be verified independently.

BIBLIOGRAPHY: Allen Ep 3052 / AK V Ep 2122 / de Vocht CTL III 394–400 and passim / H. de Vocht 'Le dernier Amanuensis d'Erasme' Revue d'histoire ecclésiastique 45 (1950) 174–86 / Cornelis Reedijk 'Das Lebensende des Erasmus' Basler Zeitschrift für Geschichte und Altertumskunde 57 (1958) 23–65, esp 27–33 / Bierlaire Familia 100

FRANZ BIERLAIRE

Guillaume COP of Basel, d 2 December 1532
Wilhelm Kopp of Basel came to prominence among the court and academic circles of Paris and is therefore best known under the French form of his name, Guillaume Cop (Copus in Latin). He matriculated at the University of Basel during the winter term of 1478–9 and graduated MA in 1483. In Basel he was tutored by another student, Johann Heberling of Schwäbisch-Gmünd, who was a few years Cop's senior and himself a pupil of *Reuchlin (RE Epp 189, 203). After his promotion to MA Cop may have visited other centres of learning before proceeding to Paris, where he received the medical baccalaureate in 1492 and became a doctor of medicine on 17 May 1496. By that time he was already married to Etiennette Turgis, who became the mother of his four sons. Before 1498 Cop was a regent of the university; he also taught the surgeons medicine and from 1497 to

1512 was physician to the German nation. From 1512 he was personal physician to King *Louis XII and the following year he participated in the Thérouanne war against the English and was apparently present at the battle of the Spurs (16 August 1513). *Francis I too retained him, at the latest from 1523, when his name appears on the roll of royal physicians, and he continued in this position until his death.

From Paris Cop maintained his connections with Basel, visiting the city from time to time, keeping an eye on Basel students in Paris, and doing favours for the Basel printers. His dominant ties, however, were with the Paris humanist circles. He studied Greek with *Lascaris and with *Aleandro, who by 1510 dedicated to him his edition of Cicero's *De divinatione* (Paris: G. de Gourmont). Around 1505 he attended *Lefèvre, who was suffering from insomnia (Rice Ep 45). He worked closely with *Budé and others to promote the establishment of a royal college of ancient languages. In 1514 he spoke up for Reuchlin, who had been condemned by the theological faculty of Paris.

By 1497 Erasmus had met Cop in Paris at a time when he is not known to have had contacts with any other native of Basel. Then and again three years later he attended Erasmus during attacks of fever; by the latter date he had become a good friend (Epp 50, 124, 126; Reedijk poem 131). In 1506 Erasmus dedicated to him his important *Carmen alpestre* on the approach of old age (Reedijk poem 83). He praised Cop again publicly in 1514 when it seems that they had met on coinciding visits to Basel (Ep 305), and analogous praise recurred in years to follow (Epp 529, 534, 862, 868, 928; LB IX 788D), especially in a preface to the edition of St Jerome, where Erasmus told an anecdote to extol Cop's human qualities (Ep 326). In 1517 Cop and Budé were instructed to convey to Erasmus a royal offer designed to attract him to Paris (Epp 522, 523), and it was to Cop that Erasmus directed his dilatory answer (Ep 537). In 1526 Erasmus again wrote to Cop to consult him about his medical problems (Ep 1735), and they were still in touch in 1534, it seems (Ep 2509 AK IV Ep 1810).

Cop published Latin translations of Greek medical works by Paul of Aegina (Paris 1511), Galen (Paris 1513, 1528), and Hippocrates

(Paris 1511–12), whom he held in particularly high esteem. Erasmus' appreciation of Cop's translations (Ep 456) was shared by others such as *Beatus Rhenanus, the Polish physician Jan *Antonin (Ep 1810), and Petrus Ramus, but they have not, it seems, been evaluated by modern scholars.

BIBLIOGRAPHY: Allen Ep 124 / DBF IX 555 / *Matrikel Basel* I 157; cf 139 / J.-C. Margolin 'Le "Chant alpestre" d'Erasme: poème sur la vieillesse' BHR 27 (1965) 37–80, esp 49–54 / AK I Ep 211 and passim / Rice *Prefatory Epistles* Epp 45, 87, and passim / P.G. Bietenholz *Basle and France in the Sixteenth Century* (Geneva-Toronto 1971) 170–2, 278–9, and passim / de Vocht MHL 445–6 / Petrus Ramus *Basilea* ed and trans H. Fleig (Basel 1944) 43, 64 / Ernest Wickenheiser *Dictionnaire biographique des médecins en France au Moyen Age* (Paris 1936) I 235–8

PGB

Nicolas COP of Paris, c 1501–40
Nicolas, the third son of Erasmus' friend Guillaume *Cop, was born in Paris and studied philosophy and medicine in his native town. From 1530 he taught philosophy at the Collège de Sainte-Barbe, and on 10 October 1533 he was elected rector of the university for a term. He used the powers of his office to rehabilitate the *Miroir de l'âme pécheresse* (1531) by *Margaret, queen of Navarre, and in a convocation held at the monastery of the Mathurins on 1 November 1533 he read an address inspired by his friend Jean Calvin. It caused a furore and forced him to flee the country. Anticipating the route later to be taken by Calvin himself, he had reached Basel by February 1534 and from there made contact with Erasmus and Ludwig *Baer, old friends of his father, at Freiburg (Ep 2906; AK III Ep 1810 correcting the date of Allen Ep 2509). At the same time he remained in touch with the Strasbourg reformers; he was also a good friend of Ludovicus *Carinus, whom he may have known from Paris.

For the next three years Cop kept a suitably low profile, and his whereabouts are uncertain. Having to choose between the examples of his brothers Jean – who was a canon and lawyer in Paris – and Michel – who was to become a pastor in Geneva – Nicolas chose to return to Paris, where in May 1536 he became medical licentiate. A year later he was dispatched to Scotland to attend the newly wed queen of *James v, Madeleine, the daughter of *Francis I, who had fallen seriously ill. He also taught medicine at the University of Paris but died suddenly towards the end of the 1539–40 term.

BIBLIOGRAPHY: Allen Ep 2906 / DBF IX 555 / Eugène and Emile Haag *La France protestante* 2nd ed by H. Bordier (Paris 1877–   ) IV 615–17 / Herminjard III Epp 445, 458, and passim / Jean Rott 'Documents strasbourgeois concernant Calvin' *Revue d'histoire et de philosophie religieuses* 44 (1964) 290–335, esp 290ff / de Vocht MHL 430–58 passim / Pierre Jourda *Marguerite d'Angoulême* (Paris 1930, repr 1966) I 178–81 / Eugénie Droz *Chemins de l'hérésie* (Geneva 1970–   ) I 93–4

PGB

Nicolas COPPIN of Mons, d 16 June 1535
Nicolas Coppin (Meuran, Nicolaus Montensis, Copinus) of Mons registered at the University of Louvain on 10 December 1494, was a student at the College of the Falcon, and received his MA in 1497. He later taught philosophy at the Falcon, and as regent of his college from about 1510 succeeded in restoring order to its finances. On 31 August 1512 he was elected rector of the university and was later re-elected for a term in both 1520 and 1528. He received his doctorate in theology on 26 January 1513 and became professor of ethics and canon of St Peter's on 2 November 1514. In 1519 he succeeded Adrian of Utrecht (later Pope *Adrian VI) as a canon of St Peter's and in 1520 as the dean, a benefice that was combined with a theological chair and the office of chancellor. Not until the beginning of 1521 did he complete his move from the regency of the Falcon to the faculty of theology, of which he was elected dean in February 1522 and 1524, in August 1527, 1528, and 1530, and in February 1532. Prudent and very able, he exerted great influence among his colleagues and often filled high offices within the university.

Initially Coppin was on good terms with Erasmus; as regent of the Falcon he attempted to reconcile Erasmus and Nicolaas *Baechem in November 1520 (Ep 1162, 1225). But at the beginning of 1525 Erasmus learned from *Dorp that Coppin had turned against him, apparently under the influence of Bishop Erard de la

*Marck (Epp 1549, 1585) and also of Jacobus *Latomus (Ep 1700). Erasmus appealed to Chancellor *Gattinara and other members of the court of *Charles v and had the satisfaction of learning that Gattinara had actually written to Coppin on his behalf (Epp 1700, 1703, 1747, 1802).

By 1526 Coppin had begun to act as inquisitor (Ep 1719) and in this capacity he examined Jacques *Lefèvre d'Etaples' French Bible (Antwerp 1529–32). He died in 1535 (Ep 3037) and in his will founded scholarships at the colleges of the Falcon and the Holy Spirit.

BIBLIOGRAPHY: Allen Ep 1162 / de Vocht CTL I 403–5 and passim / de Vocht MHL 343 and passim / H. de Jongh *L'Ancienne Faculté de théologie de Louvain* (Louvain 1911) 160–1, and passim / *Matricule de Louvain* III-1 114, 450, 626, and passim / *Correspondance de Nicolas Clénard* ed A. Roersch (Brussels 1940–1) Ep 27 and passim

CFG & PGB

Gregorius COPPUS or COPUS *See Gregor* KOPP

Hadrianus CORDATUS of Middelburg, d 1538/9
Hadrianus Cordatus, the son of Johannes, was a canon of St Peter's, Middelburg, on the island of Walcheren. In 1511 he succeeded Simon of Wissekerke as pastor of the town's *béguinage*; from 1525 he was also vicar of West-Souburg (likewise on Walcheren). On suspicion of being a Lutheran, he was imprisoned briefly in 1527 in the castle of Vilvoorden (Ep 1899). In 1532 he was appointed chaplain of the Nieuwe Kerke at Amsterdam, but in 1534 new measures in defence of Catholic teaching led to his suspension. In 1536 he was again living at Middelburg; he died there and was replaced as pastor by Johannes Valladolid (d 1541).

Cordatus' major work, on the antiquities of Zeeland, is not preserved. He also wrote commendatory poems for Adrianus Cornelii *Barlandus' *De Hollandiae principibus* (Antwerp: J. Thibault July 1519; NK 235), for Nicolaas van *Broeckhoven's edition of Plautus' *Curculio* (Antwerp: M. Hillen c 1519; NK 3743), and for Jason Pratensis' *De tuenda sanitate* (Antwerp: M. Hillen 1538; NK 1753). Erasmus probably knew Cordatus personally; Pieter *Gillis received one of Erasmus' letters through him (Ep 681, dated 27 September 1517). Cordatus was praised by Barlandus and *Alaard of Amsterdam. Gerard *Geldenhouwer, who called him his 'Maecenas,' dedicated his eighth satire to him and Jan *Becker.

BIBLIOGRAPHY: Allen Ep 681, IV xxvii / J. Fruytier in NNBW VII 323 / J.G. de Hoop Scheffer in *Kerkhistorisch Archief* 4 (1866) 191, 403–4 / P.J. Meertens *Letterkundig leven in Zeeland* (Amsterdam 1943) 32 / A.F. Mellink *Amsterdam en de wederdopers* (Nijmegen 1978) 21–4

C.G. VAN LEIJENHORST

Balthasar de CORDES d 1529
Perhaps related to, or even identical with, one Balduwinus de Corde of the diocese of Tournai who matriculated at the University of Louvain in 1470, Balthasar de Cordes was by 1503 archdeacon of Valenciennes and subsequently became official to the bishop of Tournai and may have been the 'official of Bruges' mentioned in Ep 1355 of 27 March 1523.

BIBLIOGRAPHY: Allen Ep 1355 / de Vocht *Busleyden* 35, 38–9, 129 / *Matricule de Louvain* II-1 242

PGB

Maturin CORDIER d September 1564
Cordier's name was erroneously suggested in Allen Ep 2633:42n in connection with a convocation of the University of Paris held in the monastery of the Mathurins or Trinitarians.

MICHEL REULOS

Euricius CORDUS of Frankenberg, 1484–24 December 1535
Euricius Cordus (Heinrich Ritze Solden), the son of Urban Solden, a burgher of Frankenberg, on the Eder west of Kassel, was born in Simtshausen, near Marburg. He matriculated in Erfurt in 1505, became master of a school at Kassel in 1511, married Kunigunde Dünnwald in 1514, and in 1516 was appointed rector of the school of St Mary's chapter in Erfurt, after receiving his MA degree from the university. In the faculty of arts Cordus taught poetry and rhetoric and lectured on Virgil's *Bucolica*; in 1519, however, he began to study medicine. He belonged to the circle of Erfurt humanists

and poets and was a good friend of *Eobanus Hessus. He went to Italy in 1521, studied under Niccolò *Leoniceno in Ferrara, and obtained a doctorate in medicine within six months. In 1523 Cordus returned to Erfurt but soon accepted an appointment as town physician in Brunswick. In 1527 he became professor of medicine at the newly founded University of Marburg. Six years later he was town physician and teacher at the Gymnasium of Bremen, where he remained until his death.

Cordus' importance lies first in his Latin poems and secondly in his pharmaco-medical works. After his death his collected poems were published, without place and date, around 1550. His first publication was the *Bucolicorum eclogae* (1514); his poem of thanks for escaping death by drowning in 1515 and his elegies (*Ex Nosematostichis*) in 1517 and 1519 show his gift as a poet. In his epigrams, especially in the *Antilutheromastix* (1525), Cordus advocated a science free from dogmatism and superstitions such as astrology. Subsequently he pursued the same ends in his scientific publications such as the *Botanologicon* (Cologne: J. Gymnich 1534) and *De abusu uroscopiae* (Frankfurt 1536). His collected *Opera poetica* were edited by H. Meibom (Helmstedt 1614); there is also a new edition of the *Epigrammata* of 1520 by K. Krause (Berlin 1892).

Cordus' admiration for Erasmus is shown most clearly in his *Palinodia* of 1519 (Ep 1008 introduction) and in a Christmas hymn of 1521. In 1519 Erasmus replied to a letter from Cordus (Ep 941) wishing him good luck with his school in Erfurt.

BIBLIOGRAPHY: Allen and CWE Ep 941 / NDB III 358–9 / ADB IV 476–9 / *Matrikel Erfurt* II 242 / Georg Ellinger *Geschichte der neulateinischen Literatur Deutschlands im sechzehnten Jahrhundert* (Berlin-Leipzig 1929–33) II 23–8

IG

Johannes CORICIUS *See Johannes* CORYCIUS

Janus CORNARIUS of Zwickau, c 1500–16 March 1558
Johann Hainpol (Heypol, Haynpol, Hagenbut), who called himself Janus Cornarius from 1519 or 1520, was the son of Simon, a shoemaker. After attending the Latin school in his native Zwickau, he matriculated in the

summer of 1517 at Leipzig, where he studied under Petrus *Mosellanus and obtained a BA on 13 September 1518. On 30 May 1519 he enrolled at Wittenberg; he obtained his MA on 24 January 1521 and a licence in medicine on 9 December 1523, while also teaching Greek. Subsequently he visited Livonia, Sweden, Denmark, England, and France, was in Rostock in October 1525, and stopped at Louvain, where he enjoyed the hospitality of Simon *Riquinus. He left in 1528 after a quarrel with Riquinus' wife, who, it seems, felt intimidated by her tall guest and his language (Ep 2246). He travelled up the Rhine valley as far as Strasbourg, where he obtained an introduction from Heinrich *Eppendorf to Bonifacius *Amerbach (AK III Ep 1285; cf also Ep 1321). In September 1528 he turned up in Basel, seeking employment. He had meanwhile specialized in a thorough study of Greek medicine, which he preferred to the Arabic medical tradition, and apparently gave some lectures on this topic at the University of Basel (AK III Ep 1313). While Amerbach was unable to secure employment for him at Basel and a letter to Udalricus *Zasius at Freiburg produced no results there either (AK III Epp 1296–7, 1304), Hieronymus *Froben gave him access to his library; Cornarius also worked for Johann *Bebel and established a close connection with the Basel printers which lasted until his death.

In 1530 Cornarius returned to Zwickau, set up his medical practice, and on 1 June 1530 married Anna Bärensprung, the burgomaster's daughter, who died shortly after the wedding. On 12 October 1530 he married Ursula Göpfart, an innkeeper's daughter; they had four sons, who all received a good education. Cornarius lectured in 1532 in Rostock on Hippocrates and Aristotle and was a physician in Nordhausen, in Saxony, from 1535 to 1537 and in Frankfurt am Main from 1538 to 1542. In 1543 he went to Marburg, where he became professor of medicine in 1545; in 1546 he was appointed town physician in Zwickau. In 1557 he accepted a chair of medicine at Jena and died there the following year.

Janus Cornarius was a prolific writer and editor. His *Universae rei medicae ἐπιγραφή* (Basel: H. Froben 1529) was dedicated to the citizens of Zwickau who had supported him during his studies. He edited and translated many Greek texts, primarily by medical authors, but also by other writers and even Fathers of the church. In addition to his contributions to the great Basel editions of Hippocrates (Greek and Latin, 1538) and Galen (Latin, 1549), one notes works by Dioscorides (1529) and Aetius (1542), Parthenius (1531), Artemidorus (1539), Basil (1540, 1551), Epiphanius (1543), and Chrysostom (1544). He also wrote *De peste libri duo* (Basel: J. Herwagen 1551), and edited a selection of Greek epigrams with Andrea *Alciati's translations (Basel: J. Bebel 1529), although Alciati was not entirely happy with Cornarius' efforts (AK III Epp 1347, 1400).

While in Basel, Cornarius made the acquaintance of Erasmus, who was impressed by his achievements and encouraged him, as he was preparing to leave for Wittenberg and Zwickau, to continue his translations of Hippocrates (Ep 2204).

BIBLIOGRAPHY: Allen Ep 2204 / ADB IV 481 / de Vocht CTL II 388–90 / *Matrikel Leipzig* I 557, II 530 / *Matrikel Wittenberg* I 82 / *Matrikel Rostock* II 88 / AK III Ep 1295 and passim / Pflug *Correspondance* III Ep 521 and passim

IG

Vincentius CORNELII *See Vincent* CORNELISSEN

CORNELIS of Bergen (Ep 1562 of 26 March 1525)
Cornelis of Bergen (Cornelius Bergensis), an old friend addressed by Erasmus in Ep 1562, has not been identified.

CORNELIS of Duiveland documented 1523–5
In March 1525 the Antwerp printer Simon Cocus published an *Apologia* directed against Erasmus' *Exomologesis* (1524). The *Apologia*, dedicated to Erasmus' old opponent Edward *Lee, claimed to be the work of a theologian, whose name was given as Godefridus Ruysius Taxander. Erasmus soon came to believe that it had been produced by four Dominicans of Louvain: Vicentius *Theoderici, Walter *Ruys, Govaert *Strijroy, and Cornelis of Duiveland (Duvellandius, Duvelandus, Dunelandius; Epp 1603, 1608, 1621, 1624, 2045). A friar Cornelis of Duiveland (in Zeeland) matriculated at the University of Louvain on 29 September 1523, but no more seems to be

known about him. In Ep 1655 Erasmus gave his name as Cornelius Taxander; Henry de Vocht suggested that his family name might have been van Kampen or Kempen, rendered in Greek as Taxander. In September 1528 Erasmus recalled that the Dominicans connected with the *Apologia* had dispersed soon after its appearance, one of them going to Zeeland (Ep 2045); presumably this would have been Cornelis.

BIBLIOGRAPHY: Allen Ep 1603 / *Matricule de Louvain* III-1 712 / de Vocht *Literae ad Cranevel-dium* Ep 148 / de Vocht CTL II 262

PGB

CORNELIS of Woerden documented c 1480– c 1493

Cornelis (Cornelius, Cantelius) is identified as a native of Woerden, west of Utrecht, in Ep 296. He is mentioned again, with additional detail, in Ep 447, where his name is given as 'Cantelius,' and in Erasmus' *Compendium vitae* (Allen I 46–52; CWE 4 399–410). Apart from these statements by Erasmus practically no information on Cornelis has come to light.

Cornelis was a few years older than Erasmus, who met him at the chapter school of St Lebuin in Deventer, where they shared a room (Allen Ep 447:298ff; Allen I 50; CWE 4 407). Subsequently Cornelis travelled to Italy, but his studies there were not very fruitful since his intelligence was less remarkable than his beautiful voice (hence the use of 'Cantelius' to disguise his name: CWE Ep 447:326n). After his return from Italy Cornelis entered the monastery of the canons regular of St Augustine at Steyn, near Gouda, and there made his profession. When Erasmus returned to Gouda in about 1487, he met Cornelis again and was persuaded by him to move to Steyn and eventually to make his profession, although Erasmus himself claimed later that he had been inclined to leave rather than take the irreversible vows. It seems that Cornelis was still living at Steyn by 1493; there is a letter from Willem *Hermans to Cornelis *Gerard, written at about this time and carried by a certain Cornelis. Reyner *Snoy, when copying this letter (Gouda MS 1323), identified the bearer tentatively with Cornelis of Woerden.

Cornelis of Woerden should not be identified (as tentatively suggested in CWE 4 407:91n)

with Cornelis Gerard, who had neither gone to Italy nor lived at Steyn and was, according to all testimony, highly gifted.

BIBLIOGRAPHY: Allen and CWE Ep 296 / Hermans' letter is published by P.C. Molhuysen in *Nederlandsch Archief voor Kerk-geschiedenis* n s 4 (1907) 65–8

C.J. VAN LEIJENHORST

Vincent CORNELISSEN van Mierop of The Hague, 1480–1550/1

Vincent Cornelissen van Mierop (Mijrop) entered the service of the future *Charles v in 1505 and came to fill various positions in the administration of finance; he possessed the lordship of Cabauw, north-east of Schoonhoven. When he appears in Erasmus' correspondence in the years 1533–5 he is always associated with the council of Holland in The Hague (see especially Ep 3037), and the first of two known letters Erasmus wrote to him (Epp 2819, 2923) is also addressed to Holland. Both deal with the disputed amount of a cash gift the states of Holland had granted Erasmus, a question that exercised him considerably (Epp 2896, 2913, 2922, 2924). From 1 October 1531 Cornelissen was also a member of the council of finance at the court of Brussels. In 1546 he succeeded Jean *Ruffault as treasurer-general and was in turn followed in that office by Laurens Longin in 1551. Allen refers to the epitaph Cornelissen wrote for himself in Brussels and to a prefatory letter addressed to him in an edition of Philip of Leiden's *De reipublicae cura et sorte* (Leiden: J. Severinus 1516).

BIBLIOGRAPHY: Allen Ep 2819 / Michel Baelde *De Collaterale Raden onder Karel v en Filips II* (Brussels 1965) 22, 248, and passim; cf 222, 285 / *Matricule de Louvain* IV-2 411, 428

PGB

CORNELIUS See Cornelis BATT, Jean and Aimé CORNIER, and Vincent CORNELISSEN

Adriano CORNETO, CORNETUS See Adriano CASTELLESI

Petrus de CORNIBUS of Beaune, d 21 May 1549

Petrus de Cornibus (de Cornu, Cornutus, Pierre de Cornes), a Franciscan, was born in

Beaune in the diocese of Autun. In 1519 a letter to Petrus from Friar Georgius de Raya suggests that the addressee was a student of Pierre *Tartaret. There is no evidence for the supposition that Petrus was ever a regent in the Collège de Navarre. He took his licence in theology on 15 February 1524, ranking sixth of twenty-five, and his doctorate on 6 June 1524. He was a teacher of the Spanish friar Luis de *Carjaval, who became a leading anti-Erasmian in Spain.

Petrus de Cornibus was a renowned preacher. He was called upon to harangue Cardinal Antoine *Du Prat, chancellor of France and papal legate, in his Paris entry in 1530. He preached at the funeral of Alberto *Pio in 1531 and at several other civic and religious manifestations in Paris. St Francis Xavier wrote from India that he would like to invite Petrus to join his mission. Petrus was the warden of the Paris Franciscan convent from at least 1528 to 1532. He served on committees of the faculty of theology for several important affairs and was appointed on 2 January 1534 to advise the Parlement of Paris on matters of faith. Most authors have accepted Théodore de Bèze's citation of a spurious epitaph to conclude that Petrus died in 1542, but he appeared in the faculty of theology on 1 April 1546. He died in 1549 and was buried in the Franciscan convent chapel in Paris.

Erasmus complained several times about Petrus' 'confused babbling,' especially when he linked Erasmus' name with *Luther (Epp 2126, 2205, 2466; ASD IV-2 36). *Rabelais satirized Petrus in two different passages (*Pantagruel* ch 15, *Le Tiers Livre* ch 14) but suppressed these in the 1542 edition.

BIBLIOGRAPHY: Allen Ep 2126:164n / Farge no 115

JAMES K. FARGE

Jean and Aimé CORNIER documented 1536–50

In a letter of 1536 (Ep 3123) Gilbert *Cousin reports the good progress of the Κορνηλίων school at Nozeroy, Franche-Comté. The reference no doubt concerns the brothers Jean and Aimé (Erasmus) Cornier (Cournier, Corneille, Cornelius), friends of Cousin who wrote an enthusiastic letter addressed to Jean and an epigram addressed to Aimé. On 12 April 1537 Jean, then headmaster of the Nozeroy school, was called before the Parlement of Dole to answer a charge of heresy. Released on bail, he preferred not to await the further proceedings and was last heard of teaching at the newly founded college at Lausanne (1540–5). Aimé was a schoolmaster at Montbéliard from May 1541 until 1544, when he was arrested during a temporary triumph of the Lutheran over the Calvinist faction in the county. After an interlude at Neuchâtel, he was called in 1546 to Geneva, where Calvin entrusted to him the direction of the school which became later the Collège. He died in 1550.

BIBLIOGRAPHY: Allen Ep 3123 / Eugène and Emile Haag *La France protestante* 2nd ed by H. Bordier (Paris 1877–) IV 709–10 / Gilbert Cousin *Opera* (Basel 1562) I 295–6, 406 / Lucien Febvre *Notes et documents sur la réforme et l'inquisition en Franche-Comté* (Paris 1911) 84 / E. Monot 'Gilbert Cousin et son école de Nozeroy' *Mémoires de la Société d'émulation du Jura* XII-1 (1928–9) 3–69, esp 11 / Ferdinand Buisson *Sébastien Castellion* (Paris 1892) I 233 / Herminjard VI Ep 858, VII Ep 963, VIII Ep 1225 bis, and passim / Henri Vuilleumier *Histoire de l'église réformée du pays de Vaud* (Lausanne 1927–33) I 398–9 / John Viénot *Histoire de la réforme dans le pays de Montbéliard* (Paris 1900) I 84, 106, 111 / Jean Calvin *Opera* (Brunswick 1863–1900) XII Epp 713, 756, and passim

PGB

Petrus CORNUTUS *See Petrus de* CORNIBUS

Luis Núñez CORONEL of Segovia, d c March 1531

Luis Coronel and his younger brother, Antonio, the sons of Núñez Coronel, both studied at Salamanca before going to Paris to study under John Mair (Major) at the Collège de Montaigu. Luis figures with his brother – but less prominently – in letters published in several of Mair's works. Until at least 1508 he taught arts at Montaigu, where one of his students was Eligius Hoeckaert, who later became an illustrious schoolmaster in Ghent; a letter from Hoeckaert to Coronel appears in Hoeckaert's *Commentarius super obitu Maximiliani* (Ghent: Pieter de Keysere 1519). Coronel was already a student at the Paris faculty of

theology around 1502 and was a *hospes* of the
Collège de Sorbonne in 1504 and *socius* in
1508. He obtained his licence in theology on 26
January 1514, ranking fifth of twenty-five, and
his doctorate on 29 May 1514. He remained in
Paris for three years and was moderately active
on the faculty of theology, while his brother
finished his doctorate. The latest date known
for the brothers in Paris is September 1517.

While still in Paris, Luis Coronel had held
three benefices in the diocese of Thérouanne,
in Flanders. By 1519, both brothers were
named councillors, preachers, and confessors
in the court of *Charles v, and they benefited
from his orders in 1519 and 1522 authorizing
the payment of debts owed to their deceased
father. Luis Coronel was in the service of the
inquisitor Frans van der *Hulst in Brussels in
1521 and early 1522 and served in the same
capacity in Ghent, Bruges, and Antwerp from 8
May to 3 June 1522. Coronel's name appears in
the 'Boke of the Emperor's Trayne' as accompanying Charles v to England in late May 1522
but he was obviously left behind with the
'Grande Chapelle' when England refused to
accommodate the planned retinue of 2044 persons. He returned to Spain, where he remained. On *Vives' report, Luis Coronel
became so convinced of the rightness of
Erasmus' goals and methods that he regarded
Erasmus as another Jerome or Augustine (Ep
1281). In the spring of 1522 he complimented
Erasmus on his *Paraphrasis in Matthaeum*
dedicated to Charles v (cf LB IX 801) and
pleaded with him to use great caution in his
statements on religious matters. Erasmus'
response to this was measured but generally
warm (Ep 1274; cf Ep 1285). When Coronel was
in Spain Erasmus kept in touch (Epp 1431,
1904, 1907, 2297, 2301) and was rewarded with
a written defence of the *Enchiridion* against
Spanish critics (Ep 1581), which has unfortunately not survived. As secretary to Alonso
*Manrique, archbishop of Seville and inquisitor-
general of Spain, Coronel was in an advantageous position to help Erasmus, especially
during the theological investigations of Erasmus at Valladolid in 1527 (Epp 1836, 1847,
1980). But as the anti-Erasmian spirit advanced, Coronel's influence also declined. His
death in 1531 possibly hastened the demise of
Erasmianism in Spain.

Luis Coronel had been given a living in the
abbey of San Isidro of León. A misreading of
Vives' letter to Erasmus in 1527 (Ep 1836) has
caused some modern writers to conclude
wrongly that Coronel was bishop of Las
Palmas in the Canary Islands. His works
include: *Tractatus syllogismorum* (Paris: Jean
Barbier and Denis Roce 1507, Michel Lesclan-
cher for Bernard Aubry 1518) and *Physicae
perscrutationes* (Paris: Jean Barbier 1511; Lyon:
Simon Vincent 1512, J. Giunta 1530; Alcalá
1539).

BIBLIOGRAPHY: Allen Ep 1274 / Bataillon
Erasmo y España 17 and passim / *Cartulario de
Salamanca* ed V. Beltrán de Heredia (Salamanca
1970–1) III 413–4, 421 / Farge no 117 / P.-Y. Féret
*La Faculté de théologie de Paris et ses docteurs les
plus célèbres. Epoque moderne* (Paris 1900–10) II
65 / H. Kenniston *Francisco de los Cobos*
(Pittsburgh 1959) 72 / LP III-2 967 / de Vocht CTL
III 443

JAMES K. FARGE

Dionysius CORONIUS documented 1518–51
Dionysius Coronius (Coroné, Corron, Char-
ron), a native of the diocese of Chartres, was
elected procurator of the French nation at the
University of Paris on 20 October 1518. He
attached himself to Cardinal François de
*Tournon, whom he accompanied to Bologna
in 1531. In the following year he tutored the
cardinal's nephews. From about 1543 until
after 1551 he held the royal chair of Greek at
Paris.

In 1522 Jean *Lange mentioned Coronius in a
dedicatory preface among other scholarly
recipients favoured by princes of the church
(Rice Ep 133), and in the same year Coronius
wrote to Erasmus, who acknowledged the
letter when writing to the cardinal but did not
intend to answer Coronius directly (Ep 1319).
Coronius was a good friend of Jean *Du Ruel,
whom he helped with his *De natura stirpium*
(Paris: S. de Colines 1536). He also wrote an
epitaph for Du Ruel and published or re-edited
posthumously his translations of Greek medical works by Dioscorides (1537) and Johannes
Actuarius (1539).

BIBLIOGRAPHY: Allen Ep 1319 / Michel François *Le cardinal François de Tournon* (Paris 1951)
510 / Rice *Prefatory Epistles* Ep 133

MICHEL REULOS

Denis CORRON *See Dionysius* CORONIUS

Pietro CORSI of Carpi, documented 1509–37
Corsi (Petrus Cursius) was a native of Carpi, in
Emilia, but the dates of both his birth and death
are unknown. A priest attached to the curia of
Pope *Paul III, he is given the title of canon of
Tarragona ('Petrus Cursius Carpinetanus ca-
nonicus Tarraconensis') in the dedication of
an unpublished eclogue. A typical representative of the epigonic aspects of Roman culture
at the time of the Counter-Reformation, he
was a member of the Roman Academy and
fully shared its concern for a rigorous Ciceronianism, a concern which had aroused the
scorn of Erasmus.

Apart from some unpublished letters, three
eclogues by Corsi have been preserved in
manuscript, including one that was recited in
1509 in the basilica of Santa Maria Maggiore.
Religious in scope and pagan in form and
content, it retains a certain interest for its
revelation of dramatic taste at the curia of Pope
*Julius II. Among his publications the poems
*De Civitate Castellana Faliscorum non Veientium
oppido* (Rome 1525) and *In atrocissima urbis
Romanae direptione et exidio deploratio* (Rome
1528) may be noted, while some of his epigrams
are found in two anthologies, *Coryciana* (Rome:
L. de Henricis and L. Perusinus 1524) and
Deliciae CC Italorum poetarum (Rome 1608).

If it were not for his controversy with
Erasmus, Corsi might today be largely forgotten. A tradition of Italian patriotic protest
against Erasmus had been launched by Corsi's
countryman Alberto *Pio, prince of Carpi.
Interrupted after Pio's death in 1531, this
tradition was resumed when Corsi published
his *Defensio pro Italia ad Erasmum Roterodamum*
(Rome: A. Bladus 1535, the dedicatory letter to
Paul III dated 24 November 1534). Claiming
that in the *Adagia* Erasmus had questioned the
military valour of the Italians, Corsi replied by
presenting evidence of their glorious deeds
since 1494. Erasmus was promptly informed of
Corsi's book by his Roman friends (Ep 3007); he
also received a copy but was at first reluctant to
read it (Ep 3015). In August 1535 he did,
however, produce a reply in the form of a long
letter addressed to Johann *Koler. It was
published without delay and is reprinted in
Allen as Ep 3032. The controversy is mentioned

repeatedly in Erasmus' correspondence of
1535–6.

BIBLIOGRAPHY: Allen Ep 3007 / V. Cian in
Giornale storico della letteratura italiana 11 (1888)
240 / G. Toffanin *Il Cinquecento* Storia letteraria
d'Italia VI (Milan 1929) 66 / R. Valentini 'Erasmo
da Rotterdamo e Pietro Corsi ... ' *Rendiconti
della R. Accademia dei Lincei* sixth series 12 (1936)
896–922 / D. Cantimori 'Note su Erasmo e
l'Italia' *Rivista di studi germanici* 2 (1937) 145–70
MARCO BERNUZZI

Pieter de CORTE of Bruges, 1491–17 October
1567
Pieter de Corte (Curtius), a member of an old
and distinguished Bruges family, matriculated
in Louvain on 3 September 1509 and studied at
the College of the Lily. He was a BA in 1510 and
received his MA from Maarten van *Dorp on 11
July 1513. Two years later he was appointed
professor of eloquence at the Lily, having been
admitted to the council of the faculty of arts. In
1518 he became a bachelor of divinity and a
member of the university council. From 1522 he
was regent of the Lily, at first jointly with Jan
*Heems and later on his own (Ep 1932). On 27
February 1530 he was elected rector of the
university and, when he was promoted master
of divinity on 12 July, the ceremony was
conducted with greater than usual solemnity
because of his rank.

Meanwhile de Corte had also received
several benefices, including from 1529 the
parish of St Peter's, Louvain, where he
preached forcefully against the reformers. In
1531 he became professor of theology, a post
which he retained for more than thirty years.
He was rector again in 1538 and 1548 and also
served in other administrative functions, such
as book censor, and from 1 July 1560 inquisitor.
After the council of Trent he was a member of
the commission appointed to establish new
dioceses in the Netherlands, and on 26
December 1561 he was himself consecrated first
bishop of Bruges. He promulgated the decrees
of Trent in his diocese, had to deal with a wave
of iconoclasm in 1566, and on occasion did
battle with the chapter of St Donatian and the
city council, both of which were intent on
defending their privileges.

De Corte combined his firm stand in defence
of Catholic orthodoxy with warm support for

Erasmus' Christian humanism. They must have been on intimate terms during the years 1517–21 when both lived at the Lily. When de Corte became regent after Erasmus' departure for Basel, he instituted a regular course of Greek at the college. He supported the Collegium Trilingue and was close to many of Erasmus' good friends both in Louvain and in Bruges, including Dorp, *Lips, *Vives, Marcus *Laurinus, *Fevijn, and *Cranevelt, to whom he wrote a number of letters over the years. In his only surviving letter to Erasmus (Ep 1537, 21 January 1525), a warm and spontaneous communication, de Corte informed his friend of the pressures he had to withstand in order to ensure the continued use of the *Colloquia* and the *Enchiridion* among the students of the Lily. In August 1526 he visited Bruges and reported to Vives how Erasmus' opponents at Louvain were losing, one by one, their old leaders and pillars of strength (Ep 1732). After Dorp's death he helped *Goclenius recover a manuscript provided for Dorp by Erasmus (Ep 1899). In 1530 Erasmus was promptly informed of de Corte's solemn promotion, which led to a joyful gathering of his friends from Bruges and Louvain, notwithstanding a silly speech made by the conservative Eustachius van der *Rivieren (Epp 2352, 2353). Although no subsequent traces of contact appear to exist, nothing suggests a cooling of the friendship between de Corte and Erasmus; cf also Ep 1347.

BIBLIOGRAPHY: Allen Ep 1347 / de Vocht *Literae ad Craneveldium* Ep 83 and passim / de Vocht CTL I 83–4, III 131–5, 574–5, and passim

                                                                    PGB

Theodoricus CORTEHOEVIUS documented 1530

Of Theodoricus Cortehoevius, apparently from Kortenhoef, west of Hilversum, nothing seems to be known except that he wrote a moral dialogue entitled *Bellum discors sophiae ac philautiae, veritatis ac falsitatis* (Antwerp: M. de Keyser for G. van der Haghen 12 November 1530; NK 619) and edited a selection from Erasmus' adages, *Adagiorum aureum flumen* (Antwerp: M. de Keyser for G. van der Haghen 16 February 1530; NK 772), which he dedicated to Erasmus (Ep 2265).

BIBLIOGRAPHY: Allen Ep 2265 / E. Daxhelet

Adrien Barlandus, humaniste belge, 1486–1538 (Louvain 1938, repr 1967) 144

                                                    C.G. VAN LEIJENHORST

Paolo CORTESI of San Gimignano, 1465/71–1510

Paolo Cortesi (Cortesius), a son of Antonio, head of the college of abbreviators in the Roman curia, and of Aldobrandina degli Aldobrandini of Florence, and the brother of Alessandro, Lattanzio, and Caterina, was educated in Florence and Rome. Like Alessandro, Paolo served in the curia, first as apostolic scriptor (1481) and later as apostolic secretary (1498). His home in Rome was a centre for literary discussions. Besides fellow humanists and curialists, he corresponded with cardinals, other high prelates, and secular rulers. He left Rome in 1503 as papal protonotary and retired to his villa near San Gimignano, the family home, where he died.

Cortesi's dialogue *De hominibus doctis* (1490–1, first printed 1734), dedicated to Lorenzo (I) de' *Medici, is the first critical discussion of Renaissance humanistic Latin. In a famous epistolary controversy with Angelo *Poliziano, Cortesi proposed a strict theory of Ciceronian imitation; his ideas on imitation were taken up and expanded by Pietro *Bembo. Cortesi was a leader of the Ciceronians in Rome during his residence there. In 1504 he published his *Sententiarum libri quattuor* (Rome: E. Silber) a reworking of traditional scholastic theology in strict Ciceronian Latin. It sought to return theology to an eloquent form as well to interest other humanists in theological studies. It enjoyed some popularity in northern humanistic circles and was reprinted three times (Paris: J. Bade 1513, Basel: J. Froben 1513 and H. Petri 1540, the last two with introductions by Konrad *Peutinger and *Beatus Rhenanus). The last years of his life were devoted to the composition of his *De cardinalatu* ('Castro Cortesio': S.N. Nardi 1510) which was printed after his death. Directed at the new class of higher bureaucrat represented by the cardinal, *De cardinalatu* attempted to prescribe rules for all aspects of life. Cortesi used a highly archaic Latin in the work.

Cortesi mentioned Erasmus' *Adagia* in *De cardinalatu* (f M 1 verso) and praised him for his learning (f N 14 recto). There is the possibility that Erasmus was familiar with the *Sententiarum libri quattour* (also called *In Sententias*), since Beatus Rhenanus had it reprinted in 1513. It has been suggested that some of the Ciceronian terms used for Christian ideas in the *Ciceronianus* were based on the *Sententiarum libri quattuor* (see Farris in bibliography). At any rate, in the *Ciceronianus* Erasmus shows his familiarity with Cortesi's views on imitation. Basing himself on the epistolary exchange between Poliziano and Cortesi, Erasmus presents Cortesi as inferior to Poliziano in style even though the former prided himself on imitating the Roman orator. Cortesi is thus one of Erasmus' examples of the failure of Ciceronianism as a literary movement (*Ciceronianus*, ASD I-2 667–8, 705–7).

BIBLIOGRAPHY: Older works can be found mentioned in Paolo Cortesi *De hominibus doctis dialogus* ed and trans Maria Teresa Graziosi (Rome 1972) and Roberto Weiss in *Dizionario critico della letteratura italiana* (Turin 1972) 633–36 / Carlo Dionisotti 'Umanisti dimenticati?' *Italia medioevale e umanistica* 4 (1961) 287–331 / Nino Pirotta 'Music and cultural tendencies in fifteenth century Italy' *Journal of the American Musicological Society* 19/2 (1966) 147–161 / Anna Gracci 'Studio su Paolo Cortesi da San Gimignano ed il suo *De Cardinalatu*' (thesis, University of Florence 1966–7) / Giacomo Ferraù 'Il *De hominibus doctis* di Paolo Cortesi' in *Umanità e storia: scritti in onore di Adelchi Attisani* (Naples 1971) II 261–90 / Giovanni Farris *Eloquenza e teologia del 'Prooemium in librum primum Sententiarum' di Paolo Cortese* (Savona n d) / *Renaissance Philosophy: New Translations* ed L.A. Kennedy (The Hague 1973) 29–37 / John F. D'Amico 'Humanism and theology at papal Rome, 1480–1520' (doctoral thesis, University of Rochester 1977) / Kathleen Weil-Garris and John F. D'Amico 'The Renaissance cardinal's ideal palace: a chapter from Cortesi's *De Cardinalatu*' in *Studies in Italian Art and Architecture, 15th through 18th Centuries* ed Henry A. Millon (Rome 1980) / Denys Hay 'Renaissance cardinals' *Synthesis* 3 (1976) 35–46 / Maria Teresa Graziosi 'Spigolature cortesiane' *Atti e memorie dell' Accademia dell' Arcadia* ser 3, 7 (1977) 67–84

JOHN F. D'AMICO

Franceschino CORTI of Pavia, 1463–23 June 1533
Franceschino Corti (Franciscus Curtius Junior), a nephew of the jurist Francesco Corti (d 1495), was born at Pavia and taught law there until 1512, when he left because of political turmoil. A supporter of the schismatic council of Pisa, on 2 February 1511 or 1512 he was one of three ambassadors sent to persuade the bishops of Germany of the legitimacy of the council. He was later named judge of appeals at Mantua and a councillor of *Francis I of France. He taught law at Pisa in 1514, then again at Pavia. In 1527 Pavia was sacked by the French under Lautrec, and Corti was taken hostage, according to Tiraboschi and Allen by imperial troops. He was ransomed by the Venetians to teach at Padua, where he died. Writing to Erasmus in January 1532, *Viglius Zuichemus identified him as a brother of Matteo *Corti, a professor of medicine, and as the leading jurist at Padua (Ep 2594).

Corti's works included the *Tractatus feudalis* (Venice: Gregorius de Gregoriis 1507) and various *Consilia*, which were published a number of times through the sixteenth century.

BIBLIOGRAPHY: Allen Ep 2594 / AK IV Epp 1616, 1760, and passim / Mario Ascheri *Un maestro del mos italicus: Gianfrancesco Sannazari della Ripa (1480–1535)* (Milan 1970) 13–14 and passim / Augustin Renaudet *Le Concile gallican de Pise-Milan, documents florentins* (Paris 1922) 611 / Girolamo Tiraboschi *Storia della letteratura italiana* (Rome 1782–97) VII-2 107–9

TBD

Matteo CORTI of Pavia, c 1475–1544?
Matteo Corti (Corte, Matthaeus Curtius) was apparently educated at the University of Pavia and began teaching there at the age of twenty-two. He later taught medicine at the universities of Padua, Bologna, and Pisa, by the end of his career becoming one of the most sought-after and highest paid professors of medicine in Italy. He also served for a time as the personal physician of Pope *Clement VII and of Cosimo I de' Medici. He left behind many medical works, including a large number which remain in manuscript. Writing to Erasmus from Padua, *Viglius Zuichemus mentioned him twice (Epp 2594, 2716), but there is

no evidence of any direct connection with Erasmus.

BIBLIOGRAPHY: Allen Ep 2594 / G. Tiraboschi *Storia della letteratura italiana* (Rome 1782–97) VII-2 61 / *Andreas Vesalius' First Public Anatomy at Bologna 1540* ed R. Eriksson (Uppsala-Stockholm 1959) 37–41

CHARLES B. SCHMITT

Simon CORVER documented 1519–36

No documentation is available for Simon Corver before he moved to Zwolle, in Over-ijssel, and established a printing firm, the officina Corveriana. Before that he had been a priest in Amsterdam and after 1517 he was one of the earliest adherents of *Luther in Holland. Between 1519 and 1522 he published in co-operation with Gerardus *Listrius a consid-erable number of works by Listrius himself, but also works by Wessel *Gansfort, Luther, and Erasmus, who probably sent him greetings in a letter to Listrius (CWE Ep 1013A Allen Ep 660). The officina Corveriana ceased to exist in 1522, when Listrius moved to Amersfoort, and Corver's whereabouts are no longer documen-ted. According to a plausible suggestion made by M.E. Kronenberg, he may have gone to Hamburg, where in 1522 and 1523 some fifteen heretical books were printed by someone closely connected with Corver, if indeed it was not Corver himself. Typographical material used by Corver in Zwolle was also employed in the Hamburg books and can be traced to the press of Jan Hoochstraten in Antwerp. Cor-ver's name is last found when he was detained in Amsterdam and sent to The Hague on 27 May 1536, to be sentenced as a follower of Anabaptism. The outcome of the trial is not known.

The following writings by Corver are known: two letters, 'Adolescentibus studiosis' in Listrius' *Commentarioli in dialecticen Petri Hispani* (c 1520; NK 1375) and 'Lectori' in Erasmus' *De copia*; also an 'Elegidion ad clerum Amstelredamum' in Listrius' *Elegiae II* (c 1520; NK 3405). The following works by Erasmus were published by the officina Corveriana at Zwolle: *De constructione* (September 1519; NK 2897); *Enchiridion* (7 October 1519; NK 2927; cf NK 2929); *De copia* (23 January–1 February 1520; cf NK 2916); *Dulce bellum inexpertis* (c 1520;

NK 2857); *Sileni Alcibiadis* (c 1520; NK 869); and *Novum Testamentum* (September 1522; NK 2430).

BIBLIOGRAPHY: Allen Ep 660 / CWE Ep 1013A / M.E. Kronenberg *Verboden boeken en opstandige drukkers* (Amsterdam 1948) 67–74 / M.E. Kronenberg 'Simon Corver in de gevangenis' *Het Boek* 30 (1949–51) 313–7 / A. Haga 'Nieuws over Simon Corver' *Het Boek* 3rd series, 37 (1965–6) 209–11

C.G. VAN LEIJENHORST

Antonius CORVINUS of Warburg, 11 April 1501–5 April 1553

Antonius Corvinus (Rabe), of the family of knights named Rabe von Canstein, called himself by his mother's name, Broihan (Bier-hahn or Zythogallus), until 1536. He was born at Warburg, north-west of Kassel, and proba-bly attended the school of the Dominicans there. He seems to have entered the Cistercian monastery in Loccum, west of Hannover, and may have studied briefly in Leipzig; then he lived in the monastery of Riddagshausen, near Brunswick, until he was expelled in 1523 on account of his interest in *Luther's teachings. On the recommendation of Nikolaus *Amsdorf he was appointed preacher at Goslar in 1528. A year later he became pastor in Witzenhausen on the Werra, south of Göttingen, and married Margarethe Metz. He obtained his MA from Marburg in 1536 and became an adviser to Philip of *Hesse, at whose request he went to Münster in January of 1536, trying in vain to convert the captured Anabaptist leaders *Jan of Leiden and *Knipperdolling (Ep 3031A). A text of those conversations was appended to his *Acta: Handlungen ... in der Münsterschen Sache* (Wittenberg: G. Rhau 1536) and his letter to *Spalatinus, *De miserabili Monasteriensium Anabaptistarum obsidione, excidio* (Wittenberg: G. Rhau 1536), which gave a good account of the events in Münster.

Philip of Hesse sent Corvinus to the meet-ings in Schmalkalden (1537) and Zerbst (1538) and to religious conferences in Nürnberg, Haguenau, Worms, and Regensburg (1539–41). At the same time Corvinus played a leading role in the reform of Lower Saxony, writing a church ordinance for the city of Northeim in the name of Duchess Elizabeth of Brunswick-Lüneburg. In 1542 Corvinus was asked by Franz von *Waldeck to introduce reform in his bishoprics of Minden, Osnabrück, and Münster. Together with Johann *Bugenhagen he reformed the churches of Brunswick and Hildesheim. His major achievement, however, was the establishment of a Lutheran church in the duchy of Calenberg-Göttingen by means of a church ordinance followed up by visitations in 1542 and 1543. In 1542 he moved with his family to Pattensen, near Lüneburg, and was made superintendent by Duchess Elizabeth, who ruled the duchy from 1540 as regent for her son, Eric II. Duke Eric, however, returned to the Catholic faith, and because Corvinus publicly attacked the Augsburg Interim in 1548 (*Confutatio Augustani libri*, published in 1936) he was imprisoned by the duke on 2 November 1549. When he was released on 21 October 1552 he was ill, and soon afterwards he died.

Corvinus was a friend of Johannes *Draconites and Justus *Jonas. He wrote a very popular liturgical explanation of the Gospels and the Epistles, the *Postilla, Kurtze Auslegung der Evangelien* (Wittenberg: G. Rhau 1535); highly praised by Luther, it was translated into many languages and reprinted until 1902. He also published a selection of Erasmus' *Adagia* (Magdeburg: M. Lotter 1534). As a reply to Erasmus' *De concordia* (Freiburg 1532; LB V 469–506), Corvinus wrote a dialogue, *Dissertatio quatenus expediat Erasmi de sarcienda ecclesiae concordia rationem sequi* (Wittenberg: N. Schirlentz 1534), to which Luther contributed a preface (Luther W XXXVIII 434). This work may be referred to in Epp 2993, 3127.

BIBLIOGRAPHY: Allen Ep 2993 / NDB III 371–2 / ADB IV 508–9 / Luther W *Briefwechsel* VII Ep 2148 and passim / *Der Briefwechsel des Justus Jonas* ed G. Kawerau (Halle 1884–5) Epp 311, 496, and passim

IG

Johannes CORYCIUS of Luxembourg, c 1455–1527

Johannes Corycius (Coricius, Goritz) was born in Luxembourg. After studying the liberal arts and law he entered the service of Jakob *Wimpfeling as his secretary. Wimpfeling helped him travel to Rome, where by May 1497 he was a protonotary in the curia. Under

*Julius II he was secretary of memorials. He also acted as agent or proctor in lawsuits contested at Rome, serving Jérôme de *Busleyden in this capacity in 1508. Between 1 December 1510 and 19 March 1513 he obtained the deanery of Bernkastel, in the diocese of Trier. In 1520 the Dominican order engaged him as proctor in the case of Johann *Reuchlin. Corycius was also a member of the Roman Academy and a generous friend and patron of poets. Each year on the feast of St Anne, patroness of the academy, he held festivals at his house and vineyard near Trajan's forum. Among those who attended were Pietro *Bembo, Jacopo *Sadoleto, and Marco Girolamo *Vida. However, during the Sack of Rome in 1527 Corycius was captured by imperial troops, abused, and robbed of his possessions. He managed to escape but died soon after at Verona.

Erasmus numbered Corycius among the friends he made at Rome, probably during his visit of 1509 (Epp 1342, 1479). In 1524 Blosius *Palladius edited a volume of poems entitled the *Coryciana* (Rome: L. de Henricius and L. Perusinus). In addition to verses by Bembo, Vida, Baldesar *Castiglione, and many others, the volume included a letter by Corycius himself.

BIBLIOGRAPHY: Allen Ep 1342 / H. Grimm in NDB III 372–3 / de Vocht *Busleyden* Ep 53

TBD

Jan de COSTER *See Johannes* CUSTOS

Pierre COTREL of Tournai, 1461–26 May 1545

Pierre Cotrel (Cotrellus, Coutrellus) was descended from one of the most respected families of Tournai and its territory. He studied in Louvain (although he does not seem to be mentioned in the matriculation register) and in 1489 was appointed canon of Our Lady's chapter in Tournai. From 1501 to 1508 he was chancellor of the chapter, in 1508 also archdeacon of Bruges, and from 1497 to 1545 vicargeneral to four respective bishops of Tournai, Pierre Quicke, Charles de Haultbois, Louis *Guillard, and Charles (II) de *Croy, all of whom at one time or another left him in charge of the diocese. His house on the cathedral hill, 'ou est pourtraict le grand Sainct Christofle,' was for half a century the very centre of the religious, political, and intellectual life of the principality of Tournai.

Diplomatic and unyielding at the same time, Cotrel played an important role in all developments threatening the peace and tranquillity of his fellow citizens. In 1505 he resolved the dispute over the see of Tournai between Pierre Quicke and Charles de Haultbois. It was Cotrel who persuaded *Henry VIII to grant the city honourable peace conditions when it fell to the English in 1513 and he did likewise with *Charles V when the Burgundians returned in 1521. In 1525 he ended four years of disputes between Louis Guillard, Charles de Croy, and the prince-bishop of Liège, Erard de la *Marck, by arranging Guillard's transfer from the see of Tournai to that of Chartres, the accession of Charles de Croy to Tournai, and the assignment of a substantial annuity to Erard de la Marck.

Cotrel's patronage of letters and arts bears out Erasmus, who called him a 'Maecenas' (Ep 1427). At the time of the English administration of Tournai (1513–18) he founded a college of classical languages which in 1525 he transformed into a proper university, attracting to it such talented humanists as Melchior of *Vianden, Nicolaas van *Broekhoven, and Jacobus *Ceratinus. The latter dedicated to Cotrel his translation of St John Chrysostom's *De sacerdotio* (Antwerp: M. Hillen 1526). While Cotrel's university eventually had to close in the face of unrelenting opposition from the University of Louvain, it won the admiration of Erasmus, who compared it to Louvain's Collegium Trilingue and the Collège royal in Paris (Ep 1558). In his will of January 1527 Erasmus laid down that the college should receive a copy of his collected works to be published by the *Froben press (Allen VI 505). Cotrel's own will is a final tribute to his convictions and his generosity; he left the sum of three thousand florins to the library of the Tournai chapter and used part of his fortune to endow seven scholarships in the University of Louvain.

BIBLIOGRAPHY: Allen Ep 1237 / de Vocht CTL I 522–3 and passim / J. Vos *Les Dignités et les fonctions de l'ancien chapitre de Notre Dame de Tournai* (Bruges 1898–9) I 274–7, II 78 / J. Voisin in *Analectes pour servir à l'histoire ecclésiastique de la Belgique* 9 (1872) 184–8 / A. Hocquet 'Tournai

et l'occupation anglaise' *Annales de la Société historique et archéologique de Tournai* n s 5 (1900) 384–8 / A. Hocquet 'L'Université de Tournai' *Revue tournaisienne* 5 (1909) 162 / A. Hocquet *Tournais et le Tournaisis au XVIe siècle* (Brussels 1906) 48 / L.E. Halkin *Les Conflits de juridiction entre Erard de la Marck et le chapitre cathédral de Chartres* (Liège 1933) / G. Moreau *Le Journal d'un bourgeois de Tournai: le second livre des Chroniques de Pasquier de la Barre* (Brussels 1975) 19–20 and passim

GÉRARD MOREAU

Giovanni COTTA c 1483–1509/10

Giovanni Cotta, born near Verona, was educated first at Lodi and thereafter informally at the Neapolitan Academy of Giovanni *Pontano, which he apparently entered as secretary to two noble families, the Sanseverini and the Cabavili. After Pontano's death (1503) Cotta passed into the service of Bartolomeo d'*Alviano and visited Venice at intervals as the condottiere's private secretary. He met Erasmus 'once, at dinner' (Ep 1347), probably during his master's triumphal reception in July 1508, after his victory over the imperialists four months earlier. Cotta's interests touched on both poetry and mathematics, notes of his being included in Johannes de Tridentino's edition of the Roman elegists in 1500 and in Bernardo dei Vitali's text of Ptolemy's *Geographia* in 1508. His experiments in Italian verse can also be found among the manuscripts of the Venetian coterie that included *Bembo, *Navagero, *Aleandro, and Paolo *Canal (Venice, Biblioteca Marciana, Cod. it. Cl.IX, 202, 6755–6; 213, 6881). He joined Navagero at the Academy in Pordenone, was captured with d'Alviano by the French at the battle of Agnadello (14 May 1509), and died in 1509 or 1510, at the age of 27, while trying to negotiate his master's release.

Although Erasmus named Cotta 'a man of modesty equalled by his learning,' the mistake over his first name – he called him Petrus – does not suggest a deep acquaintance, and Giovanni was used only as one in a long series of examples illustrating early death or green old age (Ep 1347).

BIBLIOGRAPHY: Allen Ep 1347 / Sanudo *Diarii* VIII and IX passim

M.J.C. LOWRY

Gilbert Cousin

Pierre de COURTEBOURNE documented
c 1502

Pierre le Bâtard de Courtebourne, as Erasmus
calls him (Petrus Nothus), was probably a
bastard brother of Florent de *Calonne, but is
not otherwise identified. There is evidence of
personal contact in a short letter (Ep 169)
Erasmus wrote him, perhaps from Saint-Omer
and conceivably before Easter 1502, after he
had spent a winter at the castle of Courtebourne, where he could have met Pierre.

ANDRÉ GODIN

Gilbert COUSIN of Nozeroy, 21 January
1506–22 May 1572

Gilbert Cousin (Cognatus) was born of a
respected family of the Hapsburg Franche-
Comté at Nozeroy, between Pontarlier and
Lons-le-Saunier. His parents, Claude Cousin
and Jeanne Daguet, had ten children, the
majority of whom chose military careers. One
brother, Hugues-le-vieux, had been captured
by the Turks and was appointed *maréchal-de-
camp* before retiring to Nozeroy after the
abdication of *Charles v. One of Gilbert's
uncles was Désiré *Morel, canon of Besançon;

another relative and benefactor of his was the
Cistercian abbot Louis de *Vers (Ep 2889).

According to his own statements Cousin
studied law for a year and a half at the
University of Dole before moving on to
theology and medicine (*Opera* i 318, 343),
which he pursued, it seems, by way of private
studies. Perhaps he went to Freiburg as a
student or a tutor, as did other young men from
the Comté. It seems that he was available when
Erasmus badly needed an amanuensis in the
summer of 1530 (Epp 2348, 2349, 2381). Thus
Cousin found a position for which he was
exceptionally well suited through his ability to
identify with the outlook of his master and to
establish amiable contacts with his friends and
visitors, as well as through his neat handwrit-
ing, his fine memory, and his reliability in
everyday matters. Erasmus later said that he
was not so much a famulus as a companion and
associate in scholarly study (Ep 2889). In return
Cousin showed how seriously he took his
position when theorizing about the office of
famulus as well as the duties of the master in
his Oἰκέτης (1535; *Opera* i 218–28).

Between October and November 1533
Cousin revisited Burgundy, accepting a benefice – or a pledge to a benefice – from Louis de
Vers and bringing back some wine for his
master (Epp 2870, 2878, 2880, 2881). Anxious to
retain his services, Erasmus sent him home
again in December with letters that pleaded for
Cousin to be allowed to hold his benefice while
remaining in Erasmus' household at Freiburg
(Epp 2889, 2890). In so doing, he made himself
a guarantor for Cousin's orthodoxy, which, he
suggested, might otherwise be in jeopardy. A
third journey to Burgundy in about December
1534 served to secure Cousin's appointment to
a canonry in the modest chapter of his native
Nozeroy (*Opera* i 332). Again Erasmus had
given him a recommendation (Ep 2985), and
again Cousin was able, for the time being, to
return to his beloved master, with whom he
moved from Freiburg to Basel in the summer of
1535. The time of his appointment to the
canonry coincided closely with the religious
persecutions following *Farel's agitation at
Neuchâtel and the placards affair in Paris, both
of which had repercussions in Burgundy.
Cousin reacted with sympathy for the victims
and with Erasmian aversion to religious strife

(AK IV Epp 1897, 1918), an attitude in which he persevered at all times.

In September 1535 Cousin was sent back to Freiburg on some business arising from the dissolution of Erasmus' household (Epp 3052, 3055, 3059). Soon thereafter he was preparing for his return to Nozeroy, pointing out the obligations he had towards his parents (Ep 3062). At the turn of the year he had settled at Nozeroy, remembering Erasmus with glowing veneration (Epp 3068, 3080). Soon he mused about returning to live at Basel. At first he planned a visit for Easter 1536 (Ep 3095), but then he thought, hesitatingly encouraged by Erasmus, that he might resign his benefice against an annual rent (Ep 3104; cf Ep 3122). He still planned his move to Basel for the autumn (Ep 3118), but Erasmus' death intervened and left him grief-stricken (AK IV Ep 2078; Opera I 233, 302, 404).

Nozeroy thus remained Cousin's home, although some more travel followed. In July 1546 he wrote from Sirod, south-west of Nozeroy, then infested by the plague (AK VI 2840); in 1555 and 1559 he expressed hopes for a visit to Paris, where he called Joachim Périon, Philippus *Montanus, and Petrus Ramus his friends (Opera I 317, II 59). In the summer of 1557 he was at Basel, seeing through the press his first edition of the homilies of Caesarius of Arles, and for a year or so from May 1558 he visited northern Italy with the youthful archbishop of Besançon, Claude de la Baume (Opera I 380–93). At Nozeroy he made his library the centre of an educated circle (Opera I 314–15, 330, 426), and he surrounded himself with paying pupils, many of whom he recommended later to his friends as they entered the universities of Dole or Basel. Topography continued to interest him (Opera I 323–99); above all, however, he remained preoccupied with the problems of religion, since they permitted him to draw continually on the inspiration he had received during his years with Erasmus. He did not adopt any Protestant doctrines and likewise remained unaffected by the spirit of the Counter-Reformation. He wished to restore the mass to its ancient dignity, not to abolish it, but, in the manner of Erasmus, he deplored and derided superstition and ecclesiastical corruption. He also continued to write freely to his many Protes-

tant friends and even published many such letters in his Opera of 1562, frequently behaving as if the denominational division had never occurred.

In the Catholic Franche-Comté, surrounded by evangelical neighbours from Montbéliard to Neuchâtel, Erasmus' Colloquia were banned, and a careful watch was kept on potential heretics. Cousin was bound to be suspect, and so was the dean of his chapter, Jean *Tornond, while the Nozeroy schoolmaster, Jean *Cornier, who was a close friend of Cousin, fled to Lausanne. As early as 1554 Cousin had to defend himself against the attacks of the canons of Salins and removed many of his books to a safe place, but he could not do without Erasmus' paraphrase of Matthew and Sebastianus Castellio's Latin Bible. Small wonder that his opponents continued to demand his suppression. On explicit orders from Rome he was kept under arrest or confinement from 1567 to his death. His friends in the Parlement of Dole and at the archiepiscopal court remained convinced of his harmlessness, but the archbishop himself, Claude de la Baume, rather than securing the freedom of his old tutor, was preoccupied with his own problems. After he had finally become a priest in 1566 his episcopal consecration was kept in suspense because of an alleged marriage, and from 1567 to 1571 he was at Rome, trying to regularize his position.

In the course of his years at Freiburg and Basel, Cousin had established links with a great many of Erasmus' friends and acquaintances, among them Bonifacius *Amerbach, Damião de *Gois, Johann *Koler, and Giovanni Angelo *Odoni. He produced a continual series of essays, commentaries, and poems, many of them circumstantial, on a variety of topics but as a whole reflecting his unfaltering commitment to the ideals of Erasmus.

BIBLIOGRAPHY: Allen Ep 2381 (with a list of Cousin's publications) / Gilbert Cousin Opera (Basel: H. Petri 1562) / Gilbert Cousin Aucunes Oeuvres ([Basel or Lyon]: Jacques Quadier [ie Parcus] 1561) (mostly translations of some Latin writings) / Gilbert Cousin La Franche-Comté au milieu du xvie siècle ed E. Monot (Lons-le-Saunier 1911) / Lucien Febvre 'Un secrétaire d'Erasme: Gilbert Cousin et la réforme en Franche-Comté' in *Bulletin de la société de l'histoire du protestantisme français* 56 (1907) 97–158 / P.-A. Pidoux *Un Humaniste comtois, Gilbert Cousin* (Lons-le-Saunier 1910) / E. Monot 'Gilbert Cousin et son école de Nozeroy' in *Mémoires de la Société d'émulation du Jura* XII-1 (1928–9) 3–69 / P.G. Bietenholz *Basle and France in the Sixteenth Century* (Geneva-Toronto 1971) 234–40, 279–82, and passim

PGB

Pierre COUSTURIER of Chêmeré-le-Roy, c1475–18 June 1537

Pierre Cousturier (Le Cousturier, Sutor) was from Chêmeré-le-Roy, near Laval (diocese of Le Mans). In Paris, he taught arts at the Collège de Sainte-Barbe, probably from about 1495 to about 1502. By 1502 he had become a *socius* of the Collège de Sorbonne, where he exercised the functions of proctor, librarian, and, in 1504–5, prior. As a theology student, he also held a living from the parish of Saint-Loyer in the diocese of Sées. Cousturier ranked third of twenty-nine in his licentiate class of 5 February 1510 and received his doctorate in theology on 16 April 1510. On 28 January 1511 he composed his last will and testament and entered the Carthusian order at Vauvert, near Paris. He frequently served his order as official visitor, and he was the prior of four Carthusian houses between 1514 and 1531: Val-Dieu (Perche region), 1514–17; Vauvert, 1517 to at least 1519; Preize (near Troyes), 1523–5; and Notre-Dame-du-Parc (Maine) in 1531. He died in this last house.

Cousturier's entry into the Carthusians must be seen as part of a significant movement of many earnest clerics at that time to revive and reform the religious orders along the lines set forth by Jan *Standonck, Jean Raulin, and Jan *Mombaer, and to effect a general reformation of the church through these reformed orders. It was natural, then, that Cousturier should ally himself with Standonck's disciple Noël *Béda to oppose the reformist goals and methods advocated by the humanists, whom Cousturier saw as radical and even heretical reformers. Cousturier rejected in principle all new versions and translations of the Bible and called Erasmus a 'little rhetorician' who was meddling incompetently in theological affairs (*De tralatione Bibliae* 1525). Erasmus, fearful that

Cousturier's ideas would prevail in Paris, tried to convince Béda that Cousturier's attack put him beyond the norms of academic controversy or traditional Christian theology (Ep 1581). Erasmus' reply to Cousturier was his *Apologia adversus debacchationes Petri Sutoris* (LB IX 737–804). Cousturier answered with his *Antapologia*, expressing surprise at Erasmus' personal attacks on him and relating the story that Etienne *Poncher, former bishop of Paris, had said that he would trust Erasmus in any point of grammar but in no point of theology. Erasmus replied again with an *Appendix respondens ad quandam antapologiam Petri Sutoris* (LB IX 805–12) and with his colloquy *Synodus grammaticorum* (1529; ASD I-3 585–90). In addition, Erasmus complained about Cousturier in some sixty different letters written between 1525 and 1531. Cousturier made two final attacks, *In damnatam Lutheri haeresim*, a defence of monastic vows, and *De potestate ecclesiae in occultis*, in which he argued that Erasmians were in the same camp as Lutherans.

Cousturier was never active on the faculty of theology of Paris, either as regent or on committees. The faculty objected to Cousturier's calling Mary the 'redemptrix et salvatrix' of the human race and demanded that he remove the phrase from his *Apologeticum in novos Anticomaritas*. The faculty also insisted on two unspecified changes before approving an unnamed book in 1528. Two other works, 'De certis christifere misteriis' (1524) and 'Expositum symboli apostolici' (posthumously approved in 1542), were apparently never published. Cousturier's *De vita cartusiana* (1522) was an exposition of Carthusian spirituality, and his chapter on contemplation has been said to have influenced the spirituality of St Ignatius of Loyola.

His works include: *La Manière de faire testament très salutaire* (Paris: Regnault Chaudière n d); *De vita cartusiana libri duo* (Paris: Jean Petit 1522; Louvain 1572; Cologne 1609, 1625); *De triplici connubio divae Annae disceptatio* (Paris: Jean Petit 1523); *De tralatione Bibliae in novarum reprobatione interpretationum* (Paris: Pierre Vidoue for Jean Petit 1525); *Apologeticum in novos Anticomaritas* (ie, heretics about the Virgin; Paris: Jean Petit 1526); *Adversus insanam Erasmi apologiam Petri Sutoris anta-*

pologia (Paris: Pierre Vidoue for Jean Petit 1526); *In damnatam Lutheri haeresim de votis monasticis* (Paris: Poncet Le Preux 1531); *De potestate ecclesiae in occultis* (Paris: Maurice de La Porte 1534, Denis Gaygnot 1535; 1546).

BIBLIOGRAPHY: Allen Ep 1591 / J.-C. Margolin in ASD I-2 195, I-5 374, 376 / H. Bernard-Maître SJ 'Un théoricien de la contemplation: Pierre Cousturier dit Sutor' *Revue d'ascétique et mystique* 32 (1956) 174–95 / DTC III-2 1987–8 / Farge no 123 / P.-Y. Féret *La Faculté de théologie de Paris et ses docteurs les plus célèbres. Epoque moderne* (Paris 1900–10) II 392–5

JAMES K. FARGE

Petrus COUTRELLUS *See Pierre* COTREL

Leonard COX of Thame, documented 1514–49
Leonard Cox (Cockes) of Thame, in Oxfordshire, matriculated on 12 June 1514 in Tübingen, where he met *Melanchthon and studied under Johann *Stöffler. In the autumn of 1518, when registering in the University of Cracow, he laid claim to the title of poet laureate. On 6 December he delivered an oration in praise of the university, which he published (Cracow: H. Wietor 1518) with a dedication to Justus Ludovicus *Decius. His other publications include two letters of Jerome taken from the edition of Erasmus. He also lectured on Jerome as well as on Livy and Quintilian. In 1520 Johann *Henckel secured his appointment as schoolmaster in Levoča (Leutschau), now in eastern Czechoslovakia, and in 1521 he directed the school of Košice (Kaschau) in the same region. After April 1524 he returned to Cracow and resumed his lectures, now with a proper academic appointment, at the same time editing some more works, including *Henry VIII's *Assertio* against *Luther and the latter's reply. His admiration for Erasmus is evident from verses in an edition of the *Hyperaspistes* (1526) and references to his works in his other publications at Cracow. Cox tutored rich students such as Andrzej *Zebrzydowski and, although he was unpopular at times, contributed substantially to the beginnings of humanistic studies at Cracow.

In 1526 Cox returned to England, where he was admitted BA at Cambridge in 1526–7 and supplicated for incorporation at Oxford and for inception as MA on 9 February 1530. In the same month he was master of the grammar school attached to the abbey of Reading. Two years later he dedicated to the abbot of Reading, Hugh of Faringdon, an edition of his *Arte and Crafte of Rhetoryke* (London: R. Redman 1532; STC 5947), the first book on this subject published in English. After the disgrace and execution in 1539 of his patron, Faringdon, he moved to the school of Caerleon in Wales and in the spring of 1540 dedicated to Thomas *Cromwell his edition of William *Lily's *De octo orationis partium constructione* (London: T. Berthelet; STC 15610.5). In another letter he stated that he had been accepted into Cromwell's service and vouched to offer the lord privy seal works at regular intervals. After Cromwell's execution Cox returned to Reading, where on 16 February 1541 the king granted him a small annuity which was paid until 1546.

Although not original, Cox showed talent and dedication in his untiring efforts to spread humanistic studies. While still at Cracow he corresponded with Erasmus in the spring of 1527 (Epp 1803, 1824) – an earlier exchange of letters is missing – and mentioned *Szydłowiecki and Jan (II) *Łaski as patrons who had helped to bring about this connection with the great humanist in Basel. He also urged Erasmus to write to his rich pupil Andrzej Zebrzydowski, a suggestion Erasmus was quick to take up with Ep 1826. The admiration for Erasmus which he had encountered and shared in Poland he took back with him to England. In 1534 he translated into English Erasmus' paraphrase and Latin version of the Epistle of Titus (London: J. Byddell n d; STC 10503). The work was presented to Cromwell in the hope of securing his appointment to the mastership of the free school at Bristol. At about the same time Erasmus himself is first known to have entered into contact with Cromwell. Cox also proposed to translate for Cromwell Erasmus' *Modus orandi Deum*, his paraphrase on Timothy, and *De pueris instituendis*, but no more is known about these projects. The paraphrase on Titus, however, was published again in the second volume of the English edition of Erasmus' complete paraphrases (1548–9; STC 2854) with a new preface, which seems to be the last reliable document of Cox's life. His other writings included a

Frans van Cranevelt by Janus Secundus

---

prefatory poem in Latin to John *Palsgrave's *L'Esclairecissement* of 1530 (STC 19166).

BIBLIOGRAPHY: Allen Ep 1803 / Stanislas Kot in PSB IV 98–9 / DNB IV 1336–7 / Emden BRUO (1501–40) 145 / McConica 62, 120, 140–1, 193–4, 247, and passim

CFG & PGB

Sebastiaan CRAEYS d 27 October 1523
Very little is known about Sebastiaan Craeys, who was the prior of the Carmelite monastery in Antwerp from 1 July 1502 to his death. At Pentecost 1517 Erasmus and Pieter *Gillis heard him preach a sermon at Antwerp in which he accused Erasmus of two sins against the Holy Spirit (Epp 948, 1967, 2045; LB VI 1052E). In 1521 Erasmus claimed that Craeys was attacking *Luther, without having read anything by him, at the sole prompting of his fellow Carmelite Nicolaas *Baechem called Egmondanus, who was professor of theology in Louvain (Ep 1196). According to Erasmus, Craeys himself possessed a theological doctorate.

BIBLIOGRAPHY: Allen Ep 948 / *Inscriptions*

funéraires de la province d'Anvers v (Antwerp 1873) 340

MARCEL A. NAUWELAERTS

Frans van CRANEVELT of Nijmegen, 3 February 1485–8 September 1564
Frans van Cranevelt (Franciscus Craneveldius Noviomagus), the son of Herman (d 1518), the secretary of Karel van *Egmond, was born at Nijmegen and shared his first lessons there with Gerard *Geldenhouwer. On 14 November 1497 he matriculated at Cologne but, being younger than twenty, could not take a degree. On 13 October 1501 he matriculated at Louvain, studying arts and law. Having attended lectures of Nicolaas *Baechem, Jan de Spouter (Despauterius), Nicolas *Coppin, Godschalk *Rosemondt, Adriaan Floriszoon (*Adrian VI), and others, he became a MA in 1505, standing first on the list of that year's promotion. He became a licentiate in civil and canon law on 30 May 1506 and a doctor on 2 October 1510. In July 1509 he had married Elisabeth van Baussele, who bore him at least eleven children. After living for some years at Louvain, perhaps as a private tutor, he was appointed pensionary of Bruges at the end of 1515; in this capacity in 1521 he addressed speeches to *Christian II of Denmark (27 July), *Charles V (7 August), and Thomas *Wolsey (14 August). Following a recommendation from Jan *Robbyns, Charles V nominated Cranevelt to a seat on the grand council of Mechelen by letters dated 27 September 1522; Cranevelt took his oath on 6 October before the president, Joost *Lauwereyns. Cranevelt remained at Mechelen until his death, outliving his first wife, Elisabeth, who died in 1545, and marrying Catherine de Plaine in or before 1560. He was buried next to Elisabeth in the chapel of Thabor, Mechelen.

Despite his political and administrative duties, Frans van Cranevelt maintained a lively interest in the scholarly community of his day and corresponded frequently with Erasmus, Jan van *Fevijn, Juan Luis *Vives, Gerard Geldenhouwer, and many others. He meticulously preserved the letters he received, and over 250 of these were published by Henry de Vocht in 1928. Cranevelt made the acquaintance of Erasmus through Maarten van *Dorp, probably in July 1517; Erasmus in turn introduced him to Thomas *More in 1520 (Epp 1145, 1173, 1220). The correspondence between Erasmus and Cranevelt concerned such matters as Erasmus' difficulties with the theologians of Louvain (Ep 1173), the imperial pension lost by Erasmus when he left Louvain, which he hoped Cranevelt could help recover (Epp 1545, 1546, 1553), *Luther's marriage (Ep 1655), and the divorce proceedings of *Henry VIII of England (Ep 1850). Although they are last known to have written to one another in 1527, there is no reason to suppose that their friendship ended. Erasmus demonstrated his appreciation for Cranevelt by including him in his will of 1527 (Allen VI app 19), and Cranevelt composed several poems on Erasmus' death (LB I preliminary pieces: Epitaphia; de Vocht Literae ad Craneveldium lxxv–lxxvi).

In addition to corresponding with Erasmus and other scholars, Cranevelt continued his own studies and literary activity. By 1525 he had attained a fair knowledge of Greek, and in 1531 he began to learn Hebrew. His Latin translations of several homilies of St Basil were printed by Rutergus *Rescius at Louvain on 15 May 1534 (NK 2382) and on 28 July 1535 (NK 254). He also translated Procopius' De aedificiis (Paris: C. Wechel 1537) and, as an act of piety, edited the De veritate fidei christianae of Juan Luis Vives (Basel: J. Oporinus January 1543). His poetic ability was praised by Erasmus (Ep 1724; see de Vocht Literae ad Craneveldium lxxiv–lxxxii for his poems). Johannes Secundus, the talented son of Nicolaas *Everaerts, portrayed Cranevelt on a fine medal in 1533, while a painting of 1559 in the town archives of Mechelen depicts an assembly of the grand council with Cranevelt taking part (de Vocht Literae ad Craneveldium xxxiii, lxvi). Cranevelt received dedications to the fifth of Geldenhouwer's Satyrae octo (1515), Rescius' Platonis Minos (1531), and Livinus Crucius' Threnodia (1540).

BIBLIOGRAPHY: Allen Ep 1145 / M.A. Nauwelaerts in NBW I 347–9 / F. Nève in BNB IV 484–6 / H.D.J. van Schevichaven in NNBW I 651 / Matricule de Louvain III-1 226 / Matrikel Köln II 433 / de Vocht CTL I 11–12, 518, III 403, 537–8, and passim / For the texts of the speeches Cranevelt delivered in 1521 see Collectanea van

Gerardus Geldenhauer Noviomagus ed J. Prinsen (Amsterdam 1901) 118–23

C.G. VAN LEIJENHORST

Thomas CRANMER of Aslockton, 2 July 1489–21 March 1556
Cranmer (Cronmarus) was born at Aslockton, Nottinghamshire, the son of the village squire, Thomas Cranmer, and Agnes Hatfield. In 1503 he was sent to Cambridge, where he studied philosophy, logic, and Latin authors including Erasmus. He received the degree of BA in July 1511 and his MA in July 1514. He was deprived of his fellowship in Jesus College upon his marriage but was reinstated after the death of his wife and child. He received the degree of bachelor of theology in 1521 and his doctorate in 1526.

In 1529 he visited Waltham Abbey and, in a famous meeting with Stephen *Gardiner and Edward *Fox, represented *Henry VIII's divorce as a purely theological matter not subject to the rules of canon law. He allegedly suggested that the universities be polled for their opinion. The king summoned Cranmer to Greenwich, adopted his suggestion, and asked him to publish his views about the 'great matter.' On the king's recommendation he was received at Durham House, the residence of Thomas *Boleyn, earl of Wiltshire. He was archdeacon of Taunton in 1530 when he accompanied Boleyn to Bologna to attend the coronation of *Charles V as Holy Roman Emperor. During this time he travelled to Rome, where he offered to speak in defence of Henry's divorce but was never given the opportunity of doing so. Pope *Clement VII appointed Cranmer grand penitentiary of England; he returned to England and moved to court as the chaplain of *Anne Boleyn. In January 1532 he was appointed English ambassador to the emperor and soon joined Charles V's court at Regensburg. He met secretly with John Frederick, elector of *Saxony, to discuss the possibility of English and French aid against Charles V. During this time he probably took the first steps towards Lutheranism. He is also reported to have expressed disapproval of Henry's treatment of *Catherine, his first queen, and her daughter, *Mary. He accompanied the imperial court to Vienna and Mantua

Thomas Cranmer by G. Flicke

but was recalled to England and nominated archbishop of Canterbury by Henry in January 1533; in order not to exacerbate relations with England further, Rome confirmed the appointment in March. Before returning to England Cranmer had secretly sent there his new German wife, Margaret, the niece of Andreas *Osiander's wife.

As Cranmer was reliable and enjoyed an upright reputation, he seemed an ideal tool for Henry and *Cromwell in their efforts to use the prestige of the see of Canterbury in the divorce matter. He was consecrated in March at Westminster and in May he declared Henry's first marriage invalid and his marriage to Anne Boleyn valid. In September 1533 he stood godfather to Princess Elizabeth. As the highest ecclesiastical authority in England Cranmer issued bulls and dispensations and in 1534 held a general visitation of the dioceses under his jurisdiction. He was the first to denounce the jurisdiction of Rome in England and was instrumental in the production of an authorized English Bible, which was ready in 1540. He interceded on behalf of John *Fisher and Thomas *More after their arrests; he also

visited Anne Boleyn in the Tower and may have heard her last confession. He had little to do with the suppression of the monasteries. In 1537 he stood godfather to the future Edward VI.

In 1537 Cranmer was prominently engaged in formulating the 'Bishops' Book,' a conservative statement of principle designed to unite the English episcopate, frequently along Erasmian lines. In 1538 he presided at conferences between English and German divines who discussed church unity. In 1539 the Act of the Six Articles forced him to send his wife back to Germany (where she remained until 1543). He escorted Anne of Cleves when she arrived in England in 1539 and later officiated at her marriage to the king. After Cromwell's fall, he intervened on his behalf. His Protestant sympathies made him chiefly responsible for the abrogation of traditional church customs; as a result several unsuccessful conspiracies were formed against him. He attended Henry VIII during his final days in 1547 and was named in the king's will among those councillors appointed to govern during Edward VI's minority.

During the reign of Edward Cranmer played a leading role in the transformation of the English church along Protestant lines. He was largely responsible for preparing the first Anglican Book of Common Prayer (1549), moderately Protestant in tone, and the second (1552), which leaned towards the Swiss reformers. Among those who assisted him were the exiles from the continent Martin *Bucer, Jan (II) *Łaski, and Peter Martyr Vermigli. In 1553 Cranmer was a reluctant member of Northumberland's plot to place Lady Jane Grey on the English throne. When Queen Mary succeeded Edward, Cranmer was arrested for disseminating 'seditious bills' and was imprisoned in the Tower. In November he was found guilty of treason, but Queen Mary's intervention delayed his execution. He was imprisoned until March 1554, when he was summoned to Oxford, with bishops Ridley and *Latimer, to face charges of heresy. In December 1555 Rome deprived him of his offices, and he was committed to the secular authority. After repeated recantations he professed his Protestant belief immediately before his execution in 1556.

When Cranmer was appointed archbishop of Canterbury, he expressed admiration for Erasmus and specifically for his *Explanatio symboli* (Epp 2815, 2831, 2879). He also continued to pay the annuity granted Erasmus by his predecessor, *Warham, and payments are mentioned repeatedly in Erasmus' correspondence until March 1536 (Ep 3104). Erasmus responded with praise in the preliminary pieces of the 1535 edition of the New Testament (LB VI).

BIBLIOGRAPHY: Jasper Ridley *Thomas Cranmer* (Oxford 1962) / DNB V 19–31 / DTC III 2026–31 / McConica 159–62 and passim

CFG

Andreas CRATANDER of Strasbourg,
d before 26 May 1540
Andreas Cratander (Cartander, Hartmann) matriculated in the University of Heidelberg on 2 March 1502 and graduated BA in the following year. For 1505 he is documented as being in Basel, where he met his first wife, Irmelin. She had died by March 1512, when Cratander was again – or still – at Basel to settle her estate. Soon thereafter he moved to Strasbourg, married Christina, a daughter of Bartholomäus Lienhart, and as her husband was received into citizenship on 20 September 1512. In the spring of 1513 he worked as a compositor for the Strasbourg printer Matthias *Schürer. By November 1515 he had returned to Basel, where he worked as a corrector for the printer Adam Petri before setting up his own business, which comprised a press as well as a bookshop, towards the end of 1518. On 2 March 1519 he became a burgher of Basel and on 27 July a member of the 'Safran' guild, while in 1530 he joined the more distinguished 'Schlüssel' guild. The name of his third wife, Veronica Renner, who survived him, first appears on a record of 1522 when he acquired the house 'zum schwarzen Bären' in the Petersgasse, henceforward the location of his business and a printer's shop for centuries after him.

As a bookseller Cratander represented great international publishing houses such as Hittorp and Horncken of Cologne in 1519 and in 1520 and 1521 Franz *Birckmann and his associates Johann *Koberger and Lukas Atlantse. This latter connection, Cratander be-

lieved, was seen with misgivings by Johann *Froben (cf Cratander's letter to *Capito, 20 September 1521, Meier 23). His press was modest in size (*Vadianische Briefsammlung* II Ep 255) and on occasion he printed in partnership with Johann *Bebel. On the whole he preferred shorter texts and titles in demand by university students, but he also produced important legal works by Claudius *Cantiuncula, Andrea *Alciati, and Udalricus *Zasius (AK II Epp 766, 944, III Ep 1021). His Latin Hippocrates of 1526 now seems far more important to medical history than it appeared at the time to one of Erasmus' correspondents (Ep 1810). He also published the earlier cosmographical works of his son-in-law, Sebastian Münster, but had to leave the fruits of Münster's Hebrew scholarship to Froben and Petri, evidently for lack of suitable type. In 1532 his dealings with *Vadianus over manuscripts taken from the abbey of St Gallen resulted in an unpleasant interview with the abbot (*Vadianische Briefsammlung* V Ep 686).

Cratander's loyalty to religious reform was never in doubt. By 1520 he was publishing such incisive works as the *Julius exclusus* and Lorenzo *Valla's exposure of the Donation of Constantine. He received in his home some men subsequently known as Anabaptists, Konrad Grebel, Hinne Rode, and Hans *Denck; but above all, he was the principal publisher of Johannes *Oecolampadius, who may have been his friend from student days in Heidelberg and took lodgings in his house at Basel. In view of Erasmus' dislike of Oecolampadius it is not surprising that in the years of Erasmus' residence in Basel and Freiburg his relations with Cratander were not significant, although in the early years Cratander printed a separate edition of Erasmus' Latin version of the New Testament (Ep 1010). He also printed German translations of the adage *Dulce bellum inexpertis*, the *Paraclesis*, and the *Consilium* concerning Luther composed jointly by Erasmus and the Dominican Johannes *Faber (Ep 1149; *Opuscula* 338–61). In 1524 Erasmus complained to the Basel council that Guillaume *Farel's pamphlet against him was for sale in Cratander's bookshop (Ep 1508). Cratander also seems to have supported Ludovicus *Carinus, who had fallen out with Erasmus, thus giving cause for further irritation, although Erasmus' famulus, Felix *Rex, had a pleasant boat trip on the Rhine with Cratander, who travelled regularly to the Frankfurt fair (Ep 2130). Erasmus' anger was renewed when, apparently through no fault of Cratander, a letter he was supposed to forward failed to reach its destination (Epp 2737, 2739, 2748, 2790).

In 1529 Cratander underwent the famous guaiac treatment (AK III Ep 1396). He sold his press in 1536; according to the well-informed Thomas Platter, his wife did not like being left in charge of the printing shop while her husband and son travelled around as booksellers. Concentrating on the book trade brought Cratander little success, however, and, according to Platter, Johann Bebel and Hieronymus *Froben had to rescue his heirs from financial ruin.

BIBLIOGRAPHY: Allen Ep 1374 / E.A. Meier et al *Andreas Cratander: ein Basler Drucker und Verleger der Reformationszeit* (Basel [1967]) / Grimm *Buchführer* 1384–7 / Benzing *Buchdrucker* 32 / Josef Benzing in NDB III 402 / AK II Ep 751, VIII xvii, and passim / Z VII Ep 87, VIII Ep 298, and passim / BRE Ep 117 and passim / BA *Oekolampads* I 66–7, 227, and passim / *Vadianische Briefsammlung* II Ep 183 and passim / Thomas Platter *Lebensbeschreibung* (Basel 1944) 118, 124 / *Matrikel Heidelberg* I 444

PGB

Francesco da CREMA of Cividale, c 1470–14 July 1525
Francesco da Crema (Franciscus Cremensis) was descended from the noble family de' Bulgari living in Cividale di Friuli. (Contrary to Henry de Vocht's assertion in CTL I 173, he cannot be identified with the Francesco da Crema whose work *Singularia et solemnia dicta* was first published at Bologna about 1472.) Bartholomaeus Megalutius dedicated to Crema the 1502 Venice edition of Fausto *Andrelini's *Livia*, and it is an attractive hypothesis that Crema secured a copy of the first edition of the *Livia* (Paris 1490) for Megalutius through his brother Bruno, who was Andrelini's famulus.

Nothing is known about Crema's studies or early career. He appears for the first time in 1490 at the court of Ercole I d'Este in Ferrara, where he met Antonius Gratia Dei. He was so fascinated by this man's erudition and eloquence that very shortly afterwards he wrote a panegyric in his praise (Florence, Biblioteca Nazionale Centrale, MS Landau Finaly 262). In 1494 he presented this work in Louvain to the Portuguese nobleman Valascus de Lucena (c 1430–31 December 1512).

On 1 December 1492, Crema had been appointed to the chair of poetry in the University of Louvain, which had remained unoccupied after Cornelio *Vitelli's departure to Paris in the summer of 1488. In Louvain Crema composed an oration on Philip the Handsome, duke of *Burgundy, which was delivered on the occasion of his solemn entry in Louvain, 9 September 1494 (Brussels, Bibliothèque royale MS 15860), and his 'De arte scribendorum versuum,' now probably lost, which was revised in 1534 by the Antwerp humanist Cornelius *Grapheus. When Erasmus first visited Louvain in June 1498, he was Crema's guest and afterwards praised his learning (Ep 76).

Crema retired from his chair in February 1499 and returned to his native town, where he wrote three more historical works: the first one, entitled *De oppugnatione Foroiulii per Germanos*, described the siege of Cividale in early August 1509 by the troops of *Maximilian I under the command of Henry of Brunswick; the second, written in 1510, dealt with the fortifications in Cividale, and in the third he described a plague epidemic in Cividale from the autumn of 1510 until the summer of 1511 and a disastrous earthquake on 26 March 1511. Crema died in Cividale and was buried in the Dominican church.

BIBLIOGRAPHY: Allen Ep 76 / Gilbert Tournoy 'Franciscus Cremensis and Antonius Gratia Dei, two Italian humanists, professors at Louvain in the fifteenth century' *Lias* 3 (1976) 33–73 (publishing all hitherto unpublished texts by Crema)

GILBERT TOURNOY

Paulus CRESCENTIUS See Pawel Sebastian KRASSOWSKI

Volphangus CRESSUS See Wolfgang KRESS

Pietro CRINITO of Florence, 9 January 1475–5 July 1507
Pietro Crinito was born at Florence to Bartolomeo del Riccio Baldi, of a branch of the Lotteringhi family, and Lisa di Beltramone. He

studied the classics under Paolo Sassi da Ronciglione and Ugolino Verino and rhetoric at the University of Florence under Angelo *Poliziano. He taught publicly and privately, at the church of Santo Spirito and for the University of Florence. He participated in scholarly discussions at the Dominican convent of San Marco, where he met notable figures such as Giovanni *Pico della Mirandola and Girolamo *Savonarola. He was known to Lorenzo (I) de' *Medici and participated in the Platonic Academy. After the invasion of Italy by *Charles VIII of France and the fall of the Medici in 1494, Crinito began a long odyssey to Naples, Rome, Venice, and numerous other Italian cities. However he returned to Florence shortly before his untimely death.

Crinito's most famous work was the *De honesta disciplina*, a collection of commonplaces first published at Florence by Filippo Giunta in 1504 and reprinted a number of times at Paris, Basel, and other centres. Erasmus cited it in his *Vita Hieronymi* (1516), taking issue with one specific passage (I 10) and claiming that Crinito was a second-rate author who did not understand what he wrote (*Opuscula* 181–3). He mentioned Crinito again in the *Ciceronianus*, this time describing him more favourably as a man of erudition, even though far from the eloquence of Cicero (ASD I-2 667–8).

Crinito's other published works include the *Libri de poetis latinis* (Florence: F. Giunta 1505), a life of Sallust, poems, and commentaries on the letters of Cicero and fables of Aesop. Unpublished letters, commentaries, and glosses are found in Munich and Florence.

BIBLIOGRAPHY: Carlo Angeleri 'Contributi biografici su l'umanista Pietro Crinito, allievo del Poliziano' *Rivista storica degli archivi toscani* 9 (1933) 41–70 / Pietro Crinito *De honesta disciplina* ed Carlo Angeleri (Rome 1955)

TBD

Andreas CRITIUS *See Andrzej* KRZYCKI

CROCUS *See Cornelis* CROOCK, *Richard* CROKE

Richard CROKE of London, c 1489–late August 1558
In the university registers Croke (Crocus) is referred to as a Londoner. He was educated at Eton and was a student at King's College, Cambridge, in 1506, after having stayed with

William *Grocyn as his servant-pupil (Ep 227). In 1511 he studied in Paris under Girolamo *Aleandro (Ep 256) and worked with Erasmus and Gilles de *Gourmont on the printing of the *Moria* (Allen I 19; Epp 221, 222). Erasmus judged him to be a promising young scholar, and after his own return from Paris to Cambridge he asked John *Colet whether he could find a subsidy for Croke (Epp 227, 230, 237).

Croke's facility in Greek ensured his welcome at other universities; after his departure from Paris in 1512, he went to teach Greek in Louvain and Cologne. In 1515 he published an edition of Ausonius (Leipzig: V. Schumann) and matriculated at Leipzig, where he taught Greek in 1516 in response to a request from the faculty (Ep 415). In 1516 Croke published his *Tabulae graecas literas impendio discere cupientibus sane quam necessariae* (Leipzig: V. Schumann) and a translation of the fourth book of Theodorus *Gaza's Greek grammar, dedicated to Archbishop Albert of *Brandenburg. Erasmus was translating the first two books. While in Germany Croke came into contact with many German scholars, notably Ulrich von *Hutten and Johann *Reuchlin. Johannes *Camerarius was one of his pupils, and Conradus *Mutianus wrote of Croke's visit with him, remarking that the visitor was 'more Greek than English.' In 1519 Croke corresponded with Guillaume *Budé in Greek.

In 1517 Croke returned to England by way of Antwerp, where he seems to have delivered to Erasmus letters from his students *Mosellanus and *Dungersheim, and also from *Emser and *Stromer (Epp 533, 534, 560, 578). In the wake of this visit Erasmus played a somewhat dubious role with regard to books belonging to Croke that were delayed or lost (Epp 712, 777, 827). After that no record of further contact survives except for Erasmus' snide remark about Croke's role in the printing of Gourmont's faulty *Moria* (1524; Allen I 19). In Cambridge Croke received his MA and thereafter was appointed reader in Greek, from 1520 with a salary paid by King *Henry VIII, to whom he later gave some Greek lessons (Epp 712, 777, 827). In 1520 he published his famous inaugural lectures at Cambridge, *Orationes duae* (Paris: S. de Colines), and his *Introductiones in rudimenta graeca* (Cologne), dedicated to William *Warham, archbishop of Canter-

Thomas Cromwell by Hans Holbein the Younger

bury. Croke was elected the first public orator at Cambridge in 1522. He received a stipend from Bishop John *Fisher for delivering Greek lectures at St John's College in 1523. Having been ordained in 1519, he received the degree of doctor of divinity in 1524 and became tutor to the king's natural son, the duke of Richmond, who lodged with him at King's College. At Thomas *Cranmer's suggestion, Croke was sent to Italy from 1529 to 1531 to poll Italian divines about the king's divorce. It appears that secrecy was necessary: Croke assumed the name of Johannes Flandrensis and later informed Henry VIII that he feared assassination. In 1531 Croke was deputy vice-chancellor of the University of Cambridge. The following year he was appointed canon and subdean of King's College, Oxford. He received another doctorate of divinity at Oxford in 1532. Cranmer failed in his attempt to have Croke, his close friend, appointed dean of King's College, and in 1545 Croke retired to Exeter College, Oxford. He was the first witness called at Cranmer's trial in 1555 and testified to his heresy.

BIBLIOGRAPHY: Allen Ep 227 / DNB V 119–21 /

Emden BRUO (1501–40) 151–2 / de Vocht CTL I 274–7 and passim / J.J. Scarisbrick *Henry VIII* (London 1971) 32, 335–8, and passim / McConica 80 and passim / *Matrikel Leipzig* I 539, II 510–11 / Rogers Ep 81 / RE Ep 224 / L. Delaruelle *Répertoire ... de la correspondance de Guillaume Budé* (Toulouse 1907) Ep 49

CFG & PGB

Thomas CROMWELL of Putney, c 1485–28 July 1540
Thomas Cromwell (Crumwell, Cronwelius, Cronuelius, Cromwellus), the son of Walter Cromwell, a smith and fuller, was born in Putney. Little is known of his early years: he may have served in the French army in Italy around 1504; he then became a merchant in the Netherlands. He also acquired a knowledge of law and of foreign languages. He returned to England about 1512 or 1513 and entered Cardinal *Wolsey's service. In 1523, probably through Wolsey's influence, he became a member of Parliament. He served Wolsey with ruthless vigour in legal matters and in the suppression of small monastic houses. After Wolsey fell from power in 1529, Cromwell helped him conclude his affairs. During the Reformation Parliament (1529–36) he played a leading role in the anti-clerical debates. In 1530 he entered the service of *Henry VIII and was sworn into the council. From this point on his rise was rapid: privy councillor in 1531, master of the jewels in 1532, principal secretary to the king and master of the rolls in 1534, and lord privy seal in 1536. However, it was not to office or title that Cromwell owed his power, but to his favour with the king. From 1532 to 1534 he masterminded the program which procured for Henry his divorce from *Catherine of Aragon, separated the English church from Rome, and established the royal supremacy. By January 1535 he was appointed vicar-general of the supreme head of the church and set in motion the visitations which culminated in the dissolution of the English monasteries. He also took steps to reform the royal bureaucracy and finances. Although he was created earl of Essex and lord great chamberlain in April 1540, the failure of his policy for a German Protestant alliance and for Henry's marriage to Anne of Cleves led to his arrest in June of the same year. He was kept alive long enough to provide

testimony for the annulment of the marriage to Anne of Cleves, then was executed on a bill of attainder.

Although there were many opportunities for the paths of Erasmus and Cromwell to cross in the Netherlands, Italy, and England, and although they shared many common contacts, including Thomas *More, Richard *Pace, Reginald *Pole, Thomas *Lupset, Richard Starkey, and perhaps John *Claymond, there is no evidence that Erasmus heard of Cromwell before December 1534, when in a letter to Erasmus *Schets he spoke of a certain nobleman who sent a package and letters to the secretary of the king (Ep 2981). In September 1535 Thomas *Bedyll, who was then in the service of Cromwell, sent Erasmus news that his master was sending a gift and would help ensure the payment of his English annuity (Ep 3058). In March 1536 Erasmus wrote to Cromwell expressing his gratitude (Ep 3107); he also mentioned Cromwell's generosity in a letter to Gilbert *Cousin (Ep 3104).

For his part, Cromwell, according to the martyrologist John Foxe, knew the whole of Erasmus' New Testament by memory. From 1530 Cromwell was increasingly interested in employing humanists in a royal propaganda campaign to back the revolution in the church; James K. McConica has argued that his program for reform was Erasmian in nature.

A portrait of Cromwell by *Holbein is now in the Frick Collection in New York.

BIBLIOGRAPHY: Allen Ep 3107 / DNB V 192–202 / R.B. Merriman *Life and Letters of Thomas Cromwell* (London 1902) / John Foxe *Ecclesiastical History* (London 1870) II 419 / McConica 160–99 and passim / W.G. Zeeveld *Foundations of Tudor Policy* (Cambridge, Mass, 1948) 5, 14, and passim / F.L. Baumer *The Early Tudor Theory of Kingship* (New Haven, Conn, 1940) 22, 168–70, and passim / S.E. Lehmberg *The Reformation Parliament, 1529–1536* (Cambridge 1970) 1–2, 26–8, and passim / D. Knowles *The Religious Orders in England* (Cambridge 1956–9) III 195–417 and passim / A.G. Dickens *Thomas Cromwell and the English Reformation* (London 1959) / A.G. Dickens *The English Reformation* (London 1964) 109–84 / G.R. Elton *Policy and Police: The Enforcement of the Reformation in the Age of Thomas Cromwell* (Cambridge 1972) / G.R. Elton *Reform and Reformation England 1509–1558*

(Cambridge, Mass, 1977) 126–295 and passim / G.R. Elton *The Tudor Revolution in Government* (Cambridge 1953) 71–159 and passim / W. Schenk *Reginald Pole, Cardinal of England* (London 1950) 37–9 and passim / R.J. Schoeck 'Duo Thomae' *Moreana* 59–60 (Dec 1978) 144–6 / P. Van Dyke *Renaissance Portraits* (London 1905, repr 1969) 138–258, 377–418

R.J. SCHOECK

Hartmuth von CRONBERG 1488–7 August 1549

Hartmuth belonged to a family of free imperial knights associated with the town of Kronberg, near Frankfurt; his father, Johann von Cronberg, was an official of the archbishop of Mainz. Hartmuth grew up at the court of the elector Palatine in Heidelberg. In 1511 he married Anna, a daughter of Phillipp von Cronberg, who was likewise in the service of Mainz and subsequently the Palatine court. Through his marriage Hartmuth was related to Franz von *Sickingen (Ep 1342). They became friends, and Cronberg took part in some of Sickingen's campaigns. He was deeply impressed with *Luther's teachings and his firm stand at the diet of Worms in 1521. Between 1521 and 1525 Cronberg wrote a number of pamphlets defending his own actions as well as Lutheran views, including *Ein christliche Schrifft und Vermanung an alle Stend dess Römischen Reychs* (Augsburg: H. Steiner 1523) and *Eyn Sendbrieff an Bapst Adrianum* (Wittenberg: H. Lufft 1523). Although Cronberg had not taken part in Sickingen's last campaign against the archbishop of Trier, he was affected by his downfall; the town of Kronberg was captured on 15 October 1522 and Cronberg lost his family estates, which were seized by Philip of *Hesse. In Sickingen's castle, the Ebernburg, he met *Oecolampadius and accompanied or followed him to Basel, late in 1522. In 1523 he went to Wittenberg and Bohemia, but in August he passed through Constance (Ep 1382) on his way back to Zürich and Basel. It seems that he then settled for some years in Basel or Strasbourg. After mediation by Martin *Bucer, Philip of Hesse agreed in 1541 to release the Cronberg estates, although under unfavourable conditions. These were not changed until after the Schmalkaldic war, when *Charles V saw to it that Cronberg was fully reinstated. Although he remained sympathetic to the Reformation, henceforward Cronberg refrained from a public commitment. He died at Kronberg.

Erasmus was favourably impressed by his modesty and good education when Cronberg visited him twice in Basel late in 1522 (Epp 1331, 1342; but cf Ep 1382).

BIBLIOGRAPHY: Allen Ep 1331 / NDB III 422 / Luther w Briefwechsel II Ep 426 / BA Oecolampads I 150–1, 204–6, 267, and passim

IG

Cornelis CROOCK of Amsterdam, d 1550

Cornelis Croock (not 'Safraen,' as de Vocht supposed; Cornelius Crocus) was born around 1500 in Amsterdam, the son of Pieter Croock, and matriculated on 31 August 1517 at Louvain, where he had *Alaard of Amsterdam and Adrianus Cornelii *Barlandus as teachers. By 1522 he was a schoolmaster in his native town. On a visit to England he received the minor orders from John *Fisher, bishop of Rochester. By 1531 he was rector of an Amsterdam school, presumably until 1537, and from 16 March 1544 to January 1549 he again directed one of Amsterdam's two municipal schools, the so-called Oudezijdsschool. In the intervening period he may have studied theology at Louvain. In Amsterdam Nicolaas *Kan taught under him, while Pieter Opmeer was one of his pupils. In 1549 he decided to join the Jesuit order, and to do so travelled via Louvain (on 14 May 1550) and Paris to Rome. He fell ill and died at the end of 1550, shortly after he had attained his goal.

Croock's first publication was a *Farrago sordidorum verborum* (Cologne: J. Gymnich 1529; many reprints). Erasmus was very displeased when he realized that his own *Paraphrasis in Elegantias Vallae* had been added to the volume (Ep 2260). He seems to have raised that matter in a letter to Croock, who disclaimed any responsibility (Ep 2354). Croock also produced other books for use in schools, prayer-books, and a sacred comedy, *Ioseph* (Antwerp: J. Grapheus for J. Steelsius 1536; NK 2728). Among the works he wrote in defence of orthodoxy, his *Ecclesia* (Antwerp: J. Grapheus for J. Steelsius 1536; NK 644) is the most important. Andreas Schottus, SJ, edited his *Opera omnia* in five volumes (Antwerp 1612–13).

BIBLIOGRAPHY: Allen Ep 2354 / NNBW III 267–8 / *Matricule de Louvain* III-1 569 / de Vocht CTL II 202–8 / J.F.M. Sterck *Onder Amsterdamsche humanisten* (Hilversum-Amsterdam 1934) / A.J. Kölker *Alardus Aemstelredamus en Cornelius Crocus* (Nijmegen-Utrecht 1963)

C.G. VAN LEIJENHORST

Johannes CROTUS Rubianus of Dornheim, 1480–c 1545

Johann Jäger (Jeger, Venatorius) was generally known under the name of Crotus Rubianus (Rubeanus), which he adopted in 1509. He was born in Dornheim, near Arnstadt, Thuringia, the son of a peasant; he matriculated in Erfurt in 1498 and obtained a BA in 1500. He belonged to the circle around Conradus *Mutianus Rufus, knew Martin *Luther from 1501, and was a friend of Ulrich von *Hutten, with whom he moved to Cologne, matriculating on 15 November 1505. A year later Crotus returned to Erfurt, obtaining his MA in 1507. He became a priest and was headmaster of the school attached to the abbey of Fulda from 1510 to 1515. A strong supporter of Johann *Reuchlin, he was the principal author of the first part of the anonymous *Epistolae obscurorum virorum*, a copy of which Wolfgang *Angst sent to Erasmus in 1515 (Ep 363). In 1517 Crotus travelled to Italy, obtained a doctorate of theology in Bologna, and returned to Germany in 1520; he met Hutten in Bamberg and became professor of theology at Erfurt. As rector of the university for the winter term 1520–1 he welcomed Luther (6 April 1521) when he was passing through Erfurt on his journey to Worms. After another stay in Fulda, Crotus entered, in 1524, the service of Albert (I) of *Brandenburg-Ansbach, the last master of the Teutonic Knights and subsequently the first duke of Prussia. Crotus remained at Kaliningrad (Königsberg) until 1530, but finally left, wishing to detach himself from the Lutheran party. In the spring of 1531 he was appointed councillor to Albert of *Brandenburg, archbishop of Mainz and Magdeburg, and became a canon in Halle. His anti-Lutheran *Apologia* (1531) caused him to lose the friendship of Helius *Eobanus Hessus and Justus *Jonas. On the other hand, he became associated with Georg *Witzel, another deserter from the Lutheran cause.

Crotus' early poems – verse in praise of the

University of Erfurt (1507) and a *Bucolicon*
(1509) – show skill and talent. His masterful use
of satire is evident in the *Epistolae obscurorum
virorum*. Crotus' joining of the Lutheran camp
was regretfully mentioned by Mutianus in Ep
1425; otherwise there is no evidence for
connections between Crotus and Erasmus.

BIBLIOGRAPHY: Allen Ep 1425 / NDB III 424–5 /
Matrikel Erfurt II 205, 317 / Knod 363–4 / W.
Krause *Helius Eobanus Hessus* (Gotha 1879) I 28,
II 164–7 / Hutten *Opera* I Ep 84 / *Der Briefwechsel
des Justus Jonas* ed G. Kawerau (Halle 1884–5) I
Ep 228 and passim / Luther w *Briefwechsel* I Ep
213, II Epp 281, 358

IG

Catherine de CROY 1470–1546
Catherine was a daughter of Philippe de Croy,
count of Chimay, and Walburge de Moers; she
was thus a sister of Charles de *Croy, prince of
Chimay, and a niece of Jacques de *Croy,
bishop of Cambrai. shortly before 1491 she
married Robert II de la *Marck, lord of Sedan;
their children were Robert III, lord of Florange;
Guillaume, lord of Jametz; Jean, lord of Saulcy;
Antoine, abbot of Beaulieu, in the Argonnes,
and archdeacon of Brabant; Philippe, archdeacon of Hesbaye; Jacques, knight of St John;
Philippine, the wife of Reinot van Brederode;
and Jacqueline, a nun.

Resolute and energetic, Catherine came to
play a significant part in the complex political
and diplomatic affairs of her husband and his
family, such as the election of her brother-in-
law, Erard de la *Marck, as prince-bishop of
Liège, the treaty of St Truiden (1518) and its
subsequent abandonment, and perhaps also
the slaughter following the surrender of
peasant rebels at Saverne, in Lower Alsace
(1525). Paschasius *Berselius did not hesitate
to call her 'in life Penelope over again, in
character Lucretia' (Ep 748), and Erasmus too
paid her a compliment (Ep 956). After the
deaths in 1536 of both her husband and her
eldest son, Catherine resided in Sedan, where
she founded the first hostel and raised her
grandson, Robert IV, the future marshal of
France. She was buried beside her husband in
the church of St Laurence, Sedan, under a
monument which no longer exists.

BIBLIOGRAPHY: J. de Chestret de Haneffe
Histoire de la maison de la Marck (Liège 1898)
152–3, 157, 162–70 / Paul Harsin *Etudes critiques*

II: *Le Règne d'Erard de la Marck* (Liège 1955) 41
and passim / P. Congar et al *Sedan et le pays
sedanais* (Paris 1969) 147 / *Le Journal d'un
bourgeois de Paris* ed V.-L. Bourrilly (Paris 1910)
415 / *Le Journal d'un bourgeois de Mons* ed A.
Louant (Brussels 1969) 46

GÉRARD MOREAU

Charles (I) de CROY 1460–11 September 1527
Charles, the eldest son of Philippe de Croy,
count of Chimay, and Walburge de Moers, and
the brother of Catherine de *Croy, was
knighted by *Maximilian I on the battlefield of
Guinegate (1479) and was created prince of
Chimay on the occasion of Maximilian's
coronation as king of the Romans at Aachen (10
April 1486). In 1489 he served under Duke
Albert of *Saxony, helping to end the revolt of
the Netherlands against Maximilian. On 24
May 1491 at Mechelen Philip the Handsome,
duke of *Burgundy, admitted him to the
prestigious order of the Golden Fleece. He was
captain-general of Hainaut and was chosen to
be a godfather and the mentor of the future
*Charles V. In the latter function he played a
leading role in the government of the
Netherlands until 1509, when he partially
retired and was succeeded as mentor by his
cousin, Guillaume de *Croy, lord of Chièvres.
He did, however, participate in the conclusion
of the treaty of St Truiden (1518) between the
Netherlands and the principality of Liège.
Charles de Croy married Louise, the sister of
Jean d'Albret, king of Navarre; they had two
daughters: Anne, the elder, who in 1520
married Philippe de *Croy, the future duke of
Aarschot, and Marguerite, who married
Charles (II) de Lalaing. Charles de Croy died
suddenly at the castle of Beaumont while
paying a visit to his daughter Anne and was
buried with great pomp at Chimay on 19
November 1527.

In 1519 Erasmus paid tribute to Charles in a
dedicatory letter addressed to Antoine de la
*Marck (Ep 956). Antoine de Lusy, the burgher
of Mons, noted in his journal that the prince
allowed himself to be controlled by his
servants, 'estranges et petites gens.'

BIBLIOGRAPHY: Allen Ep 956 / BNB IV 564–6 / L.
Devillers 'Le Hainaut sous la régence de
Maximilien d'Autriche' *Bulletins de la Commission royale d'Histoire* 14 (1887) 193, 214, 15 (1888)
158, 184, 16 (1889) 248 / *Le Journal d'un bourgeois*

Charles (1) de Croy, funeral monument at Chimay

---

de Mons ed A. Louant (Brussels 1969) 65 and passim / G. Dansaert *Guillaume de Croy-Chièvres dit Le Sage* (Paris 1942) 19, 22–3, 31, 41 / Paul Harsin *Etudes critiques* II: *Le Règne d'Erard de la Marck* (Liège 1955) 37 and passim / *Le Journal d'un bourgeois de Tournai* ed Gérard Moreau (Brussels 1975) 4 / *Chroniques de Jean Molinet* ed G. Doutrepont and O. Jodogne (Brussels 1935) II 73 and passim

GÉRARD MOREAU

Charles (II) de CROY 1507–12 December 1564
Charles, the fourth son of Henri de Croy, lord of Chateau-Porcéan (Château-Porcien), was from an early age intended for a brilliant ecclesiastical career, just like his brothers Guillaume (II) and Robert de *Croy. A Benedictine at the age of nine, he became abbot of Afflighem and Hautmont at the age of fourteen, bishop of Tournai at eighteen (29 March 1525), and abbot of Saint-Ghislain at twenty-two. In 1519 he was sent to Louvain to study under Jacobus *Latomus, and on 3 February 1522 he matriculated at the university. At the beginning of 1523 Adrianus Cornelii *Barlandus was appointed tutor of the

young prelate, of whom he wrote with great hopes (de Vocht *Literae ad Craneveldium* Ep 62). He also dedicated to Charles de Croy his *Dialogi* (Louvain: D. Martens 1524), composed to instruct him in the use of good Latin. At about this time Charles also began his theological studies under Latomus and Jan *Driedo.

In April 1526, while Barlandus was Charles' tutor, Erasmus composed a letter addressed to Charles but sent to Barlandus for personal delivery, without the knowledge of Latomus, whom Erasmus distrusted (Epp 1694, 1695). The letter solicited Charles' help in the matter of Erasmus' pension; unfortunately it is missing and no more is known about the matter. A little later, when Barlandus was appointed public orator at the University of Louvain and could no longer devote himself to Charles, the young prelate went to Italy and studied first at Pavia and subsequently at Bologna. On 13 June 1533 he was ordained priest in Rome. Another six years were to pass, however, before he held his *joyeuse entrée* as bishop of Tournai and took charge of his diocese, which thus far had been administered by Pierre *Cotrel and showed every sign of strong Protestant penetration. Although he ignored *Charles v's request that he attend the council of Trent, Charles was one of the first bishops in the Netherlands to welcome the establishment of a Jesuit college in his episcopal city. In compliance with the bull *Super universas* (12 May 1559) he was obliged to accept the partitioning of his diocese. He left it in the charge of Gilbert d'Oignies, his coadjutor since 1556, and retired to his abbey of Saint-Ghislain, where he remained until his death. Jan Driedo dedicated to him *De captivitate et redemptione humani generis* (Louvain: R. Rescius 1534) and Franciscus Sonnius the second book of *Demonstrationes religionis christianae* (Louvain: S. Valerius 1555).

BIBLIOGRAPHY: Allen Ep 1964 / NBW II 148–58 / *Matricule de Louvain* III-1 666 / Eubel III 316 / *Monasticon Belge* ed U. Berlière et al (Maredsous-Liège 1890–) I 263, IV 55 / L.-E. Halkin *Les Conflits de jurisdiction entre Erard de la Marck et le chapitre cathédral de Chartres* (Liège 1933) 64, 71, 118 / *Le Journal d'un bourgeois de Mons* ed A. Louant (Brussels 1969) 175, 290–1 / E. Daxhelet *Adrien Barlandus* (Louvain 1938) 28 and passim / *Le Journal d'un bourgeois de Tournai* ed Gérard Moreau (Brussels 1975) 65, 362, 454–5 / Gérard Moreau *Histoire du protestantisme à Tournai* (Paris 1962) 63 and passim

GÉRARD MOREAU

Eustache de CROY 1502–3 October 1538
Eustache, the younger son of Ferry de *Croy, lord of Roeulx, was already apostolic protonotary when he matriculated at the University of Louvain on 13 September 1521. In that same year he became provost of Aire and Saint-Omer, and two years later bishop of Arras (8 September 1523). Rather than take charge of his diocese, however, he went to Italy, where in November 1525 one of Erasmus' friends was hoping to meet him at Bologna (Ep 1650). A few years later he had hopes of becoming coadjutor to Erard de la *Marck, prince-bishop of Liège. Being a canon of Cambrai as well, he finally took up residence at Arras in 1536 but died two years later in the castle of Maroeuil, the summer residence of the bishops of Arras. While his heart remained at Maroeuil, where he is also remembered in an epitaph, his body was buried in the cathedral of Saint-Omer

under a monument created by Jacques de Broeucq.

BIBLIOGRAPHY: Allen Ep 1650 / *Matricule de Louvain* III-1 662 / M. de Vegiano and J.S. de Herckenrode *Nobiliaire des Pays-Bas* (Ghent 1865) I 570 / de Vocht *Busleyden* 117 / A. Berteaux *Etude historique ... sur ... la ville de Cambrai* (Cambrai 1908) I 431 / Léon-E. Halkin *Le Cardinal de la Marck ...* (Liège 1930) 244 / Léon-E. Halkin 'La coadjutorerie des princes-évêques de Liège au XVIe siècle' *Revue belge de philologie et d'histoire* 7 (1928) 1049 / E. de Marneffe *La Principauté de Liège et les Pays-Bas* (Liège 1887) I 216, 244 / J. Lestocquoy *Les Evêques d'Arras* (Fontenay-le-Comte 1942) 62–4 / J. Lestocquoy *Le Diocèse d'Arras* (Arras 1949) 84

GÉRARD MOREAU

Ferry de CROY c 1470–17 June 1524
Ferry, son of Jean de Croy, lord of Roeulx, and Jeanne de Crecque, married by 1495 Lamberte, daughter of Guy de Brimeu. They had two sons Adrien, who succeeded his father as governor of Artois, and Eustache de *Croy.

On 7 March 1500 Ferry carried in the solemn procession the alb to be used in at the christening of the future *Charles v. The following year he was chamberlain to Philip the Handsome, duke of *Burgundy, and accompanied his master to Spain. On 17 November 1505 he was admitted to the order of the Golden Fleece. Subsequently he was appointed chamberlain and court marshal to the Emperor *Maximilian; in February 1516 he and Jérôme de *Busleyden undertook an embassy to *Henry VIII in order to strengthen the Hapsburg-Tudor alliance. At the court of Charles v he occupied the positions of *grand maître d'hotel* and *maréchal de l'ost*; he was also governor of Artois. In 1521 he was at Worms for the diet when his cousin, Guillaume de *Croy, lord of Chièvres, chose him to be the executor of his will. In November of the same year his wife happened to be at Hesdin when Charles de Bourbon, constable of France, took that city by assault, but he gallantly permitted the lady to leave and take her jewels with her. From 1522 Ferry de Croy could no longer follow the emperor on his journeys as he had grown 'gros, fort gras et pesant de sa personne.' He died two years later at

Guillaume (1) de Croy

Saint-Omer and was buried in the abbey of Roeulx.

In Erasmus' correspondence Ferry is mentioned in connection with his son Eustache (Ep 1650).

BIBLIOGRAPHY: Allen Ep 1650 / M. de Vegiano and J.S. de Herckenrode *Nobiliaire des Pays-Bas* (Ghent 1865) I 570 / de Vocht *Busleyden* 87–8, 117 / *Chroniques de Jean Molinet* ed G. Doutrepont and O. Jodogne (Brussels 1935) II 469 / L.P. Gachard and C. Piot *Collection des voyages des souverains des Pays-Bas* (Brussels 1874–82) I 127, 525, II 512 / G. Dansaert *Guillaume de Croy-Chièvres dit Le Sage* (Brussels 1942) 31, 216, 292 / *Le Journal d'un bourgeois de Mons* ed A. Louant (Brussels 1969) 90 and passim

GÉRARD MOREAU

Guillaume (1) de CROY 1458–27/8 May 1521
Guillaume was the third son of Philippe de Croy, lord of Renty, and Jacqueline de Luxembourg. In 1486 he bought from his father the lordships of Chièvres and Beaumont and was knighted by *Maximilian I, then king of the Romans. He married Marie de Hamal, the widow of Adolphe de la Marck, and on 24 May 1491 was made a knight of the Golden Fleece by Philip the Handsome, duke of *Burgundy, whose chamberlain and councillor he became ten years later. Meanwhile, with his master's approval he joined the Italian expeditions of *Charles VIII and *Louis XII of France; he conducted himself valiantly and returned home to assume a command in the forces of Philip the Handsome. When the duke left in 1501 on his first journey to Spain, Chièvres was appointed to the council of regency for the Netherlands. Three years later he was president of the council of finance, and subsequently commander-in-chief, comptroller-general, and lieutenant-general of the Netherlands (26 December 1505).

On 18 March 1509 Chièvres was appointed chamberlain and mentor of the future *Charles V. Prince Charles was declared of age on 15 January 1515, and from that moment Chièvres, who strongly influenced his thinking, was the principal policy-maker for the Netherlands. A consistent advocate of peace and friendship with France, Chièvres was the chief architect of Franco-Burgundian reconciliation (cf the treaties of Noyon and Cambrai, 13 August 1516 and 11 March 1517), and was recognized as such by Erasmus (Allen I 18). Further titles and appointments followed. Chièvres was duke of Soria, admiral of the kingdom of Naples, and captain-general of the seaborne forces when he accompanied his master to Spain in 1517; there he also became *contador major*, or chief treasurer. On 18 November 1518 he was created marquis of Aarschot. In April and May 1519 he was at Montpelier for follow-up negotiations in execution of the treaty of Noyon. On 28 June 1519 Charles was elected emperor, a success which, according to Pirenne, may be considered as a personal victory for Chièvres. On 14 July 1520 he was at the side of his monarch for the signing of the secret treaty of Gravelines with *Henry VIII.

As their marriage remained childless, Chièvres and his wife extended their loving care to the children of his deceased brother Henri, in particular to the second son, Guillaume (II) de *Croy (Epp 628, 957), whose accidental death in January 1521 was a devastating blow to them. Chièvres fell ill himself and died in the night of 27/8 May. He was buried at Aarschot on 13 June, with the emperor in attendance; four years later his body was transferred to the Celestine monastery at Heverlee, which his wife had founded in accordance with his instructions. Erasmus was well aware of Chièvres' enormous influence at court (Epp 597, 628), and believed that he was not really opposed to the new learning (Ep 969). He counted on Chièvres' assistance in obtaining the arrears of his pension (Ep 1094) and later commented that Chièvres' death had deprived him of a friend at court (Ep 1342).

BIBLIOGRAPHY: Allen Ep 532 / CWE Ep 532 (with portrait) / BNB IV 528–33 / G. Dansaert *Guillaume de Croy-Chièvres dit Le Sage* (Brussels 1942) / Henri Pirenne *Histoire de Belgique* (Brussels 1902–32) III 69, 82–90, and passim / Paul Harsin *Etudes critiques* II: *Le Règne d'Erard de la Marck* (Liège 1955) 108 and passim / Michel de Vegiano and J.S. Herckenrode *Nobiliaire des Pays-Bas* (Ghent 1865) I 571–3 / M. Baelde *De collaterale raden onder Karel V en Filips II* (Brussels 1965) 9–10, 230, 253 / *Chroniques de Jean Molinet* ed G. Doutrepont and O. Jodogne (Brussels 1935) II 45 and passim / *Le Journal d'un bourgeois de Mons* ed A. Louant (Brussels 1969) 36 and passim / For Erasmus' relations with Chièvres see also Otto Herding in ASD IV-2 19
GÉRARD MOREAU

Guillaume (II) de CROY 1498–6 January 1521
Guillaume, the second son of Henri de Croy, lord of Chateau-Porcéan, and Charlotte de Chateaubriant, and the brother of Philippe, Robert, and Charles (II) de *Croy, was orphaned at the age of sixteen. Together with his brothers, Guillaume found an ideal protector in the person of his uncle, Guillaume (I) de *Croy, lord of Chièvres. Himself childless, Chièvres was eager to use his growing influence with the future *Charles V to further the advancement of his nephews; for young Guillaume he secured some of the richest ecclesiastical benefices available. When the young man matriculated at the University of Louvain on 3 September 1511 he was already an apostolic protonotary and the provost of the chapter of St Gertrude's, Nivelles. On 10 December 1512 he was appointed coadjutor to the abbot of Afflighem, Willem Machiels, and three years later coadjutor to the bishop of

Cambrai, Jacques de *Croy. When the latter died on 15 August 1516 Chièvres was returning from the peace negotiations at Noyon and happened to be passing through Cambrai that very day; he at once saw to it that his nephew took possession of the vacated see. Again it was at Chièvres' request that Pope *Leo X appointed Guillaume cardinal in 1517 with the title of Santa Maria in Aquiro; that same year Guillaume was also made abbot of St Bavo, Ghent (31 July), as well as archbishop of Toledo and primate of Spain (31 December). After receiving the abbey of Afflighem on 4 November 1518, he resigned the bishopric of Cambrai on 17 August 1519 to his brother Robert. In the following year Chièvres intervened to secure the abbey of Hautmont for Guillaume after the monks had initially elected Robert to be their next abbot.

Chièvres also found time to concern himself with Guillaume's education, appointing as his mentor Charles Carondelet, formerly chamberlain to Charles V's sister *Mary, who was to be assisted by Baudouin d'Ongnies, later secretary to Robert de Croy, while Adrianus Cornelii *Barlandus and Juan Luis *Vives were to be Guillaume's teachers at Louvain. Erasmus seems to have thought highly of Guillaume's abilities (Ep 628) and encouraged Barlandus to develop them to the full (Epp 646, 647). Vives quickly won the heart of his pupil (Ep 917), to whom he dedicated his *Meditationes* (Louvain: D. Martens) on the seven penitential Psalms in 1518. Early in 1519 Jacobus *Latomus, a colleague of Barlandus, dedicated to Guillaume his *De trium linguarum et studii theologici ratione dialogus* (Antwerp: M. Hillen 1519), which contained attacks upon Erasmus. When the latter replied with his *Apologia contra Latomi dialogum* he hastened to send a copy to Guillaume, who responded by reassuring Erasmus of his continued commitment to the new learning (Epp 945, 951). There followed a didactic exchange of letters between the young cardinal and Erasmus which to the latter seemed worthy of publication (Epp 957–9). In October 1519 Erasmus showed Guillaume his library and emptied with him the 'cup of friendship' which was a gift from Cardinal Albert of *Brandenburg (Ep 1033). They met again in February 1520 (Ep 1071), and throughout that year, except for a short visit to

Paris (Ep 1108), Vives remained attached to the cardinal, as Erasmus and Thomas *More noted with great satisfaction (Epp 1082, 1106, 1111).

In January 1521 Guillaume was in Worms for the diet; returning from a hunting trip he fell from his horse and was killed. On 16 February Erasmus informed his friend Guillaume *Budé of the sad event, paying homage to the delicate youth: 'with his whole heart he loved liberal studies, nor had he any aversion from my humble self' (Ep 1184). After a funeral at Worms (21 January) the body was taken to Aarschot for burial. Nicaise Ladam, king-at-arms to Charles V, composed an epitaph for Guillaume and a narrative about his funeral.

BIBLIOGRAPHY: Allen Ep 647 / DHGE XIII 1073 / Eubel III 148, 314 (confusing Guillaume and Jacques de Croy) / Matricule de Louvain III-1 438 / M. de Vegiano and J.S. de Herckenrode Nobiliaire des Pays-Bas (Ghent 1865) I 573 / A. Berteaux Etude historique … sur … la ville de Cambrai (Cambrai 1908) I 162–3, 409 / E.I. Strubbe and L. Voet De chronologie van de Middeleeuwen en de Moderne Tijden in de Nederlanden (Antwerp 1960) 266 / Monasticon Belge ed U. Berlière et al (Maredsous-Liège 1890–) IV 54–5 / Le Journal d'un bourgeois de Mons ed A. Louant (Brussels 1969) 102 and passim / G. Dansaert Guillaume de Croy-Chièvres dit Le Sage (Paris 1942) 153 and passim / de Vocht MHL 1–2 and passim / de Vocht CTL I 322 and passim / E. Daxhelet Adrien Barlandus (Louvain 1938) 17, 268–9 / C.G. Noreña Juan Luis Vives (The Hague 1970) 46 and passim / M.-A. Nauwelaerts 'De Spaans-Nederlandse Humanist Juan Luis Vives en Leuven' Mededelingen van de Geschied- en Oudheidkundige Kring voor Leuven en omgeving 12 (1972) 184 / Brussels, Bibliothèque Royale, MS 14864–5 f 138 verso

GÉRARD MOREAU

Jacques de CROY 1445–15 August 1516

As the younger son of Jean de Croy, count of Chimay, and Marie de Lalaing, Jacques was intended for an ecclesiastical career from early childhood. Thanks to the combined influence of his paternal and maternal families he had no trouble in becoming a canon of Cambrai, Cologne, and Liège, prior of Saint-Saulve near Valenciennes, an apostolic protonotary, and also the provost of Bonn, Masseik, and Arras. Things went less smoothly, however, in his quest for a bishopric. In 1482 he was elected bishop of Liège but failed to secure papal confirmation. In 1489 he sought recognition as 'administrator of the church and state of Liège,' but three years later he had to abandon his claims in exchange for two annuities settled on the prince-bishop and the state of Liège (as well as for endless trouble in securing the payments due to him). On 22 October 1502 he was elected bishop of Cambrai and this time was confirmed by Pope *Alexander VI on 1 February 1503, only to find his episcopal city rising in revolt against him. To break the resistance of the burghers of Cambrai he had to appeal for help to Philip the Handsome, duke of *Burgundy. Subsequently he tried in vain to challenge the claims of Erard de la *Marck for the vacated see of Liège, but on the other hand he was created duke of Cambrai by *Maximilian I on 28 June 1510. Finally, on 10 February 1511 he held his joyeuse entrée into Cambrai as bishop-duke.

On 4 December 1515 Jacques secured the appointment of his young cousin, Guillaume (II) de *Croy as his coadjutor. He died in his private residence at Dilbeek; he was buried in the church of St Géry, Cambrai, but was then transferred to the church of St Vaast in 1544. Erasmus was asked by his friend Jean *Desmarez to compose an epitaph for the bishop (Ep 497; Reedijk poem 104), the shortness of which is in noticeable contrast to another epitaph engraved on the bishop's commemorative slab in the cathedral of Cambrai.

BIBLIOGRAPHY: Allen Ep 497 / DHGE XIII 1073 / A. Berteaux Etude historique … sur … la ville de Cambrai (Cambrai 1908) I 158–62 / M. de Vegiano and J.S. de Herckenrode Nobiliaire des Pays-Bas (Ghent 1865) I 576 / de Vocht CTL I 186 / Le Journal d'un bourgeois de Mons ed A. Louant (Brussels 1969) 98, 100 / Paul Harsin Etudes critiques II: Le Règne d'Erard de la Marck (Liège 1955) 37–8 and passim / Paul Harsin 'Histoire d'une créance ou les prétentions de Jacques de Croy à l'épiscopat liégois' Anciens Pays et assemblées d'états 22 (1961) 137–68

GÉRARD MOREAU

Philippe de CROY 1496–April 1549

Philippe was the eldest son of Henri de Croy, lord of Chateau-Porcéan, and Charlotte de

Chateaubriant. The death of his father in 1514
left him lord of Chateau-Porcéan, while on 25
October 1516 he was admitted to the order of
the Golden Fleece. On 30 August 1520 at
Binche he married his cousin Anne, the
daughter and heiress of Charles (I) de *Croy,
prince of Chimay. In the following year his
father-in-law resigned in his favour his
responsibility as captain-general of Hainaut; at
the same time Philippe inherited the major part
of the lordships and titles of his uncle
Guillaume (I) de *Croy, lord of Chièvres. On
the death of his father-in-law, six years later,
he became prince of Chimay and was by then
the wealthiest lord in the Netherlands. Highly
esteemed both by *Charles v and by the regent,
his sister *Mary, he was admitted to the council
of state in 1531, became president of the council
of finance in 1532, and was created duke of
Aarschot in 1533.

In the same year Philippe de Croy came to
play a role in the efforts undertaken by
Nicolaus *Olahus, Queen Mary's secretary,
and others who wished to see Erasmus return
to the Netherlands. Following a pressing
invitation by Queen Mary herself (Ep 2820),
Philippe de Croy wrote to Erasmus in the same
vein, recalling the friendship between his late
brother, Cardinal Guillaume (II) de *Croy and
Erasmus as well as the tribute paid to the house
of Croy in the latter's publications (Ep 2822).
Olahus also emphasized the sincerity of
Philippe's admiration for the scholar (Ep 2828).
At first, however, Erasmus was prevented by
illness from undertaking the long journey from
Freiburg to the Netherlands, and later on he
abandoned this plan; by this time his relations
with Philippe were reduced to the exchange of
friendly greetings (Epp 2898, 2915, 2922, 2948).

In 1537 Philippe was appointed grand bailiff
of Hainaut, and in 1540 as well as 1549 he had
the honour of welcoming Charles v at the castle
of Chimay. On 10 July 1548 he married for the
second time; his new wife was Anne, the
widowed daughter of Duke Antoine of
*Lorraine. Guillaume Dumolin, the author of
some of the earliest French translations of
*Luther, dedicated to Philippe de Croy his Très
utile traité du vray règne de l'antichrist (Strasbourg: J. Prüss 1527) with an epistle dated from
Wittenberg, 30 December 1525.

BIBLIOGRAPHY: Allen Ep 2822 / BNB IV 537–40 /

Philippe de Croy

M. de Vegiano and J.S. Herckenrode *Nobiliaire
des Pays-Bas* (Ghent 1865) I 573 / G. Dansaert
Guillaume de Croy-Chièvres dit Le Sage (Brussels
1942) 146–7 and passim / M. Baelde *De
collaterale raden onder Karel v en Filips II* (Brussels
1965) 15 and passim / *Le Journal d'un bourgeois de
Mons* ed A. Louant (Brussels 1969) 104 and
passim / *Le Journal d'un bourgeois de Tournai* ed
Gérard Moreau (Brussels 1975) 123 / E. Mahieu
'Le protestantisme à Mons' *Annales du Cercle
archéologique de Mons* 66 (1967) 133, 148, 154 /
Gérard Moreau *Histoire du protestantisme à
Tournai* (Paris 1962) 60–1 / J.M.C. De
Caraman-Chimay 'Lettres de Charles-Quint...'
Bulletin de la Commission royale d'histoire 82
(1913) 368–88

GÉRARD MOREAU

Robert de CROY 1506–31 August 1556
Robert, the third son of Henri de Croy, lord of
Chateau-Porcéan, became bishop of Cambrai at
the age of thirteen, when that see was resigned
to him by his elder brother Guillaume (II) de
*Croy; however, he did not take possession of
his bishopric until 1526. In the meantime he
was sent to Louvain, where he matriculated on

16 March 1518. After the death of Guillaume in January 1521, Robert was tutored by Juan Luis *Vives, who had formerly been Guillaume's teacher. After Vives had left for England, some consideration was given to replacing him with Conradus *Goclenius, but in the end Goclenius continued his teaching in the Collegium Trilingue (Ep 1457). That Robert had an open mind towards the new learning is suggested by a letter from Guy *Morillon (Ep 1287), who thought that the young bishop of Cambrai might easily be persuaded to restrain the friars opposing Erasmus. It may also be noted that at this time Nicolaas van Nispen, one of the executors of the will of Jérôme de *Busleyden, was secretary to the bishops of Cambrai. On the other hand, Robert de Croy may also have received instruction from the theologian Jacobus *Latomus, a critic of Erasmus (Ep 1256).

In May 1525 Robert left Louvain and spent a few months at the nearby castle of Heverlee as the guest of his eldest brother, Philippe de *Croy; according to Antoine de Lusy, burgher of Mons, he did so 'pour oublier quelque demoiselle.' His mentor at that time was Baudouin d'Ongnies, called d'Estrées, for whom he secured a canonry at Cambrai and other benefices. In 1526 Robert de Croy moved to Cambrai and provided a canonry for Latomus, who from then on frequently resided at Cambrai. Not until 13 June 1529, however, did Robert hold his *joyeuse entrée* into his episcopal city. A few days later he played host to *Margaret of Austria and Louise of *Savoy, who arrived to negotiate the 'Ladies' Peace.' On 23 November 1532 he was at Mons for the solemn entry of Queen *Mary of Hungary (Epp 2741, 2783), and in February 1534 he departed for a pilgrimage to the Holy Land; however, he did not get further than Venice, since he failed to secure a safe conduct. From 8 June to 26 August 1546 he was at Trent to attend the council, and in 1550 he held a diocesan synod at Cambrai which was attended by Louis de Blois (Blosius), the great mystic. His tomb is in the cathedral of Cambrai in front of the Lady chapel.

BIBLIOGRAPHY: Allen Ep 1287 / BNB IV 566–7 / DHGE XIII 1073–4 / Eubel III 148–9 / de Vocht *Literae ad Craneveldium* Ep 23 and passim / de Vocht CTL I 51, 582, and passim / *Matricule de*

Louvain III-1 582 / E.I. Strubbe and L. Voet *De chronologie van de Middeleeuwen en de Moderne Tijden in de Nederlanden* (Antwerp 1960) 266 / A. Berteaux *Etude historique … sur … la ville de Cambrai* (Cambrai 1908) I 163–6, 409 / *Chartes du Chapitre de Saint-Waudru* ed E. Mathieu (Brussels 1913) IV 12 and passim / *Le Journal d'un bourgeois de Mons* ed A. Louant (Brussels 1969) 200 and passim / E. Daxhelet *Adrien Barlandus* (Louvain 1938) 251 / Hubert Jedin *Geschichte des Konzils von Trient* (Freiburg 1949–75) IV 135, 381, 430 / E. de Moreau *Histoire de l'église en Belgique* v (Brussels 1952) 32 / A. Artonne et al *Répertoire des statuts synodaux …* (Paris 1963) 173

GÉRARD MOREAU

Johannes CRUCIUS *See Jan van der* CRUYCE

Johannes CRULLUS of Antwerp, documented 1516–17

Johannes Crullus (in the vernacular no doubt Cruls, Krull, or similar) was a respected merchant and citizen of Antwerp. On 18 July 1516 the Antwerp corporation wrote to Cardinal *Wolsey in support of him and others who had been deprived of their goods (LB II 2190). On this or another occasion Thomas *More intervened in his favour (Epp 543, 545). In the early spring of 1517 Crullus asked Erasmus to dinner. He had a son who set out for England at that time and carried Ep 543 for More and a volume of writings about the *Reuchlin controversy for William *Warham, archbishop of Canterbury (Ep 545). Later the same year Erasmus expected Crullus to assist in the remittance of his annuity from Aldington, which was paid through Warham (Epp 712, 736). No more is known about Crullus and his son.

BIBLIOGRAPHY: Allen Ep 545

MARCEL A. NAUWELAERTS

CRUSIUS (Ep 3045 of [late August 1535]) Henricus *Glareanus let Erasmus know that the house of Crusius, near ('supra') the house at Freiburg formerly owned by Erasmus, had been destroyed by fire. Erasmus had owned the house 'zum Kindlein Jesu,' Schiffstrasse 7. The house 'zur Krause,' Schiffstrasse 3, was at some unspecified time between 1460 and 1565 owned by one Georg Kruss.

BIBLIOGRAPHY: A. Poinsignon, H. Flamm, et

al *Geschichtliche Ortsbeschreibung der Stadt
Freiburg i. Br.* (Freiburg 1891–1903) II 238

PGB

Jan van der CRUYCE of Bergues-Saint-
Winoc, d before 22 August 1533
Jan van der Cruyce (Crucius or Gutius,
Berganus), a native of Bergues-Saint-Winoc
(Départment du Nord), matriculated on 31
August 1514 at Louvain as a student of the
College of the Lily. He received his MA in 1517,
learnt Greek (presumably from Adrien *Amerot),
and in 1520 was appointed professor of logic in
the Lily. Erasmus, who had also lived at the
college from 1517, recommended him to
William *Blount, Lord Mountjoy, and he went
to England before November 1522 as a private
tutor to Mountjoy's children. He came to know
Richard *Pace intimately (Ep 1932). At the
request of Pieter de *Corte he returned to the
Lily in October 1527 and was appointed
professor of Greek, starting his lessons on 1
January 1528 (Ep 1932). He was still teaching
there in March 1530 (Ep 2282, LB I 1033B), but
since he probably did not hold a regular
teaching position, it is doubtful whether he
was able to continue doing so after Pieter de
Corte had left (1531). He died before 22 August
1533, when the rector allowed his will to be
executed by de Corte and Louis de Germes.
    BIBLIOGRAPHY: Allen Ep 1932 / A. Roersch in
BNB XXVI 324–5 / *Matricule de Louvain* III-1 494 /
de Vocht *Literae ad Craneveldium* Ep 257 and
passim / de Vocht CTL II 84 and passim
C.G. VAN LEIJENHORST

Elisabeth van CULEMBORG 30 March 1475–
9 December 1555
Elisabeth (Isabella) was the eldest daughter
and – after the death of three younger brothers
in their youth – the principal heiress of Jaspar,
lord of Culemborg (eighteen kilometres south-
east of Utrecht), Hoogstraten, Borssele, etc,
and of Joanna, the daughter of Anthony of
*Burgundy, 'le grand Bâtard.' She thus
belonged to the highest rank of the Burgundian nobility. Brought up at the court of young
Philip the Handsome, duke of *Burgundy,
Elisabeth in due course became lady-in-waiting
to Philip's wife, *Joanna of Castile. In 1501 she
married Jean de Luxembourg, like herself a
member of the high nobility and a knight of the

Golden Fleece. He died in 1508, and the
following year Elisabeth married Antoine de
*Lalaing, the leading politician of the Low
Countries during the regency of *Margaret of
Austria.
    In 1516 Elisabeth, who had remained
childless, transferred Hoogstraten to her
husband, who in 1518 was created count of
Hoogstraten by the future *Charles v. Praised
by her contemporaries for her beauty and
talents, Elisabeth became first lady of honour at
Margaret's court in keeping with the eminent
position occupied by her husband. After his
death in 1540 she lived in retirement at the
castle of Culemborg. Like Lalaing she took a
keen interest in art and architecture and had
important works undertaken, some of which
are still to be seen in Culemborg and
Hoogstraten. A pious lady, she endowed
numerous religious institutions and invited the
Jesuits to establish a house at Culemborg; she
also took steps to suppress heretical books,
including some by Erasmus. Thus it was not
without justification that Erasmus had feared
her influence at court when pondering the
question of a possible return to the Netherlands (Ep 1553).
    BIBLIOGRAPHY: Allen Ep 1553 / T. Ausems
and J. Lauwerys in *Jaarboek van Koninklijke
Hoogstratens Oudheidkundige Kring* 24 (1956)
5–12, 13–61 / J.D. de Jong in *Jaarboek van
Koninklijke Hoogstratens Oudheidkundige Kring*
25 (1957) 1–29
HEIDE STRATENWERTH

Valentinus CURIO of Haguenau, documented
1516–32
Valentinus Curio (Schaffner), an Alsatian, is
first recorded as a student at Freiburg, sharing
quarters with Bonifacius *Amerbach and
attending the lectures of *Zasius. After a visit
to Basel in October 1516 he moved there
permanently in 1519, matriculating at the
university for the spring term. Soon thereafter
he became a citizen at Basel and a member of
the 'Safran' guild. His acceptance by the
socially and culturally prominent circles is also
indicated by his marriage in 1520 to Anna, a
daughter of Jakob *Meyer zum Hirzen. In 1525
he purchased a house at the Heuberg. With the
encouragement of *Capito, his fellow-countryman, Curio entered the scholarly book trade.

Nicolaus Cusanus, monument in San Pietro in Vincoli, Rome

In 1519 a noteworthy Greek lexicon was produced, jointly financed by Capito, Curio, and *Cratander, another Alsatian, who did the printing while Curio contributed his solid knowledge of Greek and wrote the preface. Later both Curio and Cratander claimed the right to produce further editions of the Greek lexicon, and in 1531 litigation between them ensued.

From 1521, or perhaps earlier, to his death in 1533(?) Curio published books from his own press, specializing in Greek lexica and grammars but also printing works and pamphlets, sometimes in German, critical of the church of Rome, among them probably editions of the *Julius exclusus* and of Marsilius of Padua (1522). Although the size of his operations was modest, the scholarly quality and independent typographical style of his productions could perhaps be seen as a challenge to the *Froben press (Ep 1514). As a man of education he often accompanied his publications with prefaces of his own. He also did business as a bookseller; among his customers was *Zwingli, to whom he dedicated his edition of a Greek grammar by Jacobus Ceporinus in 1522. In the spring of

1521 Curio visited *Sickingen's castle, the Ebernburg, and was also at Avignon, calling on *Alciati. In 1524 he experienced difficulties because on his travels he had openly criticized the Swiss mercenary service. He did business with Chrétien *Wechel in Paris and with Franz *Birckmann at Antwerp. His press was eventually continued by his son Hieronymus; in 1542 his daughter Anna married the philosopher Johannes Hospinianus.

BIBLIOGRAPHY: Allen Ep 1514 / Grimm *Buchführer* 1387–9 / R. Wackernagel *Geschichte der Stadt Basel* (Basel 1907–54) III 442–3 and passim / z VII Epp 139, 156, 266 / AK II Epp 544, 571, 764; VI Ep 2732, and passim / *Aktensammlung zur Geschichte der Basler Reformation* ed E. Dürr et al (Basel 1921–50) I 120–2, II 719, V 139, 466–7 / P. Heitz and C. Bernoulli *Basler Büchermarken* (Strasbourg 1895) xxvi, 66–71

PGB

Petrus CURSIUS *See Pietro* CORSI

CURTIUS *See Pieter de* CORTE, *Franceschino and Matteo* CORTI

Nicolaus CUSANUS of Kues, 1401–11 August 1464
Nikolaus Cryfftz (Khryffz, Krebs, Cancer), who called himself Cusanus after his birthplace, Kues, on the Mosel, was the son of Johann, a sailor and boat owner, and Katharina Römer. He received instruction at the school of the Brethren of the Common Life in Deventer. Assisted by a scholarship from the count of Manderscheid, whose service he had entered, he matriculated in Heidelberg in 1416 and then went to Italy, obtaining a doctorate of laws at Padua in 1424. After his return in 1425 he took up theology and taught for a year at the University of Cologne. He discovered some valuable manuscripts of classical authors, among them one of Pliny's *Historia naturalis* and another of Plautus' comedies, some of which were hitherto unknown. He received a number of benefices, including prebends in the chapters of Trier and Koblenz and the provostship of Münstereifel. From 1431 to 1436 he attended the council of Basel on the invitation of Cardinal Giuliano Cesarini. He proved to be an efficient diplomat and mediator in various conflicts brought before the council.

He presented his views on necessary reform within the church in his fundamental *De concordantia catholica* (1433), but finally sided with the papacy when the rift between Pope Eugenius IV and the council proved irreconcilable. On 7 May 1437 he joined the minority of council fathers who departed for Italy in compliance with the pope's request. In the same year he was sent to Constantinople to negotiate with the Emperor John VIII Palaeologus about the union of the Greek and Roman churches; during his short stay in the East he was able to collect more manuscripts.

Cusanus was papal nuncio at the diet of Mainz in 1441 and at the court of King *Charles VII of France. He was appointed cardinal in 1448 and bishop of Bressanone (Brixen) in 1450. As papal legate he travelled extensively in Germany and the Low Countries in 1451 and 1452, attempting to reform the monasteries and to foster genuine devotion among lay people. A conflict with Duke Sigismund of Austria forced him to abandon his diocese after 1457; his remaining years were spent largely in Rome with his friend *Pius II. He died at Todi, in Umbria.

Cusanus was one of the most original and seminal thinkers of the late Middle Ages. An outstanding theologian, he also contributed significantly to the revival of Platonism and the development of scientific thought. Among his philosophical works are *De docta ignorantia* (1440) and *Idiota* (1450); among his scientific studies *De reparatione calendarii* (1436) and *De quadratura circuli* (1450). His collected works were edited in three volumes in Paris (J. Bade 1514) by Jacques *Lefèvre d'Etaples. Erasmus mentioned him in his *Apologia ad Fabrum* (Louvain 1517), stating that Lefèvre followed Cusanus' interpretation of a passage from Psalm 30 (LB IX 60).

BIBLIOGRAPHY: Josef Koch in *New Catholic Encyclopedia* (New York 1966–74) X 449–52 / ADB IV 655–64 / Paul E. Sigmund *Nicholas of Cusa and Medieval Political Thought* (Cambridge, Mass, 1963) / A critical edition of Cusanus' *Opera omnia* is published under the auspices of the Heidelberg Akademie der Wissenschaften by E. Hoffmann, R. Klibansky, et al (Leipzig–Hamburg 1932–); see also *Mitteilungen und Forschungsberichte der Cusanus-Gesellschaft*

(Münster 1964–) and *Bücherreihe der Cusanus-Gesellschaft* (Münster 1966–)

IG

Johannes CUSTOS of Brecht, d 20 October 1525
Johannes Custos (Jan de Coster or Brecht, Brechtius), of Brecht, between Antwerp and Breda, matriculated at Louvain on 2 November 1493 and received his MA in 1496, ranking first among all candidates. He lectured at the College of the Lily before his appointments as headmaster of the Latin school of Groningen and, by 1510, of the chapter school of Our Lady's in Antwerp. In 1515 he returned to his native Brecht and there founded a modest Latin school, which he directed until his death. He was survived by his wife, Barbara 's Hertogen, and several children.

In Louvain Custos was a pioneer in thorough and methodical study of Latin. His teaching and a Latin grammar he composed for use in the Lily laid the foundations for the work of his eminent pupil Jan de Spouter (Despauterius); also among those carrying on his tradition were Jan de *Neve, Pieter de *Corte, and Jan *Heems. His *Etymologia* (Antwerp: M. Hillen 1515) was reprinted throughout the sixteenth century, as was the *Syntaxis Brechtana*, published for the first time in Antwerp (M. Hillen), probably in the same year.

In Antwerp Custos quickly became a friend of Pieter *Gillis, who dedicated to him his edition of Angelo *Poliziano's *Epistolae* (Antwerp: D. Martens 1510). He also helped Cornelis *Batt, who owed to his recommendation an appointment at the Groningen school (Ep 573). In 1523 Juan Luis *Vives accused printers of greed because they were not touching anything except school texts such as Custos' grammar books (Ep 1362).

BIBLIOGRAPHY: CWE Ep 573 / Allen III xxvi / *Matricule de Louvain* III-1 103 / J. Theys in NBW V 266–8 / de Vocht CTL I 200–5 and passim

CFG & PGB

CYPRIANUS documented in Paris, 1510–32
Cyprianus has not been identified. He was presumably a business man and was highly respected by Girolamo *Aleandro, in whose diary he is mentioned frequently from 1510 to

1514, always in connection with financial transactions. In Ep 2679 (4 July 1532) Aleandro indicated that he was continuing to correspond with Cyprianus about the revenue of his two benefices in the region of Paris. As he calls him 'Cyprianus noster,' he probably meant to suggest that Erasmus knew him too.

BIBLIOGRAPHY: Allen Ep 2679 / *Le Carnet de voyage de Jérôme Aléandre en France et à Liège (1510–1516)* ed Jean Hoyoux (Brussels-Rome 1969) 13, 55, and passim

PGB

CYPRIANUS *See also Cyprianus* TALEUS

Petrus CYPRIUS documented 1532–3
Petrus Cyprius has not been identified. 'Cyprius' may be a form of his family name or an indication that he was a Cypriot. Erasmus spoke of him as a young man of sound judgment who had stayed in his house at Freiburg for a few months before he set out for Venice or Padua by 10 March 1532, carrying a copy of Ep 2604. In October 1533 he had delivered a letter (now missing) from Erasmus to Giambattista *Egnazio, perhaps in the course of another trip across the Alps (Ep 2871).

PGB

Marcin DĄBROWSKI *See Marcin* SŁAP

Pierre DAGUET d before the end of May 1536
Pierre Daguet was an uncle or great uncle of Gilbert *Cousin, who mentioned in Ep 3123 his recent death in the Franche-Comté. Gilbert's mother was a Jeanne Daguet of Orgelet. In his *Burgundiae descriptio* (1552) Cousin mentions a close relative, Jean Daguet, at Poligny and also a Pierre Dagay de Poligny, a student of great promise, born at Bletterans. In 1554 a Pierre Daguet was among a group of suspected heretics who had disappeared from Besançon when the magistrate decided to question them. In the second half of the sixteenth century a Jean d'Agay owned incunabula now in the Bibliothèque publique of Besançon, and around 1740 a canon Dagay built the Hôtel Boitouset at Besançon. It is possible that the names Daguet, Dagay, and d'Agay refer to individuals and branches of the same family.

BIBLIOGRAPHY: Gilbert Cousin *La Franche-*

Comté au milieu du XVIe *siècle* ed E. Monot (Lons-le-Saunier 1907) 45, 48, 109, 159, 170 / Claude Fohlen et al *Histoire de Besançon* (Paris 1965) I 626, II 169 / Auguste Castan *Catalogue des incunables de la Bibliothèque publique de Besançon* (Besançon 1893) 374, 382

PGB

Antonius DALBANUS *See Antoine d'*ALBON

Johann von DALBERG 14 August 1455–27 September 1503
Johann von Dalberg (Kämmerer, Kemmer) belonged to a noble family of the Middle Rhine which had attained prominence in the service of the counts Palatine. Johann's father, Wolf, was their marshal; his mother was Gertrud, the daughter of Friedrich von Greiffenklau. Johann matriculated at Erfurt in 1466; after obtaining a BA in 1470 he went to Pavia in 1473 to study law and obtained a doctorate in civil and canon law. In 1480 he became provost of the cathedral chapter of Worms and in 1482 bishop of Worms. Throughout his life Dalberg had contact with leading humanist scholars; owing to his efforts Rodolphus *Agricola, whom he had met in Italy, received a call to the University of Heidelberg. Dalberg was highly esteemed by Philip, the elector Palatine, and was occasionally employed in the diplomatic service of the Hapsburgs. As chancellor of the Palatinate and the University of Heidelberg he made Heidelberg and Worms into centres of humanism. He helped Konrad Celtis in founding the 'Palatina,' a literary society; Johann *Reuchlin twice received personal invitations from Dalberg before he moved to Heidelberg and was appointed Palatine councillor (December 1497).

Dalberg's rich collection of manuscripts and incunabula at the castle of Ladenburg, north of Heidelberg, was made more accessible by Henry, count *Palatine, bishop of Worms (Ep 1774), and remained a Mecca for scholars and printers throughout the sixteenth century.

BIBLIOGRAPHY: Allen Ep 1774 / NDB III 488 / ADB IV 701–3 / RE Epp 35, 55, 60 / Ludwig Geiger *Johann Reuchlin* (Leipzig 1871, repr 1964) 41–2 / *Matrikel Erfurt* I 315

IG

DAMAS, king of Persia *See* TAHMĀSP

Martinus a DAMBROWKA, DAMBROW-SKI See Marcin SŁAP

Bertram von DAMM of Brunswick, d 24 March 1542

Bertram von Damm (von dem Damme, Dam, Dham, Damus), the son of Bertram, a councillor in Brunswick, and Margarete von Huddessem, matriculated in Erfurt in 1513 and obtained a BA in 1514. He was a friend of Helius *Eobanus Hessus and also of Euricius *Cordus, who addressed an epigram to him. Damm himself composed an epigram on the subject of tippling, which was published with an anonymous oration De generibus ebriosorum et ebrietate vitanda (Erfurt 1515). By 1520 Damm began to take an interest in the cause of Martin *Luther and moved to Wittenberg, where he matriculated on 9 January 1521. In a letter of 1520 Johann *Hornburg mentioned his presence at a light-hearted poetry contest in Wittenberg; in 1521 Damm wrote from Wittenberg to Johannes *Draconites. By 1523 he had returned to Brunswick and was practising as a physician as was his friend Cordus. He sent a warm reply to a letter from Eobanus. Duke Henry of Brunswick-Wolfenbüttel had chosen the Catholic faith, and Damm, who was a Protestant, had to be very careful lest he offend the duke, who owed money to Damm's father.

Shortly before 17 June 1532, Damm travelled to Freiburg to meet Erasmus, who seems to have received him very briefly at best, in spite of a poem which Damm had composed in his praise. Erasmus subsequently sent his apologies and invited Damm to come back (Epp 2661, 2687), but he had meanwhile gone to Basel with a letter of introduction from *Zasius to Bonifacius *Amerbach (AK IV Ep 1658). While he was in Basel, Ursula *Amerbach died, and Damm addressed a consolatory poem to the grief-stricken father (AK IV Ep 1661). From Basel Damm went to the Netherlands, where he became acquainted with Damião de *Gois and probably also with Cornelius *Grapheus. Damm's verse paraphrase of the Epistle to Titus (Louvain: B. Gravius 1533) was dedicated to Gois on 27 June 1533 at Antwerp; he also wrote a poem in Gois' honour which was added to a similar one by Grapheus. After his return to Brunswick, Damm produced his major work, a verse translation of St Paul's

Epistle to the Romans: Dispositio orationis in epistola Pauli ad Romanos autore Phil. Melan-[chthonis]; item eiusdem Pauli ad Romanos epistola versu heroico ... reddita per Berthramum Damianum Brunocivanum; Urbani Rhegii judicium super hoc carmine (n p 1539). In 1537 and 1538 he is twice mentioned in letters by Antonius *Corvinus.

Since he was suffering from a lingering illness, Damm wrote his last will in 1541; he was not married at this time but mentioned a natural daughter for whose support he provided. After his death Johann Glandorp wrote two Greek epitaphs for him.

BIBLIOGRAPHY: Allen Ep 2661 / Matrikel Erfurt II 280 / Matrikel Wittenberg I 100 / AK IV Epp 1658, 1660, 1661 / Richard v. Damm 'Bertram v. Damm, ein braunschweigischer Zeit- und Streitgenosse Luthers' Zeitschrift der Gesellschaft für niedersächsische Kirchengeschichte 18 (1913) 160–205 / de Vocht MHL 613 / de Vocht CTL III 55, 110

IG

DAMIANUS See Damião de GOIS and Damiaan van VISSENAKEN

William DANCASTER documented 1490–c1530

Dancaster (Dankester), from Suffolk, was admitted as a probationary fellow to Magdalen College, Oxford, on 27 July 1490, and was a fellow from 1491 until at least 1499. He received his BA in 1490 and his MA some time later, and was subdeacon in 1497 and deacon in 1498. In 1498–99 he was senior dean of arts at Magdalen College but then moved to Eton College, where he was a fellow from 18 October 1507 probably until 1518. He may have been connected with John *Colet by 1513 (Ep 278) and was certainly a member of his household when Colet died in 1519, leaving Dancaster the sum of £6 13s 4d in his will. Erasmus wrote Dancaster in October to commiserate with him on Colet's death and to request information for his life of Colet (Ep 1027). He later sent Dancaster greetings through Thomas *Lupset (Ep 1229).

In 1527 Dancaster informed Bishop John *Fisher of Robert *Wakefield's arguments in support of *Henry VIII's divorce. In 1528 he was made rector at Ampthill, Bedfordshire, and died before 20 February 1530, when a new rector was appointed.

BIBLIOGRAPHY: Allen and CWE Ep 1027 / Emden BRUO I 540

CFG

Alessandro D'ANDREA of Naples, documented 1527–57

In 1527 Alessandro D'Andrea of Naples was at the imperial court at Valladolid, where he joined Baldesar *Castiglione and Andrea *Navagero in mocking the literary style of Erasmus (Ep 1791). In 1540 he sent Pietro Aretino two letters from Naples, where he had gone on his father's death. He wrote three *ragionamenti* or discussions of the war in the Campagna and the kingdom of Naples from 1556 to 1557, during the pontificate of *Paul IV (Venice: G.A. Valvassori 1560).

BIBLIOGRAPHY: Allen Ep 1791

TBD

Pierre DANÈS of Paris, d 23 April 1577

Born by 1497, Pierre Danès (Danesius) was a pupil of *Budé and *Lascaris and attended the Collège de Navarre. In 1519 he was teaching at another college of the University of Paris, the Collège de Lisieux. He belonged to a circle of young scholars gathered around the humanistic press of Josse *Bade, who in 1527 dedicated to him and his close companion Jacques *Toussain (Ep 1733) an edition of Priscian. In 1530 he and Toussain were appointed to teach Greek at the new college of royal lecturers (Ep 2421). In 1535 he went to Italy with his former pupil Georges, the son of Jean de *Selve, who had been appointed ambassador to Venice. In 1539 he sent a manuscript containing the last part of Paolo *Emilio's history of France to Paris from Italy.

Danès was a priest and was named rector of St Josse, Paris, in 1523. In 1546 he was provost of Sézanne (arrondissement d'Epernay, Département de la Marne) when *Francis I appointed him one of his representatives at the council of Trent. In 1549 King *Henry II named him tutor to the royal princes. In 1557 he served on a commission to reform the University of Paris and is known subsequently to have opposed Petrus Ramus. On 9 August 1557 he received papal confirmation as bishop of

Lavaur, between Toulouse and Albi, a small see that had earlier been held by Georges de Selve. He continued, however, to spend much of his time in Paris, where he died and was buried in St Germain-des-Prés. In addition to his scholarly work on several classical authors, his publications include an *Oratio* in Francis I's name to the council fathers assembled at Trent (Rome: A. Bladus 1546) and an *Apologia* and *Altera apologia* for France's co-operation with the Turks, published in Paris, 1551–2, in both Latin and French.

Erasmus' only known contacts with Danès are centred around the furore caused in France by the publication of his *Ciceronianus*. In 1528 he wrote to Danès, assuring him that no slight to Budé had been intended (Ep 2044). Danès intended to answer (Ep 2065), but no such letter is known. However, in 1530 Erasmus claimed that Danès had suggested to Budé that he moderate an offensive passage in his *Commentarii linguae graecae* (Ep 2379).

BIBLIOGRAPHY: Allen Ep 2044 / DBF X 90–1 / *Gallia christiana* XIII 346–7

MICHEL REULOS & PGB

Jacques DANIEL documented at Orléans, 1502

Jacques Daniel, who received foreign students into his household at Orléans (Ep 170), has not been identified. He was probably the tutor of Dismas van *Bergen, an arrangement which caused Erasmus great misgivings (Epp 137, 138).

HENRY HELLER

Giovanni DANIELI documented 1528–34

The information available on Giovanni Danieli (Danielis) at the present stage of research is limited to the details deducible from the colophon of some of the works of *Cajetanus. It is evident that Danieli was a member of his household. In the colophon of Josse *Bade's edition of Cajetanus' commentary on the Gospels (1532) we read that the work was revised by Danieli. In May 1534 he wrote to Erasmus from Rome (Ep 2935) referring to the *De concordia* and offering to send him a copy of Cajetanus' *Questiones et omnia (ut vocantur) quolibeta* (Venice: L. Giunta 1531).

BIBLIOGRAPHY: Allen Ep 2935

DANILO AGUZZI-BARBAGLI

Johannes DANTISCUS of Gdansk, 1 November 1485–27 October 1548
Johannes Dantiscus (von Höfen, a Curiis, Linosdemon, Jan Dantyszek) called himself after his native city, Gdansk (Danzig). He was the son of Hans, a merchant, and the grandson of a flax worker. At the age of fourteen he took part in a campaign against the Turks, and afterwards he studied in Greifswald and Cracow. He travelled to Greece, Italy, Palestine, and Arabia before studying law and theology in Cracow. In 1505 he received lower orders and in 1507 became a secretary and notary at the court of Poland. In the diplomatic service of King *Sigismund I Dantiscus frequently had occasion to travel abroad. In 1516 in Vienna *Maximilian I proclaimed him doctor of civil and canon law; he also received the poet's laurel and a diploma of nobility. The same year King Sigismund I provided him with a benefice. He was soon sent on further diplomatic missions: in 1519 he visited Spain for the first time, and from 1522 to 1523 he represented his king in the Hapsburg courts of Spain and the Netherlands. In 1524 he was sent to Spain for the third time, travelling by way of Naples; he completed the long negotiations for the recognition of Queen *Bona of Poland as duchess of Bari and remained as ambassador to the imperial court in Spain until 1530, when he followed the Emperor *Charles V through Italy and Germany, attending the coronation at Bologna and the diet at Augsburg. Thereafter he resided in the Netherlands until his recall to Poland on 12 February 1532. Dantiscus attended the diet of Regensburg in the summer of 1532 (Ep 2687) and afterwards returned to Cracow. He was made canon in 1529 and elected bishop of Chełmno (Kulm) in 1530 (Ep 2336), but he occupied his see only in 1533 after receiving higher orders. From 1537, when he became bishop of Warmia (Ermland), he resided in Lidzbark (Heilsberg), where he died. Himself a neo-Latin poet of note, Dantiscus knew how to make friends among both the culturally and politically prominent representatives of all European nations. His links with other friends and acquaintances of Erasmus, too numerous for identification in this short text, are well illustrated in a large number of manuscript letters addressed to him

between 1520 and 1546 and preserved in Hamburg, Uppsala, and Fromborg. On the basis of this correspondence Henry de Vocht was able to give a detailed account of Dantiscus' activities and interests.

Dantiscus' poems include early confessions of love, verses celebrating military deeds and acts of state, epitaphs, and epigrams. In later years his themes were increasingly moral and religious.

Dantiscus is mentioned repeatedly as a congenial courtier and a great admirer of Erasmus by some of the latter's correspondents who met him in Spain, Augsburg, and the Netherlands (Epp 2163, 2269, 2336, 2573, 2629, 2687). He never met Erasmus but in 1530 expressed his intention to write him a letter (Ep 2336). In Wrocław Henry de Vocht found the draft for a letter to Erasmus which he assigned to Dantiscus, dating it from the last half of October 1531 (de Vocht *Dantiscus* 104–8). It shows that by this time a number of friendly and candid letters had been exchanged between them. Subsequently Dantiscus sent Erasmus a medallion bearing his own effigy (Ep 2643). Erasmus' only preserved letter to Dantiscus is an elegant and warm dedication published with his Latin translation of Basil's *De Spiritu Sancto* (Basel: H. Froben 1532). At about the same time Dantiscus had reason to regret that one of Erasmus' letters to him was shown around by *Jespersen (Epp 2644, 2693). In November 1533 Erasmus mentioned a letter from Dantiscus describing a great fire at Chełmno (Epp 2876, 2877), and in August 1534 he acknowledged a gift of money (Ep 2961).

BIBLIOGRAPHY: Allen Ep 2163 / NDB III 512–13 / PSB IV 424–30 / G. Ellinger *Geschichte der neulateinischen Literatur Deutschlands im sechzehnten Jahrhundert* (Berlin 1929–33) II 295–305 and passim / H. de Vocht *John Dantiscus and his Netherlandish Friends* (Louvain 1961) / E. Boehmer 'Alfonsi Valdesii litteras XL ineditas [to Dantiscus] … ' in *Homenaje a Menéndez y Pelayo* (Madrid 1899) I 385–412 / *Nowy Korbut Pismiennietwo staropolskie* (Warsaw 1963–5) II 113–19 / Johannes Dantiscus *Carmina* ed J. Jkimina (Cracow 1950)

IG

DASSA (Ep 1488 of 4 September 1524)
Dassa, a Spanish merchant or banker, with ties
to England and conceivably located in Antwerp, has not been identified.

Agostino DATI of Siena, 1420–6 April 1478
The orator, historian, and philosopher Agostino Dati was born in Siena. Most of his active
life was spent in his native city, where he had
acquired his education, studying under Francesco *Filelfo, who taught there after 1435, and
who praised Dati's talent.

Dati was invited to teach at Urbino but
returned to Siena in 1444 because of the
turbulence following the assassination of Duke
Oddantonio da Montefeltro. There he taught
rhetoric as well as theology and preached,
even though he was married. He turned down
invitations to the papal court under *Nicholas
v but did accept civic honours in Siena,
including appointments as the city's *secretarius*
in 1457 and as a judge at Massa in 1458. He died
in Siena.

Most of Dati's surviving works were published posthumously by his son Niccolò. They
consist of a history of Siena in three books, a
history of Piombino, orations, letters, and his
*Isagogicus libellus pro conficiendis epistolis et
orationibus*. His *Opera* were published by Si-
meone di Niccolò Nardi at Siena in 1503, and
were reprinted in Venice by Agostino Zanni in
1516. His most famous work, the *Isagogicus
libellus* was first printed at Ferrara by Andrea
Belfortis in 1471, and was repeatedly re-edited
under the title *Elegantiarum libellus*.

In 1511 Dati's letters were reprinted together
with an unauthorized abridged version of
Erasmus' *De ratione studii* (Paris: G. Biermant;
(ASD I-2 89–90, 106). Although Erasmus repudi-
ated the edition, he seems to have respected
Dati's work. As early as 1489 he had praised
Dati, naming him as one of the Italian masters
of eloquence, together with Enea Silvio Picco-
lomini (*Pius II), Poggio *Bracciolini, Guarino
*Guarini of Verona, and Gasparino Barzizza
(Ep 23).

BIBLIOGRAPHY: Allen Ep 23 / Giovanni
Niccolò Bandiera *De Augustino Dato libri duo*
(Rome 1733) / C.G. Jöcher *Allgemeines Gelehrten-
Lexicon* (Leipzig 1750–1) II 38–9 / A. della Torre
Storia dell'Accademia Platonica di Firenze (Flor-
ence 1902) 142–3

EGMONT LEE

Elisabeth DAVID of Basel, d 4 August 1532
Elisabeth, a daughter of Heinrich *David, was
married to Christoph *Baumgartner. Described
as young, pregnant, and Baumgartner's wife of
seven years at the time, she is known only for
the passionate drama reported by Erasmus in
Ep 2698 which took the lives of her daughter,
Elisabeth, and herself. The chronicler Fridolin
Ryff apparently believed her to be innocent
and reported that she was given a proper
burial.

BIBLIOGRAPHY: See Christoph Baumgartner.

PGB

Heinrich DAVID of Basel, documented 1488–
1535
David was a highly respected citizen and
banker, the master of the 'Bären' guild and a
member of the great council. In 1498 he
obtained a coat of arms from the Emperor
*Maximilian. He was the Basel representative
of the *Welser company, and in 1504 his bank
received official status as the only one authorized to exchange currencies by appointment of
the Basel government. He also invested sums
of money with Basel printing firms and
maintained close business connections with
Lyon. In 1521 he was among the small minority
of councillors who refused French pensions in
exchange for permission to recruit mercenaries. He performed a pilgrimage to the Holy
Land and maintained close ties with the Basel
Dominicans, making his silver dishes available
when they played host to a provincial chapter
in 1508. In 1529 he was a member of the newly
appointed marriage court. Erasmus mentioned
him in Ep 2698 in connection with the tragic
death of his daughter Elisabeth.

BIBLIOGRAPHY: DHBS II 637 / R. Wackernagel
Geschichte der Stadt Basel (Basel 1907–54) II 503,
520, 677, III 172, 310, 473, and passim /
Wappenbuch der Stadt Basel ed W.R. Staehelin
(Basel [1917–30])

PGB

Maarten DAVIDTS documented at Brussels
from 1505, d 12 January 1535
Maarten Davidts (David, Davidis Martinus),
born in the diocese of Cambrai, was appointed
to a chaplaincy of the Brussels chapter of St
Gudula's on 27 January 1505 and became canon
on 19 December 1506. In 1531 he was also

curate of the Sterrebeck estate which Antoine *Le Sauvage had inherited from his father, Chancellor Jean *Le Sauvage (Ep 2571). The names of Davidts' relatives and details about his possessions are known from a will which he signed on 30 July 1516 and further dispositions added to it by 1532.

In the winter of 1516–17 Davidts lodged Erasmus in his house in the Stormstraat in Brussels, and to their common friends he remained known as Erasmus' former host (Epp 532, 1437, 2352, 2851, 3019). They exchanged letters in 1522 (Epp 1254, 1258), but thereafter there is no clear trace of further correspondence until about 1528 (Epp 2352, 2571, Allen Ep 1280). A last letter from Erasmus was probably on its way when Davidts died (Epp 2998, 3009). He was a faithful and outspoken supporter of Erasmus (Ep 1351), not really an intellectual and not particularly well connected, but useful in being close to the court and willing to undertake errands (Ep 1254). His friendship was rewarded by Erasmus' complete trust in his honesty (Ep 1437) and by an epitaph for the influential Philippe *Haneton which Erasmus had composed to please Davidts.

Maarten had a brother by the name of Zeger (Sigerus) Davidts, who was a priest. In 1516 Maarten appointed him executor of his will and in 1531 (Ep 2571) sent Erasmus greetings from him.

BIBLIOGRAPHY: Allen and CWE Ep 532 / Reedijk poem 120 / Placide Lefèvre in *Ephemerides theologicae Lovanienses* 42 (1966) 628–36 (publishing the will and further dispositions) / Placide Lefèvre in *Scrinium Erasmianum* I 25–7
PGB

Zeger (Sigerus) DAVIDTS *See Maarten* DAVIDTS

Ludovicus DEBERQUINUS *See Louis de* BERQUIN

Petrus DECIMARIUS documented 1526–8
Little is known so far about Petrus Decimarius. A native of the old diocese of Bazas, in the Gironde (archdiocese of Auch), he matriculated at the University of Montpellier on 29 September 1526 and was no doubt still studying at Montpellier in 1528 when Erasmus wrote to him twice (Epp 1986, 2050), in reply to letters

from Decimarius which are now missing. Erasmus' letters strongly suggest that Decimarius had earlier visited Basel and there had met the circle of Erasmus' friends. More significantly, they suggest that at Montpellier Decimarius was at the centre of a group of young medical scholars, all of whom had wished to be recommended to Erasmus and in return were greeted by him in his letters to Decimarius. They included Jacques *Ferrand, a doctor and lecturer at the university, Guillaume *Carvel, Etienne *Des Gouttes, and perhaps Antonius Cameranus (Ep 2050), also from the diocese of Bazas, who had matriculated the same day as Decimarius. One or more members of that same group came from the diocese of Burgos, in Old Castile (Ep 2050). Although the names do not seem to match, one notes three students from Burgos registering one after the other in October 1525. Two other recent arrivals among the Montpellier students were the Belgian Willem van *Schoonhove, already found in a group of admirers of Erasmus during his preceding stay at Padua, and Jean de *Boyssoné, who was later to correspond with Erasmus. It may finally be added that on 17 September 1530, just two years after Erasmus' second letter to Decimarius, another fervent admirer of his matriculated at Montpellier. He was François *Rabelais. Even Bishop Guillaume *Pellicier, who normally resided at Montpellier, was among those who wished to be recommended to Erasmus in 1528.

BIBLIOGRAPHY: *Matricule de Montpellier* 47, 49, 51, 60
PGB

Bartholomaeus DECIMATOR *See* Bartholomäus ZEHENDER

Filippo DECIO of Milan, 1454–12/13 October 1535
Filippo Decio (Decius, Detius) was born in Milan in 1454 to a family of the minor nobility from the town of Desio. Attracted to the study of law by the example of an older brother, he attended the University of Pavia, where he established a reputation as a prodigy and engaged in public disputations at an early age. In 1473 he went to Pisa, where he obtained his doctorate in 1476 and began an illustrious but stormy career as a professor of law. Despite

rivalries and constant bickering about salary and points of prestige, his income at Pisa was augmented constantly until he received more than any other professor. After the French invaded Italy in 1494 the University of Pisa fell upon difficult times, and Decio entertained offers of employment elsewhere. In 1501 he moved to Padua, and four years later, on the invitation of *Louis XII of France, to Pavia. In 1510, when Louis entered on his struggle with Pope *Julius II, Decio lent his advice to the schismatic council of Pisa, publishing an important *consilium* in its defence. In 1512, when Julius gained the ascendancy, Decio was excommunicated and fled to France, where he taught at the University of Valence. Pope *Leo X pardoned him in 1515, and he returned to Pavia, then to Pisa. He died on 12 or 13 October 1535, perhaps at Siena.

On 2 February 1530 Bonifacius *Amerbach, sending Erasmus his opinions on the proposed divorce of *Henry VIII, cited Decio as one of several jurists who opposed the opinion that a pope could dispense in all matters except articles of faith (Ep 2267).

Decio wrote commentaries on the decretals (Pavia 1483), the Digest (Milan 1507–10), the codex (Milan 1507), and other legal collections. He also wrote studies entitled *De actionibus* (Pavia 1483), *De iure emphiteutico* (Pavia 1476), and *Apophthegmata singularia iuris* (Pavia 1476). His *consilium* on the council of Pisa was published a number of times, including in the two-volume *Consilia sive responsa* (Frankfurt: S. Feyerabend 1588).

BIBLIOGRAPHY: Allen Ep 2267 / EI XII 462–3 / Myron P. Gilmore *Humanists and Jurists: Six Studies in the Renaissance* (Cambridge, Mass, 1963) 70, 82–3, and passim

TBD

Justus Ludovicus DECIUS of Wissembourg, c 1485–26 December 1545
Justus Ludovicus (or Jodocus) Decius (Dietz) was born in Wissembourg, in Alsace, the son of Jakob Dietz, mayor of the town. He did not go on to higher studies. At the age of fifteen he left his native country and travelled to Moravia, the Tirol, and Hungary, acquiring a thorough knowledge of commerce, money matters, and mining. In the fall of 1507 he was employed in Schwaz, in the Tirol, in the copper and silver

mines of the Fuggers. When the Hungarian envoy, Bishop János Filipc, came to Schwaz, Decius joined his entourage. He accompanied the bishop to Hungary and later, towards the end of 1507 or at the beginning of 1508, he travelled to Cracow, Poland. There he entered the service of the banker Jan *Boner, an associate of the Fuggers. For fourteen years he held the position of secretary to Boner and was his aide in commercial affairs and in the administration of the salt mines in Wieliczka and Bochnia, near Cracow. At Boner's request Decius made frequent journeys to foreign countries, travelling to France (in 1511), Italy (1513), and Austria (1514). Together with Boner he was engaged in the preparations for the marriage between *Sigismund I, king of Poland, and *Bona Sforza. In addition, he visited Brussels and Vienna (1516–17). In 1519, during a stay in Austria, the Emperor *Maximilian provided him with a letter of nobility, bestowing on him the title of *Sacri Lateranensis et imperialis palatii vicecomes palatinus*. Afterwards he also obtained Polish titles and was admitted to the Topor coat of arms. In 1519 he married Anna Krupka.

With the support of Piotr *Tomicki, Decius became royal secretary in May 1520. From 1528 on he was also a member of the municipal council of Cracow and master of the hospital of St Rochus. At the end of 1538 he obtained the office of *edyl* of Our Lady's in Cracow. He owned houses in Cracow and Torun as well as an estate near Cracow named after himself, Wola Justowska, with a fine Renaissance château built by Italian architects. A skilful diplomat, he was sent by the king on numerous missions. On four occasions he was sent to Italy, accompanying Isabel of Aragon, the mother of Queen Bona, to negotiate the question of the queen's dowry. In May 1521 slanderous publications accused Decius of usury and heresy, but King Sigismund I stopped their circulation by a royal decree dated 10 August 1521. In 1522 on his return from Italy, Decius visited *Luther in Wittenberg and also stopped in Basel, where he met Erasmus. Thereafter he corresponded with Erasmus, maintaining loose contact with him. By virtue of his commercial and diplomatic connections and also because of the personal interest he took in the humanities, Decius was in touch with almost all the important figures living in Poland at that time; he had contact with court and church dignitaries, with patricians in the cities, and with humanists at Cracow as well as abroad, among them *Vadianus, Girolamo *Balbi, Leonhard von *Eck, Leonard *Cox, and Anselmus *Ephorinus. He also lent his patronage to Erasmus' followers in Cracow.

Decius was a staunch supporter of the Hapsburgs and from the time when the struggle for the crown of Hungary had ended (1527), he began to play a certain role in politics. He served as intermediary and courier in the correspondence between King *Ferdinand and his followers in Poland. This did not at all hinder Decius from having friends on both sides – among the Polish followers of the Hapsburgs (like Piotr Tomicki) as well as in the opposite camp (like Jan (II) *Łaski). Decius also served as intermediary in the exchange of letters between the Prussian Duke Albert (I) of *Brandenburg-Ansbach and the leaders of the Reformation (for example, Caspar *Hedio). Decius was interested in books, both as a bibliophile – he possessed a fine library – and as an editor. Together with the Cracow printer Jan Haller he published some breviaries. It was due to his efforts that Erasmus' De epistolis conscribendis was reprinted in Cracow (H. Wietor 1523). Wishing to repay Decius for the gift of a silver cup Erasmus dedicated to him in 1523 his short Precatio dominica (Ep 1393; cf Allen I 21 and Epp 1408, 2845). In his letters Decius informed Erasmus about the political developments in Poland and gave him news about his friends (Epp 2874, 3010). He became his faithful friend (Epp 2031, 2961) and served as an intermediary in the exchange of correspondence between Erasmus and other Poles such as Jan (II) Łaski (Ep 1954), who placed great trust in Decius (Ep 2746). It was also through him that some Polish nobles, especially King Sigismund I (Ep 1958), Łaski (Ep 2862), and Johannes *Dantiscus (Ep 2961), sent money and presents to Erasmus. In turn, he conveyed to others greetings and news from Erasmus. He may have seen to it that Severyn *Boner repaid Erasmus with a suitable present for having dedicated Terence to his sons (Epp 2961, 3010). Decius also sought to gain new sponsors for Erasmus in Poland, such as Piotr *Kmita (Ep 3046).

Decius won the regard of humanist circles not only because of his friendship with Erasmus but also for his own publications. He began his literary career with Diarii et eorum quae memoratu digna in splendidissimis Sigismundi et Bonae nuptiis gesta descriptio (Cracow: H. Wietor 1518), a description of the wedding of Sigismund I and Bona. He also edited Maciej of Michow's Chronica Polonorum (Cracow: H. Wietor 1521). To this he added his own historical writings: De vetustatibus Polonorum liber I, De Jagellonum familia liber II, De Sigismundi regis temporibus liber III. In his Sendbrief von der grossen Schlacht (Nürnberg 1527) he immortalized the Polish victory over the Tartars in 1527 (Ep 1803).

It was in the field of economics, however, that Decius was most active. He advised Sigismund I on monetary matters and directed the royal exchequers in Cracow (1528–35), Toruń (1528–35), and Krolewiec (1530–40). In 1526 he submitted a proposal for reforming Poland's monetary system, 'De monetae cussione' (in manuscript). On the basis of Decius' proposal a gold currency was introduced in Poland and a monetary union established between Prussia and Poland (1528). Decius wrote another memorandum which is extant in manuscript, 'Warum das Geld im Lande teuer wurde' (1532). When accused of corruption he again sought the protection of Sigismund I, who in decrees of 1535 and 1538 dismissed the charges against him as unfounded. Towards the end of his life, after the closure of the exchequers, Decius directed his attention to mining. On 7 October 1535 he bought the Kupferberg mines in Silesia with the neighbouring villages of Janowice, Bolzeinstein, and Waltersdorf and established for them the first mining regulations in Poland, Neue Bergordnung (Cracow 1539). On 28 February 1544 Decius obtained from Sigismund I the mining rights for the region of Cracow, and formed a partnership with the Cracow councillors H. Krugel and E. Cyrus. In 1544 Decius again found himself entrusted with the administration of the exchequer in Cracow and died in that city. In the annals of Polish cultural history the name of Decius, the historian and author of economic treatises, stands in the foremost ranks beside Copernicus' name.

BIBLIOGRAPHY: Allen Ep 1393 / PSB V 42–5 (with a list of manuscript sources) / Bibliografia

polska ed K. Estreicher et al (Cracow 1870–1951)
3rd part xv 102 / *Bibliografia literatury polskiej*
'*Nowy Korbut*': *Piśmiennictwo staropolskie* (War-
saw 1963–5) II 120–3 / K. Romer *De Jodoci
Ludovici Decii vita scriptisque* (Wrocław 1874) /
A.J. Semrau *J.L. Dietz und die Münzreform unter
Sigismund I* (Toruń 1906) / W. Budka *Biblioteka
Decjuszów* (Cracow 1929) / *Korespondencja
Erazma z Polakami* trans M. Cytowska (Warsaw
1965) / *Christoph Scheurl's Briefbuch* ed F. von
Soden and J.K.F. Knaake (Potsdam 1867–72,
repr 1962) II Ep 235 / Götz von Pölnitz *Anton
Fugger* (Tübingen 1959–   ) I 298–302 and
passim

MARIA CYTOWSKA

Zacharias DEIOTARUS of Friesland, d 1533
Zacharias Deiotarus of Friesland (Diotorus,
Zacharias Phrysius) seems to have migrated to
England some time before 1519, when one of
his poems appeared in William Horman's
Vulgaria (London: R. Pynson). He was a former
servant-pupil of Erasmus (Epp 1205, 2237), and
the fact that a member of Erasmus' *familia* called
*Jan of Friesland had tried his fortune in
England a few years before led Allen to believe
that Zacharias and Jan might have been one
and the same person. By May 1521 Zacharias
entered the service of Archbishop William
*Warham (Ep 1205), and he eventually became
an apostolic notary (Ep 2530). He was
acquainted with many friends of Erasmus,
including Thomas *Lovell (Epp 1138, 1491),
Polidoro *Virgilio (Epp 1366, 1666, 1990),
Richard *Bere (Ep 1490), and Andrew *Smith
(Ep 1491). He corresponded regularly with
Erasmus and assisted his famuli when they
visited England: Lieven *Algoet (Epp 1366,
1491), Karl *Harst (Ep 1666), and Quirinius
*Talesius (Ep 2237). On occasion Zacharias
seems to have played a role in the collection of
Erasmus' annuity from Warham (Epp 2496,
2625). Zacharias' death must have been quite a
blow to Erasmus, and he referred to it in his
correspondence with *Viglius Zuichemus (Ep
2791), Piotr *Tomicki (Ep 2776), and Eustache
*Chapuys (Ep 2798).
    BIBLIOGRAPHY: Allen Ep 1205 / A.J. Van der
Aa et al *Biographisch woordenboek der Nederlanden* (Haarlem 1852–78, repr 1965) IV 99 /
Bierlaire *Familia* 52–3

C.G. VAN LEIJENHORST

Gillis van DELFT d 25/26 April 1524
Gillis van Delft (Aegidius Delphus) was born
in the diocese of Utrecht. He took his BA in
Paris on 9 February 1478 and his MA about a
year later, and he incepted on 24 March 1479.
He held several offices in the English-German
nation and taught philosophy in the colleges
of Cornouaille, Calvi, and Navarre. He was the
rector of the University of Paris from 16
December 1486 to 24 March 1487. In 1489-90
Delft sought support in obtaining a bursary at
the Collège de Sorbonne, although some
sources indicate he was already a *socius* there
since 1482. He was *lector ethicorum* in the
faculty of arts from 4 March 1491 but resigned
this position in June 1492. His licence in
theology was granted on 21 March 1492 (he
ranked fifth of eighteen) and his doctorate on 7
June 1492. Delft's whereabouts between 1494
and 1506 are not clear. If the poet 'Delius' (Epp
95, 103, 129) is Delft, then he was in Paris in
1499 and 1500. In 1501, however, he was
teaching theology in Cologne, and in the same
year he voiced support in Bruges for the refusal
of the Flemish clergy to pay a subsidy to Philip
the Handsome, duke of *Burgundy, for his
journey to Spain. On 22 May 1506 he participated in Ghent in a dispute on the pastoral
rights and prerogatives of mendicant friars and
the secular clergy. Delft returned to Paris in
1506 and presided over the *magisterium* of Josse
*Clichtove on 4 December 1506, after which he
took a hand regularly in the affairs of the
Collège de Sorbonne and the faculty of
theology until 1515. He sat on the faculty
committee which dealt with the *Reuchlin
controversy in 1514. Delft's name disappears
from all the Paris records between 1515 and
1520. It may be assumed that during this period
he was in the Netherlands and met Erasmus,
who referred to his verse paraphrases from the
Bible in 1516 (Ep 456) and did so again in the
Ciceronianus (ASD I-2 681–2). The dedication of
Delft's last work was dated from the College of
the Lily in Louvain on 31 May 1519. He
returned to Paris in 1520, where he was the
dean of the faculty of theology until his death
on 25 or 26 April 1524. A contract for his
tombstone called for delivery to the chapel of
the Collège de Sorbonne.
    Renaudet says Delft's elegant style and
poetry made him a Renaissance author as well

as a product of the scholastic tradition. Delft contributed verse to many works throughout his life. *Lefèvre d'Etaples dedicated to Delft his edition of John Damascene's *De orthodoxa fide* (Paris: Henri Estienne 1507). Erasmus, who admired Delft's style (LB IX 1115D) and his accommodation of scholasticism with humanism, invoked Delft's approval in his own defence (LB IX 753F; Epp 1581, 2379). Delft had helped Erasmus calm the storm of protest at Louvain in 1519 over Erasmus' *Encomium matrimonii*. But the theologian mentioned in Allen Ep 1196:489, in the opinion of the present writer, is probably not Delft but rather Herman *Lethmaet, who did literally rank first in his Paris class and about whom Erasmus later spoke in parallel terms (Allen Ep 1238: 22–6).

Delft's major works include: ed and comment *Opus Aristotelis de moribus a Johanne Argyropylo traductum* (Paris: Jean Higman 1489, Jean Lambert, Denis Roce 1503); ed Jean Buridan *Questiones in x libros Ethicorum Aristotelis* (Paris: Wolfgang Hopyl 1489, Poncet Le Preux 1513, Bernard Aubry, Jean Petit 1518); ed Aristotle *Libri VIII Politicorum et Oeconomicorum libri II* trans Leonardo Bruni (Paris: Georges Wolf for Durand Gerlier 1490); ed and comment Ovid *De remedio amoris* (Paris: Félix Baligault 1493, Michel Le Noir, Georg Mittelhus 1501, Nicolas de La Barre 1506); *Septem psalmi poenitentiales, noviter per E.D. metrice compilati* (Antwerp 1501); ed and comment, with Josse *Bade *Epistolae beati Pauli apostoli et beatissimorum Iacobi, Petri, Ioannis, et Iudae epistolae canonicae, cum argumentis et scholiis* (Paris: Josse Bade and Marnef brothers 1503, 1506); comment Aristotle *Aethica seu Moralia* trans Johannes *Argyropoulos (Paris: widow of Jean I Du Pré, Jean Granjon 1506, repr 1509, 1510, or 1514); *Epistola divi Pauli ad Romanos decantata. Defensio pro cleri Flandrensis libertate. Quinque psalmi Davidici decantati* (Paris: Josse Bade 1507, Jean Barbier and Marnef brothers c 1508); ed with Josse Clichtove St John Damascene *Contenta: Theologia* [seu *De orthodoxa fide liber*] trans Jacques Lefèvre d'Etaples (Paris: Henri I Estienne 1507); *Conclusiones in Sententias Magistri* (Louvain: Dirk Martens; Paris: Claude Chevallon c 1519); and *Opusculum in laudem Virginis Mariae* (n p, n d).

BIBLIOGRAPHY: Allen and CWE Ep 456 /

Auctarium chartularii universitatis parisiensis ed Charles Samaran and Emile van Moé (Paris 1935) III passim / H. Elie 'Quelques maîtres' *Archives d'histoire doctrinale et littéraire* 18 (1950–1) 200–1 / B. Moreau *Inventaire chronologique des éditions parisiennes* (Paris 1972–7) / Renaudet *Préréforme* passim / Rice *Prefatory Epistles* Ep 53 / de Vocht CTL I 313 / Paris, Archives de l'Université (Sorbonne) Registre 89 passim, Registre 90 f lxv verso

JAMES K. FARGE

DELIUS Volscus (Epp 95, 103, 129 of 1499–1500)
'Delius Volscus' is apparently not the real name of this Paris acquaintance of Erasmus; Allen wondered whether Gillis van *Delft could be intended.

Francesco Maria DELLA ROVERE duke of Urbino, 1490–20 October 1538
Francesco Maria was a son of Giovanni della Rovere, lord of Senigallia and a nephew of Pope *Sixtus IV, and Giovanna, the daughter of Federico da Montefeltro, duke of Urbino. He was educated first at Senigallia, then, after the death of his father in 1501, at the court of an uncle, Guidobaldo da Montefeltro, duke of Urbino. On 2 March 1505 he married Leonora, the daughter of Francesco Gonzaga of Mantua. In 1508 he succeeded Guidobaldo as duke of Urbino. In 1509, under another uncle, Pope *Julius II, Francesco Maria became captain-general of the papal militia and served in campaigns against Venice. In May 1511 he was in command of the papal forces encamped before Bologna when the city rose in rebellion. He and Cardinal Francesco *Alidosi, the papal legate, made an ignominious retreat, and on 24 May, after mutual recriminations, Francesco Maria murdered Alidosi. Julius II had him absolved from the crime and on 20 February 1513 gave him control of Pesaro.

Under Pope *Leo X Francesco Maria's fortunes deteriorated rapidly. Ostensibly because he refused to participate in military activities against the French in 1515, Leo stripped him of his territories in 1516 and gave them to his own nephew, Lorenzo (II) de' *Medici. Although Francesco Maria seized Urbino in February 1517 and held it until September, he spent most of Leo's pontificate in exile at Mantua. When

Leo died in 1521 Francesco Maria reconquered his former possessions, winning the recognition of *Adrian vi in 1523. Under *Clement vii he served as commander in both the papal and Venetian armies. After the battle of Pavia of 1525, his ineffectiveness and timidity in pursuing the anti-imperial goals of the League of Cognac and in protecting Rome from Spanish and German troops prompted suspicion that he was gaining revenge on the Medici for the treatment he had received under Leo x. Despite these charges and later altercations with popes Clement vii and *Paul iii, he retained his territories and in February 1538 was named commander of land forces for a crusade against the Turks. His health deteriorated before military operations could begin, and he died on 20 October.

Events involving Francesco Maria della Rovere and the troubles of the duchy of Urbino are referred to in Epp 521, 2917.

BIBLIOGRAPHY: Allen Ep 2917 / EI xv 865 / Pastor vi–xi passim

TBD

Leonardo Grosso DELLA ROVERE c 1464–17 September 1520

Leonardo was a son of Antonio Grosso and Maria della Rovere. His maternal grandmother, Lucchina della Rovere, was a sister of Pope *Sixtus iv, so that he was a great nephew of the latter and a second cousin of Cardinal Giuliano della Rovere (*Julius ii). Described as a cleric of Savona and as aged twenty-three, on 9 December 1487 Leonardo was appointed bishop of Agen. He was ill at Agen in May or June 1495 when his brother Clemente, bishop of Mende and Cardinal Giuliano's vice-legate at Avignon, took a gift of sweetmeats to him on behalf of the citizens of Avignon. Upon Julius ii's election, Leonardo came to Rome and on 17 December 1505 was appointed a cardinal, receiving the pope's former title church of Santi Apostoli. In August 1506 he set out on the papal expedition to Perugia and Bologna, but Julius created him legate to the patrimony of St Peter and left him at Viterbo; on 19 February 1507 he was appointed legate to Perugia. By the time Erasmus came to Rome in 1509 he may have been back there; he was left as legate in Rome when Julius set off again to Bologna in September 1510. According to Albertini his residence at Sant' Apollinare was ornate.

Sigismondo dei Conti described Leonardo as upright in character and dedicated to study. Andrea *Ammonio described him in a letter to Erasmus of 18 November 1511 as a friend (Ep 243) whose appointment as major penitentiary – on 5 October 1511 – had caused some surprise since a lifetime of poverty and humility had been forecast for him. His register as penitentiary survives; he held this office until his death. Among his acts was the ratification in April 1518 of the privileges of the minor penitentiaries. Probably from March 1509 Leonardo also held the office of the *signatura commissionum,* or 'signature' of justice. Julius ii named him executor of his will together with Lorenzo *Pucci. In this capacity he was much concerned with plans for the pope's monumental tomb, and the successive contracts with Michelangelo of May 1513 and July 1516 bear his name. Michelangelo referred in letters to the cardinal of Agen's efforts to make him work on the project, but after the latter's death Michelangelo tried to get the 1516 contract cancelled, claiming he had not received enough money.

Under *Leo x Leonardo retained his high position in the Roman court. He does not appear to have been involved in the conspiracy against Leo which came to light in 1517, though he did not attend the consistory on 22 June when the conspirators' sentences were announced. After the death of Cardinal Sisto *della Rovere he succeeded to the latter's title church of San Pietro in Vincoli on 8 March 1517; he resigned the bishopric of Agen on 23 March 1519 to Antonio della Rovere. Leonardo died at Rome. Cardinal Lorenzo *Campeggi wrote to *Wolsey on 10 October 1520 praising Leonardo as a religious man but also evaluating his benefices and offices and reporting that his annual income was twenty-two thousand ducats (LP iii-1 1016).

BIBLIOGRAPHY: Allen and CWE Ep 243 are very cursory / See also Eubel ii 82, iii 10, 98; Pastor vi 221 and passim; Sanudo *Diarii* vi 265, 268, and passim / F. Albertini *Opusculum de mirabilibus novae et veteris Romae* ed A. Schmarsow (Heilbronn 1866) passim / J. Burchardus *Liber notarum* ed E. Celeni (Città di Castello 1906–59) passim / *Le due spedizioni militari di Giulio ii* ed L. Frati (Bologna 1886) passim / For particular points above see F. Litta *Celebri Famiglie Italiane, Dispensa* 147 (Milan 1863) table

1 / L.H. Labande *Avignon au xve siècle* (Paris 1920) 97 / Sigismondo dei Conti *Le storie de' suoi tempi dal 1475 al 1510* (Rome 1883) II 343 / E. Göller *Die päpstlichen Pönitentiare* (Rome 1907–11) I-1 15, II-1 39–43 / W. von Hofmann *Forschungen zur Geschichte der kurialen Behörden* (Rome 1914) II 133 / E.H. Ramsden *The Letters of Michelangelo* (London 1963) I 121, 123, 149, 250–51, 255, 257, II 26–31 / Vernon Hall Jr 'Life of Julius Caesar Scaliger 1484–1558' *Transactions of the American Philosophical Society* n s 40 (1950) 90

D.S. CHAMBERS

Sisto Gara DELLA ROVERE c 1472–8 March 1517
Sisto Gara was the son of Pope *Julius II's sister Lucchina and half-brother of Cardinal Galeotto della Rovere, upon whose death he was created cardinal on 11 September 1508, receiving at the same time the administration of the bishopric of Lucca, the papal vice-chancellorship, and various other benefices, including the bishopric of Vicenza, which helped to exacerbate the pope's already bad relations with Venice. He also held the protectorship of England from 1508 to 1509, corresponding with *Henry VIII on his accession. Andrea *Ammonio mentioned him to Erasmus as a devoted friend in his letter of 18 November 1511 (Ep 243). Little information about him has survived; Paris de Grassis, mentioning his death in the palace of the papal chancery in Rome, commented that from the time he became a cardinal he had been continually ill and unable to walk. According to Grassis he was also ignorant of literature and could neither read, write, nor speak the vernacular properly.
BIBLIOGRAPHY: Allen and CWE Ep 243 / D.S. Chambers *Cardinal Bainbridge in the Court of Rome* (Oxford 1965) 10–11, 25, 43n, 47, 73, 107 / Eubel III 11 and passim / Pastor VI 222 and passim / Sanudo *Diarii* VII 629, 632, and passim
D.S. CHAMBERS

Nicaise DELORME 1438–6 January 1516
Nicaise Delorme (de L'Orme, Nicasius de Ulmo), a native of Picardy, was prior of Fleury-en-Bière when elected abbot of St Victor, Paris, as a compromise candidate. He was then in his fiftieth year and had been a canon regular of St Augustine for thirty-three years. On 12 October 1488 he was installed as

abbot and in a letter of ratification of his oath of office (6 November 1488) he criticized the abuses practised and tolerated by his predecessors. During his own tenure of office a growing number of monks came to live at St Victor, but he did not feel bound to maintain the simplicity he had pledged to observe at the time of his election. He had the abbey church sumptuously redecorated and himself lived in grand-seigniorial style in his personal residence adjacent to the walls of the monastery. His conduct led to complaints before the bishop of Paris, the reform-minded Jean *Simon, and in 1497 to the transfer to St Victor of six Netherlandish canons of the Windesheim congregation, among them Erasmus' friend Cornelis *Gerard, to whom the abbot showed special favour (Ep 74). Delorme weathered the crisis by foreaking his personal possessions and revising the St Victor book of rules, avoiding, however, copying anything from the Windesheim statutes. The six Windesheim canons withdrew, and Delorme's public appearance at the funeral of King *Charles VIII in 1498 showed he had returned to his former splendour. On 14 November 1505 he celebrated the fiftieth anniversary of his monastic vows. In 1509 a new building for St Victor's library was completed. In the church of St Victor he built a new vestry, richly adorned the altar, and replaced the organ. When his conduct was once again the subject of complaints to the bishop, now Etienne *Poncher, he finally resigned in favour of Jean Bordier on 5 July 1514: his health was failing and he was then seventy-six. The new abbot requested that he dismiss his maid and wall up the street doors to his apartment. To his death he continued to oppose adherence of St Victor to the Windesheim congregation.
BIBLIOGRAPHY: Allen and CWE Ep 74 / *Gallia christiana* VII 687–8 / Fourier Bonnard *L'Histoire de l'abbaye royale et de l'ordre des chanoines réguliers de Saint-Victor de Paris* (Paris [1904–8]) I 445ff / Renaudet *Préréforme* 50, 221–7, 449, 560–1, 567, and passim / Paris, Archives Nationales, several MSS of the series L 889
VERONIKA GERZ-VON BÜREN

François DELOYNES of Beaugency, d July 1524
François Deloynes (Deloinus) was born around 1468, the son of a bailiff of Beaugency,

near Orléans. He studied law at Orléans, like Guillaume *Budé, with whom he was very closely associated. Subsequently he taught there as *docteur-régent*, and by 1490 Jean Pyrrhus d'*Angleberme was his student. Also at Orléans Deloynes met John *Colet by 1495 (Ep 494) and Erasmus in September 1500 (Ep 480). At the end of 1500 he was appointed to the Parlement of Paris and moved to the capital. In 1522 he became *président aux enquêtes* and participated in this capacity in the trial of Saint-Villier, an accomplice of the Constable Charles de Bourbon (1523).

In Paris Deloynes was at the centre of a learned circle which included Nicolas *Bérault and other natives of Orléans. Deloynes was praised universally for his scholarship, his enlightened spirit, and his talent for friendship. Several of Josse *Bade's publications are dedicated to him: Charles *Fernand's *De animi tranquillitate* (13 November 1512), an edition of Lucretius by Nicolas Bérault which was accompanied by eight couplets from Bade's own pen, also addressed to Deloynes (10 August 1514), and an edition of the Greek grammar of *Gaza by Jean Vatel (October 1521). During his lifetime Deloynes was praised by such poets as Fausto *Andrelini (Paris, Bibliothèque Nationale, MS latin 8134 f 233 verso) and Germain de *Brie (*Poematia duo*, Paris: N. de la Barre 1520); his death inspired the latter to write *In Francisci Deloini ... obitum elegia*, (Paris: P. Vidoue September 1524). Deloynes resembled Thomas *More and Willibald *Pirckheimer in providing a humanistic education for his three daughters; the eldest, Antoinette, became the wife of Jean *Morel, an intimate friend of the poet Joachim Du Bellay.

Deloynes was the 'Pylades' of Guillaume Budé, his friend during childhood and studies, his adviser, and also his cousin by marriage. Budé immortalized him by introducing his friend in a final dialogue of the *De asse* and by proclaiming their friendship in the last lines of the book (Budé *Opera omnia*, Basel 1557, II 269, 303–15; cf Ep 403). This friendship is one of the essential factors behind the relationship between Deloynes and Erasmus.

After their first encounter at Orléans Deloynes met Erasmus again in Paris (Ep 480). An avid reader of the works of Erasmus, Deloynes showed Budé in April 1516 the page of Erasmus' *Annotationes in Novum Testamentum* on which Budé's work was mentioned with praise (Ep 403). Once Erasmus and Budé had begun to correspond, Budé immediately wished to see their correspondence expanded to include Deloynes. Only the first exchange of letters between Deloynes and Erasmus (Epp 494, 535) has been preserved, but we know that there were others (Ep 1328; LB IX 788B–C). In almost all the letters between Erasmus and Budé, Deloynes is mentioned. In 1524, at the request of Konrad *Resch, Deloynes gave Noël *Béda a copy of Erasmus' *Paraphrasis in Lucam* so as to test the reaction of the theological faculty. Shortly before his death he relayed to Erasmus the critical notes Béda had submitted to the Parlement (LB IX 447B 534A; Allen VI 66–7). Telle's view that Deloynes translated the *Moria* into French is based on a questionable reading and interpretation of Epp 597, 1599. Erasmus paid eloquent tribute to Deloynes as a protector in his *Apologia adversus Petrum Sutorem* (LB IX 738, 788; Ep 1591). In the *Ciceronianus* he expressed regret that such a man had not left any works other than a few personal letters (ASD I-2 674).

BIBLIOGRAPHY: Allen Ep 494 / Louis Delaruelle *Guillaume Budé* (Paris 1907) passim / Louis Delaruelle *Répertoire ... de la correspondance de Guillaume Budé* (Toulouse-Paris 1907) Epp 3, 46, and passim / *La Correspondance d'Erasme et de Guillaume Budé* trans M.-M. de la Garanderie (Paris 1967) 297 and passim / M.-M. de la Garanderie *Christianisme et lettres profanes* (Lille-Paris 1976) I 241–2 and passim / Louis de Berquin *Declamation des louenges de mariage* ed E.V. Telle (Geneva 1976) 67, 83, 87

MARIE-MADELEINE DE LA GARANDERIE

DELPHUS See Gillis van DELFT, Erasmus and Frans van der DILFT

Hans DENCK of Habach, c 1500–November 1527

In Ep 1962 Erasmus mentioned the recent deaths from the plague of Michael *Bentinus, his wife and child, and a house guest. This guest who is not mentioned elsewhere, may have been Hans Denck, the famous Anabaptist, who died in Basel at this time after having lived more or less clandestinely in the city and surrounding villages since the autumn of 1527.

He clearly associated with Bentinus and, according to one source (1530) had secretly come to the city a few days before his death. However, the evidence for a positive identification is insufficient.

Denck (Denk) was born in Habach, Upper Bavaria, and received a BA from the University of Ingolstadt in 1519. For a while he worked as a corrector for the Basel printers *Cratander and *Curio before being appointed rector of St Sebald's school in Nürnberg in the autumn of 1523. He was baptized by Balthasar *Hubmaier and through his proselytizing and his writings became an intellectual leader of the Anabaptist movement. In his subsequent years of wandering he returned repeatedly to the region of Strasbourg and Basel.

BIBLIOGRAPHY: Allen Ep 1962 / BA *Oekolampads* I 158, II 102–5, 112, 429, and passim / *The Mennonite Encyclopedia* (Hillboro, Kansas, 1955–9) II 32–5 / NDB III 599–600

PGB

Antoine DENIDEL documented 1495–1501
Antoine Denidel (Denydel) worked in Paris as a bookseller and printer; books in his name are known from 1495 to 1501. He produced theological, grammatical, and pedagogical treatises, usually in collaboration with other booksellers such as Nicolle de La Barre or Robert de Gourmont. Probably in January 1496 Denidel printed at his address ('ante collegium de Coqueret') Erasmus' *Carmen de casa natalitia Jesu* (Reedijk poem 33).

Conceivably he was the printer who sold books for Erasmus and kept the money for himself, as Erasmus complained in a letter dated 2 May 1499 (Ep 95). Allen unconvincingly suggested the printer Guy Marchant.

BIBLIOGRAPHY: CWE Ep 95 / Renouard *Répertoire* 109–10 / A. Claudin *Histoire de l'imprimerie en France* (Paris 1901) II 261–8 / Reedijk 224, 237–8

GENEVIÈVE GUILLEMINOT

DENIS the Carthusian of Rijkel, 1402/3–
12 March 1471
Denis (Dionysius Carthusianus), whose family name was van Leeuwen (de Leeuwis), was born at Rijkel, near St Truiden. He probably studied at the Benedictine abbey of St Truiden and at the age of thirteen entered the municipal school of Zwolle. Before he was twenty he attempted to enter the Carthusian houses of Zelem and Roermond but was rejected because of his age. Consequently from 1421 he studied arts and presumably theology at the University of Cologne, attaining the degree of MA in 1424. In the same year he was admitted to the Carthusian convent of Bethlehem Mariae at Roermond. With the notable exception of the period September 1451 to March 1452 – when he accompanied Cardinal Nicolaus *Cusanus on his legatine mission to reform the religious orders in Germany – Denis remained at Roermond. On 3 July 1467 he was appointed rector of the new convent of St Sophia, near 's Hertogenbosch, founded by the monks of Roermond. Early in 1469 he was allowed to return to Roermond because of ill health, and there he died. Among his friends had been the proverbially eloquent Franciscan preacher Jan Brugman.

Called the 'doctor ecstaticus,' Denis was the most prolific scholastic theologian of the fifteenth century. His works were edited by Dierick Loer at Cologne from 1521 to 1538 and were published in a more thorough modern edition of forty-four volumes between 1896 and 1935 (Montreuil-Tournai-Parkminster). They included a summa of theology, numerous sermons on the saints and the liturgical seasons, works of asceticism and mysticism, and commentaries on the entire Bible, the *Sentences* of Peter Lombard, the works of Dionysius the Areopagite, and the *Consolation of Philosophy* of Boethius.

Erasmus knew of Denis' commentaries *In psalmos et cantica* (Cologne: P. Quentel 1531), but evidently did not know who the author was (Ep 2616). At the request of Bishop Christoph von *Utenheim he glanced through Denis' *De vita et regimine praesulum* and a second work, perhaps *De vita et regimine curatorum*; he appreciated the content of the former but found the latter unsatisfactory in every respect (Ep 1332).

BIBLIOGRAPHY: Allen Ep 1332 / W. Mulder in NNBW II 393–6 / *Biographisch-Bibliographisches Kirchenlexikon* (Hamm, Westphalia, 1975) I 1323–4 / K. Swenden in DHGE XIV 256–60 / A. Stoelen in *Dictionnaire de spiritualité ascétique et mystique* ed Marcel Viller et al (Paris 1932–) III 430–49 / A. Mougel *Denys le Chartreux*

(Montreuil-sur-Mer 1896) / H.J.J. Scholtens 'Het Roermondse Kartuizerconvent voor de zestiende eeuw' *Publications de la Société historique et archéologique dans le Limbourg* 86–7 (1950–1) 187–245 (esp 228–44), and 'Dionysius de Karthuizer in Beeld' *Opgang* 4 (1924) 762–7, 834–6, 882–5 (on his portraits)

C.G. VAN LEIJENHORST

Maria DENYS documented at Antwerp, c 1526–30

Maria Denys (Denis, Dionysia), the daughter of Denys Adriaens, was a widow when she married Pieter *Gillis, whose first wife, Cornelia *Sandrien, had died by August 1526 (Ep 2260). Maria probably died in the winter of 1529–30, and on 28 January 1530 Erasmus wrote to Gillis to express his condolences (Ep 2260), adding to his letter three epitaphs for Gillis' two wives (Reedijk poems 126–8).

MARCEL A. NAUWELAERTS

Sebastian DERRER of Nördlingen, d 31 July 1541

The 'Doctor Sebastian' of Ep 3045 who was willing to help Erasmus' housekeeper, Margarete *Büsslin, is almost certainly Derrer. His first name and title alone are used repeatedly by *Zasius and others (AK II Ep 984, III Epp 1274, 1325, V Ep 2406).

Sebastian Derrer of Nördlingen (Swabia) matriculated at Freiburg on 17 October 1512 and was a MA in 1515–16. From 1515 he was headmaster of the Freiburg grammar school, and in 1517 he was appointed to the chair of mathematics. On 4 December 1523 he obtained his legal doctorate and soon thereafter the chair of codex which Bonifacius *Amerbach had declined. In 1535 he finally succeeded Zasius, his teacher and friend, to the most senior chair of law after Georgius *Amelius had declined the position. Derrer, who is described as a somewhat pliable man, was often dean and rector. In 1540 he published at Louvain *Jurisprudentiae liber primus*, announcing nine more books which, however, did not follow. This work, a systematic presentation of Roman law, inspired the Ramist Johannes Thomas Freigius, who posthumously published two more legal works by Derrer in the appendix of his *Trium artium ... schematismi* (Basel 1568). Derrer married Anna Scheurin of Neuenburg,

a relative of Amerbach's wife, Martha *Fuchs, in July 1528.

BIBLIOGRAPHY: ADB V 66–7 / Winterberg 26–8 / H. Schreiber *Universität Freiburg* II 330–2 / *Matrikel Freiburg* I 204 / AK II Ep 985, III Ep 1275, V Ep 2357, and passim

PGB

Etienne DES GOUTTES of Saint-Symphorien-sur-Coise, documented 1518–29

Etienne, a son of Florimond Des Gouttes (Stephanus Florimundus, de Guttis) belonged to a relatively obscure branch of a merchant family from Saint-Symphorien-sur-Coise, fifty kilometers south-east of Lyon. Like another more enduring branch, Etienne's family seems to have embraced Calvinism at an early stage. After the outbreak of the religious wars members of both branches settled in Geneva and Lausanne. Etienne matriculated at the medical school of Montpellier on 27 October 1518, using the name form Stephanus Florimundus, which is also found in the records of his subsequent trial and in the correspondence of Erasmus. It is possible that one Jean de Florimond, a priest in Montpellier, was a relative of Etienne. The latter was in no hurry to complete his studies. In May 1528 he was arrested on suspicion of heresy with his friends Guillaume *Carvel and Etienne du Temple, who is singled out for praise in the Montpellier matriculation register on account of his knowledge of Greek and Latin. Although several Lutheran writings had been found among the possessions of Etienne Des Gouttes, the case against the three defendants was finally dismissed on 7 September 1529. According to the family chronicler Etienne became physician to *Margaret of Angoulême, queen of Navarre, and died at Nantes, being survived by one daughter.

Des Gouttes and Carvel sent greetings to Erasmus through Petrus *Decimarius, which Erasmus returned in March 1528, shortly before the proceedings against the three Montpellier students got under way (Ep 1986). The links between the Des Gouttes family and Basel were renewed in 1553 when the previously mentioned family chronicler, Jérôme Des Gouttes, spent a few months there to escape religious strife in Lyon, where he lived.

BIBLIOGRAPHY: *Matricule de Montpellier* 35 /

Matrikel Basel II 79 / Paul-F. Geisendorf *Histoire d'une famille du refuge français: Les Des Gouttes* (Geneva [1943]) 26, 60, and passim / V.L. Saulnier 'Médecins de Montpellier au temps de Rabelais' BHR 19 (1957) 425–75, esp 457 / Louise Guiraud *La Réforme à Montpellier* (Montpellier 1918) I 41–5, II 331–6 and passim / P.G. Bietenholz *Basle and France in the Sixteenth Century* (Geneva-Toronto 1971) 223 and passim

PGB

Jean DESMAREZ of Cassel, d 20 February 1526

Jean Desmarez (des Marais, de Palude, Paludanus) was a native of Cassel, near Saint-Omer, then in the Netherlands. He taught Latin at the Louvain College of the Falcon for several years and was admitted to the council of the faculty of arts in 1483. He was appointed professor of eloquence or public orator, and consequently a canon of St Peter's in 1490. A fine Latin scholar, he began to teach Latin literature in a comprehensive and thorough way.

As president of the college of St Donatian Desmarez offered hospitality to Erasmus when he arrived at Louvain in September 1502 having fled the plague in Paris (Ep 175). He also introduced Erasmus to a group of congenial humanists in the College of the Lily. Erasmus remained with him until 1504, during which time he published his *Panegyricus* at Desmarez's urging (Epp 177, 180; LB X 1667C). Erasmus dedicated the work to him as well as subsequently his translation of Lucian's *De mercede conductis* in 1506. In his dedicatory letter (Ep 197) he encouraged Desmarez to undertake some translations from Greek. He also referred to his friend's personal experience of court life. In fact, Desmarez cultivated the friendship of Jacques de *Croy, bishop of Cambrai, whose epitaph he later induced Erasmus to write (Ep 497).

In November 1510 Desmarez continued his Latin lectures as professor of poetics in the faculty of law, effectively combining his new post with the chair of eloquence. He acted as dean of law for the summer term of 1519 and for the winter term of 1525.

Desmarez was a good friend of Maarten van *Dorp and in 1515 and 1516 helped to bring about the reconciliation between Dorp and

Erasmus (Epp 337, 438, 496). In 1515 Gerardus *Listrius dedicated to Desmarez his commentary on the *Moria* (published with the edition of J. Froben, Basel May 1515), and Gerard *Geldenhouwer, another old friend, dedicated to him his *Epistola ... de triumphali ingressu ... Philippi* in 1517 (Louvain: D. Martens, Epp 645, 812). Desmarez admired Thomas *More and in 1516 wrote a letter to Pieter *Gillis and a poem, both of which were printed with the first edition of More's *Utopia* (Louvain: D. Martens 1516) but later withdrawn.

From July to September 1517 Erasmus was again staying with Desmarez, who continued to be closely associated with the College of St Donatian. In 1524 Erasmus paid tribute to his old friend in the colloquy *Epithalamium Petri Aegidii* (ASD I-3 416). On the day following Desmarez's death, Adrianus Cornelii *Barlandus was appointed to succeed him in the chair of eloquence. It was in a letter of congratulation to Barlandus that Erasmus expressed his grief at Desmarez' death (Ep 1694).

BIBLIOGRAPHY: Allen and CWE Ep 180 / de Vocht CTL I 184–6, 188–90, 286–7, and passim / de Vocht *Literae ad Craneveldium* Ep 1 and passim / Reedijk poem 104

CFG & PGB

Jacques DESPARTS of Tournai, d 1458

Jacques Desparts (Despars, de Partibus) was born in Tournai around 1380. He had probably just received his MA in March 1400 when he enrolled in the faculty of medicine in Paris. He spent six months in Montpellier but returned to Paris, where he was rector of the university in 1406 and obtained his baccalaureate in medicine on 22 May 1408 and his doctorate on 7 April 1410. He was a regent in medicine in Paris until 1419. Meanwhile, he represented the University of Paris at the council of Constance in 1415 and again in 1418. He practised medicine in the Burgundian Low Countries, where his patients included Philip the Good, duke of *Burgundy, and his son Charles, later also duke of *Burgundy. From 1432 to 1453 he composed his major work, a commentary on Avicenna, and he specified that he consulted not only Latin but also Greek and Arab authors. In 1452 he returned to Paris and may have been the personal physician of King *Charles VII. He interested the king in providing a permanent locale for the faculty of medicine and personally contributed three hundred écus d'or and his library of books and manuscripts to the faculty.

Desparts was the perpetual chaplain of Cuvillers (Départment du Nord), canon of Cambrai and Cysoing, canon and treasurer of Tournai, and canon and chancellor of Notre-Dame de Paris. He died in the cloister of Notre-Dame on 3 January or 3 June 1458 and was buried in the Chapelle Saint-Jacques of the cathedral. Besides his gifts to the faculty of medicine he left legacies to Notre-Dame de Paris and to the leprosarium of Tournai, and he established three scholarships each in theology, medicine, and law for poor students from Tournai to attend any university.

His works include: *Explanatio in Avicennam, una cum textu ipsius Avicennae* 4 vols (Lyon: Jean Trechsel 1498); *Glossa interlinearis in practicam Alexandri Traliani* (Lyon 1504); *Expositio super capitulis, videlicet de regimine aquae et vini* (Venice 1518); *Summula per alphabeticum super plurimis remediis ex ipsius Mesue libris excerptis* (Lyon 1523); and *Inventarium seu collectorium receptarum omnium medicaminum* (n p, n d).

BIBLIOGRAPHY: Allen Ep 858 / *Auctarium chartularii universitatis Parisiensis* ed Charles Samaran et al (Paris 1894–1964) III 186 n 4 / DBF X 1505–6 / BNB V 774–8 / E. Wickersheimer *Dictionnaire biographique des médecins en France au Moyen Age* (Paris 1926) I 326–7

JAMES K. FARGE

Etienne DESPREZ documented at Besançon 1529–36

Etienne Desprez (Pratensis, a Prato, Pratanus) was rector of the Besançon school which was partly under the jurisdiction of the chapter. He and Erasmus corresponded from 1529, assisting each other with the shipment of wine to Freiburg and of *Froben books to Besançon (Epp 2139, 2140, 2401A, 2895, 3115). Erasmus also asked Desprez to forward his letters to other friends (Epp 3102, 3104, 3115). In his flowery answers Desprez once accused Guillaume *Guérard of having spread a malicious rumour about Erasmus' orthodoxy (Ep 2895); he also referred to Jean *Lambelin, then at the peak of his political influence, as his friend and relative (Ep 3115). He seems to have survived Lambelin's fall, however, and was probably

still alive when Ferry Julyot addressed some verses to him as his first teacher (published in 1557). An edition of Juvenal that he had owned, is now in the Bibliothèque publique of Besançon.

BIBLIOGRAPHY: Allen Ep 2140 / Claude Fohlen et al *Histoire de Besançon* (Paris 1965) I 640 / Auguste Castan *Catalogue des incunables de la Bibliothèque publique de Besançon* (Besançon 1893) 477

PGB

Tommaso DE VIO *See Cardinal* CAJETANUS

Justus DIEMUS of Bruchsal, d before 14 August 1527

Justus Diemus was born in Bruchsal, a town south of Heidelberg. Neither his family nor his date of birth is known, but a description of Diemus as a young man is extant in a letter by Stephanus Martialis (*Epistolae ad Nauseam* 57–8) dated 14 August 1527 and addressed to Fridericus *Nausea, informing him that his former student Diemus had drowned.

In October 1525 Diemus obtained recommendations from Erasmus (Ep 1630) and *Beatus Rhenanus and set out on a journey to visit his cousin Jacobus *Apocellus in Rome; on 12 January 1526 he thanked Beatus for his help and sent him a poem (BRE Ep 249). He left Rome the same year because he found the climate unbearable (Ep 1762). In Verona he was searched by the Venetians and subsequently got caught up in the tumultuous events of the peasant revolt. In Constance he obtained a position with Johannes *Fabri at the court of *Ferdinand I. On 9 September 1526 he wrote to Nausea from Tübingen describing the events of the past months (*Epistolae ad Nauseam* 38–40) and complaining that the work assigned him by Fabri occupied all his time; though disappointed with life at court he vowed to persevere until his fortune took a turn for the better. He asked Beatus to plead on his behalf with Apocellus, who wished to lure him away from court and back to Rome and was threatening to withdraw his friendship and support if Diemus failed to comply with his wishes. On 22 October 1526 he was at Speyer, having followed Ferdinand's court, and from Conradus Regius' house he wrote a letter to Erasmus in which he reported on his journey and on current political events (Ep 1762). In another letter addressed to Nausea and dated 4 January 1527 he also reported on political events and sent greetings to Johannes *Cochlaeus and his friends in Mainz (*Epistolae ad Nauseam* 46).

BIBLIOGRAPHY: Allen Ep 1762 / *Epistolae ad Nauseam* 38–40 and passim

                                   KONRAD WIEDEMANN

DIERCKX See THEODERICI

Nikolaus von DIESBACH of Bern, 22 June 1478–15 June 1550
Nikolaus, a son of Ludwig von Diesbach and Antonia von Ringoltingen, was descended from one of Bern's most powerful noble families. After studies at Paris he went to Rome and in 1498 was in the service of Cardinal Ascanio Sforza. He may have shared his time between Italy and Switzerland, being made an apostolic protonotary at Rome in 1504 and a doctor of canon law at Siena in 1509 while acquiring a long series of benefices in Switzerland, including the priorate of Grandson in 1503 and the provostship of Solothurn in 1506 (until 1527). Diplomatic opposition from Savoy prevented his appointment as bishop of Lausanne in 1510.

In 1514 Diesbach made his appearance in Basel as a canon and from 15 December 1516 he was the dean of the Basel chapter. On 28 May 1519 he was named coadjutor by Bishop Christoph von *Utenheim and soon had himself designated successor to the bishopric by Pope *Leo x. Although he was disliked by Utenheim, in view of the bishop's lack of energy Diesbach actually governed the prince-bishopric, but he was unable to prevent a further erosion of the bishop's secular powers in favour of the city council, both in the city itself and in the surrounding territory. Expecting worse to come in view of the progress of the Reformation, he entered into long and difficult negotiations about his resignation, initially asking for no less than an annual rent of six hundred florins and a lump-sum payment of three thousand florins, which, he claimed, represented the amount he had spent in order to obtain the coadjutorship. A solution was provided by *Ferdinand i, who in a personal letter of 4 March 1526 promised Diesbach a new

and better position in his lands. On 21 February 1527 he actually resigned as coadjutor in favour of Johannes *Fabri in exchange for a rent settled upon the city of Freiburg. He retired to Grandson and later to Besançon, where he died. From 1529 the Basel chapter urged him either to join them at Freiburg or to relinquish the deanship, and in 1531 he finally resigned as dean and canon.

Erasmus experienced Diesbach's friendship from his arrival at Basel in 1522 (Ep 1258). His repeated gifts of Burgundian wine (Epp 1342, 1353) proved to be an excellent cure for Erasmus' stone ailment, or so he believed (Ep 1510). Later he found an excuse for not writing to Diesbach (Ep 1780). Finally in July 1527 he dedicated to him his translation of a fragment of Origen (Ep 1844), avoiding saying anything about Diesbach and the nature of their relations.

BIBLIOGRAPHY: Allen Ep 1258 / DHBS II 670 / R. Wackernagel *Geschichte der Stadt Basel* (Basel 1905–54) III 93–4, 401, 80*, and passim / *Helvetia sacra* ed A. Bruckner (Bern 1972–   ) I-1 200–1, 293–4, I-2 514–15 / G. M[eier] 'War Bischof Nikolaus von Diesbach ein Apostat?' *Zeitschrift für schweizerische Kirchengeschichte* 8 (1914) 54–5 / J. Bücking 'Die Basler Weihbischöfe des 16. Jahrhunderts' *Zeitschrift für schweizerische Kirchengeschichte* 63 (1969) 67–91 esp 70–2 / BA Oekolampads I 250, 285–9, and passim / Herminjard I 244–5, II 95, 137, 140, 143, and passim / Gauthier 133

                                                     PGB

Johann DIETENBERGER of Frankfurt am Main, c 1475–4 September 1537
Johann Dietenberger (Phimostomus) was born in Frankfurt, the son of Henne (Hans) of Dietenbergen, in the Taunus. Around 1500 Johann entered the Dominican order. He studied in Cologne, Heidelberg, and Mainz and obtained a doctorate of theology in 1515. Thereafter he was prior or lecturer in various monasteries in southwest Germany. From 1523 he was a friend of Johannes *Cochlaeus and translated a number of Cochlaeus' polemical writings into German – for example, *Ob Sant Peter zu Rom sey gewesen* (Strasbourg: J. Grüninger 1524). He also corresponded with Cardinal *Cajetanus. At the diet at Augsburg (1530), Dietenberger was active among the

Catholic theologians. From 1532 he was a professor in Mainz, where he died.

Dietenberger wrote polemical pamphlets that remained relatively unknown, among others, *Ob der Glaube allein selig mache* (Strasbourg: J. Grüninger 1524); *Contra temerarium Martini Lutheri de votis monasticis iudicium* (Cologne: E. Cervicornus 1524); and *Fragstuck an alle Christglaubigen* (Cologne: P. Quentel 1530). His major achievement is a German translation of the Vulgate, greatly indebted to *Emser as well as *Luther; it was still being reprinted in the eighteenth century.

In 1532 Dietenberger attacked Erasmus' opinions concerning divorce in an appendix to his *Phimostomus scripturariorum* (Cologne: P. Quentel 1532), a general polemic against reformed teachings, dedicated to Johann von *Metzenhausen. Erasmus replied in his *Responsio ad disputationem cuiusdam Phimostomi de divortio* (Freiburg 1532; LB IX 955–65).

BIBLIOGRAPHY: NDB III 667–8 / *Matrikel Heidelberg* I p 486 / Nikolaus Paulus *Die deutschen Dominikaner im Kampfe gegen Luther* (Freiburg 1903) 186–9 / E.V. Telle *Erasme de Rotterdam et le septième sacrement* (Geneva 1954) 361–3 and passim / Erasmus *Dilutio eorum quae Iodocus Clithoveus scripsit* ed E.V. Telle (Paris 1968) 48, 84 / *Epistolae ad Nauseam* 94–5, 97–8

IG

Jodok or Justus DIETZ *See Justus Ludovicus DECIUS*

Erasmus van der DILFT of Antwerp, d 27 March 1540
Erasmus van der Dilft (Delft, Delphus, Dilfus) was born at Antwerp, the son of Jan and Joanna Oudaert. He matriculated at Louvain with his brother Frans van der *Dilft on 30 October 1519. He died at Padua. In 1530 he was reported to have had a packet of missing letters of Erasmus at Mechelen (Ep 2352).

BIBLIOGRAPHY: Allen Ep 2352 / *Matricule de Louvain* III-1 618 / de Vocht CTL II 171 / de Vocht *Literae ad Craneveldium* Ep 139

MARCEL A. NAUWELAERTS

Frans van der DILFT of Antwerp, d 14 June 1550
Frans van der Dilft (Delft, Dilfus), a son of a wealthy family of the Antwerp patriciate,

matriculated at Louvain on 30 October 1519 with his brother Erasmus van der *Dilft. After attending the lectures of Conradus *Goclenius (Ep 1890) in the Collegium Trilingue, he set out for Basel, where he matriculated in the university at the beginning of the winter term 1524–5 and lived in Erasmus' household until the end of December 1525. Late in February he was sent back to the Low Countries with Erasmus' letters; in April he returned to Basel, carrying the replies (Epp 1545, 1546, 1548, 1553, 1569). By the end of the year he went back to Louvain, travelling in the company of Erasmus' famulus, Karl *Harst, and warmly recommended by Erasmus (Epp 1653, 1655), who dedicated to him his translation of Plutarch's *De vitiosa verecundia* (published with the *Lingua* in February 1526; Ep 1663).

When he first went to Basel, Dilft had already been provided with a prebend of the Antwerp chapter, but by the end of February 1527 Goclenius reported that he had left Louvain several months before and was thought to be planning marriage and a career at the imperial court (Ep 1788). In August, however, he set out for Basel once more (AK III Ep 1204) and stayed with Erasmus again until February 1528 (Epp 1857, 1883, 1899). When he left he borrowed travel funds from Erasmus and Bonifacius *Amerbach, which he later repaid (Epp 2014, 2015; AK III Ep 1280). Leaving Basel, he set out on a leisurely journey through Germany, visiting many of Erasmus' friends and patrons such as Duke George of *Saxony, *Melanchthon at Jena, and *Pirckheimer and *Camerarius in Nürnberg (Epp 1942–5, 1972, 1977, 1979, 1981, 1982, 1991). By the middle of May he had still not returned to his family in Antwerp (Epp 1972, 1994A), and in August he was preparing to leave the Low Countries for the imperial court in Spain and asking Erasmus to provide him with introductions (Ep 2026). Erasmus was glad to comply (Epp 2013, 2109), and in September Dilft went to Zeeland and took ship. No suitable position was available at the court, however (Ep 2109), and by October 1529 Dilft had rejoined Erasmus' household, now at Freiburg (Ep 2222), and obliged his master by fetching wine for him from Burgundy (Epp 2225, 2241, 2242, 2348). After a visit to Basel in January 1530 (Epp 2248, 2256), he set out again for Spain by way of Genoa with a new series of recommendations from Erasmus (Epp 2251–5, 2481, 2523).

In July Erasmus replied to a letter from Dilft of 1 April, in which he had announced his entry into the service of Alonso de *Fonseca, archbishop of Toledo (Ep 2348). By the end of October 1531 Fonseca sent him to Freiburg with letters for Erasmus (Epp 2562, 2563). In May 1533 Dilft was still in Spain and corresponding with Erasmus (Ep 2876), but by July he was called back to Antwerp by his parents, who had found him a suitable bride in the person of a rich young widow. In February 1534 he wrote to Erasmus to offer him the use of a house he owned near the gates of Mechelen (Ep 2904). In September of that same year his wife died, however, and a few months later Dilft himself was near death (Ep 2998). Erasmus feared the worst (Ep 3019), but Dilft recovered and on 20 July 1535 married again (Ep 3037). His second wife was Cornelia, the daughter of Fernando Bernuy, a rich Spanish merchant who had settled in Antwerp and become an alderman, and his wife, Isabella van Bombergen. Under the impact of these events Dilft had stopped writing to Erasmus, who was annoyed, but Goclenius, still Dilft's faithful mentor, hastened to reassure Erasmus (Epp 3052, 3061).

Meanwhile Dilft had begun to succeed in his political career. Before his departure from Spain he pronounced an *Oratio gratulatoria* (Louvain 1533; NK 4329) at Barcelona before *Charles v and was rewarded with knighthood. In March 1536 he was preparing to rejoin the imperial court (Ep 3111), where he was subsequently appointed secretary of the privy council. In December 1544 he succeeded Eustache *Chapuys as Charles v's ambassador to England. In May 1550 he was recalled to the Low Countries to help in the planning and execution of a design to remove the Princess *Mary to the Netherlands, but he died unexpectedly at Antwerp the following month. He was lord of Doorne and Leverghem and had also repeatedly served as alderman and mayor of his native city of Antwerp between 1536 and 1541.

BIBLIOGRAPHY: Allen Ep 1663 / *Matricule de Louvain* III-1 618 / *Matrikel Basel* I 357 / de Vocht CTL II 171–6 and passim / de Vocht *Dantiscus* 377–8 and passim / de Vocht *Literae ad*

Craneveldium Ep 139 and passim / Bierlaire *Familia* 64–7 / P. Génard 'Naamlijst der burgemeesters van Antwerpen' *Antwerpsch archievenblad* 1st series 14 (n d) 196–209

FRANZ BIERLAIRE

DIONYSIUS (Rickel) Carthusianus *See* DENIS *the Carthusian*

Aymé de DIVONNE *See Aymon de* GINGINS

DJEM Ottoman prince, 22 December 1459–25 February 1495

Djem (Zizimus), a son of *Mehmed II and Cicek Khatun, was born in Edirne. In January 1469 he was sent with his tutors to govern Kastamonu. During Mehmed II's campaign of 1473 against Uzun Hasan he went to Edirne to safeguard Rumeli, and in December 1474 he succeeded his brother Mustafa as the governor of Karaman. When Mehmed II died on 3 May 1481, a struggle for the succession began between Djem and his elder brother, *Bayezid. The grand vizier, Karamani Mehmed Pasha, favoured Djem, but the janissaries and his other opponents eliminated Mehmed Pasha and invited Bayezid to take the throne. Djem occupied Bursa and had himself invoked as ruling sovereign in the Friday prayers; he also struck coins. His proposal that the empire should be divided between them was rejected by Bayezid, who defeated him at Yenisehir. Djem fled to Konya and then took refuge in Mameluke territory, arriving in Cairo in September 1481. Strongly influenced by the self-seeking Kasim Bey, the Karamanid pretender, and Mehmed Bey, the governor of Ankara, Djem made a new bid to secure some territory. After a fruitless campaign against Konya and Ankara, he fled to Taseli and tried once more to obtain a share of the Ottoman states by way of negotiation with Bayezid, who merely offered him an annuity on condition that he would live in Jerusalem. Djem was persuaded by Kasim Bey to cross over to Rumeli by sea. Having obtained a safe conduct from Pierre d'Aubusson, grand master of the Knights of St John in Rhodes, he arrived at Rhodes on 30 July 1482 and was promptly detained by the grand master, who regarded him as a valuable hostage. In September 1482 Bayezid agreed to a peace treaty favourable to the order, paying the knights forty-five thousand Venetian gold ducats annually for Djem's custody. In September 1482 the knights removed Djem to France and interned him at various places for seven years. His captivity caused Bayezid much anxiety, for so long as he was alive, the Christian states might invade the empire, using Djem as their instrument.

In 1489 Djem was transferred to Rome, where Pope Innocent VIII thought he could be used in a new crusade, while both Kait Bay, the Mameluke sultan, and *Matthias Corvinus of Hungary made serious efforts to obtain custody of him for their own purposes. In November 1492, at the request of the Ottomans, who paid 150,000 ducats as Djem's expenses, the new pope, *Alexander VI, confirmed the agreement originally made between Bayezid and the knights. In Rome Djem enjoyed some privileges and was even befriended by Cesare Borgia; but following the French invasion of 1494 the pope was compelled to hand Djem over to *Charles VIII. Djem accompanied Charles on his expedition against Naples, but he fell ill on the way, and died. There were rumours, probably unfounded, that he had been poisoned by Alexander VI. When surveying recent Turkish history in *De bello turcico* (LB V 353C; cf 351F) Erasmus repeated the story with a note of caution. Djem's body was taken back to the Ottoman Empire and buried at Bursa in April 1499.

Djem was considered a distinguished poet; his poems were collected in two *diwans*, one in Turkish and one in Persian.

BIBLIOGRAPHY: H. Inalcik in *Encyclopaedia of Islam* new ed (Leiden-London 1960–   ) II 529–31 (with full bibliography) / C. Baysun in *Islam Ansiklopedisi* (Istanbul 1940–   ) III 69–81 / E.H. Ertaylan *Sultan Cem* (Istanbul 1951) / L. Thuasne *Djem-Sultan* (Paris 1892)

FEHMI ISMAIL

Martin DOBERGAST documented 1517– c 1532

Martin Dobergast studied at Cologne, where he received his MA. From 1517 he was the German-speaking preacher at the church of Our Lady in Cracow, and remained in Cracow after becoming canon of Wrocław in 1520. At the request of Bishop *Tomicki he preached a series of sermons in 1524 aimed at combatting the spread of Lutheran views among the scholars of Cracow. In all likelihood while he was at Tomicki's court, he made the acquaintance of Jan *Antonin, who recommended him to Erasmus in a letter of 1 April 1527 (Epp 1810, 1825). In 1529 Dobergast went to Glogow (Glogau), in Silesia, to preach against Lutheranism at the invitation of King *Ferdinand, who in May 1531 expressed his desire for Dobergast to prolong his stay there. He died around 1532.

Dobergast's sermons against Luther were printed by M. Scharffenberg (Cracow 1525), but not a single copy is known to be extant today. In 1526 he published the bull of Pope *Leo X and the edict of King *Sigismund I against Lutheranism (Cracow: M. Scharffenberg), with a dedication to Tomicki. Mathaeus Holstein dedicated to him his *Aliquot epistolae divi Eusebii Hieronymi ... refertae saluberrimis praeceptis, ad vitam recte instituendam mire facientes, ac ab Erasmo Roterodamo pristinae integritati restitutae* (Cracow: H. Wietor n d).

BIBLIOGRAPHY: Allen Ep 1810 / H. Barycz *Historia Uniwersytetu Jagiellońskiego w epoce humanizmu* (Cracow 1935) / *Archiv für die Geschichte des Bisthums Breslau* ed A. Kastner (Neisse 1858) I 17–18, 26–7 / J.D. Janocki *Janociana sive clarorum atque illustrium Poloniae auctorum maecenatorumque memoriae miscellae* (Warsaw 1776) I 59–60 / *Acta Tomiciana* (Poznan-Wrocław 1852–   ) XI Epp 161, 204–6, XIII Ep 143 / F. Mymer *Naenia funebris* (Cracow: M. Scharffenberg 1532) f B¹ verso

HALINA KOWALSKA

Johannes DOCCUMENSIS *See* JAN *of Dokkum*

Etienne DOLET of Orléans, 3 August 1508– 3 August 1546

In his native Orléans Etienne Dolet was given a liberal education by his family, whose circumstances are otherwise unknown. At twelve he was sent to Paris, where he studied for five years. As a disciple of Simon *Villanovanus at the University of Padua (1527–30), he became a devout Ciceronian. After serving one year as secretary to Jean de Langeac, bishop of Limoges, at that time French ambassador to Venice, Dolet entered the University of Toulouse under his patronage in 1532 to study law. After being elected orator and later prior of the

French nation, Dolet delivered two orations, the first on 9 October 1533 and the second before 27 January 1534, which voiced student dissent from an edict of the Parlement (23 June 1531) suppressing the nations. His attack on the barbarity of Toulouse brought an angry reply from Pierre Pinache, orator of the Gascon nation, who denounced him to the Parlement. Dolet was arrested on 25 March 1534 but released after three days through the intercession of Jean de *Pins, bishop of Rieux. The following May he entered the 'Floral Games' and, failing to win a prize, circulated six odes against Gratien du Pont, sieur de Drusac, one of the *mainteneurs* of the games and *lieutenant-général* of the seneschalty of Toulouse. In June, Drusac obtained an edict of the Parlement banishing Dolet, who fled on foot to Lyon with a friend, Simon Finet, arriving on 1 August, dangerously ill. On his recovery he became corrector for the press of Sebastianus *Gryphius, who published Dolet's *Orationes duae in Tholosam* the same year.

Etienne Dolet

While in Paris to secure a royal licence for the publication of his *Commentarii linguae latinae* (Lyon: S. Gryphius 1536, 1538), Dolet wrote the *Dialogus de imitatione Ciceroniana* (Lyon: S. Gryphius 1535), a defence of Christophe de *Longueil against Erasmus' *Ciceronianus*. Less scurrilous than the *Oratio pro M. Tullio Cicerone* of Julius Caesar *Scaliger (Paris: Pierre Vidoue 1531), it nevertheless accused Erasmus, the 'toothless old food-for-worms,' of garrulity, shallow popularizing, and Lutheranism. Erasmus blamed both attacks on Girolamo *Aleandro and refused to answer them (Epp 3005, 3052, 3127, 3130). Dolet renewed the quarrel in several digressions in the first volume of the *Commentarii*, but in the second volume he declared a truce with the shade of Erasmus and wrote an ode on his death (LB I introductory material). Dolet was himself attacked by Scaliger, who resented his intrusion in the controversy, and by Franciscus Floridus Sabinus.

On 31 December 1536 Dolet killed a painter named Compaing who attacked him in the streets of Lyon. He fled to Paris to appeal to King *Francis I, but the royal pardon granted on 19 February was not ratified by the Parlement of Lyon, and Dolet was thrown into prison on his return. He was released provi-

sionally on 21 April 1537. In 1538, Dolet received a ten-year privilege from the king to print books which he had composed, translated, or edited in Latin, Greek, French, or Italian. The first books to bear his mark were printed at the press of Gryphius, but in 1539 he established his own shop, taking a partner, Hélouin Dulin. Able now to support a family, he married Louise Giraud in 1538 and a year later celebrated the birth of a son in a Latin poem, *Genethliacum Claudii Doleti*, translated into French as *L'Avant-naissance de Claude Dolet*. Unfortunately Dolet's *Cato christianus* and *Carmina* (1538) were denounced as heretical to the vicar-general and official of the archbishop of Lyon, and he was ordered to withdraw them from sale.

For the next three years Dolet was cautious. In addition to editing, translating, and commenting on classical authors, he published instalments of two projects which he never completed, a history of his time and a treatise on *L'Orateur françoys*. Erasmus' *De copia* (1540) was among many contemporary works to issue from his press. In 1542, however, he moved to the rue Mercière, doubled his production, and began printing and selling 'heretical' works. In a struggle which began in 1538, Dolet had sided with the journeyman printers of Lyon against their employers; as a result, in July or August 1542 the master printers denounced him to the inquisitor-general. Dolet was arrested and on 2 October declared a heretic and fomenter of heresy and delivered to the secular arm. An appeal to the Parlement of Paris won him time to obtain a royal pardon in June 1543, on condition that he abjure his errors before the official of the bishop of Paris and that the heretical books be burned, including translations of Erasmus' *Enchiridion* and *Exomologesis* (*Le Chevalier chrestien* and *Du Vrai Moyen de bien et catholiquement se confesser*). The Parlement objected that he was still under sentence of death for the murder of Compaing, and repeated letters patent from the king were necessary before the pardon was registered on 13 October 1543.

Dolet returned to Lyon but two packages bearing his name, one containing prohibited books from Geneva, the other books he had printed, were seized at the gates of Paris, and on 6 January 1544 he was arrested. Two days later he persuaded the jailer to take him to his house to collect a debt and escaped through the back door, fleeing to Piedmont. There he wrote twelve verse epistles claiming that the master printers of Lyon had framed him. Confident of their effect, he returned secretly to Lyon, where he printed them as *Le Second Enfer* with his translations of two dialogues then attributed to Plato, *Axiochus* and *Hipparchus*. Another edition of *Le Second Enfer* appeared at Troyes (N. Paris 1544), where Dolet was arrested in August or September. On 14 November 1544 the faculty of theology at the University of Paris declared that a phrase in his translation of the *Axiochus* denied the immortality of the soul and was thus heretical. On 2 August 1546 the Parlement of Paris pronounced Dolet guilty of blasphemy, sedition, and exposing for sale prohibited and condemned books. After torture, he was hanged and his body and books burned on the place Maubert on 3 August.

BIBLIOGRAPHY: Allen Ep 3005 / Although Marc Chassaigne's unsympathetic *Etienne Dolet: Portraits et documents inédits* (Paris 1930) is the most recent of many biographies, R.C.

Christie's *Etienne Dolet, the Martyr of the Renaissance* rev ed (London 1899) is still definitive / See also J.C. Dawson *Toulouse in the Renaissance* (New York 1923) 141–87 / Claude Longeon 'Etienne Dolet: années d'enfance et de jeunesse' in *Réforme et Humanisme* Actes du IVe colloque du Centre d'histoire de la réforme et du protestantisme (Montpellier 1977) 37–61 / DBF XI 441–4 follows Chassaigne / On Dolet's religious views see O. Douen 'Etienne Dolet: ses opinions religieuses' *Bulletin de la Société de l'histoire du protestantisme français* 30 (1881) 337–55, 385–408; L. Febvre 'Dolet propagateur de l'évangile' BHR 6 (1945) 98–170; C.A. Mayer 'The problem of Dolet's evangelical publications' BHR 17 (1955) 405–14; H. Busson *Le Rationalisme dans la littérature française de la Renaissance* rev ed (Paris 1957) 112–21 / On Dolet and Erasmus see E.V. Telle's excellent edition of *L'Erasmianus sive Ciceronianus d'Etienne Dolet* (Geneva 1974); P.G. Bietenholz 'Humanistic ventures into psychology: Etienne Dolet's polemic against Erasmus' in *Essays Presented to Myron P. Gilmore* ed S. Bertelli and G. Ramakus (Florence 1978) I 21–36 / For the bibliography of Dolet's works see Claude Longeon *Bibliographie des oeuvres d'Etienne Dolet* (Geneva 1980) / Etienne Dolet *Préfaces françaises* ed Claude Longeon (Geneva 1979) / Claude Longeon *Documents d'archives sur Etienne Dolet* (Saint-Etienne 1977) / Longeon also edited Dolet's *Le Second Enfer* (Geneva 1978)

JUDITH RICE HENDERSON

Judocus DONARET (Ep 472, of 29 September 1516)
This name is given by Josse *Bade to the town clerk of Ghent, whose son-in-law took Ep 435 from Paris to Erasmus. The archives of Ghent have not permitted an identification of Donaret.

MARCEL A. NAUWELAERTS

Girolamo DONATO of Venice, 1457–27 October 1511
Girolamo Donato came from a patrician family of Venice and studied Latin and Greek at Venice and Padua. He then served the Republic in the government of its subject territories and as a diplomat. He was governor of Brescia in the early 1490s, *vice-dominus* in charge of protecting Venetian interests at

Ferrara from 1498 to 1500, governor of Cremona in 1503, governor of Candia in Crete
from 1505 to 1508, and quartermaster and captain at Padua in 1509. His diplomatic posts
included embassies to Innocent VIII, to the city
of Lucca in 1496, to *Alexander VI from 1497 to
1499, to *Maximilian I in 1499, to *Louis XII of
France from 1501 to 1502, and to *Julius II in
1505 and again from 1509 to 1511. His last
mission was his most important, for it involved
making peace after the war of the League of
Cambrai, waged by Julius and his allies
against an isolated Venice. Donato died while
ambassador at Rome.

Erasmus met Donato when he visited Rome
in 1509 and later remembered him as an old but
vigorous man (Ep 1347). In the *Ciceronianus* he
described him as learned but distracted from
scholarship by the affairs of Venice (ASD I-2
668).

Donato published Latin translations of Alexander of Aphrodisias' commentary on the *De
anima* of Aristotle (Brescia: Bernardinus de
Misintis 1495) and of an *Enarratio* of Chrysostom on 1 Corinthians (Brescia: Bernardinus de
Misintis 1496). He was also interested in the
schism between the Latin and Greek churches,
composing the *De processione Spiritus Sancti
contra Graecum schisma*, dedicated to *Leo X by
his son Filippo in 1520 and published by
Angelo Mai in volume seven of *Scriptorum
veterum nova collectio* (Rome 1825–38), and the
De principatu Romanae sedis ad Graecos dedicated
by his son to *Clement VII and printed by
Francesco Giulio *Calvo at Rome in 1525. A
number of his orations were printed, including
one before Louis XII in 1501 and another on the
elevation of Julius II to the papacy (Rome
1505?). His letters to Giovanni *Pico della
Mirandola and Angelo *Poliziano were edited
by Josse *Bade in the *Illustrorum virorum
epistolae* ([Lyon] N. Wolf 1500).

BIBLIOGRAPHY: Allen Ep 1347 / Cosenza II
1253–5 / G. Fussenegger in LThK III 507 / Pastor
VI 258, 316–8 / Sanudo *Diarii* I-XII ad indicem
                                                                    TBD

Cutbertus DONSTALLUS *See Cuthbert* TUNS-
TALL

Andrea Doria by Leone Leoni

Andrea DORIA of Genoa, 30 November 1466–
25 November 1560
Andrea, the son of Cera Doria, was born at
Oneglia, in Liguria, of an ancient family which
had given Genoa many political and military
leaders; his mother was Caracosa Doria of the
Dolceaqua branch of the family. Orphaned at
an early age, Andrea became a mercenary
soldier in the papal guard and under the rulers
of Naples and Urbino. In the early 1500s he
returned to Genoa to fight Corsican rebels and
Mediterranean pirates. At the time Genoa, like
other Italian cities, was suffering from political
and military instability. In 1515 she fell under
French dominion, and Andrea Doria became a
condottiere for *Francis I. When Spanish forces
captured Genoa in 1522, Doria remained in
French pay and in 1527 helped recapture the
city. However, his relations with the French
court were strained by the slowness of the
French in paying him and by their reluctance to
give Genoa control of its rival, Savona. In the
summer of 1528 his contract with Francis I
expired, and he entered the service of the
Emperor *Charles V. He then occupied Genoa,
preserving the city's republican constitution

but becoming its first citizen and real master. Later Charles v named him prince of Melfi. One of the most brilliant admirals of his day, Doria served Charles v and Philip II against the French, the Turks, and Mediterranean pirates until his death. Although he married Peretta, the daughter of Gherardo Uso di Mare, in the late 1520s, he died childless and was succeeded by his great-nephew, Giovanni Andrea Doria.

The correspondence of Erasmus contains several reports on Doria's movements in the 1530s. In June 1533 the Dutch legal scholar *Viglius Zuichemus informed Erasmus that Doria had set out in relief of the garrison of Korone in Greece (Epp 2829, 2854), an important stronghold which Doria had captured from the Turks in 1532. Despite his mission in 1533, the fortress fell in April 1534. In November 1534 Erasmus was informed of an unsubstantiated rumour that Doria had occupied Rhodes (Ep 2977). In December 1534 Erasmus heard that Doria had been appointed leader of a fleet to conquer the Barbary pirates, who had ravaged the southern Italian coast the previous summer (Ep 2983). This expedition, in which Charles v personally took part, resulted in the conquest of Tunis in July 1535.

Meanwhile, on 8 April 1535 Luigi *Spinola, a Genoese nobleman, wrote Erasmus that he had dedicated the first two books of his 'De rei publicae institutione' to Doria (Ep 3008).

Doria's portrait, by Sebastiano del Piombo, hangs in the Palazzo Doria at Rome.

BIBLIOGRAPHY: EI XIII 166–7 / Clemente Fusero I Doria (Milan 1973) / Ivo Luzzatti Andrea Doria (Milan 1943) / V.J. Parry in The New Cambridge Modern History (Cambridge 1957–68) II 510–33 passim / J. Garcia Mercadal Juan Andrea Doria (Madrid 1944)

TBD

Filippo DORIA of Genoa, d after 1547
Filippo or Filippino Doria, the son of Bartolomeo, was a cousin of the brilliant Genoese admiral Andrea *Doria and one of his most trusted lieutenants. In the 1520s and 1530s Filippo served in most of the major campaigns of Andrea Doria, but his greatest personal triumph occurred on 28 April 1528, when he defeated a Spanish fleet off the Capo d'Orso near Capri, thus assisting the French siege of

Naples. However, the effects of this victory were undone several months later when Andrea and Filippo abandoned the service of France for that of the Emperor *Charles v. Filippo then helped Andrea capture Genoa and establish an informal rule over the Republic. He was still alive in 1547, when he played a key role in suppressing a rebellion of the Fieschi family against Andrea Doria.

On 29 March 1535 the German scholar Franciscus *Rupilius informed Erasmus of a rumour that Filippo Doria had blockaded the Hellespont, thus threatening Constantinople with famine, and had returned to Sicily with thirty prize ships and three thousand captives (Ep 3007).

BIBLIOGRAPHY: EI XIII 164–5 / Clemente Fusero I Doria (Milan 1973) / Paolo Giovio Opera: I Epistolae ed G.G. Ferrero (Rome 1956–) I Ep 31 / J. Garcia Mercadal Juan Andrea Doria (Madrid 1944) 94–5 and passim

TBD

Maarten van DORP of Naaldwijk, 1485– 31 May 1525
Maarten van Dorp (Dorpius) was born at Naaldwijk (hence Naldovicenus), near Rotterdam, and was thus able to call himself Erasmus' fellow-countryman in the famous Ep 304. His name was one of the many variant forms of a very common name in Holland and Flanders: Van Dorp(e), Vandorp, etc, meaning (the man) from the village. His father, Bartholomaeus (shortened to Mees), the son of Hendrik, was born in 1439 or 1440, as we learn from Ep 1044, written by Dorp in November 1519 when the old man was still alive. In the same letter Dorp tells us that his father had met Erasmus at Louvain in the College of Arras in the summer of 1517. Mees held an important post as steward (rentmeester) of the abbey of Egmond and was a councillor and alderman at The Hague for many years. Dorp had a brother, Willem, who succeeded their father as steward and became treasurer of the Hague council. The family used a seal representing the heads of three lions, two at the top and the third centred beneath them. Dorp remained in close touch with his native Holland and in the course of his career in Louvain he visited his homeland several times.

Dorp received his first instruction at home

and probably at Utrecht in the Hieronymus school, where his Latin teacher may well have been master Johannes Symonis of Delft (de Vocht MHL 296). On 4 December 1501 he matriculated at Louvain under the name 'Martinus filius Bartholomaei de Naeldwijk.' As registration normally took place within a fortnight, we may assume that he arrived in town a few days earlier. At Louvain Dorp was an inmate of the College of the Lily for about fourteen years. Of the four colleges in the faculty of arts the Lily was the one most favourably inclined to humanistic studies. In Dorp's student days its regent was Erasmus' old friend Leo *Outers of Hondschoote. Among the *legentes* and senior students in the college were Jan de *Neve, who succeeded Outers as regent by 1505, Johannes Despauterius, and Joost *Vroye. When Erasmus visited Louvain between 1502 and 1503 Dorp may have made his acquaintance (CWE Ep 304:8–9).

In the Lily Dorp went through the traditional courses of the trivium. On 2 April 1504 he received his MA and, having obtained a very honourable fifth place in the general classification, was able to begin professional studies in theology. He also began to teach in his college. It is fairly certain that before the end of 1504 he was appointed *legens* in philosophy (de Vocht MHL 130), a task in which he engaged enthusiastically, although in later years he sometimes regretted having spent so much time on scholastic trifles. The text of his course was edited by Nicolaas van *Broeckhoven: *Introductio facilis ... ad Aristotelis libros logice intelligendos* (Paris: H. Estienne 6 December 1512; copy in Pembroke College, Oxford). Dorp also became a successful teacher of Latin in the humanistic vein, thus dividing his time between classical Latin and scholastic philosophy. After a time this situation caused a dichotomy in his intellectual development, which was further complicated by his theological studies. At first these must have been restricted to a bare minimum, and only from about 1509 did he direct his efforts more seriously towards earning the various degrees in divinity.

As a teacher of Latin Dorp introduced bold innovations in his college. Between 1504 and 1507 he seems to have written a few didactic dialogues, of which one has survived. It is based on the classical theme of Hercules at the crossroads and is couched in the language of Roman comedy, although not in verse. Following the example set by Italian humanists and a few northern Latin schools such as those of Bruges and Ghent, he staged performances of classical comedies with his students. Plautus' *Aulularia* was done on 3 September 1508 and *Miles gloriosus* on 20(?) February 1509. For the first play he completed the missing fifth act since the supplement composed by Codro *Urceo was unavailable. Jan *Becker of Borsele sent Dorp's supplement and a few of his other verses to Jérôme de *Busleyden, and this was the beginning of a lasting friendship between the young teacher and the courtier. However, not everybody at Louvain seems to have been happy with the fact that a prospective theologian was gaining fame as a poet and humanist, and pressure was exercised on Dorp, especially by the stern theologian Jan *Briart. As the young poet was not a very strong character – Erasmus was to call him later 'more inconstant than any woman' (Ep 637) – he complied with Briart's wishes and engaged in less profane work. In 1509–10 he declined the chair of poetry in the faculty of law, which was offered to him under attractive financial conditions, and it was left to others such as his friend Adrianus Cornelii *Barlandus to continue the humanist tradition of staging plays.

At the same time Dorp began to devote himself more seriously to his theological studies, and from now on we are able to follow his career almost step by step. While still a member of the arts faculty, he entered the academic senate or university council on 28 February 1510. A few months later, on 27 June (de Vocht MHL 134, 312–13), he became *baccalaureus biblicus* and consequently was introduced into the theological faculty and put in charge of some courses of biblical exegesis. On 15 August he fulfilled a further prerequisite delivering a sermon for Assumption day, his *Concio de Divae Virginis Deiparae in coelum assumptione*. This allocution was followed on 3 December by a public *Oratio in laudem Aristotelis* in defence of the Greek philosopher against the dialectic of Lorenzo *Valla.

By the end of 1510 Dorp had obtained his second degree and became *baccalaureus sententiarius*. Possibly in March and in any case before 9 August 1511 he was *baccalaureus* *formatus.* At the latter date he received his first ecclesiastical benefice, the parish of Overschie, in Holland, granted to him by Meynard *Man, abbot of St Adalbert's at Egmond. Between 14 October 1513 and 11 February 1514 Dorp became a licentiate in theology. Shortly after 27 February a second benefice, a chaplaincy in the parish church of Noordwijk, Holland, was bestowed on him.

During the summer of 1514 Erasmus paid a short visit to Louvain around August, and Dorp was one of the few friends he expressly wanted to meet (CWE Ep 304:9–11). Perhaps they met in Dirk *Martens' press in order to discuss the publication of Erasmus' *Opuscula aliquot* (September 1514), for which Dorp did the proofreading, at least for the Cato (CWE Ep 304:173–4). When the book came off the press Dorp wrote the famous Ep 304 to Erasmus in Basel which is discussed below.

In 1515, perhaps in the late spring, Dorp travelled to his native region and was ordained in Utrecht. At Louvain he is called 'presbyter' for the first time in a university document dated 14 June 1515 (de Vocht MHL 316). After the ordination he obtained his doctorate and consequently was admitted to the council of the theological faculty as 'magister noster' on 30 August 1515 (de Vocht MHL 151). For theological studies to take eleven years was quite normal at Louvain.

The new magister now left his college in the arts faculty and on 4 September became president of the College of the Holy Ghost (de Vocht MHL 152–3). On 30 September he was appointed full professor (*ad regentiam*) and assigned a prebend in St Peter's, the principal church of Louvain. In the course of his first year as professor, he acted on 29 February 1516 as *intrans* or representative of his faculty on the academic committee in charge of the election of the rector for the next trimester (de Vocht MHL 313). Dorp had chosen a theological career under pressure and for the eminently practical reason of securing a decent income (de Vocht MHL 135); however, theology did not completely supersede his interest in humanistic literature, which was more congenial to him, nor did he sever his relations with the arts faculty, after having lived in one of its colleges until the completion of his theological studies. He maintained very friendly and scholarly

relations with grammarians and poets such as Despauterius (for whose *Syntax* he wrote a preface in March 1509), *Geldenhouwer, Neve, and Barlandus. He continued to write introductory verses or letters for such publications as Geldenhouwer's *Satyrae* (24 January 1512) or Barlandus' *Aesopus* (22 April 1512) and *Versuum ex Bucolicis Vergilii collectanea* (March 1514). On 1 October 1513, at the opening of the academic year, he delivered the traditional *Oratio de laudibus disciplinarum* on behalf of the arts faculty. A fortnight later this text, which included warm praise of humanistic eloquence and cited the examples of *Pius II, *Campano, and Rodolphus *Agricola, was published by Martens. Dorp's relations with Martens probably date back to the printer's Antwerp period. In fact, Martens' former corrector Pieter *Gillis had dedicated to Dorp Martens' edition of Agricola's *Opuscula nonnulla* (Antwerp 31 January 1511 or 1512). When the printer moved to Louvain in the summer of 1512 Dorp joined the circle of his collaborators and soon began to see his own works through the press: *Dialogus* followed by *Tomus Aululariae* and other minor texts in 1513 and February 1514; the inaugural address of 14 October 1513; the older *Concio* and the defence of Aristotle on 18 February 1514. This editorial activity may explain, at least to some extent, why Erasmus wanted Dorp's help for the edition of his *Opuscula* in the summer of 1514. A further humanist publication followed on 12 January 1515, when Dorp edited Agricola's *Dialectica* and warmly recommended it to students of eloquence. His next publication stemmed from his theological studies. With the help of Briart he published in March 1515 a collection of *Quaestiones quotlibeticae* written between 1488 and 1507 by Adriaan of Utrecht, later Pope *Adrian VI, and then circulated in manuscript among the Louvain students in theology. One can imagine that Dorp proudly took copies of the book with him when, shortly afterwards, he went to Utrecht for his ordination.

During Dorp's final year as a student and his first as professor of theology (1514–16) a scholarly controversy arose between him and Erasmus, with Thomas *More as an important third party. It is not easy to reconstruct the course of the whole affair since part of the original correspondence and other vital information on the developments day by day, and also the discussions within the theological faculty, are now lost. It is conceivable that the loss of letters as well as innuendo and rumours caused disaffection far beyond Dorp's intention. He certainly was not given to disputes; and what Erasmus wrote in 1519 about his character seems quite true: 'If Dorp makes a mistake, he does so more from over-readiness to oblige than from malice aforethought' (Ep 1002).

About the middle of September 1514, when Erasmus' *Opuscula* had come off Martens' press, Dorp wrote the long Ep 304. He wanted to give Erasmus some amicable counsel in matters which might become a source of serious trouble. It seems that for some reason no longer known but possibly connected with the repercussions of the *Reuchlin affair (cf Ep 713), a critical appraisal of the *Moria* was being made, even among Erasmus' friends at Louvain, and that Dorp was trying to prevent greater harm being done. There is no good reason to assume that Dorp had lacked the courage to discuss these problems personally with Erasmus during his visit to Louvain, as is suggested in More's letter to Dorp of 1515 (Rogers Ep 15). Nor can it be said that Dorp had completely forsaken his humanistic interests; in fact he was preparing an edition of Agricola's *Dialectica*. When Dorp suggested that Erasmus write a 'Praise of Wisdom,' he was proposing a rhetorical exercise popular with the humanists. Erasmus had more than once resorted to presenting both the case for and the case against a certain issue. Dorp also exhorted Erasmus to be very careful in his critical work on the Vulgate lest he undermine the very foundations of theology. In this context Dorp refused to credit Greek manuscripts with greater correctness than Latin ones, and this was a departure from his own earlier *Concio*, where, following the Fathers, he had said that Greek texts should be consulted whenever a Latin text is uncertain.

Not until the end of May 1515 did Erasmus get hold of a copy of Ep 304 from a friend in Antwerp (perhaps their common friend Pieter Gillis). The original letter sent to Basel had evidently been lost on the way, a frequent occurence at that time. Erasmus' answer (Ep 337) was no less friendly; he explained the true meaning and intention of his *Moria*, encouraged Dorp to learn Greek, and defended his critical approach to the Vulgate text. At the end Dorp was asked to convey greetings to some common friends.

With Ep 347 (27 August) Dorp continued the debate on a more general level, questioning whether literature and eloquence should solely occupy any one's attention. He defended scholastic philosophy and theology against the humanists' contempt and warned against the moral damage which might come from reading the classical poets (soon *Vives was to speak about poetry in the same way); he further argued that Greek manuscripts too were liable to textual corruption and maintained his view that Greek was not mandatory for western theologians.

At this point Dorp was answered by Thomas More rather than Erasmus, who did not receive his letter until much later. More was staying at Bruges and had read Dorp's printed works there; in his long letter of 21 October 1515 (Rogers Ep 15) he explained that friends had told him about two not very kind letters from Dorp to Erasmus and, at his request, had shown him these together with Erasmus' first answer (Epp 304, 337, 347). More could not find anything unfriendly in Ep 304 but noted that his friends criticized Dorp for writing it when he could have discussed the problem with Erasmus in Louvain. This would indicate that in Flanders some criticism of Dorp was being voiced (unless More's 'friends' are a fiction, in which case More would bear at least part of the responsibility for Erasmus' consequent anger against Dorp). More went on to state that he too found Dorp's second letter rather unfortunate both for its contents and for the light-hearted tone it sometimes adopted. Point by point he took issue with Dorp's views on theology, dialectic, the importance of Greek, the *Moria*, and the reading of the classics. His arguments were often personal: he said that Erasmus' criticism of churchmen and theologians was less severe than Geldenhouwer's *Satyrae*, which had Dorp's approval; he quoted Dorp's own statements in the dedication of his *Oratio de laudibus disciplinarum*; and finally he noted that only a few months earlier Dorp had seen fit to publish Plautus.

Dorp was deeply impressed with More's letter and accepted most of its arguments. Indeed he had already begun on his own initiative to withdraw from the position he had adopted in August for tactical reasons when he was about to obtain the titles of doctor and 'magister noster.' It should be noted that in October Martens published at Louvain a volume containing not only a reprint of Erasmus' *Enarratio in primum psalmum* but also Dorp's first letter and Erasmus' answer. Martens' book was undertaken for the benefit of the Louvain students of theology, so it is difficult to assume that it lacked Dorp's approval. It should therefore be noted that Erasmus was allowed the last word since Dorp's second letter was not included.

In the summer of 1516 Dorp taught a course on the Pauline Epistles. The inaugural lecture, on 6 July, was consistent with his earlier promotion of the *bonae literae*. It is true that he emphasized the necessity of studying first and foremost the Gospels and St Paul, but he also acknowledged publicly the value of eloquence for students in theology, warned against the excesses of scholastic dialectic, and deplored his own ignorance of Greek. To justify textual criticism of the Vulgate he quoted not only the Fathers but also modern authorities such as Cardinal Pierre d'Ailly, one of whose works he consulted in the library of the convent of St Maartensdal in Louvain.

When he was informed by Jean *Desmarez of Dorp's change of heart, Erasmus rejoiced (Ep 438). But the reaction of the theological faculty proves that Dorp had had good reasons for warning Erasmus in Ep 304 and for taking a scholastic stance himself at the time of his doctorate: on 30 September 1516 the faculty refused the annual renewal of Dorp's certification as an academic teacher (*regentia*; de Vocht MHL 165) and this humiliation was certainly a heavy blow for the young professor. The refusal may have come quite unexpectedly: the text of the inaugural lecture on Paul, as actually delivered, was probably less outspoken than the version printed in 1519, and in any case Dorp had continued to disagree with some of Erasmus' readings in the New Testament. They had exchanged letters on the subject which were known to some other theologians (Ep 487) and accepted by Erasmus as a proof of

Dorp's inconstancy and hostility (Epp 474, 475, 477). One wonders if Erasmus was entirely right in describing Dorp's continual reservations as a new 'tragoedia' (Epp 474, 475). In any case they can hardly have been a consequence of Dorp's humiliation of 30 September since Erasmus was venting his anger as early as 2 October, writing from Antwerp (Ep 474). Conceivably some 'friends' were adding fuel to the flames. On 11 November *Alaard of Amsterdam wrote from Louvain to warn Erasmus of Dorp's stubborness (Ep 485), whereas the next day Geldenhouwer announced that others were at fault while Dorp had done nothing to harm Erasmus (Ep 487). It is hard to believe that in a few hours he had changed completely. In November Dorp himself wrote to Erasmus (Ep 496) offering his friendship and suggesting that the past be forgotten. 'So-and-so' ('N' in the Latin text) is mentioned contemptuously in a letter to *Ammonio of 29 December (Ep 505), but it is not certain that Dorp is intended, since it can hardly be said of him that 'before this he was almost unknown in Louvain.'

Erasmus paid a short visit to Louvain at the beginning of January 1517. It is doubtful whether Dorp's invitation to dinner (Ep 509) belongs to this period. His remark 'in future, if it will not be a burden on you, I shall be with you often' rather suggests that Dorp was thinking of Erasmus as having settled in Louvain, as he was to do in July. There is no evidence to prove the assertions of de Vocht (MHL 175) about Dorp's unfriendly behaviour towards Erasmus. All points to the contrary: peace was restored between Erasmus and the Louvain theologians on that occasion (de Vocht MHL 176), and it is reasonable to assume that Dorp helped to bring it about. He may have convinced Briart, who admired his scholarly qualities, of Erasmus' good faith. We also know that about the same time Dorp regained the confidence of his faculty since on 19 February he was member of a committee (de Vocht MHL 178). Erasmus confirmed this reconciliation in a letter of 21 February (Ep 536), which also showed that the past quarrel between the two men had in large measure been caused by rumours. Dorp's rehabilitation became complete the following summer when on 31 August he was elected dean of the faculty and on 30 September he obtained the *regentia* for the new academic year. During the same meeting Erasmus was co-opted to the faculty (de Vocht MHL 190-2). A few months later, on 29 December, Dorp's remuneration as president of the College of the Holy Ghost was increased. In 1517 therefore Dorp and Erasmus were friends, and this was known outside Louvain. *Beatus Rhenanus sent greetings to Dorp on 22 March (Ep 556). For this reason it may be questioned whether the theologian, 'x,' who still opposed Erasmus in May (Ep 584), was really Dorp. During the summer of 1517 Erasmus settled at Louvain, and a warm friendship with Dorp developed, as shown by several letters of August and September (Epp 627, 641, 643, 650–2, 669). In March 1518 Erasmus mentioned Dorp as the leader of the 'Hebrew party' (Ep 794), that is, as a supporter of the Collegium Trilingue. In August Dorp was the first to visit Erasmus in Martens' house when he was suspected to be ill of the plague (Ep 867). Early in 1519 Dorp did all he could to prevent misunderstandings between Briart and Erasmus in the matter of the *De matrimonio* (Ep 946; de Vocht MHL 194). Finally Dorp published his inaugural lecture on Paul on 29 September, and Erasmus arranged to have further editions of it printed in Basel by Johann *Froben (CWE Ep 1044 introduction).

This friendship did not mean that Dorp and Erasmus now saw eye to eye in all respects. In a quarrel between Dorp and his old master and friend Jan de Neve about financial and other matters in the Lily, Erasmus did not approve all of Dorp's moves (Ep 838) and tried to prevent theological squabbles between the two men (Ep 696). The question was settled by the autumn of 1519, as is evident from Ep 1044, in which Dorp asked Erasmus to give Neve his greetings and to beg him to forget the old feud.

In the summer of 1519 Dorp seems to have considered seriously the possibility of leaving Louvain and returning to his native country. He resigned the presidency of his college and in the autumn travelled to The Hague, where he delivered an oration 'De vita Christo Domino instituenda,' now lost, before the council of Holland (de Vocht MHL 218–19). At that time he was asked by Philip (I) of *Burgundy, bishop of Utrecht, to become his suffragan, but in the end he declined and

returned to Louvain (de Vocht MHL 218, 339), where he was pained to find that he had been ejected from his college because the publication of his introductory lecture on Paul had again stirred up theological wrath (de Vocht MHL 227). Despite this new hostility on the part of the other theologians, Dorp remained a faithful friend of Erasmus (Epp 1063, 1082). For his part, Erasmus did all he could to keep it so and exhorted his friends to write friendly letters to Dorp (Ep 1044). Similiarly Erasmus was on the side of Dorp when he had to face an attack from Paris, launched by Nicolas *Bérault and Wilhelm *Nesen in August 1519 (CWE Epp 1000A, 1000B). In Nesen's libellous *Dialogus bilinguium et trilinguium* Dorp is depicted quite obviously as 'Phenacus,' the cheater (CWE 7 appendix; de Vocht CTL I 561).

After the publication of his introductory lecture on Paul, Dorp seems to have refrained from publishing further. Although some friends hoped that he would eventually become a 'new Erasmus' (de Vocht MHL 383–4), and although we know that he still was working on theological treatises such as a 'De catholicae ecclesiae ritu ac consuetudine' (de Vocht MHL 76–7), only one more text has survived. It is a short letter to Meynard Man in defence of his publication of the introductory lecture on Paul. This *Oratiunculae meae apologia* (de Vocht MHL 93) was probably written at the end of 1521 but was not published before de Vocht's edition of 1934 (MHL 75–93). From later years only a few letters survive, mainly to Frans van *Cranevelt. Another letter to Herman *Lethmaet, written on 29 December [1522], contained interesting information on *Vives and showed Dorp once more on the side of the humanistic faction in Louvain (de Vocht MHL 385–90).

The slowing down of his scholarly activity is also noticeable elsewhere. Dorp had in his possession a manuscript of Augustine's *De trinitate* that he had borrowed from Erasmus (Epp 1547, 1890, 1899), in which on Erasmus' request he had annotated variant readings from a Gembloux manuscript. For a long time Erasmus tried in vain to obtain a list of these variants from Dorp, and the manuscript returned to its owner only after Dorp's death and through the intervention of *Goclenius. There may have been several reasons for

Johannes Draconites

monument, which disappeared shortly after 1783 with the suppression of the charterhouse (de Vocht MHL 347).

BIBLIOGRAPHY: Allen and CWE Ep 304 / *Matricule de Louvain* III 228 / de Vocht MHL, with a complete survey of the older bibliography / de Vocht CTL I 214–22 and passim / Reedijk poem 113 / *555 Jaar Universiteit Leuven* (Exhibition Catalogue, Louvain 1976) / *Facultas s. theologiae Lovaniensis 1432–1797* ed E.J.M. Van Eijl (Louvain 1977) / A version in Old Dutch of Dorp's *Oratio de laudibus disciplinarum* published with a French translation in the occasional brochure *Alma Mater Lovaniensis aevi praeteriti memor* (Louvain, 2 June 1935) is a pastiche by Henry de Vocht / J.H. Bentley 'New Testament scholarship at Louvain in the early sixteenth century' *Studies in Medieval and Renaissance History* n s 2 (1979) 53–79 / J. IJsewijn 'Martinus Dorpius, *Dialogus* (ca. 1508?)' in *Charisterium H. de Vocht* ed J. IJsewijn and J. Rogiers (Louvain 1979) 74–101

JOZEF IJSEWIJN

Mees van DORP *See Maarten van* DORP

Dorp's loss of scholarly productivity, including greater involvement in administrative duties, which according to his biographer he performed exceedingly well. He was rector of the university from 28 February to 31 August 1523 (de Vocht MHL 340). Another and more important reason may have been his wish for tranquillity, as expressed in his letter to Lethmaet and reflected in Erasmus' Ep 1082. He obviously feared being involved in new theological disputes, which could be very painful and disagreeable for a man who was rather timorous by nature (Allen Ep 1437: 187–8).

In the spring of 1525 Dorp fell ill from 'cholera,' as his biographer calls the illness, aggravated by a serious tooth infection (de Vocht MHL 277). He died in May, mourned by Erasmus, Adrianus Cornelii Barlandus, and many other friends of Christian humanism (Epp 1584, 1585, 1597, 1603, 1646 – which includes an epitaph for Dorp – 1653; de Vocht MHL 253–4). Dorp was buried in the Carthusian monastery of Louvain, with which he had maintained lifelong ties of friendship. Erasmus' epitaph was inscribed on the funeral

Johannes DRACONITES of Karlstadt, 1494– 18 April 1566

Johannes Draconites (Drach, Trach, Draco) was born in Karlstadt, on the Main north of Würzburg. In 1509 he matriculated at Erfurt, described as being an orphan; he obtained his BA in 1512 and in 1514 obtained his MA and became a canon at St Severus. By 1515 he was a close friend of Helius *Eobanus Hessus. After an outbreak of the plague in 1521, Draconites resigned his canonry and went to Wittenberg to study Hebrew. There he obtained a doctorate in theology in 1523. Meanwhile, in 1522 he had been appointed as a preacher in Miltenberg, on the Main, but in 1524 he was forced to leave because of his Lutheran views. Subsequently he became the pastor of Waltershausen, near Gotha, and in 1525 he married. In 1528 Draconites left his parish in spite of Martin *Luther's advice to stay, and retired to Eisenach, devoting himself to scholarship. From 1534 to 1547 he was a professor at the University of Marburg and a pastor. In 1541 he took part in the religious colloquy during the diet of Regensburg. Draconites went to Lübeck in 1547, was at the University of Rostock from 1551 to 1560, serving twice as rector, and was appointed bishop of Pomesania by Albert of *Brandenburg, duke of Prussia. While he was at Eisenach and later during long visits to Wittenberg, he worked on his polyglot edition of the Bible, parts of which he published in Wittenberg between 1563 and 1565. His frequent absences from his residence at Kwidzyn (Marienwerder), in Pomesania, eventually caused difficulties, and he had to resign his position in 1564. He died in Wittenberg.

Apart from his work on the polyglot Bible, Draconites is the author of such pamphlets as *Epistel an die Gemeinde in Miltenberg* (Augsburg: M. Ramminger 1524); *Eine Trostpredigt ... über der Leiche Helij Eobani Hessi* (Strasbourg: W. Rihel 1541); and *Commentarius in Psalterium et Psalmorum usum* (Marburg: C. Egenolff 1543).

Like his friend Eobanus Hessus, Draconites became an ardent admirer of Erasmus in his Erfurt days. Twice his letters to Erasmus drew an appreciative reply (Epp 877, 942). In July 1520 he travelled to Louvain to visit Erasmus in person (Epp 1124, 1157). Like his Erfurt friends, Draconites composed verses to defend Erasmus against Edward *Lee (CWE Ep 1083 introduction). After 1524, however, when Erasmus had heard that Draconites had become a Lutheran (Ep 1425), all connections between them seem to have ended; on the other hand, Draconites' close friend Eobanus remained in contact with Erasmus. Eobanus visited Draconites in Eisenach in 1534 and contributed verses to Draconites' publications. After Eobanus' death, Draconites delivered the funeral oration on 4 October 1540 and subsequently edited his friend's letters (Marburg: C. Egenolff 1543).

BIBLIOGRAPHY: Allen and CWE Ep 871 / NDB IV 95 / Luther w *Briefwechsel* II Ep 410 and passim / *Der Briefwechsel des Justus Jonas* ed G. Kawerau (Halle 1884–5) I Epp 42–3 and passim / *Matrikel Erfurt* II 263 / *Matrikel Wittenberg* I 118 / *Matrikel Rostock* II 121 and passim / C. Krause *Helius Eobanus Hessus* (Gotha 1879) I 146 and passim
IG

Johannes DRIANDER *See* DRYANDER

Jan DRIEDO of Turnhout, d 4 August 1535
Jan Driedo (Driedoens, Nijs, Johannes Turen-

hout) was born in Darisdonck, which is today part of Turnhout, some forty kilometres east of Antwerp. He matriculated in the University of Louvain on 27 May 1491 and entered the College of the Falcon. He was first among those receiving the degree of MA in April 1499. He began teaching philosophy at the Falcon and was admitted to the university council for arts on 31 August 1509. Although fascinated by mathematics, he was persuaded by the future Pope *Adrian VI to take up theology. Upon the death of his friend Hendrik van Houterlee on 2 January 1511 he was appointed president of the new Houterlee College. He held this post for ten years and was eventually succeeded by his protégé Nicolaus *Clenardus.

Driedo received his doctorate in theology on 17 August 1512 and had become a priest and professor before 1515. He was elected rector in February 1518 and 1533 and dean of theology in August 1515, 1518, 1525, and 1531 as well as in February 1523 and 1528. He was rector of St James' parish in Louvain until his death. He also held some other benefices which were within the gift of the university and shortly before his death he was nominated to succeed to Nicolas *Coppin's canonry of St Peter's (Ep 3037). Among the students he had tutored were Robert and Charles (II) de *Croy, as well as the astronomer Gemma Phrysius.

Driedo abandoned traditional teaching methods and advocated the study of Scripture on the basis of a sound knowledge of the requisite languages (Ep 1167). As a result he warmly supported the Collegium Trilingue. In his *De ecclesiasticis scripturis et dogmatibus* (Louvain: R. Rescius and B. Gravius 1533) he defined the respective uses in theology and liturgy of the Vulgate and other versions of Scripture. His definitions were later incorporated verbatim in a decree of the council of Trent.

It was mainly due to Driedo's influence that Clenardus broke with the narrowly conservative approach of Jacobus *Latomus and began attending lectures at the Trilingue. Damião de *Gois and Diogo de Murça secured a subsidy for the publication of *De ecclesiasticis scripturis* from their king, *John III of Portugal, to whom the book was then dedicated. Among Driedo's other works were *De concordia liberi arbitrii et praedestinationis* (Louvain: R. Rescius 1537) and

De libertate christiana (Louvain: R. Rescius 1540).

Erasmus' correspondence and the *Acta contra Lutherum* show that in 1520 Driedo was preparing a book against *Luther's Ninety-five theses, although it was never published owing to hesitation on the part of the printers and of the author himself. The *Acta* went as far as suggesting that Driedo agreed with Luther's stand on papal supremacy. Erasmus repeatedly regretted the suppression of Driedo's book since he was convinced of his learning, fairness, and respect for Luther's person (Epp 1127A, 1163–7; *Opuscula* 325–6). On one occasion, however, he complained of Driedo's slurs against himself (Ep 1165). Driedo's firm stand against heresy was confirmed later by his attacks upon Pieter *Gherinx (Ep 2851). In the *Ecclesiastes*, published in the year of Driedo's death, Erasmus paid a final compliment to his biblical scholarship (LB V 1054C).

BIBLIOGRAPHY: Allen Ep 1163 / *Matricule de Louvain* III-1 73 / de Vocht CTL II 505–8, 543, III 372, and passim / de Vocht MHL 344–5 / de Vocht *Dantiscus* 224–5 / H. de Jongh *L'Ancienne Faculté de théologie de Louvain* (Louvain 1911) 156–9 and passim / Theodore Foley *The Doctrine of the Catholic Church in the Theology of John Driedo* (Washington 1946) / A.P. Hennessy *The Victory of Christ over Satan in John Driedo's 'De captivitate et redemptione generis humani'* (Washington 1945)

CFG & PGB

Ludwig DRINGENBERG of Dringenberg, 1410–77

Ludwig Dringenberg was the founder and first rector of the grammar school in Sélestat where many of the Alsatian humanists – *Wimpfeling (Ep 2088), Peter Schott, and Sebastian Murrh, among others – received their early education. Born in Dringenberg in Westphalia, Ludwig was sent to the school of the Brethren of the Common Life in Deventer. He was in orders when he matriculated in Heidelberg for the winter term 1430; on 13 April 1434 he earned his MA there. Recommended by young patrician students whom he had known at Heidelberg, he proceeded to Sélestat, where the city council was determined to establish a school independent of the church. Dringenberg was appointed to direct it and did so until his

death. He transmitted the ideals and methods of the Brethren of the Common Life to the new school, thus creating a link between the educational reforms of the Lower and the Upper Rhine. A humanist pedagogue, he simplified the abstruse grammatical studies of the past and extended the curriculum to include instruction in religion and morals. He broke away from the traditional glosses and commentaries and introduced the students to the church Fathers and the Latin classics. His own interest in history was communicated to his pupils and was reflected in the work of the next generation of humanists.

BIBLIOGRAPHY: Allen Ep 2088 / ADB V 411–12 / *Matrikel Heidelberg* I 186, II 382 / Schmidt *Histoire littéraire* I xiv–xv and passim / Paul Adam 'L'école humaniste de Sélestat' in *Les Lettres en Alsace* (Strasbourg 1962) / Timotheus W. Röhrich 'Die Schule von Schlettstadt, eine Vorläuferin der Reformation' *Zeitschrift für die historische Theologie* 4/2 (1834) 199–218 / Joseph Knepper *Jakob Wimpfeling* (Freiburg 1902) 6–8

MIRIAM U. CHRISMAN

Johannes DRYANDER of Wetter, 27 June 1500–20 December 1560

Johannes Dryander (Eichmann, Aichmann, Eychmann, Driander) was born in Wetter, near Marburg, and attended the local Latin school. He matriculated at Erfurt in 1518, was an amanuensis of Euricius *Cordus and may have obtained a MA. He continued his studies in Bourges and from 1528 to 1533 probably in Paris. In 1533 he obtained a doctorate of medicine in Mainz and was appointed as physician to Johann von *Metzenhausen, archbishop of Trier, who often resided in Koblenz (Ep 2984). Two years later he was called to the University of Marburg to teach medicine and mathematics. He was rector in 1548; in addition to his teaching he visited the hospitals of Haina and Merxhausen. Dryander took a special interest in anatomy and was one of the first teachers in Germany to dissect human bodies in front of his students (in 1535, 1536, 1539, and 1558). He wrote several works on mathematics, astronomy, and meteorology. His *Anatomia capitis humani* (Marburg: E. Cervicornus 1536) and *Anatomia, hoc est corporis humani dissectionis pars prima* (Marburg: E. Cervicornus 1537) are illustrated with superior woodcuts, while his edition of the *Anatomia* of Mondino de' Luzzi (Marburg: C. Egenolff 1541) plagiarized some of Andreas Vesalius' plates. Dryander, who had married Susanne Breurl and had five children, died in Marburg.

In Ep 2984 Konrad *Nyder urged Erasmus to ignore any approaches on the part of his rival, whom he described as a charlatan.

BIBLIOGRAPHY: Allen Ep 2984 / NDB IV 142–3 / *Matrikel Erfurt* II 302

IG

Jean DU BELLAY 1498–16 February 1560
Jean was the youngest son of Louis Du Bellay, a military commander in the service of *Charles VIII, and Marguerite de la Tour-Landry. His career in the service of *Francis I was intimately connected with that of his eldest brother, Guillaume Du Bellay, seigneur de Langey, who was the central brain and will of the powerful Du Bellay faction and a leading formulator of French policy. Jean received a legal licence from the University of Orléans and was given the abbey of Breteuil, in Picardy, prior to his appointment as bishop of Bayonne in 1524. In 1532 he succeeded François *Poncher as bishop of Paris. Named cardinal by Pope *Paul III in 1535, he was also appointed administrator of the bishoprics of Limoges (1541) and Bordeaux (1544); in 1542 his brother René resigned to him the archbishopric of Mans, which he held until 1556.

Du Bellay's career was primarily that of a diplomat. Between 1527 and 1530 he undertook several missions to England on behalf of Francis I, and in 1533 he returned to London at the request of Pope *Clement VII. In 1534 he went to Rome and pleaded with the assembled cardinals in favour of *Henry VIII. François *Rabelais accompanied him on this journey as a secretary and physician. Du Bellay remained one of his patrons and took him along again when he visited Rome in 1535 and early 1536 as a cardinal (Epp 3039, 3047; Scheurer II Ep 238). In 1536 Du Bellay was appointed *lieutenant-général* for Paris and the Isle-de-France, and a year later he was named to the privy council. Meanwhile he also came to play a vigorous part in his eldest brother's continued efforts to bring about an understanding between the crown of France and the German Protestants, and after Langey's death he undertook a last

diplomatic mission to Germany in 1544. After the death of Francis I Du Bellay was unable to gain the favour of the new king *Henry II. In 1551 he resigned as bishop of Paris and retired to Rome, where he remained to his death. Du Bellay shared the cultural interests of Langey and produced a book of Latin poems published with Jean *Salmon's *Odarum libri tres* (Paris: R. Estienne 1546). In response to Jacobus *Omphalius he published *Adversus Jacobi Omphalii maledicta pro rege Francorum Christianissimo defensio* ([Paris: R. Estienne 1544], also published in French). Omphalius had earlier dedicated to the cardinal his *De elocutionis imitatione* (Basel: H. Froben 1537), but when they happened to meet again at Cologne a dispute developed that caused Du Bellay to write his pamphlet.

It seems that in 1536 Erasmus wrote to Germain de *Brie, suggesting that he recommend Pierre *Vitré to the cardinal of Paris (Ep 3101).

BIBLIOGRAPHY: Allen Ep 3039 / DBF XI 892–4 / DHGE XIV 828–30 / *La Correspondance du cardinal Jean du Bellay* ed Rémy Scheurer (Paris 1969) / *Ambassades en Angleterre de Jean du Bellay* ed V.-L. Bourrilly and P. de Vaissière (Paris 1905) / V.-L. Bourrilly *Guillaume du Bellay, seigneur de Langey* (Paris 1905) / V.-L. Bourrilly and N. Weiss *Jean du Bellay, les protestants et la Sorbonne* (Paris 1904)

MICHEL REULOS & PGB

Antoine DU BLET of Lyon, d April / May 1526
Antoine Du Blet (Bletus, Dubletus) was a merchant and banker from Lyon. Nothing is known of his background except that his father, Guillaume Du Blet, was a money changer. In April 1524 *Lefèvre d'Etaples received a consignment of evangelical literature dispatched by Du Blet from Basel. Having become a friend of Guillaume *Farel, Du Blet decided to accompany the latter on a trip from Basel to Strasbourg and Wittenberg. They set out in mid-May 1524 armed with letters from *Oecolampadius to *Capito and *Luther, but went first to Constance (Ep 1454) and to Zürich, where they had meetings with *Zwingli. By the middle of June they were back in Basel, having abandoned their earlier travel plans. Du Blet returned to Lyon, from where he wrote Lefèvre once more to give him news

of the reform at Zürich. Later in the summer of 1524 he was reported to have visited Grenoble. His death is noted by Farel and Erasmus in June 1526 (Ep 1722).

Du Blet's name became entangled in the quarrel that developed between Erasmus and Farel following the latter's return to Basel. In the course of their argument Farel noted that Du Blet had called Erasmus 'Balaam,' the mercenary prophet (Ep 1510; LB X 1618A). Erasmus' subsequent references to this insult make it clear that he was deeply wounded by it.

BIBLIOGRAPHY: Allen Ep 1510 / Herminjard I 207, 214, 215, 226, and passim / Luther w *Briefwechsel* III Ep 745 / BA *Oekolampads* I 279–80 / *Guillaume Farel, 1489–1565: Biographie nouvelle, écrite d'après des documents originaux par un groupe d'historiens, professeurs et pasteurs de Suisse, de France et d'Italie* (Paris 1930) / Henri Hours 'Procès d'hérésie contre Aimé Maigret' BHR 19 (1957) 14–43, esp 16

HENRY HELLER

François DUBOIS of Amiens, c 1483–1536
François Dubois (Sylvius) was the older brother of Jacques *Dubois, who was also François' most famous student. François taught the humanities at Paris, moving from the Collège de Lisieux (1518) to that of Boncourt (1520) and to the Collège de Tournai (1526). He rose to be the principal of the latter in 1527. He published a widely used textbook on rhetoric, *Progymnasmata in arte oratoria*, and another on poetics, *Poetica*, naively claiming to acquaint the reader with the entire treasure-house of ancient poetry in a book of some twenty pages. Both were published at Paris by Jean de Gourmont, 1516, and then by Josse *Bade in 1520. He also wrote a *Defensio Macrobii* (Paris: J. Bade 1525) and *De arte dicendi* (Paris: J. Bade 1526).

From about 1516 François Dubois was one of the team of scholars assisting Bade with his editions of the classics. Among these an Ausonius, published on 3 November 1516, is the first in which François' name may be found. Later he specialized in editions of Cicero's *Orationes* with commentaries suitable for use in schools, publishing sixteen separate volumes from 1526 to 1532. He also produced commentaries on *Poliziano (in Bade's editions of *Illustrium virorum epistolae*, 13 November 1517,

and of *Opera*, February 1519) and on Sallust's *Contra Ciceronem* (Paris: J. Bade May 1532). In all these efforts he proved a serious but not exceptionally talented scholar. However, Erasmus, who in 1533 apparently recalled having met him at Louvain before October 1519 (Ep 2874), had a high opinion of him, as is shown by the familiar tone of his two letters to François (Epp 1600, 1677), the only surviving pieces of their correspondence; nor did he forget François when listing the distinguished humanist scholars of France (Epp 1407, 1600, 1713).

BIBLIOGRAPHY: Allen Ep 1600 / Philippe Renouard *Bibliographie des impressions et des oeuvres de Josse Badius* (Paris 1908) passim / M.-M. de la Garanderie *Christianisme et lettres profanes* (Lille-Paris 1976) I 109–12 / Philippe Renouard *Imprimeurs et libraires parisiens du XVIe siècle* (Paris 1964–) II passim / *Inventaire chronologique des éditions parisiennes du XVIe siècle* (Paris 1972–) II passim

MARIE-MADELEINE DE LA GARANDERIE

Jacques DUBOIS of Amiens, 1478–13 January 1555
The son of a weaver of Louvilly, near Amiens, Jacques Dubois (Sylvius) followed his elder brother, François *Dubois, to Paris and, tutored by François, acquired an impressive command of the classical languages. He was soon attracted to the Greek medical authors and studied anatomy informally under Jean Tagault. On 20 November 1529 he matriculated at the University of Montpellier, obtaining a medical doctorate the following year. From 1531 he taught medicine at Paris, where from 1550 he occupied a chair at the royal college. Even though he performed dissections himself, Dubois was a stern defender of Galen and passionately rejected the findings of Andreas Vesalius, his former student. In 1551 he launched a bitter attack against Vesalius entitled *Vaesani cuiusdam calumniarum in Hippocratis Galenique rem anatomicam depulsio* (Paris: C. Barbé). Although he on occasion preferred to assume that human anatomy had undergone structural changes over the centuries rather than acknowledge that Galen had erred, his numerous medical and anatomical works are valuable for their systematic approach. After many separate editions they

were finally collected in his *Opera medica*
(Geneva 1630). While the great reputation he
enjoyed with his contemporaries rests primarily on his medical scholarship, he also published the first grammar of the French language, *In linguam gallicam isagoge una cum
grammatica latino-gallica* (Paris: R. Estienne
1531) and showed his concern for poor
students in a work of which Erasmus might
have approved, *Victus ratio scholasticis paupe-
ribus facilis et salubris* (1540).

There is a passing reference to Jacques
Dubois in Ep 1407 and conceivably another in
Ep 2874.

BIBLIOGRAPHY: Allen Ep 1407 / DBF XI 940 /
Matricule de Montpellier 58 / C.D. O'Malley in
Dictionary of Scientific Biography ed C.C. Gillis-
pie (New York 1970–80) IV 198–9 / de Vocht CTL
III 326 and passim / M.-M. de la Garanderie
Christianisme et lettres profanes (Lille-Paris 1976)
I 110

                                                    PGB

Emeric DU CHASTEL *See Pierre* DU CHASTEL

Pierre DU CHASTEL of Arc-en-Barrois,
d 3 February 1552
Pierre Du Chastel (Castellanus, a Castello) was
born during the first years of the sixteenth
century and educated at Langres and subsequently at Dijon, where his teacher, Pierre
Turrel, read with him Erasmus' *Colloquia* (Ep
2719). By 1527 he was working in the *Froben
press at Basel and lived for several months in
Erasmus' household. In October, when he left,
Erasmus gave him an introduction to Michel
*Boudet, bishop of Langres (Ep 1894). They
remained in touch, writing each other intermittently and occasionally mentioning letters that
are now missing (Epp 2213, 2388, 2425, 2719).
After his departure from Basel Du Chastel
began to tutor the sons of several councillors of
the Parlement of Dijon, who by the autumn of
1529 were with him at Bourges, following the
lectures of Andrea *Alciati (Epp 2168, 2213,
2218–20, 2224, 2356; AK III Ep 1400). At Bourges
he met Louis de *Husson, bishop-designate of
Poitiers, who took him into his service and on
termination of his studies in 1531 took him with
him to Paris (Epp 2388, 2425, 2427). At the royal
court Du Chastel attached himself to François
de Dinteville, bishop of Auxerre and French

ambassador in Rome, who appointed him his
secretary. Before following his new master to
Rome, Du Chastel paid another visit to
Erasmus at Freiburg, matriculating at the
university on 8 June 1532. He also studied
Hebrew at Basel with Thomas Platter, but soon
left for Rome. After a few months there, he held
a teaching position in Venice and, according to
his early biographer, visited the Holy Land,
returning by way of Constantinople. Passing
through Basel, he met Thomas Platter again,
and in November 1534 he wrote to Erasmus
from Metz (Ep 2974).

By the beginning of 1537, or somewhat
earlier, Du Chastel returned to the royal court
and soon was appointed reader to King
*Francis I in succession to Jacques *Colin. After
the death of his patron, Louis de Husson, in
1537, Du Chastel was ordained and began to
accumulate ecclesiastical preferment, becoming provost of the abbey of St Pierre at Evaux
(1537), bishop of Tulle (1539), abbot of Hautvil-
lers (1543), bishop of Mâcon (1544), and abbot
of Belleperche (1545). After the death of
Guillaume *Budé in 1540, he also succeeded to
the latter's position as the king's librarian and
came to play a key role in providing contacts
between the court and humanist circles. He
also became the official patron of such scholars
as Etienne *Dolet, Petrus Ramus, and Guillaume Postel. His interventions with the Paris
faculty of theology on behalf of Robert
Estienne were ultimately not successful in
preventing official censure of Estienne's
Bibles. Cultured and mild-mannered, he initially showed some sympathy for the evangelicals and was dubbed by *Rabelais the 'plus
docte et fidèle anagnoste' in all of France. In
the reign of *Henry II he took a more
conservative stance and was appointed grand
almoner (25 November 1548), abbot of Aube-
rive (1550), and finally bishop of Orléans
(1551). In this last phase of his life he can no
longer be seen as a typical courtier-prelate.
He took his duties as grand almoner very
seriously, supervising personally, and when
necessary reforming, the charitable institutions in his charge. On his appointment as
bishop of Orléans he left the court for his
diocese, where he died. A friend of many
humanists, Du Chastel himself composed in-

different writings in humanistic style, including his funeral oration for Francis I.

Pierre had an obscure brother by the name of Emeric Du Chastel, who is mentioned in Ep 2213.

BIBLIOGRAPHY: Allen Epp 2213, 2974 / DBF XI 1174–5 / R. Doucet 'Pierre Du Chastel, grand aumônier de France' *Revue historique* 133 (1920) 212–57, 134 (1921) 1–57 / Bierlaire *Familia* 76–7 / Abel Lefranc *Histoire du Collège de France* (Paris 1893) 94, 98, and passim / Thomas Platter *Lebensbeschreibung* ed A. Hartmann (Basel 1944) 82 / *Matrikel Freiburg* I-1 282 / Reedijk poem 132 / Pierre Galland *Petri Castellani vita* (Paris 1674) / Pierre Bayle *Dictionnaire historique et critique* (Amsterdam 1740) I 87–93 / *Histoire ecclésiastique des églises réformées du royaume de France* ed G. Baum and E. Cunitz (Paris 1883) I 98–9 / François Rabelais *Le Quart Livre* ed J. Plattard (Paris 1929) 5 / Elizabeth Armstrong *Robert Estienne, Royal Printer* (Cambridge 1954) 174–83 and passim

FRANZ BIERLAIRE

Guillaume DUCHESNE of Saint-Sever, d 4 September 1525

Born at Saint-Sever, near Vire in the Calvados (LB IX 539C), Guillaume Duchesne (de Quercu) was associated first with the Collège du Maître-Gervais in Paris and in 1493 became a *socius* of the Collège de Sorbonne. He ranked second of thirty-two licentiates in theology on 27 January 1496 and obtained his doctorate on 24 March 1496. He represented the faculty of theology at the anti-papal council of Pisa-Milan in 1511 and 1512 and pleaded this council's legitimacy before the faculty. Duchesne was a regular member of faculty committees, including those on *Reuchlin in 1514, on Jacques *Merlin in 1522, and on *Lefèvre d'Etaples in 1523. According to Erasmus, Duchesne was active in the faculty's examination and condemnation of *Luther in 1520 and 1521 (Ep 1181). Erasmus frequently named Duchesne as the principal collaborator with Noël *Béda in the Paris proceedings against him (Epp 1664, 2043, 2053; LB IX 447–52, X 1670), and against Louis de *Berquin (Ep 2188).

By 1505 Duchesne was a canon of the collegiate church of St-Benoît-le-bien-tourné in Paris. By 1520 he was the curé of St-Jean-en-Greve in Paris and *provisor* of the Collège

d'Harcourt. In 1524 he was appointed by the Parlement of Paris to a special inquisitorial panel constituted by the regent Louise of *Savoy and Pope *Clement VII. On 26 June 1525, Duchesne resigned his position as canon and penitentiary of Rouen, and three months later he died. He had edited William of Auxerre's *Summa aurea in quattuor libros sententiarum* (Paris: P. Pigouchet 1500).

BIBLIOGRAPHY: Allen Ep 1188 / Clerval 111, 123, 152, 363, and passim / E. Coyecque *Recueil des actes notariés* (Paris 1905) I no 392 / P.-Y. Féret *La Faculté de théologie de Paris et ses docteurs les plus célèbres. Epoque moderne* (Paris 1900–10) II 62 / Renaudet *Préréforme* passim / Paris, Archives Nationales MS H 2875⁴ f 6 verso / Paris, Bibliothèque Nationale MS Nouvelles acquisitions latines 1782 ff 145 verso, 163 verso, 158 verso, and passim / Rouen, Archives départementales (Seine-Maritime) MS 6 F 1

JAMES F. FARGE

Guillaume DU MAINE of Loudun, d 24 November 1564

Born in Loudun in Poitou (Département de la Vienne), Guillaume Du Maine (Dumanius, Mainus) was the tutor of Guillaume *Budé's children from about 1519 as well as his disciple and associate in his Greek studies. In 1523 Du Maine collaborated with Jean Chéradame in editing a *Lexicon graeco-latinum* (Paris: G. de Gourmont) and in a dedicatory preface to François *Poncher recalled happy gatherings at Saint-Maur-les-Fossés, where Budé had a country house and Poncher was abbot. On 10 December 1524 he was nominated to a canonry of Rouen. By 1533 he was acting for the tutor of the children of *Francis I, Benedetto *Tagliacarne, who was stricken with illness, and in 1534 took his place on a permanent basis. In the same year he received the abbey of Beaulieu-les-Loches, south-east of Tours. In 1541 he was councillor and almoner to Francis I's third son, Charles, duke of Orléans, and in 1550, after Charles' death, he was reader and secretary to his sister, Marguerite, duchess of Berry. He died at Loches.

Guillaume Du Maine was a friend and patron of scholars and poets such as Nicolas *Bourbon. Josse *Bade and Pedro Juan *Olivar dedicated works to him, and Etienne *Dolet mentioned him frequently. In 1556 he published a volume of occasional verse in French, *Epître en vers ...* (Paris: M. de Vascosan), and Erasmus praised his work for *Gourmont's Greek lexicon in the preface he composed for another Greek dictionary, published by Johann *Froben in 1524 (Ep 1460).

BIBLIOGRAPHY: Allen Ep 1460 / DBF XII 94 / *Gallia christiana* XIV 286 / Louis Delaruelle *Répertoire ... de la correspondance de Guillaume Budé* (Toulouse-Paris 1907) Ep 28 and passim / David O. McNeil *Guillaume Budé and Humanism in the Reign of Francis I* (Geneva 1975) 45 and passim

MICHEL REULOS

François DU MOULIN de Rochefort d before 16 June 1526

François Du Moulin de Rochefort (Molinius, de Rupe forti) was the son of Jean Du Moulin, lord of Breuil and Rochefort, who was secretary to *Louis XI and in 1461 mayor of Poitiers. A canon of Poitiers in 1501, François became the protégé of Louise of *Savoy, who in the same year appointed him tutor to her seven-year-old son, the future *Francis I. The Bibliothèque Nationale of Paris preserves several manuscript writings by him, composed in the course of his duties; they include an ode for Francis' eighteenth birthday in 1512. When his pupil became king, Du Moulin was appointed a royal almoner and, at Louise's request, on 8 October 1519 grand almoner. In May 1522 he received the abbey of Saint-Maximin-de-Micy, near Orléans, evidently in virtue of an earlier nomination (Ep 523; Rice Ep 124). From October 1521 he pressed his claims to the newly vacated see of Condom. Du Moulin had the royal nomination, but after two years of litigation the bishopric finally went to his rival, who had been elected by the chapter.

Du Moulin was a friend of Jacques *Lefèvre d'Etaples, whom he consulted when writing a short life of St Mary Magdalen at the request of Louise of Savoy early in 1517 (the manuscript in French is in the Bibliothèque Nationale). Subsequently Lefèvre himself took up his pen to answer questions raised by Louise, and his *De Maria Magdalena et triduo Christi* is dedicated to Du Moulin, who in the following quarrel about Magdalen seems to have remained on the side of Lefèvre and *Clichtove (Rice Ep 124). Charles de Bouelles dedicated to him an

Aetatum mundi septem supputatio (Paris: J. Bade 1521).

In 1517 Du Moulin, Guillaume *Budé, and Guillaume *Cop took a leading part in promoting a royal invitation for Erasmus (Epp 523, 537, 568). Despite the failure of these early efforts, admiration for Erasmus remained strong in Du Moulin's family, as may be gathered from the attitude of an unidentified nephew (Ep 1407). It is clear that Du Moulin again lent strong support to the renewal of the royal invitation in 1523 and 1524 (Epp 1375, 1439), and Erasmus responded by dedicating to him the *Exomologesis* (Ep 1426). Du Moulin reacted with a personal invitation, which Erasmus acknowledged enthusiastically (Ep 1484), and a further exchange of letters, still in 1524, reveals plans for a visit by Du Moulin to Basel (Epp 1516, 1527). Erasmus continued to rely on him when trying to determine how he should best safeguard his interests in Paris (Epp 1711, 1719), but late in May or early in June 1526 he was informed of Du Moulin's death (Epp 1722, 1735).

BIBLIOGRAPHY: Allen Epp 523, 1426 / DBF XII 257–8 / *Gallia christiana* II 968, VIII 1536 / Rice *Prefatory Epistles* Ep 124 / Marie Holban 'François du Moulin et la querelle de la Madeleine' *Humanisme et Renaissance* 2 (1935) 26–43, 147–71

PGB

Johann DUNCKEL of Hammelburg, documented 1511–21 (?)

Very little is known about Johann Dunckel (Duncellius, Dinckellius, Durckel). A native of Hammelburg, north of Würzburg, he matriculated at the University of Freiburg in August 1511. In the spring of 1515 he was in Basel, no doubt associated with Johann *Froben, who was also from Hammelburg. In March and April he accompanied Erasmus on his journey from Basel to England (Epp 328, 330). He may have settled in England, perhaps working in the printing trade. Some verses by him are printed in the preliminary material to Augustine's *De miseria* (Cambridge: J. Siberch 1521). A Simon Tunckel was a printer at Nürnberg from 1530 to 1534.

BIBLIOGRAPHY: Allen Ep 328, IV xxiv / *Matrikel Freiburg* I-1 198 / Benzing *Buchdrucker* 336

PGB

Antoine Duprat

Hieronymus DUNGERSHEIM of Ochsenfurt, 22 April 1465–2 March 1540
Hieronymus Dungersheim of Ochsenfurt, on the Main above Würzburg, matriculated at Leipzig in the autumn of 1483 and graduated BA two years later and MA on 28 December 1488. In 1493 he was admitted to the study of theology; he took the lower orders in Merseburg on 20 December 1494 and was ordained at Würzburg in 1495. At Leipzig he became a member of the theological faculty in 1499 but left to become the preacher of the principal church of Zwickau from 1501 to 1503. He then went to Italy to study at Bologna, where he received a doctorate in canon law, and at Siena, where he obtained a theological doctorate on 24 April 1504. After his return he became a professor of theology at Leipzig from 15 January 1506, a member of the 'grosses Fürstencollegium,' and canon of Zeitz. He was vice-chancellor of the university in 1508–9 and rector for the summer term of 1510; as late as 1538 he was dean of the theological faculty. When he died he enjoyed the reputation of being a notorious miser. He opposed Luther from the beginning, and as a determined

defender of the old faith he published, mostly at Leipzig, a number of polemical treatises in German, but also some Latin works, including lives of Pope Celestine V (W. Stöckel 1518) and of St Scholastica (1515), a treatise on preaching and teaching (Landshut: J. Weissenburger 1514), and an epitome of the *Sentences* (1515) which was reprinted several times. He wrote to Erasmus in March 1517 (Ep 554), taking issue with a passage in his New Testament.

BIBLIOGRAPHY: Allen and CWE Ep 554 / *Matrikel Leipzig* I 339, 502, II xci, 15, 30, 288, 370 / Ludwig Weiss in *Würzburger Diözesanarchiv* 18/19 (1956–7) 162 / ADB V 473–4 / Luther W *Briefwechsel* I Ep 65 and passim / G.W. Panzer *Annales typographici* (Nürnberg 1793–1803) X 299–300

PGB

Henricus DUNTGINUS *See Ludwig* FURSTER

Antoine DUPRAT of Issoire, 17 January 1463–9 July 1535
Born at Issoire (Puy-de-Dome), Antoine Duprat came from a bourgeois family striving to join the office-holding class. His father, a merchant, became a consul at Issoire; his mother was from the influential Bohier family. His brother Thomas became bishop of Clermont, his half-brother, Claude, bishop of Mende, and his first cousin a cardinal and archbishop of Bourges. After acquiring a doctorate in civil and canon law he became in turn *lieutenant-général* in the *bailliage* of Montferrand (1495), *avocat général* of the Parlement of Toulouse (1495), and a *maître des requetes de l'Hôtel* (1503). In 1507 he became councillor and next year *premier président* of the Parlement of Paris. The turning point of his career came when he became the client of Louise of *Savoy and the young duke of Angoulême, later *Francis I. On the latter's accession to the throne he was made chancellor of France on 7 January 1515.

Duprat accompanied the young king into Italy, witnessed the triumph at Marignano in 1515, and played a primary role in negotiating the concordat of Bologna of 1516. In 1519 he took part in the diplomatic campaign to acquire the imperial throne for Francis. The next year he assumed responsibility for the negotiations between France and England which followed the Field of Cloth of Gold. Duprat played an important role in the trial of the Constable Bourbon (1522) and the indictment of Semblançay (1523). He helped in the reorganization of royal finances which followed, and alongside Louise of Savoy he governed the kingdom during the king's captivity (1525–6).

Having taken orders as early as 1516 Duprat was named archbishop of Sens and abbot of Saint-Benoît-sur-Loire in 1525. In 1527 he was named a cardinal and in 1528 presided over the council of Sens, at which the bishops attempted to draw a clear line between orthodox and heretical belief. That same year he became administrator of the bishopric of Albi. In 1530 he was named papal legate *a latere* and in 1534 administrator of the bishopric of Meaux. He died at the château of Nantouillet and was buried in the cathedral of Sens.

Erasmus' contact with Duprat was entirely one-sided, although hearsay evidence connected him in 1519 with the king's invitation to Erasmus (Ep 932). In 1528 Duprat had just become a cardinal and at the behest of the king virtually controlled the ecclesiastical policy of the kingdom, which he moved in a firmly conservative direction (Epp 2038, 2042). With some trepidation Erasmus attempted to approach him first indirectly and then directly to secure a privilege for his edition of the works of St Augustine. Duprat failed even to respond (Epp 2053, 2291, 2340, 2379).

Albrecht Dürer, self-portrait

BIBLIOGRAPHY: Allen Ep 2038 / Hélène Michaud *La Grande Chancellerie et les écritures royales au XVIe siècle: 1515–1589* (Paris 1967) 23–4 / A. Buisson *Le Chancelier Antoine Duprat* (Paris 1935) / R. Limouzin-Lamothe in DBF XII 503–5 / DHGE XIV, 1144–6 / M. Boudet 'Documents sur la bourgeoisie dans les deux derniers siècles du Moyen Age: Les Du Prat' *Revue de la Haute Auvergne* 28 (1926) 106–87, 29 (1927) 8–73
                                                          HENRY HELLER

Albrecht DÜRER of Nürnberg, 21 May 1471–6 April 1528

Albrecht Dürer (Durerus, noster Apelles, Durerius, Dürerus) was at first trained as a goldsmith by his father, Albrecht; on 30 November 1486 he was apprenticed for three years to the leading painter of Nürnberg, Michel Wolgemut (1434–1519). In 1490 he began travelling as a journeyman, evidently mainly in the Upper Rhineland: he was in Colmar, and apparently in Basel in 1492, and in Strasbourg from 1493 to 1494. At Pentecost 1494 he was back in Nürnberg, where he married on 7 July. Later the same year he travelled to Italy, visiting chiefly Venice (1494–5). He was again in Italy in 1505 and in Venice from 1506 to 1507, where he painted an altar-piece for the German merchants, *The Feast of the Rose-Garlands*, dated 1506, now in Prague. By February 1507 he was back in Nürnberg, where he resided, except for a visit to the Netherlands from 1520 to 1521, whose main purpose was the renewal of his imperial salary by *Charles V, *Maximilian's successor. His final masterpiece, the *Four Apostles*, which the artist presented to his native city, was inscribed with biblical texts, which, reflecting the influence of *Melanchthon, counselled the citizens against heeding extreme religious views.

Dürer met Erasmus at Antwerp and Brussels and evidently they held each other in high regard at once. The artist arrived in Antwerp at the beginning of August 1520, and at this first meeting Erasmus gave him presents (Dürer

Schriftlicher Nachlass I 152), probably in return for a portrait drawing of himself. For certainly Dürer refers to one in his diary (Dürer *Schriftlicher Nachlass* I 156), stating that he did a second drawing of Erasmus in Brussels, where he stayed between 27 August and 2 September. From Erasmus' preface (Ep 1558) to his Greek edition of Chrysostom's *De sacerdotio* (Basel: J. Froben May 1525) we learn that the sitting was interrupted by the arrival of courtiers who had come to greet him. Only one of these portrait drawings survives, that of the scholar's head and shoulders, executed in charcoal, dated 1520, now in the Louvre (Winkler 805; Allen IV 330). It has been assumed that it was used by Dürer in preparing the design of his engraved portrait of Erasmus (Dodgson 104) of 1526. It is not known whether this drawing is the first or the second Dürer did. Nikolaus *Kratzer noted on an impression he possessed of this print, recorded by Hausmann at Bonn in 1861, that he had been present when Dürer drew Erasmus in 1520. Even though the pose of each differs from that of the other, Erasmus is depicted in both looking down and wearing the same cap.

Without the other drawing, of course, it is impossible to say definitely whether Dürer worked from the extant rather than the lost one in producing the engraving. Erasmus told Willibald *Pirckheimer in his letter of 19 July 1523 (Ep 1376) that Dürer had begun to 'paint me at Brussels' (perhaps meaning 'depict me' here: 'Coeperat me pingere Bruxellae'), but like Erasmus, Dürer had been ill and was thus prevented from working on the portrait. It is not absolutely clear from this text whether Erasmus had ordered a painted or an engraved likeness at this stage, but understood literally, it would have been the former. In a letter to Pirckheimer of 8 January 1525 (Ep 1536) Erasmus, who had learned from him that Dürer had engraved his portrait (Dodgson 101), expressed his keen desire to have his own portrait done by Dürer, which he had already begun in charcoal. The use of *pingi* in this letter, however, does not necessarily mean that Erasmus was wishing to have a painted portrait. After receiving and being impressed by an example of Dürer's engraved portrait of Pirckheimer, he pressed again for his portrait to be executed by Dürer, with whom Pirckheimer as the artist's closest friend would

have had great influence (Ep 1558). At all events, to judge from Erasmus' letter to Pirckheimer of 28 August 1525 (Ep 1603), by that time Dürer had Erasmus' portrait in hand, evidently the engraving of 1526 already mentioned. Unfortunately it is perhaps the least successful of Dürer's engraved portraits. Apart from the indifferent likeness the sitter appears altogether wooden and lifeless, probably owing in the main to the long interval since Dürer had seen Erasmus. The pose adopted by Dürer, although curiously reversed, recalls that of Erasmus painted in 1517 by Quinten *Metsys. But as this portrait was sent together with a companion one of Pieter *Gillis as a gift to Sir Thomas *More from the sitters in 1517, Dürer could not have seen the original. Perhaps Dürer had seen drawings by Metsys connected with the commission when he visited Antwerp. He mentioned in his diary that he visited Metsys' house on his first trip to Antwerp in 1520 (Dürer *Schriftlicher Nachlass* I 151). Erasmus was not satisfied with the likeness, for he complained about it to Pirckheimer in his letter of 30 July 1526 (Ep 1729) but made excuses for Dürer, no doubt because of Pirckheimer's close friendship with the artist, saying that it was after all five years since Dürer had drawn him. It was, in fact, six years, and Erasmus' appearance had changed through ill health. Later in a letter to Henri de *Bottis of 29 March 1528 (Ep 1985) Erasmus again referred to this want of likeness in the print and praised by contrast his medal by Quinten Metsys.

Dürer was much affected by the ideas of the Reformation and admired *Luther. This is given vivid expression in the artist's lament written in his diary on 17 May 1521 (Dürer *Schriftlicher Nachlass* I 170–2, 196–9) on the supposed capture and possible death of Luther. He besought God to preserve the unity of Christendom, and if Luther should be dead to send someone in his place to uphold the truth and win a martyr's crown. Dürer saw Erasmus as the obvious successor. This heroic strain also found popular expression then in the idea of the Christian as a knight, which had inspired Dürer's famous engraving of 1513, *The Knight, Death, and the Devil* (Dodgson 70). The artist may have been prompted to produce it by Erasmus' *Enchiridion*. First published in 1504, it became the most influential expression of this popular theme, especially from 1521 when the German edition appeared. Erasmus took a diametrically opposed view to that of Dürer about the relation between the sacred and the profane in art. As a scholar and writer, Erasmus took a purist literary position and found it inadmissible to use classical models to represent Christ and his saints (see Panofsky 212–13). Dürer, however, as he saw all beauty as a reflection of the Divine, thought it appropriate that the Virgin should have the loveliness of Venus, the most beautiful of women.

Like many other scholars after him, Erasmus in his writings referred to Dürer's published treatises, including the *Underweyssung der Messung mit dem Zirckel und Richtscheyt* (Nürnberg: J. Petreius 1525) in his *De pronuntiatione* of 1528. *De pronuntiatione* also contained a eulogy of Dürer (ASD I-4 40) which soon proved to be an epitaph of him, because the artist died shortly after its publication.

BIBLIOGRAPHY: Allen Ep 1376 / H. Jantzen in NDB IV 164–9 / C. Dodgson *The Masters of Engraving and Etching: Albrecht Dürer* (London-Boston 1926) / A. Dürer *Schriftlicher Nachlass* ed H. Rupprich (Berlin 1956–69) / A. Gerlo *Erasme et ses portraitistes, Metsijs, Dürer, Holbein* 2nd ed (Nieuwkoop 1969) 29–44 / M. Mende *Dürer-Bibliographie* (Wiesbaden 1971) / E. Panofsky *Albrecht Dürer* (Princeton 1943, 3rd ed 1948) / E. Panofsky 'Erasmus and the visual arts' *Journal of the Warburg and Courtauld Institutes* 32 (1969) 200–27 / W.L. Strauss *The Complete Drawings of Albrecht Dürer* (New York 1974) / F. Winkler *Die Zeichnungen Albrecht Dürers* (Berlin 1936–9)

JOHN ROWLANDS

Jean DU RUEL of Soissons, 1474–24 September 1537

Born in or near Soissons, Jean Du Ruel (du Rueil, Ruell, Ruellius, a Ruella) received his medical baccalaureate at Paris in 1500 and his licence two years later. In 1506 he was appointed to lecture in the Paris faculty of medicine, of which he was dean in 1508–9. Although he did not normally attend the court, he was appointed physician to *Francis I, to whom he dedicated several works, including *De natura stirpium* (Paris: S. de Colines 1536), an important and popular manual of botany.

After the death of his wife he took the lower orders and on 12 December 1526 was admitted as a canon to the chapter of Notre-Dame. His significance rests on his translations and compilations of Greek medical works, such as his Latin version of Dioscorides' *De medicinali materia* (Paris: H. Estienne 1516; Ep 346).

Erasmus may have known Du Ruel personally in his Paris years; at any rate he saw him and Guillaume *Cop as outstanding representatives of humanistic medicine in France (Epp 541, 542). He credited Du Ruel with sound judgment (Ep 1131) and recalled his name in his correspondence with Nicolas *Bérault and Germain de *Brie (Epp 925, 1024, 1117). In 1524 Jean *Lange counted Du Ruel among the most respected friends and admirers of Erasmus in Paris (Ep 1407).

BIBLIOGRAPHY: Allen Ep 346 / DBF XII 826 / *Dictionary of Scientific Biography* ed C.C. Gillispie et al (New York 1970–80) XI 594–5 / E. Wickersheimer *Dictionnaire biographique des médecins en France au Moyen-Age* (Paris 1936) I 395 / *Commentaires de la faculté de médicine ... Université de Paris (1516–1560)* ed M.-L. Concasty (Paris 1964) / E. Deronne 'Les origines des chanoines de Notre-Dame de Paris de 1450 à 1550' *Revue d'histoire moderne et contemporaine* 18 (1971) 1–29, esp 16

MICHEL REULOS & PGB

Jacques DUSSIN documented 1530–42

Jacques Dussin (Duxin) was the teacher of *Viglius Zuichemus in Dole. After his departure from Dole Viglius addressed to him grateful letters from Bourges (26 May 1530) and from Padua (3 May 1532). From 1534 to 1536 Dussin was the provost of the chapter of St Anatole at Salins, and Gilbert *Cousin praised his 'preaching of Christ' (Ep 3123). In 1542 or 1543 his successor as provost was in office.

BIBLIOGRAPHY: Allen Ep 3123 / Lucien Febvre *Notes et documents sur la réforme et l'inquisition en Franche-Comté* (Paris 1911) 83–4, 183 / C.P. Hoynck van Papendrecht *Analecta Belgica* (The Hague 1743) I 8, 69–70, II-1 25–9, 76–7

PGB

Pierre DUVAL d 18 August 1520

The origins of Pierre Duval (Du Val, de Valle, Valla) remain unknown. He taught arts in Paris at the Collège de Sainte-Barbe and became a *bursarius* in theology at the Collège de Navarre. He ranked third of twenty-one in the licentiate class of 18 January 1498 and received his doctorate in theology on 3 April 1498. As a regent doctor of theology, Duval frequently presided over academic disputations, among them the *vesperia* of Josse *Clichtove on 17 November 1506. Duval was on the faculty committee which investigated *Reuchlin in 1514, and he and Guillaume *Petit were delegated on 9 January 1518 to write to the king about the abusive preaching of indulgences in France. In the same year Duval signed the University of Paris' appeal to the pope protesting implementation of the concordat of Bologna. He was one of three *clavigeri* of the faculty of theology at the time of his death. Duval was grand master, or principal, of the Collège de Navarre from 1503 to 1519 (Ep 444). He took part in the attempts begun by Jan *Standonck to reform monastic discipline in the Paris region. Nevertheless, he had a reputation for favouring humanistic studies. Jacques *Merlin dedicated to him the controversial *Apologia pro Origene* in his edition of Origen's *Opera* (Paris: Josse Bade 1512).

Duval was the curé of Andresy and of St Benoît-le-bien-tourné in Paris and was a canon of Notre-Dame of Paris. According to a contemporary source, his death gave rise to rumours of poisoning. At least two brothers survived him to execute his last will and testament.

BIBLIOGRAPHY: Allen and CWE Ep 444 / Clerval passim / *Mémoires de la Société de l'histoire de Paris et de l'Ile-de-France* XII: *Livre de raison de M. Nicolas Versoris, avocat au Parlement de Paris* ed G. Fagniez (Paris 1885) 108 / Jean de Launoy *Regii Navarre gymnasii Parisiensis historia* (Paris 1677) II 981 – 2 / Paris, Archives de l'Université (Sorbonne) Registre 89 f xxi recto and Registre 90 passim / Renaudet *Préréforme* passim

JAMES K. FARGE

Cornelius DUVELLANDIUS See CORNELIS of *Duiveland*

Jacques DUXIN See Jacques DUSSIN

Johann EBEL (Ep 2808 of 11 May 1533) Johann Ebel is mentioned by Johann *Löble, who stated that Ebel and Hieronymus

*Hirschkoren were holding money for Erasmus in Strasbourg. They were both business associates of Friedrich *Prechter. Johann was the husband of Prechter's daughter Susanna and conceivably a relative of Heinrich Ebel of Strasbourg, canon of St Thomas', Strasbourg, from 1518 to 1532 (see *Matrikel Freiburg* I-1 247; *Matrikel Heidelberg* I 535).

BIBLIOGRAPHY: F.J. Fuchs 'Les Prechter de Strasbourg, une famille de négociants banquiers du XVIe siècle' *Revue d'Alsace* 95 (1956) 146–94

MIRIAM U. CHRISMAN

Hans ECK von der Langenstrate d after 1536 Hans Eck (Hänsgen von der Langenstrate), a *Landsknecht*, had served in the army of Bishop Franz von *Waldeck before joining the Anabaptists in Münster and becoming a bodyguard of *Jan of Leiden. He left the besieged city in the night of 23 May 1535 with Heinrich *Gresbeck to betray the weaknesses of the defence system to the bishop's army and led the army into the city through one of the gates. For his help in the storming of the city he demanded a part of the booty, which he received more than a year later; on 5 December 1536 he acknowledged receipt of the payment of fifty Emder Gulden. He is said to have died soon afterwards from wounds received in a fight.

Eck's part in the storming of the city is described in Epp 3031 and 3041.

BIBLIOGRAPHY: Allen Ep 3031 / U. Gastaldi *Storia dell' anabaptismo dalle origini a Münster* (Turin 1972) 556 / R. Bax *Rise and Fall of the Anabaptists* (New York 1903) 303–7, 315

IG

Johann Maier of ECK 13 November 1486– 10 February 1543 Johann Maier (Mayer, Eckius, Eccius) adopted the name of his native village of Eck (Egg), on the Günz near Ottobeuren, Swabia. He was the son of a farmer and magistrate, Michael Maier (d 1524), and Anna (d 1504). In May 1498, at the age of eleven, Eck entered the University of Heidelberg, where he studied for less than a year before being sent to Tübingen in April 1499. There Eck heard the lectures of both the Scotists and Nominalists (eg, Wendelin Steinbach), receiving his BA on 1 October 1499 and his MA on 13 January 1501. In October

1501, Eck left Tübingen because of the plague
and went to Cologne, where he began studies
under the Albertist faction; however, he was
soon won over to the Thomist faction, probably
by Dietrich von Süstern's lectures on the
Summa theologiae of Thomas Aquinas. Again
because of the plague, Eck left for Freiburg in
June 1502. There he began lecturing on
Aristotle while at the same time attending
lectures in theology, law, mathematics, and
geography; it was also here that he came under
the humanist influence of Udalricus *Zasius. In
1504 Eck was made regent of the 'Pfauenburse'
aligned with the Nominalist *via moderna*. In
1506 he became *sententarius* in theology, and on
13 December 1508, by a special dispensation,
he became a secular priest at the age of
twenty-two. Eck received his doctorate in
theology on 22 October 1510, whereupon he
left Freiburg to accept the chair of theology at
the University of Ingolstadt. Apart from three
short stays in Rome (in 1520, 1521, and 1523),
Eck remained at Ingolstadt until his death.

It was from Ingolstadt that Eck conducted
the lifelong, vigorous and often vituperative
campaign against *Luther for which he is best
remembered. His initially cordial relations with
Luther deteriorated rapidly when he attacked
Luther's theses on indulgences in his *Obelisci*
of 1518. The reactions of *Karlstadt and Luther
to this attack drew Eck into the famous Leipzig
disputation (27 June to 16 July 1519). Though
the results were inconclusive, the disputation
served to confirm the enmity between Eck and
Luther. It was not without some personal
satisfaction, therefore, that Eck published the
papal bull *Exsurge Domine* in Germany in 1520
(Ep 1141). Thereafter, Eck was quickly recognized as a leading champion of the Catholic
cause, disputing with *Zwingli at Baden in
1526, representing the Catholic position along
with *Wimpina and *Cochlaeus at the diet of
Augsburg in 1530, and acting as Catholic
spokesman at the colloquies of Haguenau
(1540), Worms (1540–1), and Regensburg
(1541). His tireless efforts in writing, disputation, and church politics made him the best
known opponent of the Reformation in Germany and earned him appellations ranging
from the 'goat of Leipzig' on the Lutheran side
to the 'Catholic Achilles' on the Catholic side.

Relations between Erasmus and Eck were
unhappy from the outset. Shortly after the

Johann Maier of Eck

publication of the first edition of Erasmus' New
Testament in 1516, Eck became one of its major
critics in Germany. On 2 February 1518 Eck
wrote to Erasmus detailing his criticisms (Ep
769). Eck objected to some of Erasmus' notes
which he believed to cast a doubt on the
reliability of the Evangelists and therefore on
the Gospels. He also took exception to
Erasmus' preference for Jerome over Augustine, suggesting that his one-sided praise of
Jerome and denigration of Augustine could
only be blamed on his insufficient familiarity
with Augustine. Eck's criticisms did not go
unanswered. Erasmus' detailed reply of 15
May 1518 (Ep 844) is marked by a distinct tone
of annoyance.

This exchange marked the beginning of a
bitter, though somewhat distant, relationship.
While Eck did not, it seems, address Erasmus
again directly until 1530, Erasmus left his
defence to other humanists such as Zasius.
There is evidence, however, that each followed the other's career with some interest.
Even before the Leipzig disputation of 1519
Erasmus was aware of Eck's opposition to
Luther and expressed some surprise at it (Ep
872). Scattered references in Erasmus' corre-

spondence indicate considerable interest in Eck's part in the Leipzig disputation (Epp 911, 1020, 1141), and Eck's general polemical bent prompted Erasmus to refer to him as 'militaris theologus' (Ep 1166). Despite his disgust for Eck's personal style, Erasmus nevertheless advised his fellow humanists to be cautious about provoking Eck (Ep 1168). In 1523 Erasmus announced that he had removed himself from his polemics in order to devote himself to more important matters, adding that Pope *Adrian VI might well prefer Eck's advice to his own (Ep 1376). Erasmus then carried out his intention of ignoring Eck until 1530. Aside from several references to Eck in the second part of *Hyperaspistes* of 1527 (LB X 1339E, 1469F) and in *Responsio ad epistolam Pii* of 1529 (LB IX 1104F), which indicate Erasmus' familiarity with Eck's writings, one finds virtually no references to Eck in this period.

In 1530, however, the controversy surfaced again with new vigour. Because Erasmus' letter to Eck (answered in Ep 2387; cf Ep 2384) is not extant, it is uncertain what touched off the renewed hostilities. It seems likely, however, that the catalyst was Eck's 404 articles prepared for the diet of Augsburg, in which he listed various heretical statements of the reformers. Erasmus evidently recognized his own position in some of these statements and suspected that Eck was now attacking him, in an underhanded way, as a heretic (Ep 2371). Whether or not Eck intended such an attack he wrote to Erasmus on 18 September 1530, attempting to set his mind at rest with regard to the 404 articles (Ep 2387). Despite the conciliatory tone of this letter and its overtures of friendship, Erasmus regarded Eck's new approach as a pretence (Ep 2414) and remained confirmed in his distrust and dislike of Eck. Erasmus reported receiving many letters from friends mentioning Eck's vanity, his arrogance, his fickleness, and his drunkenness; he added that Eck had never said anything intelligent about his writings (Ep 2406). Even the efforts of friends such as Matthias *Kretz could not restore good will between the two (Ep 2437). Erasmus remained convinced that Eck was portraying him to the nobility in Germany as the arch-heretic (Ep 2462), and a letter from *Cles in 1531 confirmed that Eck was indeed publicly attacking him (Ep 2504). It was

not without good reason, therefore, that Erasmus continued to regard Eck as one of his most important enemies in Germany (Ep 2443, 2565, 2580, 2615), at least until 1532, after which Eck is no longer mentioned in Erasmus' extant letters.

Eck wrote some hundred works during his academic career spanning forty-five years. His first important theological work, the *Chrysopassus praedestinationis* (Augsburg: J. Miller November 1514), is a protracted discussion of the doctrines of predestination and justification and reveals Eck to be scholastic in his method and eclectic in his opinions. This work and his *Disputatio Viennae Pannoniae habita* (Augsburg: J. Miller, February 1517, edited in *Corpus Catholicorum* VI) are important for Eck's pre-Reformation theological views. In connection with the Leipzig disputation of 1519 three works are significant: the *Obelisci* written in February 1518 and published only after his death by Luther in the first volume of his Latin works (edited in W I 283–313, and IX 770–8); the *Defensio contra amarulentas D. Andreae Bodenstein Carolstatini invectiones* (Augsburg: S. Grimm and M. Wirsung, August 1518, edited in *Corpus Catholicorum* I); and Eck's subsequent account of the disputation, *Disputatio Iohannis Eccii et Andreae Carolstadii et Martini Lutheri* (Erfurt: M. Maler July 1519). For Eck's controversial writings against the reformers, see above all the following: *De primatu Petri adversus Ludderum* (Ingolstadt: n pr 1520); *De poenitentia et confessione contra Lutherum* (Tübingen: U. Morhart November 1522); *De purgatorio contra Ludderum* (Rome: J. Mazzocchi June 1523); *Enchiridion locorum communium adversus Lutteranos* (Landshut: J. Weyssenburger April 1525), which went through at least ninety-one editions and translations; *Verlegung der Disputation zu Bern* (Augsburg: A. Weissenhorn 1528); *Articuli 404* (Ingolstadt: n pr 1530), reprinted in W. Gussmann *D. Johann Ecks vierhundertundvier Artikel zum Reichstag von Augsburg 1530* (Cassel 1930). In addition, four short German works can be found in *Corpus Catholicorum* XIV.

Besides being a polemicist, Eck was also a noted preacher, exegete, and teacher. For these somewhat neglected aspects of his character, see the following works: *Christenliche Ausslegung der Evangelienn vonn der Zeit,*

durch das gantz Jar (Ingolstadt: G. Krapff and J.
Vogker January 1530); *Explanatio psalmi vigesimi*
(Augsburg: A. Weissenhorn March 1538,
edited in *Corpus Catholicorum* XIII and *In
primum librum Sententiarum Annotatiunculae*,
written in 1542 and first edited by Walter L.
Moore, Leiden 1976). Finally, see Eck's intellectual autobiography, *Epistola de ratione stu-
diorum suorum*, written in 1538 and published
after his death by his half-brother, Simon
Thaddeus Eck (Ingolstadt: A. Weissenhorn
1543, edited in *Corpus Catholicorum* II). For his
funeral eulogies, see *Tres orationes funebres in
exequiis Ioannis Eckii habitae* (Ingolstadt: A.
Weissenhorn 1543, edited in *Corpus Catholicorum* XVI).

BIBLIOGRAPHY: Allen and CWE Ep 769 / NDB IV
273–5 / T. Wiedemann *Dr. Johann Eck: Professor
der Theologie an der Universität Ingolstadt* (Regensburg 1865) / J. Greving *Johann Eck als junger
Gelehrter* (Münster 1906) / J. Schlecht 'Dr.
Johann Ecks Anfänge' *Historisches Jahrbuch* 36
(1915) 1–36 / Arno Seifert *Logik zwischen
Scholastik und Humanismus: Das Kommentarwerk
Johann Ecks* (Munich 1978) / See also the useful
introductions to *Corpus Catholicorum* (Münster
1919–) I, II, VI, XIII, XIV, XVI / Other
secondary works: A. Bludau *Die beiden ersten
Erasmus-Ausgaben des Neuen Testaments und ihre
Gegner* (Freiburg 1902) 68–73; H. Schauerte *Die
Busslehre des Johannes Eck* (Münster 1919); E.
Iserloh *Die Eucharistie in der Darstellung des
Johannes Eck* (Münster 1950); Walter L. Moore
'Between Mani and Pelagius: Predestination
and Justification in the Early Writings of John
Eck' (Harvard doctoral thesis 1967); S. Rowan
'Ulrich Zasius and John Eck: "Faith need not be
kept with an enemy"' *The Sixteenth Century
Journal* 8 (1977) 79–95

DENIS R. JANZ

Leonhard von ECK of Kelheim, 1480–
17 March 1550
Leonhard von Eck (Egkh) was born in Kelheim,
on the Danube west of Regensburg, the son of
Leonhard Hueber von Eck, a judge. He
studied in Ingolstadt from 1489 to 1493,
obtaining a MA, and in Siena, where he
received a doctorate of laws. On his return he
was appointed tutor to William IV, duke of
*Bavaria, and became councillor of Duke
William in 1512 and chancellor of Bavaria in

Leonhard von Eck by Barthel Beham

1519. In 1520 he married Felicitas, the widow of
the humanist Dietrich von Plieningen, whose
excellent library he inherited. An able administrator and cunning diplomat, he retained his
dominating influence on the Bavarian ruler
until his death. Not wishing to commit his
princes irreversibly to the political fortunes of
their Hapsburg cousins, Eck avoided any
systematic persecution of Lutherans and Anabaptists until the autumn of 1527, and even
though he reversed his stand in this matter, he
continued to oppose *Ferdinand's claims to
Hungary and Württemberg, while negotiating
directly with *Francis I of France. Leonhard
von Eck is mentioned as a friend by Urbanus
*Rhegius in Ep 386 (1516). Erasmus wrote to
him twice (Epp 3030 and 3035) trying to arrange
the publication of a historical work by Johannes *Aventinus through the press of Johann
*Herwagen.

BIBLIOGRAPHY: Allen and CWE Ep 386 / NDB IV
277–9 / J. von Riezler *Geschichte Baierns* 3rd ed
(Aalen 1964) IV 49–51 and passim / Max
Spindler *Handbuch der Bayerischen Geschichte*
(Munich 1967–75) II passim / Gerald Strauss
Historian in an Age of Crisis: The Life and Work of

Johannes Aventinus (Cambridge, Mass, 1963) 50–1, 162–9, 245–6, 255–7, and passim / Wilhelm Vogt *Die bayerische Politik im Bauernkrieg und der Kanzler Dr. Leonhard von Eck* (Nördlingen 1883)

IG

EDENUS (Ep 1669 of 28 February [1526]) In Ep 1669 Stephen *Gardiner reminded Erasmus that they had met in Paris in the spring of 1511 at Edenus' house, where Erasmus had apparently been a lodger. Since Gardiner himself had been a member of Edenus' household, his master may have been either Richard or Thomas Eden (Edon), both of whom were named in the will of Gardiner's father as trustees of his children.

BIBLIOGRAPHY: Allen Ep 1669 / CWE Ep 219 introduction / 'Will of John Gardener, of Bury' *Proceedings, Bury and West Suffolk Archaeological Institute* 1 (1853) 329–30 / J.A. Muller *Stephen Gardiner and the Tudor Reaction* (London 1926) 339

MORDECHAI FEINGOLD

Omaar van EDINGEN of Ghent, d 8 June 1540 Omaar van Edingen (Audomarus Edingus, Omer d'Enghien) was probably born in Ghent around 1488, the son of Frans and Clara Everwyn. His father was employed in the administrative offices of the council of Flanders and gradually rose to the position of substitute to the procurator-general. On 16 June 1517 Omaar married Maria Ymmeloot, a wealthy burgher's daughter of Ypres, and in the process acquired the citizenship of Ypres. Although he apparently had no university education, he built up a lawyer's office in Ghent which prospered, partly thanks to clients who had business with Omaar's father. During the period when Erasmus repeatedly visited Ghent (1514–17), it was the most important one in town. In 1525 Edingen succeeded Cornelis Boullin as clerk (*griffarius*) to the council of Flanders; one of the last occupants of that position to lack a university degree, he was therefore obliged to make a substantial payment for his initial six-year lease of this office. Among his duties were the supervision of the council's copyists – the most important decisions were recorded by him personally – and the collection of various fees. He retained this office until his death; he

probably died at his house in Ghent, the 'Dondersteen.' He was succeeded as clerk by a son-in-law, Filips van Steelant.

A kinsman of Karel van *Uutenhove and a good friend and frequent correspondent of Levinus *Ammonius, Edingen had probably made Erasmus' personal acquaintance and kept in touch with him, mostly through the letters of Ammonius and Uutenhove (Epp 2060, 2082, 2093, etc). After Erasmus had left Basel in 1529, Edingen eagerly offered to put him up both in his house at Ghent and on his country estate of Ophasselt, near Geraardsbergen, assembled between 1526 and 1528 (Ep 2197). Although this generous invitation was accompanied by the assurance that the entire council of Flanders was wholeheartedly on Erasmus' side, Erasmus explained in a later letter to Edingen that the Netherlands could not offer him adequate protection from his fanatical opponents (Ep 2485).

BIBLIOGRAPHY: Allen Ep 2060 / de Vocht CTL II 190 and passim / J. Decavele *De dageraad van de reformatie in Vlaanderen (1520–1565)* (Brussels 1975–) I 76 / Paul van Peteghem 'Centralisatie in Vlaanderen onder Keizer Karel (1515–1555)' doctoral thesis, Rijksuniversiteit Ghent) II 245–9 / For archival sources in Ghent see J. Buntinx *Inventaris van het archief van de Raad van Vlaanderen (1386–1795)* (Brussels 1964–79) passim

PAUL VAN PETEGHEM

EDMOND (Epp 165, 167, 168 of 1501–2) A priest and a member of the Franciscan community at Saint-Omer, Edmond (Edmondus) was as dear to Erasmus 'as a brother' (Ep 167). During his quiet winter of study at Courtebourne, Erasmus encouraged Edmond in vain to visit him (Epp 165, 168). Edmond, who helped supply Erasmus with patristic and medieval commentaries on Scriptures, has not been otherwise identified.

ANDRÉ GODIN

Nicolaus EDMONDANUS *See Nicolaas* BAE-CHEM

EDMUND Tudor 21 February 1498–12 June 1500 Edmund Tudor, the third son of *Henry VII, died at the age of two and was buried on 22 June 1500. Erasmus saw him as 'an infant in arms' during his visit with *More to Eltham Palace in the summer of 1499 (Allen I 6) and subsequently composed his *Prosopopoeia Britanniae*, which contains a fleeting allusion to Edmund (Reedijk poem 45). A painting by Frank Cadogan Cowper depicting Erasmus' meeting with the royal family is in the Houses of Parliament.

BIBLIOGRAPHY: G. Temperley *Henry VII* (London 1917) 416–17 / J.D. Mackie *The Earlier Tudors, 1485–1558* (Oxford 1952) 169

MORDECHAI FEINGOLD

Arnoldus EDUARDUS (Ep 124 of 12 April [1500])

Arnoldus Eduardus was, according to Erasmus, the name of a well-known lawyer who lived on London Bridge in the house of his father, Eduardus, a merchant. In the absence of a plausible identification it has been suggested by Allen and others that Erasmus may have reversed the names and that Edward may have been the name of an otherwise unknown son of Richard Arnold (d c 1521), the author of a chronicle and a merchant who lived in the parish of St Magnus-London Bridge. Allen also suggested that Richard Arnold may have been the Arnoldus (Allen I 6:20) who accompanied Thomas *More and Erasmus in 1499 on their visit to the royal children.

BIBLIOGRAPHY: Allen and CWE Ep 124 / DNB I 582–4

PGB

Lorenz EFFINGER of Villingen, d 21 June 1544

Said to be a native of Villingen, in the Black Forest, Lorenz Effinger (Laurentius, wrongly called Esinger) was perhaps connected with the well-known Effinger von Wildegg family from the Swiss Aargau. He was elected abbot of the Benedictine abbey of Ettenheimmünster, in the Black Forest, on 4 July 1500 and is described as learned, a good administrator, and a patron of art. During the peasants' revolt of 1525 he was compelled to seek shelter at Freiburg together with other abbots. In 1533 he relinquished the abbot's criminal jurisdiction to the bishop of Strasbourg.

Effinger and Konrad *Frick, the abbot of Schuttern, pleaded for Erasmus' support in their joint efforts to get rid of the oppressive protection of a neighbouring noble family.

Erasmus answered with a promise qualified by excuses (Epp 1120, 1148).

BIBLIOGRAPHY: G. Mezler and J.G. Mayer 'Monumenta historico-chronologica monastica' *Freiburger Diözesan-Archiv* 14 (1881) 141–167, esp 147–8 / *Germania Benedictina* V: *Baden-Württemberg* ed F. Quarthal et al (Augsburg 1975) 215–24 / J. Kindler von Knobloch *Oberbadisches Geschlechterbuch* (Heidelberg 1898–1919) I 278–9 / *Gallia christiana* V 866

PGB

Joachim EGELLIUS *See Doctor IOACINUS*

EGIDIO da Viterbo *See Egidio ANTONINI*

Fridolin EGLI of Glarus, d after 1528

Fridolin Egli (Hirudaeus), of Glarus, registered in the University of Basel in the spring of 1514 with his compatriots *Glareanus and Peter *Tschudi. At one point Erasmus sent him a short note to encourage him in his studies (Ep 405). Egli accompanied Glareanus to Paris, where he is still documented on 25 October 1518. After his return he lived in Glarus and in November 1528 took part in a Swiss diet at Einsiedeln among the delegates of the reformed party.

BIBLIOGRAPHY: Allen Ep 405 / DHBS II 789 / Z VII Epp 8, 26, and passim / E. Egli in *Zwingliana* 1 (1897–1904) 344–5 / *Matrikel Basel* I 320 / A. Büchi in *Aus Geschichte und Kunst ... Robert Durrer ... dargeboten* (Stans 1928) 378–9, 405

PGB

Floris van EGMOND 1469–14 October 1539

Floris (Florent) van Egmond (Egmont), the eldest son of Count Frederik van Buren, lord of Ysselstein, was made a Knight of the Golden Fleece in 1505. He accompanied Philip the Handsome, duke of *Burgundy, on his journey to Spain from 1501 to 1503 and in 1506 was appointed to the council of *Margaret of Austria. In 1511 he was named *onder-stadhouder* of Holland, to assist his uncle, Jan III van Egmond, in military affairs. When the Hapsburg government purchased a claim to Friesland in 1515, Floris served briefly as the *stadhouder* of the new province but in the same year was succeeded by Henry III of *Nassau. In 1518 he was appointed *stadhouder* of Holland and Zeeland, and in 1522 he served as a military commander against France. He was a

Floris van Egmond by Jan Gossaert van Mabuse

member of the council of state from its inception in 1531.

While composing his *Panegyricus*, Erasmus wrote Willem *Hermans that his work would include praise of Floris van Egmond, a victor on the jousting fields of Spain, Savoy, France, and Germany, whose patronage he encouraged Hermans to seek (Ep 178). Hermans did make contact with Count Floris and dedicated to him his translations of Greek fables (Antwerp: D. Martens 1513), but Egmond is not mentioned in the *Panegyricus* as published in 1504; this suggests that at this time Erasmus was moving from the patronage of the imperial party in the Netherlands, in which Egmond was prominent, to that of the 'national' or Francophile party, whose sentiments are in some ways reflected in the *Panegyricus*.

In later life Erasmus' known contacts with Floris van Egmond were limited to acknowledging a gift, recommending a tutor for his son, Maximiliaan van *Egmond (Ep 1018), and an occasional greeting (Ep 1192).

BIBLIOGRAPHY: Allen Ep 178 / NNBW III 324–5 / James D. Tracy *The Politics of Erasmus* (Toronto 1978) / de Vocht CTL II 125 and passim / Michel

Baelde *De collaterale raden onder Karel v en Filips II* (Brussels 1965) 257 and passim

JAMES D. TRACY

Karel van EGMOND duke of Gelderland, 9 November 1467–30 June 1538
Karel was the great-grandson of Jan II van Egmond (d 1451), whose wife, Maria van Arkel, inherited title to Gelderland from her maternal uncle, Duke Reinout IV. A bitter dispute between Jan II's son Arnout and grandson Adolf provided an occasion for Burgundian intervention and led in 1472 to the seizure of Gelderland by Charles the Rash, duke of *Burgundy. But in 1492 Adolf's son, Karel van Egmond, re-established the rule of his house in Gelderland with French assistance. For half a century this French client state, lying astride three of the great rivers which were a lifeline of Netherlands commerce, presented the Hapsburg government with one of its greatest problems. At Karel's death without issue (cf Ep 3119) Gelderland still eluded *Charles v, but in 1543 Karel's successor, William v of *Cleves, was finally compelled to surrender his claims.

There are occasional references to Karel van Egmond in Erasmus' work and correspondence (LB X 1625E; Ep 584), but he comments repeatedly and with some asperity on the incessant wars between Gelderland and the Hapsburg Netherlands (Epp 628, 1998; cf Ep 2024; *Julius exclusus, Opuscula* 113).

BIBLIOGRAPHY: Allen Ep 584 / J.M. Romein in NNBW X 442–7 / J.E.A.L. Struick *Gelre en Hapsburg, 1493–1528* (Arnhem 1960) / James D. Tracy *The Politics of Erasmus* (Toronto 1978) / G. Kalsbeek *De betrekkingen tusschen Frankrijk en Gelre* (Wageningen 1932) / A.W.E. Dek *Genealogie … Egmond* (The Hague 1958) 27–9 / P.J. May et al *Geschiedenis van Gelderland, 1492–1795* (Zutphen 1978) passim

JAMES D. TRACY

Joris and Filips van EGMOND d 26 September 1559 and 1529
In November 1522 Jan *Stercke informed Erasmus of the imminent admission to the Collegium Trilingue at Louvain of two illustrious students and boarders, the counts of Egmond (Ep 1322). They were two of the younger sons of Jan III of Egmond (d 1516),

who had been privately educated at Louvain from 1516. They received instruction from Adrianus Cornelii *Barlandus, who dedicated his *De Hollandiae principibus* (Antwerp: J. Thibault 1519) to them and their cousin, Maximiliaan van *Egmond. Joris and Filips formally matriculated at the university on 6 December 1522. Filips, lord of Baer, later continued his studies in Italy, where he died in 1529.

Joris (George) entered the church and in 1526 became a canon of St Lambert, Liège. On 10 March 1534 he succeeded to the deanship of the Liège chapter, which he held until 1543. Also in 1526 he was nominated by *Charles v to the abbacy of Saint-Amand near Tournai in succession to Cardinal Louis de Bourbon and Willem *Bollart. Holding Saint-Amand at first as an administrator, he succeeded Cardinal Willem van *Enckenvoirt as bishop of Utrecht in 1534, receiving papal confirmation on 26 February 1535. A pious man, Joris was a sincere reformer and a patron of scholars. The famous poet Janus Secundus was his secretary, while Gerard *Morinck dedicated to him his *Commentaria in librum Ecclesiastae* (Antwerp: M. Hillen 1533). Herman *Lethmaet was his vicar-general for the see of Utrecht.

BIBLIOGRAPHY: Allen Ep 1322 / NNBW III 326–9 / *Matricule de Louvain* III-1 688 / de Vocht CTL II 123–5 and passim / de Vocht MHL 478–9 / E. Daxhelet *Adrien Barlandus* (Louvain 1938, repr 1967) 270–1 and passim

PGB

Maximiliaan van EGMOND d 23 September 1548

Maximiliaan, the son of Floris van *Egmond, was studying in Louvain from 1516 and received instruction from Adrianus Cornelii *Barlandus who dedicated *De Hollandiae principibus* (Antwerp 1519) to him and his relatives Joris and Filips van *Egmond. Erasmus was induced to take a personal interest in the youth and in 1519 recommended Conradus *Goclenius as a suitable tutor for him (Ep 1018). Erasmus seems to have seen him repeatedly until his departure from Louvain; in March 1521 he mentioned how on a recent visit Maximiliaan had admirably rendered some Homeric verses from the Greek (Ep 1192). It seems that they later remembered each other

Joris van Egmond by Steven van Herwijck

with genuine affection (Ep 2843); Erasmus, at any rate, praised Maximiliaan's learning again in his preface to *De pronuntiatione* (Ep 1949), published in 1528.

By that time Maximiliaan had apparently spent three years at the court of Erard de la *Marck, prince-bishop of Liège, and had recently joined the court of *Charles v in Spain (Ep 1984). As lord of Ysselstein and count of Buren, he distinguished himself in 1537 and 1538 as a military commander against France and was made a knight of the Golden Fleece in October 1540. On 16 December 1540 he was appointed to the council of state and earlier the same year he had succeeded Georg *Schenck as governor of Friesland. In 1546 and 1547 he commanded a Netherlands army sent to join Charles v for the Schmalkaldic war. Andreas Vesalius, the famous physician, was his friend and attended him in his final sickness. Reportedly he awaited death dressed in full armour and drinking the emperor's health. He was married to Marie de Launnoy, and their only daughter, Anna, became the first wife of William the Silent, prince of Orange.

BIBLIOGRAPHY: Allen Ep 1018 / NNBW III

339–40 / de Vocht CTL II 125–6 and passim / de Vocht *Dantiscus* 43 / E. Daxhelet *Adrien Barlandus* (Louvain 1938, repr 1967) 270–1 and passim / Michel Baelde *De collaterale raden onder Karel V en Filips II* (Brussels 1965) 258–9, and passim

PGB

Nicolaus EGMONDANUS *See Nicolaas* BAE-CHEM

Giambattista EGNAZIO of Venice, 1478–4 July 1553

Born in 1478 of humble Venetian parents named Cipelli, Giambattista apparently adopted the additional name of 'Egnazio' from the village of Egna, near Bolzano, where he believed his family originated. He was educated entirely in Venice, first at the chancery school of San Marco under Benedetto Brugnolo, then under Francesco Bragadin at the school of mathematics and logic near the Rialto. Fluent in Latin and at least competent in Greek, he was soon employed by the ageing Brugnolo as an assistant, took ecclesiastical orders, and in due course was advised by his old teacher to set up a grammar school of his own. Though there is no contemporary evidence that he did this at the precocious age of seventeen given by early biographers, it is clear that Egnazio was immediately successful. Indeed by 1502 he was engaged in a sharp controversy with Venice's senior public lecturer, Marcantonio *Sabellico, whose interpretations of a number of debated passages he attacked item by item in his *Racemationes* (Venice: Pencius de Leuco 1502). This self-advertising did not secure the dead Brugnolo's post for Egnazio, but it did move him into the centre of Venetian intellectual life. In 1502 he was one of the seven named signatories of the statute of the Aldine Academy, in 1506 he was reconciled with the dying Sabellico, whose *Exempla* he edited a year later, and in 1508 he was named by Erasmus along with Aldo *Manuzio, *Aleandro, *Musurus, *Lascaris, and Fra Urbano *Valeriani as a valued helper with the *Adagia* (II i 1, 65; Ep 269; LB IX 1137).

From about this time Egnazio began to come under pressure from two patrician friends, Tommaso Giustiniani and Vicenzo Querini, to join them in their celebrated renunciation of the world for an eremitic life. But the lure of temporal success proved stronger. In 1511 Egnazio was voted *civis ab origine* of Venice, secretary to the procurators of San Marco, incumbent of the church of San Biasio, and prior of the hospital of San Marco. A benefice near Treviso was added. In 1514 he became procurator of the Venetian clergy and in 1515 accompanied an official embassy to Milan to pronounce a panegyric on *Francis I's victory at Marignano. His fame as a speaker was such that sixty similar performances, on various public or private occasions, are recorded by biographers. Over the same period he moved towards a dominant position in the revived Aldine literary circle, receiving the dedication of the third volume of the Greek orators in 1513, standing as executor to Manuzio's will in 1515, and editing the text of Lactantius' *Divine Institutions* and Aulus Gellius' *Attic Nights* later in the year. In 1516 he published at the Aldine press, *De Caesaribus*, a work which extended the *Historia Augusta* down to his contemporary, *Maximilian, and also an edition of Suetonius' *Lives* which prompted a revival of his contact with Erasmus. For the Venetian text appeared in time for Erasmus to use it in his own edition and to incorporate a flattering tribute to Egnazio's learning in his own introduction (Ep 648). Egnazio, in turn, entrusted to *Hutten (Ep 611) a letter for delivery to Erasmus: this is almost certainly Ep 588 and shows the writer acknowledging Erasmus' compliments in an earlier letter, now lost, and inviting further editorial co-operation. In view of this cordial exchange, and of the fact that Erasmus' Ep 648 was included in the new edition of Egnazio's Suetonius in 1519, it seems unlikely that the Italian critic of Erasmus mentioned in Epp 1015 and 1066 can be Egnazio. Though mainly concerned with business matters, the relationship was always friendly. Egnazio tried to calm the storm over Gianfrancesco *Torresani's refusal to publish a revised text of the *Adagia* in 1525 (Epp 1594, 1623), and Erasmus was duly grateful (Ep 1626). Several visitors to Italy, including Hieronymus *Froben (Ep 1707), Karel van *Uutenhove (Epp 2105, 2209), and Johann *Herwagen (Epp 2249, 2302), arrived in Venice with letters of introduction or requests for editorial help from Erasmus to Egnazio. Relatively little positive co-operation seems to have resulted. Erasmus repeatedly requested manuscripts of Chrysostom (Epp 2302, 2371, 2448), but Egnazio seems to have responded only by advising him not to reply to the attacks of Alberto *Pio and Aleandro on the *Colloquia* (Ep 2468). Possibly the flashy, audience-catching techniques noticed by *Viglius Zuichemus (Epp 2568, 2594) left Egnazio slightly uneasy in the realms of higher scholarship, for his Greek had never been strong, and after his appointment in December 1520 to the long-coveted public lectureship in Venice he bore an increasing load of exclusively Latin teaching. But he remained keenly aware of Erasmus' work, drawing a jovial parallel between the description of Nosoponus in *Ciceronianus* and Giulio *Camillo's labours over his memory theatre (Ep 2632). Though he failed to receive a copy of Froben's edition of St Basil from Erasmus (Ep 2871), Egnazio passed a corrected manuscript of *Institutiones graecae* (probably Fra Urbano Valeriani's grammar) to Froben through Viglius (Ep 2885), commended Viglius himself warmly (Ep 2871), and commended a protégé of his own, one Georgius *Sabinus, to Erasmus' attention (Epp 2964, 2970). Erasmus seems never to have departed from his verdict that Egnazio was a learned, upright, and straightforward character (Ep 1626; *Ciceronianus* ASD I-2 668–9), and he was regarded by others as one of the few Italian intellectuals who never abandoned their admiration for Erasmus (Ep 3002). Advancing in age and perhaps compromised by his relationship with the apostate bishop Pier Paolo *Vergerio, Egnazio resigned his lectureship in 1549 and died in 1553. His last work, a nine-book collection of largely Venetian biographies entitled *De exemplis* (Venice: N. Bevilaqua), was published the year after his death.

BIBLIOGRAPHY: E. Cicogna *Delle iscrizioni veneziane* I (Venice 1824) 341–4 / J.B. Ross 'Venetian schools and teachers, fourteenth to early sixteenth century: a survey and a study of Giovanni Battista Egnazio' *Renaissance Quarterly* 39 (1976) 521–57

M.J.C. LOWRY

Johannes Sylvius EGRANUS of Cheb, d 11 June 1535

Egranus (Johann Wildenauer) of Cheb (Eger), in Bohemia, matriculated in Leipzig in 1500 and

obtained his BA in 1501 and his MA in 1507. In 1508 and 1509 he contributed verses and prefaces to several books printed in Leipzig. Subsequently he was appointed priest of St Mary's at Zwickau, in Saxony. From there he wrote in December 1516 to Bonifacius *Amerbach, exhibiting a knowledge of Erasmus' writings (AK II Ep 560). In 1517 his sermon rejecting the traditional opinion that St Anne had married Cleopas after the death of Joachim led to a complaint to the bishop of Naumburg. Egranus replied with an *Apologia contra calumniatores suos* (Nürnberg: F. Peypus 1518) and an *Apologetica responsio* (Wittenberg: J. Rhau, early April 1518). Erasmus saw them, or at any rate the second one, at Basel in the summer of 1518. He commended the work and encouraged a new edition of it at Basel (Ep 872). *Luther likewise wrote of it with approval.

In the spring of 1520 Egranus set out to visit Luther at Wittenberg and subsequently travelled to Basel by way of Nürnberg, Augsburg, and the nearby abbey of Altomünster, where he visited *Oecolampadius. He wanted to meet *Capito in Basel but found that he had recently moved to Mainz; he may also have brought with him texts by Luther for the Basel printers (Allen Ep 1143:21n). By way of Sélestat and Strasbourg he then travelled to Louvain to meet Erasmus (Epp 1127A, 2495, 2918) before returning to Zwickau, again by way of Wittenberg, where he delivered Ep 1127A to Luther. A controversy with Thomas Münzer in 1520 caused Egranus to leave Zwickau and accept a position as the first reformed minister of Jáchymov (Joachimsthal), in the Erz mountains (1521–3). He visited Erasmus again in Basel in July 1523 and also called on Willibald *Pirckheimer in Nürnberg, taking Erasmus' side in the quarrel with *Eppendorf (Epp 1376, 1377, 1383, 1934). In 1524 he was in charge of the parish in Kulmbach, on the Main, in 1526 he went to Zagán, in Silesia, in 1530 to Karl-Marx-Stadt (Chemnitz), in Saxony, and from 1534 he was again in Jáchymov, where he died.

For a while Egranus was close to Luther, but after his visit to Louvain in 1520 he is referred to as an 'Erasmian' (Luther w *Briefwechsel* III Ep 785).

BIBLIOGRAPHY: Allen and CWE Ep 872 / NDB IV 341–2 / Luther w *Briefwechsel* I Ep 55, II Epp 282,

Eleanor of Austria by Joos van Cleve

321, 483, III Ep 785 / BA *Oekolampads* I 121,
137–9, and passim / *Matrikel Leipzig* I 433, II 381,
434

IG

Adolf EICHHOLZ of Cologne, d 1563
Adolf Eichholz (Eichholtz, Eichols, Roborius,
or Dryoxylus) was born of a patrician family of
Cologne. He matriculated at the university of
his home town on 31 March 1503, obtaining his
BA in 1504 and his MA in 1506. Subsequently he
turned to the study of law and became a
bachelor of canon law in 1509. In the same year
he matriculated at Bologna, probably having
arrived there with Hermann von *Neuenahr
and his preceptor, Johannes *Caesarius. In
1515 Eichholz matriculated at Orléans as canon
of St Mariengraden, Cologne. He studied
under Jean Pyrrhus d'*Angleberme and was
procurator of the German nation. In Orléans he
tutored Heinrich Olisleger and his two brothers as well as Karl *Harst. Subsequently he was
also connected with Johann von *Vlatten.
Three years later he returned to Cologne and
obtained a doctorate of canon law on 18 May
1521. He began to teach at the faculty of law,

becoming professor of canon law about 1535.
When canon law ceased to attract students, the
Cologne council requested him in 1552 to teach
civil law instead. He was rector in 1542 and
vice-rector in 1553, as well as repeatedly dean
of law.

Eichholz had studied Greek under Hermannus *Buschius in Cologne with Henricus
*Glareanus (AK III Ep 1188) and was connected
with many humanist scholars throughout his
life. In 1515 he was acquainted with *Hutten
and supported *Reuchlin in his controversy
with *Pfefferkorn (Hutten *Opera* I Ep 21). While
returning to Cologne in 1518 he visited Paris,
where Glareanus introduced him to Guillaume
*Budé (Ep 819). He went on to Antwerp,
carrying Ep 810 from Budé, but found that
Erasmus had gone to Basel. In the same year he
wrote Erasmus repeatedly from Cologne urging him to revise a work by Jean Pyrrhus
d'Angleberme for publication (Ep 866). A
correspondence with Bonifacius *Amerbach
began in 1526, but Eichholz seems to have
ended it in the summer of 1528, on the eve of
Basel's reformation, while continuing to exchange letters and greetings with Erasmus.
Eichholz's letter of October 1528 (Ep 2071)
refers to common friends such as Tielmannus
*Gravius and Christoph *Eschenfelder. Prior
to July 1532 Eichholz sent Erasmus a letter and
a map of Cologne for which Erasmus thanked
him in Ep 2691.

BIBLIOGRAPHY: Allen and CWE Ep 866 /
Matrikel Köln II 538 / *Matricule d'Orléans* II-1
338–43 and passim / AK III Epp 1136, 1182, 1188,
1255, 1262 / Knod 107 / Hermann Keussen
'Vertrag des Kölner Professors Adolf Eichholtz
mit seiner Dienstmagd Hilla von Hallingen
vom Jahre 1545' *Archiv für Kulturgeschichte* 10
(1912) 317–19 / *Das Stift St. Mariengraden zu Köln*
ed A.D. von den Brincken (Cologne 1969–   ) I
150, 391, and passim

IG & PGB

ELEANOR sister of Charles V, 24 November
1498–18 February 1558
Eleanor, the eldest daughter of *Joanna of
Spain and Philip the Handsome of *Burgundy,
had been reared to royalty in Mechelen by her
powerful aunt, *Margaret of Austria. As a
young princess, she had accompanied the
future *Charles V when he sailed in 1517 to

Spain to be installed as king. At one time she was promised in marriage to the young prince of Wales, the future *Henry VIII, and at another time she was forced to withdraw from a romance with the future Frederick II, elector *Palatine. In 1518 she married *Manuel I of Portugal. After being widowed in 1521, she was again played as a pawn in imperial politics with her marriage to *Francis I (4 July 1530) and her accession as queen of France (Ep 2425) under the terms of the much-abused treaty of Madrid (1526) and the treaty of Cambrai (1529). Enmeshed in the vindictive and perennial quarrels between Francis and Charles, she attempted to play the peace-maker, at one time providing, at best, a brief respite by negotiating with her sister, *Mary of Hungary (Epp 3037, 3049), and at other times reducing through personal persuasion the bellicose tensions between her husband and brother. After Francis' death she returned in 1547 to the Netherlands and in 1556 accompanied Charles on his return to Spain after his abdication; there she died shortly before the demise of him who claimed that he loved her 'best of all the world.'

BIBLIOGRAPHY: Allen Ep 3037 / DBF XII 1191–2 / K. Brandi *Kaiser Karl v.* new ed (Darmstadt 1959–67) / T. Miller *The Castles and the Crown* (New York 1963) / W. Robertson *The History of the Reign of the Emperor Charles the Fifth* (Philadelphia 1899)

ALICE TOBRINER

ELEUTHERIUS *See Sebastian* FRANCK

ELIAS or HELIAS, paternal grandfather of Erasmus *See* ERASMUS' *family*

ELIAS or ELIJA Levita *See Elias* LEVITA

ELISABETH (Ep 2 of 1487?)
In Ep 2, conjecturally dated from 1487, Erasmus answered a letter from a nun called Elisabeth. As Berta *Heyen, who was well known to Erasmus, had several daughters living in a convent at Gouda, Elisabeth may have been one of them.

BIBLIOGRAPHY: Allen and CWE Ep 2 / R.L. DeMolen 'Erasmus as Adolescent' BHR 38 (1976) 7–25, esp 10

C.G. VAN LEIJENHORST

Elizabeth of York

ELIZABETH of York queen of England, 1 February 1465–11 February 1503
Elizabeth, the mother of *Henry VIII, was the eldest daughter of Edward IV and his queen Elizabeth Woodville. She was born at Westminster Palace. When she was fifteen English ambassadors were sent to France to arrange her marriage to the dauphin, the son of *Louis XI. The French king left the arrangements unsettled, and when Edward IV died in 1483 the widowed queen and her daughters took refuge at Westminster, while Elizabeth's brothers, Edward V and Richard, were allegedly murdered upon the order of her uncle, Richard III. After ten months of confinement Richard guaranteed the safety of Elizabeth's family in return for their loyalty. There is no evidence to support the rumour which suggested a marriage between Elizabeth and Richard III. Since the earl of Richmond, later *Henry VII, hoped to marry her, Elizabeth was sent away to Yorkshire but was recalled by Henry after his victory at Bosworth. She was created duchess of York and married Henry on 18 January 1486, six weeks before Innocent VIII granted a dispensation in view of their degree of kinship.

Parliament appeared to favour the union, and Elizabeth was crowned queen in November 1487.

After the birth of Prince *Arthur in 1486 the manors and rents from dowager lands were transferred to Elizabeth. In 1489 she gave birth to *Margaret, and in 1491 to the future Henry VIII. Three other children died in infancy. In 1496 *Mary, who was later married to *Louis XII, king of France, was born. In 1500 Elizabeth accompanied the king to Calais; about this time her health began to fail, and her death was hastened by the shock of Arthur's death in 1502. She died in February 1503 and was remembered for her beauty and nobility of character. Thomas *More composed an elegy on the occasion. In 1507, when replying to Erasmus' letter from Italy, Prince Henry recalled the grief of her death (Ep 206). Erasmus praised the queen's virtues more than twenty years later in Ep 2143.

BIBLIOGRAPHY: DNB VI 618–21

CFG

Nikolaus ELLENBOG of Biberach, 18 March 1481–6 June 1543
Nikolaus Ellenbog (Cubitus, Cubitensis), the son of a humanist who was a sometime lecturer in medicine at the University of Ingolstadt, was born in Biberach, west of Memmingen (Württemberg). He studied at Heidelberg (1497), Cracow (1501), and Montpellier (1502–3). In compliance with a vow he had taken during an outbreak of plague, he entered the Benedictine monastery in Ottobeuren, near Memmingen, in 1504; there he became a priest in 1506, prior from 1508 to 1512, and steward from 1512 to 1522. Ellenbog was a humanist scholar interested in mathematics, history, theology, astronomy, geography, and medicine. From 1509 he directed a press established in the abbey and, having learnt both Greek and Hebrew, entertained a lively correspondence with *Reuchlin. In 1520 he engaged in an exchange of friendly and learned letters with *Oecolampadius, who had by then withdrawn to the abbey of Altomünster. As a result he afterwards felt obliged to demonstrate his own orthodoxy with a tract about Oecolampadius' desertion from Altomünster.

Ellenbog's years after 1522 were devoted to his studies and his correspondence, which affords an intimate picture of monastic life and events connected with the peasants' revolt. Close to a thousand letters, copied out in his own hand, have been preserved, partly in the Württembergische Landesbibliothek at Stuttgart and partly in the Bibliothèque Nationale at Paris.

In 1516, when Erasmus was at Basel, Ellenbog wrote to him, inquiring about the editions of Jerome and the New Testament. Erasmus sent a friendly reply (Epp 395, 402).

BIBLIOGRAPHY: Allen and CWE Ep 395 / NDB IV 454 / Matrikel Heidelberg I 425 / RE Epp 105–7 and passim / BA Oekolampads I 136–7, 139–40, 165–6

IG

Thomas ELRYNGTON d before 1524
Very little is known about Thomas Elryngton (Elrington), who on 21 February 1516 married Alice *Middleton, the daughter of Thomas *More's second wife. When More was in prison, his daughter Margaret *More Roper wrote to Alice that he was praying for 'the soule of mine other good sonne her first [husband]' (Rogers Ep 206). While it seems likely that Thomas may have been the son of John Elryngton (d 1504), who as a filacer was filing the writs in the Court of Common Pleas and was also a coroner for Middlesex in 1494 and Surrey in 1495, that relationship has not yet been established with certitude. What is known is that Sir Thomas More was the executor of Thomas. In September 1521 (Ep 1233) Erasmus mentioned Alice and her husband; at that time this almost certainly would have been Thomas Elryngton, rather than her second husband, Sir Giles Alington.

BIBLIOGRAPHY: LP IV-1 366 / Harpfield's Life of More ed E.V. Hitchcock (London 1936) 313 / E.M.G. Routh The Friends of Sir Thomas More (Oxford, New York, 1963) 46

R.J. SCHOECK

Jean EMERY documented 20 March 1492–1516
Jean Emery (Aymery, Emeri) was the brother of Guillaume Aymery, seigneur of Vaudray and Chevoyse. He was a bursarius of the Collège de Navarre at Paris. Launoy says that Emery studied theology under Guillaume de Châteaufort and became a theologian, but his

name is not among the list of theology licentiates and doctors. He probably went instead to the faculty of law, since he was later a *conseiller clerc* in the Parlement of Paris. Two of his nephews, however, did become doctors of theology in Paris, and the Emery cited by Renaudet on the committee of theologians investigating *Reuchlin in 1514 was his nephew Guillaume Emery. The other nephew, Jacques, was an Augustinian canon regular at Ste Geneviève and became auxiliary bishop of Sens and of Laon.

Jean Emery was appointed as a canon of Notre-Dame of Paris on 20 March 1492, just in time to protest against royal interference in the election of the bishop of Paris. He led opposition and appeals on this matter for over ten years. At the same time he became one of the most ardent supporters of Jan *Standonck's efforts to reform monastic discipline in the Paris region, descending in 1498 to the use of force and even physical brutality against recalcitrant nuns of the Hôtel-Dieu of Paris, an action which lost him his position of *provisor* at the hospital. Around this time Erasmus met him in Paris (Ep 73). In 1514 and 1516 he assisted in the reformation of the abbey of St Victor in Paris. From 1504 he was the curé of the Madeleine in Paris. The date of his death is not known.

BIBLIOGRAPHY: Allen and CWE Ep 73 / Farge nos 19, 20 / Jean de Launoy *Regii Navarrae gymnasii Parisiensis historia* (Paris 1677) II 956–7 / Renaudet *Préréforme* passim

JAMES K. FARGE

Paolo EMILIO of Verona, d 5 May 1529
Paolo Emilio (Emili, Aemilius, Paul-Emile) of Verona went to Paris in 1483 to study theology. He found a patron in Cardinal Charles de Bourbon and became a canon of the cathedral of Notre-Dame. He became royal historian, and some time before 15 May 1489 *Charles VIII rewarded him with a pension, continued by *Louis XII. In about 1516 or 1517, after twenty years of work, Emilio published the first four books of his *De rebus gestis Francorum* (Paris: J. Bade), written in imitation of ancient models. Two more books appeared in about 1519 (Paris: J. Bade), while the complete work in ten books was published in 1539 (Paris: M. de Vascosan), with the final book completed by Daniele

Zavarizzi of Verona. Emilio's history covered the course of the French monarchy from its origins until 1488. Frequently reprinted and translated in the sixteenth century, it rivalled Robert *Gaguin's *Compendium de origine et gestis Francorum* (1495) in popularity.

Erasmus probably met Emilio when he was in Paris from 1495 to 1500. Augustinus Vincentius *Caminadus sent him news of Emilio, Fausto *Andrelini, and Gaguin in Ep 136, and by 1517 Erasmus eagerly anticipated the publication of Emilio's history (Ep 534), finally obtaining a copy of the first four books in January 1518 (Ep 764). He praised Emilio's learning and piety in his letters (Epp 719, 928) and in the *Ciceronianus* (ASD I-2 668).

BIBLIOGRAPHY: Allen Ep 136 / EI XIII 898 / Cosenza I 68 / E. Fueter *Histoire de l'historiographie moderne* trans E. Jeanmaire (Paris 1914) 170–2 and passim

TBD

Johannes EMMANUEL *See Don JUAN MANUEL*

Johannes EMMEUS *See Johannes FABER Emmeus*

Hieronymus EMSER of Weidenstetten, 28 March 1479–8 December 1527
Hieronymus Emser of Weidenstetten, near Ulm, began his studies in 1493 at the University of Tübingen and moved in 1497 to Basel, where he obtained his MA in 1499 and was tutor to the sons of Johann *Amerbach in 1500. After the Swiss had defeated *Maximilian I (1499), Emser wrote some abusive verses about them and as a result had to leave Basel in 1502. He took holy orders and accompanied Cardinal Raimundus Peraudi as a secretary on his travels through Germany. In 1504 he joined the *Wimpfeling circle in Strasbourg and edited the works of Giovanni *Pico della Mirandola (Strasbourg: J. Prüss 15 March 1504). After Easter he matriculated in Erfurt, where *Mutianus Rufus and *Spalatinus became his friends. In the autumn he moved to Leipzig and graduated bachelor of canon law. While teaching theology at the University of Leipzig in 1505, he came into contact with the humanist Hermannus *Buschius. In the same year he entered the service of Duke George of *Saxony as a secretary and chaplain. In 1507 he went to Rome to promote

the canonization of Bishop Benno of Meissen (d 1105), which came about in 1524. After his return he received prebends at Dresden and Meissen and henceforward remained attached to the court of Duke George.

Emser was not at first opposed to the call for reform within the church and even received Martin *Luther as a guest in his house in Dresden in July 1518. The rift between them occurred in 1519, when Emser accompanied Johann *Eck to the Leipzig disputation and was personally insulted by Luther. From that time on he took to writing pamphlets, letters, and epigrams against Luther – for example, *An den Stier zu Wiettenberg* (Leipzig: M. Landsberg 1521) – and others against *Karlstadt – for example, *Das man der Heyligen Bilder ... nit abthon noch unehren soll* [Dresden, Emser's own press 1524?]. Emser translated a number of works, such as *Henry VIII's book on the seven sacraments, *Schutz und Handthabung der siben Sacrament* (Augsburg: J. Schönsperger 1522). His most important work, a German New Testament, edited in 1530 by his friend Augustin *Alveldt, followed Luther's version as far as it was compatible with Catholic theology. Emser died suddenly in Dresden.

When Erasmus wrote to *Cochlaeus (Ep 1974) three months after Emser's death that Emser had always been a true friend to him, he gave a simplified picture of their relationship, which, although important to both of them, did not extend over more than ten years of their lives. Emser was an admirer of Erasmus in 1515 when he prepared a new edition of Erasmus' *Enchiridion* for the Leipzig printer Valentin *Schumann (Ep 553). In 1516 or 1517 he requested his friend *Pirckheimer to extend to Erasmus an invitation to come to Leipzig at the expense of Duke George (Ep 527), and in March 1517 he repeated this invitation in an admiring letter sent with Richard *Croke, who was returning to England (Ep 553). While he expressed appreciation for this honour (Ep 809), Erasmus did not accept the invitation. No letters are known to have been exchanged between 1518 and 1524 while Emser waited for Erasmus to declare himself openly against Luther. For a while Erasmus had thought that Emser was dead (Ep 1383). Emser wrote that Erasmus was one of the scholars who had supported Luther at first but had now turned

against him (Barge II 253); he therefore did not renew contact until after the publication of Erasmus' *De libero arbitrio* against Luther. Erasmus suspected Emser of discrediting him in the eyes of Duke George and believed that he had drafted Ep 1448 (Ep 1521). He preferred to ignore (Ep 1683) or even criticize in passing (*Hyperaspistes* LB X 1249B) Emser's virulent attacks upon Luther, but despite his guarded and even cool replies (Epp 1566, 1683) Emser continued the correspondence (Epp 1551, 1773) with the same tone of reverence he had shown in his first letter. He greatly appreciated Erasmus' paraphrase of St John and especially the *Hyperaspistes*, which he translated into German (Leipzig: M. Lotter 1526), and their correspondence continued until Emser's death (Ep 1951). Emser attempted to heed Erasmus' advice that he should modify the tone of his polemic, and the latter found little to criticize in his *Apologeticon*, written in 1525 (n p) against *Zwingli's *Antibolon* (Ep 1566; LB X 1603E).

BIBLIOGRAPHY: Allen and CWE Ep 533 / NDB IV 488–9 / LThK III 855 / DHGE XV 444–5 / Luther w *Briefwechsel* IV Ep 1008 and passim / *Matrikel Tübingen* I 97 / *Matrikel Basel* I 249–50 / *Matrikel Erfurt* II 234 / *Matrikel Leipzig* I 462, II 18, 41 / AK I Ep 117 / H. Barge *Andreas Bodenstein von Karlstadt* (Leipzig 1905) I 168, 394–6, and passim

IG

Willem van ENCKENVOIRT of Mierlo, 22 January 1464–19 July 1534
Willem van Enckenvoirt (Enkevoirt) of Mierlo, in Brabant, belonged to an old family of the lesser nobility and was brought up by an uncle, Zeger van Enckenvoirt, rector of Coudewater. Intended for an ecclesiastical career, Willem was sent to Rome by 1489 or earlier. In 1505 he received a licence in canon and civil law from the Sapienza, the University of Rome. By 1495 he had entered the *familia* of Pope *Alexander VI and begun to climb the ladder of papal appointments. He was notary in the Rota in 1500, scriptor in 1503, protonotary in 1506, and collector for the dioceses of Cambrai, Liège, and Utrecht in 1507. In 1514 he was named count palatine, while from 1509 to 1517 he also served the German institution in Rome, Santa Maria dell'Anima, as provisor. Throughout these years he had been more successful than

most in gathering lucrative benefices; thus at one time or another he was appointed to canonries of Tongeren, Aachen, 's Hertogenbosch, Utrecht, Antwerp, Mechelen, Liège, Xanten, and Maastricht. As a curial lawyer he was able to render useful services to many of these chapters in the same way as he conducted the legal business of the Hapsburg government of the Low Countries.

Enckenvoirt was a personal friend of Girolamo *Aleandro, Matthäus *Schiner, and Adrian of Utrecht. When the latter ascended the papal throne as *Adrian vi, Enckenvoirt's career reached its peak. As datary he controlled appointments to papal offices and benefices. He also succeeded Adrian as bishop of the rich diocese of Tortosa and was made a cardinal shortly before the pope's death. In the sacred college he continued to represent the interests of the Hapsburgs; in particular he played an important role in negotiating the surrender of the temporalities of the princebishopric of Utrecht to *Charles v when Bishop Henry, count *Palatine, resigned the see in 1529. As a reward Enckenvoirt was himself appointed bishop of Utrecht and in 1530 he took possession of the see by procuration of his nephew Michiel van Enckenvoirt. When he returned to Rome in 1532 after a visit to the Netherlands, he took with him Lambert *Coomans, who served him faithfully until his death two years later (Ep 3037).

BIBLIOGRAPHY: Allen Ep 3037 / W.A.J. Munier in DHGE xv 452–4 / G. Brom in NNBW II 435–7 / LThK III 801 / de Vocht CTL II 63–6 and passim / de Vocht Dantiscus 154–5 / Bierlaire Familia 100
PGB

Anton ENGELBRECHT of Engen, d 1558
Anton, the older brother of Philipp *Engelbrecht, registered at the University of Leipzig in 1503 and, evidently already in orders, matriculated at Basel in the spring of 1517. In 1518 he was MA and chaplain at the cathedral of Basel. On 19 March 1518 he dedicated to Helene, countess of Lupffen, his *Andechtige Leer von dem hochwyrdigen Sacrament* (Basel: A. Petri 1518). In May 1520 he visited *Beatus Rhenanus at Sélestat and sent greetings to Erasmus through his brother (Ep 1105). On 6 June 1520 he became a doctor of theology, and four days later he was consecrated bishop in

the cathedral of Basel by Christoph von *Utenheim. Actually he was appointed suffragan bishop of Speyer with the titular see of Thermopylae and received an allowance of two hundred florins for travel to Rome to obtain papal approval. With the office of suffragan he combined that of parish priest of Bruchsal. Soon he leaned towards the Reformation; in the summer of 1524 his bishop, George, count *Palatine, dismissed him from his parish duties and as a result had to deal with the protests of his flock. Engelbrecht himself went to Strasbourg, where he was received into the house of *Capito and in October 1524 appointed to the parish of St Stephen. Until 1531 he continued to correspond with the bishop and chapter of Speyer in the matter of financial provisions; he also threatened to take legal action.

His subsequent years at Strasbourg were marked by his conflict with the city council and Martin *Bucer, whose release from the Dominican order he had helped secure a decade earlier. At a synod of 1533 he joined forces with Johannes *Sapidus and publicly opposed the power of the civic authorities in ecclesiastical matters. Requested to put his views in writing he did so, exhibiting some affinity with the mysticism of certain Anabaptists. On 27 January 1534 the Strasbourg council abolished his position and thus deprived Engelbrecht, who had recently married his housekeeper, of a livelihood.

The remainder of his life is known only incompletely. In 1536 he still was at Strasbourg and opposed the city's accession to the Wittenberg concord. In February 1544 he appeared at the diet of Speyer, accompanying Bucer's opponent, Johann *Gropper, and evidently reconciled with the church of Rome. In 1546 he published anonymously at Cologne an *Abconterfeytung ... Martin Butzers*, to which Bucer replied with his exposition of Psalm 120; neither of the two adversaries minced his words. It seems that Engelbrecht lived in Cologne until about 1549, but his family had remained in Strasbourg, and after Bucer had been exiled he returned and eventually died at Strasbourg.

BIBLIOGRAPHY: Allen Ep 1105 / Werner Bellardi 'Anton Engelbrecht (1485-1558) Helfer, Mitarbeiter und Gegner Bucers' ARG 64 (1973) 183–206 / *Matrikel Leipzig* I 452 / *Matrikel*

Basel I 334 / *Die Protokolle des Speyerer Domkapitels* (Stuttgart 1968–) II 36–7, 122–3, 304–5, 374, 395, and passim

PGB

Philipp ENGELBRECHT of Engen, c 1499–12 September 1528
Philipp Engelbrecht is better known as Engentinus, so called after his birth place, Engen, between Singen and Tuttlingen, north of Lake Constance. In the spring of 1508 he studied at Leipzig and in the autumn he matriculated at Wittenberg as a contemporary of Martin *Luther, graduating MA in 1512. In 1510 he became acquainted with Ulrich von *Hutten, to whose *Ars versificatoria* (Leipzig: W. Stöckel 1511) he contributed some obscure verses; he also met *Spalatinus (Ep 501). On 31 October 1514 he matriculated at Freiburg and there, in part on the recommendation of *Zasius, he was appointed lecturer in poetics, a position which he held from 1516 to his death. Initially, however, in 1515 he was sharing his time between the Basel press of Johann *Froben and substitute teaching at Freiburg. At this time he met Erasmus (Epp 344, 357, 366). He visited Basel again in 1520, when he contributed some distichs to the *Topica* of Claudius *Cantiuncula (Basel: A. Cratander 1520) and produced a defence of Erasmus against Edward *Lee (Ep 1105).
In 1518 he fled from the plague to Constance, the home of Thomas *Blarer, who likewise returned there from Freiburg. At Constance Engelbrecht stayed with Johannes *Fabri and was acquainted with Johann von *Botzheim. In 1521 he went to the diet of Worms and became the object of a humorous pamphlet pointing out that his purchase of a house was incompatible with the poverty befitting a poet. Engelbrecht was evidently not given to conformity and angered his academic colleagues at Freiburg with his manner of dressing. In 1522, when he finally succeeded in having his modest salary raised from forty to sixty florins annually, an admonition was added that he should have his beard trimmed. A more serious matter was that as late as 1521 he dared to defend Luther publicly, and an unpublished letter of 1526 (Basel MS) still shows him critical of Ottmar *Nachtgall and other defenders of the old faith. Having been ailing for years, he

was very sick in September 1528 but had himself carried to Strasbourg, where he underwent surgery and died. The name of his wife was Magdalene Pfister.
Engelbrecht produced editions of Valerius Flaccus and Persius as well as a life of St Lambert, the patron saint of Freiburg, but was mostly respected by his contemporaries for his Latin poems, the best of which is a hymn in praise of Freiburg. For details of his publications see NDB.

BIBLIOGRAPHY: Allen Ep 344 / NDB IV 529–30 / *Matrikel Leipzig* I 484 / *Matrikel Wittenberg* I 28 / *Matrikel Freiburg* I 217 / Schreiber *Universität Freiburg* I 85–91 / R. Wackernagel *Geschichte der Stadt Basel* (Basel 1907–54) III 194–5 / *Udalrici Zasii epistolae* (Ulm 1774) Ep 231 / BRE Ep 149 / *Vadianische Briefsammlung* II Ep 155; III Ep 349 / AK II Epp 531, 535, and passim / Z VII Ep 123 / Öffentliche Bibliothek of the University of Basel MS Fr Gr I 19 fol 46: letter to Jacobus [Bedrotus], Freiburg 16 June [1526]

PGB

ENGENTINUS *See* Philipp ENGELBRECHT

Aumar d'ENGHIEN *See Omaar van* EDINGEN

ENNO II *See Enno* II CIRKSENA, *count of Eastern Friesland*

Alonso ENRIQUEZ d January 1577
Alonso Enríquez (Henriquez) was born to a noble Spanish family and was the nephew of the admiral of Castile, Don Fadrique Enríquez. On 22 May 1523 he received a bachelor's degree in theology at the University of Alcalá. His disputation for the degree was on the topic 'An commune sit intellectui divino, angelico et humano omnia intelligere posse' and was published with a dedication to his uncle (Alcalá: A.G. Brocar 1523). On 31 January 1526 he was admitted to a higher degree of bachelor of theology, also at Alcalá. By that date he was abbot of Valladolid, a title combined with the chancellorship of the university there. As chancellor of the University of Valladolid, he was invited by the inquisitor-general, Alonso *Manrique, to take part in a conference at Valladolid in 1527 to pronounce on the orthodoxy of Erasmus. With the theologians of Alcalá, Enríquez was in the Erasmian camp and

helped overturn the charges brought against the Dutch humanist.

In 1531 Enríquez travelled to Rome to resolve difficulties over his benefices. While in Rome he composed two works, the *De matrimonio Reginae Angliae*, a short treatise attacking the proposed divorce of *Catherine of Aragon by *Henry VIII of England, and the *Defensionum pro Erasmo Roterodamo liber* in support of Erasmus' orthodoxy. This defence had been prompted by the publication by the faculty of theology of Paris of its *Determinatio* against Erasmus, accusing him of heresy and equating him with *Luther. The *De matrimonio Reginae Angliae* and the *Defensionum pro Erasmo Roterodamo liber* were published in the same volume in March 1532 (Naples: J. Sulzbach of Haguenau), along with a dedication to *Charles V and a letter of introduction to Erasmus from the German scholar Johann Albrecht *Widmanstetter (Ep 2614). There is no indication that Erasmus heard of Enríquez or his book. In 1559 the work was placed on the index of prohibited books of Pope *Paul IV.

From 1548 to 1550 Enríquez was involved in a jurisdictional conflict with the rector of the University of Valladolid, which the Roman Rota decided in favour of the rector. In 1554 an anonymous Spanish translator of Heliodorus' *Historia ethiopica* dedicated his work to the abbot of Valladolid. In 1565 the inquisitor of Toledo prosecuted Enríquez and a number of pages from his household, but there is no record of the proceedings. Enríquez died in early January 1577.

BIBLIOGRAPHY: Allen Ep 2614 / Bataillon *Erasmo y España* 243–4, 418–21, and passim

LUIS A. PÉREZ

Gerhard von ENSCHRINGEN documented 1506–49
The noble family of Enschringen (Enschryngen, Enscheringen) is found in various locations in the Rhineland and Luxembourg. Gerhard matriculated at the University of Cologne on 3 October 1506. In February 1507 he was promoted BA at the University of Trier and in the following year MA at Cologne. In 1509 he accompanied Count Hermann von *Neuenahr to Bologna, matriculating there as the count's famulus. After their return he remained in Neuenahr's service, becoming his

confidential secretary and chaplain. In May 1514 he was co-opted into the faculty of arts of the University of Trier and the same year acted as promoter of four candidates who were admitted to the degree of MA. Johann Sturm (1507–89), the famous reformer of the Strasbourg school, who was born at Schleiden, in the Eifel, fondly remembered Enschringen among his teachers, and on 16 December 1529 Neuenahr announced his intention to send Enschringen to the Strasbourg printer Johann *Schott with contributions for the great *Herbarium* then in preparation. After Neuenahr's death Enschringen was in the service of the electors of Trier. A document of 1 July 1532 indicates that he was fiscal officer (*Fiskal*) at Trier and was married to Irmgart von Rolingen. In May 1541 he presided in Trier at the promotion of three new MAS in his capacities as dean of arts and chancellor. Another document of 20 October 1549 shows him still holding an office at Trier.

Neuenahr's Ep 1078 reflects the intimacy between master and secretary in their joint pursuit of scholarship and related interests, while Erasmus' Ep 1082 would seem to indicate that he had met Enschringen in Neuenahr's company; Erasmus calls him Gerardus Episcopus, a name not found anywhere else.

BIBLIOGRAPHY: Allen and CWE Ep 1078 / *Matrikel Köln* I 145*, II 603 / Knod 115–16, 672 / Johann Maximilian Humbracht *Stammtafeln und Wapen* [sic] *der reichsfreien rheinischen Ritterschaft* (Frankfurt 1907) table 19 / Leonhard Keil *Das Promotionsbuch der Artistenfakultät* (Trier 1917; *Trierisches Archiv* Ergänzungsheft 16) 27, 39 / Koblenz, Landeshauptarchiv MS Best. 1C, no 31

HANSGEORG MOLITOR

Juan de ENZINAS (Ep 1108 of June 1520)
In a letter to Erasmus from Paris, Juan Luis *Vives mentions a promising young scholar named Juan de Enzinas (Ep 1108). Allen suggested that Juan might have been Fernando de Enzinas of Valladolid, an author of works of logic published at Paris between 1518 and 1526. Bataillon, however, argued that the humanist Francisco de Enzinas of Burgos, who became a Protestant, might have had a brother named Juan, while Maur Cocheril has

Helius Eobanus Hessus, portrait after Dürer

added that Juan might be identified with Jaime, elder brother of the same Francisco.

BIBLIOGRAPHY: Allen Ep 1108 / Bataillon *Erasmo y España* 101 / Maur Cocheril in DHGE XV 515

TBD

Helius EOBANUS Hessus of Halgehausen, 6 January 1488–4 October 1540
Eobanus Koch (Coccius) was born at Halgehausen, near Frankenberg, the son of a peasant in the service of the Cistercian abbey of Haina, north of Marburg. The father had come from the county of Wittgenstein; his mother was born in Gemünden, on the Wohra. Eobanus adopted his first name Helius on account of being born on a Sunday. He was educated at first by Abbot Dietmar of Haina and subsequently by Johann Mebes in the Latin school of Gemünden, which he attended until 1502. After further schooling at Frankenberg under Jakob Horle he registered at the University of Erfurt for the winter term of 1504. Among his teachers at Erfurt were his countrymen Ludwig Christiani of Frankenberg and Ludwig *Platz of Melsungen. Maternus Pistoris introduced

him to Latin poetry, and *Crotus Rubianus took an affectionate interest in him from the time of his arrival. A feud in 1505 between the artisans of Erfurt and the students offered Eobanus the opportunity of publishing his first poem, *De pugna studentium erphordiensium* (Erfurt: W. Stürmer, 1506; M. von Hase 97). A similar opportunity occurred later in 1505 when Eobanus followed his teachers to Frankenberg to evade an outbreak of plague at Erfurt and composed *De recessu studentium ex Erphordia* (Erfurt: W. Stürmer 1506; M. von Hase 98). Late in September 1506 he graduated BA, acquitting himself very well, and afterwards he published a poem in praise of his university, *De laudibus ... celebratissimi gymnasii litteratorii apud Erphordiam* (Erfurt: W. Stürmer 1507; M. von Hase 100). He also joined Henricus *Urbanus, Hieronymus *Emser, and others in contributing verse to Thomas Wolf's exposition of Psalm 33, edited by *Spalatinus (Erfurt: W. Stürmer 1507; M. von Hase 101). With the help of his countryman, the suffragan Johann Bonemilch of Laasphe, Eobanus was appointed headmaster of the school of St Severus in Erfurt, but he soon gave up this position and was promoted MA early in 1509. In the same year he published his *Bucolicon* (M. von Hase 251) with the foremost Erfurt printer of the time, Johann Knappe, who had also published his *De amantium infoelicitate* (1508, M. von Hase 245) which was accompanied by commendatory verse by Eobanus' friends including Crotus Rubianus and Justus *Jonas. The same Knappe had recently reprinted Erasmus' *Adagia* (M. von Hase 250). By now both *Mutianus Rufus and Ulrich von *Hutten considered Eobanus to be unrivalled among the Latin poets of Germany.

In the autumn of 1509 Eobanus entered the service of Job von Dobeneck, an alumnus of Erfurt who had since become bishop of Pomesania in East Prussia. As Dobeneck's secretary he resided in the episcopal residence of Prabutyl (Riesenburg) and in 1512 attended the wedding of *Sigismund I of Poland and *Bona Sforza at Cracow, celebrating the event in a lively poem. In the same year he met Johannes *Dantiscus who, regardless of his Catholic faith, was to remain a good friend of Eobanus when he later became bishop of Warmia (Ermland).

After his return from Pomesania Eobanus matriculated at Frankfurt an der Oder for the spring term and in Leipzig for the winter term of 1513. At Leipzig young Joachim *Camerarius was deeply impressed by his imposing appearance – he was clad in a red cloak by virtue of his episcopal office – and by his lively mind. In Leipzig he published in 1514 his *Sylvae* (M. Lotter), which had been written during the preceding years in Prussia, and also his best work of poetry, the *Heroides christianae*, which brought him general recognition as Germany's leading Latin poet.

After his return to Erfurt in July 1514 he was soon the centre of a circle of young humanists. His position as their leader was unchallengeable, and even *Reuchlin, the grand old man of German humanism, called him 'the king' in 1515. Jointly with Mutianus, Crotus, and Johannes Petrejus he spoke out in support of Reuchlin and the *bonae literae*; he also lent a hand in the composition of the *Epistolae obscurorum virorum* (Haguenau: H. Gran 1515). He sympathized with the patriotic goals of Hutten, and he enthusiastically adopted Erasmus' program of learning and religious reform. He published his *De vera nobilitate* (Erfurt: M. Maler 1514; M. von Hase 358), and thereafter, with his appointment as professor of poetry in July 1518, he came to occupy a secure and influential position in the university.

At this proud moment he set out by the end of September for a visit to Erasmus in Louvain. Travelling on foot in the company of a young nobleman, Johann *Werter, he called on Mutianus while passing through Gotha on 28 September. On 6 October they reached Frankfurt and were put up for the night by Tilomann Plettner, a friend from student days who had become the tutor of counts Wolfgang and Ludwig Stolberg. Taking a boat down the Rhine, they reached Maastricht on 14 October and Louvain on the 17th. Finding Erasmus recently recovered from illness and very busy, they received a somewhat cool welcome (Ep 870 introduction). On 20 October they started on their journey home, carrying many letters from Erasmus to their friends. Eobanus described this journey in his *Hodoeporicon*, which was being printed on 19 January 1519 (Erfurt: M. Maler; M. von Hase 394) and is dedicated to Justus Jonas, who, inspired by

Eobanus, rode to Louvain the following Easter in the company of Kaspar *Schalbe. In 1520 it was the turn of Johannes *Draconites to pay a visit to Erasmus, who was not very happy with the many callers who were following Eobanus' example. In 1520 Eobanus supported Erasmus in his quarrel with Edward *Lee; his verses against Lee were published in a collection of epigrams gathered by the humanist circle of Erfurt (CWE Ep 1083 introduction), which on this occasion is called 'sodalitas Erasmica.'

At Erfurt Eobanus' lectures on Quintilian attracted a large number of students, and his occasional orations were also received with enthusiasm. His humanistic teaching and his circle of friends set Erfurt apart from other German universities and greatly enhanced its reputation. When *Luther passed through Erfurt on his way to Worms, Eobanus greeted him on 6 April 1521 with a speech on behalf of the university; he also composed his elegies in praise and support of Luther, which he dedicated to Georg Forchheim (Erfurt: M. Maler 1521; M. von Hase 426). In later years Eobanus was saddened to see humanistic studies in Erfurt decline (cf his *De ecclesia afflicta*), and he knew that this decline, in part at least, was caused by the hostile agitation of Protestant preachers. In spite of this he never wavered in his commitment to Luther and to evangelical doctrine. Mutianus was wrong when he wrote Erasmus in 1524 (Ep 1425) that Eobanus was abiding by the old faith. It was Eobanus' *De non contemnendis studiis* (Erfurt 1523, M. von Hase 497) that inspired Luther to write his important appeal *An die Ratherren aller Städte ... dass sie christliche Schulen ... aufrichten sollen* (1524). His faithful adherence to the Lutheran movement did not, however, prevent the continuation of sincere friendship and correspondence between Eobanus and Erasmus (Epp 982, 1498, 2446, 2495).

In 1523 Eobanus took up the study of medicine, hoping to alleviate his increasing financial hardship. While they did not lead to a medical degree, his efforts produced a widely read poem, *Bonae valetudinis conservandae praecepta* (Erfurt: J. Loersfeld 1524; M. von Hase 699). In 1526 he was glad to accept an appointment at Nürnberg. Together with Camerarius he taught until 1533 (Ep 2687) at the Gymnasium of St Aegidius which had recently been founded by *Melanchthon. In 1530 he visited Augsburg at the time of the diet. Soon he longed to be back in Erfurt, especially as the Nürnberg Gymnasium failed to live up to initial expectations. Erasmus' critical comments on the teachers and students of this institution were not entirely unfounded, but they aroused Eobanus' indignation and Erasmus had to placate him (Ep 2446). During the years 1533–6 Eobanus again taught at Erfurt, but the intellectual climate had deteriorated to such a degree that he was glad to accept a position at the University of Marburg in 1536. At Marburg he was elected rector in 1538, and he completed his verse paraphrase of the Psalms (Marburg: C. Egenolff 1537), which was highly praised by Luther and reprinted more than fifty times. He also produced the only complete Latin version of the Iliad ever to be published (Basel: R. Winter 1540). When he died at Marburg he was commemorated as Germany's leading Latin poet, but his influence on later generations was surprisingly modest.

Eobanus' collected works, Operum Helii farragines duae (Schwäbisch-Hall: P. Braubach 1539), were complemented with an edition of his correspondence, undertaken by Johannes Draconites, Epistolae familiares (Marburg: C. Egenolff 1543), and enlarged by Joachim Camerarius (Leipzig 1557, 1561, and 1568). A critical edition of these letters is greatly needed today. Camerarius also published a masterly biography, Narratio de Helio Eobano Hesso (Nürnberg: V. Neuber 1553; new ed by J.T. Kreyssig 1843).

BIBLIOGRAPHY: Allen and CWE Ep 874 / NDB IV 543–5 / ADB XII 316–19 / RGG III 298 / LThK III 913–14 / The fundamental work on Eobanus still is Carl Krause Helius Eobanus Hessus: sein Leben und sein Werk (Gotha 1879, repr 1963) / C. Krause 'Eoban Hessus am Hofe des Bischofs Hiob von Dobeneck' Altpreussische Monatshefte 16 (1879) 141–58 / E. Kleineidam Universitas Studii Erffordensis (Leipzig 1964–80) II 173–268 / H.R. Abe 'Die Erfurter medizinische Fakultät in den Jahren 1392–1524' Beiträge zur Geschichte der Universität Erfurt, 1392–1816 17 (1973–4) 103ff, 122–39, 191–7 / Martin von Hase 'Bibliographie der Erfurter Drucke von 1501–1550' Archiv für Geschichte des Buchwesens 8 (1967) 655–1096

E. KLEINEIDAM

Anselmus EPHORINUS of Freideberg, c 1505–December 1566

Ephorinus was born in Freideberg in Silesia, the son of Christopher. He began his studies at the University of Cracow in 1515, graduating BA in 1522 and MA in 1527. In 1528 he was a temporary lecturer and subsequently became a member of the Collegium Minus, giving a course on St Basil's De poetis legendibus. He was associated with the Erasmian circle of Leonard *Cox and greatly contributed to the success of Cracow's printing industry. He wrote prefaces and verses for various works, publishing some of them himself, among them Erasmus' Epistola consolatoria and Precatio ad Iesum, both in 1528. He also worked as a private teacher, tutoring among others the son of Justus Ludovicus *Decius.

At the beginning of 1531 Ephorinus became the tutor of young Jan *Boner, who was setting out for study abroad in the company of Stanislaw *Aichler. They visited Erfurt and stayed for a while at Nürnberg, making the acquaintance of Helius *Eobanus, Joachim *Camerarius, and Thomas *Venatorius. In April 1531 they arrived in Freiburg and called on Erasmus, Ephorinus carrying an introduction from Eobanus (Ep 2495). They stayed in Erasmus' house for five months, and Ephorinus, to whose initiative the visit was due (Ep 2533), earned his respect and also his gratitude for rendering him some services; for example, in July he went to Strasbourg with a letter from Erasmus to Jakob *Sturm (Ep 2510). At the end of August the trio moved to Basel, where they were well received thanks to Erasmus' recommendations (Epp 2536, 2539). Their host was Johann *Gross, master of the cathedral organ. Among Ephorinus' contacts in Basel, Simon *Grynaeus, Bonifacius *Amerbach, Hieronymus *Froben and, Sigismundus *Gelenius were all to remain his friends. In April 1532 Ephorinus and his charges travelled to Konstanz and Augsburg, where they called on Anton *Fugger, presenting a letter from Erasmus; he also made the acquaintance of Johann *Koler (Ep 2658). In May or June 1532 they reached Venice (Ep 2657) and subsequently settled down in Padua, where Ephorinus began to study medicine receiving his doctorate on 11 April 1534.

For a while Ephorinus' relations with Erasmus continued to be very cordial. He sent Erasmus the latest news, delivered his letters, books, and gifts, and performed other small services (Epp 2554, 2559, 2574, 2606). In 1533, however, their relations became strained, probably because of Ephorinus' failure to forward to Severyn *Boner a copy of the Terence dedicated by Erasmus to his sons. The book had been entrusted to him early in 1532 but did not reach Boner until the spring of 1535 (Ep 3010). In February 1533 Erasmus complained to Amerbach about Ephorinus' behaviour (Ep 2770). For his part Ephorinus begged Amerbach to placate Erasmus (AK IV Ep 1761).

In the summer of 1534 Ephorinus and his two charges moved to Bologna (Ep 2961). In May 1535 they arrived in Rome, from where Ephorinus wrote to Erasmus in August congratulating him on his appointment as provost of Deventer. He also sent him a picture representing the siege of Tunis by the troops of *Charles V (Ep 3038). In November 1535 he set out for Naples but soon returned to Rome, where in April he was ennobled by Charles V. In the spring of 1537 the trio left Rome and returned to Poland by way of Paris, the Netherlands, and Germany. They reached Cracow by the autumn of 1537.

Upon his return, Ephorinus set up a medical practice and was appointed town physician. The king appointed him physician to the salt mines in Wieliczka. In May 1540 he visited Augsburg at the invitation of the Fuggers and from there wrote to Amerbach in quest of Erasmus' collected works for his library (AK V Ep 2399). His medical skills were much appreciated, and in addition he managed to keep up his contacts with many humanists, some of them Protestants. Ephorinus himself remained, however, a faithful Catholic. He married Zofia, (the daughter of the Cracow alderman Andrzej Fogelweder), who bore him five sons and six daughters. He was buried at the Franciscan church of Cracow.

Among other works, Ephorinus edited Sebastian Heyden's *Puerilium colloquiorum formulae* (Cracow: H. Wietor 1527) and compiled a *Medicinale compendium* (Cracow: H. Wietor 1542). Franciszek Mymer celebrated Ephorinus' return to Poland in a poem, *In salvum reditum Anselmi Ephoryni ...* (Cracow: H. Wietor 1538); Gelenius dedicated to him *Arriani et*

Hannonis periplus, Plutarchus de fluminibus et montibus, Strabonis epitome (Basel: H. Froben and N. Episcopius 1533). Verses by Georg von *Logau in honour of Ephorinus may be found in the collection *Pontii Paulii tres psalmi ... Item eiusdem elegiae et epigrammata aliquot* (Wrocław 1541). Books from Ephorinus' library have survived in the Camaldulensian monastery and the Biblioteka Jagiellońska in Cracow.

BIBLIOGRAPHY: Allen Ep 2539 / PSB IV 281–2 / *Korespondencja Erazma z Rotterdamu z Polakami* ed M. Cytowska (Warsaw 1965) / H. Barycz 'Die ersten wissenschaftlichen Verbindungen Polens mit Basel' *Vierteljahresschrift für Geschichte der Wissenschaft und Technik* (Warsaw) 5 (1960) Sonderheft 2, 42–5 / H. Barycz *Polacy na studiach w Rzymie w epoce Odrodzenia* (Cracow 1938) / J. Lachs 'Anselmus Ephorinus' *Archiwum Historii i Filozofii Medycyny* (Poznan) 4 (1926) 40–54, 194–209 / *Silva rerum* (Cracow) 3 (1927) 78–80 / T. Wotschke 'Zum Briefwechsel Melanchthons mit Polen' ARG 6 (1909) 354 / AK IV Ep 1546 and passim

HALINA KOWALSKA

Nicolaus EPISCOPIUS of Rittershoffen, 1501–7 March 1564

Nicolaus Episcopius (Bischoff) was born in Rittershoffen, Lower Alsace. Having apparently arrived from Montdidier, in Bresse, he is first documented in Basel when he registered in the university during the spring term of 1518. In 1520 he became a Basel citizen and belonged to the staff of the Froben press. He travelled to Chur with Hieronymus *Froben, where both obtained MA degrees from the papal legate, Antonio *Pucci. From this moment the two men are frequently mentioned together in contemporary sources. As in the case of Hieronymus, the short duration of Episcopius' academic studies is no reflection on the quality of his education. He corresponded on scholarly topics with Erasmus (Epp 1713, 1714), *Beatus Rhenanus, *Viglius Zuichemus (Ep 3116), and *Vadianus, and discussed an edition of Athenaeus with Joachim *Camerarius on 16 September 1545 and Wolfgangus Musculus on 30 May 1551 (Basel MSS). He also compiled the index to the Froben Livy in 1535.

In 1529 Episcopius married Justina *Froben, the daughter of Johann *Froben in whose house, 'zum Sessel,' the couple was to live henceforward. He became a member of the 'Safran' guild on 16 April 1529 and joined the printing firm as a partner. Thereafter the imprints of their books show his name together with that of Hieronymus Froben; no book is known to have been published by Episcopius alone. In the lifetime of Johann Froben he had travelled to Paris in 1526 (Epp 1713, 1714), and as a partner of Hieronymus Froben he continued to attend to the commercial side of the firm's operations. The *Rechnungsbuch* shows that sales at Basel were mostly his responsibility, and while a considerable volume of printing continued to be carried in the 'Sessel,' he employed rather fewer people than his partner in the house 'zum Luft.' The correspondence of *Beatus Rhenanus shows that as a native Alsatian Episcopius dealt regularly with customers in Alsace and also attended the Strasbourg fair. Freiburg too he visited repeatedly (Ep 2235; AK IV Ep 1767); in 1528 he was in Dole and in 1534 he attended the Lyon fair (Epp 2012, 2930). Episcopius, who had his coat of arms confirmed by the emperor on 27 November 1537, also held a number of civic offices; he was a member of the new matrimonial court in 1542 and in 1555 belonged to the executive of the 'Safran' guild.

Erasmus soon came to like Episcopius (Epp 1713, 1714), and their warm relations never seem to have suffered any setbacks. Episcopius visited Erasmus shortly before his death when hardly anyone was being admitted (Allen I 54). He composed an epitaph for Erasmus (LB I introductory material), and, like Hieronymus Froben, he was executor of Erasmus' will, in which he was left a gift (Allen XI 364). He died of consumption, as is learnt from the inscription of the funeral monument in St Peter's.

BIBLIOGRAPHY: Allen Ep 1714 / AK II Ep 793 and passim / BRE Ep 58, 174, and passim / *Rechnungsbuch der Froben und Episcopius ... 1557–1564* ed R. Wackernagel (Basel 1881) 82–7 and passim / ADB VI 155 / Grimm *Buchführer* 1377 / R. Wackernagel *Geschichte der Stadt Basel* (Basel 1907–54) III 440, 448, 94* / W.R. Staehelin *Basler Adels- und Wappenbriefe* [Zürich 1917–18] 20–1 / J. Tonjola *Basilea sepulta* (Basel 1661) 120 / *Vadianische Briefsammlung* VI Ep 1261, VII Ep 68
PGB

Gerardus EPISCOPUS *See Gerhard von EN-SCHRINGEN*

Heinrich EPPENDORF of Eppendorf, 1496– after 1551(?)
Apart from the years of his controversy with Erasmus, we are inadequately informed about the life of Heinrich Eppendorf (Eppendorpius, Planodorpius, 'Thraso'). He was born in Eppendorf, near Freiburg in Saxony, the son of Nikolaus Eppendorf, who was town judge and also held the hereditary office of reeve (*Erbschulze*); he was, moreover, in business as a brewer. These details about Heinrich's origin are the result of modern research (Kaegi 469–70); Eppendorf himself always claimed to be a nobleman, and contemporaries such as *Hutten (*Opera* II 185) and Otto *Brunfels (Ep 1406) actually gave him the title of knight. Erasmus too did not at first question his noble descent but after their friendship had ended he depicted Eppendorf's claim as deliberate deception (ASD I-3 612–19; Ep 1934).

After attending the Latin school of Freiburg Eppendorf matriculated in 1506 at Leipzig, where he was able to secure the patronage of Duke George of *Saxony. When he travelled to Louvain in the summer of 1520 he carried an unworked nugget of silver as a gift from the duke to Erasmus (Epp 1122, 1125). Around this time he may also have made the acquaintance of Hutten who had visited Erasmus a month earlier and later referred to Eppendorf as a common friend when addressing his *Expostulatio* to Erasmus (*Opera* II 185). A scholarship provided by Duke George (Ep 1437) permitted Eppendorf to continue his studies, and in September 1520 he matriculated at Freiburg im Breisgau; however in April or May 1522 he was forced to leave Freiburg because of his debts (cf minutes of the university council, 13 May 1522, quoted by Kaegi 471). He moved on to Basel, where he lived in close contact with Erasmus (Ep 1437), who had arrived six months earlier and was glad to avail himself of Eppendorf's services (Ep 1283). In September 1522 he accompanied Erasmus and *Beatus Rhenanus on a visit to Johann von *Botzheim in Constance (Ep 1342). It is an indication of the great confidence Erasmus placed in him that when Hutten arrived in Basel in November 1522,

Eppendorf was asked to inform him of Erasmus' desire to avoid a personal meeting (Ep 1356). Erasmus' subsequent indignation about Eppendorf's 'treachery' was commensurate with the initial trust.

In the ensuing conflict between Erasmus and Hutten Eppendorf played an important role for which Erasmus himself is our only source of information. First in Epp 1376 and 1383 to *Pirckheimer and subsequently in the *Spongia* (LB X 1631-3, 1637) – although Eppendorf's name is not mentioned in the latter – Erasmus accused him of having brought about the breach with Hutten by failing to inform Erasmus about Hutten's mood and by spurring Hutten to attack Erasmus in his *Expostulatio*. In Ep 1383 he also offered a first analysis of Eppendorf's motives, which he restated later in Ep 1437 (to *Goclenius) in a more detailed fashion, giving a highly critical assessment of his character which contrasts sharply with the praise bestowed on him in some earlier letters (Epp 1122, 1125, 1283, 1342). The grave accusation was that Eppendorf had persuaded Hutten to write his *Expostulatio* so as to blackmail Erasmus and his friends in Basel, who, to prevent the publication of Hutten's tract, would have to give Eppendorf the money to settle his debts. When they refused to be blackmailed Eppendorf allegedly caused the *Expostulatio* to be printed at Strasbourg. Four years later Erasmus had reason to repeat this account in Ep 1934 to Botzheim, indicating the precise amount allegedly demanded by Eppendorf and also suggesting that as early as 1522 Eppendorf might have purloined a gift of money entrusted to him by Duke George for remittance to Erasmus (cf Ep 1325).

In view of Erasmus' detailed indications there is little doubt that Eppendorf had contributed decisively to the rift between Erasmus and Hutten. His motives, however, were probably reported by Erasmus in a distorted fashion, for Eppendorf's admiration for Erasmus appears to have waned even before Hutten arrived in Basel. In March 1522 he obtained from Bonifacius *Amerbach a copy of Erasmus' *Epistolae ad diversos* and began to add marginal comments, some of which are clearly critical of Erasmus. Even though he quotes one such note referring to the *Spongia*,

Allen suggested that for the most part they were written in 1522 and 1523 (Allen IV 615-19).

Erasmus kept returning to Eppendorf in his letters, sometimes without mentioning his name (Epp 1804, 1893), and sometime – in the end almost exclusively – twisting his name in derogatory fashion: 'Thraso Planodorpius,' an allusion to Terence's *Eunuchus*, is first found in Ep 1496; 'Ornithoplutus ab Isocomo' appears in the *Adagia* of 1528 (I ix 44; cf Allen Ep 1168:19n) and at the same time in Ep 2129. The reason for these insults was that Eppendorf had moved to Strasbourg and was held responsible by Erasmus for a number of attacks, some of them quite virulent, that followed the publication of his *Spongia* and originated for the most part from Strasbourg (Epp 1459, 1466, 1485, 1496, 1543, 1804, 1901). Among those whom Erasmus informed of his suspicions against Eppendorf was Duke George of Saxony; Erasmus' letter is lost, but in his reply the duke stated that Eppendorf was not welcome to return to Saxony (Ep 1448). When Eppendorf managed to obtain a copy of Erasmus' letter to the duke, another violent quarrel developed, of which Erasmus gave a detailed account in Ep 1934.

At the beginning of 1528 Eppendorf returned to Basel and lodged a complaint with the city council. He argued that Erasmus' actions had caused him to lose the duke's favour and, as a result, to suffer considerable financial losses (Epp 1933, 1937). A meeting was arranged at Erasmus' house, in the course of which Erasmus refused to admit that he had written the letter to Duke George (Epp 1934, 1992; LB X 1685), but under pressure from his friends *Beatus Rhenanus and Amerbach he accepted an agreement with Eppendorf. It was signed on 3 February 1528 (LB X 1685-6; Epp 1937, 1941) and stipulated that Erasmus was to retract his charges made before the duke, to pay Eppendorf an indemnity, and to exonerate him publicly by dedicating a book to him. Eppendorf in turn promised to refrain from any publication critical of Erasmus.

This settlement brought only temporary respite, however (Ep 1943). On the day following the settlement Erasmus wrote to Duke George (Ep 1940), as he had agreed to do, but the letter merely caused the duke to convey to Eppendorf through his brother another stern admonition, lest his 'quarrelsome behaviour' disrupt Erasmus' 'Christian and wholesome work' (Saxius 56-7). On his part Eppendorf made additional demands (Ep 1950), while Erasmus noted with irritation that Eppendorf spread the news of his 'victory' all over Germany (Epp 1991, 1997). Despite repeated requests (Ep 2099) Erasmus refused to proceed with the promised dedication. When writing to Eppendorf (Ep 2086), he excused himself by claiming overwork, but in Ep 1992 to Pirckheimer he stated the true reasons for his refusal and also gave another detailed account of the entire conflict. Instead of the promised dedication he published the dialogue Ἱππεὺς ἄνιππος ('The Ignoble Knight') (ASD I-3 612-19) in a new edition of his Colloquia (Basel: H. Froben March 1529). It contained passages which agreed almost literally with his description of Eppendorf's knightly deportment in Ep 1934 (cf Ep 2216) and in general was bound to be recognized as a satirical portrait of him by anyone familiar with the events. Eppendorf reacted by trying once again to bring pressure to bear on Erasmus. He went to Augsburg and presented his case to Duke George, who was attending the diet (Ep 2333). Erasmus had several friends inform him on the developments at Augsburg (Epp 2344, 2384, 2392), and in Epp 2400 and 2406 he gave his version of Eppendorf's unsuccessful attempts to regain the confidence of his prince. Two developments caused a further reaction on the part of Erasmus; Duke George had asked Julius *Pflug to deal with Eppendorf's complaints and Erasmus feared that Pflug would be swayed by his 'lies' (Epp 2400, 2406; cf Ep 2395), and secondly Eppendorf had once again called upon Erasmus at Freiburg on his way back from Augsburg (BRE Ep 275). So, towards the end of 1530, Erasmus finally published at Freiburg (n pr) his Adversus mendacium et obtrectationem admonitio (LB X 1683-92), which he may first have allowed to circulate in manuscript (Ep 2437). A few weeks later Eppendorf replied with his Iusta querela (Haguenau: J. Setzer February 1531; reprinted in Hutten Opera II 447-54, cf BRE Ep 275). Once again he traced the quarrel back to its origins in the conflict between Erasmus and Hutten and, in doing so,

presented another defence of Hutten. This was to be the end of the public controversy since Pflug's efforts finally brought about a truce by which both protagonists agreed henceforward to keep silent (Epp 2450, 2451).

Even if due allowance is made for Erasmus' usual sensitivity to criticism, it is difficult to understand why year after year he was prepared to pit his international reputation against a man who enjoyed at best very minor status in the literary world, especially since in these same years he was involved in other controversies of a far more serious nature. In fact he went so far as to compare his quarrel with Eppendorf with the conflict between George of Saxony and Luther (Ep 2211). Some contemporaries showed their surprise at his violent reactions to such an inferior opponent (Epp 2120, 2124). Werner Kaegi was probably right when he suggested that the strength of Erasmus' reaction was an indication that Hutten's charges in the Expostulatio had struck Erasmus a more substantial blow than he was prepared to admit; in consequence he endeavoured to saddle a third party with the moral responsibility for the outbreak of the conflict with Hutten (Kaegi 474). In doing so, he helped ensure the success of Eppendorf's efforts to win fame for himself by challenging one who was already famous (Ep 2406). The fame thus won, however, was of dubious value, since in view of Erasmus' unfavourable assessments of Eppendorf's character it was easily overlooked that some other contemporaries actually had a better opinion of him. Even after his breach with Erasmus Beatus Rhenanus continued to correspond with him (BRE Epp 275, 295), and his relations with Paul *Volz also remained friendly (BRE Epp 343, 348). He subsequently achieved some recognition as an author.

After Eppendorf had settled in Strasbourg by the middle of the 1520s, he began to publish a number of German translations with local publishing houses, such as Plutarch's Apophthegmata (Kurtzweise und höffliche Sprüch) in 1534. These were followed in 1536 by a popular compilation of Roman history from Romulus to the present (Römischer Historien Bekürtzung Strasbourg: J. Schott) which was based on material gleaned from Latin and contemporary Italian historians. In the same vein he published in 1540 (J. Schott) an account of the Turkish wars (*Türckischer Kayser Ankunfft, Kryeg und Handlung gegen und wider die Christen*). His translation of Pliny's *Historia naturalis* (Strasbourg: J. Schott; cf BRE Ep 295) appeared in 1543, and in 1545–6 he produced a German translation of Albert Krantz's Latin chronicle of Sweden and Denmark (J. Schott). Their popular subjects and uncomplicated style ensured that Eppendorf's works enjoyed a relatively large circulation in Germany and thus assisted elements of humanistic education in penetrating broad segments of the population. Eppendorf was an important source for the chronicles and epigrams of Hans Sachs. No information has come to light on the last years of Eppendorf's life and his death. In view of a partial reprint of his writings at Strasbourg in 1551 it is generally assumed that he died there soon afterwards.

BIBLIOGRAPHY: Allen and CWE Ep 1122 / ADB VI 158 / NDB IV 548–9 / Christopherus Saxius *De Henrico Eppendorpio commentarius* (Leipzig 1745) / Otto Clemen 'Kleine Beiträge zur sächsischen Gelehrtengeschichte' *Neues Archiv für Sächsische Geschichte und Altertumskunde* 23 (1902) 137–44, esp 141–2 / Werner Kaegi 'Hutten und Erasmus: Ihre Freundschaft und ihr Streit' *Historische Vierteljahrschrift* 22 (1924–5) 200–78, 461–514, on Eppendorf especially 469–79

BARBARA KÖNNEKER

ERASMUS' family
Current knowledge of Erasmus' parents is largely derived from the *Compendium vitae* (Allen I 47–52; CWE 4 399–410), and any reservations the reader may have in accepting the basic correctness of the *Compendium vitae* will also apply to the following account.

The name of Erasmus' father was Gerard; he was the second youngest son of a couple named Elias and Catherine living, it seems, near Gouda. Gerard had no fewer than nine or ten brothers, among them Theobald, mentioned in Ep 76. Erasmus' mother, Margareta, was the daughter of a physician of Zevenbergen, near Breda, named Pieter. She had at least two brothers whom Erasmus met at Dordrecht, perhaps in 1498 (Ep 76), when they were very old. Seeing that in the address of a papal brief (Ep 518) Erasmus' name is given as 'Erasmus

Rogerii Roterodamensis' it has been suggested that his father's full name was Rogerius Gerardus (Allen I 577–8), but J.J. Mangan (*Life ... of Desiderius Erasmus*, New York 1926, II 63) could be right in suggesting that Rogerius would rather be the family name of Margareta. On the other hand, K.-E. Schulze (in *Gens nostra* 14, 1959, 287–90) suggests that her family name may have been Boeckel.

Margareta was a widow (Ep 187A; Allen III xxix–xxx) when she joined Gerard, whose age was similar to her own. A local tradition in Gouda recorded by 1582 held that by the time of Erasmus' birth the father was a priest and the mother his housekeeper (Allen I 47:1n). While some modern scholars have accepted this tradition it is not supported by Pope *Leo x's brief to Andrea *Ammonio (Ep 517), which is, however, quite specific in referring to a degree of kinship between Erasmus' parents that lay within the canonical prohibitions. However that may be, the *Compendium vitae* states that the family had intended Gerard for the church and that this was the reason why he found himself 'debarred by general consent from matrimony' and made his way to Rome. There he earned his living as a scribe and turned his mind to the study of Latin, Greek, and the law, and even 'heard Guarino lecture' (conceivably a son of Guarino *Guarini, teaching at Ferrara). Not until he had received false news of Margareta's death did he become a priest, according to the *Compendium vitae*. On his return home he discovered that she was alive and had borne him a son. She resolved to remain single and Gerard resolved never to 'touch her' again; he did, however, provide for the boy's education. Brought up at first by his grandmother, the child was then sent to the school of Pieter *Winckel at Gouda and subsequently to St Lebuin's school at Deventer. Margareta accompanied her son to Deventer and there was carried off by a plague epidemic in 1483. Gerard died shortly afterwards; neither was much over forty.

So far this account has not mentioned Erasmus' brother, Pieter Gerard, who was the elder of the two boys by three years (Ep 1436). The *Compendium vitae* ignores his existence except for the veiled reference to 'a companion, who betrayed his friend.' It seems that Pieter did not sufficiently support Erasmus, who wished to go to university and attempted to resist pressure for the boys to enter a monastery (Ep 447). When Erasmus joined the canons regular of St Augustine at Steyn, Pieter had already entered another house of that congregation at Sion, near Delft. Initially there are no indications that Erasmus bore his brother a grudge, his only extant letter to Pieter from about 1487 (Ep 3) is affectionate and cordial. In 1498 he still seemed to refer to his brother with genuine warmth (Epp 78, 81). Only as he grew older did his accounts of Pieter's 'betrayal' present the brother unsparingly as a tippler, wencher, and squanderer of money (Epp 447, 1436). Pieter's death, which must have occurred some time before November 1527, left Erasmus unmoved (Ep 1900). Others have judged Pieter more favourably. In his *Sylva odarum* (Paris: G. Marchand 1496) Willem *Hermans dedicated ode 17 to his friend, 'the most courteous and learned ... Pieter Gerard' (Allen I 160, 577). Pieter Opmeer of Amsterdam echoes Hermans in his *Opus chronographicum* (Antwerp: H. Verdussen 1611, I 454), saying that Pieter was a most courteous man and not a bad poet according to the canons of Gravezande (in South Holland), among whom he had lived honourably and where he was buried (Allen III xxiii).

Since all Erasmus' uncles had married, his family must have been numerous, even without considering his mother's kin. One unidentified kinsman visited Johann *Froben at Basel in April 1515 and by his looks reminded everyone of the absent Erasmus (Ep 330). Six years later Erasmus reluctantly recommended a relative in Ep 1192. P.S. Allen has drawn attention to one Gerard Gregorisz, who worked at one time as a painter in Tournus (between Dijon and Lyon), where a surviving contract of his is dated 21 April 1522. By 1581 he is referred to as 'maistre Guerard Gregoire Hollandois, compatriots et parent d'Erasme de Rotterdam' (Allen Ep 1192:1n).

BIBLIOGRAPHY: Allen I 575–81 / CWE Epp 3, 187A, 447, 517 introductions, 4 400–3, all quoting further literature

C.G. VAN LEIJENHORST & PGB

ERASMUS, abbot of Mogila *See Erazm CIOŁEK*

ERASMUS (Epp 714, 727 of November–December 1517)
Erasmus, a doctor of law apparently connected with the Burgundian court, has not been identified.

Melchior ERGESHEIMER of Sélestat, after 1460–after 1535
Melchior Ergesheimer was born to a wealthy tanner's family in Sélestat; his father was a member of the Sélestat *Magistrat*. With his older brother, Martin, he attended the Sélestat grammar school, where his schoolmates included Jakob *Wimpfeling, Jodocus Gallus, and Peter Schott. Martin became a scholar, took holy orders, and was rector of St George's at Sélestat. He later helped his younger brother to maintain the ancient independence of the city.

Melchior apparently did not continue his education after grammar school; by 1492 he had taken over his father's business. He became the chief officer of the tanner's guild in 1503, and was elected burgomaster of the city in 1500 and several years later provost, which meant that he presided over the magisterial court and pronounced the sentences. His position at the heart of the city government meant that he was able to influence the direction the city took at the time of the Reformation. A loyal Catholic, he kept his fellow-magistrates firm in the old faith, while his brother, Martin, exercised similar influence within the ecclesiastical community. Their stand attracted the hatred and scorn of the Lutherans. In 1523 the two brothers were publicly insulted and there was an outbreak of iconoclasm. A protagonist of the reform, *Schütz von Traubach, used forged documents to implicate Melchior in an attempt to turn Sélestat over to the Austrian Hapsburgs. Melchior was proved innocent and in 1524 re-elected burgomaster and provost, having resigned these posts during the dispute. Having restored order to the city, Melchior retired to live out the rest of his life in seclusion. His brother died in 1535, leaving Melchior a considerable fortune as well as his humanist library. The date of Melchior's death is unknown.

Erasmus praised Ergesheimer in the *Epistola ad fratres Inferioris Germaniae* (LB X 1614).

BIBLIOGRAPHY: Paul Adam 'Une famille bour-
geoise à Sélestat aux xve et xvie siècles' in *La
Bourgeoisie alsacienne* (Strasbourg 1967) 197–202
/ BRE Ep 134

MIRIAM U. CHRISMAN

Gotskalk ERIKSEN d 28 September 1544

Gotskalk Eriksen was born in Schleswig, the
son of Erik Clausen Rosenkrantz; later he also
styled himself Saxo Carolus or Sassenkerl. He
probably matriculated on 9 November 1507 at
the University of Cologne; by 1513 he was a MA
and secretary to King *Christian ii of Denmark.
From 1520 to 1523 he was a member of the
Danish council of the realm (*Rigsraad*). After a
pilgrimage to Santiago de Compostela (1524–
5), he shared his royal master's exile in the
Netherlands, becoming his chancellor. Unlike
the king, he was a convinced Catholic and
worked to bring about Christian's eventual
break with the Lutherans. At the request of
*Margaret of Austria he also served as a tutor to
Christian's children, apparently reading Erasmus' *Apophthegmata* with Prince *John of
Denmark (Ep 2570). After the attempted return
of Christian ii ended in his captivity, Eriksen
entered the service of *Charles v in 1532. The
following year he accompanied the imperial
court to Spain but returned subsequently on
diplomatic missions to Bavaria (1533) and
Northern Germany (1535). In 1539 he was
again in Germany, raising mercenaries for the
emperor. He died after a fall from his horse at
Valenciennes. Eriksen was closely connected
with a number of leading humanists such as
Janus Secundus and Erasmus' friends Frans
van *Cranevelt, Jan van *Fevijn, Johannes
*Dantiscus, and Cornelis de *Schepper.

BIBLIOGRAPHY: Allen Ep 2570 / *Dansk Biografisk Leksikon* (Copenhagen 1933–44) xx 68–9 /
Danmarks Adels Aarbog 27 (Copenhagen 1910)
442 / *Matrikel Köln* ii 618 / de Vocht *Literae ad
Craneveldium* Ep 67 and passim / de Vocht CTL ii
446, iii 283, and passim / de Vocht *Dantiscus* 15
and passim / A. Heise 'Mester Godskalk
Eriksen Rosenkrantz' *Personalhistorisk Tids-
skrift* 2nd series 6 (1891) 189–227

MARTIN SCHWARZ LAUSTEN

ERNST, Herzog von Bayern *See Ernest, duke of
BAVARIA*

Balthasar ESCHENFELDER *See Christoph
ESCHENFELDER*

Christoph ESCHENFELDER documented at
Boppard, 1518–46

Little is known about Erasmus' keen admirer
Christoph Eschenfelder (Eschenveldius,
Cinicampianus). As customs officer at Boppard in September 1518 he cleared a boat
descending the Rhine and entering the ecclesiastical principality of Trier. Erasmus, who was
a passenger on that boat, afterwards gave a
delightful and widely read account of Eschenfelder's overjoyed reaction to his appearance
(Ep 867) and also wrote directly to Eschenfelder (Ep 879). In 1532 Eschenfelder still held his
position as a customs official and was also a lay
judge (*Schöffe*) of the secular court at Boppard.
From 1541 to 1546 he was *Brückenmeister* in
charge of the bridge across the Rhine at
Koblenz. Erasmus remembered him faithfully
and so did his travelling friends (Ep 2071); they
also corresponded, and while some letters are
missing at least two of Eschenfelder's have
survived (Epp 2714, 3003; cf Ep 2984). In 1534
Erasmus sent Konrad *Nyder to Eschenfelder,
and the reception he received shows that the
customs official's enthusiasm for Erasmus was
as lively as ever. In January 1536 Erasmus
dedicated to him *De puritate tabernaculi*, an
exposition of Psalm 14 (Epp 3081, 3086; LB v
291–312).

In his letter of September 1532 (Ep 2714)
Eschenfelder sent greetings from his wife,
whose name we do not know. He also
answered an inquiry from Erasmus about his
two younger sons, Balthasar and Gabriel,
mentioning that Gabriel was of frail health and
intended for the church. Gabriel had actually
matriculated at the University of Heidelberg on
17 July 1526, apparently as a candidate for a
benefice requiring its holder to complete two
years of university studies. He did in fact
receive his BA on 7 July 1528.

BIBLIOGRAPHY: Allen Ep 879 / BRE Ep 319 /
Matrikel Heidelberg i 541 / A. Stollenwerk
'Christoph Eschenfelder' in *Kurzbiographien
von Mittelrhein und Moselland* (Landeskund-
liche Vierteljahrblätter, Sonderheft 1972) 325

HANSGEORG MOLITOR & PGB

Alfonso (1) d'Este and Laura Dianti(?), allegory by a follower of Titian

Gabriel ESCHENFELDER *See Christoph* ESCHENFELDER

Laurence ESINGER *See Lorenz* EFFINGER

Jan van den ESSCHEN d 1 July 1523
Jan van den Esschen was an Austin friar who had been imprisoned at Vilvoorde, near Brussels, from July 1522 and charged with Lutheranism. He was executed at Brussels on 1 July 1523 together with Hendrik *Vos, another Austin friar. Their opponents included the inquisitor Frans van der *Hulst and the Louvain theologians Jacob of *Hoogstraten and Nicolaas *Baechem Egmondanus. The execution came to the attention of *Botzheim (Ep 1382), *Zwingli, and Erasmus, who recalled it as late as 1529 (Epp 1384, 2188).
BIBLIOGRAPHY: Allen Ep 1384 / Paul Fredericq *Corpus documentorum inquisitionis haereticae pravitatis neerlandicae* (Ghent 1889–1902) IV 140–8 / *Bibliotheca reformatoria neerlandica* ed S. Cramer and F. Pijper (The Hague 1903–   ) VIII 1–114 (several contemporary accounts ed by F. Pijper) / de Vocht CTL I 425, 463
MARCEL A. NAUWELAERTS

Henry, earl of ESSEX *See Henry* BOURCHIER

Alfonso I d'ESTE duke of Ferrara, 21 July 1476–31 October 1534
Alfonso I d'Este was born at Ferrara to Ercole I, duke of Ferrara, Modena, and Reggio, and Eleanora of Aragon, granddaughter of King Alfonso I of Naples. His brothers and sisters were cardinal Ippolito d'*Este, Isabella, marquise of Mantua, Beatrice, duchess of Milan, Sigismundo, Giulio, and Ferrante. Alfonso was married at least twice: in 1491 to Anna Sforza (d 1497), the daughter of Duke Galeazzo Maria of Milan, and in 1502 to Lucrezia Borgia (d 1519), the daughter of Pope *Alexander VI. Lucrezia bore Alfonso four children: Ercole II d'*Este, later duke of Ferrara, Ippolito, later cardinal, Leonora, and Francesco. In his last years Alfonso may also have married his mistress, Laura Dianti, by whom he had an illegitimate son named Alfonsino.
When Ercole I died on 25 January 1505 Alfonso was proclaimed duke of Ferrara. In 1506 a conspiracy on the part of his brothers Ferrante and Giulio was uncovered, and Alfonso sentenced both to life imprisonment. The balance of his reign was a constant struggle to maintain his dominions against his papal overlords, *Julius II, *Leo X, and *Clement VII. Alfonso's fortunes appeared to reach a low ebb in the summer of 1529, when Pope Clement and the Emperor *Charles V agreed that he should forfeit his territories, and when King *Francis I of France, his only ally, signed the peace of Cambrai with Charles. However, through a series of diplomatic manoeuvres Alfonso won the sympathy of Charles and persuaded him to arbitrate his disputes with Clement. On 21 December 1530, to the disgust of Clement, Charles confirmed Alfonso in his possessions, in return for a payment of one hundred thousand scudi to the papal treasury and an annual tribute of seven thousand ducats.
On 2 May 1531 the Antwerp banker Erasmus *Schets informed Erasmus of the emperor's terms for the settlement between Clement VII and Alfonso (Ep 2491). Only a month earlier, on 10 April, Christoph von *Stadion, bishop of Augsburg, reported rumours that Clement and Alfonso were preparing for war against one another (Ep 2480).

Alfonso employed as his secretary Bonaventura *Pistofilo (Ep 1552). He was a patron of the poet Ludovico *Ariosto and of the painter Titian. His portrait, by Titian, hangs in the Pitti gallery in Florence.

BIBLIOGRAPHY: DBI II 332–7 / EI II 409–10 / Pastor VI–X passim

TBD

Ercole II d'ESTE duke of Ferrara, 4 April 1508–5 October 1559

Ercole II d'Este was born at Ferrara to Duke Alfonso I d'*Este and Lucrezia Borgia, the daughter of Pope *Alexander VI. On 28 January 1528, to seal an alliance between his father and King *Francis I of France, he married Renée of France, the daughter of *Louis XII. He succeeded Alfonso as duke of Ferrara on 31 October 1534. After the conflicts of his father with the papacy, Ercole's reign was a period of reconciliation culminating in the visit of Pope *Paul III to Ferrara in 1543. Meanwhile, in the 1530s and 1540s Ercole steered a middle course between France and the Emperor *Charles V. In the 1550s, however, Ercole, under pressure from his brother Cardinal Ippolito and his son Alfonso, increasingly favoured France. In 1556 he joined Pope *Paul IV and *Henry II of France in an alliance against Philip II of Spain and was named commander of the allied forces in Italy. The war went badly for the allies, and one by one they made peace: Paul IV in September 1557, Ercole on 18 May 1558, and Henry at Cateau-Cambrésis in April 1559. Ercole died a few months later.

Ercole had five children by Renée of France: Alfonso, duke of Ferrara, Luigi, bishop of Ferrara and cardinal, Anna, duchess of Guise, Lucrezia, duchess of Urbino, and Leonora. Renée's adherence to the teachings of John Calvin for a time turned Ferrara into a haven for French and Italian Protestants and caused Ercole considerable difficulty. In 1554, at his request, Henry II of France sent his chief inquisitor, Mathieu Ory, to attempt to convert Renée. After a brief imprisonment she recanted and was allowed to return to court, her influence greatly diminished.

There are only passing references to Ercole in the correspondence of Erasmus. On 17 November 1535 (Ep 3071) the Dutch legal scholar *Viglius Zuichemus informed Erasmus

of a report that the dukes of Mantua, Savoy, and Ferrara would meet Charles V at Naples. On 3 April 1536 Johannes *Sinapius sent Erasmus greetings from a number of friends at Ferrara, including the French nobleman Antoine de *Pons, whom he described as the leading figure at the court of the duke (Ep 3113).

BIBLIOGRAPHY: EI XIV 195–6 / Pastor XIII–XIV passim

TBD

Ippolito (I) d'ESTE 20 November 1479– 2 September 1520

Ippolito (I) d'Este was born at Ferrara, the third child of Duke Ercole I of Ferrara and Eleonora of Aragon, the granddaughter of Alfonso I of Aragon. From childhood he was destined for an ecclesiastical career, while his brother, Alfonso I d'*Este, was to rule the duchy. At the age of five he became commendatory abbot of Canalnovo. When he was seven Beatrice of Aragon, the wife of *Matthias Corvinus, king of Hungary, had him nominated archbishop of Estergom and primate of Hungary. Between the ages of seven and fourteen he resided in Hungary. On 20 September 1492 Pope *Alexander VI made him a cardinal. He later obtained the administration of the sees of Milan, Ferrara, Modena, Narbonne, and Capua, abbacies at Ferrara and Brescia, and many minor benefices. In 1497, because of his long absences from Hungary, he resigned the primacy for the diocese of Agram, also in Hungary.

In 1506 Cardinal Ippolito instigated an attack on his half-brother Giulio, which resulted in the loss of one of the latter's eyes. In revenge, Giulio and Ferrante, another brother, conspired to overthrow Duke Alfonso I, over whom Ippolito enjoyed great influence. The cardinal uncovered the plot, and Giulio and Ferrante were imprisoned for life.

In 1509 Cardinal Ippolito took an active role in the war against Venice and was instrumental in winning the naval battle of Polesella. In 1512 he signed the declaration calling for the council of Pisa, encouraged by *Louis XII of France to depose *Julius II, but he did not attend its sessions and was later reconciled with Julius. He travelled to Hungary in 1517 but died of stomach disorders on his return to Ferrara. He

Nicolaas Everaerts by Janus Secundus

left two illegitimate children, Ippolito and Elisabetta.

In February 1522 the astronomer Jakob *Ziegler mentioned that Cardinal Ippolito had encouraged *Leo x to invite him to Rome (Ep 1260).

Cardinal Ippolito, educated by the humanist Sebastiano da Lugo, became a patron of the poet Ludovico *Ariosto and received from him the dedication to the *Orlando furioso*.

BIBLIOGRAPHY: Allen Ep 1260 / EI XIV 397–8 / Pastor v 170 and passim / Sanudo *Diarii* I 49 and passim

TBD

Johannes EUTYCHIUS *See Johann* HUTTICH

EVANGELISTA (Ep 57 of 1497)
Evangelista, the addressee of Ep 57, has not been identified.

EVANGELISTA (Ep 864) *See Evangelista* TARASCONIO

Nicolaas EVERAERTS of Grijpskerke, 1461/2–9 August 1532
Born at Grijpskerke, near Middelburg on the island of Walcheren, Everaerts (Everts, Everardi) studied from 1479 at Louvain, where he was made doctor of both laws on 11 June 1493. He taught civil law at Louvain until 1496, when he became the official in Brussels of Erasmus' first patron, Hendrik van *Bergen, bishop of Cambrai. After Hendrik's death in 1502 he returned to the university and was rector in 1504. After a brief stint with the newly reconstituted grand council of Mechelen, he went to The Hague and served as a member and from 1509 as president of the council of Holland until he was named president of the grand council in succession to Joost *Lauwereyns and returned to Mechelen in 1528. Everaert's career both as a jurist and as an official of the Hapsburg government would amply repay study, but the only printed sources available are his own legal works, of which the posthumously published *Consilia* (Louvain 1554) are the most interesting. Henry de Vocht emphasizes the careful humanistic education Everaerts accorded to his five surviving sons and the significance of his mansion in Mechelen as a centre for a literary and artistic circle which included his sons, Frans van *Cranevelt, Maximilianus *Transsilvanus, and, on their visits to Mechelen, Cornelis de *Schepper and Johannes *Dantiscus.

The beginnings of Everaerts' acquaintance with Erasmus are not documented. Perhaps they met when Erasmus, on vacation from Paris, visited Bishop Hendrik briefly in 1498 and 1501. At any rate they shared a number of common friends and were together in Louvain during 1502 and 1503.

Maarten van *Dorp wrote from The Hague that he himself enjoyed the favour of Everaerts and certain other members of the council of Holland because he was now counted among Erasmus' partisans (Ep 1044). Some months later Erasmus sent Everaerts a copy of *Metsys' portrait medallion, together with his defences against Edward *Lee (Ep 1092), and in December 1520 he boasted, in a letter not meant for publication, that the president of Holland supported his secret project (cf the *Consilium*,

Opuscula 352–61) to delay the effect of the papal bull excommunicating *Luther by casting doubt on its authenticity (Ep 1165). Several other letters from Erasmus to Everaerts in succeeding years have survived, all testifying to his growing misgivings about Luther's precipitate course and about the greater danger posed by those who, 'from a desire for revenge,' sought to compass his ruin (Epp 1186, 1188, 1237, 1238, 1468, 1653). No letters from Everaerts to Erasmus are extant, but it is evident from Ep 1238 that he invited Erasmus to visit him in Holland or on Walcheren.

Sympathy within the council of Holland for Erasmus' position in the Reformation controversy, to which these letters testify, is especially interesting in view of the fact that during the same period the council made common cause with the states of Holland to resist the infringement on local privileges represented by the territorial Inquisition which *Charles v established in 1522, whose leaders are bitterly criticized by Erasmus (Epp 1417, 1434, 1469, the last to Everaerts). If Kalkoff is not entirely wrong in applying the term 'Counter-Reformation' to Charles' effort to stamp out heresy, the council's role in defending the legal rights of Hollanders may be regarded as an early instance of that alliance between men of state and humanist views on toleration which later came to fruition with the 'politiques' in France or the 'libertines' in the United Provinces.

Erasmus was also acquainted with three of Nicolaas' sons; see Petrus Hieronymus and Everardus *Nicolai, and Nicolaus *Grudius. His wife, Elisabeth van Bladel (d 1548), had borne him eighteen children, of whom eight survived the father. In his will of 1527 Erasmus included Everaerts among other dignitaries whom he wanted to receive a copy of his collected works to be published by Hieronymus *Froben (Allen vi 505).

BIBLIOGRAPHY: Allen and CWE Ep 1092 / NNBW iii 358–60 / NBW vii 214–31 / de Vocht CTL ii 430–44 and passim / de Vocht *Busleyden* 218, 348 / de Vocht *Literae ad Craneveldium* Ep 123 and passim / R.D. Dekkers *Humanisme en rechtswetenschap in de Nederlanden* (Antwerp 1938) / Paul Kalkoff *Die Anfänge der Gegenreformation in den Niederlanden* (Halle 1903) / J.G. de

Hoop Scheffer *Geschiendenis der kerkhervorming in Nederland van haar ontstaan tot 1531* (Amsterdam 1873)

JAMES D. TRACY

EVERAERTS or EVERARDI See also NICOLAI

Gabriel von EYB 29 September 1455–1 December 1535
Gabriel von Eyb, born in the castle of Arberg, near Feuchtwangen, Franconia, was a nephew of Albert von Eyb (cf ASD i-1 89), whose valuable library he later inherited. When he matriculated in Erfurt in 1471 he was already in possession of a number of benefices; he was a canon of Eichstätt in 1460, of Bamberg in 1467, and of Würzburg in 1473. In 1478 he registered in the University of Pavia, where he received a doctorate in canon law on 28 September 1485. From 1487 he was a councillor of the margrave of Ansbach. On 5 December 1496 he was elected bishop of Eichstätt and was installed on 16 April 1497. He endeavoured to promote a uniform liturgy by issuing a breviary (1497) and a missal (1517) for his diocese. His main interests were art and learning. He was in his seventies when the controversies around *Luther began, and he remained generally inactive although initially he had urged Johann Maier of *Eck to write his *Obelisci* against Luther's *Theses* and was the first of the German bishops to publish the Bull *Exsurge Domine* against Luther. The diocese of Eichstätt suffered considerably during the rise of Protestantism since the regions of Ansbach and Nürnberg were lost. On the other hand, Gabriel established in Eichstätt a flourishing school of sculpture influenced by the Italian Renaissance style.

Eyb is mentioned in Ep 2993 (1535) as one of the princes who concluded the pact at Donauwörth after the restoration of Württemberg.

BIBLIOGRAPHY: Allen Ep 2993 / DHGE xvi 266–8 / LThK iii 1324 / *Matrikel Erfurt* i 345

IG

Hendrik van den EYNDE See Henricus AFINIUS

WORKS FREQUENTLY CITED

SHORT TITLE FORMS FOR ERASMUS' WORKS

CONTRIBUTORS

ILLUSTRATION CREDITS

Works Frequently Cited

This list provides bibliographical information for works referred to in short title form. The reader should notice, however, that the text of certain biographies contains additional short title references to works listed in the bibliography of the specific article in question. That bibliography should be consulted in the first place. For Erasmus' writings see the short title list, pages 456–8.

ADB	*Allgemeine Deutsche Biographie* (Leipzig 1875–1912)
AK	*Die Amerbachkorrespondenz* ed A. Hartmann and B.R. Jenny (Basel 1942–)
Allen	*Opus epistolarum Des. Erasmi Roterodami* ed P.S. Allen, H.M. Allen, and H.W. Garrod (Oxford 1906–58)
ARG	*Archiv für Reformationsgeschichte. Archive for Reformation History*
ASD	*Opera Omnia Desiderii Erasmi Roterodami* (Amsterdam 1969–)
BA Oekolampads	*Briefe und Akten zum Leben Oekolampads* ed E. Staehelin, Quellen und Forschungen zur Reformationsgeschichte vols 10 and 19 (Leipzig 1927–34; repr 1971)
Basler Chroniken	*Basler Chroniken* (Leipzig-Basel 1872–)
Bataillon *Erasmo y España*	Marcel Bataillon *Erasmo y España: Estudios sobre la historia espiritual del siglo XVI* tr A. Alatorre, 2nd ed (Mexico City-Buenos Aires 1966)
Benzing *Buchdrucker*	Josef Benzing *Die Buchdrucker des 16. und 17. Jahrhunderts im deutschen Sprachgebiet* (Wiesbaden 1963)
BHR	*Bibliothèque d'Humanisme et Renaissance*
Bierlaire *Familia*	Franz Bierlaire *La familia d'Erasme* (Paris 1968)
Blarer Briefwechsel	*Briefwechsel der Brüder Ambrosius und Thomas Blaurer* ed T. Schiess (Freiburg 1908–12)
BNB	*Biographie nationale* (Académie royale des sciences, des lettres et des beaux-arts de Belgique, Brussels 1866–)
BRE	*Briefwechsel des Beatus Rhenanus* ed A. Horawitz and K. Hartfelder (Leipzig 1886, repr 1966)
Calendar of State Papers, Milan	*Calendar of State Papers and Manuscripts existing in the Archives and Collections of Milan ...* ed A.B. Hinds (Hereford 1912)
Calendar of State Papers, Spanish	*Calendar of Letters, Despatches and State Papers relating to the Negotiations between England and Spain preserved in the Archives of Simancas and elsewhere*, with supplements, ed G.A. Bergenroth et al (London 1862–)
Calendar of State Papers, Venetian	*Calendar of State Papers and Manuscripts relating to English Affairs existing in the Archives and Collections of Venice and other Libraries of*

Northern Italy, 1202–1672 ed R.L. Brown et al (London 1862–1940, repr 1970)

Clerval   *Registre des procès-verbaux de la faculté de théologie de Paris* ed J.-A. Clerval (Paris 1917)

Colloquia Erasmiana Turonensia   *Colloquia Erasmiana Turonensia* Douzième stage international d'études humanistes, Tours 1969, ed J.-C. Margolin (Paris-Toronto 1972)

Cosenza   Mario Emilio Cosenza *Biographical and Bibliographical Dictionary of the Italian Humanists and the World of Classical Scholarship in Italy, 1300–1800* (Boston, Mass 1962–7)

CWE   *Collected Works of Erasmus* (Toronto 1974–   )

DBF   *Dictionnaire de biographie française* ed J. Balteau et al (Paris 1933–   )

DBI   *Dizionario biografico degli Italiani* ed A.M. Ghisalberti et al (Rome 1960–   )

Delisle   Léopold Delisle 'Notice sur un régistre des procès-verbaux de la faculté de théologie de Paris pendant les années 1505–1533' *Notices et extraits des manuscrits de la Bibliothèque Nationale et autres bibliothèques* 36 (1899) 317–407. Offprint ed (Paris 1899)

DHBS   *Dictionnaire historique et biographique de la Suisse* (Neuchâtel 1921–34), simultaneously published in a very similar but not identical German version: *Historisch-Biographisches Lexikon der Schweiz*

DHGE   *Dictionnaire d'histoire et de géographie ecclésiastiques* ed A. Baudrillart et al (Paris 1912–   )

DNB   *Dictionary of National Biography* ed Sidney Lee et al (London 1885–   , repr 1949–50)

DS   *Dictionnaire de spiritualité ascétique et mystique, doctrine et histoire* ed M. Viller et al (Paris 1932–   )

DTC   *Dictionnaire de théologie catholique* ed A. Vacant et al (Paris 1899–1950)

EI   *Enciclopedia Italiana* ed D. Bartolini et al (Rome 1929–   , repr 1949)

Emden BRUC   A.B. Emden *A Biographical Register of the University of Cambridge to AD 1500* (Cambridge 1963)

Emden BRUO   A.B. Emden *A Biographical Register of the University of Oxford to AD 1500* (Oxford 1957–9)

Emden BRUO 1501–40   A.B. Emden *A Biographical Register of the University of Oxford, AD 1501–1540* (Oxford 1974)

Epistolae ad Nauseam   *Epistolarum miscellanearum ad Fridericum Nauseam Blancicampianum ... libri x* (Basel 1550)

Eubel   *Hierarchia catholica medii aevi summorum pontificum, S.R.E. cardinalium, ecclesiarum antistitum series* ed C. Eubel et al (Münster 1901–   )

Farge   James K. Farge *Biographical Register of Paris Doctors of Theology, 1500–1536* Subsidia Mediaevalia 10 (Toronto 1980)

Gallia christiana   *Gallia christiana in provincias ecclesiasticas distributa* ed D. Sammarthanus et al (Paris 1715–1865, repr 1970)

Gauthier   Jules Gauthier *Département du Doubs: Inventaire sommaire des archives départementales antérieures à 1790: Archives ecclésiastiques* série G I (Besançon 1900)

Grimm *Buchführer*   Heinrich Grimm 'Die Buchführer des deutschen Kulturbereichs und ihre Niederlassungsorte in der Zeitspanne 1490 bis um 1550' *Archiv für Geschichte des Buchwesens* 7 (1965–6) 1153–1772

Herminjard	*Correspondance des Réformateurs dans les pays de langue française* ed A.-L. Herminjard (Geneva-Paris 1866–97, repr 1965–6)
Hill	G.F. Hill *A Corpus of Italian Medals of the Renaissance before Cellini* (London 1930)
Hutten *Opera*	*Ulrichi Hutteni equitis Germani opera* ed E. Böcking (Leipzig 1859–61, repr 1963)
Hutten *Operum supplementum*	*Ulrichi Hutteni equitis Germani operum supplementum* ed E. Böcking (Leipzig 1869–71)
Knod	Gustav C. Knod *Deutsche Studenten in Bologna (1289-1562)* (Berlin 1899, repr 1970)
LB	*Desiderii Erasmi Roterodami opera omnia* ed J. Leclerc (Leiden 1703–6, repr 1961–2)
LP	*Letters and Papers, Foreign and Domestic, of the Reign of Henry VIII* ed J.S. Brewer et al (London 1862–1932)
LThK	*Lexikon für Theologie und Kirche* 2nd ed by J. Höfer and K. Rahner (Freiburg 1957–)
Luther w	*D. Martin Luthers Werke: Kritische Gesamtausgabe* (Weimar 1883–)
Matricule de Louvain	*Matricule de l'Université de Louvain* ed E. Reusens, A. Schillings, et al (Brussels 1903–)
Matricule de Montpellier	*Matricule de l'Université de Médecine de Montpellier (1503–1599)* ed M. Gouron (Geneva 1957)
Matricule d'Orléans	*Premier Livre des procurateurs de la nation germanique de l'ancienne Université d'Orléans, 1446–1546* ed C.M. Ridderikhoff, H. de Ridder-Symoens, et al (Leiden 1971–)
Matrikel Basel	*Die Matrikel der Universität Basel* ed H.G. Wackernagel et al (Basel 1951–)
Matrikel Erfurt	*Acten der Erfurter Universität* ed J.C.H. Weissenborn et al (Halle 1881–99, repr 1976)
Matrikel Frankfurt	*Ältere Universitäts-Matrikeln* I: *Universität Frankfurt a.O.* ed E. Friedländer et al (Leipzig 1887–91, repr 1965)
Matrikel Freiburg	*Die Matrikel der Universität Freiburg i. Br. von 1460–1656* ed H. Mayer (Freiburg 1907–10, repr 1976)
Matrikel Greifswald	*Ältere Universitäts-Matrikeln* II: *Universität Greifswald* ed E. Friedländer et al (Leipzig 1893–4, repr 1965)
Matrikel Heidelberg	*Die Matrikel der Universität Heidelberg von 1386 bis 1662* ed G. Toepke (Heidelberg 1884–93, repr 1976)
Matrikel Köln	*Matrikel der Universität Köln* ed H. Keussen (Bonn 1919–31, repr 1979)
Matrikel Leipzig	*Die Matrikel der Universität Leipzig* ed G. Erler (Leipzig 1895–1902, repr 1976)
Matrikel Rostock	*Die Matrikel der Universität Rostock* ed A. Hofmeister et al (Rostock-Schwerin 1889–1922, repr 1976)
Matrikel Tübingen	*Die Matrikeln der Universität Tübingen* ed H. Hermelink et al (Stuttgart-Tübingen 1906–)
Matrikel Wien	*Die Matrikel der Universität Wien* (Publikationen des Instituts für österreichische Geschichtsforschung VI. Reihe, 1. Abteilung, Vienna-Graz-Cologne 1954–)
Matrikel Wittenberg	*Album Academiae Vitebergensis: Ältere Reihe ... 1502–1602* ed K.E. Förstemann et al (Leipzig-Halle 1841-1905, repr 1976)
Melanchthons Briefwechsel	*Melanchthons Briefwechsel: Kritische und kommentierte Gesamtausgabe* ed Heinz Scheible (Stuttgart-Bad Cannstatt 1977–)

McConica — J.K. McConica *English Humanists and Reformation Politics under Henry VIII and Edward VI* (Oxford 1965)

More Y — *The Yale Edition of the Complete Works of St Thomas More* (New Haven-London 1961–)

NBW — *Nationaal Biografisch Woordenboek* ed J. Duverger et al (Brussels 1964–)

NDB — *Neue Deutsche Biographie* (Berlin 1953–)

NK — Wouter Nijhoff and M.E. Kronenberg *Nederlandsche Bibliographie van 1500 tot 1540* (The Hague 1923–71)

NNBW — *Nieuw Nederlandsch Biografisch Woordenboek* ed P.C. Molhuysen, P.J. Blok, et al (Leiden 1911–37, repr 1974)

Opuscula — *Erasmi opuscula: A Supplement to the Opera omnia* ed W.K. Ferguson (The Hague 1933)

Pastor — Ludwig von Pastor *The History of the Popes from the Close of the Middle Ages* ed and tr R.F. Kerr et al, 3rd ed (London 1938–53)

Pflug *Correspondance* — Julius Pflug *Correspondance* ed J.V. Pollet (Leiden 1969–)

Pirckheimer Briefwechsel — Willibald Pirckheimer *Briefwechsel* ed Emil Reicke (Munich 1940–)

PSB — *Polski Słownik Biograficzny* (Cracow, etc 1935–)

RE — *Johann Reuchlins Briefwechsel* ed Ludwig Geiger (Stuttgart 1875, repr 1962)

Reedijk — *The Poems of Desiderius Erasmus* ed C. Reedijk (Leiden 1956)

Renaudet *Préréforme* — Augustin Renaudet *Préréforme et Humanisme à Paris pendant les premières guerres d'Italie (1494-1517)* 2nd ed (Paris 1953)

Renouard *Répertoire* — Philippe Renouard *Répertoire des imprimeurs parisiens, libraires, fondeurs de caractères et correcteurs d'imprimerie ... jusqu'à la fin du seizième siècle* ed J. Veyrin-Forrer and B. Moreau (Paris 1965)

RGG — *Die Religion in Geschichte und Gegenwart* 3rd ed (Tübingen 1956–62)

Rice *Prefatory Epistles* — *The Prefatory Epistles of Jacques Lefèvre d'Etaples and Related Texts* ed Eugene F. Rice, jr (New York–London 1972)

Rogers — *The Correspondence of Sir Thomas More* ed E.F. Rogers (Princeton 1947)

Rublack *Reformation in Konstanz* — Hans-Christoph Rublack *Die Einführung der Reformation in Konstanz von den Anfängen bis zum Abschluss 1531* (Gütersloh-Karlsruhe 1971)

Sanudo *Diarii* — *I Diarii di Marino Sanuto* ed N. Barozzi et al (Venice 1879–1903, repr 1969–70)

Schmidt *Histoire littéraire* — Charles Schmidt *Histoire littéraire de l'Alsace à la fin du XVe et au commencement du XVIe siècle* (Paris 1879, repr 1966)

Scrinium Erasmianum — *Scrinium Erasmianum: Mélanges historiques publiées sous le patronage de l'Université de Louvain à l'occasion du cinquième centenaire de la naissance d'Erasme* ed J. Coppens (Leiden 1969)

Schottenloher — Karl Schottenloher *Bibliographie zur deutschen Geschichte im Zeitalter der Glaubensspaltung* 2nd ed (Stuttgart 1956–66)

Schreiber *Universität Freiburg* — Heinrich Schreiber *Geschichte der Albert-Ludwigs-Universität zu Freiburg i. Br.*: second part of his *Geschichte der Stadt und Universität Freiburg im Breisgau* (Freiburg 1857–60)

STC — *A Short-Title Catalogue of Books Printed in England, Scotland, and Ireland and of English Books Printed Abroad* ed A.W. Pollard and G.R. Redgrave (London 1926); 2nd ed revised by W.A. Jackson et al (London 1976–)

Vadianische Briefsammlung	*Vadianische Briefsammlung* ed E. Arbenz and H. Wartmann : Mitteilungen zur vaterländischen Geschichte, vols 24–5, 27–30, and supplements (St Gallen 1890–1908)
de Vocht *Busleyden*	Henry de Vocht *Jérôme de Busleyden, Founder of the Louvain Collegium Trilingue: His Life and Writings* (Turnhout 1950)
de Vocht *Dantiscus*	Henry de Vocht *John Dantiscus and his Netherlandish Friends as Revealed by their Correspondence, 1522–1546* (Louvain 1961)
de Vocht *Literae ad Craneveldium*	*Literae virorum eruditorum ad Franciscum Craneveldium, 1522–1528* ed Henry de Vocht (Louvain 1928)
de Vocht MHL	Henry de Vocht *Monumenta Humanistica Lovaniensia: Texts and Studies about Louvain Humanists in the First Half of the xvith Century* (Louvain 1934)
de Vocht CTL	Henry de Vocht *History of the Foundation and the Rise of the Collegium Trilingue Lovaniense, 1517-1550* (Louvain 1951–5)
Winterberg	Hans Winterberg *Die Schüler von Ulrich Zasius* (Stuttgart 1961)
z	*Huldreich Zwinglis Sämtliche Werke* ed E. Egli et al, Corpus Reformatorum vols 88–101 (Berlin-Leipzig-Zürich 1905–)

Short Title Forms for Erasmus' Works

Titles following colons are longer versions of the same, or are alternative titles. Items entirely enclosed in square brackets are of doubtful authorship. For abbreviations, see Works Frequently Cited, pages 451–5.

Adagia: Adagiorum chiliades 1508 (Adagiorum collectanea for the primitive form, when required) LB II / ASD II-5, 6 / CWE 30-36
Admonitio adversus mendacium: Admonitio adversus mendacium et obtrectationem LB X
Annotationes in Novum Testamentum LB VI
Antibarbari LB X / ASD I-1 / CWE 23
Apologia ad Fabrum: Apologia ad Iacobum Fabrum Stapulensem LB IX
Apologia ad Caranzam: Apologia ad Sanctium Caranzam, or Apologia de tribus locis, or Responsio ad annotationem Stunicae ... a Sanctio Caranza defensam LB IX
Apologia ad viginti et quattuor libros A. Pii LB IX
Apologia adversus Petrum Sutorem: Apologia adversus debacchationes Petri Sutoris LB IX
Apologia adversus monachos: Apologia adversus monachos quosdam hispanos LB IX
Apologia adversus rhapsodias Alberti Pii LB IX
Apologia contra Latomi dialogum: Apologia contra Iacobi Latomi dialogum de tribus linguis LB IX
Apologiae contra Stunicam: Apologiae contra Lopidem Stunicam LB IX / ASD IX-2
Apologia de 'In principio erat sermo' LB IX
Apologia de laude matrimonii: Apologia pro declamatione de laude matrimonii LB IX
Apologia de loco 'Omnes quidem': Apologia de loco 'Omnes quidem resurgemus' LB IX
Apologia invectivis Lei: Apologia qua respondet duabus invectivis Eduardi Lei Opuscula
Apophthegmata LB IV
Appendix respondens ad Sutorem LB IX
Argumenta: Argumenta in omneis epistolas apostolicas nova (with Paraphrases)
Axiomata pro causa Lutheri: Axiomata pro causa Martini Lutheri Opuscula

Carmina varia LB VIII
Catalogus lucubrationum LB I
Christiani hominis institutum, carmen LB V
Ciceronianus: Dialogus Ciceronianus LB I / ASD I-2 / CWE 28
Colloquia LB I / ASD I-3
Compendium vitae Allen I / CWE 4
[Consilium: Consilium cuiusdam ex animo cupientis esse consultum Opuscula]

De bello turcico: Consultatio de bello turcico LB V
De civilitate: De civilitate morum puerilium LB I / CWE 25
De concordia: De sarcienda ecclesiae concordia LB V

De conscribendis epistolis LB I / ASD I-2 / CWE 25
De constructione: De constructione octo partium orationis, or Syntaxis LB I / ASD I-4
De contemptu mundi: Epistola de contemptu mundi LB V / ASD V-1
De copia: De duplici copia verborum ac rerum LB I / CWE 24
De immensa Dei misericordia: Concio de immensa Dei misericordia LB V
De libero arbitrio: De libero arbitrio diatribe LB IX
De praeparatione: De praeparatione ad mortem LB V / ASD V-1
De pueris instituendis: De pueris statim ac liberaliter instituendis LB I / ASD I-2 / CWE 26
De puero Iesu: Concio de puero Iesu LB V
De ratione studii LB I / ASD I-2 / CWE 24
De recta pronuntiatione: De recta latini graecique sermonis pronuntiatione LB I / ASD I-4 / CWE 26
De tedio Iesu: Disputatiuncula de tedio, pavore, tristicia Iesu LB V
De virtute amplectenda: Oratio de virtute amplectenda LB V
Declamatio de morte LB IV
Declamatiuncula LB IV
Declarationes ad censuras Lutetiae vulgatas: Declarationes ad censuras Lutetiae vulgatas sub
  nomine facultatis theologiae Parisiensis LB IX
Detectio praestigiarum: Detectio praestigiarum cuiusdam libelli germanice scripti LB X / ASD IX-1
[Dialogus bilinguium ac trilinguium: Chonradi Nastadiensis dialogus bilinguium ac trilinguium
  Opuscula]
Dilutio: Dilutio eorum quae Iodocus Clithoveus scripsit adversus declamationem suasoriam
  matrimonii
Divinationes ad notata Bedae LB IX

Ecclesiastes: Ecclesiastes sive de ratione concionandi LB V
Elenchus in N. Bedae censuras LB IX
Enchiridion: Enchiridion militis christiani LB V
Encomium matrimonii (in De conscribendis epistolis)
Encomium medicinae: Declamatio in laudem artis medicae LB I / ASD I-4
Epigrammata LB I
Epistola ad Dorpium LB IX / CWE 3
Epistola ad fratres Inferioris Germaniae: Responsio ad fratres Germaniae Inferioris ad epistolam
  apologeticam incerto autore proditam LB X
Epistola ad graculos: Epistola ad quosdam imprudentissimos graculos LB X
Epistola apologetica de Termino LB X
Epistola consolatoria: Epistola consolatoria virginibus sacris LB V
Epistola contra pseudevangelicos: Epistola contra quosdam qui se falso iactant evangelicos LB X /
  ASD IX-1
Epistola de esu carnium: Epistola apologetica ad Christophorum episcopum Basiliensem de
  interdicto esu carnium LB IX / ASD IX-1
Exomologesis: Exomologesis sive modus confitendi LB V
Explanatio symboli: Explanatio symboli apostolorum sive catechismus LB V / ASD V-1
Expostulatio Iesu LB V

Formula: Conficiendarum epistolarum formula (see De conscribendis epistolis)

Hymni varii LB V
Hyperaspistes LB X

Institutio christiani matrimonii LB V
Institutio principis christiani LB IV / ASD IV-1 / CWE 27

[Julius exclusus: Dialogus Julius exclusus e coelis *Opuscula*] CWE 27

Lingua LB IV / ASD IV-1
Liturgia Virginis Matris: Virginis Matris apud Lauretum cultae liturgia LB V / ASD V-1

Methodus: Ratio verae theologiae LB V
Modus orandi Deum LB V / ASD V-1
Moria: Moriae encomium LB IV / ASD IV-3 / CWE 27

Novum Testamentum: Novum Testamentum 1519 and later (Novum instrumentum for the first
    edition, 1516, when required) LB VI

Obsecratio ad Virginem Mariam: Obsecratio sive oratio ad Virginem Mariam in rebus adversis
    LB V
Oratio de pace: Oratio de pace et discordia LB VIII
Oratio funebris: Oratio funebris Berthae de Heyen LB VIII

Paean Virgini Matri: Paean Virgini Matri dicendus LB V
Panegyricus: Panegyricus ad Philippum Austriae ducem LB IV / ASD IV-1 / CWE 27
Parabolae: Parabolae sive similia LB I / ASD I-5 / CWE 23
Paraclesis LB V, VI
Paraphrasis in Elegantias Vallae: Paraphrasis in Elegantias Laurentii Vallae LB I / ASD I-4
Paraphrasis in Matthaeum, etc (in Paraphrasis in Novum Testamentum)
Paraphrasis in Novum Testamentum LB VII / CWE 42-50
Peregrinatio apostolorum: Peregrinatio apostolorum Petri et Pauli LB VI, VII
Precatio ad Virginis filium Iesum (in Precatio pro pace)
Precatio dominica LB V
Precationes LB V
Precatio pro pace ecclesiae: Precatio ad Iesum pro pace ecclesiae LB IV, V
Progymnasmata: Progymnasmata quaedam primae adolescentiae Erasmi LB VIII
Psalmi: Psalmi, or Enarrationes sive commentarii in psalmos LB V
Purgatio adversus epistolam Lutheri: Purgatio adversus epistolam non sobriam Lutheri LB IX

Querela pacis LB IV / ASD IV-2 / CWE 27

Ratio verae theologiae: Methodus LB V
Responsio ad annotationes Lei: Liber quo respondet annotationibus Lei LB IX
Responsio ad collationes: Responsio ad collationes cuiusdam iuvenis gerontodidascali LB IX
Responsio ad disputationem de divortio: Responsio ad disputationem cuiusdam Phimostomi de
    divortio LB IX
Responsio ad epistolam Pii: Responsio ad epistolam paraeneticam Alberti Pii, or Responsio ad
    exhortationem Pii LB IX
Responsio ad notulas Bedaicas LB X
Responsio ad Petri Cursii defensionem: Epistola de apologia Cursii LB X
Responsio adversus febricantis libellum: Apologia monasticae religionis LB X

Spongia: Spongia adversus aspergines Hutteni LB X / ASD IX-1
Supputatio: Supputatio calumniarum Natalis Bedae LB IX

Vidua christiana LB V
Virginis et martyris comparatio LB V
Vita Hieronymi: Vita divi Hieronymi Stridonensis Opuscula

Contributors

Danilo Aguzzi-Barbagli
Rosemarie Aulinger
Kenneth R. Bartlett
Marco Bernuzzi
Franz Bierlaire
Marjorie O'Rourke Boyle
Virginia Brown
Fritz Büsser
Leo van Buyten
Virginia W. Callahan
Anna Giulia Cavagna
D.S. Chambers
Miriam U. Chrisman
Brian P. Copenhaver
Elizabeth Crittall
Maria Cytowska
John F. D'Amico
Natalie Zemon Davis
Rolf Decot
Jan De Grauwe
Rosemary Devonshire Jones
L. Domonkos
Paul J. Donelly
Richard M. Douglas
K.-H. Ducke
E.J.M. van Eijl
Edward English
Michael Erbe
Conor Fahy
James K. Farge
Mordechai Feingold
Felipe Fernández-Armesto
R.M. Flores

Inge Friedhuber
Stephan Füssel
Anton J. Gail
Marie-Madeleine de la Garanderie
Veronika Gerz-von Büren
André Godin
Frank Golczewski
Anthony Grafton
Kaspar von Greyerz
Gordon Griffiths
Hans R. Guggisberg
Geneviève Guilleminot
Léon-E. Halkin
John M. Headley
Gernot Heiss
Henry Heller
Judith Rice Henderson
Elisabeth Feist Hirsch
R. Gerald Hobbs
Eugen Hoffmann
Irmgard Höss
J. Hoyoux
Jozef IJsewijn
Marie-Thérèse Isaac
Fehmi Ismail
Denis R. Janz
William B. Jones
James M. Kittelson
Erich Kleineidam
C.S. Knighton
Alfred Kohler
Barbara Könneker
Georges Kouskoff

Halina Kowalska
Peter Krendl
Egmont Lee
Valeria Sestieri Lee
Stanford E. Lehmberg
C.G. van Leijenhorst
M.J.C. Lowry
Albrecht Luttenberger
James K. McConica
Franz Machilek
David Mackenzie
Louis P.A. Maingon
Peter Marzahl
Jean-Pierre Massaut
C. Matheeussen
Hansgeorg Molitor
Gérard Moreau
Marcel A. Nauwelaerts
José C. Nieto
John C. Olin
Arsenio Pacheco
Luis A. Pérez
Paul van Peteghem
Paolo Pissavino
Michel Reulos
Hilde de Ridder-Symoens
Dieter Riesenberger
Milagros Rivera

Steven Rowan
John Rowlands
Hans-Christoph Rublack
Gordon Rupp
Beat von Scarpatetti
Hans Schadek
Heinz Scheible
Charles B. Schmitt
R.J. Schoeck
Martin Schwarz Lausten
Harry R. Secor
Silvana Seidel Menchi
Heide Stratenwerth
Robert Stupperich
Hans Thieme
De Etta V. Thomsen
Alice Tobriner
Gilbert Tournoy
Godelieve Tournoy-Thoen
James D. Tracy
J.B. Trapp
Charles Trinkaus
Ronald W. Truman
Rainer Vinke
Hartmut Voit
Manfred E. Welti
Konrad Wiedemann
J.K. Zeman

Illustration Credits